rd University Press, Great Clarendon Street, Oxford (

Oxford New York
Athens Auckland Bangkok Bogotá Buenos Aires
Calcutta Cape Town Chennai Dar es Salaam Delhi
Florence Hong Kong Istanbul Karachi
Kuala Lumpur Mumbai Madrid Melbourne
Mexico City Nairobi Paris São Paolo Singapore
Taipei Tokyo Toronto Warsaw

and associated companies in
Berlin Ibadan

Oxford is a trade mark of Oxford University Pr

© Oxford University Press 1998

This edition based on The Concise Oxford School
5 7 9 10 8 6

ISBN 019 9103925

A CIP catalogue record for this book is av
British Library

Typeset by Pentacor PLC, High
Printed in Great Britain by Omnia
Bishopbriggs, Glasgow

OWLS

Do you have a query about words, their ori
ronunciation, or any other aspect of the En
WLS at Oxford University Press, Great Clar

All queries will be answered using
Oxford Dictionary De

The Mini
OXFORD
SCHOOL
DICTIONARY

Compiled by
Joyce M Hawkins
Andrew Delahunty
Fred McDonald

XFORD UNIVERSITY P

Contents

Preface

This dictionary has been specially written for upper primary and lower secondary school students aged 10–14 years. It should serve as a working tool in the classroom and accustom its users to the style in which most adult dictionaries are written, but at the same time be easy to use because it avoids abbreviations and similar conventions.

Inflections of all verbs and plurals of nouns are spelt out in full, and comparatives and superlatives of many adjectives and adverbs are also given. Pronunciation of difficult words is given in a simple look-and-say system without special symbols. Definitions are clearly expressed, with careful explanations of difficult concepts (e.g. *hindsight, hypothesis, irony*), and many examples of words in use are provided. There are a number of notes on correct usage, grammatical points, and words that are easily confused (e.g. *alternate/alternative*). Direct opposites or parallel terms are sometimes indicated (e.g. *maximum/minimum, optimist/pessimist, libel/slander*). Prefixes and suffixes are entered at the appropriate place in the alphabetical sequence; lists of them are contained in Appendix 1. Etymologies are given for a large number of words. The etymologies are intended to introduce the idea that words have a history as well as a meaning, to demonstrate the connection between related words and help with recognition of word elements, and to show the variety of languages that have contributed to English. It is hoped that the etymologies will also arouse the curiosity of users so that they will be encouraged to look in a larger dictionary for more detailed information.

Acknowledgements

The publisher and editors are indebted to all the people who helped in the production of this dictionary. We are grateful to the teachers who advised us in the initial stages, to John Butterworth and Clive Johnson for their helpful comments and to Richard Jeffery and Janet Foot for their careful proof-reading.

The English Language

English is the chief language of Britain, the USA, Australia, and a number of other countries. More than 300 million people speak it as their first or their only language, and millions more in all parts of the world learn it as a foreign language for use in communicating with people of other nations. It is the official language used between airline pilots and their air traffic controllers in all countries, and in shipping, and the main language of international business, science, medicine, and computing.

All languages have a history: they are constantly changing and evolving. It is probable that nearly all the languages of Europe, and some of those in the Middle East and India, came from one ancient community, who lived in Eastern Europe about 5,000 years ago. Scholars call the language of this community Indo-European. As people moved away to the east and west they lost contact with each other and developed new and different lifestyles. Naturally their language needs changed too. They invented new words and forgot old ones, and the grammar of the language also changed. Many varied languages grew from the original parent tongue, until the time came when people with the same ancestors would no longer have understood each other.

Invasions and conquests complicated the process. The English language shows this very well, for invaders brought their own languages to Britain, and British travellers took theirs to lands overseas. The earliest known inhabitants of Britain spoke a form of Celtic, related to modern Welsh and Gaelic. Very little of this Celtic survived the waves of invasion that drove its speakers into western and highland parts of the country, but the names of some cities, rivers, and hills date back to Celtic times (e.g. *Carlisle, Avon, Pendle*).

Old English

Old English, which is also called Anglo-Saxon, does not look very much like modern English (for example *Faeder ure, þu þe eart in heofonum* = Our Father, who is in heaven) but many words, especially the most frequently used ones, can be traced back to it. *Eat, drink, sleep, speak, work, play,* and *sing* are all from Old English; so are *house, door, meat, bread, milk, fish;* and *head, nose, eye, man, woman, husband, wife.* The prepositions and conjunctions that we use to join words together in sentences, such as *and, but, to, from,* come from Old English, and so do many common adverbs, for example *up, down, here, there, over, under.*

Old English did not originate in Britain. It was the language of the Angles, Saxons, and Jutes, Germanic tribes who came to Britain from the Continent in about AD 450. By about AD 700 the Anglo-Saxons had occupied most of the country and their language was the dominant one. Even the name of the country itself became 'England', which means 'land of the Angles', and from it came 'Englisc', the Old English spelling of 'English'.

The next great influence on Old English came from the Vikings, who arrived from Norway and Denmark in the 9th and 10th centuries and occupied much of northern and eastern England. They also settled in parts of Scotland, Wales, and Ireland. Their language was Old Norse, and from it we get many common words, such as *call, cast,* and *take,* and a number of words beginning with 'sc' or 'sk', including *scare, scrap, skirt,* and *sky.*

Middle English

In 1066 the Normans, led by William the Conqueror, invaded England. English life was greatly changed in the years that followed and the language changed too, so much so that, with a little practice, we can now read and understand the language of that time. These lines, for example, were written in about 1390: *This carpenter hadde wedded newe a wyf, Which that he lovede moore than his lyf.* We call this language 'Middle English' to distinguish it from Old English or Anglo-Saxon.

For much of this period the language used by the ruling classes was the French of the victorious Norman invaders, though most of the ordinary people still spoke English. Many words connected with government and law came into the language at this time through their French use, e.g. *advise, command, court, govern, people, reign, royalty, rule.*

Throughout all these centuries, although scholars in different countries spoke different languages, they all understood Latin, which had been the language of the ancient Roman Empire, and used it for writing about every subject that they studied. Some

Latin words (e.g. *mint*, *pound*, *sack*, and *street*) had already been adopted by the Anglo-Saxons before they came to Britain, because they had lived on the fringe of the Roman Empire; others (e.g. *font*, *pope*, and *school*) arrived with the spread of Christianity. Then in the 14–16th centuries (the *Renaissance*) people throughout Europe became especially interested in Greek and Roman literature, philosophy, art, and buildings, and many more words from Greek and Latin were introduced into English (e.g. *architecture*, *column*, *comedy*, *educate*, *history*, *physics*, *tributary*). The Christian Church in all western countries had always used Latin, and continued to use this (not English or other local languages) in all its services.

Modern English

From about 1500 onwards the English language continued to change, and developed enormously. It adopted words from other languages with which people came into contact through trade or travel, and it was exported to other lands when English-speaking people travelled abroad. In the early 17th century colonies began to be established, first in North America and in India, then in the West Indies, and later in Australia, New Zealand, Hong Kong, and Africa. To each country the settlers took the English language of their own time, and in each country it changed, little by little, until it differed in various ways not only from the English of other settlements but from its parent form in Britain—where, of course, the language was changing too. Some words, such as names for birds and animals found only in one country, were adopted into the form of English used there and are not known elsewhere; others (e.g. *banana*, *potato*, and *tornado*) have made their way into international English and are known everywhere.

In the 20th century, people who came from the Caribbean and Asia to settle in England brought with them their own cultures and vocabulary, and many words from these have been adopted into standard English (e.g. *chapatti*, *reggae*).

Nowadays travel is not the only way in which people acquire words from other countries. Films made in one country are shown in many others, and television programmes from all over the world are received in people's homes. The result is that while American, Australian, and other vocabulary becomes familiar in Britain, British English continues to be exported.

Dialect

There are different forms of English not only in different parts of the world but within the British Isles. People from North Yorkshire, the Midlands, East Anglia, and Somerset have different words for different things, or use different grammatical forms. The varieties of English are called dialects. Each is known, understood, and regarded as standard in its own area, but not outside it.

The way that people of an area pronounce words is called an accent, and this too varies in different parts of the country.

Every language has a number of dialects and most languages have one dialect and style of pronunciation that is regarded as standard for the whole country. In Britain, 'Standard English' is based on the form of English used in southern England. It is the basis of the written language, known (unlike other dialects) in all parts of the country, spoken by all well-educated people, used for national news bulletins on radio and television, and learned by foreigners. People from outside southern England often speak Standard English with a local accent, and use it as well as their local dialect.

Formal and informal

We wear different clothes for different kinds of occasions, and often the words that we use when writing or speaking formally are different from those that we use informally to friends.

Very informal language (e.g. *nick* = to steal, *quid* = £1, *piffle* = nonsense) is called slang. It is used either for fun, or to express something in a more vivid or picturesque way than dignified words would do, or to shock people or attract their attention. Often, special slang words are used by members of a group, and they recognize others who use them as belonging to it too.

The dictionary

There are over 500,000 words in the English language, and the total is increasing all the time. Of these, about 3,000 are known and used by almost everyone whose native language is English. Most people know the meaning of at least another 5,000 words, though they may not use all of them in everyday speech or writing. In addition, those who specialize in a particular subject (e.g. music, chemistry, medicine, computers) have a wide vocabulary of words that are used by people working in that subject but are not generally known to others.

The biggest dictionary in the world is the *Oxford English Dictionary*, which fills twenty very large volumes, and it contains most of these words. Small dictionaries can find room for only a fraction of the whole language; they include most of the words that are in common use, but (in order to make the book a convenient size and not too expensive) they have to miss out a considerable number of words, and a larger dictionary must be consulted for information about these.

Notes on the use of the dictionary

Dictionary entries

Words defined are arranged in alphabetical order. The words derived from each word (*derivatives*) are often included in the same entry without definitions if their meaning can easily be worked out from the meaning of the main word.

Words with the same spelling but with a different meaning or origin (*homographs*) are given separate entries with a space between them, and numbered with a raised figure, e.g.

peer[1] *verb* (**peers, peering, peered**) look at something closely or with difficulty.
[from *appear*]

peer[2] *noun* (**peers**) a noble. someone who is equal to another in rank, merit, or age etc., *She had no peer*. **peeress** *noun* [from Latin *par* = equal]

Pronunciation

Help is given with this when the word is difficult, or when two words with the same spelling are pronounced differently. The pronunciation is given in brackets with *say* or *rhymes with*, e.g.

toll (rhymes with *hole*) *noun*

chaos (*say* kay-oss) *noun*

Words are broken up into small units (usually of one syllable), and the syllable that is spoken with most stress is shown in thick black letters. In the pronunciation guide, note the following distinctions:

oo shows the sound as in *soon*
uu " " " " *book*
th " " " " *thin*
th " " " " *this*
zh " " " " *vision*

Parts of speech

These are printed in italic or sloping print (e.g. *noun*, *adjective*, *verb*) after the word and before its definition. Some words can be used as more than one part of speech. When these are defined, no space is left between the entries, e.g.

barricade *noun* (**barricades**) a
barrier, especially one put up
hastily across a street or door.
barricade *verb* (**barricades**,
barricading, barricaded) block
a street or door with a
barricade.

Inflections and plurals

Derived forms of verbs, plurals of nouns, and some comparative and superlative forms of adjectives and adverbs are given after the part of speech.

The first verb form given (ending in *-s*) is used for the present tense. The second form given (ending in *-ing*) is the present participle. When three verb forms are given, e.g.

admit *verb* (**admits, admitting,
admitted**)

the third form is both the past tense (as in 'he *admitted* it') and the past participle ('it was *admitted*'). When four forms are given, e.g.

come *verb* (**comes, coming,
came, come**)

freeze *verb* (**freezes, freezing,
froze, frozen**)

the third is the past tense (as in 'he *came*'; 'it *froze*'), and the fourth is the past participle ('he had *come*'; 'it was *frozen*').

Meanings

Many words have more than one meaning. Each meaning is numbered separately.

Labels

Words that are not 'Standard English' are labelled as *informal* or *slang* etc.

Examples

Examples of words in use are given in italic or sloping print *like this* to help make a definition clearer, e.g.

beware *verb* be careful,
Beware of pickpockets.

Phrases

These are listed and defined under the part of speech to which they belong, e.g.

jump *verb* (**jumps, jumping, jumped**) move up suddenly from the ground into the air.
jump at (*informal*) accept something eagerly.
jump the gun start before you should.
jump the queue not wait your turn.
jump *noun* (**jumps**) a jumping movement.

Usage notes

The dictionary includes over 200 notes on correct usage, grammatical points, and words that are easily confused, e.g.

less *adjective & adverb*

USAGE: Do not use *less* when you mean *fewer*. You should use *fewer* when you are talking about a number of individual things, and *less* when you are talking about a quantity or mass of something: *The less batter you make, the fewer pancakes you'll get.*

Origins of words

The derivation (or *etymology*) of a word is given in square brackets at the end of the entry, e.g.

alligator *noun* (**alligators**) a
large reptile of the crocodile
family. [from Spanish *el
lagarto* = the lizard]

These derivations often shed light on the word's meaning or how
its meaning has changed, or show the connection between words
that have the same set of letters in them (e.g. *attract*, *contract*,
extract, and *tractor*) and also help to indicate the number of
languages from which words have been taken into English. For
instance, *alligator* comes from Spanish, *algebra* from Arabic,
mammoth from Russian, *bungalow* from Hindi, *shawl* from
Persian or Urdu, and *skunk* from a Native American language.

Other examples:

bread [from Old English, from
Germanic]

butter [from Old English,
taken via Latin from Greek]

cake [from a Scandinavian
language]

cereal [from *Ceres*, the Roman
goddess of farming]

cheese [from Old English,
taken from Latin]

chocolate [via French or
Spanish from Nahuatl (a
Central American language
spoken by the Aztecs)]

coffee [from Arabic *kahwa*]

cream [from old French]

liquorice [from Greek *glykys*
= sweet + *rhiza* = root]

tea [via Dutch from Chinese]

No origin is given if the word is obviously related to another word
nearby, for which there is an etymology (e.g. the origin of
determine is given, but not those of *determination*, *determined*, or
determiner). Etymology is not always given for words made up of
two other words in the dictionary (e.g. *seafood*, *racecourse*), or of a
word and a prefix or suffix (e.g. *regenerate*, *radiography*, *sleepless*,
unfortunate). Some words have very complicated origins, and it is
not always possible to show all the details; users who are
interested in discovering more about word origins should look
in a larger dictionary.

Aa

a *adjective* (called the *indefinite article* and changing to **an** before most vowel sounds)
1 one (but not any special one), *Can you lend me a book?* **2** each; per, *We see it once a day* or *once an hour*. [from Old English *an* = one]

a-¹ *prefix*
1 on; to; towards (as in *afoot*, *ashore*, *aside*). **2** in the process of (as in *a-hunting*). [from the preposition *on*]

a-² *prefix* (**an-** is used before a vowel sound) not; without (as in *asymmetrical*, *anarchy*). [from Greek *a-* = not]

ab- *prefix* (changing to **abs-** before *c* and *t*) away; from (as in *abduct*, *abnormal*, *abstract*). [from Latin *ab* = away]

aback *adverb*
taken aback surprised. [from Old English *on baec* = backwards]

abacus (*say* ab-a-kus) *noun* (*plural* **abacuses**) a frame used for counting with beads sliding on wires. [from Greek]

abandon *verb* (**abandons**, **abandoning**, **abandoned**)
1 give up, *We never abandoned hope.* **2** leave something without intending to return, *Abandon ship!* **abandonment** *noun*

abandon *noun* a careless and uncontrolled manner, *dancing with great abandon*.

abbey *noun* (*plural* **abbeys**)
1 a monastery or convent.

2 a church that was once part of a monastery, *Westminster Abbey*. [same origin as *abbot*]

abbot *noun* (*plural* **abbots**) the head of an abbey. [via Latin and Greek from Aramaic (a language once spoken in the Middle East), *abba* = father]

abbreviate *verb* (**abbreviates**, **abbreviating**, **abbreviated**) shorten something. [from Latin *brevis* = short, brief]

abbreviation *noun* (*plural* **abbreviations**)
1 a shortened form of a word or words, especially one using the initial letters, such as GCSE, St., USA. **2** abbreviating something.

abdicate *verb* (**abdicates**, **abdicating**, **abdicated**)
1 resign from a throne. **2** give up an important responsibility. **abdication** *noun*

abdomen (*say* ab-dom-en) *noun* (*plural* **abdomens**)
1 the lower front part of a person's or animal's body, containing the stomach, intestines, and other digestive organs. **2** the rear section of an insect's body. **abdominal** (*say* ab-dom-in-al) *adjective*

abduct *verb* (**abducts**, **abducting**, **abducted**) take a person away illegally; kidnap. **abduction** *noun*, **abductor** *noun*

abhor *verb* (**abhors**, **abhorring**, **abhorred**) (*formal*) hate something very much. **abhorrent** *adjective*, **abhorrence** *noun* [from Latin *abhorrere* = shrink away in horror]

abide *verb* (**abides**, **abiding**, **abided**)
1 ((*old use*); *past tense* **abode**)

remain or dwell somewhere.
2 bear or tolerate, *I can't abide wasps.*
abide by keep a promise etc.

ability *noun* (*plural* **abilities**)
1 being able to do something.
2 cleverness or talent.

ablaze *adjective* blazing; on fire.

able *adjective*
1 having the power or skill or opportunity to do something.
2 skilful or clever. **ably** *adverb* [from old French]

-able *suffix* (also **-ble, -ible,** and **-uble**) forms adjectives (e.g. *readable, legible*). The nouns formed from these end in **-bility** (e.g. *readability, legibility*). [from Latin]

abnormal *adjective* not normal; unusual. **abnormally** *adverb*, **abnormality** *noun* [from *ab- + normal*]

aboard *adverb* & *preposition* on or into a ship or aircraft or train.

abolish *verb* (**abolishes, abolishing, abolished**) put an end to a law or custom etc. **abolition** (*say* ab-ol-**ish**-on) *noun*

abominable *adjective* very bad or unpleasant. **abominably** *adverb*, **abomination** *noun* [from Latin *abominari* = regard as a bad omen]

aborigine (*say* ab-er-**ij**-in-ee) *noun* (*plural* **aborigines**) one of the original inhabitants of a country. **aboriginal** *adjective* & *noun* **Aborigine** one of the original inhabitants of Australia. [from Latin *ab origine* = from the beginning]

abort *verb* (**aborts, aborting, aborted**) put an end to something before it has been completed, *They aborted the space flight because of problems.*

abortion *noun* (*plural* **abortions**) removal of a baby from the womb before it has developed enough to survive.

abortive *adjective* unsuccessful, *an abortive attempt.*

abound *verb* (**abounds, abounding, abounded**)
1 be plentiful or abundant, *Fish abound in the river.* **2** have something in great quantities, *The river abounds in fish.* [from Latin *abundare* = overflow]

about *preposition*
1 near in amount or size or time etc., *It costs about £5. Come about two o'clock.* **2** on the subject of; in connection with, *Tell me about your holiday.* **3** all round; in various parts of, *They ran about the playground.*

about *adverb*
1 in various directions, *They were running about.* **2** not far away, *He is somewhere about.* **be about to** be going to do something.
[from *a-¹* + Old English *butan* = outside]

above *preposition*
1 higher than. **2** more than.

above *adverb* at or to a higher place. [from Old English]

abrasive *adjective*
1 that scrapes things away, *an abrasive wheel.* **2** harsh, *an abrasive manner.*

abreast *adverb*
1 side by side. **2** keeping up with something. [from *a-¹* + *breast*]

bridge verb (abridges, abridging, abridged) shorten a book etc. by using fewer words, *an abridged edition.* **abridgement** noun [same origin as *abbreviate*]

broad adverb in or to another country.

abrupt adjective **1** sudden or hasty, *his abrupt departure.* **2** rather rude and unfriendly; curt, *She has quite an abrupt manner.* **abruptly** adverb, **abruptness** noun [from *ab-* + Latin *ruptum* = broken]

abs- prefix away; from. see *ab-*.

abscess (say ab-sis) noun (plural **abscesses**) an inflamed place where pus has formed in the body. [from Latin]

abscond verb (absconds, absconding, absconded) go away secretly, *The cashier had absconded with the money.* [from Latin]

absent adjective not here; not present, *absent from school.* **absence** noun

absent (say ab-sent) verb (absents, absenting, absented) **absent yourself** stay away. [from *abs-* + Latin *esse* = to be]

absentee noun (plural **absentees**) a person who is absent. **absenteeism** noun

absent-minded adjective having your mind on other things; forgetful.

absolute adjective complete; not restricted. **absolutely** adverb [same origin as *absolve*]

absolute zero noun the lowest possible temperature, calculated as −273.15°C.

absolve verb (absolves, absolving, absolved) **1** clear a person of blame or guilt. **2** release a person from a promise or obligation. [from *ab-* + Latin *solvere* = set free]

absorb verb (absorbs, absorbing, absorbed) **1** soak up a liquid or gas. **2** receive something and reduce its effects, *The buffers absorbed most of the shock.* **3** take up a person's attention or time.

absorbent adjective able to soak up liquids easily, *absorbent paper.*

abstain verb (abstains, abstaining, abstained) **1** keep yourself from doing something; refrain. **2** choose not to use your vote. **abstainer** noun, **abstention** noun

abstinence noun abstaining, especially from alcohol. **abstinent** adjective

abstract (say ab-strakt) adjective **1** concerned with ideas, not solid objects, *Truth, hope, danger are all abstract.* **2** (of a painting or sculpture) showing the artist's ideas or feelings, not showing a recognizable person or thing.

absurd adjective ridiculous or foolish. **absurdly** adverb, **absurdity** noun

abundance noun plenty. [same origin as *abound*]

abundant adjective plentiful. **abundantly** adverb

abuse (say ab-yooz) verb (abuses, abusing, abused) **1** use something badly or wrongly; misuse. **2** ill-treat a person. **3** say unpleasant things about a person or thing.

abuse (say ab-**yooss**) noun
(plural **abuses**)
1 a misuse, *the abuse of power*.
2 ill-treatment. 3 words abusing
a person or thing; insults. [from
ab- + *use*]

abusive adjective rude and
insulting, *abusive remarks*.

abysmal (say ab-**iz**-mal) adjective
extremely bad, *abysmal
ignorance*.

abyss (say ab-**iss**) noun (plural
abysses) an extremely deep pit.
[from Greek *abyssos*
= bottomless]

ac- prefix to; towards. see **ad-**.

academic adjective
1 to do with education or
studying, especially at a school or
college or university.
2 theoretical; having no practical
use, *an academic point*.
academic noun (plural
academics) a university or
college teacher.

academy noun (plural
academies)
1 a school or college, especially
one for specialized training.
2 a society of scholars or artists,
The Royal Academy. [from
Akademeia, the name of the
garden where the Greek
philosopher Plato taught his
pupils]

accelerate verb (**accelerates,
accelerating, accelerated**) make
or become quicker; increase
speed.

acceleration noun (plural
accelerations)
1 the rate at which the speed of
something increases. 2 the rate of
change of velocity.

accelerator noun (plural
accelerators)
1 the pedal that a driver presses
to make a motor vehicle go
faster. 2 a thing used to increase
the speed of something.

accent (say **ak**-sent) noun (plural
accents)
1 the way a person pronounces
words, *She has a French accent*.
2 emphasis or stress, *In 'fairy',
the accent is on 'fair-'*. 3 a mark
placed over a letter to show how
it is pronounced, e.g. on *café*.

accept verb (**accepts, accepting,
accepted**)
1 take a thing that is offered or
presented. 2 say yes to an
invitation, offer, etc. **acceptance**
noun

USAGE: Do not confuse with
except.

acceptable adjective good
enough to accept; pleasing.
acceptably adverb, **acceptability**
noun

access (say **ak**-sess) noun
1 a way to enter or reach
something. 2 the right to use or
look at something.
access verb (**accesses,
accessing, accessed**) find
information that has been stored
in a computer. [from Latin]

accessible adjective able to be
reached. **accessibly** adverb,
accessibility noun

accessory (say ak-**sess**-er-ee)
noun (plural **accessories**)
1 an extra thing that goes with
something. 2 a person who helps
another with a crime.

accident *noun* (*plural* **accidents**)
an unexpected happening,
especially one causing injury or
damage. **accidental** *adjective*,
accidentally *adverb*
by accident by chance; without
its being arranged in advance.
[from Latin *accidere* = happen]

acclaim *verb* (**acclaims**,
acclaiming, **acclaimed**) welcome
or applaud. **acclaim** *noun*,
acclamation *noun* [from *ac-*
+ Latin *clamare* = to shout]

accommodate *verb*
(**accommodates**, **accommodating**,
accommodated)
1 provide somebody with a place
to live, work, or sleep overnight.
2 help by providing something,
*We can accommodate you with
skis.* [from Latin *accommodare*
= make suitable for]

accommodation *noun*
somewhere to live, work, or sleep
overnight.

accompanist *noun* (*plural*
accompanists) a pianist etc. who
accompanies a singer or another
musician.

accompany *verb* (**accompanies**,
accompanying, **accompanied**)
1 go somewhere with somebody.
2 be present with something,
Thunder accompanied the storm.
3 play music, especially on
a piano, that supports a singer or
another player etc.
accompaniment *noun*

accomplice (*say* a-**kum**-pliss)
noun (*plural* **accomplices**)
a person who helps another in
a crime etc.

accomplish *verb* (**accomplishes**,
accomplishing, **accomplished**) do

something successfully.

accomplishment *noun* [from *ac-*
+ Latin *complere* = to complete]

accomplished *adjective* skilled.

accord *noun* agreement; consent.
of your own accord voluntarily;
without being asked or
compelled.

according *adverb*
according to 1 as stated by,
According to him, we are stupid.
2 in relation to, *Price the apples
according to their size.*

accordingly *adverb*
1 in the way that is required, *I've
given you your instructions and
I expect you to act accordingly.*
2 therefore.

accordion *noun* (*plural*
accordions) a portable musical
instrument like a large
concertina. [via German from
Italian *accordare* = to tune an
instrument]

account *noun* (*plural* **accounts**)
1 a statement of money owed,
spent, or received; a bill. **2** an
arrangement to keep money in
a bank etc. **3** a description or
report.
on account of because of.
on no account under no
circumstances; certainly not.
take something into account
consider or include it when
making a decision or calculation.

account *verb* (**accounts**,
accounting, **accounted**)
account for make it clear why
something happens.

accountable *adjective*
responsible; having to explain
why you have done something.
accountability *noun*

accountant noun (plural **accountants**) a person whose job is keeping or inspecting financial accounts. **accountancy** noun

accumulate verb (**accumulates, accumulating, accumulated**) collect; pile up. **accumulation** noun

accurate adjective correct or exact. **accurately** adverb, **accuracy** noun [from ac- + Latin cura = care]

accuse verb (**accuses, accusing, accused**) say that a person has committed a crime etc.; blame. **accusation** noun, **accuser** noun

ace noun (plural **aces**)
1 a playing card with one spot.
2 a very skilful person or thing.
3 (in tennis) a serve that is too good for the other player to reach. [from Latin as = unit]

ache noun (plural **aches**) a dull continuous pain.

ache verb (**aches, aching, ached**) have an ache. [from Old English]

achieve verb (**achieves, achieving, achieved**) succeed in doing or producing something. **achievable** adjective, **achievement** noun [from old French a chief = to a head]

acid noun (plural **acids**) a chemical substance that contains hydrogen and neutralizes alkalis. **acidic** adjective, **acidity** noun

acid adjective
1 sharp-tasting; sour. 2 looking or sounding bitter, an acid reply. **acidly** adverb

acid rain noun rain made acid by mixing with waste gases from factories etc.

acknowledge verb (**acknowledges, acknowledging, acknowledged**)
1 admit that something is true.
2 state that you have received or noticed something, Acknowledge this letter. 3 express thanks or appreciation for something. **acknowledgement** noun

acne (say **ak**-nee) noun inflamed red pimples on the face and neck.

acorn noun (plural **acorns**) the seed of the oak tree. [from Old English]

acoustic (say a-**koo**-stik) adjective
1 to do with sound or hearing.
2 (of a musical instrument) not electronic, an acoustic guitar. **acoustically** adverb [from Greek akouein = hear]

acoustics (say a-**koo**-stiks) plural noun
1 the qualities of a hall etc. that make it good or bad for carrying sound. 2 the properties of sound

acquaint verb (**acquaints, acquainting, acquainted**) tell somebody about something, Acquaint him with the facts. **be acquainted with** know slightly

acquaintance noun (plural **acquaintances**)
1 a person you know slightly.
2 being acquainted.

acquire verb (**acquires, acquiring, acquired**) obtain. **acquisition** noun [from ac- + Latin quaerere = seek]

acquit verb (**acquits, acquitting, acquitted**) decide that somebody is not guilty, The jury acquitted her. **acquittal** noun **acquit yourself well** perform or do something well. [from ac- + Latin quietus = rest]

acre (*say* ay-ker) *noun* (*plural* **acres**) an area of land measuring 4,840 square yards or 0.405 hectares. **acreage** *noun* [from Old English *aecer* = field]

acrobat *noun* (*plural* **acrobats**) a person who performs spectacular gymnastic stunts for entertainment. **acrobatic** *adjective*, **acrobatics** *plural noun*

acronym (*say* ak-ron-im) *noun* (*plural* **acronyms**) a word or name that is formed from the initial letters of other words, *Nato is an acronym of North Atlantic Treaty Organization.* [from Greek *akros* = top + *onyma* = name]

across *preposition & adverb* 1 from one side to the other, *Swim across the river. Are you across yet?* 2 on the opposite side, *the house across the street.* [from French *à croix* = crosswise]

acrylic (*say* a-kril-ik) *noun* a kind of fibre, plastic, or resin made from an organic acid.

act *noun* (*plural* **acts**) 1 an action. 2 a law passed by a parliament. 3 one of the main divisions of a play or opera. 4 a short performance in a programme of entertainment, *a juggling act.* 5 a pretence, *She is only putting on an act.*

act *verb* (**acts, acting, acted**) 1 do something; perform actions. 2 perform a part in a play or film etc. 3 function; have an effect. [from Latin *actus* = doing, performing]

action *noun* (*plural* **actions**) 1 doing something. 2 something done. 3 a battle; fighting, *He was killed in action.* 4 a lawsuit.

out of action not working or functioning.
take action do something.

activate *verb* (**activates, activating, activated**) start something working. **activation** *noun*, **activator** *noun*

active *adjective* 1 lively or energetic. 2 functioning or working; in operation, *an active volcano.* 3 radioactive. 4 (of a form of a verb) used when the subject of the verb is performing the action. In 'The shop *sells* sweets' the verb is active; in 'Sweets *are sold* by the shop' the verb is passive. **actively** *adverb*, **activeness** *noun*

activist *noun* (*plural* **activists**) a person who believes in vigorous action, especially in politics.

activity *noun* (*plural* **activities**) 1 an action or occupation, *outdoor activities.* 2 being active or lively.

actor *noun* (*plural* **actors**) a person who acts a part in a play or film etc.

actress *noun* (*plural* **actresses**) a woman who acts a part in a play or film etc.

actual *adjective* real. **actually** *adverb*, **actuality** *noun*

acupuncture (*say* ak-yoo-punk-cher) *noun* pricking parts of the body with needles to relieve pain or cure disease. **acupuncturist** *noun* [from Latin *acu* = with a needle, + *puncture*]

acute *adjective* 1 sharp or strong, *acute pain.* 2 having a sharp mind. **acutely** *adverb*, **acuteness** *noun*

acute accent noun (plural **acute accents**) a mark over a vowel, as over é in café.

acute angle noun (plural **acute angles**) an angle of less than 90˚.

AD abbreviation Anno Domini (Latin = in the year of Our Lord), used in dates counted from the birth of Jesus Christ.

ad- prefix (changing to ac-, af-, ag-, al-, an-, ap-, ar-, as-, at- before certain consonants) to; towards (as in adapt, admit). [from Latin ad = to]

adamant (say ad-am-ant) adjective firm and not giving way to requests.

adapt verb (adapts, adapting, adapted) change something so that it is suitable for a new purpose or situation. **adaptable** adjective, **adaptation** noun [from ad- + Latin aptus = suitable, apt]

adaptor noun (plural **adaptors**) a device to connect pieces of electrical or other equipment.

add verb (adds, adding, added) 1 put one thing with another. 2 make another remark. **add up** 1 make or find a total. 2 (informal) make sense; seem reasonable.

adder noun (plural **adders**) a small poisonous snake. [from Old English; originally called a nadder, which became an adder]

addict noun (plural **addicts**) a person who does or uses something that he or she cannot give up. **addicted** adjective, **addiction** noun [from Latin]

addictive adjective causing people to become addicts, an addictive drug.

addition noun (plural **additions**) 1 the process of adding. 2 something added. **additional** adjective, **additionally** adverb **in addition** also; as an extra thing.

additive noun (plural **additives**) a substance added to another in small amounts for a special purpose, e.g. as a flavouring.

address noun (plural **addresses**) 1 the details of the place where someone lives or of where letters etc. should be delivered to a person or firm. 2 a speech to an audience.

address verb (addresses, addressing, addressed) 1 write an address on a parcel etc. 2 make a speech or remark etc. to somebody.

adenoids plural noun thick spongy flesh at the back of the nose and throat, which may hinder breathing.

adept (say a-dept) adjective very skilful. [from Latin]

adequate adjective enough or good enough. **adequately** adverb, **adequacy** noun [from Latin]

adhere verb (adheres, adhering, adhered) stick to something. **adhesion** noun [from ad- + Latin haerere = to stick]

adhesive adjective sticky; causing things to stick together.

adhesive noun (plural **adhesives**) a substance used to stick things together; glue. [same origin as adhere]

adjacent adjective near or next to, I waited in an adjacent room. [from ad- + Latin jacens = lying]

adjective noun (plural **adjectives**) a word that describes a noun or adds to its meaning, e.g. *big, honest, strange, our.* **adjectival** *adjective,* **adjectivally** *adverb*

adjourn (say a-jern) *verb* (**adjourns, adjourning, adjourned**) **1** break off a meeting etc. until a later time. **2** break off and go somewhere else, *They adjourned to the library.* **adjournment** noun [from Latin, = to another day]

adjudicate (say a-joo-dik-ayt) *verb* (**adjudicates, adjudicating, adjudicated**) act as judge in a competition etc. **adjudication** noun, **adjudicator** noun

adjust *verb* (**adjusts, adjusting, adjusted**) **1** put a thing into its proper position or order. **2** alter something so that it fits or is suitable. **adjustable** *adjective,* **adjustment** noun [from *ad* + Latin *justa* = close to]

ad lib *verb* (**ad libs, ad libbing, ad libbed**) say or do something without any rehearsal or preparation. [from Latin *ad libitum* = according to pleasure]

administer *verb* (**administers, administering, administered**) **1** give or provide something, *He administered medicine.* **2** manage business affairs.

admirable *adjective* worth admiring; excellent. **admirably** *adverb*

admiral noun (plural **admirals**) a naval officer of high rank. [from Arabic *amir* = commander]

admire *verb* (**admires, admiring, admired**) **1** look at something and enjoy it.

2 think that someone or something is very good. **admiration** noun, **admirer** noun [from *ad-* + Latin *mirari* = wonder at]

admission noun (plural **admissions**) **1** admitting. **2** the charge for being allowed to go in. **3** a statement admitting something; a confession.

admit *verb* (**admits, admitting, admitted**) **1** allow someone or something to come in. **2** state reluctantly that something is true; confess, *We admit that the task is difficult. He admitted his crime.*

admittance noun being allowed to go in, especially to a private place.

admonish *verb* (**admonishes, admonishing, admonished**) advise or warn someone firmly but mildly. **admonition** noun

adolescent noun (plural **adolescents**) a young person at the age between being a child and being an adult. **adolescence** noun, **adolescent** *adjective*

adopt *verb* (**adopts, adopting, adopted**) **1** take someone into your family as your own child. **2** accept something; take something and use it, *They adopted new methods of working.* **adoption** noun

adore *verb* (**adores, adoring, adored**) love a person or thing very much. **adorable** *adjective,* **adoration** noun

adorn *verb* (**adorns, adorning, adorned**) decorate. **adornment** noun [from *ad-* + Latin *ornare* = furnish, decorate]

adrenalin (say a-dren-al-in) noun
a hormone that stimulates the
nervous system. [from ad- + renal
(because adrenalin is made by
the adrenal glands, above the
kidneys)]

adrift adjective & adverb drifting.
[from a-¹ + drift]

adulation noun very great
flattery. [from old French]

adult (say ad-ult) noun (plural
adults) a fully grown or mature
person. [from Latin adultus
= grown up]

adultery noun being unfaithful to
your wife or husband by having
sexual intercourse with someone
else. **adulterer** noun, **adulterous**
adjective [from Latin]

advance noun (plural advances)
1 a forward movement; progress.
2 an increase. 3 a loan; payment
made before it is due.
in advance beforehand; ahead.

advance verb (advances,
advancing, advanced)
1 move forward; make progress.
2 lend or pay money ahead of the
proper time, Advance her
a month's salary. **advancement**
noun [from old French]

advantage noun (plural
advantages)
1 something useful or helpful.
2 the next point won after deuce
in tennis. **advantageous** adjective
take advantage of use a person or
thing profitably or unfairly.
to advantage making a good
effect, The painting can be seen to
its best advantage here.
to your advantage profitable or
helpful to you.

Advent noun the period just
before Christmas, when
Christians celebrate the coming
of Christ.

advent noun the arrival of a new
person or thing, the advent of
computers. [from ad- + Latin
ventum = arrived]

adventure noun (plural
adventures)
1 an exciting or dangerous
experience. 2 willingness to take
risks. **adventurer** noun,
adventurous adjective [same
origin as advent]

adverb noun (plural adverbs)
a word that adds to the meaning
of a verb or adjective or another
adverb and tells how, when, or
where something happens, e.g.
gently, soon, and upstairs.
adverbial adjective, **adverbially**
adverb

adversary (say ad-ver-ser-ee)
noun (plural adversaries) an
opponent or enemy.

adverse adjective unfavourable
or harmful, adverse effects.
adversely adverb, **adversity** noun
[from Latin adversus = opposite,
from ad- + versus = turned]

advert noun (plural adverts)
(informal) an advertisement.

advertise verb (advertises,
advertising, advertised)
1 make something publicly
known, advertise a meeting.
2 praise goods etc. in order to
encourage people to buy or use
them. 3 ask or offer by a public
notice, advertise for a secretary.
advertiser noun

advertisement noun (plural
advertisements) a public notice
or announcement, especially one

advertising goods or services in newspapers, on posters, or in broadcasts.

advice noun

1 telling a person what you think he or she should do. **2** a piece of information, *We received advice that the goods had been dispatched.* [originally = opinion, point of view: from *ad-* + Latin *videre* = see]

USAGE: Do not confuse with the verb *advise*.

---

advisable adjective that is the wise thing to do. **advisability** noun

advise verb (**advises**, **advising**, **advised**)

1 give somebody advice; recommend. **2** inform. **adviser** noun, **advisory** adjective

aerial adjective

1 in or from the air. **2** to do with aircraft.

aerial noun (plural **aerials**) a wire or rod etc. for receiving or transmitting radio or television signals.

aero- prefix to do with air or aircraft (as in *aeronautics*). [from Greek *aer* = air]

aerobics plural noun exercises to stimulate breathing and strengthen the heart and lungs. **aerobic** adjective [from *aero-* + Greek *bios* = life]

aerodrome noun (plural **aerodromes**) an airfield. [from *aero-* + Greek *dromos* = running-track]

aerodynamic adjective designed to move through the air quickly and easily.

aeronautics noun the study of aircraft and flying. **aeronautic** adjective, **aeronautical** adjective

aeroplane noun (plural **aeroplanes**) a flying machine with wings.

aerosol noun (plural **aerosols**) a container that holds a liquid under pressure and can let it out in a fine spray. [from *aero-* + *solution*]

aesthetic (say iss-thet-ik) adjective to do with the appreciation of beautiful things. [from Greek *aisthesthai* = perceive]

af- prefix to; towards. see *ad-*.

afar adverb far away, *In the dim was heard from afar.* [from *a-¹* + *far*]

affair noun (plural **affairs**)

1 an event or matter, *The party was a grand affair.* **2** a temporary sexual relationship between two people who are not married to each other. [from French *à faire* = to do]

affairs plural noun the business and activities that are part of private or public life, *Keep out of my affairs*; *current affairs*.

affect verb (**affects**, **affecting**, **affected**)

1 have an effect on; influence.

2 pretend, *She affected ignorance.* [from *af-* + Latin *facere* = do]

USAGE: The word *affect* is a verb. Do not confuse it with the noun *effect*.

---

affectation noun (plural **affectations**) a pretence; behaviour that is put on for show and not natural.

affected adjective pretended and unnatural.

affection noun (plural **affections**) a strong liking for a person.

affectionate adjective showing affection; loving. **affectionately** adverb [from Latin affectionatus = devoted]

affirm verb (**affirms**, **affirming**, **affirmed**) state something definitely or firmly. **affirmation** noun

affirmative adjective that says 'yes', an affirmative reply. (Compare negative.)

afflict verb (**afflicts**, **afflicting**, **afflicted**) cause somebody to suffer, He is afflicted with arthritis. **affliction** noun

affluent (say af-loo-ent) adjective rich. **affluence** noun [from Latin affluens = overflowing, from af- + fluens = flowing]

afford verb (**affords**, **affording**, **afforded**)
1 have enough money to pay for something. **2** have enough time or resources etc. to do something.

affront verb (**affronts**, **affronting**, **affronted**) insult or offend someone.

affront noun (plural **affronts**) an insult.

afloat adjective & adverb floating; on the sea. [from a-¹ + float]

afraid adjective frightened or alarmed.
I'm afraid I regret, I'm afraid I'm late.
[past participle of an old word affray = attack, frighten]

afresh adverb again; in a new way, We must start afresh. [from a-¹ + fresh]

African adjective to do with Africa or its people.

African noun (plural **Africans**) an African person.

aft adverb at or towards the back of a ship or aircraft. [from Old English, related to after]

after preposition
1 later than, Come after tea.
2 behind in place or order, Which letter comes after H? **3** trying to catch; pursuing, Run after him. **4** in spite of, We can come after all. **5** in imitation or honour of, She is named after her aunt. **6** about or concerning, He asked after you.

after adverb
1 behind, Jill came tumbling after. **2** later, It came a week after. [from Old English]

afternoon noun (plural **afternoons**) the time from noon or lunchtime to evening.

aftershave noun a pleasant-smelling lotion that men put on their skin after shaving.

afterwards adverb at a later time. [from after + -wards]

ag- prefix to; towards. see ad-.

again adverb
1 another time; once more, try again. **2** as before, You will soon be well again. **3** besides; moreover. [from Old English ongean = in the opposite direction, back to the beginning]

against preposition
1 touching or hitting, He leant against the wall. **2** in opposition to; not in favour of, They voted against the proposal. **3** in preparation for, Protect them against the cold. [from again]

age noun (plural **ages**)
1 the length of time a person has lived or a thing has existed. **2** a special period of history or geology, the ice age.

ages plural noun (informal)
a very long time, We've been waiting for ages.

come of age reach the age at which you have an adult's legal rights and obligations (now at 18 years; formerly 21).

age verb (**ages**, **ageing**, **aged**)
make or become old. [from old French]

aged adjective
1 (say ayjd) having the age of, a girl aged 9. **2** (say ay-jid) very old, an aged man.

agency noun (plural **agencies**)
1 the office or business of an agent, a travel agency. **2** the means by which something is done, Flowers are pollinated by the agency of bees. [same origin as agent]

agenda (say a-jen-da) noun (plural **agendas**) a list of things to be done or discussed, The agenda is rather long. [Latin, = things to be done]

agent noun (plural **agents**)
1 a person who organizes things for other people. **2** a spy, a secret agent. [from Latin agens = doing things]

aggravate verb (**aggravates**, **aggravating**, **aggravated**)
1 make a thing worse or more serious. **2** annoy. **aggravation** noun

aggregate noun (plural **aggregates**) a total amount or score.

aggression noun starting an attack or war etc.; aggressive behaviour. [from Latin aggredi = attack, from ag- = against + gradi = step, move]

aggressive adjective likely to attack people; forceful. **aggressively** adverb, **aggressiveness** noun, **aggressor** noun

aggrieved (say a-greevd) adjective resentful because of being treated unfairly.

aghast adjective horrified. [from Old English]

agile adjective moving quickly or easily. **agilely** adverb, **agility** noun [from Latin agere = do]

agitate verb (**agitates**, **agitating**, **agitated**)
1 make someone feel upset or anxious. **2** stir up public interest or concern; campaign, They agitated for a new bypass. **3** shake something about. **agitation** noun, **agitator** noun [from Latin agitare = shake]

agnostic (say ag-nost-ik) noun (plural **agnostics**) a person who believes that it is impossible to know whether God exists. **agnosticism** noun [from a-² + Greek gnostikos = knowing]

ago adverb in the past, long ago. [from Middle English agone = gone by]

agog adjective eager and excited.

agony noun (plural **agonies**) extremely great pain or suffering. **agonizing** adjective

agree verb (**agrees**, **agreeing**, **agreed**)
1 think or say the same as another person etc. **2** consent, She agreed to come.

3 suit a person's health or digestion, *Curry doesn't agree with me.* **4** correspond in grammatical number, gender, or person. In 'They were good teachers', *they* agrees with *teachers* (both are plural forms) and *were* agrees with *they*; *was* would be incorrect because it is singular. [from old French]

agreeable *adjective*
1 willing, *We shall go if you are agreeable.* **2** pleasant, *an agreeable place.* **agreeably** *adverb*

agreement *noun* (plural **agreements**)
1 agreeing. **2** an arrangement that people have agreed on.

agriculture *noun* cultivating land on a large scale and rearing livestock; farming. **agricultural** *adjective*

aground *adverb & adjective* stranded on the bottom in shallow water.

ahead *adverb*
1 further forward; in front. **2** forwards, *Full steam ahead!* [from *a-¹* + *head*]

aid *noun* (plural **aids**)
1 help. **2** something that helps, *a hearing aid.* **3** money, food, etc. sent to another country to help it, *overseas aid.*
in aid of for the purpose of; to help something.

aid *verb* (**aids, aiding, aided**) help. [from old French]

Aids *noun* a disease that greatly weakens a person's ability to resist infections. [from the initial letters of 'acquired immune deficiency syndrome']

ailing *adjective*
1 ill; in poor health.
2 in difficulties; not successful, *the ailing ship industry.*

ailment *noun* (plural **ailments**) a slight illness.

aim *verb* (**aims, aiming, aimed**)
1 point a gun etc. **2** throw or kick in a particular direction. **3** try or intend to do something.

aim *noun* (plural **aims**)
1 aiming a gun etc. **2** a purpose or intention. [via old French *amer* from Latin *aestimare* = estimate]

aimless *adjective* without a purpose. **aimlessly** *adverb*

air *noun* (plural **airs**)
1 the mixture of gases that surrounds the earth and which everyone breathes. **2** the open space above the earth. **3** a tune or melody. **4** an appearance or impression of something, *an air of mystery.* **5** an impressive or haughty manner, *He puts on airs.*
by air in or by aircraft.
on the air on radio or television.

air *verb* (**airs, airing, aired**)
1 put clothes etc. in a warm place to finish drying. **2** ventilate a room. **3** express, *He aired his opinions.* [from old French]

air-conditioning *noun* a system for controlling the temperature, purity, etc. of the air in a room or building. **air-conditioned** *adjective*

aircraft *noun* (plural **aircraft**) an aeroplane, glider, or helicopter etc.

aircraft carrier *noun* (plural **aircraft carriers**) a large ship with a long deck where aircraft can take off and land.

airfield noun (plural **airfields**) an area equipped with runways etc. where aircraft can take off and land.

air force noun (plural **air forces**) the part of a country's armed forces that is equipped with aircraft.

airline noun (plural **airlines**) a company that provides a regular service of transport by aircraft.

airliner noun (plural **airliners**) a large aircraft for carrying passengers.

airlock noun (plural **airlocks**) **1** a compartment with an airtight door at each end, through which people can go in and out of a pressurized chamber. **2** a bubble of air that stops liquid flowing through a pipe.

airmail noun mail carried by air.

airman noun (plural **airmen**) a man who is a member of an air force or of the crew of an aircraft.

airport noun (plural **airports**) an airfield for aircraft carrying passengers and goods.

air raid noun (plural **air raids**) an attack by aircraft.

airstrip noun (plural **airstrips**) a strip of ground prepared for aircraft to land and take off.

airtight adjective not letting air in or out.

airy adjective **1** with plenty of fresh air. **2** light as air. **3** light-hearted and insincere, airy promises. **airily** adverb

aisle (say I'll) noun (plural **aisles**) **1** a passage between or beside rows of seats or pews. **2** a side part of a church.

ajar adverb & adjective slightly open, Leave the door ajar. [literally = turned: from a-¹ + Old English cerr = a turn]

akin adjective related or similar to, a feeling akin to regret. [from Old English a = of, + kin]

al- prefix to; towards. see ad-.

alarm noun (plural **alarms**) **1** a warning sound or signal; a piece of equipment for giving this. **2** a feeling of fear or worry. **3** an alarm clock.

alarm verb (**alarms, alarming, alarmed**) make someone frightened or anxious. **alarming** adjective [from Italian all' arme! = to arms!: compare this with alert]

alarm clock noun (plural **alarm clocks**) a clock that can be set to make a sound at a fixed time to wake a sleeping person.

alas interjection an exclamation of sorrow.

albatross noun (plural **albatrosses**) a large seabird with very long wings.

albino (say al-been-oh) noun (plural **albinos**) a person or animal with no colour in the skin and hair (which are white).

album noun (plural **albums**) **1** a book with blank pages in which to keep a collection of photographs, stamps, autographs, etc. **2** a collection of songs on a CD, record, or tape. [Latin, = white piece of stone etc. on which to write things]

alcohol noun **1** a colourless liquid made by fermenting sugar or starch. **2** drinks containing this liquid (e.g. wine, beer, whisky), that can make people drunk. [from Arabic]

alcoholic *adjective* containing alcohol.

alcoholic *noun* (*plural* **alcoholics**) a person who is seriously addicted to alcohol. **alcoholism** *noun*

ale *noun* (*plural* **ales**) beer. [from Old English]

alert *adjective* watching for something; ready to act. **alertly** *adverb*, **alertness** *noun*

alert *noun* (*plural* **alerts**) a warning or alarm.
on the alert on the lookout; watchful.

alert *verb* (**alerts**, **alerting**, **alerted**) warn someone of danger etc.; make someone aware of something. [from Italian *all'erta*! = to the watchtower!: compare this with *alarm*]

A level *noun* (*plural* **A levels**) advanced level in GCSE.

algae (*say* al-jee) *plural noun* plants that grow in water, with no true stems or leaves. [Latin, = seaweed]

algebra (*say* al-jib-ra) *noun* mathematics in which letters and symbols are used to represent quantities. **algebraic** (*say* al-jib-ray-ik) *adjective* [from Arabic *al-jabr* = putting together broken parts]

alias (*say* ay-lee-as) *noun* (*plural* **aliases**) a false or different name.

alias *adverb* also named, *Clark Kent, alias Superman.*

alibi (*say* al-ib-I) *noun* (*plural* **alibis**) evidence that a person accused of a crime was

somewhere else when it was committed. [Latin, = at another place]

alien (*say* ay-lee-en) *noun* (*plural* **aliens**)
1 a person who is not a citizen of the country where he or she is living; a foreigner. **2** a being from another world.

alien *adjective*
1 foreign. **2** unnatural, *Cruelty is alien to his nature.* [from Latin *alius* = other]

alienate (*say* ay-lee-en-ayt) *verb* (**alienates**, **alienating**, **alienated**) make a person become unfriendly or hostile. **alienation** *noun*

alight *adjective*
1 on fire. **2** lit up. [from *a-*¹ + *light*¹]

alike *adjective* & *adverb* like one another; in the same way, *The twins are very alike. Treat them alike.*

alimony *noun* money paid by someone to his or her wife or husband after they are separated or divorced; maintenance. [from Latin *alimonia* = nourishment]

alive *adjective*
1 living. **2** alert, *Be alive to the possible dangers.* [from Old English *on life* = in life]

alkali (*say* alk-al-I) *noun* (*plural* **alkalis**) a substance that neutralizes acids. **alkaline** *adjective* [from Arabic *al-kali* = the ashes (because alkali was first obtained from the ashes of seaweed)]

all *adjective* the whole number or amount of, *All my books are here; all day.*

all noun
1 everything, *That is all I know.*
2 everybody, *All are agreed.*

all adverb
1 completely, *She was dressed all in white.* 2 to each team or competitor, *The score is fifteen all.*
all in (*informal*) exhausted, *I'm all in.*
all-in adjective including or allowing everything, *an all-in price.*
all there (*informal*) having an alert mind.
all the same in spite of this; making no difference, *I like him, all the same.*

Allah noun the Muslim name of God.

allegation (say al-ig-ay-shon) noun (plural **allegations**)
a statement made without proof.

allege (say a-lej) verb (**alleges, alleging, alleged**) say something without being able to prove it, *He alleged that I had cheated.*
allegedly (say a-lej-id-lee) adverb [from old French]

allegiance (say a-lee-jans) noun (plural **allegiances**) loyalty. [from old French; related to *liege*]

allegory (say al-ig-er-ee) noun (plural **allegories**) a story in which the characters and events represent or symbolize a deeper meaning, e.g. to teach a moral lesson. **allegorical** (say al-ig-o-rik-al) adjective

alleluia interjection praise to God. [from Hebrew]

allergic adjective very sensitive to something that may make you ill, *He is allergic to pollen, which gives him hay fever.* **allergy** (say al-er-jee) noun

alley noun (plural **alleys**)
1 a narrow street or passage.
2 a place where you can play bowls or skittles. [from French *aller* = go]

alliance (say a-leye-ans) noun (plural **alliances**) an association formed by countries or groups who wish to support each other.

allied adjective
1 joined as allies; on the same side. 2 of the same kind.

alligator noun (plural **alligators**) a large reptile of the crocodile family. [from Spanish *el lagarto* = the lizard]

alliteration noun having the same letter or sound at the beginning of several words, e.g. in *Sit in solemn silence.* [from *al-* + Latin *littera* = letter]

allotment noun (plural **allotments**)
1 a small rented piece of public land used for growing vegetables, fruit, or flowers. 2 allotting; the amount allotted.

allow verb (**allows, allowing, allowed**)
1 permit, *Smoking is not allowed.*
2 permit someone to have something; provide with, *She was allowed £10 for books.* 3 agree, *I allow that you have been patient.*
allowable adjective [from old French]

allowance noun (plural **allowances**) an amount of money that is given regularly for a particular purpose.
make allowances be considerate; excuse, *Make allowances for his age.*

alloy noun (plural **alloys**) a metal formed by mixing two or more metals etc.

all right adjective & adverb
1 satisfactory. 2 in good condition. 3 as desired. 4 yes, I consent.

all-round adjective general; not specialist, an all-round athlete.
all-rounder noun

allure verb (**allures, alluring, allured**) attract or fascinate someone. **allure** noun, **alluring** adjective [from old French; related to lure]

ally (say al-eye) noun (plural **allies**)
1 a country in alliance with another. 2 a person who cooperates with another.

ally verb (**allies, allying, allied**) form an alliance. [from al- + Latin ligare = bind]

almighty adjective
1 having complete power.
2 (informal) very great, an almighty din.

almond (say ah-mond) noun (plural **almonds**) an oval edible nut. [from Greek]

almost adverb near to being something but not quite, almost ready. [from Old English]

alone adjective without any other people or things; without help. [from all one]

along preposition following the length of something, Walk along the path.

along adverb
1 on or onwards, Push it along.
2 accompanying somebody, I've brought my brother along. [from Old English]

alongside preposition & adverb next to something; beside.

aloof adverb apart; not taking part, We stayed aloof from their quarrels.

aloof adjective distant and not friendly in manner, She seemed aloof.

aloud adverb in a voice that can be heard. [from a-¹ + loud]

alpha noun the first letter of the Greek alphabet, = a.

alphabet noun (plural **alphabets**) the letters used in a language, usually arranged in a set order.
alphabetical adjective,
alphabetically adverb [from alpha, beta, the first two letters of the Greek alphabet]

already adverb by now; before now. [from all + ready]

Alsatian (say al-say-shan) noun (plural **Alsatians**) a German shepherd dog. [from Alsace, in north-eastern France: the name was adopted during the First World War, when British people disliked anything that was German]

also adverb in addition; besides.

altar noun (plural **altars**) a table or similar structure used in religious ceremonies.

USAGE: Do not confuse with the verb alter.

alter verb (**alters, altering, altered**) make or become different; change. **alteration** noun

USAGE: Do not confuse with the noun altar.

alternate (*say* ol-**tern**-at) *adjective*
1 happening or coming one after
the other, *alternate layers of
sponge and cream.* **2** one in every
two, *We meet up on alternate
Fridays.* **alternately** *adverb*

USAGE: See the note at
alternative.

alternate (*say* ol-**tern**-ayt) *verb*
(**alternates, alternating,
alternated**) use or come
alternately. **alternation** *noun,*
alternator *noun* [from Latin
alternus = every other one, from
alter = other]

alternating current *noun*
(*plural* **alternating currents**)
electric current that keeps
reversing its direction at regular
intervals.

alternative *adjective* available
instead of something else.
alternatively *adverb*

USAGE: Do not confuse
alternative with *alternate.* If
there are *alternative colours* it
means that there is a choice of
two or more colours, but
alternate colours means that
there is first one colour and
then the other.

alternative *noun* (*plural*
alternatives) one of two or more
possibilities.
no alternative no choice.

alternative medicine *noun*
types of medical treatment that
are not based on ordinary
medicine.

although *conjunction* though.
[from *all* + *though*]

altitude *noun* (*plural* **altitudes**)
the height of something,
especially above sea level. [from
Latin *altus* = high]

alto *noun* (*plural* **altos**)
1 an adult male singer with a very
high voice. **2** a contralto. [Italian,
= high]

altogether *adverb*
1 with all included; in total, *The
outfit costs £20 altogether.*
2 completely, *The stream dries up
altogether in summer.* **3** on the
whole, *Altogether, it was a good
concert.*

USAGE: Do not confuse
altogether and *all together.*

aluminium *noun* a lightweight
silver-coloured metal.

always *adverb*
1 at all times. **2** often, *You are
always crying.* **3** whatever
happens, *You can always sleep on
the floor.*

Alzheimer's disease *noun*
a serious disease of the brain
which affects some old people
and makes them confused and
forgetful.

a.m. *abbreviation* ante meridiem
[Latin, = before noon]

amalgamate *verb* (**amalgamates,
amalgamating, amalgamated**)
mix or combine. **amalgamation**
noun [from Latin]

amateur (*say* **am**-at-er) *noun*
(*plural* **amateurs**) a person who
does something as a hobby, not
as a professional. **amateurish**
adjective [from Latin *amator*
= lover]

amaze verb (amazes, amazing, amazed) surprise somebody greatly; fill with wonder. **amazement** noun

amazing adjective very surprising or remarkable.

ambassador noun (plural **ambassadors**) a person sent to a foreign country to represent his or her own government. [from old French; related to embassy]

amber noun
1 a hard clear yellowish substance used for making ornaments. 2 a yellow traffic light shown as a signal for caution, placed between red (= stop) and green (= go).

ambi- prefix both; on both sides (as in ambidextrous). [from Latin ambo = both]

ambidextrous adjective able to use either your left hand or your right hand equally well. [from ambi- + dextrous = skilful (related to dexterity)]

ambiguous adjective having more than one possible meaning; unclear. **ambiguously** adverb, **ambiguity** noun [from Latin ambiguus = doubtful, shifting, from ambi- + agere = drive, go]

ambition noun (plural **ambitions**)
1 a strong desire to achieve something. 2 the thing desired. [from Latin ambire = go around, especially to persuade people to vote for you]

ambitious adjective full of ambition.

ambivalent (say am-biv-al-ent) adjective having mixed feelings about something (e.g. liking and disliking it). **ambivalence** noun [from ambi- + Latin valens = strong]

amble verb (ambles, ambling, ambled) walk at a slow easy pace.

ambulance noun (plural **ambulances**) a vehicle equipped to carry sick or injured people. [from French hôpital ambulant, a mobile military hospital; from Latin ambulare = walk]

ambush noun (plural **ambushes**) a surprise attack from troops etc. who have concealed themselves.

ambush verb (ambushes, ambushing, ambushed) attack someone after lying in wait for them. [from old French]

amen interjection a word used at the end of a prayer or hymn, meaning 'may it be so'. [Hebrew, = certainly]

amend verb (amends, amending, amended) alter something in order to improve it. **amendment** noun

make amends make up for having done something wrong; atone.

American adjective
1 to do with the continent of America. 2 to do with the United States of America. **American** noun

amino acid (say a-meen-oh) noun (plural **amino acids**) an acid found in proteins. [from ammonia, because the amino acids contain the same group of atoms as ammonia]

amiss adjective wrong or faulty, She knew something was amiss.

ammonia noun a colourless gas or liquid with a strong smell. [from Latin]

ammunition noun a supply of bullets, shells, grenades, etc. for use in fighting. [from French *la munition*, wrongly taken as *l'ammunition*]

amnesia (say am-**nee**-zee-a) noun loss of memory. [from Greek *a-* = without + *-mnesis* = memory]

amnesty noun (plural **amnesties**) a general pardon for people who have committed a crime.

amoeba (say a-**mee**-ba) noun (plural **amoebas**) a microscopic creature consisting of a single cell which constantly changes shape. [from Greek *amoibe* = change]

among or **amongst** preposition
1 surrounded by; in, *There were weeds among the flowers.*
2 between, *Divide the sweets among the children.*

amount noun (plural **amounts**)
1 a quantity. 2 a total.

amount verb (amounts, amounting, amounted)
amount to 1 add up to. 2 be equivalent to, *Their reply amounts to a refusal.*
[from Latin *ad montem* = to the mountain, upwards]

amp noun (plural **amps**)
1 an ampere. 2 (*informal*) an amplifier.

ampere (say am-pair) noun (plural **amperes**) a unit for measuring electric current.

amphi- prefix both; on both sides; in both places (as in *amphibian*). [from Greek *amphi* = around]

amphibian noun (plural **amphibians**)
1 an amphibious animal; an animal (e.g. a frog) that at first (as a tadpole) has gills and lives

in water but later develops lungs and breathes air. 2 an amphibious aircraft or tank etc. [from *amphi-* + Greek *bios* = life]

amphibious adjective able to live or move both on land and in water.

ample adjective
1 quite enough, *ample provisions.* 2 large. **amply** adverb [from Latin *amplus* = large, plentiful]

amplifier noun (plural **amplifiers**) a piece of equipment for making a sound or electrical signal louder or stronger.

amplify verb (amplifies, amplifying, amplified)
1 make a sound or electrical signal louder or stronger. 2 give more details about something, *Could you amplify that point?*

amplitude noun
1 the strength of a sound wave or electronic signal. 2 largeness or abundance.

amputate verb (amputates, amputating, amputated) cut off an arm or leg by a surgical operation. **amputation** noun [from Latin *amb-* = around + *putare* = cut off, prune]

amuse verb (amuses, amusing, amused)
1 make a person laugh or smile. 2 make time pass pleasantly for someone. **amusing** adjective

amusement noun (plural **amusements**)
1 being amused. 2 a way of passing time pleasantly.

an adjective see **a**.

an-¹ prefix not; without. see **a-**².

an-² prefix to; towards. see **ad-**.

ana- prefix up; back (as in *analysis*). [Greek, = up]

anachronism (*say* an-**ak**-ron-izm) *noun* (*plural* **anachronisms**) something wrongly placed in a particular historical period, or regarded as out of date, *Bows and arrows would be an anachronism in modern warfare.* [from *ana-* + Greek *chronos* = time]

anaemia (*say* a-**nee**-mee-a) *noun* a poor condition of the blood that makes a person pale. **anaemic** *adjective* [from *an-*[1] + Greek *haima* = blood]

anaesthetic (*say* an-iss-**thet**-ik) *noun* (*plural* **anaesthetics**) a substance or gas that makes you unable to feel pain. **anaesthesia** *noun* [from *an-*[1] + Greek *aisthesis* = sensation]

anaesthetist (*say* an-**ees**-thet-ist) *noun* (*plural* **anaesthetists**) a person trained to give anaesthetics. **anaesthetize** *verb*

anagram *noun* (*plural* **anagrams**) a word or phrase made by rearranging the letters of another, '*Trap*' is an anagram of '*part*'.

anal (*say* **ay**-nal) *adjective* to do with the anus.

analogy (*say* a-**nal**-oj-ee) *noun* (*plural* **analogies**) comparing two things that are alike in some ways, *the analogy between the human heart and a pump.* **analogous** *adjective*

analyse *verb* (**analyses, analysing, analysed**) **1** separate something into its parts. **2** examine and interpret something, *analyse the causes.*

analysis *noun* (*plural* **analyses**) **1** a separation of something into its parts. **2** a detailed examination of something.

analytic *adjective*, **analytical** *adjective* [from Greek, = dissolving, loosening]

anarchist (*say* an-er-kist) *noun* (*plural* **anarchists**) a person who believes that all forms of government are bad and should be abolished.

anarchy (*say* an-er-kee) *noun* **1** lack of government or control, resulting in lawlessness. **2** complete disorder. [from *an-*[1] + *-archy*]

anatomy (*say* an-at-om-ee) *noun* the study of the structure of the bodies of humans or animals. **anatomical** *adjective*, **anatomist** *noun* [from *ana-* + Greek *tome* = cutting]

ancestor *noun* (*plural* **ancestors**) anyone from whom a person is descended. **ancestral** *adjective*, **ancestry** *noun* [from Latin, literally = one who goes before]

anchor *noun* (*plural* **anchors**) a heavy object joined to a ship by a chain or rope and dropped to the bottom of the sea to stop the ship from moving.

anchor *verb* (**anchors, anchoring, anchored**) **1** fix or be fixed by an anchor. **2** fix something firmly. [from Latin]

ancient *adjective* **1** very old. **2** belonging to the distant past, *ancient history.* [from old French]

and *conjunction* **1** together with; in addition to, *We had cakes and buns.* **2** so that; with this result, *Work hard and you will pass.* **3** to, *Go and buy a pen.* [from Old English]

anecdote noun (plural **anecdotes**) a short amusing or interesting story about a real person or thing. [from Greek *anekdota* = things that have not been published]

angel noun (plural **angels**)
1 an attendant or messenger of God. 2 a very kind or beautiful person. **angelic** (say an-jel-ik) adjective [from Greek *angelos* = messenger]

anger noun a strong feeling that makes you want to quarrel or fight.

anger verb (**angers, angering, angered**) make a person angry. [from Old Norse]

angle noun (plural **angles**)
1 the space between two lines or surfaces that meet; the amount by which a line or surface must be turned to make it lie along another. 2 a point of view.

angle verb (**angles, angling, angled**)
1 put something in a slanting position. 2 present news etc. from one point of view. [from Latin *angulus* = corner]

angler noun (plural **anglers**) a person who fishes with a fishing rod and line. **angling** [from Old English *angul* = fishing-hook]

Anglican adjective to do with the Church of England. **Anglican** noun

Anglo-Saxon noun (plural **Anglo-Saxons**)
1 an English person, especially of the time before the Norman conquest in 1066. 2 'Old English'. [from Old English *Angulseaxe*]

= an English Saxon (contrasted with the Old Saxons on the Continent)

angry adjective (**angrier, angriest**) feeling anger. **angrily** adverb

angular adjective
1 having angles or sharp corners. 2 (of a person) bony, not plump.

animal noun (plural **animals**)
1 a living thing that can feel and usually move about. *Horses, birds, fish, bees, and people are all animals.* 2 a brutish person; someone not worthy of being called human.

animate verb (**animates, animating, animated**)
1 make a thing lively. 2 produce something as an animated cartoon. **animation** noun, **animator** noun

ankle noun (plural **ankles**) the part of the leg where it joins the foot.

annihilate (say an-I-il-ayt) verb (**annihilates, annihilating, annihilated**) destroy something completely. **annihilation** noun [from *an-*² + Latin *nihil* = nothing]

anniversary noun (plural **anniversaries**) a day when you remember something special that happened on the same day in a previous year.

announce verb (**announces, announcing, announced**) make something known, especially by saying it publicly or to an audience. **announcement** noun, **announcer** noun [from *an-*² + Latin *nuntius* = messenger]

annoy verb (**annoys, annoying, annoyed**)
1 make a person slightly angry.

2 be troublesome to someone.

annoyance *noun* [from Latin *in odio* = hateful]

annual *adjective*
1 happening or done once a year, *her annual visit.* **2** calculated over one year, *our annual income.* **3** living for one year or one season, *an annual plant.* **annually** *adverb*

annual *noun* (*plural* **annuals**)
1 a book that comes out once a year. **2** an annual plant. [from Latin *annus* = year]

anode *noun* (*plural* **anodes**) the electrode by which electric current enters a device. (Compare *cathode.*) [from *ana-* = up + Greek *hodos* = way]

anoint *verb* (**anoints**, **anointing**, **anointed**) put oil or ointment on something, especially in a religious ceremony.

anon *adverb* (*old use*) soon, *I will say more about this anon.* [from Old English *on ane* = in one, at once]

anon. *abbreviation* anonymous.

anonymous (*say* an-**on**-im-us) *adjective* without the name of the person responsible being known or made public, *an anonymous donor.* **anonymously** *adverb*. **anonymity** (*say* an-on-**im**-it-ee) *noun* [from *an-*[1] + Greek *onyma* = name]

anorak *noun* (*plural* **anoraks**) a thick warm jacket with a hood. [from an Inuit word]

anorexia (*say* an-er-**eks**-ee-a) *noun* an illness that makes a person so anxious to lose weight that he or she refuses to eat. **anorexic** *adjective*

another *adjective & pronoun* a different or extra person or thing, *another day; choose another.*

answer *noun* (*plural* **answers**)
1 a reply. **2** the solution to a problem.

answer *verb* (**answers**, **answering**, **answered**)
1 give or find an answer to; reply. **2** respond to a signal, *Answer the telephone.*

answer back reply cheekily.

answer for be responsible for.

answer to correspond to, *This answers to the description of the stolen bag.*

ant *noun* (*plural* **ants**) a very small insect that lives as one of an organized group. [from Old English]

ant- *prefix* against; preventing. see **anti-**.

antagonism (*say* an-**tag**-on-izm) *noun* an unfriendly feeling; hostility. **antagonist** *noun*, **antagonistic** *adjective*

antagonize *verb* (**antagonizes**, **antagonizing**, **antagonized**) make a person feel hostile or angry.

ante- *prefix* before (as in *anteroom*). [from Latin]

antelope *noun* (*plural* **antelope** or **antelopes**) an animal like a deer. [from Greek]

antenatal (*say* an-tee-**nay**-tal) *adjective* before birth; during pregnancy.

antenna *noun*
1 (*plural* **antennae**) a feeler on the head of an insect or crustacean. **2** (*plural* **antennas**) an aerial. [Latin]

anthem noun (plural **anthems**)
a religious or patriotic song,
usually sung by a choir or group
of people. [from Latin]

anthology noun (plural
anthologies) a collection of
poems, stories, songs, etc. in one
book. [from Greek anthos
= flower + -logia = collection]

anthropoid adjective like
a human being, Gorillas are
anthropoid apes. [from Greek
anthropos = human being]

anthropology noun the study of
human beings and their customs.
anthropological adjective,
anthropologist noun

anti- prefix (changing to **anti-**
before a vowel) against;
preventing (as in antifreeze).
[from Greek anti = against]

antibiotic noun (plural
antibiotics) a substance (e.g.
penicillin) that destroys bacteria
or prevents them from growing.

antibody noun (plural
antibodies) a protein that forms
in the blood as a defence against
certain substances which it then
attacks and destroys. [from anti-
+ body (sense 5)]

anticipate verb (anticipates,
anticipating, anticipated)
1 do something before the proper
time or before someone else,
Others may have anticipated
Columbus in discovering America.
2 foresee, They had anticipated
our needs. **3** expect, We anticipate
that it will rain. **anticipation**
noun, **anticipatory** adjective [from
ante- + Latin capere = take]

USAGE: Many people regard
use **3** as incorrect; it is better
to avoid it and use 'expect'.

anticlimax noun (plural
anticlimaxes) a disappointing
ending or result where
something exciting had been
expected.

anticlockwise adverb & adjective
moving in the direction opposite
to clockwise.

antics plural noun funny or
foolish actions.

anticyclone noun (plural
anticyclones) an area where air
pressure is high, usually
producing fine settled weather.
[from anti- + cyclone, because the
pressure at the centre of a cyclone
is low]

antidote noun (plural **antidotes**)
something that acts against the
effects of a poison or disease.
[from anti- + Greek dotos = given]

antifreeze noun a liquid added to
water to make it less likely to
freeze.

antihistamine noun (plural
antihistamines) a drug that
protects people against
unpleasant effects when they are
allergic to something.

antimony noun a brittle silvery
metal. [from Latin]

antiquarian (say anti-kwair-ee-
an) adjective to do with the study
of antiques.

antiquated adjective old-
fashioned.

antique (say an-teek) adjective
very old; belonging to the distant
past.

antique noun (plural **antiques**)
something that is valuable
because it is very old. [from Latin
antiquus = ancient, from ante
= before]

antiquity (*say* an-tik-wit-ee) *noun* ancient times.

anti-Semitic (*say* anti-sim-it-ik) *adjective* unfriendly or hostile towards Jews. **anti-Semitism** (*say* anti-sem-it-izm) *noun*

antiseptic *adjective*
1 able to destroy bacteria, especially those that cause things to become septic or to decay.
2 thoroughly clean and free from germs.

antiseptic *noun* (*plural* **antiseptics**) a substance with an antiseptic effect.

antisocial *adjective* unfriendly or inconsiderate towards other people.

antler *noun* (*plural* **antlers**) the branching horn of a deer.

anus (*say* ay-nus) *noun* (*plural* **anuses**) the opening at the lower end of the alimentary canal, through which solid waste matter is passed out of the body.

anvil *noun* (*plural* **anvils**) a large block of iron on which a blacksmith hammers metal into shape.

anxious *adjective*
1 worried. 2 eager, *She is anxious to please us.* **anxiously** *adverb*, **anxiety** *noun*

any *adjective & pronoun*
1 one or some, *Have you any wool? There isn't any.* 2 no matter which, *Come any day you like.* 3 every, *Any fool knows that!*

any *adverb* at all; in some degree, *Is that any better?*

anybody *noun & pronoun* any person.

anyhow *adverb*
1 anyway. 2 (*informal*) carelessly, *He does his work anyhow.*

anyone *noun & pronoun* anybody.

anything *noun & pronoun* any thing.

anyway *adverb* whatever happens; whatever the situation may be.

anywhere *adverb* in or to any place.

anywhere *pronoun* any place, *Anywhere will do.*

aorta (*say* ay-or-ta) *noun* (*plural* **aortas**) the main artery that carries blood away from the left side of the heart. [from Greek]

ap-[1] *prefix* to; towards. see **ad-**.

ap-[2] *prefix* from; out or away. see **apo-**.

apart *adverb*
1 away from each other; separately, *Keep your desks apart.* 2 into pieces, *It fell apart.* 3 excluded, *Joking apart, what do you think of it?* [from French *à* = to + *part* = side]

apartheid (*say* a-part-hayt) *noun* the political policy that used to be practised in South Africa, of keeping people of different races apart. [Afrikaans, = being apart]

apartment *noun* (*plural* **apartments**)
1 a set of rooms. 2 (*American*) a flat.

apathy (*say* ap-ath-ee) *noun* lack of interest or concern. **apathetic** (*say* ap-a-thet-ik) *adjective* [from *a-*[2] + Greek *pathos* = feeling]

ape *noun* (*plural* **apes**) any of the four kinds of monkey (gorillas, chimpanzees, orang-utans, gibbons) that do not have a tail.

ape *verb* (**apes**, **aping**, **aped**) imitate or mimic. [from Old English]

aperture *noun* (*plural* **apertures**) an opening. [from Latin *aperire* = to open]

apex (*say* ay-peks) *noun* (*plural* **apexes**) the tip or highest point. [Latin]

aplomb (*say* a-plom) *noun* dignity and confidence, *She handled the press conference with aplomb.* [from French = straight as a plumb line]

apo- *prefix* (changing to **ap-** before a vowel or *h*) from; out or away (as in *Apostle*). [from Greek *apo* = away from]

apologetic *adjective* making an apology. **apologetically** *adverb*

apologize *verb* (**apologizes, apologizing, apologized**) make an apology.

apology *noun* (*plural* **apologies**) **1** a statement saying that you are sorry for having done something wrong or badly. **2** something very poor, *this feeble apology for a meal.*

apoplexy (*say* ap-o-plek-see) *noun* **1** sudden loss of the ability to feel and move, caused by the blocking or breaking of a blood vessel in the brain. **2** (*informal*) rage or anger. **apoplectic** *adjective*

Apostle *noun* (*plural* **Apostles**) any of the twelve men sent out by Christ to preach the Gospel. [from Greek *apostellein* = send out]

apostrophe (*say* a-poss-trof-ee) *noun* (*plural* **apostrophes**) the punctuation mark ' used to show that letters have been missed out (as in *I can't* = I cannot) or to show possession (as in *the boy's book; the boys' books*).

appalling *adjective* shocking; very unpleasant. [from old French *apalir* = become pale]

apparatus *noun* the equipment for a particular experiment or job etc. [from Latin *apparare* = prepare, get ready]

apparent *adjective* **1** clear or obvious, *His embarrassment was apparent to everyone.* **2** seeming; appearing to be true but not really so, *I could not understand her apparent indifference.* **apparently** *adverb* [same origin as *appear*]

apparition *noun* (*plural* **apparitions**) **1** a ghost. **2** something strange or surprising that appears.

appeal *verb* (**appeals, appealing, appealed**) **1** ask for something earnestly or formally, *They appealed for funds.* **2** ask for a decision to be changed, *He appealed against the prison sentence.* **3** seem attractive or interesting, *Cricket doesn't appeal to me.*

appeal *noun* (*plural* **appeals**) **1** the action of appealing for something or about a decision; an earnest or formal request. **2** attraction or interest.

appear *verb* (**appears, appearing, appeared**) **1** come into sight. **2** seem. **3** take part in a play, film, or show etc. [from *ap-*[1] + Latin *parere* = come into]

appearance *noun* (*plural* **appearances**) **1** appearing. **2** what somebody looks like; what something appears to be.

appease *verb* (**appeases, appeasing, appeased**) calm or pacify someone, especially by giving in to demands.
appeasement *noun* [from French *à* = to + *paix* = peace]

appendage *noun* (*plural* **appendages**) something added or attached; a thing that forms a natural part of something larger. [from *ap-*[1] + Latin *pendere* = hang]

appendicitis *noun* inflammation of the appendix.

appendix *noun*
1 (*plural* **appendixes**) a small tube leading off from the intestine. 2 (*plural* **appendices**) a section added at the end of a book. [same origin as *appendage*]

appetite *noun* (*plural* **appetites**)
1 desire for food. 2 an enthusiasm for something, *an appetite for violent films*. [from *ap-*[1] + Latin *petere* = seek]

appetizing *adjective* (of food) looking and smelling good to eat.

applaud *verb* (**applauds, applauding, applauded**) show that you like something, especially by clapping your hands.

applause *noun* clapping.

apple *noun* (*plural* **apples**) a round fruit with a red, yellow, or green skin.

appliance *noun* (*plural* **appliances**) a device or piece of equipment, *electrical appliances*. [from *apply*]

applicable (*say* ap-lik-a-bul) *adjective* able to be applied; suitable or relevant.

applicant *noun* (*plural* **applicants**) a person who applies for a job or position.

application *noun* (*plural* **applications**)
1 the action of applying. 2 a formal request. 3 the ability to apply yourself.

applied *adjective* put to practical use, *applied maths*.

apply *verb* (**applies, applying, applied**)
1 put one thing on another. 2 start using something. 3 concern; be relevant, *This rule does not apply to you.* 4 make a formal request, *apply for a job*.
apply yourself give all your attention to a job; work diligently.
[from *ap-*[1] + Latin *plicare* = to fold]

appoint *verb* (**appoints, appointing, appointed**)
1 choose a person for a job. 2 arrange something officially, *They appointed a time for the meeting.* [from old French]

appointment *noun* (*plural* **appointments**)
1 an arrangement to meet or visit somebody at a particular time. 2 choosing somebody for a job. 3 a job or position.

apposition *noun* placing things together, especially nouns and phrases in a grammatical relationship. In *the reign of Elizabeth, our Queen*, 'our Queen' is in apposition to 'Elizabeth'.

appreciable *adjective* enough to be noticed or felt; perceptible.
appreciably *adverb*

appreciate verb (appreciates, appreciating, appreciated)
1 enjoy or value something.
2 understand. 3 increase in value. **appreciation** noun, **appreciative** adjective

apprehend verb (apprehends, apprehending, apprehended)
1 seize or arrest someone.
2 understand. 3 expect something with fear or worry. [from *ap-*[1] + Latin *prehendere* = to grasp]

apprehension noun
1 fear or worry. 2 understanding.
3 the arrest of a person.

apprehensive adjective anxious or worried.

apprentice noun (plural apprentices) a person who is learning a trade or craft by a legal agreement with an employer. **apprenticeship** noun

apprentice verb (apprentices, apprenticing, apprenticed) place a person as an apprentice. [from French *apprendre* = learn]

approach verb (approaches, approaching, approached)
1 come near. 2 go to someone with a request or offer, *They approached me for help.* 3 set about doing something or tackling a problem.

approach noun (plural approaches)
1 approaching. 2 a way or road.

appropriate (say a-proh-pree-at) adjective suitable. **appropriately** adverb

appropriate (say a-proh-pree-ayt) verb (appropriates, appropriating, appropriated) take something and use it as your own. **appropriation** noun

approval noun approving somebody or something.
on approval received by a customer to examine before deciding to buy.

approve verb (approves, approving, approved) say or think that a person or thing is good or suitable. [from *ap-*[1] + Latin *probus* = good]

approximate (say a-proks-im-at) adjective almost exact or correct but not completely so.
approximately adverb

approximate (say a-proks-im-ayt) verb (approximates, approximating, approximated) make or be almost the same as something. [from *ap-*[1] + Latin *proximus* = very near]

apricot noun (plural apricots) a juicy orange-coloured fruit with a stone in it. [from Spanish or Portuguese]

apron noun (plural aprons)
1 a piece of clothing worn over the front of the body, especially to protect other clothes. 2 a hard-surfaced area on an airfield where aircraft are loaded and unloaded. [originally *a naperon*, from French *nappe* = tablecloth]

apt adjective
1 likely, *He is apt to be careless.*
2 suitable, *an apt quotation.* **aptly** adverb, **aptness** noun

aptitude noun a talent or skill, *an aptitude for languages.*

aquarium noun (plural aquariums) a tank or building in which live fish and other water animals are displayed. [from Latin *aquarius* = of water]

aquatic adjective to do with water, *aquatic sports.*

aqueduct noun (plural **aqueducts**) a bridge carrying a water-channel across low ground or a valley. [from Latin *aqua* = water + *ducere* = to lead]

ar- prefix to; towards. see **ad-**.

Arab noun (plural **Arabs**) a member of a people living in Arabia and other parts of the Middle East and North Africa. **Arabian** adjective

Arabic adjective to do with the Arabs or their language. **Arabic** noun the language of the Arabs.

arabic numerals plural noun the symbols 1, 2, 3, 4, etc. (Compare *Roman numerals*.)

arable adjective suitable for ploughing or growing crops on, *arable land*. [from Latin *arare* = to plough]

arbitrary (say ar-bit-rer-ee) adjective chosen or done on an impulse, not according to a rule or law, *an arbitrary decision*. **arbitrarily** adverb [originally = according to a judge's decision, not according to rules]

arbitration noun settling a dispute by calling in someone from outside to make a decision. **arbitrate** verb, **arbitrator** noun [from Latin *arbitrari* = to judge]

arbour (say ar-ber) noun (plural **arbours**) a shady place among trees.

arc noun (plural **arcs**)
1 a curve; part of the circumference of a circle.
2 a luminous electric current passing between two electrodes.

arcade noun (plural **arcades**) a covered passage or area, especially for shopping. [French or Italian, from Latin *arcus* = curve (because early arcades had curved roofs)]

arch[1] noun (plural **arches**)
1 a curved structure that helps to support a bridge or other building etc. 2 something shaped like this.

arch verb (**arches**, **arching**, **arched**) form something into an arch; curve, *The cat arched its back and hissed*.

arch[2] adjective pretending to be playful; mischievous, *an arch smile*. **archly** adverb [from Greek *archos* = a chief]

arch- prefix chief or principal (as in *arch-enemy*).

-arch and **-archy** suffixes form nouns meaning 'ruler' or 'rule, ruling' (e.g. *monarch*, *monarchy*). [from Greek *archein* = to rule]

archaeology (say ar-kee-ol-oj-ee) noun the study of the remains of ancient civilizations. **archaeological** adjective, **archaeologist** noun [from Greek *archaios* = old, + *-logy*]

archaic (say ar-kay-ik) adjective belonging to former or ancient times. [from Greek *arche* = beginning]

archangel noun (plural **archangels**) an angel of the highest rank.

archbishop noun (plural **archbishops**) the chief bishop of a province of the Church.

arch-enemy noun (plural **arch-enemies**) the chief enemy.

archer noun (plural **archers**) a person who shoots with a bow and arrows.

archery noun the sport of shooting at a target with a bow and arrows.

archetype (say ark-i-typ) noun (plural **archetypes**) the original form or model from which others are copied. [from *arch-* + *type*]

archipelago (say ark-i-pel-ag-oh) noun (plural **archipelagos**) a large group of islands, or the sea containing these.

architect (say ark-i-tekt) noun (plural **architects**) a person who designs buildings. [from *arch-* + Greek *tekton* = builder]

architecture noun
1 the process of designing buildings. 2 a particular style of building, *Elizabethan architecture*. **architectural** adjective

archives (say ark-I'vz) plural noun the historical documents etc. of an organization or community. [from Greek *archeia* = public records]

archway noun (plural **archways**) an arched passage or entrance.

arc lamp or **arc light** noun (plural **arc lamps**, **arc lights**) a light using an electric arc.

arctic adjective very cold, *The weather was arctic*. [from the Arctic, the area round the North Pole]

ardour (say ar-der) noun enthusiasm or passion. [from old French]

arduous adjective needing much effort; laborious. **arduously** adverb [from Latin *arduus* = steep]

area noun (plural **areas**)
1 the extent or measurement of a surface. 2 a particular region or piece of land. 3 a subject or activity.

arena (say a-reen-a) noun (plural **arenas**) the level area in the centre of an amphitheatre or sports stadium. [Latin, = sand (because the floors of Roman arenas were covered with sand)]

aren't (mainly spoken) are not. **aren't I?** (informal) am I not?

argue verb (**argues**, **arguing**, **argued**)
1 say that you disagree; exchange angry comments. 2 state that something is true and give reasons. [from Latin]

argument noun (plural **arguments**)
1 a disagreement or quarrel. 2 a reason or series of reasons put forward.

argumentative adjective fond of arguing.

aria (say ar-ee-a) noun (plural **arias**) a solo in an opera or oratorio.

-arian suffix forms nouns and adjectives (e.g. *vegetarian*) showing members of a group.

arid adjective dry and barren. [from Latin]

arise verb (**arises**, **arising**, **arose**, **arisen**)
1 come into existence; come to people's notice, *Problems arose*. 2 (old use) rise; stand up, *Arise, Sir Francis*.

aristocracy (say a-ris-tok-ra-see) noun people of the highest social rank; members of the nobility. [from Greek *aristos* = best, + *-cracy*]

aristocrat (say a-ris-tok-rat) noun (plural **aristocrats**) a member of the aristocracy. **aristocratic** adjective

arithmetic noun the science or study of numbers; calculating with numbers. **arithmetical** adjective [from Greek arithmos = number]

ark noun (plural **arks**)
1 (in the Bible) the ship in which Noah and his family escaped the Flood. **2** a wooden box in which the writings of the Jewish Law were kept. [from Latin arca = box]

arm[1] noun (plural **arms**)
1 either of the two upper limbs of the body, between the shoulder and the hand. **2** a sleeve. **3** something shaped like an arm or jutting out from a main part. **4** the raised side part of a chair. **armful** noun [Old English]

arm[2] verb (**arms, arming, armed**)
1 supply someone with weapons. **2** prepare for war. [from Latin arma = weapons]

armada (say ar-mah-da) noun (plural **armadas**) a fleet of warships.
the Armada or **Spanish Armada** the warships sent by Spain to invade England in 1588. [Spanish, = navy, from Latin armata = armed]

armadillo noun (plural **armadillos**) a small burrowing South American animal whose body is covered with a shell of bony plates. [Spanish, = little armed man]

armature noun (plural **armatures**) the current-carrying part of a dynamo or electric motor. [from Latin]

armchair noun (plural **armchairs**) a chair with arms.

armed forces or **armed services** plural noun a country's military forces; the army, navy, and air force.

armistice noun (plural **armistices**) an agreement to stop fighting in a war or battle. [from Latin arma = weapons + sistere = stop]

armour noun
1 a protective covering for the body, formerly worn in fighting. **2** a metal covering on a warship, tank, or car to protect it from missiles. **armoured** adjective

armpit noun (plural **armpits**) the hollow underneath the top of the arm, below the shoulder.

arms plural noun
1 weapons. **2** a coat of arms.
up in arms protesting vigorously.

arms race noun competition between nations in building up supplies of weapons, especially nuclear weapons.

army noun (plural **armies**)
1 a large number of people trained to fight on land. **2** a large group. [via old French armée from Latin armata = armed]

aroma (say a-roh-ma) noun (plural **aromas**) a smell, especially a pleasant one. **aromatic** (say a-ro-mat-ik) adjective [from Greek aroma = spice]

around adverb & preposition all round; about. [from a-[1] + round]

arouse verb (arouses, arousing, aroused)
1 stir up a feeling in someone, *You've aroused my curiosity.*
2 wake someone up.

arpeggio (say ar-*pej*-ee-oh) noun (plural **arpeggios**) the notes of a musical chord played one after the other instead of together. [from Italian *arpa* = harp]

arrange verb (arranges, arranging, arranged)
1 put things into a certain order; adjust. 2 form plans for something, *We arranged to be there.* 3 prepare music for a particular purpose.
arrangement noun

array noun (plural **arrays**)
1 a display. 2 an orderly arrangement. [from *ar-* + old form of *ready*]

arrears plural noun
1 money that is owing and ought to have been paid earlier.
2 a backlog of work etc.
in arrears behind with payments. [from *ar-* + Latin *retro* = behind]

arrest verb (arrests, arresting, arrested)
1 seize a person by authority of the law. 2 stop a process or movement.

arrest noun (plural **arrests**)
1 arresting somebody, *The police made several arrests.* 2 stopping something.

arrive verb (arrives, arriving, arrived)
1 reach the end of a journey or a point on it. 2 come, *The great day arrived.* **arrival** noun [from *ar-* + Latin *ripa* = shore]

arrogant adjective behaving in an unpleasantly proud way because you think you are superior to other people. **arrogantly** adverb
arrogance noun [from Latin *arrogare* = claim, demand]

arrow noun (plural **arrows**)
1 a pointed stick to be shot from a bow. 2 a sign with an outward-pointing V at the end, used to show direction or position.
arrowhead noun [from Old Norse]

arsenic noun a very poisonous metallic substance. [originally the name of arsenic sulphide, which is yellow; from Persian *zar* = gold]

arson noun the crime of deliberately setting fire to a house or building. **arsonist** noun [from Latin *ardere* = burn]

art noun (plural **arts**)
1 producing something beautiful, especially by painting or drawing; things produced in this way. 2 a skill, *the art of sailing.* [from Latin]

artery noun (plural **arteries**)
1 one of the tubes that carry blood away from the heart to all parts of the body. (Compare *vein.*)
2 an important road or route.
arterial (say ar-*teer*-ee-al) adjective

artesian well noun (plural **artesian wells**) a well that is bored straight down into a place where water will rise easily to the surface. [French *artésien* = of Artois, a region of France where wells of this type were first made]

artful adjective crafty. **artfully** adverb

arthritis (say arth-ry-tiss) noun a disease that makes joints in the body stiff and painful. **arthritic** (say arth-**rit**-ik) adjective [from Greek arthron = joint]

arthropod noun (plural **arthropods**) an animal of the group that includes insects, spiders, crabs, and centipedes. [from Greek arthron = joint + podes = feet (because arthropods have jointed limbs)]

artichoke noun (plural **artichokes**) a kind of plant with a flower head used as a vegetable. [from Arabic]

article noun (plural **articles**) 1 a piece of writing published in a newspaper or magazine. 2 an object.
definite article the word 'the'.
indefinite article the word 'a' or 'an'.

articulate adjective able to express things clearly and fluently.

articulate verb (articulates, articulating, articulated) 1 say or speak clearly. 2 connect by a joint. **articulation** noun [from Latin artus = joint]

articulated adjective (of a vehicle) in two sections that are connected by a flexible joint, an articulated lorry.

artificial adjective not natural; made by human beings in imitation of a natural thing. **artificially** adverb, **artificiality** noun [from Latin ars = art + facere = make]

artificial intelligence noun the use of computers to perform tasks normally requiring human intelligence, e.g. decision-making.

artificial respiration noun helping somebody to start breathing again after their breathing has stopped.

artillery noun 1 large guns. 2 the part of the army that uses large guns. [from old French]

artist noun (plural **artists**) 1 a person who produces works of art, especially a painter. 2 an entertainer. **artistry** noun

artistic adjective 1 to do with art or artists. 2 having a talent for art. **artistically** adverb

arts plural noun subjects (e.g. languages, literature, history) in which opinion and understanding are very important, as opposed to sciences where measurements and calculations are used.
the arts painting, music, and writing etc., considered together.

-ary suffix to do with; of that kind: forms adjectives (e.g. contrary, primary) or nouns (e.g. dictionary, January). [from Latin]

as adverb equally or similarly, This is just as easy.

as preposition in the function or role of, Use it as a handle.

as conjunction 1 when or while, She slipped as she got off the bus. 2 because, As he was late, we missed the train. 3 in a way that, Leave it as it is.
as for with regard to, As for you, I despise you.
as it were in a way, She became, as it were, her own enemy.
as well also.

as- prefix to; towards. see **ad-**.

A/S *abbreviation* advanced supplementary level in GCSE.

asbestos *noun* a soft fireproof material. [from Greek, = unquenchable]

ascend *verb* (**ascends, ascending, ascended**) go up. **ascend the throne** become king or queen.

ascent *noun* (*plural* **ascents**) 1 ascending. 2 a way up; an upward path or slope.

ascertain (*say* as-er-tayn) *verb* (**ascertains, ascertaining, ascertained**) find something out by asking. **ascertainable** *adjective* [from old French]

ascetic (*say* a-set-ik) *adjective* not allowing yourself pleasure and luxuries. **asceticism** *noun* [from Greek *asketes* = hermit]

ascribe *verb* (**ascribes, ascribing, ascribed**) regard something as belonging to or caused by; attribute, *She ascribes her success to good luck.*

asexual *adjective* (in biology, to do with reproduction) by other than sexual methods. [from *a-²* = not, + *sexual*]

ash¹ *noun* (*plural* **ashes**) the powder that is left after something has been burned. **ashy** *adjective* [from Old English *aesce*]

ash² *noun* (*plural* **ashes**) a tree with silver-grey bark. [from Old English *aesc*]

ashamed *adjective* feeling shame.

Asian *adjective* to do with Asia or its people.

Asian *noun* (*plural* **Asians**) an Asian person.

Asiatic *adjective* to do with Asia.

aside *adverb* 1 to or at one side, *pull it aside.* 2 away; in reserve.

aside *noun* (*plural* **asides**) words spoken so that only certain people will hear.

ask *verb* (**asks, asking, asked**) 1 speak so as to find out or get something. 2 invite, *Ask her to the party.*

asleep *adverb* & *adjective* sleeping.

asparagus *noun* a plant whose young shoots are eaten as a vegetable. [from Greek]

aspect *noun* (*plural* **aspects**) 1 one part of a problem or situation, *Violence was the worst aspect of the crime.* 2 a person's or thing's appearance, *The forest had a sinister aspect.* 3 the direction a house etc. faces, *This room has a southern aspect.* [from *as-* + Latin *specere* = to look]

asphalt (*say* ass-falt) *noun* a sticky black substance like tar, often mixed with gravel to surface roads, etc. [from French]

asphyxiate (*say* ass-fiks-ee-ayt) *verb* (**asphyxiates, asphyxiating, asphyxiated**) suffocate. **asphyxiation** *noun* [from Greek *asphyxia* = stopping of the pulse]

aspidistra *noun* (*plural* **aspidistras**) a house-plant with broad leaves. [from Greek *aspis* = a shield]

aspirate (*say* asp-er-at) *noun* (*plural* **aspirates**) the sound of 'h'. [same origin as *aspire*]

aspiration *noun* (*plural* **aspirations**) ambition; strong desire.

aspire verb (aspires, aspiring, aspired) have an ambition to achieve something, *He aspired to be world champion.* [from *ad-* = to + Latin *spirare* = breathe]

aspirin noun (plural **aspirins**) a medicinal drug used to relieve pain or reduce fever. [German]

ass noun (plural **asses**)
1 a donkey. 2 (*informal*) a stupid person.

assassin noun (plural **assassins**) a person who assassinates somebody. [from Arabic *hashishi* = hashish-takers, used as a name for a group of Muslims at the time of the Crusades, who were believed to take hashish before going out to kill Christian leaders]

assassinate verb (assassinates, assassinating, assassinated) kill an important person deliberately and violently, especially for political reasons. **assassination** noun

assault noun (plural **assaults**) a violent or illegal attack.

assault verb (assaults, assaulting, assaulted) make an assault on someone.

assemble verb (assembles, assembling, assembled)
1 bring or come together. 2 fit or put together the parts of something. **assemblage** noun [from *as-* + Latin *simul* = together]

assembly noun (plural assemblies)
1 assembling. 2 a regular meeting, such as when everybody in a school meets

together. 3 people who regularly meet for a special purpose; a parliament.

assent verb (assents, assenting, assented) consent; say you agree.

assent noun consent or approval.

assert verb (asserts, asserting, asserted) state something firmly. **assertion** noun
assert yourself use firmness or forcefulness.

assertive adjective asserting yourself; firm and forceful.

assess verb (assesses, assessing, assessed) decide or estimate the value or quality of a person or thing. **assessment** noun, **assessor** noun [from Latin *assessor* = an assistant judge]

asset noun (plural **assets**) something useful. [from old French]

assets plural noun a person's or firm's property, reckoned as having value.

assign verb (assigns, assigning, assigned)
1 give or allot. 2 appoint a person to perform a task.

assignment noun (plural assignments)
1 assigning. 2 something assigned; a task given to someone.

assimilate verb (assimilates, assimilating, assimilated) take in and absorb something, e.g. nourishment into the body or knowledge into the mind. **assimilation** noun

assist verb (assists, assisting, assisted) help. **assistance** noun [from Latin *assistere* = stand by]

assistant noun (plural **assistants**)
1 a person who assists another; a helper. **2** a person who serves customers in a shop.

assistant adjective helping a person and ranking next below him or her, the assistant manager.

associate verb (**associates, associating, associated**)
1 connect things in your mind, I don't associate Ryan with fitness and healthy living. **2** spend time or have dealings with a group of people.

associate noun (plural **associates**) a colleague or companion; a partner. **associate** adjective

association noun (plural **associations**)
1 an organization of people; a society. **2** associating. **3** a connection or link in your mind.

Association football noun a form of football using a round ball that may not be handled during play except by the goalkeeper.

assonance (say ass-on-ans) noun similarity of vowel sounds, e.g. in vermin and furnish. [from as- + Latin sonus = sound]

assorted adjective of various sorts put together; mixed, assorted sweets.

assortment noun (plural **assortments**) a mixed collection of things.

assume verb (**assumes, assuming, assumed**)
1 accept (without proof or question) that something is true or sure to happen. **2** take on;

undertake, She assumed the extra responsibility. **3** put on, He assumed an innocent expression.

assumption noun

assumed name noun a false name. [from as- + Latin sumere = take]

assurance noun (plural **assurances**)
1 a promise or guarantee that something is true or will happen. **2** life insurance. **3** self-confidence.

assure verb (**assures, assuring, assured**)
1 tell somebody confidently; promise. **2** make certain.

asterisk noun (plural **asterisks**) a star-shaped sign * used to draw attention to something. [from Greek asteriskos = little star]

asteroid noun (plural **asteroids**) one of the small planets found mainly between the orbits of Mars and Jupiter.

asthma (say ass-ma) noun a disease that makes breathing difficult. **asthmatic** adjective & noun [Greek]

astonish verb (**astonishes, astonishing, astonished**) surprise somebody greatly. **astonishment** noun [same origin as astound]

astound verb (**astounds, astounding, astounded**) astonish; shock somebody greatly. [from old French; related to stun]

astray adverb & adjective away from the right path or place or course of action.

astride adverb & preposition with one leg on each side of something.

astringent *adjective*
1 causing skin or body tissue to contract. **2** harsh or severe, *astringent criticism*.

astrology *noun* the study of how the stars and planets may influence people's lives.
astrologer *noun*, **astrological** *adjective* [from Greek *astron* = star, + *-logy*]

astronaut *noun* (*plural* **astronauts**) a person who travels in a spacecraft. **astronautics** *noun* [from Greek *astron* = star + *nautes* = sailor]

astronomical *adjective*
1 to do with astronomy.
2 extremely large, *The restaurant's prices are astronomical*.

astronomy *noun* the study of the stars and planets and their movements. **astronomer** *noun* [from Greek *astron* = star + *-nomia* = arrangement]

astute *adjective* clever and good at understanding situations quickly; shrewd. **astutely** *adverb*, **astuteness** *noun* [from Latin *astus* = cleverness, cunning]

asylum *noun* (*plural* **asylums**)
1 refuge and safety; a place of refuge, *The defeated rebels sought political asylum in another country*. **2** (*old use*) a mental hospital. [from Greek *asylon* = refuge]

asymmetrical (*say* ay-sim-et-rik-al) *adjective* not symmetrical. **asymmetrically** *adverb*

at *preposition* This word is used to show
1 position (*at the top*), **2** time (*at midnight*), **3** condition (*Stand at ease*), **4** direction towards something (*Aim at the target*), **5** level or price etc. (*Sell them at £1 each*), **6** cause (*We were annoyed at his failure*).
at all in any way.
at it doing or working at something.
at once 1 immediately. **2** at the same time, *It all came out at once*.

at- *prefix* to; towards. see **ad-**.

-ate *suffix* forms
1 adjectives (e.g. *passionate*),
2 nouns showing status or function (e.g. *magistrate*) or (in scientific use) nouns meaning salts of certain acids (e.g. *nitrate*; compare **-ite**), **3** verbs (e.g. *create*, *fascinate*). [from Latin]

atheist (*say* **ayth**-ee-ist) *noun* (*plural* **atheists**) a person who believes that there is no God. **atheism** *noun* [from *a-²* + Greek *theos* = god]

athlete *noun* (*plural* **athletes**) a person who is good at sport, especially athletics. [from Greek *athlein* = compete for a prize]

athletic *adjective*
1 physically strong and active.
2 to do with athletes. **athletically** *adverb*

athletics *plural noun* physical exercises and sports, e.g. running, jumping, and throwing.

-ation *suffix* forms nouns, often from verbs (e.g. *creation*, *organization*, *starvation*). [from Latin]

atlas *noun* (*plural* **atlases**) a book of maps. [named after Atlas, a giant in Greek mythology, who was made to support the universe on his shoulders]

atmosphere noun (plural **atmospheres**)
1 the air round the earth.
2 a feeling or mood given by surroundings, *the happy atmosphere of the fairground.*

atmospheric adjective [from Greek *atmos* = vapour, + *sphere*]

atom noun (plural **atoms**) the smallest particle of a substance. [from Greek *atomos* = indivisible]

atom bomb noun (plural **atom bombs**) a bomb using atomic energy.

atomic adjective
1 to do with an atom or atoms.
2 to do with atomic energy or atom bombs.

atomic number noun (plural **atomic numbers**) the number of protons in the nucleus of the atom of a chemical element.

atrocity (say a-*tross*-it-ee) noun (plural **atrocities**) something extremely bad or wicked; wickedness. [from Latin *atrox* = cruel]

attach verb (**attaches, attaching, attached**)
1 fix or join to something else.
2 regard as belonging to something, *We attach great importance to fitness.* **attachment** noun

attached to fond of.

attack noun (plural **attacks**)
1 a violent attempt to hurt or overcome somebody. 2 a piece of strong criticism. 3 sudden illness or pain.

attack verb (**attacks, attacking, attacked**) make an attack. **attacker** noun

attain verb (**attains, attaining, attained**) accomplish; succeed in doing or getting something.

attainable adjective, **attainment** noun [from at- + Latin *tangere* = touch]

attempt verb (**attempts, attempting, attempted**) make an effort to do something; try.

attempt noun (plural **attempts**) an effort to do something; a try.

attend verb (**attends, attending, attended**)
1 give care and thought to something; look and listen, *Why don't you attend to your teacher?*
2 be present somewhere; go regularly to a meeting etc. 3 look after someone; be an attendant. **attendance** noun

attendant noun (plural **attendants**) a person who helps or accompanies someone.

attention noun
1 giving concentration and careful thought, *Pay attention to what I'm saying.* 2 a position in which a soldier etc. stands with feet together and arms straight downwards.

attentive adjective giving attention to something. **attentively** adverb, **attentiveness** noun

attic noun (plural **attics**) a room in the roof of a house. [via French from Greek]

attitude noun (plural **attitudes**)
1 the position of the body or its parts; posture. 2 a way of thinking or behaving.

attract verb (**attracts, attracting, attracted**)
1 get someone's attention or interest; seem pleasant to

someone. **2** pull something by an invisible force, *Magnets attract metal pins.* **attraction** *noun* [from *at-* + Latin *tractum* = pulled]

attractive *adjective*
1 pleasant or good-looking.
2 interesting or appealing, *an attractive plan.* **attractively** *adverb*, **attractiveness** *noun*

attribute (say a-**trib**-yoot) *verb* (**attributes, attributing, attributed**) regard something as belonging to or created by, *We attribute his success to hard work.* **attribution** *noun*

attribute (say **at**-rib-yoot) *noun* (*plural* **attributes**) a quality or characteristic, *Kindness is one of his attributes.*

attributive (say a-**trib**-yoo-tiv) *adjective* expressing an attribute and placed before the word it describes, e.g. *old* in *the old dog.* (Compare **predicative**.) **attributively** *adverb*

auburn *adjective* (of hair) reddish-brown. [from old French]

auction *noun* (*plural* **auctions**) a public sale where things are sold to the person who offers the most money for them.

auction *verb* (**auctions, auctioning, auctioned**) sell something by auction. **auctioneer** *noun* [from Latin *auctum* = increased]

audacious (say aw-**day**-shus) *adjective* bold or daring. **audaciously** *adverb*, **audacity** *noun* [from Latin *audax* = bold]

audible *adjective* loud enough to be heard. **audibly** *adverb*, **audibility** *noun* [from Latin *audire* = hear]

audience *noun* (*plural* **audiences**)
1 people who have gathered to hear or watch something.
2 a formal interview with an important person.

audio *noun* reproduced sounds.

audio-visual *adjective* using both sound and pictures to give information.

audit *noun* (*plural* **audits**) an official examination of financial accounts to see that they are correct.

audit *verb* (**audits, auditing, audited**) make an audit of accounts. **auditor** *noun* [from Latin *audire* = hear (because originally the accounts were read out)]

audition *noun* (*plural* **auditions**) a test to see if an actor or musician is suitable for a job. **audition** *verb*

auditorium *noun* (*plural* **auditoriums**) the part of a building where the audience sits. [Latin, = place for hearing]

aunt *noun* (*plural* **aunts**) the sister of your father or mother; your uncle's wife. [from Latin]

au pair (say oh **pair**) *noun* (*plural* **au pairs**) a young person from overseas who works for a time in someone's home.

aura (say or-a) *noun* (*plural* **auras**) a general feeling surrounding a person or thing, *an aura of happiness.* [Greek, = breeze]

aural (say **or**-al) *adjective* to do with the ear or hearing. **aurally** *adverb* [from Latin *auris* = ear]

USAGE: Do not confuse with *oral.*

aurora (say aw-**raw**-ra) noun (plural **auroras**) bands of coloured light appearing in the sky at night, the **aurora borealis** (say bor-ee-**ay**-liss) in the northern hemisphere and the **aurora australis** (say aw-**stray**-liss) in the southern hemisphere. [Latin: aurora = dawn; borealis = of the north; australis = of the south]

auspices (say aw-**spiss**-eez) plural noun protection or support, under the auspices of the Red Cross. [originally = omens; later = influence, protection; same origin as auspicious]

auspicious (say aw-**spish**-us) adjective fortunate or favourable, an auspicious start. [from Latin auspicium = telling the future from the behaviour of birds, from avis = bird]

austere (say aw-**steer**) adjective very simple and plain; without luxuries. **austerely** adverb, **austerity** noun

aut- prefix self-; of or by yourself or itself. see **auto-**.

authentic adjective genuine, an authentic signature. **authentically** adverb, **authenticity** noun

author noun (plural **authors**) the writer of a book, play, poem, etc. **authorship** noun [from Latin auctor = originator]

authoritative adjective having proper authority or expert knowledge; official.

authority noun (plural **authorities**)
1 the right or power to give orders to other people. 2 a person or organization with the right to give orders. 3 an expert; a book etc. that gives reliable information, an authority on spiders.

authorize verb (**authorizes**, **authorizing**, **authorized**) give official permission for something. **authorization** noun

autistic (say aw-**tist**-ik) adjective unable to communicate with other people or respond to surroundings. **autism** noun [from auto-]

auto- prefix (changing to **aut-** before a vowel) self-; of or by yourself or itself (as in autograph, automatic). [from Greek autos = self]

autobiography noun (plural **autobiographies**) the story of a person's life written by himself or herself. **autobiographical** adjective

autocrat noun (plural **autocrats**) a ruler with unlimited power. **autocratic** adjective, **autocratically** adverb [from auto- + -crat]

autocue noun (plural **autocues**) (trade mark) a device that displays the script for a television presenter or newsreader to read.

autograph noun (plural **autographs**) a person's signature. **autograph** verb (**autographs**, **autographing**, **autographed**) sign your name on or in a book etc.

automatic adjective
1 working on its own without continuous attention or control by people. 2 done without thinking. **automatically** adverb [from Greek automatos = self-operating]

automation *noun* making processes automatic; using machines instead of people to do jobs.

automaton (*say* aw-tom-at-on) *noun* (*plural* **automatons**)
1 a robot. 2 a person who seems to act mechanically without thinking.

autonomy (*say* aw-ton-om-ee) *noun*
1 self-government. 2 the right to act independently without being told what to do. **autonomous** *adjective* [from *auto-* + Greek *nomia* = arrangement]

autumn *noun* (*plural* **autumns**) the season between summer and winter. **autumnal** *adjective* [from old French]

auxiliary *adjective* giving help and support, *auxiliary services.*

auxiliary *noun* (*plural* **auxiliaries**) a helper. [from Latin *auxilium* = help]

auxiliary verb *noun* (*plural* **auxiliary verbs**) a verb used in forming tenses etc. of other verbs, e.g. *have* in I have finished.

available *adjective* ready or able to be used; obtainable. **availability** *noun*

avalanche *noun* (*plural* **avalanches**) a mass of snow or rock falling down the side of a mountain. [French, from *avaler* = descend]

avenge *verb* (**avenges, avenging, avenged**) take vengeance for something done to harm you. **avenger** *noun*

avenue *noun* (*plural* **avenues**)
1 a wide street. 2 a road with trees along both sides. [from French *avenir* = approach]

average *noun* (*plural* **averages**)
1 the value obtained by adding several quantities together and dividing by the number of quantities. 2 the usual or ordinary standard.

average *adjective*
1 worked out as an average, *Their average age is ten.*
2 of the usual or ordinary standard.

average *verb* (**averages, averaging, averaged**) work out, produce, or amount to as an average. [from Arabic]

aversion *noun* a strong dislike.

avert *verb* (**averts, averting, averted**)
1 turn something away, *People averted their eyes from the accident.* 2 prevent, *We averted a disaster.*

aviary *noun* (*plural* **aviaries**) a large cage or building for keeping birds. [from Latin *avis* = bird]

aviation *noun* the flying of aircraft. **aviator** *noun* [from Latin *avis* = bird]

avocado (*say* av-ok-ah-doh) *noun* (*plural* **avocados**) a pear-shaped tropical fruit. [via Spanish from Nahuatl (a Central American language)]

avoid *verb* (**avoids, avoiding, avoided**)
1 keep yourself away from someone or something.
2 keep yourself from doing something; refrain from, *Avoid rash promises.* **avoidable** *adjective*, **avoidance** *noun* [from old French]

avoirdupois (*say* av-er-dew-**poiz**)
noun a system of weights using
the unit of 16 ounces = 1 pound.
[French, = goods of weight (goods
sold by weight)]

await *verb* (**awaits, awaiting,
awaited**) wait for. [from old
French]

awake *verb* (**awakes, awaking,
awoke, awoken**) wake up.

awake *adjective* not asleep.
[from Old English]

award *verb* (**awards, awarding,
awarded**) give something
officially as a prize, payment, or
penalty.

award *noun* (*plural* **awards**)
something awarded, such as
a prize or a sum of money. [from
old French]

aware *adjective* knowing or
realizing something, *Were you
aware of the danger?* **awareness**
noun

away *adverb*
1 to or at a distance; not at the
usual place. **2** out of existence,
The water had boiled away.
3 continuously or persistently,
We worked away at it.

away *adjective* played on an
opponent's ground, *an away
match.* [from Old English]

awe *noun* fearful or deeply
respectful wonder, *The
mountains always fill me with
awe.* **awed** *adjective*, **awesome**
adjective, **awestricken** *adjective*,
awestruck *adjective* [from Old
English]

awful
1 very bad, *an awful accident.*
2 (*informal*) very great, *That's an
awful lot of money.* **awfully** *adverb*
[from *awe* + -*ful*]

awkward *adjective*
1 difficult to use or deal with; not
convenient. **2** clumsy; not skilful.
awkwardly *adverb*, **awkwardness**
noun

awning *noun* (*plural* **awnings**)
a roof-like shelter made of canvas
etc.

axe *noun* (*plural* **axes**)
1 a tool for chopping things.
2 (*informal*) being axed.
have an axe to grind have
a personal interest in something
and want to take care of it.

axe *verb* (**axes, axing, axed**)
1 cancel or abolish something.
2 reduce something greatly.
[from Old English]

axis *noun* (*plural* **axes**)
1 a line through the centre of
a spinning object. **2** a line
dividing a thing in half. [Latin,
= axle]

axle *noun* (*plural* **axles**) the rod
through the centre of a wheel, on
which the wheel turns. [from Old
Norse]

ayatollah (*say* I-a-**tol**-a) *noun*
(*plural* **ayatollahs**) a Muslim
religious leader in Iran. [from
Arabic *ayatu-llah* = sign from
God]

aye (*say* I) *adverb* yes. [origin
unknown]

azure *adjective* sky-blue. [via old
French from Persian]

Bb

babble *verb* (**babbles, babbling,
babbled**)
1 talk very quickly without
making sense. **2** make
a murmuring sound. **babble**
noun, **babbler** *noun* [imitating the
sound]

baboon noun (plural **baboons**)
a kind of large monkey from
Africa and Asia. Baboons have
long muzzles and short tails.
[from French]

baby noun (plural **babies**) a very
young child or animal. **babyish**
adjective

babysitter noun (plural
babysitters) someone who looks
after a child while its parents are
out.

bachelor noun (plural **bachelors**)
a man who has not married.
Bachelor of Arts or **Science**
a person who has taken a first
degree in arts or science.
[from French]

back noun (plural **backs**)
1 the part that is furthest from
the front. 2 the back part of the
body from the shoulders to the
buttocks. 3 the part of a chair etc.
that your back rests against.
4 a defending player near the
goal in football, hockey, etc.

back adjective
1 placed at or near the back. 2 to
do with the back, *back pain*.

back adverb
1 to or towards the back. 2 to the
place you have come from, *Go
back home*. 3 to an earlier time or
position, *Put the clocks back one
hour*.

back verb (**backs**, **backing**,
backed)
1 move backwards. 2 give
someone support or help. 3 bet on
something. 4 cover the back of
something, *Back the rug with
canvas*. **backer** noun
back out refuse to do what you
agreed to do.

back up give support or help to
a person or thing. **back-up** noun
[from Old English]

backbencher noun (plural
backbenchers) a Member of
Parliament who does not hold an
important position.

backbone noun (plural
backbones) the column of small
bones down the centre of the
back; the spine.

backfire verb (**backfires**,
backfiring, **backfired**)
1 if a car backfires, it makes
a loud noise, caused by an
explosion in the exhaust pipe. 2 if
a plan backfires, it goes wrong.

background noun
1 the back part of a scene or view
etc. 2 the conditions influencing
something. 3 a person's family,
upbringing, and education.

backing noun
1 support. 2 material that is used
to line the back of something.
3 musical accompaniment.

backlash noun (plural
backlashes) a violent reaction to
an event.

backlog noun (plural **backlogs**)
an amount of work that should
have been finished but is still
waiting to be done.

backstroke noun a way of
swimming lying on your back.

backward adjective
1 going backwards. 2 slow at
learning or developing.
backwardness noun
backward adverb backwards.

USAGE: The adverb *backward*
is mainly used in American
English.

backwards adverb
1 to or towards the back. 2 with the back end going first. 3 in reverse order, Count backwards. **backwards and forwards** in each direction alternately; to and fro.

bacon noun smoked or salted meat from the back or sides of a pig. [via French from Germanic; related to back]

bacterium noun (plural **bacteria**) a microscopic organism. **bacterial** adjective [from Greek bakterion = little cane]

USAGE: Note that it is a mistake to use the plural form bacteria as if it were the singular. It is incorrect to say 'a bacteria' or 'this bacteria'; correct usage is this bacterium or these bacteria.

bad adjective (**worse**, **worst**)
1 not having the right qualities; not good. 2 wicked or evil. 3 serious or severe, a bad accident. 4 ill or unhealthy. 5 harmful, Sweets are bad for your teeth. 6 decayed or rotten, This meat has gone bad. **badness** noun

not bad quite good.

badge noun (plural **badges**) a button or sign that you wear to show people who you are or what school or club etc. you belong to. [origin unknown]

badger noun (plural **badgers**) a grey burrowing animal with a black and white head.

badger verb (**badgers**, **badgering**, **badgered**) keep asking someone to do something; pester.

[perhaps from badge (because of the markings on a badger's head)]

badly adverb (**worse**, **worst**)
1 in a bad way; not well. 2 severely; causing much injury, He was badly wounded. 3 very much, She badly wanted to win.

baffle verb (**baffles**, **baffling**, **baffled**) puzzle or confuse somebody. **bafflement** noun [origin unknown]

bag noun (plural **bags**) a container made of a soft material, for holding or carrying things. **bags** (informal) plenty, bags of room.

bag verb (**bags**, **bagging**, **bagged**) 1 (informal) catch or claim something. 2 put something into bags.

baggage noun luggage. [from old French]

baggy adjective (of clothes) large and loose.

bagpipes plural noun a musical instrument in which air is squeezed out of a bag into pipes. Bagpipes are played especially in Scotland.

bail[1] noun money that is paid or promised as a guarantee that a person who is accused of a crime will return for trial if he or she is released in the meantime.

bail verb (**bails**, **bailing**, **bailed**) provide bail for a person.

bail[2] noun (plural **bails**) one of the two small pieces of wood placed on top of the stumps in cricket. [from old French bail = palisade]

bail³ verb (bails, bailing, bailed)
scoop out water that has got into a boat. [from French *baille* = bucket]

bailiff noun (plural **bailiffs**)
1 a law officer who serves writs and performs arrests. 2 an official who takes people's property when they owe money.

bait noun
1 food that is put on a hook or in a trap to catch fish or animals. 2 something that is meant to tempt someone.

bait verb (baits, baiting, baited)
1 put bait on a hook or in a trap. 2 try to make someone angry by teasing them.
[from Old Norse; related to *bite*]

baize noun the thick green cloth that is used for covering snooker tables. [same origin as *bay*⁵ (because the cloth was originally reddish-brown)]

bake verb (bakes, baking, baked)
1 cook in an oven. 2 make or become very hot. 3 make a thing hard by heating it.

baker noun (plural **bakers**)
a person who bakes and sells bread or cakes. **bakery** noun

balance noun (plural **balances**)
1 a steady position, with the weight or amount evenly distributed. 2 a machine for weighing things, with two containers hanging from a bar. 3 the difference between money paid into an account and money taken out. 4 the money left after something has been paid for.

balance verb (balances, balancing, balanced) make or be steady or equal.
[from Latin]

balcony noun (plural **balconies**)
1 a platform that sticks out from an outside wall of a building. 2 the upstairs part of a theatre or cinema. [from Italian]

bald adjective
1 without hair on the top of the head. 2 with no details; blunt, *a bald statement.* **baldly** adverb, **baldness** noun

ball¹ noun (plural **balls**)
1 a round object used in many games. 2 anything that has a round shape, *a ball of string.* [from Old Norse]

ball² noun (plural **balls**) a formal party where people dance. [same origin as *ballet*]

ballad noun (plural **ballads**)
a simple song or poem that tells a story.

ballast (say bal-ast) noun heavy material that is carried in a ship to keep it steady.

ball-bearings plural noun small steel balls rolling in a groove on which machine parts can move easily.

ballerina (say bal-er-een-a) noun (plural **ballerinas**) a female ballet dancer. [Italian, = female dancing teacher]

ballet (say bal-ay) noun (plural **ballets**) a stage entertainment that tells a story with dancing, mime, and music.

ballistic missile noun (plural **ballistic missiles**) a missile that is initially powered and guided and then falls under gravity on its target. [from Greek *ballein* = to throw]

balloon noun (plural **balloons**)
1 a bag made of thin rubber that can be inflated and used as a toy

or decoration. **2** a large round bag inflated with hot air or light gases to make it rise in the air. **3** an outline round spoken words in a strip cartoon. [from French or Italian; related to **ball**[1]]

ballot noun (plural **ballots**)
1 a secret method of voting, usually by making a mark on a piece of paper. **2** a piece of paper on which a vote is made.

ballot verb (**ballots, balloting, balloted**) invite people to vote for something by a ballot.
[from Italian ballotta = small ball (because one way of voting is by placing a ball in a box; the colour of the ball shows whether you are voting for something or against it)]

ballpoint pen noun (plural **ballpoint pens**) a pen with a tiny ball round which the ink flows.

balm noun
1 a sweet-scented ointment.
2 something that soothes you.
[from Latin balsamum]

balmy adjective
1 sweet-scented like balm. **2** soft and warm, a balmy breeze.

bamboo noun (plural **bamboos**)
1 a tall plant with hard hollow stems. **2** a stem of the bamboo plant. [via Dutch from Malay (a language spoken in Malaysia)]

ban verb (**bans, banning, banned**) forbid something officially.
ban noun (plural **bans**) an order that bans something.

banana noun (plural **bananas**)
a long curved fruit with a yellow or green skin.

band[1] noun (plural **bands**)
1 a strip or loop of something.
2 a range of values, wavelengths, etc. [via French from Germanic; related to **bind**]

band[2] noun (plural **bands**)
1 an organized group of people doing something together, a band of robbers. **2** a group of people playing music together.
band verb (**bands, banding, banded**) form an organized group.
[from French]

bandage noun (plural **bandages**)
a strip of material for binding up a wound. **bandage** verb [French; related to **band**[1]]

bandit noun (plural **bandits**)
a member of a gang of robbers who attack travellers. [from Latin bannire = banish]

bandwagon noun
jump or **climb on the bandwagon** join other people in something that is successful.

bandy verb (**bandies, bandying, bandied**) if a word or story is bandied about, it is mentioned or told by a lot of different people. [probably from French]

bane noun a cause of trouble or worry etc., Exams are the bane of our lives! [from Old English]

bang noun (plural **bangs**)
1 a sudden loud noise like that of an explosion. **2** a sharp blow or knock.

bang verb (**bangs, banging, banged**)
1 hit or shut something noisily.
2 make a sudden loud noise.

bang adverb
1 with a bang; suddenly.

2 (*informal*) exactly, *bang in the middle*.
[imitating the sound]

banish verb (**banishes, banishing, banished**)
1 punish a person by ordering them to leave a place. **2** if you banish doubts or fears, you drive them away. **banishment** noun
[via French from Germanic; related to *ban*]

banisters plural noun a handrail with upright supports beside a staircase. [from Italian]

banjo noun (*plural* **banjos**) an instrument like a guitar with a round body. [a Black American word]

bank[1] noun (*plural* **banks**)
1 a slope. **2** a long piled-up mass of sand, snow, cloud, etc. **3** a row of lights or switches etc.

bank verb (**banks, banking, banked**)
1 build or form a bank. **2** tilt sideways while changing direction, *The plane banked as it prepared to land*.
[from Old Norse]

bank[2] noun (*plural* **banks**)
1 a business that looks after people's money. **2** a reserve supply, *a blood bank*.

bank verb (**banks, banking, banked**) put money in a bank. **bank on** rely on.
[from Italian]

banker noun (*plural* **bankers**) a person who runs a bank.

bank holiday noun (*plural* **bank holidays**) a public holiday, when banks are officially closed.

bankrupt adjective a person or business that is bankrupt is unable to pay debts. **bankruptcy** noun [from *bank*[2] + Latin *ruptum* = broken]

banner noun (*plural* **banners**)
1 a flag. **2** a strip of cloth with a design or slogan on it, carried on a pole or two poles in a procession or demonstration.

banquet noun (*plural* **banquets**) a formal public meal. **banqueting** noun

banter noun playful teasing or joking. **banter** verb

baptism noun (*plural* **baptisms**) baptizing.

Baptist noun (*plural* **Baptists**) a member of a group of Christians who believe that a person should not be baptized until he or she is old enough to understand what baptism means.

baptize verb (**baptizes, baptizing, baptized**) receive a person into the Christian Church in a ceremony in which he or she is sprinkled with or dipped in water, and usually given a name or names. [from Greek *baptizein* = to dip]

bar noun (*plural* **bars**)
1 a long piece of something hard, *a gold bar*. **2** a counter or room where refreshments, especially alcoholic drinks, are served.
3 a barrier or obstruction. **4** one of the small equal sections into which music is divided, *three beats to the bar*.
the Bar barristers.

bar verb (**bars, barring, barred**)
1 fasten something with a bar or bars. **2** block or obstruct, *A man with a dog barred the way*.
3 forbid or ban.

barb noun (plural **barbs**) the backward-pointing spike of a spear, arrow, or fish-hook, which makes the point stay in. [from Latin *barba* = beard]

barbarian noun (plural **barbarians**) an uncivilized or brutal person. **barbaric** adjective, **barbarous** adjective, **barbarity** noun, **barbarism** noun [from Greek *barbaros* = babbling, not speaking Greek]

barbecue noun (plural **barbecues**)
1 a metal frame for grilling food over an open fire outdoors.
2 a party where food is cooked in this way.

barbecue verb (**barbecues**, **barbecuing**, **barbecued**) cook food on a barbecue.

barbed adjective
1 having a barb or barbs.
2 a barbed comment or remark is deliberately hurtful.

barbed wire noun wire with small spikes in it, used to make fences.

barber noun (plural **barbers**) a men's hairdresser. [from Latin *barba* = beard]

bar chart noun (plural **bar charts**) a diagram that shows amounts as bars of varying width or height.

bar code noun (plural **bar codes**) a set of black lines that are printed on goods, library books, etc., and can be read by a computer to give information about the goods, books, etc.

bare adjective
1 without clothing or covering.
2 empty, *The cupboard was bare.*
3 plain; without details, *the bare facts.*

4 only just enough, *the bare necessities of life.* **barely** adverb, **bareness** noun

bare verb (**bares**, **baring**, **bared**) uncover or reveal, *The dog bared its teeth in a snarl.* [from Old English]

bargain noun (plural **bargains**)
1 an agreement about buying or selling or exchanging something.
2 something that you buy cheaply.

bargain verb (**bargains**, **bargaining**, **bargained**) argue over the price to be paid or what you will do in return for something.
bargain for be prepared for or expect, *He got more than he bargained for.*

barge noun (plural **barges**) a long flat-bottomed boat used on canals.

barge verb (**barges**, **barging**, **barged**) push or knock against roughly.
barge in rush into a room rudely. [from Latin *barca* = boat]

baritone noun (plural **baritones**) a male singer with a voice between a tenor and a bass. [from Greek *barys* = heavy, + *tone*]

barium (say **bair**-ee-um) noun a soft silvery-white metal. [from Greek]

bark¹ noun (plural **barks**) the short harsh sound made by a dog or fox. **bark** verb [from Old English *beorc*, imitating the sound]

bark² noun the outer covering of a tree's branches or trunk. [from Old Norse]

barley noun a cereal plant from which malt is made.

bar mitzvah noun (plural **bar mitzvahs**) a religious ceremony for Jewish boys aged 13. [Hebrew, = son of the commandment]

barn noun (plural **barns**) a farm building for storing hay or grain etc. **barnyard** noun [from Old English]

barnacle noun (plural **barnacles**) a shellfish that attaches itself to rocks and the bottoms of ships. [from Latin]

barometer (say ba-**rom**-it-er) noun (plural **barometers**) an instrument that measures air pressure, used in forecasting the weather. [from Greek baros = weight, + meter]

baron noun (plural **barons**) 1 a member of the lowest rank of noblemen. 2 a powerful owner of an industry or business, a newspaper baron. **barony** noun, **baronial** (say ba-**roh**-nee-al) adjective [from Latin baro = man, warrior]

baroness noun (plural **baronesses**) a female baron or a baron's wife.

baronet noun (plural **baronets**) a nobleman ranking below a baron but above a knight. **baronetcy** noun

baroque (say ba-**rok**) noun an elaborately decorated style of architecture used in the 17th and 18th centuries. [from French]

barracks noun a large building or group of buildings for soldiers to live in.

barrage (say ba-rahzh) noun (plural **barrages**) 1 a dam built across a river.

2 heavy gunfire. 3 a large amount of something, a barrage of questions.

barrel noun (plural **barrels**) 1 a large rounded container with flat ends. 2 the metal tube of a gun, through which the shot is fired. [from Latin barriculus = a small cask]

barrel organ noun (plural **barrel organs**) a musical instrument which you play by turning a handle.

barricade noun (plural **barricades**) a barrier, especially one put up hastily across a street or door.

barricade verb (barricades, barricading, barricaded) block a street or door with a barricade. [French, from Spanish barrica = barrel (because barrels were sometimes used to build barricades)]

barrier noun (plural **barriers**) something that prevents people or things from getting past; an obstacle.

barrister noun (plural **barristers**) a lawyer who represents people in the higher lawcourts. [originally one who was allowed to pass the bar, a partition separating qualified lawyers from students]

barrow noun (plural **barrows**) 1 a wheelbarrow. 2 a small cart that is pushed or pulled by hand. [from Old English; related to bear²]

barter verb (barters, bartering, bartered) trade by exchanging goods for other goods, not for money.

USAGE: This word does not mean 'to bargain'.

barter noun (plural **barters**) the system of bartering.
[probably from old French]

basalt (say bas-awlt) noun a kind of dark volcanic rock. [from Greek]

base[1] noun (plural **bases**)
1 the lowest part of something; the part on which a thing stands. **2** a starting point or foundation; a basis. **3** a headquarters. **4** each of the four corners that must be reached by a runner in baseball. **5** a substance that can combine with an acid to form a salt. **6** the number in terms of which other numbers can be expressed in a number system. 10 is the base of the decimal system and 2 is the base of the binary system.

base verb (**bases, basing, based**) use something as a starting point or foundation, The story is based on facts.
[same origin as **basis**]

base[2] adjective
1 dishonourable, base motives. **2** not of great value, base metals.
basely adverb, **baseness** noun
[from French bas = low]

baseball noun (plural **baseballs**)
1 an American ball game rather like rounders. **2** the ball used in this game.

basement noun (plural **basements**) a room or rooms below ground level.

bash verb (**bashes, bashing, bashed**) hit hard.

bash noun (plural **bashes**)
1 a hard hit. **2** (informal) a try, Have a bash at it.
[imitating the sound]

bashful adjective shy and self-conscious. **bashfully** adverb

basic adjective forming a basis or starting point; very important, Bread is a basic food. [from base[1]]

basin noun (plural **basins**)
1 a deep bowl. **2** a washbasin. **3** a sheltered area of water for mooring boats. **4** the area from which water drains into a river, the Amazon basin. [from old French]

basis noun (plural **bases**) something to start from or add to; the main principle or ingredient.
[Greek, = step, stepping]

bask verb (**basks, basking, basked**) sit or lie comfortably warming yourself in the sun.
[origin unknown]

basket noun (plural **baskets**) a container for holding or carrying things, made of strips of flexible material or wire woven together. [probably from Latin]

basketball noun (plural **basketballs**)
1 a game in which goals are scored by putting a ball through high nets. **2** the ball used in this game.

bass (say bayss) adjective deep-sounding; the bass part of a piece of music is the lowest part.

bass noun (plural **basses**)
1 a male singer with a very deep voice. **2** a bass instrument or part.
[from base[2] = low]

bassoon noun (plural **bassoons**) a bass woodwind instrument.
[from Italian basso = low]

bastard noun (plural **bastards**)
1 (old use) an illegitimate child.
2 (slang) an unpleasant or
difficult person or thing.
bastardy noun [from old French]

bat¹ noun (plural **bats**)
1 a shaped piece of wood used to
hit the ball in cricket, baseball,
etc. 2 a batsman, *their opening
bat.*
off your own bat without help
from other people.

bat verb (**bats, batting, batted**)
use a bat in cricket etc.
[from Old English]

bat² noun (plural **bats**) a flying
animal that looks like a mouse
with wings.

batch noun (plural **batches**) a set
of things or people dealt with
together. [from Old English;
related to *bake*]

bath noun (plural **baths**)
1 washing your whole body while
sitting in water. 2 a large
container for water in which to
wash your whole body; this
water, *Your bath is getting cold.*
3 a liquid in which something is
placed, *an acid bath.*

bath verb (**baths, bathing,
bathed**) wash in a bath.

bathe verb (**bathes, bathing,
bathed**)
1 go swimming. 2 wash
something gently. **bathe** noun,
bather noun, **bathing suit** noun

bathroom noun (plural
bathrooms) a room containing
a bath.

baths plural noun
1 a building with rooms where
people can bath. 2 a public
swimming pool.

batsman noun (plural **batsmen**)
a player who uses a bat in cricket
etc.

battalion noun (plural **battalions**)
an army unit containing two or
more companies. [from Italian
battaglia = battle]

batten verb (**battens, battening,
battened**) fasten something down
firmly.

batter verb (**batters, battering,
battered**) hit hard and often.

batter noun (plural **batters**)
1 a beaten mixture of flour, eggs,
and milk, used for making
pancakes etc. 2 a batsman in
baseball.
[from Latin *battuere* = to beat]

battery noun (plural **batteries**)
1 a device for storing and
supplying electricity. 2 a set of
similar pieces of equipment;
a group of large guns. 3 a series of
cages in which poultry or
animals are kept close together,
battery farming.

battle noun (plural **battles**)
1 a fight between two armies.
2 a struggle. **battlefield** noun,
battleground noun

battle verb (**battles, battling,
battled**) fight or struggle.
[same origin as *batter*]

battlements plural noun the top
of a castle wall, often with gaps
from which the defenders could
fire at the enemy.

battleship noun (plural
battleships) a heavily armed
warship.

bawl verb (**bawls, bawling,
bawled**)
1 shout. 2 cry noisily.

bay[1] noun (plural **bays**) a place where the shore curves inwards. [from Spanish]

bay[2] noun (plural **bays**) a recess. [from Latin batare = gape]

bay[3] noun (plural **bays**) the long deep cry of a hunting hound or other large dog.

at bay cornered but defiantly facing attackers, a stag at bay.

keep at bay prevent something from coming near or causing harm, We need laws to keep poverty at bay.
[from French]

bayonet noun (plural **bayonets**) a blade that can be fixed to the end of a rifle and used for stabbing. [named after Bayonne in France, where it was first used]

bay window noun (plural **bay windows**) a window that sticks out from the main wall of a house. [from bay[2]]

bazaar noun (plural **bazaars**) 1 a market place in an Eastern country. 2 a sale to raise money for a charity etc. [from Persian bazar = market]

BBC abbreviation British Broadcasting Corporation.

BC abbreviation before Christ (used with dates counting back from the birth of Jesus Christ).

be verb (**am, are, is; was, were; being, been**) 1 exist; occupy a position, The shop is on the corner. 2 happen; take place, The wedding is tomorrow. This verb is also used 3 to join subject and complement (He is my teacher). 4 to form parts of other verbs (It is raining. He was killed).

have been have gone to or come to as a visitor etc., We have been to Rome.

be- prefix used to form verbs (as in befriend, belittle) or strengthen their meaning (as in begrudge). [from Old English]

beach noun (plural **beaches**) the part of the seashore nearest to the water. [probably from Old English]

beacon noun (plural **beacons**) a light or fire used as a signal. [from Old English; related to beckon]

bead noun (plural **beads**) 1 a small piece of a hard substance with a hole in it for threading with others on a string or wire, e.g. to make a necklace. 2 a drop of liquid, a bead of sweat. [from Old English gebed = prayer (because people kept count of the prayers they said by moving the beads on a rosary)]

beady adjective (of eyes) small and bright.

beak noun (plural **beaks**) the hard horny part of a bird's mouth.

beaker noun (plural **beakers**) 1 a tall drinking-mug, often without a handle. 2 a glass container used for pouring liquids in a laboratory.

beam noun (plural **beams**) 1 a long thick bar of wood or metal. 2 a ray or stream of light or other radiation. 3 a happy smile.

beam verb (**beams, beaming, beamed**) 1 smile happily. 2 send out a beam of light or other radiation.
[from Old English]

bean noun (plural **beans**)
1 a kind of plant with seeds growing in pods. 2 its seed or pod eaten as food. 3 the seed of coffee. [from Old English]

bear[1] noun (plural **bears**) a large heavy animal with thick fur and large teeth and claws. [from Old English *bera*]

bear[2] verb (**bears, bearing, bore, borne**)
1 carry or support. 2 have a mark etc., *She still bears the scar.*
3 endure or stand, *I can't bear this pain.* 4 produce or give birth to, *She bore him two sons.* **bearer** noun

bear out support or confirm. [from Old English *beran*]

beard noun (plural **beards**) hair on a man's chin. **bearded** adjective

beard verb (**beards, bearding, bearded**) come face to face with a person and challenge him or her boldly.
[from Old English; the verb originally = to grab someone's beard]

bearing noun (plural **bearings**)
1 the way a person stands, walks, behaves, etc. 2 relevance, *My friendship with Tom has no bearing on his selection for the team.* 3 the direction or position of one thing in relation to another. 4 a device for preventing friction in a machine, *ball-bearings.*

get your bearings work out where you are in relation to things.

beast noun (plural **beasts**)
1 any large four-footed animal.
2 (*informal*) a cruel or vicious person. **beastly** adjective [from Latin *bestia*]

beat verb (**beats, beating, beat, beaten**)
1 hit often, especially with a stick.
2 shape or flatten something by beating it. 3 stir vigorously.
4 make repeated movements, *The heart beats.* 5 do better than somebody; overcome. **beater** noun

beat noun (plural **beats**)
1 a regular rhythm or stroke, *the beat of your heart.* 2 emphasis in rhythm; *the strong rhythm of pop music.* 3 a policeman's regular route.

beautiful adjective attractive to your senses or your mind. **beautifully** adverb

beautify verb (**beautifies, beautifying, beautified**) make someone beautiful. **beautification** noun

beauty noun (plural **beauties**)
1 a quality that gives pleasure to your senses or your mind. 2 a person or thing that has beauty. 3 an excellent example of something. [from old French]

beaver noun (plural **beavers**) an animal with soft brown fur and strong teeth; it builds its home in a deep pool which it makes by damming a stream.

beaver verb (**beavers, beavering, beavered**) work hard, *beavering away.*

because conjunction for the reason that.

because of for the reason of, *He limped because of his bad leg.* [from *by* + *cause*]

beck noun
at someone's beck and call always

ready and waiting to do what he
or she asks.
[from *beckon*]

beckon *verb* (**beckons, beckoning,
beckoned**) make a sign to
a person asking him or her to
come. [from Old English; related
to *beacon*]

become *verb* (**becomes,
becoming, became, become**)
1 come or grow to be; begin to be,
It became dark. **2** be suitable for;
make a person look attractive.
become of happen to, *What
became of it?*

bed *noun* (*plural* **beds**)
1 a piece of furniture that you
sleep or rest on, especially one
with a mattress and coverings.
2 a piece of a garden where plants
are grown. **3** the bottom of the sea
or of a river. **4** a flat base;
a foundation. **5** a layer of rock or
soil. [from Old English]

bedclothes *plural noun* sheets,
blankets, etc.

bedpan *noun* (*plural* **bedpans**)
a container for use as a lavatory
by a bedridden person.

bedraggled (*say* bid-**rag**-eld)
adjective very untidy; wet and
dirty.

bedridden *adjective* too weak or
ill to get out of bed.

bedrock *noun* solid rock beneath
soil.

bedroom *noun* (*plural* **bedrooms**)
a room for sleeping in.

bedtime *noun* (*plural* **bedtimes**)
the time for going to bed.

bee *noun* (*plural* **bees**) a stinging
insect with four wings that
makes honey. [from Old English]

beech *noun* (*plural* **beeches**)
a tree with smooth bark and
glossy leaves.

beef *noun* meat from an ox, bull,
or cow. [from old French]

beefy *adjective* having a solid
muscular body. **beefiness** *noun*

beehive *noun* (*plural* **beehives**)
a box or other container for bees
to live in.

beeline *noun*
make a beeline for go straight or
quickly towards something.
[because a bee was believed to fly
in a straight line back to its hive]

beer *noun* (*plural* **beers**) an
alcoholic drink made from malt
and hops. **beery** *adjective*

beet *noun* (*plural* **beet** or **beets**)
a plant with a thick root used as
a vegetable or for making sugar.

beetle *noun* (*plural* **beetles**) an
insect with hard shiny wing
covers. [from Old English;
related to *bite*]

beetroot *noun* (*plural* **beetroot**)
the dark red root of beet used as
a vegetable.

before *adverb* at an earlier time,
Have you been here before?

before *preposition & conjunction*
1 earlier than, *I was here before
you!* **2** in front of, *He came before
the judge.*

beforehand *adverb* earlier; in
readiness. [from *before* + *hand*
(suggests that your hand does something before someone else's does)]

befriend *verb* (**befriends,
befriending, befriended**) make
friends with someone.

beg *verb* (**begs, begging, begged**)
1 ask to be given money, food, etc.
2 ask earnestly or humbly or
formally.

beg the question argue in an illogical way by relying on the result that you are trying to prove.

go begging be available.

I beg your pardon I apologize; I did not hear what you said.

beggar noun (plural **beggars**)
1 a person who lives by begging.
2 (informal) a person, You lucky beggar! **beggary** noun

begin verb (**begins, beginning, began, begun**)
1 do the earliest or first part of something; start speaking. 2 come into existence, The problem began last year. 3 have something as its first part, The word begins with B. [from Old English]

beginner noun (plural **beginners**) a person who is just beginning to learn a subject.

begrudge verb (**begrudges, begrudging, begrudged**) resent having to give or allow something; grudge.

beguile (say big-I'll) verb (**beguiles, beguiling, beguiled**)
1 amuse or fascinate. 2 deceive.

behalf noun
on behalf of for the benefit of someone else.
on my behalf for me.
[from an old phrase bi halve him = on his side]

USAGE: Do not use on behalf of (= for someone else) when you mean on the part of (= by someone). For example, do not say: This was the worst performance on behalf of Arsenal that I can remember.

behave verb (**behaves, behaving, behaved**)
1 act in a particular way, They behaved badly. 2 show good manners, Behave yourself!
behaviour noun, **behavioural** adjective [from be- + have]

behead verb (**beheads, beheading, beheaded**) cut the head off a person or thing; execute a person in this way. [from Old English]

behind adverb
1 at or to the back; at a place people have left, Don't leave it behind. 2 not making good progress; late, I'm behind with my rent.

behind preposition
1 at or to the back of; on the further side of. 2 having made less progress than, He is behind the others in French. 3 supporting; causing, What is behind all this trouble?
behind a person's back kept secret from him or her deceitfully.
behind the times out of date.

behind noun (plural **behinds**) (informal) a person's bottom. [from Old English]

behindhand adverb & adjective
1 late. 2 out of date.

beige (say bayzh) noun & adjective a very light brown colour. [French]

being noun (plural **beings**)
1 existence. 2 a creature.

belated adjective coming very late or too late. **belatedly** adverb

belch verb (**belches, belching, belched**)
1 send out wind from your stomach through your mouth

noisily. **2** send out fire or smoke etc. from an opening. **belch** *noun* [from Old English]

belief *noun* (*plural* **beliefs**)
1 believing. **2** something a person believes.

believe *verb* (**believes, believing, believed**) think that something is true or that someone is telling the truth. **believable** *adjective*, **believer** *noun*
believe in think that something exists or is good or can be relied on.
[from Old English]

belittle *verb* (**belittles, belittling, belittled**) make something seem of little value, *Do not belittle their success.* **belittlement** *noun*

bell *noun* (*plural* **bells**)
1 a cup-shaped metal instrument that makes a ringing sound when struck by the clapper hanging inside it. **2** any device that makes a ringing or buzzing sound to attract attention. **3** a bell-shaped object.

belligerent (*say* bil-ij-er-ent) *adjective*
1 aggressive; eager to fight.
2 fighting; engaged in a war.
belligerently *adverb*, **belligerence** *noun* [from Latin *bellum* = war + *gerens* = waging]

bellow *noun* (*plural* **bellows**)
1 the loud deep sound made by a bull or other large animal. **2** a deep shout.

bellow *verb* (**bellows, bellowing, bellowed**) give a deep shout.

belly *noun* (*plural* **bellies**) the abdomen; the stomach.

belong *verb* (**belongs, belonging, belonged**) have a proper place,

The pans belong in the kitchen.
belong to be the property of; be a member of, *We belong to the same club.*
[from *be-* + *long* = owing to, because of]

belongings *plural noun* a person's possessions.

beloved *adjective* dearly loved.

below *adverb* at or to a lower position; underneath, *There's fire down below.*

below *preposition* lower than; under, *The temperature was ten degrees below zero.*

belt *noun* (*plural* **belts**)
1 a strip of cloth or leather etc. worn round the waist. **2** a band of flexible material used in machinery. **3** a long narrow area, *a belt of rain.*

belt *verb* (**belts, belting, belted**)
1 put a belt round something.
2 (*slang*) hit or beat. **3** (*slang*) rush along.
[via Old English from Latin]

bench *noun* (*plural* **benches**)
1 a long seat. **2** a long table for working at. **3** the seat where judges or magistrates sit; the judges or magistrates hearing a lawsuit. [from Old English]

bend *verb* (**bends, bending, bent**)
1 change from being straight.
2 turn downwards; stoop, *She bent to pick it up.*

bend *noun* (*plural* **bends**) a place where something bends; a curve or turn, *a bend in the road.*

bene- (*say* ben-ee) *prefix* well (as in *benefit, benevolent*). [from Latin *bene* = well]

beneath *preposition*
1 under. 2 unworthy of, *Cheating is beneath you.*
beneath *adverb* underneath. [from Old English]

benefactor *noun* (*plural* **benefactors**) a person who gives money or other help. [from *bene-* + Latin *factor* = doer]

beneficial *adjective* having a good or helpful effect; advantageous. [from Latin *beneficium* = favour, support]

beneficiary (*say* ben-if-ish-er-ee) *noun* (*plural* **beneficiaries**) a person who receives benefits, especially from a will. [same origin as *beneficial*]

benefit *noun* (*plural* **benefits**)
1 something that is helpful or profitable. 2 a payment to which a person is entitled from government funds or from an insurance policy.
benefit *verb* (**benefits**, **benefiting**, **benefited**)
1 do good to a person or thing. 2 receive a benefit.
[from *bene-* + Latin *facere* = do]

benevolent *adjective*
1 kind and helpful. 2 formed for charitable purposes, *a benevolent fund.* **benevolently** *adverb*, **benevolence** *noun* [from *bene-* + Latin *volens* = wishing]

benign (*say* bin-I'n) *adjective*
1 kindly. 2 favourable. 3 (of a disease) mild, not malignant. **benignly** *adverb* [from Latin *benignus* = kind-hearted]

benignant (*say* bin-ig-nant) *adjective* kindly. [same origin as *benign*]

bent *adjective* curved or crooked.
bent on intending to do something.
bent *noun* a talent for something.

bequeath *verb* (**bequeaths**, **bequeathing**, **bequeathed**) leave something to a person, especially in a will. [from *be-* + Old English *cwethan* = say]

bequest *noun* (*plural* **bequests**) something left to a person, especially in a will.

bereaved *adjective* deprived of a relative or friend who has died. **bereavement** *noun* [from *be-* + an old word *reave* = take forcibly]

berry *noun* (*plural* **berries**) any small round juicy fruit without a stone. [from Old English]

berserk (*say* ber-serk) *adjective*
go berserk become uncontrollably violent. [from Icelandic *berserkr* = wild warrior, from *ber-* = bear + *serkr* = coat]

berth *noun* (*plural* **berths**)
1 a sleeping place on a ship or train. 2 a place where a ship can moor.
give a wide berth keep at a safe distance from a person or thing.
berth *verb* (**berths**, **berthing**, **berthed**) moor in a berth. [from *be-²*]

beseech *verb* (**beseeches**, **beseeching**, **beseeched** or **besought**) ask earnestly; implore. [from *be-* + seek]

beside *preposition*
1 by the side of; near. 2 compared with.
be beside himself or **herself**, etc.,

be very excited or upset.
[from Old English *be sidan* = by
the side]

besides *preposition & adverb* in
addition to; also, *Who came
besides you? And besides, it's the
wrong colour.*

besiege *verb* (**besieges,
besieging, besieged**)
1 surround a place in order to
capture it. **2** crowd round, *Fans
besieged the singer after the
concert.*

besotted *adjective* too fond of
something; fond in a silly way.

besought *past tense* of **beseech.**

best *adjective* most excellent.

best *adverb*
1 in the best way; most. **2** most
usefully; most wisely, *We had
best go.*

best man *noun* the bridegroom's
chief attendant at a wedding.

bestow *verb* (**bestows,
bestowing, bestowed**) present to
someone. **bestowal** *noun*

best-seller *noun* (*plural* **best-
sellers**) a book sold in large
numbers.

bet *noun* (*plural* **bets**)
1 an agreement that you will pay
money etc. if you are wrong in
forecasting the result of a race
etc. **2** the money that you agree to
pay in this way.

bet *verb* (**bets, betting, bet** or
betted)
1 make a bet. **2** (*informal*) think
most likely; predict, *I bet he will
forget.*

beta (*say* beet-a) *noun* the second
letter of the Greek alphabet = b.

betray *verb* (**betrays, betraying,
betrayed**)
1 be disloyal to a person or

country etc. **2** reveal something
that should have been kept
secret. **betrayal** *noun*, **betrayer**
noun

betrothed *adjective* (*formal*)
engaged to be married. **betroth**
verb, **betrothal** *noun* [from *be-
+ troth*]

better *adjective*
1 more excellent; more
satisfactory. **2** recovered from
illness.

better *adverb*
1 in a better way; more. **2** more
usefully; more wisely, *We had
better go.*

better *verb* (**betters, bettering,
bettered**)
1 improve something. **2** do better
than. **betterment** *noun*
[from Old English]

between *preposition & adverb*
1 within two or more given
limits, *between the walls.*
2 connecting two or more people,
places, or things, *The train runs
between London and Glasgow.*
3 shared by, *Divide this money
between you.* **4** separating;
comparing, *Can you tell the
difference between them?* [from
Old English]

USAGE: The preposition
between should be followed by
the object form of the pronoun
(*me, her, him, them,* or *us*). The
expression 'between you and I'
is incorrect; say *between you
and me.*

beverage *noun* (*plural*
beverages) any kind of drink.
[from old French]

bewail *verb* (**bewails, bewailing,
bewailed**) mourn for something.

beware *verb* be careful, *Beware of pickpockets*. [from *be-* + *ware* = wary]

bewilder *verb* (**bewilders, bewildering, bewildered**) puzzle someone hopelessly.

bewilderment *noun* [from *be-* + an old word *wilder* = lose your way]

bewitch *verb* (**bewitches, bewitching, bewitched**)
1 put a magic spell on someone. 2 delight someone very much. [from *be-* + *witch* = put under a spell]

beyond *preposition & adverb*
1 further than; further on, *Don't go beyond the fence*. 2 outside the range of; too difficult for, *The problem is beyond me*.

bi- *prefix*
1 two (as in *bicycle*). 2 twice (as in *biannual*). [from Latin *bis* = twice]

bias *noun* (*plural* **biases**)
1 a feeling or influence for or against someone or something; a prejudice. 2 a tendency to swerve. 3 a slanting direction.

biased *adjective* prejudiced.

bib *noun* (*plural* **bibs**)
1 a cloth or covering put under a baby's chin during meals. 2 the part of an apron above the waist. [probably from Latin *bibere* = to drink]

Bible *noun* (*plural* **Bibles**) the sacred book of the Jews (the Old Testament) and of the Christians (the Old and New Testament). [from Greek *biblia* = books (originally = rolls of papyrus from Byblos, a port now in Lebanon)]

biblical *adjective* to do with or in the Bible.

bibliography (*say* bib-lee-og-ra-fee) *noun* (*plural* **bibliographies**)
1 a list of books about a subject or by a particular author. 2 the study of books and their history.
bibliographical *adjective* [from Greek *biblion* = book, + *-graphy*]

bicentenary (*say* by-sen-teen-er-ee) *noun* (*plural* **bicentenaries**)
a 200th anniversary. **bicentennial** (*say* by-sen-ten-ee-al) *adjective* [from *bi* + *centenary*]

biceps (*say* by-seps) *noun* (*plural* **biceps**) the large muscle at the front of the arm above the elbow. [Latin, = two-headed (because its end is attached at two points)]

bicker *verb* (**bickers, bickering, bickered**) quarrel over unimportant things; squabble.

bicycle *noun* (*plural* **bicycles**)
a two-wheeled vehicle driven by pedals. **bicyclist** *noun* [from *bi-* + Greek *kyklos* = circle, wheel]

bid *noun* (*plural* **bids**)
1 the offer of an amount you are willing to pay for something, especially at an auction. 2 an attempt.

bid *verb* (**bids, bidding, bid**) make a bid. **bidder** *noun*

bid *verb* (**bids, bidding, bid** (or *old use*) **bade**, **bid** or **bidden**)
1 command, *Do as you are bid* or *bidden*. 2 say as a greeting or farewell, *bidding them good night*.
[from two Old English words; *biddan* = to ask, and *beodan* = to announce or command]

bidding *noun* if you do someone's bidding, you do what they tell you to do.

bide verb (**bides, biding, bided**) if you bide your time, you wait for the right time to do something.

biennial noun (plural **biennials**) a plant that lives for two years, flowering and dying in the second year. [from Latin *biennis* = of two years]

bier (say beer) noun (plural **biers**) a movable stand on which a coffin or a dead body is placed before it is buried.

bifocal (say by-foh-kal) adjective (of spectacle lenses) made in two sections, with the upper part for looking at distant objects and the lower part for reading.

bifocals plural noun bifocal spectacles.

big adjective (**bigger, biggest**) 1 large. 2 important, *the big match*. 3 more grown-up; elder, *my big sister*.

bigamy (say big-a-mee) noun the crime of marrying a person when you are already married to someone else. **bigamous** adjective, **bigamist** noun [from *bi-* + Greek *-gamos* = married]

bigot noun (plural **bigots**) a bigoted person. [French]

bigoted adjective narrow-minded and intolerant. **bigotry** noun

bike noun (plural **bikes**) (*informal*) a bicycle or motorcycle. [abbreviation of *bicycle*]

bikini noun (plural **bikinis**) a woman's very small two-piece swimsuit. [named after the island of Bikini in the Pacific Ocean, where an atomic bomb test was carried out in 1946, at about the time the bikini was first worn (both caused great excitement)]

bilateral adjective 1 of or on two sides. 2 between two people or groups, *a bilateral agreement*. [from *bi-* + *lateral*]

bile noun a bitter liquid produced by the liver, helping to digest fats. [from Latin]

bilingual (say by-ling-wal) adjective 1 written in two languages. 2 able to speak two languages. [from *bi-* + Latin *lingua* = language]

bilious adjective feeling sick; sickly. **biliousness** noun [from *bile*]

-bility suffix see **-able**.

bill[1] noun (plural **bills**) 1 a written statement of charges for goods or services that have been supplied. 2 a poster. 3 a list; a programme of entertainment. 4 the draft of a proposed law to be discussed by Parliament. 5 (*American*) a banknote. **bill of fare** a menu. [same origin as *bull*[2]]

bill[2] noun (plural **bills**) a bird's beak. [from Old English]

billabong noun (plural **billabongs**) (in Australia) a backwater. [an Aboriginal word]

billiards noun a game in which three balls are struck with cues on a cloth-covered table (**billiard table**). [from French *billard* = cue]

billion noun (plural **billions**) 1 a thousand million (1,000,000,000). 2 a million million (1,000,000,000,000).

billionth *adjective & noun* [French, from *bi-* + *million*]

USAGE: Although the word originally meant a million million, nowadays it usually means a thousand million.

billow *noun* (*plural* **billows**) a huge wave.

bin *noun* (*plural* **bins**) a large or deep container.

binary (*say* by-ner-ee) *adjective* involving sets of two; consisting of two parts. [from Latin]

binary digit *noun* (*plural* **binary digits**) either of the two digits (0 and 1) used in the system of numbers known as binary notation or the binary scale.

bind *verb* (**binds, binding, bound**) 1 fasten material round something. 2 fasten the pages of a book into a cover. 3 tie up or tie together. 4 make somebody agree to do something. **binder** *noun* **bind a person over** make him or her agree not to break the law.

bind *noun* (*slang*) a nuisance; a bore. [from Old English]

binding *noun* (*plural* **bindings**) something that binds, especially the covers, glue, etc. of a book.

binding *adjective* (of an agreement or promise) that must be carried out or obeyed.

binge *noun* (*plural* **binges**) (*slang*) a time spent eating a lot of food.

bingo *noun* a game using cards on which numbered squares are crossed out as the numbers are called out at random. [origin unknown]

binoculars *plural noun* a device with lenses for both eyes, making distant objects seem nearer. [from Latin *bini* = two together + *oculus* = eye]

bio- *prefix* life (as in *biology*). [from Greek *bios* = life]

biochemistry *noun* the study of the chemical composition and processes of living things. **biochemical** *adjective*, **biochemist** *noun*

biodegradable *adjective* able to be decomposed by bacteria, *This packaging is biodegradable.*

biography (*say* by-og-ra-fee) *noun* (*plural* **biographies**) the story of a person's life. **biographical** *adjective*, **biographer** *noun*

biology *noun* the study of the life and structure of living things. **biological** *adjective*, **biologist** *noun*

bionic (*say* by-on-ik) *adjective* (of a person or parts of the body) operated by electronic devices. [from *bio-* + *electronic*]

biopsy (*say* by-op-see) *noun* (*plural* **biopsies**) examination of tissue from a living body. [from *bio-* + *autopsy*]

biped (*say* by-ped) *noun* (*plural* **bipeds**) a two-footed animal. [from *bi-* + Latin *pedes* = feet]

birch *noun* (*plural* **birches**) 1 a deciduous tree with slender branches. 2 a bundle of birch branches for flogging people. [from Old English]

bird *noun* (*plural* **birds**) 1 an animal with feathers, two wings, and two legs.

2 (*slang*) a young woman.
bird's-eye view a view from above.

birth *noun* (*plural* **births**)
1 the process by which a baby or young animal comes out from its mother's body. **2** origin; parentage, *He is of noble birth.*

birth control *noun* ways of avoiding conceiving a baby.

birthday *noun* (*plural* **birthdays**) the anniversary of the day a person was born.

birth rate *noun* (*plural* **birth rates**) the number of children born in one year for every 1,000 people.

birthright *noun* a right or privilege to which a person is entitled through being born into a particular family or country.

biscuit *noun* (*plural* **biscuits**) a small flat kind of cake that has been baked until it is crisp. [from Latin *bis* = twice + *coctus* = cooked (because originally they were baked and then dried out in a cool oven to make them keep longer)]

bisect (*say* by-**sekt**) *verb* (**bisects, bisecting, bisected**) divide something into two equal parts.
bisection *noun*, **bisector** *noun* [from *bi-* + Latin *sectum* = cut]

bishop *noun* (*plural* **bishops**)
1 an important member of the clergy in charge of all the churches in a city or district.
2 a chess piece shaped like a bishop's mitre. [via Old English from Latin *episcopus*]

bismuth *noun* a greyish-white metal.

bison (*say* by-son) *noun* (*plural* **bison**) a wild ox found in North America and Europe, with a large shaggy head.

bit[1] *noun* (*plural* **bits**)
1 a small piece or amount of something. **2** the metal part of a horse's bridle that is put into its mouth. **3** the part of a tool that cuts or grips things when twisted.
a bit 1 a short distance or time, *Wait a bit.* **2** slightly, *I'm a bit worried.*
bit by bit gradually.
[from Old English; related to *bite*]

bit[2] *past tense* of **bite**.

bit[3] *noun* (*plural* **bits**) the smallest unit of information in a computer, expressed as a choice between two possibilities. [from *binary digit*]

bitch *noun* (*plural* **bitches**)
1 a female dog, fox, or wolf.
2 (*informal*) a spiteful woman.
bitchy *adjective*

bite *verb* (**bites, biting, bit, bitten**)
1 cut or take something with your teeth. **2** penetrate; sting.
3 accept bait, *The fish are biting.*
bite the dust fall wounded and die.

bite *noun* (*plural* **bites**)
1 biting, *She took a bite.* **2** a mark or spot made by biting, *an insect bite.* **3** a snack.
[from Old English; related to *bit*[1]]

bitter *adjective*
1 tasting sharp, not sweet.
2 feeling or causing mental pain or resentment, *a bitter disappointment.* **3** very cold.
bitterly *adverb*, **bitterness** *noun* [from Old English; related to *bite*]

bivalve *noun* (*plural* **bivalves**) a shellfish (e.g. an oyster) that has a shell with two hinged parts.

bizarre (*say* biz-**ar**) *adjective* very odd in appearance or effect. [from Italian *bizarro* = angry]

Black *noun* (*plural* **Blacks**) a person with a very dark or black skin. **Black** *adjective*

USAGE: *Black* is the word generally preferred by African people and people of African descent.

black *noun* (*plural* **blacks**) the very darkest colour, like coal or soot.

black *adjective*
1 of the colour black. **2** very dirty. **3** dismal; not hopeful, *The outlook is black.* **4** hostile; disapproving, *He gave me a black look.* **5** (of coffee or tea) without milk. **blackly** *adverb*, **blackness** *noun*

black *verb* (**blacks**, **blacking**, **blacked**) make a thing black. **black out 1** cover windows etc. so that no light can penetrate. **2** faint, lose consciousness. **blackout** *noun*

blackberry *noun* (*plural* **blackberries**) a sweet black berry.

blackbird *noun* (*plural* **blackbirds**) a European songbird, the male of which is black.

blackboard *noun* (*plural* **blackboards**) a dark board for writing on with chalk.

black box *noun* (*plural* **black boxes**) a flight recorder.

blacken *verb* (**blackens**, **blackening**, **blackened**) make or become black.

black eye *noun* (*plural* **black eyes**) an eye with a bruise round it.

blackguard (*say* blag-**erd**) *noun* (*plural* **blackguards**) (*old use*) a wicked person. [originally the *black guard* = the servants who did the dirty jobs]

black hole *noun* (*plural* **black holes**) a region in outer space with such a strong gravitational field that no matter or radiation can escape from it.

blacklist *verb* (**blacklists**, **blacklisting**, **blacklisted**) put someone on a list of those who are disapproved of.

blackmail *verb* (**blackmails**, **blackmailing**, **blackmailed**) demand money etc. from someone by threats. **blackmail** *noun*, **blackmailer** *noun* [from *black* + *mail²*; literally = black armour or protection]

black market *noun* (*plural* **black markets**) illegal trading.

blacksmith *noun* (*plural* **blacksmiths**) a person who makes and repairs iron things, especially one who makes and fits horseshoes. [because of the dark colour of iron]

black spot *noun* (*plural* **black spots**) a dangerous place.

bladder *noun* (*plural* **bladders**) **1** the bag-like part of the body in which urine collects. **2** the inflatable bag inside a football. [from Old English]

blade *noun* (*plural* **blades**) **1** the flat cutting-part of a knife, sword, axe, etc. **2** the flat wide part of an oar, spade, propeller, etc. **3** a flat narrow leaf, *blades of grass.*

4 a broad flat bone, *shoulder blade*. [from Old English]

blame *verb* (**blames, blaming, blamed**)
1 say that somebody or something has caused what is wrong, *They blamed me*. **2** find fault with someone, *We can't blame them for wanting a holiday*.
blame *noun* (*plural* **blames**) responsibility for what is wrong.

blancmange (*say* bla-**monj**) *noun* (*plural* **blancmanges**) a jelly-like pudding made with milk. [from French *blanc* = white + *mange* = eat]

bland *adjective*
1 having a mild flavour rather than a strong one. **2** gentle and casual; not irritating or stimulating, *a bland manner*.
blandly *adverb*, **blandness** *noun* [from Latin *blandus* = soft, smooth]

blank *adjective*
1 not written or printed on; unmarked. **2** without interest or expression, *a blank look*. **3** empty of thoughts, *My mind's gone blank*. **blankly** *adverb*, **blankness** *noun*
blank *noun* (*plural* **blanks**)
1 an empty space. **2** a blank cartridge.
[from French *blanc* = white]

blanket *noun* (*plural* **blankets**)
1 a warm cloth covering used on a bed etc. **2** any thick soft covering, *a blanket of snow*.
blanket *adjective* covering a wide range of conditions etc., *a blanket agreement*.

[originally = woollen cloth which had not been dyed; from French *blanc* = white]

blank verse *noun* poetry without rhymes.

blare *verb* (**blares, blaring, blared**) make a loud harsh sound. **blare** *noun*

blaspheme (*say* blas-**feem**) *verb* (**blasphemes, blaspheming, blasphemed**) talk or write irreverently about sacred things.

blasphemy (*say* blas-**fim**-ee) *noun* (*plural* **blasphemies**) irreverent talk about sacred things.
blasphemous *adjective*

blast *noun* (*plural* **blasts**)
1 a strong rush of wind or air. **2** a loud noise, *the blast of the trumpets*.
blast *verb* (**blasts, blasting, blasted**) blow up with explosives.
blast off launch by the firing of rockets. **blast-off** *noun*
[from Old English; related to **blow**[1]]

blatant (*say* **blay**-tant) *adjective* very obvious, *a blatant lie*.
blatantly *adverb* [from an old word meaning 'noisy']

blaze *noun* (*plural* **blazes**) a very bright flame, fire, or light.
blaze *verb* (**blazes, blazing, blazed**)
1 burn or shine brightly. **2** show great feeling, *He was blazing with anger*.

blazer *noun* (*plural* **blazers**) a kind of jacket, often with a badge or in the colours of a school or team etc. [from *blaze*[1] (because originally blazers were made in very bright colours and were thought of as shining or 'blazing')]

-ble *suffix* see **-able**.

bleach *verb* (**bleaches, bleaching, bleached**) make or become white.

bleach *noun* (*plural* **bleaches**) a substance used to bleach things.

bleak *adjective*
1 bare and cold, *a bleak hillside*.
2 dreary or miserable, *a bleak future*. **bleakly** *adverb*, **bleakness** *noun*

bleary *adjective* watery and not seeing clearly, *bleary eyes*. **blearily** *adverb* [origin unknown]

bleat *noun* (*plural* **bleats**) the cry of a lamb, goat, or calf.

bleat *verb* (**bleats, bleating, bleated**) make a bleat. [imitating the sound]

bleed *verb* (**bleeds, bleeding, bled**)
1 lose blood. 2 draw blood or fluid from. [from Old English; related to *blood*]

blemish *noun* (*plural* **blemishes**) a flaw; a mark that spoils a thing's appearance. **blemish** *verb* [from old French]

blench *verb* (**blenches, blenching, blenched**) flinch. [from Old English]

blend *verb* (**blends, blending, blended**) mix smoothly or easily.

blend *noun* (*plural* **blends**) a mixture.

blender *noun* (*plural* **blenders**) an electric machine used to mix food or turn it into liquid.

bless *verb* (**blesses, blessing, blessed**)
1 make sacred or holy. 2 bring God's favour on a person or thing.

blessing *noun* (*plural* **blessings**)
1 a prayer that blesses a person or thing; being blessed.
2 something that people are glad of.

blind *adjective*
1 without the ability to see.
2 without any thought or understanding, *blind obedience*.
3 (of a tube, passage, or road) closed at one end. **blindly** *adverb*, **blindness** *noun*

blind *verb* (**blinds, blinding, blinded**) make a person blind.

blind *noun* (*plural* **blinds**)
1 a screen for a window.
2 a deception; something used to hide the truth, *His journey was a blind.*
[from Old English]

blind date *noun* (*plural* **blind dates**) a date between a man and woman who have not met before.

blindfold *noun* (*plural* **blindfolds**) a strip of cloth tied round someone's eyes so that they cannot see.

blindfold *verb* (**blindfolds, blindfolding, blindfolded**) cover someone's eyes with a blindfold. [from Old English *blindfeld* = struck blind, from *blind* + *fell²*]

blind spot *noun* (*plural* **blind spots**) a subject that you do not understand or know much about.

blink *verb* (**blinks, blinking, blinked**) shut and open your eyes rapidly. **blink** *noun* [from *blench*, influenced by Dutch *blinken* = shine]

bliss *noun* perfect happiness. **blissful** *adjective*, **blissfully** *adverb*

blister *noun* (*plural* **blisters**) a swelling like a bubble, especially on skin. **blister** *verb* [origin unknown]

blizzard noun (plural **blizzards**) a severe snowstorm. [origin unknown]

bloated adjective swollen by fat, gas, or liquid. [from Old Norse blautr = soft]

blob noun (plural **blobs**) a small round mass of something, blobs of paint. [because blob sounds squelchy, like liquid]

block noun (plural **blocks**)
1 a solid piece of something. 2 an obstruction. 3 a large building divided into flats or offices.
4 a group of buildings.
block verb (**blocks, blocking, blocked**) obstruct; prevent something from moving or being used. **blockage** noun

blockade noun (plural **blockades**) the blocking of a city or port etc. in order to prevent people and goods from going in or out.
blockade verb (**blockades, blockading, blockaded**) set up a blockade of a place. [from block]

block letters plural noun plain capital letters.

blond or **blonde** adjective fair-haired; fair.

blonde noun (plural **blondes**) a fair-haired girl or woman.

blood noun
1 the red liquid that flows through veins and arteries.
2 family relationship; ancestry, He is of royal blood.
in cold blood deliberately and cruelly. [from Old English; related to bleed]

blood bank noun (plural **blood banks**) a supply of blood and plasma for transfusions.

bloodbath noun (plural **bloodbaths**) a massacre.

blood donor noun (plural **blood donors**) a person who gives blood for use in transfusions.

bloodhound noun (plural **bloodhounds**) a large dog that tracks people by their scent.

bloodshed noun the killing or wounding of people.

bloodshot adjective (of eyes) streaked with red.

blood sport noun (plural **blood sports**) a sport that involves wounding or killing animals.

bloodthirsty adjective eager for bloodshed.

blood vessel noun (plural **blood vessels**) a tube carrying blood in the body; an artery, vein, or capillary.

bloody adjective (**bloodier, bloodiest**)
1 bloodstained. 2 with much bloodshed, a bloody battle.
bloody-minded adjective deliberately awkward and not helpful.

bloom noun (plural **blooms**)
1 a flower. 2 the fine powder on fresh ripe grapes etc.
bloom verb (**blooms, blooming, bloomed**) produce flowers. [from Old Norse]

blossom noun (plural **blossoms**) a flower or mass of flowers, especially on a fruit tree.
blossom verb (**blossoms, blossoming, blossomed**)
1 produce flowers. 2 develop into something, She blossomed into a fine singer.

blot noun (plural blots)
1 a spot of ink. 2 a flaw or fault; something ugly, *a blot on the landscape.*

blot verb (blots, blotting, blotted)
1 make a blot or blots on something. 2 dry with blotting paper.
blot out 1 cross out thickly. 2 obscure, *Fog blotted out the view.*

blotch noun (plural blotches) an untidy patch of colour. **blotchy** adjective

blotting paper noun absorbent paper for soaking up ink from writing.

blouse noun (plural blouses) a woman's garment like a shirt.

blow[1] verb (blows, blowing, blew, blown)
1 send out a current of air. 2 move in or with a current of air, *His hat blew off.* 3 make or sound something by blowing, *blow bubbles; blow the whistle.* 4 melt with too strong an electric current, *A fuse has blown.* 5 (slang) damn, *Blow you!*
blow up 1 inflate. 2 explode. 3 shatter by an explosion.
blow noun (plural blows) the action of blowing.
[from Old English]

blow[2] noun (plural blows)
1 a hard knock or hit. 2 a shock; a disaster. [origin unknown]

blubber noun the fat of whales. [originally = sea foam; probably related to *bubble*]

bludgeon (say bluj-on) noun (plural bludgeons) a short stick with a thickened end, used as a weapon.

bludgeon verb (bludgeons, bludgeoning, bludgeoned) hit someone several times with a heavy stick or other object. [origin unknown]

blue noun (plural blues) the colour of a cloudless sky.
out of the blue unexpectedly.

blue adjective
1 of the colour blue. 2 unhappy; depressed, *feeling blue.* 3 indecent; obscene, *blue films.* **blueness** noun
[via French from Germanic]

bluebottle noun (plural bluebottles) a large bluish fly. [origin unknown]

blueprint noun (plural blueprints) a detailed plan. [because copies of plans were made on blue paper]

blues noun a slow sad jazz song or tune.
the blues a very sad feeling; depression. [short for *blue devils*, spiteful imaginary demons that were believed to cause depression]

bluff[1] verb (bluffs, bluffing, bluffed) deceive someone, especially by pretending to be someone else or to be able to do something.
bluff noun (plural bluffs) the act of bluffing; a threat that you make but do not intend to carry out.

bluff[2] adjective frank and hearty in manner. **bluffness** noun [originally a sailor's word to describe a blunt ship's bow]

blunder noun (plural blunders) a stupid mistake.

blunder verb (blunders, blundering, blundered)
1 make a blunder. 2 move clumsily and uncertainly.

blunt adjective
1 not sharp. 2 speaking in plain terms; straightforward, *a blunt refusal.* **bluntly** adverb, **bluntness** noun

blunt verb (blunts, blunting, blunted) make a thing blunt.

blur verb (blurs, blurring, blurred) make or become indistinct or smeared.

blur noun (plural blurs) an indistinct appearance, *Without his glasses on, everything was a blur.*

blurt verb (blurts, blurting, blurted) say something suddenly or tactlessly, *He blurted it out.* [origin unknown]

blush verb (blushes, blushing, blushed) become red in the face because you are ashamed or embarrassed.

blush noun (plural blushes) reddening in the face. [from Old English]

bluster verb (blusters, blustering, blustered)
1 blow in gusts; be windy. 2 talk loudly and aggressively. **blustery** adjective

BMX abbreviation a kind of bicycle for use in racing on a dirt track. [short for bicycle motocross (x standing for cross)]

boar noun (plural boars)
1 a wild pig. 2 a male pig.

board noun (plural boards)
1 a flat piece of wood. 2 a flat piece of stiff material, e.g. a chessboard. 3 daily meals supplied in return for payment or work, *board and lodging.*
4 a committee.
on board on or in a ship, aircraft, etc.

board verb (boards, boarding, boarded)
1 go on board a ship, etc. 2 give or get meals and accommodation.
board up block with fixed boards. [from Old English]

boarder noun (plural boarders)
1 a pupil who lives at a boarding school during the term. 2 a lodger who receives meals.

boarding school noun (plural boarding schools) a school where pupils live during the term.

boast verb (boasts, boasting, boasted)
1 speak with great pride and try to impress people. 2 have something to be proud of, *The town boasts a fine park.* **boaster** noun, **boastful** adjective, **boastfully** adverb

boast noun (plural boasts) a boastful statement. [origin unknown]

boat noun (plural boats) a vehicle built to travel on water and carry people etc.
in the same boat in the same situation; suffering the same difficulties.

bob verb (bobs, bobbing, bobbed) move quickly up and down.

bobsleigh or **bobsled** noun (plural bobsleighs, bobsleds) a sledge with two sets of runners.

bodice noun (plural bodices) the upper part of a dress. [from body]

body noun (plural bodies)
1 the structure consisting of bones and flesh etc. of a person or animal; the main part of this

apart from the head and limbs.
2 a corpse. **3** the main part of
something. **4** a group or quantity
regarded as a unit, *the school's
governing body*. **5** a distinct
object or piece of matter, *Stars
and planets are heavenly bodies*.
bodily *adjective & adverb* [from
Old English]

bodyguard *noun* (*plural*
bodyguards) a guard to protect
a person's life.

bog *noun* (*plural* **bogs**) an area of
wet spongy ground. **boggy**
adjective
bogged down stuck and unable
to make any progress.
[Scottish Gaelic, = soft]

bogus *adjective* not real; sham.
[an American word; origin
unknown]

boil¹ *verb* (**boils, boiling, boiled**)
1 make or become hot enough to
bubble and give off steam. **2** cook
or wash something in boiling
water. **3** be very hot.
boil *noun* boiling point, *bring the
milk to the boil*.
[from old French]

boil² *noun* (*plural* **boils**) an
inflamed swelling under the skin.
[from Old English]

boiler *noun* (*plural* **boilers**)
a container in which water is
heated or clothes are boiled.

boisterous *adjective* noisy and
lively. [origin unknown]

bold *adjective*
1 brave; courageous. **2** impudent.
3 (of colours) strong and vivid.
boldly *adverb*, **boldness** *noun*
[from Old English]

bolster *noun* (*plural* **bolsters**)
a long pillow for placing across
a bed under other pillows.

bolster *verb* (**bolsters,
bolstering, bolstered**) add extra
support.
[from Old English]

bolt *noun* (*plural* **bolts**)
1 a sliding bar for fastening
a door. **2** a thick metal pin for
fastening things together.
3 a sliding bar that opens and
closes the breech of a rifle. **4** a
shaft of lightning. **5** an arrow
shot from a crossbow. **6** the
action of bolting.
a bolt from the blue a surprise,
usually an unpleasant one.
bolt upright quite upright.

bolt *verb* (**bolts, bolting, bolted**)
1 fasten with a bolt or bolts.
2 run away; (of a horse) run off
out of control. **3** swallow food
quickly.
[from Old English]

bomb *noun* (*plural* **bombs**) an
explosive device.
the bomb an atomic or hydrogen
bomb.

bomb *verb* (**bombs, bombing,
bombed**) attack a place with
bombs.
[probably from Greek *bombos*
= booming]

bombard *verb* (**bombards,
bombarding, bombarded**)
1 attack with gunfire or many
missiles. **2** direct a large number
of questions or comments at
somebody. **bombardment** *noun*
[same origin as *bomb*]

bomber *noun* (*plural* **bombers**)
1 someone who plants or sets off
a bomb. **2** an aeroplane from
which bombs are dropped.

bombshell *noun* (*plural*
bombshells) a great shock.

bonanza (*say* bon-**an**-za) *noun*
(*plural* **bonanzas**) sudden great
wealth or luck. [originally an
American word; from Spanish,
= good weather, prosperity]

bond *noun* (*plural* **bonds**)
1 a close friendship or
connection between two or more
people. **2** bonds ropes or chains
used to tie someone up.
3 a document stating an
agreement.

bond *verb* (**bonds, bonding,
bonded**) become closely linked or
connected.

bondage *noun* slavery; captivity.

bone *noun* (*plural* **bones**) one of
the hard parts of a person's or
animal's body (excluding teeth,
nails, horns, and cartilage).

bone *verb* (**bones, boning,
boned**) remove the bones from
meat or fish.

bonfire *noun* (*plural* **bonfires**) an
outdoor fire to burn rubbish or
celebrate something. [originally
bone fire, = a fire to dispose of
people's or animals' bones]

bonnet *noun* (*plural* **bonnets**)
1 a hat with strings that tie under
the chin. **2** a Scottish beret. **3** the
hinged cover over a car engine.
[from Latin *abonnis* = hat]

bonus (*say* **boh**-nus) *noun* (*plural*
bonuses)
1 an extra payment in addition to
a person's normal wages. **2** an
extra benefit. [from Latin *bonus*
= good]

bony *adjective*
1 with large bones; having bones
with little flesh on them. **2** full of
bones. **3** like bones.

boo *verb* (**boos, booing, booed**)
shout 'boo' in disapproval. **boo**
noun

booby *noun* (*plural* **boobies**)
a babyish or stupid person. [from
Spanish]

booby prize *noun* (*plural* **booby
prizes**) a prize given as a joke to
someone who comes last in
a contest.

booby trap *noun* (*plural* **booby
traps**) something designed to hit
or injure someone unexpectedly.

book *noun* (*plural* **books**) a set of
sheets of paper, usually with
printing or writing on them,
fastened together inside a cover.
bookseller *noun*, **bookshop** *noun*,
bookstall *noun*

book *verb* (**books, booking,
booked**)
1 reserve a place in a theatre,
hotel, train, etc. **2** enter a person
in a police record, *The police
booked him for speeding.*

bookcase *noun* (*plural*
bookcases) a piece of furniture
with shelves for books.

bookkeeping *noun* recording
details of the money that is spent
and received by a business.
bookkeeper *noun*

booklet *noun* (*plural* **booklets**)
a small thin book.

bookmaker *noun* (*plural*
bookmakers) a person whose
business is taking bets. [because
the bets used to be written down
in a notebook]

bookmark *noun* (*plural*
bookmarks) something to mark
a place in a book.

bookworm noun (plural
bookworms)
1 a grub that eats holes in books.
2 a person who loves reading.

boom verb (booms, booming,
boomed)
1 make a deep hollow sound. 2 be
growing and prospering,
Business is booming.

boom noun (plural booms)
1 a deep hollow sound.
2 prosperity; growth.
[imitating the sound]

boomerang noun (plural
boomerangs) a curved piece of
wood that can be thrown so that
it returns to the thrower,
originally used by Australian
Aborigines.

boor noun (plural boors) an ill-
mannered person. **boorish**
adjective

boost verb (boosts, boosting,
boosted)
1 increase the strength, value, or
reputation of a person or thing.
2 push something upwards.
booster noun

boost noun (plural boosts)
1 an increase. 2 an upward push.

boot noun (plural boots)
1 a shoe that covers the foot and
ankle or leg. 2 the compartment
for luggage in a car. **booted**
adjective

booty noun valuable goods taken
away by soldiers after a battle.
[from old German *buite*
= exchange, sharing out]

booze verb (boozes, boozing,
boozed) (slang) drink alcohol.

booze noun (slang) alcoholic
drink.

border noun (plural borders)
1 the boundary of a country; the
part near this. 2 an edge.
3 something placed round an
edge to strengthen or decorate it.
4 a strip of ground round a
garden or part of it.

border verb (borders, bordering,
bordered) put or be a border to
something.

borderline noun (plural
borderlines) a boundary.
borderline case something that is
on the borderline between two
different groups or kinds of
things.

bore¹ verb (bores, boring, bored)
1 drill a hole. 2 get through by
pushing.

bore² verb (bores, boring, bored)
make somebody feel uninterested
by being dull.

bore noun (plural bores) a boring
person or thing. **boredom** noun

bore³ past tense of **bear**².

bored adjective weary and
uninterested because something
is so dull.

born adjective
1 having come into existence by
birth. (See the note on **borne**.)
2 having a certain natural
quality or ability, *a born leader.*

borne past participle of **bear**².

USAGE: The word *borne* is
used before *by* or after *have*,
has, or *had*, e.g. *children borne
by Eve; she had borne him a
son.* The word *born* is used e.g.
in *a son was born.*

borrow verb (borrows,
borrowing, borrowed)
1 get something to use for a time,

with the intention to give it back afterwards. **2** obtain money as a loan. **borrower** *noun*

USAGE: Do not confuse *borrow* with *lend*, which means just the opposite.

---

bosom *noun* (*plural* **bosoms**)
a person's breast. [from Old English]

boss *noun* (*plural* **bosses**)
(*informal*) a manager; a person whose job is to give orders to workers etc.

boss *verb* (**bosses, bossing, bossed**) (*slang*) order someone about.
[from Dutch *baas* = master]

bossy *adjective* fond of ordering people about. **bossiness** *noun*

botany *noun* the study of plants. **botanical** *adjective*, **botanist** *noun*
[from Greek *botane* = a plant]

both *adjective & pronoun* the two; not only one, *Are both films good? Both are old.*

both *adverb*
both ... and not only ... but also, *The house is both small and ugly.*
[from Old Norse]

bother *verb* (**bothers, bothering, bothered**)
1 cause somebody trouble or worry; pester. **2** take trouble; feel concern, *Don't bother to reply.*

bother *noun* trouble or worry.

bottle *noun* (*plural* **bottles**)
1 a narrow-necked container for liquids. **2** (*slang*) courage, *She showed a lot of bottle.*

bottle *verb* (**bottles, bottling, bottled**) put or store something in bottles.

bottle up if you bottle up your feelings, you keep them to yourself.

bottle bank *noun* (*plural* **bottle banks**) a large container in which used glass bottles are collected for recycling.

bottleneck *noun* (*plural* **bottlenecks**) a narrow place where something, especially traffic, cannot flow freely.

bottom *noun* (*plural* **bottoms**)
1 the lowest part; the base. **2** the part furthest away, *the bottom of the garden.* **3** a person's buttocks.

bottom *adjective* lowest, *the bottom shelf.*
[from Old English]

bough *noun* (*plural* **boughs**)
a large branch coming from the trunk of a tree. [from Old English]

boulder *noun* (*plural* **boulders**)
a very large smooth stone.

bounce *verb* (**bounces, bouncing, bounced**)
1 spring back when thrown against something. **2** make a ball etc. bounce. **3** (of a cheque) be sent back by the bank because there is not enough money in the account. **4** jump suddenly; move in a lively manner.

bounce *noun* (*plural* **bounces**)
1 the action or power of bouncing. **2** a lively confident manner, *full of bounce.* **bouncy** *adjective*
[origin unknown]

bound[1] *verb* (**bounds, bounding, bounded**) jump or spring; run with jumping movements, *bounding along.*

bound *noun* (*plural* **bounds**)
a bounding movement.

bound² past tense of bind.

bound adjective
bound to certain to, He is bound to fail.
bound up with closely connected with, Happiness is bound up with success.

bound³ adjective going towards something, We are bound for Spain. [from Old Norse]

bound⁴ verb (bounds, bounding, bounded) limit; be the boundary of, Their land is bounded by the river.

boundary noun (plural boundaries)
1 a line that marks a limit. 2 a hit to the boundary of a cricket field. [from bound⁴]

bounds plural noun limits.
out of bounds where you are not allowed to go.
[from bound⁴]

bouquet (say boh-kay) noun (plural bouquets) a bunch of flowers. [French, = group of trees]

bout noun (plural bouts)
1 a boxing or wrestling contest. 2 a period of exercise or work or illness, a bout of flu.

boutique (say boo-teek) noun (plural boutiques) a small shop selling fashionable clothes.

bow¹ (rhymes with go) noun (plural bows)
1 a strip of wood curved by a tight string joining its ends, used for shooting arrows. 2 a wooden rod with horsehair stretched between its ends, used for playing a violin etc. 3 a knot made with loops.

bow² (rhymes with cow) verb (bows, bowing, bowed)
1 bend your body forwards to show respect or as a greeting. 2 bend downwards, bowed by the weight.

bow noun (plural bows) bowing your body.

bow³ (rhymes with cow) noun (plural bows) the front part of a ship.

bowel noun (plural bowels) the intestine. [from Latin botellus = little sausage]

bowl¹ noun (plural bowls)
1 a rounded usually deep container for food or liquid. 2 the rounded part of a spoon or tobacco pipe etc.
[from Old English]

bowl² noun (plural bowls) a ball used in the game of bowls or in bowling, when heavy balls are rolled towards skittles.

bowl verb (bowls, bowling, bowled)
1 send a ball to be played by a batsman. 2 get a batsman out by bowling. 3 send a ball etc. rolling.
[from old French]

bow-legged adjective having legs that curve outwards at the knees; bandy.

bowling noun
1 the game of bowls. 2 the game of knocking down skittles with a heavy ball.

bow tie noun (plural bow ties) a man's necktie tied into a bow.

bow window noun (plural bow windows) a curved window.

box¹ noun (plural boxes)
1 a container made of wood, cardboard, etc., usually with a top

box 75 **brain**

or lid. **2** a compartment in a theatre, lawcourt, etc., *witness box.* **3** a hut or shelter, *sentry box.* **4** a rectangular space to be filled in on a form or questionnaire. **5** a small evergreen shrub.
the box (*informal*) television.

box[2] *verb* (**boxes, boxing, boxed**) fight with the fists. [origin unknown]

boxer *noun* (*plural* **boxers**)
1 a person who boxes. **2** a dog that looks like a bulldog.

Boxing Day *noun* the first weekday after Christmas Day. [from the old custom of giving presents (*Christmas boxes*) to tradesmen and servants on that day]

box office *noun* (*plural* **box offices**) an office for booking seats at a theatre or cinema etc. [because boxes could be reserved there]

boy *noun* (*plural* **boys**)
1 a male child. **2** a young man.
boyhood *noun*, **boyish** *adjective*
[origin unknown]

boycott *verb* (**boycotts, boycotting, boycotted**) refuse to use or have anything to do with, *They boycotted the buses when the fares went up.* **boycott** *noun* [from the name of Captain Boycott, a harsh landlord in Ireland whose tenants in 1880 refused to deal with him]

boyfriend *noun* (*plural* **boyfriends**) a boy that a girl regularly goes out with.

bra *noun* (*plural* **bras**) a piece of underwear worn by women to support their breasts. [abbreviation of French *brassière*]

brace *verb* (**braces, bracing, braced**) support; make a thing firm against something. [from Latin *bracchia* = arms]

bracelet *noun* (*plural* **bracelets**) an ornament worn round the wrist. [same origin as *brace*]

braces *plural noun* straps to hold trousers up, passing over the shoulders.

bracing *adjective* making you feel refreshed and healthy, *the bracing sea breeze.*

bracken *noun*
1 a large fern. **2** a mass of ferns. [from Old Norse]

bracket *noun* (*plural* **brackets**)
1 a mark used in pairs to enclose words or figures, *There are round brackets ( ) and square brackets [ ].* **2** a support attached to a wall etc. **3** a group or range between certain limits, *a high income bracket.*

bracket *verb* (**brackets, bracketing, bracketed**)
1 enclose in brackets. **2** put things together because they are similar. [from Latin *bracae* = breeches]

brahmin *noun* (*plural* **brahmins**) a member of the highest Hindu class, originally priests. [from Sanskrit *brahman* = priest]

Braille (rhymes with *mail*) *noun* a system of representing letters etc. by raised dots which blind people can read by feeling them. [named after Louis Braille, a blind French teacher who invented it in about 1830]

brain *noun* (*plural* **brains**)
1 the organ inside the top of the head that controls the body. **2** the mind; intelligence.

brainwash verb (brainwashes, brainwashing, brainwashed) force a person to give up one set of ideas or beliefs and accept new ones; indoctrinate.

brainwave noun (plural brainwaves) a sudden bright idea.

brainy adjective clever; intelligent.

brake noun (plural brakes) a device for slowing or stopping something.

brake verb (brakes, braking, braked) use a brake. [origin unknown]

bramble noun (plural brambles) a blackberry bush or a prickly bush like it. [from Old English; related to broom]

bran noun ground-up husks of corn. [from old French]

branch noun (plural branches) 1 a woody arm-like part of a tree or shrub. 2 a part of a railway, road, or river etc. that leads off from the main part. 3 a shop or office etc. that belongs to a large organization.

branch verb (branches, branching, branched) form a branch.
branch out start something new. [from Latin branca = a paw]

brand noun (plural brands) a particular make of goods.

brandish verb (brandishes, brandishing, brandished) wave something about.

brand new adjective completely new.

brandy noun (plural brandies) a strong alcoholic drink, usually made from wine. [from Dutch brandewijn = burnt (distilled) wine]

brash adjective 1 impudent. 2 reckless. [origin unknown]

brass noun (plural brasses) 1 a metal that is an alloy of copper and zinc. 2 wind instruments made of brass, e.g. trumpets and trombones. **brass** adjective, **brassy** adjective

bravado (say brav-ah-doh) noun a display of boldness. [from Spanish]

brave adjective having or showing courage. **bravely** adverb, **bravery** noun

brave verb (braves, braving, braved) face and endure something bravely. [from Latin barbarus = barbarous]

brawl noun (plural brawls) a noisy quarrel or fight.

brawl verb (brawls, brawling, brawled) take part in a brawl. [origin unknown]

brawny adjective strong and muscular.

brazen verb (brazens, brazening, brazened)
brazen it out behave as if there is nothing to be ashamed of when you know you have done wrong.

breach noun (plural breaches) 1 the breaking of an agreement or rule etc. 2 a broken place; a gap.

bread noun (plural breads) a food made by baking flour and water, usually with yeast. **breadcrumbs** plural noun [from Old English]

breadth noun width; broadness. [from Old English]

break *verb* (**breaks, breaking, broke, broken**)
1 divide or fall into pieces by hitting or pressing. **2** fail to keep a promise or law etc. **3** stop for a time; end, *She broke her silence.* **4** change, *the weather broke.* **5** damage; stop working properly. **6** (of waves) fall in foam. **7** go suddenly or with force, *They broke through.* **8** appear suddenly, *Dawn had broken.* **breakage** *noun*
break a record do better than anyone else has done before.
break down 1 stop working properly. **2** collapse.
break out 1 begin suddenly. **2** escape.
break the news make something known.
break up 1 break into small parts. **2** separate at the end of a school term.

break *noun* (*plural* **breaks**)
1 a broken place; a gap. **2** an escape; a sudden dash. **3** a short rest from work. **4** a number of points scored continuously in snooker etc. **5** (*informal*) a piece of luck; an opportunity.
break of day dawn.

breakdown *noun* (*plural* **breakdowns**)
1 breaking down; failure. **2** a period of mental illness caused by anxiety or depression. **3** an analysis of accounts or statistics. **4** a sudden failure to work, esp. by a car, *We had a breakdown on the motorway; the breakdown of law and order.*

breakfast *noun* (*plural* **breakfasts**) the first meal of the day. [from *break* + *fast²*]

breakneck *adjective* dangerously fast, *He had to drive at breakneck speed to get there on time.*

breakthrough *noun* (*plural* **breakthroughs**) an important advance or achievement.

breast *noun* (*plural* **breasts**)
1 one of the two fleshy parts on the upper front of a woman's body that produce milk to feed a baby. **2** a person's or animal's chest. [from Old English]

breastplate *noun* (*plural* **breastplates**) a piece of armour covering the chest.

breath (*say* breth) *noun* (*plural* **breaths**)
1 air drawn into the lungs and sent out again. **2** a gentle blowing, *a breath of wind.*
out of breath panting.
take your breath away surprise or delight you greatly.
under your breath in a whisper.

breathalyser *noun* (*plural* **breathalysers**) a device for measuring the amount of alcohol in a person's breath. **breathalyse** *verb* [from *breath* + *analyse*]

breathe (*say* breeth) *verb* (**breathes, breathing, breathed**)
1 take air into the body and send it out again. **2** speak or utter, *Don't breathe a word of this.* [from *breath*]

breather (*say* bree-ther) *noun* (*plural* **breathers**) a pause for rest, *Let's take a breather.*

breathless *adjective* out of breath.

breed *verb* (**breeds, breeding, bred**)
1 produce young creatures. **2** keep animals in order to produce young ones from them. **3** bring

up or train. **4** create or produce. *Poverty breeds illness.* **breeder** *noun*

breed *noun* (*plural* **breeds**) a variety of animals with qualities inherited from their parents. [from Old English; related to *brood*]

breeze *noun* (*plural* **breezes**) a wind. **breezy** *adjective*

brevity *noun* shortness; briefness. [same origin as *brief*]

brew *verb* (**brews, brewing, brewed**) **1** make beer or tea. **2** develop, *Trouble is brewing.*

brew *noun* (*plural* **brews**) a brewed drink. [from Old English]

brewery *noun* (*plural* **breweries**) a place where beer is brewed.

bribe *noun* (*plural* **bribes**) money or a gift offered to a person to influence him or her.

bribe *verb* (**bribes, bribing, bribed**) give someone a bribe. **bribery** *noun* [from old French *briber* = beg]

brick *noun* (*plural* **bricks**) **1** a small hard block of baked clay etc. used to build walls. **2** a rectangular block of something.

brick *verb* (**bricks, bricking, bricked**) close something with bricks, *We bricked up the gap in the wall.*

bricklayer *noun* (*plural* **bricklayers**) a worker who builds with bricks.

bride *noun* (*plural* **brides**) a woman on her wedding day. **bridal** *adjective* [from Old English]

bridegroom *noun* (*plural* **bridegrooms**) a man on his wedding day. [from Old English *brydguma* = bride's man]

bridesmaid *noun* (*plural* **bridesmaids**) a girl or unmarried woman who attends the bride at a wedding.

bridge[1] *noun* (*plural* **bridges**) **1** a structure built over and across a river, railway, or road etc. to allow people to cross it. **2** a high platform above a ship's deck, for the officer in charge. **3** the bony upper part of the nose. **4** something that connects things.

bridge *verb* (**bridges, bridging, bridged**) make or form a bridge over something.

bridge[2] *noun* a card game rather like whist.

bridle *noun* (*plural* **bridles**) the part of a horse's harness that fits over its head.

bridle path or **bridle road** *noun* (*plural* **bridle paths, bridle roads**) a road suitable for horses but not for vehicles.

brief *adjective* short. **briefly** *adverb*, **briefness** *noun* **in brief** in a few words.

brief *noun* (*plural* **briefs**) instructions and information given to someone, especially to a barrister.

brief *verb* (**briefs, briefing, briefed**) **1** give a brief to a barrister. **2** instruct or inform someone concisely in advance. [from Latin *brevis* = short]

briefcase *noun* (*plural* **briefcases**) a flat case for carrying documents etc.

briefing *noun* (*plural* **briefings**)
a meeting to give someone
concise instructions or
information.

briefs *plural noun* very short
knickers or underpants.

brigade *noun* (*plural* **brigades**)
1 a large unit of an army.
2 a group of people organized for
a special purpose, *the fire
brigade*. [from Italian *brigata*
= a troop]

bright *adjective*
1 giving a strong light; shining.
2 clever. 3 cheerful. **brightly**
adverb, **brightness** *noun*

brighten *verb* (**brightens**,
brightening, **brightened**) make or
become brighter.

brilliant *adjective*
1 very bright; sparkling. 2 very
clever. **brilliantly** *adverb*,
brilliance *noun*

brim *noun* (*plural* **brims**)
1 the edge of a cup etc. 2 the
bottom part of a hat that sticks
out.
brim-full *adjective* completely full.

brim *verb* (**brims**, **brimming**,
brimmed) be full to the brim.
brim over overflow.

bring *verb* (**brings**, **bringing**,
brought) cause a person or thing
to come; lead; carry.
bring about cause to happen.
bring off achieve; do something
successfully.
bring up 1 look after and train
growing children. 2 mention
a subject. 3 vomit. 4 cause to stop
suddenly.

brisk *adjective* quick and lively.
briskly *adverb*, **briskness** *noun*

bristle *noun* (*plural* **bristles**)
1 a short stiff hair. 2 one of the
stiff pieces of hair, wire, or
plastic etc. in a brush. **bristly**
adjective

bristle *verb* (**bristles**, **bristling**,
bristled)
1 (of an animal) raise its bristles
in anger or fear. 2 show
indignation.
bristle with be full of, *The plan
bristled with problems.*

Britain *noun* the island made up
of England, Scotland, and Wales,
with the small adjacent islands;
Great Britain.

USAGE: Note the difference in
use between the terms *Britain*,
Great Britain, the *United
Kingdom*, and the *British Isles*.
Great Britain (or Britain) is
used to refer to the island
made up of England, Scotland,
and Wales. The United
Kingdom includes Great
Britain and Northern Ireland.
The British Isles refers to the
whole of the island group
which includes Great Britain,
Ireland, and all the smaller
nearby islands.

British Isles *plural noun* the
island group which includes
Great Britain, Ireland, and all the
smaller nearby islands.

USAGE: See note at *Britain*.

brittle *adjective* hard but easy to
break or snap. **brittleness** *noun*
[from Old English]

broad *adjective*
1 large across; wide. 2 full and
complete, *broad daylight*. 3 in
general terms; not detailed, *We*

are in broad agreement. **4** strong and unmistakable, *a broad hint; a broad accent.* **broadly** *adverb,* **broadness** *noun* [from Old English]

broad bean *noun* (*plural* **broad beans**) a bean with large flat seeds.

broadcast *noun* (*plural* **broadcasts**) a programme sent out on the radio or on television.

broadcast *verb* (**broadcasts, broadcasting, broadcast**) send out a programme on the radio or on television. **broadcaster** *noun* [originally = to scatter widely: from *broad* + *cast*]

broaden *verb* (**broadens, broadening, broadened**) make or become broader.

broad-minded *adjective* tolerant; not easily shocked.

broccoli *noun* (*plural* **broccoli**) a kind of cauliflower with greenish flowerheads. [Italian, = cabbage-heads]

brochure (*say* broh-shoor) *noun* (*plural* **brochures**) a booklet or pamphlet containing information. [from French, = stitching (because originally the pages were roughly stitched together)]

broke *adjective* (*informal*) having spent all your money. [old past participle of *break*]

broken-hearted *adjective* overwhelmed with grief.

broken home *noun* (*plural* **broken homes**) a family lacking one parent through divorce or separation.

bronchitis (*say* bronk-I-tiss) *noun* a disease with bronchial inflammation, which makes you cough a lot. [from Greek *bronchos* = windpipe, + *-itis*]

bronze *noun* (*plural* **bronzes**) **1** a metal that is an alloy of copper and tin. **2** something made of bronze. **3** a bronze medal. **4** yellowish-brown. **bronze** *adjective* [probably from Persian *birinj* = brass]

Bronze Age *noun* the time when tools and weapons were made of bronze.

brooch *noun* (*plural* **brooches**) an ornament with a hinged pin for fastening it on to clothes. [a different spelling of *broach*]

brood *noun* (*plural* **broods**) young birds that were hatched together.

brood *verb* (**broods, brooding, brooded**) **1** sit on eggs to hatch them. **2** keep thinking about something, especially with resentment. [from Old English]

brook *noun* (*plural* **brooks**) a small stream. [from Old English *broc*]

broom *noun* (*plural* **brooms**) **1** a brush with a long handle, for sweeping. **2** a shrub with yellow, white, or pink flowers.

broomstick *noun* (*plural* **broomsticks**) a broom-handle.

broth *noun* (*plural* **broths**) a kind of thin soup. [from Old English]

brother *noun* (*plural* **brothers**) **1** a son of the same parents as another person. **2** a man who is a fellow member of a Church, trade union, etc. **brotherly** *adjective* [from Old English]

brother-in-law noun (plural **brothers-in-law**) the brother of a married person's husband or wife; the husband of a person's sister.

brow noun (plural **brows**)
1 an eyebrow. **2** the forehead.
3 the ridge at the top of a hill; the edge of a cliff.

brown noun (plural **browns**) the colour of earth.

brown adjective
1 of the colour brown. **2** having a brown skin; suntanned.

Brownie noun (plural **Brownies**) a member of a junior branch of the Guides.

browse verb (**browses**, **browsing**, **browsed**)
1 read or look at something casually. **2** feed on grass or leaves. [from old French]

bruise noun (plural **bruises**) a dark mark made on the skin by hitting it.

bruise verb (**bruises**, **bruising**, **bruised**) give or get a bruise or bruises.
[from Old English]

brunette noun (plural **brunettes**) a woman with brown hair. [from French *brun* = brown, + *-ette*]

brunt noun the chief impact or strain, *They bore the brunt of the attack.* [origin unknown]

brush noun (plural **brushes**)
1 an implement used for cleaning or painting things or for smoothing the hair, usually with pieces of hair, wire, or plastic etc. set in a solid base.
2 a fox's bushy tail. **3** brushing, *Give it a good brush.* **4** a short fight, *They had a brush with the enemy.*

brush verb (**brushes**, **brushing**, **brushed**)
1 use a brush on something.
2 touch gently in passing.
brush up revise a subject.

brusque (say bruusk) adjective curt and offhand in manner.
brusquely adverb

Brussels sprouts plural noun the edible buds of a kind of cabbage.

brutal adjective very cruel.
brutally adverb, **brutality** noun

brute noun (plural **brutes**)
1 a brutal person. **2** an animal.
brutish adjective [from Latin *brutus* = stupid]

BSE abbreviation bovine spongiform encephalopathy; a fatal disease of cattle that affects the nervous system and makes the cow stagger about. BSE is sometimes known as 'mad cow disease'.

bubble noun (plural **bubbles**)
1 a thin transparent ball of liquid filled with air or gas. **2** a small ball of air in something. **bubbly** adjective

bubble verb (**bubbles**, **bubbling**, **bubbled**)
1 send up bubbles; rise in bubbles. **2** show great liveliness. [related to *burble*]

buccaneer noun (plural **buccaneers**) a pirate. [from French]

buck noun (plural **bucks**) a male deer, rabbit, or hare.

buck verb (**bucks**, **bucking**, **bucked**) (of a horse) jump with its back arched.
buck up (*informal*) **1** hurry.
2 cheer up.

bucket noun (plural **buckets**)
a container with a handle, for
carrying liquids etc. **bucketful**
noun [from French]

buckle noun (plural **buckles**)
a device through which a belt or
strap is threaded to fasten it.

buckle verb (**buckles, buckling,
buckled**) fasten something with
a buckle.

bud noun (plural **buds**) a flower or
leaf before it opens. [origin
unknown]

Buddhism (say buud-izm) noun
a faith that started in Asia and
follows the teachings of the
Indian philosopher Gautama
Buddha, who lived in the 5th
century BC. **Buddhist** noun [from
Sanskrit *Buddha* = enlightened
one]

budge verb (**budges, budging,
budged**) if you cannot budge
something, you cannot move it at
all. [from French]

budgerigar noun (plural
budgerigars) an Australian bird
often kept as a pet in a cage.
[from Australian Aboriginal
budgeri = good + *gar* = cockatoo]

budget noun (plural **budgets**)
1 a plan for spending money
wisely. **2** an amount of money set
aside for a purpose. **budgetary**
adjective
the Budget the Chancellor of the
Exchequer's statement of plans
to raise money (e.g. by taxes).

buffalo noun (plural **buffalo** or
buffaloes) a large ox. Different
kinds are found in Asia, Africa,
and North America (where they
are also called *bison*).

buffer noun (plural **buffers**)
something that softens a blow,
especially a device on a railway
engine or wagon or at the end of
a track. [from an old word *buff*
= a blow (as in *blind man's buff*):
related to *buffet*[2]]

buffet[1] (say buu-fay) noun (plural
buffets)
1 a café at a station. **2** a meal
where guests serve themselves to
food. [from French, = stool]

buffet[2] (say buf-it) noun (plural
buffets) a hit, especially with the
hand.

buffet verb (**buffets, buffeting,
buffeted**) hit or knock, *Strong
winds buffeted the aircraft.*
[from old French *buffe* = a blow]

buffoon noun (plural **buffoons**)
a person who plays the fool.
buffoonery noun [from Latin
buffo = clown]

bug noun (plural **bugs**)
1 an insect. **2** an error in
a computer program that
prevents it working properly.
3 (*informal*) a germ or virus.
4 (*informal*) a secret hidden
microphone.

bug verb (**bugs, bugging,
bugged**) (*slang*)
1 fit with a secret hidden
microphone. **2** annoy.
[origin unknown]

bugbear noun (plural **bugbears**)
something that you fear or
dislike. [from an old word *bug*
= bogy]

build verb (**builds, building, built**)
make something by putting parts
together.
build in include. **built-in** adjective

build up 1 establish gradually. **2** accumulate. **3** cover an area with buildings. **4** make stronger or more famous, *build up a reputation.* **built-up** *adjective*

build *noun* (*plural* **builds**) the shape of someone's body, *of slender build.* [from Old English]

builder *noun* (*plural* **builders**) someone who puts up buildings.

building *noun* (*plural* **buildings**) **1** the process of constructing houses etc. **2** a permanent built structure that people can go into.

building society *noun* (*plural* **building societies**) an organization that accepts deposits of money and lends to people who want to buy houses etc.

bulb *noun* (*plural* **bulbs**) **1** a thick rounded part of a plant from which a stem grows up and roots grow down. **2** a rounded part of something, *the bulb of a thermometer.* **3** a glass globe that produces electric light. **bulbous** *adjective* [from Greek *bolbos* = onion]

bulge *noun* (*plural* **bulges**) a rounded swelling; an outward curve. **bulgy** *adjective*

bulge *verb* (**bulges, bulging, bulged**) form or cause to form a bulge.

bulk *noun* (*plural* **bulks**) **1** the size of something, especially when it is large. **2** the greater portion; the majority, *The bulk of the population voted for it.*
in bulk in large amounts.

bulk *verb* (**bulks, bulking, bulked**) increase the size or thickness of

something, *bulk it out.*
[from Old English]

bulky *adjective* (**bulkier, bulkiest**) taking up a lot of space. **bulkiness** *noun*

bull *noun* (*plural* **bulls**) the fully-grown male of cattle or of certain other large animals (e.g. elephant, whale, seal). [from Old Norse]

bulldog *noun* (*plural* **bulldogs**) a dog of a powerful courageous breed with a short thick neck. [because it was used for attacking tethered bulls in the sport of 'bull-baiting']

bulldozer *noun* (*plural* **bulldozers**) a powerful tractor with a wide metal blade or scoop in front, used for shifting soil or clearing ground.

bullet *noun* (*plural* **bullets**) a small lump of metal shot from a rifle or revolver. [from French *boulet* = little ball]

bulletin *noun* (*plural* **bulletins**) a public statement giving news.

bullfight *noun* (*plural* **bullfights**) a public entertainment in which bulls are tormented and killed in an arena. **bullfighter** *noun*

bullock *noun* (*plural* **bullocks**) a young castrated bull. [from Old English *bulloc* = young bull]

bull's-eye *noun* (*plural* **bull's-eyes**) the centre of a target.

bully *verb* (**bullies, bullying, bullied**) **1** use strength or power to hurt or frighten a weaker person. **2** start play in hockey, when two opponents tap the ground and each other's sticks, *bully off.*

bully *noun* (*plural* **bullies**) someone who bullies people.

bulwark *noun* (*plural* **bulwarks**)
a wall of earth built as a defence;
a protection. [from German or
Dutch]

bumble-bee *noun* (*plural*
bumble-bees) a large bee with
a loud hum.

bump *verb* (**bumps, bumping,
bumped**)
1 knock against something.
2 move along with jolts.
bump into (*informal*) meet by
chance.
bump off (*slang*) kill.

bump *noun* (*plural* **bumps**)
1 the action or sound of bumping.
2 a swelling or lump. **bumpy**
adjective

bumper[1] *noun* (*plural* **bumpers**)
1 a bar along the front or back of
a motor vehicle to protect it in
collisions. **2** a ball in cricket that
bounces high.

bumper[2] *adjective* unusually
large or plentiful, *a bumper crop.*

bumpkin *noun* (*plural* **bumpkins**)
a country person with awkward
manners.

bun *noun* (*plural* **buns**)
1 a small round sweet cake. **2** hair
twisted into a round bunch at the
back of the head.

bunch *noun* (*plural* **bunches**)
a number of things joined or
fastened together. [origin
unknown]

bundle *noun* (*plural* **bundles**)
a number of things tied or
wrapped together.

bundle *verb* (**bundles, bundling,
bundled**)
1 make a number of things into
a bundle. **2** push hurriedly or
carelessly, *They bundled him into
a taxi.*

bungalow *noun* (*plural*
bungalows) a house without any
upstairs rooms. [from Hindi
bangla = of Bengal]

bungle *verb* (**bungles, bungling,
bungled**) make a mess of doing
something. **bungler** *noun*
[because *bungle* sounds clumsy]

bunion *noun* (*plural* **bunions**)
a swelling at the side of the joint
where the big toe joins the foot.
[origin unknown]

bunk *noun* (*plural* **bunks**) a bed
built like a shelf. [origin
unknown]

bunker *noun* (*plural* **bunkers**)
1 a container for storing fuel.
2 a sandy hollow built as an
obstacle on a golf course. **3** an
underground shelter.

bunny *noun* (*plural* **bunnies**)
(*informal*) a rabbit. [from dialect
bun = rabbit]

Bunsen burner *noun* (*plural*
Bunsen burners) a small gas
burner used in scientific work.
[named after a German scientist,
R. W. Bunsen]

bunting[1] *noun* (*plural* **buntings**)
a kind of small bird. [origin
unknown]

bunting[2] *noun* strips of small
flags hung up to decorate streets
and buildings. [origin unknown]

buoy (*say* boi) *noun* (*plural*
buoys) a floating object anchored
to mark a channel or underwater
rocks etc.

buoyant (*say* boi-ant) *adjective*
1 able to float. **2** light-hearted;
cheerful. **buoyantly** *adverb*,
buoyancy *noun* [from French or
Spanish; related to *buoy*]

bur noun (plural **burs**) a plant's seed case or flower that clings to hair or clothes.

burden noun (plural **burdens**)
1 a heavy load that you have to carry. **2** something troublesome that you have to bear, *Exams are a burden*. **burdensome** adjective

burden verb (**burdens, burdening, burdened**) put a burden on a person etc.

bureau (say bewr-oh) noun (plural **bureaux**)
1 a writing desk. **2** a business office, *They will tell you at the Information Bureau*. [French, = desk]

bureaucracy (say bewr-**ok**-ra-see) noun the use of too many rules and forms by officials, especially in government departments. **bureaucratic** (say bewr-ok-**rat**-ik) adjective

burglar noun (plural **burglars**) a person who enters a building illegally, especially in order to steal things. **burglary** noun [from French]

burgle verb (**burgles, burgling, burgled**) rob a place as a burglar. [from *burglar*]

burgundy noun (plural **burgundies**) a rich red or white wine. [originally made in Burgundy in France]

burial noun (plural **burials**) burying somebody.

burlesque (say ber-**lesk**) noun (plural **burlesques**) a comical imitation. [via French from Italian *burla* = ridicule, joke]

burly adjective (**burlier, burliest**) having a strong heavy body. [from Old English]

burn verb (**burns, burning, burned** or **burnt**)
1 blaze or glow with fire; produce heat or light by combustion. **2** damage or destroy something by fire, heat, or chemicals. **3** be damaged or destroyed by fire etc. **4** feel very hot.

USAGE: The word *burnt* (not *burned*) is always used when an adjective is required, e.g. in *burnt wood*. As parts of the verb, either *burned* or *burnt* may be used, e.g. *the wood had burned* or *had burnt completely*.

burn noun (plural **burns**)
1 a mark or injury made by burning. **2** the firing of a spacecraft's rockets. [from Old English *birnan*]

burning adjective
1 intense, *a burning ambition*. **2** very important; hotly discussed, *a burning question*.

burr noun (plural **burrs**)
1 a bur. **2** a whirring sound. **3** a soft country accent. [a different spelling of *bur*]

burrow noun (plural **burrows**) a hole or tunnel dug by a rabbit or fox etc. as a dwelling.

burrow verb (**burrows, burrowing, burrowed**)
1 dig a burrow. **2** push your way through or into something; search deeply, *She burrowed in her handbag*.

bursar noun (plural **bursars**) a person who manages the finances and other business of a school or college. [from Latin *bursa* = a bag]

burst verb (bursts, bursting, burst)
1 break or force apart. **2** come or start suddenly, *It burst into flame. They burst out laughing.* **3** be very full, *bursting with energy.*

burst noun (plural bursts)
1 bursting; a split. **2** something short and forceful, *a burst of gunfire.*

bury verb (buries, burying, buried)
1 place a dead body in the earth, a tomb, or the sea. **2** put underground; cover up.

bus noun (plural buses) a large vehicle for passengers to travel in. [short for *omnibus*]

bush noun (plural bushes)
1 a shrub. **2** wild uncultivated land, especially in Africa and Australia. **bushy** adjective [from old French or Old Norse]

bushel noun (plural bushels) a measure for grain and fruit (8 gallons or 4 pecks). [from old French]

business (say biz-ness) noun (plural businesses)
1 a person's concern or responsibilities, *Mind your own business.* **2** an affair or subject, *I'm tired of the whole business.* **3** a shop or firm. **4** buying and selling things; trade.
businessman noun, **businesswoman** noun [from Old English *bisignis* = busyness]

bust noun (plural busts)
1 a sculpture of a person's head, shoulders, and chest. **2** the upper front part of a woman's body. [from Latin]

bustle verb (bustles, bustling, bustled) hurry in a busy or excited way.

bustle noun hurried or excited activity.

busy adjective (busier, busiest)
1 having much to do; occupied. **2** full of activity. **busily** adverb, **busyness** noun

busy verb (busies, busying, busied)
busy yourself occupy yourself; keep busy.

busybody noun (plural busybodies) a person who interferes.

but conjunction however; nevertheless, *I wanted to go, but I couldn't.*

but preposition except, *There is no one here but me.*

but adverb only; no more than, *We can but try.* [from Old English]

butcher noun (plural butchers)
1 a person who cuts up meat and sells it. **2** a person who kills cruelly or needlessly. **butchery** noun

butcher verb (butchers, butchering, butchered) kill cruelly or needlessly.

butt¹ noun (plural butts)
1 the thicker end of a weapon or tool. **2** a stub, *cigarette butts.* [from Dutch *bot* = stumpy]

butt² noun (plural butts) a large cask or barrel. [from Latin *buttis* = cask]

butt³ noun (plural butts) a person or thing that is a target for ridicule or teasing, *He was the butt of their jokes.* [from old French *but* = goal]

butt⁴ verb (butts, butting, butted)
1 push or hit with the head as a ram or goat does. 2 place the edges of things together.
butt in interrupt or meddle. [from old French *buter* = hit]

butter noun a soft fatty food made by churning cream. **buttery** adjective [from Old English]

buttercup noun (plural **buttercups**) a wild plant with bright yellow cup-shaped flowers.

butterfly noun (plural **butterflies**) 1 an insect with large white or coloured wings. 2 a swimming stroke in which both arms are lifted at the same time.

buttock noun (plural **buttocks**) either of the two fleshy rounded parts of your bottom. [from Old English]

button noun (plural **buttons**) 1 a knob or disc sewn on clothes as a fastening or ornament. 2 a small knob, *Press the button.*
button verb (buttons, buttoning, buttoned) fasten something with a button or buttons.

buttonhole noun (plural **buttonholes**) 1 a slit through which a button passes to fasten clothes. 2 a flower worn on a lapel.
buttonhole verb (buttonholes, buttonholing, buttonholed) stop somebody so that you can talk to him or her.

buttress noun (plural **buttresses**) a support built against a wall.

buy verb (buys, buying, bought) get something by paying for it.
buyer noun

buy noun (plural **buys**) something that is bought.

buzz noun (plural **buzzes**) a vibrating humming sound.

buzz verb (buzzes, buzzing, buzzed) 1 make a buzz. 2 threaten an aircraft by deliberately flying close to it.

by preposition This word is used to show
1 closeness (*Sit by me*), 2 direction or route (*We got here by a short cut*), 3 time (*They came by night*), 4 manner or method (*cooking by gas*), 5 amount (*You missed it by 3 inches*).
by the way incidentally.
by yourself alone; without help.

by adverb
1 past, *I can't get by.* 2 in reserve; for future use, *Put it by.*
by and by soon; later on.
by and large on the whole.

by-election noun (plural **by-elections**) an election to replace a Member of Parliament who has died or resigned. [from *by-* = extra (an 'extra' election between general elections)]

bygone adjective belonging to the past.
let bygones be bygones forgive and forget.

bypass noun (plural **bypasses**) 1 a road taking traffic past a city etc. 2 a channel that allows something to flow when the main route is blocked.
bypass verb (bypasses, bypassing, bypassed) avoid something by means of a bypass.

by-product noun (plural **by-products**) something produced while something else is being made. [from *by-* = at the side, besides]

byroad noun (plural **byroads**)
a minor road.

bystander noun (plural **bystanders**) a person standing near but not taking part in something.

byte noun (plural **bytes**) a fixed number of bits (= binary digits) in a computer, often representing a single character. [an invented word]

byword noun (plural **bywords**) a person or thing spoken of as a famous example, *Their firm became a byword for quality.* [from Old English *biwyrde* = proverb]

Cc

cab noun (plural **cabs**)
1 a taxi. 2 a compartment for the driver of a lorry, train, bus, or crane. [short for *cabriolet* = a light horsedrawn carriage]

cabaret (say **kab**-er-ay) noun (plural **cabarets**) an entertainment, especially one provided for the customers in a restaurant or nightclub. [from old French]

cabbage noun (plural **cabbages**) a vegetable with green or purple leaves. [from old French *caboche* = head]

cabin noun (plural **cabins**)
1 a hut or shelter.
2 a compartment in a ship, aircraft, or spacecraft. 3 a driver's cab. [from Latin]

Cabinet noun the group of chief ministers, chosen by the Prime Minister, who meet to decide government policy.

cabinet noun (plural **cabinets**) a cupboard or container with drawers or shelves. [from *cabin*]

cable noun (plural **cables**)
1 a thick rope of fibre or wire; a thick chain. 2 a covered group of wires laid underground for transmitting electrical signals. 3 a telegram sent overseas. [from Latin *capulum* = halter]

cackle noun (plural **cackles**)
1 a loud silly laugh. 2 noisy chatter. 3 the loud clucking noise a hen makes. **cackle** verb [from old German or Dutch *kake* = jaw]

cactus noun (plural **cacti**) a fleshy plant, usually with prickles, from a hot dry climate. [from Greek]

cad noun (plural **cads**)
a dishonourable person. [short for *caddie* or *cadet*]

cadaverous (say kad-av-er-us) adjective pale and gaunt. [from Latin *cadaver* = corpse]

caddie noun (plural **caddies**) a person who carries a golfer's clubs during a game. [from *cadet*]

cadence (say **kay**-denss) noun (plural **cadences**)
1 rhythm; the rise and fall of the voice in speaking. 2 the final notes of a musical phrase. [via French from Latin *cadere* = fall]

cadenza (say ka-**den**-za) noun (plural **cadenzas**) an elaborate passage for a solo instrument or singer, to show the performer's skill. [via Italian from Latin *cadere* = fall]

cadet noun (plural **cadets**) a young person being trained for the armed forces or the police. [French, = younger son]

cadge verb (cadges, cadging, cadged) get something by begging for it. **cadger** noun [origin unknown]

cadmium noun a metal that looks like tin. [from Latin]

Caesarean section (say siz-air-ee-an) noun (plural **Caesarean sections**) a surgical operation for taking a baby out of the mother's womb. [so called because Julius Caesar is said to have been born in this way]

café (say kaf-ay) noun (plural **cafés**) a small restaurant. [French, = coffee, coffee house]

caffeine (say kaf-een) noun a stimulant substance found in tea and coffee. [French, from café = coffee]

cage noun (plural **cages**)
1 a container with bars or wires, in which birds or animals are kept. **2** the enclosed platform of a lift. [from French]

cairn noun (plural **cairns**) a pile of loose stones set up as a landmark or monument. [from Scottish Gaelic]

cajole verb (cajoles, cajoling, cajoled) persuade someone to do something by flattering them; coax. [from French]

cake noun (plural **cakes**)
1 a baked food made from a mixture of flour, fat, eggs, sugar, etc. **2** a shaped or hardened mass, *a cake of soap; fish cakes.*

caked adjective covered with dried mud etc.

calamine noun a pink powder used to make a soothing lotion for the skin. [from Latin]

calamity noun (plural **calamities**) a disaster. **calamitous** adjective [from Latin]

calcium noun a chemical substance found in teeth, bones, and lime. [from Latin calx = lime[1]]

calculate verb (calculates, calculating, calculated)
1 work something out by using mathematics. **2** plan something deliberately; intend, *Her remarks were calculated to hurt me.* **calculable** adjective, **calculation** noun [same origin as calculus]

calculator noun (plural **calculators**) a small electronic device for making calculations.

calculus noun mathematics for working out problems about rates of change. [from Latin calculus = small stone (used on an abacus)]

calendar noun (plural **calendars**) something that shows the dates of the month or year. [from Latin kalendae = the first day of the month]

calf[1] noun (plural **calves**) a young cow, whale, seal, etc. [from Old English]

calf[2] noun (plural **calves**) the fleshy back part of the leg below the knee. [from Old Norse]

calibre (say kal-ib-er) noun (plural **calibres**)
1 the diameter of a tube or gun barrel, or of a bullet etc. **2** ability; importance, *someone of your calibre.* [French]

call noun (plural **calls**)
1 a shout or cry. **2** a visit. **3** telephoning somebody. **4** a summons.

call verb (calls, calling, called)
1 shout or speak loudly, e.g. to

attract someone's attention.
2 telephone somebody. **3** name a person or thing, *They've decided to call the baby Alexander.* **4** tell somebody to come to you; summon. **5** make a short visit. **caller** *noun*

call a person's bluff challenge a person to do what was threatened, and expose the fact that it was a bluff.

call for 1 come and collect. **2** require, *The scandal calls for investigation.*

call up summon to join the armed forces.

calligraphy (say kal-**ig**-raf-ee) *noun* the art of beautiful handwriting. [from Greek *kalos* = beautiful, + *-graphy*]

calling *noun* (*plural* **callings**) an occupation; a profession or trade. [from the idea that God had called you to that occupation]

callous (say **kal**-us) *adjective* hard-hearted; unsympathetic. **callously** *adverb*, **callousness** *noun*

calm *adjective*
1 quiet and still; not windy. **2** not excited or agitated. **calmly** *adverb*, **calmness** *noun*
calm *verb* (**calms**, **calming**, **calmed**) make or become calm. [from Greek *kauma* = hot time of the day (when people rested)]

calorie *noun* (*plural* **calories**) a unit for measuring an amount of heat or the energy produced by food. **calorific** *adjective* [from Latin *calor* = heat]

calypso *noun* (*plural* **calypsos**) a West Indian song about current happenings. [origin unknown]

calyx (say **kay**-liks) *noun* (*plural* **calyces**) a ring of leaves (*sepals*) forming the outer case of a bud. [from Greek]

camcorder *noun* (*plural* **camcorders**) a combined video camera and sound recorder. [from *camera* + *recorder*]

camel *noun* (*plural* **camels**) a large animal with a long neck and either one or two humps on its back, used in desert countries for riding and for carrying goods. [from Greek]

cameo (say **kam**-ee-oh) *noun* (*plural* **cameos**)
1 a small hard piece of stone carved with a raised design in its upper layer. **2** a short well-performed part in a play etc.

camera *noun* (*plural* **cameras**) a device for taking photographs, films, or television pictures. **cameraman** *noun*
in camera in a judge's private room; in private. [Latin, = vault, chamber]

camouflage (say **kam**-off-lahzh) *noun* a way of hiding things by making them look like part of their surroundings.
camouflage *verb* (**camouflages**, **camouflaging**, **camouflaged**) hide by camouflage. [from French *camoufler* = disguise]

camp *noun* (*plural* **camps**) a place where people live in tents or huts etc. **campsite** *noun*
camp *verb* (**camps**, **camping**, **camped**) make a camp; live in a camp. **camper** *noun* [same origin as *campus*]

campaign noun (plural
campaigns)
1 a series of battles in one area or
with one purpose. **2** a planned
series of actions, *an advertising
campaign.*
campaign verb (campaigns,
campaigning, campaigned) take
part in a campaign. **campaigner**
noun [from Latin *campania*
= a piece of open ground]

camphor noun a strong-smelling
white substance used in
medicine, mothballs and making
plastics. **camphorated** adjective

campus noun (plural campuses)
the grounds of a university or
college. [Latin, = field]

can[1] noun **1** a sealed tin in which food or
drink is preserved. **2** a metal or
plastic container for liquids.
can verb (cans, canning, canned)
preserve in a sealed can. **canner**
noun [from Old English *canne*
= container for liquids]

can[2] auxiliary verb (past tense
could)
1 be able to, *He can play the
violin.* **2** have permission to, *You
can go.* [from Old English *cunnan*
= know, know how to do]

USAGE: Some people object to
can being used with the
meaning 'have permission to'
and insist that you should only
use *may* for this meaning. *Can*
is widely used in this meaning,
however, and in most
situations there is little reason
to prefer *may*. *May* is
appropriate, though, in formal
or official writing.

canal noun (plural canals)
1 an artificial river cut
through land so that boats can
sail along it or so that it can
drain or irrigate an area.
2 a tube through which
something passes in the
body, *the alimentary canal.*
[same origin as *channel*]

canary noun (plural canaries)
a small yellow bird that sings.
[because it came from the Canary
Islands]

cancel verb (cancels, cancelling,
cancelled)
1 say that something planned
will not be done or will not take
place. **2** stop an order or
instruction for something. **3** mark
a stamp or ticket etc. so that it
cannot be used again.
cancellation noun
cancel out stop each other's
effect, *The good and harm cancel
each other out.*

cancer noun (plural cancers)
1 a disease in which harmful
growths form in the body.
2 a tumour, especially a harmful
one. **cancerous** adjective [Latin,
= crab, creeping ulcer]

candid adjective frank. **candidly**
adverb, **candour** noun [from Latin
candidus = white]

candidate noun (plural
candidates)
1 a person who wants to be
elected or chosen for a particular
job or position etc. **2** a person
taking an examination.
candidacy noun, **candidature**
noun [from Latin *candidus*

= white (because Roman candidates for office had to wear a pure white toga)]

candle noun (plural **candles**)
a stick of wax with a wick through it, giving light when burning. **candlelight** noun [Old English from Latin, from *candere* = be white, shine]

candyfloss noun (plural **candyflosses**) a fluffy mass of very thin strands of spun sugar.

cane noun (plural **canes**)
1 the stem of a reed or tall grass etc. **2** a thin stick.

cane verb (**canes, caning, caned**) beat someone with a cane. [from Greek]

canine (say kayn-I'n) adjective to do with dogs.
canine tooth noun a pointed tooth.

canine noun (plural **canines**)
1 a dog. **2** a canine tooth. [from Latin *canis* = dog]

canker noun a disease that rots the wood of trees and plants or causes ulcers and sores on animals. [same origin as *cancer*]

cannabis noun hemp, especially when smoked as a drug. [from *Cannabis*, the Latin name of the hemp plant]

cannibal noun (plural **cannibals**)
1 a person who eats human flesh. **2** an animal that eats animals of its own kind. **cannibalism** noun

cannon noun
1 (plural **cannon**) a large heavy gun. **2** (plural **cannons**) the hitting of two balls in billiards by the third ball.

cannon verb (**cannons, cannoning, cannoned**) bump into

something heavily.
[via French from Italian *cannone* = large tube]

USAGE: Do not confuse with *canon*.

cannon ball noun (plural **cannon balls**) a large solid ball fired from a cannon.

cannot can not.

canoe noun (plural **canoes**)
a narrow lightweight boat.

canoe verb (**canoes, canoeing, canoed**) travel in a canoe.
canoeist noun

canon noun (plural **canons**)
1 a clergyman of a cathedral. **2** a general principle; a rule. [from Greek *kanon* = rule]

USAGE: Do not confuse with *cannon*.

canopy noun (plural **canopies**)
1 a hanging cover forming a shelter above a throne, bed, or person etc. **2** the part of a parachute that spreads in the air. [from Greek *konopeion* = bed with a mosquito net]

cant
1 insincere talk. **2** jargon. [from Latin *cantare* = sing]

can't (mainly spoken) cannot.

cantankerous adjective bad-tempered. [origin unknown]

canteen noun (plural **canteens**)
1 a restaurant for workers in a factory, office, etc. **2** a case or box containing a set of cutlery. **3** a soldier's or camper's water-flask. [via French from Italian]

canter noun a gentle gallop.

canter verb (**canters, cantering, cantered**) go or ride at a canter. [short for 'Canterbury gallop', the gentle pace at which pilgrims were said to travel to Canterbury in the Middle Ages]

cantilever noun (plural **cantilevers**) a beam or girder fixed at one end only and used to support a bridge etc. [origin unknown]

canvas noun (plural **canvases**) 1 a kind of strong coarse cloth. 2 a piece of canvas for painting on; a painting. [from Latin *cannabis* = hemp, from whose fibres cloth was made]

canvass verb (**canvasses, canvassing, canvassed**) visit people to ask for votes, opinions, etc. **canvasser** noun [originally = to catch in a net or bag: from *canvas*]

canyon noun (plural **canyons**) a deep valley, usually with a river running through it. [from Spanish *cañón* = tube]

cap noun (plural **caps**) 1 a soft hat without a brim but often with a peak. 2 a special headdress, e.g. that worn by a nurse. 3 a cap showing membership of a sports team. 4 a cap-like cover or top. 5 something that makes a bang when fired in a toy pistol.

cap verb (**caps, capping, capped**) 1 put a cap on or cover on something; cover. 2 award a sports cap to a person chosen as a member of a team. 3 do better than something, *Can you cap that joke?* [same origin as *cape*[1]]

capable adjective able to do something. **capably** adverb, **capability** noun [from Latin; related to *capacity*]

capacious (say ka-pay-shus) adjective roomy; able to hold a large amount.

capacity noun (plural **capacities**) 1 the amount that something can hold. 2 ability; capability. 3 the position that someone occupies, *In my capacity as your guardian I am responsible for you.* [from Latin *capere* = take, hold]

cape[1] noun (plural **capes**) a cloak. [from Latin *cappa* = hood]

cape[2] noun (plural **capes**) a large piece of high land that sticks out into the sea. [from Latin *caput* = head]

caper verb (**capers, capering, capered**) jump or run about playfully.

caper noun (plural **capers**) 1 capering. 2 (slang) an activity; an adventure. [from Latin *caper* = goat]

capillary (say ka-**pil**-er-ee) noun (plural **capillaries**) any of the very fine blood vessels that connect veins and arteries.

capital adjective 1 important. 2 (informal) excellent.

capital noun (plural **capitals**) 1 a capital city. 2 a capital letter. 3 the top part of a pillar. 4 money or property that can be used to produce more wealth. [from Latin *caput* = head]

capital city noun (plural **capital cities**) the most important city in a country.

capitalism (say **kap**-it-al-izm) noun a system in which trade and industry are controlled by private owners for profit. (Compare *Communism*.)

capitalist (say kap-it-al-ist) noun (plural **capitalists**)
1 a person who has much money or property being used to make more wealth; a very rich person. **2** a person who is in favour of capitalism.

capitalize (say kap-it-al-I'z) verb (**capitalizes, capitalizing, capitalized**)
1 write or print as a capital letter. **2** change something into capital; provide with capital (= money). **capitalization** noun
capitalize on profit by something; use it to your own advantage, *You could capitalize on your skill at drawing.*

capital letter noun (plural **capital letters**) a large letter of the kind used at the start of a name or sentence.

capital punishment noun punishing criminals by putting them to death.

capitulate verb (**capitulates, capitulating, capitulated**) admit that you are defeated and surrender. **capitulation** noun [from Latin]

capricious (say ka-prish-us) adjective deciding or changing your mind in an impulsive way. **capriciously** adverb, **capriciousness** noun

capsize verb (**capsizes, capsizing, capsized**) overturn, *the boat capsized.* [origin unknown]

capsule noun (plural **capsules**)
1 a hollow pill containing medicine. **2** a plant's seed-case that splits open when ripe.
3 a compartment that can be separated from the rest of a spacecraft. [same origin as *case*]

captain noun (plural **captains**)
1 a person in command of a ship, aircraft, sports team, etc. **2** an army officer ranking next below a major; a naval officer ranking next below a commodore. **captaincy** noun

caption noun (plural **captions**)
1 the words printed with a picture to describe it. **2** a short title or heading in a newspaper or magazine. [from Latin]

captious (say kap-shus) adjective pointing out small mistakes or faults.

captivate verb (**captivates, captivating, captivated**) charm or delight someone. **captivation** noun [same origin as *captive*]

captive noun (plural **captives**) someone taken prisoner.

captive adjective taken prisoner; unable to escape. **captivity** noun [from Latin *capere* = take, seize]

capture verb (**captures, capturing, captured**)
1 take someone prisoner. **2** take or obtain by force, trickery, skill, or attraction, *He captured her heart.*

capture noun capturing. [same origin as *captive*]

car noun (plural **cars**)
1 a motor car. **2** a carriage, *dining car.* [from old French]

caramel noun (plural **caramels**)
1 a kind of toffee tasting like burnt sugar. **2** burnt sugar used for colouring and flavouring food. [via French from Spanish]

carat noun (plural **carats**)
1 a measure of weight for precious stones. 2 a measure of the purity of gold, *Pure gold is 24 carats.* [via French and Italian from Arabic]

caravan noun (plural **caravans**)
1 an enclosed carriage equipped for living in, able to be towed by a motor vehicle or a horse.
2 a group of people travelling together across desert country.
caravanning noun [via French from Persian]

carbohydrate noun (plural **carbohydrates**) a compound of carbon, oxygen, and hydrogen (e.g. sugar or starch). [from *carbon* + *-hydrate* = combined with water]

carbolic noun a kind of disinfectant. [from *carbon* (from which it is made)]

carbon noun (plural **carbons**)
1 a substance that is present in all living things and that occurs in its pure form as diamond and graphite. 2 carbon paper.
3 a carbon copy. [from Latin *carbo* = coal]

carbonate noun (plural **carbonates**) a compound that gives off carbon dioxide when mixed with acid.

carbon dioxide noun a gas formed when things burn, or breathed out by animals.

carburettor noun (plural **carburettors**) a device for mixing fuel and air in an engine. [from *carbon* (which the fuel contains)]

carcass noun (plural **carcasses**)
1 the dead body of an animal.
2 the bony part of a bird's body after the meat has been eaten. [from French]

carcinogen noun (plural **carcinogens**) any substance that produces cancer. [from Greek *karkinoma* = tumour]

card noun (plural **cards**)
1 a small usually oblong piece of stiff paper or of plastic. 2 a playing card. 3 cardboard.
cards plural noun a game using playing cards.
on the cards likely; possible. [from Latin *charta* = papyrus leaf, paper]

cardboard noun a kind of thin board made of layers of paper or wood-fibre.

cardiac (say **kard**-ee-ak) adjective to do with the heart. [from Greek *kardia* = heart]

cardigan noun (plural **cardigans**) a knitted jacket. [named after the Earl of Cardigan, a commander in the Crimean War; cardigans were first worn by the troops in that war]

cardinal noun (plural **cardinals**) a senior priest in the Roman Catholic Church.

cardinal adjective
1 chief; most important, *the cardinal features of our plan.*
2 deep scarlet (like a cardinal's cassock).
[from old French]

cardinal numbers plural noun the whole numbers one, two, three, etc. (Compare *ordinal*.)

cardinal points plural noun the four main points of the compass (North, South, East, West).

care noun (plural **cares**)
1 serious attention and thought, *Plan your holiday with care.*
2 caution to avoid damage or loss, *Glass—handle with care.*
3 protection; supervision, *Leave the child in my care.* 4 worry; anxiety, *freedom from care.*

care verb (**cares, caring, cared**)
1 feel interested or concerned.
2 feel affection.
care for have in your care; be fond of.

career noun (plural **careers**)
1 progress through life, especially in work. 2 an occupation with opportunities for promotion.

career verb (**careers, careering, careered**) rush along wildly. [from Latin; related to *car*]

carefree adjective without worries or responsibilities.

careful adjective
1 giving serious thought and attention to something.
2 avoiding damage or danger etc.; cautious. **carefully** adverb, **carefulness** noun

careless adjective not careful. **carelessly** adverb, **carelessness** noun

caress noun (plural **caresses**)
a gentle loving touch.

caress verb (**caresses, caressing, caressed**) touch lovingly. [from Latin *carus* = dear]

caretaker noun (plural **caretakers**) a person employed to look after a school, block of flats, etc.

cargo noun (plural **cargoes**) goods carried in a ship or aircraft. [from Spanish]

Caribbean adjective to do with or from the Caribbean Sea, a part of the Atlantic Ocean east of Central America.

caricature noun (plural **caricatures**) an amusing or exaggerated picture of someone. [from Italian *caricare* = exaggerate]

carnage noun the killing of many people. [same origin as *carnal*]

carnival noun (plural **carnivals**) a festival, often with a procession in fancy dress. [from Latin *carnis* = of flesh (because originally this meant the festivities before Lent, when meat was given up until Easter)]

carnivorous (say kar-niv-er-us) adjective meat-eating. (Compare *herbivorous*.) **carnivore** noun [from Latin *carnis* = of flesh + *vorare* = devour]

carol noun (plural **carols**) a Christmas hymn. **caroller** noun, **carolling** noun [from old French]

carp[1] noun (plural **carp**) an edible freshwater fish. [from Latin *carpa*]

carp[2] verb (**carps, carping, carped**) keep finding fault. [from Latin *carpere* = slander]

car park noun (plural **car parks**) an area where cars may be parked.

carpenter noun (plural **carpenters**) a person who makes things out of wood. **carpentry** noun [from a Latin word meaning 'carriage-maker']

carpet noun (plural **carpets**) a thick soft covering for a floor. **carpeted** adjective, **carpeting** noun [from old French]

carriage noun (plural **carriages**)
1 one of the separate parts of a train, where passengers sit.
2 a passenger vehicle pulled by horses. 3 carrying goods from one place to another; the cost of carrying goods, *Carriage is extra.*
4 a moving part carrying or holding something in a machine. [same origin as *carry*]

carrier noun (plural **carriers**)
a person or thing that carries something.

carrot noun (plural **carrots**)
a plant with a thick orange-coloured root used as a vegetable. [from Greek]

carry verb (**carries, carrying, carried**)
1 take something from one place to another. 2 support the weight of something. 3 travel clearly, *Sound carries in the mountains.*
4 if a motion is carried, it is approved by most people at the meeting, *The motion was carried by ten votes to six.*
be carried away be very excited.
carry on 1 continue. 2 (*informal*) behave excitedly. 3 (*informal*) complain.
[from old French *carier*; related to *car*]

cart noun (plural **carts**) an open vehicle for carrying loads.

cart verb (**carts, carting, carted**)
1 carry in a cart. 2 (*informal*) carry something heavy or tiring, *I've carted these books all round the school.*
[from Old Norse]

carthorse noun (plural **carthorses**) a large strong horse used for pulling heavy loads.

cartilage noun tough white flexible tissue attached to a bone. [from Latin]

carton noun (plural **cartons**)
a cardboard or plastic container. [French; related to *card*]

cartoon noun (plural **cartoons**)
1 an amusing drawing. 2 a comic strip (see *comic*). 3 an animated film. **cartoonist** noun [originally = a drawing on stiff paper; from Italian, related to *card*]

cartridge noun (plural **cartridges**)
1 a case containing the explosive for a bullet or shell. 2 a container holding film for a camera, ink for a pen, etc. 3 the device that holds the stylus of a record player.

cartwheel noun (plural **cartwheels**)
1 the wheel of a cart.
2 a handstand balancing on each hand in turn with arms and legs spread like spokes of a wheel.

carve verb (**carves, carving, carved**)
1 make something by cutting wood or stone etc. 2 cut cooked meat into slices. **carver** noun [from Old English]

case[1] noun (plural **cases**)
1 a container. 2 a suitcase. [from Latin *capsa* = box]

case[2] noun (plural **cases**)
1 an example of something existing or occurring; a situation, *In every case we found that someone had cheated.* 2 something investigated by police etc. or by a lawcourt, *a murder case.* 3 a set of facts or arguments to support something, *She put forward a good case for equality.* 4 the form of a word that shows how it is related to other words. *Fred's*

is the possessive case of *Fred*;
him is the objective case of *he*.

in any case anyway.

in case because something may
happen.

[from Latin *casus* = a fall, an
occasion]

cash *noun*
1 money in coin or notes.
2 immediate payment for goods
etc.

cash *verb* (**cashes, cashing,
cashed**) change a cheque etc.
for cash.

[originally = a cash box; from
Latin *capsa* = box]

cash dispenser *noun* (*plural*
cash dispensers) a machine,
usually outside a bank, from
which people can draw out cash
by using a cash card.

cashier *noun* (*plural* **cashiers**)
a person who takes in and pays
out money in a bank or takes
payments in a shop.

cashpoint *noun* (*plural*
cashpoints) a cash dispenser.

casing *noun* (*plural* **casings**)
a protective covering. [from
case[1]]

casino *noun* (*plural* **casinos**)
a public building or room for
gambling. [Italian, = little house]

cask *noun* (*plural* **casks**) a barrel.
[from French or Spanish]

casket *noun* (*plural* **caskets**)
a small box for jewellery etc.
[origin unknown]

casserole *noun* (*plural*
casseroles)
1 a covered dish in which food is
cooked and served. 2 food cooked
in a casserole. [from Greek]

cassette *noun* (*plural* **cassettes**)
a small sealed case containing

recording tape, film, etc. [French,
= little case]

cast *verb* (**casts, casting, cast**)
1 throw. 2 shed or throw off.
3 make a vote. 4 make something
of metal or plaster in a mould.
5 choose performers for a play or
film etc.

cast *noun* (*plural* **casts**)
1 a shape made by pouring liquid
metal or plaster into a mould.
2 all the performers in a play
or film.
[from Old Norse]

castaway *noun* (*plural*
castaways) a shipwrecked
person. [originally = an outcast;
from *cast* + *away*]

caste *noun* (*plural* **castes**) (in
India) one of the social classes
into which Hindus are born.
[from Spanish or Portuguese
casta = descent (from the same
ancestors)]

casting vote *noun* (*plural*
casting votes) the vote that
decides which group wins when
the votes on each side are equal.

castle *noun* (*plural* **castles**)
1 a large old fortified building.
2 a piece in chess, also called
a *rook*.

castles in the air daydreams.
[from Latin *castellum* = fort]

castor sugar *noun* finely-ground
white sugar.

castrate *verb* (**castrates,
castrating, castrated**) remove the
testicles of a male animal.
(Compare *spay*.) **castration** *noun*

casual *adjective*
1 happening by chance; not
planned. 2 not careful; not
methodical. 3 informal; suitable
for informal occasions, *casual*

clothes. **4** not permanent, *casual work.* **casually** *adverb,* **casualness** *noun* [same origin as *case²*]

casualty *noun* (*plural* **casualties**) a person who is killed or injured in war or in an accident. [originally = chance; same origin as *case²*]

cat *noun* (*plural* **cats**)
1 a small furry domestic animal. **2** an animal of the same family as the domestic cat, *Lions and tigers are cats.* **3** (*informal*) a spiteful girl or woman.
let the cat out of the bag reveal a secret.

cata- *prefix* (becoming **cat-** before a vowel; combining with an *h* to become **cath-**)
1 down (as in *catapult*).
2 thoroughly (as in *catalogue*). [from Greek *kata* = down]

cataclysm (*say* kat-a-klizm) *noun* (*plural* **cataclysms**) a violent upheaval or disaster. [from *cata-* + Greek *klyzein* = to wash]

catalogue *noun* (*plural* **catalogues**)
1 a list of things (e.g. of books in a library), usually arranged in order. **2** a book containing a list of things that can be bought, *Christmas catalogue.*

catalogue *verb* (**catalogues, cataloguing, catalogued**) enter something in a catalogue.

catalyst (*say* kat-a-list) *noun* (*plural* **catalysts**) something that starts or speeds up a change or reaction. [from *cata-* + Greek *lysis* = loosening]

catalytic converter *noun* (*plural* **catalytic converters**) a device fitted to a car's exhaust system, with a catalyst for converting pollutant gases into less harmful ones.

catapult *noun* (*plural* **catapults**)
1 a device with elastic for shooting small stones. **2** an ancient military device for hurling stones etc.

catapult *verb* (**catapults, catapulting, catapulted**) hurl or rush violently.
[from *cata-* + Greek *pellein* = throw]

cataract *noun* (*plural* **cataracts**)
1 a large waterfall or rush of water. **2** a cloudy area that forms in the eye and prevents a person from seeing clearly.

catastrophe (*say* ka-tass-trof-ee) *noun* (*plural* **catastrophes**) a sudden great disaster.

catastrophic (*say* kat-a-strof-ik) *adjective,* **catastrophically** *adverb*
[from *cata-* + Greek *strephein* = to turn]

catch *verb* (**catches, catching, caught**)
1 take and hold something. **2** capture. **3** overtake. **4** be in time to get on a bus or train etc. **5** be infected with an illness. **6** hear, *I didn't catch what he said.* **7** surprise or detect somebody, *caught in the act.* **8** trick somebody. **9** make or become fixed or unable to move; snag; entangle, *I caught my dress on a nail.* **10** hit; strike, *The blow caught him on the nose.*
catch fire start burning.
catch it (*informal*) be scolded or punished.
catch on (*informal*) **1** become popular. **2** understand.

catch noun (plural **catches**)
1 catching something.
2 something caught or worth catching. 3 a hidden difficulty: 4 a device for fastening something. [same origin as *chase*]

catching adjective infectious.

catchment area noun (plural **catchment areas**)
1 the whole area from which water drains into a river etc. 2 the area from which a school takes pupils or a hospital takes patients.

catchphrase noun (plural **catchphrases**) a popular phrase.

catchy adjective easy to remember; soon becoming popular, *a catchy tune*.

category noun (plural **categories**) a set of people or things classified as being similar to each other. [from Greek *kategoria* = statement, accusation]

cater verb (**caters, catering, catered**)
1 provide food, especially for a lot of people. 2 provide what is needed. **caterer** noun [from old French *acatour* = a person who buys food etc.]

caterpillar noun (plural **caterpillars**) the creeping worm-like creature that will turn into a butterfly or moth. [from old French *chatepelose* = hairy cat]

cath- prefix see **cata-**.

cathedral noun (plural **cathedrals**) the most important church of a district, usually containing the bishop's throne. [from Greek *kathedra* = seat]

Catherine wheel noun (plural **Catherine wheels**) a firework that spins round. [named after St Catherine, who was martyred on a spiked wheel]

cathode noun (plural **cathodes**) the electrode by which electric current leaves a device. (Compare *anode*.) [from *cata-* = down + Greek *hodos* = way]

Catholic adjective
1 of all Christians, *the Holy Catholic Church*. 2 Roman Catholic (see *Roman*). **Catholicism** noun

Catholic noun (plural **Catholics**) a Roman Catholic.

catholic adjective including most things, *Her taste in literature is catholic*. [from Greek *katholikos* = universal]

cattle plural noun animals with horns and hoofs, kept by farmers for their milk and beef.

catty adjective (**cattier, cattiest**) speaking or spoken spitefully.

cauldron noun (plural **cauldrons**) a large deep pot for boiling things in. [from Latin *caldarium* = hot bath]

cauliflower noun (plural **cauliflowers**) a cabbage with a large head of white flowers. [from French *chou fleuri* = flowered cabbage]

cause noun (plural **causes**)
1 a person or thing that makes something happen or produces an effect. 2 a reason, *There is no cause for worry*. 3 a purpose for which people work; an organization or charity.

cause verb (**causes, causing, caused**) be the cause of; make something happen.

causeway noun (plural **causeways**) a raised road across low or marshy ground.

caustic adjective
1 able to burn or wear things away by chemical action.
2 sarcastic. **caustically** adverb
[from Greek *kaustikos* = capable of burning]

caution noun (plural **cautions**)
1 care taken in order to avoid danger etc. 2 a warning.

caution verb (**cautions, cautioning, cautioned**) warn someone.
[from Latin *cavere* = beware]

cautionary adjective giving a warning.

cautious adjective showing caution. **cautiously** adverb, **cautiousness** noun

Cavalier noun (plural **Cavaliers**) a supporter of King Charles I in the English Civil War (1642–9).
[from French *chevalier* = knight, from Latin *caballus* = horse]

cavalry noun soldiers who fight on horseback or in armoured vehicles. (Compare *infantry*.)
[from Latin *caballus* = horse]

cave noun (plural **caves**) a large hollow place in the side of a hill or cliff, or underground.

cave verb (**caves, caving, caved**) cave in fall inwards; give way in an argument.
[from Latin *cavus* = hollow]

cavern noun (plural **caverns**) a large cave. **cavernous** adjective [same origin as *cave*]

cavity noun (plural **cavities**) a hollow or hole. [same origin as *cave*]

cavort (say ka-vort) verb (**cavorts, cavorting, cavorted**) jump or run about excitedly.

caw noun (plural **caws**) the harsh cry of a crow etc.

cc abbreviation cubic centimetre(s).

CD abbreviation compact disc.

CD-ROM abbreviation compact disc read-only memory; a compact disc on which large amounts of data can be stored and then displayed on a computer screen.

cease verb (**ceases, ceasing, ceased**) stop or end.

cease noun
without cease not ceasing.

ceasefire noun (plural **ceasefires**) a signal to stop firing.

ceaseless adjective not ceasing.

cedar noun (plural **cedars**) an evergreen tree with hard fragrant wood. **cedarwood** noun [from Greek]

cedilla (say sid-il-a) noun (plural **cedillas**) a mark under *c* in certain languages to show that it is pronounced as *s*, e.g. in façade.
[from Spanish, = a little *z*]

ceiling noun (plural **ceilings**)
1 the flat surface under the top of a room. 2 the highest limit that something can reach. [origin unknown]

celebrate verb (**celebrates, celebrating, celebrated**)
1 do something special or enjoyable to show that a day or event is important. 2 perform a religious ceremony. **celebrant** noun, **celebration** noun [from Latin]

celebrated adjective famous.

celebrity noun (plural **celebrities**)
1 a famous person. 2 fame; being famous.

celery noun a vegetable with crisp white or green stems. [from Greek]

celestial (say sil-**est**-ee-al) adjective
1 to do with the sky. 2 to do with heaven; divine.

celestial bodies plural noun stars etc.

cell noun (plural **cells**)
1 a small room where a prisoner is locked up. 2 a small room in a monastery. 3 a microscopic unit of living matter. 4 a compartment of a honeycomb. 5 a device for producing electric current chemically. 6 a small group or unit in an organization etc. [from Latin *cella* = storeroom]

cellar noun (plural **cellars**) an underground room. [same origin as *cell*]

cello (say **chel**-oh) noun (plural **cellos**) a musical instrument like a large violin, played between the knees of a player. **cellist** noun [from Italian *violoncello* = small double bass]

cellulose noun
1 tissue that forms the main part of all plants and trees. 2 paint made from cellulose. [from Latin]

Celsius (say **sel**-see-us) adjective (of a temperature scale) centigrade. [named after A. Celsius, a Swedish astronomer, who invented it]

cement noun
1 a mixture of lime and clay used in building, to join bricks together, etc. 2 a strong glue. **cement** verb (**cements, cementing, cemented**)
1 put cement on something. 2 join firmly; strengthen. [from Latin]

cemetery (say **sem**-et-ree) noun (plural **cemeteries**) a place where people are buried. [from Greek *koimeterion* = dormitory]

censor noun (plural **censors**) a person who examines films, books, letters, etc. and removes or bans anything that seems harmful. **censor** verb, **censorship** noun [Latin, = magistrate with power to ban unsuitable people from ceremonies; from *censere* = to judge]

USAGE: Do not confuse with *censure*.

censure (say **sen**-sher) noun strong criticism or disapproval of something. **censure** verb [same origin as *census*]

USAGE: Do not confuse with *censor*.

census noun (plural **censuses**) an official count or survey of the population of a country or area. [from Latin *censere* = estimate, judge]

cent noun (plural **cents**) a coin worth one-hundredth of a dollar. [from Latin *centum* = 100]

centenary (say sen-**teen**-er-ee) noun (plural **centenaries**) a 100th anniversary. **centennial** (say sen-**ten**-ee-al) adjective [from Latin *centenarius* = containing a hundred]

centi- prefix
1 one hundred (as in *centipede*). 2 one-hundredth (as in *centimetre*). [from Latin *centum* = 100]

centigrade *adjective* measuring temperature on a scale using 100 degrees, where water freezes at 0° and boils at 100°. [from *centi-* + Latin *gradus* = step]

centimetre *noun* (*plural* **centimetres**) one-hundredth of a metre, about four-tenths of an inch.

centipede *noun* (*plural* **centipedes**) a small crawling creature with a long body and many legs. [from *centi-* + Latin *pedes* = feet]

central *adjective*
1 to do with or at the centre.
2 most important. **centrally** *adverb*

central heating *noun* a system of heating a building from one source by circulating hot water or hot air or steam in pipes or by linked radiators.

centre *noun* (*plural* **centres**)
1 the middle point or part. **2** an important place, e.g. from which things are organized; a place where certain things happen, *shopping centre*.

centre *verb* (**centres**, **centring**, **centred**) place something at the centre.

centre on or **centre around** be concentrated in; have as its main subject or concern.
[from Greek *kentron* = sharp point, point of a pair of compasses]

centre of gravity *noun* (*plural* **centres of gravity**) the point in an object at which it balances perfectly.

century *noun* (*plural* **centuries**)
1 a period of one hundred years.

2 a hundred runs scored by a batsman in an innings at cricket. [from Latin *centum* = 100]

ceramic *adjective* to do with or made of pottery. [from Greek]

cereal *noun* (*plural* **cereals**)
1 a grass producing seeds which are used as food, e.g. wheat, barley, rice. **2** a breakfast food made from these seeds. [from *Ceres*, the Roman goddess of farming]

USAGE: Do not confuse with *serial*.

cerebral (*say* se-rib-ral) *adjective* to do with the brain. [from Latin *cerebrum* = brain]

cerebral palsy *noun* a condition caused by brain damage before birth that makes a person suffer from spasms of the muscles and jerky movements.

ceremonial *adjective* to do with or used in a ceremony; formal. **ceremonially** *adverb*

ceremonious *adjective* full of ceremony; elaborately performed.

ceremony *noun* (*plural* **ceremonies**) the formal actions carried out on an important occasion, e.g. at a wedding or a funeral. [from Latin *caerimonia* = worship, ritual]

certain *adjective* sure; without doubt.
a certain person or **thing** a person or thing that is known but not named.

certainty *noun* (*plural* **certainties**)
1 something that is sure to happen. **2** being sure.

certificate noun (plural **certificates**) an official written or printed statement giving information about a person etc., *a birth certificate.*

certitude noun a feeling of certainty.

cervix noun (plural **cervices** (say ser-vis-ees)) the entrance to the womb. **cervical** adjective [Latin, = neck]

cesspit or **cesspool** noun (plural **cesspits, cesspools**) a covered pit where liquid waste or sewage is stored temporarily. [origin unknown]

CFC abbreviation chlorofluorocarbon; a gas containing chlorine and fluorine that is thought to be harmful to the ozone layer in the Earth's atmosphere.

chaff[1] noun husks of corn, separated from the seed. [from Old English]

chaff[2] verb tease someone. [origin unknown]

chain noun (plural **chains**)
1 a row of metal rings fastened together. 2 a connected series of things, *a chain of mountains; a chain of events.*

chain verb (**chains, chaining, chained**) fasten something with a chain or chains.

chain letter noun (plural **chain letters**) a letter that you are asked to copy and send to several other people.

chain reaction noun (plural **chain reactions**) a series of happenings in which each causes the next.

chain store noun (plural **chain stores**) one of a number of similar shops owned by the same firm.

chair noun (plural **chairs**)
1 a movable seat, with a back, for one person. 2 a position of authority at a meeting, *Mr Bloggs was in the chair.*

chair verb (**chairs, chairing, chaired**) be in control of a meeting, *Who will chair this meeting?*
[from old French; related to *cathedral*]

chairman noun (plural **chairmen**) the person who is in control of a meeting. **chairmanship** noun

USAGE: The word *chairman* may be used of a man or of a woman; they are addressed formally as *Mr Chairman* and *Madam Chairman.*

chairperson noun (plural **chairpersons**) a chairman.

chalk noun (plural **chalks**)
1 a soft white or coloured stick used for writing on blackboards or for drawing. 2 soft white limestone. **chalky** adjective

challenge noun (plural **challenges**)
1 a demand to take part in a contest. 2 a task or activity that is new and exciting but also difficult.

challenge verb (**challenges, challenging, challenged**)
1 make a challenge to someone.
2 question whether something is true or correct. **challenger** noun
[from old French]

chamber noun (plural **chambers**)
1 (old use) a room. 2 a hall used for meetings of a parliament etc.; the members of the group using it. 3 a compartment in machinery etc. [same origin as camera]

chambermaid noun (plural **chambermaids**) a woman employed to clean bedrooms at a hotel etc.

chamber music noun music for a small group of players.

chamber pot noun (plural **chamber pots**) a receptacle for urine etc., used in a bedroom.

chameleon (say kam-ee-lee-on) noun (plural **chameleons**) a small lizard that can change its colour to that of its surroundings. [from Greek khamaileon, literally = ground lion]

champagne (say sham-payn) noun a bubbly white wine, especially from Champagne in France.

champion noun (plural **champions**)
1 a person or thing that has defeated all the others in a sport or competition etc. 2 someone who supports a cause by fighting, speaking, etc. **championship** noun

champion verb (**champions**, **championing**, **championed**) support a cause by fighting or speaking for it.
[from old French]

chance noun (plural **chances**)
1 an opportunity or possibility, Now is your chance to escape. 2 the way things happen without being planned, I met her by chance.
take a chance take a risk.

chancellor noun (plural **chancellors**) an important official.
Chancellor of the Exchequer the government minister in charge of a country's finances.
[from Latin cancellarius = secretary]

change verb (**changes**, **changing**, **changed**)
1 make or become different.
2 exchange. 3 put on different clothes. 4 go from one train or bus etc. to another.

change noun (plural **changes**)
1 changing; a difference in doing something. 2 coins or notes of small values. 3 money given back to the payer when the price is less than the amount handed over. 4 a fresh set of clothes.
5 a variation in routine, Let's walk home for a change.

changeable adjective likely to change; changing frequently, changeable weather.

channel noun (plural **channels**)
1 a stretch of water connecting two seas. 2 a way for water to flow along. 3 the part of a river or sea etc. that is deep enough for ships. 4 a broadcasting wavelength.

channel verb (**channels**, **channelling**, **channelled**)
1 make a channel in something.
2 direct something through a channel or other route.
[from Latin canalis = canal]

chant noun (plural **chants**)
1 a tune to which words with no regular rhythm are fitted, e.g. one used in singing psalms.
2 a rhythmic call or shout.

chant verb (chants, chanting, chanted)
1 sing. 2 call out words in a rhythm.
[from Latin *cantare* = sing]

chaos (say **kay**-oss) noun great disorder. **chaotic** adjective, **chaotically** adverb [Greek, = bottomless pit]

chap noun (plural **chaps**) (informal) a man. [short for *chapman*, an old word for a pedlar]

chapatti noun (plural **chapattis**) a flat cake of unleavened bread, used in Indian cookery. [Hindi, from *chapana* = flatten or roll out]

chapel noun (plural **chapels**)
1 a place used for Christian worship, other than a cathedral or parish church; a religious service in this. 2 a section of a large church, with its own altar.

chaplain noun (plural **chaplains**) a member of the clergy who looks after a college or hospital or regiment etc.

chapped adjective with skin split or cracked from cold etc.

chapter noun (plural **chapters**)
1 a division of a book. 2 the clergy of a cathedral or members of a monastery. The room where they meet is called a **chapter house**. [from Latin]

character noun (plural **characters**)
1 a person in a story, film, or play. 2 all the qualities that make a person or thing what he, she, or it is. 3 a letter of the alphabet. [from Greek]

characteristic noun (plural **characteristics**) a quality that forms part of a person's or thing's character.

characteristic adjective typical of a person or thing.
characteristically adverb

charade (say sha-**rahd**) noun (plural **charades**)
1 a scene in the game of *charades*, in which people try to guess a word from other people's acting. 2 a pretence. [French]

charcoal noun a black substance made by burning wood slowly. Charcoal can be used for drawing with. [origin unknown]

charge noun (plural **charges**)
1 the price asked for something. 2 a rushing attack. 3 the amount of explosive needed to fire a gun etc. 4 electricity in something. 5 an accusation that someone has committed a crime. 6 a person or thing in someone's care.
in charge in control; deciding what shall happen to a person or thing.

charge verb (charges, charging, charged)
1 ask a particular price. 2 rush forward in an attack. 3 give an electric charge to something. 4 accuse someone of committing a crime. 5 entrust someone with a responsibility or task.
[from Latin *carcare* = to load]

chariot noun (plural **chariots**) a horse-drawn vehicle with two wheels, used in ancient times for fighting, racing, etc. **charioteer** noun [from old French; related to *car*]

charity noun (plural **charities**)
1 an organization set up to help people who are poor, ill, or disabled or have suffered a disaster. 2 giving money or help etc. to the needy. 3 kindness and sympathy towards others; being unwilling to think badly of people. **charitable** adjective, **charitably** adverb [from Latin caritas = love]

charm noun (plural **charms**)
1 the power to please or delight people; attractiveness. 2 a magic spell. 3 a small object believed to bring good luck. 4 an ornament worn on a bracelet etc.

charm verb (**charms, charming, charmed**)
1 give pleasure or delight to people. 2 put a spell on someone; bewitch. **charmer** noun [from Latin carmen = song or spell]

chart noun (plural **charts**)
1 a map for people sailing ships or flying aircraft. 2 an outline map showing special information, a weather chart. 3 a diagram or list etc. giving information in an orderly way. **the charts** a list of the records that are most popular.

chart verb (**charts, charting, charted**) make a chart of something; map. [same origin as card]

charter noun (plural **charters**)
1 an official document giving somebody certain rights etc. 2 chartering an aircraft, ship, or vehicle.

charter verb (**charters, chartering, chartered**)
1 hire an aircraft, ship, or vehicle. 2 give a charter to someone. [same origin as card]

charwoman noun (plural **charwomen**) a woman employed as a cleaner. [from Old English cerr = task]

chase verb (**chases, chasing, chased**) go quickly after a person or thing in order to capture or catch them up or drive them away. **chase** noun [from Latin captare = capture]

chasm (say kazm) noun (plural **chasms**) a deep opening in the ground. [from Greek chasma = gaping hollow]

chassis (say shas-ee) noun (plural **chassis**) the framework under a car etc., on which other parts are mounted. [originally = window frame; related to casement]

chaste adjective not having sexual intercourse at all, or only with the person to whom you are married. **chastity** noun [from Latin castus = pure]

chat noun (plural **chats**) a friendly conversation.

chat verb (**chats, chatting, chatted**) have a friendly conversation. [from chatter]

chatter verb (**chatters, chattering, chattered**)
1 talk quickly about unimportant things; keep on talking. 2 if your teeth chatter, they make a rattling sound because you are cold or frightened. **chatterer** noun

chatter noun chattering talk or sound.

chauvinism (say shoh-vin-izm) noun
1 prejudiced belief that your own country is superior to others.
2 the belief of some men that men are superior to women.
chauvinist noun, **chauvinistic** adjective

cheap adjective
1 low in price; not expensive. 2 of poor quality; of low value.
cheaply adverb, **cheapness** noun
[from Old English ceap = a bargain]

cheapen verb (cheapens, cheapening, cheapened) make or become cheap.

cheat verb (cheats, cheating, cheated)
1 trick or deceive somebody. 2 try to do well in an examination or game etc. by breaking the rules.

cheat noun (plural cheats)
a person who cheats.
[from old French]

check[1] verb (checks, checking, checked)
1 make sure that something is correct or in good condition.
2 make something stop or go slower.

check noun (plural checks)
1 checking something. 2 stopping or slowing; a pause. 3 a receipt; a bill in a restaurant. 4 the situation in chess when a king may be captured.

check[2] noun (plural checks)
a pattern of squares. **checked** adjective

checkmate noun the winning situation in chess. **checkmate** verb [from Persian shah mat = the king is dead]

checkout noun (plural checkouts) a place where goods are paid for in a self-service shop.

cheek noun (plural cheeks)
1 the side of the face below the eye. 2 rude or disrespectful behaviour; impudence.

cheeky adjective rude or disrespectful; impudent. **cheekily** adverb, **cheekiness** noun

cheer noun (plural cheers)
1 a shout of praise or pleasure or encouragement, especially 'hurray'. 2 cheerfulness, full of good cheer.

cheer verb (cheers, cheering, cheered)
1 give a cheer. 2 gladden or encourage somebody.
cheer up make or become cheerful.
[originally = a person's expression; from old French chiere = face]

cheerful adjective
1 looking or sounding happy.
2 pleasantly bright or colourful.
cheerfully adverb, **cheerfulness** noun

cheerless adjective gloomy or dreary.

cheery adjective bright and cheerful.

cheese noun (plural cheeses)
a solid food made from milk.

chemical adjective to do with or produced by chemistry.

chemical noun (plural chemicals) a substance obtained by or used in chemistry.

chemist noun (plural chemists)
1 a person who makes or sells medicines. 2 an expert in chemistry.

chemistry noun
1 the way that substances combine and react with one another. 2 the study of substances and their reactions etc.

chemotherapy noun the treatment of disease, especially cancer, by the use of chemical substances.

cheque noun (plural **cheques**) a printed form on which you write instructions to a bank to pay out money from your account. [a different spelling of check[1]]

cherish verb (**cherishes, cherishing, cherished**)
1 look after a person or thing lovingly. 2 be fond of. [from French cher = dear]

cherry noun (plural **cherries**) a small soft round fruit with a stone. [from old French]

chess noun a game for two players with sixteen pieces each (called **chessmen**) on a board of 64 squares (a **chessboard**). [from old French esches = checks]

chest noun (plural **chests**)
1 the front part of the body between the neck and the waist. 2 a large strong box for storing things in. [from Old English]

chestnut noun (plural **chestnuts**)
1 a tree that produces hard brown nuts. 2 the nut of this tree. 3 an old joke or story. [from Greek]

chest of drawers noun (plural **chests of drawers**) a piece of furniture with drawers for storing clothes etc.

chew verb (**chews, chewing, chewed**) grind food between the teeth. **chewy** adjective [from Old English]

chewing gum noun a sticky flavoured type of sweet for chewing.

chick noun (plural **chicks**) a very young bird. [shortened form of chicken]

chicken noun (plural **chickens**)
1 a young bird, especially of the domestic fowl. 2 the flesh of a domestic fowl as food.

chicken adjective (slang) afraid to do something; cowardly.

chicken verb (**chickens, chickening, chickened**)
chicken out (slang) not take part in something because you are afraid.

chickenpox noun a disease that produces red spots on the skin. [probably because the disease is mild]

chief noun (plural **chiefs**) a person with the highest rank or authority.

chief adjective most important; main. **chiefly** adverb [from French]

chieftain noun (plural **chieftains**) the chief of a tribe, band of robbers, etc.

child noun (plural **children**)
1 a young person; a boy or girl. 2 someone's son or daughter. [from Old English]

childhood noun (plural **childhoods**) the time when a person is a child.

childish adjective like a child; unsuitable for a grown person. **childishly** adverb

childminder noun (plural **childminders**) a person who looks after children for payment.

chill noun (plural **chills**)
1 unpleasant coldness. 2 an illness that makes you shiver.

chill verb (**chills, chilling, chilled**) make a person or thing very cold.

chilli noun (plural **chillies**) the hot-tasting pod of a red pepper. [via Spanish from Nahuatl (a Central American language)]

chilly adjective
1 rather cold. 2 unfriendly. **chilliness** noun

chime noun (plural **chimes**) a series of notes sounded by a set of bells each making a different musical sound.

chimney noun (plural **chimneys**) a tall pipe or structure that carries smoke away from a fire. [from French]

chimney pot noun (plural **chimney pots**) a pipe fitted to the top of a chimney.

chimpanzee noun (plural **chimpanzees**) an African ape, smaller than a gorilla. [via French from Kikongo (an African language)]

chin noun (plural **chins**) the lower part of the face below the mouth.

china noun thin delicate pottery. [from Persian *chini* = from China]

chink noun (plural **chinks**)
1 a narrow opening, *a chink in the curtains.* 2 a chinking sound.

chink verb (**chinks, chinking, chinked**) make a sound like glasses or coins being struck together. [origin unknown]

chip noun (plural **chips**)
1 a thin piece cut or broken off something hard. 2 a fried oblong strip of potato. 3 a place where a small piece has been knocked off something. 4 a small counter used in games. 5 a microchip.
a chip off the old block a child who is very like his or her father or mother.
have a chip on your shoulder have a grievance and feel bitter or resentful.

chip verb (**chips, chipping, chipped**)
1 knock small pieces off something. 2 cut a potato into chips. [from Old English]

chipolata noun (plural **chipolatas**) a small spicy sausage. [via French from Italian]

chiropody (say ki-rop-od-ee) noun medical treatment of the feet, e.g. corns. **chiropodist** noun [from Greek *cheir* = hand + *podos* = of the foot (because chiropodists originally treated hands and feet)]

chirp verb (**chirps, chirping, chirped**) make short sharp sounds like a small bird. **chirp** noun [imitating the sound]

chisel noun (plural **chisels**) a tool with a sharp end for shaping wood, stone, etc.

chisel verb (**chisels, chiselling, chiselled**) shape or cut something with a chisel.

chivalrous (say shiv-al-rus) adjective being considerate and helpful towards people less strong than yourself. **chivalry** noun [= like a perfect knight (same origin as *Cavalier*)]

chlorine (say klor-een) noun
a greenish-yellow gas used to
disinfect water etc. [from Greek
chloros = green]

chloroform (say klo-ro-form)
noun a liquid that gives off
a vapour that makes people
unconscious.

chlorophyll (say klo-ro-fil) noun
the substance that makes plants
green. [from Greek *chloros*
= green + *phyllon* = leaf]

chock-full adjective crammed
full.

chocolate noun (plural
chocolates)
1 a solid brown food or powder
made from roasted cacao seeds.
2 a drink made with this powder.
3 a sweet made of or covered with
chocolate. [via French or Spanish
from Nahuatl (a Central
American language)]

choice noun (plural choices)
1 choosing between things. **2** the
range of things from which
someone can choose, *There is
a wide choice of holidays.*
3 a person or thing chosen.

choice adjective of the best
quality, *choice bananas.*

choir noun (plural choirs) a group
of people trained to sing together,
especially in a church. **choirboy**
noun, **choirgirl** noun [from Latin
chorus = choir]

choke verb (chokes, choking,
choked)
1 cause somebody to stop
breathing properly. **2** be unable
to breathe properly. **3** clog.

choke noun (plural chokes)
a device controlling the flow of
air into the engine of a motor
vehicle.

cholera (say kol-er-a) noun an
infectious disease that is often
fatal. [from Greek]

cholesterol (say kol-est-er-ol)
noun a fatty substance that can
clog the arteries. [from Greek
chole = bile + *stereos* = stiff]

choose verb (chooses, choosing,
chose, chosen) decide which you
are going to take from among
a number of people or things.
choosy adjective [from Old
English]

chop verb (chops, chopping,
chopped) cut or hit something
with a heavy blow.

chop noun (plural chops)
1 a chopping blow. **2** a small thick
slice of meat, usually on a rib.
[origin unknown]

choppy adjective (choppier,
choppiest) (of the sea) not
smooth; full of small waves.
choppiness noun

chopsticks plural noun a pair of
thin sticks used for lifting
Chinese and Japanese food to
your mouth. [from pidgin
English, literally = quick sticks]

choral adjective to do with or
sung by a choir or chorus.

chord¹ (say kord) noun (plural
chords) a number of musical
notes sounded together. [from
accord]

chord² (say kord) noun (plural
chords) a straight line joining
two points on a curve. [a
different spelling of *cord*]

USAGE: Do not confuse with
cord.

chore (say chor) noun (plural
chores) a regular or dull task. [a
different spelling of *char*]

choreography (say ko-ree-og-ra-fee) noun the art of writing the steps for ballets or stage dances.
choreographer noun [from Greek choreia = dance, + -graphy]

chorus noun (plural **choruses**)
1 the words repeated after each verse of a song or poem. **2** music sung by a group of people. **3** a group singing together.
chorus verb (**choruses**, **chorusing**, **chorused**) sing or speak in chorus.
[Latin, from Greek choros]

christen verb (**christens**, **christening**, **christened**)
1 baptize. **2** give a name or nickname to a person or thing.
christening noun [from Old English cristnian = make someone a Christian]

Christian noun (plural **Christians**) a person who believes in Jesus Christ and his teachings.

Christian adjective to do with Christians or their beliefs.
Christianity noun

Christian name noun (plural **Christian names**) a name given to a person at his or her christening.

Christmas noun (plural **Christmases**) the day (25 December) when Christians commemorate the birth of Jesus Christ; the days round it. [from Old English Cristes maesse = the feast day of Christ]

Christmas pudding noun (plural **Christmas puddings**) a dark pudding containing dried fruit etc., eaten at Christmas.

Christmas tree noun (plural **Christmas trees**) an evergreen or artificial tree decorated at Christmas.

chromatic (say krom-at-ik) adjective to do with colours.
chromatic scale noun a musical scale going up or down in semitones.
[from Greek chroma = colour]

chromium (say kroh-mee-um) noun a shiny silvery metal. [from Greek chroma = colour (because its compounds have brilliant colours)]

chromosome (say kroh-mos-ohm) noun (plural **chromosomes**) a tiny thread-like part of an animal cell or plant cell, carrying genes. [from Greek chroma = colour + soma = body]

chronic adjective lasting for a long time, a chronic illness. **chronically** adverb [from Greek chronikos = to do with time]

chronicle noun (plural **chronicles**) a record of events in the order that they happened. [same origin as chronic]

chronology (say kron-ol-oj-ee) noun the order of events in the sequence in which they happened, e.g. in history.
chronological adjective [from Greek chronos = time, + -logy]

chrysalis noun (plural **chrysalises**) a caterpillar that is changing into a butterfly or moth. [from Greek chrysos = gold (because some are this colour)]

chrysanthemum noun (plural **chrysanthemums**) a garden flower that blooms in autumn. [originally = a kind of marigold: from Greek chrysos = gold + anthemon = flower]

chubby adjective (**chubbier**, **chubbiest**) plump. **chubbiness** noun [origin unknown]

chuckle noun (plural **chuckles**) a quiet laugh.

chuckle verb (**chuckles**, **chuckling**, **chuckled**) laugh quietly.
[origin unknown]

chum noun (plural **chums**) (informal) a friend. **chummy** adjective [short for chamber-fellow = a person you share a room with]

chunk noun (plural **chunks**) a thick piece of something. **chunky** adjective

church noun (plural **churches**)
1 a public building for Christian worship. 2 a religious service in a church, I will see you after church.

the Church all Christians; a group of these, the Church of England. [via Old English from Greek kyriakon = Lord's house]

churlish adjective ill-mannered and unfriendly; surly. [= like a churl = a peasant]

churn noun (plural **churns**)
1 a large can in which milk is carried from a farm. 2 a machine in which milk is beaten to make butter.

churn verb (**churns**, **churning**, **churned**)
1 make butter in a churn. 2 stir or swirl vigorously.

churn out produce something in large quantities.

chute (say shoot) noun (plural **chutes**) a steep channel for people or things to slide down. [French, = a fall]

chutney noun (plural **chutneys**) a strong-tasting mixture of fruit, peppers, etc., eaten with meat. [from Hindi chatni]

-cide suffix forms nouns meaning 'killing' or 'killer' (e.g. homicide). [from Latin caedere = kill]

cider noun (plural **ciders**) an alcoholic drink made from apples. [via French and Latin from Hebrew]

cigar noun (plural **cigars**) a roll of compressed tobacco leaves for smoking. [from Spanish]

cigarette noun (plural **cigarettes**) a small roll of shredded tobacco in thin paper for smoking. [French, = little cigar]

cinder noun (plural **cinders**) a small piece of partly burnt coal or wood.

cine-camera (say sin-ee) noun (plural **cine-cameras**) a camera used for taking moving pictures. [from Greek kinema = movement, + camera]

cinema noun (plural **cinemas**) a place where films are shown. [from Greek kinema = movement]

cipher (say sy-fer) noun (plural **ciphers**)
1 a kind of code. 2 the symbol 0, representing nought or zero. [from Arabic sifr = nought]

circle noun (plural **circles**)
1 a perfectly round flat shape or thing. 2 a number of people with similar interests. 3 the balcony of a cinema or theatre.

circle verb (**circles**, **circling**, **circled**) move in a circle; go round something.
[from Latin circus]

circuit (say ser-kit) noun (plural circuits)
1 a circular line or journey.
2 a motor-racing track. 3 the path of an electric current. [from Latin circum = round + itum = gone]

circular adjective
1 shaped like a circle; round.
2 moving round a circle. circularity noun

circular noun (plural circulars) a letter or advertisement etc. sent to a number of people.

circulate verb (circulates, circulating, circulated)
1 go round something continuously, Blood circulates in the body. 2 pass from place to place. 3 send something round to a number of people. circulation noun

circum- prefix around (as in circumference). [from Latin circum = around]

circumcise verb (circumcises, circumcising, circumcised) cut off the fold of skin at the tip of the penis. circumcision noun

circumference noun (plural circumferences) the line or distance round something, especially round a circle.

circumflex accent noun (plural circumflex accents) a mark over a vowel, as over e in fête.

circumnavigate verb (circumnavigates, circumnavigating, circumnavigated) sail completely round something. circumnavigation noun

circumscribe verb (circumscribes, circumscribing, circumscribed)
1 draw a line round something.

2 limit or restrict something, Her powers are circumscribed by many regulations.

circumspect adjective cautious and watchful. circumspection noun [from circum- + Latin specere = to look]

circumstance noun (plural circumstances) a fact or condition connected with an event or person or action.

circumstantial (say ser-kum-stan-shal) adjective consisting of facts that strongly suggest something but do not actually prove it, circumstantial evidence.

circus noun (plural circuses) a travelling show with clowns, acrobats, animals, etc. [Latin, = ring]

cistern noun (plural cisterns) a tank for storing water. [from Latin]

citizen noun (plural citizens) a person belonging to a particular city or country and having certain rights and duties because of this. citizenship noun [same origin as city]

citrus fruit noun (plural citrus fruits) a lemon, orange, grapefruit, or other sharp-tasting fruit. [Latin]

city noun (plural cities) a large important town, usually with special rights given by a charter. [from Latin civitas = city]

civic adjective
1 to do with a city or town. 2 to do with citizens. [from Latin civis = citizen]

civil adjective
1 to do with citizens. 2 to do with

civilians; not military, *civil aviation*. 3 polite. **civilly** *adverb* [from Latin]

civilian *noun* (*plural* **civilians**) a person who is not serving in the armed forces. [from *civil*]

civility *noun* (*plural* **civilities**) politeness.

civilization *noun* (*plural* **civilizations**)
1 a civilized condition or society. 2 making or becoming civilized.

civilize *verb* (**civilizes**, **civilizing**, **civilized**) bring culture and education etc. to a primitive community. [from French]

Civil Service *noun* people employed by the government in various departments other than the armed forces.

civil war *noun* (*plural* **civil wars**) war between groups of people of the same country.

claim *verb* (**claims**, **claiming**, **claimed**)
1 ask for something to which you believe you have a right. 2 declare; state something without being able to prove it. **claimant** *noun*

claim *noun* (*plural* **claims**)
1 claiming. 2 something claimed. 3 a piece of ground claimed or assigned to someone for mining etc.
[same origin as *clamour*]

clairvoyant *noun* (*plural* **clairvoyants**) a person who is said to be able to predict future events or know about things that are happening out of sight.
clairvoyance *noun* [from French *clair* = clear + *voyant* = seeing]

clamber *verb* (**clambers**, **clambering**, **clambered**) climb with difficulty. [from *clamb*, the old past tense of *climb*]

clammy *adjective* damp and slimy. [from Old English *claeman* = smear, make sticky]

clamour *noun* (*plural* **clamours**)
1 a loud confused noise. 2 an outcry; a loud protest or demand.
clamorous *adjective*

clamour *verb* (**clamours**, **clamouring**, **clamoured**) make a loud protest or demand.
[from Latin *clamare* = call out]

clamp *noun* (*plural* **clamps**) a device for holding things tightly.

clamp *verb* (**clamps**, **clamping**, **clamped**)
1 fix something with a clamp. 2 fix something firmly.
clamp down on 1 become stricter about something. 2 put a stop to something.

clan *noun* (*plural* **clans**) a group sharing the same ancestor, especially in Scotland. [Scottish Gaelic]

clang *noun* (*plural* **clangs**) a loud ringing sound. **clang** *verb* [imitating the sound]

clank *noun* (*plural* **clanks**) a sound like heavy pieces of metal banging together. **clank** *verb* [imitating the sound]

clap *verb* (**claps**, **clapping**, **clapped**)
1 strike the palms of the hands together loudly, especially as applause. 2 slap in a friendly way, *clapped him on the shoulder*. 3 put quickly, *They clapped him into gaol*.

clap noun (plural **claps**)
1 a sudden sharp noise, *a clap of thunder.* 2 clapping; applause. 3 a friendly slap.
[from Old English]

claret noun (plural **clarets**) a kind of red wine. [from old French *vin claret* = clear wine]

clarify verb (**clarifies, clarifying, clarified**) make or become clear or easier to understand. **clarification** noun [from Latin *clarus* = clear]

clarinet noun (plural **clarinets**) a woodwind instrument. **clarinettist** noun [from French]

clarity noun clearness. [same origin as *clarify*]

clash verb (**clashes, clashing, clashed**)
1 make a loud sound like that of cymbals banging together. 2 conflict. 3 happen inconveniently at the same time. 4 (of colours) look unpleasant together. **clash** noun [imitating the sound]

clasp noun (plural **clasps**)
1 a device for fastening things, with interlocking parts. 2 a grasp.

clasp verb (**clasps, clasping, clasped**)
1 grasp or hold tightly. 2 fasten with a clasp.
[origin unknown]

class noun (plural **classes**)
1 a group of children, students, etc. who are taught together. 2 a group of similar people, animals, or things. 3 people of the same social or economic level. 4 level of quality, *first class.*

class verb (**classes, classing, classed**) arrange things in classes or groups; classify.
[from Latin *classis* = a social division of the Roman people]

classic adjective generally agreed to be excellent or important.

classic noun (plural **classics**) a classic book, film, writer, etc. [from Latin *classicus* = of the highest class]

classical adjective
1 to do with ancient Greek or Roman literature, art. 2 serious or conventional in style, *classical music.*

classified adjective
1 put into classes or groups. 2 (of information) declared officially to be secret and available only to certain people.

classify verb (**classifies, classifying, classified**) arrange things in classes or groups. **classification** noun, **classificatory** adjective

classroom noun (plural **classrooms**) a room where a class of children or students is taught.

clatter verb & noun (**clatters, clattering, clattered**) rattle. [imitating the sound]

clause noun (plural **clauses**)
1 a single part of a treaty, law, or contract. 2 part of a complex sentence, with its own verb, *There are two clauses in 'We choose what we want'.* [from Latin]

claustrophobia noun fear of being inside an enclosed space. [from Latin *claustrum* = enclosed space, + *phobia*]

claw noun (plural **claws**)
1 a sharp nail on a bird's or

animal's foot. **2** a claw-like part or device used for grasping.

clay noun a kind of stiff sticky earth that becomes hard when baked, used for making bricks and pottery. **clayey** adjective

-cle suffix see **-cule**.

clean adjective
1 without any dirt or marks or stains. **2** fresh; not yet used. **3** honourable; not unfair, *a clean fight*. **4** not indecent. **5** a clean catch is one made skilfully with no fumbling. **cleanness** noun

clean verb (**cleans, cleaning, cleaned**) make a thing clean.

clean adverb completely, *I clean forgot*.

clear adjective
1 transparent; not muddy or cloudy. **2** easy to see or hear or understand; distinct. **3** free from obstacles or unwanted things; free from guilt, *a clear conscience*. **4** complete, *Give three clear days' notice*. **clearly** adverb, **clearness** noun

clear adverb
1 distinctly; clearly, *We heard you loud and clear*. **2** completely, *He got clear away*. **3** apart; not in contact, *Stand clear of the doors*.

clear verb (**clears, clearing, cleared**)
1 make or become clear. **2** show that someone is innocent or reliable. **3** jump over something without touching it. **4** get approval or authorization for something, *Clear this with the headmaster*.

clear away remove used plates etc. after a meal.

clear off or **out** (*informal*) go away.

clear up 1 make things tidy.
2 become better or brighter.
3 solve, *clear up the mystery*. [same origin as *clarify*]

clearing noun (plural **clearings**) an open space in a forest.

clef noun (plural **clefs**) a symbol on a stave in music, showing the pitch of the notes, *treble clef; bass clef*. [French, = key]

cleft noun (plural **clefts**) a split in something.

clemency noun gentleness or mildness; mercy.

clench verb (**clenches, clenching, clenched**) close teeth or fingers tightly.

clergy noun the people who have been ordained as priests or ministers of the Christian Church. **clergyman** noun [same origin as *clerical*]

clerical adjective
1 to do with clerks or office paperwork. **2** to do with the clergy. [via Latin from Greek *klerikos* = belonging to the Christian Church]

clerk (say klark) noun (plural **clerks**) a person employed to keep records or accounts, deal with papers in an office, etc. [originally = a Christian minister: same origin as *clerical*]

clever adjective
1 quick at learning and understanding things. **2** skilful. **cleverly** adverb, **cleverness** noun [origin unknown]

cliché (say klee-shay) noun (plural **clichés**) a phrase or idea that is used too often. [French, = stereotyped]

click noun (plural **clicks**) a short sharp sound. **click** verb [imitating the sound]

client noun (plural **clients**) a person who gets help from a lawyer, accountant, or professional person other than a doctor; a customer. [from Latin cliens = one who listens]

cliff noun (plural **cliffs**) a steep rock face, especially on a coast. [from Old English]

climate noun (plural **climates**) the regular weather conditions of an area. **climatic** (say kly-mat-ik) adjective [from Greek klima = zone, region]

climax noun (plural **climaxes**) the most interesting or important point of a story, series of events, etc. [from Greek klimax = ladder]

climb verb (climbs, climbing, climbed)
1 go up or over or down something. **2** grow upwards. **3** go higher. **climb** noun, **climber** noun **climb down** admit that you have been wrong.

cling verb (clings, clinging, clung) hold on tightly. [from Old English]

clinic noun (plural **clinics**) a place where people see doctors etc. for treatment or advice. **clinical** adjective [from Greek klinike = teaching (of medicine) at the bedside]

clink noun (plural **clinks**) a thin sharp sound like glasses being struck together. **clink** verb

clip[1] noun (plural **clips**) a fastener for keeping things together, usually worked by a spring.

clip verb (clips, clipping, clipped) fasten with a clip.
[from Old English clyppan = embrace, hug]

clip[2] verb (clips, clipping, clipped)
1 cut with shears or scissors etc. **2** (informal) hit.

clip noun (plural **clips**)
1 a short piece of film shown on its own. **2** (informal) a hit on the head.
[from Old Norse]

clippers plural noun an instrument for cutting hair.

clique (say kleek) noun (plural **cliques**) a small group of people who stick together and keep others out. [French]

cloak noun (plural **cloaks**) a sleeveless garment that hangs loosely from the shoulders.

cloak verb (cloaks, cloaking, cloaked) cover or conceal.
[from old French]

cloakroom noun (plural **cloakrooms**)
1 a place where people can leave outdoor clothes, luggage, etc. **2** a lavatory.

clock noun (plural **clocks**) a device (other than a watch) that shows what the time is.

clock verb (clocks, clocking, clocked)
clock in or **out** register the time you arrive at work or leave work.
clock up reach a certain speed.
[from Latin clocca = bell]

clockwise adverb & adjective moving round a circle in the same direction as a clock's hands. [from clock + -wise]

clockwork noun a mechanism with a spring that has to be wound up.
like clockwork very regularly.

clod noun (plural **clods**) a lump of earth or clay.

clog noun (plural **clogs**) a shoe with a wooden sole.

clog verb (**clogs, clogging, clogged**) block up.
[origin unknown]

cloister noun (plural **cloisters**) a covered path along the side of a church or monastery etc., round a courtyard. [from Latin *claustrum* = enclosed place]

clone noun (plural **clones**) an animal or plant made from the cells of another animal or plant and therefore exactly like it. [from Greek *klon* = a cutting from a plant]

close[1] (say klohss) adjective
1 near. 2 detailed or concentrated, *with close attention*. 3 tight; with little empty space, *a close fit*. 4 in which competitors are nearly equal, *a close contest*. 5 stuffy. **closely** adverb, **closeness** noun

close adverb closely, *close behind*.

close noun (plural **closes**)
1 a cul-de-sac. 2 an enclosed area, especially round a cathedral.

close[2] (say klohz) verb (**closes, closing, closed**)
1 shut. 2 end.
close in 1 get nearer. 2 if the days are closing in, they are getting shorter.

close noun end, *at the close of play*.

close-up noun (plural **close-ups**) a photograph or piece of film taken at close range.

closure noun (plural **closures**) closing.

clot noun (plural **clots**)
1 a small mass of blood, cream, etc. that has become solid.
2 (*slang*) a stupid person.

clot verb (**clots, clotting, clotted**) form clots.
[from Old English]

cloth noun (plural **cloths**)
1 woven material or felt. 2 a piece of this material. 3 a tablecloth.
[from Old English]

clothes plural noun things worn to cover the body. [from *cloth*]

clothing noun clothes.

cloud noun (plural **clouds**)
1 a mass of condensed water-vapour floating in the sky.
2 a mass of smoke, dust, etc., in the air.

cloudy adjective (**cloudier, cloudiest**)
1 full of clouds. 2 not transparent, *The liquid became cloudy*.
cloudiness noun

clover noun a small plant usually with three leaves on each stalk.
in clover in ease and luxury.

clown noun (plural **clowns**)
1 a performer who does amusing tricks and actions, especially in a circus. 2 a person who does silly things.

cloying adjective sickeningly sweet. [from an old word *accloy* = overfill, disgust]

club noun (plural **clubs**)
1 a heavy stick used as a weapon.
2 a stick with a shaped head used to hit the ball in golf. 3 a group of people who meet because they are interested in the same thing; the building where they meet.
4 a playing card with black clover leaves on it.

club verb (clubs, clubbing, clubbed) hit with a heavy stick.
club together join with other people in order to pay for something. *club together to buy a boat.*

cluck verb (clucks, clucking, clucked) make a hen's throaty cry. **cluck** noun

clue noun (plural clues) something that helps a person to solve a puzzle or a mystery.
not have a clue (informal) be stupid or helpless.

clump noun (plural clumps) 1 a cluster or mass of things. 2 a clumping sound.
clump verb (clumps, clumping, clumped) 1 form a cluster or mass. 2 walk with a heavy tread.
[from old German]

clumsy adjective (clumsier, clumsiest) 1 heavy and ungraceful; likely to knock things over or drop things. 2 not skilful; not tactful, *a clumsy apology.* **clumsily** adverb, **clumsiness** noun

cluster noun (plural clusters) a small close group.
cluster verb (clusters, clustering, clustered) form a cluster.
[from Old English]

clutch verb (clutches, clutching, clutched) grasp tightly.
clutch noun (plural clutches) 1 a tight grasp. 2 a device for connecting and disconnecting the engine of a motor vehicle from its gears.
[from Old English]

clutter noun things lying about untidily.

clutter verb (clutters, cluttering, cluttered) fill with clutter, *Piles of papers cluttered her desk.*

Co. abbreviation Company.

c/o abbreviation care of.

co- prefix 1 together, jointly (as in *coexistence, cooperate*). 2 joint (as in *co-pilot*). [same origin as *com-*]

coach noun (plural coaches) 1 a bus used for long journeys. 2 a carriage of a railway train. 3 a large horse-drawn carriage with four wheels. 4 an instructor in sports. 5 a teacher giving private specialized tuition.
coach verb (coaches, coaching, coached) instruct or train somebody, especially in sports. [from Hungarian *kocsi szekér* = cart from *Kocs*, a town in Hungary]

coagulate verb (coagulates, coagulating, coagulated) change from liquid to semi-solid; clot. **coagulant** noun, **coagulation** noun

coal noun (plural coals) a hard black mineral substance used for burning to supply heat; a piece of this.

coalesce (say koh-a-*less*) verb (coalesces, coalescing, coalesced) combine and form one whole thing. **coalescence** noun, **coalescent** adjective [from *co-* + Latin *alescere* = grow up]

coalition noun (plural coalitions) a temporary alliance, especially of two or more political parties in order to form a government. [same origin as *coalesce*]

coarse adjective 1 not smooth, not delicate; rough. 2 composed of large particles.

3 not refined; vulgar. **coarsely** *adverb*, **coarseness** *noun* [origin unknown]

coarsen *verb* (**coarsens**, **coarsening**, **coarsened**) make or become coarse.

coast *noun* (*plural* **coasts**) the seashore or the land close to it. **coastal** *adjective*, **coastline** *noun* **the coast is clear** there is no chance of being seen or hindered.

coastguard *noun* (*plural* **coastguards**) a person whose job is to keep watch on the coast, detect or prevent smuggling, etc.

coat *noun* (*plural* **coats**) **1** an outdoor garment with sleeves. **2** the hair or fur on an animal's body. **3** a coating, *a coat of paint*.

coat *verb* (**coats**, **coating**, **coated**) cover something with a coating.

coating *noun* (*plural* **coatings**) a covering layer.

coax *verb* (**coaxes**, **coaxing**, **coaxed**) persuade someone gently or patiently.

cobalt *noun* a hard silvery-white metal. [from German *Kobalt* = demon (because it was believed to harm the silver ore with which it was found)]

cobble *noun* (*plural* **cobbles**) a rounded stone used for paving streets etc. **cobbled** *adjective*

cobra (*say* koh-bra) *noun* (*plural* **cobras**) a poisonous snake that can rear up. [from Portuguese *cobra de capello* = snake with a hood]

cobweb *noun* (*plural* **cobwebs**) the thin sticky net made by a spider to trap insects. [from Old English *coppe* = spider, + *web*]

cocaine *noun* a drug made from the leaves of a tropical plant called *coca*.

cock *noun* (*plural* **cocks**) **1** a male chicken. **2** a male bird. **3** a stopcock. **4** a lever in a gun.

cock *verb* (**cocks**, **cocking**, **cocked**) **1** make a gun ready to fire by raising the cock. **2** turn something upwards or in a particular direction, *The dog cocked its ears.* [from Old English]

cockatoo *noun* (*plural* **cockatoos**) a crested parrot. [via Dutch from Malay (a language spoken in Malaysia)]

cockerel *noun* (*plural* **cockerels**) a young male chicken. [from *cock*]

cocker spaniel *noun* (*plural* **cocker spaniels**) a kind of small spaniel. [because they were used to hunt woodcock]

cockpit *noun* (*plural* **cockpits**) the compartment where the pilot of an aircraft sits. [from the pits where cock fights took place]

cockroach *noun* (*plural* **cockroaches**) a beetle-like insect. [from Spanish]

cocksure *adjective* very sure; too confident. [from *cock* (used to avoid saying *God* in oaths)]

cocoa *noun* (*plural* **cocoas**) **1** a hot drink made from a powder of crushed cacao seeds. **2** this powder.

coconut *noun* (*plural* **coconuts**) **1** a large round nut that grows on a kind of palm tree. **2** its white lining, used in sweets and cookery. [from Spanish *coco*

= grinning face (because the base of the nut looks like a monkey's face)]

cocoon noun (plural **cocoons**)
1 the covering round a chrysalis.
2 a protective wrapping.

cod noun (plural **cod**) a large edible sea fish. [origin unknown]

code noun (plural **codes**)
1 a word or phrase used to represent a message in order to keep its meaning secret. 2 a set of signs used in sending messages by machine etc., *the Morse code*. 3 a set of laws or rules, *the Highway Code*.

code verb (**codes**, **coding**, **coded**) put a message into code. [from Latin *codex* = book]

coeducation noun educating boys and girls together.
coeducational adjective [from *co- + education*]

coefficient noun (plural **coefficients**) a number by which another number is multiplied; a factor. [from *co- + efficient* (because the numbers work together)]

coexist verb (**coexists**, **coexisting**, **coexisted**) exist together or at the same time. **coexistence** noun, **coexistent** adjective

coffee noun (plural **coffees**)
1 a hot drink made from the roasted ground seeds (*coffee beans*) of a tropical plant. 2 these seeds. [from Arabic *kahwa*]

coffin noun (plural **coffins**) a long box in which a body is buried or cremated.

cog noun (plural **cogs**) one of a number of tooth-like parts

round the edge of a wheel, fitting into and pushing those on another wheel.

cogent (say koh-jent) adjective convincing, *a cogent argument*.

cogitate verb (**cogitates**, **cogitating**, **cogitated**) think deeply about something.
cogitation noun [from Latin]

coherent (say koh-heer-ent) adjective clear, reasonable, and making sense. **coherently** adverb

coil noun (plural **coils**) something wound into a spiral.

coil verb (**coils**, **coiling**, **coiled**) wind something into a coil. [same origin as *collect*]

coin noun (plural **coins**) a piece of metal, usually round, used as money.

coin verb (**coins**, **coining**, **coined**)
1 manufacture coins. 2 (*informal*) make a lot of money as profit.
3 invent a word or phrase. [French, = die for stamping coins]

coincide verb (**coincides**, **coinciding**, **coincided**)
1 happen at the same time as something else. 2 be in the same place. 3 be the same, *My opinion coincided with hers*. [from *co- + Latin incidere* = fall upon or into]

coincidence noun (plural **coincidences**) the happening of similar events at the same time by chance.

col- prefix with; together. see **com-**.

colander noun (plural **colanders**) a bowl-shaped container with holes in it, used for straining water from vegetables etc. after cooking. [from Latin *colare* = strain]

cold *adjective*
1 having or at a low temperature; not warm. **2** not friendly or loving; not enthusiastic. **coldly** *adverb*, **coldness** *noun*

cold shoulder deliberate unfriendliness. **cold-shoulder** *verb*

get cold feet feel afraid or reluctant to do something.

cold *noun* (*plural* **colds**)
1 lack of warmth; low temperature; cold weather. **2** an infectious illness that makes your nose run, your throat sore, etc.

cold-blooded *adjective*
1 having a body temperature that changes according to the surroundings. **2** callous; deliberately cruel.

collaborate *verb* (**collaborates**, **collaborating**, **collaborated**) work together on a job. **collaboration** *noun*, **collaborator** *noun* [from *col-* + Latin *laborare* = to work]

collapse *verb* (**collapses**, **collapsing**, **collapsed**)
1 fall down or inwards suddenly; break. **2** become very weak or ill. **3** fold up.

collapse *noun* (*plural* **collapses**)
1 collapsing. **2** a breakdown. [from *col-* + Latin *lapsum* = slipped]

collapsible *adjective* able to be folded up, *a collapsible umbrella.*

collar *noun* (*plural* **collars**)
1 an upright or turned-over band round the neck of a garment etc. **2** a band that goes round the neck of a dog, cat, horse, etc.

colleague *noun* (*plural* **colleagues**) a person you work with. [from Latin]

collect (*say* kol-**ekt**) *verb* (**collects**, **collecting**, **collected**)
1 bring people or things together from various places. **2** obtain examples of things as a hobby, *She collects stamps.* **3** come together. **4** ask for money or contributions etc. from people. **5** fetch, *Collect your coat from the cleaners.* **collector** *noun* [from *col-* + Latin *legere* = assemble, choose]

collection *noun* (*plural* **collections**)
1 collecting. **2** things collected. **3** money collected for a charity etc.

collective noun *noun* (*plural* **collective nouns**) a noun that is singular in form but refers to many individuals taken as a unit, e.g. *army, herd.*

college *noun* (*plural* **colleges**) a place where people can continue learning something after they have left school.

collide *verb* (**collides**, **colliding**, **collided**) crash into something. **collision** *noun* [from Latin *collidere* = clash together]

colloquial (*say* col-**oh**-kwee-al) *adjective* suitable for conversation but not for formal speech or writing. **colloquially** *adverb*, **colloquialism** *noun* [from *col-* + Latin *loqui* = speak]

colon[1] *noun* (*plural* **colons**) a punctuation mark (:), often used to introduce lists. [from Greek *kolon* = clause]

colon² noun (plural **colons**) the largest part of the intestine. [from Greek *kolon*]

colonel (say **ker**-nel) noun (plural **colonels**) an army officer in charge of a regiment. [via French from Italian]

colonial adjective to do with a colony.

colonize verb (**colonizes, colonizing, colonized**) establish a colony in a country. **colonist** noun, **colonization** noun

colony noun (plural **colonies**) 1 an area of land that the people of another country settle in and control. 2 the people of a colony. 3 a group of people or animals of the same kind living close together. [from Latin *colonia* = farm, settlement]

colossal adjective immense; enormous. [from the bronze statue of Apollo at Rhodes, called the *Colossus of Rhodes*]

colour noun (plural **colours**) 1 the effect produced by waves of light of a particular wavelength. 2 the use of various colours, not only black and white. 3 the colour of someone's skin. 4 a substance used to colour things. 5 the special flag of a ship or regiment.

colour verb (**colours, colouring, coloured**) 1 put colour on; paint or stain. 2 blush. 3 influence what someone says or believes. **colouring** noun [from Latin]

colour-blind adjective unable to see the difference between certain colours.

coloured adjective 1 having colour. 2 having a dark skin; Black.

colourful adjective 1 full of colour. 2 lively; with vivid details.

column noun (plural **columns**) 1 a pillar. 2 something long or tall and narrow, *a column of smoke*. 3 a vertical section of a page, *There are two columns on this page*. 4 a regular article in a newspaper. **columnist** noun [from Latin]

com- prefix (becoming **col-** before *l*, **cor-** before *r*, **con-** before many other consonants) with; together (as in **combine, connect**). [from Latin *cum* = with]

coma (say **koh**-ma) noun (plural **comas**) a state of deep unconsciousness, especially in someone who is ill or injured. [from Greek *koma* = deep sleep]

comb noun (plural **combs**) 1 a strip of wood or plastic etc. with teeth, used to tidy hair or hold it in place. 2 something used like this, e.g. to separate strands of wool. 3 the red crest on a fowl's head. 4 a honeycomb.

comb verb (**combs, combing, combed**) 1 tidy hair with a comb. 2 search thoroughly. [from Old English]

combat noun & verb (**combats, combating, combated**) fight. **combatant** (say **kom**-ba-tant) noun [from **com-** + Latin *batuere* = fight]

combination noun (plural **combinations**) 1 combining. 2 a number of people or things that are

combined. **3** a series of numbers
or letters used to open
a combination lock.

combine (*say* komb-I'n) *verb*
(**combines, combining, combined**)
join or mix together.

combustion *noun* the process of
burning, a chemical process
(accompanied by heat) in which
substances combine with oxygen
in air.

come *verb* (**comes, coming,
came, come**) This word is used to
show
1 movement towards somewhere
(*Come here!*), **2** arrival, reaching
a place or condition or result
(*They came to a city. We came to
a decision*), **3** happening (*How did
you come to lose it?*), **4** occurring
(*It comes on the next page*),
5 resulting (*That's what comes of
being careless*).
come by obtain.
come in for receive a share of.
come to 1 amount to. **2** become
conscious again.
come to pass happen.

comedian *noun* (*plural
comedians*) someone who
entertains people by making
them laugh. [from French]

comedy *noun* (*plural comedies*)
1 a play or film etc. that makes
people laugh. **2** humour. [from
Greek *komos* = having fun + *oide*
= song]

comet *noun* (*plural comets*) an
object moving across the sky
with a bright tail of light. [from
Greek *kometes* = long-haired
(star)]

comfort *noun* (*plural comforts*)
1 a comfortable feeling or
condition. **2** soothing somebody

who is unhappy or in pain.
3 a person or thing that gives
comfort.

comfort *verb* (**comforts,
comforting, comforted**) make
a person less unhappy; soothe.
[from Latin *confortare*
= strengthen]

comfortable *adjective*
1 at ease; relaxed. **2** making
someone feel at ease or relaxed,
comfortable shoes. **comfortably**
adverb

comic *adjective* making people
laugh. **comical** *adjective*,
comically *adverb*

comic strip *noun* a series of
drawings telling a comic story.

comic *noun* (*plural comics*)
1 a paper full of comic strips.
2 a comedian.
[from Greek; related to *comedy*]

comma *noun* (*plural commas*)
a punctuation mark (,) used to
mark a pause in a sentence or to
separate items in a list. [from
Greek *komma* = short clause]

command *noun* (*plural
commands*)
1 a statement telling somebody to
do something; an order.
2 authority; control. **3** ability to
use something; mastery, *She has
a good command of Spanish.*

command *verb* (**commands,
commanding, commanded**)
1 give a command to somebody;
order. **2** have authority over.
3 deserve and get, *They command
our respect.* **commander** *noun*
[from com- + Latin *mandare*
= entrust or impose a duty]

commandeer *verb*
(**commandeers, commandeering,
commandeered**) take or seize

something for military purposes or for your own use.

commandment noun (plural **commandments**) a sacred command, especially one of the Ten Commandments given to Moses.

commando noun (plural **commandos**) a soldier trained for making dangerous raids. [from Portuguese]

commemorate verb (**commemorates, commemorating, commemorated**) be a celebration or reminder of some past event or person etc. **commemoration** noun, **commemorative** adjective [from com- + Latin memor = memory]

commence verb (**commences, commencing, commenced**) begin. **commencement** noun [from com- + Latin initiare = initiate]

commend verb (**commends, commending, commended**) 1 praise, He was commended for bravery. 2 entrust, We commend him to your care. **commendation** noun [same origin as command]

comment noun (plural **comments**) an opinion given about an event etc. or to explain something.

comment verb (**comments, commenting, commented**) make a comment. [from Latin]

commentary noun (plural **commentaries**) a set of comments, especially describing a sports event while it is happening. **commentate** verb, **commentator** noun

commercial adjective 1 to do with commerce. 2 paid for by firms etc. whose advertisements are included, commercial radio. 3 profitable. **commercially** adverb

commercial noun (plural **commercials**) a broadcast advertisement.

commiserate verb (**commiserates, commiserating, commiserated**) sympathize. **commiseration** noun [from com- + Latin miserari = to pity]

commission noun (plural **commissions**) 1 authorization to do something; the task etc. authorized, a commission to paint a portrait. 2 an appointment to be an officer in the armed forces. 3 a group of people given authority to do or investigate something. 4 payment to someone for selling your goods etc.

commission verb (**commissions, commissioning, commissioned**) give a commission to a person or for a task etc. [same origin as commit]

commit verb (**commits, committing, committed**) 1 do or perform, commit a crime. 2 place in someone's care or custody, He was committed to prison. 3 promise that you will make your time etc. available for a particular purpose, Don't commit all your spare time to helping him. [from com- + Latin mittere = put, send]

committee noun (plural **committees**) a group of people

appointed to deal with
something.

commodity noun (plural
commodities) a useful thing;
a product. [from Latin commodus
= convenient]

commodore noun (plural
commodores)
1 a naval officer ranking next
below a rear admiral. **2** the
commander of part of a fleet.

common adjective
1 ordinary; usual; occurring
frequently, a common weed. **2** of
all or most people, They worked
for the common good. **3** shared,
Music is their common interest.
4 vulgar. **commonly** adverb,
commonness noun
in common shared by two or
more people or things.

Common Market noun a group
of European countries that trade
freely together.

commonplace adjective
ordinary; usual.

common sense noun normal
good sense in thinking or
behaviour.

Commonwealth noun
1 an association of countries, The
Commonwealth consists of Britain
and various other countries,
including Canada, Australia, and
New Zealand. **2** a federal
association of States, the
Commonwealth of Australia. **3** the
republic set up in Britain by
Cromwell, lasting from 1649 to
1660. [from common + an old
sense of wealth = welfare]

commotion noun an uproar;
a fuss. [from com- + Latin motio
= movement, motion]

commune (say kom-yoon) noun
(plural **communes**)
1 a group of people sharing
a home, food, etc. **2** a district of
local government in France and
some other countries. [from
Latin communis = common]

communicate verb
(**communicates**, **communicating**,
communicated)
1 pass news, information, etc. to
other people. **2** (of rooms etc.)
open into each other; connect.
[from Latin communicare = tell,
share]

communication noun (plural
communications)
1 communicating. **2** something
communicated; a message.
communications plural noun
links between places (e.g. roads,
railways, telephones, radio).
communicative adjective willing
to talk.

communion noun
Communion or **Holy Communion**
the Christian ceremony in which
consecrated bread and wine are
given to worshippers.
[same origin as commune]

Communism noun a political
system where the State controls
property, production, trade, etc.
(Compare capitalism.)
Communist noun

community noun (plural
communities)
1 the people living in one area.
2 a group with similar interests
or origins.

commute verb (**commutes**,
commuting, **commuted**)
1 travel a fairly long way by
train, bus, or car to and from
your daily work.

2 alter a punishment to something less severe. [from *com-* + Latin *mutare* = change]

commuter noun (plural **commuters**) a person who commutes to and from work.

compact adjective
1 closely or neatly packed together. **2** concise. **compactly** adverb, **compactness** noun

compact noun (plural **compacts**) a small flat container for face powder.

compact disc noun (plural **compact discs**) a small disc from which recorded sound etc. is reproduced by means of a laser beam.

companion noun (plural **companions**)
1 a person who accompanies another. **2** one of a matching pair of things. **3** (in book-titles) a guidebook or reference book, *The Oxford Companion to Music*. **companionship** noun [literally = someone you eat bread with: from *com-* + Latin *panis* = bread]

company noun (plural **companies**)
1 a number of people together. **2** a business firm. **3** having people with you; companionship. **4** visitors, *We've got company.* **5** a section of a battalion. [same origin as *companion*]

comparative adjective comparing a thing with something else, *They live in comparative comfort.* **comparatively** adverb

comparative noun (plural **comparatives**) the form of an adjective or adverb that expresses 'more', *The comparative of 'big' is 'bigger'.*

compare verb (**compares**, **comparing**, **compared**)
1 put things together so as to tell in what ways they are similar or different. **2** form the comparative and superlative of an adjective or adverb.
compare notes share information.
compare with 1 be similar to. **2** be as good as, *Our football pitch cannot compare with Wembley Stadium.*
[from *com-* + Latin *par* = equal]

USAGE: When *compare* is used with an object, it can be followed by either *to* or *with*. Traditionally, *to* is used when you are showing the similarity between two things: *She compared me to a pig.* With is used when you are looking at the similarities and differences between things: *Just compare this year's profits with last year's.*

comparison noun (plural **comparisons**) comparing.

compartment noun (plural **compartments**) one of the spaces into which something is divided; a separate room or enclosed space. [from Latin *compartiri* = share with someone]

compass noun (plural **compasses**) a device with a pointer that points north.
compasses or **pair of compasses** a device for drawing circles, usually with two rods hinged together at one end.

compassion noun pity or mercy. **compassionate** adjective, **compassionately** adverb [from com- + Latin passum = suffered]

compel verb (**compels**, **compelling**, **compelled**) force somebody to do something. [from com- + Latin pellere = drive]

compensate verb (**compensates**, **compensating**, **compensated**) **1** give a person money etc. to make up for a loss or injury. **2** have a balancing effect, This victory compensates for our earlier defeats. **compensation** noun, **compensatory** adjective [from Latin compensare = weigh one thing against another]

compete verb (**competes**, **competing**, **competed**) take part in a competition. [from com- + Latin petere = aim at]

competent adjective able to do a particular thing. **competently** adverb, **competence** noun [from Latin, = suitable, sufficient]

competition noun (plural **competitions**) **1** a game or race or other contest in which people try to win. **2** competing. **3** the people competing with yourself. **competitive** adjective

competitor noun (plural **competitors**) someone who competes; a rival.

compile verb (**compiles**, **compiling**, **compiled**) put things together into a list or collection, e.g. to form a book. **compiler** noun, **compilation** noun [from French]

complacent adjective self-satisfied. **complacently** adverb, **complacency** noun [from Latin]

complain verb (**complains**, **complaining**, **complained**) say that you are annoyed or unhappy about something. [from Latin]

complaint noun (plural **complaints**) **1** a statement complaining about something. **2** an illness.

complement noun (plural **complements**) **1** the quantity needed to fill or complete something, The ship had its full complement of sailors. **2** the word or words used after verbs such as be and become to complete the sense. In She was brave and He became king of England, the complements are brave and king of England.

USAGE: Do not confuse with compliment.

complementary adjective completing; forming a complement.

complementary angle noun (plural **complementary angles**) either of two angles that add up to 90°.

complete adjective **1** having all its parts. **2** finished. **3** thorough; in every way, a complete stranger. **completely** adverb, **completeness** noun

complete verb (**completes**, **completing**, **completed**) make a thing complete; add what is needed. **completion** noun [from Latin completum = filled up]

complex adjective **1** made up of parts. **2** complicated. **complexity** noun

complex noun (plural **complexes**)

1 a set of buildings made up of related parts, *a sports complex*. 2 a group of feelings or ideas that influence a person's behaviour etc., *a persecution complex*. [from Latin *complexum* = embraced, plaited]

complexion noun (plural **complexions**)
1 the natural colour and appearance of the skin of the face. 2 the way things seem, *That puts a different complexion on the matter*. [from old French]

complicated adjective
1 made up of many parts.
2 difficult to understand or do.

complication noun (plural **complications**)
1 something that complicates things or adds difficulties.
2 a complicated condition.

compliment noun (plural **compliments**) something said or done to show that you approve of a person or thing, *pay compliments*.
compliments plural noun formal greetings given in a message.
compliment verb (compliments, complimenting, complimented) pay someone a compliment; congratulate.
[via French from Italian]

USAGE: Do not confuse with *complement*.

complimentary adjective
1 expressing a compliment.
2 given free of charge, *complimentary tickets*.

component noun (plural **components**) each of the parts of which a thing is made up. [same origin as *compound*]

compose verb (composes, composing, composed)
1 form or make up, *The class is composed of 20 students*. 2 write music or poetry etc. 3 arrange in good order. 4 make calm, *compose yourself*. [from French; related to *compound*]

composer noun (plural **composers**) a person who composes music etc.

composite (say kom-poz-it) adjective made up of a number of parts or different styles. [same origin as *compose*]

composition noun (plural **compositions**)
1 composing. 2 something composed, especially a piece of music. 3 an essay or story written as a school exercise. 4 the parts that make something, *the composition of the soil*.

compost noun
1 decayed leaves and grass etc. used as a fertilizer. 2 a soil-like mixture for growing seedlings, cuttings, etc. [same origin as *compose*]

composure noun calmness of manner.

compound adjective made of two or more parts or ingredients.
compound noun (plural **compounds**) a compound substance.
compound verb (compounds, compounding, compounded) put together; combine.
[from Latin *componere* = put together]

comprehensible adjective understandable.

comprehensive *adjective*
including all or many kinds of people or things.

comprehensive *noun* (*plural* **comprehensives**)
a comprehensive school.

comprehensive school *noun* (*plural* **comprehensive schools**) a large secondary school for all or most of the children of an area.

compress (*say* kom-press) *verb* (**compresses, compressing, compressed**) press together or into a smaller space. **compression** *noun*, **compressor** *noun*

compromise (*say* kom-prom-I'z) *noun* (*plural* **compromises**) settling a dispute by each side accepting less than it asked for.

compromise *verb* (**compromises, compromising, compromised**)
1 settle by a compromise. **2** expose someone to danger or suspicion etc., *His confession compromises his sister.*
[from *com-* + Latin *promittere* = to promise]

compulsion *noun* (*plural* **compulsions**) a strong and uncontrollable desire to do something.

compulsory *adjective* that must be done; not optional. [same origin as **compel**]

compunction *noun* a guilty feeling, *She felt no compunction about hitting the burglar.* [from *com-* + Latin *punctum* = pricked (by conscience)]

compute *verb* (**computes, computing, computed**) calculate. **computation** *noun*

computer *noun* (*plural* **computers**) an electronic machine for making calculations, storing and analysing information put into it, or controlling machinery automatically.

comrade *noun* (*plural* **comrades**) a companion who shares in your activities. **comradeship** *noun* [from Spanish *camarada* = room-mate]

con- *prefix* with; together. see **com-**.

concave *adjective* curved like the inside of a ball or circle. (The opposite is **convex**.) **concavity** *noun* [from *con-* + Latin *cavus* = hollow]

conceal *verb* (**conceals, concealing, concealed**) hide; keep something secret. **concealment** *noun* [from *con-* + Latin *celare* = hide]

concede *verb* (**concedes, conceding, conceded**)
1 admit that something is true. **2** grant or allow something, *They conceded us the right to cross their land.* **3** admit that you have been defeated.

conceit *noun* being too proud of yourself; vanity. **conceited** *adjective* [originally = idea, opinion; from *conceive*]

conceive *verb* (**conceives, conceiving, conceived**)
1 become pregnant; form a baby in the womb. **2** form an idea or plan; imagine, *I can't conceive why you want to come.* [from Latin *concipere* = take in, contain]

concentrate verb (concentrates, concentrating, concentrated)
1 give your full attention or effort to something. 2 bring or come together in one place. 3 make a liquid etc. less dilute. [from French; related to *centre*]

concentration noun (plural concentrations)
1 concentrating. 2 the amount dissolved in each part of a liquid.

concentric adjective having the same centre, *concentric circles*. [from Latin; related to *centre*]

concept noun (plural concepts) an idea. [same origin as *conceive*]

conception noun (plural conceptions)
1 conceiving. 2 an idea.

concern verb (concerns, concerning, concerned)
1 be important to or affect somebody. 2 worry somebody. 3 be about; have as its subject, *The story concerns a group of rabbits.*

concern noun (plural concerns)
1 something that concerns you; a responsibility. 2 worry. 3 a business.

concert noun (plural concerts) a musical entertainment. [same origin as *concerto*]

concerto (say kon-**chert**-oh) noun (plural concertos) a piece of music for a solo instrument and an orchestra. [from Italian *concertare* = harmonize]

concession noun (plural concessions)
1 conceding. 2 something conceded. 3 a reduction in price for a certain category of person. **concessionary** adjective [same origin as *concede*]

conciliate verb (conciliates, conciliating, conciliated)
1 win over an angry or hostile person by friendliness. 2 help people who disagree to come to an agreement. **conciliation** noun [from Latin; related to *council*]

concise adjective brief; giving much information in a few words. **concisely** adverb, **conciseness** noun [from con- + Latin *caedere* = cut]

conclude verb (concludes, concluding, concluded)
1 bring or come to an end. 2 decide; form an opinion by reasoning, *The jury concluded that he was guilty.* [from con- + Latin *claudere* = shut]

conclusion noun (plural conclusions)
1 an ending. 2 an opinion formed by reasoning.

conclusive adjective putting an end to all doubt. **conclusively** adverb

concoct verb (concocts, concocting, concocted)
1 make something by putting ingredients together. 2 invent, *concoct an excuse.* **concoction** noun [from con- + Latin *coctum* = cooked]

concord noun friendly agreement or harmony. [from con- + Latin *cor* = heart]

concrete noun cement mixed with sand and gravel, used in building.

concrete adjective
1 able to be touched and felt; not abstract. 2 definite, *We need concrete evidence, not theories.* [from Latin *concretus* = stiff, hard]

concurrent *adjective* happening or existing at the same time.

concussion *noun* a temporary injury to the brain caused by a hard knock. **concussed** *adjective* [from Latin *concussum* = shaken violently]

condemn *verb* (**condemns, condemning, condemned**)
1 say that you strongly disapprove of something.
2 convict or sentence a criminal.
3 destine to something unhappy, *condemned to a lonely life*.
4 declare that houses etc. are not fit to be used. **condemnation** *noun*

condense *verb* (**condenses, condensing, condensed**)
1 make a liquid denser or more compact. 2 put something into fewer words. 3 change from gas or vapour to liquid, *Steam condenses on windows.* **condensation** *noun*, **condenser** *noun*

condescend *verb* (**condescends, condescending, condescended**)
1 behave in a way which shows that you feel superior to others.
2 allow yourself to do something that seems unsuitable for a person of your high rank. **condescension** *noun* [from Latin *condescendere* = stoop, lower yourself]

condition *noun* (*plural* **conditions**)
1 the state or fitness of a person or thing, *This bicycle is in good condition.* 2 the situation or surroundings etc. that affect something, *working conditions.*
3 something required as part of an agreement.
on condition that only if; on the

understanding that something will be done.

condition *verb* (**conditions, conditioning, conditioned**)
1 put something into a proper condition. 2 train or accustom. [from Latin]

conditional *adjective* containing a condition (see *condition* 3); depending. **conditionally** *adverb*

condom *noun* (*plural* **condoms**) a rubber sheath worn on the penis as a contraceptive. [origin unknown]

condone *verb* (**condones, condoning, condoned**) forgive or ignore wrongdoing, *Do not condone violence.*

conduct (*say* kon-**dukt**) *verb* (**conducts, conducting, conducted**)
1 lead or guide. 2 be the conductor of an orchestra or choir. 3 manage or direct something, *conduct an experiment.* 4 allow heat, light, sound, or electricity to pass along or through. 5 behave, *They conducted themselves with dignity.*

conduction *noun* the conducting of heat or electricity etc. (see *conduct* 4).

conductor *noun* (*plural* **conductors**)
1 a person who directs the performance of an orchestra or choir by movements of the arms.
2 a person who collects the fares on a bus etc. 3 something that conducts heat or electricity etc. **conductress** *noun*

cone *noun* (*plural* **cones**)
1 an object that is circular at one

end and narrows to a point at the other end. **2** the dry cone-shaped fruit of a pine, fir, or cedar tree. [from Greek]

confectioner *noun* (*plural* **confectioners**) someone who makes or sells sweets. **confectionery** *noun*

confederate *adjective* allied; joined by an agreement or treaty.

confederate *noun* (*plural* **confederates**) **1** a member of a confederacy. **2** an ally; an accomplice. [from *con-* + Latin *foederatum* = allied]

confederation *noun* (*plural* **confederations**) **1** the process of joining in an alliance. **2** a group of people, organizations, or States joined together by an agreement or treaty.

conference *noun* (*plural* **conferences**) a meeting for holding a discussion. [same origin as *confer*]

confess *verb* (**confesses, confessing, confessed**) state openly that you have done something wrong or have a weakness; admit. **confession** *noun* [from Latin]

confetti *plural noun* tiny pieces of coloured paper thrown by wedding guests at the bride and bridegroom. [Italian, = sweets (which were traditionally thrown at Italian weddings)]

confide *verb* (**confides, confiding, confided**) **1** tell confidentially, *confide a secret to someone* or *confide in someone*. **2** entrust. [from *con-* + Latin *fidere* = to trust]

confidence *noun* (*plural* **confidences**) **1** firm trust. **2** a feeling of certainty or boldness; being sure that you can do something. **3** something told confidentially. **in confidence** as a secret. **in a person's confidence** trusted with his or her secrets.

confidence trick *noun* (*plural* **confidence tricks**) swindling a person after persuading him or her to trust you.

confident *adjective* showing or feeling confidence; bold. **confidently** *adverb* [from Latin; related to *confide*]

confidential *adjective* something that is confidential is meant to be kept secret. **confidentially** *adverb*, **confidentiality** *noun*

confine *verb* (**confines, confining, confined**) **1** keep something within limits; restrict, *Please confine your remarks to the subject being discussed.* **2** keep somebody in a place. [from *con-* + Latin *finis* = limit, end]

confirm *verb* (**confirms, confirming, confirmed**) **1** prove that something is true or correct. **2** make a thing definite, *Please write to confirm your booking.* **3** make a person a full member of the Christian Church. **confirmation** *noun*, **confirmatory** *adjective* [from *con-* + Latin *firmare* = strengthen]

confiscate *verb* (**confiscates, confiscating, confiscated**) take something away as a punishment. **confiscation** *noun* [from Latin]

conflagration noun (plural **conflagrations**) a great and destructive fire.

conflict (say kon-flikt) noun (plural **conflicts**) a fight, struggle, or disagreement.

conflict (say kon-flikt) verb (**conflicts**, **conflicting**, **conflicted**) have a conflict; differ or disagree. [from con- = together + Latin flictum = struck]

conform verb (**conforms**, **conforming**, **conformed**) keep to accepted rules or customs etc. **conformist** noun, **conformity** noun [from Latin conformare = shape evenly]

confound verb (**confounds**, **confounding**, **confounded**)
1 astonish or puzzle someone.
2 confuse.

confront verb (**confronts**, **confronting**, **confronted**)
1 come or bring face to face, especially in a hostile way. 2 be present and have to be dealt with, Problems confront us. **confrontation** noun [from Latin]

confuse verb (**confuses**, **confusing**, **confused**)
1 make a person puzzled or muddled. 2 mistake one thing for another. **confusion** noun [from old French; related to confound]

confute verb (**confutes**, **confuting**, **confuted**) prove a person or statement to be wrong. **confutation** noun

congeal (say kon-jeel) verb (**congeals**, **congealing**, **congealed**) become jelly-like instead of liquid, especially in cooling, congealed blood.

congenital (say kon-jen-it-al) adjective existing in a person from birth. **congenitally** adverb [from con- + Latin genitus = born]

congested adjective crowded or blocked up, congested streets, congested lungs. **congestion** noun [from Latin congestum = heaped up]

conglomeration noun (plural **conglomerations**) a mass of different things put together. [from con- + Latin glomus = mass]

congratulate verb (**congratulates**, **congratulating**, **congratulated**) tell a person that you are pleased about his or her success or good fortune. **congratulation** noun, **congratulatory** adjective [from con- + Latin gratulari = show joy]

congregate verb (**congregates**, **congregating**, **congregated**) assemble; flock together. [from con- + Latin gregatum = herded]

congregation noun (plural **congregations**) a group who have gathered to take part in worship.

Congress noun the parliament of the USA.

congruent adjective congruent triangles have exactly the same shape and size. **congruence** noun

conic adjective to do with a cone.

conical adjective cone-shaped. **conically** adverb

conifer (say kon-if-er) noun (plural **conifers**) an evergreen tree with cones. **coniferous** adjective [from cone + Latin ferens = bearing]

conjecture noun (plural **conjectures**) a guess. **conjecture** verb, **conjectural** adjective [from Latin]

conjugate verb (**conjugates, conjugating, conjugated**) give all the different forms of a verb. **conjugation** noun

conjunction noun (plural **conjunctions**)
1 a word that joins words or phrases or sentences, e.g. *and*, but. **2** combination, *The four armies acted in conjunction.* [from Latin *conjunctum* = yoked together]

conjure verb (**conjures, conjuring, conjured**) perform puzzling tricks. **conjuror** noun
conjure up produce in your mind, *Mention of the Arctic conjures up visions of snow.*

connect verb (**connects, connecting, connected**)
1 join together; link. **2** think of as being associated with each other.

connection noun (plural **connections**)
1 a point where two things are connected; a link, *We all know there is a connection between smoking and cancer.* **2** a train, bus, etc. that leaves a station soon after another arrives, so that passengers can change from one to another.

connoisseur (say kon-a-ser) noun (plural **connoisseurs**) a person with great experience and appreciation of something, *a connoisseur of wine.* [French, = one who knows]

conquer verb (**conquers, conquering, conquered**) defeat or overcome. **conqueror** noun [from old French]

conquest noun (plural **conquests**)
1 conquering. **2** conquered territory.

conscience (say kon-shens) noun (plural **consciences**) knowing what is right and wrong, especially in your own actions. [from Latin *conscientia* = knowledge]

conscientious (say kon-shee-en-shus) adjective careful and honest, *conscientious workers.* **conscientiously** adverb

conscientious objector noun (plural **conscientious objectors**) a person who refuses to serve in the armed forces because he or she believes it is wrong.

conscious (say kon-shus) adjective awake; aware of what is happening. **consciously** adverb, **consciousness** noun [from Latin *conscius* = knowing]

conscript (say kon-skript) verb (**conscripts, conscripting, conscripted**) make a person join the armed forces. **conscription** noun

conscript (say kon-skript) noun (plural **conscripts**) a conscripted person.
[from con- + Latin *scriptus* = written in a list, enlisted]

consecrate verb (**consecrates, consecrating, consecrated**) officially say that a thing, especially a building, is holy. **consecration** noun

consecutive adjective following one after another. **consecutively** adverb [from Latin *consequi* = follow closely]

consensus noun (plural **consensuses**) general agreement; the opinion of most people. [same origin as *consent*]

consent noun agreement to what someone wishes; permission.

consent verb (**consents, consenting, consented**) say that you are willing to do or allow what someone wishes. [from con- + Latin *sentire* = feel]

consequence noun (plural **consequences**)
1 something that happens as the result of an event or action.
2 importance, *It is of no consequence.*

consequent adjective happening as a result. **consequently** adverb [same origin as *consecutive*]

conservation noun conserving; preservation, especially of the natural environment. **conservationist** noun

Conservative noun (plural **Conservatives**) a person who supports the Conservative Party, a political party that favours private enterprise and freedom from State control. **Conservative** adjective

conservative adjective
1 liking traditional ways and disliking changes. **2** (of an estimate) moderate; low. **conservatively** adverb, **conservatism** noun

conserve verb (**conserves, conserving, conserved**) prevent something valuable from being changed, spoilt, or wasted. [from con- + Latin *servare* = keep safe]

consider verb (**considers, considering, considered**)
1 think carefully about or give attention to something, especially in order to make a decision. **2** have an opinion; think to be, *Consider yourself lucky.* [from Latin]

considerable adjective fairly great, *a considerable amount.* **considerably** adverb

considerate adjective taking care not to inconvenience or hurt others. **considerately** adverb

consideration noun (plural **considerations**)
1 being considerate. **2** careful thought or attention. **3** a fact that must be kept in mind. **4** payment given as a reward.
take into consideration allow for.

considering preposition taking something into consideration, *The car runs well, considering its age.*

consist verb (**consists, consisting, consisted**) be made up or composed of, *The flat consists of three rooms.* [from Latin]

consistency noun (plural **consistencies**)
1 being consistent. **2** thickness or stiffness, especially of a liquid.

consistent adjective
1 keeping to a regular pattern or style; not changing. **2** not contradictory. **consistently** adverb

consolation noun (plural **consolations**)
1 consoling. **2** something that consoles someone.

console[1] (say kon-**sohl**) verb (**consoles, consoling, consoled**) comfort someone who is unhappy or disappointed. [from con- + Latin *solari* = soothe]

console² (say kon-sohl) noun (plural consoles)
1 a panel holding the controls of equipment. **2** a frame containing the keyboard and stops etc. of an organ. **3** a cabinet for a radio or television set. [French]

consolidate verb (consolidates, consolidating, consolidated)
1 make or become secure and strong. **2** combine two or more organizations, funds, etc. into one. **consolidation** noun [from con- + Latin solidare = make solid]

consonant noun (plural consonants) a letter that is not a vowel, B, c, d, f, etc. are consonants. [from con- + Latin sonans = sounding]

conspicuous adjective easily seen; noticeable. **conspicuously** adverb, **conspicuousness** noun [from Latin conspicere = look at carefully]

conspiracy noun (plural conspiracies) planning with others to do something illegal; a plot. **conspirator** noun

constable noun (plural constables) a police officer of the lowest rank. [from Latin, originally = officer in charge of the stable]

constant adjective
1 not changing; happening all the time. **2** faithful or loyal. **constantly** adverb, **constancy** noun

constant noun (plural constants)
1 a thing that does not vary. **2** in mathematics, a number or value that does not change.

constellation noun (plural constellations) a group of stars. [from con- + Latin stella = star]

constipated adjective unable to empty the bowels easily or regularly. **constipation** noun [from Latin constipare = cram]

constituency noun (plural constituencies) a district represented by a Member of Parliament elected by the people who live there.

constituent noun (plural constituents)
1 one of the parts that form a whole thing. **2** someone who lives in a particular constituency. **constituent** adjective

constitute verb (constitutes, constituting, constituted) make up or form something, Twelve months constitute a year. [from con- + Latin statuere = set up]

constitution noun (plural constitutions)
1 the group of laws or principles that state how a country is to be organized and governed. **2** the nature of the body in regard to healthiness, She has a strong constitution. **3** constituting. **4** the composition of something. **constitutional** adjective

constrict verb (constricts, constricting, constricted) squeeze or tighten something by making it narrower. **constriction** noun

construct verb (constructs, constructing, constructed) make something by placing parts together; build. **constructor** noun [from con- + Latin structum = built]

construction noun (plural **constructions**)
1 constructing. 2 something constructed; a building. 3 two or more words put together to form a phrase or clause or sentence. 4 an explanation or interpretation, *They put a bad construction on our refusal.*

constructive adjective constructing; being helpful, *constructive suggestions.*

consult verb (**consults, consulting, consulted**) go to a person or book etc. for information or advice. **consultation** noun [from Latin *consulere* = take advice or counsel]

consultant noun (plural **consultants**) a person who is qualified to give expert advice.

consume verb (**consumes, consuming, consumed**)
1 eat or drink something. 2 use up, *Much time was consumed in waiting.* 3 destroy, *Fire consumed the building.* [from con- + Latin *sumere* = take up]

consumer noun (plural **consumers**) a person who buys or uses goods or services.

consummate (say kon-**sum**-at) adjective perfect; highly skilled, *a consummate artist.* [from con- + Latin *summus* = highest]

consumption noun
1 consuming. 2 (old use) tuberculosis of the lungs.

contact noun (plural **contacts**)
1 touching. 2 being in touch; communication. 3 a person to communicate with when you need information or help.

contact verb (**contacts,**

contacting, contacted) get in touch with a person. [from con- + Latin *tactum* = touched]

contact lens noun (plural **contact lenses**) a tiny lens worn against the eyeball, instead of spectacles.

contagious adjective spreading by contact with an infected person, *a contagious disease.* [from con- + Latin *tangere* = to touch]

contain verb (**contains, containing, contained**)
1 have inside, *The box contains chocolates.* 2 consist of, *A gallon contains 8 pints.* 3 restrain; hold back, *Try to contain your laughter.* [from con- + Latin *tenere* = hold]

container noun (plural **containers**)
1 a box or bottle etc. designed to contain something. 2 a large box-like object of standard design in which goods are transported.

contaminate verb (**contaminates, contaminating, contaminated**) make a thing dirty or impure or diseased etc.; pollute. **contamination** noun [from Latin; related to *contagion*]

contemplate verb (**contemplates, contemplating, contemplated**)
1 look at something thoughtfully. 2 consider or think about doing something, *We are contemplating a visit to London.* **contemplation** noun **contemplative** adjective [from Latin]

contemporary adjective
1 belonging to the same period, *Dickens was contemporary with*

Thackeray. **2** modern; up-to-date, *contemporary furniture.*

contemporary *noun* (*plural* **contemporaries**) a person who is contemporary with another or who is about the same age, *She was my contemporary at college.* [from *con-* + Latin *tempus* = time]

contempt *noun* a feeling of despising a person or thing.

contemptible *adjective* deserving contempt, *Hurting her feelings like that was a contemptible thing to do.*

contemptuous *adjective* feeling or showing contempt, *She gave me a contemptuous look.* **contemptuously** *adverb*

content[1] (*say* kon-**tent**) *adjective* contented. **contentment** *noun*

content[2] (*say* **kon**-tent) *noun or* **contents** *plural noun* what something contains. [from Latin *contenta* = things contained]

contented *adjective* happy with what you have; satisfied. **contentedly** *adverb*

contest (*say* **kon**-test) *noun* (*plural* **contests**) a competition; a struggle in which rivals try to obtain something or to do best.

contestant *noun* (*plural* **contestants**) a person taking part in a contest; a competitor.

context *noun* (*plural* **contexts**) **1** the words that come before and after a particular word or phrase and help to fix its meaning. **2** the background to an event that helps to explain it. [from *con-* + Latin *textum* = woven]

continent *noun* (*plural* **continents**) one of the main masses of land in the world, *The continents are Europe, Asia,* *Africa, North America, South America, Australia, and Antarctica.* **continental** *adjective* **the Continent** the mainland of Europe, not including the British Isles. [from Latin *terra continens* = continuous land]

continual *adjective* happening all the time, usually with breaks in between, *Stop this continual quarrelling!* **continually** *adverb*

USAGE: Do not confuse with *continuous*. *Continual* is used to describe something that happens very frequently (*there were continual interruptions*) while *continuous* is used to describe something that happens without a pause (*there was continuous rain all day*).

---

continue *verb* (**continues, continuing, continued**) **1** do something without stopping. **2** begin again after stopping, *The game will continue after lunch.* **continuation** *noun*

continuous *adjective* going on and on; without a break. **continuously** *adverb*, **continuity** *noun*

USAGE: See note at *continual*.

---

contort *verb* (**contorts, contorting, contorted**) twist or force out of the usual shape or meaning. **contortion** *noun* [from *con-* + Latin *tortum* = twisted]

contortionist *noun* (*plural* **contortionists**) a person who can twist his or her body into unusual positions.

contour noun (plural **contours**)
1 a line on a map joining the points that are the same height above sea level. 2 an outline.

contra- prefix against. [Latin]

contraband noun smuggled goods. [from contra- + Italian banda = a ban]

contraception noun preventing conception; birth control. [from contra- + conception]

contraceptive noun (plural **contraceptives**) a substance or device that prevents conception.

contract (say **kon**-trakt) noun (plural **contracts**)
1 a formal agreement to do something. 2 a document stating the terms of an agreement.

contract (say kon-**trakt**) verb (**contracts, contracting, contracted**)
1 make or become smaller. 2 make a contract. 3 get an illness, She contracted measles. [from con- + Latin tractum = pulled]

contraction noun (plural **contractions**)
1 contracting. 2 a shortened form of a word or words. Can't is a contraction of cannot.

contractor noun (plural **contractors**) a person who makes a contract, especially for building.

contradict verb (**contradicts, contradicting, contradicted**)
1 say that something said is not true or that someone is wrong. 2 say the opposite of, These rumours contradict previous ones. **contradiction** noun, **contradictory** adjective [from contra- + Latin dicere = say]

contraflow noun (plural **contraflows**) a flow of road traffic travelling in the opposite direction to the usual flow and close beside it. [from contra- + flow]

contralto noun (plural **contraltos**) a female singer with a low voice. [Italian, from contra- + alto]

contraption noun (plural **contraptions**) a strange-looking device or machine. [origin unknown]

contrary adjective
1 (say **kon**-tra-ree) of the opposite kind or direction etc.; opposed; unfavourable.
2 (say kon-**trair**-ee) awkward and obstinate.

contrary (say **kon**-tra-ree) noun the opposite.
on the contrary the opposite is true.

contrast noun (plural **contrasts**)
1 a difference clearly seen when things are compared. 2 something showing a clear difference.

contrast verb (**contrasts, contrasting, contrasted**)
1 compare or oppose two things in order to show that they are clearly different. 2 be clearly different when compared. [from contra- + Latin stare = to stand]

contravene verb (**contravenes, contravening, contravened**) act against a rule or law. **contravention** noun [from contra- + Latin venire = come]

contribute verb (**contributes, contributing, contributed**)
1 give money or help etc. when others are doing the same.

2 write something for a newspaper or magazine etc. **3** help to cause something.
contribution noun, **contributor** noun, **contributory** adjective [from con- + Latin tribuere = bestow]

contrite adjective very sorry for having done wrong. [from Latin contritus = ground down]

contrive verb (**contrives**, **contriving**, **contrived**) plan cleverly; find a way of doing or making something. [from old French]

control verb (**controls**, **controlling**, **controlled**)
1 have the power to make someone or something do what you want. **2** hold something, especially anger, in check; restrain. **controller** noun
control noun controlling a person or thing; authority.
out of control no longer able to be controlled.
[from old French]

controls plural noun the switches etc. used to control a machine.

controversial adjective causing controversy.

controversy (say kon-tro-ver-see or kon-**trov**-er-see) noun (plural **controversies**) a long argument or disagreement. [from contra- + Latin versum = turned]

conundrum noun (plural **conundrums**) a riddle; a hard question. [origin unknown]

convalesce verb (**convalesces**, **convalescing**, **convalesced**) be recovering from an illness.
convalescence noun,

convalescent adjective & noun [from con- + Latin valescere = grow strong]

convection noun the passing on of heat within liquid, air, or gas by circulation of the warmed parts. [from con- + Latin vectum = carried]

convenience noun (plural **conveniences**)
1 being convenient. **2** something that is convenient. **3** a public lavatory.
at your convenience whenever you find convenient; as it suits you.

convenient adjective easy to use or deal with or reach.
conveniently adverb [from Latin convenire = to suit]

conventional adjective
1 done or doing things in the accepted way; traditional. **2** (of weapons) not nuclear.
conventionally adverb, **conventionality** noun

conversation noun (plural **conversations**) talk between people. **conversational** adjective

convert (say kon-**vert**) verb (**converts**, **converting**, **converted**)
1 change. **2** cause a person to change his or her beliefs. **3** kick a goal after scoring a try at Rugby football. **converter** noun, **conversion** noun

convex adjective curved like the outside of a ball or circle. (The opposite is concave.) **convexity** noun [from Latin convexus = arched]

convey verb (**conveys**, **conveying**, **conveyed**)
1 transport. **2** communicate

a message or idea etc. **conveyor** *noun* [from old French *conveier* = lead, escort]

conveyor belt *noun* (*plural* **conveyor belts**) a continuous moving belt for conveying objects.

convict (*say* kon-**vikt**) *verb* (**convicts, convicting, convicted**) prove or declare that a certain person is guilty of a crime.

convict (*say* **kon**-vikt) *noun* (*plural* **convicts**) a convicted person who is in prison. [from *con-* + Latin *victum* = conquered]

conviction *noun* (*plural* **convictions**)
1 convicting or being convicted of a crime. 2 being convinced. 3 a firm opinion or belief.
carry conviction be convincing.

convince *verb* (**convinces, convincing, convinced**) make a person feel certain that something is true. [from *con-* + Latin *vincere* = conquer]

convoy *noun* (*plural* **convoys**) a group of ships or lorries travelling together. [same origin as *convey*]

convulsion *noun* (*plural* **convulsions**)
1 a violent movement of the body. 2 a violent upheaval.

coo *verb* (**coos, cooing, cooed**) make a dove's soft murmuring sound. **coo** *noun*

cook *verb* (**cooks, cooking, cooked**) make food ready to eat by heating it.
cook up (*informal*) if you cook up a story or plan, you invent it.

cook *noun* (*plural* **cooks**) a person who cooks. [from Latin]

cookery *noun* the skill of cooking food.

cool *adjective*
1 fairly cold; not hot or warm. 2 calm; not enthusiastic. **coolly** *adverb*, **coolness** *noun*

cool *verb* (**cools, cooling, cooled**) make or become cool. **cooler** *noun*

cooperate *verb* (**cooperates, cooperating, cooperated**) work helpfully with other people. **cooperation** *noun*, **cooperative** *adjective*

coordinate *verb* (**coordinates, coordinating, coordinated**) organize people or things to work properly together. **coordination** *noun*, **coordinator** *noun*

coordinate *noun* (*plural* **coordinates**) either of the pair of numbers or letters used to fix the position of a point on a graph or map.
[from *co-* + Latin *ordinare* = arrange]

cope *verb* (**copes, coping, coped**) manage or deal with something successfully. [from French; related to *coup*]

copious *adjective* plentiful; in large amounts. **copiously** *adverb* [same origin as *copy*]

copper *noun* (*plural* **coppers**)
1 a reddish-brown metal used to make wire, coins, etc. 2 a reddish-brown colour. 3 a coin made of copper or metal of this colour.
copper *adjective* [via Old English from Latin *cyprium* = Cyprus metal (because the Romans got most of their copper from Cyprus)]

copse noun (plural **copses**)
a small group of trees.

copulate verb (**copulates**, **copulating**, **copulated**) have sexual intercourse with someone. **copulation** noun [from Latin copulare = link or join together]

copy noun (plural **copies**)
1 a thing made to look like another. **2** something written or typed out again from its original form. **3** one of a number of specimens of the same book or newspaper etc.

copy verb (**copies**, **copying**, **copied**)
1 make a copy of something. **2** do the same as someone else; imitate. **copyist** noun [from Latin copia = plenty, abundance]

copyright noun the legal right to print a book, reproduce a picture, record a piece of music, etc.

cor- prefix with; together. see **com-**.

coral noun
1 a hard red, pink, or white substance formed by the skeletons of tiny sea-creatures massed together. **2** a pink colour.

cord noun (plural **cords**)
1 a long thin flexible strip of twisted threads or strands. **2** a piece of flex. **3** a cord-like structure in the body, the spinal cord. **4** corduroy. [from Greek]

USAGE: Do not confuse with chord.

cordial adjective warm and friendly. **cordially** adverb, **cordiality** noun [from Latin cordis

= of the heart (a cordial was originally a drink given to stimulate the heart)]

corduroy noun cotton cloth with velvety ridges. [from cord + duroy = a kind of woollen material]

core noun (plural **cores**)
1 the part in the middle of something. **2** the hard central part of an apple or pear etc., containing the seeds. [origin unknown]

corgi noun (plural **corgis**) a small dog with short legs and upright ears. [from Welsh cor = dwarf + ci = dog]

cork noun (plural **corks**)
1 the lightweight bark of a kind of oak tree. **2** a stopper for a bottle, made of cork or other material.

cork verb (**corks**, **corking**, **corked**) close something with a cork.

corkscrew noun (plural **corkscrews**)
1 a device for removing corks from bottles. **2** a spiral.

corn[1] noun
1 the seed of wheat and similar plants. **2** a plant, such as wheat, grown for its grain. [from Old English]

corn[2] noun (plural **corns**) a small hard lump on the foot. [from Latin cornu = horn]

cornea noun (plural **corneas**) the transparent covering over the pupil of the eye. **corneal** adjective [from Latin]

corner noun (plural **corners**)
1 the angle or area where two lines or sides or walls meet or where two streets join. **2** a free hit or kick from the corner of a hockey or football field.

3 a region, *a quiet corner of the world.*

corner *verb* (**corners, cornering, cornered**)
1 drive someone into a corner or other position from which it is difficult to escape. **2** travel round a corner. **3** obtain possession of all or most of something, *corner the market.*
[from Latin *cornu* = horn, tip]

cornet *noun* (*plural* **cornets**)
1 a cone-shaped wafer etc. holding ice cream. **2** a musical instrument rather like a trumpet. [French, = small horn]

cornflakes *plural noun* toasted maize flakes eaten as a breakfast cereal.

cornucopia *noun*
1 a horn-shaped container overflowing with fruit and flowers. **2** a plentiful supply of good things. [from Latin *cornu* = horn + *copiae* = of plenty]

corny *adjective* (**cornier, corniest**) (*informal*)
1 repeated so often that people are bored, *corny jokes.*
2 sentimental. [originally = rustic, simple: from *corn*[1]]

corollary (*say* ker-ol-er-ee) *noun* (*plural* **corollaries**) a fact etc. that logically results from another, *The work is difficult and, as a corollary, tiring.* [from Latin]

coronary *noun* (*plural* **coronaries**) short for **coronary thrombosis**, blockage of an artery carrying blood to the heart. [from *corona* (because the coronary arteries encircle the heart like a crown)]

coronation *noun* (*plural* **coronations**) the crowning of a king or queen.

corporal *noun* (*plural* **corporals**) a soldier ranking next below a sergeant.

corporal punishment *noun* punishment by being whipped or beaten.

corps (*say* kor) *noun* (*plural* **corps** (*say* korz))
1 a special army unit, *the Medical Corps.* **2** a large group of soldiers. **3** a set of people doing the same job, *the diplomatic corps.* [French, from Latin *corpus* = body]

corpse *noun* (*plural* **corpses**) a dead body. [from Latin *corpus* = body]

corpuscle *noun* (*plural* **corpuscles**) one of the red or white cells in blood. [from Latin *corpusculum* = little body]

correct *adjective*
1 true; accurate; without any mistakes. **2** proper; done or said in an approved way. **correctly** *adverb,* **correctness** *noun*

correct *verb* (**corrects, correcting, corrected**)
1 make a thing correct by altering or adjusting it. **2** mark the mistakes in something.
3 point out or punish a person's faults. **correction** *noun,* **corrective** *adjective,* **corrector** *noun*
[from *cor-* + Latin *rectus* = straight]

correspond *verb* (**corresponds, corresponding, corresponded**)
1 write letters to each other.
2 agree; match, *Your story corresponds with his.* **3** be similar or equivalent, *Their assembly corresponds to our parliament.*

correspondence *noun*
1 letters; writing letters.
2 similarity; agreement.

corridor *noun* (*plural* **corridors**)
a passage in a building. [via
French from Italian]

corroborate *verb* (**corroborates,
corroborating, corroborated**) help
to confirm a statement etc.
corroboration *noun* [from *cor-*
+ Latin *roborare* = strengthen]

corrode *verb* (**corrodes,
corroding, corroded**) destroy
metal gradually by chemical
action. **corrosion** *noun*, **corrosive**
adjective [from *cor-* + Latin *rodere*
= gnaw]

corrugated *adjective* shaped into
alternate ridges and grooves,
corrugated iron. [from *cor-* + Latin
ruga = wrinkle]

corrupt *adjective*
1 dishonest; accepting bribes.
2 wicked. 3 decaying.

corrupt *verb* (**corrupts,
corrupting, corrupted**)
1 cause someone to become
dishonest or wicked. 2 spoil;
cause something to decay.
corruption *noun*, **corruptible**
adjective
[from *cor-* + Latin *ruptum*
= broken]

cosine *noun* (*plural* **cosines**) (in
a right-angled triangle) the ratio
of the length of a side adjacent to
one of the acute angles to the
length of the hypotenuse.
(Compare *sine*.) [from *co-* + *sine*]

cosmetic *noun* (*plural*
cosmetics) a substance (e.g. face
powder, lipstick) put on the skin
to make it look more attractive.
[from Greek *kosmein* = arrange,
decorate]

cosmetic surgery *noun* surgery
carried out to make people look
more attractive.

cosmic *adjective*
1 to do with the universe. 2 to do
with outer space, *cosmic rays*.
[from *cosmos*]

cosmopolitan *adjective* from
many countries; containing
people from many countries.
[from *cosmos* + Greek *polites*
= citizen]

cosmos (*say* koz-moss) *noun* the
universe. [from Greek, = the
world]

cost *noun* (*plural* **costs**) the price
of something.

cost *verb* (**costs, costing, cost**)
1 have a certain price. 2 (*past
tense* is **costed**) estimate the cost
of something.

costly *adjective* (**costlier, costliest**)
expensive. **costliness** *noun*

costume *noun* (*plural* **costumes**)
clothes, especially for a particular
purpose or of a particular place
or period. [via French from
Italian; related to *custom*]

cosy *adjective* (**cosier, cosiest**)
warm and comfortable. **cosily**
adverb, **cosiness** *noun*

cot *noun* (*plural* **cots**) a baby's
bed with high sides. [from Hindi
khat = bedstead]

cottage *noun* (*plural* **cottages**)
a small simple house, especially
in the country. [from Old
English]

cotton *noun*
1 a soft white substance covering
the seeds of a tropical plant; the
plant itself. 2 thread made from
this substance. 3 cloth made from
cotton thread. [via French from
Arabic]

cotton wool *noun* soft fluffy wadding originally made from cotton.

couch *noun* (*plural* **couches**)
1 a long soft seat like a sofa but with only one end raised. **2** a sofa or settee.

couch *verb* (**couches**, **couching**, **couched**) express in words of a certain kind, *The request was couched in polite terms.*
[from French *coucher* = lay down flat]

cough (*say* kof) *verb* (**coughs**, **coughing**, **coughed**) send out air from the lungs with a sudden sharp sound.

cough *noun* (*plural* **coughs**)
1 the act or sound of coughing. **2** an illness that makes you cough.

could past tense of **can**².

couldn't (*mainly spoken*) could not.

council *noun* (*plural* **councils**) a group of people chosen or elected to organize or discuss something, especially those elected to organize the affairs of a town or county. [from Latin *concilium* = assembly]

USAGE: Do not confuse with *counsel.*

councillor *noun* (*plural* **councillors**) a member of a town or county council.

council tax *noun* (*plural* **council taxes**) a tax paid to a local authority to pay for local services, based on the estimated value of someone's house or flat.

counsel *noun* (*plural* **counsels**)
1 advice, *give counsel.* **2** a barrister or group of barristers

representing someone in a lawsuit.

take counsel with consult.

USAGE: Do not confuse with *council.*

counsel *verb* (**counsels**, **counselling**, **counselled**) give advice to someone; recommend. [from Latin *consulere* = consult]

count¹ *verb* (**counts**, **counting**, **counted**)
1 say numbers in their proper order. **2** find the total of something by using numbers. **3** include in a total, *There are six of us, counting the dog.* **4** be important, *It's what you do that counts.* **5** regard; consider, *I should count it an honour to be invited.*

count on rely on.

count *noun* (*plural* **counts**)
1 counting. **2** a number reached by counting; a total. **3** any of the points being considered, e.g. in accusing someone of crimes, *guilty on all counts.*
[via French from Latin *computare* = compute]

count² *noun* (*plural* **counts**) a foreign nobleman. [from old French]

countdown *noun* (*plural* **countdowns**) counting numbers backwards to zero before an event, especially the launching of a space rocket.

counter¹ *noun* (*plural* **counters**)
1 a flat surface over which customers are served in a shop, bank, etc. **2** a small round playing piece used in certain board games. **3** a device for counting things.

under the counter sold or obtained in an underhand way. [same origin as *count*[1]]

counter[2] *verb* (**counters, countering, countered**)
1 counteract. 2 counter-attack; return an opponent's blow by hitting back. [via old French from Latin *contra* = against]

counter- *prefix*
1 against; opposing; done in return (as in *counter-attack*). 2 corresponding (as in *countersign*). [from Latin *contra* = against]

counteract *verb* (**counteracts, counteracting, counteracted**) act against something and reduce or prevent its effects. **counteraction** *noun*

counterbalance *noun* (*plural* **counterbalances**) a weight or influence that balances another. **counterbalance** *verb*

counterfeit (*say* **kownt**-er-feet) *adjective* fake; not genuine.

counterfeit *verb* (**counterfeits, counterfeiting, counterfeited**) forge or make an imitation of something. [from old French *countrefait* = made in opposition]

counterfoil *noun* (*plural* **counterfoils**) a section of a cheque or receipt etc. that is torn off and kept as a record. [from *counter-* + an old sense of *foil*[1] = sheet of paper]

counterpart *noun* (*plural* **counterparts**) a person or thing that corresponds to another, *Their President is the counterpart of our Prime Minister.*

countless *adjective* too many to count.

country *noun* (*plural* **countries**)
1 the land occupied by a nation. 2 all the people of a country. 3 the countryside.

countryside *noun* an area with fields, woods, villages, etc. away from towns.

county *noun* (*plural* **counties**) each of the main areas that a country is divided into for local government. [originally = the land of a count (*count*[2])]

coup (*say* koo) *noun* (*plural* **coups**) a sudden action taken to win power; a clever victory. [French, = a blow]

couple *noun* (*plural* **couples**) two people or things considered together; a pair.

couple *verb* (**couples, coupling, coupled**) fasten or link two things together. [same origin as *copulate*]

couplet *noun* (*plural* **couplets**) a pair of lines in rhyming verse.

coupon *noun* (*plural* **coupons**) a piece of paper that gives you the right to receive or do something. [French, = piece cut off]

courage *noun* the ability to face danger or difficulty or pain even when you are afraid; bravery. **courageous** *adjective* [from Latin *cor* = heart]

courier (*say* koor-ee-er) *noun* (*plural* **couriers**)
1 a messenger. 2 a person employed to guide and help a group of tourists. [old French, = runner]

course *noun* (*plural* **courses**)
1 the direction in which something goes; a route, *the ship's course.* 2 a series of events

or actions etc., *Your best course is to start again.* **3** a series of lessons, exercises, etc. **4** part of a meal, *the meat course.*

5 a racecourse. **6** a golf course.

of course without a doubt; as we expected.

court noun (plural **courts**)
1 the royal household.
2 a lawcourt; the judges etc. in a lawcourt. **3** an enclosed area for games such as tennis or netball.
4 a courtyard.

court verb (**courts, courting, courted**) try to win somebody's love or support. **courtship** noun [from old French]

courteous (*say* ker-tee-us) adjective polite. **courteously** adverb, **courtesy** noun [from old French, = having manners suitable for a royal court]

courtier noun (plural **courtiers**) (*old use*) one of a king's or queen's companions at court.

courtly adjective dignified and polite.

courtyard noun (plural **courtyards**) a space surrounded by walls or buildings.

cousin noun (plural **cousins**) a child of your uncle or aunt. [from old French]

cover verb (**covers, covering, covered**)
1 place one thing over or round another; conceal. **2** travel a certain distance, *We covered ten miles a day.* **3** aim a gun at somebody, *I've got you covered.*
4 protect by insurance or a guarantee, *These goods are covered against fire or theft.* **5** be enough to pay for something, *£5 should cover my*

fare. **6** deal with or include, *The book covers all kinds of farming.*
coverage noun

cover noun (plural **covers**)
1 a thing used for covering something else; a lid, wrapper, envelope, etc. **2** the binding of a book. **3** something that hides or shelters or protects you.
[from old French]

cow noun (plural **cows**) the fully-grown female of cattle or of certain other large animals (e.g. elephant, whale, seal). [from Old English]

coward noun (plural **cowards**) a person who has no courage and shows fear in a shameful way.
cowardice noun, **cowardly** adjective [from old French]

cowboy noun (plural **cowboys**) a man in charge of grazing cattle on a ranch in the USA.

cower verb (**cowers, cowering, cowered**) crouch or shrink back in fear.

coy adjective pretending to be shy or modest; bashful. **coyly** adverb, **coyness** noun [from old French; related to *quiet*]

crab noun (plural **crabs**) a shellfish with ten legs. [from Old English]

crab apple noun (plural **crab apples**) a small sour apple. [probably from a Scandinavian language]

crack noun (plural **cracks**)
1 a line on the surface of something where it has broken but not come completely apart.
2 a narrow gap. **3** a sudden sharp noise. **4** a knock, *a crack on the head.* **5** (*informal*) a joke;

a wisecrack. **6** a drug made from cocaine.

crack adjective (informal) first-class, *He is a crack shot.*

crack verb (**cracks, cracking, cracked**)
1 make or get a crack; split. **2** make a sudden sharp noise. **3** break down, *He cracked under the strain.*
crack a joke tell a joke.
crack down on (informal) stop something that is illegal or against rules.
get cracking (informal) get busy.

cracker noun (plural **crackers**)
1 a paper tube that bangs when pulled apart. **2** a firework that explodes with a crack. **3** a thin biscuit.

crackle verb (**crackles, crackling, crackled**) make small cracking sounds, *The fire crackled in the grate.* **crackle** noun

-cracy suffix forms nouns meaning 'ruling' or 'government' (e.g. *democracy*). [from Greek *-kratia* = rule]

cradle noun (plural **cradles**)
1 a small cot for a baby.
2 a supporting framework.

cradle verb (**cradles, cradling, cradled**) hold gently.
[from Old English]

craft noun (plural **crafts**)
1 a job that needs skill, especially with the hands. **2** skill. **3** cunning; trickery. **4** (plural **craft**) a ship or boat; an aircraft or spacecraft.
[from Old English]

craftsman noun (plural **craftsmen**) a person who is good at a craft. **craftsmanship** noun

crafty adjective (**craftier, craftiest**) cunning. **craftily** adverb, **craftiness** noun [originally = skilful: from *craft*]

crag noun (plural **crags**) a steep piece of rough rock. **craggy** adjective, **cragginess** noun [a Celtic word]

cram verb (**crams, cramming, crammed**)
1 push many things into something so that it is very full. **2** learn as many facts as you can in a short time just before an examination. [from Old English]

cramp noun (plural **cramps**) pain caused by a muscle tightening suddenly.

cramp verb (**cramps, cramping, cramped**)
1 keep in a space that is too small. **2** hinder someone's freedom or growth etc.

crane noun (plural **cranes**)
1 a machine for lifting and moving heavy objects. **2** a large wading bird with long legs and neck.

crane verb (**cranes, craning, craned**) stretch your neck to try and see something.

crank noun (plural **cranks**)
1 an L-shaped part used for changing the direction of movement in machinery.
2 a person with strange or fanatical ideas. **cranky** adjective

cranny noun (plural **crannies**) a crevice. [from old French]

crash noun (plural **crashes**)
1 the loud noise of something breaking or colliding. **2** a violent collision or fall. **3** a sudden drop or failure.

crash verb (crashes, crashing, crashed)
1 make or have a crash; cause to crash. 2 move with a crash.

crash adjective intensive, a crash course.

crash helmet noun (plural crash helmets) a padded helmet worn to protect the head in a crash.

crass adjective
1 very obvious or shocking; gross, crass ignorance. 2 very stupid. [from Latin crassus = thick]

-crat suffix forms nouns meaning 'ruler' or 'believer in some type of government'. [same origin as -cracy]

crate noun (plural crates)
1 a packing case made of strips of wood. 2 an open container with compartments for carrying bottles. [origin unknown]

crater noun (plural craters)
1 a bowl-shaped cavity or hollow. 2 the mouth of a volcano. [from Greek krater = bowl]

craving noun (plural cravings) a strong desire; a longing.

crawl verb (crawls, crawling, crawled)
1 move with the body close to the ground or other surface, or on hands and knees. 2 move slowly. 3 be covered with crawling things. **crawler** noun

crawl noun
1 a crawling movement. 2 a very slow pace. 3 an overarm swimming stroke.

crayon noun (plural crayons) a stick or pencil of coloured wax etc. for drawing. [French]

craze noun (plural crazes) a temporary enthusiasm.

crazy adjective (crazier, craziest)
1 insane. 2 very foolish, this crazy idea. **crazily** adverb, **craziness** noun [from craze]

crazy paving noun paving made of oddly-shaped pieces of stone etc.

creak noun (plural creaks) a harsh squeak like that of a stiff door-hinge. **creaky** adjective

creak verb (creaks, creaking, creaked) make a creak. [imitating the sound]

cream noun (plural creams)
1 the fatty part of milk. 2 a yellowish-white colour. 3 a food containing or looking like cream, chocolate cream. 4 a soft substance, shoe cream. 5 the best part. **creamy** adjective

cream verb (creams, creaming, creamed) make creamy; beat butter etc. until it is soft like cream.

cream off remove the best part of something.

crease noun (plural creases)
1 a line made in something by folding, pressing, or crushing it. 2 a line on a cricket pitch marking a batsman's or bowler's position.

crease verb (creases, creasing, creased) make a crease or creases in something.

create verb (creates, creating, created)
1 bring into existence; make or produce, especially something that no one has made before. 2 (slang) make a fuss; grumble. **creation** noun, **creative** adjective, **creativity** noun, **creator** noun [from Latin]

creature noun (plural **creatures**)
a person or animal. [from Latin
creatura = a created being]

crèche (say kresh) noun (plural
crèches) a place where babies
and young children are looked
after while their parents are at
work. [French]

credentials plural noun
documents showing a person's
identity, qualifications, etc.

credible adjective able to be
believed; convincing. **credibly**
adverb, **credibility** noun [same
origin as *credit*]

USAGE: Do not confuse with
creditable or *credulous*.

credit noun (plural **credits**)
1 honour; acknowledgement. 2 an
arrangement trusting a person to
pay for something later on. 3 an
amount of money in someone's
account at a bank etc., or entered
in an account-book as paid in.
(Compare *debit*.) 4 belief or trust,
I put no credit in this rumour.
credits or **credit titles** plural noun
a list of people who have helped
to produce a film or television
programme.

credit verb (**credits**, **crediting**,
credited)
1 believe. 2 attribute; say that
a person has done or achieved
something, *Columbus is credited
with the discovery of America*.
3 enter something as a credit in
an account-book. (Compare
debit.)
[from Latin *credere* = believe,
trust]

credit card noun (plural **credit
cards**) a card authorizing a person
to buy on credit.

creditor noun (plural **creditors**)
a person to whom money is owed.

credulous adjective too ready to
believe things; gullible. [from
Latin *credulus* = trusting]

USAGE: Do not confuse with
credible.

creed noun (plural **creeds**) a set
or formal statement of beliefs.
[from Latin *credo* = I believe]

creep verb (**creeps**, **creeping**,
crept)
1 move along close to the ground.
2 move quietly. 3 come gradually.
4 prickle with fear, *It makes my
flesh creep*.

creep noun (plural **creeps**)
1 a creeping movement. 2 (slang)
an unpleasant person, especially
one who seeks to win favour.
the creeps (informal) a nervous
feeling caused by fear or dislike.

creeper noun (plural **creepers**)
a plant that grows along the
ground or up a wall etc.

creepy adjective (**creepier**,
creepiest) frightening and
sinister.

cremate verb (**cremates**,
cremating, **cremated**) burn a dead
body to ashes. **cremation** noun
[from Latin *cremare* = to burn]

crematorium noun (plural
crematoria) a place where
corpses are cremated.

crescendo (say krish-end-oh)
noun (plural **crescendos**)
a gradual increase in loudness.
[Italian, = increasing]

crescent noun (plural **crescents**)
1 a narrow curved shape coming
to a point at each end. 2 a curved

street. [originally = the new moon: from Latin *crescens* = growing]

cress noun a plant with hot-tasting leaves, used in salads and sandwiches. [from Old English]

crest noun (plural **crests**)
1 a tuft of hair, skin, or feathers on an animal's or bird's head.
2 the top of a hill or wave etc.
3 a design used on notepaper etc. **crested** adjective

crestfallen adjective disappointed or dejected.

crevasse (say kri-**vass**) noun (plural **crevasses**) a deep open crack, especially in a glacier. [same origin as *crevice*]

crevice noun (plural **crevices**) a narrow opening, especially in a rock or wall. [from old French *crever* = burst, split]

crew[1] noun (plural **crews**)
1 the people working in a ship or aircraft. **2** a group working together, *the camera crew*. [from old French]

crew[2] past tense of **crow**[2].

crib noun (plural **cribs**)
1 a baby's cot. **2** a framework holding fodder for animals.
3 a model representing the Nativity of Jesus Christ.
4 something cribbed. **5** a translation for use by students.

crib verb (**cribs**, **cribbing**, **cribbed**) copy someone else's work.

crick noun (plural **cricks**) painful stiffness in the neck or back.

cricket[1] noun a game played outdoors between teams with a ball, bats, and two wickets.

cricketer noun [origin unknown]

cricket[2] noun (plural **crickets**) a brown insect like a grasshopper. [from old French *criquer* = crackle (imitating the sound it makes)]

crime noun (plural **crimes**)
1 an action that breaks the law.
2 law-breaking. [from Latin]

criminal noun (plural **criminals**) a person who has committed a crime or crimes. **criminal** adjective, **criminally** adverb

crimson adjective deep-red.

crimson noun [from Arabic *kirmiz* = an insect which was used to make crimson dye]

cringe verb (**cringes**, **cringing**, **cringed**) shrink back in fear; cower. [from Old English *crincan* = yield, fall in battle]

cripple noun (plural **cripples**) a person who is permanently lame.

cripple verb (**cripples**, **crippling**, **crippled**)
1 make a person lame. **2** weaken or damage something seriously.

crisis noun (plural **crises**) an important and dangerous or difficult situation. [from Greek]

crisp adjective
1 very dry so that it breaks with a snap. **2** fresh and stiff, *a crisp £5 note*. **3** cold and dry, *a crisp morning*. **4** brisk and sharp, *a crisp manner*. **crisply** adverb, **crispness** noun

crisp noun (plural **crisps**) a very thin fried slice of potato. Crisps are usually sold in packets. [from Latin]

criss-cross adjective & adverb with crossing lines. [from *Christ-cross* (the cross on which Christ died)]

criterion (say kry-teer-ee-on)
noun (plural **criteria**) a standard
by which something is judged.
[from Greek, = means of judging]

critic noun (plural **critics**)
1 a person who gives opinions on
books, plays, films, music, etc.
2 a person who criticizes. [from
Greek krites = judge]

critical adjective
1 criticizing. **2** to do with critics
or criticism. **3** to do with or at
a crisis; very serious. **critically**
adverb

criticism noun (plural **criticisms**)
1 criticizing; pointing out faults.
2 the work of a critic.

criticize verb (**criticizes**,
criticizing, **criticized**) say that
a person or thing has faults.

croak noun (plural **croaks**) a deep
hoarse sound like that of a frog.
croak verb [imitating the sound]

crockery noun household china.

crocodile noun (plural
crocodiles)
1 a large tropical reptile with
a thick skin, long tail, and huge
jaws. **2** a long line of
schoolchildren walking in pairs.
crocodile tears sorrow that is not
sincere (so called because the
crocodile was said to weep while
it ate its victim).

crocus noun (plural **crocuses**)
a small plant with yellow, purple,
or white flowers. [from Greek]

crony noun (plural **cronies**) a close
friend or companion. [from
Greek]

crook noun (plural **crooks**)
1 a shepherd's stick with a curved
end. **2** something bent or curved.
3 (informal) a person who makes
a living dishonestly.

crooked adjective
1 bent or twisted; not straight.
2 dishonest.

croon verb (**croons**, **crooning**,
crooned) sing softly and gently.

crop noun (plural **crops**)
1 something grown for food,
a good crop of wheat. **2** a whip
with a loop instead of a lash.
3 part of a bird's throat. **4** a very
short haircut.

crop verb (**crops**, **cropping**,
cropped)
1 cut or bite off, sheep were
cropping the grass. **2** produce
a crop.
crop up happen unexpectedly.

croquet (say kroh-kay) noun
a game played with wooden balls
and mallets. [origin unknown]

cross noun (plural **crosses**)
1 a mark or shape made like + or
×. **2** an upright post with another
piece of wood across it, used in
ancient times for crucifixion; **the
Cross** the cross on which Christ
was crucified, used as a symbol of
Christianity. **3** a mixture of two
different things.

cross verb (**crosses**, **crossing**,
crossed)
1 go across something. **2** draw
a line or lines across something.
3 make the sign or shape of
a cross, Cross your fingers for
luck. **4** produce something from
two different kinds.
cross out draw a line across
something because it is
unwanted, wrong, etc.

cross adjective
1 going from one side to another.
2 annoyed; bad-tempered. **crossly**

adverb, crossness noun
[via Old Norse and old Irish from
Latin]

cross- prefix
1 across; crossing something (as
in *crossbar*). **2** from two different
kinds (as in *cross-breed*).

crossbar noun (plural **crossbars**)
a horizontal bar, especially
between two uprights.

cross-breed verb (**cross-breeds,
cross-breeding, cross-bred**) breed
by mating an animal with one of
a different kind. **cross-breed**
noun (Compare *hybrid*.)

cross-examine verb (**cross-
examines, cross-examining,
cross-examined**) cross-question
someone, especially in
a lawcourt. **cross-examination**
noun

cross-eyed adjective with eyes
that look or seem to look towards
the nose.

crossing noun (plural **crossings**)
a place where people can cross
a road, railway, etc.

cross-legged adjective & adverb
with ankles crossed and knees
spread apart.

cross-question verb (**cross-
questions, cross-questioning,
cross-questioned**) question
someone carefully in order to test
answers given to previous
questions.

cross-reference noun (plural
cross-references) a note telling
people to look at another part of
a book etc. for more information.

crossroads noun (plural
crossroads) a place where two or
more roads cross one another.

cross-section noun (plural
cross-sections)
1 a drawing of something as if it
has been cut through. **2** a typical
sample.

crossword noun (plural
crosswords) short for **crossword
puzzle**, a puzzle in which words
have to be guessed from clues
and then written into the blank
squares in a diagram.

crotchet noun (plural **crotchets**)
a note in music, which usually
represents one beat (written ♩).
[from French, = small hook]

crouch verb (**crouches, crouching,
crouched**) lower your body, with
your arms and legs bent. [origin
unknown]

crow[1] noun (plural **crows**) a large
black bird.

as the crow flies in a straight line.
[from Old English]

crow[2] verb (**crows, crowing,
crowed** or **crew**)
1 make a shrill cry as a cock does.
2 boast; be triumphant. **crow**
noun [imitating the sound]

crowbar noun (plural **crowbars**)
an iron bar used as a lever.
[because the end is shaped like
a crow's beak]

crowd noun (plural **crowds**)
a large number of people in one
place.

crowd verb (**crowds, crowding,
crowded**)
1 come together in a crowd.
2 cram; fill uncomfortably full.
[from Old English]

crown noun (plural **crowns**)
1 an ornamental headdress worn
by a king or queen. **2** (often
Crown) the sovereign, *This land
belongs to the Crown.*

3 the highest part, *the crown of the road.* **4** a former coin worth 5 shillings (25p).

Crown Prince or **Crown Princess** the heir to the throne.

crown verb (**crowns, crowning, crowned**)
1 place a crown on someone as a symbol of royal power or victory. **2** form or cover or decorate the top of something. **3** reward; make a successful end to something, *Our efforts were crowned with victory.* **4** (*slang*) hit someone on the head.
[from Latin *corona* = garland or crown]

crucial (*say* kroo-shal) *adjective*
most important. **crucially** *adverb*
[from Latin *crux* = of a cross]

crucifix noun (plural **crucifixes**)
a model of the Cross or of Jesus Christ on the Cross. [same origin as *crucify*]

crucify verb (**crucifies, crucifying, crucified**) put a person to death by nailing or binding the hands and feet to a cross. **crucifixion** noun
[from Latin *crucifigere* = fix to a cross]

crude adjective
1 in a natural state; not yet refined, *crude oil.* **2** not well finished; rough, *a crude carving.* **3** vulgar. **crudely** adverb, **crudity** noun [from Latin *crudus* = raw, rough]

cruel adjective (**crueller, cruellest**)
causing pain or suffering. **cruelly** adverb, **cruelty** noun [from old French; related to *crude*]

cruise noun (plural **cruises**)
a pleasure trip in a ship.

cruise verb (**cruises, cruising, cruised**)
1 sail or travel at a moderate speed. **2** have a cruise.
[from Dutch *kruisen* = to cross]

cruiser noun (plural **cruisers**)
1 a fast warship. **2** a large motor boat.

crumb noun (plural **crumbs**)
a tiny piece of bread, etc.

crumble verb (**crumbles, crumbling, crumbled**) break or fall into small fragments.
crumbly adjective

crumpet noun (plural **crumpets**)
a soft flat cake made with yeast, eaten toasted with butter. [origin unknown]

crumple verb (**crumples, crumpling, crumpled**)
1 crush or become crushed into creases. **2** collapse loosely. [from Old English *crump* = crooked]

crunch verb (**crunches, crunching, crunched**) crush something noisily, for example between your teeth.

crunch noun (plural **crunches**)
a crunching sound. **crunchy** adjective
the crunch (*informal*) a crucial event or turning point.

Crusade noun (plural **Crusades**)
a military expedition made by Christians in the Middle Ages to recover Palestine from the Muslims who had conquered it. **Crusader** noun

crusade noun (plural **crusades**)
a campaign against something bad. [from Latin *crux* = cross]

crush verb (**crushes, crushing, crushed**)
1 press something so that it gets

broken or harmed. **2** squeeze tightly. **3** defeat.

crush noun (plural **crushes**)
1 a crowd of people pressed together. **2** a drink made with crushed fruit.

crust noun (plural **crusts**)
1 the hard outer layer of something, especially bread. **2** the rocky outer layer of the earth. [from Latin *crusta* = rind, shell]

crustacean (say krust-ay-shon) noun (plural **crustaceans**) an animal with a shell, e.g. a crab. [same origin as *crust*]

crutch noun (plural **crutches**) a support like a long walking stick for helping a lame person to walk.

cry noun (plural **cries**)
1 a loud wordless sound expressing pain, grief, joy, etc. **2** a shout. **3** crying, *Have a good cry.*

cry verb (**cries, crying, cried**)
1 shed tears; weep. **2** call out loudly.

cryptic adjective hiding its meaning in a puzzling way. **cryptically** adverb [from Greek *kryptos* = hidden]

crystal noun (plural **crystals**)
1 a transparent colourless mineral rather like glass. **2** very clear high-quality glass. **3** a small solid piece of certain substances, *crystals of snow and ice.* **crystalline** adjective [from Greek *krystallos* = ice]

crystallize verb (**crystallizes, crystallizing, crystallized**)
1 form into crystals. **2** become definite in form. **crystallization** noun

cub noun (plural **cubs**) a young lion, tiger, fox, bear, etc.

Cub or **Cub Scout** noun (plural **Cubs, Cub Scouts**) a member of the junior branch of the Scout Association.

cubby hole noun (plural **cubby holes**) a small compartment. [from an old word *cub* = coop, hutch]

cube noun (plural **cubes**)
1 something that has six equal square sides. **2** the number produced by multiplying something by itself twice, *The cube of 3 is $3 \times 3 \times 3 = 27$.*

cube verb (**cubes, cubing, cubed**)
1 multiply a number by itself twice, *4 cubed is $4 \times 4 \times 4 = 64$.* **2** cut something into small cubes. [from Greek]

cube root noun (plural **cube roots**) the number that gives a particular number if it is multiplied by itself twice, *The cube root of 27 is 3.*

cubic adjective three-dimensional. **cubic foot, cubic metre,** etc., the volume of a cube with sides that are one foot or one metre etc. long.

cubicle noun (plural **cubicles**) a compartment of a room. [originally = bedroom: from Latin *cubare* = lie down]

cuckoo noun (plural **cuckoos**) a bird that makes a sound like 'cuck-oo'.

cucumber noun (plural **cucumbers**) a long green-skinned vegetable eaten raw or pickled. [from Latin]

cuddle verb (**cuddles, cuddling, cuddled**) put your arms closely round a person or animal that you love. **cuddly** adjective

cue[1] noun (plural **cues**) something said or done that acts as a signal for an actor etc. to say or do something. [origin unknown]

cue[2] noun (plural **cues**) a long stick for striking the ball in billiards or snooker. [a different spelling of queue (because of its long, thin shape)]

cuff noun (plural **cuffs**)
1 the end of a sleeve that fits round the wrist. 2 hitting somebody with your hand; a slap.

cuff verb (**cuffs, cuffing, cuffed**) hit somebody with your hand.

cul-de-sac noun (plural **culs-de-sac**) a street with an opening at one end only; a dead end. [French, = bottom of a sack]

-cule suffix forms diminutives (e.g. molecule = little mass). [from Latin]

cull verb (**culls, culling, culled**)
1 select and use, culling lines from several poems. 2 pick out and kill surplus animals from a flock. **cull** noun [from Latin colligere = collect]

culpable adjective deserving blame. [from Latin culpare = to blame]

culprit noun (plural **culprits**) the person who has done something wrong.

cult noun (plural **cults**)
1 a religious sect. 2 devotion to a person or a thing by a lot of people. [from Latin cultus = worship]

cultivate verb (**cultivates, cultivating, cultivated**)
1 use land to grow crops. 2 grow or develop things by looking after them. **cultivation** noun, **cultivator** noun

culture noun (plural **cultures**)
1 appreciation and understanding of literature, art, music, etc. 2 customs and traditions, West Indian culture.
3 improvement by care and training, physical culture.
4 cultivating things. **cultural** adjective [from Latin colere = cultivate, look after; worship]

cumbersome adjective clumsy to carry or manage. [from encumber + -some]

cumulative adjective accumulating; increasing by continuous additions. [from Latin cumulus = heap]

cunning adjective
1 clever at deceiving people.
2 cleverly designed or planned.

cunning noun
1 skill in deceiving people; craftiness. 2 skill or ingenuity. [from Old Norse]

cup noun (plural **cups**)
1 a small bowl-shaped container for drinking from. 2 anything shaped like a cup. 3 a goblet-shaped ornament given as a prize. **cupful** noun

cup verb (**cups, cupping, cupped**) form into the shape of a cup, cup your hands. [from Latin]

cupboard noun (plural **cupboards**) a piece of furniture with a door, for storing things. [originally = sideboard: from cup + board]

cur noun (plural **curs**) a scruffy or bad-tempered dog.

curate noun (plural **curates**) a member of the clergy who helps a vicar. [from Latin *cura* = care]

curator (say kewr-ay-ter) noun (plural **curators**) a person in charge of a museum or other collection. [same origin as *cure*]

curb verb (**curbs, curbing, curbed**) restrain, *curb your impatience*.

curb noun (plural **curbs**) a restraint, *Put a curb on spending*.

USAGE: Do not confuse with *kerb*.

curd noun or **curds** plural noun a thick substance formed when milk turns sour. [origin unknown]

curdle verb (**curdles, curdling, curdled**) form into curds.
make someone's blood curdle horrify or terrify them.

cure verb (**cures, curing, cured**)
1 get rid of someone's illness.
2 stop something bad. 3 treat something in order to preserve it, *Fish can be cured in smoke*.

cure noun (plural **cures**)
1 something that cures a person or thing; a remedy. 2 curing; being cured, *We cannot promise a cure*.
[from Latin *curare* = care for, cure]

curfew noun (plural **curfews**) a time or signal after which people must remain indoors until the next day.

curiosity noun (plural **curiosities**)
1 being curious. 2 something unusual and interesting.

curious adjective
1 wanting to find out about things; inquisitive. 2 strange; unusual. **curiously** adverb

curl noun (plural **curls**) a curve or coil, e.g. of hair.

curl verb (**curls, curling, curled**) form into curls.
curl up sit or lie with knees drawn up.

curly adjective having curls.

currant noun (plural **currants**)
1 a small black dried grape used in cookery. 2 a small round red, black, or white berry. [from old French *raisins de Courauntz* = grapes from Corinth (a city in Greece)]

USAGE: Do not confuse with *current*.

currency noun (plural **currencies**)
1 the money in use in a country.
2 the general use of something, *Some words have no currency now*. [from *current*]

current adjective happening now; used now. **currently** adverb

current noun (plural **currents**)
1 water or air etc. moving in one direction. 2 the flow of electricity along a wire etc. or through something.
[from Latin *currens* = running]

USAGE: Do not confuse with *currant*.

curriculum noun (plural **curricula**) a course of study in a school or university. [Latin, = running, course]

curry[1] noun (plural **curries**) food cooked with spices that taste hot.
curried adjective [from Tamil *kari* = sauce]

curry[2] *verb* (**curries, currying, curried**)
curry favour seek to win favour by flattering someone.
[from old French]

curse *noun* (*plural* **curses**)
1 a call or prayer for a person or thing to be harmed; the evil produced by this. 2 something very unpleasant. 3 an angry word or words.

curse *verb* (**curses, cursing, cursed**)
1 make a curse. 2 use a curse against a person or thing.
be cursed with something suffer from it.

cursor *noun* (*plural* **cursors**)
a movable indicator, usually a flashing light, on a VDU screen. [Latin, = runner]

curt *adjective* brief and hasty or rude, *a curt reply*. **curtly** *adverb*, **curtness** *noun* [from Latin *curtus* = cut short]

curtain *noun* (*plural* **curtains**)
1 a piece of material hung at a window or door. 2 the large cloth screen hung at the front of a stage. [from old French]

curtsy *noun* (*plural* **curtsies**)
a movement of respect made by women and girls, putting one foot behind the other and bending the knees.

curtsy *verb* (**curtsies, curtsying, curtsied**)
make a curtsy.
[a different spelling of *courtesy*]

curvature *noun* (*plural* **curvatures**)
curving; a curved shape.

curve *verb* (**curves, curving, curved**)
bend smoothly.

curve *noun* (*plural* **curves**)
a curved line or shape. **curvy** *adjective*

cushion *noun* (*plural* **cushions**)
1 a bag, usually of cloth, filled with soft material so that it is comfortable to sit on or lean against. 2 anything soft or springy that protects or supports something, *The hovercraft travels on a cushion of air*.

cushion *verb* (**cushions, cushioning, cushioned**)
1 supply with cushions, *cushioned seats*. 2 protect from the effects of a knock or shock etc., *His fur hat cushioned the blow*.

custard *noun* (*plural* **custards**)
1 a sweet yellow sauce made with milk. 2 a pudding made with beaten eggs and milk. [from old French]

custody *noun*
1 care and supervision; guardianship. 2 imprisonment.
take into custody arrest.
[from Latin *custos* = guardian]

custom *noun* (*plural* **customs**)
1 the usual way of behaving or doing something. 2 regular business from customers. [from Latin *consuescere* = become accustomed]

customary *adjective* according to custom; usual. **customarily** *adverb*

customer *noun* (*plural* **customers**) a person who uses a shop, bank, or other business. [originally a person who customarily used the same shop etc.]

customs *plural noun*
1 taxes charged on goods brought into a country. **2** the place at a port or airport where officials examine your luggage. [= taxes customarily charged, from *custom*]

cut *verb* (**cuts, cutting, cut**)
1 divide or wound or separate something by using a knife, axe, scissors, etc. **2** make a thing shorter or smaller; remove part of something, *They are cutting all their prices.* **3** divide a pack of playing cards. **4** hit a ball with a chopping movement. **5** go through or across something. **6** stay away from something deliberately, *She cut her music lesson.* **7** make a sound recording. **8** switch off electrical power or an engine etc.
cut a corner pass round it very closely.
cut and dried already decided.
cut in interrupt.

cut *noun* (*plural* **cuts**)
1 cutting; the result of cutting. **2** a small wound. **3** (*slang*) a share.
be a cut above something be superior.

cute *adjective* (*informal*)
1 attractive. **2** clever. **cutely** *adverb*, **cuteness** *noun* [from *acute*]

cutlass *noun* (*plural* **cutlasses**) a short sword with a broad curved blade. [same origin as *cutlery*]

cutlery *noun* knives, forks, and spoons. [from Latin *culter* = knife]

cutlet *noun* (*plural* **cutlets**) a thick slice of meat for cooking.

cutting *noun* (*plural* **cuttings**)
1 a steep-sided passage cut through high ground for a road or railway. **2** something cut out of a newspaper or magazine. **3** a piece cut from a plant to form a new plant.

-cy *suffix* forms nouns showing action or condition etc. (e.g. *piracy*, *infancy*). [from Latin or Greek]

cycle *noun* (*plural* **cycles**)
1 a bicycle or motorcycle.
2 a series of events that are regularly repeated in the same order. **cyclic** *adjective*, **cyclical** *adjective*
cycle *verb* (**cycles, cycling, cycled**) ride a bicycle or tricycle. **cyclist** *noun*
[from Greek *kyklos* = circle]

cyclone *noun* (*plural* **cyclones**) a wind that rotates round a calm central area. **cyclonic** *adjective* [from Greek *kykloma* = wheel]

cygnet (*say* **sig**-nit) *noun* (*plural* **cygnets**) a young swan. [from Latin *cycnus* = swan]

cylinder *noun* (*plural* **cylinders**) an object with straight sides and circular ends. **cylindrical** *adjective* [from Greek *kylindros* = roller]

cymbal *noun* (*plural* **cymbals**) a percussion instrument consisting of a metal plate that is hit to make a ringing sound. [from Greek]

USAGE: Do not confuse with *symbol*.

cynic (*say* **sin**-ik) *noun* (*plural* **cynics**) a person who believes that people's reasons for doing things are selfish or bad, and shows this by sneering at them.

cynical *adjective*, **cynically** *adverb*, **cynicism** *noun* [from Greek *kynikos* = surly]

cypress *noun* (*plural* **cypresses**) an evergreen tree with dark leaves.

Dd

dab *noun* (*plural* **dabs**)
1 a quick gentle touch, usually with something wet. 2 a small lump, *a dab of butter.*

dab *verb* (**dabs, dabbing, dabbed**) touch something quickly and gently.

dabble *verb* (**dabbles, dabbling, dabbled**)
1 splash something about in water. 2 do something as a hobby, *dabble in chemistry.*

dachshund (*say* daks-huund) *noun* (*plural* **dachshunds**) a small dog with a long body and very short legs. [German, = badger-dog (because dachshunds were used to dig badgers out of their sets)]

daffodil *noun* (*plural* **daffodils**) a yellow flower that grows from a bulb. [from *asphodel*, another plant with yellow flowers]

daft *adjective* (*informal*) silly or stupid. [from Old English]

dagger *noun* (*plural* **daggers**) a pointed knife with two sharp edges, used as a weapon. [from old French]

daily *adverb* & *adjective* every day.

dainty *adjective* (**daintier, daintiest**) small, delicate, and pretty. **daintily** *adverb*, **daintiness** *noun* [via old French from Latin *dignitas* = value, beauty]

dairy *noun* (*plural* **dairies**) a place where milk, butter, etc. are produced or sold. [from Old English]

daisy *noun* (*plural* **daisies**) a small flower with white petals and a yellow centre. [from *day's eye* (because the daisy opens in daylight and closes at night)]

dam¹ *noun* (*plural* **dams**) a wall built to hold water back.

dam *verb* (**dams, damming, dammed**) hold water back with a dam.
[from Old English]

dam² *noun* (*plural* **dams**) the mother of a horse or dog etc. (Compare *sire*.) [from *dame*]

damage *noun* harm or injury done to something.

damage *verb* (**damages, damaging, damaged**) harm or spoil something.
[from Latin *damnum* = loss]

damages *plural noun* money paid as compensation for an injury or loss.

Dame *noun* (*plural* **Dames**) the title of a lady who has been given the equivalent of a knighthood.

dame *noun* (*plural* **dames**) a comic middle-aged woman in a pantomime, usually played by a man. [from Latin *domina* = lady]

damn *verb* (**damns, damning, damned**) curse. [from Latin *damnare* = condemn]

damnation *noun* being condemned to hell.

damned *adjective* hateful or annoying.

damp *adjective* slightly wet; not quite dry. **damply** *adverb*, **dampness** *noun*

damp *noun* moisture in the air or on a surface or all through something.

damp course *noun* (*plural* **damp courses**) a layer of material built into a wall to prevent dampness in the ground from rising.

dampen *verb* (**dampens, dampening, dampened**) 1 make something damp. 2 reduce the strength of something.

damsel *noun* (*plural* **damsels**) (*old use*) a young woman. [from old French]

dance *verb* (**dances, dancing, danced**) move about in time to music.

dance *noun* (*plural* **dances**) 1 a set of movements used in dancing. 2 a piece of music for dancing to. 3 a party or gathering where people dance. **dancer** *noun* [from old French]

dandelion *noun* (*plural* **dandelions**) a yellow wild flower with jagged leaves. [from French *dent-de-lion* = tooth of a lion (because the jagged edges of the leaves looked like lions' teeth)]

dandruff *noun* tiny white flakes of dead skin in a person's hair. [origin unknown]

danger *noun* (*plural* **dangers**) something that is not safe or could harm you. [from old French]

dangerous *adjective* likely to kill or harm you. **dangerously** *adverb*

dangle *verb* (**dangles, dangling, dangled**) hang or swing loosely.

dappled *adjective* marked with patches of a different colour. [probably from Old Norse *depill* = spot]

dare *verb* (**dares, daring, dared**) 1 be brave or bold enough to do something. 2 challenge a person to do something risky.

dare *noun* (*plural* **dares**) a challenge to do something risky.

dark *adjective* 1 with little or no light. 2 not light in colour, *a dark suit.* 3 having dark hair. 4 sinister or evil. **darkly** *adverb*, **darkness** *noun*

dark *noun* 1 absence of light, *Cats can see in the dark.* 2 the time when darkness has come, *She went out after dark.* [from Old English]

darken *verb* (**darkens, darkening, darkened**) make or become dark.

darling *noun* (*plural* **darlings**) someone who is loved very much. [from Old English *deorling* = little dear]

darn *verb* (**darns, darning, darned**) mend a hole by weaving threads across it.

darn *noun* (*plural* **darns**) a place that has been darned. [from Old English *diernan* = hide]

dart *noun* (*plural* **darts**) 1 an object with a sharp point, thrown at a target. 2 a darting movement. 3 a tapering tuck stitched in something to make it fit.

dart *verb* (**darts, darting, darted**) run suddenly and quickly.

darts noun a game in which darts are thrown at a circular board (**dartboard**).

dash verb (**dashes, dashing, dashed**)
1 run quickly; rush. 2 throw a thing violently against something, *The storm dashed the ship against the rocks.*

dash noun (plural **dashes**)
1 a short quick run; a rush. 2 energy or liveliness. 3 a small amount, *Add a dash of brandy.* 4 a short line (—) used in writing or printing. [origin unknown]

dashboard noun (plural **dashboards**) a panel with dials and controls in front of the driver of a car etc. [originally a board on the front of a carriage to keep out mud, which dashed against it]

dashing adjective lively and showy.

data (say **day**-ta) noun pieces of information.

USAGE: Strictly speaking, this word is a plural noun (the singular is *datum*), so it should be used with a plural verb: *Here are the data.* However, the word is widely used nowadays as if it were a singular noun and most people do not regard this as wrong: *Here is the data.*

database noun (plural **databases**) a store of information held in a computer.

date[1] noun (plural **dates**)
1 the time when something happens or happened or was written, stated as the day, month, and year (or any of these). 2 an appointment to meet someone,

especially someone of the opposite sex.

date verb (**dates, dating, dated**)
1 give a date to something. 2 have existed from a particular time, *The church dates from 1684.* 3 seem old-fashioned.
[from Latin *data* = given (at a certain time)]

date[2] noun (plural **dates**) a small sweet brown fruit that grows on a kind of palm tree. [from Greek]

daub verb (**daubs, daubing, daubed**) paint or smear something clumsily. **daub** noun [from Latin *dealbare* = whitewash, plaster]

daughter noun (plural **daughters**) a girl or woman who is someone's child.

daughter-in-law noun (plural **daughters-in-law**) a son's wife.

daunt verb (**daunts, daunting, daunted**) make somebody afraid or discouraged. [from Latin *domitare* = to tame]

dawdle verb (**dawdles, dawdling, dawdled**) go slowly and lazily. **dawdler** noun

dawn noun (plural **dawns**) the time when the sun rises.

dawn verb (**dawns, dawning, dawned**)
1 begin to grow light in the morning. 2 begin to be realized, *The truth dawned on them.* [from Old English]

day noun (plural **days**)
1 the 24 hours between midnight and the next midnight. 2 the light part of this time. 3 a particular day, *sports day.* 4 a period of time, *in Queen Victoria's day.*

daybreak noun dawn.

daydream noun (plural **daydreams**) pleasant thoughts of something you would like to happen.

daydream verb (**daydreams**, **daydreaming**, **daydreamed**) have daydreams.

dazed adjective unable to think or see clearly. **daze** noun [from Old Norse *dasathr* = weary]

dazzle verb (**dazzles**, **dazzling**, **dazzled**)
1 make a person unable to see clearly because of too much bright light. **2** amaze or impress a person by a splendid display. [from *daze*]

de- prefix
1 removing (as in *defrost*). **2** down, away (as in *descend*). **3** completely (as in *denude*). [from old French; related to *dis-*]

dead adjective
1 no longer alive. **2** not lively. **3** not functioning; no longer in use. **4** exact or complete, *a dead loss*. [from Old English]

deaden verb (**deadens**, **deadening**, **deadened**) make pain or noise etc. weaker.

dead end noun (plural **dead ends**)
1 a road or passage with one end closed. **2** a situation where there is no chance of making progress.

dead heat noun (plural **dead heats**) a race in which two or more winners finish exactly together.

deadline noun (plural **deadlines**) a time limit. [originally this meant a line round an American military prison; if prisoners went beyond it they could be shot]

deadlock noun (plural **deadlocks**) a situation in which no progress can be made. [from *dead* + *lock*[1]]

deadly adjective (**deadlier**, **deadliest**) likely to kill.

deaf adjective
1 unable to hear. **2** unwilling to hear. **deafness** noun [from Old English]

deafen verb (**deafens**, **deafening**, **deafened**) make somebody become deaf, especially by a very loud noise.

deal verb (**deals**, **dealing**, **dealt**)
1 hand something out; give. **2** give out cards for a card game. **3** do business; trade, *He deals in scrap metal*. **dealer** noun

deal with 1 be concerned with, *This book deals with words and meanings*. **2** do what is needed, *deal with the problem*.

deal noun (plural **deals**)
1 an agreement or bargain.
2 someone's turn to deal at cards.
a good deal or **a great deal** a large amount.
[from Old English *daelan* = divide, share out]

dear adjective
1 loved very much. **2** a polite greeting in letters, *Dear Sir*. **3** expensive. **dearly** adverb [from Old English]

death noun (plural **deaths**) dying; the end of life. [from Old English]

debatable adjective questionable; that can be argued against.

debate noun (plural **debates**) a formal discussion.

debate verb (**debates**, **debating**, **debated**) hold a debate. **debater** noun

debilitating *adjective* causing weakness.

debit *noun* (*plural* **debits**) an entry in an account-book showing how much money is owed. (Compare *credit*.)

debris (*say* deb-ree) *noun* scattered broken pieces of something; rubbish left behind. [from French *débris* = broken down]

debt (*say* det) *noun* (*plural* **debts**) something that you owe someone.
in debt owing money etc.
[same origin as *debit*]

debtor (*say* det-or) *noun* (*plural* **debtors**) a person who owes money to someone.

deca- *prefix* ten (as in *decathlon*). [from Greek]

decade (*say* dek-ayd) *noun* (*plural* **decades**) a period of ten years. [from old French]

decadent (*say* dek-a-dent) *adjective* falling to a lower standard of morality. **decadence** *noun* [same origin as *decay*]

decaffeinated *adjective* (of coffee or tea) with the caffeine removed.

decapitate *verb* (**decapitates, decapitating, decapitated**) cut someone's head off; behead.
decapitation *noun* [from *de-* + Latin *caput* = head]

decathlon *noun* (*plural* **decathlons**) an athletic contest in which each competitor takes part in ten events. [from *deca-* + Greek *athlon* = contest]

decay *verb* (**decays, decaying, decayed**)
1 go bad; rot. **2** become less good or less strong. **decay** *noun* [from old French *decair* = fall down]

deceased *adjective* dead.

deceit (*say* dis-eet) *noun* (*plural* **deceits**) making a person believe something that is not true.
deceitful *adjective*, **deceitfully** *adverb*

deceive *verb* (**deceives, deceiving, deceived**) make a person believe something that is not true.
deceiver *noun* [from Latin]

decent *adjective*
1 respectable and honest.
2 reasonable or adequate.
3 (*informal*) kind. **decently** *adverb*, **decency** *noun* [from Latin]

deception *noun* (*plural* **deceptions**) deceiving someone.
deceptive *adjective*, **deceptively** *adverb*

deci- (*say* dess-ee) *prefix* one-tenth (as in *decimetre*). [same origin as *decimal*]

decibel (*say* dess-ib-el) *noun* (*plural* **decibels**) a unit for measuring the loudness of sound. [originally one-tenth of the unit called a *bel*]

decide *verb* (**decides, deciding, decided**)
1 make up your mind; make a choice. **2** settle a contest or argument. **decider** *noun* [from Latin]

decided *adjective*
1 having clear and definite opinions. **2** noticeable, *a decided difference*. **decidedly** *adverb*

deciduous (say dis-**id**-yoo-us) *adjective* a deciduous tree is one that loses its leaves in autumn. [from Latin *decidere* = fall off]

decimal *adjective* using tens or tenths.

decimal *noun* (*plural* **decimals**) a decimal fraction. [from Latin *decimus* = tenth]

decimal fraction *noun* (*plural* **decimal fractions**) a fraction with tenths shown as numbers after a dot ($\frac{3}{10}$ is 0.3; $1\frac{1}{2}$ is 1.5).

decimal point *noun* (*plural* **decimal points**) the dot in a decimal fraction.

decipher (say dis-**I**-fer) *verb* (**deciphers**, **deciphering**, **deciphered**) 1 decode. 2 work out the meaning of something written badly.

decision *noun* (*plural* **decisions**) 1 deciding; what you have decided. 2 determination.

decisive (say dis-**I**-siv) *adjective* 1 that settles or ends something, *a decisive battle*. 2 full of determination; resolute. **decisively** *adverb*, **decisiveness** *noun*

deck *noun* (*plural* **decks**) 1 a floor on a ship or bus. 2 a pack of playing cards. 3 a turntable on a record player.

deckchair *noun* (*plural* **deckchairs**) a folding chair with a canvas or plastic seat. [because they were used on the decks of passenger ships]

declaim *verb* (**declaims**, **declaiming**, **declaimed**) make a speech etc. loudly and dramatically. **declamation** *noun* [from *de-* + Latin *clamare* = to shout]

declare *verb* (**declares**, **declaring**, **declared**) 1 say something clearly or firmly. 2 tell customs officials that you have goods on which you ought to pay duty. 3 end a cricket innings before all the batsmen are out. **declaration** *noun*

declare war announce that you are starting a war against someone. [from *de-* + Latin *clarare* = make clear]

decline *verb* (**declines**, **declining**, **declined**) 1 refuse. 2 become weaker or smaller. 3 slope downwards. 4 state the forms of a noun, pronoun, or adjective that correspond to particular cases, numbers, and genders.

decline *noun* (*plural* **declines**) a gradual decrease or loss of strength. [from *de-* + Latin *clinare* = bend]

decode *verb* (**decodes**, **decoding**, **decoded**) work out the meaning of something written in code. **decoder** *noun*

decompose *verb* (**decomposes**, **decomposing**, **decomposed**) decay. **decomposition** *noun*

decorate *verb* (**decorates**, **decorating**, **decorated**) 1 make something look more beautiful or colourful. 2 put fresh paint or paper on walls. 3 give somebody a medal. **decoration** *noun*, **decorator** *noun*, **decorative** *adjective* [from Latin *decor* = beauty]

decorous (say **dek**-er-us) *adjective* polite and dignified.

decorously adverb [from Latin decorus = suitable, proper]

decoy (say dee-koi) noun (plural **decoys**) something used to tempt a person or animal into a trap or into danger.

decoy (say dik-oi) verb (**decoys, decoying, decoyed**) tempt a person or animal into a trap etc.

decrease verb (**decreases, decreasing, decreased**) make or become smaller or fewer.

decrease noun (plural **decreases**) decreasing; the amount by which something decreases.
[from de- + Latin crescere = grow]

decree noun (plural **decrees**) an official order or decision.

decree verb (**decrees, decreeing, decreed**) make a decree.
[from Latin decretum = what has been decided]

decrepit (say dik-rep-it) adjective old and weak. **decrepitude** noun [from Latin decrepitus = creaking]

dedicate verb (**dedicates, dedicating, dedicated**)
1 devote to a special use, She dedicated herself to her work.
2 name a person as a mark of respect, e.g. at the beginning of a book. **dedication** noun [from Latin]

deduce verb (**deduces, deducing, deduced**) work something out by reasoning. **deducible** adjective [from de- + Latin ducere = to lead]

deduct verb (**deducts, deducting, deducted**) subtract part of something. [same origin as deduce]

deduction noun (plural **deductions**)
1 deducting; something deducted.
2 deducing; something deduced.

deed noun (plural **deeds**)
1 something that someone has done; an act. 2 a legal document. [from Old English]

deep adjective
1 going a long way down or back or in, a deep well; deep cupboards.
2 measured from top to bottom or front to back, a hole six feet deep.
3 intense or strong, deep colours; deep feelings. 4 low-pitched, not shrill, a deep voice. **deeply** adverb, **deepness** noun

deepen verb (**deepens, deepening, deepened**) make or become deeper.

deer noun (plural **deer**) a fast-running graceful animal, the male of which usually has antlers. [from Old English deor = an animal]

deface verb (**defaces, defacing, defaced**) spoil the surface of something, e.g. by scribbling on it. **defacement** noun

defeat verb (**defeats, defeating, defeated**)
1 win a victory over someone.
2 baffle; be too difficult for someone.

defeat noun (plural **defeats**)
1 defeating someone. 2 being defeated; a lost game or battle. [from Latin disfacere = undo, destroy]

defect (say dee-ekt or dee-fekt) noun (plural **defects**) a flaw.

defect (say dif-ekt) verb (**defects, defecting, defected**) desert your own country etc. and join the enemy. **defection** noun,

defector noun
[from Latin *deficere* = fail, leave, undo]

defective adjective having defects; incomplete.
defectiveness noun

defence noun (plural **defences**)
1 defending something.
2 something that defends or protects. 3 a reply put forward by a defendant.

defend verb (defends, defending, defended)
1 protect, especially against an attack. 2 try to prove that a statement is true or that an accused person is not guilty.
defender noun [from Latin]

defendant noun (plural **defendants**) a person accused of something in a lawcourt.

defensive adjective used or done for defence; protective.
defensively adverb
on the defensive ready to defend yourself.

defer[1] verb (defers, deferring, deferred) postpone. **deferment** noun, **deferral** noun [from old French; related to *differ*]

defer[2] verb (defers, deferring, deferred) give way to a person's wishes or authority; yield. [from Latin]

deference (say def-er-ens) noun polite respect. **deferential** (say def-er-en-shal) adjective, **deferentially** adverb [from *defer*[2]]

defiant adjective defying; openly disobedient. **defiantly** adverb, **defiance** noun

deficiency noun (plural **deficiencies**)
1 a lack or shortage. 2 a defect.
deficient adjective [same origin as *defect*]

defile verb (defiles, defiling, defiled) make a thing dirty or impure. **defilement** noun [from an old word *defoul*]

define verb (defines, defining, defined)
1 explain what a word or phrase means. 2 show clearly what something is; specify. 3 show a thing's outline. **definable** adjective [from de- + Latin *finis* = limit]

definite adjective
1 clearly stated; exact, *Fix a definite time.* 2 certain or settled, *Is it definite that we are to move?* **definitely** adverb
definite article the word 'the'.
[from Latin *definitus* = defined]

definition noun (plural **definitions**)
1 a statement of what a word or phrase means or of what a thing is. 2 being distinct; clearness of outline (e.g. in a photograph).

deflate verb (deflates, deflating, deflated)
1 let out air from a tyre or balloon etc. 2 make someone feel less proud or less confident.
3 reduce or reverse inflation.
deflation noun, **deflationary** adjective [from de- + *inflate*]

deflect verb (deflects, deflecting, deflected) make something turn aside. **deflection** noun, **deflector** noun [from de- + Latin *flectere* = bend]

deforest verb (**deforests, deforesting, deforested**) clear away the trees from an area. **deforestation** noun

deform verb (**deforms, deforming, deformed**) spoil a thing's shape or appearance. **deformation** noun [from de- + Latin forma = shape, form]

deft adjective skilful and quick. **deftly** adverb, **deftness** noun [from Old English]

defuse verb (**defuses, defusing, defused**)
1 remove the fuse from a bomb etc. 2 make a situation less dangerous or tense.

defy verb (**defies, defying, defied**)
1 resist something openly; refuse to obey, They defied the law.
2 challenge a person to do something you believe cannot be done, I defy you to prove this.
3 prevent something being done, The door defied all efforts to open it. [from de- + Latin fidus = faithful]

degenerate verb (**degenerates, degenerating, degenerated**) become worse, especially morally. **degeneration** noun

degenerate adjective having become immoral or bad. **degeneracy** noun [from Latin]

degrade verb (**degrades, degrading, degraded**)
1 humiliate or dishonour someone. 2 reduce to a simpler molecular form. **degradation** (say deg-ra-**day**-shon) noun [from de- + Latin gradus = grade]

degree noun (plural **degrees**)
1 a unit for measuring temperature. 2 a unit for measuring angles. 3 extent, to some degree. 4 an award to someone at a university or college who has successfully finished a course. [from de- + Latin gradus = grade]

dehydrated adjective dried up, with all moisture removed. **dehydration** noun [from de- + Greek hydor = water]

deity (say dee-it-ee or day-it-ee) noun (plural **deities**) a god or goddess. [from Latin deus = god]

dejected adjective sad or depressed. **dejectedly** adverb, **dejection** noun [from de- + Latin -jectum = cast]

delay verb (**delays, delaying, delayed**)
1 make someone or something late. 2 postpone.

delay noun (plural **delays**) delaying; the time for which something is delayed, a two-hour delay.

delegate (say del-ig-at) noun (plural **delegates**) a person who represents others and acts on their instructions.

delegate (say del-ig-ayt) verb (**delegates, delegating, delegated**)
1 appoint someone as a delegate, We delegated Jones to represent us. 2 entrust, We delegated the work to Jones.
[from Latin delegare = entrust]

delegation (say del-ig-ay-shon) noun (plural **delegations**)
1 delegating. 2 a group of delegates.

deliberate (say dil-ib-er-at) adjective
1 done on purpose; intentional.
2 slow and careful. **deliberately** adverb

deliberate (say dil-**ib**-er-ayt) *verb* (**deliberates, deliberating, deliberated**) discuss or think carefully. **deliberation** *noun* [from *de-* + Latin *librare* = weigh]

delicacy *noun* (*plural* **delicacies**) 1 being delicate. 2 a delicious food.

delicate *adjective* 1 fine and graceful, *delicate embroidery*. 2 fragile and easily damaged. 3 pleasant and not strong or intense. 4 becoming ill easily. 5 using or needing great care, *a delicate situation*. **delicately** *adverb*, **delicateness** *noun* [from Latin]

delicious *adjective* tasting or smelling very pleasant. **deliciously** *adverb* [from Latin]

delight *verb* (**delights, delighting, delighted**) 1 please someone greatly. 2 take great pleasure in something.

delight *noun* (*plural* **delights**) great pleasure. **delightful** *adjective*, **delightfully** *adverb* [from Latin *delectare* = entice]

delinquent (say dil-**ing**-kwent) *noun* (*plural* **delinquents**) someone who breaks the law or commits an offence. **delinquent** *adjective*, **delinquency** *noun* [from Latin *delinquere* = offend]

delirium (say dil-**irri**-um) *noun* 1 a state of mental confusion and agitation during a feverish illness. 2 wild excitement. **delirious** *adjective*, **deliriously** *adverb* [Latin, = deranged]

deliver *verb* (**delivers, delivering, delivered**) 1 take letters or goods etc. to someone's house or place of work. 2 give a speech or lecture etc.

3 help with the birth of a baby. 4 aim or strike a blow or an attack. 5 rescue; set free. **deliverer** *noun*, **deliverance** *noun*, **delivery** *noun* [from *de-* + Latin *liberare* = set free]

delta *noun* (*plural* **deltas**) a triangular area at the mouth of a river where it spreads into branches. [shaped like the Greek letter delta (= D), written Δ]

delude *verb* (**deludes, deluding, deluded**) deceive or mislead someone. [from Latin *deludere* = play unfairly]

deluge *noun* (*plural* **deluges**) 1 a large flood. 2 a heavy fall of rain. 3 something coming in great numbers, *a deluge of questions*.

deluge *verb* (**deluges, deluging, deluged**) overwhelm by a deluge. [from old French]

delusion *noun* (*plural* **delusions**) a false belief.

demagogue (say **dem**-a-gog) *noun* (*plural* **demagogues**) a leader who wins support by making emotional speeches rather than by careful reasoning. [from Greek *demos* = people + *agogos* = leading]

demand *verb* (**demands, demanding, demanded**) 1 ask for something firmly or forcefully. 2 need, *It demands skill*.

demand *noun* (*plural* **demands**) 1 a firm or forceful request. 2 a desire to have or buy something, *There is a great demand for computers*. **in demand** wanted or needed. [from *de-* + Latin *mandare* = to order]

demarcation (say dee-mar-**kay**-shon) noun marking the boundary or limits of something. [from Spanish]

demented adjective driven mad; crazy. [from de- + Latin mentis = of the mind]

demi- prefix half (as in demisemiquaver). [from French]

demigod noun (plural demigods) a partly divine being.

democracy noun (plural democracies)
1 government of a country by representatives elected by the whole people. 2 a country governed in this way. **democrat** noun, **democratic** adjective, **democratically** adverb [from Greek demos = people, + -cracy]

Democrat noun (plural Democrats) a member of the Democratic Party in the USA.

demolish verb (demolishes, demolishing, demolished)
1 knock a building down and break it up. 2 destroy something completely. **demolition** noun [from de- + Latin moliri = build]

demon noun (plural demons)
1 a devil; an evil spirit. 2 a fierce or forceful person. **demonic** (say dim-on-ik) adjective [from Greek daimon = a spirit]

demonstrate verb (demonstrates, demonstrating, demonstrated)
1 show or prove something. 2 take part in a demonstration. **demonstrator** noun [from de- + Latin monstrare = to show]

demonstration noun (plural demonstrations)
1 demonstrating; showing how to do or work something. 2 a meeting or procession etc. held to show everyone what you think about something.

demonstrative (say dim-on-strat-iv) adjective
1 showing or proving something. 2 showing feelings or affections openly. 3 (in grammar) pointing out the person or thing referred to. This, that, these, and those are demonstrative adjectives and pronouns. **demonstratively** adverb, **demonstrativeness** noun

demoralize verb (demoralizes, demoralizing, demoralized) dishearten someone; weaken someone's confidence or morale. **demoralization** noun [from de- + morale]

demote verb (demotes, demoting, demoted) reduce a person to a lower position or rank. **demotion** noun [from de- + promote]

demure adjective shy and modest. **demurely** adverb, **demureness** noun [origin unknown]

den noun (plural dens)
1 a lair. 2 a person's private room. 3 a place where something illegal happens, a gambling den. [from Old English]

denial noun (plural denials) denying or refusing something.

denim noun a kind of strong, usually blue, cotton cloth used to make jeans etc. [from French serge de Nim = serge from Nimes (a town in southern France)]

denomination noun (plural denominations)
1 a name or title. 2 a religious group with a special name, Baptists, Methodists, and other denominations. 3 a unit of weight

or of money, *coins of small denomination.* [from *de-* + Latin *nominare* = to name]

denominator *noun (plural* **denominators)** the number below the line in a fraction, showing how many parts the whole is divided into, e.g. 4 in ¼. (Compare *numerator.*)

denounce *verb* (**denounces, denouncing, denounced**) speak strongly against something; accuse, *They denounced him as a spy.* **denunciation** *noun* [from *de-* + Latin *nuntiare* = announce]

dense *adjective*
1 thick; packed close together, *dense fog.* **2** stupid. **densely** *adverb* [from Latin]

density *noun (plural* **densities)**
1 thickness. **2** (in physics) the proportion of mass to volume.

dent *noun (plural* **dents)** a hollow left in a surface where something has pressed or hit it.

dent *verb* (**dents, denting, dented**) make a dent in something.

dental *adjective* to do with the teeth or with dentistry. [from Latin *dentalis* = to do with a tooth]

dentist *noun (plural* **dentists)** a person who is trained to treat teeth, fill or extract them, fit false ones, etc. **dentistry** *noun* [from French *dent* = tooth]

denture *noun (plural* **dentures)** a set of false teeth. [French]

denude *verb* (**denudes, denuding, denuded**) make bare or naked; strip something away. **denudation** *noun* [from *de-* + Latin *nudare* = to bare]

denunciation *noun (plural* **denunciations)** denouncing.

deny *verb* (**denies, denying, denied**)
1 say that something is not true. **2** refuse to give or allow something, *deny a request.* [from *de-* + Latin *negare* = say no]

deodorant *(say* dee-**oh**-der-ant*)* *noun (plural* **deodorants)** a substance that removes smells.

depart *verb* (**departs, departing, departed**) go away; leave.

departure *noun* [from old French *départir* = separate]

department *noun (plural* **departments)** one section of a large organization or shop. **departmental** *adjective* [from French *département* = division]

depend *verb* (**depends, depending, depended**)
depend on 1 rely on, *We depend on your help.* **2** be controlled by something else, *Whether we can picnic depends on the weather.* [from *de-* + Latin *pendere* = hang]

dependant *noun (plural* **dependants)** a person who depends on another, especially financially, *She has two dependants.*

USAGE: Note that the spelling ends in -*ant* for this noun but -*ent* for the adjective *dependent.*

---

dependent *adjective* depending, *She has two dependent children; they are dependent on her.* **dependence** *noun*

deplore *verb* (**deplores, deploring, deplored**) be very upset or annoyed by something.

deplorable *adjective*, **deplorably** *adverb* [from *de-* + Latin *plorare* = weep]

deport *verb* (**deports**, **deporting**, **deported**) send an unwanted foreign person out of a country. **deportation** *noun* [from *de-* + Latin *portare* = carry]

depose *verb* (**deposes**, **deposing**, **deposed**) remove a person from power. [from old French *deposer* = put down]

deposit *noun* (*plural* **deposits**) 1 an amount of money paid into a bank etc. 2 money paid as a first instalment. 3 a layer of solid matter in or on the earth.

deposit *verb* (**deposits**, **depositing**, **deposited**) 1 put something down. 2 pay money as a deposit. **depositor** *noun* [from *de-* + Latin *positum* = placed]

depot (*say* **dep**-oh) *noun* (*plural* **depots**) 1 a place where things are stored. 2 a headquarters. [same origin as *deposit*]

depraved *adjective* behaving wickedly; of bad character. **depravity** *noun* [from *de-* + Latin *pravus* = perverse, wrong]

depress *verb* (**depresses**, **depressing**, **depressed**) 1 make somebody sad. 2 lower the value of something, *Threat of war depressed prices.* 3 press down, *Depress the lever.* **depressive** *adjective*

depression *noun* (*plural* **depressions**) 1 a great sadness or feeling of hopelessness. 2 a long period when trade is very slack because fewer people can afford to buy things. 3 a shallow hollow in the ground or on a surface. 4 an area of low air pressure which may bring rain. 5 pressing something down.

deprive *verb* (**deprives**, **depriving**, **deprived**) take or keep something away from somebody. **deprival** *noun*, **deprivation** *noun* [from *de-* + Latin *privare* = rob]

depth *noun* (*plural* **depths**) 1 being deep; how deep something is. 2 the deepest or lowest part.
in depth thoroughly.
out of your depth 1 in water that is too deep to stand in. 2 trying to do something that is too difficult for you. [from *deep*]

deputation *noun* (*plural* **deputations**) a group of people sent as representatives of others.

deputy *noun* (*plural* **deputies**) a person appointed to act as a substitute for another.

deranged *adjective* insane. **derangement** *noun* [from *de-* + French *rang* = rank]

derelict (*say* derri-likt) *adjective* abandoned and left to fall into ruin. **dereliction** *noun* [from *de-* + Latin *relictum* = left behind]

deride *verb* (**derides**, **deriding**, **derided**) laugh at with contempt or scorn; ridicule. **derision** *noun* [from *de-* + Latin *ridere* = to laugh]

derive *verb* (**derives**, **deriving**, **derived**) 1 obtain something from a source, *She derived great enjoyment from music.* 2 form or originate from something, *Some English words are derived from Latin words.*

derivation *noun*, **derivative**
adjective [from *de-* + Latin *rivus*
= a stream]

descend *verb* (**descends**,
descending, **descended**) go down.
descent *noun*

be descended from have as an
ancestor; come by birth from
a certain person or family.
[from *de-* + Latin *scandere*
= climb]

descendant *noun* (*plural*
descendants) a person who is
descended from someone.

describe *verb* (**describes**,
describing, **described**)
1 say what someone or
something is like. **2** draw in
outline; move in a pattern, *The
orbit of the Earth around the Sun
describes an ellipse*. **description**
noun, **descriptive** *adjective* [from
de- + Latin *scribere* = write]

desert (*say* dez-ert) *noun* (*plural*
deserts) a large area of dry often
sandy land.

desert (*say* diz-ert) *verb* (**deserts**,
deserting, **deserted**) abandon;
leave a person or place without
intending to return. **deserter**
noun, **desertion** *noun*
[from Latin *desertus*
= abandoned]

desert island *noun* (*plural* **desert
islands**) an uninhabited island.

deserve *verb* (**deserves**,
deserving, **deserved**) have a right
to something; be worthy of
something. **deservedly** *adverb*
[from Latin *deservire* = serve
someone well]

design *noun* (*plural* **designs**)
1 a drawing that shows how
something is to be made.

2 the way something is made or
arranged. **3** lines and shapes that
form a decoration; a pattern. **4** a
mental plan or scheme.
have designs on plan to get hold
of.

design *verb* (**designs**, **designing**,
designed)
1 draw a design for something.
2 plan or intend something for a
special purpose. **designer** *noun*
[from *de-* + Latin *signare* = mark
out]

desirable *adjective*
1 causing people to desire it;
worth having. **2** worth doing;
advisable. **desirability** *noun*

desire *noun* (*plural* **desires**)
a feeling of wanting something
very much. **desirous** *adjective*

desire *verb* (**desires**, **desiring**,
desired) have a desire for
something.
[from Latin]

desk *noun* (*plural* **desks**)
1 a piece of furniture with a flat
top and often drawers, used when
writing or reading etc. **2** a counter
at which a cashier or receptionist
sits. [from Latin]

desolate *adjective*
1 lonely and sad. **2** uninhabited.
desolation *noun* [from Latin
desolare = abandon]

despair *noun* a feeling of
hopelessness.

despair *verb* (**despairs**,
despairing, **despaired**) feel
despair.
[from *de-* + Latin *sperare* = to
hope]

desperate *adjective*
1 extremely serious; hopeless,
a desperate situation. **2** reckless

and ready to do anything.
desperately adverb, **desperation**
noun [same origin as despair]

despise verb (**despises**, **despising**,
despised) think someone or
something is inferior or
worthless. [from de- + Latin
-spicere = to look]

despite preposition in spite of.
[same origin as despise]

despondent adjective sad or
gloomy. **despondently** adverb,
despondency noun [from Latin
despondere = give up, resign]

dessert (say diz-ert) noun (plural
desserts) fruit or a sweet food
served as the last course of
a meal. [from French desservir
= clear the table]

destination noun (plural
destinations) the place to which
a person or thing is travelling.
[same origin as destiny]

destined adjective having as
a destiny; intended.

destiny noun (plural **destinies**)
what will happen or has
happened to somebody or
something; fate. [from Latin
destinare = fix, settle]

destitute adjective left without
anything; living in extreme
poverty. **destitution** noun [from
Latin destitutus = left in the
lurch]

destroy verb (**destroys**,
destroying, **destroyed**) ruin or
put an end to something.
destruction noun, **destructive**
adjective [from de- + Latin struere
= pile up]

destroyer noun (plural
destroyers) a fast warship.

detach verb (**detaches**, **detaching**,
detached) unfasten or separate.
detachable adjective, **detachment**
noun [from de- + attach]

detached adjective
1 separated. 2 not prejudiced; not
involved in something.

detail noun (plural **details**)
1 a very small part of a design or
plan or decoration etc. 2 a small
piece of information. **detailed**
adjective [from de- + French
tailler = cut in pieces]

detain verb (**detains**, **detaining**,
detained)
1 keep someone waiting. 2 keep
someone at a place. **detention**
noun [from de- + Latin tenere
= hold]

detect verb (**detects**, **detecting**,
detected) discover. **detection**
noun, **detector** noun [from de-
+ Latin tegere = cover]

detective noun (plural
detectives) a person who
investigates crimes.

detention noun (plural
detentions)
1 detaining; being detained.
2 being made to stay late in
school as a punishment. [same
origin as detain]

deter verb (**deters**, **deterring**,
deterred) discourage or prevent
a person from doing something.
deterrent noun [from de- + Latin
terrere = frighten]

detergent noun (plural
detergents) a substance used for
cleaning or washing things.
[from de- + Latin tergere
= to clean]

deteriorate (say dit-**eer**-ee-er-ayt) verb (deteriorates, deteriorating, deteriorated) become worse.
deterioration noun [from Latin *deterior* = worse]

determination noun
1 the firm intention to achieve what you have decided to achieve. 2 determining or deciding something.

determine verb (determines, determining, determined)
1 decide, *determine what is to be done*. 2 find out; calculate, *determine the height of the mountain*. [from *de-* + Latin *terminare* = to limit]

determined adjective full of determination; with your mind firmly made up.

detest verb (detests, detesting, detested) dislike something very much; loathe. **detestable** adjective, **detestation** noun

detonate (say **det**-on-ayt) verb (detonates, detonating, detonated) explode or cause something to explode. **detonation** noun, **detonator** noun [from *de-* + Latin *tonare* = to thunder]

detour (say **dee**-toor) noun (plural detours) a roundabout route instead of the normal one. [from French *détourner* = turn away]

detriment (say **det**-rim-ent) noun harm or disadvantage, *She worked long hours, to the detriment of her health.* [from Latin *detrimentum* = worn away]

detrimental (say det-rim-**en**-tal) adjective harmful or disadvantageous. **detrimentally** adverb

deuce noun (plural deuces) a score in tennis where both sides have 40 points and must gain two consecutive points to win. [from old French *deus* = two]

devalue verb (devalues, devaluing, devalued)
1 reduce a thing's value. 2 reduce the value of a country's currency in relation to other currencies or to gold. **devaluation** noun

devastate verb (devastates, devastating, devastated) ruin or cause great destruction to something. **devastation** noun [from Latin]

develop verb (develops, developing, developed)
1 make or become bigger or better. 2 come gradually into existence, *Storms developed.* 3 begin to have or use, *They developed bad habits.* 4 use an area of land for building houses, shops, factories, etc. 5 treat photographic film with chemicals so that pictures appear. **developer** noun, **development** noun [from French]

deviate (say **dee**-vee-ayt) verb (deviates, deviating, deviated) turn aside from a course or from what is usual or true. **deviation** noun [from *de-* + Latin *via* = way]

device noun (plural devices)
1 something made for a particular purpose, *a device for opening tins.* 2 a design used as a decoration or emblem.
leave someone to their own devices leave them to do as they wish.
[same origin as *devise*]

devil noun (plural **devils**)
1 an evil spirit. 2 a wicked, cruel, or annoying person. **devilish** adjective, **devilry** noun [via Old English from Latin]

devilment noun mischief.

devious (say dee-vee-us) adjective
1 roundabout; not direct, a devious route. 2 not straightforward; underhand. **deviously** adverb, **deviousness** noun [same origin as deviate]

devise verb (**devises**, **devising**, **devised**) invent or plan. [from old French]

devoid adjective lacking or without something, His work is devoid of merit. [from de- + old French voider = make void]

devolution noun handing over power from central government to local or regional government. [same origin as devolve]

devolve verb (**devolves**, **devolving**, **devolved**) pass or be passed to a deputy or successor. [from Latin devolvere = roll down]

devote verb (**devotes**, **devoting**, **devoted**) give completely, He devoted his time to sport. [from de- + Latin vovere = to vow]

devoted adjective very loving or loyal.

devotee (say dev-o-tee) noun (plural **devotees**) a person who is devoted to something; an enthusiast.

devotion noun great love or loyalty.

devotions plural noun prayers.

devour verb (**devours**, **devouring**, **devoured**) eat or swallow something hungrily or greedily. [from de- + Latin vorare = to swallow]

devout adjective earnestly religious or sincere. **devoutly** adverb, **devoutness** noun [same origin as devote]

dew noun tiny drops of water that form during the night on surfaces of things in the open air. **dewdrop** noun, **dewy** adjective [from Old English]

dexterity (say deks-terri-tee) noun skill in handling things. [from Latin dexter = on the right-hand side]

dhoti noun (plural **dhotis**) the loincloth worn by male Hindus. [Hindi]

di-¹ prefix two; double (as in dioxide). [from Greek dis = twice]

di-² prefix
1 not; the reverse of. 2 apart; separated. see dis-.

dia- prefix through (as in diarrhoea); across (as in diagonal). [from Greek dia = through]

diabetes (say dy-a-bee-teez) noun a disease in which there is too much sugar in a person's blood. **diabetic** (say dy-a-bet-ik) adjective & noun [from Greek]

diabolical adjective
1 like a devil; very wicked. 2 very clever or annoying. [from Latin diabolus = devil]

diadem (say dy-a-dem) noun (plural **diadems**) a crown or headband worn by a royal person. [from Greek]

diagnose verb (diagnoses, diagnosing, diagnosed) find out what disease a person has or what is wrong. **diagnosis** noun, **diagnostic** adjective [from dia- + Greek gignoskein = know]

diagonal (say dy-ag-on-al) noun (plural diagonals) a straight line joining opposite corners. **diagonal** adjective, **diagonally** adverb [from dia- + Greek gonia = angle]

diagram noun (plural diagrams) a kind of drawing or picture that shows the parts of something or how it works. [from dia- + -gram]

dial noun (plural dials) a circular object with numbers or letters round it.

dial verb (dials, dialling, dialled) telephone a number by turning a telephone dial or pressing numbered buttons. [from Latin diale = clock-face, from dies = day]

dialect noun (plural dialects) the words and pronunciations used by people in one district but not in the rest of a country. [from Greek dialektos = way of speaking]

dialogue noun (plural dialogues) a conversation. [from Greek]

dialysis (say dy-al-iss-iss) noun a way of removing harmful substances from the blood by letting it flow through a machine. [from dia- + Greek lysis = loosening]

diameter (say dy-am-it-er) noun (plural diameters) 1 a line drawn straight across a circle or sphere and passing through its centre. 2 the length of this line. [from Greek diametros = measuring across]

diametrically adverb completely, diametrically opposite.

diamond noun (plural diamonds) 1 a very hard precious stone, a form of carbon, that looks like clear glass. 2 a shape with four equal sides and four angles that are not right angles. 3 a playing card with red diamond shapes on it. [from Greek adamas = adamant (= a very hard stone)]

diaper noun (plural diapers) (American) a baby's nappy. [from Greek diaspros = made of white cloth]

diaphanous (say dy-af-an-us) adjective (of fabric) almost transparent. [from dia- + Greek phainein = to show]

diaphragm (say dy-a-fram) noun (plural diaphragms) 1 the muscular layer inside the body that separates the chest from the abdomen and is used in breathing. 2 a dome-shaped contraceptive device that fits over the cervix. [from dia- + Greek phragma = fence]

diarist noun (plural diarists) a person who keeps a diary.

diarrhoea (say dy-a-ree-a) noun too frequent and too watery emptying of the bowels. [from dia- + Greek rhoia = a flow]

diary noun (plural diaries) a book in which someone writes down what happens each day. [from Latin dies = day]

diatribe noun (plural diatribes) a strong verbal attack. [French]

dice noun (strictly this is the plural of **die²**, but it is often used as a singular, plural **dice**) a small cube marked with dots (1 to 6) on its sides, used in games.

dice verb (**dices, dicing, diced**)
1 cut meat, vegetables, etc. into small cubes. **2** gamble or take risks with, *dice with death*. [plural of *die²*]

dictate verb (**dictates, dictating, dictated**)
1 speak or read something aloud for someone else to write down. **2** give orders in a bossy way.
dictation noun [from Latin *dictare* = keep saying]

dictates (say **dik**-tayts) plural noun orders or commands.

dictator noun (plural **dictators**) a ruler who has unlimited power.
dictatorial (say dik-ta-**tor**-ee-al) adjective, **dictatorship** noun

diction noun a person's way of speaking words, *clear diction*. [from Latin *dictio* = saying, word]

dictionary noun (plural **dictionaries**) a book that contains words in alphabetical order so that you can find out how to spell them and what they mean. [same origin as *diction*]

didactic (say dy-**dak**-tik) adjective having the manner of someone who is lecturing people.
didactically adverb [from Greek *didaktikos* = teaching]

diddle verb (**diddles, diddling, diddled**) (slang) cheat or swindle. [origin unknown]

didn't (mainly spoken) did not.

die¹ verb (**dies, dying, died**)
1 stop living or existing. **2** stop burning or functioning, *The fire had died down*. [from Old Norse]

die² noun singular of **dice**. [from old French]

die³ noun (plural **dies**) a device that stamps a design on coins etc. or that cuts or moulds metal. [from old French]

diehard noun (plural **diehards**) a person who obstinately refuses to give up old ideas or policies. [from *die hard* = die painfully]

diesel (say **dee**-zel) noun (plural **diesels**)
1 an engine that works by burning oil in compressed air.
2 fuel for this kind of engine. [named after R. Diesel, a German engineer, who invented it]

diet¹ noun (plural **diets**)
1 special meals that someone eats in order to be healthy or to lose weight. **2** the sort of foods usually eaten by a person or animal.
diet verb (**diets, dieting, dieted**) keep to a diet.
[from Greek *diaita* = way of life]

diet² noun (plural **diets**) the parliament of certain countries (e.g. Japan). [from Latin *dieta* = day's business]

dietitian (say dy-it-**ish**-an) noun (plural **dietitians**) an expert in diet and nutrition.

dif- prefix
1 not; the reverse of. **2** apart; separated. see **dis-**.

differ verb (**differs, differing, differed**)
1 be different. **2** disagree. [from *dif-* + Latin *ferre* = carry]

difference noun (plural **differences**)
1 being different; the way in which things differ. **2** the remainder left after one number

is subtracted from another, *The difference between 8 and 3 is 5.* **3** a disagreement.

different *adjective* unlike; not the same. **differently** *adverb*

USAGE: It is regarded as more acceptable to say *different from* rather than *different to*, which is common in less formal use. The phrase *different than* is used in American English but not in standard British English.

differential *noun* (*plural* **differentials**)
1 a difference in wages between one group of workers and another. **2** a differential gear.

differential gear *noun* (*plural* **differential gears**) a system of gears that makes a vehicle's driving wheels revolve at different speeds when going round corners.

differentiate *verb* (**differentiates, differentiating, differentiated**)
1 make different, *These things differentiate one breed from another.* **2** distinguish; recognize differences, *We do not differentiate between them.* **differentiation** *noun*

difficult *adjective* needing a lot of effort or skill; not easy. **difficulty** *noun* [from *dif-* + Latin *facilis* = easy]

diffident (*say* dif-id-ent) *adjective* shy and not self-confident; hesitating to put yourself or your ideas forward. **diffidently** *adverb*, **diffidence** *noun* [from *dif-* + Latin *fidentia* = confidence]

diffract *verb* (**diffracts, diffracting, diffracted**) break up a beam of light etc. **diffraction** *noun* [from *dif-* + Latin *fractum* = broken]

diffuse (*say* dif-yooz) *verb* (**diffuses, diffusing, diffused**)
1 spread something widely or thinly, *diffused lighting.* **2** mix slowly, *diffusing gases.* **diffusion** *noun*

diffuse (*say* dif-yooss) *adjective*
1 spread widely; not concentrated. **2** using many words; not concise. **diffusely** *adverb*, **diffuseness** *noun* [from *dif-* + Latin *fusum* = poured]

dig *verb* (**digs, digging, dug**)
1 break up soil and move it; make a hole or tunnel by moving soil. **2** poke something in, *Dig a knife into it.* **3** seek or discover by investigating, *We dug up some facts.* **digger** *noun*

dig *noun* (*plural* **digs**)
1 a piece of digging, especially an archaeological excavation. **2** a poke.
[probably from Old English]

digest (*say* dy-jest) *verb* (**digests, digesting, digested**)
1 soften and change food in the stomach etc. so that the body can absorb it. **2** take information into your mind and think it over. **digestible** *adjective*, **digestion** *noun*

digest (*say* dy-jest) *noun* (*plural* **digests**) a summary of news, information, etc.
[from Latin]

digestive *adjective* to do with digestion, *the digestive system.*

digestive biscuit *noun* (*plural* **digestive biscuits**) a wholemeal biscuit (because it is supposed to be easy to digest).

digit (say **dij**-it) noun (plural **digits**)
1 any of the numbers from 0 to 9. 2 a finger or toe. [from Latin *digitus* = finger or toe]

digital adjective to do with or using digits.

digital clock noun (plural **digital clocks**) a clock that shows the time with a row of figures.

digital watch noun (plural **digital watches**) a watch that shows the time with a row of figures.

dignified adjective having dignity.

dignitary noun (plural **dignitaries**) an important official. [same origin as *dignity*]

dignity noun a calm and serious manner.
beneath your dignity not considered worthy enough for you to do. [from Latin *dignus* = worthy]

dilapidated adjective falling to pieces. **dilapidation** noun [from Latin]

dilemma (say dil-**em**-a) noun (plural **dilemmas**) a situation where someone has to choose between two or more possible actions, each of which will bring difficulties. [from Greek, = double proposal]

USAGE: Do not use *dilemma* to mean simply a problem or difficult situation. There should be some idea of choosing between two (or perhaps more) things.

diligent (say **dil**-ij-ent) adjective hard-working. **diligently** adverb, **diligence** noun [from Latin *diligens* = careful, conscientious]

dilute verb (dilutes, diluting, diluted) make a liquid weaker by adding water or other liquid. **dilution** noun
dilute adjective diluted, *a dilute acid*. [from Latin *diluere* = wash away]

dim adjective (dimmer, dimmest)
1 not bright or clear; only faintly lit. 2 (informal) stupid. **dimly** adverb, **dimness** noun
dim verb (dims, dimming, dimmed) make or become dim. **dimmer** noun

dimension noun (plural **dimensions**)
1 a measurement such as length, width, area, or volume. 2 size or extent. **dimensional** adjective [from Latin *dimensio* = measuring out]

diminish verb (diminishes, diminishing, diminished) make or become smaller. **diminution** noun [same origin as *diminutive*]

diminutive (say dim-**in**-yoo-tiv) adjective very small. [from Latin *diminuere* = lessen]

dimple noun (plural **dimples**) a small hollow or dent, especially in the skin. **dimpled** adjective

din noun a loud annoying noise.

dine verb (dines, dining, dined) (formal) have dinner. **diner** noun [from old French *disner*]

dinghy (say **ding**-ee) noun (plural **dinghies**) a kind of small boat. [from Hindi *dingi* = a small river boat]

dingy (say **din**-jee) adjective dirty-looking. **dingily** adverb, **dinginess** noun [origin unknown]

dinner noun (plural **dinners**) the main meal of the day, either at midday or in the evening. [same origin as *dine*]

dinosaur (say **dy**-noss-or) noun (plural **dinosaurs**) a prehistoric lizard-like animal, often of enormous size. [from Greek *deinos* = terrible + *sauros* = lizard]

diocese (say **dy**-oss-iss) noun (plural **dioceses**) a district under the care of a bishop.

dioxide noun an oxide with two atoms of oxygen to one of another element, carbon dioxide. [from *di-*[1] + *oxide*]

dip verb (**dips**, **dipping**, **dipped**) put down or go down, especially into a liquid.

dip noun (plural **dips**)
1 dipping. 2 a downward slope.
3 a quick swim. 4 a substance into which things are dipped. [from Old English]

diploma noun (plural **diplomas**) a certificate awarded by a college etc. for skill in a particular subject. [Latin, from Greek, literally = folded paper]

diplomacy noun
1 the work of making agreements with other countries. 2 skill in dealing with people and gently persuading them to agree to things; tact.

diplomat noun (plural **diplomats**)
1 a person employed in diplomacy on behalf of his or her country. 2 a tactful person.
diplomatic adjective [from Latin

diploma = an official letter given to travellers, saying who they were]

direct adjective
1 as straight as possible. 2 going straight to the point; frank.
3 exact, *the direct opposite*.
directly adverb & conjunction, **directness** noun

direct verb (**directs**, **directing**, **directed**)
1 tell someone the way. 2 guide or aim in a certain direction.
3 control or manage. 4 order, *He directed his troops to advance*.
director noun
[from Latin *directum* = kept straight]

direct current noun electric current flowing only in one direction.

direction noun (plural **directions**)
1 directing. 2 the line along which something moves or faces.
directional adjective

direct object noun (plural **direct objects**) the word that receives the action of the verb. In *'she hit him'*, 'him' is the direct object.

directory noun (plural **directories**) a book containing a list of people with their telephone numbers, addresses, etc. [from Latin *directorius* = guiding]

dirge noun (plural **dirges**) a slow sad song. [from the first word of a song that used to be part of the Roman Catholic service for a dead person]

dirt noun earth, soil; anything that is not clean.

dirty *adjective* (**dirtier, dirtiest**)
1 not clean; soiled. **2** unfair; dishonourable, *a dirty trick*. **3** indecent; obscene. **dirtily** *adverb*, **dirtiness** *noun*

dis- *prefix* (changing to **dif-** before words beginning with *f*, and to **di-** before some consonants)
1 not; the reverse of (as in *dishonest*). **2** apart; separated (as in *disarm, disperse*). [from Latin]

disabled *adjective* unable to use part of your body properly because of illness or injury.
disability *noun*, **disablement** *noun*

disadvantage *noun* (*plural* **disadvantages**) something that hinders or is unhelpful.

disagree *verb* (**disagrees, disagreeing, disagreed**)
1 have or express a different opinion from someone. **2** have a bad effect, *Rich food disagrees with me.* **disagreement** *noun*

disagreeable *adjective* unpleasant. [from old French]

disappear *verb* (**disappears, disappearing, disappeared**) stop being visible; vanish.
disappearance *noun*

disappoint *verb* (**disappoints, disappointing, disappointed**) fail to do what someone hopes for.
disappointment *noun* [originally = to dismiss someone from an important position: from *dis-* + *appoint*]

disapprove *verb* (**disapproves, disapproving, disapproved**) have an unfavourable opinion of something; not approve.
disapproval *noun*

disarm *verb* (**disarms, disarming, disarmed**)
1 reduce the size of armed forces.
2 take away someone's weapons.
3 overcome a person's anger or doubt, *Her friendliness disarmed their suspicions.* **disarmament** *noun* [from old French]

disaster *noun* (*plural* **disasters**)
1 a very bad accident or misfortune. **2** a complete failure.
disastrous *adjective*, **disastrously** *adverb*

disbelief *noun* refusal or unwillingness to believe something.

disc *noun* (*plural* **discs**)
1 any round flat object. **2** (in computers, usually **disk**) a storage device consisting of magnetically coated plates. **3** a gramophone record. [from Latin *discus* = disc]

discerning *adjective* perceptive; showing good judgement.

discharge *verb* (**discharges, discharging, discharged**)
1 release a person. **2** send something out, *discharge smoke.* **3** pay or do what was agreed, *discharge the debt.*

disciple *noun* (*plural* **disciples**)
1 a person who accepts the teachings of another whom he or she regards as a leader. **2** any of the original followers of Jesus Christ. [from Latin *discipulus* = learner]

discipline *noun* (*plural* **disciplines**)
1 orderly and obedient behaviour. **2** a subject for study.
disciplinary (*say* dis-ip-lin-er-ee) *adjective* [from Latin *disciplina* = training]

disco *noun* (*plural* **discos**) a place where CDs or records are played for dancing. [from French *discothèque* = record-library]

discolour verb (**discolours, discolouring, discoloured**) spoil a thing's colour; stain.
discoloration noun [from dis- + Latin colorare = to colour]

disconcert (say dis-kon-sert) verb (**disconcerts, disconcerting, disconcerted**) make a person feel uneasy. [from dis- + French concerter = make harmonious]

disconnect verb (**disconnects, disconnecting, disconnected**) break a connection; detach.
disconnection noun

disconsolate (say dis-kon-sol-at) adjective disappointed. [from dis- + Latin consolatus = consoled]

discontent noun lack of contentment; dissatisfaction.
discontented adjective,
discontentment noun

discontinue verb (**discontinues, discontinuing, discontinued**) put an end to something. [from dis- + Latin continuare = continue]

discord noun (plural **discords**)
1 disagreement; quarrelling.
2 musical notes sounded together and producing a harsh or unpleasant sound. **discordant** adjective [from dis- + Latin cordis = of the heart]

discount noun (plural **discounts**) an amount by which a price is reduced.

discount verb (**discounts, discounting, discounted**) ignore or disregard something, *We cannot discount the possibility.* [from old French]

discourage verb (**discourages, discouraging, discouraged**)
1 take away someone's enthusiasm or confidence. 2 try

to persuade someone not to do something. **discouragement** noun [from old French]

discover verb (**discovers, discovering, discovered**)
1 find. 2 be the first person to find something. **discoverer** noun,
discovery noun [from dis- + Latin cooperire = to cover]

discredit verb (**discredits, discrediting, discredited**)
1 destroy people's confidence in a person or thing; disgrace.
2 distrust.

discredit noun
1 disgrace. 2 distrust.
discreditable adjective
[from dis- + credit]

discreet adjective
1 not giving away secrets. 2 not showy. **discreetly** adverb [from Latin discernere = be discerning]

USAGE: Do not confuse with discrete.

discrepancy (say dis-krep-an-see) noun (plural **discrepancies**) difference; lack of agreement, *There are several discrepancies in the two accounts.* [from Latin discrepantia = discord]

discrete adjective separate; distinct from each other. [from Latin discretus = separated]

USAGE: Do not confuse with discreet.

discretion (say dis-kresh-on) noun
1 being discreet; keeping secrets.
2 power to take action according to your own judgement, *The treasurer has full discretion.* [from discreet]

discriminate verb (discriminates, discriminating, discriminated) 1 notice the differences between things; distinguish; prefer one thing to another. 2 treat people differently or unfairly, e.g. because of their race, sex, or religion. **discrimination** noun

discus noun (plural **discuses**) a thick heavy disc thrown in athletic contests. [Latin]

discuss verb (discusses, discussing, discussed) talk with other people about a subject. **discussion** noun [from Latin]

disease noun (plural **diseases**) an unhealthy condition; an illness. **diseased** adjective [from dis- + ease]

disembark verb (disembarks, disembarking, disembarked) put or go ashore. **disembarkation** noun

disentangle verb (disentangles, disentangling, disentangled) free from tangles or confusion.

disfigure verb (disfigures, disfiguring, disfigured) spoil the appearance of a person or thing. **disfigurement** noun [from dis- + Latin figura = a shape]

disgrace noun 1 shame; loss of approval or respect. 2 something that causes shame. **disgraceful** adjective, **disgracefully** adverb

disgrace verb (disgraces, disgracing, disgraced) bring disgrace upon someone. [from dis- + Latin gratia = grace]

disguise verb (disguises, disguising, disguised) make

a person or thing look different in order to deceive people.

disguise noun (plural **disguises**) something used for disguising.

disgust noun a feeling that something is very unpleasant or disgraceful.

disgust verb (disgusts, disgusting, disgusted) cause disgust. **disgusted** adjective, **disgusting** adjective [from dis- + Latin gustare = to taste]

dish noun (plural **dishes**) 1 a plate or bowl for food. 2 food prepared for eating. 3 a satellite dish.

dish verb (dishes, dishing, dished) (informal) **dish out** give out portions of something to people.

dishevelled (say dish-ev-eld) adjective ruffled and untidy. **dishevelment** noun [from dis- + old French chevel = hair]

dishonest adjective not honest. **dishonestly** adverb, **dishonesty** noun [from old French]

dishonour noun & verb (dishonours, dishonouring, dishonoured) disgrace. **dishonourable** adjective

disillusion verb (disillusions, disillusioning, disillusioned) get rid of someone's pleasant but wrong beliefs. **disillusionment** noun

disinclined adjective unwilling to do something.

disinfect verb (disinfects, disinfecting, disinfected) destroy the germs in something. **disinfection** noun [from French]

disinfectant noun (plural disinfectants) a substance used for disinfecting things.

disintegrate verb (disintegrates, disintegrating, disintegrated) break up into small parts or pieces. **disintegration** noun

disinterested adjective impartial; not biased; not influenced by hope of gaining something yourself, *She gave us some disinterested advice.*

USAGE: It is not accepted as part of standard English to use this word as if it meant 'not interested' or 'bored'. If this is what you mean, use *uninterested*.

disjointed adjective disconnected. [from dis- + Latin *jungere* = join]

disk noun (plural disks) a disc. [the American spelling of *disc*]

dislike verb (dislikes, disliking, disliked) not to like somebody or something.

dislocate verb (dislocates, dislocating, dislocated) 1 move or force a bone from its proper position in one of the joints. 2 disrupt, *Fog dislocated the traffic.* **dislocation** noun [from dis- + Latin *locare* = to place]

dislodge verb (dislodges, dislodging, dislodged) move or force something from its place. [from French]

disloyal adjective not loyal. **disloyally** adverb, **disloyalty** noun [from French]

dismal adjective 1 gloomy. 2 of poor quality. **dismally** adverb [from Latin *dies mali* = unlucky days]

dismantle verb (dismantles, dismantling, dismantled) take something to pieces. [from dis- + old French *manteler* = fortify]

dismay noun a feeling of surprise and discouragement. **dismayed** adjective [from dis- + *may*[1]]

dismiss verb (dismisses, dismissing, dismissed) 1 send someone away. 2 tell a person that you will no longer employ him or her. 3 stop considering an idea etc. 4 get a batsman or cricket side out. **dismissal** noun, **dismissive** adjective [from dis- + Latin *missum* = sent]

dismount verb (dismounts, dismounting, dismounted) get off a horse or bicycle.

disobey verb (disobeys, disobeying, disobeyed) not to obey; disregard orders. **disobedient** adjective, **disobedience** noun

disorder noun (plural disorders) 1 untidiness. 2 a disturbance. 3 an illness. **disorderly** adjective

disorganized adjective muddled and badly organized. **disorganization** noun [from French]

dispatch verb (dispatches, dispatching, dispatched) 1 send off to a destination. 2 kill.

dispatch noun (plural dispatches) 1 dispatching. 2 a report or message sent. 3 promptness; speed.

dispel verb (dispels, dispelling, dispelled) drive away; scatter, *Wind dispels fog.* [from dis- + Latin *pellere* = to drive]

dispensary noun (plural **dispensaries**) a place where medicines are dispensed.

dispense verb (dispenses, dispensing, dispensed) **1** distribute; deal out. **2** prepare medicine according to prescriptions. **dispensation** noun, **dispenser** noun

dispense with do without something.
[from Latin dispensare = weigh out]

disperse verb (disperses, dispersing, dispersed) scatter. **dispersal** noun, **dispersion** noun
[from Latin dispersum = scattered]

displace verb (displaces, displacing, displaced) **1** shift from its place. **2** take a person's or thing's place. **displacement** noun

display verb (displays, displaying, displayed) show; arrange something so that it can be clearly seen.

display noun (plural **displays**) **1** the displaying of something; an exhibition. **2** something displayed.
[from dis- = separately + Latin plicare = to fold]

disposable adjective made to be thrown away after it has been used.

dispose verb (disposes, disposing, disposed) **1** place in position; arrange, Dispose your troops in two lines. **2** make a person ready or willing to do something, I feel disposed to help him.

be well disposed be friendly.

dispose of get rid of.
[from old French; related to deposit]

disposition noun (plural **dispositions**) **1** a person's nature or qualities. **2** arrangement.

disproportionate adjective out of proportion; too large or too small.

disprove verb (disproves, disproving, disproved) show that something is not true.

dispute verb (disputes, disputing, disputed) **1** argue; debate. **2** quarrel. **3** raise an objection to, We dispute their claim.

dispute noun (plural **disputes**) **1** an argument or debate. **2** a quarrel.
in dispute being argued about.
[from dis- + Latin putare = settle]

disqualify verb (disqualifies, disqualifying, disqualified) bar someone from a competition etc. because he or she has broken the rules or is not properly qualified to take part. **disqualification** noun

disregard verb (disregards, disregarding, disregarded) ignore.

disregard noun the act of ignoring something.

disrepair noun bad condition caused by not doing repairs, The old mill is in a state of disrepair.

disreputable adjective not respectable. [from disrepute]

disrespect noun lack of respect; rudeness. **disrespectful** adjective, **disrespectfully** adverb

disrupt verb (disrupts, disrupting, disrupted) put into disorder; interrupt a continuous flow, Fog

disrupted traffic. **disruption** noun,
disruptive adjective [from dis-
+ Latin ruptum = broken]

dissatisfied adjective not
satisfied. **dissatisfaction** noun

dissect (say dis-sekt) verb
(**dissects, dissecting, dissected**)
cut something up in order to
examine it. **dissection** noun [from
dis- + Latin sectum = cut]

dissent noun disagreement over
an idea, proposal, etc..

dissent verb (**dissents,
dissenting, dissented**) disagree.
[from dis- + Latin sentire = feel]

dissident noun (plural
dissidents) a person who
disagrees, especially someone
who opposes their government.
dissident adjective, **dissidence**
noun [from Latin dissidere = sit
by yourself]

dissolute adjective having an
immoral way of life. [from Latin
dissolutus = loose]

dissolution noun (plural
dissolutions)
1 putting an end to a marriage or
partnership etc. 2 the formal
ending of a parliament or
assembly. [from Latin]

dissolve verb (**dissolves,
dissolving, dissolved**)
1 mix something with a liquid so
that it becomes part of the liquid.
2 make or become liquid; melt.
3 put an end to a marriage or
partnership etc. 4 formally end
a parliament, assembly, or other
gathering, Parliament was
dissolved and a general election
was held. [from dis- = separate
+ Latin solvere = loosen]

dissuade verb (**dissuades,
dissuading, dissuaded**) persuade
somebody not to do something.
dissuasion noun [from dis- + Latin
suadere = persuade]

distance noun (plural **distances**)
the amount of space between two
places.
in the distance far away.

distant adjective
1 far away. 2 not friendly; not
sociable. **distantly** adverb [from
dis- + Latin stans = standing]

distaste noun dislike.

distasteful adjective unpleasant.

distemper noun
1 a disease of dogs and certain
other animals. 2 a kind of paint.
[from Latin]

distil verb (**distils, distilling,
distilled**) purify a liquid by
boiling it and condensing the
vapour. **distillation** noun [from
dis- + Latin stillare = drip down]

distinct adjective
1 easily heard or seen;
noticeable. 2 clearly separate or
different. **distinctly** adverb,
distinctness noun [from Latin
distinctus = separated]

USAGE: See note at distinctive.

distinction noun (plural
distinctions)
1 a difference. 2 excellence or
honour. 3 an award for
excellence; a high mark in an
examination.

distinctive adjective that
distinguishes one thing from
another or others, The school has
a distinctive uniform. **distinctively**
adverb

USAGE: Do not confuse this word with *distinct*. A *distinct* mark is a clear mark; a *distinctive* mark is one that is not found anywhere else.

distinguish verb (distinguishes, distinguishing, distinguished)
1 make or notice differences between things. 2 see or hear something clearly. 3 bring honour to, *He distinguished himself by his bravery.*
distinguishable adjective [from Latin *distinguere* = to separate]

distort verb (distorts, distorting, distorted)
1 pull or twist out of its normal shape. 2 misrepresent; give a false account of something, *distort the truth.* **distortion** noun [from dis- + Latin *tortum* = twisted]

distract verb (distracts, distracting, distracted) take a person's attention away from something. [from dis- + Latin *tractum* = pulled]

distraction noun (plural distractions)
1 something that distracts attention. 2 an amusement. 3 great worry or distress.

distress noun (plural distresses) great sorrow, pain, or trouble.

distribute verb (distributes, distributing, distributed)
1 deal or share out. 2 spread or scatter. **distribution** noun, **distributor** noun [from dis- = separate + Latin *tributum* = given]

district noun (plural districts) part of a town or country.

distrust noun lack of trust; suspicion. **distrustful** adjective

distrust verb (distrusts, distrusting, distrusted) not to trust.

disturb verb (disturbs, disturbing, disturbed)
1 spoil someone's peace or rest. 2 cause someone to worry. 3 move a thing from its position.
disturbance noun [from dis- = thoroughly + Latin *turbare* = confuse, upset]

disuse noun the state of being no longer used. **disused** adjective

ditch noun (plural ditches) a trench dug to hold water or carry it away, or to serve as a boundary.

ditto noun (used in lists) the same again. [from Italian *detto* = said]

dive verb (dives, diving, dived)
1 go under water, especially head first. 2 move down quickly. **dive** noun [from Old English]

diverse (say dy-verss) adjective varied; of several different kinds. **diversity** noun

diversify verb (diversifies, diversifying, diversified) make or become varied; involve yourself in different kinds of things. **diversification** noun

diversion noun (plural diversions)
1 diverting something from its course. 2 an alternative route for traffic when a road is closed. 3 a recreation or entertainment.

divert verb (diverts, diverting, diverted)
1 turn something aside from its course. 2 entertain or amuse. [from di-² + Latin *vertere* = to turn]

divide verb (divides, dividing, divided)
1 separate from something or into smaller parts; split up. 2 find how many times one number is contained in another, *Divide six by three (6 ÷ 3 = 2).* **divider** noun

divine adjective
1 belonging to or coming from God. 2 like a god. 3 (*informal*) excellent; extremely beautiful. **divinely** adverb [from Latin *divus* = god]

division noun (*plural* divisions)
1 dividing. 2 a dividing line; a partition. 3 one of the parts into which something is divided. 4 (in Parliament) separation of members into two sections for counting votes. **divisional** adjective [from Latin *dividere* = divide]

divisive (*say* div-I-siv) adjective causing disagreement within a group.

divorce noun (*plural* divorces) the legal ending of a marriage.

divorce verb (divorces, divorcing, divorced)
1 end a marriage by divorce. 2 separate; think of things separately.
[French; related to *divert*]

Diwali (*say* di-wah-lee) noun a Hindu religious festival at which lamps are lit, held in October or November. [from Sanskrit *dipavali* = row of lights]

DIY abbreviation do-it-yourself.

dizzy adjective (dizzier, dizziest) having or causing the feeling that everything is spinning round; giddy. **dizzily** adverb, **dizziness** noun [from Old English]

DJ abbreviation disc jockey.

DNA abbreviation deoxyribonucleic acid; a substance in chromosomes that stores genetic information.

do verb (does, doing, did, done)
This word has many different uses, most of which mean performing or dealing with something (*Do your best. I can't do this. She is doing well at school*) or being suitable or enough (*This will do*). The verb is also used with other verbs 1 in questions (*Do you want this?*), 2 in statements with 'not' (*He does not want it*), 3 for emphasis (*I do like nuts*), 4 to avoid repeating a verb that has just been used (*We work as hard as they do*).

do away with get rid of.

do up 1 fasten, *Do your coat up.* 2 repair or redecorate, *Do up the spare room.*

dock¹ noun (*plural* docks) a part of a harbour where ships are loaded, unloaded, or repaired.

dock verb (docks, docking, docked)
1 bring or come into a dock. 2 when two spacecraft dock, they join together in space.
[from old German or old Dutch]

dock² noun an enclosure for the prisoner on trial in a lawcourt. [from Flemish *dok* = cage]

dock³ noun a weed with broad leaves. [from Old English]

dock⁴ verb (docks, docking, docked)
1 cut short an animal's tail. 2 reduce or take away part of someone's wages or supplies etc. [origin unknown]

docker noun (plural **dockers**)
a labourer who loads and
unloads ships.

doctor noun (plural **doctors**)
1 a person who is trained to treat
sick or injured people. **2** a person
who holds an advanced degree (a
doctorate) at a university, *Doctor
of Music*. [Latin, = teacher]

doctrine noun (plural **doctrines**)
a belief held by a religious,
political, or other group.
doctrinal adjective [from Latin
doctrina = teaching]

document noun (plural
documents) a written or printed
paper giving information or
evidence about something.
documentation noun [from Latin
documentum = lesson, official
paper]

documentary adjective
1 consisting of documents,
documentary evidence. **2** showing
real events or situations.

documentary noun (plural
documentaries) a film giving
information about real events.
[same origin as *document*]

dodge verb (dodges, dodging,
dodged) move quickly to avoid
someone or something.

dodge noun (plural **dodges**)
1 a dodging movement.
2 (*informal*) a trick; a clever way
of doing something.

dodgy adjective (*informal*)
1 awkward or tricky. **2** not
working properly. **3** dishonest.

dodo noun (plural **dodos**) a large
heavy bird that used to live on an
island in the Indian Ocean but
has been extinct for over 200

years. [from Portuguese *doudo*
= fool (because the bird had no
fear of man)]

doe noun (plural **does**) a female
deer, rabbit, or hare. [from Old
English]

doesn't (*mainly spoken*) does not.

dog noun (plural **dogs**) a four-
legged animal that barks, often
kept as a pet.

dog verb (dogs, dogging,
dogged) follow closely or
persistently, *Reporters dogged
his footsteps.*
[from Old English]

dog-eared adjective (of a book)
having the corners of the pages
bent from constant use.

dogged (*say* dog-id) adjective
persistent or obstinate. **doggedly**
adverb

dogma noun (plural **dogmas**)
a belief or principle that a Church
or other authority declares is
true and must be accepted.
[Greek, = opinion, decree]

dogmatic adjective expressing
ideas in a very firm authoritative
way. **dogmatically** adverb

do-it-yourself adjective suitable
for an amateur to do or make at
home.

dole verb (doles, doling, doled)
dole out distribute.

dole noun (*informal*) money paid
by the State to unemployed
people.
[from Old English]

doll noun (plural **dolls**) a toy
model of a person. [pet form of
Dorothy]

dollar noun (plural **dollars**) a unit
of money in the USA and some
other countries. [from German
thaler = a silver coin]

dolphin noun (plural **dolphins**)
a sea animal like a small whale with a beak-like snout.
[from Greek]

-dom suffix forms nouns showing rank, office, territory, or condition (e.g. kingdom, freedom).
[from Old English]

domain (say dom-ayn) noun (plural **domains**)
1 a kingdom. **2** an area of knowledge, interest, etc. [from French; related to dominion]

dome noun (plural **domes**) a roof shaped like the top half of a ball. **domed** adjective [via French from Italian]

domestic adjective
1 to do with the home or household. **2** (of animals) kept by people, not wild. **domestically** adverb, **domesticated** adjective [from Latin domesticus = to do with the home]

dominate verb (**dominates**, **dominating**, **dominated**)
1 control by being stronger or more powerful. **2** be conspicuous or prominent, The mountain dominated the whole landscape. **dominant** adjective, **domination** noun [from Latin dominus = master]

domineer verb (**domineers**, **domineering**, **domineered**)
behave in a dominating way. **domineering** adjective [same origin as dominate]

dominion noun (plural **dominions**)
1 authority to rule others; control. **2** an area over which someone rules; a domain. [from Latin dominium = property]

domino noun (plural **dominoes**)
a small flat oblong piece of wood or plastic with dots (1 to 6) or a blank space at each end, used in the game of dominoes.

donkey noun (plural **donkeys**) an animal that looks like a small horse with long ears. [origin unknown]

donor noun (plural **donors**)
someone who gives something, a blood donor. [from old French]

don't (mainly spoken) do not.

doom noun a grim fate that you cannot avoid, especially death or destruction, a sense of impending doom.

doom verb (**dooms**, **dooming**, **doomed**) destine to a grim fate. [from Old English]

door noun (plural **doors**)
a movable barrier on hinges (or one that slides or revolves), used to open or close an entrance. **doorknob** noun, **doormat** noun

doorstep noun (plural **doorsteps**)
the step or piece of ground just outside a door.

doorway noun (plural **doorways**)
the opening into which a door fits.

dope noun (plural **dopes**)
1 (informal) a drug, especially one taken or given illegally. **2** (informal) a stupid person. **dopey** adjective

dope verb (**dopes**, **doping**, **doped**) (informal) give a drug to a person or animal.
[from Dutch doop = sauce]

dormant adjective
1 sleeping. **2** living or existing but not active; not extinct, a dormant volcano. [French, = sleeping]

dormitory noun (plural dormitories) a room for several people to sleep in, especially in a school or institution.

dormitory town or **suburb** a place from which people travel to work elsewhere.
[from Latin *dormire* = to sleep]

dormouse noun (plural dormice) an animal like a large mouse that hibernates in winter. [origin unknown]

dose noun (plural doses) an amount of medicine etc. taken at one time. [from Greek *dosis* = something given]

dot noun (plural dots) a tiny spot.

dot verb (dots, dotting, dotted) mark something with dots.

double adjective
1 twice as much; twice as many.
2 having two things or parts that form a pair, *a double-barrelled gun*. 3 suitable for two people, *a double bed*. **doubly** adverb

double noun (plural doubles)
1 a double quantity or thing.
2 a person or thing that looks exactly like another.

double verb (doubles, doubling, doubled)
1 make or become twice as much or as many. 2 bend or fold in two.
3 turn back sharply, *The fox doubled back on its tracks.*
[from old French]

double bass noun (plural double basses) a musical instrument with strings, like a large cello.
[from *double* + *bass*¹]

double-cross verb (double-crosses, double-crossing, double-crossed) deceive or cheat someone who thinks you are working with them.

doubt noun (plural doubts) a feeling of not being sure about something.

doubt verb (doubts, doubting, doubted) feel doubt. **doubter** noun
[from Latin *dubitare* = hesitate]

doubtful adjective
1 feeling doubt. 2 making you feel doubt. **doubtfully** adverb

dough noun
1 a thick mixture of flour and water used for making bread, pastry, etc. 2 (*slang*) money.
doughy adjective

doughnut noun (plural doughnuts) a round bun that has been fried and covered in sugar.

dour (say doo-er) adjective stern and gloomy-looking. **dourly** adverb [from Scottish Gaelic *dur* = dull, obstinate]

dove noun (plural doves) a kind of pigeon. [from Old Norse]

dovetail noun (plural dovetails) a wedge-shaped joint used to join two pieces of wood.

dovetail verb (dovetails, dovetailing, dovetailed)
1 join pieces of wood with a dovetail. 2 fit neatly together, *My plans dovetailed with hers.*
[because the wedge-shape looks like a dove's tail]

dowager noun (plural dowagers) a woman who holds a title or property after her husband has died, *the dowager duchess*. [from old French *douage* = widow's share]

dowdy adjective (dowdier, dowdiest) shabby; unfashionable. **dowdily** adverb

down¹ adverb
1 to or in a lower place or position or level, *It fell down.* **2** to a source or place etc., *Track them down.* **3** in writing, *Take down these instructions.* **4** as a payment, *We will pay £5 down and the rest later.*

be down on disapprove of, *She is down on smoking.*

down preposition downwards through or along or into, *Pour it down the drain.*
[from Old English *adune*]

down² noun very fine soft feathers or hair. **downy** adjective
[from Old Norse]

down³ noun (plural **downs**) a grass-covered hill, *the South Downs.* **downland** noun [from Old English *dun*]

downhill adverb & adjective down a slope.

download verb (**downloads**, **downloading**, **downloaded**) transfer data from a large computer system to a smaller one.

downright adverb & adjective complete or completely, *a downright lie.*

Down's syndrome noun a medical condition caused by a chromosome defect in which a baby is born with reduced intelligence and physical abnormalities.

downward adjective & adverb going towards what is lower. **downwards** adverb

dowry noun (plural **dowries**) property or money brought by a bride to her husband when she marries him. [from old French; related to *endow*]

doze verb (**dozes**, **dozing**, **dozed**) sleep lightly.

doze noun a light sleep. **dozy** adjective

dozen noun (plural **dozens**) a set of twelve. [from old French]

USAGE: Correct use is *ten dozen* (not *ten dozens*).

drab adjective (**drabber**, **drabbest**) **1** not colourful. **2** dull or uninteresting, *a drab life.* **drably** adverb, **drabness** noun

draft noun (plural **drafts**) **1** a rough sketch or plan. **2** a written order for a bank to pay out money.

draft verb (**drafts**, **drafting**, **drafted**) **1** prepare a draft. **2** select for a special duty, *She was drafted to our office in Paris.* [a different spelling of *draught*]

USAGE: This is also the American spelling of *draught.*

drag verb (**drags**, **dragging**, **dragged**) **1** pull something heavy along. **2** search a river or lake etc. with nets and hooks. **3** continue slowly and dully.

drag noun **1** a hindrance; something boring. **2** (slang) women's clothes worn by men.

dragon noun (plural **dragons**) **1** a mythological monster, usually with wings and able to breathe out fire. **2** a fierce person. [from Greek *drakon* = serpent]

dragonfly noun (plural **dragonflies**) an insect with a long thin body and two pairs of transparent wings.

drain noun (plural **drains**)
1 a pipe or ditch etc. for taking away water or other liquid.
2 something that takes away strength or resources. **drainpipe** noun

drain verb (**drains**, **draining**, **drained**)
1 take away water etc. through a drain. 2 flow or trickle away.
3 empty liquid out of a container.
4 take away strength etc.; exhaust. **drainage** noun [from Old English]

drake noun (plural **drakes**) a male duck. [from West Germanic]

drama noun (plural **dramas**)
1 a play. 2 writing or performing plays. 3 a series of exciting events. **dramatic** adjective, **dramatist** noun, **dramatize** verb [from Greek]

drape verb (**drapes**, **draping**, **draped**) hang cloth etc. loosely over something. [from French drap = cloth]

draper noun (plural **drapers**) a shopkeeper who sells cloth or clothes. [same origin as **drape**]

drastic adjective having a strong or violent effect. **drastically** adverb [from Greek]

draught (say drahft) noun (plural **draughts**)
1 a current of usually cold air indoors. 2 a haul of fish in a net.
3 the depth of water needed to float a ship. 4 a swallow of liquid. **draughty** adjective [from Old Norse]

draughts noun a game played with 24 round pieces on a chessboard. [from draught in an old sense = way of moving]

draw verb (**draws**, **drawing**, **drew**, **drawn**)
1 produce a picture or outline by making marks on a surface. 2 pull. 3 take out, draw water.
4 attract, The fair drew large crowds. 5 end a game or contest with the same score on both sides. 6 move or come, The ship drew nearer. 7 write out a cheque to be cashed.

draw a conclusion form an opinion about something by thinking about the evidence.

draw noun (plural **draws**)
1 the drawing of lots (see lot).
2 the drawing out of a gun etc., He was quick on the draw. 3 an attraction. 4 a drawn game. [from Old English]

USAGE: Do not confuse this word with drawer.

drawback noun (plural **drawbacks**) a disadvantage. [from draw back = hesitate]

drawbridge noun (plural **drawbridges**) a bridge over a moat, hinged at one end so that it can be raised or lowered.

drawer noun (plural **drawers**)
1 a sliding box-like compartment in a piece of furniture. 2 a person who draws something. 3 someone who draws (= writes out) a cheque.

drawing noun (plural **drawings**) a picture or outline drawn.

drawing pin noun (plural drawing pins) a short pin with a flat top to be pressed with your thumb, used for fastening paper etc. to a surface.

drawing room noun (plural drawing rooms) a sitting room. [short for *withdrawing room* = a private room in a hotel etc., to which guests could withdraw]

drawl verb (drawls, drawling, drawled) speak very slowly or lazily.

drawl noun (plural drawls) a drawling way of speaking. [from old German or old Dutch *dralen* = delay]

dread noun great fear.

dread verb (dreads, dreading, dreaded) fear something greatly. [from Old English]

dreadful adjective (*informal*) very bad, *dreadful weather*. **dreadfully** adverb

dreadlocks plural noun hair worn in many ringlets or plaits, especially by Rastafarians. [from *dread* + *lock*[2] (because the style was copied from pictures of Ethiopian warriors)]

dream noun (plural dreams) 1 things a person seems to see while sleeping. 2 something imagined; an ambition or ideal. **dreamy** adjective, **dreamily** adverb

dream verb (dreams, dreaming, dreamt or dreamed) 1 have a dream or dreams. 2 have an ambition. 3 think something might happen, *I never dreamt she would leave*. **dreamer** noun [from Middle English]

dreary adjective (drearier, dreariest) 1 dull or boring. 2 gloomy. **drearily** adverb, **dreariness** noun [from Old English]

dredge verb (dredges, dredging, dredged) drag something up, especially by scooping at the bottom of a river or the sea. **dredger** noun [origin unknown]

dregs plural noun worthless bits that sink to the bottom of a liquid.

drench verb (drenches, drenching, drenched) make wet all through; soak.

dress noun (plural dresses) 1 a woman's or girl's garment with a bodice and skirt. 2 clothes; costume, *fancy dress*.

dress verb (dresses, dressing, dressed) 1 put clothes on. 2 arrange a display in a window etc.; decorate, *dress the shop windows*. 3 prepare food for cooking or eating. 4 put a dressing on a wound. **dresser** noun [from French *dresser* = prepare]

dresser noun (plural dressers) a sideboard with shelves at the top for dishes etc. [same origin as *dress*]

dressing noun (plural dressings) 1 a bandage, plaster, or ointment etc. for a wound. 2 a sauce of oil, vinegar, etc. for a salad. 3 manure or other fertilizer for spreading on the soil.

dressing gown noun (plural dressing gowns) a loose garment for wearing when you are not fully dressed.

dress rehearsal noun (plural **dress rehearsals**) a rehearsal at which the cast wear their costumes.

dribble verb (**dribbles**, **dribbling**, **dribbled**)
1 let saliva trickle out of your mouth. 2 move the ball forward in football or hockey with slight touches of your feet or stick.
[from *drib*, a different spelling of *drip*]

drift verb (**drifts**, **drifting**, **drifted**)
1 be carried gently along by water or air. 2 move along slowly and casually. 3 live casually with no definite objective. **drifter** noun

drift noun (plural **drifts**)
1 a drifting movement. 2 a mass of snow or sand piled up by the wind. 3 the general meaning of a speech etc.
[from Old Norse]

driftwood noun wood floating on the sea or washed ashore by it.

drill noun (plural **drills**)
1 a tool for making holes; a machine for boring holes or wells. 2 repeated exercises in gymnastics, military training, etc.

drill verb (**drills**, **drilling**, **drilled**)
1 make a hole etc. with a drill. 2 do repeated exercises; make people do exercises.
[from Dutch]

drink verb (**drinks**, **drinking**, **drank**, **drunk**)
1 swallow liquid. 2 drink a lot of alcoholic drinks. **drinker** noun

drink noun (plural **drinks**)
1 a liquid for drinking; an amount of liquid swallowed. 2 an alcoholic drink.

drip verb (**drips**, **dripping**, **dripped**)
fall or let something fall in drops.

drip noun (plural **drips**)
1 liquid falling in drops; the sound it makes. 2 apparatus for dripping liquid into the veins of a sick person.
[from Old English]

drip-dry adjective made of material that dries easily and does not need ironing.

dripping noun fat melted from roasted meat and allowed to set.

drive verb (**drives**, **driving**, **drove**, **driven**)
1 make something or someone move. 2 operate a motor vehicle or a train etc. 3 force or compel someone to do something, *Hunger drove them to steal.* 4 force someone into a state, *She is driving me crazy.* 5 rush; move rapidly, *Rain drove against the window.* **driver** noun

drive noun (plural **drives**)
1 a journey in a vehicle. 2 a hard stroke in cricket or golf etc. 3 the transmitting of power to machinery, *four-wheel drive.* 4 energy or enthusiasm. 5 an organized effort, *a sales drive.* 6 a track for vehicles through the grounds of a house.
[from Old English]

drive-in adjective that you can use without getting out of your car.

drivel noun silly talk; nonsense.
[from Old English *dreflian* = dribble]

drizzle noun very fine rain. [from Old English *dreosan* = to fall]

drone verb (**drones**, **droning**, **droned**)
1 make a deep humming sound. 2 talk in a boring voice.

drone noun (plural **drones**)
1 a droning sound. 2 a male bee.

drool verb (**drools, drooling, drooled**) dribble.
drool over be very emotional about liking something.
[from *drivel*]

droop verb (**droops, drooping, drooped**) hang down weakly.
[from Old Norse]

drop noun (plural **drops**)
1 a tiny amount of liquid. 2 a fall or decrease. 3 a descent. 4 a small round sweet. 5 a hanging ornament.

drop verb (**drops, dropping, dropped**)
1 fall. 2 let something fall. 3 put down a passenger etc., *Drop me at the station.*
drop in visit someone casually.
drop out stop taking part in something. **drop-out** noun

drought (say drout) noun (plural **droughts**) a long period of dry weather. [from Old English]

drown verb (**drowns, drowning, drowned**)
1 die or kill by suffocation under water. 2 flood or drench. 3 make so much noise that another sound cannot be heard. [from Old Norse]

drowsy adjective sleepy. **drowsily** adverb, **drowsiness** noun

drudge noun (plural **drudges**) a person who does dull work.
drudgery noun [origin unknown]

drug noun (plural **drugs**)
1 a substance used in medicine. 2 a substance that affects your senses or your mind, *a drug addict.*

drug verb (**drugs, drugging, drugged**) give a drug to someone, especially to make them unconscious.
[from French]

drum noun (plural **drums**)
1 a musical instrument made of a cylinder with a skin or parchment stretched over one or both ends. 2 a cylindrical object or container, *an oil drum.*

drum verb (**drums, drumming, drummed**)
1 play a drum or drums. 2 tap repeatedly on something.
drummer noun

drumstick noun (plural **drumsticks**)
1 a stick for beating a drum. 2 the lower part of a cooked bird's leg.

drunk adjective not able to control your behaviour through drinking too much alcohol.

drunk noun (plural **drunks**) a person who is drunk.
[past participle of *drink*]

drunkard noun (plural **drunkards**) a person who is often drunk.

drunken adjective
1 drunk, *a drunken man.* 2 caused by drinking alcohol, *a drunken brawl.*

dry adjective (**drier, driest**)
1 without water or moisture. 2 thirsty. 3 boring or dull. 4 (of remarks or humour) said in a matter-of-fact or ironical way, *dry wit.* **drily** adverb, **dryness** noun

dry verb (**dries, drying, dried**) make or become dry.
[from Old English]

dry-cleaning noun a method of cleaning clothes etc. using a liquid that evaporates quickly.

dual carriageway noun (plural **dual carriageways**) a road with a dividing strip between lanes of traffic in opposite directions.

dubious (say dew-bee-us) adjective doubtful. **dubiously** adverb [from Latin dubium = doubt]

duchess noun (plural **duchesses**) a duke's wife or widow. [from Latin]

duchy noun (plural **duchies**) the territory of a duke, the duchy of Cornwall. [from old French]

duck noun (plural **ducks**)
1 a swimming bird with a flat beak; the female of this.
2 a batsman's score of nought at cricket. 3 a ducking movement.

duck verb (**ducks, ducking, ducked**)
1 bend down quickly to avoid something. 2 go or push quickly under water. 3 dodge; avoid doing something.
[from Old English]

duckling noun (plural **ducklings**) a young duck.

duct noun (plural **ducts**) a tube or channel through which liquid, gas, air, or cables can pass. [from Latin ductus = leading]

ductile adjective (of metal) able to be drawn out into fine strands. [from Latin]

due adjective
1 expected; scheduled to do something or to arrive, The train is due in ten minutes. 2 owing; needing to be paid. 3 that ought to be given; rightful, Treat her with due respect.

due to as a result of.

USAGE: Traditionally, correct use is as in His lateness was due to an accident. Some people object to the use of 'due to' without a preceding noun (e.g. 'lateness') to which it refers. However, such uses as 'He was late, due to an accident' are nowadays widely regarded as acceptable. But if you prefer, you can use because of or owing to instead.

due adverb exactly, We sailed due east.

due noun (plural **dues**)
1 something you deserve or have a right to; proper respect, Give him his due. 2 a fee, harbour dues. [from French dû = what is owed]

duel noun (plural **duels**) a fight between two people, especially with pistols or swords. **duelling** noun, **duellist** noun [from Italian]

duet noun (plural **duets**) a piece of music for two players or singers. [from Italian duo = two]

duffel coat noun (plural **duffel coats**) a thick overcoat with a hood, fastened with toggles. [named after Duffel, a town in Belgium, where the cloth for it was made]

duffer noun (plural **duffers**) a person who is stupid or not good at doing something. [origin unknown]

duke noun (plural **dukes**) a member of the highest rank of noblemen. **dukedom** noun [from Latin dux = leader]

dull adjective
1 not bright or clear, dull weather.
2 stupid. 3 boring, a dull concert.

not sharp, *a dull pain; a dull thud.* **dully** *adverb,* **dullness** *noun* [from Old English]

dumb *adjective*
1 without the ability to speak.
2 silent. **3** (*informal*) stupid.
dumbly *adverb,* **dumbness** *noun* [from Old English]

dumbfound *verb* (**dumbfounds, dumbfounding, dumbfounded**) astonish; strike a person dumb with surprise. [from *dumb* + *confound*]

dummy *noun* (*plural* **dummies**)
1 something made to look like a person or thing. **2** an imitation teat given to a baby to suck. [from *dumb*]

dump *noun* (*plural* **dumps**)
1 a place where something (especially rubbish) is left or stored. **2** (*informal*) a dull or unattractive place.

dump *verb* (**dumps, dumping, dumped**)
1 get rid of something that is not wanted. **2** put something down carelessly.

dumpling *noun* (*plural* **dumplings**) a lump of dough cooked in a stew etc. or baked with fruit inside. [same origin as *dumpy*]

dumpy *adjective* short and fat. [from an old word *dump* = dumpy person]

dunce *noun* (*plural* **dunces**) a person who is slow at learning. [from John Duns Scotus, a Scottish philosopher in the Middle Ages (because his opponents said that his followers could not understand new ideas)]

dune *noun* (*plural* **dunes**) a mound of loose sand shaped by the wind.

dung *noun* solid waste matter excreted by an animal.

dungarees *plural noun* overalls made of thick strong cloth. [from Hindi *dungri* = the cloth they were made of]

dungeon (*say* dun-jon) *noun* (*plural* **dungeons**) an underground cell for prisoners. [from old French]

duodenum (*say* dew-o-deen-um) *noun* (*plural* **duodenums**) the part of the small intestine that is just below the stomach. **duodenal** *adjective* [from Latin *duodecim* = twelve (because its length is about twelve times the breadth of a finger)]

dupe *verb* (**dupes, duping, duped**) deceive. [French]

duplicate (*say* dyoop-lik-at) *noun* (*plural* **duplicates**)
1 something that is exactly the same as something else. **2** an exact copy.

duplicate (*say* dyoop-lik-ayt) *verb* (**duplicates, duplicating, duplicated**) make or be a duplicate. **duplication** *noun,* **duplicator** *noun* [from Latin *duplex* = double]

duplicity (*say* dew-plis-it-ee) *noun* deceitfulness. [same origin as *duplicate*]

durable *adjective* strong and likely to last. **durably** *adverb,* **durability** *noun* [from Latin *durare* = endure]

during *preposition* while something else is going on. [from Latin *durans* = lasting, enduring]

dusk *noun* (*plural* **dusks**) twilight in the evening. [from Old English]

dust *noun* tiny particles of earth or other solid material.

dust *verb* (**dusts, dusting, dusted**)
1 wipe away dust. 2 sprinkle with dust or something powdery. [from Old English]

dustbin *noun* (*plural* **dustbins**) a bin for household rubbish.

dustman *noun* (*plural* **dustmen**) a person employed to empty dustbins and cart away rubbish.

dustpan *noun* (*plural* **dustpans**) a pan in which dust is brushed from a floor.

dusty *adjective* (**dustier, dustiest**)
1 covered with dust. 2 like dust.

dutiful *adjective* doing your duty; obedient. **dutifully** *adverb* [from *duty* + *-ful*]

duty *noun* (*plural* **duties**)
1 what you ought to do or must do. 2 a task that must be done. 3 a tax charged on imports and on certain other things.
on duty actually doing what is your regular work.
[same origin as *due*]

duvet (*say* doo-vay) *noun* (*plural* **duvets**) a kind of quilt used instead of other bedclothes. [French, = *down²*]

dwarf *noun* (*plural* **dwarfs** or **dwarves**) a very small person or thing.

dwarf *verb* (**dwarfs, dwarfing, dwarfed**) make something seem small by contrast, *The ocean liner dwarfed the tugs that were towing it.*
[from Old English]

dwelling *noun* (*plural* **dwellings**) a house etc. to live in.

dwindle *verb* (**dwindles, dwindling, dwindled**) get smaller gradually. [from Old English]

dye *verb* (**dyes, dyeing, dyed**) colour something by putting it into a liquid. **dyer** *noun*

dye *noun* (*plural* **dyes**) a substance used to dye things. [from Old English]

dynamic *adjective* energetic or forceful. **dynamically** *adverb* [from Greek *dynamis* = power]

dynamite *noun*
1 a powerful explosive. 2 something likely to make people very excited or angry. [same origin as *dynamic*]

dynamo *noun* (*plural* **dynamos**) a machine that makes electricity.

dynasty (*say* din-a-stee) *noun* (*plural* **dynasties**) a succession of rulers all from the same family. **dynastic** *adjective* [same origin as *dynamic*]

dys- *prefix* bad; difficult. [from Greek]

dyslexia (*say* dis-leks-ee-a) *noun* unusually great difficulty in being able to read and spell. **dyslexic** *adjective* [from *dys-* + Greek *lexis* = speech (which was confused with Latin *legere* = read)]

dystrophy (*say* dis-trof-ee) *noun* a disease that weakens the muscles. [from *dys-* + Greek *-trophia* = nourishment]

Ee

E. *abbreviation* east; eastern.

e- *prefix*
1 out; away. 2 up, upwards; thoroughly. 3 formerly. see *ex-*.

each *adjective & pronoun* every; every one, *each child; each of you.* [from Old English]

USAGE: In standard English, the pronoun *each* should be used with a singular verb and singular pronouns: *Each has chosen her own outfit.*

eager *adjective* strongly wanting to do something; enthusiastic. **eagerly** *adverb*, **eagerness** *noun* [from Latin]

eagle *noun (plural eagles)* a large bird of prey with very strong sight.

ear¹ *noun (plural ears)*
1 the organ of the body that is used for hearing. 2 hearing ability, *She has a good ear for music.* [from Old English *eare*]

ear² *noun (plural ears)* the spike of seeds at the top of a stalk of corn. [from Old English *ear*]

eardrum *noun (plural eardrums)* a membrane in the ear that vibrates when sounds reach it.

earl *noun (plural earls)* a British nobleman. **earldom** *noun*

early *adjective & adverb (earlier, earliest)*
1 before the usual or expected time. 2 near the beginning, *early in the book.* **earliness** *noun* [from *ere* + *-ly*]

earmark *verb (earmarks, earmarking, earmarked)* put something aside for a particular purpose. [from the custom of marking an animal's ear to identify it]

earn *verb (earns, earning, earned)* get something by working or in return for what you have done. [from Old English]

earnest *adjective* showing serious feelings or intentions. **earnestly** *adverb*, **earnestness** *noun*

earshot *noun* the distance within which a sound can be heard. [from *ear* + *shot* in the sense 'as far as something can reach']

earth *noun (plural earths)*
1 the planet (*Earth*) that we live on. 2 the ground; soil. 3 the hole where a fox or badger lives. 4 connection to the ground to complete an electrical circuit.

earth *verb (earths, earthing, earthed)* connect an electrical circuit to the ground.

earthenware *noun* pottery made of coarse baked clay.

earthly *adjective* concerned with life on earth rather than with life after death.

earthquake *noun (plural earthquakes)* a violent movement of part of the earth's surface.

earthy *adjective*
1 like earth or soil. 2 crude and vulgar.

earwig *noun (plural earwigs)* a crawling insect with pincers at the end of its body. [so named because it was thought to crawl into people's ears]

ease *noun* freedom from trouble or effort or pain, *She climbed the tree with ease.*

easel *noun (plural easels)* a stand for supporting a blackboard or a painting. [from Dutch *ezel* = donkey (which carries a load)]

easily *adverb*
1 without difficulty; with ease. 2 by far, *easily the best.* 3 very likely, *He could easily be lying.*

east noun
1 the direction where the sun rises. 2 the eastern part of a country, city, etc.

east adjective & adverb towards or in the east; coming from the east. **easterly** adjective, **eastern** adjective, **easterner** noun, **easternmost** adjective
[from Old English]

Easter noun the Sunday (in March or April) when Christians commemorate the resurrection of Christ; the days around it. [named after *Eastre*, an Anglo-Saxon goddess whose feast was celebrated in spring]

eastward adjective & adverb towards the east. **eastwards** adverb

easy adjective (**easier**, **easiest**) able to be done or used or understood without trouble. **easiness** noun

easy adverb with ease; comfortably, *Take it easy!*

eat verb (**eats**, **eating**, **ate**, **eaten**)
1 chew and swallow as food. 2 have a meal, *When do we eat?* 3 use up; destroy gradually, *Extra expenses ate up our savings.*
[from Old English]

eaves plural noun the overhanging edges of a roof.

eavesdrop verb (**eavesdrops**, **eavesdropping**, **eavesdropped**) listen secretly to a private conversation. **eavesdropper** noun [as if you are listening outside a wall, where water drops from the eaves]

ebb noun (plural **ebbs**)
1 the movement of the tide when it is going out, away from the land. 2 a low point, *Our courage was at a low ebb.*

EC abbreviation European Community.

eccentric (say ik-sen-trik) adjective behaving strangely. **eccentrically** adverb, **eccentricity** (say ek-sen-**triss**-it-ee) noun [from Greek *ekkentros* = away from the centre]

ecclesiastical (say ik-lee-zee-ast-ik-al) adjective to do with the Church or the clergy. [from Greek *ekklesia* = church]

echo noun (plural **echoes**) a sound that is heard again as it is reflected off something.

echo verb (**echoes**, **echoing**, **echoed**)
1 make an echo. 2 repeat a sound or saying.
[from Greek *eche* = sound]

éclair (say ay-**klair**) noun (plural **éclairs**) a finger-shaped cake of pastry with a creamy filling. [French]

eclipse noun (plural **eclipses**) the blocking of the sun's or moon's light when the moon or the earth is in the way.

eco- prefix to do with ecology or the environment. [from *ecology*]

ecology (say ee-**kol**-o-jee) noun the study of living things in relation to each other and to where they live. **ecological** adjective, **ecologically** adverb, **ecologist** noun [from Greek *oikos* = house, + *-logy*]

economic (say ee-kon-**om**-ik) adjective
1 to do with economy or economics. 2 profitable.

economical adjective using as little as possible. **economically** adverb

economics *noun* the study of how money is used and how goods and services are provided and used. **economist** *noun*

economize *verb* (economizes, economizing, economized) be economical; use or spend less.

economy *noun* (plural **economies**)
1 a country's or household's income (e.g. from what it sells or earns) and the way this is spent (e.g. on goods and services). 2 being economical. 3 a saving, *We made economies*. [from Greek *oikos* = house + *-nomia* = management]

ecstasy (say ek-sta-see) *noun*
1 a feeling of great delight. 2 an illegal drug that makes people feel very energetic and can cause hallucinations. **ecstatic** (say ik-stat-ik) *adjective*, **ecstatically** *adverb* [from Greek, = standing outside yourself]

-ed *suffix* can form a past tense or past participle of a verb (e.g. *paint/painted*), or an adjective (e.g. *diseased*). [from Old English]

eddy *noun* (plural **eddies**) a swirling patch of water or air or smoke etc.

edge *noun* (plural **edges**)
1 the part along the side or end of something. 2 the sharp part of a knife or axe or other cutting instrument.
be on edge be tense and irritable.

edgy *adjective* tense and irritable. **edginess** *noun*

edible *adjective* suitable for eating, not poisonous, *edible fruits*. [from Latin *edere* = eat]

edit *verb* (edits, editing, edited)
1 be the editor of a newspaper or other publication. 2 make written material ready for publishing. 3 choose and put the parts of a film or tape recording etc. into order. [from *editor*]

edition *noun* (plural **editions**)
1 the form in which something is published, *a paperback edition*. 2 all the copies of a book etc. issued at the same time, *the first edition*. 3 an individual television or radio programme in a series.

editor *noun* (plural **editors**)
1 the person in charge of a newspaper or a section of it. 2 a person who edits something. [Latin, = producer]

editorial *adjective* to do with editing or editors.

editorial *noun* (plural **editorials**) a newspaper article giving the editor's comments on something.

educate *verb* (educates, educating, educated) provide people with education. **educative** *adjective*, **educator** *noun* [from Latin]

education *noun* the process of training people's minds and abilities so that they acquire knowledge and develop skills. **educational** *adjective*, **educationally** *adverb*, **educationist** *noun*

-ee *suffix* forms nouns meaning 'person affected by or described as' (e.g. *absentee, employee, refugee*). [from French]

EEC *abbreviation* European Economic Community (= the Common Market).

eel *noun* (plural **eels**) a long fish that looks like a snake.

eerie *adjective* (**eerier, eeriest**) strange in a frightening or mysterious way. **eerily** *adverb*, **eeriness** *noun*

ef- *prefix*
1 out; away. **2** up, upwards; thoroughly. **3** formerly. see **ex-**.

effect *noun* (*plural* **effects**)
1 a change that is produced by an action or cause; a result. **2** an impression that is produced by something, *a cheerful effect*.

USAGE: Do not confuse with *affect*.

effective *adjective*
1 producing the effect that is wanted. **2** impressive and striking. **effectively** *adverb*, **effectiveness** *noun*

effeminate *adjective* (of a man) having qualities that are thought to be feminine. **effeminacy** *noun*

efficient *adjective* doing work well; effective. **efficiently** *adverb*, **efficiency** *noun*

effort *noun* (*plural* **efforts**)
1 the use of energy; the energy used. **2** something difficult or tiring. **3** an attempt, *This painting is a good effort*.

e.g. *abbreviation* for example. [short for Latin *exempli gratia* = for the sake of an example]

egg[1] *noun* (*plural* **eggs**)
1 a more or less round object produced by the female of birds, fishes, reptiles, and insects, which may develop into a new individual if fertilized. **2** a hen's or duck's egg used as food. **3** an ovum. [from Old Norse]

egg[2] *verb* (**eggs, egging, egged**)
encourage someone with taunts or dares etc., *We egged him on*. [from Old Norse *eggja* = sharpen]

ego (*say* eeg-oh) *noun* (*plural* **egos**) a person's self or self-respect. [Latin, = I]

Eid (*say* eed) *noun* a Muslim festival. Eid ul-Fitr marks the end of the fast of Ramadan. [from Arabic *'id* = feast]

eiderdown *noun* (*plural* **eiderdowns**) a quilt stuffed with soft material. [originally the soft down of the *eider*, a kind of duck]

eight *adjective* & *noun* (*plural* **eights**) the number 8. **eighth** *adjective* & *noun*

eighteen *adjective* & *noun* the number 18. **eighteenth** *adjective* & *noun*

eighty *adjective* & *noun* (*plural* **eighties**) the number 80. **eightieth** *adjective* & *noun*

either *adjective* & *pronoun*
1 one or the other of two, *Either team can win; either of them*. **2** both of two, *There are fields on either side of the river*.

either *adverb* also; similarly, *If you won't go, I won't either*.

either *conjunction* (used with *or*) the first of two possibilities, *He is either ill or drunk. Either come right in or go away*.

ejaculate *verb* (**ejaculates, ejaculating, ejaculated**)
1 (of a man) produce semen from the penis. **2** suddenly say something. **ejaculation** *noun* [from *e-* + Latin *jacere* = to throw]

eject *verb* (**ejects, ejecting, ejected**)
1 send something out forcefully. **2** force someone to leave.

3 (of a pilot) be thrown out of an aircraft in a special seat in an emergency. **ejection** *noun*, **ejector** *noun* [from *e-* + Latin *-jectum* = thrown]

elaborate (*say* il-ab-er-at) *adjective* having many parts or details; complicated. **elaborately** *adverb*, **elaborateness** *noun*

elaborate (*say* il-ab-er-ayt) *verb* (**elaborates, elaborating, elaborated**) explain or work something out in detail. **elaboration** *noun* [from *e-* + Latin *laborare* = to work]

elastic *noun* cord or material woven with strands of rubber etc. so that it can stretch.

elastic *adjective* able to be stretched or squeezed and then go back to its original length or shape. **elasticity** *noun* [from Greek]

elbow *noun* (*plural* **elbows**) the joint in the middle of the arm.

elbow *verb* (**elbows, elbowing, elbowed**) push with the elbow. [from Old English]

elder[1] *adjective* older, *my elder brother*.

elder *noun* (*plural* **elders**)
1 an older person, *Respect your elders!* **2** an official in certain Churches.
[an old spelling of *older*]

elder[2] *noun* (*plural* **elders**) a tree with white flowers and black berries. **elderberry** *noun* [from Old English]

elderly *adjective* rather old. [from *elder*[1] + *-ly*]

eldest *adjective* oldest. [an old spelling of *oldest*]

elect *verb* (**elects, electing, elected**)
1 choose by voting. **2** choose to do something; decide. [from *e-* + Latin *lectum* = chosen]

election *noun* (*plural* **elections**) electing; the process of electing Members of Parliament.

electorate *noun* (*plural* **electorates**) all the electors.

electric *adjective*
1 to do with or worked by electricity. **2** causing sudden excitement, *The news had an electric effect*. **electrical** *adjective*, **electrically** *adverb* [from Greek *elektron* = amber (which is easily given a charge of static electricity)]

electric chair *noun* an electrified chair used for capital punishment in the USA.

electrician *noun* (*plural* **electricians**) a person whose job is to deal with electrical equipment.

electricity *noun* a form of energy carried by certain particles of matter (electrons and protons), used for lighting and heating and for making machines work.

electrify *verb* (**electrifies, electrifying, electrified**)
1 give an electric charge to something. **2** supply something with electric power; cause something to work with electricity. **3** thrill with sudden excitement. **electrification** *noun*

electro- *prefix* to do with or using electricity.

electrocute *verb* (**electrocutes, electrocuting, electrocuted**) kill by electricity. **electrocution** *noun* [from *electro-* + *execute*]

electrode noun (plural **electrodes**) a solid conductor through which electricity enters or leaves a vacuum tube. [from *electro-* + Greek *hodos* = way]

electromagnet noun (plural **electromagnets**) a magnet worked by electricity. **electromagnetic** adjective

electron noun (plural **electrons**) a particle of matter with a negative electric charge. [same origin as *electric*]

electronic adjective produced or worked by a flow of electrons. **electronically** adverb

electronic mail noun messages sent from one computer to others.

electronics noun the use or study of electronic devices.

elegant adjective graceful and dignified. **elegantly** adverb, **elegance** noun [from Latin]

element noun (plural **elements**) **1** each of the parts that make up a whole thing. **2** each of about 100 substances composed of atoms that have the same number of protons. **3** a basic or elementary principle, *the elements of algebra.* **4** a wire or coil that gives out heat in an electric fire or cooker etc. **5** the environment or circumstances that suit you best, *Karen is really in her element at parties.*
the elements the forces of weather, such as rain, wind, and cold.

elementary adjective dealing with the simplest stages of something; easy.

elephant noun (plural **elephants**) a very large animal with a trunk and tusks. [from Greek *elephas* = ivory (which its tusks are made of)]

elevate verb (**elevates**, **elevating**, **elevated**) lift or raise something to a higher position. **elevation** noun [from *e-* + Latin *levare* = to lift]

eleven adjective & noun (plural **elevens**) the number 11. **eleventh** adjective & noun

elicit (say ill-**iss**-it) verb (**elicits**, **eliciting**, **elicited**) draw out information by reasoning or questioning. [from Latin]

eligible (say **el**-ij-ib-ul) adjective qualified or suitable for something. **eligibility** noun [from Latin *eligere* = choose]

eliminate verb (**eliminates**, **eliminating**, **eliminated**) get rid of something. **elimination** noun [from *e-* + Latin *limen* = entrance]

elision (say il-**lizh**-on) noun omitting part of a word in pronouncing it, e.g. in saying *I'm* for *I am.* [from Latin *elidere* = to push out]

élite (say ay-**leet**) noun a group of people given privileges which are not given to others. [from old French *élit* = chosen]

ellipse (say il-**ips**) noun (plural **ellipses**) an oval shape. [same origin as *elliptical*]

elliptical (say il-**ip**-tik-al) adjective **1** shaped like an ellipse. **2** with some words omitted, *an elliptical phrase.* **elliptically** adverb [from Greek *elleipsis* = fault]

elm noun (plural **elms**) a tall tree with rough leaves.

elocution (say el-o-kew-shon) *noun* the art of speaking clearly and correctly. [same origin as *eloquent*]

elongated *adjective* made longer; lengthened. **elongation** *noun* [from *e-* + Latin *longus* = long]

elope *verb* (**elopes, eloping, eloped**) run away secretly to get married. **elopement** *noun* [from old French]

eloquent *adjective* speaking fluently and expressing ideas vividly. **eloquently** *adverb*, **eloquence** *noun* [from *e-* + Latin *loqui* = speak]

else *adverb*
1 besides; other, *Nobody else knows.* **2** otherwise; if not, *Run or else you'll be late.* [from Old English]

elsewhere *adverb* somewhere else.

elude (say il-ood) *verb* (**eludes, eluding, eluded**) avoid being caught by someone, *The fox eluded the hounds.* **elusive** *adjective* [from *e-* + Latin *ludere* = to play]

USAGE: Do not confuse with *allude*.

em- *prefix*
1 in; into. **2** on. see **en-**.

e-mail *noun* electronic mail.

emancipate (say im-an-sip-ayt) *verb* (**emancipates, emancipating, emancipated**) set free from slavery or other restraints. **emancipation** *noun* [from *e-* + Latin *mancipium* = slave]

embalm *verb* (**embalms, embalming, embalmed**) preserve a corpse from decay by using spices or chemicals. [from *em-* + *balm*]

embankment *noun* (*plural* **embankments**) a long bank of earth or stone to hold back water or support a road or railway. [from *em-* + *bank*]

embargo *noun* (*plural* **embargoes**) a ban. [from Spanish *embargar* = restrain]

embark *verb* (**embarks, embarking, embarked**) put or go on board a ship or aircraft. **embarkation** *noun*
embark on begin, *They embarked on a dangerous exercise.* [from *em-* + French *barque* = a sailing ship]

embarrass *verb* (**embarrasses, embarrassing, embarrassed**) make someone feel awkward or ashamed. **embarrassment** *noun*

embassy *noun* (*plural* **embassies**)
1 an ambassador and his or her staff. **2** the building where they work. [from old French; related to *ambassador*]

embellish *verb* (**embellishes, embellishing, embellished**) ornament something; add details to it. **embellishment** *noun* [from *em-* + French *bel* = beautiful]

embers *plural noun* small pieces of glowing coal or wood in a dying fire. [from Old English]

embezzle *verb* (**embezzles, embezzling, embezzled**) take dishonestly money that was left in your care. **embezzlement** *noun*

emblem *noun* (*plural* **emblems**) a symbol that represents something, *The crown is a royal emblem*. **emblematic** *adjective* [from Latin]

embody *verb* (**embodies, embodying, embodied**)
1 express principles or ideas in a visible form, *The house embodies our idea of a modern home*. 2 include or contain, *Parts of the old treaty are embodied in the new one*. **embodiment** *noun*

embrace *verb* (**embraces, embracing, embraced**)
1 hold someone closely in your arms. 2 include a number of things. 3 accept or adopt a cause or belief.

embrace *noun* (*plural* **embraces**) a hug.
[from *em-* + Latin *bracchium* = an arm]

embroider *verb* (**embroiders, embroidering, embroidered**)
1 decorate cloth with needlework. 2 add made-up details to a story to make it more interesting. **embroidery** *noun*

embryo (say em-bree-oh) *noun* (*plural* **embryos**)
1 a baby or young animal as it starts to grow in the womb; a young bird growing in an egg. 2 anything in its earliest stages of development. **embryonic** (say embre-**on**-ik) *adjective* [from *em-* + Greek *bryein* = grow]

emend *verb* (**emends, emending, emended**) remove errors from a piece of writing. [from *e-* + Latin *menda* = a fault]

emerald *noun* (*plural* **emeralds**)
1 a bright-green precious stone. 2 its colour. [from old French]

emerge *verb* (**emerges, emerging, emerged**)
1 come out or appear. 2 become known. **emergence** *noun*, **emergent** *adjective* [from *e-* + Latin *mergere* = plunge]

emergency *noun* (*plural* **emergencies**) a sudden serious happening needing prompt action. [same origin as *emerge*]

emigrate *verb* (**emigrates, emigrating, emigrated**) leave your own country and go and live in another. **emigration** *noun*, **emigrant** *noun* [from *e-* + Latin *migrare* = migrate]

USAGE: People are *emigrants* from the country they leave and *immigrants* in the country where they settle.

eminent *adjective* famous and respected. **eminence** *noun*, **eminently** *adverb*

emit *verb* (**emits, emitting, emitted**) send out light, heat, fumes, etc. **emission** *noun* [from *e-* + Latin *mittere* = send]

emotion *noun* (*plural* **emotions**) a strong feeling in the mind, such as love or hate. **emotional** *adjective*, **emotionally** *adverb* [from French]

emperor *noun* (*plural* **emperors**) a man who rules an empire. [from Latin *imperator* = commander]

emphasis (say em-fa-sis) *noun* (*plural* **emphases**)
1 special importance given to something. 2 stress put on a word or part of a word. **emphasize** *verb* [from *em-* + Greek *phainein* = to show]

emphatic (say im-fat-ik) adjective
using emphasis. **emphatically**
adverb

empire noun (plural **empires**)
1 a group of countries controlled
by one person or government.
2 a set of shops or firms under
one control. [from Latin]

employ verb (**employs**,
employing, **employed**)
1 pay a person to work for you.
2 make use of, Our doctor employs
the most modern methods.
employer noun, **employment**
noun

employee noun (plural
employees) a person employed
by someone (who is the
employer).

empress noun (plural **empresses**)
1 a woman who rules an empire.
2 an emperor's wife. [from old
French]

empty adjective
1 with nothing in it. 2 with
nobody in it. 3 with no meaning
or no effect, empty promises.
emptily adverb, **emptiness** noun

empty verb (**empties**, **emptying**,
emptied) make or become empty.
[from Old English]

en- prefix (changing to **em-** before
words beginning with b, m, or p)
1 in; into. 2 on. [from Latin or
Greek, = in]

enable verb (**enables**, **enabling**,
enabled) give the means or
ability to do something.

enamel noun (plural **enamels**)
1 a shiny substance for coating
metal. 2 paint that dries hard and
shiny. 3 the shiny surface of
teeth.

encamp verb (**encamps**,
encamping, **encamped**) settle in
a camp.

encampment noun (plural
encampments) a camp.

enchant verb (**enchants**,
enchanting, **enchanted**)
1 put someone under a magic
spell. 2 fill someone with intense
delight. **enchanter** noun,
enchantment noun, **enchantress**
noun [from old French; related to
incantation]

encircle verb (**encircles**,
encircling, **encircled**) surround.
encirclement noun

enclose verb (**encloses**, **enclosing**,
enclosed)
1 put a wall or fence round; shut
in on all sides. 2 put something
into a box or envelope etc. [from
old French; related to include]

enclosure noun (plural
enclosures)
1 enclosing. 2 an enclosed area.
3 something enclosed with
a letter or parcel.

encore (say on-kor) noun (plural
encores) an extra item performed
at a concert etc. after previous
items have been applauded.

encounter verb (**encounters**,
encountering, **encountered**)
1 meet someone unexpectedly.
2 experience, We encountered
some difficulties.

encounter noun (plural
encounters)
1 an unexpected meeting.
2 a battle.
[from en- + Latin contra = against]

encourage verb (**encourages**,
encouraging, **encouraged**)
1 give confidence or hope;
hearten. 2 try to persuade; urge.

3 stimulate; help to develop, *Encourage healthy eating.*

encouragement *noun* [from *en-* + old French *corage* = courage]

encroach *verb* (**encroaches, encroaching, encroached**) intrude upon someone's rights; go further than the proper limits, *The extra work would encroach on their free time.* **encroachment** *noun*

encrust *verb* (**encrusts, encrusting, encrusted**) cover with a crust or layer. **encrustation** *noun* [from Latin]

encumber *verb* (**encumbers, encumbering, encumbered**) be a burden to; hamper.

encumbrance *noun* [from *en-* + old French *combre* = dam]

encyclopedia *noun* (*plural* **encyclopedias**) a book or set of books containing all kinds of information. **encyclopedic** *adjective* [from Greek *enkyklopaideia* = general education]

end *noun* (*plural* **ends**)
1 the last part or extreme point of something. **2** the half of a sports pitch or court defended or occupied by one team or player. **3** destruction or death. **4** purpose, *She did it to gain her own ends.*

end *verb* (**ends, ending, ended**) bring or come to an end.

endanger *verb* (**endangers, endangering, endangered**) cause danger to.

endless *adjective*
1 never stopping. **2** with the ends joined to make a continuous strip for use in machinery etc., *an endless belt.* **endlessly** *adverb*

endow *verb* (**endows, endowing, endowed**)
1 provide a source of income to establish something, *She endowed a scholarship.* **2** provide with an ability or quality, *He was endowed with great talent.*

endowment *noun* [from old French; related to *dowry*]

endure *verb* (**endures, enduring, endured**)
1 suffer or put up with pain or hardship etc. **2** continue to exist; last. **endurable** *adjective*, **endurance** *noun* [from *en-* + Latin *durus* = hard]

enemy *noun* (*plural* **enemies**)
1 one who hates and opposes or seeks to harm another. **2** a nation or army etc. at war with another. [from old French]

energetic *adjective* full of energy. **energetically** *adverb*

energy *noun* (*plural* **energies**)
1 strength to do things, liveliness. **2** the ability of matter or radiation to do work. Energy is measured in joules. [from *en-* + Greek *ergon* = work]

enforce *verb* (**enforces, enforcing, enforced**) compel people to obey a law or rule. **enforcement** *noun*, **enforceable** *adjective*

engage *verb* (**engages, engaging, engaged**)
1 arrange to employ or use, *Engage a typist.* **2** occupy the attention of, *They engaged her in conversation.* **3** begin a battle with, *We engaged the enemy.*

engaged *adjective*
1 having promised to marry somebody. **2** in use; occupied.

engagement *noun* (*plural* **engagements**)
1 engaging something. 2 a promise to marry somebody. 3 an arrangement to meet somebody or do something. 4 a battle.

engaging *adjective* attractive or charming.

engine *noun* (*plural* **engines**)
1 a machine that provides power. 2 a vehicle that pulls a railway train; a locomotive. [from old French; related to *ingenious*]

engineer *noun* (*plural* **engineers**) an expert in engineering.

engineer *verb* (**engineers, engineering, engineered**) plan and construct or cause to happen, *He engineered a meeting between them.*

engineering *noun* the design and building or control of machinery or of structures such as roads and bridges.

engrave *verb* (**engraves, engraving, engraved**) carve words or lines etc. on a surface. **engraver** *noun*, **engraving** *noun* [from *en-* + Old English *grafan* = carve]

enigma (*say* in-ig-ma) *noun* (*plural* **enigmas**) something very difficult to understand; a puzzle. [from Greek]

enigmatic (*say* en-ig-mat-ik) *adjective* mysterious and puzzling. **enigmatically** *adverb*

enjoy *verb* (**enjoys, enjoying, enjoyed**) get pleasure from something. **enjoyable** *adjective*, **enjoyment** *noun* [from *en-* + old French *joir* = rejoice]

enlarge *verb* (**enlarges, enlarging, enlarged**) make or become bigger. **enlargement** *noun*

enlighten *verb* (**enlightens, enlightening, enlightened**) give more knowledge or information to a person. **enlightenment** *noun*

enlist *verb* (**enlists, enlisting, enlisted**)
1 join the armed forces. 2 obtain someone's support or services etc., *enlist their help.* **enlistment** *noun*

enmity *noun* being somebody's enemy; hostility.

enormous *adjective* very large; huge. **enormously** *adverb*, **enormousness** *noun* [from *e-* + Latin *norma* = standard]

enough *adjective, noun & adverb* as much or as many as necessary, *enough food*; *I have had enough*; *Are you warm enough?* [from Old English]

enquire *verb* (**enquires, enquiring, enquired**)
1 ask for information, *He enquired if I was well.* 2 investigate something carefully. [same origin as *inquire*]

USAGE: See the note at *inquire*.

enquiry *noun* (*plural* **enquiries**)
1 a question. 2 an investigation.

enrage *verb* (**enrages, enraging, enraged**) make someone very angry.

enrich *verb* (**enriches, enriching, enriched**) make richer. **enrichment** *noun*

enrol *verb* (**enrols, enrolling, enrolled**)
1 become a member of a society etc. 2 make someone into a member. **enrolment** *noun* [from *en-* + old French *rolle* = roll]

ensemble (say on-**sombl**) noun
(plural **ensembles**)
1 a group of things that go
together. 2 a group of musicians.
3 a matching outfit of clothes.
[French]

enslave verb (enslaves, enslaving,
enslaved) make a slave of
someone; force someone into
slavery. **enslavement** noun

ensure verb (ensures, ensuring,
ensured) make certain of;
guarantee, Good will ensure
good health. [from old French]

USAGE: Do not confuse with
insure.

entail verb (entails, entailing,
entailed) make a thing necessary;
involve, This plan entails danger.
entailment noun [from en- + old
French taillir = bequeath]

entangle verb (entangles,
entangling, entangled) tangle.
entanglement noun

enter verb (enters, entering,
entered)
1 come in or go in. 2 put
something into a list or book.
3 type something into a computer.
4 register as a competitor. [from
Latin intra = within]

enterprise noun (plural
enterprises)
1 being enterprising;
adventurous spirit. 2 an
undertaking or project.
3 business activity, private
enterprise. [from en- + Latin
prehendere = take]

enterprising adjective willing to
undertake new or adventurous
projects.

entertain verb (entertains,
entertaining, entertained)
1 amuse. 2 have people as guests
and give them food and drink.
3 consider, He refused to entertain
the idea. **entertainer** noun

entertainment noun (plural
entertainments)
1 entertaining; being
entertained. 2 something
performed before an audience to
amuse or interest them.

enthusiasm noun (plural
enthusiasms) a strong liking,
interest, or excitement.
enthusiast noun, **enthusiastic**
adjective [from Greek
enthousiazein = be possessed by
a god]

entire adjective whole or
complete. **entirely** adverb [from
old French; related to integer]

entirety (say int-I-rit-ee) noun the
whole of something.
in its entirety in its complete
form.

entitle verb (entitles, entitling,
entitled) give the right to have
something, This coupon entitles
you to a ticket. **entitlement** noun
[from old French]

entitled adjective having as a title,
a short poem entitled 'Spring'.

entomology (say en-tom-ol-o-jee)
noun the study of insects.
entomologist noun [from Greek
entomon = insect, + -logy]

entrance[1] (say en-trans) noun
(plural entrances)
1 the way into a place. 2 entering,
Her entrance is the signal for
applause. [from old French]

entrance² (say in-**trahns**) verb (**entrances, entrancing, entranced**) fill with intense delight; enchant. [from en- + trance]

entrant noun (plural **entrants**) someone who enters for an examination or contest etc. [from French]

entrench verb (**entrenches, entrenching, entrenched**) 1 fix or establish firmly, These ideas are entrenched in his mind. 2 settle in a well-defended position. **entrenchment** noun

entrust verb (**entrusts, entrusting, entrusted**) place a person or thing in someone's care.

entry noun (plural **entries**) 1 an entrance. 2 something entered in a list or in a diary etc.

entwine verb (**entwines, entwining, entwined**) twine round.

enumerate verb (**enumerates, enumerating, enumerated**) count; list one by one. [from e- + Latin numerare = to number]

envelop (say en-**vel**-op) verb (**envelops, enveloping, enveloped**) cover or wrap round something completely. [from old French]

envelope (say en-vel-ohp) noun (plural **envelopes**) a wrapper or covering, especially a folded cover for a letter. [from French]

envious adjective feeling envy. **enviously** adverb

environment noun (plural **environments**) 1 surroundings, especially as they affect people's lives. 2 the natural world of the land, sea, and air. **environmental** adjective [from old French environer = surround, enclose]

environmentalist noun (plural **environmentalists**) a person who wishes to protect or improve the environment.

environmentally-friendly adjective not harmful to the environment.

envy noun 1 a feeling of discontent you have when someone possesses things that you would like to have for yourself. 2 something causing this, Their car is the envy of all their friends.

envy verb (**envies, envying, envied**) feel envy towards someone. [from French; related to invidious]

enzyme noun (plural **enzymes**) a kind of substance that assists chemical processes. [from Greek enzymos = leavened]

epi- prefix on; above; in addition. [from Greek epi = on]

epic noun (plural **epics**) 1 a long poem or story about heroic deeds or history. 2 a spectacular film. [from Greek epos = song]

epicentre noun (plural **epicentres**) the point where an earthquake reaches the earth's surface. [from epi- + Greek kentros = centre]

epidemic noun (plural **epidemics**) an outbreak of a disease that spreads quickly among the people of an area. [from epi- + Greek demos = people]

epigram noun (plural **epigrams**) a short witty saying. [from epi- + -gram]

epilepsy noun a disease of the nervous system, causing convulsions. **epileptic** adjective & noun [from Greek epilambanein = seize, attack]

epilogue (say ep-il-og) noun (plural **epilogues**) a short section at the end of a book or play etc. [from epi- + Greek logos = speech]

episode noun (plural **episodes**) **1** one event in a series of happenings. **2** one programme in a radio or television serial.

epitaph noun (plural **epitaphs**) words written on a tomb or describing a person who has died. [from epi- + Greek taphos = tomb]

epithet noun (plural **epithets**) an adjective; words expressing something special about a person or thing, e.g. 'the Great' in Alfred the Great. [from Greek epithetos = attributed]

equal adjective **1** the same in amount, size, or value etc. **2** having the necessary strength, courage, or ability etc., She was equal to the task. **equally** adverb

equal noun (plural **equals**) a person or thing that is equal to another, She has no equal.

equal verb (**equals**, **equalling**, **equalled**) be the same in amount, size, or value etc.

equality noun being equal.

equalize verb (**equalizes**, **equalizing**, **equalized**) make things equal. **equalization** noun

equation noun (plural **equations**) a statement that two amounts etc. are equal, e.g. $3 + 4 = 2 + 5$.

equator noun (plural **equators**) an imaginary line round the Earth at an equal distance from the North and South Poles. [from Latin circulus aequator diei et noctis = circle equalizing day and night]

equatorial (say ek-wa-tor-ee-al) adjective to do with or near the equator.

equi- prefix equal; equally. [from Latin aequus = equal]

equilateral (say ee-kwi-lat-er-al) adjective (of a triangle) having all sides equal.

equilibrium (say ee-kwi-lib-ree-um) noun **1** a balance between different forces, influences, etc. **2** a balanced state of mind. [from equi- + Latin libra = balance]

equinox (say ek-win-oks) noun (plural **equinoxes**) the time of year when day and night are equal in length (about 20 March in spring, about 22 September in autumn). **equinoctial** adjective [from equi- + Latin nox = night]

equip verb (**equips**, **equipping**, **equipped**) supply with what is needed. [from French]

equipment noun the things needed for a particular purpose.

equivalent adjective equal in importance, meaning, value, etc. **equivalence** noun [from equi- + Latin valens = worth]

-er[1] and **-ier** suffix can form the comparative of adjectives and adverbs (e.g. high/higher, lazy/lazier). [from Old English -re]

-er⁴ *suffix* can form nouns meaning 'a person or thing that does something' (e.g. *farmer, computer*). [from Old English *-ere*; in a few words (e.g. *butler, mariner*) from Latin: compare *-or*]

era (say **eer**-a) *noun* (*plural* **eras**) a period of history. [from Latin]

eradicate *verb* (**eradicates, eradicating, eradicated**) get rid of something; remove all traces of it. **eradication** *noun* [from Latin *eradicare* = root out]

erase *verb* (**erases, erasing, erased**) 1 rub something out. 2 wipe out a recording on magnetic tape. **eraser** *noun* [from *e-* + Latin *rasum* = scraped]

erect *adjective* standing straight up.

erect *verb* (**erects, erecting, erected**) set up or build something. **erection** *noun*, **erector** *noun* [from Latin]

erosion *noun* the wearing away of the earth's surface by the action of water, wind, etc.

erotic *adjective* arousing sexual feelings. **erotically** *adverb* [from Greek *eros* = sexual love]

errand *noun* (*plural* **errands**) a short journey to take a message or fetch goods etc. [from Old English]

erratic (say ir-**at**-ik) *adjective* 1 not regular. 2 not reliable. **erratically** *adverb* [from Latin *erraticus* = wandering]

error *noun* (*plural* **errors**) a mistake. [same origin as *err*]

erupt *verb* (**erupts, erupting, erupted**) 1 burst out. 2 when a volcano erupts, it shoots out lava. **eruption** *noun* [from *e-* + Latin *ruptum* = burst]

escalate *verb* (**escalates, escalating, escalated**) make or become greater, more serious or more intense, *The riots escalated into a war.* **escalation** *noun* [from *escalator*]

escalator *noun* (*plural* **escalators**) a staircase with an endless line of steps moving up or down. [from French *escalade* = scaling a wall with ladders]

escapade (say es-ka-**paid**) *noun* (*plural* **escapades**) a reckless adventure. [French, = an escape]

escape *verb* (**escapes, escaping, escaped**) 1 get yourself free; get out or away. 2 avoid something, *He escaped punishment.*

escape *noun* (*plural* **escapes**) 1 escaping. 2 a way to escape. [from French]

escapist *noun* (*plural* **escapists**) a person who likes to avoid thinking about serious matters by occupying his or her mind in entertainments, daydreams, etc. **escapism** *noun*

escort¹ (say **ess**-kort) *noun* (*plural* **escorts**) a person or group accompanying a person or thing, especially as a protection.

escort² (say iss-**kort**) *verb* (**escorts, escorting, escorted**) act as an escort to somebody or something.

especial *adjective* special. [from French]

especially *adverb* specially; more than anything else.

espionage (*say* ess-pee-on-ahzh) *noun* spying. [from French *espion* = spy]

espresso *noun* (*plural* **espressos**) coffee made by forcing steam through ground coffee beans. [Italian, = pressed out]

Esq. *abbreviation* (short for **Esquire**) a title written after a man's surname where no title is used before his name. [an *esquire* was originally a knight's attendant; from Latin *scutarius* = shield-bearer)]

-esque *suffix* forms adjectives meaning 'like' or 'in the style of' (e.g. *picturesque*). [French]

-ess *suffix* forms feminine nouns (e.g. *lioness*, *princess*). [from French]

essay (*say* ess-ay) *noun* (*plural* **essays**)
1 a short piece of writing in prose. 2 an attempt.

essence *noun* (*plural* **essences**)
1 the most important quality or element of something.
2 a concentrated liquid. [from Latin *esse* = to be]

essential *adjective* not able to be done without. **essentially** *adverb*

essential *noun* (*plural* **essentials**) an essential thing. [same origin as *essence*]

-est and **-iest** *suffix* can form the superlative of adjectives and adverbs (e.g. *high/highest, lazy/laziest*). [from Old English]

establish *verb* (**establishes, establishing, established**)
1 set up a business, government, or relationship etc. on a firm basis. 2 show something to be true; prove, *He established his innocence.*

the established Church a country's national Church, established by law. [from old French; related to *stable*[1]]

establishment *noun* (*plural* **establishments**)
1 establishing something.
2 a business firm or other institution.
the Establishment people who are established in positions of power and influence.

estate *noun* (*plural* **estates**)
1 an area of land with a set of houses or factories on it. 2 a large area of land owned by one person. 3 all that a person owns when he or she dies. 4 (*old use*) a condition or status, *the holy estate of matrimony*. [from old French; related to *state*]

estate agent *noun* (*plural* **estate agents**) a person whose business is selling or letting houses and land.

esteem *verb* (**esteems, esteeming, esteemed**) think that a person or thing is excellent.

esteem *noun* respect and admiration. [same origin as *estimate*]

estimable *adjective* worthy of esteem.

estimate (*say* ess-tim-at) *noun* (*plural* **estimates**) a rough calculation or guess about an amount or value.

estimate (*say* ess-tim-ayt) *verb* (**estimates, estimating, estimated**) make an estimate.

estimation noun
[from Latin aestimare = to put
a value on something]

estuary (say ess-tew-er-ee) noun
(plural estuaries) the mouth of
a river where it reaches the sea
and the tide flows in and out.
[from Latin aestus = tide]

etc. abbreviation (short for et
cetera) and other similar things;
and so on. [from Latin et = and,
+ cetera = the other things]

etch verb (etches, etching, etched)
1 engrave a picture with acid on
a metal plate, especially for
printing. 2 if something is etched
on your mind or memory, it has
made a deep impression and you
will never forget it. **etcher** noun
[from Dutch]

eternal adjective lasting for ever;
not ending or changing. **eternally**
adverb, **eternity** noun [from old
French]

ether (say ee-ther) noun
1 a colourless liquid that
evaporates easily into fumes that
are used as an anaesthetic. 2 the
upper air. [from Greek]

ethereal (say ith-eer-ee-al)
adjective light and delicate.
ethereally adverb [from Latin
aetherius = belonging to the
upper air]

ethical (say eth-ik-al) adjective
1 to do with ethics. 2 morally
right; honourable. **ethically**
adverb

ethics (say eth-iks) plural noun
standards of right behaviour;
moral principles. [from Greek
ethos = character]

ethnic adjective belonging to
a particular racial group within
a larger set of people. [from
Greek ethnos = nation]

ethnic cleansing noun the mass
killing of people from other
ethnic or religious groups within
a certain area.

etiquette (say et-ik-et) noun the
rules of correct behaviour.

-ette suffix forms diminutives
which mean 'little' (e.g. cigarette,
kitchenette). [from French]

etymology (say et-im-ol-oj-ee)
noun (plural etymologies)
1 an account of the origin of
a word and its meaning. 2 the
study of the origins of words.
etymological adjective [from
Greek etymon = original word,
+ -logy]

EU abbreviation European Union.

eu- (say yoo) prefix well. [from
Greek]

eucalyptus (say yoo-kal-ip-tus)
noun (plural eucalyptuses)
1 a kind of evergreen tree.
2 a strong-smelling oil obtained
from its leaves.

Eucharist (say yoo-ker-ist) noun
the Christian sacrament in
which bread and wine are
consecrated and swallowed,
commemorating the Last Supper
of Christ and his disciples. [from
Greek eucharistia
= thanksgiving]

eulogy (say yoo-loj-ee) noun
(plural eulogies) a piece of praise
for a person or thing. [from eu-
+ Greek -logia = speaking]

euphemism (say yoo-fim-izm)
noun (plural euphemisms) a mild
word or phrase used instead of
an offensive or frank one; 'to pass

away' is a euphemism for *'to die'*.
euphemistic *adjective*,
euphemistically *adverb* [from *eu-* + Greek *pheme* = speech]

European *adjective* to do with Europe or its people. **European** *noun*

euthanasia (*say* yooth-an-ay-zee-a) *noun* the act of causing somebody to die gently and without pain, especially when they are suffering from a painful incurable disease. [from *eu-* + Greek *thanatos* = death]

evacuate *verb* (**evacuates**, **evacuating**, **evacuated**)
1 move people away from a dangerous place. **2** make a thing empty of air or other contents.
evacuation *noun* [from *e-* + Latin *vacuus* = empty]

evacuee *noun* (*plural* **evacuees**) a person who has been evacuated.

evade *verb* (**evades**, **evading**, **evaded**) avoid a person or thing by cleverness or trickery. [from *e-* + Latin *vadere* = go]

evaluate *verb* (**evaluates**, **evaluating**, **evaluated**) estimate the value of something; assess.
evaluation *noun* [from French]

evaporate *verb* (**evaporates**, **evaporating**, **evaporated**)
1 change from liquid into steam or vapour. **2** cease to exist, *Their enthusiasm had evaporated.*
evaporation *noun* [from *e-* = out + Latin *vapor* = steam]

evasion *noun* (*plural* **evasions**)
1 evading. **2** an evasive answer or excuse.

evasive *adjective* evading something; not frank or

straightforward. **evasively** *adverb*, **evasiveness** *noun*

even[1] *adjective*
1 level and smooth. **2** not varying. **3** calm; not easily upset, *an even temper.* **4** equal, *Our scores were even.* **5** able to be divided exactly by two, *Six and fourteen are even numbers.* (Compare *odd*.) **evenly** *adverb*, **evenness** *noun*

even *verb* (**evens**, **evening**, **evened**) make or become even.

even *adverb* (used to emphasize a word or statement) *She ran even faster.*
even so although that is correct.

evening *noun* (*plural* **evenings**) the time at the end of the day before most people go to bed. [from Old English]

event *noun* (*plural* **events**)
1 something that happens, especially something important. **2** a race or competition that forms part of a sports contest. [from Latin *evenire* = happen]

eventful *adjective* full of happenings.

eventual *adjective* happening at last, *his eventual success.*
eventually *adverb* [from Latin *eventus* = result, event]

ever *adverb*
1 at any time, *the best thing I ever did.* **2** always, *ever hopeful.* **3** (*informal*, used for emphasis) *Why ever didn't you tell me?*

evergreen *adjective* having green leaves all the year. **evergreen** *noun*

every *adjective* each without any exceptions, *We enjoyed every minute.*
every one each one.

every other day or week etc., each alternate one; every second one.

USAGE: Follow with a singular verb, e.g. *Every one of them is growing* (not 'are growing').

---

everybody *pronoun* every person.

everyday *adjective* ordinary; usual, *everyday clothes.*

everyone *pronoun* everybody.

everything *pronoun*
1 all things; all. 2 the only or most important thing, *Beauty is not everything.*

everywhere *adverb* in every place.

evict *verb* (evicts, evicting, evicted) make people move out from where they are living. **eviction** *noun* [from Latin *evictum* = expelled]

evidence *noun*
1 anything that gives people reason to believe something.
2 statements made or objects produced in a lawcourt to prove something. [same origin as *evident*]

evident *adjective* obvious; clearly seen. **evidently** *adverb* [from *e-* + Latin *videre* = see]

evil *adjective* morally bad; wicked. **evilly** *adverb*

evil *noun* (plural **evils**)
1 wickedness. 2 something unpleasant or harmful. [from Old English]

evolution (say ee-vol-oo-shon) *noun*
1 evolving; gradual change into something different.

2 the development of animals and plants from earlier or simpler forms. **evolutionary** *adjective*

evolve *verb* (evolves, evolving, evolved) develop gradually or naturally. [from *e-* + Latin *volvere* = to roll]

ewe (say yoo) *noun* (plural **ewes**) a female sheep. [from Old English]

ex- *prefix* (changing to ef- before words beginning with *f*; shortened to **e-** before many consonants)
1 out; away (as in *extract*). 2 up, upwards; thoroughly (as in *extol*). 3 formerly (as in *ex-president*). [from Latin *ex* = out of]

exact *adjective*
1 correct. 2 clearly stated; giving all details, *exact instructions.* **exactly** *adverb*, **exactness** *noun*

exact *verb* (exacts, exacting, exacted) insist on something and obtain it, *He exacted obedience from the recruits.* **exaction** *noun* [from *ex-* + Latin *actum* = performed]

exaggerate *verb* (exaggerates, exaggerating, exaggerated) make something seem bigger, better, or worse etc. than it really is. **exaggeration** *noun* [from *ex-* + Latin *aggerare* = heap up]

examination *noun* (plural **examinations**)
1 a test of a person's knowledge or skill. 2 examining something; an inspection.

examine *verb* (examines, examining, examined)
1 test a person's knowledge or skill.
2 inspect; look at something

example 222 **excite**

closely. **examiner** noun [from Latin *examinare* = weigh accurately]

example noun (plural **examples**) **1** anything that shows what others of the same kind are like or how they work. **2** a person or thing good enough to be worth imitating. [from Latin]

exasperate verb (**exasperates**, **exasperating**, **exasperated**) annoy someone. **exasperation** noun [from *ex-* + Latin *asper* = rough]

excavate verb (**excavates**, **excavating**, **excavated**) dig out; uncover by digging. **excavation** noun, **excavator** noun [from *ex-* + Latin *cavus* = hollow]

exceed verb (**exceeds**, **exceeding**, **exceeded**) **1** be greater than; surpass. **2** do more than you need or ought to do; go beyond its limits, *He has exceeded his authority.* [from *ex-* + Latin *cedere* = go]

excel verb (**excels**, **excelling**, **excelled**) be better than others at doing something. [from *ex-* + Latin *celsus* = lofty]

Excellency noun (plural **Excellencies**) the title of high officials such as ambassadors and governors. [from Latin]

excellent adjective extremely good. **excellently** adverb, **excellence** noun [from Latin]

except preposition excluding; not including, *They all left except me.*

except verb (**excepts**, **excepting**, **excepted**) exclude; leave out, *I blame you all, no one is excepted.* [from *ex-* + Latin *-ceptum* = taken]

USAGE: Do not confuse with *accept.*

exception noun (plural **exceptions**) a person or thing that is left out or does not follow the general rule.

take exception raise objections to something.

with the exception of except.

exceptional adjective **1** forming an exception; very unusual. **2** outstandingly good. **exceptionally** adverb

excess noun (plural **excesses**) too much of something. **excessive** adjective [same origin as *exceed*]

exchange verb (**exchanges**, **exchanging**, **exchanged**) give something and receive something else for it. **exchangeable** adjective

exchange noun (plural **exchanges**) **1** exchanging. **2** a place where things (especially stocks and shares) are bought and sold, *a stock exchange.* **3** a place where telephone lines are connected to each other when a call is made. [from old French]

exchequer noun (plural **exchequers**) a national treasury into which public funds (such as taxes) are paid. [from Latin *scaccarium* = chessboard (because the Norman kings kept their accounts by means of counters placed on a chequered tablecloth)]

excitable adjective easily excited.

excite verb (**excites**, **exciting**, **excited**) **1** rouse a person's feelings; make eager, *The thought of finding gold excited them.* **2** cause a feeling; arouse, *The invention excited*

great interest. **excitedly** *adverb*
[from *ex-* + Latin *citum* = woken,
stirred]

excitement *noun* (*plural*
excitements) a strong feeling of
eagerness or pleasure.

exclaim *verb* (**exclaims,
exclaiming, exclaimed**) shout or
cry out in eagerness or surprise.
[from *ex-* + Latin *clamare* = cry]

exclamation *noun* (*plural*
exclamations)
1 exclaiming. **2** a word or words
cried out expressing joy or pain
or surprise etc.

exclamation mark *noun* (*plural*
exclamation marks) the
punctuation mark (!) placed after
an exclamation.

exclude *verb* (**excludes,
excluding, excluded**)
1 keep somebody or something
out. **2** leave something out, *Do not
exclude the possibility of rain.*
exclusion *noun* [from *ex-* + Latin
claudere = shut]

exclusive *adjective*
1 allowing only certain people to
be members etc., *an exclusive
club.* **2** not shared with others,
*This newspaper has an exclusive
report.* **exclusively** *adverb*,
exclusiveness *noun*
exclusive of excluding, not
including, *This is the price
exclusive of meals.*

excrete *verb* (**excretes, excreting,
excreted**) get rid of waste matter
from the body. **excretion** *noun*,
excretory *adjective* [from *ex-*
+ Latin *cretum* = separated]

excruciating (say iks-**kroo**-shee-
ayt-ing) *adjective*

extremely painful; agonizing.
excruciatingly *adverb* [from *ex-*
+ Latin *cruciatum* = tortured]

excursion *noun* (*plural*
excursions) a short journey made
for pleasure. [from *ex-* + Latin
cursus = course]

excuse (say iks-**kewz**) *verb*
(**excuses, excusing, excused**)
1 forgive. **2** allow someone not to
do something or to leave a room
etc., *Please may I be excused
swimming?*
excuse (say iks-**kewss**) *noun*
(*plural* **excuses**) a reason given to
explain why something wrong
has been done.
[from *ex-* + Latin *causa*
= accusation]

execute *verb* (**executes,
executing, executed**)
1 put someone to death as
a punishment. **2** perform or
produce something, *She executed
the somersault perfectly.*
execution *noun* [from Latin
executare = to carry out]

executive (say ig-**zek**-yoo-tiv)
noun (*plural* **executives**) a senior
person with authority in
a business or government
organization.

exempt *adjective* not having to do
something that others have to do,
*Charities are exempt from paying
tax.* **exemption** *noun*

exercise *noun* (*plural* **exercises**)
1 using your body to make it
strong and healthy. **2** a piece of
work done for practice.
exercise *verb* (**exercises,
exercising, exercised**)
1 do exercises. **2** give exercise to
an animal etc.

3 use, *exercise patience.*
[from Latin *exercere* = keep someone working]

exert *verb* (exerts, exerting, exerted) use power or influence etc., *He exerted all his strength.* **exertion** *noun*

exert yourself make an effort.

exhale *verb* (exhales, exhaling, exhaled) breathe out. **exhalation** *noun* [from *ex-* + Latin *halare* = breathe]

exhaust *verb* (exhausts, exhausting, exhausted)
1 make somebody very tired.
2 use up something completely. **exhaustion** *noun*

exhaust *noun* (plural exhausts)
1 the waste gases or steam from an engine. **2** the pipe etc. through which they are sent out.
[from *ex-* + Latin *haustum* = drained]

exhaustive *adjective* thorough; trying everything possible, *We made an exhaustive search.* **exhaustively** *adverb*

exhibit *verb* (exhibits, exhibiting, exhibited) show or display something in public. **exhibitor** *noun*

exhibit *noun* (plural exhibits) something on display in a gallery or museum.
[from *ex-* + Latin *habere* = hold]

exhibition *noun* (plural exhibitions) a collection of things put on display for people to look at.

exhilarate (say ig-**zil**-er-ayt) *verb* (exhilarates, exhilarating, exhilarated) make someone very happy and excited. **exhilaration** *noun* [from *ex-* + Latin *hilaris* = cheerful]

exhort (say ig-**zort**) *verb* (exhorts, exhorting, exhorted) urge someone earnestly. **exhortation** *noun* [from *ex-* + Latin *hortari* = encourage]

exile *verb* (exiles, exiling, exiled) banish.

exile *noun* (plural exiles)
1 a banished person. **2** having to live away from your own country, *He was in exile for ten years.*
[from Latin]

exist *verb* (exists, existing, existed)
1 be present as part of what is real, *Do ghosts exist?* **2** stay alive, *We cannot live without food.* **existence** *noun*, **existent** *adjective* [from *ex-* + Latin *sistere* = stand]

exit *noun* (plural exits)
1 the way out of a building.
2 going off the stage, *The actress made her exit.*

exit *verb* (in stage directions) he or she leaves the stage.
[Latin, = he or she goes out]

exorcize *verb* (exorcizes, exorcizing, exorcized) get rid of an evil spirit. **exorcism** *noun*, **exorcist** *noun* [from Greek]

exotic *adjective*
1 very unusual, *exotic clothes.*
2 from another part of the world, *exotic plants.* **exotically** *adverb* [from Greek *exo* = outside]

expand *verb* (expands, expanding, expanded) make or become larger or fuller. **expansion** *noun*, **expansive** *adjective* [from *ex-* + Latin *pandere* = to spread]

expect *verb* (expects, expecting, expected)
1 think or believe that something

will happen or that someone will come. **2** think that something ought to happen, *She expects obedience*. [from *ex-* + Latin *spectare* = to look]

expectant *adjective*
1 expecting something to happen; hopeful. **2** an expectant mother is a woman who is pregnant.
expectantly *adverb*, **expectancy** *noun*

expectation *noun* (*plural* **expectations**)
1 expecting something; being hopeful. **2** something you expect to happen or get.

expedient (*say* iks-**pee**-dee-ent) *adjective*
1 suitable or convenient. **2** useful and practical though perhaps unfair. **expediently** *adverb*, **expediency** *noun*
expedient *noun* (*plural* **expedients**) a means of doing something, especially when in difficulty.

expedition *noun* (*plural* **expeditions**)
1 a journey made in order to do something. **2** speed or promptness. **expeditionary** *adjective* [from French; related to *expedite*]

expel *verb* (**expels**, **expelling**, **expelled**)
1 send or force something out, *This fan expels stale air*. **2** make a person leave a school or country etc. **expulsion** *noun* [from *ex-* + Latin *pellere* = drive]

expendable *adjective* able to be sacrificed or got rid of in order to gain something.

expenditure *noun* (*plural* **expenditures**) the spending or using up of money or effort etc.

expense *noun* (*plural* **expenses**) the cost of doing something.

expensive *adjective* costing a lot.
expensively *adverb*, **expensiveness** *noun*

experience *noun* (*plural* **experiences**)
1 what you learn from doing or seeing things. **2** something that has happened to you.
experience *verb* (**experiences**, **experiencing**, **experienced**) have something happen to you. [same origin as *experiment*]

experienced *adjective* having great skill or knowledge from much experience.

experiment *noun* (*plural* **experiments**) a test made in order to find out what happens or to prove something. **experimental** *adjective*, **experimentally** *adverb*
experiment *verb* (**experiments**, **experimenting**, **experimented**) carry out an experiment.
experimentation *noun* [from Latin *experiri* = to test]

expert *noun* (*plural* **experts**) a person with great knowledge or skill in something.
expert *adjective* having great knowledge or skill. **expertly** *adverb*, **expertness** *noun* [from Latin *expertus* = experienced]

expire *verb* (**expires**, **expiring**, **expired**)
1 come to an end; stop being usable, *Your season ticket has expired*. **2** die. **3** breathe out air.

expiration noun, **expiry** noun
[from *ex-* + Latin *spirare*
= breathe]

explain verb (**explains**, **explaining**,
explained)
1 make something clear to
somebody else; show its
meaning. **2** account for
something, *That explains his
absence.* **explanation** noun [from
ex- + Latin *planare* = make level
or plain]

explicit (say iks-**pliss**-it) adjective
stated or stating something
openly and exactly. (Compare
implicit.) **explicitly** adverb [from
Latin *explicitus* = unfolded]

explode verb (**explodes**,
exploding, **exploded**)
1 burst or suddenly release
energy with a loud noise. **2** cause
a bomb to go off. **3** increase
suddenly or quickly. [originally
= to drive a player off the stage
by clapping or hissing; from *ex-*
+ Latin *plaudere* = clap]

exploit (say iks-**ploit**) verb
(**exploits**, **exploiting**, **exploited**)
1 use or develop resources. **2** use
a person or thing selfishly.
exploitation noun

explore verb (**explores**, **exploring**,
explored)
1 travel through a country etc. in
order to learn about it. **2** examine
a subject or idea carefully, *We
explored the possibilities.*
exploration noun, **explorer** noun,
exploratory adjective [from Latin
explorare = search out]

explosion noun (plural
explosions)
1 the exploding of a bomb etc.;
the noise made by exploding.
2 a sudden great increase.

explosive adjective able to
explode.

explosive noun (plural
explosives) an explosive
substance.

exponent noun (plural
exponents)
1 a person who expounds
something. **2** someone who uses
a certain technique. **3** the raised
number etc. written to the right
of another (e.g. 3 in 2^3) showing
how many times the first one is
to be multiplied by itself; index.

export verb (**exports**, **exporting**,
exported) send goods abroad to
be sold. **exportation** noun,
exporter noun

export noun (plural **exports**)
1 exporting things. **2** something
exported.
[from *ex-* + Latin *portare* = carry]

expose verb (**exposes**, **exposing**,
exposed)
1 reveal or uncover. **2** allow light
to reach a photographic film so
as to take a picture. **exposure**
noun [from old French]

express adjective
1 going or sent quickly. **2** clearly
stated, *This was done against my
express orders.*

express noun (plural **expresses**)
a fast train stopping at only a few
stations.

express verb (**expresses**,
expressing, **expressed**)
1 put ideas etc. into words; make
your feelings known. **2** press or
squeeze out, *Express the juice.*
[from old French]

expression noun (plural
expressions)
1 the look on a person's face that
shows his or her feelings. **2** a word

or phrase etc. **3** a way of speaking or of playing music etc. so as to show your feelings. **4** expressing, *this expression of opinion.*

expressive *adjective* full of expression.

expulsion *noun* (*plural* **expulsions**) expelling or being expelled.

exquisite (*say* eks-kwiz-it) *adjective* very beautiful.
exquisitely *adverb* [from Latin *exquisitus* = sought out]

extend *verb* (**extends, extending, extended**)
1 stretch out. **2** make something become longer or larger. **3** offer or give, *Extend a warm welcome to our friends.* **extendible** *adjective*, **extensible** *adjective* [from *ex-* + Latin *tendere* = to stretch]

extension *noun* (*plural* **extensions**)
1 extending or being extended. **2** something added on; an addition to a building. **3** one of a set of telephones in an office or house etc.

extensive *adjective* covering a large area or range, *extensive gardens.* **extensively** *adverb*, **extensiveness** *noun*

extent *noun* (*plural* **extents**)
1 the area or length over which something extends. **2** the amount, level, or scope of something, *the full extent of his power.* [from Latin *extenta* = extended]

exterior *adjective* outer.
exterior *noun* (*plural* **exteriors**) the outside of something. [Latin, = further out]

exterminate *verb* (**exterminates, exterminating, exterminated**) destroy or kill all the members or examples. **extermination** *noun*, **exterminator** *noun* [originally = banish; from *ex-* + Latin *terminus* = boundary]

external *adjective* outside.
externally *adverb* [from Latin]

extinct *adjective*
1 not existing any more, *The dodo is an extinct bird.* **2** not burning; not active, *an extinct volcano.* [same origin as *extinguish*]

extinction *noun*
1 making or becoming extinct. **2** extinguishing; being extinguished.

extinguish *verb* (**extinguishes, extinguishing, extinguished**)
1 put out a fire or light. **2** put an end to; destroy, *Our hopes of victory were extinguished.* [from *ex-* + Latin *stinguere* = quench]

extort *verb* (**extorts, extorting, extorted**) obtain something by force or threats. **extortion** *noun* [from *ex-* + Latin *tortum* = twisted]

extortionate *adjective* charging or demanding far too much. [from *extort*]

extra *adjective* additional; more than is usual, *extra strength.*

extra *adverb* more than usually, *extra strong.*

extra *noun* (*plural* **extras**)
1 an extra person or thing. **2** a person acting as part of a crowd in a film or play. [probably from *extraordinary*]

extra- *prefix* outside; beyond (as in *extraterrestrial*). [from Latin]

extract (say iks-**trakt**) *verb* (**extracts, extracting, extracted**) take out; remove. **extractor** *noun*

extract (say **eks**-trakt) *noun* (*plural* **extracts**)
1 a passage taken from a book, speech, film, etc. **2** a substance separated or obtained from another.
[from *ex-* + Latin *tractum* = pulled]

extraction *noun*
1 extracting. **2** someone's descent, *He is of Chinese extraction.*

extraordinary *adjective* very unusual or strange.
extraordinarily *adverb* [from Latin *extra ordinem* = out of the ordinary]

extrasensory *adjective* outside the range of the known human senses.

extraterrestrial *adjective* from beyond the earth's atmosphere; from outer space.

extraterrestrial *noun* (*plural* **extraterrestrials**) a being from outer space.

extravagant *adjective* spending or using too much. **extravagantly** *adverb*, **extravagance** *noun* [from *extra-* + Latin *vagans* = wandering]

extreme *adjective*
1 very great or intense, *extreme cold.* **2** furthest away, *the extreme north.* **3** going to great lengths in actions or opinions; not moderate. **extremely** *adverb*

extreme *noun* (*plural* **extremes**)
1 something extreme. **2** either end of something. [from Latin *extremus* = furthest out]

extricate (say **eks**-trik-ayt) *verb* (**extricates, extricating, extricated**) release from a difficult position. **extrication** *noun* [from *ex-* + Latin *tricae* = entanglements]

extrovert *noun* (*plural* **extroverts**) a person who is generally friendly and likes company. (The opposite is *introvert.*)

exuberant (say ig-**zew**-ber-ant) *adjective* very lively. **exuberantly** *adverb*, **exuberance** *noun* [from Latin *exuberare* = grow thickly]

exude *verb* (**exudes, exuding, exuded**)
1 give off like sweat or a smell etc. **2** ooze out. [from *ex-* + Latin *sudare* = to sweat]

exult *verb* (**exults, exulting, exulted**) rejoice greatly. **exultant** *adjective*, **exultation** *noun* [from Latin *exsilire* = leap up]

eye *noun* (*plural* **eyes**)
1 the organ of the body that is used for seeing. **2** the power of seeing, *She has sharp eyes.* **3** the small hole in a needle. **4** the centre of a storm.

eye *verb* (**eyes, eyeing, eyed**) look at something with interest.
[from Old English]

eyeball *noun* (*plural* **eyeballs**) the ball-shaped part of the eye inside the eyelids.

eyebrow *noun* (*plural* **eyebrows**) the fringe of hair growing on the face above the eye.

eyelash *noun* (*plural* **eyelashes**) one of the short hairs that grow on an eyelid.

eyelid *noun* (*plural* **eyelids**) either of the two folds of skin that can close over the eyeball.

eyepiece noun (plural **eyepieces**) the lens of a telescope or microscope etc. that you put to your eye.

eyesight noun the ability to see.

eyewitness noun (plural **eyewitnesses**) a person who actually saw an accident or crime etc.

Ff

fable noun (plural **fables**) a short story that teaches about behaviour, often with animals as characters. [from Latin *fabula* = story]

fabric noun (plural **fabrics**) 1 cloth. 2 the framework of a building (walls, floors, and roof). [from Latin]

fabricate verb (**fabricates, fabricating, fabricated**) 1 construct or manufacture something. 2 invent, *fabricate an excuse.* **fabrication** noun [from Latin *fabricare* = to make or forge]

fabulous adjective 1 wonderful. 2 incredibly great, *fabulous wealth.* 3 told of in fables. **fabulously** adverb [same origin as *fable*]

façade (say fas-ahd) noun (plural **façades**) 1 the front of a building. 2 an outward appearance, especially a deceptive one. [French; related to *face*]

face noun (plural **faces**) 1 the front part of the head. 2 the expression on a person's face. 3 the front or upper side of something. 4 a surface, *A cube has six faces.*

face verb (**faces, facing, faced**) 1 look or have the front towards something, *Our room faced the sea.* 2 meet and have to deal with something; encounter, *Explorers face many dangers.* 3 cover a surface with a layer of different material. [from Latin *facies* = appearance]

facetious (say fas-ee-shus) adjective trying to be funny at an unsuitable time, *facetious remarks.* **facetiously** adverb [from Latin *facetus* = witty]

facilitate (say fas-il-it-ayt) verb (**facilitates, facilitating, facilitated**) make something easy or easier. **facilitation** noun

facility (say fas-il-it-ee) noun (plural **facilities**) 1 something that provides you with the means to do things, *There are sports facilities.* 2 easiness.

facsimile (say fak-sim-il-ee) noun (plural **facsimiles**) 1 an exact reproduction of a document etc. 2 a fax. [from Latin *fac* = make + *simile* = a likeness]

fact noun (plural **facts**) something that is certainly true. **the facts of life** information about how babies are conceived. [from Latin *factum* = thing done]

faction noun (plural **factions**) a small united group within a larger one, especially in politics. [from Latin]

-faction suffix forms nouns (e.g. *satisfaction*) from verbs that end in *-fy*. [from Latin]

factor noun (plural **factors**)
1 something that helps to bring about a result, *Hard work was a factor in her success.* 2 a number by which a larger number can be divided exactly, *2 and 3 are factors of 6.* [from Latin *facere* = do or make]

factory noun (plural **factories**)
a large building where machines are used to make things. [from Latin *factorium* = place where things are made]

faculty noun (plural **faculties**)
1 any of the powers of the body or mind (e.g. sight, speech, understanding). 2 a department teaching a particular subject in a university, *the faculty of music.*

fad noun (plural **fads**)
1 a person's particular like or dislike. 2 a temporary fashion or craze. **faddy** adjective [originally a dialect word; origin unknown]

fade verb (**fades, fading, faded**)
1 lose or cause to lose colour or freshness or strength. 2 disappear gradually. 3 make a sound etc. become gradually weaker (*fade it out*) or stronger (*fade it in* or *up*).

faeces (say **fee**-seez) plural noun
solid waste matter passed out of the body. [plural of Latin *faex* = dregs]

Fahrenheit adjective measuring temperature on a scale where water freezes at 32° and boils at 212°. [named after G. D. Fahrenheit, a German scientist, who invented the mercury thermometer]

fail verb (**fails, failing, failed**)
1 try to do something but be unable to do it. 2 become weak or useless; break down, *The brakes failed.* 3 not do something, *He failed to warn me.* 4 not get enough marks to pass an examination. 5 judge that someone has not passed an examination.

fail noun
without fail for certain; whatever happens.
[from Latin *fallere* = disappoint, deceive]

failing noun (plural **failings**)
a weakness or a fault.

failure noun (plural **failures**)
1 not being able to do something. 2 a person or thing that has failed.

faint adjective
1 pale or dim; not distinct. 2 weak or giddy; nearly unconscious. 3 slight, *a faint hope.* **faintly** adverb, **faintness** noun

faint verb (**faints, fainting, fainted**) become unconscious. [same origin as *feint*]

USAGE: Do not confuse with *feint*.

fair[1] adjective
1 right or just; according to the rules, *a fair fight.* 2 (of hair or skin) light in colour; (of a person) having fair hair. 3 (*old use*) beautiful. 4 fine or favourable, *fair weather.* 5 moderate; quite good, *a fair number of people.* **fairness** noun

fair adverb fairly, *Play fair!* [from Old English]

fair[2] noun (plural **fairs**)
1 a group of entertainments such as roundabouts and sideshows. 2 an exhibition or market. [from Latin *feriae* = holiday]

fairly *adverb*
1 justly; according to the rules.
2 moderately, *It is fairly hard.*

fairy *noun* (*plural* **fairies**) an imaginary very small creature with magic powers. **fairyland** *noun*, **fairy tale** *noun* [from an old word *fay*, from Latin *fata* = the Fates, three goddesses who were believed to control people's lives]

faith *noun* (*plural* **faiths**) strong belief; trust.
in good faith with honest intentions.
[from old French; related to *fidelity*]

faithful *adjective*
1 loyal and trustworthy.
2 sexually loyal to one partner. **faithfully** *adverb*, **faithfulness** *noun*
Yours faithfully see *yours*.

fake *noun* (*plural* **fakes**) something that looks genuine but is not; a forgery.
fake *verb* (**fakes, faking, faked**)
1 make something that looks genuine, in order to deceive people. 2 pretend, *They faked illness.* **faker** *noun*

falcon *noun* (*plural* **falcons**) a kind of hawk often used in the sport of hunting other birds or game. **falconry** *noun*

fall *verb* (**falls, falling, fell, fallen**)
1 come or go down without being pushed or thrown etc. 2 decrease; become lower, *Prices fell.* 3 be captured or overthrown, *The city fell.* 4 die in battle. 5 happen, *Silence fell.* 6 become, *She fell asleep.*
fall back retreat.
fall back on use for support or in an emergency.

fall for 1 be attracted by a person.
2 be taken in by a deception.
fall out quarrel.
fall through fail, *plans fell through.*

fall *noun* (*plural* **falls**)
1 the action of falling.
2 (*American*) autumn, when leaves fall.

fallacy (*say* fal-a-see) *noun* (*plural* **fallacies**) a false idea or belief. **fallacious** (*say* fal-ay-shus) *adjective* [same origin as *fail*]

Fallopian tube *noun* (*plural* **Fallopian tubes**) one of the two tubes in a woman's body along which the eggs travel from the ovaries to the uterus.

fallout *noun* particles of radioactive material carried in the air after a nuclear explosion.

false *adjective*
1 untrue or incorrect. 2 not genuine; faked. 3 treacherous or deceitful. **falsely** *adverb*, **falseness** *noun*, **falsity** *noun* [same origin as *fail*]

falter *verb* (**falters, faltering, faltered**)
1 hesitate when you move or speak. 2 become weaker; begin to give way, *His courage faltered.* [origin unknown]

fame *noun* being famous. **famed** *adjective* [from Latin *fama* = report, rumour]

familiar *adjective*
1 well-known; often seen or experienced. 2 knowing something well, *Are you familiar with this book?* 3 very friendly. **familiarly** *adverb*, **familiarity** *noun* [from Latin *familias* = family]

family noun (plural **families**)
1 parents and their children, sometimes including grandchildren and other relations. 2 a group of things that are alike in some way. [from Latin]

family planning noun birth control.

family tree noun (plural **family trees**) a diagram showing how people in a family are related.

famine noun (plural **famines**) a very bad shortage of food in an area. [from Latin *fames* = hunger]

famished adjective very hungry. **famishing** adjective [same origin as *famine*]

famous adjective known to very many people. [same origin as *fame*]

famously adverb (informal) very well, *They get on famously*.

fan[1] noun (plural **fans**) an object or machine for making air move about so as to cool people or things.
fan verb (**fans, fanning, fanned**) send a current of air on something.
fan out spread out in the shape of a fan.

fan[2] noun (plural **fans**) an enthusiast; a great admirer or supporter. [short for *fanatic*]

fanatic noun (plural **fanatics**) a person who is very enthusiastic or too enthusiastic about something. **fanatical** adjective, **fanatically** adverb, **fanaticism** noun [from Latin *fanaticus* = inspired by a god]

fanciful adjective
1 imagining things. 2 imaginary.

fancy noun (plural **fancies**)
1 a liking or desire for something. 2 imagination.

fancy adjective decorated or elaborate; not plain.

fancy verb (**fancies, fancying, fancied**)
1 believe, *I fancy it's raining.* 2 imagine. 3 have a liking or desire for something. [short for *fantasy*]

fancy dress noun unusual costume worn for a party, often to make you look like a famous person.

fantastic adjective
1 (informal) excellent. 2 designed in a very fanciful way. **fantastically** adverb [from Greek *phantazesthai* = imagine]

fantasy noun (plural **fantasies**) something imaginary or fantastic. [same origin as *fantastic*]

far adverb
1 at or to a great distance, *We didn't go far.* 2 much; by a great amount, *This is far better.*

far adjective distant or remote, *On the far side of the river.* [from Old English]

fare noun (plural **fares**)
1 the price charged for a passenger to travel. 2 food and drink, *There was only very plain fare.*

farewell interjection & noun (plural **farewells**) goodbye.

farm noun (plural **farms**)
1 an area of land where someone grows crops or keeps animals for food or other use. 2 the farmer's house. **farmhouse** noun, **farmyard** noun

farm verb (farms, farming, farmed)
1 grow crops or keep animals for food etc. 2 use land for growing crops; cultivate.

farmer noun (plural farmers)
a person who owns or manages a farm.

farther adverb & adjective at or to a greater distance; more distant. [a different spelling of *further*]

USAGE: *Farther* and *farthest* are used only in connection with distance (e.g. *She lives farther from the school than I do*), but even in such cases many people prefer to use *further*. Only *further* can be used to mean 'additional', e.g. in *We must make further inquiries*. If you are not sure which is right, use *further*.

farthest adverb & adjective at or to the greatest distance; most distant.

USAGE: See the note at *farther*.

farthing noun (plural farthings)
a former British coin worth one-quarter of a penny. [from Old English *feorthing* = one-fourth]

fascinate verb (fascinates, fascinating, fascinated) be very attractive or interesting to somebody. **fascination** noun, **fascinator** noun [from Latin *fascinum* = a spell]

fashion noun (plural fashions)
1 the style of clothes or other things that most people like at a particular time. 2 a way of

doing something, *Continue in the same fashion.* **fashionable** adjective, **fashionably** adverb

fast[1] adjective
1 moving or done quickly; rapid. 2 allowing fast movement, *a fast road.* 3 showing a time later than the correct time, *Your watch is fast.* 4 firmly fixed or attached. 5 not likely to fade, *fast colours.* **fastness** noun

fast adverb
1 quickly, *Run fast!* 2 firmly, *His leg was stuck fast in the mud.* **fast asleep** in a deep sleep. [from Old English *faest*]

fast[2] verb (fasts, fasting, fasted) go without food. **fast** noun [from Old English *faestan*]

fasten verb (fastens, fastening, fastened) fix one thing firmly to another. **fastener** noun, **fastening** noun [from Old English]

fat noun (plural fats)
1 the white greasy part of meat. 2 oil or grease used in cooking. **the fat of the land** the best food.

fat adjective (fatter, fattest)
1 having a very thick round body. 2 thick, *a fat book.* 3 full of fat. **fatness** noun

fatal adjective causing death or disaster, *a fatal accident.* **fatally** adverb [from Latin *fatalis* = by fate]

fate noun (plural fates)
1 a power that is thought to make things happen. 2 what will happen or has happened to somebody or something; destiny. [from Latin *fatum*, literally = that which has been spoken]

father noun (plural fathers)
1 a male parent. 2 the title of certain priests. **fatherly** adjective

father-in-law noun (plural **fathers-in-law**) the father of a married person's husband or wife.

fatigue noun
1 tiredness. 2 weakness in metals, caused by stress. **fatigued** adjective [from Latin *fatigare* = make weary]

fatten verb (**fattens, fattening, fattened**) make or become fat.

fatty adjective like fat; containing fat.

fatuous adjective silly or foolish. **fatuously** adverb, **fatuousness** noun, **fatuity** noun [from Latin]

fault noun (plural **faults**)
1 anything that makes a person or thing imperfect; a flaw or mistake. 2 the responsibility for something wrong, *It wasn't your fault.* 3 a break in a layer of rock. **faulty** adjective

fault verb (**faults, faulting, faulted**)
1 find faults in something. 2 form a fault.
[from old French; related to *fail*]

fauna noun the animals of a certain area or period of time. (Compare *flora*.) [from the name of Fauna, an ancient Roman country goddess, sister of Faunus (see *faun*)]

favour noun (plural **favours**)
1 a kind or helpful act. 2 approval; goodwill. 3 friendly support shown to one person or group but not to another, *without fear or favour.*

favour verb (**favours, favouring, favoured**) be in favour of something; show favour to a person.
[from Latin]

favourable adjective
1 showing approval. 2 helpful or advantageous. **favourably** adverb

favourite adjective liked more than others. **favourite** noun

fax noun (plural **faxes**)
1 a machine that sends an exact copy of a document electronically. 2 a copy produced by this.

fax verb (**faxes, faxing, faxed**) send a copy of a document using a fax machine.
[from *facsimile*]

fear noun (plural **fears**) a feeling that something unpleasant may happen.

fear verb (**fears, fearing, feared**) feel fear; be afraid of somebody or something.
[from Old English]

fearful adjective
1 feeling fear; afraid. 2 causing fear or horror, *a fearful monster.* 3 (*informal*) very great or bad. **fearfully** adverb

fearsome adjective frightening.

feasible adjective
1 able to be done; possible. 2 likely or probable, *a feasible explanation.* **feasibly** adverb, **feasibility** noun [from French *faire* = do]

USAGE: The use of *feasible* to mean 'likely or probable' has not become generally accepted in standard English, so it is better to avoid it in writing or formal situations.

feast noun (plural **feasts**)
1 a large splendid meal. 2 a religious festival. **feast** verb [from old French; related to *fête*]

feather noun (plural **feathers**)
one of the very light coverings
that grow from a bird's skin.
feathery adjective

feather verb (**feathers,
feathering, feathered**) cover or
line something with feathers.

feature noun (plural **features**)
1 any part of the face (e.g. mouth,
nose, eyes). 2 an important or
noticeable part; a characteristic.
3 a special newspaper article or
programme that deals with
a particular subject. 4 the main
film in a cinema programme.
[from Latin *factura* = a creation]

fed past tense of **feed**.
fed up (informal) discontented.

federal adjective to do with
a system in which several States
are ruled by a central
government but are responsible
for their own internal affairs.
federation noun [from Latin
foederis = of a treaty]

fee noun (plural **fees**) a charge for
something. [from old French]

feeble adjective weak; without
strength. **feebly** adverb,
feebleness noun [from Latin
flebilis = wept over]

feed verb (**feeds, feeding, fed**)
1 give food to a person or animal.
2 take food. 3 supply something
to a machine etc. **feeder** noun

feed noun food for animals or
babies.

feedback noun
1 the response you get from
people to something you have
done. 2 the harsh noise produced
when some of the sound from an
amplifier goes back into it.

feel verb (**feels, feeling, felt**)
1 touch something to find out
what it is like. 2 be aware of
something; have an opinion.
3 experience an emotion. 4 give
a certain sensation, *It feels warm.*
feel like want.

feeler noun (plural **feelers**)
1 a long thin projection on an
insect's or crustacean's body,
used for feeling; an antenna.
2 a cautious question or
suggestion etc. to test people's
reactions.

feeling noun (plural **feelings**)
1 the ability to feel things; the
sense of touch. 2 what a person
feels.

feint (say faynt) noun (plural
feints) a pretended attack or
punch meant to deceive an
opponent.

feint verb (**feints, feinting,
feinted**) make a feint.
[old French, = feigned]

USAGE: Do not confuse with
faint.

fell[1] past tense of **fall**.

fell[2] verb (**fells, felling, felled**)
make something fall; cut or
knock down, *They were felling the
trees.*

fellow noun (plural **fellows**)
1 a friend or companion; one who
belongs to the same group.
2 a man or boy. 3 a member of
a learned society.

fellow adjective of the same
group or kind, *Her fellow teachers
supported her.*
[from Old Norse]

fellowship *noun* (*plural* **fellowships**)
1 friendship. 2 a group of friends; a society.

felt[1] *past tense* of **feel**.

felt[2] *noun* a thick fabric made of fibres of wool or fur etc. pressed together. [from Old English]

female *adjective* of the sex that can bear offspring or produce eggs or fruit.

female *noun* (*plural* **females**) a female person, animal, or plant. [from Latin *femina* = woman]

feminine *adjective*
1 to do with or like women; suitable for women. 2 (in some languages) belonging to the class of words which includes the words referring to women. **femininity** *noun* [same origin as *female*]

feminist *noun* (*plural* **feminists**) a person who believes that women should be given the same rights and status as men. **feminism** *noun*

fence *noun* (*plural* **fences**)
1 a barrier made of wood or wire etc. round an area. 2 a structure for a horse to jump over. 3 a person who buys stolen goods and sells them again.

fence *verb* (**fences**, **fencing**, **fenced**)
1 put a fence round or along something. 2 fight with long narrow swords (called *foils*) as a sport. **fencer** *noun* [shortened from *defence*]

fend *verb* (**fends**, **fending**, **fended**)
fend for provide things for someone.

fend off keep a person or thing away from yourself. [shortened from *defend*]

ferment (*say* fer-ment) *verb* (**ferments**, **fermenting**, **fermented**) bubble and change chemically by the action of a substance such as yeast. **fermentation** *noun*

ferment (*say* fer-ment) *noun*
1 fermenting. 2 an excited or agitated condition. [from Latin *fermentum* = yeast]

fern *noun* (*plural* **ferns**) a plant with feathery leaves and no flowers. [from Old English]

ferocious *adjective* fierce or savage. **ferociously** *adverb*, **ferocity** *noun* [from Latin *ferox* = fierce]

-ferous and **-iferous** *suffix* form nouns meaning 'carrying' or 'providing' (e.g. *carboniferous*). [from Latin *ferre* = carry]

ferry *verb* (**ferries**, **ferrying**, **ferried**) transport people or things, especially across water.

ferry *noun* (*plural* **ferries**) a boat or aircraft used in ferrying.

fertile *adjective*
1 producing good crops, *fertile soil*. 2 able to produce offspring. 3 able to produce ideas, *a fertile imagination*. **fertility** *noun*

fertilize *verb* (**fertilizes**, **fertilizing**, **fertilized**)
1 add substances to the soil to make it more fertile. 2 put pollen into a plant or sperm into an egg or female animal so that it develops seed or young. **fertilization** *noun*, **fertilizer** *noun*

festival *noun* (*plural* **festivals**) a time when people arrange special celebrations, performances, etc. [from Latin]

festivity noun (plural **festivities**)
a festive occasion or celebration.

festoon noun (plural **festoons**)
a chain of flowers or ribbons etc.
hung as a decoration.

festoon verb (**festoons**,
festooning, **festooned**) decorate
something with ornaments.
[via French from Italian *festone*
= festive ornament]

fetch verb (**fetches**, **fetching**,
fetched)
1 go for and bring back, *fetch
some milk; fetch a doctor.* **2** be sold
for a particular price, *The chairs
fetched £20.*

fête (say fayt) noun (plural **fêtes**)
an outdoor entertainment with
stalls and sideshows. [from old
French *feste* = feast]

fetter noun (plural **fetters**) a chain
or shackle put round a prisoner's
ankle.

feud (say fewd) noun (plural
feuds) a long-lasting quarrel,
especially between two families.
[via Old French from Germanic;
related to *foe*]

feudal (say few-dal) adjective to
do with the system used in the
Middle Ages in which people
could farm land in exchange for
work done for the owner.
feudalism noun [from Latin]

fever noun (plural **fevers**)
1 an abnormally high body
temperature, usually with an
illness. **2** excitement or agitation.
fevered adjective, **feverish**
adjective, **feverishly** adverb [from
Latin]

few adjective not many. **fewness**
noun

few noun a small number of
people or things.

fiancé (say fee-ahn-say) noun
(plural **fiancés**) a man who is
engaged to be married. [French,
= betrothed]

fiancée (say fee-ahn-say) noun
(plural **fiancées**) a woman who is
engaged to be married. [same
origin as *fiancé*]

fiasco (say fee-as-koh) noun
(plural **fiascos**) a complete
failure. [Italian]

fibre noun (plural **fibres**)
1 a very thin thread. **2** a substance
made of thin threads.
3 indigestible material in certain
foods that stimulates the action
of the intestines. **fibrous** adjective

fibreglass noun
1 fabric made from glass fibres.
2 plastic containing glass fibres.

fickle adjective constantly
changing; not loyal to one person
or group etc. **fickleness** noun

fiction noun (plural **fictions**)
1 writings about events that have
not really happened; stories and
novels. **2** something imagined or
untrue. **fictional** adjective

fiddle noun (plural **fiddles**)
1 (*informal*) a violin. **2** (*slang*)
a swindle.

fiddle verb (**fiddles**, **fiddling**,
fiddled)
1 (*informal*) play the violin.
2 fidget or tinker with
something, using your fingers.
3 (*slang*) swindle; get or change
something dishonestly.
fiddler noun
[from Old English]

fidget verb (**fidgets**, **fidgeting**,
fidgeted) make small restless
movements. **fidgety** adjective

field noun (plural **fields**)
1 a piece of land with grass or crops growing on it. **2** an area of interest or study, *recent advances in the field of science.* **3** those who are taking part in a race or outdoor game etc.

field verb (**fields, fielding, fielded**)
1 stop or catch the ball in cricket etc. **2** be on the side not batting in cricket etc. **3** put a team into a match, contest, etc., *They fielded their best players for the final.* **fielder** noun, **fieldsman** noun

fieldwork noun practical work or research done in various places, not in a library or museum or laboratory etc.

fiend (say feend) noun (plural **fiends**)
1 an evil spirit; a devil. **2** a very wicked or cruel person. **3** an enthusiast, *a fresh-air fiend.* **fiendish** adjective [from Old English]

fierce adjective
1 angry and violent or cruel. **2** intense, *fierce heat.* **fiercely** adverb, **fierceness** noun [from Latin *ferus =* untamed]

fifteen adjective & noun
1 the number 15. **2** a team in Rugby Union football. **fifteenth** adjective & noun [from Old English]

fifth adjective & noun (plural **fifths**) next after the fourth. **fifthly** adverb [from Old English]

fifty adjective & noun (plural **fifties**) the number 50. **fiftieth** adjective & noun [from Old English]

fifty-fifty adjective & adverb
1 shared equally between two people or groups. **2** evenly balanced, *a fifty-fifty chance.*

fig noun (plural **figs**) a soft fruit full of small seeds. [from Latin]

fight noun (plural **fights**)
1 a struggle against somebody using hands, weapons, etc. **2** an attempt to achieve or overcome something, *the fight against poverty.*

fight verb (**fights, fighting, fought**)
1 have a fight. **2** attempt to achieve or overcome something. **fighter** noun

figure noun (plural **figures**)
1 the symbol of a number. **2** an amount or value. **3** a diagram or illustration. **4** a shape. **5** the shape of a person's, especially a woman's, body. **6** a person. **7** a representation of a person or animal in painting, sculpture, etc.

figure verb (**figures, figuring, figured**) appear or take part in something.
figure out work something out.

figurehead noun (plural **figureheads**)
1 a carved figure decorating the prow of a sailing ship. **2** a person who is head of a country or organization but has no real power.

figure of speech noun (plural **figures of speech**) a word or phrase used for dramatic effect and not intended literally, e.g. 'a *flood* of letters'.

filament noun (plural **filaments**)
a thread or thin wire, especially one in a light bulb. [from Latin *filum* = thread]

file[1] noun (plural **files**) a metal tool with a rough surface that is rubbed on things to shape them or make them smooth.

file verb (**files, filing, filed**) shape or smooth something with a file. [from Old English]

file[2] noun (plural **files**)
1 a folder or box etc. for keeping papers in order. 2 a collection of data stored under one name in a computer. 3 a line of people one behind the other.

file verb (**files, filing, filed**)
1 put something into a file. 2 walk in a file, *They filed out.* [from Latin *filum* = thread (because a string or wire was put through papers to hold them in order)]

filings plural noun tiny pieces of metal rubbed off by a file, *iron filings.*

fill verb (**fills, filling, filled**)
1 make or become full. 2 block up a hole or cavity. **filler** noun

fill noun enough to fill a person or thing, *We ate our fill.* [from Old English]

film noun (plural **films**)
1 a motion picture, such as those shown in cinemas or on television. 2 a rolled strip or sheet of thin plastic coated with material that is sensitive to light, used for taking photographs or making a motion picture. 3 a very thin layer, *a film of grease.*

film verb (**films, filming, filmed**)

make a film of a story etc. [from Old English *filmen* = thin skin]

filter noun (plural **filters**)
1 a device for holding back dirt or other unwanted material from a liquid or gas etc. passing through it. 2 a system for filtering traffic.

filter verb (**filters, filtering, filtered**)
1 pass through a filter. 2 move gradually, *They filtered into the hall.* 3 move in a particular direction while other traffic is held up. [from old French]

filth noun disgusting dirt. [from Old English]

filthy adjective (**filthier, filthiest**) disgustingly dirty. **filthiness** noun

fin noun (plural **fins**)
1 a thin flat part sticking out from a fish's body, that helps it to swim. 2 a small part that sticks out on an aircraft or rocket etc., for helping its balance. [from Old English]

final adjective
1 coming at the end; last. 2 that puts an end to an argument etc., *You must go, and that's final!*
finally adverb, **finality** noun

final noun (plural **finals**) the last in a series of contests.
[from Latin *finis* = end]

finalist noun (plural **finalists**) a competitor in a final.

finance noun the use or management of money. **financial** adjective

finances plural noun money resources; funds.

finance verb (**finances, financing, financed**) provide the money for

something. **financier** noun
[from old French *finer* = settle
a debt]

find verb (**finds, finding, found**)
1 get or see something by looking
for it or by chance. **2** learn
something by experience, *He
found that digging was hard
work.*

find out get or discover some
information.

find noun (plural **finds**)
something found.
[from Old English]

fine¹ adjective
1 of high quality; excellent. **2** dry
and clear; sunny, *fine weather.*
3 very thin; consisting of small
particles. **4** in good health; well,
I'm fine. **finely** adverb, **fineness**
noun

fine adverb
1 finely, *chop it fine.* **2** (informal)
very well, *That will suit me fine.*
[same origin as *finish*]

fine² noun (plural **fines**) money
which has to be paid as
a punishment.

fine verb (**fines, fining, fined**)
make somebody pay a fine.
[from Latin *finis* = end (in the
Middle Ages it referred to the
sum paid to settle a lawsuit)]

finger noun (plural **fingers**)
1 one of the separate parts of the
hand. **2** a narrow piece of
something, *fish fingers.*

finger verb (**fingers, fingering,
fingered**) touch or feel something
with your fingers.

fingerprint noun (plural
fingerprints) a mark made by the
tiny ridges on the fingertip, used
as a way of identifying someone.

finish verb (**finishes, finishing,
finished**) bring or come to an end.

finish noun (plural **finishes**)
1 the last stage of something; the
end. **2** the surface or coating on
woodwork etc.
[from Latin *finis* = end]

finite (say **fy**-nyt) adjective
limited; not infinite, *We have only
a finite supply of coal.* [from Latin
finitus = finished]

finite verb noun (plural **finite
verbs**) a verb that agrees with its
subject in person and number;
'was', 'went', and 'says' are finite
verbs; 'going' and 'to say' are not.

fir noun (plural **firs**) an evergreen
tree with needle-like leaves, that
produces cones. [from Old Norse]

fire noun (plural **fires**)
1 the process of burning that
produces light and heat. **2** coal
and wood etc. burning in a grate
or furnace to give heat. **3** a device
using electricity or gas to heat
a room. **4** the shooting of guns,
Hold your fire!

on fire burning.

set fire to start something
burning.

fire verb (**fires, firing, fired**)
1 set fire to. **2** bake pottery or
bricks etc. in a kiln. **3** shoot a gun;
send out a bullet or missile.
4 dismiss someone from a job.
5 excite, *fire them with
enthusiasm.* **firer** noun
[from Old English]

firearm noun (plural **firearms**)
a small gun; a rifle, pistol, or
revolver.

fire brigade noun (plural **fire
brigades**) a team of people
organized to fight fires.

fire engine noun (plural **fire engines**) a large vehicle that carries firefighters and equipment to put out large fires.

fire escape noun (plural **fire escapes**) a special staircase by which people may escape from a burning building etc.

fire extinguisher noun (plural **fire extinguishers**) a metal cylinder from which water or foam can be sprayed to put out a fire.

firefighter noun (plural **firefighters**) a member of a fire brigade.

fireplace noun (plural **fireplaces**) an open structure for holding a fire in a room.

firewood noun wood for use as fuel.

firework noun (plural **fireworks**) a device containing chemicals that burn or explode attractively and noisily.

firing squad noun (plural **firing squads**) a group ordered to shoot a condemned person.

firm noun (plural **firms**) a business organization.

firm adjective
1 not giving way when pressed; hard or solid. **2** steady; not shaking or moving. **3** definite and not likely to change, *a firm belief*. **firmly** adverb, **firmness** noun

firm verb (**firms, firming, firmed**) make something become firm. [from Latin]

first adjective coming before all others in time or order or importance. **firstly** adverb

first adverb before everything else, *Finish this work first.*

first aid noun treatment given to an injured person before a doctor comes.

fish noun (plural **fish** or **fishes**) an animal with gills and fins that always lives and breathes in water.

fish verb (**fishes, fishing, fished**) **1** try to catch fish. **2** search for something; try to get something, *He is only fishing for praise.* [from Old English]

fisherman noun (plural **fishermen**) a person who tries to catch fish.

fishmonger noun (plural **fishmongers**) a shopkeeper who sells fish. [from *fish* + an old word *monger* = trader]

fishy adjective (**fishier, fishiest**) **1** smelling or tasting of fish. **2** (*informal*) causing doubt or suspicion, *a fishy excuse.* **fishily** adverb, **fishiness** noun

fission noun
1 splitting something. **2** splitting the nucleus of an atom so as to release energy. **fissionable** adjective [from Latin *fissum* = split]

fist noun (plural **fists**) a tightly closed hand with the fingers bent into the palm. [from Old English]

fit¹ adjective (**fitter, fittest**) **1** suitable or good enough, *a meal fit for a king.* **2** healthy, *Keep fit!* **3** ready or likely, *They worked till they were fit to collapse.* **fitly** adverb, **fitness** noun

fit² verb (**fits, fitting, fitted**) **1** be the right size and shape for something; be suitable. **2** put something into place, *Fit a lock on the door.* **3** alter something to make it the right size and shape.

4 make suitable for something, *His training fits him for the job.* **fitter** *noun*

fit *noun* the way something fits, *a good fit.*
[origin unknown]

fit² *noun* (*plural* **fits**)
1 a sudden illness, especially one that makes you move violently or become unconscious. **2** an outburst, *a fit of rage.* [from Old English]

fitful *adjective* happening in short periods, not steadily. **fitfully** *adverb* [from *fit²* + *-ful*]

fitting *adjective* proper or appropriate, *This statue is a fitting memorial to an extraordinary woman.*

five *adjective & noun* (*plural* **fives**) the number 5. [from Old English]

fix *verb* (**fixes, fixing, fixed**)
1 fasten or place firmly. **2** make permanent and unable to change. **3** decide or arrange, *We fixed a date for the party.* **4** repair; put into working condition, *He is fixing my bike.* **fixer** *noun*
fix up arrange or organize something.

fixedly *adverb* in a fixed way.

fixture *noun* (*plural* **fixtures**)
1 something fixed in its place. **2** a sports event planned for a particular day.

fizz *verb* (**fizzes, fizzing, fizzed**) make a hissing or spluttering sound; produce a lot of small bubbles. [imitating the sound]

fizzy *adjective* (of a drink) having a lot of small bubbles. **fizziness** *noun*

flabby *adjective* fat and soft, not firm. **flabbily** *adverb*, **flabbiness** *noun* [related to *flap*]

flag¹ *noun* (*plural* **flags**)
1 a piece of cloth with a coloured pattern or shape on it, used as a sign or signal. **2** a small piece of paper or plastic that looks like a flag. **flagpole** *noun*, **flagstaff** *noun*

flag *verb* (**flags, flagging, flagged**)
1 become weak; droop. **2** signal with a flag or by waving.
[from an old word *flag* = drooping]

flag² *noun* (*plural* **flags**) a flat slab of stone used for paving. [from Old Norse *flaga* = slab of stone]

flagrant (*say* **flay**-grant) *adjective* very bad and noticeable, *flagrant disobedience.* **flagrantly** *adverb*, **flagrancy** *noun* [from Latin *flagrans* = blazing]

flagship *noun* (*plural* **flagships**)
1 a ship that carries an admiral and flies his flag. **2** the best and most important product that a company produces.

flair *noun* a natural ability or talent, *Ian has a flair for languages.* [French, = power to smell things]

USAGE: Do not confuse with *flare*.

flake *noun* (*plural* **flakes**)
1 a very light thin piece of something. **2** a small flat piece of falling snow. **flaky** *adjective*

flamboyant *adjective* very showy in appearance or manner.
[French, = blazing]

flame *noun* (*plural* **flames**) a tongue-shaped portion of fire or burning gas.

flame verb (flames, flaming, flamed)
1 produce flames. 2 become bright red.

flamingo noun (plural flamingoes) a wading bird with long legs, a long neck, and pinkish feathers. [from Spanish]

flammable adjective able to be set on fire. **flammability** noun [from Latin flamma = flame]

USAGE: See note at inflammable.

flank noun (plural flanks) the side of something, especially an animal's body or an army.

flannel noun (plural flannels)
1 a soft cloth for washing yourself. 2 a soft woollen material. [from Welsh gwlanen = woollen]

flap verb (flaps, flapping, flapped)
1 wave about. 2 (slang) panic or fuss about something.

flap noun (plural flaps)
1 a part that is fixed at one edge onto something else, often to cover an opening. 2 the action or sound of flapping. 3 (slang) a panic or fuss, in a flap.

flare verb (flares, flaring, flared)
1 blaze with a sudden bright flame. 2 become angry suddenly. 3 become gradually wider, flaring nostrils.

flare noun (plural flares)
1 a sudden bright flame or light, especially one used as a signal. 2 a gradual widening. [origin unknown]

USAGE: Do not confuse with flair.

flash noun (plural flashes)
1 a sudden bright flame or light. 2 a device for making a sudden bright light for taking photographs. 3 a sudden display of anger, wit, etc. 4 a short item of news.

flash verb (flashes, flashing, flashed)
1 make a flash. 2 appear suddenly; move quickly, The train flashed past us.

flashback noun (plural flashbacks) going back in a film or story to something that happened earlier.

flashy adjective gaudy or showy.

flask noun (plural flasks)
1 a bottle with a narrow neck. 2 a vacuum flask.

flat adjective (flatter, flattest)
1 with no curves or bumps; smooth and level. 2 spread out; lying at full length, Lie flat on the ground. 3 (of a tyre) with no air inside. 4 (of feet) without the normal arch underneath.
5 absolute, a flat refusal. 6 dull; not changing. 7 (of a drink) no longer fizzy. 8 (of a battery) unable to produce any more electric current. 9 (in music) one semitone lower than the natural note, E flat. **flatly** adverb, **flatness** noun

flat noun (plural flats)
1 a set of rooms for living in, usually on one floor of a building. 2 (in music) a note one semitone lower than the natural note; the sign (♭) that indicates this. 3 a punctured tyre. [from Old Norse]

flatten verb (flattens, flattening, flattened) make or become flat.

flatter verb (flatters, flattering, flattered)
1 praise somebody more than he or she deserves. 2 make a person or thing seem better or more attractive than they really are.
flatterer noun, **flattery** noun [from old French *flater* = smooth down]

flaunt verb (flaunts, flaunting, flaunted) display something proudly in a way that annoys people; show it off, *He liked to flaunt his expensive clothes and cars.*

USAGE: Do not confuse this word with *flout*, which has a different meaning.

flavour noun (plural **flavours**) the taste of something.
flavour verb (flavours, flavouring, flavoured) give something a flavour; season it.
flavouring noun
[from old French]

flaw noun (plural **flaws**) something that makes a person or thing imperfect. **flawed** adjective

flea noun (plural **fleas**) a small jumping insect that sucks blood.

fleck noun (plural **flecks**)
1 a very small patch of colour. 2 a particle; a speck, *flecks of dirt.*
flecked adjective

fledged adjective (of young birds) having grown feathers and able to fly.
fully-fledged adjective fully trained, *a fully-fledged engineer.*

fledgeling noun (plural **fledgelings**) a young bird that is just fledged. [from *fledge* = become fledged, + *-ling*]

fleece noun (plural **fleeces**) the woolly hair of a sheep or similar animal. **fleecy** adjective
fleece verb (fleeces, fleecing, fleeced)
1 shear the fleece from a sheep. 2 swindle a person out of some money.

fleet noun (plural **fleets**) a number of ships, aircraft, or vehicles owned by one country or company.

fleeting adjective passing quickly; brief.

flesh noun
1 the soft substance of the bodies of people and animals, consisting of muscle and fat. 2 the pulpy part of fruits and vegetables.
fleshy adjective [from Old English]

flex verb (flexes, flexing, flexed) bend or stretch something that is flexible, *flex your muscles.*
flex noun (plural **flexes**) flexible insulated wire for carrying electric current.
[from Latin *flexum* = bent]

flexible adjective
1 easy to bend or stretch. 2 able to be changed or adapted, *Our plans are flexible.* **flexibility** noun

flick noun (plural **flicks**) a quick light hit or movement.
flick verb (flicks, flicking, flicked) hit or move with a flick.

flicker verb (flickers, flickering, flickered)
1 burn or shine unsteadily. 2 move quickly to and fro.
flicker noun (plural **flickers**) a flickering light or movement.

flight[1] *noun* (*plural* **flights**)
1 flying. 2 a journey in an aircraft etc. 3 a series of stairs. 4 the feathers or fins on a dart or arrow. [from Old English]

flight[2] *noun* (*plural* **flights**)
fleeing; an escape. [from Middle English]

flimsy *adjective* (**flimsier, flimsiest**) made of something thin or weak. **flimsily** *adverb*, **flimsiness** *noun* [origin unknown]

flinch *verb* (**flinches, flinching, flinched**) move or shrink back because you are afraid; wince. **flinch** *noun*

fling *verb* (**flings, flinging, flung**) throw something violently or carelessly.

fling *noun* (*plural* **flings**)
1 the movement of flinging.
2 a vigorous dance, *the Highland fling*. 3 a short time of enjoyment, *have a fling*.
[origin unknown]

flint *noun* (*plural* **flints**)
1 a very hard kind of stone.
2 a piece of flint or hard metal used to produce sparks. **flinty** *adjective* [from Old English]

flip *verb* (**flips, flipping, flipped**)
1 flick. 2 (*slang*) become crazy or very angry.

flip *noun* (*plural* **flips**) a flipping movement.
[origin unknown]

flippant *adjective* not showing proper seriousness. **flippantly** *adverb*, **flippancy** *noun* [from *flip*]

flirt *verb* (**flirts, flirting, flirted**) behave lovingly towards somebody to amuse yourself. **flirtation** *noun*

flirt *noun* (*plural* **flirts**) a person who flirts. **flirtatious** *adjective*, **flirtatiously** *adverb* [origin unknown]

float *verb* (**floats, floating, floated**)
1 stay or move on the surface of a liquid or in air. 2 make something float. **floater** *noun*

float *noun* (*plural* **floats**)
1 a device designed to float.
2 a vehicle with a platform used for delivering milk or for carrying a display in a parade etc. 3 a small amount of money kept for paying small bills or giving change etc.

flock *noun* (*plural* **flocks**) a group of sheep, goats, or birds.

flock *verb* (**flocks, flocking, flocked**) gather or move in a crowd.

flog *verb* (**flogs, flogging, flogged**)
1 beat a person or animal hard with a whip or stick as a punishment. 2 (*slang*) sell. **flogging** *noun* [from Latin]

flood *noun* (*plural* **floods**)
1 a large amount of water spreading over a place that is usually dry. 2 a great amount, *a flood of requests*. 3 the movement of the tide when it is coming in towards the land.

flood *verb* (**floods, flooding, flooded**)
1 cover with a flood. 2 come in great amounts, *Letters flooded in.*

floodlight *noun* (*plural* **floodlights**) a lamp that makes a broad bright beam to light up a stage, stadium, important building, etc. **floodlit** *adjective*

floor *noun* (*plural* **floors**)
1 the part of a room that people

walk on. **2** a storey of a building; all the rooms at the same level.

USAGE: In Britain, the *ground floor* of a building is the one at street level, and the one above it is the *first floor*. In the USA, the *first floor* is the one at street level, and the one above it is the *second floor*.

floor verb (floors, flooring, floored)
1 put a floor into a building. **2** knock a person down. **3** baffle somebody.
[from Old English]

flop verb (flops, flopping, flopped)
1 fall or sit down clumsily. **2** hang or sway heavily and loosely. **3** (*slang*) be a failure. **floppy** adjective

floppy disk noun (plural **floppy disks**) a flexible disc holding data for use in a computer.

flora noun the plants of a particular area or period. (Compare *fauna*.) [from the name of *Flora*, the ancient Roman goddess of flowers; her name comes from Latin *flores* = flowers]

florist noun (plural **florists**) a shopkeeper who sells flowers. [same origin as *flora*]

flotsam noun wreckage or cargo found floating after a shipwreck. **flotsam and jetsam** odds and ends.
[from old French *floter* = float]

flounce verb (flounces, flouncing, flounced) go in an impatient or annoyed manner, *She flounced out of the room*. **flounce** noun

flounder verb (flounders, floundering, floundered)
1 move clumsily and with difficulty. **2** make mistakes or become confused when trying to do something. [from old French]

flour noun a fine powder of wheat or other grain, used in cooking. **floury** adjective [old spelling of *flower*]

flourish verb (flourishes, flourishing, flourished)
1 grow or develop strongly. **2** be successful; prosper. **3** wave something about dramatically.

flourish noun (plural **flourishes**) a showy or dramatic sweeping movement, curve, or passage of music.
[from Latin *florere* = to flower]

flout verb (flouts, flouting, flouted) disobey a rule or instruction openly and scornfully, *She shaved her head one day, just because she loved to flout convention*. [probably from Dutch *fluiten* = whistle, hiss]

USAGE: Do not confuse this word with *flaunt*, which has a different meaning.

flow verb (flows, flowing, flowed)
1 move along smoothly or continuously. **2** gush out, *Water flowed from the tap*. **3** hang loosely, *flowing hair*. **4** (of the tide) come in towards the land.

flow noun (plural **flows**)
1 a flowing movement or mass. **2** the movement of the tide when it is coming in towards the land, *the ebb and flow of the tide*.

flower noun (plural **flowers**)
1 the part of a plant from which seed and fruit develops.
2 a blossom and its stem used for decoration, usually in groups. (Compare *flora*.)

flower verb (flowers, flowering, flowered) produce flowers. [from old French; related to *flora*]

flowery adjective
1 full of flowers. 2 full of ornamental phrases.

flu noun influenza.

fluctuate verb (fluctuates, fluctuating, fluctuated) rise and fall; vary, *Prices fluctuated.* **fluctuation** noun [from Latin *fluctus* = a wave]

fluent (say floo-ent) adjective
1 skilful at speaking clearly and without hesitating. 2 able to speak a foreign language easily and well. **fluently** adverb, **fluency** noun [from Latin *fluens* = flowing]

fluff noun a fluffy substance. [probably from Flemish]

fluffy adjective having a mass of soft fur or fibres. **fluffiness** noun

fluid noun (plural fluids) a substance that is able to flow freely as liquids and gases do.

fluid adjective
1 able to flow freely. 2 not fixed, *My plans for Christmas are fluid.* **fluidity** noun
[from Latin *fluere* = to flow]

fluke noun (plural flukes) a piece of good luck that makes you able to do something you thought you could not do. [origin unknown]

fluorescent (say floo-ess-ent) adjective creating light from radiation, *a fluorescent lamp.* **fluorescence** noun [from *fluorspar*, a fluorescent mineral]

fluoridation noun adding fluoride to drinking water in order to help prevent tooth decay.

fluoride noun a chemical substance that is thought to prevent tooth decay. [from Latin]

flurry noun (plural flurries)
1 a sudden whirling gust of wind, rain, or snow. 2 an excited or flustered disturbance. [from an old word *flurr* = to throw about]

flush[1] verb (flushes, flushing, flushed)
1 blush. 2 clean or remove something with a fast flow of water.

flush noun (plural flushes)
1 a blush. 2 a fast flow of water. [imitating the sound of water]

flush[2] adjective
1 level with the surrounding surface, *The doors are flush with the walls.* 2 having plenty of money. [origin unknown]

fluster verb (flusters, flustering, flustered) make somebody nervous and confused. **fluster** noun [origin unknown]

flute noun (plural flutes) a musical instrument consisting of a long pipe with holes that are stopped by fingers or keys. [from old French]

flutter verb (flutters, fluttering, fluttered)
1 flap wings quickly. 2 move or flap quickly and irregularly.

flutter noun (plural flutters)
1 a fluttering movement.
2 a nervously excited condition.
3 (informal) a small bet, *Have a flutter!*
[from Old English]

fly[1] noun (plural flies)
1 a small flying insect with two wings. 2 a real or artificial fly used as bait in fishing. [from Old English *flycge*]

fly[2] *verb* (**flies, flying, flew, flown**)
1 move through the air by means of wings or in an aircraft. **2** travel through the air or through space. **3** wave in the air, *Flags are flying.* **4** make something fly, *They flew model aircraft.* **5** move or pass quickly, *Time flies.* **6** flee from, *You must fly the country!* **flyer** *noun*

fly *noun* (*plural* **flies**) the front opening of a pair of trousers. [from Old English *fleogan*]

flying saucer *noun* (*plural* **flying saucers**) a mysterious saucer-shaped object reported to have been seen in the sky and believed by some people to be an alien spacecraft.

flyleaf *noun* (*plural* **flyleaves**) a blank page at the beginning or end of a book.

flyover *noun* (*plural* **flyovers**) a bridge that carries one road or railway over another.

flywheel *noun* (*plural* **flywheels**) a heavy wheel used to regulate machinery.

foal *noun* (*plural* **foals**) a young horse.

foam *noun*
1 a white mass of tiny bubbles on a liquid; froth. **2** a spongy kind of rubber or plastic. **foamy** *adjective*

foam *verb* (**foams, foaming, foamed**) form foam.
[from Old English]

fob *verb* (**fobs, fobbing, fobbed**)
fob off get rid of someone by an excuse or a trick.

focal *adjective* to do with or at a focus.

focus *noun* (*plural* **focuses** or **foci**)
1 the distance from an eye or lens at which an object appears clearest. **2** the point at which rays etc. seem to meet. **3** something that is a centre of interest or attention etc.
in focus appearing clearly.
out of focus not appearing clearly.

focus *verb* (**focuses, focusing, focused**)
1 use or adjust a lens so that objects appear clearly. **2** concentrate, *She focused her attention on it.*
[Latin, = hearth (the central point of a household)]

fodder *noun* food for horses and farm animals.

foetus (*say* fee-tus) *noun* (*plural* **foetuses**) a developing embryo, especially an unborn human baby. **foetal** *adjective* [Latin]

fog *noun* thick mist. **foggy** *adjective*

foghorn *noun* (*plural* **foghorns**) a loud horn for warning ships in fog.

foil[1] *noun* (*plural* **foils**)
1 a very thin sheet of metal, *cooking foil.* **2** a person or thing that makes another look better in contrast.

foil[2] *noun* (*plural* **foils**) a long narrow sword used in the sport of fencing. [origin unknown]

foil[3] *verb* (**foils, foiling, foiled**) prevent something from being successful, *We foiled his evil plan.* [from old French *fouler* = trample]

foist *verb* (**foists, foisting, foisted**) make a person accept something inferior or unwelcome, *They foisted the job on me.*

fold *verb* (**folds, folding, folded**)
bend or move so that one part
lies on another part.

fold *noun* (*plural* **folds**) a line
where something is folded.
[from Old English *fealdan*]

-fold *suffix* adjectives and
adverbs meaning 'multiplied by'
(e.g *twofold, fourfold, manifold*).
[from Old English]

folder *noun* (*plural* **folders**)
a folding cover for loose papers.

folk *noun* people. [from Old
English]

folk dance *nouns* (*plural* **folk
dances**) a dance in the traditional
style of a country.

folklore *noun* old beliefs and
legends.

folk song *noun* (*plural* **folk
songs**) a song in the traditional
style of a country.

follow *verb* (**follows, following,
followed**)
1 go or come after. 2 do a thing
after something else. 3 take
a person or thing as a guide or
example. 4 take an interest in the
progress of events or a sport or
team etc. 5 understand, *Did you
follow what he said?* 6 result from
something. **follower** *noun* [from
Old English]

following *preposition* after, as
a result of, *Following the
burglary, we had new locks fitted.*

folly *noun* (*plural* **follies**)
foolishness; a foolish action etc.
[from French *folie* = madness]

fond *adjective*
1 loving or liking a person or
thing. 2 foolishly hopeful, *fond
hopes.* **fondly** *adverb*, **fondness**
noun [from an old word *fon* = fool]

fondle *verb* (**fondles, fondling,
fondled**) touch or stroke lovingly.
[from *fond*]

food *noun* (*plural* **foods**) any
substance that a plant or animal
can take into its body to help it to
grow and be healthy. [from Old
English]

food chain *noun* (*plural* **food
chains**) a series of plants and
animals each of which serves as
food for the one above it in the
series.

fool *noun* (*plural* **fools**)
1 a stupid person; someone who
acts unwisely. 2 a jester or clown,
Stop playing the fool. 3 a creamy
pudding with crushed fruit in it,
gooseberry fool.
fool's errand a useless errand.
fool's paradise happiness that
comes only from being mistaken
about something.

fool *verb* (**fools, fooling, fooled**)
1 behave in a joking way; play
about. 2 trick or deceive
someone.

foolish *adjective* without good
sense or judgement; unwise.
foolishly *adverb*, **foolishness** *noun*

foolproof *adjective* easy to use or
do correctly.

foot *noun* (*plural* **feet**)
1 the lower part of the leg below
the ankle. 2 any similar part, e.g.
one used by certain animals to
move or attach themselves to
things. 3 the lowest part, *the foot
of the hill.* 4 a measure of length,
12 inches or about 30
centimetres, *a ten-foot pole; it is
ten feet long.* 5 a unit of rhythm in
a line of poetry, e.g. each of the

four divisions in *Jack / and Jill / went up / the hill*.

on foot walking.

foot-and-mouth disease *noun* a serious contagious disease that affects cattle, sheep, and other animals.

football *noun* (*plural* **footballs**) 1 a game played by two teams which try to kick an inflated leather ball into their opponents' goal. 2 the ball used in this game. **footballer** *noun*

foothill *noun* (*plural* **foothills**) a low hill near the bottom of a mountain or range of mountains.

foothold *noun* (*plural* **footholds**) 1 a place to put your foot when climbing. 2 a small but firm position from which you can advance in business etc.

footing *noun* 1 having your feet placed on something; a foothold, *He lost his footing and slipped*. 2 the status or nature of a relationship, *We are on a friendly footing with that country*.

footlights *plural noun* a row of lights along the front of the floor of a stage.

footnote *noun* (*plural* **footnotes**) a note printed at the bottom of the page.

footpath *noun* (*plural* **footpaths**) a path for pedestrians.

footprint *noun* (*plural* **footprints**) a mark made by a foot or shoe.

footstep *noun* (*plural* **footsteps**) 1 a step taken in walking or running. 2 the sound of this.

for *preposition* This word is used to show 1 purpose or direction (*This letter is for you; We set out for home*), 2 distance or time (*Walk for six miles or two hours*), 3 price or exchange (*We bought it for £2; New lamps for old*), 4 cause (*She was fined for speeding*), 5 defence or support (*He fought for his country; Are you for us or against us?*), 6 reference (*For all her wealth, she is bored*), 7 similarity or correspondence (*We took him for a fool*).

for ever for all time; always.

for *conjunction* because, *They hesitated, for they were afraid.* [from Old English]

for- *prefix* 1 away, off (as in *forgive*). 2 prohibiting (as in *forbid*). 3 abstaining or neglecting (as in *forgo, forsake*). [from Old English]

forbear *verb* (**forbears, forbearing, forbore, forborne**) 1 refrain from something, *We forbore to mention it.* 2 be patient or tolerant. **forbearance** *noun* [from Old English]

forbid *verb* (**forbids, forbidding, forbade, forbidden**) 1 order someone not to do something. 2 refuse to allow, *We shall forbid the marriage.* [from Old English]

forbidding *adjective* looking stern or unfriendly.

force *noun* (*plural* **forces**) 1 strength or power. 2 (in science) an influence, which can be measured, that causes something to move. 3 an organized group of police, soldiers, etc.

in or **into force** in or into effectiveness, *The new law comes* *into force next week.*

the forces a country's armed forces.

force *verb* (**forces, forcing, forced**)
1 use force in order to get or do something, or to make somebody obey. **2** break something open by force. **3** cause plants to grow or bloom earlier than is normal, *You can force them in a greenhouse.*
[from Latin *fortis* = strong]

forceful *adjective* strong and vigorous. **forcefully** *adverb*

forcible *adjective* done by force; forceful. **forcibly** *adverb*

ford *noun* (*plural* **fords**) a shallow place where you can walk across a river.

ford *verb* (**fords, fording, forded**) cross a river at a ford.
[from Old English]

fore *adjective & adverb* at or towards the front, *fore and aft.*

fore *noun* the front part.

to the fore to or at the front; in or to a prominent position.

fore- *prefix* before (as in *forecast*); in front (as in *foreleg*).

forearm[1] *noun* (*plural* **forearms**) the arm from the elbow to the wrist or fingertips. [from *fore-* + *arm*[1]]

forearm[2] *verb* (**forearms, forearming, forearmed**) prepare in advance against possible danger. [from *fore-* + *arm*[2]]

forecast *noun* (*plural* **forecasts**) a statement that tells in advance what is likely to happen.

forecast *verb* (**forecasts, forecasting, forecast**) make a forecast. **forecaster** *noun*
[from *fore-* + *cast*]

forefinger *noun* (*plural* **forefingers**) the finger next to the thumb.

foregone conclusion *noun* (*plural* **foregone conclusions**) a result that can be foreseen easily and with certainty.

foreground *noun* the front part of a scene or view etc.

forehand *noun* (*plural* **forehands**) a stroke made in tennis etc. with the palm of the hand turned forwards.

forehead (*say* forrid or for-hed) *noun* (*plural* **foreheads**) the part of the face above the eyes.

foreign *adjective*
1 belonging to or in another country. **2** not belonging naturally to a place or to someone's nature, *Lying is foreign to her nature.* [from old French]

foreigner *noun* (*plural* **foreigners**) a person from another country.

foreman *noun* (*plural* **foremen**) **1** a worker in charge of a group of other workers. **2** a member of a jury who is in charge of the jury's discussions and who speaks on its behalf.

foremost *adjective & adverb* first in position or rank; most important.

forensic (*say* fer-en-sik) *adjective* to do with or used in lawcourts. [from Latin; related to *forum*]

forensic medicine *noun* medical knowledge needed in legal matters.

forerunner *noun* (*plural* **forerunners**) a person or thing that comes before another; a sign of what is to come.

foresee verb (foresees, foreseeing, foresaw, foreseen) realize what is going to happen.

foreshadow verb (foreshadows, foreshadowing, foreshadowed) be a sign of something that is to come.

foreshorten verb (foreshortens, foreshortening, foreshortened) show an object in a drawing etc. with some lines shortened to give an effect of distance or depth.

foresight noun the ability to foresee and prepare for future needs.

forest noun (plural forests) trees and undergrowth covering a large area. **forested** adjective [from old French]

forestry noun planting forests and looking after them. **forester** noun

foretaste noun (plural foretastes) an experience of something that is to come in the future.

foretell verb (foretells, foretelling, foretold) tell in advance; prophesy.

forethought noun careful thought and planning for the future.

foreword noun (plural forewords) a preface.

forfeit (say for-fit) verb (forfeits, forfeiting, forfeited) pay or give up something as a penalty. **forfeiture** noun

forfeit noun (plural forfeits) something forfeited. [from old French]

forge[1] noun (plural forges) a place where metal is heated and shaped; a blacksmith's workshop.

forge verb (forges, forging, forged) **1** shape metal by heating and hammering. **2** copy something in order to deceive people. **forger** noun, **forgery** noun [from old French]

forge[2] verb (forges, forging, forged) **forge ahead** move forward by a strong effort. [probably a different spelling of force]

forget verb (forgets, forgetting, forgot, forgotten) **1** fail to remember. **2** stop thinking about, Forget your troubles.

forget yourself behave rudely or thoughtlessly.

forgetful adjective tending to forget. **forgetfully** adverb, **forgetfulness** noun

forgive verb (forgives, forgiving, forgave, forgiven) stop feeling angry with somebody about something. **forgiveness** noun

fork noun (plural forks) **1** a small device with prongs for lifting food to your mouth. **2** a large device with prongs used for digging or lifting things. **3** a place where something separates into two or more parts, a fork in the road.

fork verb (forks, forking, forked) **1** lift or dig with a fork. **2** form a fork by separating into two branches. **3** follow one of these branches, Fork left.

fork out (slang) pay out money. [via Old English from Latin]

fork-lift truck noun (plural fork-lift trucks) a truck with two metal bars at the front for lifting and moving heavy loads.

forlorn *adjective* left alone and unhappy.
forlorn hope the only faint hope left.
[from *for-* + *an old word lorn* = lost]

form *noun* (*plural* **forms**)
1 the shape, appearance, or condition of something. 2 the way something exists, *Ice is a form of water.* 3 a class in school. 4 a bench. 5 a piece of paper with spaces to be filled in.

form *verb* (**forms, forming, formed**)
1 shape or construct something; create. 2 come into existence; develop, *Icicles formed.*
[from Latin]

formal *adjective*
1 strictly following the accepted rules or customs; ceremonious, *a formal occasion; formal dress.*
2 rather serious and stiff in your manner. **formally** *adverb* [from Latin *formalis* = having a set form]

format *noun* (*plural* **formats**) the shape and size of something; the way it is arranged. [from Latin *formatus* = formed, shaped]

formation *noun* (*plural* **formations**)
1 the act of forming something.
2 a thing formed. 3 a special arrangement or pattern, *flying in formation.* [from Latin *formare* = to mould]

former *adjective* of an earlier time. **formerly** *adverb*
the former the first of two people or things just mentioned.
[from Old English; related to *fore*]

formidable (*say* for-mid-a-bul) *adjective*
1 frightening. 2 difficult to deal with or do, *a formidable task.*
formidably *adverb* [from Latin *formidare* = to fear]

formula *noun* (*plural* **formulae**)
1 a set of chemical symbols showing what a substance consists of. 2 a rule or statement expressed in symbols or numbers. 3 a list of substances needed for making something.
4 a fixed wording for a ceremony etc. 5 one of the groups into which racing cars are placed according to the size of their engines, *Formula One.* [Latin, = small form]

formulate *verb* (**formulates, formulating, formulated**) express an idea or plan clearly and exactly. **formulation** *noun* [from *formula*]

fort *noun* (*plural* **forts**) a fortified building. [from Latin *fortis* = strong]

forth *adverb*
1 out; into view. 2 onwards or forwards, *from this day forth.*
and so forth and so on.

forthcoming *adjective*
1 happening soon, *forthcoming events.* 2 made available when needed, *Money for the trip was not forthcoming.* 3 willing to give information.

forthright *adjective* frank and outspoken.

fortification *noun* (*plural* **fortifications**)
1 fortifying something. 2 a wall or building constructed to make a place strong against attack.

fortify verb (fortifies, fortifying, fortified)
1 make a place strong against attack, especially by building fortifications. **2** strengthen. [same origin as *fort*]

fortnight noun (plural **fortnights**) a period of two weeks. **fortnightly** adverb & adjective [from Old English *feowertene niht* = fourteen nights]

fortress noun (plural **fortresses**) a fortified building or town. [from French *forteresse* = strong place]

fortunate adjective lucky. **fortunately** adverb [same origin as *fortune*]

fortune noun (plural **fortunes**)
1 luck, especially good luck.
2 a great amount of money.
tell someone's fortune predict what will happen to them in the future. [from Latin *fortuna* = luck]

forty adjective & noun (plural **forties**) the number 40. **fortieth** adjective & noun
forty winks a short sleep; a nap.

forward adjective
1 going forwards. **2** placed in the front. **3** having made more than the normal progress. **4** too eager or bold. **forwardness** noun

forward adverb forwards.

forward noun (plural **forwards**) a player in the front line of a team in football, hockey, etc.

forwards adverb
1 to or towards the front. **2** in the direction you are facing.

fossil noun (plural **fossils**) the remains or traces of a prehistoric animal or plant that has been buried in the ground for a very long time and become hardened in rock. **fossilized** adjective [from Latin *fossilis* = dug up]

foul adjective
1 disgusting; tasting or smelling unpleasant. **2** (of weather) rough; stormy. **3** unfair; breaking the rules of a game. **4** colliding or entangled with something. **foully** adverb, **foulness** noun

foul noun (plural **fouls**) an action that breaks the rules of a game.

foul verb (fouls, fouling, fouled)
1 make or become foul, *Smoke had fouled the air.* **2** commit a foul against a player in a game. [from Old English]

found¹ past tense of **find**.

found² verb (founds, founding, founded)
1 establish; provide money for starting, *They founded a hospital.*
2 base, *This novel is founded on fact.* [from Latin *fundus* = bottom]

foundation noun (plural **foundations**)
1 the founding of something.
2 a base or basis. **3** the solid base on which a building is built up. **foundation stone** noun

founder¹ noun (plural **founders**) a person who founds something, *the founder of the hospital.*

founder² verb (founders, foundering, foundered)
1 fill with water and sink, *The ship foundered.* **2** stumble or fall.
3 fail completely, *Their plans foundered.* [same origin as *found*²]

fountain noun (plural **fountains**) an ornamental structure in which a jet of water shoots up into the air.

four adjective & noun (plural fours) the number 4.
on all fours on hands and knees.

fourteen adjective & noun the number 14.
fourteenth adjective & noun

fourth adjective next after the third. **fourthly** adverb
fourth noun (plural fourths) 1 the fourth person or thing. 2 one of four equal parts; a quarter.

fowl noun (plural fowls) a bird, especially one kept on a farm etc. for its eggs or meat. [from Old English]

fox noun (plural foxes) a wild animal that looks like a dog with a long furry tail. **foxy** adjective

fraction noun (plural fractions) 1 a number that is not a whole number, e.g. ½, 0.5. 2 a tiny part. **fractional** adjective, **fractionally** adverb [Latin, = breaking]

fracture noun (plural fractures) the breaking of something, especially of a bone.
fracture verb (fractures, fracturing, fractured) break. [from Latin fractus = broken]

fragile adjective easy to break or damage. **fragilely** adverb, **fragility** noun [from Latin]

fragment noun (plural fragments) 1 a small piece broken off. 2 a small part. **fragmentary** adjective, **fragmentation** noun, **fragmented** adjective [from Latin]

fragrant adjective having a pleasant smell. **fragrance** noun [from Latin fragrare = smell sweet]

frail adjective 1 (of things) fragile. 2 (of people) not strong or healthy, a frail old man. **frailty** noun [from Latin fragilis = fragile]

frame noun (plural frames) 1 a holder that fits round the outside of a picture. 2 a rigid structure that supports something. 3 a human or animal body, He has a small frame. 4 a single exposure on a cinema film.
frame of mind the way you think or feel for a while.
frame verb (frames, framing, framed) 1 put a frame on or round. 2 construct, They framed the question badly. 3 make an innocent person seem guilty by arranging false evidence. **frame-up** noun

framework noun (plural frameworks) 1 a frame supporting something. 2 a basic plan or system.

franc noun (plural francs) a unit of money in France, Switzerland, and many other countries. [from Latin Francorum rex = King of the Franks, which was stamped on French gold coins in the Middle Ages]

frank adjective making your thoughts and feelings clear to people; candid. **frankly** adverb, **frankness** noun

frantic adjective wildly agitated or excited. **frantically** adverb [from old French; related to frenzy]

fraud noun (plural frauds) 1 a dishonest trick; a swindle. 2 an impostor; a person or thing that is not what it pretends to be. **fraudulent** *adjective*, **fraudulently** *adverb*, **fraudulence** *noun*

fray[1] *noun* (*plural* **frays**) a fight or conflict, *ready for the fray*. [shortened from *affray*; compare *afraid*]

fray[2] *verb* (**frays, fraying, frayed**) **1** make or become ragged so that loose threads show. **2** (of tempers or nerves) become strained or upset. [from French; related to *friction*]

freak *noun* (*plural* **freaks**) a very strange or abnormal person, animal, or thing. **freakish** *adjective*

freckle *noun* (*plural* **freckles**) a small brown spot on the skin. **freckled** *adjective* [from Old Norse]

free *adjective* (**freer, freest**)
1 able to do what you want to do or go where you want to go. **2** not costing anything. **3** not fixed, *Leave one end free.* **4** not having or being affected by something, *The harbour is free of ice.* **5** available; not being used or occupied. **6** generous, *She is very free with her money.* **freely** *adverb*

free *verb* (**frees, freeing, freed**) set free.
[from Old English]

freedom *noun* (*plural* **freedoms**) being free; independence.

freehand *adjective* (of a drawing) done without a ruler or compasses etc.

free-range *adjective*
1 free-range hens are not kept in small cages but are allowed to move about freely. **2** free-range eggs are ones laid by these hens.

freewheel *verb* (**freewheels, freewheeling, freewheeled**) ride a bicycle without needing to pedal.

freeze *verb* (**freezes, freezing, froze, frozen**)
1 turn into ice; become covered with ice. **2** make or be very cold. **3** keep wages or prices etc. at a fixed level. **4** suddenly stand completely still.

freezer *noun* (*plural* **freezers**) a refrigerator in which food can be frozen quickly and stored.

French window *noun* (*plural* **French windows**) a long window that serves as a door on an outside wall.

frenzy *noun* wild excitement or agitation. **frenzied** *adjective*, **frenziedly** *adverb* [from Greek *phren* = the mind]

frequency *noun* (*plural* **frequencies**)
1 being frequent. **2** how often something happens. **3** the number of oscillations per second of a wave of sound or light etc.

frequent (*say* freek-went) *adjective* happening often. **frequently** *adverb*

frequent (*say* frik-went) *verb* (**frequents, frequenting, frequented**) be in or go to a place often, *They frequented the club.* [from Latin *frequens* = crowded]

fresh *adjective*
1 newly made or produced or arrived; not stale, *fresh bread.* **2** not tinned or preserved, *fresh fruit.* **3** cool and clean, *fresh air.* **4** (of water) not salty. **freshly** *adverb*, **freshness** *noun* [from Old English]

freshen verb (freshens, freshening, freshened) make or become fresh.

fret[1] verb (frets, fretting, fretted) worry about something. **fretful** adjective, **fretfully** adverb [from Old English]

fret[2] noun (plural frets) a bar or ridge on the fingerboard of a guitar etc. [origin unknown]

friar noun (plural friars) a man who is a member of certain Roman Catholic religious orders, who has vowed to live a life of poverty. **friary** noun [from French *frère* = brother]

friction noun
1 rubbing. **2** bad feeling between people; quarrelling. **frictional** adjective [from Latin *fricare* = to rub]

fridge noun (plural fridges) (*informal*) a refrigerator.

friend noun (plural friends)
1 a person you like who likes you. **2** a helpful or kind person.

friendly adjective (friendlier, friendliest) behaving like a friend. **friendliness** noun

friendship noun (plural friendships) being friends.

frieze (say freez) noun (plural friezes) a strip of designs or pictures round the top of a wall. [from Latin]

fright noun (plural frights)
1 sudden great fear. **2** a person or thing that looks ridiculous. [from Old English]

frighten verb (frightens, frightening, frightened) make or become afraid.
be frightened of be afraid of.

frightful adjective awful; very great or bad. **frightfully** adverb

frill noun (plural frills)
1 a decorative gathered or pleated trimming on a dress, curtain, etc. **2** something extra that is pleasant but unnecessary, *a simple life with no frills.* **frilled** adjective, **frilly** adjective

fringe noun (plural fringes)
1 a decorative edging with many threads hanging down loosely. **2** a straight line of hair hanging down over the forehead. **3** the edge of something. **fringed** adjective

frisk verb (frisks, frisking, frisked)
1 jump or run about playfully. **2** search somebody by running your hands over his or her clothes. **frisky** adjective, **friskily** adverb, **friskiness** noun [from old French *frisque* = lively]

fritter[1] noun (plural fritters) a slice of meat or fruit or potato etc. coated in batter and fried. [from Latin *frictum* = fried]

fritter[2] verb (fritters, frittering, frittered) waste something gradually; spend money or time on trivial things. [from an old word *fritters* = fragments]

frivolous adjective seeking pleasure in a light-hearted way; not serious. **frivolously** adverb, **frivolity** noun [from Latin]

frizzy adjective (of hair) in tight curls. **frizziness** noun

fro adverb
to and fro backwards and forwards.

frock noun (plural frocks) a girl's or woman's dress.

frog noun (plural frogs) a small jumping animal that can live both in water and on land.
a frog in your throat hoarseness.

frolic noun (plural **frolics**) a lively cheerful game or entertainment. **frolicsome** adjective

frolic verb (**frolics**, **frolicking**, **frolicked**) play about in a lively cheerful way.
[from Dutch *vrolijk* = joyously]

from preposition This word is used to show
1 starting point in space or time or order (*We flew from London to Paris. We work from 9 to 5 o'clock. Count from one to ten*), **2** source or origin (*Get water from the tap*), **3** separation or release (*Take the gun from him. She was freed from prison*), **4** difference (*Can you tell margarine from butter?*), **5** cause (*I suffer from headaches*). [from Old English]

frond noun (plural **fronds**) a leaf-like part of a fern, palm tree, etc. [from Latin *frondis* = of a leaf]

front noun (plural **fronts**)
1 the part or side that comes first or is the most important or furthest forward. **2** a road or promenade along the seashore. **3** the place where fighting is happening in a war. **frontal** adjective

front adjective of the front; in front.
[from Latin *frons* = forehead, front]

frontier noun (plural **frontiers**) the boundary between two countries or regions. [from old French; related to *front*]

frontispiece noun (plural **frontispieces**) an illustration opposite the title-page of a book. [from French]

frost noun (plural **frosts**)
1 powdery ice that forms on things in freezing weather.
2 weather with a temperature below freezing point.

frost verb (**frosts**, **frosting**, **frosted**) cover with frost or frosting.
[from Old English]

frostbite noun harm done to the body by very cold weather. **frostbitten** adjective

frosty adjective (**frostier**, **frostiest**) **1** cold with frost. **2** unfriendly and unwelcoming, *a frosty look*. **frostily** adverb

froth noun a white mass of tiny bubbles on a liquid. **frothy** adjective [from Old Norse]

frown verb (**frowns**, **frowning**, **frowned**) wrinkle your forehead because you are angry or worried.

frown noun (plural **frowns**) a frowning movement or look. [from Old French]

fruit noun (plural **fruits** or **fruit**) **1** the seed-container that grows on a tree or plant and is often used as food. **2** the result of doing something, *the fruits of his efforts*. **fruity** adjective

fruit verb (**fruits**, **fruiting**, **fruited**) produce fruit.

fruitful adjective producing good results, *fruitful discussions*. **fruitfully** adverb

fruitless adjective producing no results. **fruitlessly** adverb

frustrate verb (**frustrates**, **frustrating**, **frustrated**) prevent somebody from doing something; prevent something from being successful, *frustrate their wicked plans.* **frustration** noun [from Latin *frustra* = in vain]

fry verb (**fries, frying, fried**) cook something in very hot fat. **fryer** noun

fudge noun a soft sugary sweet. [origin unknown]

fuel noun (*plural* **fuels**) something that is burnt to produce heat or power.

fuel verb (**fuels, fuelling, fuelled**) supply something with fuel. [from old French; related to *focus*]

fugitive (*say* few-jit-iv) noun (*plural* **fugitives**) a person who is running away from something. [from Latin *fugere* = flee]

-ful suffix forms
1 adjectives meaning 'full of' or 'having this quality' (e.g. *beautiful, truthful*), **2** nouns meaning 'the amount required to fill something' (e.g. *handful*). [from *full*]

fulcrum noun (*plural* **fulcrums** or **fulcra**) the point on which a lever rests. [Latin]

fulfil verb (**fulfils, fulfilling, fulfilled**)
1 do what is required; satisfy; carry out, *You must fulfil your promises.* **2** make something come true, *It fulfilled an ancient prophecy.* **3** give you satisfaction. **fulfilment** noun [from Old English *fullfyllan* = fill up, satisfy]

full adjective
1 containing as much or as many as possible. **2** having many people or things, *full of ideas.* **3** complete, *the full story.* **4** the greatest possible, *at full speed.* **5** fitting loosely; with many folds, a full skirt. **6** when there is a full moon, you can see its whole disc. **fully** adverb, **fullness** noun

full adverb completely and directly, *It hit him full in the face.* [from Old English]

full-blown adjective fully developed.

full stop noun (*plural* **full stops**) the dot used as a punctuation mark at the end of a sentence or an abbreviation.

fully adverb completely.

fumble verb (**fumbles, fumbling, fumbled**) hold or handle something clumsily.

fume noun or **fumes** plural noun strong-smelling smoke or gas.

fume verb (**fumes, fuming, fumed**)
1 give off fumes. **2** be very angry. [from Latin *fumus* = smoke]

fumigate (*say* few-mig-ayt) verb (**fumigates, fumigating, fumigated**) disinfect something by fumes. **fumigation** noun

fun noun amusement or enjoyment.
make fun of make people laugh at a person or thing.

function noun (*plural* **functions**)
1 what somebody or something is there to do, *The function of a knife is to cut things.* **2** an important event or party. **3** a basic operation in a computer. **4** a variable quantity whose value depends on the value of other variable quantities, *X is a function of Y and Z.*

function verb (**functions, functioning, functioned**) perform a function; work properly. [from Latin *functum* = performed]

fund noun (plural **funds**)
1 money collected or kept for a special purpose. 2 a stock or supply.

fund verb (**funds, funding, funded**) supply with money. [same origin as **found²**]

fundamental adjective basic. **fundamentally** adverb [from Latin *fundamentum* = foundation]

funeral noun (plural **funerals**) the ceremony when a dead person is buried or cremated. [from Latin *funeris* = of a burial]

fungus noun (plural **fungi** (say fung-I)) a plant without leaves or flowers that grows on other plants or on decayed material, *Mushrooms are fungi.* [Latin]

funnel noun (plural **funnels**)
1 a metal chimney on a ship or steam engine. 2 a tube that is wide at the top and narrow at the bottom to help you pour things into a narrow opening. [from Latin *fundere* = pour]

funny adjective (**funnier, funniest**)
1 that makes you laugh or smile. 2 strange or odd, *a funny smell.* **funnily** adverb

fur noun (plural **furs**)
1 the soft hair that covers some animals. 2 animal skin with the fur on it, used for clothing; fabric that looks like animal fur.

furious adjective
1 very angry. 2 violent or intense, *furious heat.* **furiously** adverb [from Latin]

furnace noun (plural **furnaces**) a device in which great heat can be produced, e.g. for melting metals or making glass. [from Latin *furnus* = oven]

furnish verb (**furnishes, furnishing, furnished**)
1 provide a place with furniture. 2 provide or supply with something.

furniture noun tables, chairs, and other movable things that you need in a house or school or office etc.

furrow noun (plural **furrows**)
1 a long cut in the ground made by a plough or other implement. 2 a groove. 3 a deep wrinkle in the skin.

furry adjective like fur; covered with fur.

further adverb & adjective
1 at or to a greater distance; more distant. 2 more; additional, *We made further enquiries.*

USAGE: See the note at **farther**.

further verb (**furthers, furthering, furthered**) help something to progress, *This success will further your career.* **furtherance** noun

further education noun education for people above school age.

furthest adverb & adjective at or to the greatest distance; most distant.

fury noun (plural **furies**) wild anger; rage. [from Latin *furia* = rage; an avenging spirit]

fuse¹ noun (plural **fuses**) a safety device containing a short piece of wire that melts if too much electricity is passed through it.

fuse verb (**fuses, fusing, fused**)
1 stop working because a fuse has melted. 2 blend together, especially through melting. [from Latin *fusum* = melted]

fuse[2] *noun* (*plural* **fuses**) a length of material that burns easily, used for setting off an explosive. [from Latin *fusus* = spindle (because originally the material was put in a tube)]

fusion *noun*
1 the action of blending or uniting things. **2** the uniting of atomic nuclei, usually releasing energy.

fuss *noun* (*plural* **fusses**)
1 unnecessary excitement or bustle. **2** an agitated protest.

fuss *verb* (**fusses, fussing, fussed**) make a fuss about something.

fussy *adjective* (**fussier, fussiest**)
1 fussing; inclined to make a fuss. **2** choosing very carefully; hard to please. **3** full of unnecessary details or decorations. **fussily** *adverb*, **fussiness** *noun*

future *noun* the time that will come; what is going to happen then.

future *adjective* belonging to or referring to the future.

fuzz *noun* something fluffy or frizzy.

fuzzy *adjective*
1 like fuzz; covered with fuzz. **2** blurred; not clear. **fuzzily** *adverb*, **fuzziness** *noun*

-fy *suffix* forms verbs meaning 'make' or 'bring into a certain condition' (e.g. *beautify, purify*). [from Latin *-ficare* = make]

Gg

gabble *verb* (**gabbles, gabbling, gabbled**) talk so quickly that it is difficult to know what is being said. [from old Dutch]

gadget *noun* (*plural* **gadgets**) any small useful tool. **gadgetry** *noun*

Gaelic (*say* **gay**-lik) *noun* the Celtic languages of Scotland and Ireland.

gag *noun* (*plural* **gags**)
1 something put into a person's mouth or tied over it to prevent him or her speaking. **2** a joke.

gag *verb* (**gags, gagging, gagged**)
1 put a gag on a person. **2** prevent someone from making comments, *We cannot gag the press.* **3** retch. [imitating the sound of someone retching]

gaiety *noun*
1 cheerfulness. **2** brightly coloured appearance. (See *gay* for origin and usage note.)

gaily *adverb* in a cheerful way.

gain *verb* (**gains, gaining, gained**)
1 get something that you did not have before; obtain. **2** a clock or watch gains when it becomes ahead of the correct time. **3** reach; arrive at, *At last we gained the shore.*

gain on come closer to a person or thing when chasing them or in a race.

gain *noun* (*plural* **gains**) something gained; a profit or improvement. **gainful** *adjective*

galaxy *noun* (*plural* **galaxies**) a very large group of stars. **galactic** (*say* ga-**lak**-tik) *adjective* [originally = the Milky Way: from Greek *galaxias* = milky]

gale *noun* (*plural* **gales**) a very strong wind. [origin unknown]

gallant (*say* **gal**-ant) *adjective*
1 brave or chivalrous. **2** fine and stately, *our gallant ship.* **gallantly**

adverb, **gallantry** *noun* [originally = spendidly dressed: from old French *galant* = celebrating]

gallery *noun* (*plural* **galleries**)
1 a platform jutting out from the wall in a church or hall. **2** the highest balcony in a cinema or theatre. **3** a long room or passage. **4** a room or building for showing works of art. [from Italian *galleria* = gallery, church porch, perhaps from *Galilee* (a church porch furthest from the altar was called a *galilee*, as Galilee was the province furthest from Jerusalem)]

gallon *noun* (*plural* **gallons**) a unit used to measure liquids, 8 pints or 4.546 litres. [from old French]

gallop *noun* (*plural* **gallops**)
1 the fastest pace that a horse can go. **2** a fast ride on a horse.

gallop *verb* (**gallops, galloping, galloped**) go or ride at a gallop. [from old French; related to *wallop*]

gallows *noun* (*plural* **gallows** or **gallowses**) a framework with a noose for hanging criminals. [from Old English]

galoshes *plural noun* a pair of waterproof shoes worn over ordinary shoes. [from old French]

galvanize *verb* (**galvanizes, galvanizing, galvanized**)
1 stimulate someone into sudden activity. **2** coat iron with zinc to protect it from rust. **galvanization** *noun* [named after an Italian scientist, Luigi Galvani, who discovered that muscles move because of electricity in the body]

gambit *noun* (*plural* **gambits**)
1 a kind of opening move in chess. **2** an action or remark intended to gain an advantage. [from Italian *gambetto* = tripping up]

gamble *verb* (**gambles, gambling, gambled**)
1 bet on the result of a game, race, or other event. **2** take great risks in the hope of gaining something. **gambler** *noun*

gamble *noun* (*plural* **gambles**)
1 a bet or chance, *a gamble on the lottery*. **2** a risky attempt. [from Old English *gamenian* = play games]

gambol *verb* (**gambols, gambolling, gambolled**) jump or skip about in play. [from French]

game *noun* (*plural* **games**)
1 a form of play or sport, especially one with rules, *a game of football, a computer game*. **2** a section of a long game such as tennis or whist. **3** a scheme or plan; a trick, *Whatever his game is, he won't succeed*. **4** wild animals or birds hunted for sport or food.
give the game away reveal a secret.

game *adjective*
1 able and willing to do something, *'Shall we swim to the island?' 'I'm game!'* **2** brave. **gamely** *adverb*
[from Old English]

gamekeeper *noun* (*plural* **gamekeepers**) a person employed to protect game birds and animals, especially from poachers.

gamma *noun* the third letter of the Greek alphabet, = g.

gamma rays *plural noun* very short X-rays.

gander *noun* (*plural* **ganders**) a male goose. [from Old English]

gang *noun* (*plural* **gangs**) a number of people who do things together, *a gang of criminals, a roadmending gang.*

gang *verb* (**gangs, ganging, ganged**) join in a gang, *gang up.* [from Old Norse]

gangling *adjective* tall, thin, and awkward-looking.

gangplank *noun* (*plural* **gangplanks**) a plank placed so that people can walk into or out of a boat. [from Old Norse *gangr* = walking, going]

gangrene (*say* gang-green) *noun* decay of body tissue in a living person.

gangster *noun* (*plural* **gangsters**) a member of a gang of violent criminals.

gangway *noun* (*plural* **gangways**)
1 a gap left for people to pass between rows of seats or through a crowd. **2** a movable bridge placed so that people can walk into or out of a ship. [same origin as *gangplank*]

gaol (*say* jayl) *noun* (*plural* **gaols**) a different spelling of *jail.* **gaol** *verb*, **gaoler** *noun*

gap *noun* (*plural* **gaps**)
1 a break or opening in something continuous such as a hedge or fence. **2** an interval. **3** a wide difference in ideas.

gape *verb* (**gapes, gaping, gaped**)
1 have your mouth open. **2** stare with your mouth open. **3** be open wide.

garage (*say* ga-rahzh or ga-rij) *noun* (*plural* **garages**)
1 a building in which a motor vehicle or vehicles may be kept. **2** a place where motor vehicles are repaired or serviced and where petrol is sold. [French; = a shelter]

garbage *noun* rubbish, especially household rubbish.

garble *verb* (**garbles, garbling, garbled**) give a confused account of a story or message so that it is misunderstood. [from Arabic *garbala* = sift, select (because the real facts are 'sifted out')]

garden *noun* (*plural* **gardens**) a piece of ground where flowers, fruit, or vegetables are grown. **gardener** *noun*, **gardening** *noun*

gargle *verb* (**gargles, gargling, gargled**) hold a liquid at the back of the mouth and breathe air through it to wash the inside of the throat. **gargle** *noun* [from French *gargouille* = throat]

gargoyle *noun* (*plural* **gargoyles**) an ugly or comical face or figure carved on a building, especially on a waterspout. [from French *gargouille* = throat (because the water passes through the throat of the figure)]

garland *noun* (*plural* **garlands**) a wreath of flowers worn or hung as a decoration. **garland** *verb* [from old French]

garlic *noun* a plant with a bulb divided into smaller bulbs (cloves), which have a strong smell and taste and are used for flavouring food.

garment *noun* (*plural* **garments**) a piece of clothing. [from French *garnement* = equipment]

garnish verb (garnishes, garnishing, garnished) decorate something, especially food.

garnish noun something used to decorate food or give it extra flavour.

garret noun (plural garrets) an attic. [from old French *garite* = watchtower]

garrison noun (plural garrisons) **1** troops who stay in a town or fort to defend it. **2** the building they occupy. **garrison** verb [from old French *garison* = defence]

garter noun (plural garters) a band of elastic to hold up a sock or stocking. [from old French]

gas¹ noun (plural gases) **1** a substance that (like air) can move freely and is not liquid or solid at ordinary temperatures. **2** a gas that can be burned, used for lighting, heating, or cooking.

gas verb (gasses, gassing, gassed) **1** kill or injure someone with gas. **2** (*informal*) talk idly for a long time. [an invented word suggested by the Greek word *chaos*]

gas² noun (*American*) gasoline. [abbreviation]

gaseous (*say* gas-ee-us) adjective in the form of a gas.

gash noun (plural gashes) a long deep cut or wound.

gash verb (gashes, gashing, gashed) make a gash in something.

gasoline noun (*American*) petrol. [from *gas* + Latin *oleum* = oil]

gasp verb (gasps, gasping, gasped) **1** breathe in suddenly when you are shocked or surprised.

2 struggle to breathe with your mouth open when you are tired or ill. **3** speak in a breathless way. **gasp** noun [from Old Norse]

gassy adjective fizzy.

gastric adjective to do with the stomach. [from Greek *gaster* = stomach]

gastronomy (*say* gas-tron-om-ee) noun the art or science of good eating. **gastronomic** adjective [from Greek *gaster* = stomach + -*nomia* = management]

gastropod noun (plural gastropods) an animal (e.g. a snail) that moves by means of a fleshy 'foot' on its stomach. [from Greek *gaster* = stomach + *podos* = of the foot]

gate noun (plural gates) **1** a movable barrier, usually on hinges, used as a door in a wall or fence. **2** the opening it covers. **3** a barrier for controlling the flow of water in a dam or lock. **4** the number of people attending a football match etc. [from Old English]

gatecrash verb (gatecrashes, gatecrashing, gatecrashed) go to a private party without being invited. **gatecrasher** noun

gateway noun (plural gateways) **1** an opening containing a gate. **2** a way to reach something, *The gateway to success.*

gather verb (gathers, gathering, gathered) **1** come or bring together. **2** collect; obtain gradually, *gather information.* **3** collect as harvest; pluck, *Gather the corn when it is ripe; gather flowers.* **4** understand or learn, *We gather you have been on holiday.* **5** pull cloth into folds

by running a thread through it.
6 a sore gathers when it swells up
and forms pus. [from Old
English]

gathering *noun* (*plural*
gatherings)
1 an assembly of people.
2 a swelling that forms pus.

gaudy *adjective* too showy and
bright. **gaudily** *adverb*, **gaudiness**
noun [from Latin *gaudere*
= rejoice!]

gauge (*say* gayj) *noun* (*plural*
gauges)
1 a standard measurement. **2** the
distance between a pair of rails
on a railway. **3** a measuring
instrument.

gauge *verb* (**gauges**, **gauging**,
gauged)
1 measure. **2** estimate; form
a judgement.

gaunt *adjective*
1 a gaunt person is lean and
haggard. **2** a gaunt place is grim
or desolate-looking. **gauntness**
noun [origin unknown]

gauntlet *noun*
run the gauntlet have to suffer
continuous severe criticism or
risk.
[from a former military and
naval punishment in which the
victim was made to pass between
two rows of men who struck him
as he passed; the word is from
Swedish *gatlopp* = passage]

gauze *noun*
1 thin transparent woven
material. **2** fine wire mesh. **gauzy**
adjective [from *Gaza*, a town in
Palestine, where it was first
made]

gay *adjective*
1 homosexual. **2** cheerful.

3 brightly coloured. **gayness**
noun [from French]

USAGE: Nowadays the most
common meaning of *gay* is
'homosexual'. The older
meanings 'cheerful' and
'brightly coloured' can still be
used but are becoming less and
less common in everyday use.
Gayness is the noun from
meaning 1 of *gay*. The noun
that relates to the other two
meanings is *gaiety*.

gaze *verb* (**gazes**, **gazing**, **gazed**)
look at something steadily for
a long time.
gaze *noun* (*plural* **gazes**) a long
steady look.
[origin unknown]

gazetteer (*say* gaz-it-eer) *noun*
(*plural* **gazetteers**) a list of place
names. [originally = journalist;
the first gazetteer was intended
to help journalists]

GCSE *abbreviation* General
Certificate of Secondary
Education.

gear *noun* (*plural* **gears**)
1 a cogwheel, especially one of
a set in a motor vehicle that turn
power from the engine into
movement of the wheels.
2 equipment or apparatus,
camping gear.

gear *verb* (**gears**, **gearing**,
geared)
gear to make something match
something else, *Health care
should be geared to people's needs,
not to whether they can pay.*
gear up get ready for, *We were all
geared up to play cricket, but then
it rained.*

Geiger counter (say gy-ger) noun (plural **Geiger counters**) an instrument that detects and measures radioactivity. [named after a German scientist, H. W. Geiger, who helped to develop it]

gelatine noun a clear jelly-like substance made by boiling animal tissue and used to make jellies and other foods and in photographic film. **gelatinous** (say jil-**at**-in-us) adjective [from Italian gelata = jelly]

gem noun (plural **gems**)
1 a precious stone. 2 an excellent person or thing. [via Old English from Latin]

-gen suffix used in scientific language to form nouns meaning 'producing' or 'produced' (e.g. oxygen, hydrogen).

gender noun (plural **genders**)
1 the group in which a noun is classed in the grammar of some languages (e.g. masculine, feminine, neuter). 2 a person's sex, Jobs should be open to all, regardless of race or gender. [from Latin genus = a kind]

gene (say jeen) noun (plural **genes**) the part of a living cell that controls which characteristics (such as the colour of hair or eyes) are inherited from parents. [from Greek genos = kind, race]

genealogy (say jeen-ee-**al**-o-jee) noun (plural **genealogies**)
1 a statement or diagram showing how people are descended from an ancestor; a pedigree. 2 the study of family history and ancestors.

genealogical (say jeen-ee-a-**loj**-ik-al) adjective [from Greek genea = race of people, + -logy]

genera (say **jen**-e-ra) plural noun plural of **genus**.

general adjective
1 to do with or involving most people or things, This drug is now in general use. 2 not detailed; broad, I've got the general idea. 3 chief or head, the general manager.

general noun (plural **generals**) a senior army officer. [from Latin]

general election noun (plural **general elections**) an election of Members of Parliament for the whole country.

generally adverb
1 usually. 2 in a general sense; without regard to details, I was speaking generally.

general practitioner noun (plural **general practitioners**) a doctor who treats all kinds of diseases. He or she is the first doctor that people see when they are ill.

generate verb (**generates**, **generating**, **generated**) produce or create. [from Latin generatus = fathered]

generation noun (plural **generations**)
1 generating. 2 a single stage in a family, Three generations were included: children, parents, and grandparents. 3 all the people born at about the same time, our parents' generation.

generator noun (plural **generators**)
1 an apparatus for producing

gases or steam. **2** a machine for converting mechanical energy into electricity.

generous *adjective*
1 willing to give things or share them. **2** given freely; plentiful, *a generous helping*. **generously** *adverb*, **generosity** *noun* [from Latin *generosus* = noble]

genetic (say jin-**et**-ik) *adjective*
1 to do with genes. **2** to do with characteristics inherited from parents or ancestors. **genetically** *adverb* [from *genesis*]

genial (say **jee**-nee-al) *adjective* kindly and cheerful. **genially** *adverb*, **geniality** (say jee-nee-**al**-it-ee) [from Latin *genialis* = joyous]

genital (say **jen**-it-al) *adjective* to do with animal reproduction or reproductive organs. [from old French; related to *generate*]

genitals (say **jen**-it-alz) *plural noun* external sexual organs.

genius *noun* (*plural* **geniuses**)
1 an unusually clever person. **2** a very great natural ability, *He has a real genius for music.* [Latin, = a spirit]

genocide (say **jen**-o-syd) *noun* deliberate extermination of a race of people. [from Greek *genos* = race, + -*cide*]

gentle *adjective* kind and quiet; not rough or severe. **gently** *adverb*, **gentleness** *noun* [from Latin *gentilis* = from a good family]

gentleman *noun* (*plural* **gentlemen**)
1 a well-mannered or honourable man. **2** a man of good social position. **3** (*in polite use*) a man.

genuine *adjective* real; not faked or pretending. **genuinely** *adverb*, **genuineness** *noun* [from Latin *genu* = knee (because a father would take a baby onto his knee to show that he accepted it as his)]

genus (say **jee**-nus) *noun* (*plural* **genera** (say **jen**-er-a)) a group of similar animals or plants, *Lions and tigers belong to the same genus.* [Latin, = family or race]

geo- *prefix* earth. [from Greek *ge* = earth]

geography (say jee-**og**-ra-fee) *noun* the study of the earth's surface and of its climate, peoples, and products. **geographer** *noun*, **geographical** *adjective*, **geographically** *adverb* [from *geo-* + -*graphy*]

geology (say jee-**ol**-o-jee) *noun* the study of the structure of the earth's crust and its layers. **geological** *adjective*, **geologically** *adverb*, **geologist** *noun* [from *geo-* + -*logy*]

geometry (say jee-**om**-it-ree) *noun* the study of lines, angles, surfaces, and solids in mathematics. **geometric** *adjective*, **geometrical** *adjective*, **geometrically** *adverb* [from *geo-* + Greek -*metria* = measurement]

gerbil (say **jer**-bil) *noun* (*plural* **gerbils**) a small brown animal with long hind legs, from Africa and Asia. One sort of gerbil, which originally came from Mongolia, is often kept as a pet. [from Latin]

geriatric (say je-ree-**at**-rik) *adjective* to do with the care of old people and their health. [from Greek *geras* = old age + *iatros* = doctor]

germ noun (plural **germs**)
1 a micro-organism, especially one that can cause disease.
2 a tiny living structure from which a plant or animal may develop. 3 part of the seed of a cereal plant. [from Latin *germen* = seed or sprout]

German measles noun rubella.

German shepherd dog noun (plural **German shepherd dogs**) a large strong dog, often used by the police.

germinate verb (**germinates**, **germinating**, **germinated**) when a seed germinates, it begins to develop, and roots and shoots grow from it. **germination** noun [same origin as *germ*]

gesticulate (say jes-**tik**-yoo-layt) verb (**gesticulates**, **gesticulating**, **gesticulated**) make expressive movements with your hands and arms. **gesticulation** noun [same origin as *gesture*]

gesture (say **jes**-cher) noun (plural **gestures**)
1 a movement that expresses what a person feels. 2 an action that shows goodwill, *It would be a nice gesture to send her some flowers.*

gesture verb (**gestures**, **gesturing**, **gestured**) tell a person something by making a gesture, *She gestured me to be quiet.* [from Latin *gestus* = action, way of standing or moving]

get verb (**gets**, **getting**, **got**) This word has many different uses, including
1 obtain or receive, *She got first*

prize. 2 become, *Don't get angry!*
3 reach a place, *We got there by midnight.* 4 put or move, *I can't get my shoe on.* 5 prepare, *Will you get the tea?* 6 persuade or order, *Get him to wash up.* 7 catch or suffer from an illness.
8 (informal) understand, *Do you get what I mean?*

get away with 1 escape with something. 2 avoid being punished for what you have done.

get by (informal) manage.

get on 1 make progress. 2 be friendly with somebody.

get over recover from an illness etc.

get up 1 stand up. 2 get out of your bed in the morning.
3 prepare or organize, *We got up a concert.*

get your own back (informal) have your revenge.

have got to must.

geyser (say **gee**-zer or **gy**-zer) noun (plural **geysers**)
1 a natural spring that shoots up columns of hot water. 2 a kind of water heater. [from *Geysir* = gusher, the name of a geyser in Iceland]

ghastly adjective
1 very unpleasant or bad.
2 looking pale and ill. **ghastliness** noun [from Old English *gaestan* = terrify]

ghost noun (plural **ghosts**) the spirit of a dead person that appears to the living. **ghostly** adjective

ghoulish (say **gool**-ish) adjective enjoying things that are grisly or unpleasant. **ghoulishly** adverb,

ghoulishness noun [from Arabic *gul* = a demon that eats dead bodies]

giant noun (plural **giants**)
1 (in myths or fairy tales) a creature like a huge man.
2 a man, animal, or plant that is much larger than the usual size.

gibberish (say jib-er-ish) noun meaningless speech; nonsense.

gibbet (say jib-it) noun (plural **gibbets**)
1 a gallows. 2 an upright post with an arm from which a criminal's body was hung after execution, as a warning to others.

gibbon noun (plural **gibbons**)
a small ape from south-east Asia. Gibbons have very long arms to help them swing through the trees where they live. [French]

giddy adjective
1 feeling that everything is spinning round and that you might fall. 2 causing this feeling, *We looked down from the giddy height of the cliff.* **giddily** adverb, **giddiness** noun [from Old English]

gift noun (plural **gifts**)
1 a present. 2 a talent, *She has a gift for music.* [from Old Norse]

gigantic (say jy-gan-tik) adjective
extremely large; huge. [from Latin *gigantis* = of a giant]

giggle verb (**giggles**, **giggling**, **giggled**) laugh in a silly way.

giggle noun (plural **giggles**)
1 a silly laugh. 2 (informal) something amusing; a bit of fun. [imitating the sound]

gild verb (**gilds**, **gilding**, **gilded**)
cover something with a thin layer of gold or gold paint. [from Old English]

gills plural noun the part of the body through which fishes and certain other water animals breathe.

gilt noun a thin covering of gold or gold paint.

gimmick noun (plural **gimmicks**)
something unusual or silly done or used just to attract people's attention.

gin noun a colourless alcoholic drink flavoured with juniper berries. [from the name of Geneva, a city in Switzerland]

ginger noun
1 the hot-tasting root of a tropical plant, or a flavouring made from this root, used especially in drinks and Eastern cooking. 2 liveliness or energy. 3 a reddish-yellow colour. **ginger** adjective

ginger verb (**gingers**, **gingering**, **gingered**) make something more lively, *This will ginger things up!* [via Old English, Latin, and Greek from Dravidian (a group of languages spoken in southern India)]

gingerly adverb cautiously. [origin unknown]

giraffe noun (plural **giraffe** or **giraffes**) an African animal, the world's tallest mammal, which reaches up to 5.5 metres in height. The giraffe's neck makes up nearly half its height. [from Arabic]

girder noun (plural **girders**)
a metal beam supporting part of a building or a bridge.

girdle noun (plural **girdles**) a belt or cord worn round the waist.

girl noun (plural **girls**)
1 a female child. **2** a young woman. **girlhood** noun, **girlish** adjective

giro (say **jy**-roh) noun a system of arranging payment for customers, run by a post office or bank.

gist (say jist) noun the essential points or general sense of a speech, conversation, etc.

give verb (**gives**, **giving**, **gave**, **given**)
1 let someone have something. **2** make or do something, *He gave a laugh*. **3** be flexible or springy; bend or collapse when pressed. **giver** noun
give in acknowledge that you are defeated; yield.
give up 1 stop trying. **2** end a habit.

given adjective named or stated in advance, *All the people in a given area*.

glacial (say **glay**-shal) adjective icy; made of or produced by ice. **glacially** adverb [from Latin glacies = ice]

glacier (say **glas**-ee-er) noun (plural **glaciers**) a mass of ice that moves very slowly down a mountain valley. [same origin as glacial]

glad adjective
1 pleased; expressing joy. **2** giving pleasure, *We brought the glad news*. **gladly** adverb, **gladness** noun
glad of grateful for or pleased with something.

gladden verb (**gladdens**, **gladdening**, **gladdened**) make a person glad.

glade noun (plural **glades**) an open space in a forest. [origin unknown]

gladiator (say glad-ee-ay-ter) noun (plural **gladiators**) a man trained to fight for public entertainment in ancient Rome. **gladiatorial** (say glad-ee-at-or-ee-al) adjective [from Latin gladius = sword]

glamorous adjective excitingly attractive.

glamour noun attractiveness, romantic charm. [from an old meaning of grammar = magic]

glance verb (**glances**, **glancing**, **glanced**)
1 look at something briefly. **2** strike something at an angle and slide off it. *The ball glanced off his bat.* **glance** noun

gland noun (plural **glands**) an organ of the body that separates substances from the blood so that they can be used or secreted (passed out of the body). **glandular** adjective [from Latin]

glare verb (**glares**, **glaring**, **glared**)
1 shine with an unpleasant dazzling light. **2** stare angrily or fiercely. **glare** noun

glasnost noun the open reporting of news or giving of information, especially in the former Soviet Union. [Russian, = openness]

glass noun (plural **glasses**)
1 a hard brittle substance that is usually transparent. **2** a container made of glass for drinking from. **3** a mirror. **4** a lens. **glassy** adjective [from Old English]

glasses *plural noun*
1 spectacles. 2 binoculars.

glaze *verb* (**glazes, glazing, glazed**)
1 fit a window or building with glass. 2 give a shiny surface to something. 3 become glassy.
[from *glass*]

gleam *noun* (*plural* **gleams**)
1 a beam of soft light, especially one that comes and goes. 2 a small amount of hope, humour, etc.

gleam *verb* (**gleams, gleaming, gleamed**) shine brightly, especially after cleaning or polishing.
[from Old English]

glib *adjective* speaking or writing readily but not sincerely or thoughtfully. **glibly** *adverb*, **glibness** *noun* [from an old word *glibbery* = slippery]

glide *verb* (**glides, gliding, glided**)
1 move along smoothly. 2 fly without using an engine. 3 birds glide when they fly without beating their wings. **glide** *noun*

glider *noun* (*plural* **gliders**) an aeroplane without an engine that flies by floating on warm air currents called thermals.

glimmer *noun* (*plural* **glimmers**)
1 a faint light. 2 a small sign or trace of something, *a glimmer of hope.*

glimmer *verb* (**glimmers, glimmering, glimmered**) shine with a faint, flickering light.

glimpse *noun* (*plural* **glimpses**) a brief view.

glimpse *verb* (**glimpses, glimpsing, glimpsed**) see something briefly.

glint *noun* (*plural* **glints**) a very brief flash of light.

glint *verb* (**glints, glinting, glinted**) shine with a flash of light.
[probably from a Scandinavian language]

glisten (*say* glis-en) *verb* (**glistens, glistening, glistened**) shine like something wet or oily.

glitter *verb* (**glitters, glittering, glittered**) shine with tiny flashes of light; sparkle.

glitter *noun* tiny sparkling pieces used for decoration.

gloat *verb* (**gloats, gloating, gloated**) be pleased in an unkind way that you have succeeded or that someone else has been hurt or upset. [origin unknown]

global *adjective*
1 to do with the whole world; worldwide. 2 to do with the whole of a system. **globally** *adverb* [from *globe*]

global warming *noun* the increase in the temperature of the earth's atmosphere, caused by the greenhouse effect.

globe *noun* (*plural* **globes**)
1 something shaped like a ball, especially one with a map of the whole world on it. 2 the world, *She has travelled all over the globe.* 3 a hollow round glass object.

gloom *noun*
1 darkness. 2 sadness or despair.

gloomy *adjective* (**gloomier, gloomiest**)
1 almost dark. 2 depressed or depressing. **gloomily** *adverb*, **gloominess** *noun*

glorify verb (glorifies, glorifying, glorified)
1 give great praise or great honour to. **2** make a thing seem more splendid or attractive than it really is, *It is a film that glorifies war.* **glorification** noun

glorious adjective splendid or magnificent. **gloriously** adverb

glory noun (plural glories)
1 fame and honour. **2** praise.
3 beauty or magnificence.

glory verb (glories, glorying, gloried) rejoice; pride yourself, *They gloried in victory.*
[from Latin]

gloss[1] noun (plural glosses) the shine on a smooth surface.

gloss verb (glosses, glossing, glossed) make a thing glossy. [origin unknown]

gloss[2] verb (glosses, glossing, glossed)
gloss over mention a fault or mistake etc. only briefly to make it seem less serious than it really is. [from old French *gloser* = flatter or deceive]

glossary noun (plural glossaries) a list of difficult words with their meanings explained. [from Greek *glossa* = tongue, language]

glossy adjective (glossier, glossiest) smooth and shiny. **glossily** adverb, **glossiness** noun

glove noun (plural gloves) a covering for the hand, usually with separate divisions for each finger and thumb. **gloved** adjective [from Old English]

glow noun
1 brightness and warmth without flames. **2** a warm or cheerful feeling, *We felt a glow of pride.*

glow verb (glows, glowing, glowed) shine with a soft, warm light.

glue noun (plural glues) a sticky substance used for joining things together. **gluey** adjective

glue verb (glues, gluing, glued)
1 stick with glue. **2** attach or hold closely, *His ear was glued to the keyhole.*
[from French]

glum adjective miserable or depressed. **glumly** adverb, **glumness** noun [from dialect *glum* = to frown]

glut noun (plural gluts) an excessive supply. [from Latin *gluttire* = to swallow]

glutinous (say gloo-tin-us) adjective glue-like or sticky.

glutton noun (plural gluttons) a person who eats too much. **gluttonous** adjective, **gluttony** noun
glutton for punishment a person who seems to enjoy doing something difficult or unpleasant.
[from old French; related to *glut*]

gm abbreviation gram.

GMT abbreviation Greenwich Mean Time.

gnarled (say narld) adjective twisted and knobbly, like an old tree.

gnash (say nash) verb (gnashes, gnashing, gnashed) grind your teeth together.

gnat (say nat) noun (plural gnats) a tiny fly that bites. [from Old English]

gnaw (say naw) verb (gnaws, gnawing, gnawed) keep on biting something hard so that it wears away. [from Old English]

gnome *(say* nohm) *noun (plural* **gnomes)** a kind of dwarf in fairy tales, usually living underground. [from Latin]

go *verb* **(goes, going, went, gone)** This word is used to show **1** movement, especially away from somewhere *(Where are you going?),* **2** direction *(The road goes to Bristol),* **3** change, **4** progress or result *(The gun went bang),* **5** place *(Plates go on that shelf),* **6** sale *(The house went very cheaply).*

go off 1 explode. **2** become stale. **3** stop liking something.

go on continue.

go out stop burning or shining.

go *noun (plural* **goes)**
1 a turn or try, *May I have a go?* **2** *(informal)* energy or liveliness, *She is full of go.*

make a go of make a success of something.

on the go active; always working or moving.

goad *noun (plural* **goads)** a stick with a pointed end for prodding cattle to move onwards.

goad *verb* **(goads, goading, goaded)** stir into action by being annoying, *He goaded me into fighting.*
[from Old English]

goal *noun (plural* **goals)**
1 the place where a ball must go to score a point in football, hockey, etc. **2** a point scored in this way. **3** something that you are trying to reach or achieve.

goalkeeper *noun (plural* **goalkeepers)** the player who stands in the goal to try and keep the ball from entering.

goat *noun (plural* **goats)** a mammal with horns and a beard, closely related to the sheep. Domestic goats are kept for their milk. [from Old English]

gobble *verb* **(gobbles, gobbling, gobbled)** eat quickly and greedily. [from old French *gober* = to swallow]

go-between *noun (plural* **go-betweens)** a person who acts as a messenger or negotiator between others.

God *noun* the creator of the universe in Christian, Jewish, and Muslim belief.

god *noun (plural* **gods)** a male being that is worshipped, *Mars was a Roman god.*

goddess *noun (plural* **goddesses)** a female being that is worshipped.

godparent *noun (plural* **godparents)** a person at a child's christening who promises to see that it is brought up as a Christian. **godchild** *noun,* **goddaughter** *noun,* **godfather** *noun,* **godmother** *noun,* **godson** *noun*

godsend *noun (plural* **godsends)** a piece of unexpected good luck. [from an old phrase *God's send* = what God has sent]

goggle *verb* **(goggles, goggling, goggled)** stare with wide-open eyes.

going *present participle* of **go.**
be going to do something be ready or likely to do it.

gold *noun (plural* **golds)**
1 a precious yellow metal. **2** a deep yellow colour. **3** a gold medal, usually given as first prize. **gold** *adjective*

golden *adjective*
1 made of gold. 2 coloured like gold. 3 precious or excellent, *a golden opportunity*.

golden wedding *noun* (*plural* **golden weddings**) a couple's fiftieth wedding anniversary.

goldfish *noun* (*plural* **goldfish**) a small red or orange fish, often kept as a pet.

golf *noun* an outdoor game played by hitting a small white ball with a club into a series of holes on a specially prepared ground (a **golf course** or **golf links**) and taking as few strokes as possible.
golfer *noun*, **golfing** *noun*

-gon *suffix* used to form nouns meaning 'having a certain number of angles (and sides)' (e.g. *hexagon*). [from Greek *gonia* = angle]

gong *noun* (*plural* **gongs**) a large metal disc that makes an echoing sound when it is hit. [from Malay (a language spoken in Malaysia)]

good *adjective* (**better, best**)
1 having the right qualities; of the kind that people like, *a good book*. 2 kind, *It was good of you to help us*. 3 well-behaved, *Be a good boy*. 4 skilled or talented, *a good pianist*. 5 healthy; giving benefit, *Exercise is good for you*.
6 thorough, *Give it a good clean*. 7 large; considerable, *It's a good distance from the shops*.
good *noun*
1 something good, *Do good to others*. 2 benefit, *It's for your own good*.

for good for ever.
no good useless.

USAGE: In standard English, *good* cannot be used as an adverb. You can say *She's a good player* but not *She played good*. The adverb that goes with *good* is *well*.

goodbye *interjection* a word used when you leave somebody or at the end of a phone call. [short for *God be with you*]

goods *plural noun*
1 things that are bought and sold. 2 things that are carried on trains or lorries.

goose *noun* (*plural* **geese**) a long-necked water bird with webbed feet, larger than a duck. [from Old English]

gooseberry *noun* (*plural* **gooseberries**)
1 a small green fruit that grows on a prickly bush. 2 (*informal*) an unwanted extra person. [probably from French dialect *gozell*]

goose-flesh *plural noun* or **goose pimples** *plural noun* skin that has turned rough with small bumps on it because a person is cold or afraid. [because it looks like the skin of a plucked goose]

gorge *noun* (*plural* **gorges**) a narrow valley with steep sides.
gorge *verb* (**gorges, gorging, gorged**) eat greedily; stuff with food.
[French, = throat]

gorgeous *adjective* magnificent or beautiful. **gorgeously** *adverb* [from old French]

gorilla noun (plural **gorillas**) an African ape, the largest of all the apes. Males are about 1.8 metres tall and can weigh up to 300kg. [from Latin, probably from an African word = hairy woman]

USAGE: Do not confuse with *guerrilla*, which can be pronounced in the same way.

gospel noun
the Gospels the first four books of the New Testament, telling of the life and teachings of Jesus Christ. [from Old English *god* = good + *spel* = news]

gossip verb (**gossips**, **gossiping**, **gossiped**) talk a lot about other people.

gossip noun (plural **gossips**)
1 talk, especially rumours, about other people. 2 a person who enjoys gossiping. **gossipy** adjective
[from Old English *godsibb* = close friend (literally = god-brother or sister), someone to gossip with]

got past tense of **get**.
have got possess, *Have you got a car?*
have got to must.

Gothic noun the style of building common in Europe in the 12th–16th centuries, with pointed arches and much decorative carving. [from the Goths, whom the Romans regarded as barbarians (because some people thought this style was barbaric compared to Greek or Roman styles)]

gouge (say gowj) verb (**gouges**, **gouging**, **gouged**) scoop or force out by pressing. [from Latin *gubia* = a kind of chisel]

gourmet (say goor-may) noun (plural **gourmets**) a person who understands and appreciates good food and drink. [French, = wine taster]

govern verb (**governs**, **governing**, **governed**) be in charge of the public affairs of a country or region. [from Latin *gubernare* = steer or direct]

governess noun (plural **governesses**) a woman employed to teach children in a private household.

government noun (plural **governments**)
1 the group of people who are in charge of the public affairs of a country. 2 the process of governing. **governmental** adjective

governor noun (plural **governors**)
1 a person who governs a State or a colony etc. 2 a member of the governing body of a school or other institution. 3 the person in charge of a prison.

gown noun (plural **gowns**) a loose flowing garment. [from Latin *gunna* = a fur-lined robe]

GP abbreviation general practitioner.

grab verb (**grabs**, **grabbing**, **grabbed**) take hold of something suddenly or greedily. [from old German or old Dutch]

grace noun
1 beauty, especially of movement. 2 goodwill or favour. 3 dignity or good manners, *At least he had the grace to apologize.* 4 a short prayer of thanks before or after a meal. 5 the title of

a duke, duchess, or archbishop, *His Grace the Duke of Kent.*

grace *verb* (**graces, gracing, graced**) bring honour or dignity to something, *The mayor himself graced us with his presence.* [from Latin *gratus* = pleasing]

graceful *adjective* beautiful and elegant in movement or shape. **gracefully** *adverb,* **gracefulness** *noun*

gracious *adjective* behaving kindly and honourably. **graciously** *adverb,* **graciousness** *noun*

grade *noun* (*plural* **grades**) 1 a step in a scale of quality or value or rank. 2 a mark showing the quality of a student's work.

grade *verb* (**grades, grading, graded**) arrange in grades. [from Latin *gradus* = a step]

gradient (*say* gray-dee-ent) *noun* (*plural* **gradients**) a slope or the steepness of a slope.

gradual *adjective* happening slowly but steadily. **gradually** *adverb*

graduate (*say* grad-yoo-at) *noun* (*plural* **graduates**) a person who has a university or college degree. [same origin as *grade*]

graffiti *noun* words or drawings scribbled or sprayed on a wall. [Italian, = scratchings]

USAGE: Strictly speaking, this word is a plural noun (the singular is *graffito*), so it should be used with a plural verb: *There are graffiti all over the wall.* However, the word is widely used nowadays as if it were a singular noun and most people do not regard this as wrong: *There is graffiti all over the wall.*

graft *noun* (*plural* **grafts**) 1 a shoot from one plant or tree fixed into another to form a new growth. 2 a piece of living tissue transplanted by a surgeon to replace what is diseased or damaged, *a skin graft.*

graft *verb* (**grafts, grafting, grafted**) insert or transplant as a graft. [from Greek *grapheion* = pointed writing stick (because of the pointed shape of the end of the shoot)]

grain *noun* (*plural* **grains**) 1 a small hard seed or similar particle. 2 cereal plants when they are growing or after being harvested. 3 a very small amount, *a grain of truth.* 4 the pattern of lines made by the fibres in a piece of wood or paper. **grainy** *adjective* [from Latin]

gram *noun* (*plural* **grams**) a unit of mass or weight in the metric system. [from Latin *gramma* = a small weight]

-gram *suffix* used to form nouns meaning something written or drawn etc. (e.g. *diagram*). [from Greek *gramma* = thing written]

grammar *noun* (*plural* **grammars**) 1 the rules for using words correctly. 2 a book about these rules. **grammatical** *adjective* [from Greek, = the art of letters]

grammar school *noun* (*plural* **grammar schools**) a secondary

school for children with
academic ability.

grand *adjective*
1 splendid and impressive. **2** most
important or highest-ranking.
3 including everything; complete.
grandly *adverb*, **grandness** *noun*
[from Latin *grandis* = fully-
grown]

grandchild *noun* (*plural*
grandchildren) the child of
a person's son or daughter.
granddaughter *noun*, **grandson**
noun

grandeur (*say* grand-yer) *noun*
impressive beauty; splendour.

grandfather *noun* (*plural*
grandfathers) the father of
a person's father or mother.

grandiose (*say* grand-ee-ohss)
adjective large and impressive;
trying to seem impressive. [via
French from Italian]

grandmother *noun* (*plural*
grandmothers) the mother of
a person's father or mother.

grandparent *noun* (*plural*
grandparents) a grandfather or
grandmother.

grand piano *noun* (*plural* **grand
pianos**) a large piano with the
strings fixed horizontally.

grandstand *noun* (*plural*
grandstands) a building with
a roof and rows of seats for
spectators at a racecourse or
sports ground.

grand total *noun* the sum of
other totals.

granite *noun* a very hard kind of
rock used for building. [from
Italian *granito* = like grains
(because of the small particles
you can see in the rock)]

grant *verb* (**grants**, **granting**,
granted)
1 give or allow someone what he
or she has asked for, *grant
a request*. **2** admit; agree that
something is true.
take for granted assume that
something is true or will always
be available.

grant *noun* (*plural* **grants**)
something granted, especially
a sum of money.
[from old French]

Granth (*say* grunt) *noun* the
sacred scriptures of the Sikhs.
[from Sanskrit]

grape *noun* (*plural* **grapes**) a small
green or purple berry that grows
in bunches on a vine. Grapes are
used to make wine. [from old
French]

grapefruit *noun* (*plural*
grapefruit) a large round yellow
citrus fruit. [because they grow
in clusters, like grapes]

grapevine *noun* (*plural*
grapevines)
1 a vine on which grapes grow.
2 a way by which news spreads
unofficially, with people passing
it on from one to another.

graph *noun* (*plural* **graphs**)
a diagram showing how two
quantities or variables are
related. [from Greek *graphein*
= to write or draw]

-graph *suffix* used to form nouns
and verbs meaning
1 something written, drawn, or
recorded in some way (e.g.
photograph). **2** a machine which
records (e.g. *telegraph*,
seismograph). [same origin as
graph]

graphic *adjective*
1 to do with drawing or painting, *a graphic artist*. 2 giving a lively description. **graphically** *adverb* [same origin as *graph*]

-graphy *suffix* used to form names of
1 sciences (e.g. *geography*), 2 methods of writing, drawing, or recording (e.g. *photography*). [same origin as *graph*]

grapple *verb* (**grapples, grappling, grappled**)
1 struggle or wrestle. 2 seize or hold firmly. 3 try to deal with a problem etc., *I've been grappling with this essay all day.*

grasp *verb* (**grasps, grasping, grasped**)
1 seize and hold firmly. 2 understand.

grasp *noun*
1 the power of understanding something. 2 a firm hold.

grasping *adjective* greedy for money or possessions.

grass *noun* (*plural* **grasses**)
1 a plant with green blades and stalks. 2 ground covered with grass; lawn. **grassy** *adjective*

grasshopper *noun* (*plural* **grasshoppers**) a jumping insect that makes a shrill noise.

grass roots *plural noun* the ordinary people in a political party or other group.

grate¹ *noun* (*plural* **grates**)
1 a metal framework that keeps fuel in a fireplace. 2 a fireplace. [from old French or Spanish]

grate² *verb* (**grates, grating, grated**)
1 shred something into small pieces by rubbing it on a rough surface.
2 make an unpleasant noise by rubbing. 3 sound harshly.
grate on have an irritating effect. [via old French from Germanic]

grateful *adjective* feeling or showing that you are thankful for something that has been done for you. **gratefully** *adverb* [from Latin *gratus* = thankful, pleasing]

gratify *verb* (**gratifies, gratifying, gratified**)
1 give pleasure. 2 satisfy a feeling or desire, *Please gratify our curiosity*. **gratification** *noun* [from Latin *gratus* = pleasing]

grating *noun* (*plural* **gratings**) a framework of metal bars placed across an opening. [from *grate¹*]

gratitude *noun* being grateful.

grave¹ *noun* (*plural* **graves**) the place where a dead body is buried. [from Old English]

grave² *adjective* serious or solemn. **gravely** *adverb* [from Latin *gravis* = heavy]

grave accent (rhymes with *starve*) *noun* (*plural* **grave accents**) a mark over a vowel, as over *a* in *vis-à-vis*. [from French; related to *grave²*]

gravel *noun* small stones mixed with coarse sand, used to make paths. **gravelled** *adjective*, **gravelly** *adjective* [from old French]

graveyard *noun* (*plural* **graveyards**) a burial ground.

gravity *noun*
1 the force that pulls all objects in the universe towards each other. 2 the force that pulls everything towards the earth. 3 seriousness. [same origin as *grave²*]

gravy *noun* a hot brown sauce made from meat juices.

graze *verb* (**grazes, grazing, grazed**)
1 feed on growing grass. 2 scrape your skin slightly. *I grazed my elbow on the wall.* 3 touch something lightly in passing.

graze *noun* (*plural* **grazes**) a raw place where skin has been scraped.
[from Old English *graes* = grass]

grease *noun* melted fat; any thick oily substance. **greasy** *adjective*

grease *verb* (**greases, greasing, greased**) put grease on something.
[from Latin *crassus* = thick, fat]

great *adjective*
1 very large; much above average. 2 very important or talented. *a great composer.*
3 (*informal*) very good or enjoyable. *It's great to see you again.* 4 older or younger by one generation. *great-grandfather.*
greatly *adverb*, **greatness** *noun*

Great Britain *noun* the island made up of England, Scotland, and Wales, with the small adjacent islands.

USAGE: See the note at *Britain.*

greed *noun* being greedy. [from *greedy*]

greedy *adjective* (**greedier, greediest**) wanting more food, money, or other things than you need. **greedily** *adverb*, **greediness** *noun* [from Old English]

green *noun* (*plural* **greens**)
1 the colour of grass, leaves, etc.
2 an area of grassy land. *the village green; a putting green.*

green *adjective*
1 of the colour green. 2 concerned with protecting the natural environment. 3 inexperienced and likely to make mistakes.
greenness *noun*

green belt *noun* (*plural* **green belts**) an area kept as open land round a city.

greenery *noun* green leaves or plants.

greengrocer *noun* (*plural* **greengrocers**) a person who keeps a shop that sells fruit and vegetables. **greengrocery** *noun*

greenhouse *noun* (*plural* **greenhouses**) a glass building where plants are protected from cold.

greenhouse effect *noun* the warming of the earth's surface when radiation from the sun is trapped by the atmosphere.

greens *plural noun* green vegetables, such as cabbage and spinach.

Greenwich Mean Time (*say* **gren**-ich) *noun* the time on the line of longitude which passes through Greenwich in London, used as a basis for calculating time throughout the world.

greet *verb* (**greets, greeting, greeted**)
1 speak to a person who arrives. 2 receive. *They greeted the song with applause.* 3 present itself to. *A strange sight greeted our eyes.*
[from Old English]

greeting *noun* (*plural* **greetings**) words or actions used to greet somebody.

grey noun (plural **greys**) the colour between black and white, like ashes or dark clouds. **grey** adjective, **greyness** noun [from Old English]

greyhound noun (plural **greyhounds**) a slender dog with smooth hair, used in racing. [from Old English *grighund*, probably = bitch-hound]

grid noun (plural **grids**) a framework or pattern of bars or lines crossing each other.

grid reference noun (plural **grid references**) a set of numbers that allows you to describe the exact position of something on a map.

grief noun deep sorrow, especially at a person's death. **come to grief** suffer a disaster. [same origin as *grieve*]

grievance noun (plural **grievances**) something that people are discontented about. [old French, = injury or hardship]

grieve verb (**grieves**, **grieving**, **grieved**)
1 feel deep sorrow, especially at a person's death. **2** make a person feel very sad. [from old French *grever* = to burden; related to *grave*²]

grill noun (plural **grills**)
1 a heated element on a cooker, for sending heat downwards.
2 food cooked under this.
3 a grille.

grill verb (**grills**, **grilling**, **grilled**)
1 cook under a grill. **2** question closely and severely, *The police grilled him for an hour.*

grim adjective (**grimmer**, **grimmest**)
1 stern or severe. **2** unpleasant or

unattractive, *a grim prospect.* **grimly** adverb, **grimness** noun [from Old English]

grimace (say grim-**ayss** or grim-as) noun (plural **grimaces**) a twisted expression on the face made in pain or disgust.

grimace verb (**grimaces**, **grimacing**, **grimaced**) make a grimace. [from Spanish *grima* = fright]

grime noun dirt in a layer on a surface or on the skin. **grimy** adjective [from old German or old Dutch]

grin noun (plural **grins**) a broad smile showing your teeth.

grin verb (**grins**, **grinning**, **grinned**) smile broadly showing your teeth. [from Old English]

grind verb (**grinds**, **grinding**, **ground**)
1 crush something into tiny pieces or powder. **2** sharpen or smooth something by rubbing it on a rough surface. **3** rub harshly in fury, *He ground his teeth in fury.* **4** move with a harsh grating noise, *The bus ground to a halt.* **grinder** noun

grip verb (**grips**, **gripping**, **gripped**)
1 hold something firmly. **2** hold a person's attention, *The opening chapter really gripped me.*

grip noun (plural **grips**)
1 a firm hold. **2** a handle, especially on a sports racket, etc. **3** (*American*) a travelling bag. **4** control or power, *The country is in the grip of lottery fever.* **get to grips with** begin to deal with successfully.

gristle noun tough rubbery tissue in meat. **gristly** adjective [from Old English]

grit noun
1 tiny pieces of stone or sand.
2 courage and endurance. **gritty** adjective, **grittiness** noun

grit verb (**grits, gritting, gritted**)
1 spread a road or path with grit.
2 clench your teeth when in pain or trouble.

grizzled adjective streaked with grey hairs. [from old French grisel = grey]

grizzly bear noun (plural **grizzly bears**) a large fierce bear of North America. [from grizzled (the bear has brown fur with white-tipped hairs)]

groan verb (**groans, groaning, groaned**)
1 make a long deep sound in pain, distress, or disapproval.
2 creak loudly under a heavy load. **groan** noun, **groaner** noun

grocer noun (plural **grocers**) a person who keeps a shop that sells food and household goods. [originally = wholesaler; from Latin grossus = gross (because a wholesaler buys goods in the gross = in large quantities)]

groceries plural noun goods sold by a grocer.

groom noun (plural **grooms**)
1 a person whose job is to look after horses. 2 a bridegroom.

groom verb (**grooms, grooming, groomed**)
1 clean and brush a horse or other animal. 2 make something neat and trim. 3 train a person for a certain job or position, Evans is being groomed for the captaincy.

groove noun (plural **grooves**) a long narrow furrow or channel cut in the surface of something. **grooved** adjective [from old Italian groeve = furrow or ditch]

grope verb (**gropes, groping, groped**) feel about for something you cannot see.

gross (say grohss) adjective
1 fat and ugly. 2 having bad manners; vulgar. 3 very obvious or shocking, gross stupidity. 4 total; without anything being deducted, our gross income. (Compare net².) **grossly** adverb, **grossness** noun

gross noun (plural **gross**) twelve dozen (144) of something, ten gross = 1440. [from Latin]

grotesque (say groh-tesk) adjective fantastically ugly or very strangely shaped. **grotesquely** adverb, **grotesqueness** noun

ground¹ past tense of **grind**.

ground² noun (plural **grounds**)
1 the solid surface of the earth.
2 a sports field.

ground verb (**grounds, grounding, grounded**)
1 prevent a plane from flying, All aircraft are grounded because of the fog. 2 give a good basic training, Ground them in the rules of spelling. 3 base, This theory is grounded on reliable evidence.

grounds plural noun
1 the gardens of a large house.
2 solid particles that sink to the bottom, coffee grounds. 3 reasons, There are grounds for suspicion.

group noun (plural **groups**)
1 a number of people, animals, or things that come together or belong together in some way.
2 a band of musicians.

group verb (**groups, grouping, grouped**) put together or come together in a group or groups.

grouse[1] noun (plural **grouse**)
a bird with feathered feet, hunted as game. [origin unknown]

grouse[2] verb (**grouses, grousing, groused**) (informal) grumble or complain. **grouse** noun, **grouser** noun [origin unknown]

grove noun (plural **groves**)
a group of trees; a small wood.

grovel verb (**grovels, grovelling, grovelled**)
1 crawl on the ground, especially in a show of fear or humility.
2 act in an excessively humble way, for example by apologizing a lot. **groveller** noun [from Old Norse a grufu = face downwards]

grow verb (**grows, growing, grew, grown**)
1 become bigger or greater.
2 develop. 3 cultivate; plant and look after, He grows roses.
4 become, He grew rich. **grower** noun

growl verb (**growls, growling, growled**) make a deep angry sound in the throat. **growl** noun [imitating the sound]

grown-up noun (plural **grown-ups**) an adult person.
grown-up adjective like or suitable for an adult.

growth noun (plural **growths**)
1 growing or developing.
2 something that has grown.
3 a lump that has grown on or inside a person's body; a tumour.

grub noun (plural **grubs**)
1 a tiny worm-like creature that will become an insect; a larva.
2 (slang) food.

grub verb (**grubs, grubbing, grubbed**)
1 dig up by the roots. 2 turn things over or move them about while looking for something; rummage.
[origin unknown]

grubby adjective (**grubbier, grubbiest**) rather dirty.
grubbiness noun

grudge noun (plural **grudges**)
a feeling of resentment or ill will, She isn't the sort of person who bears a grudge.

grudge verb (**grudges, grudging, grudged**) resent having to give or allow something.
[from old French grouchier = grumble]

gruff adjective having a rough unfriendly voice or manner.
gruffly adverb, **gruffness** noun [from Italian grof = coarse or rude]

grumble verb (**grumbles, grumbling, grumbled**) complain in a bad-tempered way. **grumble** noun, **grumbler** noun [origin unknown]

grunt verb (**grunts, grunting, grunted**)
1 make a pig's gruff snort. 2 speak or say gruffly. **grunt** noun [from Old English grunnettan, imitating the sound]

guarantee noun (plural **guarantees**) a formal promise to do something or to repair an object if it breaks or goes wrong.

guarantee verb (**guarantees**, **guaranteeing**, **guaranteed**) give a guarantee; promise. **guarantor** noun

guard verb (**guards**, **guarding**, **guarded**)
1 protect; keep safe. 2 watch over and prevent from escaping.

guard noun (plural **guards**)
1 guarding; protection, *Keep the prisoners under close guard.*
2 someone who guards a person or place. 3 a group of soldiers or police officers etc. acting as a guard. 4 a railway official in charge of a train. 5 a protecting device, *a fireguard.*
[via old French from Germanic; related to *ward*]

guardian noun (plural **guardians**)
1 someone who guards. 2 a person who is legally in charge of a child whose parents cannot look after him or her. **guardianship** noun
[via old French from Germanic; related to *warden*]

guerrilla (say ger-**il**-a) noun (plural **guerrillas**) a member of a small unofficial army who fights by making surprise attacks. [Spanish, = little war]

USAGE: Do not confuse with *gorilla.*

guess noun (plural **guesses**) an opinion or answer that you give without making careful calculations or without certain knowledge.

guess verb (**guesses**, **guessing**, **guessed**) make a guess. **guesser** noun

guest noun (plural **guests**)
1 a person who is invited to visit or stay at another's house.

2 a person staying at a hotel.
3 a person who takes part in another's show as a visiting performer.

guidance noun
1 guiding. 2 advising or advice on problems.

Guide noun (plural **Guides**) a member of the Girl Guides Association, an organization for girls.

guide noun (plural **guides**)
1 a person who shows others the way or points out interesting sights. 2 a book giving information about a place or subject.

guide verb (**guides**, **guiding**, **guided**) show someone the way or how to do something.
[via old French from Germanic; related to *wit*]

guide dog noun (plural **guide dogs**) a dog trained to lead a blind person.

guile (rhymes with *mile*) noun craftiness. [via old French from Old Norse]

guillotine (say **gil**-ot-een) noun (plural **guillotines**) a machine with a heavy blade for beheading criminals, used in France.
[named after Dr Guillotin, who suggested its use in France in 1789]

guilt noun
1 the fact that you have committed an offence. 2 a feeling that you are to blame for something that has happened.
[from Old English *gylt* = a crime or sin]

guilty adjective
1 having done wrong. 2 feeling or showing guilt. **guiltily** adverb

guinea pig noun (plural **guinea pigs**)
1 a small furry animal without a tail. **2** a person who is used as the subject of an experiment. [from *Guinea* in west Africa, probably by mistake for Guiana, in South America, where the guinea pig comes from]

guitar noun (plural **guitars**) a musical instrument played by plucking its strings. **guitarist** noun [from Greek *kithara*, a small harp]

gulf noun (plural **gulfs**)
1 a large area of the sea that is partly surrounded by land. **2** a wide gap; a great difference. [from Greek]

gull noun (plural **gulls**) a seagull. [a Celtic word]

gullible adjective easily deceived. [from an old word *gull* = fool or deceive]

gulp verb (gulps, gulping, gulped)
1 swallow hastily or greedily.
2 make a loud swallowing noise, especially because of fear.

gulp noun (plural **gulps**)
1 the act of gulping. **2** a large mouthful of liquid. [imitating the sound]

gum[1] noun (plural **gums**) the firm flesh in which your teeth are rooted. [from Old English]

gum[2] noun (plural **gums**)
1 a sticky substance produced by some trees and shrubs, used as glue. **2** a sweet made with gum or gelatine, *a fruit gum*. **3** chewing gum. **4** a gum tree. **gummy** adjective

gum verb (gums, gumming, gummed) cover or stick something with gum. [via old French, Latin, and Greek from Egyptian]

gum tree noun (plural **gum trees**) a eucalyptus.

gun noun (plural **guns**)
1 a weapon that fires shells or bullets from a metal tube.
2 a starting pistol. **3** a device that forces a substance out of a tube, *a grease gun*. **gunfire** noun, **gunshot** noun

gun verb (guns, gunning, gunned)
gun down shoot someone with a gun. [probably from the Swedish girl's name *Gunnhildr*, from *gunnr* = war]

gunpowder noun an explosive made from a powdered mixture of potassium nitrate, charcoal, and sulphur.

gurgle verb (gurgles, gurgling, gurgled) make a low bubbling sound. **gurgle** noun

guru noun (plural **gurus**)
1 a Hindu religious leader. **2** an influential teacher; a mentor. [from Sanskrit]

gush verb (gushes, gushing, gushed)
1 flow suddenly or quickly. **2** talk too enthusiastically or emotionally. **gush** noun

gust noun (plural **gusts**) a sudden rush of wind, rain, or smoke. **gusty** adjective, **gustily** adverb

gust verb (gusts, gusting, gusted) blow in gusts. [from Old Norse]

gut noun (plural **guts**) the lower part of the digestive system; the intestine.

gut verb (**guts, gutting, gutted**)
1 remove the guts from a dead fish or other animal. **2** remove or destroy the inside of something, *The fire gutted the factory.*

guts plural noun
1 the digestive system; the inside parts of a person or thing. **2** (*informal*) courage.

gutted adjective (*informal*) extremely disappointed or upset.

gutter noun (*plural* **gutters**) a long narrow channel at the side of a street, or along the edge of a roof, for carrying away rainwater.

gutter verb (**gutters, guttering, guttered**) a candle gutters when it burns unsteadily so that melted wax runs down. [from Latin *gutta* = a drop]

guttural (*say* gut-er-al) adjective throaty and harsh-sounding, *a guttural voice.* [from Latin *guttur* = throat]

guy¹ noun (*plural* **guys**)
1 a figure representing Guy Fawkes, burnt on 5 November in memory of the Gunpowder Plot which planned to blow up Parliament on that day in 1605. **2** (*informal*) a man.

guy² or **guy-rope** noun (*plural* **guys, guy-ropes**) a rope used to hold something in place, especially a tent. [probably from old German]

gym (*say* jim) noun (*plural* **gyms**) (*informal*)
1 a gymnasium. **2** gymnastics.

gymkhana (*say* jim-kah-na) noun (*plural* **gymkhanas**) a series of horse-riding contests and other sports events. [from Urdu]

gymnasium noun (*plural* **gymnasia, gymnasiums**) a place equipped for gymnastics. [from Greek *gymnos* = naked (because Greek men exercised naked)]

gymnastics plural noun exercises performed to develop the muscles or to show the performer's agility. **gymnastic** adjective

gypsy noun (*plural* **gypsies**) a member of a people who live in caravans and wander from place to place, especially a Romany. [from *Egyptian*, because gypsies were originally thought to have come from Egypt]

gyrate (*say* jy-rayt) verb (**gyrates, gyrating, gyrated**) revolve; move in circles or spirals. **gyration** noun [from Greek *gyros* = a ring or circle]

gyroscope (*say* jy-ro-skohp) noun (*plural* **gyroscopes**) a device that keeps steady because of a heavy wheel spinning inside it. [same origin as *gyrate*]

Hh

haberdashery noun small articles used in sewing, e.g. ribbons, buttons, thread. [origin unknown]

habit noun (*plural* **habits**)
1 something that you do without thinking because you have done it so often; a settled way of behaving. **2** the long dress worn by a monk or nun. **habitual** adjective, **habitually** adverb [from Latin]

habitat noun (plural **habitats**) where an animal or plant lives naturally. [Latin, literally = inhabits]

habitation noun (plural **habitations**)
1 a dwelling. 2 inhabiting a place. [from Latin *habitare* = inhabit]

hack verb (**hacks**, **hacking**, **hacked**)
1 chop or cut roughly.
2 (*informal*) break into a computer system. [from Old English]

hackles plural noun
with his or **her hackles up** angry and ready to fight. [*hackles* are the long feathers on some birds' necks]

haddock noun (plural **haddock**) a sea fish like cod but smaller, used as food.

hadn't (*mainly spoken*) had not.

haemoglobin (say heem-a-gloh-bin) noun the red substance that carries oxygen in the blood. [from Greek *haima* = blood + *globule* (because of the shape of haemoglobin cells)]

haemophilia (say heem-o-fil-ee-a) noun a disease that causes people to bleed dangerously from even a slight cut. **haemophiliac** noun [from Greek *haima* = blood + *philia* = loving]

haemorrhage (say hem-er-ij) noun bleeding, especially inside a person's body. [from Greek *haima* = blood + *rhegnunai* = burst]

hag noun (plural **hags**) an ugly old woman. [from Old English]

haggard adjective looking ill or very tired. [from old French]

haggis noun (plural **haggises**) a Scottish food made from sheep's offal.

hail[1] noun frozen drops of rain. **hail** verb, **hailstone** noun, **hailstorm** noun [from Old English]

hail[2] interjection an exclamation of greeting.
hail verb (**hails**, **hailing**, **hailed**) call out to somebody.
hail from come from, *He hails from Ireland.*
[from Old Norse]

hair noun (plural **hairs**)
1 a soft covering that grows on the heads and bodies of people and animals. 2 one of the threads that make up this covering.
hairbrush noun, **haircut** noun
keep your hair on (*informal*) do not lose your temper.
split hairs make petty or unimportant distinctions of meaning. **hair-splitting** noun

hairdresser noun (plural **hairdressers**) a person whose job is to cut and arrange people's hair.

hairpin noun (plural **hairpins**) a U-shaped pin for keeping hair in place.

hairpin bend noun (plural **hairpin bends**) a sharp bend in a road.

hair-raising adjective terrifying.

hairy adjective
1 with a lot of hair. 2 (*informal*) dangerous or risky.

halal noun meat prepared according to Muslim law. [Arabic, = according to religious law]

halcyon (say **hal**-see-on) adjective happy and peaceful, halcyon days. [from Greek alkyon = a bird which was once believed to build its nest on the sea, which magically stayed calm]

half noun (plural **halves**) one of the two equal parts or amounts into which something is or can be divided.

half adverb partly; not completely, This meat is only half cooked.
not half (slang) extremely, Was she cross? Not half!

half-brother noun (plural **half-brothers**) a brother to whom you are related by one parent but not by both parents.

half-hearted adjective not very enthusiastic. **half-heartedly** adverb

half-life noun (plural **half-lives**) the time taken for the radioactivity of a substance to fall to half its original value.

halfpenny (say **hayp**-nee) noun (plural **halfpennies** for separate coins, **halfpence** for a sum of money) a former coin worth half a penny.

half-sister noun (plural **half-sisters**) a sister to whom you are related by one parent but not by both parents.

half-term noun (plural **half-terms**) a short holiday in the middle of a term.

halfway adjective & adverb between two others and equally distant from each.

hall noun (plural **halls**)
1 a space or passage into which the front entrance of a house etc.
opens. 2 a very large room or building used for meetings, concerts, etc. [from Old English]

Hallowe'en noun 31 October, traditionally a time when ghosts and witches are believed to appear. [from All Hallow Even, the evening before the Christian festival honouring all the hallows = saints]

hallucination noun (plural **hallucinations**) something you think you can see or hear that is not really there. [from Latin alucinari = wander in your mind]

halo noun (plural **haloes**) a circle of light round something, especially round the head of a saint etc. in paintings. [from Greek]

halt verb (**halts, halting, halted**) stop.

halt noun (plural **halts**)
1 a stop, Work came to a halt.
2 a small stopping place on a railway.

halve verb (**halves, halving, halved**)
1 divide something into halves.
2 reduce something to half its size. [from half]

ham noun (plural **hams**)
1 meat from a pig's leg. 2 (slang) an actor who overacts.
3 (informal) someone who operates a radio to send and receive messages as a hobby. [from Old English]

hamburger noun (plural **hamburgers**) a flat round cake of minced beef served fried, often in a bread roll. [named after Hamburg in Germany (not after ham)]

hammer noun (plural **hammers**)
a tool with a heavy metal head
used for driving nails in,
breaking things, etc.

hammer verb (**hammers,
hammering, hammered**)
1 hit something with a hammer.
2 strike loudly. **3** (informal)
defeat.

hammock noun (plural
hammocks) a bed made of
a strong net or piece of cloth
hung by cords. [via Spanish from
Taino (a South American
language)]

hamper¹ noun (plural **hampers**)
a large box-shaped basket with
a lid. [from old French]

hamper² verb (**hampers,
hampering, hampered**) hinder;
prevent from moving or working
freely. [origin unknown]

hamster noun (plural **hamsters**)
a small furry animal with cheek
pouches for carrying grain. [from
German]

hand noun (plural **hands**)
1 the end part of the arm below
the wrist. **2** a pointer on a clock
or dial. **3** a worker; a member of
a ship's crew, *All hands on deck!*
4 the cards held by one player in
a card game. **5** side or direction,
on the other hand. **6** help or aid,
Give me a hand with these boxes.
at hand near.
by hand using your hand or
hands.
give or **receive a big hand**
applaud; be applauded.
hands down winning easily.
in good hands in the care or
control of someone who can be
trusted.
in hand in your possession; being

dealt with.
on hand available.
out of hand out of control.

hand verb (**hands, handing,
handed**) give or pass something
to somebody, *Hand it over.*
hand down pass something from
one generation to another.

handbag noun (plural **handbags**)
a small bag for holding a purse
and personal articles.

handbook noun (plural
handbooks) a small book that
gives useful facts about
something.

handcuff noun (plural **handcuffs**)
one of a pair of metal rings linked
by a chain, for fastening wrists
together.

handcuff verb (**handcuffs,
handcuffing, handcuffed**) fasten
with handcuffs.

handful noun (plural **handfuls**)
1 as much as can be carried in
one hand. **2** a few people or
things. **3** (informal) a troublesome
person or task.

handicap noun (plural
handicaps)
1 a disadvantage. **2** a physical or
mental disability. **handicapped**
adjective [from *hand in cap* (from
an old game in which forfeit
money was deposited in a cap)]

handkerchief noun (plural
handkerchiefs) a small square of
cloth for wiping the nose or face.

handle noun (plural **handles**) the
part of a thing by which it is
carried or controlled.

handle verb (**handles, handling,
handled**)
1 touch or feel something with
your hands. **2** deal with; manage,

Will you handle the catering?

handler *noun*

[from Old English]

handlebar *noun* or **handlebars** *plural noun* the bar, with a handle at each end, that steers a bicycle or motorcycle etc.

handsome *adjective*
1 good-looking. **2** generous. **handsomely** *adverb* [originally = easy to handle or use: from *hand* + *-some*]

handstand *noun* (*plural* **handstands**) balancing on your hands with your feet in the air.

handwriting *noun* writing done by hand. **handwritten** *adjective*

handy *adjective* (**handier**, **handiest**)
1 convenient or useful. **2** good at using the hands. **handily** *adverb*, **handiness** *noun*

hang *verb* (**hangs**, **hanging**, **hung**)
1 fix the top or side of something to a hook or nail etc.; be supported in this way. **2** stick wallpaper to a wall. **3** decorate with drapery or hanging ornaments etc., *The tree was hung with lights.* **4** droop or lean, *People hung over the gate.* **5** (with past tense & past participle **hanged**) execute somebody by hanging them from a rope that tightens round the neck, *He was hanged in 1950.*

hang about 1 loiter. **2** not go away.

hang back hesitate to go forward or to do something.

hang on 1 hold tightly.
2 (*informal*) wait.

hang up end a telephone conversation by putting back the receiver.

hang *noun*
get the hang of (*informal*) learn how to do or use something.

hang-glider *noun* (*plural* **hang-gliders**) a framework in which a person can glide through the air. **hang-gliding** *noun*

hangover *noun* (*plural* **hangovers**) an unpleasant feeling after drinking too much alcohol.

hank *noun* (*plural* **hanks**) a coil or piece of wool, thread, etc.

hanker *verb* (**hankers**, **hankering**, **hankered**) feel a longing for something.

haphazard *adjective* done or chosen at random, not by planning. [from an old word *hap* = luck, + *hazard*]

happen *verb* (**happens**, **happening**, **happened**)
1 take place; occur. **2** do something by chance, *I happened to see him.* [from an old word *hap* = luck]

happy *adjective* (**happier**, **happiest**)
1 pleased or contented.
2 fortunate, *a happy coincidence.* **happily** *adverb*, **happiness** *noun* [same origin as **happen**]

harangue (*say* ha-**rang**) *verb* (**harangues**, **haranguing**, **harangued**) make a long speech to somebody. **harangue** *noun* [from Latin]

harass (*say* **ha**-ras) *verb* (**harasses**, **harassing**, **harassed**) trouble or annoy somebody often. **harassment** (*say* **ha**-ras-ment) *noun* [from French *harer* = set a dog on someone]

harbour *noun* (*plural* **harbours**) a place where ships can shelter or unload.

hard adjective
1 firm or solid; not soft. 2 difficult, hard sums. 3 severe or stern. 4 causing suffering, hard luck. 5 using great effort, a hard worker. 6 hard drugs are strong and addictive ones. **hardness** noun

hard of hearing slightly deaf.

hard up (informal) short of money.

hard adverb
1 so as to be hard, The ground froze hard. 2 with great effort; intensively, We worked hard. It is raining hard. 3 with difficulty, hard-earned.
[from Old English]

hard disk noun (plural **hard disks**) a disk fixed inside a computer, able to store large amounts of data.

harden verb (**hardens, hardening, hardened**) make or become hard or hardy. **hardener** noun

hardly adverb only just; only with difficulty, She can hardly walk.

USAGE: It is not acceptable in standard English to use 'not' with hardly, as in 'she can't hardly walk'.

hardship noun (plural **hardships**) difficult conditions that cause discomfort or suffering, a life of hardship.

hardware noun
1 metal implements and tools etc.; machinery. 2 the machinery of a computer as opposed to the software. (Compare software.)

hard water noun water containing minerals that prevent soap from making much lather.

hardy adjective (**hardier, hardiest**) able to endure cold or difficult conditions. **hardiness** noun [from French hardi = bold or daring]

hare noun (plural **hares**) an animal like a rabbit but larger.

harm verb (**harms, harming, harmed**) damage or injure.

harm noun damage or injury. **harmful** adjective, **harmless** adjective
[from Old English]

harmonica noun (plural **harmonicas**) a mouth organ. [from Latin harmonicus = to do with melody]

harmonious adjective
1 combining together in a pleasant and attractive way. 2 peaceful and friendly.

harmony noun (plural **harmonies**)
1 a pleasant combination, especially of musical notes. 2 being friendly to each other. [from Latin harmonia = agreement]

harness noun (plural **harnesses**) the straps put round a horse's head and neck for controlling it.

harness verb (**harnesses, harnessing, harnessed**)
1 put a harness on a horse. 2 control and use something, Could we harness the power of the wind?
[via French from Old Norse]

harp noun (plural **harps**) a musical instrument with strings stretched across a frame and plucked by the fingers. **harpist** noun

harpoon noun (plural **harpoons**) a spear attached to a rope, used for catching whales etc.
harpoon verb

harrowing *adjective* very upsetting or distressing.

harsh *adjective*
1 rough and unpleasant. 2 severe or cruel. **harshly** *adverb*, **harshness** *noun* [from old German *horsch* = rough or hairy]

harvest *noun* (*plural* **harvests**)
1 the time when farmers gather in the corn, fruit, or vegetables that they have grown. 2 the crop that is gathered in.

hash *noun* a mixture of small pieces of meat and vegetables, usually fried.
make a hash of (*informal*) make a mess of something; bungle. [from French *hacher* = cut up small]

hasn't (*mainly spoken*) has not.

haste *noun* a hurry.
make haste act quickly.

hasten *verb* (**hastens**, **hastening**, **hastened**) hurry.

hasty *adjective* hurried; done too quickly. **hastily** *adverb*, **hastiness** *noun*

hat *noun* (*plural* **hats**) a shaped covering for the head.
keep it under your hat keep it secret.

hatch[1] *noun* (*plural* **hatches**) an opening in a floor, wall, or door, usually with a covering. [from Old English]

hatch[2] *verb* (**hatches**, **hatching**, **hatched**)
1 break out of an egg. 2 keep an egg warm until a baby bird comes out. 3 plan, *They hatched a plot.* [origin unknown]

hatchet *noun* (*plural* **hatchets**) a small axe.

hate *verb* (**hates**, **hating**, **hated**) dislike very strongly.

hate *noun* extreme dislike. [from Old English]

hatred *noun* extreme dislike.

hat-trick *noun* (*plural* **hat-tricks**) getting three goals, wickets, victories, etc. one after the other.

haughty *adjective* (**haughtier**, **haughtiest**) proud of yourself and looking down on other people. **haughtily** *adverb*, **haughtiness** *noun* [from French *haut* = high]

haul *verb* (**hauls**, **hauling**, **hauled**) pull or drag with great effort.
haulage *noun*

haul *noun* (*plural* **hauls**)
1 hauling. 2 the amount obtained by an effort; booty, *The robbers made a good haul.* 3 a distance to be covered, *a long haul.*

haunt *verb* (**haunts**, **haunting**, **haunted**)
1 (of ghosts) appear often in a place or to a person. 2 visit a place often. 3 stay in your mind, *Memories haunt me.*

haunt *noun* (*plural* **haunts**) a place that you often visit, *My favourite haunt.*

have *verb* (**has**, **having**, **had**) This word has many uses, including
1 possess or own, *We have two dogs.* 2 contain, *This tin has sweets in it.* 3 experience, *He had a shock.* 4 be obliged to do something, *We have to go now.* 5 allow, *I won't have him bullied.* 6 receive or accept, *Will you have a sweet?* 7 get something done, *I'm having my watch mended.* 8 (*slang*) cheat or deceive, *We've been had!*
have somebody on (*informal*) fool him or her.

have *auxiliary verb* used to form the past tense of verbs, e.g. *He has gone.*
[from Old English]

haven *noun* (*plural* **havens**) a refuge. [from Old Norse]

haven't (*mainly spoken*) have not.

havoc *noun* great destruction or disorder. [from old French *havot*, an order to begin looting]

hawk *noun* (*plural* **hawks**) a bird of prey with very strong eyesight.

hawthorn *noun* (*plural* **hawthorns**) a thorny tree with small red berries (called *haws*).

hay *noun* dried grass for feeding to animals.

hay fever *noun* irritation of the nose, throat, and eyes, caused by pollen or dust.

hazard *noun* (*plural* **hazards**)
1 a danger or risk. 2 an obstacle.
hazardous *adjective* [via French from Persian or Turkish *zar* = dice]

hazy *adjective*
1 misty. 2 vague or uncertain.
hazily *adverb*, **haziness** *noun*

he *pronoun*
1 the male person or animal being talked about. 2 a person (male or female), *He who hesitates is lost.* [from Old English]

head *noun* (*plural* **heads**)
1 the part of the body containing the brains, eyes, and mouth.
2 your brains or mind; intelligence, *Use your head!*
3 a talent or ability, *She has a good head for figures.* 4 the side of a coin on which someone's head is shown. 5 a person, *It costs £2 per head.* 6 the top, *a pinhead*; the leading part of something, *at the head of the procession.* 7 the chief; the person in charge.
8 a headteacher.
come to a head reach a crisis point.
keep your head stay calm.

head *verb* (**heads**, **heading**, **headed**)
1 be at the top or front of something. 2 hit a ball with your head. 3 move in a particular direction, *We headed for the coast.*
4 force someone to turn by getting in front, *head him off.*
[from Old English]

headache *noun* (*plural* **headaches**)
1 a pain in the head. 2 (*informal*) a worrying problem.

heading *noun* (*plural* **headings**) a word or words put at the top of a piece of printing or writing.

headland *noun* (*plural* **headlands**) a large piece of high land that sticks out into the sea; a promontory.

headlight *noun* (*plural* **headlights**) a powerful light at the front of a car, engine, etc.

headline *noun* (*plural* **headlines**) a heading in a newspaper.
the headlines the main items of news.

headlong *adverb* & *adjective*
1 head first. 2 in a hasty or thoughtless way.

headmaster *noun* (*plural* **headmasters**) a male headteacher.

headmistress *noun* (*plural* **headmistresses**) a female headteacher.

head-on *adverb* & *adjective* with the front parts colliding, *a head-on collision.*

headquarters *noun & plural noun* the place from which an organization is controlled.

headstrong *adjective* determined to do as you want.

headteacher *noun (plural headteachers)* the person in charge of a school.

headway *noun*
make headway make progress.

heal *verb* (**heals, healing, healed**)
1 make or become healthy flesh again, *The wound healed.* 2 *(old use)* cure, *healing the sick.*

health *noun*
1 the condition of a person's body or mind, *His health is bad.* 2 being healthy, *in sickness and in health.*

healthy *adjective* (**healthier, healthiest**)
1 being well; free from illness. 2 producing good health, *Fresh air is healthy.* **healthily** *adverb*, **healthiness** *noun*

heap *noun (plural heaps)* a pile, especially an untidy one.
heaps *plural noun (informal)* a great amount; plenty, *There's heaps of time.*

heap *verb* (**heaps, heaping, heaped**)
1 make things into a heap. 2 put on large amounts, *She heaped the plate with food.*

hear *verb* (**hears, hearing, heard**)
1 take in sounds through the ears. 2 receive news or information etc. **hearer** *noun*
hear! hear! (in a debate) I agree.

hearing *noun (plural hearings)*
1 the ability to hear. 2 a chance to be heard; a trial in a lawcourt.

hearing aid *noun (plural hearing aids)* a device to help a deaf person to hear.

heart *noun (plural hearts)*
1 the organ of the body that makes the blood circulate. 2 a person's feelings or emotions; sympathy. 3 enthusiasm; courage, *Take heart.* 4 the middle or most important part. 5 a curved shape representing a heart. 6 a playing card with red heart shapes on it.
break a person's heart make him or her very unhappy.
heartbroken *adjective*
by heart memorized.

heart attack *noun (plural heart attacks)* a sudden failure of the heart to work properly, which results in great pain or sometimes death.

hearten *verb* (**heartens, heartening, heartened**) make a person feel encouraged.

heartfelt *adjective* felt deeply.

hearth *noun (plural hearths)* the floor of or near a fireplace.

heartless *adjective* without pity or sympathy.

hearty *adjective*
1 strong and vigorous. 2 enthusiastic and sincere, *hearty congratulations.* 3 (of a meal) large. **heartily** *adverb*, **heartiness** *noun*

heat *noun (plural heats)*
1 hotness or (in scientific use) the form of energy causing this. 2 hot weather. 3 a race or contest to decide who will take part in the final.

heat *verb* (**heats, heating, heated**) make or become hot.
[from Old English]

heathen noun (plural **heathens**)
a person who does not believe in
one of the chief religions. [from
Old English]

heather noun an evergreen plant
with small purple, pink, or white
flowers. [from Old English]

heatwave noun (plural
heatwaves) a long period of hot
weather.

heave verb (**heaves, heaving,
heaved**)
1 lift or move something heavy.
2 (informal) throw. **3** rise and fall.
4 if your stomach heaves, you
feel like vomiting. **heave** noun
heave a sigh utter a deep sigh.

heaven noun (plural **heavens**)
1 the place where God and angels
are thought to live. **2** a very
pleasant place or condition.
the heavens the sky.

heavy adjective (**heavier, heaviest**)
1 having great weight; difficult to
lift or carry. **2** great in amount or
force etc., heavy rain; a heavy
penalty. **3** needing much effort,
heavy work. **4** full of sadness or
worry, with a heavy heart. **heavily**
adverb, **heaviness** noun [from Old
English]

heavyweight noun (plural
heavyweights)
1 a heavy person. **2** a boxer of the
heaviest weight. **heavyweight**
adjective

Hebrew noun the language of the
Jews in ancient Palestine and
modern Israel.

hectare (say **hek**-tar) noun (plural
hectares) a unit of area equal to
10,000 square metres or nearly 2½
acres. [from Greek hekaton
= hundred, + French are
= a hundred square metres]

hecto- prefix one hundred (as in
hectogram = 100 grams). [from
Greek]

hedge noun (plural **hedges**) a row
of bushes forming a barrier or
boundary.

hedgehog noun (plural
hedgehogs) a small animal
covered with long prickles.
[because of the grunting noises it
makes]

heed noun
take or **pay heed** give attention to
something. **heedful** adjective,
heedless adjective [from Old
English]

heel noun (plural **heels**)
1 the back part of the foot. **2** the
part round or under the heel of
a sock or shoe etc.
take to your heels run away.
[from Old English hela]

hefty adjective (**heftier, heftiest**)
large and strong. **heftily** adverb

height noun (plural **heights**)
1 how high something is; the
distance from the base to the top
or from head to foot. **2** a high
place. **3** the highest or most
intense part, at the height of the
holiday season.

heighten verb (**heightens,
heightening, heightened**) make or
become higher or more intense.

heir (say as air) noun (plural
heirs) a person who inherits
something.

heiress (say **air**-ess) noun (plural
heiresses) a female heir,
especially of great wealth.

heirloom (say **air**-loom) noun
(plural **heirlooms**) a valued
possession that has been handed

down in a family for several generations. [from *heir* + Old English *geloma* = tool]

helicopter noun (plural **helicopters**) a kind of aircraft with a large horizontal propeller or rotor. [from *helix* + Greek *pteron* = wing]

helium (say hee-lee-um) noun a light colourless gas that does not burn. [from Greek *helios* = sun]

helix (say hee-liks) noun (plural **helices** (say hee-liss-eez)) a spiral. [Greek, = coil]

hell noun
1 a place where wicked people are thought to be punished after they die. 2 a very unpleasant place.
hell for leather (*informal*) at high speed.

hello interjection a word used to greet somebody or to attract their attention.

helmet noun (plural **helmets**) a strong covering worn to protect the head.

help verb (helps, helping, helped)
1 do part of another person's work for him or her. 2 benefit; make something better or easier, *This will help you to sleep.* 3 if you cannot help doing something, you cannot avoid doing it, *I can't help coughing.* 4 serve food etc. to somebody, *just help yourself.*
helper noun, **helpful** adjective, **helpfully** adverb

help noun
1 helping somebody. 2 a person or thing that helps.
[from Old English]

helping noun (plural **helpings**) a portion of food.

helpless adjective not able to do things. **helplessly** adverb, **helplessness** noun

helpline noun (plural **helplines**) a telephone service providing help with problems.

hem noun (plural **hems**) the edge of a piece of cloth that is folded over and sewn down.

hem verb (hems, hemming, hemmed) put a hem on something.
hem in surround and restrict.

hemisphere noun (plural **hemispheres**)
1 half a sphere. 2 half the earth.
hemispherical adjective [from Greek *hemi-* = half, + *sphere*]

hen noun (plural **hens**)
1 a female bird. 2 a female fowl.

hence adverb
1 henceforth. 2 therefore. 3 (*old use*) from here. [from Old English]

henchman noun (plural **henchmen**) a trusty supporter. [origin unknown]

hepta- prefix seven. [from Greek]

her pronoun the form of *she* used as the object of a verb or after a preposition.

her adjective belonging to her, *her book.*

herald noun (plural **heralds**) an official in former times who made announcements and carried messages for a king or queen.

heraldry noun the study of coats of arms. **heraldic** (say hir-al-dik) adjective [because a herald decided who could have a coat of arms and what should be on it]

herb noun (plural **herbs**) a plant used for flavouring or for making medicine. **herbal** adjective [from Latin]

herbivorous (say her-biv-er-us) adjective plant-eating. (Compare carnivorous.) **herbivore** noun [from Latin herba = grass, + -vorous]

herd noun (plural **herds**)
1 a group of cattle or other animals that feed together.
2 a mass of people; a mob. **herdsman** noun

herd verb (**herds, herding, herded**)
1 gather or move or send in a herd, We all herded into the dining room. 2 look after a herd of animals.

here adverb in or to this place etc. **here and there** in various places or directions.

hereby adverb by this act or decree etc.

hereditary adjective
1 inherited, a hereditary disease.
2 inheriting a position, Our Queen is a hereditary monarch.

heredity (say hir-ed-it-ee) noun inheriting characteristics from parents or ancestors. [from Latin heredis = to do with an heir]

heresy (say herri-see) noun (plural **heresies**) an opinion that disagrees with the beliefs accepted by the Christian Church or other authority. [from Greek hairesis = choice]

heretic (say herri-tik) noun (plural **heretics**) a person who supports a heresy. **heretical** (say hi-ret-ik-al) adjective

heritage noun the things that someone has inherited. [from Latin hereditare = inherit]

hermetically adverb so as to be airtight, The tin is hermetically sealed. [from Latin]

hermit noun (plural **hermits**) a person who lives alone and keeps away from people. [from Greek eremos = alone or deserted]

hero noun (plural **heroes**)
1 a man or boy who is admired for doing something very brave or great. 2 the chief male character in a story etc. **heroic** adjective, **heroically** adverb, **heroism** noun [from Greek heros = a very strong or brave man, whom the gods love]

heroin noun a very strong drug, made from morphine.

heroine noun (plural **heroines**)
1 a woman or girl who is admired for doing something very brave or great. 2 the chief female character in a story etc. [Greek, feminine of heros = hero]

heron noun (plural **herons**) a wading bird with long legs and a long neck. [via old French from Germanic]

herring noun (plural **herring** or **herrings**) a sea fish used as food.

hers possessive pronoun belonging to her, Those books are hers. [from her]

USAGE: It is incorrect to write her's.

herself pronoun she or her and nobody else. The word is used to refer back to the subject of a sentence (e.g. She cut herself) or for emphasis (e.g. *She herself has said it*).

by herself alone; on her own.

hertz *noun* (*plural* **hertz**) a unit of frequency of electromagnetic waves, = one cycle per second. [named after a German scientist, H. R. Hertz, who discovered radio waves]

hesitate *verb* (**hesitates, hesitating, hesitated**) be slow or uncertain in speaking, moving, etc. **hesitant** *adjective*, **hesitation** *noun* [from Latin *haesitare* = get stuck]

hetero- *prefix* other; different. [from Greek *heteros* = other]

heterogeneous (*say* het-er-o-jeen-ee-us) *adjective* composed of people or things of different kinds. [from *hetero-* + Greek *genos* = a kind]

heterosexual *adjective* attracted to people of the opposite sex; not homosexual. **heterosexual** *noun*

hexa- *prefix* six. [from Greek]

hexagon *noun* (*plural* **hexagons**) a flat shape with six sides and six angles. **hexagonal** *adjective* [from *hexa-* + Greek *gonia* = angle]

hibernate *verb* (**hibernates, hibernating, hibernated**) spend the winter in a state like deep sleep. **hibernation** *noun* [from Latin *hibernus* = wintry]

hiccup *noun* (*plural* **hiccups**)
1 a high gulping sound made when your breath is briefly interrupted. **2** a brief hitch. **hiccup** *verb* [imitating the sound]

hide[1] *verb* (**hides, hiding, hid, hidden**)
1 keep a person or thing from being seen; conceal. **2** get into

a place where you cannot be seen. **3** keep a thing secret. [from Old English *hydan*]

hide[2] *noun* (*plural* **hides**) an animal's skin. [from Old English *hyd*]

hide-and-seek *noun* a game in which one person looks for others who are hiding.

hideous *adjective* very ugly or unpleasant. **hideously** *adverb*

hiding[1] *noun* being hidden, *She went into hiding*. **hiding place** *noun*

hiding[2] *noun* (*plural* **hidings**) a thrashing or beating. [from an old word *hide* = to beat the hide (skin)]

hierarchy (*say* hyr-ark-ee) *noun* (*plural* **hierarchies**) an organization that ranks people one above another according to the power or authority that they hold. [from Greek *hieros* = sacred, + *-archy*]

hieroglyphics (*say* hyr-o-glif-iks) *plural noun* pictures or symbols used in ancient Egypt to represent words. [from Greek *hieros* = sacred + *glyphe* = carving]

hi-fi *noun* (*plural* **hi-fis**) (*informal*)
1 high fidelity. **2** equipment for reproducing recorded sound with very little distortion.

higgledy-piggledy *adverb* & *adjective* completely mixed up; in great disorder. [nonsense word based on *pig* (because of the way pigs huddle together)]

high *adjective*
1 reaching a long way upwards, *high hills*. **2** far above the ground or above sea level, *high clouds*. **3** measuring from top to bottom,

two metres high. **4** above average level in importance, quality, amount, etc., *high rank; high prices.* **5** (of meat) beginning to go bad. **6** (slang) affected by a drug.
high time fully time, *it's high time we left.*

high *adverb* at or to a high level or position etc., *They flew high above us.*
[from Old English]

highbrow *adjective* intellectual. [from *highbrowed* = having a high forehead (thought to be a sign of intelligence)]

higher education *noun* education at a university, polytechnic, or college.

high fidelity *noun* reproducing recorded sound with very little distortion.

high jump *noun* an athletic contest in which competitors try to jump over a high bar.

highlight *noun* (*plural* **highlights**) **1** the most interesting part of something, *The highlight of the holiday was the trip to Pompeii.* **2** a light area in a painting etc. **3** a light-coloured streak in a person's hair.

highly *adverb* **1** extremely, *highly amusing.* **2** very favourably, *We think highly of her.*

Highness *noun* (*plural* **Highnesses**) the title of a prince or princess.

high road *noun* (*plural* **high roads**) the main road.

high school *noun* (*plural* **high schools**) a secondary school.

high street *noun* (*plural* **high streets**) a town's main street.

high tea *noun* an evening meal with tea and meat or other cooked food.

highway *noun* (*plural* **highways**) a main road or route.

highwayman *noun* (*plural* **highwaymen**) a man who robbed travellers on highways in former times.

hijack *verb* (**hijacks, hijacking, hijacked**) seize control of an aircraft or vehicle during a journey. **hijack** *noun*, **hijacker** *noun*

hike *noun* (*plural* **hikes**) a long walk. **hike** *verb*, **hiker** *noun*

hilarious *adjective* very funny. **hilariously** *adverb*, **hilarity** *noun* [from Greek *hilaros* = cheerful]

hill *noun* (*plural* **hills**) a piece of land that is higher than the ground around it. **hillside** *noun*, **hilly** *adjective* [from Old English]

hilt *noun* (*plural* **hilts**) the handle of a sword or dagger etc.
to the hilt completely.

him *pronoun* the form of *he* used as the object of a verb or after a preposition. [from Old English]

himself *pronoun* he or him and nobody else. (Compare *herself.*)

hind *adjective* at the back, *the hind legs.* [probably from *behind*]

hinder *verb* (**hinders, hindering, hindered**) get in someone's way; make it difficult for a person to do something quickly or for something to happen. **hindrance** *noun*

hindquarters *plural noun* an animal's hind legs and rear parts.

hindsight *noun* looking back on an event with knowledge or understanding that you did not have at the time.

Hindu noun (plural **Hindus**)
a person who believes in Hinduism, which is one of the religions of India.

hinge noun (plural **hinges**)
a joining device on which a lid or door etc. turns when it opens.

hinge verb (**hinges, hinging, hinged**)
1 fix something with a hinge.
2 depend, *Everything hinges on this meeting.*

hint noun (plural **hints**)
1 a slight indication or suggestion, *Give me a hint of what you want.* 2 a useful suggestion, *household hints.*

hint verb (**hints, hinting, hinted**)
make a hint.
[from an old word *hent* = getting hold, especially of an idea]

hip[1] noun (plural **hips**) the bony part at the side of the body between the waist and the thigh. [from Old English *hype*]

hip[2] noun (plural **hips**) the fruit of the wild rose. [from Old English *heope*]

hippopotamus noun (plural **hippopotamuses**) a very large African animal that lives near water. [from Greek *hippos ho potamios* = horse of the river]

hire verb (**hires, hiring, hired**)
1 pay to borrow something. 2 lend for payment, *He hires out bicycles.*
hirer noun

hire noun hiring, *for hire.* [from Old English]

hire purchase noun buying something by paying in instalments.

his adjective & possessive pronoun belonging to him, *That is his book. That book is his.* [from Old English]

hiss verb (**hisses, hissing, hissed**)
make a sound like an *s*, *The snakes were hissing.* **hiss** noun [imitating the sound]

histogram noun (plural **histograms**) a chart consisting of rectangles of varying sizes. [from Greek *histos* = mast, + *-gram*]

historian noun (plural **historians**) a person who writes or studies history.

historic adjective famous or important in history; likely to be remembered, *a historic town; a historic event.*

USAGE: Do not confuse with *historical*.

historical adjective
1 to do with history. 2 that actually existed or took place in the past, *The novel is based on historical events.*

USAGE: Do not confuse with *historic*.

history noun (plural **histories**)
1 what happened in the past.
2 study of past events.
3 a description of important events. [from Greek *historia* = learning or finding out]

hit verb (**hits, hitting, hit**)
1 come forcefully against a person or thing; knock or strike. 2 have a bad effect on, *Famine has hit the poor countries.* 3 reach, *I can't hit that high note.*
hit on discover something by chance.

hit noun (plural **hits**)
1 hitting; a knock or stroke. **2** a shot that hits the target. **3** a success. **4** a successful song, show, etc.

hitch verb (**hitches, hitching, hitched**)
1 raise or pull with a slight jerk. **2** fasten with a loop or hook etc. **3** hitch-hike.

hitch noun (plural **hitches**)
1 a hitching movement. **2** a knot. **3** a difficulty causing delay.

hitch-hike verb (**hitch-hikes, hitch-hiking, hitch-hiked**) travel by getting lifts from passing vehicles. **hitch-hiker** noun

hi-tech adjective using the most advanced technology, especially electronic devices and computers.

hither adverb to or towards this place.

hitherto adverb until this time.

HIV abbreviation human immunodeficiency virus; a virus that causes Aids. [from the initial letters of *human immunodeficiency virus*]

hive noun (plural **hives**)
1 a beehive. **2** the bees living in a beehive.
hive of industry a place full of people working busily.

hoard noun (plural **hoards**)
a carefully saved store of money, treasure, food, etc.

hoard verb (**hoards, hoarding, hoarded**) store something away.
hoarder noun

USAGE: Do not confuse with *horde*.

hoarding noun (plural **hoardings**)
a tall fence covered with advertisements.

hoar frost noun a white frost. [from Old English *har* = grey-haired, + *frost*]

hoarse adjective with a rough voice. **hoarsely** adverb, **hoarseness** noun [from Old English]

hoax verb (**hoaxes, hoaxing, hoaxed**) deceive somebody as a joke. **hoax** noun, **hoaxer** noun [probably from *hocus-pocus*, used by conjurors as a 'magic' word]

hobble verb (**hobbles, hobbling, hobbled**) limp. [probably from old German]

hobby noun (plural **hobbies**)
something you do for pleasure in your spare time. [from *hobby horse*]

hobby horse noun (plural **hobby horses**)
1 a stick with a horse's head, used as a toy. **2** a subject that a person likes to talk about whenever he or she gets the chance.

hobgoblin noun (plural **hobgoblins**) a mischievous or evil spirit.

hockey noun a game played by two teams with curved sticks and a hard ball. [origin unknown]

hoe noun (plural **hoes**) a tool for scraping up weeds.

hoe verb (**hoes, hoeing, hoed**) scrape or dig with a hoe.

hog noun (plural **hogs**)
1 a male pig. **2** (*informal*) a greedy person.
go the whole hog (*slang*) do something completely or thoroughly.

Hogmanay noun New Year's Eve in Scotland.

hoist verb (hoists, hoisting, hoisted) lift; raise something by using ropes and pulleys etc. [probably from Dutch]

hold verb (holds, holding, held) This word has many uses, including

1 have and keep, especially in your hands, **2** have room for (*The jug holds two pints*), **3** support (*This plank won't hold my weight*), **4** stay unbroken; continue (*Will the fine weather hold?*), **5** believe or consider (*We shall hold you responsible*), **6** cause something to take place (*hold a meeting*), **7** restrain or stop (*Hold everything!*).

hold forth make a long speech.

hold out refuse to give in.

hold up 1 hinder. **2** stop and rob somebody by threats or force.

hold with approve of, *We don't hold with bullying.*

hold your tongue (*informal*) stop talking.

hold noun (plural holds)

1 holding something; a grasp. **2** something to hold on to for support. **3** the part of a ship where cargo is stored, below the deck.

get hold of 1 grasp. **2** obtain. **3** make contact with a person.

hold-up noun (plural hold-ups) **1** a delay. **2** a robbery with threats or force.

hole noun (plural holes) **1** a hollow place; a gap or opening. **2** a burrow. **3** one of the small holes into which you have to hit the ball in golf. **4** (*informal*) an unpleasant place.

holey adjective in a hole in an awkward situation.

hole verb (holes, holing, holed) **1** make a hole or holes in something. **2** hit a golf ball into one of the holes.

holiday noun (plural holidays) **1** a day or week etc. when people do not go to work or to school. **2** a time when you go away to enjoy yourself. [from holy + day (because holidays were originally religious festivals)]

holiness noun being holy or sacred.

His Holiness the title of the pope.

hollow adjective with an empty space inside; not solid. **hollowly** adverb

hollow noun (plural hollows) a hollow or sunken place.

hollow verb (hollows, hollowing, hollowed) make a thing hollow. [from Old English]

holly noun (plural hollies) an evergreen bush with shiny prickly leaves and red berries. [from Old English]

holocaust noun (plural holocausts) an immense destruction, especially by fire, *the nuclear holocaust.*

the Holocaust the mass murder of the Jews by the Nazis from 1939 to 1945.

[from Greek *holos* = whole + *kaustos* = burnt]

hologram noun (plural holograms) a type of photograph made by laser beams that produces a three-dimensional image.

holy adjective (holier, holiest) **1** belonging or devoted to God.

2 consecrated, *holy water.*
holiness *noun*

homage *noun (plural* **homages)**
an act or expression of respect or
honour, *We paid homage to his
achievements.*

home *noun (plural* **homes)**
1 the place where you live. **2** the
place where you were born or
where you feel you belong.
3 a place where those who need
help are looked after, *an old
people's home.* **4** the place to be
reached in a race or in certain
games.

home *adjective*
1 of a person's own home or
country, *home industries.* **2** played
on a team's own ground, *a home
match.*

home *adverb*
1 to or at home, *Is she home yet?*
2 to the point aimed at, *Push the
bolt home.*
**bring something home to
somebody** make him or her
realize it.

home *verb* (**homes, homing,
homed**) make for a target, *The
missile homed in.*

home economics *noun* the
study of household management.

homely *adverb* simple and
ordinary, *a homely meal.*
homeliness *noun*

home-made *adjective* made at
home, not bought from a shop.

homeopathy *noun* the treatment
of disease by tiny doses of drugs
that in a healthy person would
produce symptoms of the disease.
homeopathic *adjective* [from
Greek *homoios* = similar +
-pathos = suffering]

homesick *adjective* sad because
you are away from home.
homesickness *noun*

homeward *adjective & adverb*
going towards home. **homewards**
adverb

homework *noun* school work
that has to be done at home.

homicide *noun (plural*
homicides) the killing of one
person by another. **homicidal**
adjective [from Latin *homo*
= person, + *-cide*]

homo- *prefix* same. [from Greek]

homogeneous (say hom-o-jeen-
ee-us) *adjective* composed of
people or things of the same kind.
[from *homo-* + Greek *genos*
= a kind]

homograph *noun (plural*
homographs) a word that is spelt
like another but has a different
meaning or origin, e.g. *bat* (a
flying animal) and *bat* (for
hitting a ball). [from *homo-* +
-graph]

homonym (say hom-o-nim) *noun
(plural* **homonyms)** a homograph
or homophone. [from *homo-*
+ Greek *onyma* = name]

homophone *noun (plural*
homophones) a word with the
same sound as another, e.g. *son,
sun.* [from *homo-* + Greek *phone*
= sound]

Homo sapiens *noun* human
beings regarded as a species of
animal. [Latin, = wise man or
person]

homosexual *adjective* attracted
to people of the same sex.
homosexual *noun,* **homosexuality**
noun

honest adjective not stealing or cheating or telling lies; truthful.
honestly adverb, **honesty** noun [from old French; related to honour]

honey noun a sweet sticky food made by bees.

honeycomb noun (plural **honeycombs**) a wax structure of small six-sided sections made by bees to hold their honey and eggs.

honeycombed adjective with many holes or tunnels.

honeymoon noun (plural **honeymoons**) a holiday spent together by a newly-married couple. [from honey + moon (because the first intensely passionate feelings gradually wane)]

honeysuckle noun a climbing plant with fragrant yellow or pink flowers. [because people sucked the flowers for their sweet nectar]

honk noun (plural **honks**) a loud sound like that made by a goose or an old-fashioned car horn.
honk verb

honorary adjective
1 given or received as an honour, an honorary degree. **2** unpaid, the honorary treasurer of the club.

USAGE: Do not confuse with honourable.

honour noun (plural **honours**)
1 great respect. **2** a person or thing that brings honour. **3** honesty and loyalty, a man of honour. **4** an award for distinction.
honour verb (honours, honouring, honoured)

1 feel or show honour for a person. **2** acknowledge and pay a cheque etc. **3** keep to the terms of an agreement or promise. [from Latin]

honourable adjective deserving honour; honest and loyal.
honourably adverb

USAGE: Do not confuse with honorary.

hood noun (plural **hoods**)
1 a covering of soft material for the head and neck. **2** a folding roof or cover. **hooded** adjective

-hood suffix forms nouns meaning condition or quality (e.g. childhood). [from Old English]

hoodwink verb (hoodwinks, hoodwinking, hoodwinked) deceive. [originally = to blindfold with a hood: from hood + an old sense of wink = close the eyes]

hoof noun (plural **hoofs** or **hooves**) the horny part of the foot of a horse etc.

hook noun (plural **hooks**) a bent or curved piece of metal etc. for hanging things on or for catching hold of something.
hook verb (hooks, hooking, hooked)
1 catch something with a hook. **2** fasten something with or on a hook. **3** send a ball in a curving direction.
be hooked on something (slang) be addicted to it.
hooked adjective hook-shaped.

hooligan noun (plural **hooligans**) a rough and violent young person. **hooliganism** noun [the surname of a rowdy Irish family in a cartoon]

hoop noun (plural **hoops**) a ring made of metal or wood.

hoot noun (plural **hoots**)
1 the sound made by an owl or a vehicle's horn or a steam whistle. 2 a cry of scorn or disapproval. 3 laughter. 4 something funny. **hoot** verb, **hooter** noun

hop¹ verb (**hops, hopping, hopped**)
1 jump on one foot. 2 (of an animal) spring from all feet at once. 3 (informal) move quickly, Here's the car—hop in! **hop it** (slang) go away.
hop noun (plural **hops**) a hopping movement.
[from Old English]

hop² noun (plural **hops**) a climbing plant used to give beer its flavour. [from old German or old Dutch]

hope noun (plural **hopes**)
1 a wish for something to happen. 2 a person or thing that gives hope, You are our only hope.
hope verb (**hopes, hoping, hoped**) feel hope; want and expect something.

hopeful adjective
1 feeling hope. 2 likely to be good or successful.

hopefully adverb
1 it is to be hoped; I hope that. 2 in a hopeful way.

USAGE: Some people say it is incorrect to use hopefully to mean 'I hope that' or 'let's hope', and say that it should only be used to mean 'in a hopeful way'. This first use is

very common in informal language but you should probably avoid it when you are writing or speaking formally.

hopeless adjective
1 without hope. 2 very bad at something. **hopelessly** adverb, **hopelessness** noun

hopscotch noun a game of hopping into squares drawn on the ground. [from hop + an old word scotch = a cut or scratch]

horde noun (plural **hordes**) a large group or crowd. [via Polish from Turkish ordu = royal camp]

USAGE: Do not confuse with hoard.

horizon noun (plural **horizons**) the line where the earth and the sky seem to meet. [from Greek horizein = form a boundary]

horizontal adjective level, so as to be parallel to the horizon; going across from left to right. (The opposite is vertical.) **horizontally** adverb

hormone noun (plural **hormones**) a substance that stimulates an organ of the body or of a plant. **hormonal** adjective [from Greek horman = set something going]

horn noun (plural **horns**)
1 a hard substance that grows into a point on the head of a bull, cow, ram, etc. 2 a pointed part. 3 a brass instrument played by blowing. 4 a device for making a warning sound. **horned** adjective, **horny** adjective [from Old English]

horoscope noun (plural **horoscopes**) an astrologer's

forecast of future events. [from Greek *hora* = hour (of birth) + *skopos* = observer]

horrendous *adjective* horrifying. [from Latin *horrendus* = making your hair stand on end]

horrible *adjective*
1 horrifying. **2** very unpleasant. **horribly** *adverb* [from Latin]

horrid *adjective* horrible. **horridly** *adverb* [from Latin *horridus* = rough, shaggy, or wild]

horrify *verb* (**horrifies, horrifying, horrified**)
1 make somebody feel great fear and dislike. **2** shock. [from Latin *horrificare* = make someone shiver with cold or fear]

horror *noun* (*plural* **horrors**)
1 great fear and dislike or dismay. **2** a person or thing causing horror.

horse *noun* (*plural* **horses**)
1 a large four-legged animal used for riding and for pulling carts etc. **2** a framework for hanging clothes on to dry. **3** a vaulting horse.
on horseback mounted on a horse.

horse chestnut *noun* (*plural* **horse chestnuts**) a large tree that produces dark-brown nuts (conkers).

horsepower *noun* a unit for measuring the power of an engine. [because the unit was based on the amount of work a horse could do]

horseshoe *noun* (*plural* **horseshoes**) a U-shaped piece of metal nailed to a horse's hoof.

horticulture *noun* the art of cultivating gardens. **horticultural** *adjective* [from Latin *hortus* = garden, + *culture*]

hose *noun* (*plural* **hoses**)
1 (also **hosepipe**) a flexible tube for taking water to something.
2 (*old use*) breeches, *doublet and hose*.

hospitable *adjective* welcoming; liking to give hospitality. **hospitably** *adverb* [from Latin]

hospital *noun* (*plural* **hospitals**) a place providing medical and surgical treatment for people who are ill or injured. [from Latin *hospitalis* = hospitable]

hospitality *noun* welcoming people and giving them food and entertainment. [from Latin]

host¹ *noun* (*plural* **hosts**) a person who has guests and looks after them. [from Latin *hospes*]

host² *noun* (*plural* **hosts**) a large number of people or things. [from Latin *hostis* = enemy or army]

host³ *noun* (*plural* **hosts**) the bread consecrated at Holy Communion. [from Latin *hostia* = sacrifice]

hostage *noun* (*plural* **hostages**) a person who is held prisoner until the holder gets what he or she wants.

hostel *noun* (*plural* **hostels**) a building where travellers, students, or other groups can stay or live. [from old French; related to *hospital*]

hostess *noun* (*plural* **hostesses**) a woman who has guests and looks after them. [from old French]

hostile *adjective*
1 to do with an enemy.
2 unfriendly, *a hostile glance*. **hostility** *noun* [same origin as *host*²]

hot adjective (**hotter, hottest**)
1 having great heat or a high temperature. **2** giving a burning sensation when tasted. **3** passionate or excitable, *a hot temper.* **hotly** adverb, **hotness** noun
in hot water (*informal*) in trouble or disgrace.

hotel noun (*plural* **hotels**) a building where people pay to have meals and stay for the night. [from French; related to **hostel**]

hound noun (*plural* **hounds**) a dog used in hunting or racing.

hour noun (*plural* **hours**)
1 one twenty-fourth part of a day and night; sixty minutes. **2** a time, *Why are you up at this hour?*
hours plural noun a fixed period for work, *Office hours are 9 a.m. to 5 p.m.*

hourly adverb & adjective every hour.

house (*say* howss) noun (*plural* **houses**)
1 a building made for people to live in, usually designed for one family. **2** a building or establishment for a special purpose, *the opera house.*
3 a building for a government assembly; the assembly itself, *the House of Commons; the House of Lords.* **4** each of the divisions of a school for sports competitions etc. **5** a family or dynasty, *the royal house of Tudor.*

house (*say* howz) verb (**houses, housing, housed**) provide accommodation or room for someone or something.

household noun (*plural* **households**) all the people who live together in the same house. [from **house** + an old sense of **hold** = possession]

householder noun (*plural* **householders**) a person who owns or rents a house.

housekeeper noun (*plural* **housekeepers**) a person employed to look after a household.

housekeeping noun
1 looking after a household. **2** (*informal*) the money for a household's food and other necessities.

housemaid noun (*plural* **housemaids**) a woman servant in a house, especially one who cleans rooms.

house-proud adjective very careful to keep a house clean and tidy.

house-trained adjective (of an animal) trained to be clean in the house.

housewife noun (*plural* **housewives**) a woman who does the housekeeping for her family.

housework noun the cleaning and cooking etc. done in housekeeping.

housing noun (*plural* **housings**)
1 accommodation; houses. **2** a stiff cover or guard for a piece of machinery.

housing estate noun (*plural* **housing estates**) a set of houses planned and built together in one area.

hovel noun (*plural* **hovels**) a small shabby house. [origin unknown]

hover verb (hovers, hovering, hovered)
1 stay in one place in the air.
2 wait about near someone or something; linger.

hovercraft noun (plural hovercraft) a vehicle that travels just above the surface of land or water, supported by a strong current of air sent downwards from its engines.

how adverb
1 in what way; by what means, *How did you do it?* 2 to what extent or amount etc., *How high can you jump?* 3 in what condition, *How are you?*
how about would you like, *How about a game of football?*
how do you do? a formal greeting.

however adverb
1 in whatever way; to whatever extent, *You will never catch him, however hard you try.* 2 all the same; nevertheless, *Later, however, he decided to go.*

howl noun (plural howls) a long loud sad-sounding cry or sound, such as that made by a dog or wolf.

howl verb (howls, howling, howled)
1 make a howl. 2 weep loudly.

howler noun (plural howlers) (*informal*) a foolish mistake.

hub noun (plural hubs)
1 the central part of a wheel. 2 the central point of interest or activity.

hubbub noun a loud confused noise of voices. [probably from Irish]

huddle verb (huddles, huddling, huddled)
1 crowd together into a small space. 2 curl your body closely.
huddle noun

huff noun
in a huff offended or sulking about something, *She went away in a huff.* **huffy** adjective

hug verb (hugs, hugging, hugged)
1 clasp someone tightly in your arms; embrace. 2 keep close to something, *The ship hugged the shore.*
hug noun (plural hugs) a tight embrace.

huge adjective extremely large; enormous. **hugely** adverb, **hugeness** noun [from old French]

hulk noun (plural hulks)
1 the body or wreck of an old ship. 2 a large clumsy person or thing. **hulking** adjective [from Old English]

hull noun (plural hulls) the framework of a ship.

hullabaloo noun (plural hullabaloos) an uproar. [origin unknown]

hum verb (hums, humming, hummed)
1 sing a tune with your lips closed. 2 make a low continuous sound as some flying insects do.

human adjective to do with human beings. [from Latin]

human being noun (plural human beings) a creature distinguished from other animals by its better mental development, power of speech, and upright posture.

humane (*say* hew-*mayn*) *adjective*
kind-hearted and merciful.
humanely *adverb* [old spelling of
human]

humanitarian *adjective*
concerned with people's welfare
and the reduction of suffering.
humanitarian *noun*

humanity *noun*
1 human beings; people. **2** being
human. **3** being humane.
humanities *plural noun* arts
subjects.

humble *adjective*
1 modest; not proud or showy. **2** of
low rank or importance. **humbly**
adverb, **humbleness** *noun* [from
Latin *humilis* = near the ground,
low]

humbug *noun* (*plural* **humbugs**)
1 insincere or dishonest talk or
behaviour. **2** a hard peppermint
sweet.

humdrum *adjective* dull and not
exciting; commonplace.

humid (*say* hew-*mid*) *adjective* (of
air) moist. **humidity** *noun* [from
Latin]

humiliate *verb* (**humiliates**,
humiliating, **humiliated**) make
a person feel disgraced.
humiliation *noun* [same origin as
humble]

humility *noun* being humble.
[same origin as *humble*]

hummingbird *noun* (*plural*
hummingbirds) a small tropical
bird that makes a humming
sound by moving its wings
rapidly.

humorous *adjective* full of
humour.

humour *noun*
1 being amusing; what makes
people laugh. **2** the ability to

enjoy comical things, *a sense of
humour*. **3** a mood, *in a good
humour*.

humour *verb* (**humours**,
humouring, **humoured**) keep
a person contented by doing what
he or she wants.
[from Latin]

hump *noun* (*plural* **humps**)
1 a rounded lump or mound. **2** an
abnormal outward curve at the
top of a person's back.

humpback bridge *noun* (*plural*
humpback bridges) a small bridge
that steeply curves upwards in
the middle.

humus (*say* hew-*mus*) *noun* rich
earth made by decayed plants.
[Latin, = soil]

hunch[1] *noun* (*plural* **hunches**)
a feeling that you can guess what
will happen. [origin unknown]

hunch[2] *verb* (**hunches**, **hunching**,
hunched) bend into a hump, *He
hunched his shoulders*. [origin
unknown]

hunchback *noun* (*plural*
hunchbacks) someone with
a hump on their back.
hunchbacked *adjective*

hundred *noun & adjective* (*plural*
hundreds) the number 100.
hundredth *adjective & noun* [from
Old English]

hundredweight *noun* (*plural*
hundredweight) a unit of weight,
112 pounds (= 50.8 kilograms).
[probably originally = 100
pounds]

hunger *noun* the feeling that you
have when you have not eaten
for some time; need for food.

hunger strike *noun* (*plural*
hunger strikes) refusing to eat, as
a way of making a protest.

hungry adjective (**hungrier**, **hungriest**) feeling hunger. **hungrily** adverb

hunk noun (plural **hunks**)
1 a large piece of something.
2 (informal) a muscular, good-looking man.

hunt verb (**hunts**, **hunting**, **hunted**)
1 chase and kill animals for food or as a sport. 2 search for something. **hunter** noun, **huntsman** noun

hurdle noun (plural **hurdles**)
1 an upright frame to be jumped over in hurdling. 2 an obstacle. [from Old English]

hurdling noun racing in which the runners jump over hurdles. **hurdler** noun

hurl verb (**hurls**, **hurling**, **hurled**) throw something violently.

hurrah or **hurray** interjection a shout of joy or approval; a cheer.

hurricane noun (plural **hurricanes**) a storm with violent wind.

hurry verb (**hurries**, **hurrying**, **hurried**)
1 move quickly; do something quickly. 2 try to make somebody or something be quick. **hurried** adjective, **hurriedly** adverb

hurry noun hurrying; a need to hurry.

hurt verb (**hurts**, **hurting**, **hurt**) cause pain or damage or injury. **hurt** noun pain or injury. **hurtful** adjective

hurtle verb (**hurtles**, **hurtling**, **hurtled**) move rapidly, *The train hurtled along.* [from an old sense of *hurt* = knock or dash against something]

husband noun (plural **husbands**) the man to whom a woman is married. [from Old Norse *husbondi* = master of the house]

husk noun (plural **husks**) the dry outer covering of some seeds and fruits. [probably from old German]

husky adjective (**huskier**, **huskiest**)
1 hoarse. 2 big and strong; burly. **huskily** adverb, **huskiness** noun

hustle verb (**hustles**, **hustling**, **hustled**) hurry or bustle. **hustle** noun, **hustler** noun [from Italian *husselen* = shake or toss]

hut noun (plural **huts**) a small roughly-made house or shelter.

hutch noun (plural **hutches**) a box-like cage for a pet rabbit etc.

hybrid noun (plural **hybrids**)
1 a plant or animal produced by combining two different species or varieties. 2 something that combines parts or characteristics of two different things.

hydr- prefix
1 water. 2 containing hydrogen. see **hydro-**.

hydrant noun (plural **hydrants**) a special water-tap to which a large hose can be attached for fire-fighting or street-cleaning etc. [same origin as *hydro*]

hydraulic adjective worked by the force of water or other fluid, *hydraulic brakes.* [from *hydr-* + Greek *aulos* = pipe]

hydro- prefix (**hydr-** before a vowel)
1 water (as in *hydroelectric*). 2 (in chemical names) containing hydrogen (as in *hydrochloric*). [from Greek *hydor* = water]

hydrochloric acid noun
a colourless acid containing
hydrogen and chlorine.

hydroelectric adjective using
water-power to produce
electricity. **hydroelectricity** noun

hydrogen noun a lightweight gas
that combines with oxygen to
form water. [from hydro- + -gen
= producing]

hydrogen bomb noun (plural
hydrogen bombs) a very
powerful bomb using energy
created by the fusion of hydrogen
nuclei.

hyena noun (plural **hyenas**) a wild
animal that looks like a wolf and
makes a shrieking howl. [from
Greek]

hygiene (say hy-jeen) noun
keeping things clean in order to
remain healthy and prevent
disease. **hygienic** adjective,
hygienically adverb [from Greek
hygies = healthy]

hymn noun (plural **hymns**)
a religious song, usually praise
to God. **hymn book** noun [from
Greek]

hyper- prefix over or above;
excessive. [from Greek hyper
= over]

hyperbola (say hy-per-bol-a) noun
(plural **hyperbolas**) a kind of
curve.

hyphen noun (plural **hyphens**)
a short dash used to join words
or parts of words together (e.g. in
hitch-hiker). [from Greek,
= together]

hypnosis (say hip-noh-sis) noun
a condition like a deep sleep in
which a person's actions may be
controlled by someone else. [from
Greek hypnos = sleep]

hypnotize verb (**hypnotizes**,
hypnotizing, **hypnotized**) produce
hypnosis in somebody.
hypnotism noun, **hypnotic**
adjective, **hypnotist** noun

hypo- prefix below; under. [from
Greek hypo = under]

hypochondriac (say hy-po-kon-
dree-ak) noun (plural
hypochondriacs) a person who
constantly imagines that he or
she is ill. **hypochondria** noun
[from Greek hypochondrios
= under the breastbone (because
the organs there were once
thought to be the source of
depression and anxiety)]

hypocrite (say hip-o-krit) noun
(plural **hypocrites**) a person who
pretends to be more virtuous
than he or she really is. **hypocrisy**
(say hip-ok-riss-ee) noun,
hypocritical adjective [from Greek
hypokrites = actor or pretender]

hypodermic adjective injecting
something under the skin,
a hypodermic syringe. [from hypo-
+ Greek derma = skin]

hypotenuse (say hy-pot-i-newz)
noun (plural **hypotenuses**) the
side opposite the right angle in
a right-angled triangle. [from
Greek]

hypothermia noun being too
cold; the condition in which
someone's temperature is below
normal. [from hypo- + Greek
therme = heat]

hypothesis (say hy-poth-i-sis)
noun (plural **hypotheses**)
a suggestion or guess that tries to
explain something. **hypothetical**
adjective [from hypo- + Greek
thesis = placing]

hysteria noun wild uncontrollable excitement, panic, or emotion. **hysterics** noun [from Greek hystera = womb (once thought to be the cause of hysteria)]

hysterical adjective
1 in a state of hysteria.
2 (informal) extremely funny. **hysterically** adverb

Ii

I pronoun a word used by a person to refer to himself or herself. [from Old English]

-ible see **-able**.

-ic suffix forms
1 adjectives, some of which are used as nouns (e.g. comic, domestic, public). 2 names of arts (e.g. music, magic). [from Latin -icus or Greek -ikos]

-ical suffix forms adjectives from or similar to words ending in -ic (e.g. comical, musical).

ice noun (plural **ices**)
1 frozen water, a brittle transparent solid substance. 2 an ice cream.

ice age noun (plural **ice ages**) a period in the past when most of the earth's surface was covered with ice.

iceberg noun (plural **icebergs**) a large mass of ice floating in the sea with most of it under water. [from Dutch]

ice cream noun (plural **ice creams**) a sweet creamy frozen food.

ice hockey noun a form of hockey played on ice.

ice rink noun (plural **ice rinks**) a place made for skating.

-ician suffix forms nouns meaning 'person skilled in something' (e.g. musician).

icicle noun (plural **icicles**) a pointed hanging piece of ice formed when dripping water freezes. [from Old English]

icing noun a sugary substance for decorating cakes.

-icity suffix forms nouns (e.g. publicity) from words ending in -ic.

-ics suffix forms nouns which are plural in form but are often used with a singular verb (e.g. mathematics, gymnastics).

icy adjective (**icier, iciest**)
1 covered with ice. 2 very cold. **icily** adverb, **iciness** noun

idea noun (plural **ideas**)
1 a plan or thought formed in the mind. 2 an opinion or belief. [Greek]

ideal adjective perfect; completely suitable. **ideally** adverb

ideal noun (plural **ideals**) a person or thing regarded as perfect or as worth trying to achieve. [from Latin, related to idea]

identical adjective exactly the same. **identically** adverb [same origin as identity]

identify verb (**identifies, identifying, identified**)
1 recognize as being a certain person or thing. 2 treat something as being identical to something else, Don't identify wealth with happiness. 3 think of yourself as sharing someone's

feelings etc., *We can identify with the hero of this play*. **identification** *noun*

identity *noun* (*plural* **identities**)
1 who or what a person or thing is. **2** being identical; sameness. **3** distinctive character. [from Latin *idem* = same]

idiom *noun* (*plural* **idioms**)
a phrase that means something different from the meanings of the words in it, e.g. *in hot water* (= in disgrace), *hell for leather* (= at high speed). **idiomatic** *adjective*, **idiomatically** *adverb* [from Greek *idios* = your own]

idiosyncrasy (*say* id-ee-o-sink-ra-see) *noun* (*plural* **idiosyncrasies**)
one person's own way of behaving or doing something. [from Greek *idios* = your own + *syn-* + *krasis* = mixture]

idiot *noun* (*plural* **idiots**)
1 a stupid or foolish person. **2** a person who is mentally deficient. **idiocy** *noun*, **idiotic** *adjective*, **idiotically** *adverb* [from Greek *idiotes* = private citizen, uneducated person]

idle *adjective*
1 doing no work; lazy. **2** not in use, *The machines were idle.* **3** useless; with no special purpose, *idle gossip.* **idly** *adverb*, **idleness** *noun*

idol *noun* (*plural* **idols**)
1 a statue or image that is worshipped as a god. **2** a person who is admired intensely. [from Greek *eidolon* = image]

idolize *verb* (**idolizes**, **idolizing**, **idolized**) admire someone intensely. **idolization** *noun*

i.e. *abbreviation* that is, *The world's highest mountain (i.e. Mount Everest) is in the Himalayas.* [short for Latin *id est* = that is]

USAGE: Do not confuse with *e.g.*

-ie see **-y.**

-ier see **-er.**

-iest see **-est.**

if *conjunction*
1 on condition that; supposing that, *He will do it if you pay him.* **2** even though, *I'll finish this job if it kills me.* **3** whether, *Do you know if dinner is ready?* **if only** I wish, *If only I were rich!*

-iferous see **-ferous.**

-ification *suffix* forms nouns of action (e.g. *purification*) from verbs that end in *-ify.* [from Latin *-ficare* = make]

ignition *noun* (*plural* **ignitions**)
1 igniting. **2** the part of a motor engine that starts the fuel burning.

ignominious *adjective*
humiliating; with disgrace. **ignominy** *noun*

ignorant *adjective* not knowing about something or about many things. **ignorantly** *adverb*, **ignorance** *noun* [same origin as *ignore*]

ignore *verb* (**ignores**, **ignoring**, **ignored**) take no notice of a person or thing. [from Latin *ignorare* = not know]

il- *prefix*
1 in; into. **2** on; towards. **3** not. see **in-.**

ilk *noun*
of that ilk (*informal*) of that kind. [from Old English *ilca* = same]

ill *adjective*
1 unwell; in bad health. 2 bad or harmful, *There were no ill effects.*

ill *adverb* badly, *She was ill-treated.*

ill at ease uncomfortable or embarrassed.

illegal *adjective* not legal; against the law. **illegally** *adverb*, **illegality** *noun*

illegible *adjective* impossible to read. **illegibly** *adverb*, **illegibility** *noun*

illegitimate *adjective* born when the parents are not married to each other. **illegitimately** *adverb*, **illegitimacy** *noun*

illiterate *adjective* unable to read or write. **illiterately** *adverb*, **illiteracy** *noun*

illness *noun* (*plural* **illnesses**)
1 being ill. 2 a particular form of bad health; a disease.

illogical *adjective* not logical; not reasoning correctly. **illogically** *adverb*, **illogicality** *noun*

illuminate *verb* (**illuminates, illuminating, illuminated**)
1 light something up. 2 decorate streets etc. with lights. 3 decorate a manuscript with coloured designs. 4 clarify or help to explain something. **illumination** *noun* [from *il-* + Latin *lumen* = light]

illusion *noun* (*plural* **illusions**) something unreal or imaginary; a false impression. *The train went so fast that we had the illusion that it was flying.* (Compare **delusion**.) **illusive** *adjective*, **illusory** *adjective* [from Latin *illudere* = mock]

illustrate *verb* (**illustrates, illustrating, illustrated**)
1 show something by pictures, examples, etc. 2 put illustrations in a book. **illustrator** *noun* [from Latin *illustrare* = add light or brilliance]

illustration *noun* (*plural* **illustrations**)
1 a picture in a book etc. 2 illustrating something. 3 an example that helps to explain something.

illustrious *adjective* famous and distinguished. [from Latin]

im- *prefix*
1 in; into. 2 on; towards. 3 not. see **in-**.

image *noun* (*plural* **images**)
1 a picture or statue of a person or thing. 2 the appearance of something as seen in a mirror or through a lens etc. 3 a person or thing that is very much like another, *He is the image of his father.* 4 a person's public reputation. [from Latin]

imaginary *adjective* existing only in the imagination; not real.

imagination *noun* (*plural* **imaginations**) the ability to imagine things, especially in a creative or inventive way. **imaginative** *adjective*

imagine *verb* (**imagines, imagining, imagined**) form pictures or ideas in your mind.

imitate *verb* (**imitates, imitating, imitated**) copy or mimic something. **imitation** *noun*, **imitator** *noun*, **imitative** *adjective*

immaculate *adjective*
1 perfectly clean; spotless. 2 without any fault or blemish.

immaculately adverb [from im- + Latin macula = spot or blemish]

immature adjective not mature. **immaturity** noun

immediate adjective
1 happening or done without any delay. **2** nearest; with nothing or no one between, our immediate neighbours. **immediately** adverb, **immediacy** noun [from im- + Latin mediatus = coming between]

immense adjective exceedingly great; huge. **immensely** adverb, **immensity** noun [from im- + Latin mensum = measured]

immersion heater noun (plural **immersion heaters**) a device that heats up water by means of an electric element in the water in a tank etc. [from im- + Latin mersum = dipped]

immigrate verb (immigrates, immigrating, immigrated) come into a country to live there. **immigration** noun, **immigrant** noun

USAGE: See the note at emigrate.

imminent adjective likely to happen at any moment, an imminent storm. **imminence** noun [from Latin imminere = hang over]

immobilize verb (immobilizes, immobilizing, immobilized) stop a thing from moving or working. **immobilization** noun

immoral adjective morally wrong; wicked. **immorally** adverb, **immorality** noun

immortal adjective
1 living for ever; not mortal.

2 famous for all time. **immortal** noun, **immortality** noun, **immortalize** verb

immune adjective safe from or protected against something, immune from (or against or to) infection etc. **immunity** noun [from Latin immunis = exempt]

immunize verb (immunizes, immunizing, immunized) make a person immune from a disease etc., e.g. by vaccination. **immunization** noun

impact noun (plural **impacts**)
1 a collision; the force of a collision. **2** an influence or effect, the impact of computers on our lives. [from im- + Latin pactum = driven]

impale verb (impales, impaling, impaled) pierce or fix something on a sharp pointed object. **impalement** noun [from im- + Latin palus = a stake]

impartial adjective not favouring one side more than the other; not biased. **impartially** adverb, **impartiality** noun

impatient adjective not patient. **impatiently** adverb, **impatience** noun

impel verb (impels, impelling, impelled)
1 urge or drive someone to do something, Curiosity impelled her to investigate. **2** drive forward; propel. [from im- + Latin pellere = to drive]

impending adjective soon to happen; imminent. [from im- + Latin pendere = hang]

impenetrable adjective
1 impossible to get through.
2 incomprehensible.

imperative *adjective*
1 expressing a command.
2 essential, *Speed is imperative.*

imperative *noun* (*plural*
imperatives) a command; the
form of a verb used in making
commands (e.g. 'come' in
Come here!).
[from Latin *imperare* = to
command]

imperceptible *adjective* if
something is imperceptible it is
so slight or gradual that it is
almost impossible to notice.

imperfect *adjective*
1 not perfect. 2 (of a tense of
a verb) showing a continuous
action, e.g. *She was singing.*
imperfectly *adverb*, **imperfection**
noun

imperial *adjective*
1 to do with an empire or its
rulers. 2 (of weights and
measures) fixed by British law;
non-metric, *an imperial gallon.*
imperially *adverb* [from Latin
imperium = supreme power]

imperious *adjective* haughty and
bossy. [same origin as *imperial*]

impermeable *adjective* not
allowing liquid to pass through
it.

impersonal *adjective*
1 not affected by personal
feelings; showing no emotion.
2 not referring to a particular
person. **impersonally** *adverb*

impersonal *noun* (*plural*
impersonal verbs) a verb used
only with 'it', e.g. in *It is raining*
or *It is hard to find one.*

impertinent *adjective* insolent;
not showing proper respect.
impertinently *adverb*,
impertinence *noun*

imperturbable *adjective* not
excitable; calm. **imperturbably**
adverb

impervious *adjective*
1 not allowing water, heat, etc. to
pass through, *impervious to
water.* 2 not able to be affected by
something, *impervious to
criticism.* [from *im-* + Latin *per*
= through + *via* = way]

impetuous *adjective* acting
hastily without thinking; rash.
[same origin as *impetus*]

impetus *noun*
1 the force that makes an object
start moving and that keeps it
moving. 2 the influence that
causes something to develop
more quickly. [Latin, = an attack]

implacable *adjective* not able to
be placated; relentless.
implacably *adverb* [from *im-*
+ *placate* + *-able*]

implant *verb* (**implants**,
implanting, **implanted**) insert; fix
something in. **implantation** *noun*

implant *noun* (*plural* **implants**)
an organ or piece of tissue
inserted in the body.
[from *im-* + Latin *plantare* = to
plant]

implement *noun* (*plural*
implements) a tool.

implicate *verb* (**implicates**,
implicating, **implicated**) involve
a person in a crime etc.; show
that a person is involved, *His
evidence implicates his sister.*
[from Latin *implicare* = to fold in]

implication *noun* (*plural*
implications)
1 implicating. 2 implying;
something that is implied.

implicit (say im-pliss-it) adjective
1 implied but not stated openly.
(Compare explicit.) **2** absolute;
unquestioning, She expects
implicit obedience. **implicitly**
adverb [from Latin implicitus
= entangled]

implore verb (implores,
imploring, implored) beg
somebody to do something;
entreat. [from Latin implorare
= ask tearfully]

imply verb (implies, implying,
implied) suggest something
without actually saying it.
implication noun [from old
French; related to implicate]

impolite adjective not polite.

import verb (imports, importing,
imported) bring in goods etc.
from another country.

import noun (plural imports)
1 importing; something
imported. **2** (formal) meaning or
importance, The message was of
great import.
[from im- + Latin portare = carry]

important adjective
1 having or able to have a great
effect. **2** having great authority
or influence. **importantly** adverb,
importance noun

impose verb (imposes, imposing,
imposed) put or inflict, It imposes
a strain upon us.
impose on somebody put an
unfair burden on him or her.
[from im- + Latin positum
= placed]

imposing adjective impressive.

imposition noun (plural
impositions)
1 something imposed; an unfair
burden or inconvenience.
2 imposing something.

impossible adjective
1 not possible. **2** (informal) very
annoying; unbearable, He really
is impossible! **impossibly** adverb,
impossibility noun

impostor noun (plural
impostors) a person who
dishonestly pretends to be
someone else. [from French]

impotent adjective
1 powerless; unable to take
action. **2** (of a man) unable to
have sexual intercourse.
impotently adverb, **impotence**
noun

impoverish verb (impoverishes,
impoverishing, impoverished)
1 make a person poor. **2** make
a thing poor in quality,
impoverished soil.
impoverishment noun [from im-
+ old French povre = poor]

impracticable adjective not able
to be done in practice.

impractical adjective not
practical.

imprecise adjective not precise.

impregnable adjective strong
enough to be safe against attack.
[from im- + old French prendre
= take]

impregnate verb (impregnates,
impregnating, impregnated)
1 fertilize; make pregnant.
2 saturate; fill throughout, The
air was impregnated with the
scent. **impregnation** noun [from
im- + Latin pregnare = be
pregnant]

impress verb (impresses,
impressing, impressed)
1 make a person admire
something or think it is very
good. **2** fix something firmly in
the mind, He impressed on them

the need for secrecy. **3** press
a mark into something. [from *im-*
+ old French *presser* = to press]

impression *noun* (*plural*
impressions)
1 an effect produced on the mind.
2 a vague idea. **3** an imitation of
a person or a sound etc. **4** a reprint
of a book.

impressionable *adjective* easily
influenced or affected.

impressive *adjective* making
a strong impression; seeming to
be very good.

imprison *verb* (**imprisons,
imprisoning, imprisoned**) put
someone in prison; shut someone
up in a place. **imprisonment** *noun*

improbable *adjective* unlikely.
improbably *adverb*, **improbability**
noun

impromptu *adjective* & *adverb*
done without any rehearsal or
preparation. [from Latin *in
promptu* = in readiness]

improper *adjective*
1 unsuitable or wrong. **2** indecent.
improperly *adverb*, **impropriety**
(*say* im-pro-pry-it-ee) *noun*

improper fraction *noun* (*plural*
improper fractions) a fraction
that is greater than 1, with the
numerator greatery than the
denominator, e.g. $\frac{5}{3}$.

improve *verb* (**improves,
improving, improved**) make or
become better. **improvement**
noun [from old French *emprouer*
= make a profit]

improvise *verb* (**improvises,
improvising, improvised**)
1 compose or perform something
without any rehearsal or
preparation. **2** make something
quickly with whatever is

available. **improvisation** *noun*
[from *im-* + Latin *provisus*
= provided for]

imprudent *adjective* unwise.

impudent *adjective* cheeky or
disrespectful. **impudently** *adverb*,
impudence *noun* [from *im-* + Latin
pudens = ashamed]

impulse *noun* (*plural* **impulses**)
1 a sudden desire to do
something; a push; impetus.
3 (in physics) a force acting for
a very short time, *electrical
impulses.* [same origin as *impel*]

impulsive *adjective* done or
acting on impulse, not after
careful thought. **impulsively**
adverb, **impulsiveness** *noun*

impure *adjective* not pure.
impurity *noun*

in *preposition* This word is used to
show position or condition, e.g.
1 at or inside; within the limits of
something (*in a box*; *in two
hours*), **2** into (*He fell in a puddle*),
3 arranged as; consisting of (*a
serial in four parts*), **4** occupied
with; a member of (*He is in the
army*), **5** by means of (*We paid in
cash*).
in all in total number; altogether.

in *adverb*
1 so as to be in something or
inside (*Get in*), **2** inwards (*The top
caved in*), **3** at home; indoors (*Is
anybody in?*), **4** in action; (in
cricket) batting; (of a fire)
burning, **5** having arrived (*The
train is in*).
in for likely to get, *You're in for
a shock.*
in on (*informal*) aware of or
sharing in, *I want to be in on this
project.*

in- *prefix* (changing to **il-** before *l*, **im-** before *b, m, p,* **ir-** before *r*)
1 in; into; on; towards (as in *include, invade*). **2** not (as in *incorrect, indirect*). [sense **1** from Latin; sense **2** usually from Latin; in a few words from Germanic *un-*]

inability *noun* being unable.

inaccessible *adjective* not accessible.

inaccurate *adjective* not accurate.

inadequate *adjective*
1 not enough. **2** not capable enough. **inadequately** *adverb*, **inadequacy** *noun*

inadvisable *adjective* not advisable.

inanimate *adjective*
1 not living. **2** not moving.

inappropriate *adjective* not appropriate.

inarticulate *adjective*
1 not able to speak or express yourself clearly, *inarticulate with rage.* **2** not expressed in words, *an inarticulate cry.*

inaudible *adjective* unable to be heard. **inaudibly** *adverb*, **inaudibility** *noun*

inaugurate *verb* (**inaugurates, inaugurating, inaugurated**)
1 start or introduce something new and important. **2** formally establish a person in office, *inaugurate a new President.* **inaugural** *adjective*, **inauguration** *noun*, **inaugurator** *noun* [from Latin]

inborn *adjective* present in a person or animal from birth, *an inborn ability.*

inbred *adjective*
1 inborn. **2** produced by inbreeding.

inbreeding *noun* breeding from closely related individuals.

incalculable *adjective* not able to be calculated or predicted. [from *in-* + *calculate* + *-able*]

incandescent *adjective* giving out light when heated; shining. **incandescence** *noun* [from *in-* + Latin *candescere* = become white]

incantation *noun* (*plural* **incantations**) a spoken spell or charm; the chanting of this. [from *in-* = in, + Latin *cantare* = sing]

incapable *adjective* not able to do something, *incapable of working alone.*

incapacitate *verb* (**incapacitates, incapacitating, incapacitated**) make a person or thing unable to do something; disable. [from *in-* + *capacity* + *-ate*]

incarnate *adjective* having a body or human form, *a devil incarnate.*

incarnation *noun*
the Incarnation the embodiment of God in human form as Jesus Christ. [from *in-* + Latin *carnis* = of flesh]

incautious *adjective* rash.

incendiary *adjective* starting or designed to start a fire, *an incendiary bomb.* [same origin as *incense*]

incentive *noun* (*plural* **incentives**) something that encourages a person to do something or to work harder. [from Latin *incentivus* = setting the tune]

incest *noun* sexual intercourse between two people who are so closely related that they cannot marry each other. **incestuous** *adjective* [from *in-* + Latin *castus* = pure]

inch *noun* (*plural* **inches**) a measure of length, one-twelfth of a foot (about 2½ centimetres). [from Old English]

incident *noun* (*plural* **incidents**) an event. [from Latin *incidere* = fall upon or happen to]

incidental *adjective* happening as a minor part of something else, *incidental expenses*. [from *incident*]

incidentally *adverb* by the way.

incinerate *verb* (**incinerates, incinerating, incinerated**) destroy something by burning. **incineration** *noun* [from *in-* + Latin *cineris* = of ashes]

incinerator *noun* (*plural* **incinerators**) a device for burning rubbish.

incision *noun* (*plural* **incisions**) a cut, especially one made in a surgical operation. [from *in-* + Latin *caesum* = cut]

incisive *adjective* clear and sharp, *incisive comments*.

incisor (say in-sy-zer) *noun* (*plural* **incisors**) each of the sharp-edged front teeth in the upper and lower jaws.

incite *verb* (**incites, inciting, incited**) urge a person to do something; stir up, *They incited a riot.* **incitement** *noun* [from *in-* = towards + Latin *citare* = rouse]

inclination *noun* (*plural* **inclinations**)
1 a tendency. 2 a liking or preference. 3 a slope or slant.

incline *verb* (**inclines, inclining, inclined**)
1 lean or slope. 2 bend the head or body forward, as in a nod or bow. 3 cause or influence, *Her frank manner inclines me to believe her.*
be inclined have a tendency, *The door is inclined to bang.*
[from Latin *inclinare* = to bend]

include *verb* (**includes, including, included**) make or consider something as part of a group of things. [from Latin *includere* = enclose]

incoherent *adjective* not speaking or reasoning in an orderly way.

income *noun* (*plural* **incomes**) money received regularly from wages, investments, etc. [from *in* (adverb) + *come*]

income tax *noun* tax charged on income.

incomparable *adjective* without an equal; unsurpassed, *incomparable beauty.* [from *in-* + Latin *comparabilis* = comparable].

incompetent *adjective* not competent.

incomplete *adjective* not complete.

incomprehensible *adjective* not able to be understood.
incomprehension *noun* [from *in-* + Latin *comprehensibilis* = comprehensible]

incongruous *adjective* out of place or unsuitable.
incongruously *adverb*,
incongruity *noun* [from *in-* + Latin *congruus* = agreeing or suitable]

inconsiderate *adjective* not considerate.

inconsistent *adjective* not consistent. **inconsistently** *adverb*, **inconsistency** *noun*

inconspicuous *adjective* not conspicuous. **inconspicuously** *adverb*

incontinent *adjective* not able to control the bladder or bowels. **incontinence** *noun* [from *in-* + Latin *continentia* = restraining, keeping in]

incontrovertible *adjective* unable to be denied; indisputable. [from *in-* + Latin *controversus* = disputed]

inconvenience *noun* (*plural* **inconveniences**) being inconvenient.

inconvenience *verb* (**inconveniences**, **inconveniencing**, **inconvenienced**) cause inconvenience or slight difficulty to someone.

inconvenient *adjective* not convenient.

incorporate *verb* (**incorporates**, **incorporating**, **incorporated**) include something as a part. **incorporation** *noun* [from *in-* + Latin *corpus* = body]

incorporated *adjective* (of a business firm) formed into a legal corporation.

incorrect *adjective* not correct. **incorrectly** *adverb*

incorruptible *adjective* **1** not able to decay. **2** not able to be bribed.

increase *verb* (**increases**, **increasing**, **increased**) make or become larger or more.

increase *noun* (*plural* **increases**) increasing; the amount by which a thing increases.

[from *in-* + Latin *crescere* = grow]

incredible *adjective* unbelievable. **incredibly** *adverb*, **incredibility** *noun*

USAGE: Do not confuse with *incredulous*.

incredulous *adjective* not believing somebody; showing disbelief. **incredulously** *adverb*, **incredulity** *noun*

USAGE: Do not confuse with *incredible*.

incriminate *verb* (**incriminates**, **incriminating**, **incriminated**) show a person to have been involved in a crime etc. **incrimination** *noun* [from *in-* + Latin *criminare* = accuse of a crime]

incubate *verb* (**incubates**, **incubating**, **incubated**) **1** hatch eggs by keeping them warm. **2** cause bacteria or a disease etc. to develop. **incubation** *noun* [from *in-* + Latin *cubare* = lie]

incubator *noun* (*plural* **incubators**) **1** a device for incubating eggs etc. **2** a device in which a baby born prematurely can be kept warm and supplied with oxygen.

indebted *adjective* owing money or gratitude to someone.

indecent *adjective* not decent; improper. **indecently** *adverb*, **indecency** *noun*

indecisive *adjective* not decisive.

indeed *adverb* **1** really; truly, *I am indeed surprised*; (used to strengthen a meaning), *very nice indeed*. **2** admittedly, *It is, indeed, his first attempt*. [from *in deed* = in action or fact]

indefensible *adjective* unable to be defended or justified, *an indefensible decision*.

indefinite *adjective* not definite; vague.

indefinite article the word 'a' or 'an'.

indefinitely *adverb* for an indefinite or unlimited time.

indelible *adjective* impossible to rub out or remove. **indelibly** *adverb* [from *in-* + Latin *delere* = destroy]

indelicate *adjective*
1 slightly indecent. 2 tactless.
indelicacy *noun*

independent *adjective*
1 not dependent; not controlled by any other person or thing. 2 (of a country) governing itself. 3 (of broadcasting) not financed by money from licences.
independently *adverb*,
independence *noun*

indestructible *adjective* unable to be destroyed. **indestructibility** *noun* [from *in-* + Latin *destruere* = destroy]

indeterminate *adjective* not fixed or decided exactly; left vague. [from *in-* + Latin *determinare* = define or determine]

index *noun*
1 (*plural* **indexes**) an alphabetical list of things, especially at the end of a book. 2 a number showing how prices or wages have changed from a previous level. 3 (*plural* **indices**) the raised number etc. written to the right of another (e.g. 3 in 2^3) showing how many times the first one is to be multiplied by itself. [Latin, = pointer]

Indian *adjective*
1 to do with India or its people.
2 to do with Native Americans.
Indian *noun*

USAGE: The preferred term for the descendants of the original inhabitants of North and South America is **Native American**. **American Indian** is usually acceptable but the term **Red Indian** is now regarded as offensive and should not be used.

india rubber *noun* (*plural* **india rubbers**) a rubber. [because it was made of rubber from India]

indicate *verb* (**indicates**, **indicating**, **indicated**)
1 point something out or make it known. 2 be a sign of. 3 when drivers indicate, they signal which direction they are turning by using their indicators.
indication *noun* [from Latin; related to *index*]

indicative *adjective* giving an indication.

indicative *noun* the form of a verb used in making a statement (e.g. 'he said' or 'he is coming'), not in a command or question etc.

indicator *noun* (*plural* **indicators**)
1 a thing that indicates or points to something. 2 a flashing light used to signal that a motor vehicle is turning.

indifferent *adjective*
1 not caring about something; not interested. 2 not very good, *an indifferent cricketer*.
indifferently *adverb*, **indifference** *noun* [from *in-* + Latin *differre* = recognize differences]

indigenous (say in-dij-in-us) *adjective* growing or originating in a particular country; native, *The koala bear is indigenous to Australia.* [from Latin *indigena* = born in a country]

indigestible *adjective* difficult or impossible to digest.

indigestion *noun* pain caused by difficulty in digesting food. [from *in-* + Latin *digerere* = digest]

indignant *adjective* angry at something that seems unfair or wicked. **indignantly** *adverb*, **indignation** *noun* [from Latin *indignari* = regard as unworthy]

indignity *noun* (*plural* **indignities**) treatment that makes a person feel undignified or humiliated; an insult. [from *in-* + Latin *dignus* = worthy]

indirect *adjective* not direct. **indirectly** *adverb*

indiscreet *adjective*
1 not discreet; revealing secrets.
2 not cautious; rash. **indiscreetly** *adverb*, **indiscretion** *noun*

indiscriminate *adjective* showing no discrimination; not making a careful choice. **indiscriminately** *adverb*

indispensable *adjective* not able to be dispensed with; essential. **indispensability** *noun*

indisputable *adjective* undeniable. [from *in-* + Latin *disputare* = dispute]

indistinct *adjective* not distinct. **indistinctly** *adverb*, **indistinctness** *noun*

indistinguishable *adjective* not able to be told apart; not distinguishable.

individual *adjective*
1 of or for one person. 2 single or separate, *Count each individual word.* **individually** *adverb*

individual *noun* (*plural* **individuals**) one person, animal, or plant. [from *in-* + Latin *dividuus* = able to be divided]

individuality *noun* the things that make one person or thing different from another; distinctive identity.

indivisible *adjective* not able to be divided or separated. **indivisibly** *adverb* [from *in-* + Latin *divisum* = divided]

indoctrinate *verb* (**indoctrinates**, **indoctrinating**, **indoctrinated**) fill a person's mind with particular ideas or beliefs, especially so that he or she comes to accept them without thinking. **indoctrination** *noun* [from *in-* = in, + *doctrine*]

indomitable *adjective* not able to be overcome or conquered. [from *in-* + Latin *domitare* = to tame]

indoor *adjective* used or placed or done etc. inside a building, *indoor games.*

indoors *adverb* inside a building.

induce *verb* (**induces**, **inducing**, **induced**)
1 persuade. 2 produce or cause, *Some substances induce sleep.* 3 if a pregnant woman is induced, labour is brought on artificially with drugs. **induction** *noun* [from *in-* + Latin *ducere* = to lead]

indulge *verb* (**indulges**, **indulging**, **indulged**) allow a person to have or do what he or she wishes. **indulgence** *noun*, **indulgent** *adjective*

indulge in allow yourself to have or do something that you like.

industrial *adjective* to do with industry; working or used in industry. **industrially** *adverb*

industrial action *noun* striking or working to rule.

industrialized *adjective* (of a country or district) having many industries. **industrialization** *noun*

Industrial Revolution *noun* the rapid expansion of British industry by the use of machines during the late 18th and early 19th centuries.

industrious *adjective* working hard. **industriously** *adverb*

industry *noun* (*plural* **industries**) 1 making or producing goods etc., especially in factories. 2 a particular branch of this, *the motor industry*. 3 being industrious. [from Latin *industria* = hard work]

ineffective *adjective* not effective; inefficient. **ineffectively** *adverb*

ineffectual *adjective* not achieving anything.

inefficient *adjective* not efficient. **inefficiently** *adverb*, **inefficiency** *noun*

inert *adjective* not moving or reacting. **inertly** *adverb* [from Latin *iners* = idle]

inert gas *noun* (*plural* **inert gases**) a gas that almost never combines with other substances.

inertia (*say* in-er-sha) *noun* 1 inactivity; being inert or slow to take action. 2 the tendency for a moving thing to keep moving in a straight line. [same origin as *inert*]

inevitable *adjective* unavoidable; sure to happen. **inevitably** *adverb*, **inevitability** *noun* [from *in-* + Latin *evitare* = avoid]

inexhaustible *adjective* so great that it cannot be used up completely, *Ben has an inexhaustible supply of jokes.*

inexorable (*say* in-eks-er-a-bul) *adjective* 1 relentless. 2 not able to be persuaded by requests or entreaties. **inexorably** *adverb* [from *in-* + Latin *exorare* = plead]

inexperience *noun* lack of experience. **inexperienced** *adjective*

infallible *adjective* 1 never wrong. 2 never failing, *an infallible remedy.* **infallibly** *adverb*, **infallibility** *noun* [from *in-* + Latin *fallere* = deceive]

infancy *noun* 1 early childhood; babyhood. 2 an early stage of development.

infant *noun* (*plural* **infants**) a baby or young child. [from Latin *infans* = unable to speak]

infantile *adjective* 1 to do with infants. 2 very childish.

infantry *noun* soldiers who fight on foot. (Compare *cavalry*.) [from Italian *infante* = a youth]

infatuated *adjective* filled with foolish or unreasoning love. **infatuation** *noun* [from *in-* + Latin *fatuus* = foolish]

infect *verb* (**infects**, **infecting**, **infected**) pass on a disease or bacteria etc. to a person, animal, or plant. [from Latin *infectum* = tainted]

infection noun (plural **infections**)
1 infecting. **2** an infectious disease or condition.

infectious adjective
1 (of a disease) able to be spread by air or water etc. (Compare **contagious**.) **2** quickly spreading to others, *His fear was infectious.*

inferior adjective less good or less important; low or lower in position, quality, etc. **inferiority** noun [Latin, = lower]

infernal adjective
1 to do with or like hell, *the infernal regions.* **2** (*informal*) detestable or tiresome, *that infernal noise.* **infernally** adverb [from Latin *infernus* = below, used by Christians to mean 'hell']

inferno noun (plural **infernos**) a terrifying fire. [same origin as *infernal*]

infertile adjective not fertile. **infertility** noun

infest verb (**infests**, **infesting**, **infested**) (of pests) be numerous and troublesome in a place. **infestation** noun [from Latin *infestus* = hostile]

infidelity noun unfaithfulness.

infiltrate verb (**infiltrates**, **infiltrating**, **infiltrated**) get into a place or organization gradually and without being noticed. **infiltration** noun, **infiltrator** noun [from *in-* + Latin *filtrare* = to filter]

infinite adjective
1 endless; without a limit. **2** too great to be measured. **infinitely** adverb [from Latin *infinitus* = unlimited]

infinitesimal adjective extremely small. **infinitesimally** adverb

infinitive noun (plural **infinitives**) a form of a verb that does not indicate a particular tense or number or person, in English used with or without *to*, e.g. *go* in 'Let him go' or 'Allow him to go'. [from *in-* + Latin *finitivus* = definite]

infinity noun an infinite number or distance or time.

inflame verb (**inflames**, **inflaming**, **inflamed**)
1 produce strong feelings or anger in people. **2** cause redness, heat, and swelling in a body part. [from *in-* + Latin *flamma* = flame]

inflammable adjective able to be set on fire. [same origin as *inflame*]

USAGE: This word means the same as *flammable*. If you want to say that something is not able to be set on fire, use *non-flammable*.

---

inflammation noun painful redness or swelling in a part of the body.

inflate verb (**inflates**, **inflating**, **inflated**)
1 fill something with air or gas so that it expands. **2** increase something too much. **3** raise prices or wages etc. more than is justifiable. [from *in-* + Latin *flatum* = blown]

inflation noun
1 inflating. **2** a general rise in prices and fall in the purchasing power of money. **inflationary** adjective

inflect verb (**inflects**, **inflecting**, **inflected**)
1 change the ending or form of a word to show its tense or its

grammatical relation to other words, e.g. *sing* changes to *sang* or *sung*, *child* changes to *children*. **2** alter the voice in speaking. [originally = bend inwards: from *in-* + Latin *flectere* = to bend]

inflection *noun* (*plural* **inflections**) an ending or form of a word used to inflect, e.g. *-ed*.

inflexible *adjective* not able to be bent or changed or persuaded. **inflexibly** *adverb*, **inflexibility** *noun* [from *in-* + Latin *flexibilis* = flexible]

influence *noun* (*plural* **influences**)
1 the power to produce an effect. **2** a person or thing with this power.
influence *verb* (**influences**, **influencing**, **influenced**) have influence on a person or thing; affect.
[from *in-* + Latin *fluentia* = flowing]

influential *adjective* having influence.

influenza *noun* an infectious disease that causes fever, catarrh, and pain. [Italian, literally = influence]

inform *verb* (**informs**, **informing**, **informed**) give information to somebody. **informant** *noun* [from Latin *informare* = form an idea]

informal *adjective* not formal. **informally** *adverb*, **informality** *noun*

USAGE: In this dictionary, words marked *informal* are used in talking but not when you are writing or speaking formally.

information *noun* facts told or heard or discovered, or put into a computer etc. [from Latin *informatio* = idea]

informative *adjective* giving a lot of useful information.

informed *adjective* knowing about something.

infra- *prefix* below. [Latin]

infra-red *adjective* below or beyond red in the colour spectrum.

infuriate *verb* (**infuriates**, **infuriating**, **infuriated**) make a person very angry; enrage. **infuriation** *noun* [from *in-* + Latin *furia* = fury]

-ing *suffix* forms nouns and adjectives showing the action of a verb (e.g. *hearing*, *tasting*, *telling*).

ingenious *adjective*
1 clever at inventing things. **2** cleverly made or thought out. **ingeniously** *adverb*, **ingenuity** *noun* [from Latin *ingenium* = genius]

ingrained *adjective*
1 (of dirt) marking a surface deeply. **2** (of feelings or habits etc.) firmly fixed. [from *in the grain* (of wood)]

ingratiate *verb* (**ingratiates**, **ingratiating**, **ingratiated**) **ingratiate yourself** get yourself into favour with someone, especially by flattering them or always agreeing with their ideas or opinions. **ingratiation** *noun* [from Latin *in gratiam* = into favour]

ingratitude *noun* lack of gratitude.

ingredient *noun* (*plural* **ingredients**) one of the parts of a mixture; one of the things used in a recipe. [from Latin *ingrediens* = going in]

inhabit *verb* (**inhabits, inhabiting, inhabited**) live in a place. **inhabitant** *noun* [from *in-* + Latin *habitare* = occupy]

inhale *verb* (**inhales, inhaling, inhaled**) breathe in. **inhalation** *noun* [from *in-* + Latin *halare* = breathe]

inhaler *noun* (*plural* **inhalers**) a device used for relieving asthma etc. by inhaling.

inherent (*say* in-heer-ent) *adjective* existing in something as one of its natural or permanent qualities. **inherently** *adverb*, **inherence** *noun* [from *in-* + Latin *haerere* = to stick]

inherit *verb* (**inherits, inheriting, inherited**)
1 receive money, property, or a title etc. when its previous owner dies. **2** get certain qualities etc. from parents or predecessors. **inheritance** *noun*, **inheritor** *noun* [from *in-* + Latin *heres* = heir]

inhibition *noun* (*plural* **inhibitions**) a feeling of embarrassment or worry that prevents you from doing something or expressing your emotions. **inhibited** *adjective* [from *in-* + Latin *habere* = to hold]

inhuman *adjective* cruel; without pity or kindness. **inhumanity** *noun* [from *in-* + Latin *humanus* = human]

inimitable *adjective* impossible to imitate.

initial *noun* (*plural* **initials**) the first letter of a word or name.

initial *adjective* at the beginning, *the initial stages.* **initially** *adverb* [from Latin *initium* = the beginning]

initiative (*say* in-ish-a-tiv) *noun* the power or courage to get something started; enterprising ability.
take the initiative take action to start something happening.

inject *verb* (**injects, injecting, injected**)
1 put a medicine or drug into the body by means of a hollow needle. **2** put liquid into something by means of a syringe etc. **3** add a new quality, *Inject some humour into the story.* **injection** *noun* [from *in-* + Latin *jacere* = to throw]

injure *verb* (**injures, injuring, injured**) harm or hurt someone. **injury** *noun*, **injurious** (*say* in-joor-ee-us) *adjective* [originally = treat someone unfairly: from *in-* + Latin *juris* = of right]

injustice *noun* (*plural* **injustices**)
1 lack of justice. **2** an unjust action or treatment.

ink *noun* (*plural* **inks**) a black or coloured liquid used in writing and printing. [from Greek]

inky *adjective*
1 stained with ink. **2** black like ink, *inky darkness.*

inland *adjective* & *adverb* in or towards the interior of a country; away from the coast.

Inland Revenue *noun* the government department responsible for collecting taxes and similar charges inland (not at a port).

in-laws plural noun (informal) relatives by marriage. [from French en loi de mariage = in law of marriage]

inlet noun (plural **inlets**)
1 a strip of water reaching into the land from a sea or lake.
2 a passage that lets something in (e.g. to a tank).

inmost adjective most inward.

inn noun (plural **inns**) a hotel or public house, especially in the country. **innkeeper** noun

inner adjective inside; nearer to the centre. **innermost** adjective

innings noun (plural **innings**) the time when a cricket team or player is batting. [from an old verb in = put or get in, + -ing]

innocent adjective
1 not guilty. 2 not wicked.
3 harmless. **innocently** adverb, **innocence** noun [from in- + Latin nocens = doing harm]

innocuous adjective harmless. [from in- + Latin nocuus = harmful]

innovation noun (plural **innovations**)
1 introducing new things or new methods. 2 something newly introduced. **innovative** adjective, **innovator** noun [from in- + Latin novus = new]

innumerable adjective countless. [from in- + Latin numerare = to count or number]

inoculate verb (inoculates, inoculating, inoculated) inject or treat someone with a vaccine or serum as a protection against a disease. **inoculation** noun [from Latin inoculare = implant]

USAGE: Note the spelling of this word. It has one 'n' and one 'c'.

inoffensive adjective harmless.

inorganic adjective not of living organisms; of mineral origin.

input noun what is put into something (e.g. data into a computer). **input** verb

inquest noun (plural **inquests**) an official inquiry to find out how a person died. [from old French; related to inquire]

inquire verb (inquires, inquiring, inquired)
1 investigate something carefully. 2 ask for information. [from in- + Latin quaerere = seek]

USAGE: You can spell this word inquire or enquire in either of its meanings. It is probably more common for inquire to be used for 'investigate' and enquire to be used for 'ask for information', but there is no real need to follow this distinction.

inquiry noun (plural **inquiries**)
1 an investigation. 2 a question.

inquisitive adjective always asking questions or trying to look at things; prying. **inquisitively** adverb [same origin as inquire]

inroads plural noun
make inroads on or into use up large quantities of stores etc. [from in (adverb) + an old sense of road = riding]

insane adjective not sane; mad. **insanely** adverb, **insanity** noun

insanitary *adjective* unclean and likely to be harmful to health.

insatiable (say in-**say**-sha-bul) *adjective* impossible to satisfy, *an insatiable appetite*. [from *in-* + Latin *satiare* = satiate]

inscribe *verb* (inscribes, inscribing, inscribed) write or carve words etc. on something. [from *in-* + Latin *scribere* = write]

inscription *noun* (plural inscriptions)
1 words or names inscribed on a monument, coin, stone, etc.
2 inscribing.

insect *noun* (plural insects) a small animal with six legs, no backbone, and a body divided into three parts (head, thorax, abdomen). [from Latin *insectum* = cut up]

insecticide *noun* (plural insecticides) a substance for killing insects. [from *insect* + *-cide*]

insectivorous *adjective* feeding on insects and other small invertebrate creatures.
insectivore *noun*

insecure *adjective* not secure; unsafe. **insecurely** *adverb*, **insecurity** *noun*

inseminate *verb* (inseminates, inseminating, inseminated) insert semen into the womb.
insemination *noun* [from *in-* + Latin *seminare* = to sow]

insensitive *adjective* not sensitive. **insensitively** *adverb*, **insensitivity** *noun*

inseparable *adjective*
1 not able to be separated. **2** liking to be constantly together, *inseparable friends.*
inseparably *adverb*

insert *verb* (inserts, inserting, inserted) put a thing into something else. **insertion** *noun* [from *in-* + Latin *serere* = to plant]

inside *noun* (plural insides) the inner side, surface, or part.
inside out with the inside turned to face outwards.

inside *adverb* & *preposition* on or to the inside of something; in, *Come inside. It's inside that box.*

insider *noun* (plural insiders) a member of a certain group, especially someone with access to private information.

insight *noun* (plural insights) being able to perceive the truth about things; understanding.

insignificant *adjective* not important or influential.
insignificance *noun*

insincere *adjective* not sincere.
insincerely *adverb*, **insincerity** *noun*

insinuate *verb* (insinuates, insinuating, insinuated)
1 hint something unpleasant.
2 introduce a thing or yourself gradually or craftily into a place.
insinuation *noun* [from *in-* + Latin *sinuare* = to curve]

insist *verb* (insists, insisting, insisted) be very firm in saying or asking for something. **insistent** *adjective*, **insistence** *noun* [from *in-* + Latin *sistere* = to stand]

insolent *adjective* very impudent; insulting. **insolently** *adverb*, **insolence** *noun* [from Latin *insolentia* = pride]

insoluble *adjective*
1 impossible to solve, *an insoluble problem*. **2** impossible

to dissolve. **insolubility** *noun*
[from *in-* + Latin *solubilis*
= soluble]

insomnia *noun* being unable to
sleep. **insomniac** *noun* [from *in-*
+ Latin *somnus* = sleep]

inspect *verb* (**inspects, inspecting,
inspected**) examine something
carefully and critically.
inspection *noun* [from *in-* + Latin
specere = to look]

inspector *noun* (*plural*
inspectors)
1 a person whose job is to inspect
or supervise things. **2** a police
officer ranking next above
a sergeant.

inspiration *noun* (*plural*
inspirations)
1 a sudden brilliant idea.
2 inspiring; an inspiring
influence.

inspire *verb* (**inspires, inspiring,
inspired**) fill a person with
enthusiasm or creative feelings
or ideas, *The applause inspired us
with confidence.* [from *in-* + Latin
spirare = breathe]

install *verb* (**installs, installing,
installed**)
1 put something in position and
ready to use, *They installed
central heating.* **2** put a person
into an important position with
a ceremony, *He was installed as
pope.* **installation** *noun* [from *in-*
+ Latin *stallum* = a place or
position]

instalment *noun* (*plural*
instalments) each of the parts in
which something is given or paid
for gradually, *an instalment of
a serial.* [from old French]

instance *noun* (*plural* **instances**)
an example, *for instance.* [from
Latin]

instant *adjective*
1 happening immediately, *instant
success.* **2** (of food) designed to be
prepared quickly and easily,
instant coffee. **instantly** *adverb*

instant *noun* (*plural* **instants**)
a moment, *not an instant too soon.*
[from Latin *instans* = urgent]

instantaneous *adjective*
happening immediately.
instantaneously *adverb*

instead *adverb* in place of
something else. [from *in-* + *stead*
= a place]

instinct *noun* (*plural* **instincts**)
a natural tendency or ability,
Birds fly by instinct. **instinctive**
adjective, **instinctively** *adverb*
[from Latin *instinguere* = urge
on]

institute *noun* (*plural* **institutes**)
a society or organization; the
building used by this.

institution *noun* (*plural*
institutions)
1 an institute; a public
organization, e.g. a hospital or
university. **2** a habit or custom.
3 instituting something.
institutional *adjective*

instruct *verb* (**instructs,
instructing, instructed**)
1 teach a person a subject or skill.
2 inform. **3** tell a person what he
or she must do. **instruction** *noun,*
instructional *adjective,* **instructor**
noun [from Latin *instruere* = to
build up or prepare]

instrument *noun* (*plural*
instruments)
1 a device for producing musical

sounds. **2** a tool used for delicate or scientific work. **3** a measuring-device. [same origin as *instruct*]

instrumental *adjective*
1 performed on musical instruments, without singing.
2 being the means of doing something, *She was instrumental in getting me a job.*

insubordinate *adjective*
disobedient or rebellious.
insubordination *noun*

insufferable *adjective*
unbearable.

insular *adjective*
1 to do with or like an island.
2 narrow-minded. [same origin as *insulate*]

insulate *verb* (**insulates, insulating, insulated**) cover or protect something to prevent heat, cold, or electricity etc. from passing in or out. **insulation** *noun*, **insulator** *noun* [from Latin *insula* = island]

insulin *noun* a substance that controls the amount of sugar in the blood. The lack of insulin causes diabetes. [from Latin]

insult (*say* in-sult) *verb* (**insults, insulting, insulted**) hurt a person's feelings or pride.

insult (*say* in-sult) *noun* (*plural* **insults**) an insulting remark or action.
[from Latin]

insuperable *adjective* unable to be overcome, *an insuperable difficulty.* [from *in-* + Latin *superare* = to overcome]

insurance *noun* an agreement to compensate someone for a loss, damage, or injury etc., in return for a payment (called a *premium*) made in advance.

insure *verb* (**insures, insuring, insured**) protect with insurance, *Is your jewellery insured?* [a different spelling of *ensure*]

USAGE: Do not confuse with *ensure*.

intact *adjective* not damaged; complete. [from *in-* + Latin *tactum* = touched]

intake *noun* (*plural* **intakes**)
1 taking something in. **2** the number of people or things taken in.

integer *noun* (*plural* **integers**) a whole number (e.g. 0, 3, 19), not a fraction. [Latin, = whole]

integral (*say* in-tig-ral) *adjective*
1 being an essential part of a whole thing, *An engine is an integral part of a car.* **2** whole or complete. [same origin as *integer*]

integrate *verb* (**integrates, integrating, integrated**)
1 make parts into a whole; combine. **2** join together harmoniously into a single community. **integration** *noun* [from Latin *integrare* = make whole]

integrity (*say* in-teg-rit-ee) *noun* honesty. [from Latin *integritas* = wholeness or purity]

intellect *noun* (*plural* **intellects**) the ability to think (contrasted with *feeling* and *instinct*). [same origin as *intelligent*]

intellectual *adjective*
1 to do with or using the intellect.
2 having a good intellect and a liking for knowledge.
intellectually *adverb*

intellectual *noun* (*plural* **intellectuals**) an intellectual person.

intelligence *noun*
1 being intelligent. 2 information, especially of military value; the people who collect and study this information.

intelligent *adjective* able to learn and understand things; having great mental ability. **intelligently** *adverb* [from Latin *intelligere* = understand]

intend *verb* (**intends, intending, intended**) have something in mind as what you want to do; plan. [from Latin *intendere* = stretch, aim]

intense *adjective*
1 very strong or great. 2 feeling things very strongly and seriously, *He's a very intense young man.* **intensely** *adverb*, **intensity** *noun* [from Latin *intensus* = stretched tight]

intent *noun* (*plural* **intents**) intention.

intent *adjective* with concentrated attention; very interested. **intently** *adverb* [same origin as *intend*]

intention *noun* (*plural* **intentions**) what a person intends; a purpose or plan.

intentional *adjective* deliberate, not accidental. **intentionally** *adverb*

inter- *prefix* between; among. [from Latin]

interact *verb* (**interacts, interacting, interacted**) have an effect upon one another. **interaction** *noun*

interbreed *verb* (**interbreeds, interbreeding, interbred**) breed with each other; cross-breed.

intercept *verb* (**intercepts, intercepting, intercepted**) stop or catch a person or thing that is going from one place to another. **interception** *noun* [from *inter-* + Latin *captum* = seized]

interchange *verb* (**interchanges, interchanging, interchanged**)
1 put each of two things into the other's place. 2 exchange things. 3 alternate. **interchangeable** *adjective*

interchange *noun* (*plural* **interchanges**)
1 interchanging. 2 a road junction where vehicles can move from one motorway etc. to another.

intercourse *noun*
1 communication or dealings between people. 2 sexual intercourse. [from Latin *intercursus* = running between]

interdependent *adjective* dependent upon each other.

interest *noun* (*plural* **interests**)
1 a feeling of wanting to know about or help with something.
2 a thing that interests somebody, *Science fiction is one of my interests.* 3 an advantage or benefit, *She looks after her own interests.* 4 money paid regularly in return for money lent or deposited.

interest *verb* (**interests, interesting, interested**) attract a person's interest. **interested** *adjective*, **interesting** *adjective* [Latin, = it matters]

interfere *verb* (**interferes, interfering, interfered**)
1 take part in something that has nothing to do with you. 2 get in

the way; obstruct. **interference**
noun [from *inter-* + Latin *ferire*
= to strike]

interior adjective inner.

interior noun (plural **interiors**)
the inside of something; the
central or inland part of
a country.
[Latin, = further in]

interjection noun (plural
interjections) a word or words
exclaimed expressing joy or pain
or surprise, such as *oh!* or *wow!*
or *good heavens!* [from *inter-*
+ Latin *jactum* = thrown]

interlude noun (plural **interludes**)
1 an interval. **2** something
happening in an interval or
between other events. [from
inter- + Latin *ludus* = game]

intermediate adjective coming
between two things in time,
place, or order. [from *inter-*
+ Latin *medius* = middle]

interminable adjective endless;
long and boring. **interminably**
adverb [from *in-* + Latin
terminare = to limit or end]

intermission noun (plural
intermissions) an interval,
especially between parts of a film.
[same origin as *intermittent*]

intermittent adjective happening
at intervals; not continuous.
intermittently adverb [from *inter-*
+ Latin *mittere* = to let go]

internal adjective inside.
internally adverb [from Latin]

internal-combustion engine
noun (plural **internal-combustion
engines**) an engine that produces
power by burning fuel inside the
engine itself.

international adjective to do with
or belonging to more than one
country; agreed between nations.
internationally adverb

international noun (plural
internationals)
1 a sports contest between teams
representing different countries.
2 a sports player who plays for
his or her country.

Internet noun an international
computer network that allows
users all over the world to
exchange information.

interplanetary adjective between
planets.

interpolate verb (interpolates,
interpolating, interpolated)
1 interject a remark in
a conversation. **2** insert words;
put terms into a mathematical
series. **interpolation** noun [from
Latin *interpolare* = redecorate or
smarten up]

interpose verb (interposes,
interposing, interposed) place
something between two things.
[from *inter-* + Latin *positum* = put]

interpret verb (interprets,
interpreting, interpreted)
1 explain what something means.
2 translate what someone says
into another language orally.
interpretation noun, **interpreter**
noun

interrogate verb (interrogates,
interrogating, interrogated)
question someone closely or
formally. **interrogation** noun,
interrogator noun [from *inter-*
+ Latin *rogare* = ask]

interrogative adjective
questioning; expressing
a question. **interrogatory**
adjective

interrupt verb (interrupts, interrupting, interrupted)
1 break in on a person's speech etc. by inserting a remark.
2 prevent something from continuing. **interruption** noun [from inter- + Latin ruptum = broken]

intersect verb (intersects, intersecting, intersected)
1 divide a thing by passing or lying across it. 2 (of lines or roads etc.) cross each other. **intersection** noun [from inter- + Latin sectum = cut]

interval noun (plural intervals)
1 a time between two events or parts of a play etc. 2 a space between two things.
at intervals with some time or distance between each one. [from Latin intervallum = space between ramparts]

intervene verb (intervenes, intervening, intervened)
1 come between two events, in the intervening years. 2 interrupt a discussion or fight etc. to try and stop it or change its result. **intervention** noun [from inter- + Latin venire = come]

interview noun (plural interviews) a formal meeting with someone in which you ask him or her questions or to obtain information.

interview verb (interviews, interviewing, interviewed) hold an interview with someone. **interviewer** noun [from inter- + French voir = see]

intestine noun (plural intestines) the long tube along which food passes while being absorbed by the body, between the stomach and the anus. **intestinal** adjective [from Latin intestinus = internal]

intimate (say in-tim-at) adjective
1 very friendly with someone.
2 private and personal, intimate thoughts. 3 detailed, an intimate knowledge of the country.
intimately adverb, **intimacy** noun [from Latin intimus = close friend]

intimidate verb (intimidates, intimidating, intimidated) frighten a person by threats into doing something. **intimidation** noun [from in- + Latin timidus = timid]

into preposition used to express 1 movement to the inside (Go into the house), 2 change of condition or occupation etc. (It broke into pieces. She went into politics), 3 (in division) 4 into 20 = 20 divided by 4.

intolerable adjective unbearable. **intolerably** adverb

intoxicate verb (intoxicates, intoxicating, intoxicated) make a person drunk or very excited. **intoxication** noun [from in- + Latin toxicum = poison]

intra- prefix within. [from Latin]

intransitive adjective (of a verb) used without a direct object after it, e.g. hear in we can hear (but not in we can hear you). (Compare transitive.)
intransitively adverb [from in- + Latin transitivus = passing over]

intravenous (say in-tra-veen-us) adjective into a vein. [from intra- + Latin vena = vein]

intricate *adjective* very complicated. **intricately** *adverb*, **intricacy** *noun* [from Latin *intricatus* = entangled]

intrigue (*say* in-treeg) *verb* (**intrigues, intriguing, intrigued**) **1** plot with someone in an underhand way. **2** interest someone very much, *The subject intrigues me.* [from Italian; related to *intricate*]

intro- *prefix* into; inwards. [from Latin]

introduce *verb* (**introduces, introducing, introduced**) **1** make a person known to other people. **2** announce a broadcast, speaker, etc. **3** bring something into use or for consideration. [from *intro-* + Latin *ducere* = to lead]

introduction *noun* (*plural* **introductions**) **1** introducing somebody or something. **2** an explanation put at the beginning of a book or speech etc. **introductory** *adjective*

introvert *noun* (*plural* **introverts**) a shy person who does not like to talk about his or her own thoughts and feelings with other people. (The opposite is *extrovert*.)

intrude *verb* (**intrudes, intruding, intruded**) come in or join in without being wanted. **intrusion** *noun*, **intrusive** *adjective* [from *in-* + Latin *trudere* = to push]

intruder *noun* (*plural* **intruders**) **1** someone who intrudes. **2** a burglar.

intuition *noun* the power to know or understand things without having to think hard or without

being taught. **intuitive** *adjective*, **intuitively** *adverb* [from *in-* + Latin *tueri* = to look]

Inuit (*say* in-yoo-it) *noun* (*plural* **Inuit**) **1** a member of a people living in northern Canada and Greenland; an Eskimo. **2** the language of the Inuit. [Inuit, = people]

USAGE: See note at *Eskimo*.

inundate *verb* (**inundates, inundating, inundated**) flood or overwhelm a place, *We've been inundated with letters about the programme.* **inundation** *noun* [from *in-* + Latin *unda* = a wave]

invade *verb* (**invades, invading, invaded**) **1** attack and enter a country etc. **2** crowd into a place, *Tourists invade Oxford in summer.* **invader** *noun* [from *in-* + Latin *vadere* = go]

invalid (*say* in-va-leed) *noun* (*plural* **invalids**) a person who is ill or who is weakened by illness.

invalid (*say* in-val-id) *adjective* not valid, *This passport is invalid.* **invalidity** *noun* [from *in-* + Latin *validus* = strong or powerful]

invaluable *adjective* having a value that is too great to be measured; extremely valuable. [from *in-* + *value* + *-able*]

invariable *adjective* not variable; never changing. **invariably** *adverb*

invasion *noun* (*plural* **invasions**) attacking and entering a country etc. [same origin as *invade*]

invent *verb* (**invents, inventing, invented**) **1** be the first person to make or

think of a particular thing.
2 make up a false story etc.,
invent an excuse. **invention** *noun*,
inventor *noun*, **inventive** *adjective*
[from *in-* + Latin *venire* = come]

invertebrate *noun* (*plural*
invertebrates) an animal without
a backbone. **invertebrate** *adjective*

inverted commas *plural noun*
punctuation marks " " or ' ' put
round quotations and spoken
words.

invest *verb* (**invests**, **investing**,
invested)
1 use money to make a profit, e.g.
by lending it in return for
interest to be paid, or by buying
stocks and shares or property.
2 give somebody a rank, medal,
etc. in a formal ceremony.
investment *noun*, **investor** *noun*
[from Latin *investire* = to clothe]

investigate *verb* (**investigates**,
investigating, **investigated**) find
out as much as you can about
something; make a systematic
inquiry. **investigation** *noun*,
investigator *noun*, **investigative**
adjective [from Latin]

invigilate *verb* (**invigilates**,
invigilating, **invigilated**) supervise
candidates at an examination.
invigilation *noun*, **invigilator** *noun*
[from *in-* + Latin *vigilare* = to
watch]

invigorate *verb* (**invigorates**,
invigorating, **invigorated**) give
a person strength or courage.
(Compare *vigour*.) [from *in-*
+ Latin *vigor* = vigour]

invincible *adjective* not able to be
defeated; unconquerable.
invincibly *adverb*, **invincibility**
noun [from *in-* + Latin *vincere*
= conquer]

invisible *adjective* not visible; not
able to be seen. **invisibly** *adverb*,
invisibility *noun*

invite *verb* (**invites**, **inviting**,
invited)
1 ask a person to come or do
something. **2** be likely to cause
something to happen, *You are
inviting disaster.* **invitation** *noun*

invoice *noun* (*plural* **invoices**)
a list of goods sent or work done,
with the prices charged. [from
French *envoyer* = send]

involuntary *adjective* not
deliberate; unintentional.
involuntarily *adverb*

involve *verb* (**involves**, **involving**,
involved)
1 have as a part; make a thing
necessary, *The job involves hard
work.* **2** make someone share in
something, *They involved us in
their charity work.* **involvement**
noun [from *in-* + Latin *volvere* =
roll]

inward *adjective*
1 on the inside. **2** going or facing
inwards.
inward *adverb* inwards.
[from Old English]

inwards *adverb* towards the
inside.

iodine *noun* a chemical substance
used as an antiseptic. [from
Greek *iodes* = violet-coloured
(because it gives off violet-
coloured vapour)]

ion *noun* (*plural* **ions**) an
electrically charged particle.

-ion, **-sion**, **-tion**, **-xion**
suffixes form nouns meaning
'condition or action' (e.g.
dominion, *dimension*, *attraction*,
pollution, *inflexion*).

ionosphere (say I-on-os-feer)
noun a region of the upper
atmosphere, containing ions.

IQ *abbreviation* intelligence
quotient; a number showing how
a person's intelligence compares
with that of an average person.

ir- *prefix*
1 in; into. **2** on; towards. **3** not. see
in-.

IRA *abbreviation* Irish Republican
Army.

iridescent *adjective* showing
rainbow-like colours. **iridescence**
noun [from Greek *iris* = iris or
rainbow]

iron *noun* (*plural* **irons**)
1 a hard grey metal. **2** a device
with a flat base that is heated for
smoothing clothes or cloth.
3 a tool etc. made of iron. **iron**
adjective

iron *verb* (**irons**, **ironing**, **ironed**)
smooth clothes or cloth with an
iron.

Iron Age *noun* the time when
tools and weapons were made of
iron.

ironic (say I-ron-ik) *adjective*
using irony; full of irony. **ironical**
adjective, **ironically** *adverb*

ironmonger *noun* (*plural*
ironmongers) a shopkeeper who
sells irons and other metal
objects. **ironmongery** *noun* [from
iron + an old word *monger*
= trader]

irony (say I-ron-ee) *noun* (*plural*
ironies)
1 saying the opposite of what you
mean in order to emphasize it,
e.g. saying 'What a lovely day'
when it is pouring with rain. **2** an
oddly contradictory situation,
The irony of it is that I tripped

*while telling someone else to be
careful.* [from Greek *eiron*
= someone who pretends not to
know]

irrational *adjective* not rational;
illogical. **irrationally** *adverb*

irregular *adjective*
1 not regular; uneven. **2** against
the rules or usual custom. **3** (of
troops) not in the regular armed
forces. **irregularly** *adverb*,
irregularity *noun*

irrepressible *adjective* unable to
be repressed; always lively and
cheerful. **irrepressibly** *adverb*

irreproachable *adjective*
blameless or faultless.
irreproachably *adverb* [from *ir-*
+ French *reprocher* = reproach]

irresistible *adjective* unable to be
resisted; very attractive.
irresistibly *adverb*

irrespective *adjective* not taking
something into account, *Prizes
are awarded to winners,
irrespective of age.*

irresponsible *adjective* not
showing a proper sense of
responsibility. **irresponsibly**
adverb, **irresponsibility** *noun*

irrigate *verb* (**irrigates**, **irrigating**,
irrigated) supply land with water
so that crops etc. can grow.
irrigation *noun* [from *ir-* + Latin
rigare = to water]

irritable *adjective* easily annoyed;
bad-tempered. **irritably** *adverb*,
irritability *noun*

irritate *verb* (**irritates**, **irritating**,
irritated)
1 annoy. **2** cause itching.
irritation *noun*, **irritant** *adjective* &
noun [from Latin]

-ise *suffix* see **-ize**.

-ish *suffix* forms nouns meaning 1 'of a certain nature' (e.g. *foolish*), 2 'rather' (e.g. *greenish*, *yellowish*).

Islam *noun* the religion of Muslims. **Islamic** *adjective* [Arabic, = submission to God]

island *noun* (*plural* **islands**) 1 a piece of land surrounded by water. 2 something that resembles an island because it is isolated. [from Old English]

-ism *suffix* forms nouns showing action from verbs ending in *-ize* (e.g. *baptism*, *criticism*), or condition (e.g. *heroism*).

isn't (mainly spoken) is not.

iso- *prefix* equal (as in *isobar*). [from Greek]

isobar (say I-so-bar) *noun* (*plural* **isobars**) a line (on a map) connecting places that have the same atmospheric pressure. [from *iso-* + Greek *baros* = weight]

isolate *verb* (**isolates**, **isolating**, **isolated**) place a person or thing apart or alone; separate. **isolation** *noun* [from Latin *insulatus* = made into an island]

isosceles (say I-soss-il-eez) *adjective* an isosceles triangle has two sides of equal length. [from *iso-* + Greek *skelos* = leg]

isotope *noun* (*plural* **isotopes**) a form of an element that differs from other forms in its nuclear properties but not in its chemical properties. [from *iso-* + Greek *topos* = place (because they appear in the same place in the table of chemical elements)]

issue *verb* (**issues**, **issuing**, **issued**) 1 come or go out; flow out. 2 supply; give out, *We issued one blanket to each refugee.* 3 put out

for sale; publish. 4 send out, *They issued a gale warning.* 5 result.

issue *noun* (*plural* **issues**) 1 a subject for discussion or concern, *What are the real issues?* 2 a result, *Await the issue of the trial.* 3 a particular edition of a newspaper or magazine, *The Christmas issue of Radio Times.* 4 issuing something, *The issue of passports is held up.* [from old French; related to *exit*]

-ist *suffix* forms nouns meaning 'person who does something or believes in or supports something' (e.g. *cyclist*, *Communist*).

isthmus (say iss-mus) *noun* (*plural* **isthmuses**) a narrow strip of land connecting two larger pieces of land. [from Greek]

IT *abbreviation* information technology.

it *pronoun* 1 the thing being talked about. 2 the player who has to catch others in a game. The word is also used 1 in statements about the weather (*It is raining*) or about circumstances etc. (*It is six miles to York*), 2 as an indefinite object (*Run for it!*), 3 to refer to a phrase (*It is unlikely that she will fail*).

italic (say it-al-ik) *adjective* printed with sloping letters (called *italics*) like this. [because this style was first used in Italy]

itch *verb* (**itches**, **itching**, **itched**) 1 have or feel a tickling sensation in the skin that makes you want to scratch it. 2 long to do something.

-ite *suffix* (in scientific use) forms names of minerals (e.g. *anthracite*), explosives (e.g. *dynamite*), and salts of certain acids (e.g. *nitrite*; compare **-ate**).

item *noun* (*plural* **items**)
1 one thing in a list or group of things. **2** one piece of news, article etc. in a newspaper or bulletin. [Latin, = just so, similarly (used to introduce each item on a list)]

-itis *suffix* forms nouns meaning inflammation of part of the body (as in *bronchitis*). [Greek]

its *possessive pronoun* belonging to it, *The cat hurt its paw.*

USAGE: Do not put an apostrophe into *its* unless you mean 'it is' or 'it has' (see the next entry).

it's (*mainly spoken*)
1 it is, *It's very hot.* **2** it has, *It's broken all records.*

USAGE: Do not confuse with *its.*

itself *pronoun* it and nothing else. (Compare *herself*.)
by itself on its own; alone.

ITV *abbreviation* Independent Television.

-ive *suffix* forms adjectives, chiefly from verbs (e.g. *active*, *explosive*).

ivory *noun*
1 the hard creamy-white substance that forms elephants' tusks. **2** a creamy-white colour. [from Latin]

ivy *noun* (*plural* **ivies**) a climbing evergreen plant with shiny leaves. [from Old English]

-ize or **-ise** *suffix* forms verbs meaning 'bring or come into a certain condition' (e.g. *civilize*), or 'treat in a certain way' (e.g. *pasteurize*), or 'have a certain feeling' (e.g. *sympathize*). [from the Greek verb-ending *-izein*, or French *-iser*]

Jj

jab *verb* (**jabs, jabbing, jabbed**) poke roughly; push a thing into something.

jack *noun* (*plural* **jacks**)
1 a device for lifting something heavy off the ground. **2** a playing card with a picture of a young man. **3** a small white ball aimed at in bowls.
jack of all trades someone who can do many different kinds of work. [the name *Jack*, used for various sorts of tool (as though it was a person helping you)]

jackdaw *noun* (*plural* **jackdaws**) a kind of small crow. [from the name *Jack* + Middle English *dawe* = jackdaw]

jacket *noun* (*plural* **jackets**)
1 a short coat, usually reaching to the hips. **2** a cover to keep the heat in a water-tank etc. **3** a paper wrapper for a book. **4** the skin of a potato that is baked without being peeled. [from old French]

jackpot *noun* (*plural* **jackpots**) an amount of prize money that increases until someone wins it.
hit the jackpot 1 win a large prize. **2** have remarkable luck or success.

[originally = a kitty which could be won only by playing a pair of jacks or cards of higher value: from *jack* + *pot*[1]]

jagged (say jag-id) *adjective* having an uneven edge with sharp points. [from Scots *jag* = stab]

jaguar *noun* (*plural* **jaguars**) a large fierce South American animal rather like a leopard. [via Portuguese from a South American language]

jail *noun* (*plural* **jails**) a prison. [from old French *jaiole* = cage or prison]

jam *noun* (*plural* **jams**)
1 a sweet food made of fruit boiled with sugar until it is thick. **2** a lot of people, cars, or logs etc. crowded together so that movement is difficult.
in a jam in a difficult situation.

jam *verb* (**jams**, **jamming**, **jammed**)
1 crowd or squeeze into a space. **2** make or become fixed and difficult to move. **3** push something forcibly, *jam the brakes on*. **4** block a broadcast by causing interference with the transmission.

jamboree *noun* (*plural* **jamborees**) a large party or celebration

jangle *verb* (**jangles**, **jangling**, **jangled**) make a loud harsh ringing sound. **jangle** *noun* [from old French]

janitor *noun* (*plural* **janitors**) a caretaker. [originally = doorkeeper: from Latin *janua* = door]

jar[1] *noun* (*plural* **jars**) a container made of glass or pottery. [via French from Arabic]

jar[2] *verb* (**jars**, **jarring**, **jarred**)
1 cause an unpleasant jolt or shock. **2** sound harshly.
jar *noun* (*plural* **jars**) a jarring effect.
[imitating the sound]

jargon *noun* special words used by a group of people, *scientists' jargon*. [from French]

jaunt *noun* (*plural* **jaunts**) a short trip. **jaunting** *noun*

jaunty *adjective* (**jauntier**, **jauntiest**) lively and cheerful. **jauntily** *adverb*, **jauntiness** *noun*
[originally = stylish, elegant: from French, related to *gentle*]

javelin *noun* (*plural* **javelins**) a lightweight spear. [from French]

jaw *noun* (*plural* **jaws**)
1 either of the two bones that form the framework of the mouth. **2** the lower part of the face. **3** something shaped like the jaws or used for gripping things. **4** (*slang*) talking. [from old French]

jazz *noun* a kind of music with strong rhythm. **jazzy** *adjective*

jealous *adjective*
1 unhappy or resentful because you feel that someone is your rival or is better or luckier than yourself. **2** careful in keeping something, *He is very jealous of his own rights.* **jealously** *adverb*, **jealousy** *noun*

jeans *plural noun* trousers made of strong cotton fabric. [from *Genoa*, a city in Italy, where such a cloth was once made]

jeer verb (jeers, jeering, jeered)
laugh or shout at somebody
rudely or scornfully. **jeer** noun
[origin unknown]

jelly noun (plural **jellies**)
1 a soft transparent food. **2** any
soft slippery substance. **jellied**
adjective [from Latin gelare
= freeze]

jellyfish noun (plural **jellyfish**)
a sea animal with a body like
jelly.

jerk verb (jerks, jerking, jerked)
1 make a sudden sharp
movement. **2** pull something
suddenly.

jerk noun (plural **jerks**)
1 a sudden sharp movement.
2 (slang) a stupid person. **jerky**
adjective, **jerkily** adverb

jerkin noun (plural **jerkins**)
a sleeveless jacket. [origin
unknown]

jersey noun (plural **jerseys**)
1 a pullover with sleeves. **2** a plain
machine-knitted material used
for making clothes. [originally
= a woollen cloth made in Jersey,
one of the Channel Islands]

jest noun (plural **jests**) a joke.
[from Middle English gest
= a story]

jester noun (plural **jesters**)
a professional entertainer at
a royal court in the Middle Ages.

jet noun (plural **jets**)
1 a stream of water, gas, flame,
etc. shot out from a narrow
opening. **2** a spout or nozzle from
which a jet comes. **3** an aircraft
driven by engines that send out
a high-speed jet of hot gases at
the back. [from French jeter = to
throw]

jet lag noun extreme tiredness
that a person feels after a long
flight between different time
zones.

jettison verb (jettisons,
jettisoning, jettisoned)
1 throw something overboard.
2 get rid of something that is no
longer wanted. **3** release or drop
something from an aircraft or
spacecraft in flight. [same origin
as jet]

jetty noun (plural **jetties**) a small
landing stage. [same origin as jet]

Jew noun (plural **Jews**) a member
of a people descended from the
ancient tribes of Israel, or who
believes in the religion of this
people. **Jewish** adjective [from
Hebrew yehudi = belonging to the
tribe of Judah (the founder of one
of the ten tribes of ancient
Israel)]

jewel noun (plural **jewels**)
1 a precious stone. **2** an ornament
containing precious stones.
jewelled adjective [from old
French]

jewellery noun jewels and
similar ornaments for wearing.

jigsaw noun (plural **jigsaws**)
1 a saw that can cut curved
shapes. **2** a jigsaw puzzle.

jigsaw puzzle noun (plural
jigsaw puzzles) a picture cut into
irregular pieces which are then
shuffled and fitted together again
for amusement.

jilt verb (jilts, jilting, jilted)
abandon a boyfriend or
girlfriend, especially after
promising to marry him or her.
[origin unknown]

jingle verb (**jingles, jingling, jingled**) make or cause to make a tinkling sound.

jingle noun (plural **jingles**)
1 a jingling sound. 2 a very simple verse or tune, especially one used in advertising.

jitters plural noun (informal) nervousness. **jittery** adjective

job noun (plural **jobs**)
1 work that someone does regularly to earn a living. 2 a piece of work to be done. 3 (informal) a difficult task, You'll have a job to lift that box. 4 (informal) a thing; a state of affairs, It's a good job you're here.

jockey noun (plural **jockeys**) a person who rides horses in races. [pet form of the name Jock]

jodhpurs (say jod-perz) plural noun trousers for horse riding, fitting closely from the knee to the ankle. [named after Jodhpur, a city in India, where similar trousers are worn]

jog verb (**jogs, jogging, jogged**)
1 run or trot slowly, especially for exercise. 2 give something a slight push. **jogger** noun
jog someone's memory help him or her to remember something. [same origin as jagged]

jogtrot noun a slow steady trot.

join verb (**joins, joining, joined**)
1 put or come together; fasten or connect. 2 do something together with others, We all joined in the chorus. 3 become a member of a group or organization etc., Join the Navy.
join up enlist in the armed forces.

joint noun (plural **joints**)
1 a join. 2 the place where two

bones fit together. 3 a large piece of meat cut ready for cooking.

joint adjective shared or done by two or more people, nations, etc., a joint project. **jointly** adverb

joke noun (plural **jokes**) something said or done to make people laugh.

joker noun (plural **jokers**)
1 someone who jokes. 2 an extra playing card with a jester on it.

jolly adjective (**jollier, jolliest**) cheerful and good-humoured. **jollity** noun

jolly adverb (informal) very, jolly good.

jolt verb (**jolts, jolting, jolted**)
1 shake or dislodge something with a sudden sharp movement. 2 move along jerkily, e.g. on a rough road. 3 give someone a shock.

jolt noun (plural **jolts**)
1 a jolting movement. 2 a shock.

jostle verb (**jostles, jostling, jostled**) push roughly, especially in a crowd.

jot verb (**jots, jotting, jotted**) write something quickly, jot it down.

jotter noun (plural **jotters**) a notepad or notebook.

joule (say jool) noun (plural **joules**) a unit of work or energy. [named after an English scientist, James Joule]

journal noun (plural **journals**)
1 a newspaper or magazine. 2 a diary. [from Latin, = by day]

journalist noun (plural **journalists**) a person who writes for a newspaper or magazine. **journalism** noun, **journalistic** adjective

journey *noun* (*plural* **journeys**)
1 going from one place to another. **2** the distance or time taken to travel somewhere, *two days' journey*.

journey *verb* (**journeys, journeying, journeyed**) make a journey.
[from French *journée* = a day's travel, from *jour* = day]

jovial *adjective* cheerful and good-humoured. **jovially** *adverb*, **joviality** *noun* [from Latin *jovialis* = to do with Jupiter (because people born under its influence were said to be cheerful)]

joy *noun* (*plural* **joys**)
1 a feeling of great pleasure; gladness. **2** a thing that causes joy. **joyful** *adjective*, **joyfully** *adverb*, **joyfulness** *noun*, **joyous** *adjective*, **joyously** *adverb*

joyride *noun* (*plural* **joyrides**) a drive in a stolen car for amusement. **joyrider** *noun*, **joyriding** *noun*

joystick *noun* (*plural* **joysticks**)
1 the control lever of an aircraft. **2** a device for moving a cursor etc. on a VDU screen.

JP *abbreviation* Justice of the Peace.

jubilant *adjective* rejoicing or triumphant. **jubilantly** *adverb*, **jubilation** *noun* [from Latin *jubilans* = shouting for joy]

jubilee *noun* (*say* joo-bil-ee) (*plural* **jubilees**) a special anniversary, *silver* (25th), *golden* (50th), *and diamond* (60th) *jubilee*. [from Hebrew *yobel* = a year when slaves were freed and property returned to its owners, held in ancient Israel every 50 years]

Judaism (*say* joo-day-izm) *noun* the religion of the Jewish people. [from Greek *Ioudaios* = Jew]

judge *noun* (*plural* **judges**)
1 a person appointed to hear cases in a lawcourt and decide what should be done. **2** a person deciding who has won a contest or competition, or the value or quality of something.

judge *verb* (**judges, judging, judged**)
1 act as a judge. **2** form and give an opinion. **3** estimate, *He judged the distance carefully*.
[from Latin *judex* = a judge, from *jus* = law + *-dicus* = saying]

judgement *noun* (*plural* **judgements**)
1 judging. **2** the decision made by a lawcourt. **3** someone's opinion. **4** the ability to judge wisely. **5** something considered as a punishment from God, *It's a judgement on you!*

judicial *adjective* to do with lawcourts, judges, or judgements, *the British judicial system*. **judicially** *adverb*

USAGE: Do not confuse with *judicious*.

judicious (*say* joo-dish-us) *adjective* having or showing good sense or good judgement. **judiciously** *adverb* [same origin as *judge*]

USAGE: Do not confuse with *judicial*.

judo *noun* a Japanese method of self-defence without using weapons. [from Japanese *ju* = gentle + *do* = way]

jug noun (plural **jugs**) a container for holding and pouring liquids, with a handle and a lip. [pet form of *Joan* or *Jenny*]

juggernaut noun (plural **juggernauts**) a huge lorry. [named after a Hindu god whose image was dragged in procession on a huge wheeled vehicle]

juggle verb (**juggles, juggling, juggled**)
1 toss and keep a number of objects in the air, for entertainment. 2 rearrange or alter things skilfully or in order to deceive people. **juggler** noun [from old French]

jugular adjective to do with the throat or neck, *the jugular veins.* [from Latin *jugulum* = throat]

juice noun (plural **juices**)
1 the liquid from fruit, vegetables, or other food.
2 a liquid produced by the body, *the digestive juices.* **juicy** adjective [from Latin]

jukebox noun (plural **jukeboxes**) a machine that automatically plays a record that you have selected when you put a coin in.

jumble verb (**jumbles, jumbling, jumbled**) mix things up into a confused mass.

jumble noun a confused mixture of things; a muddle.

jumble sale noun (plural **jumble sales**) a sale of second-hand goods.

jumbo noun (plural **jumbos**)
1 something very large; a jumbo jet. 2 an elephant. [the name of a very large elephant in London Zoo]

jumbo jet noun (plural **jumbo jets**) a very large jet aircraft.

jump verb (**jumps, jumping, jumped**)
1 move up suddenly from the ground into the air. 2 go over something by jumping, *jump the fence.* 3 pass over something; miss out part of a book etc.
4 move suddenly in surprise.
5 pass quickly to a different place or level.
jump at (*informal*) accept something eagerly.
jump the gun start before you should.
jump the queue not wait your turn.

jump noun (plural **jumps**)
1 a jumping movement. 2 an obstacle to jump over. 3 a sudden rise or change.

jumper noun (plural **jumpers**) a jersey. [from French *jupe* = tunic]

jumpy adjective nervous.

junction noun (plural **junctions**)
1 a join. 2 a place where roads or railway lines meet. [from Latin *junctum* = joined]

jungle noun (plural **jungles**) a thick tangled forest, especially in the tropics. **jungly** adjective [from Hindi]

junior adjective
1 younger. 2 for young children, *a junior school.* 3 lower in rank or importance, *junior officers.* [Latin, = younger]

junk noun rubbish; things of no value.

junk food noun food that is not nourishing.

jury noun (plural **juries**) a group of people (usually twelve) appointed to give a verdict about a case in a lawcourt. **juryman** noun, **jurywoman** noun [from Latin jurare = take an oath]

just adjective
1 giving proper consideration to everyone's claims. **2** deserved; right in amount etc., *a just reward*. **justly** adverb, **justness** noun

just adverb
1 exactly, *It's just what I wanted.* **2** only; simply, *I just wanted to see him.* **3** barely; by only a small amount, *just below the knee.* **4** at this moment or only a little while ago, *She has just gone.* [from Latin justus = rightful]

justice noun (plural **justices**)
1 being just; fair treatment. **2** legal proceedings, *a court of justice.* **3** a judge or magistrate.

jut verb (**juts, jutting, jutted**) stick out. [a different spelling of *jet*]

jute noun fibre from tropical plants, used for making sacks etc. [from Bengali (a language spoken in Bangladesh and West Bengal)]

juvenile adjective to do with or for young people. [from Latin juvenis = young person]

juvenile delinquent noun (plural **juvenile delinquents**) a young person who has broken the law.

Kk

kaleidoscope (say kal-I-dos-kohp) noun (plural **kaleidoscopes**) a tube that you look through to see brightly coloured patterns which change as you turn the end of the tube.

kaleidoscopic adjective [from Greek kalos = beautiful + eidos = form + skopein = look at]

kangaroo noun (plural **kangaroos**) an Australian animal that jumps along on its strong hind legs. (See *marsupial*.) [an Australian Aboriginal word]

karaoke noun a form of entertainment in which people sing well-known songs against a pre-recorded backing. [Japanese]

karate (say ka-rah-tee) noun a Japanese method of self-defence in which the hands and feet are used as weapons. [from Japanese kara = empty + te = hand]

keel noun (plural **keels**) the long piece of wood or metal along the bottom of a boat. **on an even keel** steady.

keel verb (**keels, keeling, keeled**) **keel over** fall down or overturn, *The ship keeled over.*

keen adjective
1 enthusiastic; very interested in or eager to do something, *a keen swimmer.* **2** sharp, *a keen edge.* **3** piercingly cold, *a keen wind.* **keenly** adverb, **keenness** noun

keep verb (**keeps, keeping, kept**) This word has many uses, including
1 have something and look after it or not get rid of it, **2** stay or cause to stay in the same condition etc. (*keep still; keep it hot*), **3** do something continually (*She keeps laughing*), **4** respect and not break (*keep a promise*), **5** make entries in (*keep a diary*),

keep up 1 make the same progress as others. **2** continue something.

keep noun (plural **keeps**)
1 maintenance; the food etc. that you need to live, *She earns her keep.* **2** a strong tower in a castle.
for keeps (informal) permanently; to keep, *Is this football mine for keeps?*

keeper noun (plural **keepers**)
1 a person who looks after an animal, building, etc., *the park keeper.* **2** a goalkeeper or wicketkeeper.

keeping noun care; looking after something, *in safe keeping.*

keg noun (plural **kegs**) a small barrel. [from Old Norse]

kelvin noun (plural **kelvins**) the SI unit of thermodynamic temperature. [named after a British scientist, Lord Kelvin, who invented it]

kennel noun (plural **kennels**) a shelter for a dog. [from Latin *canis* = dog]

kerb noun (plural **kerbs**) the edge of a pavement. [a different spelling of *curb*]

kernel noun (plural **kernels**) the part inside the shell of a nut etc.

ketchup noun a thick sauce made from tomatoes and vinegar etc. [probably from Chinese *k'e chap* = tomato juice]

kettle noun (plural **kettles**) a container with a spout and handle, for boiling water in. [from Old English]

key noun (plural **keys**)
1 a piece of metal shaped so that it will open a lock. **2** a device for winding up a clock or clockwork toy etc. **3** a small lever to be pressed by a finger, e.g. on a piano, typewriter, or computer. **4** a system of notes in music, *the key of C major.* **5** a fact or clue that explains or solves something, *the key to the mystery.*

key verb (**keys, keying, keyed**)
key in type information into a computer using a keyboard.

keyboard noun (plural **keyboards**) the set of keys on a piano, typewriter, computer, etc.

keyhole noun (plural **keyholes**) the hole through which a key is put into a lock.

kg abbreviation kilogram.

khaki noun a dull yellowish-brown colour, used for military uniforms. [from Urdu *khaki* = dust-coloured]

kibbutz noun (plural **kibbutzim**) a commune in Israel, especially for farming. [from Hebrew *qibbus* = gathering]

kick verb (**kicks, kicking, kicked**)
1 hit or move a person or thing with your foot. **2** move your legs about vigorously. **3** (of a gun) recoil when fired.
kick out get rid of; dismiss.
kick up (informal) make a noise or fuss.

kick noun (plural **kicks**)
1 a kicking movement. **2** the recoiling movement of a gun. **3** (informal) a thrill. **4** (informal) an interest or activity, *He's on a health kick.*
[origin unknown]

kid noun (plural **kids**)
1 (informal) a child. **2** a young goat. **3** fine leather made from goatskin.

kidnap verb (**kidnaps, kidnapping, kidnapped**) take someone away by force, especially in order to obtain a ransom. **kidnapper** noun [from *kid* + an old word *napper* = thief]

kidney noun (plural **kidneys**) either of the two organs in the body that remove waste products from the blood and excrete urine into the bladder.

kill verb (**kills, killing, killed**)
1 make a person or thing die.
2 destroy or put an end to something. **killer** noun
kill time occupy time idly while waiting.

kilo noun (plural **kilos**) a kilogram.

kilo- prefix one thousand (as in *kilolitre* = 1,000 litres, *kilohertz* = 1,000 hertz). [from Greek *chilioi* = thousand]

kilogram noun (plural **kilograms**) a unit of mass or weight equal to 1,000 grams (about 2.2 pounds).

kilometre (say kil-o-meet-er or kil-om-it-er) noun (plural **kilometres**) a unit of length equal to 1,000 metres (about ⅝ of a mile).

kilowatt noun (plural **kilowatts**) a unit of electrical power equal to 1,000 watts.

kilt noun (plural **kilts**) a kind of pleated skirt worn especially by Scotsmen. **kilted** adjective [probably from a Scandinavian language]

-kin suffix forms diminutives (e.g. *lambkin* = little lamb). [from old Dutch]

kind¹ noun (plural **kinds**) a class of similar things or animals; a sort or type.

payment in kind payment in goods not in money.
[from Old English *cynd* = nature]

USAGE: Correct use is *this kind of thing* or *these kinds of things* (not 'these kind of things').

kind² adjective friendly and helpful; considerate. **kind-hearted** adjective, **kindness** noun [from Old English *gecynd* = natural or proper]

kindergarten noun (plural **kindergartens**) a school or class for very young children. [from German *Kinder* = children + *Garten* = garden]

kindle verb (**kindles, kindling, kindled**)
1 start a flame; set light to something. 2 begin burning.
[from Old Norse]

kinetic adjective to do with or produced by movement, *kinetic energy*. [from Greek *kinetikos* = moving]

king noun (plural **kings**)
1 a man who is the ruler of a country through inheriting the position. 2 a person or thing regarded as supreme, *the lion is the king of beasts*. 3 the most important piece in chess.
4 a playing card with a picture of a king. **kingly** adjective, **kingship** noun [from Old English]

kingdom noun (plural **kingdoms**) a country ruled by a king or queen.

kingfisher noun (plural **kingfishers**) a small bird with blue feathers that dives to catch fish.

kink noun (plural **kinks**)
1 a short twist in a rope, wire, piece of hair, etc. 2 a peculiarity. [from old German]

kinky adjective involving peculiar sexual behaviour.

kiosk noun (plural **kiosks**)
1 a telephone box. 2 a small hut or stall where newspapers, sweets, etc. are sold. [via French and Turkish from Persian]

kiss noun (plural **kisses**) touching somebody with your lips as a sign of affection.

kiss verb (**kisses, kissing, kissed**) give somebody a kiss. [from Old English]

kiss of life noun blowing air from your mouth into another person's to help the other person to start breathing again, especially after an accident.

kit noun (plural **kits**)
1 equipment or clothes for a particular occupation. 2 a set of parts sold ready to be fitted together. [from old Dutch]

kitchen noun (plural **kitchens**) a room in which meals are prepared and cooked. [from Old English]

kite noun (plural **kites**)
1 a light framework covered with cloth, paper, etc. and flown in the wind on the end of a long piece of string. 2 a large hawk. [from Old English]

kitten noun (plural **kittens**) a very young cat. [from old French chitoun = small cat]

kleptomania noun an uncontrollable urge to steal things. **kleptomaniac** noun [from Greek kleptes = thief, + mania]

km abbreviation kilometre.

knack noun a special skill, There's a knack to putting up a deckchair.

knapsack noun (plural **knapsacks**) a bag carried on the back by soldiers, hikers, etc. [from Dutch]

knave noun (plural **knaves**)
1 (old use) a dishonest man; a rogue. 2 a jack in playing cards. [from Old English cnafa = a boy or male servant]

knead verb (**kneads, kneading, kneaded**) press and stretch something soft (especially dough) with your hands.

knee noun (plural **knees**) the joint in the middle of the leg.

kneecap noun (plural **kneecaps**) the small bone covering the front of the knee joint.

kneel verb (**kneels, kneeling, knelt**) be or get yourself in a position on your knees. [from Old English]

knickers plural noun a woman's or girl's undergarment worn on the lower part of the body.

knife noun (plural **knives**) a cutting instrument consisting of a sharp blade set in a handle.

knight noun (plural **knights**)
1 a man who has been given the rank that allows him to put 'Sir' before his name. 2 a piece in chess, with a horse's head. **knighthood** noun [from Old English cniht = young man]

knit verb (**knits, knitting, knitted** or **knit**) make something by looping together wool or other yarn, using long needles or a machine. **knitter** noun, **knitting needle** noun

knit your brow frown.
[from Old English *cnyttan* = tie in knots]

knob *noun* (*plural* **knobs**)
1 the round handle of a door, drawer, etc. **2** a round lump on something. **3** a small round piece of something, *a knob of butter*.
knobbly *adjective*, **knobby** *adjective*

knock *verb* (**knocks**, **knocking**, **knocked**)
1 hit a thing hard or so as to make a noise. **2** produce by hitting, *knock a hole in it*. **3** (*slang*) criticize unfavourably, *Stop knocking Britain!*
knock off 1 (*informal*) stop working. **2** deduct something from a price. **3** (*slang*) steal.
knock out make a person unconscious, especially by a blow to the head.

knockout *noun* (*plural* **knockouts**)
1 knocking somebody out. **2** a contest in which the loser in each round has to drop out. **3** (*slang*) an amazing person or thing.

knot *noun* (*plural* **knots**)
1 a place where a piece of string, rope, or ribbon etc. is twisted round itself or another piece. **2** a tangle; a lump. **3** a round spot on a piece of wood where a branch joined it. **4** a cluster of people or things. **5** a unit for measuring the speed of ships and aircraft, 2,025 yards (= 1,852 metres or 1 nautical mile) per hour.

knot *verb* (**knots**, **knotting**, **knotted**)
1 tie or fasten with a knot.
2 entangle.

know *verb* (**knows**, **knowing**, **knew**, **known**)
1 have something in your mind that you have learnt or discovered. **2** recognize or be familiar with a person or place, *I've known him for years*. **3** understand, *She knows how to please us*. [from Old English]

knowing *adjective* showing that you know something, *a knowing look*.

knowingly *adverb*
1 in a knowing way.
2 deliberately.

knowledge *noun*
1 knowing. **2** all that a person knows. **3** all that is known.
to my knowledge as far as I know. [from *know* + Old English *lac* = practice]

knowledgeable *adjective* well-informed. **knowledgeably** *adverb*

knuckle *noun* (*plural* **knuckles**) a joint in the finger.

knuckle *verb* (**knuckles**, **knuckling**, **knuckled**)
knuckle down to buckle down to.
knuckle under be submissive.

koala (*say* koh-ah-la) *noun* (*plural* **koalas**) an Australian animal that looks like a small bear. [an Australian Aboriginal word]

Koran (*say* kor-ahn) *noun* the sacred book of Islam, written in Arabic, believed by Muslims to contain the words of Allah revealed to the prophet Muhammad. [from Arabic *kur'an* = reading]

kosher *adjective* keeping to Jewish laws about food, *kosher meat*. [from Hebrew *kasher* = suitable or proper]

kw *abbreviation* kilowatt.

Ll

label *noun* (*plural* **labels**) a small piece of paper, cloth, or metal etc. fixed on or beside something to show what it is or what it costs, or its owner or destination, etc.

label *verb* (**labels**, **labelling**, **labelled**) put a label on something.
[from old French]

laboratory *noun* (*plural* **laboratories**) a room or building equipped for scientific experiments. [from Latin *laboratorium* = workplace]

laborious *adjective*
1 needing or using a lot of hard work. 2 explaining something at great length and with obvious effort. **laboriously** *adverb*

Labour *noun* the Labour Party, a socialist political party.

labour *noun* (*plural* **labours**)
1 hard work. 2 a task. 3 the contractions of the womb when a baby is being born.

labour *verb* (**labours**, **labouring**, **laboured**)
1 work hard. 2 explain something at great length and with obvious effort, *Don't labour the point*.
[from Latin *labor* = work, trouble, or suffering]

labourer *noun* (*plural* **labourers**) a person who does hard manual work, especially outdoors.

laburnum *noun* (*plural* **laburnums**) a tree with hanging yellow flowers. [Latin]

labyrinth *noun* (*plural* **labyrinths**) a complicated arrangement of passages or paths; a maze. [from Greek]

lace *noun* (*plural* **laces**)
1 net-like material with decorative patterns of holes in it.
2 a piece of thin cord or leather for fastening a shoe, etc.

lack *noun* being without something.

lack *verb* (**lacks**, **lacking**, **lacked**) be without something, *He lacks courage*.

lacquer *noun* a hard glossy varnish. **lacquered** *adjective*

lacrosse *noun* a game in which players use a stick with a net on it (a *crosse*) to catch and throw a ball. [from French *la crosse* = the crosse]

lacy *adjective* made of lace or like lace.

lad *noun* (*plural* **lads**) a boy or youth. [origin unknown]

ladder *noun* (*plural* **ladders**)
1 two upright pieces of wood or metal etc. and crosspieces (*rungs*), for use in climbing.
2 a vertical ladder-like flaw in a stocking etc. where a stitch has become undone.

ladle *noun* (*plural* **ladles**) a large deep spoon with a long handle, used for lifting and pouring liquids.

lady *noun* (*plural* **ladies**)
1 a well-mannered woman.
2 a woman of good social position. 3 (in polite use) a woman. **ladylike** *adjective*, **ladyship** *noun*

Lady noun the title of a noblewoman.
[from Old English *hlaefdige* = person who makes the bread (compare *lord*)]

ladybird noun (plural **ladybirds**) a small flying beetle, usually red with black spots.

lag[1] verb (**lags, lagging, lagged**) go too slowly and fail to keep up with others. [origin unknown]

lag[2] verb (**lags, lagging, lagged**) wrap pipes or boilers etc. in insulating material (**lagging**) to keep them warm. [probably from a Scandinavian language]

lager (say **lah**-ger) noun (plural **lagers**) a light beer. [from German *Lager* = storehouse (because the beer was kept to mature)]

lagoon noun (plural **lagoons**) a salt-water lake separated from the sea by sandbanks or reefs. [from Latin *lacuna* = pool]

laid past tense of **lay**.

lain past participle of **lie**[2].

lair noun (plural **lairs**) a sheltered place where a wild animal lives. [from Old English]

lake noun (plural **lakes**) a large area of water entirely surrounded by land. [from Latin]

lamb noun (plural **lambs**)
1 a young sheep. **2** meat from a lamb. **lambswool** noun [from Old English]

lame adjective
1 unable to walk normally.
2 weak; not convincing, *a lame excuse*. **lamely** adverb, **lameness** noun [from Old English]

lament verb (**laments, lamenting, lamented**) express grief or regret about something. **lamentation** noun
[from Latin *lamentari* = weep]

lamentable (say lam-**in**-ta-bul) adjective regrettable or deplorable.

lamp noun (plural **lamps**) a device for producing light from electricity, gas, or oil. **lamplight** noun, **lampshade** noun [from Greek *lampas* = torch]

lamp-post noun (plural **lamp-posts**) a tall post in a street etc., with a lamp at the top.

lance noun (plural **lances**) a long spear.

lance corporal noun (plural **lance corporals**) a soldier ranking between a private and a corporal. [origin unknown]

land noun (plural **lands**)
1 the part of the earth's surface not covered by sea. **2** the ground or soil; an area of country, *forest land*. **3** the area occupied by a nation; a country.

land verb (**lands, landing, landed**)
1 arrive or put on land from a ship or aircraft etc. **2** reach the ground after jumping or falling.
3 bring a fish out of the water.
4 obtain, *She landed an excellent job.* **5** arrive or cause to arrive at a certain place or position etc., *They landed up in gaol.* **6** present with a problem, *He landed me with this task.*
[from Old English]

landing noun (plural **landings**)
1 bringing or coming to land.
2 a place where people can get on and off a boat. **3** the level area at the top of stairs.

landing stage noun (plural landing stages) a platform on which people and goods are taken on and off a boat.

landlady noun (plural landladies) 1 a woman who lets rooms to lodgers. 2 a woman who looks after a public house.

landlord noun (plural landlords) 1 a person who lets a house, room, or land to a tenant. 2 a person who looks after a public house.

landmark noun (plural landmarks) 1 an object that is easily seen in a landscape. 2 an important event in the history of something.

landowner noun (plural landowners) a person who owns a large amount of land.

landscape noun (plural landscapes) the scenery or a picture of the countryside.

landslide noun (plural landslides) 1 a huge mass of soil and rocks sliding down a slope. 2 an overwhelming victory in an election, *She won the General Election by a landslide.*

lane noun (plural lanes) 1 a narrow road, especially in the country. 2 a strip of road for a single line of traffic. 3 a strip of track or water for one runner, swimmer, etc. in a race. [from Old English]

language noun (plural languages) 1 words and their use. 2 the words used in a particular country or by a particular group of people. [from Latin *lingua* = tongue]

languid adjective slow because of tiredness, weakness, or laziness. **languidly** adverb, **languor** noun [same origin as *languish*]

languish verb (languishes, languishing, languished) 1 become weak or listless and depressed. 2 live in miserable conditions; be neglected. [from Latin *languere* = be faint or weak]

lank adjective (of hair) long and limp. [from Old English]

lanky adjective (lankier, lankiest) awkwardly thin and tall. **lankiness** noun

lantern noun (plural lanterns) a transparent case for holding a light and shielding it from the wind. [from Latin; related to *lamp*]

lap¹ noun (plural laps) 1 the level place formed by the front of the legs above the knees when a person is sitting down. 2 going once round a racecourse. 3 one section of a journey, *the last lap.*
lap verb (laps, lapping, lapped) be a lap ahead of someone in a race. [from Old English *laeppa*]

lap² verb (laps, lapping, lapped) 1 take up liquid by moving the tongue, as a cat does. 2 make a gentle splash against something, *Waves lapped the shore.* [from Old English *lapian*]

lapel (say la-pel) noun (plural lapels) a flap folded back at the front edge of a coat etc. [from *lap*¹]

lapse noun (plural lapses) 1 a slight mistake or failure, *a lapse of memory.* 2 an amount of time elapsed, *after a lapse of six months.*

lapse *verb* (**lapses, lapsing, lapsed**)
1 pass or slip gradually, *He lapsed into unconsciousness.* **2** be no longer valid, through not being renewed, *My insurance policy has lapsed.*
[from Latin *lapsus* = sliding]

larch *noun* (*plural* **larches**) a tall deciduous tree that bears small cones. [via old German from Latin]

lard *noun* a white greasy substance prepared from pig-fat and used in cooking. [French, = bacon]

larder *noun* (*plural* **larders**) a cupboard or small room for storing food. [from Latin]

large *adjective* of more than the ordinary or average size; big.
largeness *noun*
at large 1 free to roam about, not captured, *The escaped prisoners are still at large.* **2** in general, as a whole, *She is respected by the country at large.*
[from Latin *largus* = abundant or generous]

largely *adverb* to a great extent, *You are largely responsible for the accident.*

lark[1] *noun* (*plural* **larks**) a small sandy-brown bird; the skylark. [from Old English]

lark[2] *noun* (*plural* **larks**) (*informal*) something amusing; a bit of fun, *We did it for a lark.* [origin unknown]

larva *noun* (*plural* **larvae**) an insect in the first stage of its life, after it comes out of the egg.
larval *adjective* [Latin, = ghost or mask]

laser *noun* (*plural* **lasers**) a device that makes a very strong narrow beam of light or other electromagnetic radiation. [from the initials of 'light amplification (by) stimulated emission (of) radiation']

lash *noun* (*plural* **lashes**)
1 a stroke with a whip etc. **2** the cord or cord-like part of a whip. **3** an eyelash.

lash *verb* (**lashes, lashing, lashed**)
1 strike with a whip; beat violently. **2** tie with cord etc., *Lash the sticks together.*
lash down (of rain or wind) pour or beat down forcefully.
lash out 1 speak or hit out angrily. **2** spend money extravagantly.

lass *noun* (*plural* **lasses**) a girl or young woman. **lassie** *noun*

lasso *noun* (*plural* **lassoes** or **lassos**) a rope with a sliding noose at the end, used for catching cattle etc. [from Spanish]

last[1] *adjective & adverb*
1 coming after all others; final.
2 latest; most recent, *last night.*
3 least likely, *She is the last person I'd have chosen.*
the last straw a final thing that makes problems unbearable.

last *noun*
1 a person or thing that is last.
2 the end, *He was brave to the last.*
at last or **at long last** finally; after much delay.
[from Old English *latost*]

last[2] *verb* (**lasts, lasting, lasted**)
1 continue; go on existing or living or being usable. **2** be enough for, *The food will last us for three days.* [from Old English *laestan*]

lasting *adjective* able to last for a long time, *a lasting peace.*

lastly *adverb* in the last place; finally.

latch *noun* (*plural* **latches**) a small bar fastening a door or gate, lifted by a lever or spring.
latchkey *noun*
latch *verb* (**latches, latching, latched**) fasten with a latch.
latch onto 1 meet someone and follow them around all the time.
2 understand something.

late *adjective & adverb*
1 after the usual or expected time. **2** near the end, *late in the afternoon.* **3** recent, *the latest news.* **4** who has died recently, *the late king.*
of late recently.

lately *adverb* recently.

latent heat *noun* the heat needed to change a solid into a liquid or vapour, or a liquid into a vapour, without a change in temperature. [from Latin *latens* = lying hidden]

lathe (*say* layth) *noun* (*plural* **lathes**) a machine for holding and turning pieces of wood while they are being shaped.

lather *noun* a mass of froth.
lather *verb* (**lathers, lathering, lathered**)
1 cover with lather. **2** form a lather.

Latin *noun* the language of the ancient Romans. [from *Latium*, an ancient district of Italy including Rome]

Latin America *noun* the parts of Central and South America where the main language is Spanish or Portuguese. [because these languages developed from Latin]

latitude *noun* (*plural* **latitudes**)
1 the distance of a place from the equator, measured in degrees.
2 freedom from restrictions on what people can do or believe.
[from Latin *latitudo* = breadth]

latrine (*say* la-treen) *noun* (*plural* **latrines**) a lavatory in a camp or barracks etc. [French, related to *lavatory*]

latter *adjective* later, *the latter part of the year.*
the latter the second of two people or things just mentioned. (Compare *former.*)

lattice *noun* (*plural* **lattices**) a framework of crossed laths or bars with spaces between. [from French]

laugh *verb* (**laughs, laughing, laughed**) make the sounds that show you think something is funny.
laugh *noun* (*plural* **laughs**) the sound of laughing.
[from Old English]

laughable *adjective* deserving to be laughed at.

laughing stock *noun* (*plural* **laughing stocks**) a person or thing that is the object of ridicule and scorn.

laughter *noun* the act, sound, or manner of laughing.

launch[1] *verb* (**launches, launching, launched**)
1 send a ship from the land into the water. 2 set a thing moving by throwing or pushing it. 3 send a rocket etc. into space. 4 start into action, *launch an attack*. [from old French]

launch[2] *noun* (*plural* **launches**) a large motor boat. [from Spanish]

launderette *noun* (*plural* **launderettes**) a place fitted with washing machines that people pay to use. [from *laundry* + *-ette*]

laundry *noun* (*plural* **laundries**)
1 a place where clothes etc. are washed and ironed for customers. 2 clothes etc. sent to or from a laundry. [from Latin *lavandaria* = things to be washed]

laureate (*say* lorri-at) *adjective*
Poet Laureate a person appointed to write poems for national occasions. [from *laurel*, because a laurel wreath was worn in ancient times as a sign of victory]

laurel *noun* (*plural* **laurels**) an evergreen shrub with smooth shiny leaves. [from Latin]

lava *noun* molten rock that flows from a volcano; the solid rock formed when it cools. [from Latin *lavare* = to wash]

lavatory *noun* (*plural* **lavatories**)
1 a toilet. 2 a room containing a toilet. [from Latin *lavatorium* = a basin or bath for washing]

lavender *noun*
1 a shrub with sweet-smelling purple flowers. 2 a light-purple colour. [from Latin]

lavish *adjective*
1 generous. 2 plentiful. **lavishly** *adverb*, **lavishness** *noun* [from old French *lavasse* = heavy rain]

law *noun* (*plural* **laws**)
1 a rule or set of rules that everyone must obey. 2 (*informal*) the police. 3 a scientific statement of something that always happens, *the law of gravity*.

law-abiding *adjective* obeying the law.

lawcourt *noun* (*plural* **lawcourts**) a room or building in which a judge or magistrate hears evidence and decides whether someone has broken the law.

lawful *adjective* allowed or accepted by the law. **lawfully** *adverb*

lawless *adjective*
1 not obeying the law. 2 without proper laws, *a lawless country*. **lawlessly** *adverb*, **lawlessness** *noun*

lawn *noun* (*plural* **lawns**) an area of closely-cut grass in a garden or park. [from old French]

lawnmower *noun* (*plural* **lawnmowers**) a machine for cutting the grass of lawns.

lawn tennis *noun* tennis played on an outdoor grass or hard court.

lawsuit *noun* (*plural* **lawsuits**) a dispute or claim etc. that is brought to a lawcourt to be settled.

lawyer *noun* (*plural* **lawyers**) a person who is qualified to give advice in matters of law.

laxative noun (plural **laxatives**)
a medicine that stimulates the
bowels to empty. [from Latin
laxare = loosen]

lay[1] verb (**lays, laying, laid**)
1 put something down in
a particular place or way.
2 arrange things, especially for
a meal, *lay the table*. **3** place, *He
laid the blame on his sister*.
4 prepare or arrange, *We laid our
plans*. **5** produce an egg.
lay off 1 stop employing
somebody for a while.
2 (*informal*) stop doing
something.
lay on supply or provide.
lay out 1 arrange or prepare.
2 knock a person unconscious.
3 prepare a corpse for burial.
[from Old English]

USAGE: Do not confuse *lay/
laid/laying* = 'put down', with
lie/lay/lain/lying = 'be in a flat
position'. Correct uses are as
follows: *Go and lie down; she
went and lay down; please lay it
on the floor*. 'Go and lay down'
is incorrect.

lay[2] past tense of **lie**[2].

lay[3] adjective
1 not belonging to the clergy, *a lay
preacher*. **2** not professionally
qualified, *lay opinion*. [from
Greek *laos* = people]

lay-by noun (plural **lay-bys**)
a place where vehicles can stop
beside a main road.

layer noun (plural **layers**) a single
thickness or coating. [from *lay*[1]]

layman noun (plural **laymen**)
1 a person who does not have
specialized knowledge or
training (e.g. as a doctor or

lawyer). **2** a person who is not
ordained as a member of the
clergy. [from *lay*[3] + *man*]

layout noun (plural **layouts**) an
arrangement of parts of
something according to a plan.

lazy adjective (**lazier, laziest**) not
wanting to work; doing little
work. **lazily** adverb, **laziness** noun

lead[1] (say leed) verb (**leads,
leading, led**)
1 take or guide someone,
especially by going in front. **2** be
winning in a race or contest etc.;
be ahead. **3** be in charge of
a group of people. **4** be a way or
route, *This path leads to the
beach*. **5** play the first card in
a card game. **6** live or experience,
He leads a dull life.
lead to result in; cause.

lead[1] (say leed) noun (plural
leads)
1 guidance or example, *Give us
a lead*. **2** a leading place or part or
position, *She took the lead*.
3 a strap or cord for leading a dog
or other animal. **4** an electrical
wire attached to something.
[from Old English *laedan*]

lead[2] (say led) noun (plural **leads**)
1 a soft heavy grey metal. **2** the
writing substance (graphite) in
a pencil. **lead** adjective [from Old
English *lead*]

leader noun (plural **leaders**)
1 the person in charge of a group
of people; a chief. **2** the person
who is winning. **leadership** noun

leaf noun (plural **leaves**)
1 a flat usually green part of
a plant, growing from its stem,
branch, or root. **2** the paper forming one page of a book. **3** a very
thin sheet of metal, *gold leaf*.

4 a flap that makes a table larger.
leafy *adjective*, **leafless** *adjective*
turn over a new leaf make a fresh
start and improve your
behaviour.
[from Old English]

leaflet *noun* (*plural* **leaflets**)
1 a piece of paper printed with
information. **2** a small leaf.

league[1] *noun* (*plural* **leagues**)
1 a group of people or nations
who agree to work together.
2 a group of teams who compete
against each other for
a championship.
in league with working or
plotting together.
[from Latin *legare* = bind]

league[2] *noun* (*plural* **leagues**) an
old measure of distance, about 3
miles. [from Greek]

leak *noun* (*plural* **leaks**)
1 a hole or crack etc. through
which liquid or gas accidentally
escapes. **2** the revealing of secret
information. **leaky** *adjective*

leak *verb* (**leaks**, **leaking**, **leaked**)
1 get out or let out through a leak.
2 reveal secret information.
leakage *noun*

lean[1] *adjective*
1 with little or no fat, *lean meat.*
2 thin, *a lean body.* [from Old
English *hlaene*]

lean[2] *verb* (**leans**, **leaning**, **leaned**
or **leant**)
1 bend your body towards or over
something. **2** put or be in
a sloping position. **3** rest against
something. [from Old English
hleonian]

leaning *noun* (*plural* **leanings**)
a tendency or preference.

leap *verb* (**leaps**, **leaping**, **leaped** or
leapt) jump vigorously. **leap** *noun*

leapfrog *noun* a game in which
each player jumps with legs
apart over another who is
bending down.

leap year *noun* (*plural* **leap years**)
a year with an extra day in it (29
February). [probably because the
dates from March onwards 'leap'
a day of the week; a date which
would fall on a Monday in an
ordinary year will be on Tuesday
in a leap year]

learn *verb* (**learns**, **learning**,
learned or **learnt**) get knowledge
or skill; find out about
something. [from Old English]

USAGE: It is not acceptable in
standard English to use *learn*
to mean 'to teach'.

learned (*say* ler-nid) *adjective*
having much knowledge
obtained by study.

learner *noun* (*plural* **learners**)
a person who is learning
something, especially to drive
a car.

learning *noun* knowledge
obtained by study.

lease *noun* (*plural* **leases**) an
agreement to allow someone to
use a building or land etc. for
a fixed period in return for
payment. **leaseholder** *noun*

lease *verb* (**leases**, **leasing**,
leased) allow or obtain the use of
something by lease.
[from French]

leash *noun* (*plural* **leashes**) a dog's
lead. [from French]

least *adjective* & *adverb* very
small in amount etc., *the least bit;
the least expensive bike.*

leather noun material made from
animal skins. **leathery** adjective
[from Old English]

leave verb (**leaves, leaving, left**)
1 go away from a person or place.
2 stop belonging to a group.
3 cause or allow something to
stay where it is or as it is, *You left
the door open*. **4** go away without
taking something, *I left my book
at home*. **5** put something to be
collected or passed on, *leave
a message*.
leave off cease.
leave out omit; not include.

leave noun
1 permission. **2** official
permission to be away from
work; the time for which this
permission lasts, *three days' leave*.

lecture noun (*plural* **lectures**)
1 a talk about a subject to an
audience or a class. **2** a long
serious warning or rebuke.
lecture verb (**lectures, lecturing,
lectured**) give a lecture. **lecturer**
noun
[from Latin *lectura* = reading, or
something to be read]

led past tense of **lead**[1].

ledge noun (*plural* **ledges**)
a narrow shelf, *a window ledge*;
a mountain ledge. [origin
unknown]

ledger noun (*plural* **ledgers**) an
account-book. [probably from
Dutch]

leech noun (*plural* **leeches**)
a small blood-sucking worm that
lives in water. [from Old English]

leek noun (*plural* **leeks**) a long
green and white vegetable of the
onion family. [from Old English]

leer verb (**leers, leering, leered**)
look at someone in an insulting,
sly, or unpleasant way. **leer** noun

leeway noun
1 extra space or time available.
2 a drift to leeward or off course.
make up leeway make up lost
time; regain a lost position.

left[1] adjective & adverb
1 on or towards the west if you
think of yourself as facing north.
2 (of political groups) in favour of
socialist reforms. **left-hand**
adjective
left noun the left-hand side or
part etc.
[from Old English *lyft* = weak]

left[2] past tense of **leave**.

left-handed adjective using the
left hand in preference to the
right hand.

leg noun (*plural* **legs**)
1 one of the limbs on a person's
or animal's body, on which it
stands or moves. **2** the part of
a piece of clothing covering a leg.
3 each of the supports of a chair
or other piece of furniture. **4** one
part of a journey. **5** one of a pair
of matches between the same
teams. [from Old Norse]

legacy noun (*plural* **legacies**)
something left to a person in
a will.

legal adjective
1 lawful. **2** to do with the law or
lawyers. **legally** adverb, **legality**
noun [from Latin]

legend noun (*plural* **legends**) an
old story handed down from the
past, which may or may not be
true. (Compare *myth*.) **legendary**
adjective [from Latin *legenda*
= things to be read]

legible *adjective* clear enough to read. **legibly** *adverb*, **legibility** *noun* [from Latin *legere* = to read]

legion *noun* (*plural* **legions**)
1 a division of the ancient Roman army. 2 a group of soldiers or former soldiers.

legislate *verb* (**legislates, legislating, legislated**) make laws. **legislation** *noun*, **legislator** *noun* [from Latin *legis* = of a law + *latio* = proposing]

legitimate *adjective*
1 lawful. 2 born when parents are married to each other. **legitimately** *adverb*, **legitimacy** *noun* [from Latin *legitimare* = make something lawful]

leisure *noun* time that is free from work, when you can do what you like. **leisured** *adjective*, **leisurely** *adjective*
at leisure having leisure; not hurried.
at your leisure when you have time.

lemming *noun* (*plural* **lemmings**) a small mouse-like animal of Arctic regions that migrates in large numbers and is said to run headlong into the sea and drown.

lemon *noun* (*plural* **lemons**)
1 an oval yellow citrus fruit with a sour taste. 2 a pale-yellow colour. [same origin as *lime²*]

lemonade *noun* a lemon-flavoured drink.

lemur (*say* **lee**-mer) *noun* (*plural* **lemurs**) a monkey-like animal. [from Latin]

lend *verb* (**lends, lending, lent**)
1 allow a person to use something of yours for a short time.
2 provide someone with money that they must repay, usually in return for payments (called *interest*). **lender** *noun*
lend a hand help somebody. [from Old English]

USAGE: Do not confuse *lend* with *borrow*, which means just the opposite.

length *noun* (*plural* **lengths**)
1 how long something is. 2 a piece of cloth, rope, wire, etc. cut from a larger piece. 3 the amount of thoroughness in an action, *They went to great lengths to make us comfortable.*
at length 1 after a long time.
2 taking a long time; in detail.

lengthen *verb* (**lengthens, lengthening, lengthened**) make or become longer.

lengthy *adjective*
1 very long. 2 long and boring. **lengthily** *adverb*

lenient (*say* **lee**-nee-ent) *adjective* merciful; not severe. **leniently** *adverb*, **lenience** *noun* [from Latin *lenis* = gentle]

lens *noun* (*plural* **lenses**)
1 a curved piece of glass or plastic used to focus things. 2 the transparent part of the eye, immediately behind the pupil. [Latin, = lentil (because of its shape)]

Lent *noun* a time of fasting and penitence observed by Christians for about six weeks before Easter. **Lenten** *adjective* [from Old English *lencten* = the spring]

lent *past tense* of **lend**.

lentil *noun* (*plural* **lentils**) a kind of small bean. [from old French; related to *lens*]

leopard (*say* lep-erd) *noun* (*plural* **leopards**) a large lion-like spotted wild animal, also called a panther. **leopardess** *noun*

leper *noun* (*plural* **lepers**) a person who has leprosy.

leprosy *noun* an infectious disease that makes parts of the body waste away. **leprous** *adjective* [from Greek *lepros* = scaly (because white scales form on the skin)]

lesbian *noun* (*plural* **lesbians**) a homosexual woman. [named after the Greek island of Lesbos (because Sappho, a poetess who lived there about 600BC, was said to be homosexual)]

less *adjective & adverb* smaller in amount; not so much, *Make less noise. It is less important.*

USAGE: Do not use *less* when you mean *fewer*. You should use *fewer* when you are talking about a number of individual things, and *less* when you are talking about a quantity or mass of something: *The less batter you make, the fewer pancakes you'll get.*

less *noun* a smaller amount.

less *preposition* minus; deducting, *She earned £100, less tax.*

-less *suffix* forms adjectives meaning 'without' (e.g. *colourless*) or 'unable to be ...' (e.g. *countless*). [from Old English]

lesser *adjective* not so great as the other, *the lesser evil.*

lesson *noun* (*plural* **lessons**) 1 an amount of teaching given at one time. 2 something to be

learnt by a pupil. 3 an example or experience from which you should learn, *Let this be a lesson to you!* 4 a passage from the Bible read aloud as part of a church service. [from old French; related to *lecture*]

lest *conjunction* (*old use*) so that something should not happen, *Remind us, lest we forget.*

let *verb* (**lets**, **letting**, **let**) 1 allow somebody or something to do something; not prevent or forbid, *Let me see it.* 2 cause to, *Let us know what happens.* 3 allow or cause to come or go or pass, *Let me out!* 4 allow someone to use a house or building etc. in return for payment (*rent*). 5 leave, *Let it alone.*

let down 1 deflate. 2 disappoint somebody.

let off 1 cause to explode. 2 excuse somebody from a duty or punishment etc.

let up (*informal*) relax. **let-up** *noun*

lethal (*say* lee-thal) *adjective* deadly; causing death. **lethally** *adverb* [from Latin *letum* = death]

lethargy (*say* leth-er-jee) *noun* extreme lack of energy or vitality; sluggishness. **lethargic** (*say* lith-ar-jik) *adjective* [from Greek *lethargos* = forgetful]

letter *noun* (*plural* **letters**) 1 a symbol representing a sound used in speech. 2 a written message, usually sent by post. [from Latin]

letter box *noun* (*plural* **letter boxes**) 1 a slot in a door, through which letters are delivered. 2 a postbox.

lettering noun letters drawn or painted.

lettuce noun (plural **lettuces**) a garden plant with broad crisp leaves used in salads. [from Latin]

leukaemia (say lew-kee-mee-a) noun a disease in which there are too many white corpuscles in the blood. [from Greek *leukos* = white + *haima* = blood]

level adjective
1 flat or horizontal. **2** at the same height or position etc. as others.

level noun (plural **levels**)
1 height, depth, position, or value etc., *Fix the shelves at eye level.* **2** a level surface. **3** a device that shows whether something is level.

on the level (informal) honest.

level verb (**levels, levelling, levelled**)
1 make or become level. **2** aim a gun or missile. **3** direct an accusation at a person. [from Latin *libra* = balance]

level crossing noun (plural **level crossings**) a place where a road crosses a railway at the same level.

lever noun (plural **levers**)
1 a bar that turns on a fixed point (the *fulcrum*) in order to lift something or force something open. **2** a bar used as a handle to operate machinery etc., *a gear lever.*

lever verb (**levers, levering, levered**) lift or move something by means of a lever. [from Latin *levare* = raise]

leverage noun
1 the force you need when you use a lever. **2** influence.

levity noun being humorous, especially at an unsuitable time; frivolity. [from Latin *levis* = lightweight]

levy verb (**levies, levying, levied**)
1 impose or collect a tax or other payment by the use of authority or force. **2** enrol, *levy an army.*

levy noun (plural **levies**) an amount of money paid in tax. [same origin as *lever*]

liability noun (plural **liabilities**)
1 being liable. **2** a debt or obligation. **3** a disadvantage or handicap.

liable adjective
1 likely to do or get something, *She is liable to colds. The cliff is liable to crumble.* **2** legally responsible for something.

liaison (say lee-ay-zon) noun (plural **liaisons**)
1 communication and cooperation between people or . groups. **2** a person who is a link or go-between. [from French *lier* = bind]

liar noun (plural **liars**) a person who tells lies. [from Old English]

libel (say ly-bel) noun (plural **libels**) an untrue written, printed, or broadcast statement that damages a person's reputation. (Compare *slander.*) **libellous** adjective

libel verb (**libels, libelling, libelled**) make a libel against someone.
[from Latin *libellus* = little book]

liberal adjective
1 giving generously. **2** given in large amounts. **3** not strict; tolerant. **liberally** adverb, **liberality** noun [same origin as *liberty*]

Liberal Democrat noun (plural Liberal Democrats) a member of the Liberal Democrat political party.

liberate verb (liberates, liberating, liberated) set free. **liberation** noun, **liberator** noun

liberty noun (plural **liberties**) freedom.

take liberties behave too casually or in too familiar a way. [from Latin *liber* = free]

librarian noun (plural **librarians**) a person in charge of or assisting in a library. **librarianship** noun

library (say ly-bra-ree) noun (plural **libraries**)

1 a place where books are kept for people to use or borrow. 2 a collection of books, records, films, etc. [from Latin *libraria* = bookshop]

lice plural of **louse**.

licence noun (plural **licences**)

1 an official permit to do or use or own something, *a driving licence.* 2 special freedom to avoid the usual rules or customs. [from Latin *licere* = be allowed]

license verb (licenses, licensing, licensed) give a licence to a person; authorize, *We are licensed to sell tobacco.*

lichen (say ly-ken or lich-en) noun (plural **lichens**) a dry-looking plant that grows on rocks, walls, trees, etc.

lick verb (licks, licking, licked)

1 move your tongue over something. 2 (of a wave or flame) move like a tongue; touch lightly. 3 (*slang*) defeat.

lid noun (plural **lids**)

1 a cover for a box or pot etc. 2 an eyelid.

lie[1] noun (plural **lies**) a statement that the person who makes it knows to be untrue.

lie verb (lies, lying, lied) tell a lie or lies; be deceptive. [from Old English *leogan*]

lie[2] verb (lies, lying, lay, lain)

1 be or get in a flat or resting position, *He lay on the grass. The cat has lain here all night.* 2 be or remain, *The island lies near the coast. The machinery lay idle.*

lie low keep yourself hidden. [from Old English *licgan*]

USAGE: See the note at **lay**[1].

lieutenant (say lef-ten-ant) noun (plural **lieutenants**)

1 an officer in the army or navy. 2 a deputy or chief assistant. [from French *lieu* = place + *tenant* = holding]

life noun (plural **lives**)

1 the ability to function and grow. 2 the period between birth and death. 3 living things, *Is there life on Mars?* 4 liveliness, *full of life.* 5 a biography.

lifebelt noun (plural **lifebelts**) a ring of material that will float, used to support someone's body in water.

lifeboat noun (plural **lifeboats**) a boat for rescuing people at sea.

life cycle noun (plural **life cycles**) the series of changes in the life of a living thing.

lifeguard noun (plural **lifeguards**) someone whose job is to rescue swimmers who are in difficulty.

life jacket noun (plural **life jackets**) a jacket of material that will float, used to support someone's body in water.

lifeless *adjective*
1 without life. 2 unconscious.
lifelessly *adverb*

lifelike *adjective* looking exactly
like a real person or thing.

lifetime *noun* (*plural* **lifetimes**)
the time for which someone is
alive.

lift *verb* (**lifts, lifting, lifted**)
1 raise or pick up something.
2 rise or go upwards. 3 (*informal*)
steal. 4 remove or abolish
something, *The ban has been
lifted.*

lift *noun* (*plural* **lifts**)
1 lifting. 2 a device for taking
people or goods from one floor or
level to another in a building.
3 a free ride in somebody else's
vehicle, *Can you give me a lift to
the station?*

ligament *noun* (*plural* **ligaments**)
a piece of the tough flexible
tissue that holds your bones
together. [from Latin *ligare*
= bind]

light¹ *noun* (*plural* **lights**)
1 radiation that stimulates the
sense of sight and makes things
visible. 2 something that
provides light, especially an
electric lamp. 3 a flame.
bring or **come to light** make or
become known.

light *adjective*
1 full of light; not dark. 2 pale,
light blue.

light *verb* (**lights, lighting, lit** or
lighted)
1 start a thing burning; kindle.
2 provide the light.
light up 1 put lights on, especially
at dusk. 2 make or become light

or bright.
[from Old English *leoht*]

USAGE: Say *He lit the lamps;
the lamps were lit* (not
'lighted'), but *She carried a
lighted torch* (not 'a lit torch').

light² *adjective*
1 having little weight; not heavy.
2 small in amount or force etc.,
light rain; a light punishment.
3 needing little effort, *light work.*
4 cheerful, not sad, *with a light
heart.* 5 not serious or profound,
light music. **lightly** *adverb*,
lightness *noun*

light *adverb* lightly; with only
a small load, *We were travelling
light.*
[from Old English *liht*]

lighten¹ *verb* (**lightens, lightening,
lightened**) make or become
lighter or brighter.

lighten² *verb* (**lightens, lightening,
lightened**) make or become
lighter or less heavy.

light-hearted *adjective*
1 cheerful and free from worry.
2 not serious.

lighthouse *noun* (*plural*
lighthouses) a tower with a bright
light at the top to guide or warn
ships.

lightning *noun* a flash of bright
light produced by natural
electricity during
a thunderstorm.
like lightning with very great
speed.

lightning conductor *noun*
(*plural* **lightning conductors**)
a metal rod or wire fixed on
a building to divert lightning
into the earth.

light year noun (plural **light years**) the distance that light travels in one year (about 9.5 million million km).

like[1] verb (**likes, liking, liked**) **1** think a person or thing is pleasant or satisfactory. **2** wish, *I should like to come.* [from Old English]

like[2] adjective similar; having some or all of the qualities of another person or thing, *They are as like as two peas.*

like noun a similar person or thing, *We shall not see his like again.*

like preposition **1** similar to; in the manner of, *He swims like a fish.* **2** in a suitable state for, *It looks like rain. I feel like a cup of tea.* [from Old Norse]

likelihood noun being likely; probability.

likely adjective (**likelier, likeliest**) **1** probable; expected to happen or be true etc., *Rain is likely.* **2** expected to be successful, *a likely lad; a likely spot.* [from **like**[2]]

liken verb (**likens, likening, likened**) compare, *He likened the human heart to a pump.*

likeness noun (plural **likenesses**) **1** a similarity in appearance; a resemblance. **2** a portrait.

liking noun a feeling that you like something, *She has a liking for ice cream.*

lilac noun **1** a bush with fragrant purple or white flowers. **2** pale purple. [from Persian *lilak* = bluish]

lilt noun (plural **lilts**) a light pleasant rhythm. **lilting** adjective

lily noun (plural **lilies**) a garden plant with trumpet-shaped flowers, growing from a bulb. [from Greek]

limb noun (plural **limbs**) **1** a leg, arm, or wing. **2** a large branch of a tree.

out on a limb isolated; without any support.

limber verb (**limbers, limbering, limbered**)

limber up exercise in preparation for an athletic activity.

lime[1] noun a white substance (calcium oxide) used in making cement and as a fertilizer. [from Old English *lim*]

lime[2] noun (plural **limes**) a green fruit like a small round lemon. **lime juice** noun [from Arabic *lima* = citrus fruit]

lime[3] noun (plural **limes**) a tree with yellow flowers. [from Old English *lind*]

limelight noun

in the limelight receiving a lot of publicity and attention. [from *lime*[1] which gives a bright light when heated, formerly used to light up the stage of a theatre]

limerick noun (plural **limericks**) a type of amusing poem with five lines. [named after Limerick, a town in Ireland]

limestone noun a kind of rock from which lime (calcium oxide) is obtained.

limit noun (plural **limits**) **1** a line, point, or level where something ends. **2** the greatest amount allowed, *the speed limit.*

limit verb (**limits, limiting, limited**) **1** keep something within certain

limits. **2** be a limit to something.
limitation noun
[from Latin limes = boundary]

limited company noun (plural
limited companies) a business
company whose shareholders
would have to pay only some of
its debts.

limp[1] verb (**limps, limping, limped**)
walk lamely.

limp[1] noun (plural **limps**)
a limping walk.

limp[2] adjective
1 not stiff or firm. **2** without
strength or energy. **limply**
adverb, **limpness** noun

limpet noun (plural **limpets**)
a small shellfish that attaches
itself firmly to rocks. [via Old
English from Latin]

line[1] noun (plural **lines**)
1 a long thin mark. **2** a row or
series of people or things; a row
of words. **3** a length of rope,
string, wire, etc. used for a special
purpose, a fishing line.
4 a railway; a line of railway
track. **5** a system of ships,
aircraft, buses, etc. **6** a way of
doing things or behaving; a type
of business.
in line 1 forming a straight line.
2 conforming.

line[1] verb (**lines, lining, lined**)
1 mark something with lines, Use
lined paper. **2** form something
into a line or lines, Line them up.
[from Old English]

line[2] verb (**lines, lining, lined**)
cover the inside of something.
[from linen (used for linings)]

lineage (say **lin**-ee-ij) noun (plural
lineages) ancestry; a line of
descendants from an ancestor.

linear (say **lin**-ee-er) adjective
1 arranged in a line. **2** to do with
a line or length.

linen noun
1 cloth made from flax. **2** shirts,
sheets, and tablecloths etc.
(which were formerly made of
linen). [from Latin linum = flax]

liner noun (plural **liners**) a large
ship or aircraft on a regular
route, usually carrying
passengers. [from line[1]]

-ling suffix forms nouns meaning
'having a certain quality' (e.g.
weakling) or diminutives
meaning 'little' (e.g. duckling).
[from Old English]

linger verb (**lingers, lingering,
lingered**) stay for a long time, as
if unwilling to leave; be slow to
leave. [from Old English]

lingerie (say **lan**-zher-ee) noun
women's underwear. [French,
from linge = linen]

linguistics noun the study of
languages. **linguistic** adjective

lining noun (plural **linings**) a layer
that covers the inside of
something. [from line[2]]

link noun (plural **links**)
1 one ring or loop of a chain.
2 a connection.

link verb (**links, linking, linked**)
join things together; connect.
linkage noun

links noun & plural noun a golf
course. [from Old English hlinc
= sandy ground near the
seashore (where golf was often
played)]

linoleum noun a stiff shiny floor
covering. [from Latin linum = flax
+ oleum = oil (because linseed oil
is used to make linoleum)]

linseed noun the seed of flax, from which oil is obtained. [from Latin *linum* = flax, + *seed*]

lint noun a soft material for covering wounds. [probably from old French *lin* = flax (from which lint was originally made)]

lion noun (plural **lions**) a large strong flesh-eating animal found in Africa and India. **lioness** noun [from Greek]

lip noun (plural **lips**)
1 either of the two fleshy edges of the mouth. **2** the edge of something hollow, such as a cup or crater. **3** the pointed part at the top of a jug etc., from which you pour things. [from Old English]

lip-reading noun understanding what a person says by watching the movements of his or her lips, not by hearing.

lipstick noun (plural **lipsticks**) a stick of a waxy substance for colouring the lips.

liqueur (say lik-yoor) noun (plural **liqueurs**) a strong sweet alcoholic drink. [French, = liquor]

liquid noun (plural **liquids**) a substance (such as water or oil) that flows freely but is not a gas.

liquid adjective
1 in the form of a liquid; flowing freely. **2** easily converted into cash, *the firm's liquid assets*. **liquidity** noun
[from Latin *liquidus* = flowing]

liquor noun
1 alcoholic drink. **2** juice produced in cooking; liquid in which food has been cooked. [from Latin]

liquorice (say lick-er-iss) noun
1 a black substance used in medicine and as a sweet. **2** the plant from whose root this substance is obtained. [from Greek *glykys* = sweet + *rhiza* = root]

lisp noun (plural **lisps**) a fault in speech in which *s* and *z* are pronounced like *th*. **lisp** verb

list noun (plural **lists**) a number of names, items, or figures etc. written or printed one after another.

list verb (**lists**, **listing**, **listed**) make a list of people or things.

listen verb (**listens**, **listening**, **listened**) pay attention in order to hear something. **listener** noun [from Old English]

listless adjective too tired to be active or enthusiastic. **listlessly** adverb, **listlessness** noun [from an old word *list* = desire, + *-less*]

lit past tense of **light**[1].

literacy noun the ability to read and write.

literal adjective
1 meaning exactly what is said, not metaphorical or exaggerated. **2** word for word, *a literal translation*. [from Latin *littera* = letter]

literally adverb really; exactly as stated, *The noise made me literally jump out of my seat.*

literature noun books and other writings, especially those considered to have been written well. [same origin as *literal*]

litigation noun (plural **litigations**) a lawsuit; the process of carrying on a lawsuit.

litmus *noun* a blue substance that is turned red by acids and can be turned back to blue by alkalis. [from Old Norse *litr* = dye + *mosi* = moss (because litmus is obtained from some kinds of moss)]

litmus paper *noun* paper stained with litmus.

litre *noun* (*plural* **litres**) a measure of liquid, about 1¾ pints.

litter *noun* (*plural* **litters**)
1 rubbish or untidy things left lying about. **2** straw etc. put down as bedding for animals. **3** the young animals born to one mother at one time. **4** a kind of stretcher.

litter *verb* (**litters, littering, littered**)
1 make a place untidy with litter. **2** spread straw etc. for animals. [from old French *litière* = bed]

little *adjective* (**less, least**) small in amount or size or intensity etc.; not great or big or much.
little by little gradually; by a small amount at a time.

little *adverb* not much, *I eat very little.*

live[1] (rhymes with *give*) *verb* (**lives, living, lived**)
1 have life; be alive. **2** have your home, *She lives in Glasgow.* **3** pass your life in a certain way, *He lived as a hermit.*
live down if you cannot live down a mistake or embarrassment, you cannot make people forget it.
live on use something as food; depend on for your living. [from Old English]

live[2] (rhymes with *hive*) *adjective*
1 alive. **2** burning, *live coals.*
3 carrying electricity. **4** broadcast while it is actually happening, not from a recording. [from *alive*]

livelihood *noun* (*plural* **livelihoods**) a way of earning money or providing enough food to support yourself. [from Old English *lif* = life + *lad* = course or way]

lively *adjective* (**livelier, liveliest**) full of life or action; vigorous and cheerful. **liveliness** *noun*

liver *noun* (*plural* **livers**)
1 a large organ of the body, found in the abdomen, that processes digested food and purifies the blood. **2** an animal's liver used as food. [from Old English]

livestock *noun* farm animals.

livid *adjective*
1 bluish-grey, *a livid bruise.* **2** furiously angry. [from Latin]

living *noun*
1 being alive. **2** the way that a person lives, *a good standard of living.* **3** a way of earning money or providing enough food to support yourself.

living room *noun* (*plural* **living rooms**) a room for general use during the day.

lizard *noun* (*plural* **lizards**) a reptile with a rough or scaly skin, four legs, and a long tail. [from Latin]

load *noun* (*plural* **loads**)
1 something carried; a burden. **2** the quantity that can be carried. **3** the total amount of electric current supplied. **4** (*informal*) a large amount, *It's a load of nonsense. You could earn loads of money.*

load *verb* (**loads, loading, loaded**)
1 put a load in or on something.

2 fill heavily. **3** weight with something heavy, *loaded dice.* **4** put a bullet or shell into a gun; put a film into a camera. **5** enter data etc. into a computer.
[from Old English]

loaf[1] *noun* (*plural* **loaves**)
1 a shaped mass of bread baked in one piece. **2** minced or chopped meat etc. moulded into an oblong shape.
use your loaf think; use common sense.
[from Old English]

loaf[2] *verb* (**loafs, loafing, loafed**) spend time idly; loiter or stand about. **loafer** *noun* [probably from German *Landläufer* = a tramp]

loam *noun* rich soil containing clay, sand, and decayed leaves etc. **loamy** *adjective*

loan *noun* (*plural* **loans**)
1 something lent, especially money. **2** lending; being lent, *These books are on loan from the library.*

loathe (rhymes with *clothe*) *verb* (**loathes, loathing, loathed**) feel great hatred and disgust for something; detest. **loathing** *noun*

loathsome *adjective* making you feel great hatred and disgust; detestable.

lobby *noun* (*plural* **lobbies**)
1 an entrance hall. **2** a group who lobby Members of Parliament etc.

lobby *verb* (**lobbies, lobbying, lobbied**) try to influence a Member of Parliament etc. in favour of a special interest.
[same origin as *lodge*: the lobby of the Houses of Parliament is where members of the public can meet Members]

lobster *noun* (*plural* **lobsters**) a large shellfish with eight legs and two long claws. [via Old English from Latin]

local *adjective* belonging to a particular place or a small area.
locally *adverb*

local *noun* (*plural* **locals**) (*informal*)
1 someone who lives in a particular district. **2** a public house near a person's home.
[from Latin *locus* = a place]

local anaesthetic *noun* (*plural* **local anaesthetics**) an anaesthetic affecting only the part of the body where it is applied.

localized *adjective* restricted to a particular place, *localized showers.*

locate *verb* (**locates, locating, located**)
1 discover where something is, *locate the electrical fault.* **2** situate something in a particular place, *The cinema is located in High Street.* [from Latin *locare* = to place]

location *noun* (*plural* **locations**)
1 the place where something is situated. **2** discovering where something is; locating.
on location filmed in natural surroundings, not in a studio.

lock[1] *noun* (*plural* **locks**)
1 a fastening that is opened with a key or other device. **2** a section of a canal or river fitted with gates and sluices so that boats can be raised or lowered to the level beyond each gate.
3 a wrestling-hold that keeps an opponent's arm or leg from moving.
lock, stock, and barrel completely.

lock verb (locks, locking, locked)
1 fasten or secure something by means of a lock. **2** store something away securely. **3** become fixed in one place; jam. [from Old English *loc*]

lock² noun (plural **locks**) a clump of hair. [from Old English *locc*]

locker noun (plural **lockers**) a small cupboard or compartment where things can be stowed safely.

locket noun (plural **lockets**) a small ornamental case for holding a portrait or lock of hair etc., worn on a chain round the neck. [from old French *locquet* = small latch or lock]

locks plural noun the hair of the head.

locomotive noun (plural **locomotives**) a railway engine.

locomotive adjective to do with movement or the ability to move, *locomotive power*. **locomotion** noun [from Latin *locus* = place + *motivus* = moving]

locus (say loh-kus) noun (plural **loci** (say loh-ky))
1 the exact place of something. **2** (in geometry) the path traced by a moving point, or made by points placed in a certain way. [Latin, = place]

locust noun (plural **locusts**) a kind of grasshopper that travels in large swarms which eat all the plants in an area.

lodge noun (plural **lodges**)
1 a small house, especially at the gates of a park. **2** a porter's room at the entrance to a college, factory, etc. **3** a beaver's or otter's lair.

lodge verb (lodges, lodging, lodged)
1 stay somewhere as a lodger. **2** provide a person with somewhere to live temporarily. **3** become stuck or caught somewhere, *The ball lodged in the tree*. **lodging house** noun **lodge a complaint** complain formally. [from old French *loge* = hut, from Germanic]

lodger noun (plural **lodgers**) a person who pays to live in another person's house.

loft noun (plural **lofts**) a room or storage space under the roof of a house or barn etc. [from Old Norse]

lofty adjective
1 tall. **2** noble. **3** haughty. **loftily** adverb, **loftiness** noun [from an old sense of *loft* = sky]

log¹ noun (plural **logs**)
1 a large piece of a tree that has fallen or been cut down; a piece cut off this. **2** a detailed record of a ship's voyage, aircraft's flight, etc. kept in a logbook.

log verb (logs, logging, logged) enter facts in a logbook.
log in (or **on**), **log out** (or **off**) connect and disconnect a terminal correctly to or from a computer system.

log² noun (plural **logs**) a logarithm, *log tables*.

logarithm noun (plural **logarithms**) one of a series of numbers set out in tables which make it possible to do sums by adding and subtracting instead of multiplying and dividing. [from Greek *logos* = reckoning + *arithmos* = number]

loggerheads *plural noun*
at loggerheads disagreeing or quarrelling.
[from an old word *loggerhead* = a stupid person]

logic *noun*
1 reasoning; a system of reasoning. **2** the principles used in designing a computer; the circuits involved in this. [from Greek *logos* = word, reason]

logical *adjective* using logic; reasoning or reasoned correctly.
logically *adverb*, **logicality** *noun*

-logical *suffix* forms adjectives (e.g. *biological*) from nouns ending in *-logy*.

-logist *suffix* forms nouns meaning 'an expert in or student of something' (e.g. *biologist*).
[same origin as *-logy*]

logo (*say* loh-goh or log-oh) *noun* (*plural* logos) a printed symbol used by a business company etc. as its emblem. [short for *logograph*, from Greek *logos* = word, + *-graph*]

-logy or **-ology** *suffixes* form nouns meaning a subject of study (e.g. *biology*). [from Greek *-logia* = study]

loiter *verb* (loiters, loitering, loitered) linger or stand about idly. **loiterer** *noun*

lollipop *noun* (*plural* lollipops) a large round hard sweet on a stick. [origin unknown]

lonely *adjective* (lonelier, loneliest) **1** sad because you are on your own. **2** solitary. **3** far from inhabited places; not often visited or used, *a lonely road*. **loneliness** *noun* [from *lone*]

long[1] *adjective*
1 measuring a lot from one end to the other. **2** taking a lot of time, *a long holiday*. **3** having a certain length, *The river is 10 miles long*.

long *adverb*
1 for a long time, *Have you been waiting long?* **2** at a long time before or after, *They left long ago*. **3** throughout a time, *all night long*.
as long as or **so long as** provided that; on condition that.
[from Old English *lang*]

long[2] *verb* (longs, longing, longed) feel a strong desire. [from Old English *langian*]

long division *noun* dividing one number by another and writing down all the calculations.

longing *noun* (*plural* longings) a strong desire.

longitude *noun* (*plural* longitudes) the distance east or west, measured in degrees, from the Greenwich meridian. [from Latin *longitudo* = length]

long jump *noun* an athletic contest in which competitors jump as far as possible along the ground in one leap.

long-sighted *adjective* able to see distant things clearly but not things close to you.

long-winded *adjective* talking or writing at great length.

look *verb* (looks, looking, looked) **1** use your eyes; turn your eyes in a particular direction. **2** face in a particular direction. **3** have a certain appearance; seem, *You look sad*.
look after 1 protect or take care of someone. **2** be in charge of something.

look down on despise.

look forward to be waiting eagerly for something you expect.

look into investigate.

look out be careful.

look up 1 search for information about something. **2** improve in prospects, *Things are looking up.*

look up to admire or respect.

look noun (plural **looks**)
1 the act of looking; a gaze or glance. **2** appearance, *I don't like the look of this place.*
[from Old English]

looking-glass noun (plural **looking-glasses**) a glass mirror.

lookout noun (plural **lookouts**)
1 looking out or watching for something. **2** a place from which you can keep watch. **3** a person whose job is to keep watch.
4 a future prospect, *It's a poor lookout for us.* **5** (informal) a person's own concern, *If he wastes his money, that's his lookout.*

loom[1] noun (plural **looms**)
a machine for weaving cloth.
[from Old English]

loom[2] verb (**looms**, **looming**, **loomed**) appear suddenly; seem large or close and threatening, *An iceberg loomed up through the fog.* [probably from old Dutch]

loop noun (plural **loops**) the shape made by a curve crossing itself; a piece of string, ribbon, wire, etc. made into this shape.

loophole noun (plural **loopholes**)
1 a way of avoiding a law or rule or promise etc. without actually breaking it. **2** a narrow opening in the wall of a fort etc.

loose adjective
1 not tight; not firmly fixed, *a loose tooth.* **2** not tied up or shut in, *There's a lion loose!* **3** not packed in a box or packet etc. **4** not exact, *a loose translation.*
loosely adverb, **looseness** noun
at a loose end with nothing to do.

loosen verb (**loosens**, **loosening**, **loosened**) make or become loose or looser.

loot noun stolen things; goods taken from an enemy.

loot verb (**loots**, **looting**, **looted**)
1 rob a place or an enemy, especially in a time of war or disorder. **2** take something as loot. **looter** noun
[from Hindi]

lop verb (**lops**, **lopping**, **lopped**) cut away branches or twigs; cut off.

lopsided adjective with one side lower than the other; uneven.

lord noun (plural **lords**)
1 a nobleman, especially one who is allowed to use the title 'Lord' in front of his name. **2** a master or ruler. **lordly** adjective, **lordship** noun
Lord Mayor the mayor of a large city.
Our Lord Jesus Christ.
the Lord God.
[from Old English *hlaford* = person who keeps the bread (compare *lady*)]

lorry noun (plural **lorries**) a large strong motor vehicle for carrying heavy goods or troops. [origin unknown]

lose verb (**loses**, **losing**, **lost**)
1 be without something that you once had, especially because you cannot find it. **2** fail to keep or obtain something, *We lost control*

3 be defeated in a contest or argument etc. **4** cause the loss of, *That fall lost us the game.* **5** (of a clock or watch) become behind the correct time. **loser** *noun*

be lost or **lose your way** not know where you are or which is the right path.

lose your life be killed.

lost cause an idea or policy etc. that is failing.

loss *noun* (*plural* **losses**)
1 losing something. **2** something lost.

be at a loss not know what to do or say.

lot *noun* (*plural* **lots**)
1 a number of people or things. **2** one of a set of objects used in choosing or deciding something by chance, *We drew lots to see who should go first.* **3** a person's share or fate. **4** something for sale at an auction. **5** a piece of land.

the lot or **the whole lot** everything; all.
[from Old English]

lotion *noun* (*plural* **lotions**)
a liquid for putting on the skin.
[from Latin *lotio* = washing]

lottery *noun* (*plural* **lotteries**)
a way of raising money by selling numbered tickets and giving prizes to people who hold winning numbers, which are chosen by a method depending on chance (compare *lot* 2).

loud *adjective*
1 easily heard; producing much noise. **2** unpleasantly bright; gaudy, *loud colours.* **loudly** *adverb*, **loudness** *noun*

loudspeaker *noun* (*plural* **loudspeakers**) a device that changes electrical signals into sound.

lounge *noun* (*plural* **lounges**)
a sitting room.

lounge *verb* (**lounges, lounging, lounged**) sit or stand in a lazy and relaxed way.

louse *noun* (*plural* **lice**) a small insect that lives as a parasite on animals or plants. [from Old English]

lousy *adjective* (**lousier, lousiest**)
1 full of lice. **2** (*slang*) very bad or unpleasant.

lout *noun* (*plural* **louts**) a bad-mannered man. [origin unknown]

lovable *adjective* easy to love.

love *noun* (*plural* **loves**)
1 great liking or affection. **2** sexual affection or passion. **3** a loved person; a sweetheart. **4** (in tennis) no score; nil.

in love feeling strong love.

make love have sexual intercourse.

love *verb* (**loves, loving, loved**)
feel love for a person or thing. **lover** *noun*, **lovingly** *adverb*
[from Old English]

love affair *noun* (*plural* **love affairs**) a romantic or sexual relationship between two people in love.

lovely *adjective* (**lovelier, loveliest**)
1 beautiful. **2** very pleasant or enjoyable. **loveliness** *noun*

lover *noun* (*plural* **lovers**) a person who someone is having a sexual relationship with but is not married to.

lovesick *adjective* longing for someone you love, especially someone who does not love you.

low *adjective* not high. **lowness** *noun*

low *adverb* at or to a low level or position etc., *The plane was flying low.*
[from Old Norse]

lower *adjective & adverb* less high.

lower *verb* (**lowers, lowering, lowered**) make or become lower.

loyal *adjective* always firmly supporting your friends or group or country etc. **loyally** *adverb*, **loyalty** *noun* [from old French]

lozenge *noun* (*plural* **lozenges**)
1 a small flavoured tablet, especially one containing medicine. 2 a diamond shape.

Ltd. *abbreviation* limited.

lubricant *noun* (*plural* **lubricants**) a lubricating substance.

lubricate *verb* (**lubricates, lubricating, lubricated**) oil or grease something so that it moves smoothly. **lubrication** *noun* [from Latin *lubricus* = slippery]

lucid *adjective*
1 clear and easy to understand. 2 sane. **lucidly** *adverb*, **lucidity** *noun* [from Latin *lucidus* = bright]

luck *noun*
1 the way things happen without being planned; chance. 2 good fortune, *It will bring you luck.*
[from old German]

lucky *adjective* (**luckier, luckiest**) having or bringing or resulting from good luck. **luckily** *adverb*

ludicrous *adjective* ridiculous. **ludicrously** *adverb* [from Latin *ludere* = to play or have fun]

luggage *noun* suitcases and bags etc. holding things for taking on a journey. [from *lug*]

lukewarm *adjective*
1 only slightly warm; tepid. 2 not very enthusiastic, *lukewarm applause.* [from an old word *luke* = tepid, + *warm*]

lull *verb* (**lulls, lulling, lulled**) soothe or calm; send someone to sleep.

lull *noun* (*plural* **lulls**) a short period of quiet or inactivity. [imitating the sounds you make to soothe a child]

lullaby *noun* (*plural* **lullabies**) a song that is sung to send a baby to sleep. [from *lull* + baby or bye-byes, a child's word for bed or sleep]

lumbago *noun* pain in the muscles of the lower back.

lumber *noun*
1 unwanted furniture etc.; junk.
2 (*American*) timber.

lumber *verb* (**lumbers, lumbering, lumbered**)
1 leave someone with an unwanted or unpleasant task. 2 move in a heavy clumsy way. [origin unknown]

luminous *adjective* glowing in the dark. **luminosity** *noun*

lump¹ *noun* (*plural* **lumps**)
1 a solid piece of something. 2 a swelling. **lumpy** *adjective*

lump *verb* (**lumps, lumping, lumped**) put or treat things together in a group because you regard them as alike in some way.
[origin unknown]

lump² *verb* (**lumps, lumping, lumped**)

lump it (*informal*) put up with something you dislike.
[from an old word *lump* = look sulky]

magazine

lump

...g a number

...acies)

insanity... great foolishness.

lunatic noun (plural **lunatics**) an insane person. **lunatic** adjective [from Latin *luna* = moon (because formerly people were thought to be affected by changes of the moon)]

lunch noun (plural **lunches**) a meal eaten in the middle of the day. **lunch** verb [short for **luncheon**]

lung noun (plural **lungs**) either of the two parts of the body, in the chest, used in breathing.

lunge verb (**lunges**, **lunging**, **lunged**) thrust the body forward suddenly. **lunge** noun [from French *allonger* = lengthen]

lupin noun (plural **lupins**) a garden plant with tall spikes of flowers.

lurch[1] verb (**lurches**, **lurching**, **lurched**) stagger; lean suddenly to one side. **lurch** noun [originally a sailor's word: origin unknown]

lurch[2] noun
leave somebody in the lurch leave somebody in difficulties. [from old French]

lure verb (**lures**, **luring**, **lured**) tempt a person or animal into a trap; entice. **lure** noun

lurid (say **lewr-id**) adjective
1 in very bright colours; gaudy.
2 sensational and shocking, *the lurid details of the murder*. **luridly** adverb, **luridness** noun [from Latin]

lurk verb (**lurks**, **lurking**, **lurked**) wait where you cannot be seen.

luscious (say **lush-us**) adjective delicious. **lusciously** adverb, **lusciousness** noun [origin unknown]

lush adjective
1 growing thickly and strongly, *lush grass*. 2 luxurious. **lushly** adverb, **lushness** noun

lust noun (plural **lusts**) powerful desire, especially sexual desire. **lustful** adjective

lust verb (**lusts**, **lusting**, **lusted**) have a powerful desire for a person or thing, *people who lust after power*.
[Old English, = pleasure]

lusty adjective (**lustier**, **lustiest**) strong and vigorous. **lustily** adverb, **lustiness** noun [originally = lively and cheerful: same origin as *lust*]

luxuriant adjective growing abundantly. [same origin as *luxury*]

USAGE: Do not confuse with *luxurious*.

luxury noun (plural **luxuries**)
1 something expensive that you enjoy but do not really need.
2 expensive and comfortable surroundings, *a life of luxury*. **luxurious** adjective, **luxuriously** adverb [from Latin *luxus* = plenty]

-ly suffix forms
1 adjectives (e.g. *friendly, heavenly, sickly*), 2 adverbs from adjectives (e.g. *boldly, sweetly, thoroughly*). [from Old English]

lying present participle of **lie**[1] and **lie**[2].

lynch verb (**lynches**, **lynching**, **lynched**) join together to execute or punish someone violently without a proper trial, especially by hanging them. [named after William Lynch, an American judge who allowed this kind of punishment in about 1780]

lyric (say **li**-rik) noun (plural **lyrics**)
1 a short poem that expresses thoughts and feelings. **2** the words of a song. **lyrical** adjective, **lyrically** adverb [from Greek lyrikos = to be sung to a kind of small harp called a lyre]

Mm

MA abbreviation Master of Arts.

mac noun (plural **macs**) (informal) a mackintosh.

macaroni noun flour-paste (pasta) formed into tubes.

macaroon noun (plural **macaroons**) a small sweet cake or biscuit made with ground almonds.

machine noun (plural **machines**) something with parts that work together to do a job. [from Greek mechane = device]

machine-gun noun (plural **machine-guns**) a gun that can keep firing bullets quickly one after another.

machinery noun
1 machines. **2** mechanism. **3** an organized system for doing something.

mackerel noun (plural **mackerel**) a sea fish used as food. [from old French]

mackintosh noun (p. **mackintoshes**) a raincoa [named after the Scottish inventor of a waterproof material, C. Macintosh]

mad adjective (**madder**, **maddest**)
1 having something wrong with the mind; insane. **2** extremely foolish. **3** very keen, He is mad about football. **4** (informal) very excited or annoyed. **madly** adverb, **madness** noun, **madman** noun

like mad (informal) with great speed, energy, or enthusiasm.

madam noun a word used when speaking politely to a woman, Can I help you, madam? [from French ma dame = my lady]

mad cow disease noun BSE.

madden verb (**maddens**, **maddening**, **maddened**) make a person mad or angry.

mafia noun
1 a large organization of criminals in Italy, Sicily, and the United States of America. **2** any group of people believed to act together in a sinister way. [Italian, = bragging]

magazine noun (plural **magazines**)
1 a paper-covered publication that comes out regularly, with articles or stories etc. by a number of writers. **2** the part of a gun that holds the cartridges. **3** a store for weapons and ammunition or for explosives. **4** a device that holds film for a camera or slides for a projector. [from Arabic makhazin = storehouses]

magenta (*say* ma-**jen**-ta) *noun*
a colour between bright red and
purple. [named after Magenta, a
town in north Italy, where
Napoleon III won a battle in the
year when the dye was
discovered (1859)]

maggot *noun* (*plural* **maggots**)
the larva of some kinds of fly.
maggoty *adjective* [origin
unknown]

magic *noun* the art or pretended
art of making things happen by
secret or unusual powers. **magic**
adjective, **magical** *adjective*,
magically *adverb* [from old
Persian *magus* = priest; later
= astrologer or wizard]

magician *noun* (*plural*
magicians)
1 a person who does magic tricks.
2 a wizard.

magistrate *noun* (*plural*
magistrates) an official who
hears and judges minor cases in
a local court. **magistracy** *noun*
[from Latin *magister* = master]

magnanimous (*say* mag-**nan**-im-
us) *adjective* generous and
forgiving, not petty-minded.
magnanimously *adverb*,
magnanimity *noun* [from Latin
magnus = great + *animus* = mind]

magnate *noun* (*plural* **magnates**)
a wealthy influential person,
especially in business. [from
Latin *magnus* = great]

magnesium *noun* a silvery-white
metal that burns with a very
bright flame.

magnet *noun* (*plural* **magnets**)
a piece of iron or steel that can
attract iron and that points north
and south when it is hung up.
magnetism *noun*

magnetic *adjective* having the
powers of a magnet. **magnetically**
adverb

magnetize *verb* (**magnetizes**,
magnetizing, **magnetized**)
1 make into a magnet. 2 attract
like a magnet. **magnetization**
noun

magneto (*say* mag-**neet**-oh) *noun*
(*plural* **magnetos**) a small
electric generator using magnets.

magnificent *adjective*
1 grand or splendid in
appearance etc. 2 excellent.
magnificently *adverb*,
magnificence *noun* [from Latin
magnificus = splendid]

magnify *verb* (**magnifies**,
magnifying, **magnified**) make
something look or seem bigger
than it really is. **magnification**
noun, **magnifier** *noun* [from Latin
magnus = great + *facere* = make]

magnifying glass *noun* (*plural*
magnifying glasses) a lens that
magnifies things.

magnitude *noun* (*plural*
magnitudes)-
1 size or extent. 2 importance.
[from Latin *magnus* = great]

magpie *noun* (*plural* **magpies**)
a noisy bird with black and white
feathers, related to the crow.
[from *Mag* (short for Margaret)
+ an old word *pie* = magpie]

mahogany *noun* a hard brown
wood. [origin unknown]

maid *noun* (*plural* **maids**)
1 a female servant. 2 (*old use*)
a girl. **maidservant** *noun* [short
for *maiden*]

maiden *noun* (*plural* **maidens**)
(*old use*) a girl. **maidenhood** *noun*

maiden adjective
1 not married, *a maiden aunt.*
2 first, *a maiden voyage.*
[from Old English]

maiden name noun (plural
maiden names) a woman's family
name before she married.

maiden over noun (plural
maiden overs) a cricket over in
which no runs are scored.

mail[1] noun letters or parcels etc.
sent by post.

mail order ordering goods by
post.
[from old French *male* = a bag]

mail[2] noun armour made of metal
rings joined together, *a suit of
chain mail.*
[from Latin *macula* = mesh]

mailing list noun (plural **mailing
lists**) a list of names and
addresses of people to whom an
organization sends information
from time to time.

mail order noun a system for
buying and selling goods by post.

main adjective largest or most
important.

main noun
1 the main pipe or cable in
a public system carrying water,
gas, or (usually called **mains**)
electricity to a building. 2 (*old
use*) the seas, *Drake sailed the
Spanish main.*

main clause noun (plural **main
clauses**) a clause that can be used
as a complete sentence.
(Compare *subordinate clause.*)

mainland noun the main part of
a country or continent, not the
islands round it.

mainly adverb
1 chiefly. 2 almost completely.
3 usually.

mainstream noun the most
widely accepted ideas or
opinions about something,
*Fascism is not in the mainstream
of British politics.*

maintain verb (**maintains,
maintaining, maintained**)
1 cause something to continue;
keep in existence. 2 keep a thing
in good condition. 3 provide
money for a person to live on.
4 state that something is true.

maintenance noun [from Latin
manu = by hand + *tenere* = to
hold]

maize noun a tall kind of corn
with large seeds on cobs.

majestic adjective
1 stately and dignified.
2 imposing. **majestically** adverb

majesty noun (plural **majesties**)
1 the title of a king or queen, *Her
Majesty the Queen.* 2 being
majestic. [from old French;
related to *major*]

major adjective
1 greater; very important, *major
roads.* 2 of the musical scale that
has a semitone after the 3rd and
7th notes. (Compare *minor.*)

major noun (plural **majors**) an
army officer ranking next above
a captain.
[Latin, = larger, greater]

majority noun (plural **majorities**)
1 the greatest part of a group of
people or things. (Compare
minority.) 2 the difference
between numbers of votes, *She
had a majority of 25 over her
opponent.* 3 the age at which
a person becomes an adult
according to the law (now 18,

formerly 21 years of age), *He attained his majority.* [same origin as *major*]

make *verb* (**makes, making, made**)
1 bring something into existence, especially by putting things together. **2** gain or earn, *She makes £5,000 a year.* **3** cause or compel, *Make him repeat it.* **4** achieve, *The swimmer just made the shore.* **5** reckon, *What do you make the time?* **6** perform an action etc., *make an effort.* **7** arrange for use, *make the beds.* **8** cause to be successful or happy, *Her visit made my day.*
make do manage with something that is not what you really want.
make for go towards.
make love 1 have sexual intercourse. **2** (*old use*) try to win someone's love.
make off go away quickly.
make out 1 manage to see, hear, or understand something. **2** claim or pretend that something is true.
make up 1 build or put together. **2** invent a story etc. **3** compensate for something. **4** put on make-up.
make up your mind decide.
make *noun* (*plural* **makes**)
1 making; how something is made. **2** a brand of goods; something made by a particular firm.
makeshift *adjective* improvised or used because you have nothing better, *We used a box as a makeshift table.* [from an old phrase *make shift* = manage somehow, put up with]
make-up *noun*
1 cosmetics. **2** the way something is made up. **3** a person's character.

mal- *prefix*
1 bad. **2** badly (as in *malnourished*). [from Latin *male* = badly]

maladjusted *adjective* unable to fit in or cope with other people or your own circumstances. [from *mal-* + *adjusted*]

malapropism *noun* (*plural* **malapropisms**) a comical confusion of words, e.g. using *hooligan* instead of *hurricane*. [named after Mrs Malaprop in Sheridan's play *The Rivals*, who made mistakes of this kind]

malaria *noun* a feverish disease spread by mosquitoes. **malarial** *adjective* [from Italian *mala aria* = bad air, which was once thought to cause the disease]

male *adjective*
1 belonging to the sex that reproduces by fertilizing egg-cells produced by the female. **2** of men, *a male voice choir.*
male *noun* (*plural* **males**) a male person, animal, or plant. [from old French; related to *masculine*]

male chauvinist *noun* (*plural* **male chauvinists**) a man who thinks that women are not as good as men.

malevolent (*say* ma-lev-ol-ent) *adjective* wishing to harm people. **malevolently** *adverb*, **malevolence** *noun* [from *mal-* + Latin *volens* = wishing]

malfunction *noun* (*plural* **malfunctions**) faulty functioning, *a malfunction in the computer.*
malfunction *verb* (**malfunctions, malfunctioning, malfunctioned**) fail to work properly.

malice noun the desire to harm others or to tease. **malicious** adjective, **maliciously** adverb [from Latin malus = evil]

malign (say mal-I'n) adjective
1 harmful, a malign influence.
2 showing malice. **malignity** (say mal-**ig**-nit-ee) noun [from Latin malignare = plot wickedly]

malignant adjective
1 (of a tumour) growing uncontrollably. 2 full of malice. **malignantly** adverb, **malignancy** noun [same origin as malign]

malleable adjective
1 able to be pressed or hammered into shape. 2 easy to influence; adaptable. **malleability** noun [from Latin malleare = to hammer]

mallet noun (plural **mallets**)
1 a large hammer, usually made of wood. 2 an implement with a long handle, used in croquet or polo for striking the ball. [from Latin malleus = a hammer]

malnutrition noun bad health because you do not have enough food or the right kind of food. **malnourished** adjective

malt noun dried barley used in brewing, making vinegar, etc. **malted** adjective

maltreat verb (**maltreats, maltreating, maltreated**) ill-treat. **maltreatment** noun

mammal noun (plural **mammals**) any animal which gives birth to live babies which are fed with milk from the mother's body. **mammalian** (say mam-**ay**-lee-an) adjective [from Latin mamma = breast]

mammoth noun (plural **mammoths**) an extinct elephant with a hairy skin and curved tusks.

mammoth adjective huge. [from Russian]

man noun (plural **men**)
1 a grown-up male human being.
2 an individual person.
3 mankind. 4 a piece used in chess etc.

man verb (**mans, manning, manned**) supply with people to work something, Man the pumps! [from Old English]

manacle noun (plural **manacles**) a fetter or handcuff.

manacle verb (**manacles, manacling, manacled**) fasten with manacles. [from Latin manus = hand]

manage verb (**manages, managing, managed**)
1 be able to cope with something difficult. 2 be in charge of a shop, factory, etc. **manageable** adjective [from Italian maneggiare = to handle]

management noun
1 managing. 2 managers; the people in charge.

manager noun (plural **managers**) a person who manages something. **manageress** noun, **managerial** (say man-a-**jeer**-ee-al) adjective

mandarin noun (plural **mandarins**)
1 an important official. 2 a kind of small orange. [via Portuguese and Malay (a language spoken in Malaysia) from Sanskrit]

mane noun (plural **manes**) the long hair on a horse's or lion's neck.

manganese noun a hard brittle metal.

manger noun (plural **mangers**) a trough in a stable etc., for horses or cattle to feed from. [from French *manger* = eat]

mangle verb (**mangles, mangling, mangled**) damage something by crushing or cutting it roughly. [from old French]

mango noun (plural **mangoes**) a tropical fruit with yellow pulp.

manhandle verb (**manhandles, manhandling, manhandled**) treat or push roughly.

manhole noun (plural **manholes**) a space or opening, usually with a cover, by which a person can get into a sewer or boiler etc. to inspect or repair it.

manhood noun
1 the condition of being a man.
2 manly qualities.

mania noun (plural **manias**)
1 violent madness. 2 great enthusiasm, *a mania for sport*. **maniac** noun, **manic** adjective [Greek, = madness]

manicure noun (plural **manicures**) care and treatment of the hands and nails. **manicure** verb, **manicurist** noun [from Latin *manus* = hand + *cura* = care]

manifest adjective clear and obvious. **manifestly** adverb

manifesto noun (plural **manifestos**) a public statement of a group's or person's policy or principles.

manifold adjective of many kinds; very varied. [from *many* + *-fold*]

manipulate verb (**manipulates, manipulating, manipulated**) handle or arrange something cleverly or cunningly. **manipulation** noun, **manipulator** noun [from Latin *manus* = hand]

mankind noun human beings in general.

manly adjective
1 suitable for a man. 2 brave and strong. **manliness** noun

manner noun
1 the way something happens or is done. 2 a person's way of behaving. 3 sort, *all manner of things*. [from old French]

mannerism noun (plural **mannerisms**) a person's own particular gesture or way of speaking.

manners plural noun how a person behaves with other people; politeness.

manoeuvre (say man-**oo**-ver) noun (plural **manoeuvres**) a difficult or skilful or cunning action.

manoeuvre verb (**manoeuvres, manoeuvring, manoeuvred**) move carefully and skilfully. **manoeuvrable** adjective [via French from Latin *manu operari* = work by hand]

manor noun (plural **manors**)
1 a manor house. 2 the land belonging to a manor house. **manorial** adjective [from old French; related to *mansion*]

manor house noun (plural **manor houses**) a large important house in the country.

manpower noun the number of people who are working or needed or available for work on something.

mansion noun (plural **mansions**)
a large stately house. [from Latin
mansio = a place to stay,
a dwelling]

manslaughter noun killing
a person unlawfully but without
meaning to.

mantelpiece noun (plural
mantelpieces) a shelf above
a fireplace.

mantle noun (plural **mantles**)
1 a cloak. 2 a covering, a mantle
of snow.

manual adjective worked by or
done with the hands, a manual
typewriter, manual work.
manually adverb

manual noun (plural **manuals**)
a handbook containing
instructions etc..
[from Latin manus = hand]

manufacture verb
(**manufactures**, **manufacturing**,
manufactured) make things,
especially on a large scale.
manufacture noun, **manufacturer**
noun [from Latin manu = by
hand + facere = make]

manure noun fertilizer,
especially dung.

manuscript noun (plural
manuscripts) something written
or typed but not printed. [from
Latin manu = by hand + scriptum
= written]

Manx adjective to do with the Isle
of Man.

many adjective (**more**, **most**) great
in number; numerous, many
people.

many noun many people or
things, Many were found.

Maori (rhymes with flowery) noun
(plural **Maoris**)
1 a member of the aboriginal
people of New Zealand. 2 their
language.

map noun (plural **maps**)
a diagram of part or all of the
earth's surface or of the sky.

map verb (**maps**, **mapping**,
mapped) make a map of an area.
map out plan the details of
something.
[from Latin mappa mundi = sheet
of the world]

marathon noun (plural
marathons) a long-distance race
for runners. [named after
Marathon in Greece, from which
a messenger is said to have run
to Athens (about 40 kilometres)
to announce that the Greeks had
defeated the Persian army]

marauding adjective going about
in search of plunder or prey.
marauder noun [from French
maraud = rogue]

marble noun (plural **marbles**)
1 a small glass ball used in
games. 2 a kind of limestone
polished and used in sculpture or
building. [from Greek marmaros
= shining stone]

march verb (**marches**, **marching**,
marched)
1 walk with regular steps. 2 make
somebody walk somewhere, He
marched them up the hill. **marcher**
noun

march noun (plural **marches**)
1 marching. 2 music suitable for
marching to.
[from old French]

mare noun (plural **mares**) a female
horse or donkey.

mare's nest *noun* a discovery that seems interesting but turns out to be false or worthless.

margarine (*say* mar-ja-**reen** or mar-ga-**reen**) *noun* a substance used like butter, made from animal or vegetable fats. [from French]

margin *noun* (*plural* **margins**)
1 an edge or border. **2** the blank space between the edge of a page and the writing or pictures etc. on it. **3** the difference between two scores or prices etc., *She won by a narrow margin.* [from Latin]

marginal *adjective*
1 in a margin, *marginal notes.* **2** very slight, *a marginal difference.* **marginally** *adverb*

marginal seat *noun* (*plural* **marginal seats**) a constituency where a Member of Parliament was elected with only a small majority and may be defeated in the next election.

marine (*say* ma-**reen**) *adjective* of or concerned with the sea.

marine *noun* (*plural* **marines**) a member of the troops who are trained to serve at sea as well as on land.
[from Latin *mare* = sea]

marionette *noun* (*plural* **marionettes**) a puppet worked by strings or wires. [French, = little Mary]

maritime *adjective*
1 to do with the sea or ships. **2** found near the sea. [same origin as *marine*]

mark[1] *noun* (*plural* **marks**)
1 a spot, dot, line, or stain etc. on something. **2** a number or letter etc. put on a piece of work to show how good it is.
3 a distinguishing feature.
4 a symbol, *They all stood as a mark of respect.* **5** a target.
on your marks! a command to runners to get ready to begin a race.
up to the mark of the normal or expected standard.

mark *verb* (**marks, marking, marked**)
1 put a mark on something. **2** give a mark to a piece of work; correct. **3** pay attention to something, *Mark my words!*
4 keep close to an opposing player in football etc.
marker *noun*
[from Old English *merc*]

mark[2] *noun* (*plural* **marks**) a German unit of money.

marked *adjective* noticeable, *a marked improvement.* **markedly** *adverb*

market *noun* (*plural* **markets**)
1 a place where things are bought and sold, usually from stalls in the open air. **2** demand for things; trade. **market place** *noun*
[via Old English from Latin *merx* = goods, merchandise]

market research *noun* the study of what people need or want to buy.

marksman *noun* (*plural* **marksmen**) an expert in shooting at a target. **marksmanship** *noun*

mark time *verb*
1 march on one spot without moving forward. **2** occupy your time without making any progress.

marmalade *noun* jam made from oranges, lemons, or other citrus fruit. [via French from

Portuguese *marmelo* = quince (from which marmalade was first made)]

maroon verb (**maroons, marooning, marooned**) abandon or isolate somebody in a deserted place; strand. [via French from Spanish *cimarrón* = runaway slave]

marquee (say mar-**kee**) noun (plural **marquees**) a large tent used for a party or exhibition etc. [from French; related to *marquis*]

marquis noun (plural **marquises**) a nobleman ranking next above an earl.

marriage noun (plural **marriages**) **1** the state of being married. **2** a wedding.

marrow noun (plural **marrows**) **1** a large gourd eaten as a vegetable. **2** the soft substance inside bones.

marry verb (**marries, marrying, married**) **1** become a person's husband or wife. **2** unite a man and woman legally for the purpose of living together. [from Latin *maritus* = husband]

marsh noun (plural **marshes**) an area of very wet ground. **marshy** adjective [from Old English]

marshal noun (plural **marshals**) **1** an official who supervises a contest or ceremony etc. **2** an officer of very high rank, *a Field Marshal*.

marshmallow noun (plural **marshmallows**) a soft spongy sweet, usually pink or white. [originally made from the root of the marshmallow, a pink flower that grows in marshes]

marsupial (say mar-**soo**-pee-al) noun (plural **marsupials**) an animal such as a kangaroo or wallaby. The female has a pouch on the front of its body in which its babies are carried. [from Greek *marsypion* = pouch]

martial adjective to do with war; warlike. [Latin, = belonging to Mars, the Roman god of war]

martial arts plural noun fighting sports, such as judo and karate.

martial law noun government of a country by the armed forces during a crisis.

martyr noun (plural **martyrs**) a person who is killed or made to suffer because of his or her beliefs. **martyrdom** noun

marvel noun (plural **marvels**) a wonderful thing. **marvellous** adjective [from old French; related to *miracle*]

marzipan noun a soft sweet food made of ground almonds, eggs, and sugar. [via German from Italian]

mascot noun (plural **mascots**) a person, animal, or thing that is believed to bring good luck. [from French]

masculine adjective **1** to do with men. **2** typical of or suitable for men. **3** (in some languages) belonging to the class of words which includes the words referring to men, such as *garçon* and *livre* in French. **masculinity** noun [from Latin *masculus* = male]

mash verb (**mashes, mashing, mashed**) crush into a soft mass.

mask noun (plural **masks**) a covering worn over the face to disguise or protect it.

masochist (say mas-ok-ist) noun (plural **masochists**) a person who enjoys things that seem painful or tiresome. **masochism** noun [named after an Austrian novelist, L. von Sacher-Masoch, who wrote about masochism]

mason noun (plural **masons**) a person who builds or works with stone.

masonry noun
1 the stone parts of a building; stonework. **2** a mason's work.

masquerade noun (plural **masquerades**) a pretence.

masquerade verb (**masquerades, masquerading, masqueraded**) pretend to be something, He masqueraded as a policeman.
[via French from Italian mascara = mask]

Mass noun (plural **Masses**) the Communion service in a Roman Catholic church.

mass noun (plural **masses**)
1 a large amount. **2** a heap or other collection of matter. **3** (in scientific use) the quantity of matter that a thing contains. In non-scientific use this is called weight.

mass adjective involving a large number of people, mass murder.

massacre noun (plural **massacres**) the killing of a large number of people. **massacre** verb [from French, = butchery]

massage (say mass-ahzh) verb (**massages, massaging, massaged**) rub and press the body to make it less stiff or less painful. **massage** noun, **masseur** noun, **masseuse** noun [from French]

massive adjective large and heavy; huge. [from French; related to mass]

mass media noun the media.

mass production noun manufacturing goods in large quantities. **mass-produced** adjective

mast noun (plural **masts**) a tall pole that holds up a ship's sails or a flag or an aerial. [from Old English]

master noun (plural **masters**)
1 a man who is in charge of something. **2** a male teacher. **3** a great artist, composer, sportsman, etc. **4** something from which copies are made. **5** Master a title put before a boy's name. [same origin as magistrate]

masterful adjective
1 domineering. **2** very skilful. **masterfully** adverb

master key noun (plural **master keys**) a key that will open several different locks.

masterly adjective very skilful.

Master of Arts noun (plural **Masters of Arts**) a person who has taken the next degree after Bachelor of Arts.

master of ceremonies noun (plural **masters of ceremonies**) a person who introduces the speakers at a formal event, or the entertainers at a variety show.

Master of Science noun (plural **Masters of Science**) a person who has taken the next degree after Bachelor of Science.

masterpiece noun (plural **masterpieces**)
1 an excellent piece of work. **2** a person's best piece of work.

mastery noun complete control or thorough knowledge or skill in something.

mastiff noun (plural **mastiffs**) a large kind of dog. [from old French]

masturbate verb (**masturbates**, **masturbating**, **masturbated**) excite yourself by fingering your genitals. **masturbation** noun [from Latin]

mat noun (plural **mats**)
1 a small carpet. 2 a doormat. 3 a small piece of material put on a table to protect the surface. [from Old English]

matador noun (plural **matadors**) a bullfighter who fights on foot. [Spanish, from *matar* = kill]

match[1] noun (plural **matches**) a small thin stick with a head made of a substance that gives a flame when rubbed on something rough. **matchbox** noun, **matchstick** noun [from old French]

match[2] noun (plural **matches**)
1 a game or contest between two teams or players. 2 one person or thing that matches another. 3 a marriage.
match verb (**matches**, **matching**, **matched**)
1 be equal or similar to another person or thing. 2 put teams or players to compete against each other. 3 find something that is similar or corresponding. [from Old English]

mate[1] noun (plural **mates**)
1 a companion or friend. 2 one of a mated pair. 3 an officer on a merchant ship.

mate verb (**mates**, **mating**, **mated**)
1 come or put together so as to have offspring. 2 put things together as a pair or because they correspond. [from old German]

mate[2] noun & verb (in chess) checkmate.

material noun (plural **materials**)
1 anything used for making something else. 2 cloth or fabric. [from Latin *materia* = matter]

materialize verb (**materializes**, **materializing**, **materialized**)
1 become visible; appear, *The ghost didn't materialize.* 2 become a fact; happen, *The trip did not materialize.* **materialization** noun

maternal adjective
1 to do with a mother. 2 motherly. **maternally** adverb [from Latin *mater* = mother]

maternity noun motherhood.

maternity adjective to do with having a baby, *maternity ward.* [same origin as *maternal*]

mathematics noun the study of numbers, measurements, and shapes. **mathematical** adjective, **mathematically** adverb, **mathematician** noun [from Greek *mathema* = science]

matriarch (say **may**-tree-ark) noun (plural **matriarchs**) a woman who is head of a family or tribe. (Compare *patriarch*.) **matriarchal** adjective, **matriarchy** noun [from Latin *mater* = mother, + *-arch*]

matrix (say **may**-triks) noun (plural **matrices** (say **may**-tri-seez))
1 an array of mathematical

quantities etc. in rows and columns. **2** a mould or framework in which something is made or allowed to develop. [from Latin]

matron *noun* (*plural* **matrons**)
1 a mature married woman.
2 a woman in charge of nursing in a school etc. or (formerly) of the nursing staff in a hospital. **matronly** *adjective*

matted *adjective* tangled into a mass. [from *mat*]

matter *noun* (*plural* **matters**)
1 something you can touch or see, not spirit or mind or qualities etc. **2** things of a certain kind, *printed matter*. **3** something to be thought about or done, *It's a serious matter*. **4** a quantity, *in a matter of minutes*.
no matter it does not matter.
what is the matter? what is wrong?

matter *verb* (**matters, mattering, mattered**) be important.
[same origin as *material*]

matter of course *noun* the natural or expected thing, *I always lock my bike up, as a matter of course*.

matter-of-fact *adjective* keeping to facts; not imaginative or emotional, *She talked about death in a very matter-of-fact way*.

mattress *noun* (*plural* **mattresses**) soft or springy material in a fabric covering, used on or as a bed. [via French from Arabic]

mature *adjective*
1 fully grown or developed.
2 grown-up. **maturely** *adverb*, **maturity** *noun*

mature *verb* (**matures, maturing,**

matured) make or become mature.
[from Latin *maturus* = ripe]

maul *verb* (**mauls, mauling, mauled**) injure by handling or clawing, *He was mauled by a lion*. [originally = knock down: from Latin *malleus* = a hammer]

mauve (*say* mohv) *noun* pale purple. [from Latin *malva* = a plant with mauve flowers]

maxim *noun* (*plural* **maxims**) a short saying giving a general truth or rule of behaviour, e.g. 'Waste not, want not'. [from Latin *maxima propositio* = greatest statement]

maximize *verb* (**maximizes, maximizing, maximized**) increase something to a maximum.

maximum *noun* (*plural* **maxima** or **maximums**) the greatest possible number or amount. (The opposite is *minimum*.) [Latin, = greatest thing]

may[1] *auxiliary verb* (**may, might**) used to express
1 permission (*You may go now*),
2 possibility (*It may be true*),
3 wish (*Long may she reign*),
4 uncertainty (*whoever it may be*). [from Old English]

USAGE: See note at *can*.

may[2] *noun* hawthorn blossom. [because the hawthorn blooms in the month of May]

maybe *adverb* perhaps; possibly.

mayfly *noun* (*plural* **mayflies**) an insect that lives for only a short time, in spring.

mayhem *noun* violent confusion or damage, *The mob caused mayhem*.

mayonnaise noun a creamy sauce made from eggs, oil, vinegar, etc., eaten with salad or in a sandwich. [French, named after Mahón on Minorca, which the French had just captured when mayonnaise was invented]

mayor noun (plural **mayors**) the person in charge of the council in a town or city. **mayoral** adjective, **mayoress** noun [from old French; related to major]

maze noun (plural **mazes**) a network of paths, especially one designed as a puzzle in which to try and find your way. [from amaze]

me pronoun the form of I used as the object of a verb or after a preposition. [from Old English]

meadow (say med-oh) noun (plural **meadows**) a field of grass. [from Old English]

meagre adjective scanty in amount; barely enough, a meagre diet. [from French]

meal[1] noun (plural **meals**) food served and eaten at one sitting. [from Old English mael]

meal[2] noun coarsely-ground grain. **mealy** adjective [from Old English melu]

mean[1] verb (**means, meaning, meant**) (say ment)
1 have as an equivalent, 'Maybe' means 'perhaps'. 2 have as a purpose; intend, I mean to win. 3 indicate, Dark clouds mean rain. [from Old English maenan]

mean[2] adjective (**meaner, meanest**)
1 not generous; miserly. 2 unkind or spiteful, a mean trick. 3 poor in quality or appearance, a mean little house. **meanly** adverb, **meanness** noun [from Old English maene]

mean[3] noun (plural **means**) a middle point or condition. **mean** adjective average.

meander (say mee-an-der) verb (**meanders, meandering, meandered**) take a winding course; wander. **meander** noun [named after the Meander, a river in Turkey (now Mendere or Menderes)]

meaning noun (plural **meanings**) what something means. **meaningful** adjective, **meaningless** adjective

means noun a way of achieving something or producing a result, a means of transport.
by all means certainly.
by means of by this method; using this.
by no means not at all.
means plural noun money or other wealth.
live beyond your means spend more than you can afford. [from mean[3], in an old sense = someone in the middle, a go-between]

meantime noun
in the meantime the time between two events or while something else is happening. [from mean[3] + time]

meanwhile adverb in the time between two events or period of time while something else is happening. [from mean[3] + while]

measles *noun* an infectious disease that causes small red spots on the skin. [probably from old German *masele* = pimple]

measure *verb* (**measures, measuring, measured**)
1 find how big or heavy something is by comparing it with a unit of standard size or weight. 2 be a certain size, *The room measures 3 × 4 metres.* **measurable** *adjective*, **measurement** *noun*

measure *noun* (*plural* **measures**)
1 a unit used for measuring, *A kilometre is a measure of length.* 2 a device used in measuring. 3 the size or quantity of something. 4 something done for a particular purpose, *We took measures to stop vandalism.* [from Latin]

meat *noun* (*plural* **meats**) animal flesh used as food. **meaty** *adjective* [from Old English *mete* = food]

mechanic *noun* (*plural* **mechanics**) a person who maintains or repairs machinery.

mechanical *adjective*
1 to do with machines. 2 produced or worked by machines. 3 done or doing things without thought. **mechanically** *adverb* [from Greek *mechane* = machine]

mechanics *noun*
1 the study of movement and force. 2 the study or use of machines.

mechanism *noun* (*plural* **mechanisms**)
1 the moving parts of a machine. 2 the way a machine works.

medal *noun* (*plural* **medals**) a piece of metal shaped like a coin, star, or cross, given to a person for bravery or for achieving something. [from French]

meddle *verb* (**meddles, meddling, meddled**)
1 interfere. 2 tinker, *Don't meddle with it.* **meddler** *noun*, **meddlesome** *adjective* [from old French; related to *mix*]

media *plural* of **medium** *noun* **the media** newspapers, radio, and television, which convey information and ideas to the public. (See **medium**.)

USAGE: This word is a plural. Although it is commonly used with a singular verb, this is not generally approved of. Say *The media are* (not 'is') *very influential.* It is incorrect to speak of one of them (e.g. television) as 'this media'.

mediate *verb* (**mediates, mediating, mediated**) negotiate between the opposing sides in a dispute. **mediation** *noun*, **mediator** *noun*

medical *adjective* to do with the treatment of disease. **medically** *adverb* [from Latin *medicus* = doctor]

medicine *noun* (*plural* **medicines**)
1 a substance, usually swallowed, used to try to cure a disease. 2 the study and treatment of diseases. **medicinal** (*say* med-**iss**-in-al) *adjective*, **medicinally** *adverb* [same origin as *medical*]

medieval (*say* med-ee-ee-val) *adjective* belonging to or to do with the Middle Ages. [from Latin *medius* = middle + *aevum* = age]

mediocre (*say* mee-dee-**oh**-ker) *adjective* not very good; of only medium quality. **mediocrity** *noun* [from Latin *mediocris* = of medium height]

meditate *verb* (**meditates, meditating, meditated**) think deeply and quietly. **meditation** *noun*, **meditative** *adjective* [from Latin]

Mediterranean *adjective* to do with the Mediterranean Sea (which lies between Europe and Africa) or the countries round it. [from Latin *Mare Mediterraneum* = sea in the middle of land, from *medius* = middle + *terra* = land]

medium *adjective* neither large nor small; moderate.

medium *noun* (*plural* **media**)
1 a thing in which something exists, moves, or is expressed, *Air is the medium in which sound travels. Television is used as a medium for advertising.* (See **media**.) **2** (*plural* **mediums**) a person who claims to be able to communicate with the dead. [Latin, = middle thing]

meek *adjective* (**meeker, meekest**) quiet and obedient. **meekly** *adverb*, **meekness** *noun* [from Old Norse]

meet *verb* (**meets, meeting, met**) **1** come together from different places. **2** get to know someone, *We met at a party.* **3** come into contact; touch. **4** go to receive an arrival, *We will meet your train.* **5** pay a bill or the cost of something. **6** satisfy, *I hope this meets your needs.*

meet *noun* (*plural* **meets**) a gathering of riders and hounds for a hunt. [from Old English *metan*]

meeting *noun* (*plural* **meetings**) **1** coming together. **2** a number of people who have come together for a discussion, contest, etc.

mega- *prefix* **1** large or great (as in *megaphone*). **2** one million (as in *megahertz* = one million hertz). [from Greek *megas* = great]

megalomania *noun* an exaggerated idea of your own importance. **megalomaniac** *noun* [from *mega-* + *mania*]

megaphone *noun* (*plural* **megaphones**) a funnel-shaped device for amplifying a person's voice. [from *mega-* + Greek *phone* = voice]

melancholy *adjective* sad; gloomy.

melancholy *noun* sadness or depression. [from Greek *melas* = black + *chole* = bile (because black bile in the body was once thought to cause melancholy)]

mellow *adjective* (**mellower, mellowest**) **1** not harsh; soft and rich in flavour, colour, or sound. **2** kindly and genial. **mellowness** *noun*

mellow *verb* (**mellows, mellowing, mellowed**) make or become mellow. [origin unknown]

melodious *adjective* like a melody; pleasant to listen to.

melodrama *noun* (*plural* **melodramas**) a play full of dramatic excitement and emotion. **melodramatic** *adjective* [from Greek *melos* = music + French *drame* = drama (because melodramas were originally musicals)]

melody *noun* (*plural* **melodies**) a tune, especially a pleasing tune. [from Greek *melos* = music + *oide* = song]

melt *verb* (**melts, melting, melted**) **1** make or become liquid by heating. **2** disappear slowly. **3** soften.

melting pot *noun* (*plural* **melting pots**) a place where people of many different races and cultures live and influence each other.

member *noun* (*plural* **members**) **1** a person or thing that belongs to a particular society or group. **2** a part of something. **membership** *noun* [from Latin *membrum* = limb]

membrane *noun* (*plural* **membranes**) a thin skin or similar covering. **membranous** *adjective* [from Latin]

memoir (*say* mem-wahr) *noun* (*plural* **memoirs**) a biography, especially one written by someone who knew the person. [from French *mémoire* = memory]

memorable *adjective* **1** worth remembering. **2** easy to remember. **memorably** *adverb*

memorandum *noun* (*plural* **memoranda** or **memorandums**) **1** a note to remind yourself of something. **2** a note from one person to another in the same firm. [Latin, = thing to be remembered]

memorial *noun* (*plural* **memorials**) something to remind people of a person or event, *a war memorial.* **memorial** *adjective* [from Latin *memoria* = memory]

memorize *verb* (**memorizes, memorizing, memorized**) get something into your memory. [from *memory*]

memory *noun* (*plural* **memories**) **1** the ability to remember things. **2** something that you remember. **3** the part of a computer where information is stored. [from Latin *memor* = remembering]

menace *noun* (*plural* **menaces**) **1** a threat or danger. **2** a troublesome person or thing.

menace *verb* (**menaces, menacing, menaced**) threaten with harm or danger. [from Latin *minax* = threatening]

mend *verb* (**mends, mending, mended**) **1** repair. **2** make or become better; improve. **mender** *noun*

mend *noun* (*plural* **mends**) a repair.

menopause *noun* the time of life when a woman gradually ceases to menstruate. [from Greek *menos* = of a month + *pausis* = stopping]

menstruate *verb* (**menstruates, menstruating, menstruated**) bleed from the womb about once a month, as girls and women normally do from their teens until middle age. **menstruation** *noun*. **menstrual** *adjective* [from Latin *menstruus* = monthly]

mental *adjective*
1 to do with or in the mind.
2 (*informal*) mad. **mentally** *adverb* [from Latin *mentis* = of the mind]

mentality *noun* (*plural* **mentalities**) a person's mental ability or attitude.

mention *verb* (**mentions, mentioning, mentioned**) speak or write about a person or thing briefly; refer to.

mention *noun* (*plural* **mentions**) an example of mentioning something, *Our school got a mention in the local paper.*

menu (*say* men-yoo) *noun* (*plural* **menus**)
1 a list of the food available in a restaurant or served at a meal.
2 a list of things, shown on a screen, from which you decide what you want a computer to do.

MEP *abbreviation* Member of the European Parliament.

mercenary *adjective* working only for money or some other reward.

mercenary *noun* (*plural* **mercenaries**) a soldier hired to serve in a foreign army. [from Latin *merces* = wages]

merchandise *noun* goods for sale. [from French *marchand* = merchant]

merchant *noun* (*plural* **merchants**) a person involved in trade. [from Latin *mercari* = to trade]

merchant navy *noun* the ships and sailors that carry goods for trade.

merciful *adjective* showing mercy. **mercifully** *adverb*

mercury *noun* a heavy silvery metal (also called *quicksilver*) that is usually liquid, used in thermometers. **mercuric** *adjective* [from the name of the planet Mercury]

mercy *noun* (*plural* **mercies**)
1 kindness or pity shown in not punishing a wrongdoer severely or not harming a defeated enemy etc. 2 something to be thankful for. [from old French]

mere *adjective* not more than, *He's a mere child.*

merely *adverb* only; simply.

merge *verb* (**merges, merging, merged**) combine or blend. [from Latin *mergere* = dip]

merger *noun* (*plural* **mergers**) the combining of two business companies etc. into one.

meridian *noun* (*plural* **meridians**) a line on a map or globe from the North Pole to the South Pole. The meridian that passes through Greenwich is shown on maps at 0° longitude. [from Latin]

meringue (*say* mer-ang) *noun* (*plural* **meringues**) a crisp cake made from egg white and sugar. [French]

merit *noun* (*plural* **merits**)
1 a quality that deserves praise.
2 excellence. **meritorious** *adjective* [from Latin *meritum* = value]

mermaid *noun* (*plural* **mermaids**) a mythical sea creature with a woman's body but with a fish's tail instead of legs. **merman** *noun* [from Old English *mere* = sea, + *maid*]

merry adjective (**merrier, merriest**)
cheerful and lively. **merrily**
adverb, **merriment** noun [from
Old English]

merry-go-round noun (plural
merry-go-rounds) a roundabout
at a fair.

mesh noun (plural **meshes**)
1 the open spaces in a net, sieve,
or other criss-cross structure.
2 material made like a net;
network.

mesmerize verb (**mesmerizes,
mesmerizing, mesmerized**)
1 (old use) hypnotize. 2 fascinate
or hold a person's attention
completely. **mesmerism** noun
[named after an Austrian doctor,
F. A. Mesmer, who made
hypnosis famous]

mess noun (plural **messes**)
1 a dirty or untidy condition or
thing. 2 a difficult or confused
situation; trouble. 3 (in the
armed forces) a dining room.
make a mess of bungle.

mess verb (**messes, messing,
messed**)
mess about 1 behave stupidly.
2 potter.
mess up 1 make a thing dirty or
untidy. 2 bungle; spoil by
muddling, *They messed up our
plans.*
mess with interfere or tinker
with.
[from old French *mes* = a portion
of food]

message noun (plural **messages**)
a piece of information etc. sent
from one person to another.
[from old French; related to
missile]

messenger noun (plural
messengers) a person who
carries a message.

Messiah (say mis-I-a) noun
(plural **Messiahs**)
1 the saviour of the world
expected by the Jewish people.
2 Jesus Christ, whom Christians
believe to be this saviour.
Messianic adjective [from Hebrew
mashiah = anointed]

messy adjective (**messier,
messiest**) dirty and untidy.
messily adverb, **messiness** noun

metabolism (say mit-ab-ol-izm)
noun the process by which food is
built up into living material in
a plant or animal, or used to
supply it with energy. **metabolic**
adjective, **metabolize** verb [from
Greek *metabole* = change]

metal noun (plural **metals**) a hard
mineral substance (e.g. gold,
silver, copper, iron) that melts
when it is heated. **metallic**
adjective [from Latin]

metamorphosis (say met-a-mor-
fo-sis) noun (plural
metamorphoses (say met-a-mor-
fo-seez)) a change of form or
character. **metamorphose** verb

metaphor noun (plural
metaphors) using a word or
phrase in a way that is not
literal, e.g. 'The pictures of
starving people *touched our
hearts*'. **metaphorical** adjective,
metaphorically adverb [from
Greek *metapherein* = transfer]

meteor (say meet-ee-er) noun
(plural **meteors**) a piece of rock
or metal that moves through
space and burns up when it

enters the earth's atmosphere.
[from Greek *meteoros* = high in
the air]

meteorite noun (*plural*
meteorites) the remains of
a meteor that has landed on the
earth.

meter noun (*plural* **meters**)
a device for measuring
something, e.g. the amount
supplied, *a gas meter*. **meter** verb
[from *mete*]

USAGE: Do not confuse with
metre.

methane (*say* mee-thayn) noun
an inflammable gas produced by
decaying matter. [from *methyl*,
a chemical which methane
contains]

method noun (*plural* **methods**)
1 a procedure or way of doing
something. **2** methodical
behaviour; orderliness. [from
Greek *methodos* = pursuit of
knowledge]

methodical adjective doing
things in an orderly or
systematic way. **methodically**
adverb

methylated spirit and **spirits**
noun a liquid fuel made from
alcohol. [from *methyl*, a chemical
added to make alcohol nasty to
drink]

metre noun (*plural* **metres**)
1 a unit of length in the metric
system, about 39¼ inches.
2 rhythm in poetry. [from Greek
metron = a measure]

USAGE: Do not confuse with
meter.

metric adjective
1 to do with the metric system.
2 to do with metre in poetry.
metrically adverb

metric system noun a measuring
system based on decimal units
(the metre, litre, and gram).

metric ton noun (*plural* **metric
tons**) 1,000 kilograms.

metronome noun (*plural*
metronomes) a device that
makes a regular clicking noise to
help a person keep in time when
practising music. [from Greek
metron = measure + *nomos* = law]

mew verb (**mews, mewing,
mewed**) make a cat's cry. **mew**
noun

mice *plural of* **mouse**.

micro- prefix very small (as in
microfilm). [from Greek *mikros*
= small]

microbe noun (*plural* **microbes**)
a micro-organism. [from *micro-*
+ Greek *bios* = life]

microchip noun (*plural*
microchips) a very small piece of
silicon etc. made to work like
a complex wired electric circuit.

microcosm noun (*plural*
microcosms) a world in
miniature; something regarded
as resembling something else on
a very small scale. [from Greek
mikros kosmos = little world]

microfilm noun a length of film
on which written or printed
material is photographed in
greatly reduced size.

micron noun (*plural* **microns**)
a unit of measurement, one
millionth of a metre. [same
origin as *micro-*]

microphone noun (plural **microphones**) an electrical device that picks up sound waves for recording, amplifying, or broadcasting. [from *micro-* + Greek *phone* = sound]

microscope noun (plural **microscopes**) an instrument with lenses that magnify tiny objects or details. [from *micro-* + Greek *skopein* = look at]

microscopic adjective
1 extremely small; too small to be seen without the aid of a microscope. 2 to do with a microscope.

microwave noun (plural **microwaves**)
1 a very short electromagnetic wave. 2 a microwave oven.

microwave oven noun (plural **microwave ovens**) an oven that uses microwaves to heat or cook food very quickly.

midday noun the middle of the day; noon.

middle noun (plural **middles**)
1 the place or part of something that is at the same distance from all its sides or edges or from both its ends. 2 someone's waist.

middle adjective
1 placed or happening in the middle. 2 moderate in size or rank etc.

Middle Ages noun the period in history from about AD1000 to 1400.

middle class and **classes** noun the class of people between the upper class and the working class, including business and professional people such as teachers, doctors, and lawyers.

middle-class adjective

Middle East noun the countries from Egypt to Iran inclusive.

Middle English noun the English language from about 1150 to 1500.

middle school noun (plural **middle schools**) a school for children aged from about 9 to 13.

middling adjective of medium size or quality.

middling adverb fairly or moderately.

midge noun (plural **midges**) a small insect like a gnat.

midget noun (plural **midgets**) an extremely small person or thing.

midget adjective [from *midge*]

midland adjective
1 to do with the middle part of a country. 2 to do with the Midlands.

Midlands plural noun the central part of England.

midnight noun twelve o'clock at night.

midst noun
in the midst of in the middle of or surrounded by.
in our midst among us.

midsummer noun the middle of summer, about 21 June in the northern hemisphere.

midway adverb halfway.

midwife noun (plural **midwives**) a person trained to look after a woman who is giving birth to a baby. **midwifery** noun [from Old English *mid* = with + *wif* = woman]

might¹ noun great strength or power.
with all your might using all your strength and determination. [from Old English]

might² *auxiliary verb* used
1 as the past tense of *may¹* (*We told her she might go*), **2** to express possibility (*It might be true*).

mighty *adjective* very strong or powerful. **mightily** *adverb*, **mightiness** *noun*

migraine (say mee-grayn or my-grayn) *noun* (*plural* **migraines**) a severe kind of headache. [French]

migrate *verb* (**migrates**, **migrating**, **migrated**)
1 leave one place or country and settle in another. **2** (of birds or animals) move periodically from one area to another. **migration** *noun*, **migratory** *adjective*

mild *adjective* (**milder**, **mildest**)
1 gentle; not harsh or severe.
2 not strongly flavoured. **mildly** *adverb*, **mildness** *noun* [from Old English]

mildew *noun* a tiny fungus that forms a white coating on things kept in damp conditions. **mildewed** *adjective* [from Old English]

mile *noun* (*plural* **miles**) a measure of distance, 1,760 yards (about 1.6 kilometres). [from Latin *mille* = thousand (paces)]

milestone *noun* (*plural* **milestones**)
1 a stone of a kind that used to be fixed beside a road to mark the distance between towns. **2** an important event in life or history.

militant *adjective*
1 eager to fight. **2** forceful or aggressive, *a militant protest.* **militant** *noun*, **militancy** *noun*

military *adjective* to do with soldiers or the armed forces. [from Latin *miles* = soldier]

milk *noun*
1 a white liquid that female mammals produce in their bodies to feed their babies. **2** the milk of cows, sheep, or goats used as food by human beings. **3** a milky liquid, e.g. that in a coconut.

milk *verb* (**milks**, **milking**, **milked**) get the milk from a cow or other animal.

milkman *noun* (*plural* **milkmen**) a man who delivers milk to customers' houses.

milky *adjective* (**milkier**, **milkiest**)
1 like milk. **2** white.

Milky Way *noun* the broad band of stars formed by our galaxy.

mill *noun* (*plural* **mills**)
1 machinery for grinding corn to make flour; a building containing this machinery.
2 a grinding machine, *a coffee mill.* **3** a factory for processing certain materials, *a paper mill.* [via Old English from Latin *molere* = grind]

millennium *noun* (*plural* **millenniums**) a period of 1,000 years. [from Latin *mille* = thousand + *annus* = year]

milli- *prefix*
1 one thousand (as in *millepede*).
2 one-thousandth (as in *milligram*, *millilitre*, *millimetre*). [from Latin *mille* = thousand]

million noun (plural **millions**) one thousand thousand (1,000,000).
millionth adjective & noun [French; related to **milli-**]

millionaire noun (plural **millionaires**) an extremely rich person.

millstone noun (plural **millstones**) either of a pair of large circular stones between which corn is ground.
a millstone around someone's neck a heavy responsibility or burden.

mimic verb (**mimics, mimicking, mimicked**) imitate. **mimicry** noun
mimic noun (plural **mimics**) a person who mimics others, especially to amuse people.

mince verb (**minces, mincing, minced**)
1 cut into very small pieces in a machine. 2 walk in an affected way. **mincer** noun
not to mince matters speak bluntly.
mince noun minced meat. [from French; related to **minute**²]

mincemeat noun a sweet mixture of currants, raisins, apple, etc. used in pies. [from *mince* + an old sense of *meat* = food]

mince pie noun (plural **mince pies**) a pie containing mincemeat, traditionally eaten at Christmas.

mind noun (plural **minds**)
1 the ability to think, feel, understand, and remember, originating in the brain.
2 a person's thoughts and feelings or opinion, *I changed my mind*.

mind verb (**minds, minding, minded**)
1 look after, *He was minding the baby*. 2 be careful about, *Mind the step*. 3 be sad or upset about something; object to, *We don't mind waiting*. **minder** noun

mine¹ possessive pronoun belonging to me. [from Old English]

mine² noun (plural **mines**)
1 a place where coal, metal, precious stones, etc. are dug out of the ground. 2 an explosive placed in or on the ground or in the sea etc. to destroy people or things that come close to it.
mine verb (**mines, mining, mined**)
1 dig from a mine. 2 lay explosive mines in a place.
[from old French]

minefield noun (plural **minefields**)
1 an area where explosive mines have been laid. 2 something with hidden dangers or problems.

miner noun (plural **miners**) a person who works in a mine.

mineral noun (plural **minerals**)
1 a hard inorganic substance found in the ground. 2 a cold fizzy non-alcoholic drink. [from Latin *minera* = ore]

mingle verb (**mingles, mingling, mingled**) mix. [from Old English]

mingy adjective (**mingier, mingiest**) (*informal*) not generous; mean. [probably from *mean*² + *stingy*]

mini- prefix miniature; very small. [short for *miniature*]

miniature adjective
1 very small. 2 copying

something on a very small scale, *a miniature railway.*

miniature noun (plural **miniatures**)
1 a very small portrait. 2 a small-scale model.
[from Italian]

minim noun (plural **minims**)
a note in music, lasting twice as long as a crotchet (written ♩). [same origin as *minimum*]

minimize verb (**minimizes**, **minimizing**, **minimized**) reduce something to a minimum.

minimum noun (plural **minima** or **minimums**) the lowest possible number or amount. (The opposite is *maximum*.) **minimal** *adjective* [Latin, = least thing]

minister noun (plural **ministers**)
1 a person in charge of a government department. 2 a member of the clergy. **ministerial** *adjective* [Latin, = servant]

ministry noun (plural **ministries**)
1 a government department, *the Ministry of Defence.* 2 the work of the clergy. [same origin as *minister*]

minnow noun (plural **minnows**)
a tiny freshwater fish.

minor *adjective*
1 not very important, especially when compared to something else. 2 to do with the musical scale that has a semitone after the second note. (Compare *major*.) [Latin, = smaller, lesser]

minority noun (plural **minorities**)
1 the smallest part of a group of people or things. 2 a small group that is different from others. (Compare *majority*.) [same origin as *minor*]

minstrel noun (plural **minstrels**)
a travelling singer and musician in the Middle Ages.

mint¹ noun (plural **mints**)
1 a plant with fragrant leaves that are used for flavouring things. 2 peppermint or a sweet flavoured with this. [from Latin *mentha* = mint]

mint² noun (plural **mints**) the place where a country's coins are made.
in mint condition in perfect condition, as though it had never been used.

mint verb (**mints**, **minting**, **minted**) make coins.
[from Latin *moneta* = coins; a mint]

minus *preposition* with the next number or thing subtracted, *Ten minus four equals six* (10 − 4 = 6).

minus *adjective* less than zero, *temperatures of minus ten degrees* (−10°).
[Latin, = less]

minute¹ (say min-it) noun (plural **minutes**)
1 one-sixtieth of an hour. 2 a very short time; a moment. 3 a particular time, *Come here this minute!* 4 one-sixtieth of a degree (used in measuring angles). [from Latin *pars minuta prima* = first little part]

minute² (say my-newt) *adjective*
1 very small, *a minute insect.* 2 very detailed, *a minute examination.* **minutely** *adverb*
[from Latin *minutus* = little]

minutes plural noun a written summary of what was said at a meeting. [probably from Latin *minuta scriptura* = small writing]

miracle noun (plural **miracles**)
something wonderful and good
that happens, especially
something believed to have
a supernatural or divine cause.
miraculous adjective,
miraculously adverb [same origin
as *mirror*]

mirage (say mi-rahzh) noun
(plural **mirages**) an illusion;
something that seems to be there
but is not, especially when a lake
seems to appear in a desert.
[French, from *se mirer* = be
reflected or mirrored]

mirror noun (plural **mirrors**)
a device or surface of reflecting
material, usually glass.

mirror verb (**mirrors, mirroring,
mirrored**) reflect in or like
a mirror.
[from Latin *mirari* = to look at or
wonder at]

mis- prefix badly or wrongly.
(Compare *amiss*.) [from Old
English *mis-* (related to *amiss*), or
old French *mes-* (related to
minus)]

misbehave verb (**misbehaves,
misbehaving, misbehaved**)
behave badly. **misbehaviour** noun

miscalculate verb (**miscalculates,
miscalculating, miscalculated**)
calculate incorrectly.
miscalculation noun

miscarriage noun (plural
miscarriages)
1 the birth of a baby before it has
developed enough to live.
2 failure to achieve the right
result, *a miscarriage of justice*.
[from *miscarry* = to be lost,
destroyed, or badly managed]

miscellaneous (say mis-el-ay-
nee-us) adjective of various kinds;
mixed. **miscellany** (say mis-el-an-
ee) noun [from Latin *miscellus*
= mixed]

mischief noun
1 naughty or troublesome
behaviour. **2** trouble caused by
this. **mischievous** adjective,
mischievously adverb [from old
French *meschever* = come to a bad
end]

misconception noun (plural
misconceptions) a mistaken idea.

misconduct noun bad behaviour
by someone in a responsible
position, *professional misconduct*.

miser noun (plural **misers**)
a person who hoards money and
spends as little as possible.
miserly adjective, **miserliness**
noun [same origin as *misery*]

miserable adjective
1 full of misery; very unhappy,
poor, or uncomfortable.
2 disagreeable or unpleasant,
miserable weather. **miserably**
adverb [same origin as *misery*]

misery noun (plural **miseries**)
1 great unhappiness or
discomfort or suffering,
especially lasting for a long time.
2 (*informal*) a discontented or
disagreeable person. [from Latin
miser = wretched]

misfire verb (**misfires, misfiring,
misfired**)
1 fail to fire. **2** fail to function
correctly or to have the required
effect, *The joke misfired.*

misfit noun (plural **misfits**)
a person who does not fit in well
with other people or who is not
well suited to his or her work.

misfortune noun (plural misfortunes)
1 bad luck. **2** an unlucky event or accident.

misgiving noun (plural misgivings) a feeling of doubt or slight fear or mistrust. [from an old word misgive = give someone bad feelings about something]

misguided adjective guided by mistaken ideas or beliefs.

mishap (say mis-hap) noun (plural mishaps) an unlucky accident. [from mis- + Middle English hap = luck]

misinterpret verb (misinterprets, misinterpreting, misinterpreted) interpret incorrectly. **misinterpretation** noun

mislay verb (mislays, mislaying, mislaid) lose something for a short time because you cannot remember where you put it.

mislead verb (misleads, misleading, misled) give somebody a wrong idea; deceive.

misnomer noun (plural misnomers) an unsuitable name for something. [from mis- + Latin nomen = name]

misogynist (say mis-oj-in-ist) noun (plural misogynists) a person who hates women. **misogyny** noun [from Greek misos = hatred + gyne = woman]

misplaced adjective
1 placed wrongly.
2 inappropriate, misplaced sympathy. **misplacement** noun

misprint noun (plural misprints) a mistake in printing.

misrepresent verb (misrepresents, misrepresenting, misrepresented) represent in a false or misleading way. **misrepresentation** noun

Miss noun (plural Misses) a title put before a girl's or unmarried woman's name. [short for mistress]

miss verb (misses, missing, missed)
1 fail to hit, reach, catch, see, hear, or find something. **2** be sad because someone or something is not with you. **3** notice that something has gone.

miss noun (plural misses) missing something, Was that shot a hit or a miss? [from Old English]

misshapen adjective badly shaped. [from mis- + shapen, the old past participle of shape]

missile noun (plural missiles) a weapon or other object for firing or throwing at a target. [from Latin missum = sent]

missing adjective
1 lost; not in the proper place.
2 absent.

mission noun (plural missions)
1 an important job that somebody is sent to do or feels he or she must do. **2** a place or building where missionaries work. [from Latin missio = sending someone out]

missionary noun (plural missionaries) a person who is sent to another country to spread a religious faith.

mist noun (plural mists)
1 damp cloudy air near the

ground. **2** condensed water vapour on a window, mirror, etc. [from Old English]

mistake noun (plural **mistakes**) **1** something done wrongly. **2** an incorrect action.

mistake verb (**mistakes, mistaking, mistook, mistaken**) **1** misunderstand, *Don't mistake my meaning.* **2** choose or identify wrongly, *We mistook her for her sister.* [from *mis-* + Old Norse *taka* = take]

mistaken adjective **1** incorrect. **2** having an incorrect opinion.

mistletoe noun a plant with white berries that grows as a parasite on trees. [from Old English]

mistress noun (plural **mistresses**) **1** a woman who is in charge of something. **2** a woman teacher. **3** a woman who is a man's lover but not his wife. [from Old French *maistresse*, feminine form of *maistre* = master]

mistrust verb (**mistrusts, mistrusting, mistrusted**) feel no trust in somebody or something. **mistrust** noun

misty adjective (**mistier, mistiest**) **1** full of mist. **2** not clear or distinct. **mistily** adverb, **mistiness** noun

misunderstand verb (**misunderstands, misunderstanding, misunderstood**) get a wrong idea or impression of something.

mitigating circumstances plural noun facts that may

partially excuse wrongdoing. [from Latin *mitigare* = make mild]

mitten noun (plural **mittens**) a kind of glove without separate parts for the fingers. [from French]

mix verb (**mixes, mixing, mixed**) **1** put different things together so that the substances etc. are no longer distinct; blend or combine. **2** (of a person) get together with others. **mixer** noun **mix up 1** mix thoroughly. **2** confuse.

mix noun (plural **mixes**) a mixture. [from *mixed*]

mixed adjective containing two or more kinds of things or people. [from Latin *mixtus* = mingled]

mixture noun (plural **mixtures**) **1** something made of different things mixed together. **2** the process of mixing.

mnemonic (say nim-**on**-ik) noun (plural **mnemonics**) a verse or saying that helps you to remember something. [from Greek *mnemonikos* = for the memory]

moan verb (**moans, moaning, moaned**) **1** make a long low sound of pain or suffering. **2** grumble. **moan** noun

moat noun (plural **moats**) a deep wide ditch round a castle, usually filled with water. **moated** adjective

mob noun (plural **mobs**) **1** a large disorderly crowd; a rabble. **2** a gang. [from Latin *mobile vulgus* = excitable crowd]

mobile adjective moving easily.
mobility noun
mobile noun (plural **mobiles**)
a decoration for hanging up so
that its parts move in currents
of air.
[from Latin movere = move]
mobile home noun (plural
mobile homes) a large caravan
permanently parked and used for
living in.
mobilize verb (mobilizes,
mobilizing, mobilized) assemble
people or things for a particular
purpose, especially for war.
mobilization noun
mock verb (mocks, mocking,
mocked)
1 make fun of a person or thing.
2 imitate someone or something
to make people laugh. **mockery**
noun
mock adjective imitation, not
real, mock exams.
mock-up noun (plural **mock-ups**)
a model of something, made in
order to test or study it.
mode noun (plural **modes**)
1 the way a thing is done. 2 what
is fashionable. [from Latin]
model noun (plural **models**)
1 a copy of an object, usually on
a smaller scale. 2 a particular
design. 3 a person who poses for
an artist or displays clothes by
wearing them. 4 a person or
thing that is worth copying.
model verb (models, modelling,
modelled)
1 make a model of something.
2 make according to a model.
3 work as an artist's model or
a fashion model.
[from Latin modulus = a small
measure]

modem (say moh-dem) noun
(plural **modems**) a device that
links a computer to a telephone
line. [from modulator
+ demodulator]
moderate adjective
1 medium; not extremely small
or great or hot etc., a moderate
climate. 2 not extreme or
unreasonable, moderate opinions.
moderately adverb
moderate (say mod-er-ayt) verb
(moderates, moderating,
moderated) make or become
moderate. **moderation** noun
in moderation in moderate
amounts.
[from Latin moderari = restrain]
modern adjective
1 belonging to the present or
recent times. 2 in fashion now.
modernity noun [from Latin modo
= just now]
modernize verb (modernizes,
modernizing, modernized) make
a thing more modern.
modernization noun
modest adjective
1 not vain or boastful. 2 moderate,
a modest income. 3 not showy or
splendid. 4 behaving or dressing
decently or decorously. **modestly**
adverb, **modesty** noun [from
Latin, = keeping the proper
measure]
modify verb (modifies, modifying,
modified)
1 change something slightly.
2 describe a word or limit its
meaning, Adjectives modify
nouns. **modification** noun [from
Latin modificare = to limit]
modulate verb (modulates,
modulating, modulated)
1 adjust or regulate. 2 vary in

pitch or tone etc. **3** alter an electronic wave to allow signals to be sent. **modulation** *noun*, **modulator** *noun* [same origin as *model*]

module *noun* (*plural* **modules**)
1 an independent part of a spacecraft, building, etc.
2 a unit; a section of a course of study. **modular** *adjective* [same origin as *model*]

moist *adjective* slightly wet; damp. **moistly** *adverb*, **moistness** *noun* [from old French]

moisten *verb* (**moistens**, **moistening**, **moistened**) make or become moist.

moisture *noun* water in the air or making a thing moist.

mole[1] *noun* (*plural* **moles**)
1 a small furry animal that burrows under the ground.
2 a person who secretly gives confidential information to an enemy or rival. [probably from old Dutch]

mole[2] *noun* (*plural* **moles**) a small dark spot on skin. [from Old English]

molecule *noun* (*plural* **molecules**) the smallest part into which a substance can be divided without changing its chemical nature; a group of atoms. **molecular** *adjective* [from Latin *molecula* = little mass]

molehill *noun* (*plural* **molehills**) a small pile of earth thrown up by a burrowing mole.

mollusc *noun* (*plural* **molluscs**) an animal with no backbone and a soft body protected by a shell; snails and many shellfish are molluscs. [from Latin *molluscus* = soft thing]

molten *adjective* melted; made liquid by great heat. [the old past participle of *melt*]

moment *noun* (*plural* **moments**)
1 a very short time. **2** a particular time, *Call me the moment she arrives.* [from Latin *movere* = move]

momentary *adjective* lasting for only a moment. **momentarily** *adverb*

momentous (*say* mo-ment-us) *adjective* very important. [from an old sense of *moment* = importance]

momentum *noun* amount or force of movement, *The stone gathered momentum as it rolled downhill.* [Latin, = movement]

monarch *noun* (*plural* **monarchs**) a king, queen, emperor, or empress ruling a country. **monarchic** *adjective* [from Greek *monos* = alone + *archein* = to rule]

monarchy *noun* (*plural* **monarchies**) a country ruled by a monarch. **monarchist** *noun*

monastery *noun* (*plural* **monasteries**) a building where monks live and work. **monastic** *adjective* [from Greek *monazein* = live alone]

monetary *adjective* to do with money.

money *noun*
1 coins and banknotes. **2** wealth. [same origin as *mint*[2]]

mongrel (*say* mung-rel) *noun* (*plural* **mongrels**) a dog of mixed breeds. [related to *mingle*]

monitor *noun* (*plural* **monitors**)
1 a device for watching or testing how something is working.

2 a pupil who is given a special responsibility in a school.

monitor verb (**monitors, monitoring, monitored**) watch or test how something is working. [from Latin monere = warn]

monk noun (plural **monks**) a member of a community of men who live according to the rules of a religious organization. (Compare **nun**.) [via Old English from Greek monachos = single or solitary]

monkey noun (plural **monkeys**) **1** an animal with long arms, hands with thumbs, and often a tail. **2** a mischievous person. [origin unknown]

mono- prefix **1** one. **2** single. [from Greek monos = alone]

monocle noun (plural **monocles**) a lens worn over one eye, like half of a pair of spectacles. [from mono- + Latin oculus = eye]

monogram noun (plural **monograms**) a design made up of a letter or letters, especially a person's initials. **monogrammed** adjective [from mono- + -gram]

monolith noun (plural **monoliths**) a large single upright block of stone. [from mono- + Greek lithos = stone]

monolithic adjective **1** consisting of monoliths. **2** to do with or like a monolith. **3** huge and difficult to move or change.

monologue noun (plural **monologues**) a speech by one person. [from mono- + Greek logos = word]

monopolize verb (**monopolizes, monopolizing, monopolized**) take the whole of something for yourself, One girl monopolized my attention. **monopolization** noun [from monopoly]

monopoly noun (plural **monopolies**) complete possession or control of something by one group, The company had a monopoly in supplying electricity. [from mono- + Greek polein = sell]

monosyllable noun (plural **monosyllables**) a word with only one syllable. **monosyllabic** adjective

monotone noun a level unchanging tone of voice in speaking or singing.

monotonous adjective boring because it does not change. **monotonously** adverb, **monotony** noun [from mono- + Greek tonos = tone]

monsoon noun (plural **monsoons**) **1** a strong wind in and near the Indian Ocean, bringing heavy rain in summer. **2** the rainy season brought by this wind. [via Dutch from Arabic mawsim = a season]

monster noun (plural **monsters**) **1** a large frightening creature. **2** a huge thing. **3** a wicked or cruel person.

monster adjective huge. [from Latin monstrum = marvel]

monstrosity noun (plural **monstrosities**) a monstrous thing.

monstrous adjective **1** like a monster; huge. **2** very shocking or outrageous.

month noun (plural **months**) each of the twelve parts into which a year is divided. [from Old English; related to *moon* (because time was measured by the changes in the moon's appearance)]

monthly adjective & adverb happening or done once a month.

monument noun (plural **monuments**) a statue, building, or column etc. put up as a memorial of some person or event. [from Latin *monumentum* = a memorial]

monumental adjective
1 built as a monument. 2 very large or important.

moo verb (**moos, mooing, mooed**) make the low deep sound of a cow. **moo** noun [imitating the sound]

mood noun (plural **moods**) the way someone feels, *She is in a cheerful mood.* [from Old English]

moody adjective (**moodier, moodiest**)
1 gloomy or sullen. 2 having sudden changes of mood for no apparent reason. **moodily** adverb, **moodiness** noun

moon noun (plural **moons**)
1 the natural satellite of the earth that can be seen in the sky at night. 2 a satellite of any planet.
moonbeam noun, **moonlight** noun, **moonlit** adjective

moor[1] noun (plural **moors**) an area of rough land covered with heather, bracken, and bushes.
moorland noun [from Old English]

moor[2] verb (**moors, mooring, moored**) fasten a boat etc. to a fixed object by means of a cable. [probably from old German]

mooring noun (plural **moorings**) a place where a boat can be moored.

mop noun (plural **mops**)
1 a bunch or pad of soft material fastened on the end of a stick, used for cleaning floors etc. 2 a thick mass of hair.

mop verb (**mops, mopping, mopped**) clean or wipe with a mop etc.
mop up 1 wipe or soak up liquid. 2 deal with the last parts of something, *The army is mopping up the last of the rebels.*

mope verb (**mopes, moping, moped**) be sad.

moped (say **moh**-ped) noun (plural **mopeds**) a kind of small motorcycle that can be pedalled. [from *motor* + *pedal*]

moral adjective
1 connected with what is right and wrong in behaviour.
2 virtuous. **morally** adverb, **morality** noun
moral support encouragement.

moral noun (plural **morals**) a lesson in right behaviour taught by a story or event. [from Latin *mores* = customs]

USAGE: Do not confuse with *morale*.

morale (say mor-**ahl**) noun the level of confidence and good spirits in a person or group of people, *Morale was high after the victory.* [same origin as *moral*]

USAGE: Do not confuse with *moral*.

morals *plural noun* standards of behaviour.

morbid *adjective*
1 thinking about gloomy or unpleasant things. **2** unhealthy. **morbidly** *adverb*, **morbidity** *noun* [from Latin *morbus* = disease]

more *adjective* (comparative of **much** and **many**) greater in amount etc.

more *noun* a greater amount.

more *adverb*
1 to a greater extent, *more beautiful*. **2** again, *once more*. **more or less 1** approximately. **2** nearly or practically.

moreover *adverb* besides; in addition to what has been said.

Mormon *noun* (*plural* **Mormons**) a member of a religious group founded in the USA. [the name of a prophet whom they believe wrote their sacred book]

morning *noun* (*plural* **mornings**) the early part of the day, before noon or before lunchtime. [from *morn*]

moron *noun* (*plural* **morons**) (*informal*) a very stupid person. **moronic** *adjective* [from Greek *moros* = foolish]

morose (*say* mo-rohss) *adjective* bad-tempered and miserable. **morosely** *adverb*, **moroseness** *noun* [from Latin]

Morse code *noun* a signalling code using short and long sounds or flashes of light (dots and dashes) to represent letters. [named after its American inventor, S. F. B. Morse]

morsel *noun* (*plural* **morsels**) a small piece of food. [from old French]

mortal *adjective*
1 not living for ever, *All of us are mortal.* **2** causing death; fatal, *a mortal wound.* **3** deadly, *mortal enemies.* **mortally** *adverb*, **mortality** *noun*

mortal *noun* (*plural* **mortals**) a human being, as compared to a god or immortal spirit. [from Latin *mortis* = of death]

mortar *noun* (*plural* **mortars**)
1 a mixture of sand, cement, and water used in building to stick bricks together. **2** a hard bowl in which substances are pounded with a pestle. **3** a short cannon.

mortgage (*say* mor-gij) *noun* (*plural* **mortgages**) an arrangement to borrow money to buy a house, with the house as security for the loan.

mortgage *verb* (**mortgages**, **mortgaging**, **mortgaged**) offer a house etc. as security in return for a loan. [from old French]

mortify *verb* (**mortifies**, **mortifying**, **mortified**) humiliate someone or make them feel very ashamed. **mortification** *noun* [originally = kill or destroy: from Latin *mors* = death]

mortuary *noun* (*plural* **mortuaries**) a place where dead bodies are kept before being buried. [from Latin *mortuus* = dead]

mosaic (*say* mo-zay-ik) *noun* (*plural* **mosaics**) a picture or design made from small coloured pieces of stone or glass. [via old French from Italian]

mosque (*say* mosk) *noun* (*plural* **mosques**) a building where

Muslims worship. [via French and Italian from Arabic]

mosquito noun (plural **mosquitoes**) a kind of gnat that sucks blood. [Spanish or Portuguese, = little fly]

moss noun (plural **mosses**) a plant that grows in damp places and has no flowers. **mossy** adjective

most adjective (superlative of **much** and **many**) greatest in amount etc., Most people came by bus.

most noun the greatest amount, Most of the food was eaten.

most adverb
1 to the greatest extent; more than any other, most beautiful. 2 very or extremely, most impressive.
[from Old English]

-most suffix forms superlative adjectives (e.g. hindmost, uppermost). [from Old English -mest]

mostly adverb mainly.

motel noun (plural **motels**) a hotel providing accommodation for motorists and their cars. [from motor + hotel]

moth noun (plural **moths**) an insect rather like a butterfly, that usually flies at night. [from Old English]

mother noun (plural **mothers**) a female parent. **motherhood** noun

mother verb (**mothers**, **mothering**, **mothered**) look after someone in a motherly way.

mother-in-law noun (plural **mothers-in-law**) the mother of a married person's husband or wife.

motherly adjective kind and gentle like a mother. **motherliness** noun

motion noun (plural **motions**)
1 a way of moving; movement.
2 a formal statement to be discussed and voted on at a meeting.

motion verb (**motions**, **motioning**, **motioned**) signal by a gesture, She motioned him to sit beside her.
[from Latin motio = movement]

motive noun (plural **motives**) what makes a person do something, a motive for murder.
[from Latin motivus = moving]

motor noun (plural **motors**) a machine providing power to drive machinery etc.; an engine.

motor verb (**motors**, **motoring**, **motored**) go or take someone in a car.
[Latin, = mover]

motorist noun (plural **motorists**) a person who drives a car.

motorway noun (plural **motorways**) a wide road for fast long-distance traffic.

motto noun (plural **mottoes**)
1 a short saying used as a guide for behaviour, Their motto is 'Who dares, wins'. 2 a short verse or riddle etc. found inside a cracker. [Italian]

mould[1] noun (plural **moulds**) a hollow container of a particular shape, in which a liquid or soft substance is put to set into this shape.

mould verb (**moulds**, **moulding**, **moulded**) make something have a particular shape or character.
[from Latin modulus = little measure]

mould² noun a fine furry growth of very small fungi. **mouldy** adjective [from Old Norse]

moulder verb (moulders, mouldering, mouldered) rot away or decay into dust.

moult verb (moults, moulting, moulted) shed feathers, hair, or skin etc. while a new growth forms. [from Latin mutari = to change, probably via Old English]

mound noun (plural mounds) 1 a pile of earth or stones etc. 2 a small hill.

mount verb (mounts, mounting, mounted) 1 climb or go up; ascend. 2 get on a horse or bicycle etc. 3 increase in amount, Our costs mounted. 4 place or fix in position for use or display, Mount your photos in an album.

mount noun (plural mounts) 1 a mountain, Mount Everest. 2 something on which an object is mounted. 3 a horse etc. for riding.
[from Latin mons = mountain]

mountain noun (plural mountains) 1 a very high hill. 2 a large heap or pile or quantity. **mountainous** adjective [from old French; related to mount]

mountaineer noun (plural mountaineers) a person who climbs mountains. **mountaineering** noun

mounted adjective serving on horseback, mounted police.

mourn verb (mourns, mourning, mourned) be sad, especially because someone has died. **mourner** noun [from Old English]

mournful adjective sad and sorrowful. **mournfully** adverb

mouse noun (plural mice) 1 a small animal with a long thin tail and a pointed nose. 2 (plural mouses or mice) a small device which you move around on a mat to control a computer. **mousetrap** noun, **mousy** adjective [from Old English]

mousse (say mooss) noun (plural mousses) 1 a creamy pudding flavoured with fruit or chocolate. 2 a frothy creamy substance put on the hair so that it can be styled more easily. [French, = froth]

moustache (say mus-tahsh) noun (plural moustaches) hair allowed to grow on a man's upper lip.

mouth noun (plural mouths) 1 the opening through which food is taken into the body. 2 the place where a river enters the sea. 3 an opening or outlet. **mouthful** noun

mouth organ noun (plural mouth organs) a small musical instrument that you play by blowing and sucking while passing it along your lips.

move verb (moves, moving, moved) 1 take or go from one place to another; change a person's or thing's position. 2 affect a person's feelings, Their sad story moved us deeply. 3 put forward a formal statement (a motion) to be discussed and voted on at a meeting. **mover** noun

move noun (plural moves) 1 a movement. 2 a player's turn to move a piece in chess etc.

get a move on (*informal*) hurry up.

on the move moving or making progress.

movement *noun* (*plural* **movements**)
1 moving or being moved.
2 a group of people working together to achieve something.
3 one of the main divisions of a symphony or other long musical work.

mow *verb* (**mows, mowing, mowed, mown**) cut down grass etc. **mower** *noun*

mow down knock down and kill.

MP *abbreviation* Member of Parliament.

Mr (*say* mist-er) *noun* (*plural* **Messrs**) a title put before a man's name. [short for *mister*]

Mrs (*say* mis-iz) *noun* (*plural* **Mrs**) a title put before a married woman's name. [short for *mistress*]

Ms (*say* miz) *noun* a title put before a woman's name. [from *Mrs* and *Miss*]

USAGE: You put *Ms* before the name of a woman if she does not wish to be called 'Miss' or 'Mrs', or if you do not know whether she is married.

M.Sc. *abbreviation* Master of Science.

Mt *abbreviation* mount or mountain.

much *adjective* (**more, most**) existing in a large amount, *much noise*.

much *noun* a large amount of something.

much *adverb*
1 greatly or considerably, *much to my surprise*. 2 approximately, *It is much the same*.
[from Old English]

muck *noun*
1 farmyard manure. 2 (*informal*) dirt or filth. 3 (*informal*) a mess. **mucky** *adjective*

muck *verb*

muck about (*informal*) mess about.

muck out clean out the place where an animal is kept.

muck up (*informal*) 1 make dirty. 2 make a mess of; spoil.
[probably from a Scandinavian language]

mud *noun* wet soft earth. **muddy** *adjective*, **muddiness** *noun*
[probably from old German]

muddle *verb* (**muddles, muddling, muddled**)
1 jumble or mix things up.
2 confuse. **muddler** *noun*

muddle *noun* (*plural* **muddles**) a muddled condition or thing; confusion or disorder.
[origin unknown]

mudguard *noun* (*plural* **mudguards**) a curved cover over the top part of the wheel of a bicycle etc. to protect the rider from the mud and water thrown up by the wheel.

muff *noun* (*plural* **muffs**) a short tube-shaped piece of warm material into which the hands are pushed from opposite ends.
[from Dutch]

muffin *noun* (*plural* **muffins**)
1 a flat bun eaten toasted and buttered. 2 a small sponge cake, usually containing fruit, chocolate chips, etc.

muffle *verb* (**muffles, muffling, muffled**)
1 cover or wrap something to protect it or keep it warm.
2 deaden the sound of something, *a muffled scream.*

muffler *noun* (*plural* **mufflers**) a warm scarf. [from *muffle*]

mug *noun* (*plural* **mugs**)
1 a kind of large cup, usually used without a saucer. 2 (*slang*) a fool; a person who is easily deceived. 3 (*slang*) a person's face.

mug *verb* (**mugs, mugging, mugged**) attack and rob somebody in the street. **mugger** *noun*

mule *noun* (*plural* **mules**) an animal that is the offspring of a donkey and a mare, known for being stubborn. **mulish** *adjective* [from Old English]

mull[1] *verb* (**mulls, mulling, mulled**) heat wine or beer with sugar and spices, as a drink, *mulled ale.* [origin unknown]

mull[2] *verb* (**mulls, mulling, mulled**) **mull something over** think about something carefully; ponder. [probably related to *mill*]

multi- *prefix* many (as in *multicoloured* = with many colours). [from Latin *multus* = many]

multicultural *adjective* made up of people of many different races, religions, and cultures.

multilateral *adjective* (of an agreement or treaty) made between three or more people or countries etc. [from Latin *multilaterus* = many sided]

multimedia *adjective* using more than one medium, *a multimedia show with pictures, lights, and music.*

multimedia *noun* a computer program with sound and still and moving pictures linked to the text.

multimillionaire *noun* (*plural* **multimillionaires**) a person with a fortune of several million pounds.

multinational *noun* (*plural* **multinationals**) a large business company which works in several countries.

multiple *adjective* having many parts.

multiple *noun* (*plural* **multiples**) a number that contains another number (a *factor*) an exact amount of times with no remainder, *8 and 12 are multiples of 4.*
[same origin as *multiply*]

multiple sclerosis *noun* a disease of the nervous system which makes a person unable to control their movements, and may affect their sight.

multiply *verb* (**multiplies, multiplying, multiplied**)
1 take a number a given quantity of times, *Five multiplied by four equals twenty (5 × 4 = 20).* 2 make or become many; increase. **multiplication** *noun*, **multiplier** *noun* [from Latin *multiplex* = many-sided]

multiracial *adjective* consisting of people of many different races.

multitude *noun* (*plural* **multitudes**) a great number of

people or things. **multitudinous**
adjective [from Latin *multus*
= many]

mumble *verb* (**mumbles,**
mumbling, mumbled) speak
indistinctly so that you are not
easy to hear. **mumble** *noun*,
mumbler *noun*

mumbo-jumbo *noun* talk or
ceremony that has no real
meaning. [probably from a West
African language]

mummy *noun* (*plural* **mummies**)
a corpse wrapped in cloth and
treated with oils etc. before being
buried so that it does not decay,
as was the custom in ancient
Egypt. **mummify** *verb* [from
Arabic]

mumps *noun* an infectious
disease that causes the neck to
swell painfully. [from an old
word *mump* = pull a face
(because the glands in the face
sometimes swell)]

munitions *plural noun* military
weapons and ammunition etc.
[from Latin *munitum* = fortified]

mural *adjective* on or to do with
a wall.
mural *noun* (*plural* **murals**) a wall
painting.
[from Latin *murus* = wall]

murder *verb* (**murders,**
murdering, murdered) kill
a person unlawfully and
deliberately. **murderer** *noun*,
murderess *noun*
murder *noun* (*plural* **murders**)
the murdering of somebody.
murderous *adjective*
[from Old English]

murky *adjective* (**murkier,**
murkiest) dark and gloomy. **murk**
noun, **murkiness** *noun* [from Old
English]

murmur *verb* (**murmurs,**
murmuring, murmured)
1 make a low continuous sound.
2 speak in a soft voice. **murmur**
noun [from Latin]

muscle *noun* (*plural* **muscles**)
1 a band or bundle of fibrous
tissue that can contract and relax
and so produce movement in
parts of the body. **2** the power of
muscles; strength. **muscular**
adjective, **muscularity** *noun* [from
Latin]

museum *noun* (*plural* **museums**)
a place where interesting, old, or
valuable objects are displayed for
people to see. [from Greek
mouseion = place of Muses
(goddesses of the arts and
sciences)]

mush *noun* soft pulp. **mushy**
adjective [different spelling of
mash]

mushroom *noun* (*plural*
mushrooms) an edible fungus
with a stem and a dome-shaped
top.

music *noun*
1 a pattern of pleasant or
interesting sounds made by
instruments or by the voice.
2 printed or written symbols
which stand for musical sounds.
[from Greek *mousike* = of the
Muses (see **museum**)]

musical *adjective*
1 to do with music. **2** producing
music. **3** good at music or
interested in it. **musically** *adverb*

musical noun (plural **musicals**)
a play or film containing a lot of
songs.

musician noun (plural **musicians**)
someone who plays a musical
instrument.

Muslim noun (plural **Muslims**)
a person who follows the
religious teachings of
Muhammad (who lived in about
570–632), set out in the Koran.
[Arabic, = someone who submits
to God]

must auxiliary verb used to
express
1 necessity or obligation (You
must go). 2 certainty (You must be
joking!) [from Old English]

mustard noun a yellow paste or
powder used to give food a hot
taste.
mustard and cress small green
plants eaten in salads.

muster noun (plural **musters**) an
assembly of people or things.
pass muster be up to the required
standard.
[from Latin monstrare = to show]

mustn't (mainly spoken) must
not.

musty adjective (**mustier**,
mustiest) smelling or tasting
mouldy or stale. **mustiness** noun
[probably from moist]

mutation noun (plural
mutations) a change in the form
of a living creature because of
changes in its genes.

mute adjective
1 silent; not speaking or able to
speak. 2 not pronounced, The g in
'gnat' is mute. **mutely** adverb,
muteness noun

mutilate verb (**mutilates**,
mutilating, **mutilated**) damage
something by breaking or cutting
off part of it. **mutilation** noun
[from Latin mutilus = maimed]

mutineer noun (plural **mutineers**)
a person who mutinies.

mutiny noun (plural **mutinies**)
rebellion against authority,
especially refusal by members of
the armed forces to obey orders.
mutinous adjective, **mutinously**
adverb

mutiny verb (**mutinies**,
mutinying, **mutinied**) take part in
a mutiny.
[from old French]

mutter verb (**mutters**, **muttering**,
muttered)
1 speak in a low voice. 2 grumble.
mutter noun [related to mute]

mutton noun meat from a sheep.
[from old French]

mutual (say **mew**-tew-al) adjective
1 given or done to each other,
mutual destruction. 2 felt by each
for the other, mutual affection.
mutually adverb

muzzle noun (plural **muzzles**)
1 an animal's nose and mouth.
2 a cover put over an animal's
nose and mouth so that it cannot
bite. 3 the open end of a gun.

muzzle verb (**muzzles**, **muzzling**,
muzzled)
1 put a muzzle on an animal.
2 silence; prevent a person from
expressing opinions.
[from old French]

my adjective belonging to me.
[originally, the form of mine'
used before consonants]

myself pronoun I or me and
nobody else. (Compare herself.)

mysterious *adjective* full of mystery; puzzling. **mysteriously** *adverb*

mystery *noun* (*plural* **mysteries**) something that cannot be explained or understood; something puzzling. [from Greek *mysterion* = a secret thing or ceremony]

mystic *adjective*
1 having a spiritual meaning.
2 mysterious and filling people with wonder. **mystical** *adjective*, **mystically** *adverb*, **mysticism** *noun*

mystic *noun* (*plural* **mystics**) a person who seeks to obtain spiritual contact with God by deep religious meditation. [from Greek *mystikos* = secret]

mystify *verb* (**mystifies**, **mystifying**, **mystified**) puzzle or bewilder. **mystification** *noun*

myth (*say* mith) *noun* (*plural* **myths**)
1 an old story containing ideas about ancient times or about supernatural beings. (Compare *legend*.) 2 an untrue story or belief. [from Greek *mythos* = story]

mythical *adjective* imaginary; found only in myths, *a mythical animal.*

mythology *noun* myths or the study of myths. **mythological** *adjective*

Nn

N. *abbreviation*
1 north. 2 northern.

nag *verb* (**nags**, **nagging**, **nagged**)
1 pester a person by keeping on criticizing, complaining, or asking for things. 2 keep on hurting, *a nagging pain.*

nail *noun* (*plural* **nails**)
1 the hard covering over the end of a finger or toe. 2 a small sharp piece of metal hammered in to fasten pieces of wood etc. together.

nail *verb* (**nails**, **nailing**, **nailed**)
1 fasten with a nail or nails.
2 catch; arrest.
[from Old English]

naked *adjective* without any clothes or coverings on. **nakedly** *adverb*, **nakedness** *noun*

naked eye *noun* the eye when it is not helped by a telescope or microscope etc.

name *noun* (*plural* **names**)
1 the word or words by which a person, animal, place, or thing is known. 2 a reputation.

name *verb* (**names**, **naming**, **named**)
1 give a name to. 2 state the name or names of.
name the day decide when something, especially a wedding, is to take place or happen, *Have you two named the day yet?*

namely *adverb* that is to say, *My two favourite subjects are sciences, namely chemistry and biology.*

nap noun (plural **naps**) a short sleep.

catch a person napping catch a person unprepared for something or not alert.

napkin noun (plural **napkins**)
1 a piece of cloth or paper used to keep your clothes clean or to wipe your lips or fingers; a serviette, *a table napkin*.
2 a nappy. [from French *nappe* = tablecloth, + *-kin*]

nappy noun (plural **nappies**) a piece of cloth or other fabric put round a baby's bottom.

narcotic noun (plural **narcotics**) a drug that makes a person sleepy or unconscious. **narcotic** *adjective*, **narcosis** noun [from Greek *narke* = numbness]

narrative noun (plural **narratives**) a spoken or written account of something.

narrow *adjective*
1 not wide or broad.
2 uncomfortably close; with only a small margin of safety, *a narrow escape*. **narrowly** *adverb*

narrow-minded *adjective* not tolerant of other people's beliefs and ways.

nasty *adjective* (**nastier, nastiest**)
1 unpleasant. **2** unkind. **nastily** *adverb*, **nastiness** noun [origin unknown]

nation noun (plural **nations**) a large community of people most of whom have the same ancestors, language, history, and customs, and who usually live in the same part of the world under one government. **national** *adjective* & noun, **nationally** *adverb* [from Latin *natio* = birth or race]

national anthem noun (plural **national anthems**) a nation's official song, which is played or sung on important occasions.

national curriculum noun an official list of the subjects that must be taught by state schools.

nationalist noun (plural **nationalists**)
1 a person who is very patriotic.
2 a person who wants his or her country to be independent, rather than being a part of another country, *Scottish Nationalists*. **nationalism** noun, **nationalistic** *adjective*

nationality noun (plural **nationalities**) the condition of belonging to a particular nation, *What is his nationality?*

nationalize *verb* (**nationalizes, nationalizing, nationalized**) put an industry etc. under public or government ownership. **nationalization** noun

national park noun (plural **national parks**) an area of natural beauty which is protected by the government and which the public may visit.

native noun (plural **natives**) a person born in a particular place, *He is a native of Sweden*.

native *adjective*
1 belonging to a person because of the place of his or her birth, *my native country*. **2** natural or instinctive; belonging to a person by nature, *native wit, native ability*. [from Latin *nativus* = natural or innate]

Native American noun (plural **Native Americans**) one of the original inhabitants of North and South America.

USAGE: See note at **Indian**.

natural adjective
1 produced or done by nature, not by people or machines. **2** normal; not surprising. **3** (of a note in music) neither sharp nor flat. **naturally** adverb, **naturalness** noun

natural noun (plural **naturals**)
1 a person who is naturally good at something. **2** a natural note in music; a sign (♮) that shows this.

natural history noun the study of plants and animals.

naturalist noun (plural **naturalists**) an expert in natural history.

natural science noun the study of physics, chemistry, and biology.

natural selection noun Charles Darwin's theory that only the plants and animals best suited to their surroundings will survive and breed.

nature noun (plural **natures**)
1 everything in the world that was not made by people. **2** the characteristics of a person or thing, *She has a loving nature.*
3 a kind or sort of thing, *He likes things of that nature.*

naughty adjective (**naughtier, naughtiest**)
1 badly behaved or disobedient.
2 slightly rude or indecent, *naughty pictures.* **naughtily** adverb, **naughtiness** noun
[originally = poor: from *naught*]

nausea (say naw-zee-a) noun a feeling of sickness or disgust. **nauseous** adjective, **nauseating** adjective [from Greek *nausia* = seasickness]

nautical adjective of ships or sailors. [from Greek *nautes* = sailor]

nautical mile noun (plural **nautical miles**) a measure of distance used at sea, 2,025 yards (1.852 kilometres).

naval adjective to do with a navy. [from Latin *navis* = ship]

navel noun (plural **navels**) the small hollow in the centre of the abdomen, where the umbilical cord was attached. [from Old English]

navigate verb (**navigates, navigating, navigated**)
1 sail in or through a river or sea etc., *The ship navigated the Suez Canal.* **2** make sure that a ship, aircraft, or vehicle is going in the right direction. **navigation** noun, **navigator** noun [from Latin *navis* = ship + *agere* = to drive]

navy noun (plural **navies**)
1 a country's warships and the people trained to use them. **2** (also **navy blue**) a very dark blue, the colour of naval uniform. [from old French *navie* = a ship or fleet; related to *naval*]

Nazi (say nah-tsee) noun (plural **Nazis**) a member of the National Socialist Party in Germany in Hitler's time, with Fascist beliefs. **Nazism** noun [from the German pronunciation of *Nationalsozialist*]

NB abbreviation take note that (Latin *nota bene* = note well).

NE *abbreviation*
1 north-east. 2 north-eastern.

near *adverb & adjective* not far away.
  near by not far away, *They live near by.*
  near *preposition* not far away from, *near the shops.*

nearby *adjective* near, *a nearby house.*

nearly *adverb*
1 almost, *We have nearly finished.* 2 closely, *They are nearly related.*

neat *adjective* (**neater, neatest**)
1 simple and clean and tidy. 2 skilful. 3 undiluted, *neat whisky.* **neatly** *adverb,* **neatness** *noun* [from Latin *nitidus* = clean, shining]

neaten *verb* (**neatens, neatening, neatened**) make or become neat.

nebula *noun* (*plural* **nebulae**) a bright or dark patch in the sky, caused by a distant galaxy or a cloud of dust or gas. [Latin, = mist]

nebulous *adjective* indistinct or vague, *nebulous ideas.* [same origin as *nebula*]

necessary *adjective* not able to be done without; essential.
  necessarily *adverb* [from Latin]

necessity *noun* (*plural* **necessities**)
1 need, *the necessity of buying food and clothing.* 2 something necessary.

neck *noun* (*plural* **necks**)
1 the part of the body that joins the head to the shoulders. 2 the part of a garment round the neck. 3 a narrow part of something, especially of a bottle.

necklace *noun* (*plural* **necklaces**) an ornament worn round the neck.

necktie *noun* (*plural* **neckties**) a strip of material worn passing under the collar of a shirt and knotted in front.

need *verb* (**needs, needing, needed**)
1 be without something you should have; require, *We need two more chairs.* 2 (as an *auxiliary verb*) have to do something, *You need not answer.*

need *noun* (*plural* **needs**)
1 something needed; a necessary thing. 2 a situation where something is necessary, *There is no need to cry.* 3 great poverty or hardship. **needful** *adjective,* **needless** *adjective* [from Old English]

needle *noun* (*plural* **needles**)
1 a very thin pointed piece of steel used in sewing. 2 something long and thin and sharp, *a knitting needle, pine needles.* 3 the pointer of a meter or compass.

needlework *noun* sewing or embroidery.

needy *adjective* (**needier, neediest**) very poor; lacking things necessary for life. **neediness** *noun*

negative *adjective*
1 that says 'no', *a negative answer.* 2 not definite or positive. 3 less than nought; minus. 4 to do with the kind of electric charge carried by electrons. **negatively** *adverb*

USAGE: The opposite of sense 1 is *affirmative,* and of senses 2, 3, 4 *positive.*

negative noun (plural **negatives**)
1 a negative statement.
2 a photograph on film with the dark parts light and the light parts dark, from which a positive print (with the dark and light or colours correct) can be made.

neglect verb (**neglects**, **neglecting**, **neglected**)
1 not look after or attend to a person or thing. 2 not do something; forget, He neglected to shut the door.

neglect noun neglecting or being neglected. **neglectful** adjective
[from Latin nec = not + legere = choose]

negligence noun lack of proper care or attention; carelessness. **negligent** adjective, **negligently** adverb [same origin as neglect]

negligible adjective not big enough or important enough to be worth bothering about. [from French négliger = neglect]

negotiable adjective
1 able to be changed after being discussed, The salary is negotiable. 2 (of a cheque) able to be changed for cash or transferred to another person. [from negotiate]

negotiate verb (**negotiates**, **negotiating**, **negotiated**)
1 bargain or discuss with others in order to reach an agreement.
2 arrange after discussion, They negotiated a treaty. 3 get over an obstacle or difficulty. **negotiation** noun, **negotiator** noun [from Latin negotium = business]

neigh verb (**neighs**, **neighing**, **neighed**) make the high-pitched cry of a horse. **neigh** noun

neighbour noun (plural **neighbours**) a person who lives next door or near to another. **neighbouring** adjective, **neighbourly** adjective [from Old English neahgebur = near dweller]

neighbourhood noun (plural **neighbourhoods**)
1 the surrounding district or area. 2 a part of a town where people live, a quiet neighbourhood.

neither (say ny-ther or nee-ther) adjective & pronoun not either.

USAGE: Correct use is Neither of them likes it. Neither he nor his children like it. Use a singular verb (e.g. likes) unless one of its subjects is plural (e.g. children).

neither adverb & conjunction neither ... nor not one thing and not the other, She neither knew nor cared.
[from Old English]

USAGE: Say I don't know that either (not 'neither').

neo- prefix new. [from Greek]

neolithic (say nee-o-lith-ik) adjective belonging to the later part of the Stone Age. [from neo- + Greek lithos = stone]

neon noun a gas that glows when electricity passes through it, used in glass tubes to make illuminated signs. [from Greek neos = new]

nephew noun (plural **nephews**)
the son of a person's brother or sister.

nerve noun (plural **nerves**)
1 any of the fibres in the body that carry messages to and from the brain, so that parts of the body can feel and move.
2 courage; calmness in a dangerous situation, *Don't lose your nerve.* **3** impudence, *You've got a nerve!*
nerves plural noun nervousness.

nerve verb (**nerves, nerving, nerved**) give strength or courage to someone.
[from Latin *nervus* = sinew]

nervous adjective
1 easily upset or agitated; excitable. **2** slightly afraid; timid. **3** of the nerves, *a nervous illness.*
nervously adverb, **nervousness** noun

nervous breakdown noun (plural **nervous breakdowns**)
a state of severe depression and anxiety, so that the person cannot cope with life.

nervous system noun (plural **nervous systems**) the system, consisting of the brain, spinal cord, and nerves, which sends electrical messages from one part of the body to another.

-ness suffix forming nouns from adjectives (e.g. *kindness, sadness*). [from Old English]

nest noun (plural **nests**)
1 a structure or place in which a bird lays its eggs and feeds its young. **2** a place where some small creatures (e.g. mice, wasps) live. **3** a set of similar things that fit inside each other, *a nest of tables.*

nest verb (**nests, nesting, nested**)
1 have or make a nest. **2** fit inside something.
[from Old English]

nest egg noun (plural **nest eggs**)
a sum of money saved up for future use. [originally = an egg left in the nest to encourage a hen to lay more]

nestle verb (**nestles, nestling, nestled**) curl up comfortably.
[from Old English *nestlian* = to nest]

net¹ noun (plural **nets**)
1 material made of pieces of thread, cord, or wire etc. joined together in a criss-cross pattern with holes between. **2** something made of this.

net verb (**nets, netting, netted**) cover or catch with a net.
[from Old English]

net² adjective remaining when nothing more is to be deducted, *The net weight, without the box, is 100 grams.* (Compare *gross.*)

net verb (**nets, netting, netted**) obtain or produce as net profit.
[from French *net* = neat]

netball noun a game in which two teams try to throw a ball into a high net hanging from a ring.

netting noun a piece of net.

nettle noun (plural **nettles**) a wild plant with leaves that sting when they are touched.

nettle verb (**nettles, nettling, nettled**) annoy or provoke someone.

network noun (plural **networks**)
1 a net-like arrangement of connected lines or parts, *the railway network.* **2** a group of radio or television stations

which broadcast the same programmes. **3** a set of computers which are linked to each other.

neurotic (say newr-**ot**-ik) *adjective* always very worried about something. [from Greek *neuron* = nerve]

neuter *adjective*
1 neither masculine nor feminine. **2** (in some languages) belonging to the class of words which are neither masculine nor feminine, such as *Fenster* in German.

neuter *verb* (neuters, neutering, neutered) remove an animal's sex organs so that it cannot breed. [Latin, = neither]

neutral *adjective*
1 not supporting either side in a war or quarrel. **2** not very distinctive, *a neutral colour such as grey*. **3** neither acid nor alkaline. **neutrally** *adverb*, **neutrality** *noun* [same origin as *neuter*]

neutral gear *noun* a gear that is not connected to the driving parts of an engine.

neutron *noun* (*plural* neutrons) a particle with no electric charge. [from *neutral*]

never *adverb*
1 at no time; not ever. **2** not at all. [from Old English *naefre* = not ever]

nevertheless *adverb* & *conjunction* in spite of this; although this is a fact.

new *adjective* not existing before; just made, invented, discovered, or received etc. **newly** *adverb*, **newness** *noun*

new *adverb* newly, *newborn*; *new-laid*.

newcomer *noun* (*plural* **newcomers**) a person who has arrived recently.

newfangled *adjective* disliked because it is new in method or style. [from *new* + Middle English *fang* = seize]

newly *adverb*
1 recently. **2** in a new way.

new moon *noun* (*plural* **new moons**) the moon at the beginning of its cycle, when only a thin crescent can be seen.

news *noun*
1 information about recent events or a broadcast report of this. **2** a piece of new information.

newsagent *noun* (*plural* **newsagents**) a shopkeeper who sells newspapers.

newspaper *noun* (*plural* **newspapers**)
1 a daily or weekly publication on large sheets of paper, containing news reports, articles, etc. **2** the sheets of paper forming a newspaper, *Wrap it in newspaper.*

newt *noun* (*plural* **newts**) a small animal rather like a lizard, that lives near or in water. [from Old English: originally *an ewt*]

newton *noun* (*plural* **newtons**) a unit for measuring force. [named after an English scientist, Isaac Newton]

New Year's Day *noun* 1 January.

next *adjective* nearest; coming immediately after, *on the next day.*

next *adverb*
1 in the next place. **2** on the next occasion, *What happens next?* [from Old English]

next door adverb & adjective in the next house or room.

nib noun (plural **nibs**) the pointed metal part of a pen.

nibble verb (**nibbles, nibbling, nibbled**) take small, quick, or gentle bites.

nice adjective (**nicer, nicest**)
1 pleasant or kind. **2** precise or careful, *Dictionaries make nice distinctions between meanings of words*. **nicely** adverb **niceness** noun [originally = stupid: from Latin *nescius* = ignorant]

nick noun (plural **nicks**)
1 a small cut or notch. **2** (slang) a police station or prison.
in good nick (informal) in good condition.
in the nick of time only just in time.

nickel noun (plural **nickels**)
1 a silvery-white metal.
2 (American) a 5-cent coin. [from German]

nickname noun (plural **nicknames**) a name given to a person instead of his or her real name. [originally *an eke-name*: from Middle English *eke* = addition, + *name*]

nicotine noun a poisonous substance found in tobacco. [from the name of J. Nicot, who introduced tobacco into France in 1560]

niece noun (plural **nieces**) the daughter of a person's brother or sister. [from French; related to *nephew*]

niggardly adjective mean or stingy. **niggardliness** noun [from Middle English *nig* = a mean person]

night noun (plural **nights**)
1 the dark hours between sunset and sunrise. **2** a particular night or evening, *the first night of the play*.

nightclub noun (plural **nightclubs**) a place that is open at night where people go to drink and dance.

nightdress noun (plural **nightdresses**) a loose dress that girls or women wear in bed.

nightingale noun (plural **nightingales**) a small brown bird that sings sweetly. [from Old English *nihtegala* = night-singer (because it often sings until late in the evening)]

nightmare noun (plural **nightmares**)
1 a frightening dream. **2** an unpleasant experience, *the journey was a nightmare*.

nightmarish adjective [from *night* + Middle English *mare* = an evil spirit]

nil noun nothing or nought. [from Latin *nihil* = nothing]

nimble adjective able to move quickly; agile. **nimbly** adverb

nine adjective & noun (plural **nines**) the number 9. **ninth** adjective & noun

nineteen adjective & noun the number 19. **nineteenth** adjective & noun

ninety adjective & noun (plural **nineties**) the number 90. **ninetieth** adjective & noun

nip verb (**nips, nipping, nipped**)
1 pinch or bite quickly.
2 (informal) go quickly.

nip noun (plural **nips**)
1 a quick pinch or bite. **2** sharp

coldness, *There's a nip in the air.*
3 a small drink of a spirit, *a nip of brandy.*

nippers *plural noun* pincers.

nipple *noun* (*plural* **nipples**)
a small projecting part, especially at the front of a person's breast.

nirvana *noun* (in Buddhism and Hinduism) the highest state of knowledge and understanding, achieved by meditation. [Sanskrit]

nit *noun* (*plural* **nits**) a parasitic insect or its egg, found in people's hair. [from Old English]

nit-picking *noun* pointing out very small faults.

nitrate *noun* (*plural* **nitrates**)
1 a chemical compound containing nitrogen. **2** potassium or sodium nitrate, used as a fertilizer.

nitrogen (*say* ny-tro-jen) *noun*
a gas that makes up about four-fifths of the air. [from *nitre* = a substance once thought to be a vital part of the air]

no *adjective* not any, *We have no money.*

no *adverb*
1 used to deny or refuse something, *Will you come? No.*
2 not at all, *She is no better.*
[from *none*]

No. or **no.** *abbreviation* (*plural* **Nos.** or **nos.**) number. [from Latin *numero* = by number]

noble *adjective* (**nobler**, **noblest**)
1 of high social rank; aristocratic. **2** having a very good character or qualities, *a noble king.* **3** stately or impressive, *a noble building.* **nobly** *adverb*, **nobility** *noun*

noble *noun* (*plural* **nobles**)
a person of high social rank.
nobleman *noun*, **noblewoman** *noun*
[from Latin]

nobody *pronoun* no person; no one.

nobody *noun* (*plural* **nobodies**)
(*informal*) an unimportant or unimpressive person; a nonentity.

nocturnal *adjective*
1 happening at night. **2** active at night, *nocturnal animals.* [from Latin *noctis* = of night]

nod *verb* (**nods**, **nodding**, **nodded**)
1 move the head up and down, especially as a way of agreeing with somebody or as a greeting.
2 be drowsy. **nod** *noun*

noise *noun* (*plural* **noises**)
a sound, especially one that is loud or unpleasant. **noisy** *adjective*, **noisily** *adverb*, **noiseless** *adjective* [from French]

nomad *noun* (*plural* **nomads**)
a member of a tribe that moves from place to place looking for pasture for their animals.
nomadic *adjective* [from Greek *nomas* = roaming]

no man's land *noun* an area that does not belong to anybody, especially the land between opposing armies.

nominate *verb* (**nominates**, **nominating**, **nominated**) name a person or thing to be appointed or chosen. **nomination** *noun*, **nominator** *noun* [from Latin *nominare* = to name]

non- *prefix* not. [from Latin]

non-commissioned officer *noun* (*plural* **non-commissioned officers**) a member of the armed forces, such as a corporal or sergeant, who has not been commissioned as an officer but has been promoted from the ranks of ordinary soldiers.

non-committal *adjective* not committing yourself; not showing what you think.

nondescript *adjective* having no special or distinctive qualities and therefore difficult to describe.

none *pronoun*
1 not any. **2** no one, *None can tell.* [from Old English *nan* = not one]

USAGE: It is better to use a singular verb (e.g. *None of them is here*), but the plural is not incorrect (e.g. *None of them are here*).

nonentity (*say* non-en-tit-ee) *noun* (*plural* **nonentities**) an unimportant person. [from *non-* + *entity*]

non-existent *adjective* not existing or unreal.

non-fiction *noun* writings that are not fiction; books about real people and things and true events.

non-flammable *adjective* not able to be set on fire.

USAGE: See note at *inflammable*.

nonplussed *adjective* puzzled or confused. [from Latin *non plus* = not further]

nonsense *noun*
1 words put together in a way that does not mean anything. **2** stupid ideas or behaviour.
nonsensical (*say* non-sens-ik-al) *adjective* [from *non-* + *sense*]

non-stop *adjective* & *adverb*
1 not stopping, *They talked non-stop for hours.* **2** not stopping between two main stations, *a non-stop train.*

noodles *plural noun* pasta made in narrow strips, used in soups etc. [from German]

nook *noun* (*plural* **nooks**) a sheltered corner; a recess.

noon *noun* twelve o'clock midday. [via Old English from Latin]

no one *noun* no person; nobody.

noose *noun* (*plural* **nooses**) a loop in a rope that gets smaller when the rope is pulled. [origin unknown]

nor *conjunction* and not, *She cannot do it; nor can I.*

normal *adjective*
1 usual or ordinary. **2** natural and healthy; without a physical or mental illness. **normally** *adverb*, **normality** *noun*

Norman *noun* (*plural* **Normans**) a member of the people of Normandy in northern France, who conquered England in 1066. **Norman** *adjective* [from Old Norse *northmathr* = man from the north (because the Normans were partly descended from the Vikings)]

north *noun*
1 the direction to the left of a person who faces east. **2** the northern part of a country, city, etc.

north *adjective* & *adverb* towards or in the north. **northerly** *adjective*, **northern** *adjective*, **northerner** *noun*, **northernmost** *adjective* [from Old English]

north-east noun, adjective & adverb midway between north and east. **north-easterly, north-eastern** adjective

northward adjective & adverb towards the north. **northwards** adverb

north-west noun, adjective & adverb midway between north and west. **north-westerly, north-western** adjective

Nos. or **nos.** plural of **No.** or **no.**

nose noun (plural **noses**)
1 the part of the face that is used for breathing and for smelling things. 2 the front end or part.

nosedive noun (plural **nosedives**) a steep downward dive, especially of an aircraft. **nosedive** verb

nostalgia (say nos-**tal**-ja) noun sentimental remembering or longing for the past. **nostalgic** adjective, **nostalgically** adverb [originally = homesickness: from Greek nostos = return home + algos = pain]

nostril noun (plural **nostrils**) either of the two openings in the nose. [from Old English nosthryl = nose-hole]

nosy adjective (**nosier, nosiest**) inquisitive. **nosily** adverb, **nosiness** noun [from sticking your nose in = being inquisitive]

not adverb used to change the meaning of something to its opposite or absence. [from nought]

notation noun (plural **notations**) a system of symbols representing numbers, quantities, musical notes, etc.

notch noun (plural **notches**) a small V-shape cut into a surface.

note noun (plural **notes**)
1 something written down as a reminder or as a comment or explanation. 2 a short letter. 3 a banknote, a £5 note. 4 a single sound in music. 5 any of the black or white keys on a piano etc. (see key 3). 6 a sound or quality that indicates something, a note of warning. 7 notice or attention, Take note.

note verb (**notes, noting, noted**)
1 make a note about something; write down. 2 notice or pay attention to, Note what we say. [from Latin nota = a mark]

notebook noun (plural **notebooks**) a book with blank pages on which to write notes.

notepaper noun paper for writing letters.

nothing noun
1 no thing; not anything. 2 no amount; nought.
for nothing 1 without payment, free. 2 without a result. [from no thing]

notice noun (plural **notices**)
1 something written or printed and displayed for people to see. 2 attention, It escaped my notice. 3 information that something is going to happen; warning that you are about to end an agreement or a person's employment etc., We gave him a month's notice.

notice verb (**notices, noticing, noticed**) see or become aware of something. [from Latin notus = known]

noticeable adjective easily seen or noticed. **noticeably** adverb

notion noun (plural **notions**) an idea, especially one that is vague or incorrect. [from Latin notio = getting to know]

notorious adjective well-known for something bad. **notoriously** adverb, **notoriety** (say noh-ter-I-it-ee) noun [same origin as notice]

notwithstanding preposition in spite of.

nought (say nawt) noun
1 the figure 0. **2** nothing. [from Old English nowiht = not anything]

noun noun (plural **nouns**) a word that stands for a person, place, or thing. Common nouns are words such as boy, dog, river, sport, table, which are used of a whole kind of people or things; proper nouns are words such as Charles, Thames, and London which name a particular person or thing. [from Latin nomen = name]

nourish verb (**nourishes**, **nourishing**, **nourished**) keep a person, animal, or plant alive and well by means of food. **nourishment** noun [from old French; related to nutrient]

novel noun (plural **novels**) a story that fills a whole book.

novel adjective of a new and unusual kind, a novel experience. [from Latin novus = new]

novelist noun (plural **novelists**) a person who writes novels.

novelty noun (plural **novelties**)
1 newness and originality. **2** something new and unusual. **3** a small and unusual object, suitable as a small gift.

novice noun (plural **novices**)
1 a beginner. **2** a person preparing to be a monk or nun. [from French; related to novel]

now adverb
1 at this time. **2** by this time. **3** immediately, You must go now. **4** I wonder, or I am telling you, Now why didn't I think of that? **now and again** or **now and then** sometimes; occasionally.

now conjunction as a result of or at the same time as something, Now that you have come, we'll start.

now noun this moment, They will be at home by now.

nowadays adverb at the present time, as contrasted with years ago.

nowhere adverb not anywhere.

nowhere noun no place, Nowhere is as beautiful as Scotland.

nozzle noun (plural **nozzles**) the spout of a hose or pipe etc. [= little nose]

nuclear adjective
1 to do with a nucleus or nuclei. **2** using the energy that is created by reactions in the nuclei of atoms.

nucleus noun (plural **nuclei**)
1 the part in the centre of something, round which other things are grouped. **2** the central part of an atom or of a seed or a biological cell. [Latin, = kernel]

nude adjective not wearing any clothes; naked. **nudity** noun [from Latin nudus = bare]

nudge verb (**nudges**, **nudging**, **nudged**)
1 poke a person gently with your elbow. **2** push slightly or gradually. **nudge** noun [origin unknown]

nugget noun (plural **nuggets**)
a rough lump of gold or platinum
found in the earth. [origin
unknown]

nuisance noun (plural **nuisances**)
an annoying person or thing.
[from French nuire = to hurt
someone]

numb adjective unable to feel or
move. **numbly** adverb, **numbness**
noun

number noun (plural **numbers**)
1 a symbol or word indicating
how many; a numeral or figure.
2 a numeral given to a thing to
identify it, a telephone number.
3 a quantity of people or things,
the number of people present. **4** one
issue of a magazine or
newspaper. **5** a song or piece of
music.

USAGE: Note that a number of,
meaning 'several', should be
followed by a plural verb: A
number of problems remain.

number verb (**numbers**,
numbering, **numbered**)
1 mark with numbers. **2** count.
3 amount to. The crowd
numbered 10,000.
[from old French; related to
numeral]

numeral noun (plural **numerals**)
a symbol that represents a certain
number; a figure. [from Latin
numerus = number]

numerate (say new-mer-at)
adjective having a good basic
knowledge of mathematics.
numeraoy noun [same origin as
numeral]

numerator noun (plural
numerators) the number above
the line in a fraction, showing

how many parts are to be taken,
e.g. 2 in ⅜. (Compare
denominator.)

numerical (say new-merri-kal)
adjective of a number or series of
numbers, in numerical order.
numerically adverb [same origin
as numeral]

numerous adjective many. [same
origin as numeral]

nun noun (plural **nuns**) a member
of a community of women who
live according to the rules of
a religious organization.
(Compare monk.) [via Old
English from Latin nonna,
feminine of nonnus = monk]

nunnery noun (plural **nunneries**)
a convent.

nurse noun (plural **nurses**)
1 a person trained to look after
people who are ill or injured.
2 a woman employed to look after
young children.

nurse verb (say **nurses**, **nursing**,
nursed)
1 look after someone who is ill or
injured. **2** hold carefully.
3 feed a baby.
[from nourish]

nursemaid noun (plural
nursemaids) a young woman
employed to look after young
children.

nursery noun (plural **nurseries**)
1 a place where young children
are looked after or play. **2** a place
where young plants are grown
and usually for sale.

nursery rhyme noun (plural
nursery rhymes) a simple rhyme
or song of the kind that young
children like.

nursery school noun (plural
nursery schools) a school for
children below primary school
age.

nursing home noun (plural
nursing homes) a small hospital
or home for invalids.

nut noun (plural **nuts**)
1 a fruit with a hard shell.
2 a kernel. 3 a small piece of
metal with a hole in the middle,
for screwing onto a bolt. 4 (slang)
the head. 5 (slang) a mad or
eccentric person. **nutty** adjective
[from Old English]

nutcrackers plural noun pincers
for cracking nuts.

nutrition (say new-trish-on) noun
1 nourishment. 2 the study of
what nourishes people.
nutritional adjective, **nutritionally**
adverb

nutritious (say new-trish-us)
adjective nourishing; giving good
nourishment. **nutritiousness**
noun

nutshell noun (plural **nutshells**)
the shell of a nut.
in a nutshell stated very briefly.

nuzzle verb (**nuzzles**, **nuzzling**,
nuzzled) rub gently with the
nose. [from *nose*]

NW abbreviation
1 north-west. 2 north-western.

nylon noun a synthetic, strong,
lightweight cloth or fibre.
[invented to go with *rayon* and
cotton]

NZ abbreviation New Zealand.

Oo

O interjection oh.

oaf noun (plural **oafs**) a stupid
lout. [from Old Norse]

oak noun (plural **oaks**) a large
deciduous tree with seeds called
acorns. **oaken** adjective [from Old
English]

oar noun (plural **oars**) a pole with
a flat blade at one end, used for
rowing a boat. **oarsman** noun,
oarsmanship noun [from Old
English]

oasis (say oh-ay-sis) noun (plural
oases) a fertile place in a desert,
with a spring or well of water.
[from Greek]

oath noun (plural **oaths**)
1 a solemn promise to do
something or that something is
true, appealing to God or a holy
person as witness. 2 a swear
word.

oats plural noun a cereal used to
make food (*oats* for horses,
oatmeal for people). [from Old
English]

ob- prefix (changing to **oc-** before
c, **of-** before f, **op-** before p)
1 to; towards (as in *observe*).
2 against (as in *opponent*). 3 in
the way; blocking (as in *obstruct*).
[from Latin *ob* = towards,
against]

obedient adjective doing what
you are told; willing to obey.
obediently adverb, **obedience**
noun

obey verb (**obeys**, **obeying**,
obeyed) do what you are told to
do by a person, law, etc. [from *ob*-
+ Latin *audire* = listen or hear]

obituary noun (plural **obituaries**)
a notice in a newspaper of
a person's death, often with
a short account of his or her life.
[from Latin *obitus* = death]

object (say ob-jikt) noun (plural
objects)
1 something that can be seen or
touched. **2** a purpose or
intention. **3** (in grammar) the
word or words naming who or
what is acted upon by a verb or
by a preposition, e.g. *him* in *the
dog bit him* and *against him*.

object (say ob-jekt) verb (**objects,
objecting, objected**) say that you
are not in favour of something or
do not agree; protest.
objector noun
[from *ob-* + Latin *-jectum*
= thrown]

objection noun (plural
objections)
1 objecting to something.
2 a reason for objecting.

objectionable adjective
unpleasant or nasty.
objectionably adverb

objective noun (plural
objectives) what you are trying to
reach or do; an aim.

objective adjective
1 real or actual, *Dreams have no
objective existence.* **2** not
influenced by personal feelings
or opinions, *an objective account
of the quarrel.* (Compare
subjective.) **objectively** adverb,
objectivity noun

obligation noun (plural
obligations)
1 being obliged to do something.
2 what you are obliged to do;
a duty.

under an obligation owing
gratitude to someone who has
helped you.

obligatory (say ob-**lig**-a-ter-ee)
adjective compulsory, not
optional.

oblige verb (**obliges, obliging,
obliged**)
1 force or compel. **2** help and
please someone, *Can you oblige
me with a loan?*
be obliged to someone feel
gratitude to a person who has
helped you. [from *ob-* + Latin
ligare = bind]

obliging adjective polite and
helpful.

oblique (say ob-**leek**) adjective
1 slanting. **2** not saying
something straightforwardly, *an
oblique reply.* **obliquely** adverb
[from Latin]

obliterate verb (**obliterates,
obliterating, obliterated**) blot out;
destroy and remove all traces of
something. **obliteration** noun
[from Latin *obliterare* = cross
out, from *ob-* + *littera* = letter]

oblong adjective rectangular in
shape and longer than it is wide.
oblong noun [from Latin]

obnoxious adjective very
unpleasant; objectionable. [from
ob- + Latin *noxa* = harm]

oboe noun (plural **oboes**) a high-
pitched woodwind instrument.
oboist noun [from French *haut*
= high + *bois* = wood]

obscene (say ob-**seen**) adjective
indecent in a very offensive way.
obscenely adverb, **obscenity** noun
[from Latin]

obscure adjective
1 difficult to see or to understand;
not clear. **2** not well-known.

obscurely *adverb*, **obscurity** *noun*

obscure *verb* (**obscures**, **obscuring**, **obscured**) make a thing obscure; darken or conceal, *Clouds obscured the sun.* [from Latin *obscurus* = dark]

observant *adjective* quick at observing or noticing things. **observantly** *adverb*

observation *noun* (*plural* **observations**)
1 observing or watching. 2 a comment or remark.

observatory *noun* (*plural* **observatories**) a building with telescopes. etc. for observing the stars or weather.

observe *verb* (**observes**, **observing**, **observed**)
1 see and notice; watch carefully. 2 obey a law. 3 keep or celebrate a custom or religious festival etc. 4 make a remark. **observer** *noun* [from *ob-* + Latin *servare* = to watch or keep]

obsolescent *adjective* becoming obsolete; going out of use or fashion. **obsolescence** *noun*

obsolete *adjective* not used any more; out of date. [from Latin *obsoletus* = worn out]

obstacle *noun* (*plural* **obstacles**) something that stands in the way or obstructs progress. [from *ob-* + Latin *stare* = to stand]

obstinate *adjective* keeping firmly to your own ideas or ways, even though they may be wrong. **obstinately** *adverb*, **obstinacy** *noun* [from Latin *obstinare* = keep on, persist]

obstreperous (*say* ob-strep-er-us) *adjective* noisy and unruly. [from *ob-* + Latin *strepere* = make a noise]

obstruct *verb* (**obstructs**, **obstructing**, **obstructed**) stop a person or thing from getting past; hinder. **obstruction** *noun*, **obstructive** *adjective* [from *ob-* + Latin *structum* = built]

obtain *verb* (**obtains**, **obtaining**, **obtained**) get something by buying, taking, or being given it. **obtainable** *adjective* [from *ob-* + Latin *tenere* = to hold]

obtrusive *adjective* unpleasantly noticeable. **obtrusiveness** *noun*

obtuse angle *noun* (*plural* **obtuse angles**) an angle of more than 90° but less than 180°. (Compare *acute angle*.)

obvious *adjective* easy to see or understand. **obviously** *adverb* [from Latin *ob viam* = in the way]

oc- *prefix*
1 to; towards. 2 against. 3 in the way; blocking. see **ob-**.

occasion *noun* (*plural* **occasions**)
1 the time when something happens. 2 a special event. 3 a suitable time; an opportunity.

occasional *adjective*
1 happening at intervals. 2 for special occasions, *occasional music.* **occasionally** *adverb*

occult *adjective* to do with the supernatural or magic, *occult powers.* [from Latin *occultum* = hidden]

occupation *noun* (*plural* **occupations**)
1 a person's job or profession. 2 something you do to pass your time. 3 capturing a country etc. by military force.

occupational *adjective* caused by an occupation, *an occupational disease.*

occupational therapy noun
creative work designed to help
people to recover from certain
illnesses.

occupy verb (occupies,
occupying, occupied)
1 live in a place; inhabit. 2 fill
a space or position. 3 capture
a country etc. and place troops
there. 4 keep somebody busy.
occupier noun [from Latin]

occur verb (occurs, occurring,
occurred)
1 happen or exist. 2 be found;
appear, *These plants occur in
ponds.* 3 come into a person's
mind, *An idea occurred to me.*

ocean noun (plural oceans) the
seas that surround the
continents of the earth,
especially one of the large named
areas of this, *the Pacific Ocean.*
oceanic adjective [from Oceanus,
the river that the ancient Greeks
thought surrounded the world]

o'clock adverb by the clock,
Lunch is at one o'clock. [short for
of the clock]

octa- or **octo-** prefix eight. [from
Greek]

octagon noun (plural octagons)
a flat shape with eight sides and
eight angles. **octagonal** adjective
[from *octa-* + Greek *gonia* = angle]

octave noun (plural octaves) the
interval of eight steps between
one musical note and the next
note of the same name above or
below it. [from Latin *octavus*
= eighth]

octo- prefix eight. see **octa-**.

octopus noun (plural octopuses)
a sea creature with eight long
tentacles. [from *octo-* + Greek
pous = foot]

oculist noun (plural oculists)
a doctor who treats diseases of
the eye.

odd adjective
1 strange or unusual. 2 (of
a number) not able to be divided
exactly by 2; not even. 3 left over
from a pair or set, *I've got one odd
sock.* 4 of various kinds; not
regular, *odd jobs.* **oddly** adverb,
oddness noun, **oddity** noun [from
Old Norse]

oddments plural noun small
things of various kinds.

odds plural noun the chances
that a certain thing will happen;
a measure of this, *When the odds
are 10 to 1, you will win £10 if you
bet £1.*

odds and ends oddments.

odious (say oh-dee-us) adjective
hateful. **odiously** adverb,
odiousness noun

odour noun (plural odours)
a smell. **odorous** adjective,
odourless adjective [Latin *odor*
= smell]

odyssey (say od-iss-ee) noun
(plural odysseys) a long
adventurous journey. [named
after the *Odyssey*, a Greek poem
telling of the wanderings of
Odysseus]

o'er preposition & adverb (poetic)
over.

oesophagus (say ee-sof-a-gus)
noun (plural oesophagi) the tube
from the throat to the stomach.

of preposition (used to indicate
relationships)
1 belonging to, *the mother of the
child.* 2 concerning; about, *news
of the disaster.* 3 made from, *built
of stone.* 4 from, *north of the town.*
[from Old English]

of- *prefix*
1 to; towards. **2** against. **3** in the way; blocking. see **ob-**.

off *preposition*
1 not on; away or down from, *He fell off the ladder*. **2** not taking or wanting, *She is off her food*. **3** deducted from, *£5 off the price*.

off *adverb*
1 away or down from something, *His hat blew off*. **2** not working or happening, *The heating is off. The match is off because of snow*. **3** to the end; completely, *Finish it off*. **4** as regards money or supplies, *How are you off for cash?* **5** behind or at the side of a stage, *There were noises off*. **6** (of food) beginning to go bad.

offal *noun* the organs of an animal (e.g. liver, kidneys) sold as food. [originally = waste products: from *off* + *fall*]

offence *noun* (*plural* **offences**)
1 an illegal action. **2** a feeling of annoyance or resentment.

offend *verb* (**offends, offending, offended**)
1 cause offence to someone; hurt a person's pride. **2** do wrong, *offend against the law*. **offender** *noun* [from *ob-* + Latin *fendere* = to strike]

offensive *adjective*
1 causing offence; insulting.
2 disgusting, *an offensive smell*.
3 used in attacking, *offensive weapons*. **offensively** *adverb*, **offensiveness** *noun*
offensive *noun* (*plural* **offensives**) an attack.
take the offensive be the first to attack.

offer *verb* (**offers, offering, offered**)
1 present something so that people can accept it if they want to. **2** say that you are willing to do or give something or to pay a certain amount.

offer *noun* (*plural* **offers**)
1 offering something. **2** an amount offered.

offhand *adjective*
1 said or done without preparation. **2** (of a remark etc.) rather casual and rude; curt. **offhanded** *adjective*

office *noun* (*plural* **offices**)
1 a room or building used for business, especially for clerical work; the people who work there. **2** a government department, *the Foreign and Commonwealth Office*. **3** an important job or position.
be in office hold an official position. [from Latin *officium* = a service or duty]

officer *noun* (*plural* **officers**)
1 a person who is in charge of others, especially in the armed forces. **2** an official. **3** a member of the police.

official *adjective*
1 done or said by someone with authority. **2** done as part of your job or position, *official duties*. **officially** *adverb*
official *noun* (*plural* **officials**) a person who holds a position of authority.

offing *noun*
in the offing likely to happen soon.

off-licence *noun* (*plural* **off-licences**) a shop with a licence to sell alcohol to be drunk somewhere else.

offshoot *noun* (*plural* **offshoots**) **1** a side shoot on a plant. **2** a by-product.

offside *adjective & adverb* (of a player in football etc.) in a position where the rules do not allow him or her to play the ball.

often *adverb* many times; in many cases.

ogre *noun* (*plural* **ogres**) **1** a cruel giant in fairy tales. **2** a terrifying person. [French]

oh *interjection* an exclamation of pain, surprise, delight, etc., or used for emphasis (*Oh yes I will!*).

ohm *noun* (*plural* **ohms**) a unit of electrical resistance. [named after a German scientist, G. S. Ohm, who studied electric currents]

oil *noun* (*plural* **oils**) **1** a thick slippery liquid that will not dissolve in water. **2** a kind of petroleum used as fuel. **oil well** *noun*

oil *verb* (**oils**, **oiling**, **oiled**) put oil on something, especially to make it work smoothly. [from Latin]

oilfield *noun* an area where oil is found.

oily *adjective* **1** containing or like oil; covered or soaked with oil. **2** behaving in an insincerely polite way. **oiliness** *noun*

ointment *noun* (*plural* **ointments**) a cream or slippery paste for putting on sore skin and cuts. [from old French]

OK or **okay** *adverb & adjective* (*informal*) all right. [perhaps from the initials of *oll* (or *orl*)

korrect, a humorous spelling of *all correct*, first used in the USA in 1839]

old *adjective* **1** not new; born or made or existing from a long time ago. **2** of a particular age, *I'm ten years old*. **3** former or original, *in its old place*. **4** (*informal*) used casually or for emphasis, *good old mum!* **oldness** *noun*

Old English *noun* the English language from about 700 to 1150, also called *Anglo-Saxon*.

old-fashioned *adjective* of the kind that was usual a long time ago; no longer fashionable.

Old Norse *noun* the language spoken by the Vikings, the ancestor of modern Scandinavian languages.

olive *noun* (*plural* **olives**) **1** an evergreen tree with a small bitter fruit. **2** this fruit, from which an oil (*olive oil*) is made. **3** a shade of green like an unripe olive. [from Greek]

olive branch *noun* (*plural* **olive branches**) something you do or offer that shows you want to make peace. [from a story in the Bible, where the dove brings Noah an olive branch as a sign that God is no longer angry with mankind]

-ology *suffix* see **-logy**.

Olympic Games or **Olympics** *plural noun* a series of international sports contests held every fourth year in a different part of the world. [from the name of Olympia, a city in Greece where they were held in ancient times]

omega (say oh-meg-a) noun the last letter of the Greek alphabet, a long *o*. [from Greek *o mega* = big O]

omelette noun (plural **omelettes**) eggs beaten together and cooked in a pan, often with a filling. [French]

omen noun (plural **omens**) an event regarded as a sign of what is going to happen. [Latin]

ominous adjective suggesting that trouble is coming. **ominously** adverb [from Latin *ominosus* = acting as an omen]

omit verb (**omits**, **omitting**, **omitted**)
1 miss something out. 2 fail to do something. **omission** noun [from Latin]

omni- prefix all. [from Latin]

omnibus noun (plural **omnibuses**)
1 a book containing several stories or books that were previously published separately. 2 (old use) a bus. [Latin, = for everybody]

omniscient (say om-niss-ee-ent) adjective knowing everything. **omniscience** noun [from *omni-* + Latin *sciens* = knowing]

omnivorous (say om-niv-er-us) adjective feeding on all kinds of food. (Compare *carnivorous*, *herbivorous*.) [from *omni-* + Latin *vorare* = devour]

on preposition
1 supported by; covering; added or attached to, *the sign on the door*. 2 close to; towards, *The army advanced on Paris*. 3 during; at the time of, *on my birthday*. 4 by reason of, *Arrest him on suspicion*. 5 concerning, *a book on*

butterflies. 6 in a state of; using or showing, *The house was on fire*.

on adverb
1 so as to be on something, *Put it on*. 2 further forward, *Move on*. 3 working; in action, *Is the heater on?*

on and off not continually.

once adverb
1 for one time or on one occasion only, *They came only once*. 2 formerly, *They once lived here*.

once noun one time, *Once is enough*.

once conjunction as soon as, *You can go once I have taken your names*.
[from *one*]

oncoming adjective approaching; coming towards you, *oncoming traffic*.

one adjective
1 single. 2 individual or united.

one noun
1 the smallest whole number, 1. 2 a person or thing alone. **one another** each other.

one pronoun a person; any person, *One likes to help*. **oneself** pronoun

one-sided adjective
1 with one side or person in a contest, conversation etc. being much stronger or doing a lot more than the other, *a one-sided match*. 2 showing only one point of view in an unfair way, *This is a very one-sided account of the conflict*.

onion noun (plural **onions**) a round vegetable with a strong flavour. **oniony** adjective [from old French]

onlooker noun (plural **onlookers**) a spectator.

only *adjective* being the one person or thing of a kind; sole, *my only wish*.

only child a child who has no brothers or sisters.

only *adverb* no more than; and that is all, *There are only three cakes left*.

only *conjunction* but then; however, *He makes promises, only he never keeps them*. [from Old English]

onomatopoeia (say on-om-at-o-**pee**-a) *noun* the formation of words that imitate what they stand for; e.g. cuckoo, plop. **onomatopoeic** *adjective* [from Greek *onoma* = name + *poiein* = make]

onshore *adjective* from the sea towards the land, *an onshore breeze*.

onslaught *noun* (*plural* **onslaughts**) a fierce attack. [from old Italian *aan* = on + *slag* = a blow]

onto *preposition* to a position on.

onward *adverb* & *adjective* going forward; further on. **onwards** *adverb*

ooze *verb* (**oozes**, **oozing**, **oozed**) 1 flow out slowly; trickle. 2 allow something to flow out slowly, *The wound oozed blood*.

ooze *noun* mud at the bottom of a river or sea.

op- *prefix* 1 to; towards. 2 against. 3 in the way; blocking. see **ob-**.

opal *noun* (*plural* **opals**) a kind of stone with a rainbow sheen. **opalescent** *adjective*

opaque (say o-**payk**) *adjective* not able to be seen through; not transparent or translucent. [from Latin *opacus* = shady or dark]

open *adjective* 1 allowing people or things to go in and out; not closed or fastened. 2 not covered or blocked up. 3 spread out; unfolded. 4 not limited or restricted, *an open championship*. 5 letting in visitors or customers. 6 with wide empty spaces, *open country*. 7 honest and frank; not secret or secretive, *Be open about the danger*. 8 not decided, *an open mind*. **openness** *noun* **in the open air** not inside a house or building. **open-air** *adjective*

open *verb* (**opens**, **opening**, **opened**) 1 make or become open or more open. 2 begin. **opener** *noun* [from Old English]

opencast *adjective* (of a mine) worked by removing layers of earth from the surface, not underground.

opening *noun* (*plural* **openings**) 1 a space or gap; a place where something opens. 2 the beginning of something. 3 an opportunity.

openly *adverb* without secrecy.

opera *noun* (*plural* **operas**) a play in which all or most of the words are sung. **operatic** *adjective* [Latin = work]

operate *verb* (**operates**, **operating**, **operated**) 1 make a machine work. 2 be in action; work. 3 perform a surgical operation on somebody. **operable** *adjective* [from Latin *operari* = to work]

operation noun (plural operations)
1 a piece of work or method of working. 2 something done to the body to take away or repair a part of it. 3 a planned military activity. **operational** adjective
in operation working or in use, When does the new system come into operation?

operator noun (plural operators) a person who works something, especially a telephone switchboard or exchange.

opinion noun (plural opinions) what you think of something; a belief or judgement. [from Latin opinari = believe]

opinion poll noun (plural opinion polls) an estimate of what people think, made by questioning a sample of them.

opium noun a drug made from the juice of certain poppies, used in medicine. [from Greek opion = poppy juice]

opponent noun (plural opponents) a person or group opposing another in a contest or war. [from Latin opponere = to set against]

opportunist noun (plural opportunists) a person who is quick to seize opportunities.

opportunity noun (plural opportunities) a good chance to do a particular thing.

oppose verb (opposes, opposing, opposed)
1 argue or fight against; resist. 2 contrast, 'Soft' is opposed to 'hard'. [from French; related to opponent]

opposite adjective
1 placed on the other or further side; facing, on the opposite side of the road. 2 moving away from or towards each other, The trains were travelling in opposite directions. 3 completely different, opposite characters.

opposite noun (plural opposites) an opposite person or thing.

opposite preposition opposite to, They live opposite the school. [from Latin oppositus = set or placed against]

opposition noun
1 opposing something; resistance. 2 the people who oppose something; **the Opposition** the chief political party opposing the one that is in power.

oppress verb (oppresses, oppressing, oppressed)
1 govern or treat somebody cruelly or unjustly. 2 weigh somebody down with worry or sadness. **oppression** noun, **oppressive** adjective, **oppressor** noun [from op- + Latin pressus = pressed]

opt verb (opts, opting, opted) choose.
opt out decide not to take part in something.
[from Latin optare = wish for]

optical adjective to do with sight; aiding sight, optical instruments. **optically** adverb [from Greek optos = seen]

optical illusion noun (plural optical illusions) a deceptive appearance that makes you see something wrongly.

optician *noun* (*plural* **opticians**)
a person who makes or sells
spectacles etc.

optimist *noun* (*plural* **optimists**)
a person who expects that things
will turn out well. (Compare
pessimist.) **optimism** *noun*,
optimistic *adjective*, **optimistically**
adverb [from French, related to
optimum]

optimum *adjective* best; most
favourable. **optimum** *noun*,
optimal *adjective* [Latin, = best
thing]

option *noun* (*plural* **options**)
1 the right or power to choose
something. **2** something chosen
or that may be chosen. [same
origin as *opt*]

optional *adjective* that you can
choose, not compulsory.
optionally *adverb*

or *conjunction* used to show that
there is a choice or an
alternative, *Do you want a bun or
a biscuit?* [from *other*]

-or *suffix* forms nouns meaning 'a
person or thing that does
something' (e.g. *tailor*,
refrigerator). [from Latin or old
French]

oracle *noun* (*plural* **oracles**)
1 a shrine where the ancient
Greeks consulted one of their
gods for advice or a prophecy.
2 a wise or knowledgeable
adviser. **oracular** (*say* or-**ak**-yoo-
ler) *adjective* [from Latin *orare*
= speak]

oral *adjective*
1 spoken, not written. **2** to do

with or using the mouth. **orally**
adverb [from Latin *oris* = of the
mouth]

USAGE: Do not confuse with
aural.

orange *noun* (*plural* **oranges**)
1 a round juicy citrus fruit with
reddish-yellow peel. **2** a reddish-
yellow colour.

orangeade *noun* an orange-
flavoured drink.

orang-utan *noun* (*plural* **orang-
utans**) a large ape of Borneo and
Sumatra. [from Malay *orang
hutan* = man of the forest (Malay
is spoken in Malaysia)]

orator *noun* (*plural* **orators**)
a person who makes speeches.
oratorical *adjective*

orbit *noun* (*plural* **orbits**)
1 the curved path taken by
something moving round a planet
etc. in space. **2** the range of
someone's influence or control.
orbital *adjective*

orbit *verb* (**orbits**, **orbiting**,
orbited) move in an orbit round
something, *The spacecraft orbited
the earth.*

orchard *noun* (*plural* **orchards**)
a piece of ground planted with
fruit trees.

orchestra *noun* (*plural*
orchestras) a large group of
people playing various musical
instruments together. **orchestral**
adjective [Greek, = the space
where the chorus danced during
a play]

orchid *noun* (*plural* **orchids**)
a kind of flower, often with
unevenly shaped petals. [from
Latin]

ordain verb (ordains, ordaining, ordained)
1 make a person a member of the clergy in the Christian Church, *He was ordained in 1981.* 2 declare or order something by law. [from old French; related to *order*]

ordeal noun (plural **ordeals**)
a difficult or horrific experience.

order noun (plural **orders**)
1 a command. 2 a request for something to be supplied. 3 the way things are arranged, *in alphabetical order.* 4 a neat arrangement; a proper arrangement or condition, *in working order.* 5 obedience to rules or laws, *law and order.* 6 a kind or sort, *She showed courage of the highest order.* 7 a group of monks or nuns who live by certain religious rules.
in order that or **in order to** for the purpose of.

order verb (orders, ordering, ordered)
1 command. 2 ask for something to be supplied. 3 put something into order; arrange neatly. [from Latin *ordo* = a row, series, or arrangement]

orderly adjective
1 arranged neatly or well; methodical. 2 well-behaved and obedient. **orderliness** noun

ordinal number noun (plural **ordinal numbers**) a number that shows a thing's position in a series, e.g. *first, fifth, twentieth.* (Compare *cardinal numbers.*) [from Latin *ordinalis* = showing the order]

ordinary adjective normal or usual; not special. **ordinarily** adverb [from Latin *ordinarius* = orderly or usual]

ordination noun (plural **ordinations**) ordaining or being ordained as a member of the clergy.

Ordnance Survey noun an official survey organization that makes detailed maps of the British Isles.

ore noun (plural **ores**) rock with metal or other useful substances in it, *iron ore.* [from Old English]

organ noun (plural **organs**)
1 a musical instrument from which sounds are produced by air forced through pipes, played by keys and pedals. 2 a part of the body with a particular function, *the digestive organs.* [from Greek *organon* = tool]

organic adjective.
1 to do with the organs of the body, *organic diseases.* 2 to do with or formed from living things, *organic matter.* 3 organic food is grown or produced without the use of chemical fertilizers, pesticides, etc., *organic farming.* **organically** adverb

organism noun (plural **organisms**) a living thing; an individual animal or plant. [from Greek]

organist noun (plural **organists**) a person who plays the organ.

organization noun (plural **organizations**)
1 an organized group of people, such as a business, charity,

government department, etc.
2 the organizing of something.
organizational *adjective*

organize *verb* (**organizes,
organizing, organized**)
1 plan and prepare something,
We organized a picnic. **2** form
people into a group to work
together. **3** put things in order.
organizer *noun* [same origin as
organ]

orgasm *noun* (*plural* **orgasms**)
the climax of sexual excitement.

orgy *noun* (*plural* **orgies**)
1 a wild party that involves a lot
of drinking and sex. **2** an
extravagant activity, *an orgy of
spending.* [from Latin *orgia*
= secret rites (held in honour of
Bacchus, the Greek and Roman
god of wine)]

oriental *adjective* to do with the
countries east of the
Mediterranean Sea, especially
China and Japan.

orientate *verb* (**orientates,
orientating, orientated**) place
something or face in a certain
direction. **orientation** *noun*

origami *noun* (*say* o-rig-ah-mee) *noun*
folding paper into decorative
shapes. [from Japanese *ori* = fold
+ *kami* = paper]

origin *noun* (*plural* **origins**)
1 the start of something; the
point or cause from which
something began. **2** the point
where two or more axes on
a graph meet. [from Latin *oriri*
= to rise]

original *adjective*
1 existing from the start; earliest,
the original inhabitants. **2** new in
its design etc.; not a copy.

3 producing new ideas;
inventive. **originally** *adverb,*
originality *noun*

originate *verb* (**originates,
originating, originated**)
1 cause something to begin;
create. **2** have its origin, *The
quarrel originated in rivalry.*
origination *noun,* **originator** *noun*

ornament *noun* (*plural*
ornaments) an object displayed
or worn as a decoration.
ornamental *adjective*

ornament *verb* (**ornaments,
ornamenting, ornamented**)
decorate something with
beautiful things. **ornamentation**
noun

ornithology *noun* the study of
birds. **ornithologist** *noun,*
ornithological *adjective* [from
Greek *ornithos* = of a bird, +
-logy]

orphan *noun* (*plural* **orphans**)
a child whose parents are dead.

ortho- *prefix* right; straight;
correct. [from Greek *orthos*
= straight]

orthodox *adjective* holding
beliefs that are correct or
generally accepted. **orthodoxy**
noun [from *ortho-* + Greek *doxa*
= opinion]

Orthodox Church *noun* the
Christian Churches of eastern
Europe.

orthopaedics (*say* orth-o-pee-
diks) *noun* the treatment of
deformities and injuries to bones
and muscles. **orthopaedic**
adjective [from *ortho-* + Greek
paideia = rearing of children
(because the treatment was
because of children)]

oscillate verb (**oscillates**, **oscillating**, **oscillated**)
1 move to and fro like a pendulum; vibrate. **2** waver or vary. **oscillation** noun, **oscillator** noun [from Latin *oscillare* = to swing]

-osis suffix
1 a diseased condition (as in *tuberculosis*). **2** an action or process (as in *metamorphosis*). [from Latin or Greek]

osmosis noun the passing of fluid through a porous partition into another more concentrated fluid. [from Greek *osmos* = a push]

ostentatious adjective making a showy display of something to impress people. **ostentatiously** adverb, **ostentation** noun

osteopath noun (plural **osteopaths**) a person who treats certain medical conditions, diseases etc. by manipulating a patient's bones and muscles. **osteopathy** noun, **osteopathic** adjective [from Greek *osteon* = bone + *-patheia* = suffering]

ostrich noun (plural **ostriches**) a large long-legged African bird that can run very fast but cannot fly. It was said to bury its head in the sand when pursued, believing that it cannot then be seen.

other adjective
1 different, *some other tune*. **2** remaining, *Try the other shoe*. **3** additional, *my other friends*. **4** just recent or past, *I saw him the other day*.
other pronoun & noun (plural **others**) the other person or thing, *Where are the others?* [from Old English]

otherwise adverb
1 if things happen differently; if you do not, *Write it down, otherwise you'll forget*. **2** in other ways, *It rained, but otherwise the holiday was good*. **3** differently, *We could not do otherwise*. [from *other* + *-wise*]

otter noun (plural **otters**) a fish-eating animal with webbed feet, a flat tail, and thick brown fur, living near water. [from Old English]

ought auxiliary verb expressing duty (*We ought to feed them*), rightness or advisability (*You ought to take more exercise*), or probability (*At this speed, we ought to be there by noon*). [from Old English *ahte* = owed]

oughtn't (mainly spoken) ought not.

ounce noun (plural **ounces**) a unit of weight equal to ⅟₁₆ of a pound (about 28 grams). [from Latin]

our adjective belonging to us. [from Old English]

ours possessive pronoun belonging to us, *These seats are ours*. [from *our*]

USAGE: It is incorrect to write *our's*.

ourselves pronoun we or us and nobody else. (Compare *herself*.)

out adverb
1 away from or not in a particular place or position or state etc.; not at home. **2** into the open; into existence or sight etc., *The sun came out*. **3** not in action or use etc.; (of a batsman) having had

the innings ended; (of a fire) not burning. **4** to or at an end; completely, *sold out; tired out.* **5** without restraint; boldly or loudly, *Speak out!*

be out for or **out to** be seeking or wanting, *They are out to make trouble.*

out of date 1 old-fashioned. **2** not valid any more.

out of doors in the open air.

out of the way remote.

out- *prefix* **1** out of; away from (as in *outcast*). **2** external; separate (as in *outhouse*). **3** more than; so as to defeat or exceed (as in *outdo*).

out and out *adjective* thorough or complete, *an out and out villain.*

outboard motor *noun (plural* **outboard motors)** a motor fitted to the outside of a boat's stern.

outbreak *noun (plural* **outbreaks)** the start of a disease or war or anger etc.

outburst *noun (plural* **outbursts)** the bursting out of anger or laughter etc.

outcast *noun (plural* **outcasts)** a person who has been rejected by family, friends, or society.

outcrop *noun (plural* **outcrops)** a piece of rock from a lower level that sticks out on the surface of the ground. [from *out*, + *crop* = outcrop]

outcry *noun (plural* **outcries)** a strong protest.

outdo *verb (outdoes, outdoing, outdid, outdone)* do better than another person etc.

outdoors *adverb* in the open air.

outer *adjective* outside or external; nearer to the outside.

outermost *adjective*

outer space *noun* the universe beyond the earth's atmosphere.

outfit *noun (plural* **outfits)** **1** a set of clothes worn together. **2** a set of equipment. **3** *(informal)* a team or organization.

outgrow *verb (outgrows, outgrowing, outgrew, outgrown)* **1** grow out of clothes or habits etc. **2** grow faster or larger than another person or thing.

outhouse *noun (plural* **outhouses)** a small building (e.g. a shed or barn) that belongs to a house but is separate from it.

outing *noun (plural* **outings)** a journey for pleasure.

outlandish *adjective* looking or sounding strange or foreign. [from Old English *utland* = a foreign land]

outlast *verb (outlasts, outlasting, outlasted)* last longer than something else.

outlaw *noun (plural* **outlaws)** a person who is punished by being excluded from legal rights and the protection of the law.

outlay *noun (plural* **outlays)** what is spent on something.

outlet *noun (plural* **outlets)** **1** a way for something to get out. **2** a market for goods.

outline *noun (plural* **outlines)** **1** a line round the outside of something, showing its boundary or shape. **2** a summary.

outlook *noun (plural* **outlooks)** **1** a view on which people look out. **2** a person's mental attitude to something. **3** future prospects, *The outlook is bleak.*

outlying *adjective* far from the centre; remote, *the outlying districts.*

outmoded *adjective* out of date.

outnumber *verb* (**outnumbers, outnumbering, outnumbered**) be more numerous than another group.

outpatient *noun* (*plural* **outpatients**) a person who visits a hospital for treatment but does not stay there.

outpost *noun* (*plural* **outposts**) a distant settlement. [from *out* + *post*²]

output *noun* (*plural* **outputs**) 1 the amount produced. 2 the information or results produced by a computer.

outrage *noun* (*plural* **outrages**) 1 something that shocks people by being very wicked or cruel. 2 great anger. **outrageous** *adjective*, **outrageously** *adverb*

outrage *verb* (**outrages, outraging, outraged**) shock and anger people greatly. [from old French *outrer* = go beyond, exaggerate, influenced by *rage*]

outright *adverb* 1 completely; not gradually, *This drug should be banned outright.* 2 frankly, *We told him this outright.*

outright *adjective* thorough or complete, *an outright fraud.*

outset *noun* the beginning of something, *from the outset of his career.*

outside *noun* (*plural* **outsides**) the outer side, surface, or part. **at the outside** at the most, *a mile at the outside.*

outside *adjective* 1 on or coming from the outside, *the outside edge.* 2 greatest possible, *the outside price.* 3 remote or slight, *an outside chance.*

outside *adverb* on or to the outside; outdoors, *Leave it outside. It's cold outside.*

outside *preposition* on or to the outside of, *Leave it outside the door.*

outside broadcast *noun* (*plural* **outside broadcasts**) a broadcast made on location and not in a studio.

outsider *noun* (*plural* **outsiders**) 1 a person who does not belong to a certain group. 2 a horse or person thought to have no chance of winning a race or competition.

outsize *adjective* much larger than average.

outskirts *plural noun* the outer parts or districts, especially of a town.

outspoken *adjective* speaking or spoken very frankly.

outstanding *adjective* 1 extremely good or distinguished. 2 not yet paid or dealt with.

outstrip *verb* (**outstrips, outstripping, outstripped**) 1 run faster or further than another; outrun. 2 surpass in achievement or success. [from *out-* + Middle English *strypen* = move quickly]

outward *adjective* 1 going outwards. 2 on the outside. **outwardly** *adverb*, **outwards** *adverb*

outwit verb (outwits, outwitting, outwitted) deceive somebody by being crafty.

ova plural of ovum.

oval adjective shaped like a 0, rounded and longer than it is broad. **oval** noun [from Latin ovum = egg]

ovary noun (plural ovaries) 1 either of the two organs in which ova or egg-cells are produced in a woman's or female animal's body. 2 part of the pistil in a plant, from which fruit is formed. [from Latin ovum = egg]

oven noun (plural ovens) a closed space in which things are cooked or heated.

over preposition 1 above. 2 more than, It's over a mile away. 3 concerning, They quarrelled over money. 4 across the top of; on or to the other side of, They rowed the boat over the lake. 5 during, We can talk over dinner. 6 in superiority or preference to, their victory over United.

over adverb 1 out and down from the top or edge; from an upright position, He fell over. 2 so that a different side shows, Turn it over. 3 at or to a place; across, Walk over to our house. 4 remaining, There is nothing left over. 5 all through; thoroughly, Think it over. 6 at an end, The lesson is over.
over and over many times; repeatedly.

over noun (plural overs) a series of six balls bowled in cricket.

over- prefix 1 over (as in overturn). 2 too much; too (as in over-anxious).

overact verb (overacts, overacting, overacted) (of an actor) act in an exaggerated manner.

overall adjective including everything; total, the overall cost.

overalls plural noun a garment, like a shirt and trousers combined, worn over other clothes to protect them.

overarm adjective & adverb with the arm lifted above shoulder level and coming down in front of the body, bowling overarm.

overawe verb (overawes, overawing, overawed) overcome a person with awe.

overbalance verb (overbalances, overbalancing, overbalanced) lose balance and fall over.

overbearing adjective domineering.

overblown adjective 1 exaggerated or pretentious. 2 (of a flower) too fully open; past its best.

overboard adverb from in or on a ship into the water, She jumped overboard.

overcast adjective covered with cloud.

overcoat noun (plural overcoats) a warm outdoor coat.

overcome verb (overcomes, overcoming, overcame, overcome) 1 win a victory over somebody; defeat. 2 make a person helpless, He was overcome by the fumes. 3 find a way of dealing with a problem etc.

overdo verb (overdoes, overdoing, overdid, overdone) 1 do something too much. 2 cook food for too long.

overdose noun (plural **overdoses**) too large a dose of a drug.

overdraft noun (plural **overdrafts**) the amount by which a bank account is overdrawn.

overdraw verb (**overdraws**, **overdrawing**, **overdrew**, **overdrawn**) draw more money from a bank account than the amount you have in it.

overdue adjective late; not paid or arrived etc. by the proper time.

overhaul verb (**overhauls**, **overhauling**, **overhauled**)
1 examine something thoroughly and repair it if necessary.
2 overtake. **overhaul** noun

overhead adjective & adverb
1 above the level of your head.
2 in the sky.

overheads plural noun the expenses of running a business.

overhear verb (**overhears**, **overhearing**, **overheard**) hear something accidentally or without the speaker intending you to hear it.

overjoyed adjective filled with great joy.

overlap verb (**overlaps**, **overlapping**, **overlapped**)
1 lie across part of something.
2 happen partly at the same time. **overlap** noun [from over + lap¹]

overlay verb (**overlays**, **overlaying**, **overlaid**) cover with a layer; lie on top of something.

overlook verb (**overlooks**, **overlooking**, **overlooked**)
1 not notice or consider something. 2 not punish an offence. 3 have a view over something.

overpower verb (**overpowers**, **overpowering**, **overpowered**) overcome.

overpowering adjective very strong.

overrate verb (**overrates**, **overrating**, **overrated**) have too high an opinion of something.

override verb (**overrides**, **overriding**, **overrode**, **overridden**)
1 overrule. 2 be more important than, *Safety overrides all other considerations.*

overrule verb (**overrules**, **overruling**, **overruled**) reject a suggestion etc. by using your authority, *We voted for having a disco but the headteacher overruled the idea.*

overrun verb (**overruns**, **overrunning**, **overran**, **overrun**)
1 spread over and occupy or harm something, *Mice overran the place.* 2 go on for longer than it should, *The broadcast overran its time.*

oversee verb (**oversees**, **overseeing**, **oversaw**, **overseen**) watch over or supervise people working. **overseer** noun

oversight noun (plural **oversights**) a mistake made by not noticing something.

overtake verb (**overtakes**, **overtaking**, **overtook**, **overtaken**)
1 pass a moving vehicle or person etc. 2 catch up with someone.

overthrow verb (**overthrows**, **overthrowing**, **overthrew**, **overthrown**) remove someone from power by force, *They overthrew the king.*

overtime noun time spent working outside the normal hours; payment for this.

overture *noun* (*plural* **overtures**)
1 a piece of music written as an introduction to an opera, ballet, etc. **2** a friendly attempt to start a discussion, *They made overtures of peace.* [from old French, = opening]

overturn *verb* (**overturns, overturning, overturned**)
1 turn over or upside down.
2 reverse a legal decision.

overwhelm *verb* (**overwhelms, overwhelming, overwhelmed**)
1 bury or drown beneath a huge mass. **2** overcome completely.

ovum (*say* oh-vum) *noun* (*plural* **ova**) a female cell that can develop into a new individual when it is fertilized. [Latin, = egg]

owe *verb* (**owes, owing, owed**)
1 have a duty to pay or give something to someone, especially money. **2** have something because of the action of another person or thing, *They owed their lives to the pilot's skill.*

owing to because of; caused by.

USAGE: The use of *owing to* as a preposition meaning 'because of' is entirely acceptable, unlike this use of *due to*, which some people object to. See note at *due.*

owl *noun* (*plural* **owls**) a bird of prey with large eyes, usually flying at night.

own *adjective* belonging to yourself or itself.
get your own back get revenge.
on your own alone.

own *verb* (**owns, owning, owned**)
1 possess; have something as your property. **2** acknowledge or

admit something, *I own that I made a mistake.*
own up confess; admit guilt.

owner *noun* (*plural* **owners**) the person who owns something.

ownership *noun*

ox *noun* (*plural* **oxen**) a large animal kept for its meat and for pulling carts.

oxide *noun* (*plural* **oxides**) a compound of oxygen and one other element.

oxygen *noun* a colourless odourless tasteless gas that exists in the air and is essential for living things. [from French]

oyster *noun* (*plural* **oysters**) a kind of shellfish whose shell sometimes contains a pearl.

ozone *noun* a form of oxygen with a sharp smell. [from Greek *ozein* = to smell]

ozone layer *noun* a layer of ozone high in the atmosphere, protecting the world from harmful amounts of the sun's rays.

Pp

p *abbreviation* penny or pence.

p. *abbreviation* (*plural* **pp.**) page.

pace *noun* (*plural* **paces**)
1 one step in walking, marching, or running. **2** speed, *He set a fast pace.* [from Latin *passus*, literally = a stretch of the leg]

pacemaker *noun* (*plural* **pacemakers**)
1 a person who sets the pace for another in a race. **2** an electrical device to keep the heart beating.

pacifist (say pas-if-ist) noun (plural **pacifists**) a person who believes that war is always wrong. **pacifism** noun

pacify verb (pacifies, pacifying, pacified)
1 calm a person down. 2 bring peace to a country etc. **pacification** noun [from Latin pacis = of peace]

pack noun (plural **packs**)
1 a bundle; a collection of things wrapped or tied together. 2 a set of playing cards (usually 52). 3 a group of hounds or wolves etc. 4 a group of people; a group of Brownies or Cub Scouts. 5 a large amount, a pack of lies. 6 a mass of pieces of ice floating in the sea, pack ice.

pack verb (packs, packing, packed)
1 put things into a suitcase, bag, or box etc. in order to move or store them. 2 crowd together; fill tightly.
pack off send a person away.
send a person packing dismiss him or her.

package noun (plural **packages**)
1 a parcel or packet. 2 a number of things offered or accepted together. **packaging** noun [from pack]

package holiday noun (plural **package holidays**) a holiday with everything arranged and included in the price.

packet noun (plural **packets**) a small parcel. [from pack]

pad noun (plural **pads**)
1 a soft thick mass of material, used e.g. to protect or stuff something. 2 a piece of soft material worn to protect your leg in cricket and other games. 3 a set of sheets of paper fastened together at one edge. 4 the soft fleshy part under an animal's foot or the end of a finger or toe. 5 a flat surface from which rockets are launched or where helicopters take off and land.

pad verb (pads, padding, padded) put a pad on or in something.

padding noun material used to pad things.

paddle¹ verb (paddles, paddling, paddled) walk about in shallow water. **paddle** noun [probably from old Dutch]

paddle² noun (plural **paddles**) a short oar with a broad blade; something shaped like this.

paddle verb (paddles, paddling, paddled) move a boat along with a paddle or paddles; row gently. [origin unknown]

paddock noun (plural **paddocks**) a small field where horses are kept.

padlock noun (plural **padlocks**) a detachable lock with a metal loop that passes through a ring or chain etc.

paediatrics (say peed-ee-at-riks) noun the study of children's diseases. **paediatric** adjective, **paediatrician** noun [from Greek paidos = of a child + iatros = doctor]

pagan (say pay-gan) noun (plural **pagans**) a person who does not believe in one of the chief religions; a heathen. **pagan** adjective [same origin as peasant]

page¹ noun (plural **pages**) a piece of paper that is part of a book or newspaper etc.; one side of this. [from Latin]

page² noun (plural **pages**) a boy or man employed to go on errands or be an attendant. [from Greek paidion = small boy]

pageant noun (plural **pageants**)
1 a play or entertainment about historical events and people.
2 a procession of people in costume as an entertainment.
pageantry noun [origin unknown]

pagoda (say pag-oh-da) noun (plural **pagodas**) a Buddhist tower, or a Hindu temple shaped like a pyramid, in India and the Far East. [via Portuguese from Persian]

paid past tense of **pay**.
put paid to (informal) put an end to someone's activity or hope etc.

pail noun (plural **pails**) a bucket. [from Old English]

pain noun (plural **pains**)
1 an unpleasant feeling caused by injury or disease. 2 suffering in the mind. **painful** adjective, **painfully** adverb, **painless** adjective
take pains make a careful effort with work etc.
[from Latin poena = punishment]

painkiller noun (plural **painkillers**) a medicine or drug that relieves pain.

painstaking adjective very careful and thorough.

paint noun (plural **paints**) a liquid substance put on something to colour it. **paintbox** noun, **paintbrush** noun

paint verb (**paints**, **painting**, **painted**)
1 put paint on something. 2 make

a picture with paints.
[from Latin]

painting noun (plural **paintings**) a painted picture.

pair noun (plural **pairs**)
1 a set of two things or people; a couple. 2 something made of two joined parts, a pair of scissors. [from Latin paria = equal things]

palace noun (plural **palaces**) a mansion where a king, queen, or other important person lives. [from Palatium, the name of a hill on which the house of the emperor Augustus stood in ancient Rome]

palatable adjective tasting pleasant.

palate noun (plural **palates**)
1 the roof of your mouth.
2 a person's sense of taste. [from Latin]

pale¹ adjective
1 almost white, a pale face. 2 not bright in colour or light, pale green; the pale moonlight. **palely** adverb, **paleness** noun [from Latin pallidus = pallid]

pale² noun (plural **pales**) a boundary.
beyond the pale beyond the limits of good taste or behaviour etc.
[from Latin palus = a stake or fence post]

palindrome noun (plural **palindromes**) a word or phrase that reads the same backwards as forwards, e.g. radar. [from Greek palindromos = running back again]

paling noun (plural **palings**)
a fence made of wooden posts or railings; one of its posts. [from *pale*]

pall[1] (say pawl) noun (plural **palls**)
1 a cloth spread over a coffin.
2 a dark covering, *A pall of smoke lay over the town.* [from Latin *pallium* = cloak]

pall[2] (say pawl) verb (**palls, palling, palled**) become uninteresting or boring to someone, *The novelty of the new computer game soon began to pall.* [from *appal*]

palliative noun (plural **palliatives**) something that lessens pain or suffering.
palliative adjective

palm noun (plural **palms**)
1 the inner part of the hand, between the fingers and the wrist. 2 a palm tree.
palm off deceive a person into accepting something.

palm tree noun (plural **palm trees**) a tropical tree with large leaves and no branches.

palpitate verb (**palpitates, palpitating, palpitated**)
1 (of the heart) beat hard and quickly. 2 (of a person) quiver with fear or excitement.
palpitation noun [from Latin]

pampas noun wide grassy plains in South America.

pamper verb (**pampers, pampering, pampered**) treat or look after someone very kindly and indulgently; coddle.

pamphlet noun (plural **pamphlets**) a leaflet or booklet giving information on a subject. [from *Pamphilet*, the name of a long 12th-century poem in Latin]

pan noun (plural **pans**)
1 a wide container with a flat base, used for cooking etc.
2 something shaped like this.
3 the bowl of a lavatory. [from Old English]

pan- prefix
1 all (as in *panorama*). 2 to do with the whole of a continent or group etc. (as in *pan-African*). [from Greek]

pancake noun (plural **pancakes**) a thin round cake of batter fried on both sides. [from *pan* + *cake*]

panda noun (plural **pandas**) a large bear-like black-and-white animal found in China. [from the name given to a related animal in Nepal]

pandemonium noun uproar and complete confusion. [from *pan-* + *demon*]

pane noun (plural **panes**) a sheet of glass in a window. [from Latin]

panel noun (plural **panels**)
1 a long flat piece of wood, metal, etc. that is part of a door, wall, piece of furniture, etc. 2 a group of people chosen to discuss or decide something. **panelled** adjective, **panelling** noun [from old French, related to *pane*]

pang noun (plural **pangs**) a sudden sharp pain. [from *prong*]

panic noun sudden uncontrollable fear. **panic-stricken** adjective, **panicky** adjective

panic verb (**panics, panicking, panicked**) fill or be filled with panic.
[from the name of Pan, an ancient Greek god thought to be able to cause sudden fear]

panorama noun (plural **panoramas**) a view or picture of a wide area. **panoramic** adjective [from pan- + Greek horama = view]

pant verb (**pants, panting, panted**) take short quick breaths, usually after running or working hard.

panther noun (plural **panthers**) a leopard. [from Greek]

pantomime noun (plural **pantomimes**)
1 a Christmas entertainment, usually based on a fairy tale.
2 mime. [from pan- + mime (because in its most ancient form an actor mimed the different parts)]

pantry noun (plural **pantries**) a small room for storing food; a larder. [from old French paneterie, literally = bread-store]

pants plural noun (informal)
1 trousers. 2 underpants or knickers.

paper noun (plural **papers**)
1 a substance made in thin sheets from wood, rags, etc. and used for writing or printing or drawing on or for wrapping things.
2 a newspaper. 3 wallpaper.
4 a document.

paper verb (**papers, papering, papered**) cover a wall or room with wallpaper.

paperback noun (plural **paperbacks**) a book with a thin flexible cover.

papier mâché (say pap-yay mash-ay) noun paper made into pulp and moulded to make models, ornaments, etc. [French, = chewed paper]

para-¹ prefix
1 beside (as in parallel). 2 beyond (as in paradox). [from Greek]

para-² prefix protecting from (as in parasol). [from Italian]

parable noun (plural **parables**) a story told to teach people something, especially one of those told by Jesus Christ. [from Greek paraballein = put beside or compare: related to parabola]

parabola (say pa-rab-ol-a) noun (plural **parabolas**) a curve like the path of an object thrown into the air and falling down again. **parabolic** adjective [from para-¹ + Greek bole = a throw]

parachute noun (plural **parachutes**) an umbrella-like device on which people or things can float slowly to the ground from an aircraft. **parachuting** noun, **parachutist** noun [from para-² + French chute = a fall]

parade noun (plural **parades**)
1 a procession that displays people or things. 2 an assembly of troops for inspection, drill, etc.; a ground for this. 3 a public square, promenade, or row of shops.

parade verb (**parades, parading, paraded**)
1 move in a parade. 2 assemble for a parade.
[from Spanish or Italian, = display]

paradise noun
1 heaven; a heavenly place. 2 the Garden of Eden. [from ancient Persian pairidaeza = garden]

paradox noun (plural **paradoxes**) a statement that seems to contradict itself but which contains a truth, e.g. 'More haste, less speed'. **paradoxical** *adjective*, **paradoxically** *adverb* [from *para-*[1] + Greek *doxa* = opinion]

paraffin *noun* a kind of oil used as fuel. [via German from Latin *parum* = hardly + *affinis* = related (because paraffin does not combine readily with other substances)]

paragraph *noun* (*plural* **paragraphs**) one or more sentences on a single subject, forming a section of a piece of writing and beginning on a new line, usually slightly in from the margin of the page. [from *para-*[1] + *-graph*]

parallel *adjective*
1 (of lines etc.) always at the same distance from each other, like the rails on which a train runs. **2** similar or corresponding, *When petrol prices rise there is a parallel rise in bus fares.* **parallelism** *noun*

parallel *noun* (*plural* **parallels**)
1 something similar or corresponding. **2** a comparison, *You can draw a parallel between the two situations.* **3** a line etc. that is parallel to another. **4** a line of latitude.
[from *para-*[1] + Greek *allelos* = one another]

USAGE: Take care with the spelling of this word: one 'r', two 'l's, then one 'l'.

parallelogram *noun* (*plural* **parallelograms**) a quadrilateral with its opposite sides equal and parallel. [from *parallel* + *-gram*]

paralyse *verb* (**paralyses**, **paralysing**, **paralysed**)
1 cause paralysis in a person etc.

2 make something be unable to move, *She was paralysed with fear.* [from French, related to *paralysis*]

paralysis *noun* being unable to move, especially because of a disease or an injury to the nerves. **paralytic** (*say* pa-ra-**lit**-ik) *adjective* [from Greek *para* = on one side + *lysis* = loosening]

parameter (*say* pa-**ram**-it-er) *noun* (*plural* **parameters**) a quantity or quality etc. that is variable and affects other things by its changes. [from *para-*[1] + Greek *metron* = measure]

USAGE: Do not confuse with *perimeter*.

paramount *adjective* more important than anything else, *Secrecy is paramount.* [from old French *paramont* = above]

parapet *noun* (*plural* **parapets**) a low wall along the edge of a balcony, bridge, roof, etc. [via French from Italian]

paraphernalia *noun* numerous pieces of equipment, belongings, etc. [originally = the personal belongings a woman could keep after her marriage (as opposed to her dowry, which went to her husband): from *para-*[1] + Greek *pherne* = dowry]

paraphrase *verb* (**paraphrases**, **paraphrasing**, **paraphrased**) give the meaning of something by using different words. **paraphrase** *noun* [from *para-*[1] + *phrase*]

parasite *noun* (*plural* **parasites**) an animal or plant that lives in or on another, from which it gets its food. **parasitic** adjective [from Greek parasitos = guest at a meal]

paratroops plural noun troops trained to be dropped from aircraft by parachute. **paratrooper** noun [from parachute + troops]

parcel noun (plural **parcels**) something wrapped up to be sent by post or carried. **parcel** verb (**parcels, parcelling, parcelled**) 1 wrap something up as a parcel. 2 divide something into portions, parcel out the work. [from old French, related to particle]

parched adjective very dry or thirsty. [origin unknown]

parchment noun (plural **parchments**) a kind of heavy paper, originally made from animal skins. [from the city of Pergamum, now in Turkey, where parchment was made in ancient times]

pardon noun forgiveness. **pardon** verb (**pardons, pardoning, pardoned**) 1 forgive somebody. 2 excuse somebody kindly. **pardonable** adjective, **pardonably** adverb **pardon** interjection used to mean 'I didn't hear or understand what you said' or 'I apologize'.

parent noun (plural **parents**) 1 a father or mother; a living thing that has produced others of its kind. 2 a source from which others are derived, the parent company. **parenthood** noun,

parenting noun, **parental** (say pa-rent-al) adjective [from Latin parens = producing offspring]

parenthesis (say pa-ren-thi-sis) noun (plural **parentheses**) 1 something extra that is inserted in a sentence, usually between brackets or dashes. 2 either of the pair of brackets (like these) used to mark off words from the rest of a sentence. **parenthetical** adjective [Greek, = putting in besides]

parish noun (plural **parishes**) a district with its own church. **parishioner** noun [from Greek paroikia = neighbourhood, from para-¹ = beside + oikos = house]

park noun (plural **parks**) 1 a large garden or recreation ground for public use. 2 an area of grassland or woodland belonging to a country house. **park** verb (**parks, parking, parked**) leave a vehicle somewhere for a time.

parliament noun (plural **parliaments**) the assembly that makes a country's laws. **parliamentary** adjective [same origin as parley]

parlour noun (plural **parlours**) (old use) a sitting room. [originally = a room in a monastery where the monks were allowed to talk: from French parler = speak]

parody noun (plural **parodies**) an imitation that makes fun of a person or thing. **parody** verb (**parodies, parodying, parodied**) make or be a parody of a person or thing. [from para-¹ + Greek oide = song]

parole noun the release of a prisoner before the end of his or her sentence on condition of good behaviour, *He was on parole.* [French, = word of honour]

paroxysm (*say* pa-roks-izm) noun (*plural* **paroxysms**) a sudden outburst of rage, jealousy, laughter, etc. [from Greek *paroxynein* = to annoy or exasperate]

parrot noun (*plural* **parrots**) a brightly-coloured tropical bird that can learn to repeat words etc. [from French]

parsley noun a plant with crinkled green leaves used to flavour and decorate food.

parsnip noun (*plural* **parsnips**) a plant with a pointed pale-yellow root used as a vegetable. [from old French]

parson noun (*plural* **parsons**) a member of the clergy, especially a rector or vicar. [from old French *persone* = person]

part noun (*plural* **parts**)
1 some but not all of a thing or number of things; anything that belongs to something bigger. **2** the character played by an actor or actress. **3** the words spoken by a character in a play. **4** one side in an agreement or in a dispute or quarrel.
take in good part not be offended at something.
take part join in an activity.
part verb (**parts, parting, parted**) separate or divide.
part with give away or get rid of something.

part exchange noun giving something that you own, as part of the price of what you are buying.

partial adjective
1 not complete or total, *a partial eclipse.* **2** favouring one side more than the other; biased or unfair. **partially** adverb, **partiality** noun
be partial to be fond of something.

participate verb (**participates, participating, participated**) take part or have a share in something. **participant** noun, **participation** noun, **participator** noun [from Latin *pars* = part + *capere* = take]

participle noun (*plural* **participles**) a word formed from a verb (e.g. *gone, going; guided, guiding*) and used with an auxiliary verb to form certain tenses (e.g. *It has gone. It is going*) or the passive (e.g. *We were guided to our seats*), or as an adjective (e.g. *a guided missile; a guiding light*). The **past participle** (e.g. *gone, guided*) describes a completed action or past condition. The **present participle** (which ends in *-ing*) describes a continuing action or condition. [from Latin *particeps* = taking part]

particle noun (*plural* **particles**) a very small portion or amount. [from Latin, = little part]

particular adjective
1 of this one and no other; individual, *This particular stamp is very rare.* **2** special, *Take particular care of it.* **3** giving something close attention; choosing carefully, *He is very*

particular about his clothes.
particularly *adverb,* **particularity**
noun
particular *noun (plural*
particulars) a single fact; a detail,
*Can you give me the particulars of
the case?*

in particular 1 especially, *We liked
this one in particular.* **2** special,
We did nothing in particular.
[same origin as *particle*]

parting *noun (plural* **partings**)
1 leaving or separation. **2** a line
where hair is combed away in
different directions.

partisan *noun (plural* **partisans**)
1 a strong supporter of a party or
group etc. **2** a member of an
organization resisting the
authorities in a conquered
country.

partition *noun (plural* **partitions**)
1 a thin wall that divides a room
or space. **2** dividing something,
especially a country, into
separate parts.

partition *verb* (**partitions,
partitioning, partitioned**)
1 divide something into separate
parts. **2** divide a room or space by
means of a partition.
[from Latin *partitio* = division]

partly *adverb* to some extent but
not completely.

partner *noun (plural* **partners**)
1 one of a pair of people who do
something together, e.g. in
business or dancing or playing
a game. **2** the person that
someone is married to or is
having a sexual relationship
with. **partnership** *noun* [from
Latin *partiri* = to divide or share]

part of speech *noun (plural*
parts of speech) any of the groups
into which words are divided in
grammar (noun, pronoun,
adjective, verb, adverb,
preposition, conjunction,
interjection).

partridge *noun (plural*
partridges) a game bird with
brown feathers.

part-time *adjective & adverb*
working for only some of the
normal hours. **part-timer** *noun*

party *noun (plural* **parties**)
1 a gathering of people to enjoy
themselves, *a birthday party.*
2 a group working or travelling
together. **3** an organized group of
people with similar political
beliefs, *the Labour Party.*
4 a person who is involved in an
action or lawsuit etc., *the guilty
party.* [from old French; related
to *part*]

pass *verb* (**passes, passing,
passed**)
1 go past something; go onwards.
2 move something in a certain
direction, *Pass the cord through
the ring.* **3** give or transfer
something to another person,
Pass the butter to your father. **4** be
successful in a test or
examination. **5** approve or
accept, *They passed a law.*
6 occupy time. **7** happen, *We
heard what passed when they met.*
8 come to an end. **9** utter, *Pass
a remark.* **10** let your turn go by
at cards or in a competition etc.,
Pass!

pass out 1 complete your
military training. **2** faint.

pass *noun (plural* **passes**)
1 passing something.

2 a permit to go in or out of a place. **3** a route through a gap in a range of mountains. **4** a critical state of affairs, *Things have come to a pretty pass!*
[from Latin *passus* = pace]

passage noun (plural **passages**)
1 a way through something; a corridor. **2** a journey by sea or air. **3** a section of a piece of writing or music. **4** passing, *the passage of time.* **passageway** noun [old French; *from* passing]

passenger noun (plural **passengers**) a person who is driven or carried in a car, train, ship, or aircraft etc. [same origin as *passage*]

passer-by noun (plural **passers-by**) a person who happens to be going past something.

passion noun (plural **passions**)
1 strong emotion. **2** great enthusiasm.
the Passion the sufferings of Jesus Christ at the Crucifixion. [from Latin *passio* = suffering]

passionate adjective full of passion. **passionately** adverb

passive adjective
1 not resisting or fighting against something. **2** acted upon and not active. **3** (of a form of a verb) used when the subject of the sentence receives the action, e.g. *was hit* in 'She was hit on the head'. (Compare *active.*) **passively** adverb, **passiveness** noun, **passivity** noun [from Latin *passivus* = capable of suffering]

Passover noun a Jewish religious festival commemorating the freeing of the Jews from slavery in Egypt. [from *pass over*,

because God spared the Jews from the fate which affected the Egyptians]

passport noun (plural **passports**) an official document that entitles the person holding it to travel abroad. [from *pass* + *port*[1]]

password noun (plural **passwords**)
1 a secret word or phrase used to distinguish friends from enemies. **2** a word you need to key in to gain access to certain computer files.

past adjective of the time gone by, *during the past week.*

past noun the time gone by.

past preposition **1** beyond, *Walk past the school.* **2** after, *It is past midnight.*
past it (slang) too old to be able to do something.
[the old past participle of *pass*]

paste noun (plural **pastes**)
1 a soft and moist or gluey substance. **2** a hard glassy substance used to make imitation jewellery.

paste verb (**pastes**, **pasting**, **pasted**)
1 stick something onto a surface by using paste. **2** coat something with paste. **3** (slang) beat or thrash someone.

pastel noun (plural **pastels**)
1 a crayon that is like chalk. **2** a light delicate colour. [from Latin *pastellus* = woad]

pasteurize verb (**pasteurizes**, **pasteurizing**, **pasteurized**) purify milk by heating and then cooling it. [named after a French scientist, Louis Pasteur, who invented the process]

pastille noun (plural **pastilles**)
a small flavoured sweet for
sucking. [from Latin *pastillus*
= lozenge]

pastime noun (plural **pastimes**)
something you do to make time
pass pleasantly; a hobby or game.

pastoral adjective to do with
country life, *a pastoral scene.*

pastry noun (plural **pastries**)
1 dough made with flour, fat, and
water, rolled flat and baked.
2 something made of pastry.
[from *paste*]

pasture noun (plural **pastures**)
land covered with grass etc. that
cattle, sheep, or horses can eat.

pasture verb (**pastures**,
pasturing, **pastured**) put animals
to graze in a pasture.
[from Latin *pastum* = fed]

pasty[1] (say **pas**-tee) noun (plural
pasties) pastry with a filling of
meat and vegetables, baked
without a dish to shape it. [from
old French *pasté* = paste or
pastry]

pasty[2] (say **pay**-stee) adjective
looking pale and unhealthy.
[from *paste*]

pat verb (**pats**, **patting**, **patted**) tap
gently with the open hand or
with something flat.

pat noun (plural **pats**)
1 a patting movement or sound.
2 a small piece of butter or other
soft substance.

a pat on the back praise.

patch noun (plural **patches**)
1 a piece of material or metal etc.
put over a hole or damaged place.
2 an area that is different from
its surroundings. **3** a piece of
ground, *the cabbage patch.*
4 a small area or piece of

something, *There are patches of
fog.*

not a patch on (informal) not
nearly as good as.

patch verb (**patches**, **patching**,
patched) put a patch on
something.

patch up 1 repair something
roughly. **2** settle a quarrel.
[probably from old French *pieche*
= piece]

patchwork noun needlework in
which small pieces of different
cloth are sewn edge to edge.

patchy adjective occurring in
patches; uneven. **patchily** adverb,
patchiness noun

pâté (say **pat**-ay) noun (plural
pâtés) paste made of meat or fish.
[French]

pâté de foie gras (say **pat**-ay der
fwah **grah**) noun a paste or pie of
goose-liver. [French, = paste of
fat liver]

patent (say **pat**-ent or **pay**-tent)
noun (plural **patents**) the official
right given to an inventor to
make or sell his or her invention
and to prevent other people from
copying it.

patent verb (**patents**, **patenting**,
patented) get a patent for
something.
[originally, in *letters patent*, an
open letter from a monarch or
government recording a contract
or granting a right: from Latin
patens = lying open]

paternalistic adjective treating
people in a paternal way,
providing for their needs but
giving them no responsibility.
paternalism noun

paternity noun
1 fatherhood. 2 being the father of a particular baby. [from Latin *pater* = father]

path noun (plural **paths**)
1 a narrow way along which people or animals can walk. 2 a line along which a person or thing moves. [from Old English]

pathetic adjective
1 making you feel pity or sympathy. 2 miserably inadequate or useless, *a pathetic attempt*. **pathetically** adverb [same origin as *pathos*]

pathos (say pay-thoss) noun
a quality of making people feel pity or sympathy. [Greek, = feeling or suffering]

-pathy suffix forms nouns meaning 'feeling or suffering something' (e.g. *sympathy*, *telepathy*). [from Greek *patheia* = feeling or suffering]

patience noun
1 being patient. 2 a card game for one person.

patient adjective
1 able to wait or put up with annoyances without becoming angry. 2 able to persevere. **patiently** adverb

patient noun (plural **patients**)
a person who has treatment from a doctor or dentist etc. [from Latin *patiens* = suffering]

patio noun (plural **patios**) a paved area beside a house. [Spanish, = courtyard]

patriarch (say pay-tree-ark) noun (plural **patriarchs**)
1 the male who is head of a family or tribe. 2 a bishop of high rank in the Orthodox Christian churches. **patriarchal** adjective [from Greek *patria* = family + *archein* = to rule]

patriot (say pay-tree-ot or pat-ree-ot) noun (plural **patriots**) a person who loves his or her country and supports it loyally. **patriotic** adjective, **patriotically** adverb, **patriotism** noun [from Greek *patris* = fatherland]

patrol verb (patrols, patrolling, patrolled) walk or travel regularly over an area in order to guard it and see that all is well.

patrol noun (plural **patrols**)
1 a patrolling group of people, ships, aircraft, etc. 2 a group of Scouts or Guides.
on patrol patrolling.
[from French *patrouiller* = paddle in mud]

patron (say pay-tron) noun (plural **patrons**)
1 someone who supports a person or cause with money or encouragement. 2 a regular customer. **patronage** (say pat-ron-ij) noun [from Latin *patronus* = protector]

patronize (say pat-ron-I'z) verb (patronizes, patronizing, patronized)
1 be a regular customer of a particular shop, restaurant, etc. 2 talk to someone in a way that shows you think they are stupid or inferior to you.

patter[1] noun a series of light tapping sounds.

patter verb (patters, pattering, pattered) make light tapping sounds. *Rain pattered on the window panes*. [from *pat*]

patter[2] noun the quick talk of a comedian, conjuror, salesperson, etc. [originally = recite a prayer: from Latin *pater noster* = Our Father, the first words of a Christian prayer]

pattern noun (plural **patterns**)
1 a repeated arrangement of lines, shapes, or colours etc. 2 a thing to be copied in order to make something, *a dress pattern*. 3 the regular way in which something happens, *James Bond films follow a set pattern*. 4 an excellent example or model. [same origin as *patron*]

paunch noun (plural **paunches**) a large belly. [from old French]

pauper noun (plural **paupers**) a person who is very poor. [Latin, = poor]

pause noun (plural **pauses**) a temporary stop in speaking or doing something.

pause verb (pauses, pausing, paused) stop speaking or doing something for a short time. [from Greek *pauein* = to stop]

pave verb (paves, paving, paved) lay a hard surface on a road or path etc. **paving-stone** noun **pave the way** prepare for something. [from Latin *pavire* = ram down]

pavement noun (plural **pavements**) a paved path along the side of a street.

pavilion noun (plural **pavilions**)
1 a building for use by players and spectators etc., especially at a cricket ground. 2 an ornamental building or shelter used for dances, concerts, exhibitions, etc. [from French *pavillon* = tent]

paw noun (plural **paws**) the foot of an animal that has claws.

paw verb (paws, pawing, pawed) touch or scrape something with a hand or foot. [from old French]

pawn[1] noun (plural **pawns**)
1 the least valuable piece in chess. 2 a person whose actions are controlled by somebody else. [from Latin *pedo* = foot-soldier]

pawn[2] verb (pawns, pawning, pawned) leave something with a pawnbroker as security for a loan. [from old French *pan* = pledge]

pawnbroker noun (plural **pawnbrokers**) a shopkeeper who lends money to people in return for objects that they leave as security. **pawnshop** noun

pay verb (pays, paying, paid)
1 give money in return for goods or services. 2 give what is owed, *pay your debts; pay the rent*. 3 be profitable or worthwhile, *It pays to advertise*. 4 give or express, *pay attention; pay them a visit; pay compliments*. 5 suffer a penalty. 6 let out a rope by loosening it gradually. **payer** noun
pay off 1 pay in full what you owe. 2 be worthwhile or have good results, *All the preparation she did really paid off*.
pay up pay the full amount you owe.

pay noun salary or wages. [from Latin *pacare* = appease]

payable adjective that must be paid.

payment noun (plural **payments**) 1 paying. 2 money paid.

PC *abbreviation*
1 personal computer. **2** police constable.

PE *abbreviation* physical education.

pea *noun* (*plural* **peas**) the small round green seed of a climbing plant, growing inside a pod and used as a vegetable. [via Old English from Greek]

peace *noun*
1 a time when there is no war, violence, or disorder. **2** quietness and calm.

peaceable *adjective* fond of peace; not quarrelsome or warlike. **peaceably** *adverb*

peaceful *adjective* quiet and calm. **peacefully** *adverb*, **peacefulness** *noun*

peach *noun* (*plural* **peaches**)
1 a round soft juicy fruit with a pinkish or yellowish skin and a large stone. **2** (*informal*) a thing of great quality, *a peach of a shot.* [from Old French]

peacock *noun* (*plural* **peacocks**) a male bird with a long brightly-coloured tail that it can spread out like a fan. **peahen** *noun* [via Old English from Latin]

peak *noun* (*plural* **peaks**)
1 a pointed top, especially of a mountain. **2** the highest or most intense part of something, *Traffic reaches its peak at 5 p.m.* **3** the part of a cap that sticks out in front. **peaked** *adjective*

peak *verb* (**peaks, peaking, peaked**) reach its highest point or value.

peal *noun* (*plural* **peals**)
1 the loud ringing of a bell or set of bells. **2** a loud burst of thunder or laughter.

peal *verb* (**peals, pealing, pealed**) (of bells) ring loudly. [from *appeal*]

peanut *noun* (*plural* **peanuts**) a small round nut that grows in a pod in the ground.

pear *noun* (*plural* **pears**) a juicy fruit that gets narrower near the stalk. [via Old English from Latin]

pearl *noun* (*plural* **pearls**) a small shiny white ball found in the shells of some oysters and used as a jewel. **pearly** *adjective* [from French]

peasant *noun* (*plural* **peasants**) a person who belongs to a farming community, especially in poor areas of the world. **peasantry** *noun* [from Latin *paganus* = villager]

peat *noun* rotted plant material that can be dug out of the ground and used as fuel or in gardening. **peaty** *adjective* [from Latin *peta*, probably from a Celtic word]

pebble *noun* (*plural* **pebbles**) a small round stone. **pebbly** *adjective* [origin unknown]

peck *verb* (**pecks, pecking, pecked**)
1 bite at something quickly with the beak. **2** kiss someone lightly on the cheek.

peck *noun* (*plural* **pecks**)
1 a quick bite by a bird. **2** a light kiss on the cheek. [probably from old German]

peckish *adjective* (*informal*) hungry. [from *peck* + *-ish*]

peculiar *adjective*
1 strange or unusual. **2** belonging to a particular person, place, or thing; restricted, *This custom is peculiar to this tribe.* **3** special,

This point is of peculiar interest.
peculiarly *adverb*, **peculiarity**
noun [from Latin *peculium*
= private property]

pedal *noun* (*plural* **pedals**) a lever
pressed by the foot to operate
a bicycle, car, machine, etc. or in
certain musical instruments.

pedal *verb* (**pedals, pedalling,
pedalled**) use a pedal; move or
work something, especially
a bicycle, by means of pedals.
[from Latin *pedis* = of a foot]

pedantic *adjective* being very
careful and strict about exact
meanings and facts etc. in
learning. **pedantically** *adverb*

peddle *verb* (**peddles, peddling,
peddled**)
1 go from house to house selling
small things. **2** sell illegal drugs.
3 try to get people to accept an
idea, way of life, etc. [from
pedlar]

pedestal *noun* (*plural* **pedestals**)
the raised base on which a statue
or pillar etc. stands.
put someone on a pedestal
admire him or her greatly.
[from Italian *piede* = foot, + *stall*[1]]

pedestrian *noun* (*plural*
pedestrians) a person who is
walking.

pedestrian *adjective* ordinary
and dull.
[same origin as *pedal*]

pedestrian crossing *noun*
(*plural* **pedestrian crossings**)
a place where pedestrians can
cross the road safely.

pedigree *noun* (*plural* **pedigrees**)
a list of a person's or animal's
ancestors, especially to show how
well an animal has been bred.
[from old French *pé de grue*

= crane's foot (from the shape
made by the lines on a family
tree)]

pedlar *noun* (*plural* **pedlars**)
a person who goes from house to
house selling small things. [from
Middle English *ped* = a hamper
or basket (in which a pedlar
carried his goods)]

peel *noun* (*plural* **peels**) the skin
of certain fruits and vegetables.

peel *verb* (**peels, peeling, peeled**)
1 remove the peel or covering
from something. **2** come off in
strips or layers. **3** lose a covering
or skin.
[Middle English; related to Latin
pilare = cut off the hair]

peelings *plural noun* strips of
skin peeled from potatoes etc.

peep *verb* (**peeps, peeping,
peeped**)
1 look quickly or secretly. **2** look
through a narrow opening.
3 come slowly or briefly into
view, *The moon peeped out from
behind the clouds.* **peep** *noun*,
peephole *noun* [origin unknown]

peer[1] *verb* (**peers, peering, peered**)
look at something closely or with
difficulty. [origin unknown]

peer[2] *noun* (*plural* **peers**)
1 a noble. **2** someone who is equal
to another in rank, merit, or age
etc., *She had no peer.* **peeress**
noun, **peerage** *noun* [from Latin
par = equal]

peerless *adjective* without an
equal; better than the others.

peevish *adjective* irritable.
[origin unknown]

peg *noun* (*plural* **pegs**) a piece of
wood or metal or plastic for
fastening things together or for
hanging things on.

peg *verb* (**pegs, pegging, pegged**)
1 fix something with pegs. **2** keep wages or prices at a fixed level.
peg away work diligently; persevere.
peg out (*slang*) die.

Pekingese *noun* (*plural* **Pekingese**) a small kind of dog with short legs, a flat face, and long silky hair. [from *Peking*, the old name of Beijing, the capital of China (where the breed came from)]

pelican *noun* (*plural* **pelicans**) a large bird with a pouch in its long beak for storing fish. [from Greek]

pelican crossing *noun* (*plural* **pelican crossings**) a place where pedestrians can cross a street safely by operating lights that signal traffic to stop.

pellet *noun* (*plural* **pellets**) a tiny ball of metal, food, paper, etc. [from Latin *pila* = ball]

pelt[1] *verb* (**pelts, pelting, pelted**) **1** throw a lot of things at someone. **2** run fast. **3** rain very hard. [origin unknown]

pelt[2] *noun* (*plural* **pelts**) an animal skin, especially with the fur still on it. [from Latin *pellis* = skin or leather]

pen[1] *noun* (*plural* **pens**) an instrument with a point for writing with ink. [from Latin *penna* = feather (because a pen was originally a sharpened quill)]

pen[2] *noun* (*plural* **pens**) an enclosure for cattle, sheep, hens, or other animals.

pen *verb* (**pens, penning, penned**) shut animals etc. into a pen or other enclosed space. [from Old English]

penalize *verb* (**penalizes, penalizing, penalized**) punish; put a penalty on someone.
penalization *noun*

penalty *noun* (*plural* **penalties**) **1** a punishment. **2** a point or advantage given to one side in a game when a member of the other side has broken a rule.

pence *plural noun* see **penny**. [from *pennies*]

pencil *noun* (*plural* **pencils**) an instrument for drawing or writing, made of a thin stick of graphite or coloured chalk etc. enclosed in a cylinder of wood or metal. [from Latin *penicillum* = paintbrush]

pendant *noun* (*plural* **pendants**) an ornament worn hanging on a cord or chain round the neck. [from Latin *pendens* = hanging]

pending *preposition*
1 until, *Please take charge, pending his return.* **2** during, *pending these discussions.*
pending *adjective* waiting to be decided or settled.

pendulum *noun* (*plural* **pendulums**) a weight hung so that it can swing to and fro, especially in the works of a clock. [from Latin, = something hanging down]

penetrate *verb* (**penetrates, penetrating, penetrated**) make or find a way through or into something; pierce. **penetration** *noun*, **penetrative** *adjective* [from Latin *penitus* = inside]

penfriend noun (plural penfriends) a friend to whom you write without meeting.

penguin noun (plural penguins) an Antarctic seabird that cannot fly but uses its wings as flippers for swimming. [origin unknown]

penicillin noun an antibiotic obtained from mould. [from the Latin name of the mould used]

peninsula noun (plural peninsulas) a piece of land that is almost surrounded by water. **peninsular** adjective [from Latin paene = almost + insula = island]

penis (say peen-iss) noun (plural penises) the part of the body with which a male urinates and has sexual intercourse. [Latin, = tail]

penitence noun regret for having done wrong. **penitent** adjective, **penitently** adverb [from Latin paenitere = to make someone sorry]

penknife noun (plural penknives) a small folding knife. [originally used for sharpening quill pens]

pen-name noun (plural pen-names) a name used by an author instead of his or her real name.

penniless adjective having no money; very poor.

penny noun (plural pennies for separate coins, pence for a sum of money)
1 a British coin worth 1/100 of a pound. **2** a former coin worth 1/12 of a shilling. [from Old English]

pension noun (plural pensions) an income consisting of regular payments made by a government or firm to someone who is retired, widowed, or disabled. [from Latin pensio = payment]

pensioner noun (plural pensioners) a person who receives a pension.

penta- prefix five. [from Greek]

pentagon noun (plural pentagons) a flat shape with five sides and five angles. **pentagonal** (say pent-**ag**-on-al) adjective **the Pentagon** a five-sided building in Washington, headquarters of the leaders of the American armed forces. [from penta- + Greek gonia = angle]

pentameter noun (plural pentameters) a line of verse with five rhythmic beats. [from penta- + Greek metron = measure]

pentathlon noun (plural pentathlons) an athletic contest consisting of five events. [from penta- + Greek athlon = contest]

Pentecost noun
1 the Jewish harvest festival, fifty days after Passover. **2** Whit Sunday. [from Greek pentekoste = fiftieth (day)]

pent-up adjective shut in, pent-up feelings. [old past participle of pen²]

penultimate adjective last but one. [from Latin paene = almost, + ultimate]

peony noun (plural peonies) a plant with large round red, pink, or white flowers. [named after Paion, physician of the Greek gods (because the plant was once used in medicines)]

people plural noun human beings; persons, especially those belonging to a particular country, area, or group etc.

people noun (plural **peoples**) a community or nation, *a warlike people; the English-speaking peoples.*

pepper noun (plural **peppers**)
1 a hot-tasting powder used to flavour food. 2 a bright green, red, or yellow vegetable. **peppery** adjective

pepper verb (**peppers, peppering, peppered**)
1 sprinkle with pepper. 2 pelt with many small objects. [from Old English]

peppermint noun (plural **peppermints**)
1 a kind of mint used for flavouring. 2 a sweet flavoured with this mint. [because of its sharp taste]

per preposition for each, *The charge is £2 per person.* [from Latin, = through]

per- prefix
1 through (as in *perforate*).
2 thoroughly (as in *perturb*).
3 away entirely; towards badness (as in *pervert*). [from Latin]

perceive verb (**perceives, perceiving, perceived**) see, notice, or understand something. [from Latin *percipere* = seize, understand]

per cent adverb for or in every hundred, *three per cent (3%).* [from *per* + Latin *centum* = hundred]

percentage noun (plural **percentages**) an amount or rate expressed as a proportion of 100.

perceptible adjective able to be seen or noticed. **perceptibly** adverb, **perceptibility** noun

perception noun (plural **perceptions**) the ability to see, notice, or understand something. [same origin as *perceive*]

perceptive adjective quick to notice or understand things.

perch¹ noun (plural **perches**)
1 a place where a bird sits or rests. 2 a seat high up.

perch verb (**perches, perching, perched**) rest or place on a perch. [from Latin *pertica* = pole]

perch² noun (plural **perch**) an edible freshwater fish. [from Greek]

percolate verb (**percolates, percolating, percolated**) flow through small holes or spaces. **percolation** noun [from *per-* + Latin *colum* = strainer]

percolator noun (plural **percolators**) a pot for making coffee, in which boiling water percolates through coffee grounds.

percussion noun
1 musical instruments (e.g. drums, cymbals) played by being struck or shaken. 2 the striking of one thing against another. **percussive** adjective [from Latin *percussum* = hit]

perdition noun eternal damnation. [from Latin *perditum* = destroyed]

peregrine noun (plural **peregrines**) a kind of falcon. [from Latin *peregrinus* = travelling (because it migrates)]

perennial adjective lasting for many years; keeping on recurring. **perennially** adverb

perennial noun (plural
perennials) a plant that lives for
many years.
[from per- + Latin annus = year]

perfect (say per-fikt) adjective
1 so good that it cannot be made
any better. **2** complete, a perfect
stranger. **perfectly** adverb

perfect (say per-fekt) verb
(perfects, perfecting, perfected)
make a thing perfect. **perfection**
noun

to perfection perfectly.
[from Latin perfectum
= completed]

perfectionist noun (plural
perfectionists) a person who likes
everything to be done perfectly.

perfect tense noun a tense of
a verb showing a completed
action, e.g. He has arrived.

perforate verb (perforates,
perforating, perforated)
1 make tiny holes in something,
especially so that it can be torn
off easily. **2** pierce. **perforation**
noun [from per- + Latin forare
= bore through]

perform verb (performs,
performing, performed)
1 do something in front of an
audience, perform a play. **2** do
something, perform an operation.
performance noun, **performer**
noun [from old French]

perfume noun (plural perfumes)
1 a pleasant smell. **2** a liquid for
giving something a pleasant
smell; scent. **perfume** verb,
perfumery noun [originally used
of smoke from something
burning: via French from old
Italian parfumare = to smoke
through]

perfunctory adjective done
without much care or interest,
a perfunctory glance.
perfunctorily adverb [from Latin]

perhaps adverb it may be;
possibly. [from per + Middle
English hap = luck]

peri- prefix around (as in
perimeter). [from Greek]

peril noun (plural perils) danger.
perilous adjective, **perilously**
adverb [from Latin periculum
= danger]

perimeter noun (plural
perimeters)
1 the outer edge or boundary of
something. **2** the distance round
the edge. [from peri- + Greek
metron = measure]

USAGE: Do not confuse with
parameter.

period noun (plural periods)
1 a length of time. **2** the time
when a woman menstruates. **3** (in
punctuation) a full stop. [from
Greek periodos = course or cycle
(of events)]

periodic adjective occurring at
regular intervals. **periodically**
adverb

periodical noun (plural
periodicals) a magazine
published at regular intervals
(e.g. monthly).

periodic table noun a table in
which the chemical elements are
arranged in order of increasing
atomic number.

periscope noun (plural
periscopes) a device with a tube
and mirrors with which a person
in a trench or submarine etc. can

see things that are otherwise out of sight. [from *peri-* + Greek *skopein* = look at]

perish *verb* (**perishes, perishing, perished**)
1 die; be destroyed. **2** rot, *The rubber ring has perished.*
perishable *adjective* [from *per-* + Latin *ire* = go]

perjure *verb* (**perjures, perjuring, perjured**)
perjure yourself commit perjury.

perjury *noun* telling a lie while you are on oath to speak the truth. [from Latin *perjurare* = break an oath]

perk[1] *verb* (**perks, perking, perked**)
perk up make or become more cheerful.
[from *perch*[1]]

perk[2] *noun* (*plural* **perks**) (*informal*) something extra given to a worker, *Free bus travel is one of the perks of the job.* [from *perquisite*, from Latin]

perky *adjective* lively and cheerful. **perkily** *adverb* [from *perk*[1]]

permanent *adjective* lasting for always or for a very long time. **permanently** *adverb*, **permanence** *noun* [from *per-* + Latin *manens* = remaining]

permanent wave *noun* (*plural* **permanent waves**) treatment of the hair to give it long-lasting waves.

permeate *verb* (**permeates, permeating, permeated**) spread into every part of something; pervade, *Smoke had permeated the hall.* **permeation** *noun* [from *per-* + Latin *meare* = to pass]

permissible *adjective* allowable.

permission *noun* the right to do something, given by someone in authority; authorization. [same origin as *permit*]

permissive *adjective* letting people do what they wish; tolerant or liberal.

permit (*say* per-**mit**) *verb* (**permits, permitting, permitted**) give permission or consent or a chance to do something; allow.

permit (*say* **per**-mit) *noun* (*plural* **permits**) written or printed permission to do something or go somewhere. [from *per-* + Latin *mittere* = send or let go]

permutation *noun* (*plural* **permutations**)
1 changing the order of a set of things. **2** a changed order, *3, 1, 2 is a permutation of 1, 2, 3.* [from *per-* + Latin *mutare* = to change]

peroxide *noun* a chemical used for bleaching hair. [from *per-* + *oxide*]

perpendicular *adjective* upright; at a right angle (90°) to a line or surface. [from Latin *perpendiculum* = plumb line]

perpetrate *verb* (**perpetrates, perpetrating, perpetrated**) commit or be guilty of, *perpetrate a crime or an error.* **perpetration** *noun*, **perpetrator** *noun* [from *per-* + Latin *patrare* = make something happen]

perpetual *adjective* lasting for a long time; continual. **perpetually** *adverb* [from Latin *perpes* = uninterrupted]

perplex *verb* (**perplexes, perplexing, perplexed**) bewilder or puzzle somebody. **perplexity** noun [from per- + Latin plexus = twisted together]

persecute verb (persecutes, persecuting, persecuted) be continually cruel to somebody, especially because you disagree with his or her beliefs. **persecution** noun, **persecutor** noun [from Latin persecutum = pursued]

persevere verb (perseveres, persevering, persevered) go on doing something even though it is difficult. **perseverance** noun [from per- + Latin severus = strict]

Persian adjective to do with or belonging to Persia, a country in the Middle East now called Iran. **Persian** noun the language of Persia.

persist verb (persists, persisting, persisted)
1 continue firmly or obstinately, She persists in breaking the rules. 2 continue to exist, The custom persists in some countries. **persistent** adjective, **persistently** adverb, **persistence** noun, **persistency** noun [from per- + Latin sistere = to stand]

person noun (plural **people** or **persons**)
1 a human being; a man, woman, or child. 2 (in Grammar) any of the three groups of personal pronouns and forms taken by verbs. The **first person** (= I, me, we, us) refers to the person(s) speaking; the **second person** (= you) refers to the person(s) spoken to; the **third person** (= he, him, she, her, it, they, them) refers to the person(s) spoken about.
in person being actually present

oneself, She was there in person. [from Latin persona = mask used by an actor]

personal adjective
1 belonging to, done by, or concerning a particular person, personal belongings. 2 criticizing a person, making personal remarks. **personally** adverb

USAGE: Do not confuse with personnel.

personality noun (plural **personalities**)
1 a person's character, She has a cheerful personality. 2 a well-known person, a TV personality.

personify verb (personifies, personifying, personified) represent a quality or idea etc. as a person. **personification** noun

personnel noun the people employed by a firm or other large organization. [French, = personal]

USAGE: Do not confuse with personal.

perspective noun (plural **perspectives**) the impression of depth and space in a picture or scene.
in perspective giving a well-balanced view of things. [from Latin perspicere = look at closely]

perspire verb (perspires, perspiring, perspired) sweat. **perspiration** noun [from per- + Latin spirare = breathe]

persuade verb (persuades, persuading, persuaded) make someone believe or agree to do something. **persuasion** noun,

persuasive *adjective* [from *per-* + Latin *suadere* = advise or induce]

pert *adjective* cheeky. **pertly** *adverb*, **pertness** *noun*

perturb *verb* (**perturbs, perturbing, perturbed**) worry someone. **perturbation** *noun* [from *per-* + Latin *turbare* = disturb]

pervade *verb* (**pervades, pervading, pervaded**) spread all through something; permeate. **pervasion** *noun*, **pervasive** *adjective* [from *per-* + Latin *vadere* = go]

perverse *adjective* obstinately doing something different from what is reasonable or required. **perversely** *adverb*, **perversity** *noun* [same origin as *pervert*]

pervert (*say* per-**vert**) *verb* (**perverts, perverting, perverted**)
1 turn something from the right course of action, *By false evidence they perverted the course of justice.*
2 cause a person to behave wickedly or abnormally. **perversion** *noun*

pervert (*say* **per**-vert) *noun* (*plural* **perverts**) a person whose sexual behaviour is thought to be unnatural or disgusting. [from *per-* + Latin *vertere* = to turn]

pessimist *noun* (*plural* **pessimists**) a person who expects that things will turn out badly. (Compare *optimist*.) **pessimism** *noun*, **pessimistic** *adjective*, **pessimistically** *adverb* [from Latin *pessimus* = worst]

pest *noun* (*plural* **pests**)
1 a destructive insect or animal, such as a locust or a mouse.
2 a nuisance. [from Latin *pestis* = plague]

pester *verb* (**pesters, pestering, pestered**) keep annoying someone by frequent questions or requests. [from French *empestrer* = infect with plague]

pesticide *noun* (*plural* **pesticides**) a substance for killing harmful insects and other pests. [from *pest* + *-cide*]

pestilence *noun* (*plural* **pestilences**) a deadly epidemic. [same origin as *pest*]

pet *noun* (*plural* **pets**)
1 a tame animal kept for companionship and pleasure.
2 a person treated as a favourite, *teacher's pet.*

pet *adjective* favourite, *Science fiction is my pet subject.*

pet *verb* (**pets, petting, petted**) treat or fondle someone affectionately.

petal *noun* (*plural* **petals**) one of the separate coloured outer parts of a flower. [from Greek *petalos* = spread out, unfolded]

peter *verb* (**peters, petering, petered**)
peter out become gradually less and cease to exist. [origin unknown]

petition *noun* (*plural* **petitions**) a formal request for something, especially a written one signed by many people. [from Latin *petere* = claim or ask for]

petrify *verb* (**petrifies, petrifying, petrified**)
1 make someone so terrified that

he or she cannot move. **2** turn to stone. **petrifaction** noun [from Greek *petra* = rock]

petrol noun a liquid made from petroleum, used as fuel for engines.

petroleum noun an oil found underground that is refined to make fuel (e.g. petrol, paraffin) or for use in dry-cleaning etc. [from Greek *petra* = rock + Latin *oleum* = oil]

petticoat noun (plural **petticoats**) a woman's or girl's dress-length undergarment. [from *petty* = little, + *coat*]

petting noun affectionate touching or fondling.

petty adjective (**pettier, pettiest**) **1** unimportant or trivial, *petty regulations.* **2** mean and small-minded. **pettily** adverb, **pettiness** noun [from French *petit* = small]

petty cash noun cash kept by an office for small payments.

pew noun (plural **pews**) a long wooden seat, usually fixed in rows, in a church. [from old French; related to *podium*]

pewter noun a grey alloy of tin and lead.

pH noun a measure of the acidity or alkalinity of a solution. Pure water has a pH of 7, acids have a pH between 0 and 7, and alkalis have a pH between 7 and 14. [from the initial letter of German *Potenz* = power, + H, the symbol for hydrogen]

phantom noun (plural **phantoms**) a ghost; something that is not real.

Pharaoh (say fair-oh) noun (plural **Pharaohs**) the title of the king of ancient Egypt. [from ancient Egyptian *pr-'o* = great house]

pharmacy noun (plural **pharmacies**)
1 a shop selling medicines; a dispensary. **2** the job of preparing medicines. [from Greek *pharmakon* = drug]

phase noun (plural **phases**) a stage in the progress or development of something.

phase verb (**phases, phasing, phased**) do something in stages, not all at once, *a phased withdrawal.* [from Latin]

Ph.D. abbreviation Doctor of Philosophy; a university degree awarded to someone who has done advanced research in their subject.

pheasant (say fez-ant) noun (plural **pheasants**) a game bird with a long tail. [from Greek]

phenomenal adjective amazing or remarkable. **phenomenally** adverb

phenomenon noun (plural **phenomena**) an event or fact, especially one that is remarkable. [from Greek *phainomenon* = something appearing]

USAGE: Note that *phenomena* is a plural. It is incorrect to say 'this phenomena' or 'these phenomenas'.

phial noun (plural **phials**) a small glass bottle. [from Greek]

phil- prefix **1** fond of. **2** a lover of. see **philo-**.

philanthropy *noun* love of mankind, especially as shown by kind and generous acts that benefit large numbers of people.
philanthropist *noun*, **philanthropic** *adjective* [from *phil-* + Greek *anthropos* = mankind]

philistine (*say* fil-ist-I'n) *noun* (*plural* **philistines**) a person who dislikes art, poetry, etc. [from the Philistines in the Bible, who were enemies of the Israelites]

philo- *prefix*
1 fond of. **2** a lover of. [from Greek *philein* = to love]

philosopher *noun* (*plural* **philosophers**) an expert in philosophy.

philosophical *adjective*
1 to do with philosophy. **2** calm and not upset after a misfortune or disappointment, *Be philosophical about losing.*
philosophically *adverb*

philosophy *noun* (*plural* **philosophies**)
1 the study of truths about life, morals, etc. **2** a set of ideas or principles or beliefs. [from *philo-* + Greek *sophia* = wisdom]

phobia (*say* foh-bee-a) *noun* (*plural* **phobias**) great or abnormal fear of something. [from Greek *phobos* = fear]

-phobia *suffix* forms nouns meaning 'fear or great dislike of something' (e.g. *hydrophobia*).

phone *noun* (*plural* **phones**) a telephone.

phone *verb* (**phones**, **phoning**, **phoned**) telephone. [short for *telephone*]

phonetic (*say* fon-et-ik) *adjective*
1 to do with speech-sounds.
2 representing speech-sounds.
phonetically *adverb* [from Greek *phonein* = speak]

phosphorus *noun* a chemical substance that glows in the dark. [from Greek *phos* = light + *-phoros* = bringing]

photo *noun* (*plural* **photos**) a photograph.

photo- *prefix* light (as in *photograph*). [from Greek]

photograph *noun* (*plural* **photographs**) a picture made by the effect of light or other radiation on film or special paper.

photograph *verb* (**photographs**, **photographing**, **photographed**) take a photograph of a person or thing. **photographer** *noun*

photography *noun* taking photographs. **photographic** *adjective*

photosynthesis *noun* the process by which green plants use sunlight to turn carbon dioxide and water into complex substances, giving off oxygen.

phrase *noun* (*plural* **phrases**)
1 a group of words that form a unit in a sentence or clause, e.g. *in the garden* in 'The Queen was in the garden'. **2** a short section of a tune. [from Greek *phrazein* = declare]

physical *adjective*
1 to do with the body rather than the mind or feelings. **2** to do with things that you can touch or see. **3** to do with physics. **physically** *adverb* [same origin as *physics*]

physical education or **physical training** *noun* gymnastics or other exercises done to keep the body healthy.

physician noun (plural **physicians**) a doctor, especially one who is not a surgeon. [from old French *fisicien* = physicist]

physicist (say fiz-i-sist) noun (plural **physicists**) an expert in physics.

physics (say fiz-iks) noun the study of the properties of matter and energy (e.g. heat, light, sound, movement). [from Greek *physikos* = natural]

physiotherapy (say fiz-ee-o-th'erra-pee) noun the treatment of a disease or weakness by massage, exercises, etc.

physiotherapist noun [from Greek *physis* = nature, + *therapy*]

physique (say fiz-eek) noun (plural **physiques**) a person's build. [French, = physical]

pi noun the symbol (π) of the ratio of the circumference of a circle to its diameter. The value of pi is approximately 3.142. [the name of the sixteenth letter (π) of the Greek alphabet]

pianist noun (plural **pianists**) a person who plays the piano.

piano noun (plural **pianos**) a large musical instrument with a keyboard. [short for *pianoforte*, from Italian *piano* = soft + *forte* = loud (because it can produce soft notes and loud notes)]

piccolo noun (plural **piccolos**) a small high-pitched flute. [Italian, = small]

pick¹ verb (**picks, picking, picked**)
1 separate a flower or fruit from its plant, *We picked apples.*
2 choose; select carefully. 3 pull bits off or out of something.
4 open a lock by using something pointed, not with a key.

pick a quarrel deliberately provoke a quarrel with somebody.

pick holes in find fault with.

pick on keep criticizing or harassing a particular person.

pick someone's pocket steal from it.

pick up 1 lift or take up. 2 collect. 3 take someone into a vehicle. 4 manage to hear something. 5 get better or recover.

pick noun
1 choice, *take your pick.* 2 the best of a group.
[origin unknown]

pick² noun (plural **picks**)
1 a pickaxe. 2 a plectrum. [a different spelling of *pike*]

pickaxe noun (plural **pickaxes**) a heavy pointed tool with a long handle, used for breaking up hard ground etc. [from old French *picois*, later confused with *axe*]

picket noun (plural **pickets**)
1 a striker or group of strikers who try to persuade other people not to go into a place of work during a strike. 2 a pointed post as part of a fence.

picket verb (**pickets, picketing, picketed**) stand outside a place of work to try to persuade other people not to go in during a strike.
[from French *picquet* = small pike]

pickle noun (plural **pickles**)
1 a strong-tasting food made of pickled vegetables. 2 (*informal*) a mess.

pickle verb (**pickles, pickling, pickled**) preserve food in vinegar or salt water.

pickpocket noun (plural pickpockets) a thief who steals from people's pockets or bags.

pick-up noun (plural pick-ups)
1 the part of a record player that holds the stylus. 2 an open truck for carrying small loads.

picnic noun (plural picnics) a meal eaten in the open air away from home.

picnic verb (picnics, picnicking, picnicked) have a picnic.
picnicker noun
[from French]

picture noun (plural pictures)
1 a representation of a person or thing made by painting, drawing, or photography. 2 a film at the cinema. 3 how something seems; an impression.

picture verb (pictures, picturing, pictured)
1 show in a picture. 2 imagine. [from Latin pictum = painted]

picturesque adjective
1 forming an attractive scene, a picturesque village. 2 vividly described; expressive, picturesque language.
picturesquely adverb

pie noun (plural pies) a baked dish of meat, fish, or fruit covered with pastry. [perhaps from magpie (because the contents of a pie look like the bits and pieces a magpie collects in its nest)]

piece noun (plural pieces)
1 a part or portion of something; a fragment. 2 a separate thing or example, a fine piece of work. 3 something written, composed, or painted etc., a piece of music. 4 one of the objects used to play a game on a board, a chess-piece.

piece verb (pieces, piecing, pieced) put pieces together to make something.

piecemeal adjective & adverb done or made one piece at a time. [from piece + Old English mael = a measure]

pie chart noun (plural pie charts) a circle divided into sectors to represent the way in which a quantity is divided up.

pier noun (plural piers)
1 a long structure built out into the sea for people to walk on. 2 a pillar supporting a bridge or arch. [from Latin]

pierce verb (pierces, piercing, pierced) make a hole through something; penetrate.

piety noun being very religious and devout; piousness. [from Latin pietas = dutiful behaviour]

pig noun (plural pigs)
1 a fat animal with short legs and a blunt snout, kept for its meat. 2 (informal) someone greedy, dirty, or unpleasant. **piggy** adjective & noun [origin unknown]

pigeon noun (plural pigeons) a bird with a fat body and a small head. [from old French pijon = young bird]

pigeon-hole noun (plural pigeon-holes) a small compartment above a desk etc., used for holding letters or papers.

pigeon-hole verb (pigeon-holes, pigeon-holing, pigeon-holed) decide that a person belongs to a particular category, She doesn't want to be pigeon-holed simply as a pop singer.

piggyback *adverb* carried on somebody else's back or shoulders. **piggyback** *noun* [from *pick-a-back*]

pig-headed *adjective* obstinate.

piglet *noun* (*plural* **piglets**) a young pig.

pigment *noun* (*plural* **pigments**) a substance that colours something. **pigmented** *adjective*, **pigmentation** *noun* [from Latin *pingere* = to paint]

pigsty *noun* (*plural* **pigsties**) 1 a partly-covered pen for pigs. 2 a filthy room or house.

pigtail *noun* (*plural* **pigtails**) a plait of hair worn hanging at the back of the head.

pike *noun* (*plural* **pikes**) 1 a heavy spear. 2 (*plural* **pike**) a large freshwater fish. [origin unknown]

pile¹ *noun* (*plural* **piles**) 1 a number of things on top of one another. 2 (*informal*) a large quantity; a lot of money. 3 a tall building.

pile *verb* (**piles, piling, piled**) put things into a pile; make a pile. [from Latin *pila* = pillar]

pile² *noun* (*plural* **piles**) a heavy beam made of metal, concrete, or timber driven into the ground to support something. [from Old English]

pile³ *noun* a raised surface on fabric, made of upright threads, *a carpet with a thick pile.* [from Latin *pilus* = hair]

pile-up *noun* (*plural* **pile-ups**) a road accident that involves a number of vehicles.

pilfer *verb* (**pilfers, pilfering, pilfered**) steal small things.

pilferer *noun*, **pilferage** *noun* [from old French]

pilgrim *noun* (*plural* **pilgrims**) a person who travels to a holy place for religious reasons. **pilgrimage** *noun*

pill *noun* (*plural* **pills**) a small solid piece of medicine for swallowing.
the pill a contraceptive pill. [from Latin *pila* = ball]

pillage *verb* (**pillages, pillaging, pillaged**) carry off goods using force, especially in a war; plunder. **pillage** *noun* [from Latin *pilare* = cut the hair from]

pillar *noun* (*plural* **pillars**) a tall stone or wooden post. [same origin as *pile*¹]

pillar box *noun* (*plural* **pillar boxes**) a postbox standing in a street. [because many of them are shaped like a short pillar]

pillion *noun* (*plural* **pillions**) a seat behind the driver on a motorcycle. [from Scottish Gaelic *pillean* = cushion]

pillow *noun* (*plural* **pillows**) a cushion for a person's head to rest on, especially in bed.

pillowcase or **pillowslip** *noun* (*plural* **pillowcases, pillowslips**) a cloth cover for a pillow.

pilot *noun* (*plural* **pilots**) 1 a person who works the controls for flying an aircraft. 2 a person qualified to steer a ship in and out of a port or through a difficult stretch of water. 3 a guide.

pilot *verb* (**pilots, piloting, piloted**) 1 be pilot of an aircraft or ship. 2 guide or steer.

pilot *adjective* testing on a small scale how something will work, *a pilot scheme*.
[from Greek *pedon* = oar or rudder]

pilot light *noun* (*plural* **pilot lights**)
1 a small flame that lights a larger burner on a gas cooker etc. 2 an electric indicator light.

pimp *noun* (*plural* **pimps**) a man who gets clients for prostitutes and lives off their earnings. [origin unknown]

pimple *noun* (*plural* **pimples**) a small round raised spot on the skin. **pimply** *adjective*

PIN *abbreviation* personal identification number; a number used as a person's password so that he or she can use a cash dispenser, computer, etc.

pin *noun* (*plural* **pins**)
1 a short thin piece of metal with a sharp point and a rounded head, used to fasten pieces of cloth or paper etc. together. 2 a pointed device for fixing or marking something.
pins and needles a prickling feeling.

pin *verb* (**pins, pinning, pinned**)
1 fasten something with a pin or pins. 2 make a person or thing unable to move, *He was pinned under the wreckage.* 3 fix, *They pinned the blame on her.*

pincer *noun* (*plural* **pincers**) the claw of a shellfish such as a lobster. [from old French *pincier* = to pinch]

pincers *plural noun* a tool with two parts that are pressed together for gripping and holding things.

pinch *verb* (**pinches, pinching, pinched**)
1 squeeze something tightly or painfully between two things, especially between the finger and thumb. 2 (*informal*) steal.

pinch *noun* (*plural* **pinches**)
1 a pinching movement. 2 the amount that can be held between the tips of the thumb and forefinger, *a pinch of salt.*
at a pinch in time of difficulty; if necessary.
feel the pinch suffer from lack of money.
[same origin as *pincer*]

pincushion *noun* (*plural* **pincushions**) a small pad into which pins are stuck to keep them ready for use.

pine[1] *noun* (*plural* **pines**) an evergreen tree with needle-shaped leaves. [from Latin]

pine[2] *verb* (**pines, pining, pined**)
1 feel an intense longing for somebody or something.
2 become weak through longing for somebody or something.
[from Old English]

pineapple *noun* (*plural* **pineapples**) a large tropical fruit with a tough prickly skin and yellow flesh. [from *pine*[1] + *apple* (because it looks like a pine cone)]

ping-pong *noun* table tennis. [from the sound of the bats hitting the ball]

pinion *noun* (*plural* **pinions**) a bird's wing, especially the outer end.

pinion *verb* (**pinions, pinioning, pinioned**)
1 clip a bird's wings to prevent it from flying. 2 hold or fasten

someone's arms or legs in order to prevent them from moving. [from Latin *pinna* = pin, arrow, or feather]

pink *adjective* pale red. **pinkness** *noun*

pink *noun* (*plural* **pinks**)
1 a pink colour. 2 a garden plant with fragrant flowers, often pink or white.

pinnacle *noun* (*plural* **pinnacles**)
1 a pointed ornament on a roof. 2 a high mountain top. 3 the highest point of something, *It was the pinnacle of her career.*

pinpoint *adjective* exact or precise, *with pinpoint accuracy.*

pinpoint *verb* (**pinpoints**, **pinpointing**, **pinpointed**) find or identify something precisely.

pinstripe *noun* (*plural* **pinstripes**) one of the very narrow stripes that form a pattern in cloth. **pinstriped** *adjective*

pint *noun* (*plural* **pints**) a measure for liquids, one-eighth of a gallon. [from old French]

pin-up *noun* (*plural* **pin-ups**) (*informal*) a picture of an attractive or famous person for pinning on a wall.

pioneer *noun* (*plural* **pioneers**) one of the first people to go to a place or do or investigate something. **pioneer** *verb* [from French *pionnier* = foot soldier, later = one of the troops who went ahead of the army to prepare roads etc.]

pious *adjective* very religious; devout. **piously** *adverb*, **piousness** *noun* [from Latin *pius* = dutiful]

pip *noun* (*plural* **pips**)
1 a small hard seed of an apple, pear, orange, etc. 2 one of the

stars on the shoulder of an army officer's uniform. 3 a short high-pitched sound, *She heard the six pips of the time signal on the radio.*

pip *verb* (**pips**, **pipping**, **pipped**) (*informal*) defeat someone by a small amount.

pipe *noun* (*plural* **pipes**)
1 a tube through which water or gas etc. can flow from one place to another. 2 a short narrow tube with a bowl at one end in which tobacco can burn for smoking. 3 a tube forming a musical instrument or part of one.
the pipes bagpipes.

pipe *verb* (**pipes**, **piping**, **piped**)
1 send something along pipes. 2 transmit music or other sound by wire or cable. 3 play music on a pipe or the bagpipes. 4 decorate a cake with thin lines of icing, cream, etc.
pipe down (*informal*) be quiet.
pipe up begin to say something.

pipe dream *noun* (*plural* **pipe dreams**) an impossible wish. [perhaps from dreams produced by smoking opium]

pipeline *noun* (*plural* **pipelines**) a pipe for carrying oil or water etc. a long distance.
in the pipeline in the process of being made or organized.

piping *noun*
1 pipes; a length of pipe. 2 a decorative line of icing, cream, etc. on a cake or other dish. 3 a long narrow pipe-like fold decorating clothing, upholstery, etc.

piping *adjective* shrill, *a piping voice.*
piping hot very hot.

pirate noun (plural **pirates**)
1 a person on a ship who robs other ships at sea or makes a plundering raid on the shore.
2 someone who produces or publishes or broadcasts without authorization, *a pirate radio station; pirate videos.* **piratical** *adjective,* **piracy** *noun* [from Greek *peirain* = to attack]

pirouette (say pir-oo-et) *noun* (plural **pirouettes**) a spinning movement of the body made while balanced on the point of the toe or on one foot. **pirouette** *verb* [French, = spinning top]

pistol *noun* (plural **pistols**) a small handgun.

piston *noun* (plural **pistons**) a disc or cylinder that fits inside a tube in which it moves up and down as part of an engine or pump etc. [via French from Italian *pestone* = pestle]

pit *noun* (plural **pits**)
1 a deep hole. 2 a hollow. 3 a coal mine. 4 the part of a racecourse where racing cars are refuelled and repaired during a race.

pit *verb* (**pits, pitting, pitted**)
1 make holes or hollows in something, *The ground was pitted with holes.* 2 put somebody in competition with somebody else, *He was pitted against the champion.*

pitch[1] *noun* (plural **pitches**)
1 a piece of ground marked out for cricket, football, or another game. 2 the highness or lowness of a voice or a musical note.
3 intensity or strength, *Excitement was at fever pitch.*
4 the steepness of a slope, *the pitch of the roof.*

pitch *verb* (**pitches, pitching, pitched**)
1 throw or fling. 2 fix a tent etc.
3 fall heavily, *He pitched forward as the bus braked suddenly.*
4 move up and down on a rough sea. 5 set something at a particular level, *They pitched their hopes high.* 6 (of a bowled ball in cricket) strike the ground. **pitch in** (*informal*) start working or eating vigorously.

pitch[2] *noun* a black sticky substance rather like tar. **pitch-black** or **pitch-dark** *adjectives* very black or very dark.

pitched battle *noun* (plural **pitched battles**) a battle between troops in prepared positions.

pitcher *noun* (plural **pitchers**) a large jug. [from old French *pichier* = pot]

pitchfork *noun* (plural **pitchforks**) a large fork with two prongs, used for lifting hay.

pitchfork *verb* (**pitchforks, pitchforking, pitchforked**)
1 lift something with a pitchfork.
2 put a person somewhere suddenly.
[originally *pickfork*: from *pick*[1]]

pitfall *noun* (plural **pitfalls**) an unsuspected danger or difficulty.

pitiable *adjective* making you feel pity; pitiful.

pitiful *adjective* making you feel pity; pathetic. **pitifully** *adverb*

pity *noun*
1 the feeling of being sorry because someone is in pain or trouble. 2 a cause for regret, *It's a pity that you can't come.* **take pity on** feel sorry for someone and help them.

pity verb (**pities, pitying, pitied**) feel pity for someone. [same origin as *piety*]

pivot noun (plural **pivots**) a point or part on which something turns or balances. **pivotal** adjective

pivot verb (**pivots, pivoting, pivoted**) turn or place something to turn on a pivot.

pixie noun (plural **pixies**) a small fairy; an elf. [origin unknown]

pizza (say peets-a) noun (plural **pizzas**) an Italian food that consists of a layer of dough baked with a savoury topping. [Italian, = pie]

pizzicato (say pits-i-kah-toh) adjective & adverb plucking the strings of a musical instrument. [Italian, = pinched or twitched]

placard noun (plural **placards**) a poster or notice, especially one carried at a demonstration. [from old French *plaquier* = to lay flat]

place noun (plural **places**)
1 a particular part of space, especially where something belongs; an area or position.
2 a seat, *Save me a place.* 3 a job; employment. 4 a building; a home, *Come round to our place.*
5 a duty or function, *It's not my place to interfere.* 6 a point in a series of things, *In the first place, the date is wrong.*
in place 1 in the right position.
2 suitable.
out of place 1 in the wrong position. **2** unsuitable.

place verb (**places, placing, placed**) put something in a particular place. **placement** noun
[from Greek *plateia* = broad way]

placid adjective calm and peaceful; not easily made anxious or upset. **placidly** adverb, **placidity** noun [from Latin *placidus* = gentle]

plagiarize (say play-jee-er-I'z) verb (**plagiarizes, plagiarizing, plagiarized**) copy and use someone else's writings or ideas etc. as if they were your own. **plagiarism** noun, **plagiarist** noun [from Latin *plagiarius* = kidnapper]

plague noun (plural **plagues**)
1 a dangerous illness that spreads very quickly. 2 a large number of pests, *a plague of locusts.*

plague verb (**plagues, plaguing, plagued**) pester or annoy, *We've been plagued by wasps all afternoon.*
[from Latin]

plain adjective
1 simple; not decorated or elaborate. 2 not beautiful. 3 easy to see or hear or understand. 4 frank and straightforward.
plainly adverb, **plainness** noun

plain noun (plural **plains**) a large area of flat country.
[from Latin *planus* = flat]

USAGE: Do not confuse with *plane.*

plain clothes noun civilian clothes worn instead of a uniform, e.g. by police.

plaintiff noun (plural **plaintiffs**) the person who brings a complaint against somebody else to a lawcourt. (Compare *defendant.*) [same origin as *plaintive*]

plaintive adjective sounding sad. [from French plaintif = grieving or complaining]

plait (say plat) verb (**plaits, plaiting, plaited**) weave three or more strands of hair or rope to form one length.

plait noun (plural **plaits**) a length of hair or rope that has been plaited.
[from Latin plicatum = folded]

plan noun (plural **plans**)
1 a way of doing something thought out in advance.
2 a drawing showing the arrangement of parts of something. 3 a map of a town or district.

plan verb (**plans, planning, planned**) make a plan for something. **planner** noun
[French, = flat surface, plan of a building: related to plain]

plane¹ noun (plural **planes**)
1 an aeroplane. 2 a tool for making wood smooth by scraping its surface. 3 a flat or level surface.

plane verb (**planes, planing, planed**) smooth wood with a plane.

plane adjective flat or level, a plane surface.
[same origin as plain]

USAGE: Do not confuse with plain.

plane² noun (plural **planes**) a tall tree with broad leaves. [from Greek]

planet noun (plural **planets**) one of the bodies that move in an orbit round the sun. The main planets are Mercury, Venus, Earth, Mars, Jupiter, Saturn, Uranus, Neptune, and Pluto.

planetary adjective [from Greek planetes = wanderer (because planets seem to move in relation to the stars)]

plank noun (plural **planks**) a long flat piece of wood. [from Latin]

plankton noun microscopic plants and animals that float in the sea, lakes, etc. [Greek, = wandering or drifting]

plant noun (plural **plants**)
1 a living thing that cannot move and that makes its food from chemical substances, Flowers, trees, and shrubs are plants.
2 a small plant, not a tree or shrub. 3 a factory or its equipment. 4 (slang) something planted to deceive people (see plant verb 3).

plant verb (**plants, planting, planted**)
1 put something in soil for growing. 2 fix something firmly in place. 3 place something where it will be found, usually to mislead people or cause trouble. **planter** noun
[from Latin]

plantation noun (plural **plantations**)
1 a large area of land where cotton, tobacco, or tea etc. is planted. 2 a group of planted trees.

plaque (say plak) noun (plural **plaques**)
1 a flat piece of metal or porcelain fixed on a wall as an ornament or memorial. 2 a filmy substance that forms on teeth and gums, where bacteria can live.

plaster noun (plural **plasters**)
1 a mixture of lime, sand, and water etc. for covering walls and ceilings. 2 plaster of Paris.
3 a piece of sticking plaster.

plaster verb (**plasters, plastering, plastered**)
1 cover a wall etc. with plaster.
2 cover something thickly; daub.

plastic noun (plural **plastics**)
a strong light synthetic substance that can be moulded into a permanent shape.

plastic adjective
1 made of plastic. 2 soft and easy to mould. Clay is a plastic substance. **plasticity** noun
[from Greek plastos = moulded or formed]

plastic surgery noun surgery to repair deformed or injured parts of the body. **plastic surgeon** noun

plate noun (plural **plates**)
1 an almost flat usually circular object from which food is eaten or served. 2 a thin flat sheet of metal, glass, or other hard material. 3 an illustration on special paper in a book. **plateful** noun

plate verb (**plates, plating, plated**)
1 coat metal with a thin layer of gold, silver, tin, etc. 2 cover something with sheets of metal. [from Latin platus = broad or flat]

plateau (say plat-oh) noun (plural **plateaux** (say plat-ohz)) a flat area of high land. [French, related to plate]

platform noun (plural **platforms**)
1 a flat surface that is above the level of the ground or the rest of the floor, e.g. in a hall or beside a railway line at a station. 2 the policies that a political party puts forward when there is an election. [from French plateforme = a flat surface]

platinum noun a valuable silver-coloured metal that does not tarnish. [from Spanish plata = silver]

platitude noun (plural **platitudes**) a trite or hackneyed remark. **platitudinous** adjective [French, from plat = flat]

plausible adjective seeming to be honest or worth believing but perhaps deceptive, a plausible excuse. **plausibly** adverb, **plausibility** noun [from Latin plausibilis = deserving applause]

play verb (**plays, playing, played**)
1 take part in a game, sport, or other amusement. 2 make music or sound with a musical instrument, record player, etc.
3 perform a part in a play or film. **player** noun
play down give people the impression that something is not important.
play up (informal) be mischievous or annoying.

play noun (plural **plays**)
1 a story acted on a stage or on radio or television. 2 playing. [from Old English]

playful adjective
1 wanting to play; full of fun.
2 done in fun; not serious. **playfully** adverb, **playfulness** noun

playground noun (plural **playgrounds**) a piece of ground for children to play on.

playgroup noun (plural **playgroups**) a group of very young children who play together regularly, supervised by adults.

playing card noun (plural **playing cards**) each of a set of cards (usually 52) used for playing games.

playing field noun (plural **playing fields**) a field used for outdoor games.

playmate noun (plural **playmates**) a person you play games with.

play-off noun (plural **play-offs**) a match that is played to decide a draw or tie.

plaything noun (plural **playthings**) a toy.

playwright noun (plural **playwrights**) a dramatist. [from play + wright = maker]

PLC or **p.l.c.** abbreviation public limited company.

plea noun (plural **pleas**)
1 a request or appeal, a plea for mercy. 2 an excuse, He stayed at home on the plea of a headache. 3 a formal statement of 'guilty' or 'not guilty' made in a lawcourt by someone accused of a crime.

plead verb (pleads, pleading, pleaded)
1 beg someone to do something. 2 state formally in a lawcourt that you are guilty or not guilty of a crime. 3 give something as an excuse, She didn't come on holiday with us, pleading poverty.

pleasant adjective pleasing; giving pleasure. **pleasantly** adverb, **pleasantness** noun [from French plaisant = pleasing]

please verb (pleases, pleasing, pleased)
1 make a person feel satisfied or glad. 2 (used to make a request or an order polite), Please ring the bell. 3 like; think suitable, Do as you please. [from Latin placere = satisfy]

pleasure noun (plural **pleasures**)
1 a feeling of satisfaction or gladness; enjoyment. 2 something that pleases you. [from French plaisir = to please]

plectrum noun (plural **plectra**) a small piece of metal or bone etc. for plucking the strings of a musical instrument. [from Greek plektron = something to strike with]

pledge noun (plural **pledges**)
1 a solemn promise. 2 a thing handed over as security for a loan or contract.

pledge verb (pledges, pledging, pledged)
1 promise solemnly to do or give something. 2 hand something over as security. [from old French]

plenty noun quite enough; as much as is needed or wanted.

plenty adverb (informal) quite or fully, It's plenty big enough. [from Latin plenitas = fullness]

pliable adjective
1 easy to bend; flexible. 2 easy to influence or control. **pliability** noun [French, from plier = to bend]

pliers plural noun pincers that have jaws with flat surfaces for gripping things. [from ply²]

plight noun (plural **plights**) a difficult situation. [from old French]

plimsoll noun (plural **plimsolls**)
a canvas sports shoe with
a rubber sole. [same origin as
Plimsoll line (because the thin
sole reminded people of a Plimsoll
line)]

Plimsoll line noun (plural
Plimsoll lines) a mark on a ship's
side showing how deeply it may
legally go down in the water
when loaded. [named after an
English politician, S. Plimsoll,
who in the 1870s protested about
ships being overloaded]

PLO abbreviation Palestine
Liberation Organization.

plod verb (**plods, plodding,
plodded**)
1 walk slowly and heavily. 2 work
slowly but steadily. **plodder** noun

plop noun (plural **plops**) the
sound of something dropping
into water. **plop** verb [imitating
the sound]

plot noun (plural **plots**)
1 a secret plan. 2 the story in
a play, novel, or film. 3 a small
piece of land.

plot verb (**plots, plotting,
plotted**)
1 make a secret plan. 2 make
a chart or graph of something,
*We plotted the ship's route on our
map.*
[origin unknown]

plough noun (plural **ploughs**)
a farming implement for turning
the soil over.

plough verb (**ploughs,
ploughing, ploughed**)
1 turn over soil with a plough.
2 go through something with
great effort or difficulty, *He
ploughed through the book.*

ploughman noun
plough back reinvest profits in
the business that produced them.

pluck verb (**plucks, plucking,
plucked**)
1 pick a flower or fruit. 2 pull the
feathers off a bird. 3 pull
something up or out. 4 pull
a string (e.g. on a guitar) and let
it go again.
pluck up courage summon up
courage and overcome fear.

plucky adjective (**pluckier,
pluckiest**) brave or spirited.
pluckily adverb

plug noun (plural **plugs**)
1 something used to stop up
a hole. 2 a device that fits into
a socket to connect wires to
a supply of electricity.
3 (*informal*) a piece of publicity
for something.

plug verb (**plugs, plugging,
plugged**)
1 stop up a hole. 2 (*informal*)
publicize something.
plug in put a plug into an
electrical socket.

plum noun (plural **plums**)
1 a soft juicy fruit with a pointed
stone in the middle. 2 (*old use*)
a dried grape or raisin used in
cooking, *plum pudding*. 3 a red-
dish-purple colour. 4 (*informal*)
something good, *a plum job*. [via
Old English from Latin]

plumb verb (**plumbs, plumbing,
plumbed**)
1 measure how deep something
is. 2 get to the bottom of a matter,
We could not plumb the mystery.
3 fit a room or building with
a plumbing system.

plumb adjective exactly upright;
vertical, *The wall was plumb.*

plumb adverb (informal) exactly, It fell plumb in the middle. [from Latin plumbum = lead² (originally plumb = the lead weight on a plumb line)]

plumber noun (plural **plumbers**) a person who fits and mends plumbing.

plumbing noun
1 the water pipes, water tanks, and drainage pipes in a building. 2 the work of a plumber. [from plumb (because water pipes used to be made of lead)]

plume noun (plural **plumes**)
1 a large feather. 2 something shaped like a feather, a plume of smoke.

plume verb (plumes, pluming, plumed) if a bird plumes its feathers, it smooths them with its beak; preen. [from Latin pluma = feather]

plummet noun (plural **plummets**) a plumb line or the weight on its end.

plummet verb (plummets, plummeting, plummeted) drop downwards quickly. [from old French; related to plumb]

plump¹ adjective slightly fat; rounded. **plumpness** noun

plump verb (plumps, plumping, plumped) make something rounded, plump up a cushion. [from old German plumpich = bulky]

plump² verb (plumps, plumping, plumped)
plump for (informal) choose. [from old German plompen = to plop]

plunder verb (plunders, plundering, plundered) rob a person or place using force; loot. **plunderer** noun

plunder noun
1 plundering. 2 goods etc. that have been plundered; loot. [from old German]

plunge verb (plunges, plunging, plunged)
1 go or push forcefully into something; dive. 2 fall or go downwards suddenly. 3 go or force into action etc., They plunged the world into war.

plunge noun (plural **plunges**) a sudden fall or dive.
take the plunge start a bold course of action. [from old French; related to plumb]

plural noun (plural **plurals**) the form of a noun or verb used when it stands for more than one person or thing, The plural of 'child' is 'children'. (Compare singular.) **plural** adjective, **plurality** noun [from Latin pluralis = of many]

plus preposition with the next number or thing added, 2 plus 2 equals four (2 + 2 = 4). [Latin, = more]

plush noun a thick velvety cloth used in furnishings. **plushy** adjective [from Latin pilus = hair]

plutonium noun a radioactive substance used in nuclear weapons and reactors. [named after the planet Pluto]

ply¹ noun (plural **plies**)
1 a thickness or layer of wood or cloth etc. 2 a strand in yarn, 4-ply wool. [from French pli = a fold]

ply[2] *verb* (**plies, plying, plied**)

1 use or wield a tool or weapon. **2** work at, *Tailors plied their trade.* **3** keep offering, *They plied her with food* or *with questions.* **4** go regularly, *The boat plies between the two harbours.* **5** drive or wait about looking for custom, *Taxis are allowed to ply for hire.* [from *apply*]

plywood *noun* strong thin board made of layers of wood glued together.

PM *abbreviation* Prime Minister.

p.m. *abbreviation* post meridiem (Latin, = after noon).

pneumatic (*say* new-mat-ik) *adjective* filled with or worked by compressed air, *a pneumatic drill.* **pneumatically** *adverb* [from Greek *pneuma* = wind]

pneumonia (*say* new-moh-nee-a) *noun* a serious illness caused by inflammation of one or both lungs. [from Greek *pneumon* = lung]

PO *abbreviation*

1 Post Office. **2** postal order.

poach *verb* (**poaches, poaching, poached**)

1 cook an egg (removed from its shell) in or over boiling water. **2** cook fish or fruit etc. in a small amount of liquid. **3** steal game or fish from someone else's land or water. **4** take something unfairly, *One club was poaching members from another.* **poacher** *noun* [same origin as *pouch*]

pocket *noun* (*plural* **pockets**)

1 a small bag-shaped part, especially in a garment. **2** a person's supply of money, *The expense is beyond my pocket.* **3** an isolated part or area, *small*

pockets of rain. **pocketful** *noun*

be out of pocket have spent more money than you have gained.

pocket *adjective* small enough to carry in a pocket, *a pocket calculator.*

pocket *verb* (**pockets, pocketing, pocketed**) put something into a pocket.

[from old French *pochet* = little pouch]

pocket money *noun* money given to a child to spend as he or she likes.

pod *noun* (*plural* **pods**) a long seed-container of the kind found on a pea or bean plant. [origin unknown]

poem *noun* (*plural* **poems**) a piece of poetry. [from Greek *poiema* = thing made]

poet *noun* (*plural* **poets**) a person who writes poetry. **poetess** *noun* [from Greek *poietes* = maker]

poetry *noun* writing arranged in short lines, usually with a particular rhythm and sometimes with rhymes. **poetic** *adjective*, **poetical** *adjective*, **poetically** *adverb*

poignant (*say* poin-yant) *adjective* very distressing; affecting the feelings, *poignant memories.* **poignancy** *noun* [from French, = pricking]

point *noun* (*plural* **points**)

1 the narrow or sharp end of something. **2** a dot, *the decimal point.* **3** a particular place or time, *At this point she was winning.* **4** a detail or characteristic, *He has his good points.* **5** the important or essential idea, *Keep to the point!* **6** purpose or value, *There is no* *point in hurrying.* **7** an electrical socket. **8** a device for changing a train from one track to another.

point *verb* (points, pointing, pointed)

1 aim or direct, *She pointed a gun at me.* **2** show where something is, especially by holding out a finger etc. towards it. **3** fill in the parts between bricks with mortar or cement.

point out draw attention to something.

[from Latin *punctum* = pricked]

point-blank *adjective*

1 aimed or fired from close to the target. **2** direct and straightforward, *a point-blank refusal.*

point-blank *adverb* in a point-blank manner, *He refused point-blank.*

[from to *point* + *blank* = the white centre of a target]

pointed *adjective*

1 with a point at the end. **2** clearly directed at a person, *a pointed remark.* **pointedly** *adverb*

pointer *noun* (*plural* pointers)

1 a stick, rod, or mark etc. used to point at something. **2** a dog that points with its muzzle towards birds that it scents. **3** an indication or hint.

pointless *adjective* without a point; with no purpose. **pointlessly** *adverb*

poise *verb* (poises, poising, poised) balance.

poise *noun*

1 a dignified self-confident manner. **2** balance.

[from old French]

poison *noun* (*plural* poisons) a substance that can harm or kill a living thing. **poisonous** *adjective*

poison *verb* (poisons, poisoning, poisoned)

1 give poison to; kill somebody with poison. **2** put poison in something. **3** corrupt or spoil something, *He poisoned their minds.* **poisoner** *noun*

poke *verb* (pokes, poking, poked)

1 prod or jab. **2** push out or forward; stick out. **3** search, *I was poking about in the attic.*

poke fun at ridicule.

poke *noun* (*plural* pokes) a poking movement; a prod.

poker[1] *noun* (*plural* pokers) a stiff metal rod for poking a fire.

poker[2] *noun* a card game in which players bet on who has the best cards. [probably from German *pochen* = to brag]

polar *adjective*

1 to do with or near the North Pole or South Pole. **2** to do with either pole of a magnet. **polarity** *noun*

polar bear *noun* (*plural* polar bears) a white bear living in Arctic regions.

polarize *verb* (polarizes, polarizing, polarized)

1 keep vibrations of light-waves etc. to a single direction. **2** divide into two groups of completely opposite extremes of feeling or opinion, *Opinions had polarized.* **polarization** *noun* [from *pole*[2]]

Polaroid camera *noun* (*plural* Polaroid cameras) (*trade mark*) a camera that takes a picture and produces the finished photograph a few seconds later.

pole[1] *noun* (*plural* **poles**) a long slender rounded piece of wood or metal. [same origin as *pale*[2]]

pole[2] *noun* (*plural* **poles**)
1 a point on the earth's surface that is as far north (**North Pole**) or as far south (**South Pole**) as possible. **2** either of the ends of a magnet. **3** either terminal of an electric cell or battery. [from Greek *polos* = axis]

pole star *noun* the star above the North Pole.

pole vault *noun* an athletic contest in which competitors jump over a high bar with the help of a long pole.

police *noun* the people whose job is to catch criminals and make sure that the law is kept.

policeman *noun*, **policewoman** *noun*

police *verb* (**polices, policing, policed**) keep order in a place by means of police.
[same origin as *political*]

policy[1] *noun* (*plural* **policies**) the aims or plan of action of a person or group. [same origin as *political*]

policy[2] *noun* (*plural* **policies**) a document stating the terms of a contract of insurance. [from Greek *apodeixis* = evidence]

polish *verb* (**polishes, polishing, polished**)
1 make a thing smooth and shiny by rubbing. **2** make a thing better by making corrections and alterations. **polisher** *noun*
polish off finish off.

polish *noun* (*plural* **polishes**)
1 a substance used in polishing. **2** a shine. **3** elegance of manner. [from Latin]

polite *adjective* having good manners. **politely** *adverb*, **politeness** *noun* [from Latin *politus* = polished]

political *adjective* connected with the governing of a country, city, or county. **politically** *adverb* [from Greek *politeia* = citizenship or government]

politician *noun* (*plural* **politicians**) a person who is involved in politics.

politics *noun* political matters.

poll (*say as* pole) *noun* (*plural* **polls**)
1 voting or votes at an election. **2** an opinion poll. **3** (*old use*) the head.

poll *verb* (**polls, polling, polled**)
1 vote at an election. **2** receive a stated number of votes in an election. **polling booth** *noun*, **polling station** *noun*
[probably from old Dutch word *polle* = head. In some polls those voting yes stand apart from those voting no, and the decision is reached by counting the heads in the two groups]

pollen *noun* powder produced by the anthers of flowers, containing male cells for fertilizing other flowers. [Latin, = fine flour]

pollen count *noun* (*plural* **pollen counts**) a measurement of the amount of pollen in the air, given as a warning for people who are allergic to pollen.

pollinate *verb* (**pollinates, pollinating, pollinated**) fertilize a plant with pollen. **pollination** *noun*

poll tax noun (plural **poll taxes**) a tax on each person; the community charge.

pollute verb (**pollutes, polluting, polluted**) make a place or thing dirty or impure. **pollutant** noun, **pollution** noun [from Latin]

poly- prefix many (as in polytechnic). [from Greek]

polygamy (say pol-**ig**-ă-mee) noun having more than one wife at a time. **polygamous** adjective [from poly- + Greek gamos = marriage]

polygon noun (plural **polygons**) a shape with many sides, Hexagons and octagons are polygons. **polygonal** adjective [from poly- + Greek gonia = corner]

polyhedron noun (plural **polyhedrons**) a solid shape with many sides. [from poly- + Greek hedra = base]

polytechnic noun (plural **polytechnics**) a college giving instruction in many subjects at degree level or below. In 1992 the British polytechnics were able to change their names and call themselves universities. [from poly- + Greek techne = skill]

polythene noun a lightweight plastic used to make bags, wrappings, etc. [from polyethylene, a polymer from which it is made]

pomegranate noun (plural **pomegranates**) a tropical fruit with many seeds. [from Latin pomum = apple + granatum = having many seeds]

pomp noun the ceremonial splendour that is traditional on important public occasions. [from Greek pompe = solemn procession]

pompous adjective full of excessive dignity and self-importance. **pompously** adverb, **pomposity** noun [from pomp]

pond noun (plural **ponds**) a small lake. [from pound²]

ponder verb (**ponders, pondering, pondered**) think deeply and seriously; muse. [from Latin ponderare = weigh]

ponderous adjective
1 heavy and awkward.
2 laborious and dull, He writes in a ponderous style. **ponderously** adverb [from Latin ponderis = of weight]

pontificate verb (**pontificates, pontificating, pontificated**) speak or write pompously. **pontification** noun

pony noun (plural **ponies**) a small horse. [from French poulenet = small foal]

ponytail noun (plural **ponytails**) a bunch of long hair tied at the back of the head.

poodle noun (plural **poodles**) a dog with thick curly hair. [from German Pudelhund = water-dog]

pooh interjection an exclamation of contempt.

pool¹ noun (plural **pools**)
1 a pond. 2 a puddle. 3 a swimming pool. [from Old English]

pool² noun (plural **pools**)
1 the fund of money staked in a gambling game. 2 a group of things shared by several people.
the pools gambling based on the results of football matches.

pool verb (pools, pooling, pooled) put money or things together for sharing. [from French]

poor adjective
1 with very little money or other resources. 2 not good; inadequate, *A poor piece of work.* 3 unfortunate; deserving pity, *Poor fellow!* **poorness** noun [from old French; related to *pauper*]

poorly adverb
1 in a poor way, *We've played poorly this season.* 2 rather ill.

pop[1] noun (plural pops)
1 a small explosive sound. 2 a fizzy drink.

pop verb (pops, popping, popped)
1 make a pop. 2 (*informal*) go or put quickly, *Pop down to the shop. I'll just pop this pie into the microwave.* [imitating the sound]

pop[2] noun modern popular music. [short for *popular*]

Pope noun (plural Popes) the leader of the Roman Catholic Church. [from Greek *papas* = father]

pop-eyed adjective with bulging eyes.

poplar noun (plural poplars) a tall slender tree. [from Latin]

poppy noun (plural poppies) a plant with large red flowers.

popular adjective
1 liked or enjoyed by many people. 2 intended for the general public. **popularly** adverb, **popularity** noun [from Latin *populus* = people]

populate verb (populates, populating, populated) supply with a population; inhabit. [same origin as *popular*]

population noun (plural populations) the people who live in a district or country; the total number of these people.

porcelain noun the finest kind of china. [from French]

porch noun (plural porches) a shelter outside the entrance to a building.

porcupine noun (plural porcupines) a small animal covered with long prickles. [from old French *porc espin* = spiny pig]

pore[1] noun (plural pores) a tiny opening on the skin through which moisture can pass in or out. [from Greek *poros* = passage]

pore[2] verb (pores, poring, pored) **pore over** study with close attention, *He was poring over his books.* [origin unknown]

USAGE: Do not confuse with *pour*.

pork noun meat from a pig. [from Latin *porcus* = pig]

pornography (*say* porn-og-ra-fee) noun obscene pictures or writings. **pornographic** adjective [from Greek *porne* = prostitute, + -*graphy*]

porpoise (*say* por-pus) noun (plural porpoises) a sea animal rather like a small whale. [from Latin *porcus* = pig + *piscis* = fish]

porridge noun a food made by boiling oatmeal to a thick paste. [from an old word *pottage* = soup]

port¹ noun (plural **ports**)
1 a harbour. 2 a city or town with a harbour. 3 the left-hand side of a ship or aircraft when you are facing forward. (Compare *starboard*.) [from Latin *portus* = harbour]

port² noun a strong red Portuguese wine. [from the city of Oporto in Portugal]

portable adjective able to be carried. [from Latin *portare* = carry]

portcullis noun (plural **portcullises**) a strong heavy vertical grating that can be lowered in grooves to block the gateway to a castle. [from old French *porte coleice* = sliding door]

porter¹ noun (plural **porters**) a person whose job is to carry luggage or other goods. [from Latin *portare* = carry]

porter² noun (plural **porters**) a person whose job is to look after the entrance to a large building. [from Latin *porta* = gate]

porthole noun (plural **portholes**) a small window in the side of a ship or aircraft. [from Latin *porta* = gate, + *hole*]

portion noun (plural **portions**) a part or share given to somebody.

portion verb (**portions, portioning, portioned**) divide something into portions, *Portion it out.*
[from Latin]

portly adjective (**portlier, portliest**) stout and dignified.

portliness noun [originally = dignified: from Middle English *port* = bearing, deportment]

portrait noun (plural **portraits**) a picture of a person or animal.

pose noun (plural **poses**)
1 a position or posture of the body, e.g. for a portrait or photograph. 2 a pretence; unnatural and affected behaviour to impress people.

pose verb (**poses, posing, posed**)
1 take up a pose. 2 put someone into a pose. 3 pretend. 4 put forward or present, *It poses several problems for us.*

posh adjective (*informal*)
1 very smart; high-class, *a posh restaurant.* 2 upper-class, *a posh accent.*

position noun (plural **positions**)
1 the place where something is or should be. 2 the way a person or thing is placed or arranged, *in a sitting position.* 3 a situation or condition, *I am in no position to help you.* 4 paid employment; a job. **positional** adjective

positive adjective
1 definite or certain, *We have positive proof that he is guilty.* 2 agreeing; saying 'yes', *We received a positive reply.* 3 greater than nought. 4 of the kind of electric charge that lacks electrons. 5 (of an adjective or adverb) in the simple form, not comparative or superlative, *The positive form is 'big', the comparative is 'bigger', the superlative is 'biggest'.* **positively** adverb

USAGE: The opposite of senses 1–4 is *negative.*

possess *verb* (**possesses, possessing, possessed**)
1 have or own something.
2 control someone's thoughts or behaviour, *I don't know what possessed you to do such a thing!*
possessor *noun* [from Latin]

possessed *adjective* seeming to be controlled by strong emotion or an evil spirit, *He fought like a man possessed.*

possession *noun* (*plural* **possessions**)
1 something you possess or own.
2 possessing.

possessive *adjective*
1 wanting to possess and keep things for yourself. 2 showing that somebody owns something, *a possessive pronoun* (see *pronoun*).

possibility *noun* (*plural* **possibilities**)
1 being possible. 2 something that may exist or happen etc.

possible *adjective* able to exist, happen, be done, or be used. [from Latin *posse* = be able]

possibly *adverb*
1 in any way, *I can't possibly do it.* 2 perhaps.

post¹ *noun* (*plural* **posts**)
1 an upright piece of wood, concrete, or metal etc. set in the ground. 2 the starting point or finishing point of a race, *He was left at the post.*

post *verb* (**posts, posting, posted**) put up a notice or poster etc. to announce something. [from Latin *postis* = post]

post² *noun*
1 the collecting and delivering of letters, parcels, etc. 2 these letters and parcels etc.

post *verb* (**posts, posting, posted**) put a letter or parcel etc. into a postbox for collection.
keep me posted keep me informed.
[from French; related to *post³* (because originally mail was carried in relays by riders posted along the route)]

post³ *noun* (*plural* **posts**)
1 a position of paid employment; a job. 2 the place where someone is on duty, *a sentry-post.* 3 a place occupied by soldiers, traders, etc.

post *verb* (**posts, posting, posted**) place someone on duty, *We posted sentries.*
[from Latin *positum* = placed]

post- *prefix* after (as in *post-war*). [from Latin]

postage *noun* the charge for sending something by post.

postage stamp *noun* (*plural* **postage stamps**) a stamp for sticking on things to be posted, showing the amount paid.

postal *adjective* to do with or by the post.

postal order *noun* (*plural* **postal orders**) a document bought from a post office for sending money by post.

postbox *noun* (*plural* **postboxes**) a box into which letters are put for collection.

postcard *noun* (*plural* **postcards**) a card for sending messages by post without an envelope.

postcode *noun* (*plural* **postcodes**) a group of letters and numbers included in an address to help in sorting them.

poster noun (plural **posters**)
a large sheet of paper
announcing or advertising
something, for display in a public
place. [from post¹]

posterity noun future
generations of people, *These
letters and diaries should be
preserved for posterity.* [from
Latin *posterus* = following,
future]

postman noun (plural **postmen**)
a person who delivers or collects
letters etc.

postmark noun (plural
postmarks) an official mark put
on something sent by post to
show where and when it was
posted.

post-mortem noun (plural **post-
mortems**) an examination of
a dead body to discover the cause
of death. [Latin, = after death]

post office noun (plural **post
offices**) a building or room where
postal business is carried on.

postpone verb (**postpones**,
postponing, **postponed**) fix a later
time for something, *They
postponed the meeting for
a fortnight.* **postponement** noun
[from post- + Latin *ponere* = to
place]

postscript noun (plural
postscripts) something extra
added at the end of a letter (after
the writer's signature) or at the
end of a book. [from post- + Latin
scriptum = written]

posture noun (plural **postures**)
the way a person stands, sits, or
walks; a pose.

posture verb (**postures**,
posturing, **postured**) pose,

especially to impress people.
[from Latin *positura* = position
or situation]

post-war adjective happening
during the time after a war.

pot¹ noun (plural **pots**)
1 a deep usually round container.
2 (informal) a lot of something,
He has got pots of money.
go to pot (informal) lose quality;
be ruined.
take pot luck (informal) take
whatever is available.

pot verb (**pots**, **potting**, **potted**)
put into a pot.
[from Old English]

pot² noun (slang) marijuana.
[short for Spanish *potiguaya*
= drink of grief]

potassium noun a soft silvery-
white metal substance that is
essential for living things.

potato noun (plural **potatoes**)
a starchy white tuber growing
underground, used as a vegetable.
[from Old English]

potentate (say poh-ten-tayt) noun
(plural **potentates**) a powerful
monarch or ruler. [from Latin
potentatus = power or rule]

potential (say po-ten-shal)
adjective capable of happening or
being used or developed,
a potential winner. **potentially**
adverb, **potentiality** noun

potential noun the ability of
a person or thing to develop in
the future.
[from Latin *potentia* = power]

pothole noun (plural **potholes**)
1 a deep natural hole in the
ground. **2** a hole in a road.

potion noun (plural **potions**)
a liquid for drinking as
a medicine etc. [from Latin *potio*
= a drink]

potted adjective shortened or abridged, a potted account of the story.

potter¹ noun (plural **potters**) a person who makes pottery.

potter² verb (**potters, pottering, pottered**) work or move about in a leisurely way, I spent the afternoon pottering around in the garden. [from an old word pote = push or poke]

pottery noun (plural **potteries**) 1 cups, plates, ornaments, etc. made of baked clay. 2 a place where a potter works.

pouch noun (plural **pouches**) 1 a small bag. 2 something shaped like a bag. [from French poche = bag or pocket]

poultry noun birds (e.g. chickens, geese, turkeys) kept for their eggs and meat. [from old French poulet = pullet]

pounce verb (**pounces, pouncing, pounced**) jump or swoop down quickly on something. **pounce** noun [from old French]

pound¹ noun (plural **pounds**) 1 a unit of money (in Britain = 100 pence). 2 a unit of weight equal to 16 ounces or about 454 grams. [from Old English pund]

pound² noun (plural **pounds**) 1 a place where stray animals are taken. 2 a public enclosure for vehicles officially removed. [origin unknown]

pound³ verb (**pounds, pounding, pounded**) 1 hit something often, especially in order to crush it. 2 run or go heavily, pounding along. 3 thump, My heart was pounding. [from Old English punian]

pour verb (**pours, pouring, poured**) 1 flow or make something flow. 2 rain heavily, It rained all day. 3 come or go in large amounts, Letters poured in. **pourer** noun [origin unknown]

USAGE: Do not confuse with pore.

pout verb (**pouts, pouting, pouted**) push out your lips when you are annoyed or sulking. **pout** noun [probably from a Scandinavian language]

poverty noun being poor. [from old French; related to pauper]

powder noun (plural **powders**) 1 a mass of fine dry particles of something. 2 a medicine or cosmetic etc. made as a powder. 3 gunpowder, Keep your powder dry. **powdery** adjective

powder verb (**powders, powdering, powdered**) 1 put powder on something. 2 make something into powder. [from old French; related to pulverize]

power noun (plural **powers**) 1 strength or energy. 2 the ability to do something, the power of speech. 3 political authority or control. 4 a powerful country, person, or organization. 5 mechanical or electrical energy; the electricity supply, There was a power failure after the storm. 6 (in mathematics) the product of a number multiplied by itself a given number of times, The third power of 2 = 2 × 2 × 2 = 8. **powered** adjective, **powerless** adjective

powerful *adjective* having great power, strength, or influence.
powerfully *adverb*

power station *noun* (*plural* **power stations**) a building where electricity is produced.

pp. *abbreviation* pages.

practicable *adjective* able to be done. [French, from *pratiquer* = put into practice]

USAGE: Do not confuse with *practical*.

practical *adjective*
1 able to do useful things, *a practical person.* 2 likely to be useful, *a very practical invention.* 3 actually doing something, *She has had practical experience.*
practicality *noun*

USAGE: Do not confuse with *practicable*.

practical *noun* (*plural* **practicals**) a lesson or examination in which you actually do or make something rather than reading or writing about it, *a chemistry practical.*
[from Greek *prattein* = do]

practical joke *noun* (*plural* **practical jokes**) a trick played on somebody.

practically *adverb*
1 in a practical way. 2 almost, *I've practically finished.*

practice *noun* (*plural* **practices**)
1 practising, *Have you done your piano practice?* 2 actually doing something; action, not theory, *It works well in practice.* 3 the professional business of a doctor, dentist, lawyer, etc. 4 a habit or custom, *It is his practice to work until midnight.*

out of practice no longer skilful because you have not practised recently.
[from *practise*]

USAGE: See the note on *practise*.

practise *verb* (**practises**, **practising**, **practised**)
1 do something repeatedly in order to become better at it. 2 do something actively or habitually, *Practise what you preach.* 3 work as a doctor, dentist, or lawyer.
[from Latin *practicare* = carry out, perform]

USAGE: Note the spelling: *practice* is a noun, *practise* is a verb.

practised *adjective* experienced or expert.

prairie *noun* (*plural* **prairies**) a large area of flat grass-covered land in North America. [French, from Latin *pratum* = meadow]

praise *verb* (**praises**, **praising**, **praised**)
1 say that somebody or something is very good. 2 honour God in words.

praise *noun* words that praise somebody or something.
praiseworthy *adjective*
[from Latin *pretium* = value]

pram *noun* (*plural* **prams**) a four-wheeled carriage for a baby, pushed by a person walking.

prance *verb* (**prances**, **prancing**, **pranced**) move about in a lively or happy way.

prank *noun* (*plural* **pranks**) a trick played for mischief; a practical joke. **prankster** *noun*

prattle verb (prattles, prattling, prattled) chatter like a young child. **prattle** noun

prawn noun (plural **prawns**) an edible shellfish like a large shrimp.

pray verb (prays, praying, prayed) 1 talk to God. 2 ask earnestly for something. 3 (formal) please, Pray be seated. [from old French]

prayer noun (plural **prayers**) praying; words used in praying.

pre- prefix before (as in prehistoric). [from Latin]

preach verb (preaches, preaching, preached) give a religious or moral talk. **preacher** noun [from old French]

precarious (say pri-kair-ee-us) adjective not very safe or secure. **precariously** adverb [from Latin precarius = uncertain]

precaution noun (plural **precautions**) something done to prevent future trouble or danger. **precautionary** adjective [from pre- + Latin cavere = take care]

precede verb (precedes, preceding, preceded) come or go before or in front of another thing. [from pre- + Latin cedere = go]

USAGE: Do not confuse with proceed.

---

precedent (say press-i-dent) noun (plural **precedents**) a previous case that is taken as an example to be followed.

precinct (say pree-sinkt) noun (plural **precincts**) 1 the area round a place, especially round a cathedral. 2 a part of a town where traffic is not allowed, a shopping precinct. [from pre- + Latin cinctum = surrounded]

precious adjective 1 very valuable. 2 greatly loved. **preciousness** noun

precious adverb (informal) very, We have precious little time. [from Latin pretium = value]

precipice noun (plural **precipices**) a very steep place, such as the face of a cliff. [from Latin praeceps = headlong]

précis (say pray-see) noun (plural **précis** (say pray-seez)) a summary. [French, = precise]

precise adjective exact; clearly stated. **precisely** adverb, **precision** noun [from Latin praecisum = cut short]

precocious (say prik-oh-shus) adjective (of a child) very advanced or developed for his or her age. **precociously** adverb, **precocity** noun [from Latin praecox = ripe very early]

predator (say pred-a-ter) noun (plural **predators**) an animal that hunts or preys upon others. **predatory** adjective [from Latin praedator = plunderer]

predecessor (say pree-dis-ess-er) noun (plural **predecessors**) an earlier person or thing, e.g. an ancestor or the former holder of a job. [from pre- + Latin decessor = person departed]

predicate noun (plural **predicates**) the part of a sentence that says something about the subject, e.g. 'is short' in life is short. [from Latin praedicare = proclaim]

predicative (say prid-ik-a-tiv)
adjective forming part of the
predicate, e.g. *old* in *The dog is
old*. (Compare *attributive*.)
predicatively *adverb*

predict *verb* (predicts, predicting,
predicted) say what will happen
in the future; foretell or
prophesy. **predictable** *adjective*,
prediction *noun*, **predictor** *noun*
[from *pre-* + Latin *dicere* = say]

predispose *verb* (predisposes,
predisposing, predisposed)
influence you in advance so that
you are likely to do or be in
favour of something, *We are
predisposed to pity the refugees.*
predisposition *noun*

predominate *verb*
(predominates, predominating,
predominated) be the largest or
most important or most
powerful. **predominant** *adjective*,
predominance *noun* [from *pre-*
+ Latin *dominari* = rule,
dominate]

pre-eminent *adjective* excelling
others; outstanding. **pre-
eminently** *adverb*, **pre-eminence**
noun

preen *verb* (preens, preening,
preened)
1 (of a bird) smooth its feathers
with its beak. **2** (of a person)
smarten.
preen yourself congratulate
yourself.

preface (say pref-as) *noun* (plural
prefaces) an introduction at the
beginning of a book or speech.
preface *verb* [from Latin *praefatio*
= something said beforehand]

prefect *noun* (plural prefects)
1 a school pupil given authority
to help to keep order. **2** a district

official in France, Japan, and
other countries. [from Latin
praefectus = overseer]

prefer *verb* (prefers, preferring,
preferred)
1 like one person or thing more
than another. **2** put forward,
*They preferred charges of forgery
against him.* **preference** *noun*
[from *pre-* + Latin *ferre* = carry]

preferable (say pref-er-a-bul)
adjective liked better; more
desirable. **preferably** *adverb*

prefix *noun* (plural prefixes)
a word or syllable joined to the
front of a word to change or add
to its meaning, as in *dis*order,
*out*stretched, *un*happy.

pregnant *adjective* having a baby
developing in the womb.
pregnancy *noun* [from *pre-* + Latin
gnasci = be born]

prehensile *adjective* (of an
animal's foot or tail etc.) able to
grasp things. [from Latin
prehendere = seize]

prehistoric *adjective* belonging to
very ancient times, before
written records of events were
made. **prehistory** *noun*

prejudice *noun* (plural
prejudices) a fixed opinion
formed without examining the
facts fairly. **prejudiced** *adjective*
[from *pre-* + Latin *judicium*
= judgement]

preliminary *adjective* coming
before an important action or
event and preparing for it. [from
pre- + Latin *limen* = threshold]

prelude *noun* (plural preludes)
1 a thing that introduces or leads
up to something else. **2** a short
piece of music. [from *pre-* + Latin
ludere = to play]

premature *adjective* too early;
coming before the usual or
proper time. **prematurely** *adverb*
[from *pre-* + Latin *maturus*
= mature]

premeditated *adjective* planned
beforehand, *a premeditated
crime.* [from *pre-* + Latin *meditare*
= meditate]

premier *noun* (*plural* **premiers**)
a prime minister or other head of
government. [French, = first]

première (*say* prem-**yair**) *noun*
(*plural* **premières**) the first public
performance of a play or film.
[French, feminine of *premier*
= first]

premises *plural noun* a building
and its grounds. [originally, the
buildings etc. previously
mentioned on a deed: from Latin
praemittere = put before]

premium *noun* (*plural* **premiums**)
1 an amount or instalment paid
to an insurance company. **2** an
extra payment; a bonus.
at a premium above the normal
price; highly valued.
[from Latin *praemium* = reward]

Premium Bond *noun* (*plural*
Premium Bonds) a savings
certificate that gives the person
who holds it a chance to win
a prize of money.

premonition *noun* (*plural*
premonitions) a feeling that
something is about to happen,
especially something bad. [from
pre- + Latin *monere* = warn]

preoccupied *adjective* having
your thoughts completely busy
with something. **preoccupation**
noun

prep *noun* homework. [short for
preparation]

preparation *noun* (*plural*
preparations)
1 preparing. **2** something
prepared.

preparatory school *noun*
(*plural* **preparatory schools**)
a school that prepares pupils for
a higher school.

prepare *verb* (**prepares,
preparing, prepared**) make ready;
get ready.
be prepared to be ready and
willing to do something.
[from *pre-* + Latin *parare* = get
something ready]

preposition *noun* (*plural*
prepositions) a word used with
a noun or pronoun to show place,
position, time, or means, e.g. *at*
home, *in* the hall, *on* Sunday, *by*
train. [from *pre-* + Latin *positio*
= placing]

preposterous *adjective* very
absurd; outrageous. [from Latin
praeposterus = back to front,
from *prae* = before + *posterus*
= behind]

prep school *noun* (*plural* **prep
schools**) a preparatory school.

Presbyterian (*say* prez-bit-**eer**-ee-
an) *noun* (*plural* **Presbyterians**)
a member of a Church that is
governed by people called *elders*
or *presbyters* who are chosen by
the congregation. [from Greek
presbyteros = elder]

prescribe *verb* (**prescribes,
prescribing, prescribed**)
1 advise a person to use
a particular medicine or
treatment etc. **2** say what should
be done. [from *pre-* + Latin
scribere = write]

prescription noun (plural **prescriptions**)
1 a doctor's written order for a medicine. 2 the medicine prescribed. 3 prescribing.

presence noun
1 being present in a place, *Your presence is required.* 2 if someone has presence, they have an impressive personality or manner.

presence of mind noun the ability to act quickly and sensibly in an emergency.

present[1] adjective
1 in a particular place, *No one else was present.* 2 belonging or referring to what is happening now; existing now, *the present Queen.*

present noun present times or events.
[from Latin *praesens* = being at hand]

present[2] noun (plural **presents**) something given or received without payment; a gift.

present (say priz-ent) verb (presents, presenting, presented)
1 give something, especially with a ceremony, *Who is to present the prizes?* 2 introduce someone to another person or to an audience. 3 put on a play or other entertainment. 4 show. 5 cause or provide something, *Writing a dictionary presents many problems.* **presentation** noun, **presenter** noun
[from Latin *praesentare* = place before someone]

presently adverb
1 soon, *I shall be with you presently.* 2 now, *the person who is presently in charge.* [from present[1]]

preserve verb (preserves, preserving, preserved) keep something safe or in good condition. **preserver** noun, **preservation** noun, **preservative** adjective & noun

preserve noun (plural **preserves**)
1 jam. 2 an activity that belongs to a particular person or group. [from pre- + Latin *servare* = keep]

preside verb (presides, presiding, presided) be in charge of a meeting etc. [from pre- + Latin -*sidere* = sit]

president noun (plural **presidents**)
1 the person in charge of a club, society, or council etc. 2 the head of a republic. **presidency** noun, **presidential** adjective [from Latin *praesidens* = sitting in front]

press verb (presses, pressing, pressed)
1 put weight or force steadily on something; squeeze. 2 make something by pressing. 3 make clothes smooth by ironing them. 4 urge; make demands, *They pressed for an increase in wages.*

press noun (plural **presses**)
1 a device for pressing things, *a trouser press.* 2 a machine for printing things. 3 a firm that prints or publishes books etc., *Oxford University Press.* 4 newspapers; journalists.
[from Latin *pressum* = squeezed]

pressure noun (plural **pressures**)
1 continuous pressing. 2 the force with which something presses.

3 an influence that persuades or compels you to do something. [from Latin]

pressure cooker noun (plural **pressure cookers**) a large air-tight pan used for cooking food quickly under steam pressure.

prestige (say pres-**teej**) noun good reputation. **prestigious** adjective [from Latin praestigium = an illusion]

presumably adverb according to what you may presume.

presume verb (**presumes, presuming, presumed**)
1 suppose; assume something to be true. **2** take the liberty of doing something; venture, May we presume to advise you? **presumption** noun [from pre- + Latin sumere = take]

presumptuous adjective too bold or confident. **presumptuously** adverb

presuppose verb (**presupposes, presupposing, presupposed**) suppose or assume something beforehand. **presupposition** noun [from French]

pretence noun (plural **pretences**) an attempt to pretend that something is true.

false pretences pretending to be something that you are not, in order to deceive people, You've invited me here under false pretences.

pretend verb (**pretends, pretending, pretended**)
1 behave as if something is true or real when you know that it is not, either in play or so as to deceive people. **2** put forward a claim, The son of King James II was called the Old Pretender because he pretended to the British throne. **pretender** noun [from Latin praetendere = put forward or claim]

pretentious adjective
1 showy or ostentatious. **2** claiming to have great merit or importance. **pretentiously** adverb, **pretentiousness** noun [from French; related to pretend]

pretext noun (plural **pretexts**) a reason put forward to conceal the true reason. [from Latin praetextus = an outward display]

pretty adjective (**prettier, prettiest**) attractive in a delicate way. **prettily** adverb, **prettiness** noun

pretty adverb quite, It's pretty cold.
[from Old English]

prevent verb (**prevents, preventing, prevented**)
1 stop something from happening. **2** stop a person from doing something. **preventable** adjective, **prevention** noun, **preventive** or **preventative** adjective & noun [from Latin praevenire = come first, anticipate]

preview noun (plural **previews**) a showing of a film or play etc. before it is shown to the general public.

previous adjective coming before this; preceding. **previously** adverb [from pre- + Latin via = way]

prey (say as pray) noun an animal that is hunted or killed by another for food.

bird or **beast of prey** one that kills and eats other birds or four-footed animals.

prey verb (preys, preying,
preyed)
prey on 1 hunt or take as prey.
2 cause to worry, *The problem
preyed on his mind.*

price noun (plural prices)
1 the amount of money for which
something is bought or sold.
2 what must be given or done in
order to achieve something.
[from old French: related to
praise]

priceless adjective
1 very valuable. **2** (*informal*) very
amusing.

prick verb (pricks, pricking,
pricked)
1 make a tiny hole in something.
2 hurt somebody with a pin or
needle etc. **prick** noun
prick up your ears start listening
suddenly.

prickle noun (plural prickles)
1 a small thorn. **2** a sharp spine
on a hedgehog or cactus etc.
3 a feeling that something is
pricking you. **prickly** adjective

prickle verb (prickles, prickling,
prickled) feel or cause a pricking
feeling.

pride noun (plural prides)
1 being proud. **2** something that
makes you feel proud. **3** a group
of lions.
pride of place the most important
or most honoured position.

pride verb (prides, priding,
prided)
pride yourself on be proud of.
[from *proud*]

priest noun (plural priests)
1 a member of the clergy.
2 a person who conducts

religious ceremonies. **priestess**
noun, **priesthood** noun, **priestly**
adjective

prig noun (plural prigs) a self-
righteous person. **priggish**
adjective

prim adjective (primmer,
primmest) formal and correct in
manner; disliking anything
rough or rude. **primly** adverb,
primness noun [origin unknown]

primary adjective first; most
important. (Compare *secondary*.)
primarily (say pry-mer-il-ee)
adverb [same origin as *prime*]

primary colour noun (plural
primary colours) one of the
colours from which all others can
be made by mixing (red, yellow,
and blue for paint; red, green,
and blue for light).

primary school noun (plural
primary schools) a school for the
first stage of a child's education.

primate (say pry-mat) noun
(plural primates)
1 an archbishop. **2** an animal of
the group that includes human
beings, apes, and monkeys. [from
Latin *primas* = of the first rank]

prime adjective
1 chief; most important, *the
prime cause.* **2** excellent; first-
rate, *prime beef.*

prime noun the best time or
stage of something, *in the prime
of life.*

prime verb (primes, priming,
primed)
1 prepare something for use or
action. **2** put a coat of liquid on
something to prepare it for
painting. **3** equip a person with
information.
[from Latin *primus* = first]

prime minister noun (plural **prime ministers**) the leader of a government.

prime number noun (plural **prime numbers**) a number (e.g. 2, 3, 5, 7, 11) that can be divided exactly only by itself and one.

primeval (say pry-mee-val) adjective belonging to the earliest times of the world. [from Latin primus = first + aevum = age]

primitive adjective
1 at an early stage of civilization.
2 at an early stage of development; not complicated or sophisticated.

primrose noun (plural **primroses**) a pale-yellow flower that blooms in spring. [from Latin prima rosa = first rose]

prince noun (plural **princes**)
1 the son of a king or queen.
2 a man or boy in a royal family. **princely** adjective [from Latin princeps = chieftain]

princess noun (plural **princesses**)
1 the daughter of a king or queen.
2 a woman or girl in a royal family. **3** the wife of a prince. [from French]

principal adjective chief; most important. **principally** adverb

principal noun (plural **principals**) the head of a college or school.
[from Latin principalis = first or chief]

USAGE: Do not confuse with principle.

principle noun (plural **principles**)
1 a general truth, belief, or rule, She taught me the principles of geometry. **2** a rule of conduct, Cheating is against his principles.

in principle in general, not in details.

on principle because of your principles of behaviour.
[from Latin principium = source]

USAGE: Do not confuse with principal.

print verb (**prints, printing, printed**)
1 put words or pictures on paper by using a machine. **2** write with letters that are not joined together. **3** press a mark or design etc. on a surface. **4** make a picture from the negative of a photograph. **printer** noun

print noun (plural **prints**)
1 printed lettering or words.
2 a mark made by something pressing on a surface. **3** a printed picture, photograph, or design.
[from old French priente = pressed]

printout noun (plural **printouts**) information etc. produced in printed form by a computer.

priority noun (plural **priorities**)
1 being earlier or more important than something else; precedence. **2** something considered more important than other things, Safety is a priority.

prise verb (**prises, prising, prised**) lever something out or open, Prise the lid off the crate. [French, = seized]

prism (say prizm) noun (plural **prisms**)
1 a solid shape with ends that are triangles or polygons which are equal and parallel. **2** a glass prism that breaks up light into the colours of the rainbow. **prismatic** adjective [from Greek]

prison noun (plural **prisons**)
a place where criminals are kept
as a punishment. [from old
French]

prisoner noun (plural **prisoners**)
1 a person kept in prison.
2 a captive.

private adjective
1 belonging to a particular
person or group, *private property*.
2 confidential, *private talks*.
3 secluded. **4** not holding public
office, *a private citizen*.
5 independent; not organized by
a government, *private medicine*;
a private detective. **privately**
adverb, **privacy** (say priv-a-see)
noun
in private where only particular
people can see or hear; not in
public.

private noun (plural **privates**)
a soldier of the lowest rank.
[from Latin *privus* = single or
individual]

privatize verb (**privatizes,
privatizing, privatized**) transfer
a nationalized industry etc. to
a private organization.
privatization noun

privilege noun (plural **privileges**)
a special right or advantage
given to one person or group.
privileged adjective [from Latin
privus = an individual + *legis* =
law]

Privy Council noun a group of
distinguished people who advise
the sovereign.

prize noun (plural **prizes**) an
award given to the winner of
a game or competition etc.

prize verb (**prizes, prizing, prized**)
value something greatly.
[a different spelling of *price*]

pro noun (plural **pros**) (*informal*)
a professional.

pro- prefix
1 favouring or supporting (as in
pro-British). **2** deputizing or
substituted for (as in *pronoun*).
3 onwards; forwards (as in
proceed). [from Latin *pro* = for; in
front of]

probable adjective likely to
happen or be true. **probably**
adverb, **probability** noun [from
Latin *probare* = prove]

probation noun the testing of
a person's character and
abilities. **probationary** adjective
on probation being supervised by
a probation officer instead of
being sent to prison.
[same origin as *prove*]

probation officer noun (plural
probation officers) an official who
supervises the behaviour of
a convicted criminal who is not
in prison.

probe noun (plural **probes**)
1 an instrument for exploring
something. **2** an investigation.

probe verb (**probes, probing,
probed**)
1 explore something with a probe.
2 investigate.
[from Latin *proba* = proof]

problem noun (plural **problems**)
1 something difficult to deal with
or understand. **2** something that
has to be done or answered.
problematic or **problematical**
adjective [from Greek]

procedure noun (plural
procedures) an orderly way of
doing something. [French, from
procéder = proceed]

proceed verb (proceeds, proceeding, proceeded)
1 go forward or onward.
2 continue; go on to do something, *She proceeded to explain the plan.* [from *pro-* + Latin *cedere* = go]

USAGE: Do not confuse with *precede*.

proceedings plural noun
1 things that happen; activities.
2 a lawsuit.

proceeds plural noun the money made from a sale or show etc.; profit.

process (say proh-sess) noun (plural **processes**) a series of actions for making or doing something.
in the process of in the course of doing something.

process verb (processes, processing, processed) put something through a manufacturing or other process, *processed cheese.* [same origin as *proceed*]

procession noun (plural **processions**) a number of people or vehicles etc. moving steadily forward following each other. [from Latin *processio* = an advance]

processor noun (plural **processors**)
1 a machine that processes things. 2 the part of a computer that controls all its operations.

proclaim verb (proclaims, proclaiming, proclaimed) announce something officially or publicly. **proclamation** noun [from *pro-* + Latin *clamare* = to shout]

prod verb (prods, prodding, prodded)
1 poke. 2 stimulate someone into action. **prod** noun [origin unknown]

prodigal adjective wasteful or extravagant. **prodigally** adverb, **prodigality** noun [from Latin *prodigus* = lavish, generous]

prodigious adjective wonderful or enormous. **prodigiously** adverb [same origin as *prodigy*]

prodigy noun (plural **prodigies**)
1 a person with wonderful abilities. 2 a wonderful thing. [from Latin *prodigium* = good omen]

produce verb (produces, producing, produced)
1 make or create something; bring something into existence.
2 bring something out so that it can be seen. 3 organize the performance of a play, making of a film, etc. 4 extend a line further, *Produce the base of the triangle.* **producer** noun

produce (say prod-yooss) noun things produced, especially by farmers. [from *pro-* + Latin *ducere* = to lead]

product noun (plural **products**)
1 something produced. 2 the result of multiplying two numbers. (Compare *quotient*.) [from Latin *productum* = produced]

production noun (plural **productions**)
1 producing. 2 the thing or amount produced.

productive adjective producing a lot of things. **productivity** noun

profanity noun (plural **profanities**) words or language that show disrespect for religion.

profession noun (plural **professions**)
1 an occupation that needs special education and training, *The professions include being a doctor, nurse, or lawyer.* 2 a declaration, *They made professions of loyalty.* [from Latin *professio* = public declaration]

professional adjective
1 to do with a profession. 2 doing a certain kind of work as a full-time job for payment, not as an amateur, *a professional footballer.* **professional** noun, **professionally** adverb

professor noun (plural **professors**) a university lecturer of the highest rank. **professorship** noun [same origin as **profess**]

profile noun (plural **profiles**)
1 a side view of a person's face. 2 a short description of a person's character or career.
keep a low profile not make yourself noticeable.
[from old Italian *profilare* = draw in outline]

profit noun (plural **profits**)
1 the extra money obtained by selling something for more than it cost to buy or make. 2 an advantage gained by doing something. **profitable** adjective, **profitably** noun

profit verb (**profits**, **profiting**, **profited**) gain an advantage or benefit from something.
[from old French]

profiteer noun (plural **profiteers**) a person who makes a great profit unfairly. **profiteering** noun

profound adjective
1 very deep or intense, *We take a profound interest in it.* 2 showing considerable thought or needing great study.
profoundly adverb, **profundity** noun [from pro- + Latin *fundus* = bottom]

prognosis (say prog-**noh**-sis) noun (plural **prognoses**) a forecast or prediction, especially about a disease.
prognostication noun [from Greek *pro-* = before + *gnosis* = knowing]

program noun (plural **programs**) a series of coded instructions for a computer to carry out.

program verb (**programs**, **programming**, **programmed**) prepare a computer by means of a program. **programmer** noun [the American spelling of *programme*]

programme noun (plural **programmes**)
1 a list of planned events. 2 a leaflet giving details of a play, concert, etc. 3 a show, play, or talk etc. on radio or television.
[from Greek *programma* = public notice]

progress (say **proh**-gress) noun
1 forward movement; an advance. 2 a development or improvement.

progress (say pro-**gress**) verb (**progresses**, **progressing**, **progressed**)
1 move forward. 2 improve.
progression noun, **progressive** adjective [from pro- + Latin *gressus* = going]

prohibit verb (prohibits,
prohibiting, prohibited) forbid or
ban, *Smoking is prohibited.*
prohibition noun [from Latin]

prohibitive adjective
1 prohibiting. 2 (of prices) so
high that people will not buy
things.

project (say proj-ekt) noun (plural
projects)
1 a plan or scheme. 2 the task of
finding out as much as you can
about something and writing
about it.

project (say pro-jekt) verb
(projects, projecting, projected)
1 stick out. 2 show a picture on
a screen. 3 give people
a particular impression, *He likes
to project an image of absent-
minded brilliance.* **projection**
noun
[from *pro-* + Latin *-jectum*
= thrown]

projectile noun (plural
projectiles) a missile.

projector noun (plural
projectors) a machine for
showing films or photographs on
a screen.

prolific adjective producing a lot,
a prolific author. **prolifically**
adverb

prologue (say proh-log) noun
(plural prologues) an
introduction to a poem or play
etc. [from Greek *pro-* = before
+ *logos* = speech]

prolong verb (prolongs,
prolonging, prolonged) make
a thing longer or make it last for
a long time. **prolongation** noun
[from *pro-* + Latin *longus* = long]

prom noun (plural proms)
(informal)
1 a promenade. 2 a promenade
concert.

promenade (say prom-in-ahd)
noun (plural promenades)
1 a place suitable for walking,
especially beside the seashore.
2 a leisurely walk. **promenade**
verb [French, from *se promener*
= to walk]

promenade concert (plural
promenade concerts) a concert
where part of the audience may
stand or walk about.

prominent adjective
1 sticking out; projecting.
2 conspicuous. 3 important.
prominently adverb, **prominence**
noun [from Latin]

promiscuous adjective
1 having many casual sexual
relationships. 2 indiscriminate.
promiscuously adverb,
promiscuity noun

promise noun (plural promises)
1 a statement that you will
definitely do or not do
something. 2 an indication of
future success or good results,
His work shows promise.
promise verb (promises,
promising, promised) make
a promise.
[from Latin]

promote verb (promotes,
promoting, promoted)
1 move a person to a higher rank
or position. 2 help the progress or
sale of something, *He has done
much to promote the cause of
peace.* **promoter** noun, **promotion**
noun [from *pro-* + Latin *motum*
= moved]

prompt *adjective*
1 without delay, *a prompt reply.*
2 punctual. **promptly** *adverb*, **promptness** *noun*, **promptitude** *noun*

prompt *verb* (**prompts**, **prompting**, **prompted**)
1 cause or encourage a person to do something. **2** remind an actor or speaker of words when he or she has forgotten them. **prompter** *noun*
[from Latin *promptus* = produced]

prong *noun* (*plural* **prongs**) one of the spikes on a fork. **pronged** *adjective*

pronoun *noun* (*plural* **pronouns**) a word used instead of a noun. **demonstrative pronouns** are *this, that, these, those;* **interrogative pronouns** are *who? what? which?,* etc.; **personal pronouns** are *I, me, we, us, thou, thee, you, ye, he, him, she, her, it, they, them;* **possessive pronouns** are *mine, yours, theirs,* etc.; **reflexive pronouns** are *myself, yourself,* etc.; **relative pronouns** are *who, what, which, that.* [from *pro-* = in place of, + *noun*]

pronounce *verb* (**pronounces**, **pronouncing**, **pronounced**)
1 say a sound or word in a particular way, *'Two' is pronounced like 'too'.* **2** declare something formally, *I now pronounce you man and wife.* [from *pro-* + Latin *nuntiare* = announce]

pronounced *adjective* noticeable, *This street has a pronounced slope.*

pronunciation *noun* (*plural* **pronunciations**)
1 the way a word is pronounced.
2 the way a person pronounces words.

USAGE: Note the spelling; this word should not be written or spoken as 'pronounciation'.

proof *noun* (*plural* **proofs**)
1 a fact or thing that shows something is true. **2** a printed copy of a book or photograph etc. made for checking before other copies are printed.

proof *adjective* able to resist something or not be penetrated, *a bulletproof jacket.*
[from old French; related to *prove*]

prop[1] *noun* (*plural* **props**) a support, especially one made of a long piece of wood or metal.

prop *verb* (**props**, **propping**, **propped**) support something by leaning it against something else. [probably from old Dutch]

prop[2] *noun* (*plural* **props**) an object or piece of furniture used on a theatre stage or in a film. [from *property*]

propaganda *noun* publicity intended to make people believe something. [Italian, = propagating, spreading]

propel *verb* (**propels**, **propelling**, **propelled**) push something forward. [from *pro-* + Latin *pellere* = to drive]

propeller *noun* (*plural* **propellers**) a device with blades that spin round to drive an aircraft or ship.

proper *adjective*
1 suitable or right, *the proper way to hold a bat.* **2** respectable, *prim and proper.* **3** (*informal*) complete or thorough, *You're a proper*

nuisance! **properly** *adverb* [from Latin *proprius* = your own, special]

proper fraction *noun* (*plural* **proper fractions**) a fraction that is less than 1, with the numerator less than the denominator, e.g. ⅓.

proper noun *noun* (*plural* **proper nouns**) the name of one person or thing, e.g. *Mary, London, Spain.*

property *noun* (*plural* **properties**) 1 a thing or things that belong to somebody. 2 a building or someone's land. 3 a quality or characteristic, *It has the property of becoming soft when heated.* [same origin as *proper*]

prophecy *noun* (*plural* **prophecies**) 1 a statement that prophesies something. 2 the action of prophesying.

prophesy *verb* (**prophesies, prophesying, prophesied**) say what will happen in the future; foretell. [from Greek *pro* = before + *phanai* = speak]

prophet *noun* (*plural* **prophets**) 1 a person who makes prophecies. 2 a religious teacher who is believed to be inspired by God. **prophetess** *noun*, **prophetic** *adjective*

the Prophet Muhammad, who founded the Muslim faith. [from Greek *prophetes* = someone who speaks for a god]

proportion *noun* (*plural* **proportions**) 1 a part or share of a whole thing. 2 a ratio. 3 the correct relationship in size, amount, or importance between two things, *You've drawn his head out of proportion.* **proportional** *adjective*,

proportionally *adverb*, **proportionate** *adjective*

proportions *plural noun* size, *a ship of large proportions.* [from *pro*- + Latin *portio* = portion or share]

proportional representation *noun* a system in which each political party has a number of Members of Parliament in proportion to the number of votes for all its candidates.

propose *verb* (**proposes, proposing, proposed**) 1 suggest an idea or plan etc. 2 ask a person to marry you. **proposal** *noun* [from old French; related to *proponent*]

proposition *noun* (*plural* **propositions**) 1 a suggestion or offer. 2 a statement. 3 (*informal*) an undertaking or problem, *a difficult proposition.* [same origin as *proponent*]

proprietor *noun* (*plural* **proprietors**) the owner of a shop or business. **proprietress** *noun* [from *proprietary*]

prosaic *adjective* plain or dull and ordinary. **prosaically** *adverb* [from *prose*]

prose *noun* writing or speech that is not in verse. [from Latin *prosa* = straightforward, plain]

prosecute *verb* (**prosecutes, prosecuting, prosecuted**) 1 make someone go to a lawcourt to be tried for a crime. 2 continue with something; pursue, *prosecuting their trade.* **prosecution** *noun*, **prosecutor** *noun* [from Latin *prosecutus* = pursued]

prospect noun (plural **prospects**)
1 a possibility or expectation of something, *There is no prospect of success.* **2** a wide view.

prospect (say pro-**spekt**) verb (**prospects, prospecting, prospected**) explore in search of something, *prospecting for gold.*
prospector noun
[from pro- + Latin -*spicere* = to look]

prospective adjective expected to be or to happen; possible, *prospective customers.*

prospectus noun (plural **prospectuses**) a booklet describing and advertising a school, business company, etc. [Latin, = view or prospect]

prosperous adjective successful or rich. **prosperity** noun

prostitute noun (plural **prostitutes**) a person who takes part in sexual acts for payment. **prostitution** noun [from Latin *prostitutus* = for sale]

protect verb (**protects, protecting, protected**) keep safe from harm or injury. **protection** noun, **protective** adjective, **protector** noun [from pro- + Latin *tectum* = covered]

protein noun (plural **proteins**) a substance that is found in all living things and is an essential part of the food of animals. [from Greek *proteios* = primary, most important]

protest (say proh-test) noun (plural **protests**) a statement or action showing that you disapprove of something.

protest (say pro-test) verb (**protests, protesting, protested**) **1** make a protest. **2** declare firmly, *They protested their innocence.* **protestation** noun [from pro- + Latin *testari* = say on oath]

Protestant noun (plural **Protestants**) a member of any of the western Christian Churches separated from the Roman Catholic Church. [because in the 16th century many people protested (= declared firmly) their opposition to the Catholic Church]

proto- prefix
1 first. **2** at an early stage of development. [from Greek *protos* = first or earliest]

proton noun (plural **protons**) a particle of matter with a positive electric charge. [same origin as proto-]

prototype noun (plural **prototypes**) the first model of something, from which others are copied or developed.

protractor noun (plural **protractors**) a device for measuring angles, usually a semicircle marked off in degrees.

proud adjective
1 very pleased with yourself or with someone else who has done well. **2** causing pride, *This is a proud moment for us.* **3** full of self-respect and independence, *They were too proud to ask for help.* **proudly** adverb [via Old English from old French *prud* = brave]

prove verb (**proves, proving, proved**)
1 show that something is true.

turn out, *The forecast proved to be correct*. **provable** *adjective* [from Latin *probare* = to test]

proverb *noun* (*plural* **proverbs**) a short well-known saying that states a truth, e.g. 'Many hands make light work'. [from *pro-* + Latin *verbum* = word]

proverbial *adjective*
1 referred to in a proverb. 2 well-known.

provide *verb* (**provides, providing, provided**)
1 make something available; supply. 2 prepare for something, *Try to provide against emergencies*. **provider** *noun* [from Latin *providere* = foresee]

provided *conjunction* on condition, *You can stay provided that you help*.

providing *conjunction* provided.

province *noun* (*plural* **provinces**)
1 a section of a country. 2 the area of a person's special knowledge or responsibility, *Repairing stereos is outside my province, I'm afraid*. **provincial** *adjective*
the provinces the parts of a country outside its capital city. [from Latin]

provision *noun* (*plural* **provisions**)
1 providing something.
2 a statement in a document, *the provisions of the treaty*. [from Latin *provisum* = provided]

provisional *adjective* arranged or agreed upon temporarily but possibly to be altered later. **provisionally** *adverb*

provisions *plural noun* supplies of food and drink.

provoke *verb* (**provokes, provoking, provoked**)
1 make a person angry. 2 cause or give rise to something, *The joke provoked laughter*.

provocation *noun*, **provocative** *adjective* [from *pro-* + Latin *vocare* = summon]

prow *noun* (*plural* **prows**) the front end of a ship. [from French]

prowl *verb* (**prowls, prowling, prowled**) move about quietly or cautiously, like a hunter. **prowl** *noun*, **prowler** *noun*

proxy *noun* (*plural* **proxies**) a person authorized to represent or act for another person, *I will be abroad, so I have arranged to vote by proxy*. [from Latin]

prude *noun* (*plural* **prudes**) a person who is easily shocked. **prudish** *adjective*, **prudery** *noun* [from old French]

prudent *adjective* careful, not rash or reckless. **prudently** *adverb*, **prudence** *noun*, **prudential** *adjective* [from French; related to *provide*]

prune¹ *noun* (*plural* **prunes**) a dried plum. [from Greek]

prune² *verb* (**prunes, pruning, pruned**) cut off unwanted parts of a tree or bush etc. [from old French]

pry *verb* (**pries, prying, pried**) look or ask inquisitively.

PS *abbreviation* postscript.

psalm (*say* sahm) *noun* (*plural* **psalms**) a religious song, especially one from the Book of Psalms in the Bible. **psalmist** *noun* [via Old English from Greek *psalmos* = song sung to the harp]

pseudo- (say s'yood-oh) prefix false; pretended. [from Greek]

pseudonym noun (plural **pseudonyms**) a false name used by an author. [from pseudo- + Greek onyma = name]

psychiatrist (say sy-ky-a-trist) noun (plural **psychiatrists**) a doctor who treats mental illnesses. **psychiatry** noun, **psychiatric** adjective [from psycho- + Greek iatreia = healing]

psychic (say sy-kik) adjective 1 supernatural. 2 having supernatural powers, especially being able to predict the future. 3 to do with the mind or soul. **psychical** adjective [same origin as psycho-]

psycho- prefix to do with the mind. [from Greek psyche = life or soul]

psychoanalysis noun investigation of a person's mental processes, especially in psychotherapy.

psychology noun the study of the mind and how it works. **psychological** adjective, **psychologist** noun [from psycho- + -logy]

PT abbreviation physical training.

pterodactyl (say te-ro-dak-til) noun (plural **pterodactyls**) an extinct flying reptile. [from Greek pteron = wing + daktylos = finger (because one of the 'fingers' on its front leg was enlarged to support its wing)]

PTO abbreviation please turn over.

pub noun (plural **pubs**) (informal) a public house.

puberty (say pew-ber-tee) noun the time when a young person is developing physically into an adult.

public adjective belonging to or known by everyone, not private. **publicly** adverb

public noun people in general. **in public** openly, not in private. [from Latin publicus = of the people]

publication noun (plural **publications**) 1 publishing. 2 a published book or newspaper etc.

public house noun (plural **public houses**) a building licensed to serve alcoholic drinks to the public.

publicity noun public attention; doing things (e.g. advertising) to draw people's attention to something.

public school noun (plural **public schools**) 1 a secondary school that charges fees. 2 (in Scotland and the USA) a school run by a local authority or by the State.

publish verb (**publishes**, **publishing**, **published**) 1 have something printed and sold to the public. 2 announce something in public. **publisher** noun [from Latin publicare = make public]

pucker verb (**puckers**, **puckering**, **puckered**) wrinkle. [origin unknown]

pudding noun (plural **puddings**) 1 a food made in a soft mass, especially in a mixture of flour and other ingredients. 2 the sweet course of a meal. [from French]

puddle noun (plural **puddles**)
a shallow patch of liquid,
especially of rainwater on a road.
[from Old English]

puff noun (plural **puffs**)
1 a short blowing of breath, wind,
or smoke etc. **2** a soft pad for
putting powder on the skin.
3 a cake of very light pastry filled
with cream.

puff verb (**puffs, puffing, puffed**)
1 blow out puffs of smoke etc.
2 breathe with difficulty; pant.
3 inflate or swell something, *He
puffed out his chest.*

puffy adjective puffed out;
swollen. **puffiness** noun

pugnacious adjective wanting to
fight; aggressive. **pugnaciously**
adverb, **pugnacity** noun [from
Latin *pugnare* = to fight]

pull verb (**pulls, pulling, pulled**)
1 make a thing come towards or
after you by using force on it.
2 move by a driving force, *The
car pulled out into the road.* **pull**
noun
pull a face make a strange face.
pull off achieve something.
pull somebody's leg tease him or
her.
pull through recover from an
illness.
pull yourself together become
calm or sensible.

pulley noun (plural **pulleys**)
a wheel with a rope, chain, or
belt over it, used for lifting or
moving heavy things.

pullover noun (plural **pullovers**)
a knitted piece of clothing for the
top half of the body.

pulp noun
1 the soft moist part of fruit. **2** any
soft moist mass. **pulpy** adjective
[from Latin]

pulpit noun (plural **pulpits**)
a small enclosed platform for the
preacher in a church or chapel.
[from Latin *pulpitum* = a platform,
stage, or scaffold]

pulsate verb (**pulsates, pulsating,
pulsated**) expand and contract
rhythmically; vibrate. **pulsation**
noun [from Latin]

pulse[1] noun (plural **pulses**)
1 the rhythmical movement of
the arteries as blood is pumped
through them by the beating of
the heart, *The pulse can be felt in
a person's wrists.* **2** a throb.

pulse verb (**pulses, pulsing,
pulsed**) throb or pulsate.
[from Latin *pulsum* = driven,
beaten]

pulse[2] noun (plural **pulses**) the
edible seed of peas, beans, lentils,
etc. [from Latin]

pulverize verb (**pulverizes,
pulverizing, pulverized**) crush
something into powder.
pulverization noun [from Latin
pulveris = of dust]

pump[1] noun (plural **pumps**)
a device that pushes air or liquid
into or out of something, or along
pipes.

pump verb (**pumps, pumping,
pumped**)
1 move air or liquid with a pump.
2 (*informal*) question a person to
obtain information.
pump up inflate.
[originally a sailors' word:
origin unknown]

pump² noun (plural **pumps**)
a canvas sports shoe with a rubber sole. [origin unknown]

pumpkin noun (plural **pumpkins**)
a very large round fruit with a hard orange skin. [from Greek pepon, a kind of large melon]

pun noun (plural **puns**) a joking use of a word sounding the same as another, e.g. 'Deciding where to bury him was a grave decision'.

punch¹ verb (**punches**, **punching**, **punched**)
1 hit someone with your fist. 2 make a hole in something.

punch noun (plural **punches**)
1 a hit with a fist. 2 a device for making holes in paper, metal, leather, etc. 3 vigour, delivered with punch.

punch² noun a drink made by mixing wine or spirits and fruit juice in a bowl. [from Sanskrit pañca = five (the number of ingredients in the traditional recipe: spirits, fruit juice, water, sugar, and spice)]

punchline noun (plural **punchlines**) words that give the climax of a joke or story.

punctual adjective doing things exactly at the time arranged; not late. **punctually** adverb, **punctuality** noun [from Latin punctum = a point]

punctuate verb (**punctuates**, **punctuating**, **punctuated**)
1 put punctuation marks into something. 2 put something in at intervals, His speech was punctuated by cheers. [from Latin punctuare = mark with points or dots]

punctuation noun marks such as commas, full stops, and brackets put into a piece of writing to make it easier to read.

puncture noun (plural **punctures**) a small hole made by something sharp, especially in a tyre.

puncture verb (**punctures**, **puncturing**, **punctured**) make a puncture in something.

pungent (say pun-jent) adjective
1 having a strong taste or smell. 2 (of remarks) sharp. **pungently** adverb, **pungency** noun [from Latin pungere = to prick]

punish verb (**punishes**, **punishing**, **punished**) make a person suffer because he or she has done something wrong. **punishable** adjective, **punishment** noun [same origin as pain]

punk noun (plural **punks**)
1 (also **punk rock**) a loud aggressive style of rock music. 2 a person who likes this music. [origin unknown]

punt¹ noun (plural **punts**) a flat-bottomed boat, usually moved by pushing a pole against the bottom of a river while standing in the punt.

punt verb (**punts**, **punting**, **punted**) move a punt with a pole. [from Latin ponto = pontoon']

punt² verb (**punts**, **punting**, **punted**) kick a football after dropping it from your hands and before it touches the ground. [origin unknown]

pupa (say pew-pa) noun (plural **pupae**) a chrysalis. [from Latin; related to pupil]

pupil noun (plural **pupils**)
1 someone who is being taught by

another person, especially at school. **2** the opening in the centre of the eye. [from Latin *pupilla* = little girl or doll (the use in sense 2 refers to the tiny images of people and things that can be seen in the eye)]

puppet *noun* (*plural* **puppets**)
1 a kind of doll that can be made to move by fitting it over your hand or working it by strings or wires. **2** a person whose actions are controlled by someone else. **puppetry** *noun* [probably related to *pupil*]

puppy *noun* (*plural* **puppies**)
a young dog. [from old French; related to *pupil*]

purchase *verb* (**purchases,** **purchasing, purchased**) buy. **purchaser** *noun*

purchase *noun* (*plural* **purchases**)
1 something bought. **2** buying. **3** a firm hold to pull or raise something.

pure *adjective*
1 not mixed with anything else; clean. **2** mere; nothing but, *pure nonsense*. **purely** *adverb*, **pureness** *noun*, **purity** *noun* [from Latin]

purée (*say* pewr-ay) *noun* (*plural* **purées**) fruit or vegetables made into pulp. [French; = squeezed]

purge *verb* (**purges, purging,** **purged**) get rid of unwanted people or things. **purge** *noun* [from Latin *purgare* = make pure]

purify *verb* (**purifies, purifying,** **purified**) make a thing pure. **purification** *noun*, **purifier** *noun*

Puritan *noun* (*plural* **Puritans**)
a Protestant in the 16th and 17th centuries who wanted simpler religious ceremonies and strictly moral behaviour.

purple *noun* deep reddish-blue colour.

purpose *noun* (*plural* **purposes**)
1 what you intend to do; a plan or aim. **2** determination, *walk with purpose*. **purposeful** *adjective*, **purposefully** *adverb*
on purpose by intention, not by accident. [from old French; related to *propose*]

purr *verb* (**purrs, purring, purred**)
make the low murmuring sound that a cat does when it is pleased. **purr** *noun*

purse *noun* (*plural* **purses**) a small pouch for carrying money.

purse *verb* (**purses, pursing,** **pursed**) draw something into folds, *She pursed up her lips.* [from Latin *bursa* = a bag]

pursue *verb* (**pursues, pursuing,** **pursued**)
1 chase someone in order to catch them. **2** continue with something; work at, *We are pursuing our enquiries.* **pursuer** *noun* [from old French; related to *prosecute*]

pursuit *noun* (*plural* **pursuits**)
1 pursuing. **2** a regular activity.

pus *noun* a thick yellowish substance produced in inflamed or infected tissue, e.g. in an abscess or boil. [Latin]

push *verb* (**pushes, pushing,** **pushed**)
1 make a thing go away from you by using force on it. **2** move yourself by using force, *He pushed in front of me.* **3** try to

force someone to do or use
something; urge.

push off (slang) go away.

push noun (plural **pushes**) a
pushing movement or effort.

at a push if necessary but only
with difficulty.

[from French; related to *pulse¹*]

pusher noun (plural **pushers**)
a person who sells illegal drugs.

pushy adjective unpleasantly self-
confident and eager to do things.

puss noun (informal) a cat.

put verb (**puts, putting, put**) This
word has many uses, including
1 move a person or thing to
a place or position (*Put the lamp
on the table*), **2** cause a person or
thing to do or experience
something or be in a certain
condition (*Put the light on. Put
her in a good mood*), **3** express in
words (*She put it tactfully*).

be hard put have difficulty in
doing something.

put off 1 postpone. **2** dissuade.
3 stop someone wanting
something, *The smell puts me off.*

put out 1 stop a fire from burning
or a light from shining. **2** annoy
or inconvenience, *Our lateness
has put her out.*

put up 1 build. **2** raise. **3** give
someone a place to sleep;
provide, *Who will put up the
money?*

put up with endure or tolerate.

putt verb (**putts, putting, putted**)
hit a golf ball gently towards the
hole. **putt** noun, **putter** noun,
putting green noun [a different
spelling of *put*]

putty noun a soft paste that sets
hard, used for fitting the glass
into a window frame.

puzzle noun (plural **puzzles**)
1 a difficult question or problem.
2 a game or toy that sets
a problem or difficult task.
3 a jigsaw puzzle.

puzzle verb (**puzzles, puzzling,
puzzled**)
1 give someone a problem so that
they have to think hard. **2** think
patiently about how to solve
something. **puzzlement** noun
[origin unknown]

pygmy (say pig-mee) noun (plural
pygmies)
1 a very small person or thing.
2 a member of a race of very
small people in Central Africa.
[from Greek]

pyjamas plural noun a loose
jacket and trousers worn in bed.
[from Persian or Urdu *pay* = leg
+ *jamah* = clothing]

pylon noun (plural **pylons**) a tall
framework made of strips of
steel, supporting electric cables.
[from Greek]

pyramid noun (plural **pyramids**)
1 a structure with a square base
and with sloping sides that meet
in a point at the top. **2** an ancient
Egyptian tomb shaped like this.
pyramidal (say pir-am-id-al)
adjective [from Greek]

python noun (plural **pythons**)
a large snake that kills its prey
by coiling round and crushing it.
[the name of a large serpent or
monster in Greek legend, killed
by Apollo]

Qq

QC *abbreviation* Queen's Counsel.

QED *abbreviation* quod erat demonstrandum (Latin, = which was the thing that had to be proved).

quack[1] *verb* (**quacks, quacking, quacked**) make the harsh cry of a duck. **quack** *noun* [imitating the sound]

quack[2] *noun* (*plural* **quacks**) a person who falsely claims to have medical skill or have remedies to cure diseases. [from Italian *quacken* = to boast]

quadratic equation *noun* (*plural* **quadratic equations**) an equation that involves quantities or variables raised to the power of two, but no higher than two. [from Latin *quadrare* = to square]

quadri- *prefix* four. [from Latin]

quadrilateral *noun* (*plural* **quadrilaterals**) a flat geometric shape with four sides.

quadruped *noun* (*plural* **quadrupeds**) an animal with four feet. [from *quadri-* + Latin *pedis* = of a foot]

quagmire *noun* (*plural* **quagmires**) a bog or marsh. [from an old word *quag* = marsh, + *mire*]

quail[1] *noun* (*plural* **quail** or **quails**) a bird related to the partridge. [from old French]

quail[2] *verb* (**quails, quailing, quailed**) flinch; feel or show fear. [origin unknown]

quaint *adjective* attractively odd or old-fashioned. **quaintly** *adverb*, **quaintness** *noun*

quake *verb* (**quakes, quaking, quaked**) tremble; shake with fear.

Quaker *noun* (*plural* **Quakers**) a member of a religious group called the Society of Friends, founded by George Fox in the 17th century. [originally an insult, probably from George Fox's saying that people should 'tremble at the name of the Lord']

qualify *verb* (**qualifies, qualifying, qualified**)
1 make or become able to do something through having certain qualities or training, or by passing a test. 2 make a statement less extreme; limit its meaning. 3 (of an adjective) add meaning to a noun. **qualification** *noun* [from Latin *qualis* = of what kind?, of a particular kind]

quality *noun* (*plural* **qualities**)
1 how good or bad something is. 2 a characteristic; something that is special in a person or thing. [same origin as *qualify*]

qualm (*say* kwahm) *noun* (*plural* **qualms**) a misgiving or scruple. [origin unknown]

quandary *noun* (*plural* **quandaries**) a difficult situation where you are uncertain what to do. [origin unknown]

quantity *noun* (*plural* **quantities**)
1 how much there is of something; how many there are of one sort. 2 a large amount. [from Latin *quantus* = how big?, how much?]

quarantine *noun* keeping a person or animal isolated in case they have a disease which could spread to others. [from

Italian *quaranta* = forty (the original period of isolation was 40 days)]

quarrel noun (plural **quarrels**) an angry disagreement.

quarrel verb (**quarrels, quarrelling, quarrelled**) have a quarrel. **quarrelsome** adjective [from Latin *querela* = complaint]

quarry[1] noun (plural **quarries**) an open place where stone or slate is dug or cut out of the ground.

quarry verb (**quarries, quarrying, quarried**) dig or cut from a quarry.
[from Latin]

quarry[2] noun (plural **quarries**) an animal etc. being hunted or pursued. [from old French]

quart noun (plural **quarts**) two pints, a quarter of a gallon. [from French; related to *quarter*]

quarter noun (plural **quarters**)
1 each of four equal parts into which a thing is or can be divided. 2 three months, one-fourth of a year. 3 a district or region, *People came from every quarter.*
at close quarters very close together.
give no quarter show no mercy.

quarter verb (**quarters, quartering, quartered**)
1 divide something into quarters.
2 put soldiers etc. into lodgings.
[from Latin *quartus* = fourth]

quarters plural noun lodgings.

quartet noun (plural **quartets**)
1 a group of four musicians.
2 a piece of music for four musicians. 3 a set of four people or things. [via French from Italian *quarto* = fourth]

quartz noun a hard mineral. [via German from Polish]

quasi- (say kwayz-I) prefix seeming to be something but not really so, *a quasi-scientific explanation.* [from Latin *quasi* = as if]

quaver verb (**quavers, quavering, quavered**) tremble or quiver.

quaver noun (plural **quavers**)
1 a quavering sound. 2 a note in music (♪) lasting half as long as a crotchet.

quay (say kee) noun (plural **quays**) a landing-place where ships can be tied up for loading and unloading; a wharf. **quayside** noun [from old French]

queasy adjective feeling slightly sick. **queasily** adverb, **queasiness** noun [origin unknown]

queen noun (plural **queens**)
1 a woman who is the ruler of a country through inheriting the position. 2 the wife of a king.
3 a female bee or ant that produces eggs. 4 an important piece in chess. 5 a playing card with a picture of a queen on it. **queenly** adjective

Queen's Counsel noun (plural **Queen's Counsels**) a senior barrister.

queer adjective
1 strange or eccentric. 2 slightly ill or faint. **queerly** adverb, **queerness** noun

queer verb (**queers, queering, queered**)
queer a person's pitch spoil his or her chances beforehand.

quell verb (**quells, quelling, quelled**)
1 crush a rebellion. 2 stop

yourself from feeling fear, anger etc.; suppress. [from Old English]

quench verb (**quenches, quenching, quenched**)
1 satisfy your thirst by drinking.
2 put out a fire or flame. [from Old English]

query (say **kweer**-ee) noun (plural **queries**)
1 a question. 2 a question mark. [from Latin *quaere* = ask!]

quest noun (plural **quests**) a long search for something, *the quest for gold*. [same origin as *question*]

question noun (plural **questions**)
1 a sentence asking something.
2 a problem to be discussed or solved, *Parliament debated the question of education.* 3 doubt, *Whether we shall win is open to question.*

in question being discussed or disputed, *His honesty is not in question.*

out of the question impossible.

question verb (**questions, questioning, questioned**)
1 ask someone questions. 2 say that you are doubtful about something. **questioner** noun [from Latin *quaesitum* = sought for]

questionable adjective causing doubt; not certainly true or honest or advisable.

question mark noun (plural **question marks**) the punctuation mark ? placed after a question.

questionnaire noun (plural **questionnaires**) a list of questions.

queue (say **kew**) noun (plural **queues**) a line of people or vehicles waiting for something.

queue verb (**queues, queueing, queued**) wait in a queue. [French]

quibble noun (plural **quibbles**) a trivial complaint or objection.

quibble verb (**quibbles, quibbling, quibbled**) make trivial complaints or objections. [probably from Latin *quibus* = what?, for which, for whom (because *quibus* often appeared in legal documents)]

quick adjective
1 taking only a short time to do something. 2 done in a short time. 3 able to notice or learn or think quickly. 4 (old use) alive, *the quick and the dead*. **quickly** adverb, **quickness** noun [from Old English]

quicksand noun (plural **quicksands**) an area of loose wet sand which is so deep that heavy objects sink into it. [from *quick* in sense 4 (because the sand moves as if it were alive and 'eats' things)]

quid noun (plural **quid**) (slang) £1. [origin unknown]

quiet adjective
1 silent, *Be quiet!* 2 with little sound; not loud or noisy. 3 calm and peaceful; without disturbance, *a quiet life.* 4 (of colours) not bright. **quietly** adverb, **quietness** noun

quiet noun quietness. [from Latin *quietus* = calm]

quieten verb (**quietens, quietening, quietened**) make or become quiet.

quill noun (plural **quills**)
1 a large feather. 2 a pen made from a large feather. 3 one of the spines on a hedgehog.

quilt *noun* (*plural* **quilts**) a padded bedcover. [from Latin *culcita* = mattress or cushion]

quintet *noun* (*plural* **quintets**)
1 a group of five musicians.
2 a piece of music for five musicians. [from Italian *quinto* = fifth]

quirk *noun* (*plural* **quirks**)
1 a peculiarity of a person's behaviour. 2 a trick of fate. [origin unknown]

quit *verb* (**quits, quitting, quitted** or **quit**)
1 leave or abandon. 2 (*informal*) stop doing something. **quitter** *noun* [same origin as *quiet*]

quite *adverb*
1 completely or entirely, *I am quite all right.* 2 somewhat; to some extent, *She is quite a good swimmer.* 3 really, *It's quite a change.* [same origin as *quiet*]

quits *adjective* even or equal after retaliating or paying someone, *I think you and I are quits now.*

quiver[1] *noun* (*plural* **quivers**) a container for arrows. [via old French from Germanic]

quiver[2] *verb* (**quivers, quivering, quivered**) tremble. **quiver** *noun* [from Old English]

quiz *noun* (*plural* **quizzes**) a series of questions, especially as an entertainment or competition.
quiz *verb* (**quizzes, quizzing, quizzed**) question someone closely.

quoit (*say* koit) *noun* (*plural* **quoits**) a ring thrown at a peg in the game of **quoits**. [origin unknown]

quota *noun* (*plural* **quotas**)
1 a fixed share that must be given or received or done. 2 a limited amount. [from Latin *quot* = how many?]

quotation *noun* (*plural* **quotations**)
1 quoting. 2 something quoted.
3 a statement of the price.

quotation marks *plural noun* inverted commas.

quote *verb* (**quotes, quoting, quoted**)
1 repeat words that were first written or spoken by someone else. 2 mention something as proof. 3 state the price of goods or services that you can supply.
quote *noun* (*plural* **quotes**) a quotation.
[from Latin *quotare* = to number]

quotient (*say* kwoh-shent) *noun* (*plural* **quotients**) the result of dividing one number by another. (Compare *product*.) [from Latin *quoties* = how many times?]

Rr

rabbi (*say* rab-I) *noun* (*plural* **rabbis**) a Jewish religious leader. [Hebrew, = my master]

rabbit *noun* (*plural* **rabbits**) a furry animal with long ears that digs burrows. [origin unknown]

rabble *noun* (*plural* **rabbles**) a disorderly crowd; a mob.

rabid (*say* rab-id) *adjective*
1 fanatical, *a rabid tennis fan.*
2 suffering from rabies.

rabies (*say* ray-beez) *noun* a fatal disease that affects dogs, cats, etc. and can infect people. [Latin, from *rabere* = to be mad]

race¹ *noun* (*plural* **races**)
1 a competition to be the first to reach a particular place or to do something. 2 a strong fast current of water, *the tidal race.*

race *verb* (**races, racing, raced**)
1 compete in a race. 2 move very fast. **racer** *noun*
[from Old Norse]

race² *noun* (*plural* **races**) a very large group of people thought to have the same ancestors and with physical characteristics (e.g. colour of skin and hair, shape of eyes and nose) that differ from those of other groups.
racial *adjective* [via French from Italian]

racism (*say* ray-sizm) *noun*
1 belief that a particular race of people is better than others.
2 hostility towards people of other races. **racist** *noun*

rack¹ *noun* (*plural* **racks**)
1 a framework used as a shelf or container. 2 a bar or rail with cogs into which the cogs of a gear or wheel etc. fit. 3 an ancient device for torturing people by stretching them.

rack *verb* (**racks, racking, racked**) torment, *He was racked with pain.*
rack your brains think hard in trying to solve a problem.
[from old German or old Dutch]

rack² *noun* destruction, *The place has gone to rack and ruin.* [a different spelling of *wreck*]

racket¹ *noun* (*plural* **rackets**) a bat with strings stretched across a frame, used in tennis and similar games. [from Arabic *rahat* = palm of the hand]

racket² *noun* (*plural* **rackets**)
1 a loud noise; a din. 2 a dishonest business; a swindle. [origin unknown]

racy *adjective* (**racier, raciest**) lively and slightly shocking in style, *She gave a racy account of her travels.* [originally = having a particular quality: from *race*²]

radar *noun* a system or apparatus that uses radio waves to show on a screen etc. the position of objects that cannot be seen because of darkness, fog, distance, etc. [from the initial letters of *radio detection and ranging*]

radiant *adjective*
1 radiating light or heat etc.
2 radiated, *radiant heat.* 3 looking very bright and happy. **radiantly** *adverb*, **radiance** *noun*

radiate *verb* (**radiates, radiating, radiated**)
1 send out light, heat, or other energy in rays. 2 spread out from a central point like the spokes of a wheel. [same origin as *radium*]

radiation *noun*
1 the process of radiating. 2 light, heat, or other energy radiated.
3 the energy or particles sent out by a radioactive substance.

radiator *noun* (*plural* **radiators**)
1 a device that gives out heat, especially a metal case that is heated electrically or through which steam or hot water flows.
2 a device that cools the engine of a motor vehicle. [from *radiate*]

radical *adjective*
1 basic and thorough, *radical changes*. **2** wanting to make great reforms, *a radical politician*.
radically *adverb*

radical *noun* (*plural* **radicals**)
a person who wants to make great reforms.
[from Latin *radicis* = of a root]

radio *noun* (*plural* **radios**) (also called *wireless*)
1 the process of sending and receiving sound or pictures by means of electromagnetic waves without a connecting wire. **2** an apparatus for receiving sound (a *receiver*) or sending it out (a *transmitter*) in this way. **3** sound broadcasting. [same origin as *radium*]

radio- *prefix*
1 to do with rays or radiation. **2** to do with radio.

radioactive *adjective* having atoms that break up and send out radiation which produces electrical and chemical effects and penetrates things.
radioactivity *noun*

radiocarbon dating *noun* the use of a kind of radioactive carbon that decays at a steady rate, to find out how old something is.

radio telescope *noun* (*plural* **radio telescopes**) an instrument that can detect radio waves from space.

radiotherapy *noun* the use of radioactive substances in treating diseases.

radish *noun* (*plural* **radishes**) a small hard round red vegetable, eaten raw in salads. [from Latin *radix* = root]

radium *noun* a radioactive metal, often used in radiotherapy. [from Latin *radius* = a ray]

radius *noun* (*plural* **radii** or **radiuses**)
1 a straight line from the centre of a circle or sphere to the circumference; the length of this line. **2** a range or distance from a central point, *The school takes pupils living within a radius of ten kilometres*. [Latin, = a spoke or ray]

raffle *noun* (*plural* **raffles**) a kind of lottery, usually to raise money for a charity.

raffle *verb* (**raffles**, **raffling**, **raffled**) offer something as a prize in a raffle.

raft *noun* (*plural* **rafts**) a flat floating structure made of wood etc., used as a boat. [from Old Norse]

rafter *noun* (*plural* **rafters**) any of the long sloping pieces of wood that hold up a roof. [from Old English]

rag[1] *noun* (*plural* **rags**)
1 an old or torn piece of cloth. **2** a piece of ragtime music. [from *ragged*]

rag[2] *noun* (*plural* **rags**) a carnival held by students to collect money for charity.

rag *verb* (**rags**, **ragging**, **ragged**) (*slang*) tease.
[origin unknown]

rage *noun* (*plural* **rages**)
1 great or violent anger. **2** a craze, *Skateboarding was all the rage*.

rage *verb* (**rages**, **raging**, **raged**)
1 be very angry. **2** be violent or noisy, *A storm was raging*.
[from old French; related to *rabies*]

ragged adjective
1 torn or frayed. 2 wearing torn clothes. 3 jagged. 4 irregular or uneven, *a ragged performance.*
[from Old Norse *roggvathr* = tufted]

raid noun (plural **raids**)
1 a sudden attack. 2 a surprise visit by police etc. to arrest people or seize illegal goods.

raid verb (**raids, raiding, raided**) make a raid on a place. **raider** noun

rail[1] noun (plural **rails**)
1 a level or sloping bar for hanging things on or forming part of a fence, banisters, etc. 2 a long metal bar forming part of a railway track.
by rail on a train.
[from old French; related to *rule*]

rail[2] verb (**rails, railing, railed**) protest angrily or bitterly. [via French from Portuguese]

railings plural noun a fence made of metal bars.

railway noun
1 the parallel metal bars that trains travel on. 2 (plural **railways**) a system of transport using rails.

rain noun drops of water that fall from the sky. **rainy** adjective

rain verb (**rains, raining, rained**)
1 fall as rain or like rain. 2 send down like rain, *They rained blows on him.*

rainbow noun (plural **rainbows**) a curved band of colours seen in the sky when the sun shines through rain.

rainfall noun the amount of rain that falls in a particular place or time.

rainforest noun (plural **rainforests**) a dense tropical forest in an area of very heavy rainfall.

raise verb (**raises, raising, raised**)
1 move something to a higher place or an upright position. 2 increase the amount or level of something. 3 collect; manage to obtain, *They raised £100 for Oxfam.* 4 bring up young children or animals, *raise a family.* 5 rouse or cause, *She raised a laugh with her joke.* 6 put forward, *We raised objections.* 7 end a siege. [from Old Norse]

raisin noun (plural **raisins**) a dried grape. [French, = grape]

rake noun (plural **rakes**) a gardening tool with a row of short spikes fixed to a long handle.

rake verb (**rakes, raking, raked**)
1 gather or smooth with a rake. 2 search. 3 gather; collect, *raking it in.*
rake up 1 collect. 2 remind people of an old scandal etc., *Don't rake that up.*

rally noun (plural **rallies**)
1 a large meeting to support something or share an interest. 2 a competition to test skill in driving, *the Monte Carlo Rally.* 3 a series of strokes in tennis before a point is scored. 4 a recovery.

rally verb (**rallies, rallying, rallied**)
1 bring or come together for a united effort, *They rallied support. People rallied round.* 2 revive; recover strength.

RAM abbreviation random-access memory (in a computer), with contents that can be retrieved or stored directly without having to read through items already stored.

ram noun (plural **rams**)
1 a male sheep. 2 a device for ramming things.

ram verb (**rams, ramming, rammed**) push one thing hard against another.

Ramadan noun the ninth month of the Muslim year, when Muslims do not eat or drink between sunrise and sunset. [Arabic, from *ramida* = to be parched]

ramble noun (plural **rambles**) a long walk in the country.

ramble verb (**rambles, rambling, rambled**)
1 go for a ramble; wander. 2 talk or write a lot without keeping to the subject. **rambler** noun [origin unknown]

ramifications plural noun
1 the branches of a structure.
2 the many effects of a plan or action. [from Latin *ramificare* = to branch out]

ramp noun (plural **ramps**) a slope joining two different levels. [from French *ramper* = to climb]

rampage verb (**rampages, rampaging, rampaged**) rush about wildly or destructively. **on the rampage** rampaging.

rampant adjective
1 growing or increasing unrestrained, *Disease was rampant in the poorer districts.*
2 (of an animal on coats of arms) standing upright on a hind leg, *a lion rampant.* [same origin as *ramp*]

rampart noun (plural **ramparts**) a wide bank of earth built as a fortification or a wall on top of this. [from French *remparer* = fortify]

ramshackle adjective badly made and rickety, *a ramshackle hut.* [from *ransack*]

ranch noun (plural **ranches**) a large cattle-farm in America.

rancid adjective smelling or tasting unpleasant like stale fat. [from Latin]

random noun
at random using no particular order or method, *In bingo, numbers are chosen at random.*

random adjective done or taken at random, *a random sample.*

range noun (plural **ranges**)
1 a line or series of things, *a range of mountains.* 2 the limits between which things exist or are available; an extent, *a wide range of goods.* 3 the distance that a gun can shoot, an aircraft can travel, a sound can be heard, etc. 4 a place with targets for shooting-practice. 5 a large open area of grazing-land or hunting-ground. 6 a kitchen fireplace with ovens.

range verb (**ranges, ranging, ranged**)
1 exist between two limits; extend, *Prices ranged from £1 to £50.* 2 arrange. 3 move over a wide area; wander.
[from old French; related to *rank*¹]

ranger noun (plural **rangers**) someone who looks after or patrols a park, forest, etc. [from *range*]

rank¹ noun (plural **ranks**)
1 a line of people or things.
2 a place where taxis stand to await customers. 3 a position in a series of different levels, *He holds the rank of sergeant.*

rank verb (**ranks, ranking, ranked**)
1 arrange in a rank or ranks.
2 have a certain rank or place, *She ranks among the greatest novelists.* [via old French from Germanic]

rank² adjective (**ranker, rankest**)
1 growing too thickly and coarsely. 2 smelling very unpleasant. 3 unmistakably bad, *rank injustice.* **rankly** adverb, **rankness** noun [from Old English]

rank and file noun the ordinary people or soldiers, not the leaders.

ransack verb (**ransacks, ransacking, ransacked**)
1 search thoroughly or roughly.
2 rob or pillage a place. [from Old Norse]

ransom noun (plural **ransoms**) money that has to be paid for a prisoner to be set free.

hold to ransom hold someone captive or in your power and demand ransom.

ransom verb (**ransoms, ransoming, ransomed**)
1 free someone by paying a ransom. 2 get a ransom for someone. [from old French; related to *redeem*]

rant verb (**rants, ranting, ranted**) speak loudly and violently. [from Dutch]

rap verb (**raps, rapping, rapped**)
1 knock loudly. 2 (*informal*) reprimand. 3 (*slang*) chat.
4 speak rhymes with a backing of rock music.

rap noun (plural **raps**)
1 a rapping movement or sound.
2 (*informal*) blame or punishment, *take the rap.*
3 (*slang*) a chat. 4 rhymes spoken with a backing of rock music.

rapacious (*say* ra-**pay**-shus) adjective
1 greedy. 2 using threats or force to get everything you can. **rapaciously** adverb, **rapacity** noun [from Latin *rapax* = grasping]

rape noun (plural **rapes**) the act of having sexual intercourse with a person without her or his consent.

rape verb (**rapes, raping, raped**) force someone to have sexual intercourse. **rapist** noun [from Latin *rapere* = take by force]

rapid adjective moving very quickly; swift. **rapidly** adverb, **rapidity** noun [from Latin]

rapids plural noun part of a river where the water flows very quickly.

rapt adjective very intent and absorbed; enraptured. **raptly** adverb [from Latin *raptum* = seized]

rapture noun very great delight. **rapturous** adjective, **rapturously** adverb [from old French; related to *rapt*]

rare¹ adjective (**rarer, rarest**)
1 unusual; not often found or happening. 2 (of air) thin; below normal pressure. **rarely** adverb, **rareness** noun, **rarity** noun [from Latin]

rare[2] *adjective* (of meat) only
lightly cooked; undercooked.
[from Old English]

rarefied *adjective*
1 (of air) rare. 2 remote from
everyday life, *the rarefied
atmosphere of the university.*

rascal *noun* (*plural* **rascals**)
a dishonest or mischievous
person; a rogue. **rascally** *adjective*
[from old French]

rash[1] *adjective* doing something or
done without thinking of the
possible risks or effects. **rashly**
adverb, **rashness** *noun* [probably
from Old English]

rash[2] *noun* (*plural* **rashes**)
1 an outbreak of spots or patches
on the skin. 2 a number of
(usually unwelcome) events
happening in a short time, *a rash
of accidents.* [probably from old
French]

rasher *noun* (*plural* **rashers**)
a slice of bacon. [origin
unknown]

rasp *noun* (*plural* **rasps**)
1 a file with sharp points on its
surface. 2 a rough grating sound.

rasp *verb* (**rasps**, **rasping**, **rasped**)
1 scrape roughly. 2 make a rough
grating sound or effect.

raspberry *noun* (*plural*
raspberries) a small soft red fruit.
[origin unknown]

Rastafarian *noun* (*plural*
Rastafarians) a member of
a religious group that started in
Jamaica. [from *Ras Tafari* (*ras*
= chief), the title of a former
Ethiopian king whom the
group reveres]

rat *noun* (*plural* **rats**)
1 an animal like a large mouse.
2 an unpleasant or treacherous
person.

rate *noun* (*plural* **rates**)
1 speed, *The train travelled at
a great rate.* 2 a measure of cost,
value, etc., *Postage rates went up.*
3 quality or standard, *first-rate.*
at any rate anyway.

rate *verb* (**rates**, **rating**, **rated**)
1 put a value on something.
2 regard as, *He rated me among
his friends.*
[from Latin *ratum* = reckoned]

rather *adverb*
1 slightly or somewhat, *It's rather
dark.* 2 preferably or more
willingly, *I would rather not go.*
3 more exactly, *He is lazy rather
than stupid.* 4 (*informal*)
definitely, yes, *'Will you come?'
'Rather!'* [from Old English]

rating *noun* (*plural* **ratings**)
1 the way something is rated.
2 a sailor who is not an officer.
[from *rate*]

ratio (*say* ray-shee-oh) *noun*
(*plural* **ratios**)
1 the relationship between two
numbers, given by the quotient,
The ratio of 2 to 10 = 2:10 = $\frac{2}{10} = \frac{1}{5}$.
2 proportion, *Mix flour and
butter in the ratio of two to one*
(= two measures of flour to one
measure of butter). [Latin,
= reasoning, reckoning]

ration *noun* (*plural* **rations**) an
amount allowed to one person.

ration *verb* (**rations**, **rationing**,
rationed) share something out in
fixed amounts.
[French; related to *ratio*]

rational *adjective*
1 reasonable or sane. **2** able to reason, *Plants are not rational.*
rationally *adverb*, **rationality** *noun* [same origin as *ratio*]

rationalize *verb* (**rationalizes**, **rationalizing**, **rationalized**)
1 make a thing logical and consistent, *Attempts to rationalize English spelling have failed.* **2** invent a reasonable explanation of something, *She rationalized her meanness by calling it economy.* **3** make an industry etc. more efficient by reorganizing it. **rationalization** *noun*

rations *plural noun* a fixed daily amount of food issued to a soldier etc.

rattle *verb* (**rattles**, **rattling**, **rattled**)
1 make a series of short sharp hard sounds. **2** make a person nervous or flustered.
rattle off say or recite rapidly.

rattle *noun* (*plural* **rattles**)
1 a rattling sound. **2** a device or baby's toy that rattles.
[imitating the sound]

rattlesnake *noun* (*plural* **rattlesnakes**) a poisonous American snake with a tail that rattles.

raucous (*say* raw-kus) *adjective* loud and harsh, *a raucous voice.*
[from Latin *raucus* = hoarse]

rave *verb* (**raves**, **raving**, **raved**)
1 talk wildly or angrily or madly. **2** talk rapturously about something.

rave *noun* (*plural* **raves**) a big party or event with loud fast music and flashing lights.
[from old French]

ravenous *adjective* very hungry.
ravenously *adverb* [from French *raviner* = rush, ravage]

ravine (*say* ra-veen) *noun* (*plural* **ravines**) a deep narrow gorge or valley. [French, = a rush of water (because a ravine is cut by rushing water)]

ravishing *adjective* very beautiful.

raw *adjective*
1 not cooked. **2** in the natural state; not yet processed, *raw materials.* **3** without experience, *raw recruits.* **4** with the skin removed, *a raw wound.* **5** cold and damp, *a raw morning.*
rawness *noun*

raw material *noun* (*plural* **raw materials**) natural substances used in industry, *rich in iron ore, coal, and other raw materials.*

ray *noun* (*plural* **rays**)
1 a thin line of light, heat, or other radiation. **2** each of a set of lines or parts extending from a centre. [from Latin *radius*]

razor *noun* (*plural* **razors**) a device with a very sharp blade, especially one used for shaving. [same origin as *raze*]

re- *prefix*
1 again (as in *rebuild*). **2** back again, to an earlier condition (as in *reopen*). **3** in return; to each other (as in *react*). **4** against (as in *rebel*). **5** away or down (as in *recede*). [from Latin]

reach *verb* (**reaches**, **reaching**, **reached**)
1 go as far as; arrive at a place or thing. **2** stretch out your hand to get or touch something.
reachable *adjective*

reach noun (plural **reaches**)
1 the distance a person or thing can reach. **2** a distance you can easily travel, *We live within reach of the sea.* **3** a straight stretch of a river or canal.
[from Old English]

react verb (**reacts, reacting, reacted**) respond to something; have a reaction. [from *re-* + Latin *agere* = act or do]

reaction noun (plural **reactions**)
1 an effect or feeling etc. produced in one person or thing by another. **2** a chemical change caused when substances act upon each other.

reactionary adjective opposed to progress or reform.

reactor noun (plural **reactors**) an apparatus for producing nuclear power in a controlled way.

read verb (**reads, reading, read** (say as red))
1 look at something written or printed and understand it or say it aloud. **2** (of a computer) copy, search, or extract data. **3** indicate or register, *The thermometer reads 20° Celsius.* **readable** adjective

reader noun (plural **readers**)
1 a person who reads. **2** a book that helps you learn to read.

readily (say red-il-ee) adverb
1 willingly. **2** easily; without any difficulty.

reading noun (plural **readings**)
1 reading books. **2** the figure shown on a meter or gauge. **3** a gathering of people at which something is read aloud, *a poetry reading.*

ready adjective (**readier, readiest**) able or willing to do something or be used immediately; prepared. **readiness** noun
at the ready ready for use or action.

ready adverb beforehand, *This meat is ready cooked.* **ready-made** adjective
[from Old English]

real adjective
1 existing or true; not imaginary. **2** genuine; not an imitation, *real pearls.* **3** (of food) regarded as superior because it is produced by traditional methods, *real ale.* [from Latin]

realism noun seeing or showing things as they really are. **realist** noun, **realistic** adjective, **realistically** adverb

reality noun (plural **realities**)
1 what is real, *You must face reality.* **2** something real, *Her worst fears had become a reality.*

realize verb (**realizes, realizing, realized**)
1 be fully aware of something; accept something as true. **2** make a hope or plan etc. happen, *She realized her ambition to become a racing driver.* **3** obtain money in exchange for something by selling it. **realization** noun [from *real* + *-ize*]

really adverb
1 truly or in fact. **2** very, *She's really clever.*

realm (say relm) noun (plural **realms**)
1 a kingdom. **2** an area of knowledge, interest, etc., *in the realms of science.* [from old French; related to *regiment*]

reams *plural noun* a large quantity of writing.

reap *verb* (**reaps, reaping, reaped**) **1** cut down and gather corn when it is ripe. **2** obtain as the result of something done, *They reaped great benefit from their training.* **reaper** *noun* [from Old English]

rear¹ *noun* the back part.

rear *adjective* placed at the rear. [from Latin *retro-* = back]

rear² *verb* (**rears, rearing, reared**) **1** bring up young children or animals. **2** rise up; raise itself on hind legs, *The horse reared in fright.* **3** build or set up a monument etc. [from Old English]

rearguard *noun* (*plural* **rearguards**) troops protecting the rear of an army.

fight a rearguard action go on defending or resisting something even though you are losing.

rearrange *verb* (**rearranges, rearranging, rearranged**) arrange in a different way or order. **rearrangement** *noun*

reason *noun* (*plural* **reasons**) **1** a cause or explanation of something. **2** reasoning; common sense, *Listen to reason.*

USAGE: Do not use the phrase *the reason is* with the word *because* (which means the same thing). Correct usage is *We cannot come. The reason is that we both have flu* (not 'The reason is because …').

reason *verb* (**reasons, reasoning, reasoned**) **1** use your ability to think and draw conclusions. **2** try to persuade someone by giving reasons, *We reasoned with the rebels.* [from French; related to *ratio*]

reasonable *adjective* **1** ready to use or listen to reason; sensible or logical. **2** fair or moderate; not expensive, *reasonable prices.* **3** acceptable or fairly good, *a reasonable standard of living.* **reasonably** *adverb*

reassure *verb* (**reassures, reassuring, reassured**) restore someone's confidence by removing doubts and fears. **reassurance** *noun*

rebel (*say* rib-el) *verb* (**rebels, rebelling, rebelled**) refuse to obey someone in authority, especially the government; fight against the rulers of your own country.

rebel (*say* reb-el) *noun* (*plural* **rebels**) someone who rebels against the government, or against accepted standards of behaviour. **rebellion** *noun*, **rebellious** *adjective* [from *re-* + Latin *bellum* = war (originally referring to a defeated enemy who began to fight again)]

rebound *verb* (**rebounds, rebounding, rebounded**) bounce back after hitting something. **rebound** *noun*

rebuff *noun* (*plural* **rebuffs**) an unkind refusal; a snub. **rebuff** *verb* [from *re-* + Italian *buffo* = a gust]

rebuke *verb* (**rebukes, rebuking, rebuked**) speak severely to a person who has done wrong. **rebuke** *noun* [originally = to force back: from *re-* + old French *buker* = to hit]

recalcitrant *adjective*
disobedient or uncooperative.
recalcitrance *noun* [from Latin
recalcitrare = to kick back]

recall *verb* (**recalls, recalling,
recalled**)
1 ask a person to come back. **2** ask
for something to be returned.
3 bring back into the mind;
remember.

recapitulate *verb* (**recapitulates,
recapitulating, recapitulated**)
state again the main points of
what has been said.
recapitulation *noun* [from *re-*
+ Latin *capitulare* = arrange
under headings]

recapture *verb* (**recaptures,
recapturing, recaptured**)
1 capture again; recover. **2** bring
or get back a mood or feeling.
recapture *noun*

receipt (say ris-**eet**) *noun* (*plural*
receipts)
1 a written statement that money
has been paid or something has
been received. **2** receiving
something.

receive *verb* (**receives, receiving,
received**)
1 take or get something that is
given or sent. **2** greet someone
who comes. [from *re-* + Latin
capere = take]

receiver *noun* (*plural* **receivers**)
1 a person or thing that receives
something. **2** a person who buys
and sells stolen goods. **3** an
official who takes charge of
a bankrupt person's property.
4 a radio or television set that
receives broadcasts. **5** the part of
a telephone that receives the
sound and is held to a
person's ear.

recent *adjective* happening or
made or done a short time ago.
recently *adverb* [from Latin]

reception *noun* (*plural*
receptions)
1 the way a person or thing is
received. **2** a formal party to
receive guests, *a wedding
reception*. **3** a place in a hotel or
office etc. where visitors are
received and registered.

receptionist *noun* (*plural*
receptionists) a person whose job
is to receive and direct visitors,
patients, etc.

receptive *adjective* quick or
willing to receive ideas etc.

recession *noun* (*plural*
recessions)
1 receding from a point.
2 a reduction in trade or
prosperity.

recipe (say **ress**-ip-ee) *noun*
(*plural* **recipes**) instructions for
preparing or cooking food.
[Latin, = take (used at the
beginning of a list of
ingredients)]

reciprocal (say ris-**ip**-rok-al)
adjective given and received;
mutual, *reciprocal help*.
reciprocally *adverb*, **reciprocity**
noun

reciprocal *noun* (*plural*
reciprocals) a reversed fraction,
$\frac{2}{3}$ *is the reciprocal of* $\frac{3}{2}$.
[from Latin *reciprocus* = moving
backwards and forwards]

recital *noun* (*plural* **recitals**)
1 reciting something. **2** a musical
entertainment given by one
performer or group.

recite verb (recites, reciting, recited) say a poem etc. aloud from memory. **recitation** noun [from Latin *recitare* = to read aloud]

reckless adjective rash; ignoring risk or danger. **recklessly** adverb, **recklessness** noun [from an old word reck = heed, + -less]

reckon verb (reckons, reckoning, reckoned)
1 calculate or count up. 2 have as an opinion; feel confident, *I reckon we shall win*.
reckon with think about or deal with, *We didn't reckon with the train strike when we planned our journey*.

reclaim verb (reclaims, reclaiming, reclaimed)
1 claim or get something back. 2 make a thing usable again, *reclaimed land*. **reclamation** noun

recognize verb (recognizes, recognizing, recognized)
1 know who someone is or what something is because you have seen that person or thing before. 2 realize, *We recognize the truth of what you said*. 3 accept something as genuine, welcome, or lawful etc., *Nine countries recognized the island's new government*. **recognition** noun, **recognizable** adjective [from re- + Latin *cognoscere* = know]

recoil verb (recoils, recoiling, recoiled)
1 move back suddenly in shock or disgust. 2 (of a gun) jerk backwards when it is fired.

recollect verb (recollects, recollecting, recollected) remember.

recollection noun [from re- + Latin *colligere* = collect]

recommend verb (recommends, recommending, recommended) say that a person or thing would be a good one to do a job or achieve something.
recommendation noun [from re- + Latin *commendare* = commend]

reconcile verb (reconciles, reconciling, reconciled)
1 make people who have quarrelled become friendly again. 2 persuade a person to put up with something, *New frames reconciled him to wearing glasses*. 3 make things agree, *I cannot reconcile what you say with what you do*. **reconciliation** noun [from re- + Latin *conciliare* = conciliate]

recondition verb (reconditions, reconditioning, reconditioned) overhaul and repair.

reconnaissance (say rik-on-i-sans) noun an exploration of an area, especially in order to gather information about it for military purposes. [French, = recognition]

reconstruct verb (reconstructs, reconstructing, reconstructed)
1 construct or build something again. 2 create or act past events again, *Police reconstructed the robbery*. **reconstruction** noun

record (say rek-ord) noun (plural records)
1 information kept in a permanent form, e.g. written or printed. 2 a disc on which sound has been recorded. 3 facts known about a person's past life or career etc., *She has a good school record*. 4 the best performance in a sport etc., or the most

remarkable event of its kind, *He holds the record for the high jump.*

record (say rik-ord) *verb*
(**records, recording, recorded**)
1 put something down in writing or other permanent form. **2** store sounds or scenes (e.g. television pictures) on a disc or magnetic tape etc. so that you can play or show them later.
[from French]

recorder *noun* (*plural* **recorders**)
1 a kind of flute held downwards from the player's mouth.
2 a person or thing that records something.

recover *verb* (**recovers, recovering, recovered**)
1 get something back again after losing it; regain. **2** get well again after being ill or weak. **recovery** *noun* [from old French; related to *recuperate*]

recreation *noun* (*plural* **recreations**)
1 refreshing your mind or body after work through an enjoyable pastime. **2** a game or hobby etc. that is an enjoyable pastime. **recreational** *adjective* [from *re-* + Latin *creatio* = creation]

recruit *noun* (*plural* **recruits**)
1 a person who has just joined the armed forces. **2** a new member of a society or group etc.
recruit *verb* (**recruits, recruiting, recruited**) enlist recruits. **recruitment** *noun*
[from French *recroître* = to increase again]

rectangle *noun* (*plural* **rectangles**) a shape with four sides and four right angles. **rectangular** *adjective* [from Latin *rectus* = straight or right, + *angle*]

rectum *noun* (*plural* **rectums** or **recta**) the last part of the large intestine, ending at the anus.
[Latin, = straight (intestine)]

recuperate *verb* (**recuperates, recuperating, recuperated**) get better after an illness.
recuperation *noun* [from Latin]

recur *verb* (**recurs, recurring, recurred**) happen again; keep on happening. **recurrent** *adjective*, **recurrence** *noun* [from *re-* + Latin *currere* = to run]

recycle *verb* (**recycles, recycling, recycled**) convert waste material into a form in which it can be reused.

red *adjective* (**redder, reddest**)
1 of the colour of blood or a colour rather like this. **2** to do with Communists; favouring Communism. **redness** *noun*
red *noun*
1 red colour. **2** a Communist. **in the red** in debt (because debts were entered in red in account-books).

redden *verb* (**reddens, reddening, reddened**) make or become red.

redeem *verb* (**redeems, redeeming, redeemed**)
1 buy something back or pay off a debt. **2** save a person from damnation, *Christians believe that Christ redeemed us all.*
3 make up for faults, *His one redeeming feature is his kindness.*
redeemer *noun*, **redemption** *noun* [from *re-* + Latin *emere* = buy]

red-handed *adjective*
catch red-handed catch while actually committing a crime.

red herring *noun* (*plural* **red herrings**) something that draws attention away from the main

subject; a misleading clue.
[because a red herring (= a
kipper) drawn across a fox's path
put hounds off the scent]

red-hot *adjective* very hot; so hot
that it has turned red.

Red Indian *noun* (*plural* **Red
Indians**) (*old use*) a Native
American from North America.

USAGE: See note at *Indian*.

red tape *noun* use of too many
rules and forms in official
business. [because bundles of
official papers are tied up with
red or pink tape]

reduce *verb* (**reduces, reducing,
reduced**)
1 make or become smaller or less.
2 force someone into a condition
or situation, *He was reduced to
borrowing the money.* **reduction**
noun [from *re-* + Latin *ducere*
= bring]

redundant *adjective* not needed,
especially for a particular job.
redundancy *noun*

re-echo *verb* (**re-echoes, re-
echoing, re-echoed**) echo; go on
echoing.

reed *noun* (*plural* **reeds**)
1 a tall plant that grows in water
or marshy ground. **2** a thin strip
that vibrates to make the sound
in a clarinet, saxophone, oboe,
etc. [from Old English]

reef *noun* (*plural* **reefs**) a ridge of
rock or sand etc., especially one
near the surface of the sea. [via
old German or old Dutch from
Old Norse]

reek *verb* (**reeks, reeking, reeked**)
smell strongly or unpleasantly.
reek *noun*

reel *noun* (*plural* **reels**)
1 a spool. **2** a lively Scottish
dance.

reel *verb* (**reels, reeling, reeled**)
1 wind something onto or off
a reel. **2** stagger.
reel off say something quickly.

refer *verb* (**refers, referring,
referred**) pass a problem etc. to
someone else, *My doctor referred
me to a specialist.* **referral** *noun*
refer to 1 mention or speak about,
I wasn't referring to you. **2** look in
a book etc. for information, *We
referred to our dictionary.*
[from *re-* + Latin *ferre* = bring]

referee *noun* (*plural* **referees**)
someone appointed to see that
people keep to the rules of a game.
[literally = someone who is
referred to]

reference *noun* (*plural*
references)
1 referring to something, *There
was no reference to recent events.*
2 a direction to a book or page or
file etc. where information can
be found. **3** a testimonial.
in or **with reference to** concerning
or about.

reference book *noun* (*plural*
reference books) a book (such as
a dictionary or encyclopedia)
that gives information
systematically.

referendum *noun* (*plural*
referendums or **referenda**) voting
by all the people of a country (not
by Parliament) to decide whether
something shall be done. It is also
called a *plebiscite*. [Latin,
= referring]

refill *verb* (**refills, refilling, refilled**)
fill again.

refill noun (plural **refills**) a container holding a substance which is used to refill something, *This pen needs another refill.*

refine verb (**refines, refining, refined**)
1 purify. **2** improve something, especially by making small changes. [from *re-* + Middle English *fine* = make pure]

refined adjective
1 purified. **2** cultured; having good taste or good manners.

refinement noun (plural **refinements**)
1 the action of refining. **2** being refined. **3** something added to improve a thing.

refinery noun (plural **refineries**) a factory for refining something, *an oil refinery.*

reflect verb (**reflects, reflecting, reflected**)
1 send back light, heat, or sound etc. from a surface. **2** form an image of something as a mirror does. **3** think something over; consider. **4** be influenced by something, *Prices reflect the cost of producing things.* **reflection** noun, **reflective** adjective, **reflector** noun [from *re-* + Latin *flectere* = to bend]

reflex noun (plural **reflexes**) a movement or action done without any conscious thought. [same origin as *reflect*]

reflexive pronoun noun (plural **reflexive pronouns**) any of the pronouns *myself, herself, himself,* etc. (as in 'She cut *herself*'), which refer back to the subject of the verb.

reflexive verb noun (plural **reflexive verbs**) a verb where the subject and the object are the same person or thing, as in 'She cut *herself*', 'The cat *washed itself*'.

reform verb (**reforms, reforming, reformed**) make or become better by removing faults. **reformer** noun, **reformative** adjective, **reformatory** adjective

reform noun (plural **reforms**)
1 reforming. **2** a change made in order to improve something. [from *re-* + Latin *formare* = to form]

reformation noun reforming. **the Reformation** a religious movement in Europe in the 16th century intended to reform certain teachings and practices of the Roman Catholic Church, which resulted in the establishment of the Reformed or Protestant Churches.

refract verb (**refracts, refracting, refracted**) bend a ray of light at the point where it enters water or glass etc. at an angle. **refraction** noun, **refractor** noun, **refractive** adjective [from *re-* + Latin *fractum* = broken]

refrain[1] verb (**refrains, refraining, refrained**) stop yourself from doing something, *Refrain from talking.* [from Latin *refrenare* = to bridle]

refrain[2] noun (plural **refrains**) the chorus of a song. [from French]

refresh verb (**refreshes, refreshing, refreshed**) make a tired person etc. feel fresh and strong again.

refreshing adjective
1 producing new strength, a refreshing sleep. **2** pleasantly different or unusual, refreshing honesty.

refreshments plural noun
drinks and snacks provided at an event.

refrigerator noun (plural **refrigerators**) a cabinet or room in which food is stored at a very low temperature. [from re- + Latin frigus = cold]

refuge noun (plural **refuges**) a place where a person is safe from pursuit or danger.
take refuge go somewhere or do something so that you are protected. [from re- + Latin fugere = flee]

refugee noun (plural **refugees**) a person who has had to leave home and seek refuge somewhere, e.g. because of war or persecution or famine.

refund verb (refunds, refunding, refunded) pay money back.

refund noun (plural **refunds**) money paid back. [from Latin refundere = pour back]

regain verb (regains, regaining, regained)
1 get something back after losing it. **2** reach a place again.

regalia (say rig-**ayl**-i-a) plural noun the emblems of royalty or rank, The royal regalia include the crown, sceptre, and orb.

regard verb (regards, regarding, regarded)
1 look or gaze at. **2** think of in a certain way; consider to be, We regard the matter as serious.

regard noun
1 a gaze. **2** consideration; heed, You acted without regard to people's safety. **3** respect, We have a great regard for her.
with regard to concerning.
[from re- + French garder = to guard]

regarding preposition
concerning, There are laws regarding drugs.

regardless adverb without considering something, Do it, regardless of the cost.

regards plural noun kind wishes sent in a message, Give him my regards.

regatta noun (plural **regattas**) a meeting for boat or yacht races. [from Italian]

regenerate verb (regenerates, regenerating, regenerated) give new life or strength to something. **regeneration** noun

regent noun (plural **regents**) a person appointed to rule a country while the monarch is too young or unable to rule. [from Latin regens = ruling]

reggae (say **reg**-ay) noun a West Indian style of music with a strong beat. [origin unknown]

regime (say ray-**zheem**) noun (plural **regimes**) a system of government or organization, a Communist regime. [French; related to regiment]

refuse (say ri-**fewz**) verb (refuses, refusing, refused) say that you are unwilling to do or give or accept something. **refusal** noun

refuse (say **ref**-yooss) noun waste material, Lorries collected the refuse.

regiment noun (plural **regiments**) an army unit, usually divided into battalions or companies.
regimental adjective [from Latin regimentum = rule, governing]

region noun (plural **regions**) an area; a part of a country or of the world, in tropical regions.
regional adjective, **regionally** adverb
in the region of near, The cost will be in the region of £100.
[from Latin regio = boundary]

register noun (plural **registers**)
1 an official list of things or names etc. 2 a book in which information about school attendances is recorded. 3 the range of a voice or musical instrument.

register verb (**registers, registering, registered**)
1 list something in a register. 2 indicate; show, The thermometer registered 100°. 3 make an impression on someone's mind. 4 pay extra for a letter or parcel to be sent with special care. **registration** noun

regret noun (plural **regrets**) a feeling of sorrow or disappointment about something that has happened or been done.
regretful adjective, **regretfully** adverb

regret verb (**regrets, regretting, regretted**) feel regret about something. **regrettable** adjective, **regrettably** adverb
[from old French regreter = mourn for the dead]

regular adjective
1 always happening or doing something at certain times. 2 even or symmetrical, regular teeth. 3 normal, standard, or correct, the regular procedure. 4 belonging to a country's permanent armed forces, a regular soldier. **regularly** adverb, **regularity** noun [from Latin regula = a rule]

regulate verb (**regulates, regulating, regulated**)
1 control, especially by rules. 2 make a machine work at a certain speed. **regulator** noun [same origin as regular]

regulation noun
1 regulating. 2 a rule or law.

rehabilitation noun restoring a person to a normal life or a building etc. to a good condition. **rehabilitate** verb [from re- + Latin habilitare = enable]

rehearse verb (**rehearses, rehearsing, rehearsed**) practise something before performing to an audience. **rehearsal** noun

reign verb (**reigns, reigning, reigned**)
1 rule a country as king or queen. 2 be supreme; be the strongest influence, Silence reigned.

reign noun the time when someone reigns.
[from Latin regnum = royal authority]

reimburse verb (**reimburses, reimbursing, reimbursed**) repay money that has been spent, Your expenses will be reimbursed.
reimbursement noun [from re- + an old word imburse = pay]

rein noun (plural **reins**) a strap used to guide a horse. [from old French; related to retain]

reincarnation noun being born again into a new body. [from re- + incarnation (see incarnate)]

reindeer noun (plural **reindeer**)
a kind of deer that lives in Arctic
regions.

reinforce verb (reinforces,
reinforcing, reinforced)
strengthen by adding extra
people or supports etc. [from *re-*
+ old French *enforcer* = enforce]

reinforcements plural noun
extra troops or ships etc. sent to
strengthen a force.

reiterate verb (reiterates,
reiterating, reiterated) say
something again and again.
reiteration noun [from *re-* + Latin
iterare = repeat]

reject verb (rejects, rejecting,
rejected)
1 refuse to accept a person or
thing. 2 throw away or discard.
rejection noun [from *re-* + Latin
-jectum = thrown]

rejoice verb (rejoices, rejoicing,
rejoiced) feel or show great joy.
[from old French]

rejuvenate verb (rejuvenates,
rejuvenating, rejuvenated) make
a person seem young again.
rejuvenation noun [from *re-* +
Latin *juvenis* = young]

relapse verb (relapses, relapsing,
relapsed) return to a previous
condition; become worse after
improving. **relapse** noun [from *re-*
+ Latin *lapsum* = slipped]

relate verb (relates, relating,
related)
1 narrate. 2 connect or compare
one thing with another.
3 understand and get on well
with, *Some people cannot relate to
animals.*

related adjective belonging to the
same family.

relation noun (plural **relations**)
1 a relative. 2 the way one thing
is related to another.

relationship noun (plural
relationships)
1 how people or things are
related. 2 how people get on with
each other. 3 a close association
with strong feelings.

relative noun (plural **relatives**)
a person who is related to
another.

relative adjective connected or
compared with something;
compared with the average, *They
live in relative comfort.* **relatively**
adverb

relative pronoun see *pronoun*.

relax verb (relaxes, relaxing,
relaxed)
1 become less strict or stiff. 2 stop
working; rest. **relaxation** noun
[from *re-* + Latin *laxus* = loose]

relay (say ri-lay) verb (relays,
relaying, relayed) pass on
a message or broadcast.

relay (say re-lay) noun (plural
relays)
1 a fresh group taking the place
of another, *The firemen worked in
relays.* 2 a relay race. 3 a device
for relaying a broadcast.

relay race noun (plural **relay
races**) a race between teams in
which each person covers part of
the distance.

release verb (releases, releasing,
released)
1 set free or unfasten. 2 let a thing
fall or fly or go out. 3 make a film
or record etc. available to the
public.

release noun (plural **releases**)
1 being released. 2 something
released. 3 a device that

unfastens something.
[from old French; related to *relax*]

relegate verb (**relegates, relegating, relegated**)
1 put into a less important place.
2 put a sports team into a lower division of a league. **relegation** noun [from *re-* + Latin *legatum* = sent]

relent verb (**relents, relenting, relented**) become less severe or more merciful. [from *re-* + Latin *lentare* = bend, soften]

relentless adjective not stopping or relenting; pitiless. **relentlessly** adverb

relevant adjective connected with what is being discussed or dealt with. (The opposite is *irrelevant*.) **relevance** noun [from Latin]

reliable adjective able to be relied on; trustworthy. **reliably** adverb, **reliability** noun

relic noun (plural **relics**) something that has survived from an earlier period of history. [from Latin *reliquus* = remaining]

relief noun (plural **reliefs**)
1 the ending or lessening of pain, trouble, boredom, etc.
2 something that gives relief or help. 3 a person who takes over a turn of duty when another finishes. 4 a method of making a design etc. that stands out from a surface.

relief map noun (plural **relief maps**) a map that shows hills and valleys by shading or moulding.

relieve verb (**relieves, relieving, relieved**) give relief to a person or thing.
relieve of take something from

a person, *The thief relieved him of his wallet.* [from *re-* + Latin *levare* = raise, lighten]

religion noun (plural **religions**)
1 what people believe about God or gods, and how they worship.
2 a particular system of beliefs and worship. [from Latin *religio* = reverence]

religious adjective
1 to do with religion. 2 believing firmly in a religion and taking part in its customs. **religiously** adverb

relish noun (plural **relishes**)
1 great enjoyment. 2 something tasty that adds flavour to plainer food.

relish verb (**relishes, relishing, relished**) enjoy greatly.
[from old French]

reluctant adjective unwilling or not keen. **reluctantly** adverb, **reluctance** noun [from *re-* + Latin *luctatus* = struggling]

rely verb (**relies, relying, relied**)
rely on trust a person or thing to help or support you.
[from old French *relier* = bind together]

remain verb (**remains, remaining, remained**)
1 be there after other parts have gone or been dealt with; be left over. 2 continue to be in the same place or condition; stay. [from *re-* + Latin *manere* = to stay]

remainder noun
1 the remaining part or people or things. 2 the number left after subtraction or division.

remains plural noun
1 all that is left over after other

parts have been removed or destroyed. **2** ancient ruins or objects; relics. **3** a dead body.

remand verb (remands, remanding, remanded) send a prisoner back into custody while further evidence is sought. **remand** noun **on remand** in prison while waiting for a trial. [from re- + Latin mandare = entrust]

remark noun (plural remarks) something said; a comment.

remark verb (remarks, remarking, remarked) **1** make a remark; say. **2** notice. [from French]

remarkable adjective unusual or extraordinary. **remarkably** adverb [from remark]

remedy noun (plural remedies) something that cures or relieves a disease etc. or that puts a matter right. [from re- + Latin mederi = heal]

remember verb (remembers, remembering, remembered) **1** keep something in your mind. **2** bring something back into your mind. **remembrance** noun [from re- + Latin memor = mindful, remembering]

remind verb (reminds, reminding, reminded) help or make a person remember something. **reminder** noun [from re- + an old sense of mind = put into someone's mind, mention]

reminisce (say rem-in-iss) verb (reminisces, reminiscing, reminisced) think or talk about things that you remember.

reminiscence noun, **reminiscent** adjective [from Latin reminisci = remember]

remiss adjective negligent; careless about doing what you ought to do. [same origin as remit]

remnant noun (plural remnants) a part or piece left over from something. [from old French; related to remain]

remonstrate verb (remonstrates, remonstrating, remonstrated) make a protest, We remonstrated with him about his behaviour. [from re- + Latin monstrare = to show]

remorse noun deep regret for having done wrong. **remorseful** adjective, **remorsefully** adverb [from re- + Latin morsum = bitten]

remote adjective **1** far away or isolated. **2** some but very little; unlikely, a remote chance. **remotely** adverb, **remoteness** noun [from Latin remotum = removed]

remote control noun controlling something from a distance, usually by electricity or radio.

removal noun removing or moving something.

remove verb (removes, removing, removed) take something away or off.

remove noun (plural removes) a distance or degree away from something, That is several removes from the truth. [from re- + Latin movere = move]

Renaissance (say ren-ay-sans) noun the revival of classical

styles of art and literature in
Europe in the 14th–16th
centuries. [French, = rebirth]

render verb (renders, rendering,
rendered)
1 (formal) give or perform
something, Render help to the
victims. **2** cause to become, The
shock rendered us speechless.

rendezvous (say rond-ay-voo)
noun (plural **rendezvous** (say
rond-ay-vooz))
1 a meeting with somebody.
2 a place arranged for this.
[French, = present yourselves]

renew verb (renews, renewing,
renewed)
1 restore something to its
original condition or replace it
with something new. **2** begin or
make or give again, We renewed
our request. **renewal** noun

renewable resource noun
(plural **renewable resources**)
a resource (such as power from
the sun, wind, or waves) that can
never be used up, or which can
be renewed.

renounce verb (renounces,
renouncing, renounced) give up
or reject. **renunciation** noun [from
re- + Latin nuntiare = announce]

renovate verb (renovates,
renovating, renovated) repair
a thing and make it look new.
renovation noun [from re- + Latin
novus = new]

renowned adjective well-known
because of something good. [from
re- + French nomer = to name]

rent¹ noun (plural **rents**) a regular
payment for the use of
something, especially a house
that belongs to another person.

rent verb (rents, renting, rented)
have or allow the use of
something in return for rent.
[from French]

rent² noun (plural **rents**) a torn
place; a split.

repair verb (repairs, repairing,
repaired) put something into
good condition after it has been
damaged or broken etc.
repairable adjective

repair noun (plural **repairs**)
1 repairing, closed for repair.
2 a mended place, the repair is
hardly visible.

in good repair in good condition;
well maintained.
[from re- + Latin parare = get
something ready]

repartee noun witty replies and
remarks. [from French repartir
= answer back]

repatriate verb (repatriates,
repatriating, repatriated) send
a person back to his or her own
country. **repatriation** noun [from
re- + Latin patria = native
country]

repeal verb (repeals, repealing,
repealed) cancel a law officially.
repeal noun [from re- + French
appeler = to appeal]

repeat verb (repeats, repeating,
repeated) say or do the same
thing again. **repeatedly** adverb
repeat noun (plural **repeats**)
1 the action of repeating.
2 something that is repeated.
[from re- + Latin petere = seek]

repel verb (repels, repelling,
repelled)
1 drive away or repulse, repel the
attack. **2** disgust somebody.
repellent adjective & noun [from
re- + Latin pellere = to drive]

repent verb (repents, repenting, repented) be sorry for what you have done. **repentance** noun, **repentant** adjective [from old French; related to *penitent*]

repercussion noun (plural repercussions) a result or reaction produced indirectly by something. [from re- + Latin percutere = to strike]

repertoire (say rep-er-twahr) noun a stock of songs or plays etc. that a person or company knows and can perform. [French; related to *repertory*]

repetition noun (plural repetitions)
1 repeating. 2 something repeated. **repetitious** adjective

repetitive adjective full of repetitions. **repetitively** adverb

replace verb (replaces, replacing, replaced)
1 put a thing back in its place.
2 take the place of another person or thing. 3 put a new or different thing in place of something. **replacement** noun

replica noun (plural replicas) an exact copy. [from Italian]

reply noun (plural replies) something said or written to deal with a question, letter, etc.; an answer.

reply verb (replies, replying, replied) give a reply to; answer. [from old French]

report verb (reports, reporting, reported)
1 describe something that has happened or that you have done or studied. 2 make a complaint or accusation against somebody.
3 go and tell somebody that you have arrived or are ready for work.

report noun (plural reports)
1 a description or account of something. 2 a regular statement of how someone has worked or behaved, e.g. at school. 3 an explosive sound.
[from re- + Latin portare = carry]

reporter noun (plural reporters) a person whose job is to collect and report news for a newspaper, radio or television programme, etc.

repose noun calm, rest, or sleep.

repose verb (reposes, reposing, reposed) rest or lie somewhere. [from re- + Latin pausare = to pause]

repossess verb (repossesses, repossessing, repossessed) take something back because it has not been paid for.

reprehensible adjective extremely bad and deserving blame or rebuke. [from Latin reprehendere = blame, rebuke]

represent verb (represents, representing, represented)
1 show a person or thing in a picture or play etc. 2 symbolize or stand for, *In Roman numerals, V represents 5.* 3 be an example or equivalent of something. 4 help someone by speaking or doing something on their behalf. **representation** noun [from re- + Latin praesentare = to present]

representative noun (plural representatives) a person or thing that represents another or others.

representative adjective
1 representing others. 2 typical of a group.

repress verb (represses, repressing, repressed)
1 keep down; control by force.
2 restrain or suppress. **repression** noun, **repressive** adjective [from Latin]

reprieve noun (plural reprieves) postponement or cancellation of a punishment etc., especially the death penalty. [from old French]

reprimand noun (plural reprimands) a rebuke, especially a formal or official one.

reprimand verb (reprimands, reprimanding, reprimanded) give someone a reprimand.
[from French; related to repress]

reprisal noun (plural reprisals) an act of revenge. [from old French]

reproach verb (reproaches, reproaching, reproached) tell someone you are upset and disappointed by something he or she has done. **reproach** noun, **reproachful** adjective, **reproachfully** adverb [from old French]

reproduce verb (reproduces, reproducing, reproduced)
1 cause to be seen or heard or happen again. **2** make a copy of something. **3** produce offspring. **reproduction** noun, **reproductive** adjective

reprove verb (reproves, reproving, reproved) rebuke or reproach. **reproof** noun [from Latin reprobare = disapprove]

reptile noun (plural reptiles) a cold-blooded animal that has a backbone and very short legs or no legs at all, e.g. a snake, lizard, crocodile, or tortoise. [from Latin reptilis = crawling]

republic noun (plural republics) a country that has a president, especially one who is elected. (Compare monarchy.) **republican** adjective [from Latin res publica = public affairs]

repudiate verb (repudiates, repudiating, repudiated) reject or deny. **repudiation** noun [from Latin repudiare = to divorce]

repulsive adjective
1 disgusting. **2** repelling things. (The opposite is attractive.) **repulsively** adverb, **repulsiveness** noun

reputable (say rep-yoo-ta-bul) adjective having a good reputation; respected. **reputably** adverb

reputation noun (plural reputations) what people say about a person or thing. [from Latin reputare = consider]

reputed adjective said or thought to be something, This is reputed to be the best hotel. **reputedly** adverb

request verb (requests, requesting, requested)
1 ask for a thing. **2** ask a person to do something.

request noun (plural requests)
1 asking for something. **2** a thing asked for.
[from old French; related to require]

require verb (requires, requiring, required)
1 need. **2** make somebody do something; oblige, Drivers are required to pass a test. [from re- + Latin quaerere = seek]

requirement noun (plural requirements) what is required; a need.

rescue verb (rescues, rescuing, rescued) save from danger, harm, etc.; free from captivity. **rescuer** noun

rescue noun (plural rescues) the action of rescuing.
[from old French]

research noun careful study or investigation to discover facts or information.

research (say ri-serch) verb (researches, researching, researched) do research into something.
[from old French recerche = careful search]

resemblance noun (plural resemblances) likeness or similarity.

resemble verb (resembles, resembling, resembled) be like another person or thing. [from old French; related to similar]

resent verb (resents, resenting, resented) feel indignant about or insulted by something. **resentful** adjective, **resentfully** adverb, **resentment** noun [from re- + Latin sentire = feel]

reservation noun (plural reservations)
1 reserving. 2 something reserved. 3 an area of land kept for a special purpose. 4 a limit on how far you agree with something, I believe most of his story, but I have some reservations.

reserve verb (reserves, reserving, reserved)
1 keep or order something for a particular person or a special use. 2 postpone, reserve judgement.

reserve noun (plural reserves)
1 a person or thing kept ready to be used if necessary. 2 an area of land kept for a special purpose, a nature reserve. 3 shyness; being reserved.
[from re- + Latin servare = keep]

reservoir (say rez-er-vwar) noun (plural reservoirs) a place where water is stored, especially an artificial lake. [from French réservoir; related to reserve]

residence noun (plural residences) a place where a person lives.

resident noun (plural residents) a person living in a particular place. **resident** adjective [from re- + Latin -sidens = sitting]

residential adjective
1 containing people's homes, a residential area. 2 making it necessary to live in a particular place, residential care.

residue noun (plural residues) what is left over. **residual** adjective [from Latin residuus = remaining]

resign verb (resigns, resigning, resigned) give up your job or position. **resignation** noun
be resigned or **resign yourself to something** accept that you must put up with it.
[from Latin resignare = unseal]

resist verb (resists, resisting, resisted) oppose; fight or act against something. [from re- + Latin sistere = stand firmly]

resistance noun
1 resisting. 2 the ability of a substance to hinder the flow of electricity. **resistant** adjective

resolute *adjective* showing great determination. **resolutely** *adverb* [same origin as *resolve*]

resolution *noun* (*plural* **resolutions**)
1 being resolute. 2 something you have resolved to do, *New Year resolutions*. 3 a formal decision made by a committee etc. 4 the solving of a problem etc.

resolve *verb* (**resolves**, **resolving**, **resolved**)
1 decide firmly or formally. 2 solve a problem etc. 3 overcome doubts or disagreements.

resolve *noun*
1 something you have decided to do; a resolution. 2 great determination.
[from *re-* + Latin *solvere* = loosen]

resort *verb* (**resorts**, **resorting**, **resorted**) turn to or make use of something, *They resorted to violence.*

resort *noun* (*plural* **resorts**)
1 a place where people go for relaxation or holidays.
2 resorting, *without resort to cheating.*
the last resort something to be tried when everything else has failed.
[from *re-* + French *sortir* = go out]

resounding *adjective*
1 loud and echoing. 2 very great; outstanding, *a resounding victory.*

resource *noun* (*plural* **resources**)
1 something that can be used; an asset, *The country's natural resources include coal and oil.* 2 an ability; ingenuity. [from Old French; related to *resurgence*]

resourceful *adjective* clever at finding ways of doing things. **resourcefully** *adverb*, **resourcefulness** *noun*

respect *noun* (*plural* **respects**)
1 admiration for a person's or thing's good qualities.
2 politeness or consideration, *Have respect for people's feelings.*
3 a detail or aspect, *In this respect he is like his sister.* 4 reference, *The rules with respect to bullying are quite clear.*

respect *verb* (**respects**, **respecting**, **respected**) have respect for a person or thing.
[from Latin *respicere* = look back at, consider]

respectable *adjective*
1 having good manners and character etc. 2 fairly good, *a respectable score.* **respectably** *adverb*, **respectability** *noun*

respectful *adjective* showing respect. **respectfully** *adverb*

respective *adjective* of or for each individual, *We went to our respective rooms.* **respectively** *adverb*

respiration *noun* breathing. **respiratory** *adjective*

respirator *noun* (*plural* **respirators**)
1 a device that fits over a person's nose and mouth to purify air before it is breathed. 2 an apparatus for giving artificial respiration.

resplendent *adjective* brilliant with colour or decorations. [from *re-* + Latin *splendens* = glittering]

respond *verb* (**responds**, **responding**, **responded**)
1 reply. 2 act in answer to, or

because of, something; react. [from *re-* + Latin *spondere* = to promise]

response *noun* (*plural* **responses**)
1 a reply. 2 a reaction.

responsibility *noun* (*plural* **responsibilities**)
1 being responsible. 2 something for which a person is responsible.

responsible *adjective*
1 looking after a person or thing and having to take the blame if something goes wrong. 2 reliable and trustworthy. 3 with important duties, *a responsible job*. 4 causing something, *His carelessness was responsible for their deaths.* **responsibly** *adverb* [same origin as *respond*]

rest[1] *noun* (*plural* **rests**)
1 a time of sleep or freedom from work as a way of regaining strength. 2 a support, *an armrest*. 3 an interval of silence between notes in music.

rest *verb* (**rests, resting, rested**)
1 have a rest; be still. 2 allow to rest, *Sit down and rest your feet.* 3 support; be supported. 4 be left without further investigation etc., *And there the matter rests.* [from Old English]

rest[2] *noun*
the rest the remaining part; the others.

rest *verb* (**rests, resting, rested**)
remain, *Rest assured, it will be a success.*
rest with be left to someone to deal with, *It rests with you to suggest a date.*
[from Latin *restare* = stay behind]

restaurant *noun* (*plural* **restaurants**) a place where you can buy a meal and eat it. [French, literally = restoring]

restful *adjective* giving rest or a feeling of rest.

restive *adjective* restless or impatient because of delay, boredom, etc. [earlier (of a horse) = refusing to move: from *rest*[1]]

restless *adjective* unable to rest or keep still. **restlessly** *adverb*

restore *verb* (**restores, restoring, restored**) put something back to its original place or condition. **restoration** *noun* [from Latin]

restrain *verb* (**restrains, restraining, restrained**) hold a person or thing back; keep under control. **restraint** *noun* [from Latin *restringere* = tie up firmly, confine]

restrict *verb* (**restricts, restricting, restricted**) limit or control. **restriction** *noun*, **restrictive** *adjective* [from Latin *restrictus* = restrained]

result *noun* (*plural* **results**)
1 something produced by an action or condition etc.; an effect or consequence. 2 the score or situation at the end of a game, competition, or race etc. 3 the answer to a sum or calculation.

result *verb* (**results, resulting, resulted**)
1 happen as a result. 2 have a particular result. **resultant** *adjective*
[from Latin]

resurrect *verb* (**resurrects, resurrecting, resurrected**) bring back into use or existence, *resurrect an old custom.* [from *resurrection*]

resurrection *noun*
1 coming back to life after being dead. 2 the revival of something. **the Resurrection** in the Christian religion, the resurrection of Jesus Christ three days after his death.

resuscitate *verb* (**resuscitates, resuscitating, resuscitated**) revive a person from unconsciousness or apparent death. **resuscitation** *noun* [from *re-* + Latin *suscitare* = revive]

retail *noun* selling to the general public. (Compare *wholesale*.) **retailer** *noun* [from old French *retaille* = a piece cut off]

retain *verb* (**retains, retaining, retained**)
1 continue to have something; keep in your possession or memory etc. 2 hold something in place. [from *re-* + Latin *tenere* = to hold]

retaliate *verb* (**retaliates, retaliating, retaliated**) repay an injury or insult etc. with a similar one; counter-attack. **retaliation** *noun* [from *re-* + Latin *talis* = the same kind]

reticent (*say* ret-i-sent) *adjective* not telling people what you feel or think; discreet. **reticence** *noun* [from Latin *reticere* = keep silent]

retina *noun* (*plural* **retinas**) a layer of membrane at the back of the eyeball, sensitive to light. [from Latin]

retinue *noun* (*plural* **retinues**) a group of people accompanying an important person. [from old French *retenue* = restrained, in someone's service]

retire *verb* (**retires, retiring, retired**)
1 give up your regular work because you are getting old. 2 retreat. 3 go to bed or to your private room. **retirement** *noun* [from *re-* + French *tirer* = to draw]

retiring *adjective* shy; avoiding company.

retort *noun* (*plural* **retorts**)
1 a quick or witty or angry reply. 2 a glass bottle with a long downward-bent neck, used in distilling liquids. 3 a receptacle used in making steel etc.

retort *verb* (**retorts, retorting, retorted**) make a quick, witty, or angry reply.
[from *re-* + Latin *tortum* = twisted]

retract *verb* (**retracts, retracting, retracted**)
1 pull back or in, *The snail retracts its horns.* 2 withdraw an offer or statement. **retraction** *noun*, **retractable** *adjective*, **retractile** *adjective* [from *re-* + Latin *tractum* = pulled]

retreat *verb* (**retreats, retreating, retreated**) go back after being defeated or to avoid danger or difficulty etc.; withdraw.

retreat *noun* (*plural* **retreats**)
1 retreating. 2 a quiet place to which someone can withdraw. [from old French; related to *retract*]

retribution *noun* (*plural* **retributions**) a deserved punishment. [from *re-* + Latin *tributum* = assigned]

retrieve *verb* (**retrieves, retrieving, retrieved**)
1 bring or get something back.

2 rescue. **retrievable** adjective, **retrieval** noun [from old French *retrover* = find again]

retriever noun (plural **retrievers**) a kind of dog that is often trained to retrieve game.

retro- prefix
1 back. **2** backward (as in *retrograde*). [from Latin]

retrograde adjective
1 going backwards. **2** becoming less good. [from *retro-* + Latin *gradus* = a step]

retrospect noun
in retrospect when you look back at what has happened.
[from *retro-* + *prospect*]

retrospective adjective
1 looking back on the past.
2 applying to the past as well as the future, *The law could not be made retrospective.* **retrospection** noun

return verb (**returns, returning, returned**)
1 come back or go back. **2** bring, give, put, or send back.

return noun (plural **returns**)
1 returning. **2** something returned. **3** profit, *He gets a good return on his savings.* **4** a return ticket.
[from *re-* + Latin *tornare* = to turn]

return ticket noun (plural **return tickets**) a ticket for a journey to a place and back again.

reunion noun (plural **reunions**)
1 reuniting. **2** a meeting of people who have not met for some time.

reunite verb (**reunites, reuniting, reunited**) unite again after being separated.

reuse verb (**reuses, reusing, reused**) use again. **reusable** adjective

reuse noun using again.

reveal verb (**reveals, revealing, revealed**) let something be seen or known. [from Latin *revelare* = unveil]

revel verb (**revels, revelling, revelled**)
1 take great delight in something.
2 hold revels. **reveller** noun [from old French; related to *rebel*]

revelation noun (plural **revelations**)
1 revealing. **2** something revealed, especially something surprising.

revels plural noun noisy festivities.

revenge noun harming somebody in return for harm that they have caused.

revenge verb (**revenges, revenging, revenged**) avenge; take vengeance.
[from old French; related to *vindicate*]

revenue noun (plural **revenues**)
1 a country's income from taxes etc., used for paying public expenses. **2** a company's income.
[French, = returned]

reverberate verb (**reverberates, reverberating, reverberated**) resound or re-echo. **reverberation** noun [from *re-* + Latin *verberare* = to beat]

reverence noun a feeling of awe and deep or religious respect.

Reverend noun the title of a member of the clergy, *the Reverend John Smith.* [from Latin *reverendus* = someone to be respected]

USAGE: Do not confuse with *reverent.*

reverent adjective feeling or showing reverence. **reverently** adverb

USAGE: Do not confuse with *Reverend.*

reverie (say rev-er-ee) noun (plural **reveries**) a daydream. [from French]

reversal noun (plural **reversals**)
1 reversing or being reversed.
2 a piece of bad luck; a reverse.

reverse adjective opposite in direction, order, or manner etc.

reverse noun (plural **reverses**)
1 the reverse side, order, manner, etc. 2 a piece of misfortune, *They suffered several reverses.*
in reverse the opposite way round.

reverse verb (**reverses, reversing, reversed**)
1 turn in the opposite direction or order etc.; turn something inside out or upside down. 2 move backwards. 3 cancel a decision or decree. **reversible** adjective

reverse gear noun a gear that allows a vehicle to be driven backwards.

review noun (plural **reviews**)
1 an inspection or survey.
2 a published description and opinion of a book, film, play, etc.

review verb (**reviews, reviewing, reviewed**) make a review of something. **reviewer** noun

USAGE: Do not confuse with *revue.*

revise verb (**revises, revising, revised**)
1 go over work that you have already done, especially in preparing for an examination.
2 alter or correct something.
revision noun [from *re-* + Latin *visere* = examine]

revive verb (**revives, reviving, revived**) come or bring back to life, strength, activity, or use etc.
revival noun [from *re-* + Latin *vivere* = to live]

revolt verb (**revolts, revolting, revolted**)
1 rebel. 2 disgust somebody.

revolt noun (plural **revolts**)
1 a rebellion. 2 a feeling of disgust.
[same origin as *revolve*]

revolting adjective disgusting.

revolution noun (plural **revolutions**)
1 a rebellion that overthrows the government. 2 a complete change. 3 revolving; rotation; one complete turn of a wheel, engine, etc. **revolutionary** adjective

revolve verb (**revolves, revolving, revolved**) turn or keep on turning round. [from *re-* + Latin *volvere* = to roll]

revolver noun (plural **revolvers**) a pistol with a revolving mechanism that makes it possible to fire it a number of times without reloading.

revue noun (plural **revues**) an entertainment consisting of songs, sketches, etc., often about current events. [French, = review]

USAGE: Do not confuse with review.

reward noun (plural **rewards**) something given in return for a useful action or a merit.

reward verb (**rewards**, **rewarding**, **rewarded**) give a reward to someone. [originally = consider, take notice; related to regard]

rewarding adjective giving satisfaction and a feeling of achievement, a rewarding job.

rhetorical question noun (plural **rhetorical questions**) something put as a question so that it sounds dramatic, not to get an answer, e.g. 'Who cares?' (= nobody cares).

rheumatism noun a disease that causes pain and stiffness in joints and muscles. **rheumatic** adjective, **rheumatoid** adjective [from Greek rheuma, a substance in the body which was once believed to cause rheumatism]

rhinoceros noun (plural **rhinoceros** or **rhinoceroses**) a large heavy animal with a horn or two horns on its nose. [from Greek rhinos = of the nose + keras = horn]

rhododendron noun (plural **rhododendrons**) an evergreen shrub with large trumpet-shaped flowers. [from Greek rhodon = rose + dendron = tree]

rhombus noun (plural **rhombuses**) a shape with four equal sides but no right angles, like the diamond on playing cards. [from Greek]

rhubarb noun a plant with thick reddish stalks that are used as fruit. [from Latin]

rhyme noun (plural **rhymes**) 1 a similar sound in the endings of words, e.g. bat/fat/mat, batter/fatter/matter. 2 a poem with rhymes. 3 a word that rhymes with another.

rhyme verb (**rhymes**, **rhyming**, **rhymed**) 1 form a rhyme. 2 have rhymes. [from old French; related to rhythm (originally used of a kind of rhythmic verse which was usually rhymed)]

rhythm noun (plural **rhythms**) a regular pattern of beats, sounds, or movements. **rhythmic** adjective, **rhythmical** adjective, **rhythmically** adverb [from Greek]

rib noun (plural **ribs**) 1 each of the curved bones round the chest. 2 a curved part that looks like a rib or supports something, the ribs of an umbrella. **ribbed** adjective

ribbon noun (plural **ribbons**) 1 a narrow strip of silk or nylon etc. used for decoration or for tying something. 2 a long narrow strip of inked material used in a typewriter etc.

rice noun a cereal plant grown in flooded fields in hot countries, or its seeds. [from Greek]

rich adjective 1 having a lot of money or property or resources etc.; wealthy. 2 full of goodness, quality, etc. **3** expensive or luxurious. **richly** adverb, **richness** noun

rickety adjective shaky; likely to break or fall down.

rickshaw noun (plural **rickshaws**) a two-wheeled carriage pulled by one or more people, used in the Far East. [from Japanese jin-riki-sha = person-power-vehicle]

ricochet (say rik-osh-ay) verb (**ricochets, ricocheting, ricocheted**) bounce off something; rebound, The bullets ricocheted off the wall. **ricochet** noun [French, = the skipping of a flat stone on water]

rid verb (**rids, ridding, rid**) make a person or place free from something unwanted, He rid the town of rats.

get rid of cause to go away.

riddle[1] noun (plural **riddles**) a puzzling question, especially as a joke. [from Old English raedels]

riddle[2] verb (**riddles, riddling, riddled**) pierce with many holes, They riddled the target with bullets.

ride verb (**rides, riding, rode, ridden**) **1** sit on a horse, bicycle, etc. and be carried along on it. **2** travel in a car, bus, train, etc. **3** float or be supported on something, The ship rode the waves.

ride noun (plural **rides**) **1** a journey on a horse, bicycle, etc. or in a vehicle. **2** a roundabout etc. that you ride on at a fair. [from Old English]

ridge noun (plural **ridges**) a long narrow part higher than the rest of something. **ridged** adjective

ridicule verb (**ridicules, ridiculing, ridiculed**) make fun of a person or thing. **ridicule** noun [from Latin ridere = to laugh]

ridiculous adjective so silly that it makes people laugh or despise it. **ridiculously** adverb

rifle noun (plural **rifles**) a long gun with spiral grooves (called rifling) inside the barrel that make the bullet spin and so travel more accurately.

rifle verb (**rifles, rifling, rifled**) search and rob, They rifled his desk.

rift valley noun (plural **rift valleys**) a steep-sided valley formed where the land has sunk.

rig verb (**rigs, rigging, rigged**) **1** provide a ship with ropes, spars, sails, etc. **2** set something up quickly or out of makeshift materials. **rig-out** noun

rig out provide with clothes or equipment.

rig noun (plural **rigs**) **1** a framework supporting the machinery for drilling an oil well. **2** the way a ship's masts and sails etc. are arranged. **3** (informal) an outfit of clothes. [probably from a Scandinavian language]

rigging noun the ropes etc. that support a ship's mast and sails.

right adjective **1** on or towards the east, if you think of yourself as facing north. **2** correct; true, the right answer. **3** morally good; fair or just, Is it right to cheat? **4** (of political groups) conservative; not in favour of socialist reforms. **right-hand** adjective, **rightly** adverb, **rightness** noun

right *adverb*
1 on or towards the right-hand side, *Turn right.* **2** straight, *Go right on.* **3** completely, *Go right round it.* **4** exactly, *right in the middle.* **5** rightly, *You did right to tell me.*

right away immediately.

right *noun* (*plural* **rights**)
1 the right-hand side or part etc. **2** what is morally good or fair or just. **3** something that people are allowed to do or have, *People over 18 have the right to vote in elections.*

right *verb* (**rights, righting, righted**) make a thing right or upright, *They righted the boat.* [from Old English]

right angle *noun* an angle of 90°.

rightful *adjective* deserved or proper, *in her rightful place.* **rightfully** *adverb*

right hand *noun* (*plural* **right hands**) the hand that most people use more than the left, on the right side of the body.

right-handed *adjective* using the right hand in preference to the left hand.

right of way *noun* (*plural* **rights of way**)
1 a public path across private land. **2** the right of one vehicle to pass or cross a junction etc. before another.

rigid *adjective*
1 stiff or firm; not bending, *a rigid support.* **2** strict, *rigid rules.* **rigidly** *adverb*, **rigidity** *noun* [from Latin]

rigmarole *noun* (*plural* **rigmaroles**)
1 a long rambling statement.

2 a complicated procedure. [from Middle English *ragman* = a legal document]

rigorous *adjective*
1 strict or severe. **2** careful and thorough. **rigorously** *adverb*

rim *noun* (*plural* **rims**) the outer edge of a cup, wheel, or other round object. [from Old English]

rind *noun* the tough skin on bacon, cheese, or fruit.

ring[1] *noun* (*plural* **rings**)
1 a circle. **2** a thin circular piece of metal worn on a finger. **3** the space where a circus performs. **4** a square area in which a boxing match or wrestling match takes place.

ring *verb* (**rings, ringing, ringed**) put a ring round something; encircle. [from Old English *hring*]

ring[2] *verb* (**rings, ringing, rang, rung**)
1 cause a bell to sound. **2** make a loud clear sound like that of a bell. **3** be filled with sound, *The hall rang with cheers.* **4** telephone, *Please ring me tomorrow.* **ringer** *noun*

ring *noun* (*plural* **rings**) the act or sound of ringing.

give someone a ring (*informal*) telephone someone. [from Old English *hringan*]

ringleader *noun* (*plural* **ringleaders**) a person who leads others in rebellion, mischief, crime, etc. [from *ring*[1]]

ringmaster *noun* (*plural* **ringmasters**) the person in charge of a performance in a circus ring.

ring road noun (plural **ring roads**)
a road that runs around the edge
of a town so that traffic does not
have to go through the centre.

rink noun (plural **rinks**) a place
made for skating. [origin
unknown]

rinse verb (**rinses**, **rinsing**, **rinsed**)
1 wash something lightly. 2 wash
in clean water to remove soap.

rinse noun (plural **rinses**)
1 rinsing. 2 a liquid for colouring
the hair.

riot noun (plural **riots**) wild or
violent behaviour by a crowd of
people.

riot verb (**riots**, **rioting**, **rioted**)
take part in a riot.
[from old French *rihoter* = to
quarrel]

riotous adjective
1 disorderly or unruly.
2 boisterous, *riotous laughter*.

RIP abbreviation may he or she
(or they) rest in peace. [short for
Latin *requiescat* (or *requiescant*)
in pace]

rip verb (**rips**, **ripping**, **ripped**)
1 tear roughly. 2 rush.

rip noun a torn place.
[origin unknown]

ripe adjective (**riper**, **ripest**)
1 ready to be harvested or eaten.
2 ready and suitable, *The time is
ripe for revolution*. **ripeness** noun
a ripe old age a great age.

ripen verb (**ripens**, **ripening**,
ripened) make or become ripe.

ripple noun (plural **ripples**) a small
wave or series of waves.

ripple verb (**ripples**, **rippling**,
rippled) form ripples.
[origin unknown]

rise verb (**rises**, **rising**, **rose**, **risen**)
1 go upwards. 2 get up from lying,
sitting, or kneeling. 3 get out of
bed. 4 rebel, *They rose in revolt
against the tyrant*. 5 (of a river)
begin its course. 6 (of the wind)
begin to blow more strongly.

rise noun (plural **rises**)
1 the action of rising; an upward
movement. 2 an increase in
amount etc. or in wages. 3 an
upward slope.
give rise to cause.

rising noun (plural **risings**)
a revolt.

risk noun (plural **risks**) a chance
of danger or loss.

risk verb (**risks**, **risking**, **risked**)
take the chance of damaging or
losing something.
[via French from Italian]

risky adjective (**riskier**, **riskiest**)
full of risk.

rissole noun (plural **rissoles**)
a fried cake of minced meat or
fish.

ritual noun (plural **rituals**) the
series of actions used in
a religious or other ceremony.
ritual adjective, **ritually** adverb
[from Latin *ritus*]

rival noun (plural **rivals**) a person
or thing that competes with
another or tries to do the same
thing. **rivalry** noun [from Latin
rivalis = someone using the same
stream (from *rivus* = stream)]

river noun (plural **rivers**) a large
stream of water flowing in
a natural channel. [from Latin
ripa = bank]

rivet noun (plural **rivets**) a strong
nail or bolt for holding pieces of
metal together. The end opposite

the head is flattened to form another head when it is in place.

rivet verb (**rivets, riveting, riveted**)
1 fasten with rivets. 2 hold firmly, *He stood riveted to the spot.* 3 fascinate, *The concert was riveting.* **riveter** noun
[from old French]

road noun (plural **roads**)
1 a level way with a hard surface made for traffic to travel on. 2 a way or course, *the road to success.* [from Old English]

roadworthy adjective safe to be used on roads.

roam verb (**roams, roaming, roamed**) wander. **roam** noun
[origin unknown]

roar noun (plural **roars**) a loud deep sound like that made by a lion.

roar verb (**roars, roaring, roared**) make a roar.
a roaring trade brisk selling of something.

roast verb (**roasts, roasting, roasted**)
1 cook meat etc. in an oven or by exposing it to heat. 2 make or be very hot.

roast adjective roasted, *roast beef.*

roast noun (plural **roasts**)
1 meat for roasting. 2 roast meat.
[via old French from Germanic]

rob verb (**robs, robbing, robbed**) take or steal from somebody, *He robbed me of my watch.* **robber** noun, **robbery** noun

robe noun (plural **robes**) a long loose garment.

robin noun (plural **robins**) a small brown bird with a red breast.
[from old French, = Robert]

robot noun (plural **robots**)
1 a machine that looks or acts like a person. 2 a machine operated by remote control.
robotic adjective [from Czech *robota* = forced labour]

robust adjective strong and vigorous. **robustly** adverb, **robustness** noun [from Latin *robur* = strength, an oak tree]

rock[1] noun (plural **rocks**)
1 a large stone or boulder. 2 the hard part of the earth's crust, under the soil. 3 a hard sweet usually shaped like a stick and sold at the seaside. [from old French]

rock[2] verb (**rocks, rocking, rocked**)
1 move gently backwards and forwards while supported on something. 2 shake violently, *The earthquake rocked the city.*

rock noun
1 a rocking movement. 2 rock music.
[from Old English]

rock-bottom adjective at the lowest level, *rock-bottom prices.*

rockery noun (plural **rockeries**) a mound or bank in a garden, where plants are made to grow between large rocks.

rocket noun (plural **rockets**)
1 a firework that shoots high into the air. 2 a structure that flies by expelling burning gases, used to send up a missile or a spacecraft.
rocketry noun

rocket verb (**rockets, rocketing, rocketed**) move quickly upwards or away.
[from Italian *rocchetto* = small distaff (because of the shape)]

rocking horse noun (plural rocking horses) a model of a horse that can be rocked by a child sitting on it.

rock music noun popular music with a heavy beat.

rocky[1] adjective (rockier, rockiest) 1 like rock. 2 full of rocks.

rocky[2] adjective (rockier, rockiest) unsteady. **rockiness** noun

rod noun (plural rods) 1 a long thin stick or bar. 2 a stick with a line attached for fishing.

rodent noun (plural rodents) an animal that has large front teeth for gnawing things, Rats, mice, and squirrels are rodents. [from Latin rodens = gnawing]

rodeo (say roh-day-oh) noun (plural rodeos) a display of cowboys' skill in riding, controlling horses, etc. [Spanish, from rodear = go round]

roe[1] noun a mass of eggs or reproductive cells in a fish's body. [from old German or old Dutch]

roe[2] noun (plural roes or roe) a kind of small deer of Europe and Asia. The male is called a roebuck. [from Old English]

rogue noun (plural rogues) 1 a dishonest person. 2 a mischievous person. **roguery** noun [origin unknown]

role noun (plural roles) 1 a performer's part in a play or film etc. 2 someone's or something's purpose or function, the role of computers in education. [from French rôle = roll (originally the roll of paper on which an actor's part was written)]

role model noun (plural role models) a person who is regarded as an example of how to behave, Fathers are role models to their sons.

roll verb (rolls, rolling, rolled) 1 move along by turning over and over, like a ball or wheel. 2 form something into the shape of a cylinder or ball. 3 flatten something by rolling a rounded object over it. 4 rock from side to side. 5 pass steadily, The years rolled on. 6 make a long vibrating sound, The thunder rolled.

roll noun (plural rolls) 1 a cylinder made by rolling something up. 2 a small individual portion of bread baked in a rounded shape. 3 an official list of names. 4 a long vibrating sound, a drum roll. [from Latin rotula = little wheel]

roll-call noun (plural roll-calls) the calling of a list of names to check that everyone is present.

roller noun (plural rollers) 1 a cylinder for rolling over things, or on which something is wound. 2 a long swelling sea-wave.

Rollerblade noun (plural Rollerblades) (trade mark) a boot like an ice-skating boot, with a line of wheels in place of the skate, for rolling smoothly on hard ground. **rollerblading** noun

roller coaster noun (plural roller coasters) a switchback at a fair etc.

roller skate noun (plural roller skates) a framework with wheels, fitted under a shoe so that the wearer can roll smoothly over the ground. **roller-skating** noun

rolling pin noun a heavy cylinder for rolling over pastry to flatten it.

ROM abbreviation read-only memory (in a computer), with contents that can be searched or copied but not changed.

Roman adjective
1 of ancient or modern Rome or its people. 2 Roman Catholic.
Roman noun

Roman alphabet noun this alphabet, in which most European languages are written.

Roman Catholic adjective belonging to or to do with the Church that has the Pope (bishop of Rome) as its leader.
Roman Catholic noun (plural Roman Catholics) a member of this Church.

romance (say ro-manss) noun (plural romances)
1 tender feelings, experiences, and qualities connected with love. 2 a love story. 3 a love affair. 4 an imaginative story about the adventures of heroes, a romance of King Arthur's court.

Roman numerals plural noun letters that represent numbers (I = 1, V = 5, X = 10, etc.), used by the ancient Romans. (Compare arabic numerals.)

romantic adjective
1 to do with romance.
2 sentimental or idealistic; not realistic or practical.
romantically adverb

romp verb (romps, romping, romped) play in a lively way.
romp noun

roof noun (plural roofs)
1 the part that covers the top of a building, shelter, or vehicle.
2 the top inside surface of something, the roof of the mouth.

rook[1] noun (plural rooks) a black crow that nests in large groups.
rook verb (rooks, rooking, rooked) (informal) swindle; charge people an unnecessarily high price.
[from Old English]

rook[2] noun (plural rooks) a chess piece shaped like a castle. [from Arabic]

room noun (plural rooms)
1 a part of a building with its own walls and ceiling. 2 enough space, Is there room for me? **roomful** noun [from Old English]

roost verb (roosts, roosting, roosted) (of birds) perch or settle for sleep.
roost noun (plural roosts) a place where birds roost.

root[1] noun (plural roots)
1 that part of a plant that grows under the ground and absorbs water and nourishment from the soil. 2 a source or basis, The love of money is the root of all evil.
3 a number in relation to the number it produces when multiplied by itself, 9 is the square root of 81 (9 × 9 = 81).
take root 1 grow roots. **2** become established.
root verb (roots, rooting, rooted)
1 take root; cause something to take root. 2 fix firmly, Fear rooted us to the spot.
root out get rid of something.
[from Old Norse]

root² verb (roots, rooting, rooted) rummage; (of an animal) turn up ground in search of food. [from Old English]

rope noun (plural ropes) a strong thick cord made of twisted strands of fibre.

show someone the ropes show him or her how to do something.

rope verb (ropes, roping, roped) fasten with a rope.

rope in persuade a person to take part in something.

rose¹ noun (plural roses)
1 a shrub that has showy flowers often with thorny stems. **2** a deep pink colour. **3** a sprinkling-nozzle with many holes, e.g. on a watering can or hosepipe. [via Old English from Greek]

rose² past tense of rise.

roster noun (plural rosters) a list showing people's turns to be on duty etc.

rosy adjective (rosier, rosiest)
1 deep pink. **2** hopeful or cheerful, a rosy future. **rosiness** noun

rot verb (rots, rotting, rotted) go soft or bad and become useless; decay.

rot noun
1 rotting or decay. **2** (informal) nonsense.

rota (say roh-ta) noun (plural rotas) a list of people to do things or of things to be done in turn. [Latin, = wheel]

rotate verb (rotates, rotating, rotated)
1 go round like a wheel; revolve. **2** arrange or happen in a series; take turns at doing something.

rotation noun, **rotary** adjective, **rotatory** adjective [same origin as rota]

rote noun
by rote from memory or by routine, without full understanding of the meaning, We used to learn French songs by rote. [origin unknown]

rotor noun (plural rotors) a rotating part of a machine or helicopter. [from rotate]

rotten adjective
1 rotted, rotten apples. **2** (informal) worthless or unpleasant. **rottenness** noun

rouble (say roo-bul) noun (plural roubles) the unit of money in Russia.

rouge (say roozh) noun a reddish cosmetic for colouring the cheeks. **rouge** verb [French, = red]

rough adjective (rougher, roughest)
1 not smooth; uneven. **2** not gentle or careful; violent, a rough push. **3** not exact, a rough guess. **roughly** adverb, **roughness** noun

rough verb (roughs, roughing, roughed)
rough it do without ordinary comforts.
rough out draw or plan something roughly.
rough up (slang) treat a person violently.

roughen verb (roughens, roughening, roughened) make or become rough.

round adjective
1 shaped like a circle or ball or cylinder; curved. **2** full or complete, a round dozen. **3** returning to the start, a round

trip. **roundness** *noun*

in round figures approximately, without giving exact units.

round *adverb*

1 in a circle or curve; round something, *Go round to the back of the house.* **2** in every direction, *Hand the cakes round.* **3** in a new direction, *Turn your chair round.* **4** to someone's house or office etc., *Go round after dinner.*

come round become conscious again.

round about 1 near by. **2** approximately.

round *preposition*

1 on all sides of, *Put a fence round the field.* **2** in a curve or circle at an even distance from, *The earth moves round the sun.* **3** to all parts of, *Show them round the house.* **4** on the further side of, *The shop is round the corner.*

round *noun (plural* **rounds)**

1 a round object. **2** a whole slice of bread; a sandwich made with two slices of bread. **3** a series of visits made by a doctor, postman, etc. **4** one section or stage in a competition, *Winners go on to the next round.* **5** a shot or volley of shots from a gun; ammunition for this. **6** a song in which people sing the same words but start at different times.

round *verb (* **rounds, rounding, rounded)**

1 make or become round. **2** travel round, *The car rounded the corner.*

round off finish something.

round up gather people or animals together.

[from Old French; related to *rotund*]

roundabout *noun (plural* **roundabouts)**

1 a road junction where traffic has to pass round a circular structure in the road. **2** a circular revolving ride at a fair.

roundabout *adjective* indirect; not using the shortest way of going or of saying or doing something, *I heard the news in a roundabout way.*

rounders *noun* a game in which players try to hit a ball and run round a circuit.

round-the-clock *adjective* lasting or happening all day and all night.

round trip *noun (plural* **round trips)** a trip to one or more places and back to where you started.

round-up *noun (plural* **round-ups)**

1 a gathering up of cattle or people, *a police round-up of suspects.* **2** a summary, *a round-up of the news.*

rouse *verb (* **rouses, rousing, roused)**

1 make or become awake. **2** cause to become active or excited.

rousing *adjective* loud or exciting, *three rousing cheers.*

rout *verb (* **routs, routing, routed)** defeat and chase away an enemy.

rout *noun*

route *(say as* root*) noun (plural* **routes)** the way taken to get to a place.

routine *(say* roo-teen*) noun (plural* **routines)** a regular way of doing things. **routinely** *adverb* [French; related to *route*]

row[1] *(rhymes with* go*) noun (plural* **rows)** a line of people or things. [from Old English *raw*]

row² (rhymes with *go*) *verb* (**rows, rowing, rowed**) make a boat move by using oars. **rower** *noun*, **rowing boat** *noun* [from Old English *rowan*]

row³ (rhymes with *cow*) *noun* (*plural* **rows**)
1 a loud noise. 2 a quarrel. 3 a scolding. [origin unknown]

rowdy *adjective* (**rowdier, rowdiest**) noisy and disorderly. **rowdiness** *noun*

royal *adjective* to do with a king or queen. **royally** *adverb*

royalty *noun*
1 being royal. 2 a royal person or persons, *in the presence of royalty*. 3 (*plural* **royalties**) a payment made to an author or composer etc. for each copy of a work sold or for each performance.

RSVP *abbreviation* répondez s'il vous plaît (French, = please reply).

rub *verb* (**rubs, rubbing, rubbed**) move something backwards and forwards while pressing it on something else. **rub** *noun* **rub out** remove something by rubbing.

rubber *noun* (*plural* **rubbers**)
1 a strong elastic substance used for making tyres, balls, hoses, etc. 2 a piece of rubber for rubbing out pencil or ink marks. **rubbery** *adjective*

rubbish *noun*
1 things that are worthless or not wanted. 2 nonsense. [from old French]

rubble *noun* broken pieces of brick or stone.

ruby *noun* (*plural* **rubies**) a red jewel. [from Latin *rubeus* = red]

rucksack *noun* (*plural* **rucksacks**) a bag on straps for carrying on the back. [from German *Rücken* = back + *Sack* = sack¹]

rudder *noun* (*plural* **rudders**) a hinged upright piece at the back of a ship or aircraft, used for steering.

ruddy *adjective* (**ruddier, ruddiest**) red and healthy-looking, *a ruddy complexion*. [from Old English]

rude *adjective* (**ruder, rudest**)
1 impolite. 2 indecent or improper. 3 roughly made; crude, *a rude shelter*. 4 vigorous and hearty, *in rude health*. **rudely** *adverb*, **rudeness** *noun* [from Latin *rudis* = raw, wild]

rudimentary *adjective*
1 to do with rudiments; elementary. 2 not fully developed, *Penguins have rudimentary wings*.

rudiments (*say* rood-i-ments) *plural noun* the elementary principles of a subject, *Learn the rudiments of chemistry*. [same origin as *rude*]

ruff *noun* (*plural* **ruffs**)
1 a starched pleated frill worn round the neck in the 16th century. 2 a collar-like ring of feathers or fur round a bird's or animal's neck. [a different spelling of *rough*]

ruffian *noun* (*plural* **ruffians**) a violent lawless person. **ruffianly** *adjective*

ruffle *verb* (**ruffles, ruffling, ruffled**)
1 disturb the smoothness of a thing. 2 upset or annoy someone.

ruffle *noun* (*plural* **ruffles**) a gathered ornamental frill.

rug noun (plural **rugs**)
1 a thick mat for the floor.
2 a piece of thick fabric used as a blanket.

Rugby or **Rugby football** noun
a kind of football game using an oval ball that players may carry or kick. [named after Rugby School in Warwickshire, where it was first played]

rugged adjective
1 having an uneven surface or outline; craggy. 2 sturdy.

rugger noun Rugby football.

ruin noun (plural **ruins**)
1 severe damage or destruction to something. 2 a building that has fallen down.

ruin verb (**ruins, ruining, ruined**)
damage a thing so severely that it is useless; destroy. **ruination** noun
[from Latin *ruere* = to fall]

ruinous adjective
1 causing ruin. 2 in ruins; ruined.

rule noun (plural **rules**)
1 something that people have to obey. 2 ruling; governing, *under French rule*. 3 a carpenter's ruler.
as a rule usually; more often than not.

rule verb (**rules, ruling, ruled**)
1 govern; reign. 2 make a decision, *The referee ruled that it was a foul.* 3 draw a straight line with a ruler or other straight edge.
[from old French; related to *regulate*]

ruler noun (plural **rulers**)
1 a person who governs. 2 a strip of wood, metal, or plastic with straight edges, used for measuring and drawing straight lines.

ruling noun (plural **rulings**)
a judgement.

rum noun a strong alcoholic drink made from sugar or molasses.

rumble verb (**rumbles, rumbling, rumbled**) make a deep heavy continuous sound like thunder.
rumble noun

ruminant adjective ruminating.

ruminant noun (plural **ruminants**) an animal that chews the cud (see *cud*).

ruminate verb (**ruminates, ruminating, ruminated**)
1 chew the cud. 2 meditate or ponder. **rumination** noun, **ruminative** adjective

rummage verb (**rummages, rummaging, rummaged**) turn things over or move them about while looking for something.
rummage noun

rumour noun (plural **rumours**) information that spreads to a lot of people but may not be true.
rumour verb
be rumoured be spread as a rumour.
[from Latin *rumor* = noise]

rump noun (plural **rumps**) the hind part of an animal.

rumple verb (**rumples, rumpling, rumpled**) crumple; make a thing untidy.

rump steak noun (plural **rump steaks**) a piece of meat from the rump of a cow.

rumpus noun (plural **rumpuses**) (*informal*) an uproar; an angry protest.

run verb (**runs, running, ran, run**)
1 move with quick steps so that both or all feet leave the ground at each stride. 2 go or travel; flow, *Tears ran down his cheeks.*

3 produce a flow of liquid, *Run some water into it.* **4** work or function, *The engine was running smoothly.* **5** manage or organize, *She runs a grocery shop.* **6** compete in a contest, *He ran for President.* **7** extend, *A fence runs round the estate.* **8** go or take in a vehicle, *I'll run you to the station.*

run away leave a place secretly or quickly.

run down 1 run over. **2** stop gradually; decline. **3** (*informal*) say unkind or unfair things about someone.

run into 1 collide with. **2** happen to meet.

run out 1 have used up your stock of something. **2** knock over the wicket of a running batsman.

run over knock down or crush with a moving vehicle.

run through examine or rehearse.

run *noun* (*plural* **runs**)
1 the action of running; a time spent running, *Go for a run.* **2** a point scored in cricket or baseball. **3** a continuous series of events, etc., *She had a run of good luck.* **4** an enclosure for animals, *a chicken run.* **5** a track, *a ski run.* **on the run** running away from pursuit or capture.

runaway *noun* (*plural* **runaways**) someone who has run away.

runaway *adjective*
1 having run away or out of control. **2** won easily, *a runaway victory.*

rundown *adjective*
1 tired and in bad health. **2** in bad condition; dilapidated.

rung[1] *noun* (*plural* **rungs**) a crosspiece in a ladder. [from Old English]

rung[2] *past participle of* **ring**[2].

runner *noun* (*plural* **runners**)
1 a person or animal that runs, especially in a race. **2** a stem that grows away from a plant and roots itself. **3** a groove, rod, or roller for a thing to move on; each of the long strips under a sledge. **4** a long narrow strip of carpet or covering.

runner bean *noun* (*plural* **runner beans**) a kind of climbing bean with long green pods which are eaten.

runner-up *noun* (*plural* **runners-up**) someone who comes second in a competition.

running *present participle of* **run**.
in the running competing and with a chance of winning.

running *adjective* continuous or consecutive; without an interval, *It rained for four days running.*

runny *adjective* (**runnier, runniest**)
1 flowing like liquid, *runny honey.* **2** producing a flow of liquid, *a runny nose.*

runway *noun* (*plural* **runways**) a long hard surface on which aircraft take off and land.

rural *adjective* to do with or belonging to the countryside. [from Latin *ruris* = of the country]

ruse *noun* (*plural* **ruses**) a deception or trick. [from French]

rush[1] *verb* (**rushes, rushing, rushed**)
1 hurry. **2** move or flow quickly. **3** attack or capture by rushing.

rush *noun* (*plural* **rushes**)

1 a hurry. 2 a sudden movement towards something. 3 a sudden great demand for something. [from old French]

rush² noun (plural **rushes**) a plant with a thin stem that grows in marshy places. [from Old English]

rush hour noun (plural **rush hours**) the time when traffic is busiest.

rusk noun (plural **rusks**) a kind of hard, dry biscuit, especially for feeding babies.

rust noun
1 a red or brown substance that forms on iron or steel exposed to damp and corrodes it. 2 a reddish-brown colour.
rust verb (**rusts, rusting, rusted**) make or become rusty. [from Old English]

rustic adjective
1 rural. 2 made of rough timber or branches, *a rustic bridge*. [same origin as *rural*]

rustle verb (**rustles, rustling, rustled**)
1 make a sound like paper being crumpled. 2 (*American*) steal horses or cattle, *cattle rustling*. **rustle** noun, **rustler** noun

rustle up (*informal*) produce, *rustle up a meal*.

rusty adjective (**rustier, rustiest**)
1 coated with rust. 2 weakened by lack of use or practice, *My French is a bit rusty*. **rustiness** noun

rut noun (plural **ruts**)
1 a deep track made by wheels in soft ground. 2 a settled and usually dull way of life, *We are getting into a rut*. **rutted** adjective [probably related to *route*]

ruthless adjective pitiless, merciless, or cruel. **ruthlessly** adverb, **ruthlessness** noun [from Middle English *ruth* = pity]

rye noun a cereal used to make bread, biscuits, etc.

Ss

S. abbreviation
1 south. 2 southern.

sabbath noun (plural **sabbaths**) a weekly day for rest and prayer, Saturday for Jews, Sunday for Christians. [from Hebrew *shabat* = rest]

sabotage noun deliberate damage or disruption to hinder an enemy, employer, etc.
sabotage verb, **saboteur** noun [from French *saboter* = make a noise with *sabots* (= wooden clogs)]

saccharin (say sak-er-in) noun a very sweet substance used as a substitute for sugar. [from Greek *saccharon* = sugar]

sack¹ noun (plural **sacks**) a large bag made of strong material.
sacking noun
the sack (*informal*) dismissal from a job, *He got the sack*.
sack verb (**sacks, sacking, sacked**) (*informal*) dismiss someone from a job. [via Old English from Latin]

sack² verb (**sacks, sacking, sacked**) (*old use*) plunder a captured town in a violent destructive way. **sack** noun [from French *mettre à sac* = put in a sack]

sacrament noun (plural **sacraments**) an important Christian religious ceremony

such as baptism or Holy
Communion. [same origin as
sacred]

sacred *adjective* holy; to do with
God or a god. [from Latin]

sacrifice *noun* (*plural* **sacrifices**)
1 giving something that you
think will please a god. **2** giving
up a thing you value, so that
something good may happen.
3 a thing sacrificed. **sacrificial**
adjective

sacrifice *verb* (**sacrifices,
sacrificing, sacrificed**) give
something as a sacrifice.
[from Latin *sacrificare* = make
something holy]

sacrilege (*say* sak-ril-ij) *noun*
disrespect or damage to
something people regard as
sacred. **sacrilegious** *adjective*
[from Latin *sacer* = sacred
+ *legere* = take away]

sad *adjective* (**sadder, saddest**)
unhappy; showing or causing
sorrow. **sadly** *adverb*, **sadness**
noun [from Old English]

sadden *verb* (**saddens, saddening,
saddened**) make a person sad.

saddle *noun* (*plural* **saddles**)
1 a seat for putting on the back of
a horse or other animal. **2** the
seat of a bicycle. **3** a ridge of high
land between two peaks.

saddle *verb* (**saddles, saddling,
saddled**) put a saddle on a horse
etc.

sadist (*say* say-dist) *noun* (*plural*
sadists) a person who enjoys
hurting or humiliating other
people. **sadism** *noun*, **sadistic**
adjective [named after a French
novelist, the Marquis de Sade,
noted for the cruelties in his
stories]

safari *noun* (*plural* **safaris**) an
expedition to see or hunt wild
animals. [from Arabic *safar*
= a journey]

safe *adjective*
1 not in danger. **2** not dangerous.
safely *adverb*, **safeness** *noun*,
safety *noun*

safe *noun* (*plural* **safes**) a strong
cupboard or box in which
valuables can be locked safely.
[from old French; related to *save*]

safeguard *noun* (*plural*
safeguards) a protection.

safety pin *noun* (*plural* **safety
pins**) a U-shaped pin with a clip
fastening over the point.

sag *verb* (**sags, sagging, sagged**)
go down in the middle because
something heavy is pressing on
it; droop. **sag** *noun*

sage[1] *noun* a kind of herb used in
cooking and formerly used in
medicine. [from Latin *salvia*
= healing plant]

sage[2] *adjective* wise. **sagely**
adverb

sage *noun* (*plural* **sages**) a wise
and respected person.
[from Latin *sapere* = to be wise]

sago *noun* a starchy white food
used to make puddings. [from
Malay (a language spoken in
Malaysia)]

said *past tense* of **say**.

sail *noun* (*plural* **sails**)
1 a large piece of strong cloth
attached to a mast etc. to catch
the wind and make a ship or boat
move. **2** a short voyage. **3** an arm
of a windmill.

sail *verb* (**sails, sailing, sailed**)
1 travel in a ship or boat. **2** start
a voyage, *We sail at noon.*
3 control a ship or boat.

4 move quickly and smoothly.
sailing ship noun
[from Old English]

sailor noun (plural **sailors**)
a person who sails; a member of
a ship's crew or of a navy.

saint noun (plural **saints**) a holy
or very good person. **saintly**
adverb, **saintliness** noun [via Old
English from Latin sanctus
= holy]

sake noun
for the sake of so as to help or
please a person, get a thing, etc.

salad noun (plural **salads**)
a mixture of vegetables eaten
raw or cold.

salary noun (plural **salaries**)
a regular wage, usually for
a year's work, paid in monthly
instalments. **salaried** adjective
[from Latin salarium = salt-
money, money given to Roman
soldiers to buy salt]

sale noun (plural **sales**)
1 selling. **2** a time when things
are sold at reduced prices. [from
Old Norse]

salient (say say-lee-ent) adjective
1 jutting out; projecting. **2** most
noticeable, the salient features of
the plan. [from Latin saliens
= leaping]

saliva noun the natural liquid in
a person's or animal's mouth.
salivary adjective [Latin]

sallow adjective (of the skin)
slightly yellow. **sallowness** noun
[from Old English]

salmon (say sam-on) noun (plural
salmon) a large edible fish with
pink flesh.

salon noun (plural **salons**)
1 a large elegant room. **2** a room
or shop where a hairdresser etc.
receives customers. [French]

saloon noun (plural **saloons**)
1 a car with a hard roof and
a separate boot. **2** a room where
people can sit, drink, etc. [from
French salon]

salt noun (plural **salts**)
1 sodium chloride, the white
substance that gives sea water its
taste and is used for flavouring
food. **2** a chemical compound of
a metal and an acid. **salty**
adjective
salt verb (**salts**, **salting**, **salted**)
flavour or preserve food with
salt.

salt cellar noun (plural **salt
cellars**) a small dish or perforated
pot holding salt for use at meals.
[cellar from old French salier
= salt-box]

salute verb (**salutes**, **saluting**,
saluted)
1 raise your right hand to your
forehead as a sign of respect.
2 greet. **3** say that you respect or
admire something, We salute this
achievement.
salute noun (plural **salutes**)
1 the act of saluting. **2** the firing
of guns as a sign of greeting or
respect.

salvage verb (**salvages**, **salvaging**,
salvaged) save or rescue
something so that it can be used
again. **salvage** noun [from Latin
salvare = save]

salvation noun
1 saving from loss or damage etc.
2 (in Christian teaching) saving

the soul from sin and its consequences. [same origin as *salvage*]

same *adjective*
1 of one kind, exactly alike or equal. **2** not changing; not different. **sameness** *noun*

sample *noun* (*plural* **samples**) a small amount that shows what something is like; a specimen.

sample *verb* (**samples, sampling, sampled**) take a sample of something.
[from old French *essample* = example]

sanatorium *noun* (*plural* **sanatoriums** or **sanatoria**) a hospital for treating chronic diseases or convalescents. [from Latin *sanare* = heal]

sanctimonious *adjective* making a show of being virtuous or pious. [from Latin *sanctimonia* = holiness, piety]

sanction *noun* (*plural* **sanctions**)
1 permission or authorization.
2 action taken against a nation that is considered to have broken an international law etc., *Sanctions against that country include refusing to trade with it.*

sanction *verb* (**sanctions, sanctioning, sanctioned**) permit or authorize.
[from Latin *sancire* = make holy]

sanctity *noun* being sacred; holiness.

sanctuary *noun* (*plural* **sanctuaries**)
1 a safe place; a refuge. **2** a sacred place; the part of a church where the altar stands.

sand *noun* the tiny particles that cover the ground in deserts, seashores, etc.

sand *verb* (**sands, sanding, sanded**) smooth or polish with sandpaper or some other rough material. **sander** *noun*
[from Old English]

sandal *noun* (*plural* **sandals**) a lightweight shoe with straps over the foot. **sandalled** *adjective*
[from Greek *sandalon* = wooden shoe]

sandpaper *noun* strong paper coated with sand or a similar substance, rubbed on rough surfaces to make them smooth.

sandwich *noun* (*plural* **sandwiches**) two or more slices of bread with jam, meat, or cheese etc. between them.

sandwich *verb* (**sandwiches, sandwiching, sandwiched**) put a thing between two other things. [invented by the Earl of Sandwich (1718–92) so that he could eat while gambling]

sandy *adjective*
1 like sand. **2** covered with sand. **3** yellowish-red, *sandy hair*. **sandiness** *noun*

sane *adjective*
1 having a healthy mind; not mad. **2** sensible. **sanely** *adverb*, **sanity** *noun* [from Latin *sanus* = healthy]

sanitary *adjective*
1 free from germs and dirt; hygienic. **2** to do with sanitation. [from Latin *sanitas* = health]

sanitary towel *noun* (*plural* **sanitary towels**) an absorbent pad worn during menstruation.

sanitation *noun* arrangements for drainage and the disposal of sewage. [from *sanitary*]

sanity *noun* being sane.

sap noun the liquid inside a plant, carrying food to all its parts.

sap verb (**saps, sapping, sapped**) take away a person's strength gradually.

sapling noun (plural **saplings**) a young tree. [from *sap*]

sapphire noun (plural **sapphires**) a bright-blue jewel. [from Latin]

sarcastic adjective saying amusing or contemptuous things that hurt someone's feelings. **sarcastically** adverb, **sarcasm** noun [from Greek *sarkazein* = tear the flesh]

sardine noun (plural **sardines**) a small sea fish, usually sold in tins, packed tightly in oil. [from French]

sari noun (plural **saris**) a length of cloth worn wrapped round the body as a dress, especially by Indian women and girls. [from Hindi]

sash noun (plural **sashes**) a strip of cloth worn round the waist or over one shoulder. [from Arabic *shash* = turban]

satchel noun (plural **satchels**) a bag worn on the shoulder or the back, especially for carrying books to and from school. [from Latin *saccellus* = little sack]

satellite noun (plural **satellites**)
1 a planet or spacecraft etc. that moves in an orbit round a planet, *The moon is a satellite of the earth.* **2** a country that is under the influence of a more powerful country; a hanger-on. [from Latin *satelles* = a guard]

satin noun a silky material that is shiny on one side. **satiny** adjective

satire noun (plural **satires**)
1 using humour or exaggeration to show what is bad about a person or thing. **2** a play or poem etc. that does this. **satirical** adjective, **satirically** adverb, **satirist** noun, **satirize** verb [from Latin]

satisfaction noun
1 satisfying. **2** being satisfied and pleased because of this.
3 something that satisfies a desire etc. [from Latin *satis* = enough + *facere* = make]

satisfactory adjective good enough; sufficient. **satisfactorily** adverb

satisfy verb (**satisfies, satisfying, satisfied**)
1 give a person etc. what is needed or wanted. **2** make someone feel certain; convince, *The firemen were satisfied that the fire was out.* [same origin as *satisfaction*]

saturate verb (**saturates, saturating, saturated**)
1 make a thing very wet. **2** make something take in as much as possible of a substance or goods etc. **saturation** noun [from Latin *satur* = full, satiated]

sauce noun (plural **sauces**)
1 a thick liquid served with food to add flavour. **2** (*informal*) being cheeky; impudence. [from Latin *salsus* = salted]

saucepan noun (plural **saucepans**) a metal cooking pan with a handle at the side.

saucer noun (plural **saucers**) a small shallow object on which a cup etc. is placed. [from old French *saussier* = container for sauce]

saucy *adjective* (**saucier, sauciest**) cheeky or impudent. **saucily** *adverb*, **sauciness** *noun*

sauna *noun* (*plural* **saunas**) a room or compartment filled with steam, used as a kind of bath. [Finnish]

saunter *verb* (**saunters, sauntering, sauntered**) walk slowly and casually. **saunter** *noun*

sausage *noun* (*plural* **sausages**) a tube of skin or plastic stuffed with minced meat and other filling. [from old French; related to *sauce*]

savage *adjective* wild and fierce; cruel. **savagely** *adverb*, **savageness** *noun*, **savagery** *noun*

savage *noun* (*plural* **savages**)
1 a savage person. 2 (*old use*) a member of a primitive people.

savage *verb* (**savages, savaging, savaged**) attack by biting, scratching, or trampling, *The sheep was savaged by a dog.* [from Latin *silvaticus* = of the woods, wild]

save *verb* (**saves, saving, saved**)
1 keep safe; free a person or thing from danger or harm. 2 keep something, especially money, so that it can be used later. 3 avoid wasting something, *This will save time.* 4 (in sports) prevent an opponent from scoring. **save** *noun*, **saver** *noun* [from old French; related to *salvage*]

savings *plural noun* money saved.

saviour *noun* (*plural* **saviours**) a person who saves someone. **the** or **our Saviour** (in Christianity) Jesus Christ.

savoury *adjective*
1 tasty but not sweet. 2 having an appetizing taste or smell.

saw¹ *noun* (*plural* **saws**) a tool with a zigzag edge for cutting wood or metal etc.

saw *verb* (**saws, sawing, sawed, sawn**)
1 cut something with a saw.
2 move to and fro as a saw does. [from Old English]

saw² *past tense* of **see**.

sawdust *noun* powder that comes from wood cut by a saw.

saxophone *noun* (*plural* **saxophones**) a brass wind instrument with a reed in the mouthpiece. **saxophonist** *noun* [named after a Belgian instrument maker, Adolphe Sax, who invented it]

say *verb* (**says, saying, said**)
1 speak or express something in words. 2 give an opinion.

say *noun* the power to decide something, *I have no say in the matter.*
[from Old English]

saying *noun* (*plural* **sayings**) a well-known phrase or proverb or other statement.

scab *noun* (*plural* **scabs**)
1 a hard crust that forms over a cut or graze while it is healing.
2 (*offensive*) a blackleg. **scabby** *adjective* [from Old Norse]

scaffold *noun* (*plural* **scaffolds**) a platform on which criminals are executed.

scaffolding *noun* a structure of poles or tubes and planks making platforms for workers to stand on while building or repairing a house etc.

scald *verb* (**scalds, scalding, scalded**)
1 burn yourself with very hot liquid or steam. **2** heat milk until it is nearly boiling. **3** clean pans etc. with boiling water. **scald** *noun* [from Latin *excaldare* = wash in hot water]

scale[1] *noun* (*plural* **scales**)
1 a series of units, degrees, or qualities etc. for measuring something. **2** a series of musical notes going up or down in a fixed pattern. **3** proportion or ratio, *The scale of this map is one centimetre to the kilometre.* **4** the relative size or importance of something, *They entertain friends on a large scale.*
to scale with the parts in the same proportions as those of an original, *The architect's plans were drawn to scale.*
scale *verb* (**scales, scaling, scaled**) climb, *She scaled the ladder.*
scale down or **up** reduce or increase at a fixed rate, or in proportion to something else. [from Latin *scala* = ladder]

scale[2] *noun* (*plural* **scales**)
1 each of the thin overlapping parts on the outside of fish, snakes, etc.; a thin flake or part like this. **2** a hard substance formed in a kettle or boiler by hard water, or on teeth. **scaly** *adjective*
scale *verb* (**scales, scaling, scaled**) remove scales or scale from something.
[from old French; related to *scales*]

scale model *noun* (*plural* **scale models**) a model of something, made to scale.

scales *plural noun* a device for weighing things. [from Old Norse *skal* = ˈbowl]

scalp *noun* (*plural* **scalps**) the skin on the top of the head.

scamp *noun* (*plural* **scamps**) a rascal. [same origin as *scamper*]

scamper *verb* (**scampers, scampering, scampered**) run quickly, lightly, or playfully.
scamper *noun* [originally = run away, decamp; probably via old Dutch from Latin *ex-* = away + *campus* = field]

scan *verb* (**scans, scanning, scanned**)
1 look at every part of something. **2** glance at something. **3** count the beats of a line of poetry; be correct in rhythm, *This line doesn't scan.* **4** sweep a radar or electronic beam over an area to examine it or in search of something.
scan *noun* (*plural* **scans**)
1 scanning. **2** an examination using a scanner.
[from Latin]

scandal *noun* (*plural* **scandals**)
1 something shameful or disgraceful. **2** gossip about people's faults and wrongdoing.
scandalous *adjective* [from Greek *skandalon* = stumbling block]

scandalize *verb* (**scandalizes, scandalizing, scandalized**) shock a person by something considered shameful or disgraceful.

scanner *noun* (*plural* **scanners**)
1 a machine that examines things by means of light or other rays.

2 a machine that converts printed text, pictures, etc. into machine-readable form.

scanty *adjective* (**scantier, scantiest**) small in amount or extent; meagre, *a scanty harvest*. **scantily** *adverb*, **scantiness** *noun*

scapegoat *noun* (*plural* **scapegoats**) a person who is made to bear the blame or punishment for what others have done. [named after the *goat* which the ancient Jews allowed to *escape* into the desert after the priest had symbolically laid the people's sins upon it]

scar *noun* (*plural* **scars**) the mark left by a cut or burn etc. after it has healed.

scar *verb* (**scars, scarring, scarred**) make a scar or scars on skin etc.

scarce *adjective* (**scarcer, scarcest**) **1** not enough to supply people. **2** rare. **scarcity** *noun*
make yourself scarce (*informal*) go away; keep out of the way.

scarcely *adverb* only just; only with difficulty, *She could scarcely walk.*

scare *verb* (**scares, scaring, scared**) frighten.

scare *noun* (*plural* **scares**) **1** a fright. **2** alarm, mistaken or unnecessary anxiety. [from Old Norse]

scarecrow *noun* (*plural* **scarecrows**) a figure of a person dressed in old clothes, set up to frighten birds away from crops.

scarf *noun* (*plural* **scarves**) a strip of material worn round the neck or head. [from old French]

scarlet *adjective* & *noun* bright red.

scathing (*say* skayth-ing) *adjective* severely criticizing a person or thing. [from Old Norse *skatha* = injure or damage]

scatter *verb* (**scatters, scattering, scattered**) throw or send or move in various directions. [a different spelling of *shatter*]

scavenge *verb* (**scavenges, scavenging, scavenged**) **1** search for useful things amongst rubbish. **2** (of a bird or animal) search for decaying flesh as food. **scavenger** *noun*

scene *noun* (*plural* **scenes**) **1** the place where something has happened, *the scene of the crime.* **2** a part of a play or film. **3** a view as seen by a spectator. **4** an angry or noisy outburst, *He made a scene about the money.* **5** stage scenery. [from Greek *skene* = stage]

scenery *noun* **1** the natural features of a landscape. **2** things put on a stage to make it look like a place.

scent *noun* (*plural* **scents**) **1** a pleasant smell. **2** a liquid perfume. **3** an animal's smell that other animals can detect. **scented** *adjective* [from Latin]

sceptical (*say* skep-tik-al) *adjective* inclined to question things; not believing easily. **sceptically** *adverb*, **scepticism** *noun* [from Greek *skeptikos* = thoughtful]

sceptre *noun* (*plural* **sceptres**) a rod carried by a king or queen as a symbol of power. [from old French]

schedule (say shed-yool) noun (plural schedules) a programme or timetable of planned events or work. [from Latin scedula = little piece of paper]

schematic (say skee-mat-ik) adjective in the form of a diagram or chart. [same origin as scheme]

scheme noun (plural schemes) a plan of action.

scheme verb (schemes, scheming, schemed) make plans; plot. **schemer** noun [from Greek schema = form]

scholar noun (plural scholars) 1 a person who has studied a subject thoroughly. 2 a person who has been awarded a scholarship. **scholarly** adjective [from Latin scholaris = to do with a school]

scholarship noun (plural scholarships) 1 a grant of money given to someone to help to pay for his or her education. 2 scholars' knowledge or methods; advanced study.

school[1] noun (plural schools) 1 a place where teaching is done, especially of pupils aged 5–18. 2 the pupils in a school. 3 the time when teaching takes place in a school, School begins at 9 a.m. 4 a group of people who have the same beliefs or style of work etc.

school verb (schools, schooling, schooled) train, She was schooling her horse for the competition. [from Greek]

school[2] noun (plural schools) a shoal of fish or whales etc. [from old German or old Italian schole = a troop]

schoolchild noun (plural schoolchildren) a child who goes to school. **schoolboy** noun, **schoolgirl** noun

schooling noun 1 training. 2 education, especially in a school.

schoolteacher noun (plural schoolteachers) a person who teaches in a school. **schoolmaster** noun, **schoolmistress** noun

science noun the study of chemistry, physics, plants and animals, etc. [from Latin scientia = knowledge]

science fiction noun stories about imaginary scientific discoveries or space travel and life on other planets.

scientific adjective 1 to do with science or scientists. 2 studying things systematically and testing ideas carefully. **scientifically** adverb

scientist noun (plural scientists) 1 an expert in science. 2 someone who uses scientific methods.

scintillate verb (scintillates, scintillating, scintillated) 1 sparkle. 2 be lively and witty. **scintillation** noun [from Latin scintilla = spark]

scissors plural noun a cutting instrument used with one hand, with two blades pivoted so that they can close against each other. [from Latin scissum = cut]

scoff verb (scoffs, scoffing, scoffed) jeer; speak contemptuously. **scoffer** noun

scold verb (scolds, scolding, scolded) to speak angrily; to tell someone off. **scolding** noun [probably from Old Norse]

scone (say skon or skohn) noun (plural scones) a soft flat cake, usually eaten with butter.

scoop noun (plural scoops) 1 a kind of deep spoon for serving ice cream etc. 2 a deep shovel for lifting grain, sugar, etc. 3 a scooping movement. 4 an important piece of news published by only one newspaper.

scoop verb (scoops, scooping, scooped) lift or hollow something out with a scoop.

scoot verb (scoots, scooting, scooted) 1 propel a bicycle or scooter by sitting or standing on it and pushing it along with one foot. 2 run or go away quickly.

scooter noun (plural scooters) 1 a kind of motorcycle with small wheels. 2 a board with wheels and a long handle, which you ride on by scooting. [from scoot]

scope noun 1 opportunity to work, This job gives scope for your musical abilities. 2 the range or extent of a subject. [from Greek skopos = target]

scorch verb (scorches, scorching, scorched) make something go brown by burning it slightly. [origin unknown]

scorched-earth policy noun the burning of crops and destruction of anything that might be useful to an opposing army.

score noun (plural scores or, in sense 2, score) 1 the number of points or goals made in a game; a result. 2 (old use) twenty, 'Three score years and ten' means $3 \times 20 + 10 = 70$ years. 3 written or printed music. **on that score** for that reason, because of that, You needn't worry on that score.

score verb (scores, scoring, scored) 1 get a point or goal in a game. 2 keep a count of the score. 3 mark with lines or cuts. 4 write out a musical score. **scorer** noun [from Old Norse]

scores plural noun many; a large number.

scorn noun contempt. **scornful** adjective, **scornfully** adverb

scorn verb (scorns, scorning, scorned) 1 treat someone with contempt. 2 refuse something scornfully.

scorpion noun (plural scorpions) an animal that looks like a tiny lobster, with a poisonous sting. [from Greek]

Scot noun (plural Scots) a person who comes from Scotland.

scotch[1] noun whisky made in Scotland. [from Scottish]

scotch[2] verb (scotches, scotching, scotched) put an end to an idea or rumour etc. [origin unknown]

scot-free adjective without harm or punishment. [from scot = a form of tax, + free]

Scots adjective from or belonging to Scotland.

USAGE: See note at Scottish.

Scottish *adjective* to do with or belonging to Scotland.

USAGE: *Scottish* is the most widely used word for describing things to do with Scotland: *Scottish education, Scottish mountains.* *Scots* is less common and is mainly used to describe people: *a Scots girl.* *Scotch* is only used in fixed expressions like *Scotch egg* and *Scotch terrier.*

scoundrel *noun* (*plural* **scoundrels**) a wicked or dishonest person.

scour[1] *verb* (**scours, scouring, scoured**)
1 rub something until it is clean and bright. 2 clear a channel or pipe by the force of water flowing through it. **scourer** *noun* [from *ex- + curare* = take care of, clean]

scour[2] *verb* (**scours, scouring, scoured**) search thoroughly. [origin unknown]

scourge (*say* skerj) *noun* (*plural* **scourges**)
1 a whip for flogging people. 2 something that inflicts suffering or punishment. [from *ex- + Latin corrigia* = whip]

Scout *noun* (*plural* **Scouts**) a member of the Scout Association, an organization for boys.

scout *noun* (*plural* **scouts**) someone sent out to collect information.

scout *verb* (**scouts, scouting, scouted**)
1 act as a scout. 2 search an area thoroughly.
[from Latin *auscultare* = listen]

scowl *noun* (*plural* **scowls**) a bad-tempered frown.

scowl *verb* (**scowls, scowling, scowled**) make a scowl.

scrabble *verb* (**scrabbles, scrabbling, scrabbled**)
1 scratch or claw at something with the hands or feet. 2 grope or struggle to get something. [from old Dutch]

scraggy *adjective* thin and bony. [origin unknown]

scramble *verb* (**scrambles, scrambling, scrambled**)
1 move quickly and awkwardly. 2 struggle to do or get something. 3 (of aircraft or their crew) hurry and take off quickly. 4 cook eggs by mixing them up and heating them in a pan. 5 mix things together. 6 alter a radio or telephone signal so that it cannot be used without a decoding device. **scrambler** *noun*

scramble *noun* (*plural* **scrambles**)
1 a climb or walk over rough ground. 2 a struggle to do or get something. 3 a motor-cycle race over rough ground.

scrap[1] *noun* (*plural* **scraps**)
1 a small piece. 2 rubbish; waste material, especially metal that is suitable for reprocessing.

scrap *verb* (**scraps, scrapping, scrapped**) get rid of something that is useless or unwanted. [from Old Norse]

scrap[2] *noun* (*plural* **scraps**) (*informal*) a fight.

scrap *verb* (**scraps, scrapping, scrapped**) (*informal*) fight. [probably from *scrape*]

scrape verb (scrapes, scraping, scraped)
1 clean or smooth or damage something by passing something hard over it. 2 remove by scraping, *Scrape the mud off your shoes.* 3 pass with difficulty, *We scraped through.* 4 get something by great effort or care, *They scraped together enough money for a holiday.* **scraper** noun

scrape noun (plural scrapes)
1 a scraping movement or sound.
2 a mark etc. made by scraping.
3 an awkward situation caused by mischief or foolishness.
[from Old English]

scrappy adjective
1 made of scraps or bits or disconnected things. 2 carelessly done. **scrappiness** noun

scratch verb (scratches, scratching, scratched)
1 mark or cut the surface of a thing with something sharp.
2 rub the skin with fingernails or claws because it itches.
3 withdraw from a race or competition.

scratch noun (plural scratches)
1 a mark made by scratching.
2 the action of scratching. **scratchy** adjective
start from scratch start from the beginning or with nothing prepared.
up to scratch up to the proper standard.

scrawl noun (plural scrawls) untidy handwriting.

scrawl verb (scrawls, scrawling, scrawled) write in a scrawl.
[origin unknown]

scrawny adjective scraggy.

scream noun (plural screams)
1 a loud cry of pain, fear, anger, or excitement. 2 a loud piercing sound. 3 (*informal*) a very amusing person or thing.

scream verb (screams, screaming, screamed) make a scream.
[origin unknown]

screech noun (plural screeches) a harsh high-pitched scream or sound. **screech** verb [imitating the sound]

screen noun (plural screens)
1 a thing that protects, hides, or divides something. 2 a surface on which films or television pictures are shown.
3 a windscreen.

screen verb (screens, screening, screened)
1 protect, hide, or divide with a screen. 2 show a film or television pictures on a screen.
3 examine carefully, e.g. to check whether a person is suitable for a job or whether a substance is present in something. 4 sift gravel etc.

screenplay noun (plural screenplays) the script of a film, with instructions to the actors etc.

screw noun (plural screws)
1 a metal pin with a spiral ridge (the **thread**) round it, holding things together by being twisted in. 2 a twisting movement.
3 something twisted. 4 a propeller, especially for a ship or motor boat.

screw verb (screws, screwing, screwed)
1 fasten with a screw or screws.
2 twist.

screwdriver noun (plural **screwdrivers**) a tool for turning screws.

scribble verb (**scribbles**, **scribbling**, **scribbled**)
1 write quickly or untidily or carelessly. 2 make meaningless marks. **scribble** noun [from Latin *scribere* = write]

script noun (plural **scripts**)
1 handwriting. 2 the text of a play, film, broadcast talk, etc. [from Latin *scriptum* = written]

scripture noun (plural **scriptures**)
1 sacred writings. 2 (in Christianity) the Bible. [same origin as *script*]

scroll noun (plural **scrolls**)
1 a roll of paper or parchment used for writing on. 2 a spiral design.

scroll verb (**scrolls**, **scrolling**, **scrolled**) move the display on a computer screen up or down to see what comes before or after it. [from old French]

scrounge verb (**scrounges**, **scrounging**, **scrounged**) cadge. **scrounger** noun [from an old word *scringe* = squeeze roughly]

scrub[1] verb (**scrubs**, **scrubbing**, **scrubbed**)
1 rub with a hard brush, especially to clean something. 2 (informal) cancel. **scrub** noun [probably from old German or old Dutch]

scrub[2] noun
1 low trees and bushes. 2 land covered with these. [from *shrub*]

scrubby adjective undersized and shabby or wretched. [from *scrub*[2]]

scruff noun the back of the neck. [from Old Norse]

scruffy adjective shabby and untidy. **scruffily** adverb, **scruffiness** noun [a different spelling of *scurfy*]

scrum noun (plural **scrums**)
1 (also **scrummage**) a group of players from each side in Rugby football who push against each other and try to heel out the ball which is thrown between them.
2 a crowd pushing against each other.

scruple noun (plural **scruples**) a feeling of doubt or hesitation when your conscience tells you that an action would be wrong.

scruple verb (**scruples**, **scrupling**, **scrupled**) have scruples, *He would not scruple to betray us.* [from Latin]

scrupulous adjective
1 very careful and conscientious.
2 strictly honest or honourable. **scrupulously** adverb [from *scruple*]

scrutinize verb (**scrutinizes**, **scrutinizing**, **scrutinized**) examine or look at something carefully.

scrutiny noun [from Latin *scrutari* = examine, (originally) = sort rags]

scuba diving noun swimming underwater using a tank of air strapped to your back. [from the initials of *self-contained underwater breathing apparatus*]

scuff verb (**scuffs**, **scuffing**, **scuffed**)
1 drag your feet while walking.
2 scrape with your foot; mark or damage something by doing this. [origin unknown]

scuffle noun (plural **scuffles**) a confused fight or struggle.

scuffle verb (**scuffles**, **scuffling**, **scuffled**) take part in a scuffle. [probably from a Scandinavian language]

scullery noun (plural **sculleries**) a room where dishes etc. are washed up. [from Latin *scutella* = small dish]

sculptor noun (plural **sculptors**) a person who makes sculptures.

sculpture noun (plural **sculptures**)
1 making shapes by carving wood or stone or casting metal.
2 a shape made in this way.
sculpture verb [from Latin *sculpere* = carve]

scum noun
1 froth or dirt on top of a liquid.
2 worthless people.

scuttle¹ noun (plural **scuttles**) a bucket or container for coal in a house. [via Old Norse from Latin *scutella* = dish]

scuttle² verb (**scuttles**, **scuttling**, **scuttled**) scurry; hurry away. [from *scud*]

scuttle³ verb (**scuttles**, **scuttling**, **scuttled**) sink a ship deliberately by letting water into it. [probably from Spanish *escotar* = cut out]

scythe noun (plural **scythes**) a tool with a long curved blade for cutting grass or corn.
scythe verb (**scythes**, **scything**, **scythed**) cut with a scythe. [from Old English]

SE abbreviation
1 south-east. 2 south-eastern.

se- prefix
1 apart or aside (as in *secluded*).
2 without (as in *secure*). [Latin]

sea noun (plural **seas**)
1 the salt water that covers most of the earth's surface; a part of

this. 2 a large lake, *the Sea of Galilee*. 3 a large area of something, *a sea of faces*.
at sea 1 on the sea. **2** not knowing what to do.

sea anemone noun (plural **sea anemones**) a sea creature with short tentacles round its mouth.

seaboard noun (plural **seaboards**) a coastline or coastal region.

sea breeze noun (plural **sea breezes**) a breeze blowing from the sea onto the land.

seafaring adjective & noun working or travelling on the sea.
seafarer noun

seafood noun fish or shellfish from the sea eaten as food.

seagull noun (plural **seagulls**) a seabird with long wings.

seal¹ noun (plural **seals**) a sea mammal with thick fur or bristles, that breeds on land. [from Old English]

seal² noun (plural **seals**)
1 a piece of metal with an engraved design for pressing on a soft substance to leave an impression. 2 this impression.
3 something designed to close an opening and prevent air or liquid etc. from getting in or out.
4 a small decorative sticker, *Christmas seals*.
seal verb (**seals**, **sealing**, **sealed**). 1 close something by sticking two parts together. 2 close securely; stop up. 3 press a seal on something.
seal off prevent people getting to an area.
[from old French; related to *sign*]

sea level *noun* the level of the sea halfway between high and low tide.

sealing-wax *noun* a substance that is soft when heated but hardens when cooled, used for sealing documents or for marking with a seal.

sea lion *noun* (*plural* **sea lions**) a kind of large seal that lives in the Pacific Ocean.

seam *noun* (*plural* **seams**)
1 the line where two edges of cloth or wood etc. join. **2** a layer of coal in the ground. [from Old English]

seamanship *noun* skill in seafaring.

seamy *adjective*
seamy side the less attractive side or part, *Police see a lot of the seamy side of life.*
[originally, the 'wrong' side of a piece of sewing, where the rough edges of the seams show]

sear *verb* (**sears**, **searing**, **seared**) scorch or burn the surface of something.

search *verb* (**searches**, **searching**, **searched**) look very carefully in a place etc. in order to find something. **search** *noun*, **searcher** *noun* [from old French]

searchlight *noun* (*plural* **searchlights**) a light with a strong beam that can be turned in any direction.

search party *noun* (*plural* **search parties**) a group of people organized to search for a missing person or thing.

search warrant *noun* (*plural* **search warrants**) an official document giving the police permission to search private property.

seasick *adjective* sick because of the movement of a ship.
seasickness *noun*

seaside *noun* a place by the sea where people go for holidays.

season *noun* (*plural* **seasons**)
1 each of the four main parts of the year (spring, summer, autumn, winter). **2** the time of year when something happens, *the football season.*
in season available and ready for eating, *Strawberries are in season in the summer.*

season *verb* (**seasons**, **seasoning**, **seasoned**)
1 give extra flavour to food by adding salt, pepper, or other strong-tasting substances. **2** dry and treat timber etc. to make it ready for use.
[from Latin *satio* = time for sowing seed]

seasonable *adjective* suitable for the season, *Hot weather is seasonable in summer.*
seasonably *adverb*

USAGE: Do not confuse with *seasonal.*

seasonal *adjective*
1 for or to do with a season.
2 happening in a particular season, *Fruit-picking is seasonal work.* **seasonally** *adverb*

USAGE: Do not confuse with *seasonable.*

seasoning *noun* (*plural* **seasonings**) a substance used to season food.

season ticket *noun* (*plural* **season tickets**) a ticket that can be used as often as you like throughout a period of time.

seat *noun* (*plural* **seats**)
1 a thing made or used for sitting on. 2 the right to be a member of a council, committee, parliament, etc., *She won the seat ten years ago.* 3 the buttocks; the part of a skirt or trousers covering these. 4 the place where something is based or located, *London is the seat of our government.*

seat *verb* (**seats, seating, seated**)
1 place in or on a seat. 2 have seats for, *The theatre seats 3,000 people.*

seat belt *noun* (*plural* **seat belts**) a strap to hold a person securely in a seat.

seating *noun*
1 the seats in a place, *seating for 400.* 2 the arrangement of seats, *a seating plan.*

seaweed *noun* a plant or plants that grow in the sea.

seaworthy *adjective* (of a ship) fit for a sea voyage. **seaworthiness** *noun*

secateurs *plural noun* clippers held in the hand for pruning plants. [French, from Latin *secare* = to cut]

secluded *adjective* screened or sheltered from view. **seclusion** *noun* [from *se-* + Latin *claudere* = shut]

second[1] *adjective*
1 next after the first. 2 another, *a second chance.* 3 less good, *second quality.* **secondly** *adverb*

second *noun* (*plural* **seconds**)
1 a person or thing that is second.

2 an attendant of a fighter in a boxing match, duel, etc. 3 a thing that is of second (not the best) quality. 4 one-sixtieth of a minute of time or of a degree used in measuring angles.

second *verb* (**seconds, seconding, seconded**)
1 assist someone. 2 support a proposal, motion, etc. **seconder** *noun*
[from Latin *secundus* = next]

second[2] (*say* sik-ond) *verb* (**seconds, seconding, seconded**) transfer a person temporarily to another job or department etc. **secondment** *noun* [from French *en second* = in the second rank (because officers seconded to another company served under officers who belonged to that company)]

secondary *adjective*
1 coming after or from something. 2 less important. 3 (of education etc.) for children of more than about 11 years old, *a secondary school.* (Compare *primary*.)

second-hand *adjective*
1 bought or used after someone else has owned it. 2 selling second-hand goods, *a second-hand shop.*

second nature *noun* behaviour that has become automatic or a habit, *Lying is second nature to him.*

second-rate *adjective* inferior; not very good.

secret *adjective*
1 that must not be told or shown to other people. 2 not known by everybody. 3 working secretly. **secretly** *adverb*, **secrecy** *noun*

secret noun (plural **secrets**)
something secret.
[from Latin *secretum* = set apart]

secretary (say sek-rit-ree) noun
(plural **secretaries**)
1 a person whose job is to help
with letters, answer the
telephone, and make business
arrangements for a person or
organization. **2** the chief
assistant of a government
minister or ambassador.
secretarial adjective [from Latin
secretarius = an officer or servant
allowed to know your secrets]

secrete (say sik-reet) verb
(**secretes**, **secreting**, **secreted**)
1 hide something. **2** produce
a substance in the body, *Saliva is
secreted in the mouth.* **secretion**
noun [same origin as *secret*]

secretive (say seek-rit-iv)
adjective liking or trying to keep
things secret. **secretively** adverb,
secretiveness noun

secret police noun a police force
which works in secret for
political purposes, not to deal
with crime.

secret service noun
a government department
responsible for espionage.

sect noun (plural **sects**) a group
whose beliefs differ from those of
others in the same religion;
a faction.

section noun (plural **sections**)
1 a part of something. **2** a cross-
section. [from Latin *sectum* = cut]

sector noun (plural **sectors**)
1 one part of an area. **2** a part of
something, *the private sector of
industry.* [from Latin *secare*
= to cut]

secular adjective to do with
worldly affairs, not spiritual or
religious matters. [from Latin
saecularis = worldly]

secure adjective
1 safe, especially against attack.
2 certain not to slip or fail.
3 reliable. **securely** adverb

secure verb (**secures**, **securing**,
secured)
1 make a thing secure. **2** obtain,
*We secured two tickets for the
show.*
[from *se-* + Latin *cura* = care]

security noun (plural **securities**)
1 being secure; safety.
2 precautions against theft or
spying etc. **3** something given as
a guarantee that a promise will
be kept or a debt repaid.
4 investments such as stocks and
shares.

security guard noun (plural
security guards) a person
employed to guard a building or
its contents against theft and
vandalism.

security risk noun (plural
security risks) a person or
sequence of events thought likely
to threaten the security of
a project, country etc..

sedate adjective calm and
dignified. **sedately** adverb,
sedateness noun

sedate verb (**sedates**, **sedating**,
sedated) give a sedative to.
sedation noun [from Latin
sedatum = made calm]

sedative (say sed-a-tiv) noun
(plural **sedatives**) a medicine that
makes a person calm. [from Latin
sedare = settle]

sedentary (say sed-en-ter-ee) *adjective* done sitting down, *sedentary work*. [from Latin *sedens* = sitting]

sedge *noun* a grass-like plant growing in marshes or near water. [from Old English]

sediment *noun* fine particles of solid matter that float in liquid or sink to the bottom of it. [from Latin *sedere* = sit]

sedimentary *adjective* formed from particles that have settled on a surface, *sedimentary rocks*.

sedition *noun* speeches or actions intended to make people rebel against the authority of the State. **seditious** *adjective* [from *se-* + Latin *itio* = going]

seduce *verb* (**seduces, seducing, seduced**)
1 persuade a person to have sexual intercourse. 2 attract or lead astray by offering temptations. **seducer** *noun*, **seduction** *noun*, **seductive** *adjective* [from *se-* + Latin *ducere* = to lead]

see *verb* (**sees, seeing, saw, seen**)
1 perceive with the eyes. 2 meet or visit somebody, *See a doctor about your cough.* 3 understand, *She saw what I meant.* 4 imagine, *Can you see yourself as a teacher?* 5 consider, *I will see what can be done.* 6 make sure, *See that the windows are shut.* 7 discover, *See who is at the door.* 8 escort, *See her to the door.*
see through not be deceived by something.
see to attend to.

seed *noun* (*plural* **seeds** or **seed**)
1 a fertilized part of a plant, capable of growing into a new plant. 2 (*old use*) descendants. 3 a seeded player.

seed *verb* (**seeds, seeding, seeded**)
1 plant or sprinkle seeds in something. 2 name the best players and arrange for them not to play against each other in the early rounds of a tournament.

seedling *noun* (*plural* **seedlings**) a very young plant growing from a seed.

seedy *adjective* (**seedier, seediest**)
1 full of seeds. 2 shabby and disreputable. **seediness** *noun*

seeing *conjunction* considering, *Seeing that we have all finished, let's go.*

seek *verb* (**seeks, seeking, sought**)
1 search for. 2 try to obtain.

seem *verb* (**seems, seeming, seemed**) give the impression of being something, *She seems worried about her work.*
seemingly *adverb* [from Old Norse]

seemly *adjective* (*old use*) (of behaviour etc.) proper or suitable. **seemliness** *noun* [from an old sense of *seem* = be suitable]

seep *verb* (**seeps, seeping, seeped**) ooze slowly out or through something. **seepage** *noun* [probably from Old English]

see-saw *noun* (*plural* **see-saws**) a plank balanced in the middle so that two people can sit, one on each end, and make it go up and down. [from an old rhyme which imitated the rhythm of a saw going to and fro, later used by children on a see-saw]

seethe *verb* (seethes, seething, seethed)
1 bubble and surge like water boiling. 2 be very angry or excited. [from Old English]

segment *noun* (plural **segments**)
a part that is cut off or separates naturally from other parts, *the segments of an orange.*
segmented *adjective* [from Latin]

segregate *verb* (segregates, segregating, segregated)
1 separate people of different religions, races, etc. 2 isolate a person or thing. **segregation** *noun* [from *se-* + Latin *gregis* = from a flock]

seismic (*say* sy-zmik) *adjective* to do with earthquakes or other vibrations of the earth. [from Greek *seismos* = earthquake]

seize *verb* (seizes, seizing, seized)
1 take hold of a person or thing suddenly or forcibly. 2 take eagerly, *Seize your chance!* 3 have a sudden effect on, *Panic seized us.*
seize up become jammed, especially because of friction or overheating.
[via old French from Germanic]

seizure *noun* (plural **seizures**)
1 seizing. 2 a sudden fit, as in epilepsy or a heart attack.

seldom *adverb* rarely; not often. [from Old English]

select *verb* (selects, selecting, selected) choose a person or thing. **selector** *noun*

select *adjective*
1 carefully chosen, *a select group.*
2 (of a club etc.) choosing its members carefully; exclusive. [from *se-* + Latin *lectus* = collected]

selection *noun* (plural **selections**)
1 selecting; being selected. 2 a person or thing selected. 3 a group selected from a larger group. 4 a range of goods from which to choose.

self *noun* (plural **selves**)
1 a person as an individual. 2 a person's particular nature, *She has recovered and is her old self again.* 3 a person's own advantage, *He always puts self first.* [from Old English]

self- *prefix*
1 of or to or done by yourself or itself. 2 automatic (as in *self-loading*).

self-assured *adjective* confident.

self-centred *adjective* selfish.

self-confident *adjective* confident of your own abilities.

self-conscious *adjective* embarrassed or unnatural because you know that people are watching you.

self-contained *adjective* (of accommodation) complete in itself; containing all the necessary facilities.

self-control *noun* the ability to control your own behaviour. **self-controlled** *adjective*

self-denial *noun* deliberately going without things you would like to have.

self-determination *noun* a country's right to rule itself and to choose its own method of government.

self-employed *adjective* working independently, not for an employer.

self-esteem *noun* your own opinion of yourself and your own worth.

self-evident *adjective* obvious and not needing proof or explanation.

self-important *adjective* pompous.

selfish *adjective* doing what you want and not thinking of other people; keeping things for yourself. **selfishly** *adverb*, **selfishness** *noun*

selfless *adjective* unselfish.

self-made *adjective* rich or successful because of your own efforts.

self-pity *noun* too much sorrow and pity for yourself and your own problems.

self-possessed *adjective* calm and dignified.

self-raising *adjective* (of flour) making cakes rise without needing to have baking powder etc. added.

self-respect *noun* your own proper respect for yourself.

self-righteous *adjective* smugly sure that you are behaving virtuously.

self-service *adjective* where customers help themselves to things and pay a cashier for what they have taken.

self-sufficient *adjective* able to produce or provide what you need without help from others.

self-supporting *adjective* earning enough to keep yourself without needing money from others.

sell *verb* (**sells, selling, sold**) exchange something for money. **seller** *noun*

sell out 1 sell all your stock of something. **2** (*informal*) betray someone.

sell *noun*
1 (*informal*) a deception. **2** the manner of selling something.
hard sell *noun* forceful selling; putting pressure on someone to buy.
soft sell selling by suggestion or gentle persuasion.

sell-out *noun* (*plural* **sell-outs**) an entertainment, sporting event, etc. for which all the tickets have been sold.

selves *plural* of **self**.

semaphore *noun* a system of signalling by holding the arms in positions that indicate letters of the alphabet. [from Greek *sema* = sign + *-phoros* = carrying]

semen (*say* seem-en) *noun* a white liquid produced by males and containing sperm. [Latin, from *semere* = to sow]

semi *noun* (*plural* **semis**) (*informal*) a semi-detached house.

semi- *prefix*
1 half. **2** partly. [from Latin]

semibreve *noun* (*plural* **semibreves**) the longest musical note normally used (𝅝), lasting four times as long as a crotchet.

semicircle *noun* (*plural* **semicircles**) half a circle. **semicircular** *adjective*

semicolon *noun* (*plural* **semicolons**) a punctuation mark (;) used to mark a break that is more than that marked by a comma.

semiconductor noun (plural semiconductors) a substance that can conduct electricity but not as well as most metals do.

semi-detached adjective (of a house) joined to another house on one side only.

semifinal noun (plural semifinals) a match or round whose winner will take part in the final.

seminar noun (plural seminars) a meeting for advanced discussion and research on a subject. [German; related to seminary]

semiquaver noun (plural semiquavers) a note in music (♬), equal in length to one quarter of a crotchet.

Semitic (say sim-it-ik) adjective to do with the Semites, the group of people that includes the Jews and Arabs. **Semite** (say see-myt) noun

semitone noun (plural semitones) half a tone in music.

semolina noun hard round grains of wheat used to make milk puddings and pasta. [from Italian semola = bran]

senate noun (plural senates) 1 the governing council in ancient Rome. 2 the upper house of the parliament of the United States, France, and certain other countries. **senator** noun [from Latin senatus = council of elders]

send verb (sends, sending, sent) 1 make a person or thing go somewhere. 2 cause to become, It sent them mad. **sender** noun **send for** order a person or thing

to come or be brought to you.
send up (informal) make fun of something by imitating it.

senile (say seen-I'll) adjective weak or confused and forgetful because of old age. **senility** noun [from Latin senilis = old]

senior adjective 1 older than someone else. 2 higher in rank. 3 for older children, a senior school. **seniority** noun

senior noun (plural seniors) 1 a person who is older or higher in rank than you are, He is my senior. 2 a member of a senior school. [Latin, = older]

senior citizen noun (plural senior citizens) an elderly person, especially a pensioner.

sensation noun (plural sensations) 1 a feeling, a sensation of warmth. 2 a very excited condition; something causing this, The news caused a great sensation. [from Latin sensus = sense]

sensational adjective 1 causing great excitement, interest, or shock. 2 (informal) very good; wonderful. **sensationally** adverb

sense noun (plural senses) 1 the ability to see, hear, smell, touch, or taste things. 2 the ability to feel or appreciate something; awareness, a sense of humour. 3 the power to think or make wise decisions, He hasn't got the sense to come in out of the rain. 4 meaning, The word 'run' has many senses. **make sense 1** have a meaning. **2** be a sensible idea.

sense verb (senses, sensing, sensed)
1 feel; get an impression, *I sensed that she did not like me.* 2 detect something, *This device senses radioactivity.*
[from Latin]

senseless adjective
1 stupid; not showing good sense. 2 unconscious.

senses plural noun sanity, *He is out of his senses.*

sensible adjective wise; having or showing good sense. **sensibly** adverb

sensitive adjective
1 receiving impressions quickly and easily, *sensitive fingers.*
2 easily hurt or offended, *She is very sensitive about her age.*
3 affected by something, *Photographic paper is sensitive to light.* **sensitively** adverb, **sensitivity** noun

sensor noun (plural sensors)
a device or instrument for detecting a physical property such as light, heat, or sound.

sentence noun (plural sentences)
1 a group of words that express a complete thought and form a statement, question, exclamation, or command. 2 the punishment announced to a convicted person in a lawsuit.

sentence verb (sentences, sentencing, sentenced) give someone a sentence in a lawcourt, *The judge sentenced him to a year in prison.*
[from Latin *sententia* = opinion]

·ntentious adjective giving
··al advice in a pompous way.
·· ing as *sentence*]

sentiment noun (plural sentiments)
1 an opinion. 2 sentimentality.

sentimental adjective showing or arousing tenderness or romantic feeling or foolish emotion. **sentimentally** adverb, **sentimentality** noun

sentinel noun (plural sentinels)
a sentry. [via French from Italian]

sentry noun (plural sentries)
a soldier guarding something.

separate adjective
1 not joined to anything. 2 not shared. **separately** adverb

separate verb (separates, separating, separated)
1 make or keep separate; divide. 2 become separate. 3 stop living together as a married couple. **separation** noun, **separator** noun
[from *se-* + Latin *parare* = prepare]

septic adjective infected with harmful bacteria that cause pus to form. [from Greek *septikos* = made rotten]

sepulchre (say sep-ul-ker) noun (plural sepulchres) a tomb. [from Latin *sepultum* = buried]

sequel noun (plural sequels)
1 a book or film etc. that continues the story of an earlier one. 2 something that follows or results from an earlier event. [from Latin *sequi* = follow]

sequence noun (plural sequences)
1 the following of one thing after another; the order in which things happen. 2 a series of things. [from Latin *sequens* = following]

seraph *noun* (*plural* **seraphim** or **seraphs**) a kind of angel. [from Hebrew]

serenade *noun* (*plural* **serenades**) a song or tune played by a lover to his lady.

serenade *verb* (**serenades, serenading, serenaded**) sing or play a serenade to someone. [via French from Italian *sereno* = serene]

serene *adjective* calm and cheerful. **serenely** *adverb*, **serenity** *noun*

serf *noun* (*plural* **serfs**) a farm labourer who worked for a landowner in the Middle Ages, and who was not allowed to leave. **serfdom** *noun* [same origin as *servant*]

sergeant (*say* sar-jent) *noun* (*plural* **sergeants**) a soldier or policeman who is in charge of others. [from old French; related to *serve*]

sergeant major *noun* (*plural* **sergeant majors**) a soldier who is one rank higher than a sergeant. [from *sergeant* + *major* = greater]

serial *noun* (*plural* **serials**) a story or film etc. that is presented in separate parts. [from *series*]

USAGE: Do not confuse with *cereal*.

serial killer *noun* (*plural* **serial killers**) a person who commits a series of murders for no apparent reason.

serial number *noun* (*plural* **serial numbers**) a number put onto an object, usually by the manufacturers, to distinguish it from other identical objects.

series *noun* (*plural* **series**)
1 a number of things following or connected with each other.
2 a number of games or matches between the same competitors.
3 a number of separate radio or television programmes with the same characters or on the same subject. [Latin, = row or chain]

serious *adjective*
1 solemn and thoughtful; not smiling. 2 sincere; not casual; not light-hearted, *a serious attempt*.
3 causing anxiety, not trivial, *a serious accident*. **seriously** *adverb*, **seriousness** *noun* [from Latin]

sermon *noun* (*plural* **sermons**) a talk given by a preacher, especially as part of a religious service. [from Latin *sermo* = talk, conversation]

serpent *noun* (*plural* **serpents**) a snake. [from Latin *serpens* = creeping]

serried *adjective* arranged in rows close together, *serried ranks of troops*. [from Latin *serere* = join together]

servant *noun* (*plural* **servants**) a person whose job is to work or serve in someone else's house. [from Latin *servus* = slave]

serve *verb* (**serves, serving, served**)
1 work for a person or organization or country etc. 2 sell things to people in a shop. 3 give out food to people at a meal. 4 spend time in something; undergo, *He served a prison sentence*. 5 be suitable for something, *This will serve our purpose*. 6 start play in tennis etc.

by hitting the ball. **server** *noun*
it serves you right you deserve it.
serve *noun* (*plural* **serves**) a
service in tennis etc.
[same origin as *servant*]

service *noun* (*plural* **services**)
1 working for a person or
organization or country etc. **2**
something that helps people or
supplies what they want, *a bus
service*. **3** the army, navy, or air
force, *the armed services*.
4 a religious ceremony.
5 providing people with goods,
food, etc., *quick service*. **6** a set of
dishes and plates etc. for a meal,
a dinner service. **7** the servicing of
a vehicle or machine etc. **8** the
action of serving in tennis etc.
service *verb* (**services, servicing,
serviced**)
1 repair or keep a vehicle or
machine etc. in working order.
2 supply with services.
[from Latin *servitium* = slavery]

serviceable *adjective* usable;
suitable for ordinary use or
wear.

services *plural noun* an area
beside a main road with a garage,
shop, restaurant, lavatories, etc.
for travellers to use.

serviette *noun* (*plural* **serviettes**)
a piece of cloth or paper used to
keep your clothes or hands clean
at a meal. [French, from *servir*
= to serve]

serving *noun* (*plural* **servings**)
a helping of food.

session *noun* (*plural* **sessions**)
1 a meeting or series of meetings,
*The Queen will open the next
session of Parliament*. **2** a time

spent doing one thing, *a recording
session*. [from Latin *sessio*
= sitting]

set *verb* (**sets, setting, set**) This
word has many uses, including
1 put or fix (*Set the vase on the
table. Set a date for the wedding*),
2 make or become firm or hard
(*Leave the jelly to set*), **3** give
someone a task (*This sets us
a problem*), **4** put into a condition
(*Set them free*), **5** go down below
the horizon (*The sun was setting*).
set about 1 start doing
something. **2** (*informal*) attack
somebody.
set off 1 begin a journey. **2** start
something happening. **3** cause
something to explode.
set out 1 begin a journey.
2 display or make known.
set sail begin a voyage.
set to 1 begin doing something
vigorously. **2** begin fighting or
arguing.
set up 1 place in position.
2 establish, *set up house*. **3** cause
or start, *set up a din*.

set *noun* (*plural* **sets**)
1 a group of people or things that
belong together. **2** a radio or
television receiver. **3** the way
something is placed, *the set of his
jaw*. **4** a badger's burrow. **5** the
scenery or stage for a play or
film. **6** a group of games in
a tennis match.
[from Old English]

setback *noun* (*plural* **setbacks**)
something that stops progress or
slows it down.

set book *noun* (*plural* **set books**)
a book that must be studied for
a literature examination.

set square noun (plural **set squares**) a device shaped like a right-angled triangle, used in drawing lines parallel to each other etc.

settee noun (plural **settees**) a long soft seat with a back and arms.

setter noun (plural **setters**) a dog of a long-haired breed that can be trained to stand rigid when it scents game.

setting noun (plural **settings**) **1** the way or place in which something is set. **2** music for the words of a song etc.

settle verb (**settles, settling, settled**)
1 arrange; decide or solve something, *That settles the problem.* **2** make or become calm or comfortable or orderly; stop being restless, *Stop chattering and settle down!* **3** go and live somewhere, *They settled in Canada.* **4** sink; come to rest on something, *Dust had settled on his books.* **5** pay a bill or debt.

settlement noun (plural **settlements**)
1 settling something. **2** the way something is settled. **3** a small number of people or houses established in a new area.

set-up noun (*informal*) the way something is organized or arranged.

seven adjective & noun (plural **sevens**) the number 7. **seventh** adjective & noun

seventeen noun & adjective the number 17. **seventeenth** adjective & noun

seventy adjective & noun (plural **seventies**) the number 70. **seventieth** adjective & noun

several adjective & noun more than two but not many.

severe adjective
1 strict; not gentle or kind. **2** intense or forceful, *severe gales.* **3** very plain, *a severe style of dress.* **severely** adverb, **severity** noun

sew verb (**sews, sewing, sewed, sewn** or **sewed**)
1 join things together by using a needle and thread. **2** work with a needle and thread or with a sewing machine. [from Old English]

USAGE: Do not confuse with *sow.*

sewage (*say* soo-ij) noun liquid waste matter carried away in drains.

sewer (*say* soo-er) noun (plural **sewers**) a large underground drain for carrying away sewage. [from old French]

sewing machine noun (plural **sewing machines**) a machine for sewing things.

sex noun (plural **sexes**)
1 each of the two groups (**male** and **female**) into which living things are placed according to their functions in the process of reproduction. **2** the instinct that causes members of the two sexes to be attracted to one another. **3** sexual intercourse.

sexism noun discrimination against people of a particular sex, especially women. **sexist** adjective & noun

sexual *adjective*
1 to do with sex or the sexes. **2** (of reproduction) happening by the fusion of male and female cells.
sexually *adverb*, **sexuality** *noun*

sexual intercourse *noun* an intimate act between two people, in which the man puts his penis into the woman's vagina, to express love, for pleasure, or to conceive a child.

sexy *adjective* (**sexier, sexiest**) (*informal*)
1 sexually attractive. **2** concerned with sex.

SF *abbreviation* science fiction.

shabby *adjective* (**shabbier, shabbiest**)
1 in a poor or worn-out condition; dilapidated. **2** poorly dressed. **3** unfair or dishonourable, *a shabby trick.* **shabbily** *adverb*, **shabbiness** *noun* [from Old English *sceabb* = scab]

shack *noun* (*plural* **shacks**) a roughly-built hut. [probably from a Mexican word]

shackle *noun* (*plural* **shackles**) an iron ring for fastening a prisoner's wrist or ankle to something.
shackle *verb* (**shackles, shackling, shackled**) put shackles on a prisoner.

shade *noun* (*plural* **shades**)
1 slight darkness produced where something blocks the sun's light. **2** a device that reduces or shuts out bright light. **3** a colour; how light or dark a colour is. **4** a slight difference, *The word had several shades of meaning.* **5** (*poetical*) a ghost.

shade *verb* (**shades, shading, shaded**)
1 shelter something from bright light. **2** make part of a drawing darker than the rest. **3** move gradually from one state or quality to another, *evening shading into night.*
[from Old English *sceadu*]

shadow *noun* (*plural* **shadows**)
1 the dark shape that falls on a surface when something is between the surface and a light. **2** an area of shade. **shadowy** *adjective*

shadow *verb* (**shadows, shadowing, shadowed**)
1 cast a shadow on something. **2** follow a person secretly.
[same origin as *shade*]

Shadow Cabinet *noun* members of the Opposition in Parliament who act as spokesmen on important matters.

shady *adjective* (**shadier, shadiest**)
1 giving shade, *a shady tree.* **2** in the shade, *a shady place.* **3** not completely honest; disreputable, *a shady deal.*

shaft *noun* (*plural* **shafts**)
1 a long slender rod or straight part, *the shaft of an arrow.* **2** a ray of light. **3** a deep narrow hole, *a mine shaft.*

shaggy *adjective* (**shaggier, shaggiest**)
1 having long rough hair or fibre. **2** rough, thick, and untidy, *shaggy hair.*

shake *verb* (**shakes, shaking, shook, shaken**)
1 move quickly up and down or from side to side. **2** disturb; shock; upset, *The news shook us.* **3** tremble; be unsteady, *His voice*

was shaking. **shaker** *noun*
shake hands clasp a person's
right hand with yours in greeting
or parting or as a sign of
agreement.
shake *noun (plural* **shakes**)
1 shaking; a shaking movement.
2 *(informal)* a moment, *I'll be
there in two shakes.* **shaky**
adjective, **shakily** *adverb*
shall *auxiliary verb*
1 used with *I* and *we* to express
the ordinary future tense, e.g.
I shall arrive tomorrow, and in
questions, e.g. *Shall I shut the
door?* (but *will* is used with other
words, e.g. *they will arrive; will
you shut the door?*). **2** used with
words other than *I* and *we* in
promises, e.g. *Cinderella, you
shall go to the ball!* (but *I will go*
= I promise or intend to go).
[from Old English]

USAGE: If you want to be
strictly correct, keep to the
rules given here, but
nowadays many people use
will after *I* and *we* and it is not
usually regarded as wrong.

shallow *adjective (***shallower,
shallowest***)*
1 not deep, *shallow water.* **2** not
capable of deep feelings, *a shallow
character.* **shallowness** *noun*
[origin unknown]

sham *noun (plural* **shams**)
something that is not genuine;
a pretence. **sham** *adjective*
sham *verb (***shams, shamming,
shammed***)* pretend.
[probably from *shame*]

shamble *verb (***shambles,
shambling, shambled***)* walk or
run in a lazy or awkward way.

shame *noun*
1 a feeling of great sorrow or
guilt because you have done
wrong. **2** dishonour or disgrace.
3 something you regret, *It's
a shame that it rained.* **shameful**
adjective, **shamefully** *adverb*
shame *verb (***shames, shaming,
shamed***)* make a person feel
ashamed.

shameless *adjective* not feeling
or looking ashamed. **shamelessly**
adverb

shampoo *noun (plural*
shampoos)
1 a liquid substance for washing
the hair. **2** a substance for
cleaning a carpet etc. or washing
a car. **3** a wash with shampoo,
a shampoo and set.
shampoo *verb (***shampoos,
shampooing, shampooed***)* wash
or clean with a shampoo.
[originally = to massage: from
Hindi *champo* = press]

shan't *(mainly spoken)* shall not.

shanty[1] *noun (plural* **shanties**)
a shack. [from Canadian French]
shanty[2] *noun (plural* **shanties**)
a sailors' song with a chorus.
[probably from French *chanter*
= sing]

shanty town *noun (plural* **shanty
towns**) a settlement consisting of
shanties.

shape *noun (plural* **shapes**)
1 a thing's outline; the
appearance an outline produces.
2 proper form or condition, *Get it
into shape.* **3** the general form or
condition of something, *the shape
of British industry.*
shape *verb (***shapes, shaping,
shaped***)*
1 make into a particular shape.

2 develop, *It's shaping up nicely.*
[from Old English]

shapeless *adjective* having no definite shape.

shapely *adjective* (**shapelier**, **shapeliest**) having an attractive shape.

share *noun* (*plural* **shares**)
1 a part given to one person or thing out of something that is being divided. 2 each of the equal parts forming a business company's capital, giving the person who holds it the right to receive a portion (a *dividend*) of the company's profits.

share *verb* (**shares**, **sharing**, **shared**)
1 give portions of something to two or more people. 2 have or use or experience something that others have too, *share a room*; *share the responsibility.*

shark *noun* (*plural* **sharks**) a large sea fish with sharp teeth.

sharp *adjective*
1 with an edge or point that can cut or make holes. 2 quick at noticing or learning things, *sharp eyes.* 3 steep or pointed; not gradual, *a sharp bend.* 4 forceful or severe, *a sharp frost.* 5 distinct; loud and shrill, *a sharp cry.* 6 slightly sour. 7 (in music) one semitone higher than the natural note, *C sharp.* **sharply** *adverb*, **sharpness** *noun*

sharp *adverb*
1 sharply, *turn sharp right.* 2 punctually, *at six o'clock sharp.* 3 (in music) above the correct pitch, *You were singing sharp.*

sharp *noun* (*plural* **sharps**) (in music) a note one semitone

higher than the natural note; the sign (#) that indicates this. [from Old English]

sharpen *verb* (**sharpens**, **sharpening**, **sharpened**) make or become sharp. **sharpener** *noun*

sharp practice *noun* dishonest or barely honest dealings in business.

shatter *verb* (**shatters**, **shattering**, **shattered**)
1 break violently into small pieces. 2 destroy, *It shattered our hopes.* 3 upset greatly, *We were shattered by the news.*

shave *verb* (**shaves**, **shaving**, **shaved**)
1 scrape growing hair off the skin. 2 cut or scrape a thin slice off something. **shaver** *noun*

shave *noun* (*plural* **shaves**) the act of shaving the face.
close shave (*informal*) a narrow escape.

shavings *plural noun* thin strips shaved off a piece of wood or metal.

shawl *noun* (*plural* **shawls**) a large piece of material worn round the shoulders or head or wrapped round a baby. [from Persian or Urdu]

she *pronoun* the female person or animal being talked about. [Middle English; related to *he*]

sheaf *noun* (*plural* **sheaves**)
1 a bundle of cornstalks tied together. 2 a bundle of arrows, papers, etc. held together. [from Old English]

shear *verb* (**shears**, **shearing**, **sheared**, **sheared** or, in sense 1, **shorn**)
1 cut or trim; cut the wool off a sheep. 2 break because of

a sideways or twisting force, *the bolts sheared off.* **shearer** noun [from Old English]

USAGE: Do not confuse with *sheer.*

shears plural noun a cutting tool shaped like a very large pair of scissors and worked with both hands.

sheath noun (plural **sheaths**)
1 a close-fitting cover. **2** a cover for the blade of a knife or sword etc. **3** a condom.

shed[1] noun (plural **sheds**)
a simply-made building used for storing things or sheltering animals, or as a workshop. [from *shade*]

shed[2] verb (**sheds, shedding, shed**)
1 let something fall or flow, *The tree shed its leaves. We shed tears.*
2 give off, *A heater sheds warmth.*
3 get rid of, *The company has shed 200 workers.* [from Old English]

sheen noun a shine or gloss. [from Old English *sciene* = beautiful]

sheep noun (plural **sheep**) an animal that eats grass and has a thick fleecy coat, kept in flocks for its wool and its meat. [from Old English]

sheepdog noun (plural **sheepdogs**) a dog trained to guard and herd sheep.

sheepish adjective
1 bashful. **2** embarrassed or shamefaced. **sheepishly** adverb, **sheepishness** noun [originally = innocent or silly: from *sheep* + *-ish*]

sheer[1] adjective
1 complete or thorough, *sheer stupidity.* **2** vertical, with almost no slope, *a sheer drop.*
3 (of material) very thin; transparent. [from Old English *scir* = shining, noble, or pure]

sheer[2] verb (**sheers, sheering, sheered**) swerve; move sharply away. [probably from old German]

USAGE: Do not confuse with *shear.*

sheet noun (plural **sheets**)
1 a large piece of lightweight material used on a bed in pairs for a person to sleep between.
2 a whole flat piece of paper, glass, or metal. **3** a wide area of water, ice, flame, etc. [from Old English *scete*]

sheikh (say shayk or sheek) noun (plural **sheikhs**) the leader of an Arab tribe or village. [from Arabic *shaykh* = elder, old man]

shelf noun (plural **shelves**)
1 a flat piece of wood, metal, or glass etc. fixed to a wall or in a piece of furniture so that things can be placed on it. **2** a flat level surface that sticks out; a ledge.

shell noun (plural **shells**)
1 the hard outer covering of a nut, egg, snail, tortoise, etc. **2** the walls or framework of a building, ship, etc. **3** a metal case filled with explosive, fired from a large gun.

shell verb (**shells, shelling, shelled**)
1 take something out of its shell.
2 fire explosive shells at something.
shell out (*informal*) pay out money.

shellfish noun (plural **shellfish**) a sea animal that has a shell.

shelter noun (plural **shelters**)
1 something that protects people from rain, wind, danger, etc.
2 protection, Seek shelter from the rain.

shelter verb (**shelters, sheltering, sheltered**)
1 provide with shelter. 2 protect. 3 find a shelter, They sheltered under the trees.

shelve verb (**shelves, shelving, shelved**)
1 put things on a shelf or shelves. 2 fit a wall or cupboard etc. with shelves. 3 postpone or reject a plan etc. 4 slope, The bed of the river shelves steeply. [from shelf]

shepherd noun (plural **shepherds**) a person whose job is to look after sheep.

shepherd verb (**shepherds, shepherding, shepherded**) guide or direct people.
[from sheep + herd]

sheriff noun (plural **sheriffs**) the chief law officer of a county, whose duties vary in different countries. [from Old English scir = shire + refa = officer]

sherry noun (plural **sherries**) a kind of strong wine. [named after Jerez de la Frontera, a town in Spain, where it was first made]

Shetland pony noun (plural **Shetland ponies**) a kind of small, strong, shaggy pony, originally from the Shetland Isles.

shield noun (plural **shields**)
1 a large piece of metal, wood, etc. carried to protect the body. 2 a model of a triangular shield used as a trophy. 3 a protection.

shield verb (**shields, shielding, shielded**) protect from harm or from being discovered.

shift verb (**shifts, shifting, shifted**)
1 move or cause to move. 2 (of an opinion or situation) change slightly.

shift for yourself manage without help; rely on your own efforts.

shift noun (plural **shifts**)
1 a change of position or condition etc. 2 a group of workers who start work as another group finishes; the time when they work, the night shift. 3 a straight dress with no waist. [from Old English]

shifty adjective evasive, not straightforward; untrustworthy.
shiftily adverb; **shiftiness** noun

shilling noun (plural **shillings**) a former British coin, = 5p.

shilly-shally verb (**shilly-shallies, shilly-shallying, shilly-shallied**) be unable to make up your mind. [from shall I? shall I?]

shimmer verb (**shimmers, shimmering, shimmered**) shine with a quivering light, The sea shimmered in the moonlight.
shimmer noun

shin noun (plural **shins**) the front of the leg between the knee and the ankle.

shin verb (**shins, shinning, shinned**) climb by using the arms and legs, not on a ladder. [from Old English]

shine verb (**shines, shining, shone, or in sense 4, shined**)
1 give out or reflect light; be bright. 2 be excellent, He doesn't shine in maths. 3 aim a light, Shine your torch on it. 4 polish, Have you shined your shoes?

shingle noun pebbles on a beach. [origin unknown]

shiny *adjective* (**shinier, shiniest**) shining or glossy.

ship *noun* (*plural* **ships**) a large boat, especially one that goes to sea.

ship *verb* (**ships, shipping, shipped**) transport goods etc., especially by ship.

-ship *suffix* forms nouns meaning 'condition' (e.g. *friendship, hardship*), position (e.g. *chairmanship*), or skill (e.g. *seamanship*). [from Old English]

shipping *noun*
1 ships, *Britain's shipping*.
2 transporting goods by ship.

shipshape *adjective* in good order; tidy.

shipwreck *noun* (*plural* **shipwrecks**)
1 the wrecking of a ship by storm or accident. 2 a wrecked ship.
shipwrecked *adjective*

shipyard *noun* (*plural* **shipyards**) a place where ships are built or repaired.

shire *noun* (*plural* **shires**) a county.
the Shires the country areas of (especially central) England, away from the cities.

shirk *verb* (**shirks, shirking, shirked**) avoid a duty or work etc. selfishly or unfairly. **shirker** *noun* [probably from German *Schurke* = scoundrel]

shirt *noun* (*plural* **shirts**) a piece of clothing for the top half of the body, made of light material and with a collar and sleeves.
in your shirtsleeves not wearing a jacket over your shirt.

shiver *verb* (**shivers, shivering, shivered**) tremble with cold or fear. **shiver** *noun*, **shivery** *adjective* [origin unknown]

shoal[1] *noun* (*plural* **shoals**) a large number of fish swimming together. [same origin as *school*[2]]

shoal[2] *noun* (*plural* **shoals**)
1 a shallow place. 2 an underwater sandbank. [from Old English]

shock[1] *noun* (*plural* **shocks**)
1 a sudden unpleasant surprise.
2 great weakness caused by pain or injury etc. 3 the effect of a violent shake or knock. 4 an effect caused by electric current passing through the body.

shock *verb* (**shocks, shocking, shocked**)
1 give someone a shock; surprise or upset a person greatly. 2 seem very improper or scandalous to a person.
[from French]

shock[2] *noun* (*plural* **shocks**) a bushy mass of hair. [origin unknown]

shocking *adjective*
1 causing indignation or disgust.
2 (*informal*) very bad, *shocking weather*.

shock wave *noun* (*plural* **shock waves**) a sharp change in pressure in the air around an explosion or an object moving very quickly.

shod *past tense* of **shoe**.

shoddy *adjective* (**shoddier, shoddiest**) of poor quality; badly made or done, *shoddy work*.
shoddily *adverb*, **shoddiness** *noun*

shoe *noun* (*plural* **shoes**)
1 a strong covering for the foot.
2 a horseshoe. 3 something

shaped or used like a shoe.
be in somebody's shoes be in his or her situation.

shoe verb (**shoes, shoeing, shod**) fit with a shoe or shoes.
[from Old English]

shoelace noun (plural **shoelaces**) a cord for lacing up and fastening a shoe.

shoot verb (**shoots, shooting, shot**)
1 fire a gun or missile etc. 2 hurt or kill by shooting. 3 move or send very quickly, *The car shot past us.* 4 kick or hit a ball at a goal. 5 (of a plant) put out buds or shoots. 6 slide the bolt of a door into or out of its fastening. 7 film or photograph something, *They shot the film in Africa.*

shoot noun (plural **shoots**)
1 a young branch or new growth of a plant. 2 an expedition for shooting animals.

shooting star noun (plural **shooting stars**) a meteor.

shop noun (plural **shops**)
1 a building or room where goods or services are on sale to the public. 2 a workshop. 3 talk that is about your own work or job, *She is always talking shop.*

shop verb (**shops, shopping, shopped**) go and buy things at shops. **shopper** noun
shop around compare goods and prices in several shops before buying.

shop floor noun
1 the workers in a factory, not the managers. 2 the place where they work.

shopkeeper noun (plural **shopkeepers**) a person who owns or manages a shop.

shoplifter noun (plural **shoplifters**) a person who steals goods from a shop after entering as a customer. **shoplifting** noun

shopping noun 1 buying goods in shops. 2 the goods bought.

shore¹ noun (plural **shores**) the land along the edge of a sea or of a lake. [from old German or old Italian *schore*]

shore² verb (**shores, shoring, shored**) prop something up with a piece of wood etc. [from old German or old Italian *schoren*]

shorn past participle of **shear**.

short adjective
1 not long; occupying a small distance or time, *a short walk.*
2 not tall, *a short person.* 3 not enough; not having enough of something, *We are short of water.*
4 curt. 5 (of pastry) rich and crumbly because it contains a lot of fat. **shortness** noun
for short as an abbreviation, *Raymond is called Ray for short.*
short for an abbreviation of, *'Ray' is short for Raymond.*

short adverb suddenly, *She stopped short.*

shortage noun (plural **shortages**) lack or scarcity of something; insufficiency.

shortbread noun a rich sweet biscuit, made with butter.

short circuit noun (plural **short circuits**) a fault in an electrical circuit in which current flows along a shorter route than the normal one. **short-circuit** verb

shortcoming noun (plural **shortcomings**) a fault or failure to reach a good standard.

short cut *noun (plural* **short cuts)**
a route or method that is quicker
than the usual one.

shorten *verb* (**shortens,**
shortening, shortened) make or
become shorter.

shorthand *noun* a set of special
signs for writing words down as
quickly as people say them.

short-handed *adjective* not
having enough workers or staff.

shortly *adverb*
1 in a short time; soon, *They will
arrive shortly.* 2 in a few words.
3 curtly.

shorts *plural noun* trousers with
legs that do not reach to the knee.

short-sighted *adjective*
1 unable to see things clearly.
2 lacking imagination or
foresight.

short-tempered *adjective* easily
becoming angry.

shot[1] *past tense of* **shoot.**

shot[2] *noun (plural* **shots)**
1 the firing of a gun or missile
etc.; the sound of this.
2 something fired from a gun;
lead pellets for firing from small
guns. 3 a person judged by skill
in shooting, *He's a good shot.*
4 a heavy metal ball thrown as
a sport. 5 a stroke in tennis,
cricket, billiards, etc.
6 a photograph; a filmed scene.
7 an attempt, *Have a shot at the
crossword.* 8 an injection of a drug
or vaccine.

shot *adjective* (of fabric) woven
so that different colours show at
different angles, *shot silk.*

should *auxiliary verb* used to
express
1 obligation or duty, = ought to
(*You should have told me*),

2 something expected (*They
should be here by ten o'clock*),
3 a possible event (*if you should
happen to see him*), 4 with *I* and
we to make a polite statement (*I
should like to come*) or in
a conditional clause (*If they had
supported us we should have
won*). [past tense of *shall*]

USAGE: In sense **4**, although
should is strictly correct,
many people nowadays use
would and this is not regarded
as wrong.

shoulder *noun (plural* **shoulders)**
1 the part of the body between
the neck and the arm, foreleg, or
wing. 2 a side that juts out, *the
shoulder of the bottle.*

shoulder *verb* (**shoulders,**
shouldering, shouldered)
1 take something on your
shoulder or shoulders. 2 push
with your shoulder. 3 accept
responsibility or blame.

shoulder blade *noun (plural*
shoulder blades) either of the two
large flat bones at the top of your
back.

shouldn't (*mainly spoken*) should
not.

shout *noun (plural* **shouts**) a loud
cry or call.

shout *verb* (**shouts, shouting,**
shouted) give a shout; speak or
call loudly.

shove *verb* (**shoves, shoving,**
shoved) push roughly. ● *noun*

shove off (*informal*) go away.

shovel *noun (plural* **shovels)**
a tool like a spade with the sides
turned up, used for lifting coal,
earth, snow, etc.

shovel verb (shovels, shovelling, shovelled)
1 move or clear with a shovel.
2 scoop or push roughly, *He was shovelling food into his mouth.*
[from Old English]

show verb (shows, showing, showed, shown)
1 allow or cause something to be seen, *Show me your new bike.*
2 make a person understand; demonstrate, *Show me how to use it.* 3 guide, *Show him in.* 4 treat in a certain way, *She showed us much kindness.* 5 be visible, *That scratch won't show.* 6 prove your ability to someone, *We'll show them!*
show off 1 show something proudly. 2 try to impress people.
show up 1 make or be clearly visible; reveal a fault etc.
2 (informal) arrive.
show noun (plural shows)
1 a display or exhibition, *a flower show.* 2 an entertainment.
3 (slang) something that happens or is done, *He runs the whole show.*
[from Old English]

showdown noun (plural showdowns) a final test or confrontation.

shower noun (plural showers)
1 a brief fall of rain or snow. 2 a lot of small things coming or falling like rain, *a shower of stones.*
3 a device or cabinet for spraying water to wash a person's body; a wash in this.
shower verb (showers, showering, showered)
1 fall or send things in a shower.
2 wash under a shower.
[from Old English]

showman noun (plural showmen)
1 a person who presents entertainments. 2 someone who is good at attracting attention. **showmanship** noun

showpiece noun (plural showpieces) a fine example of something for people to see and admire.

showy adjective (showier, showiest) likely to attract attention; brightly or highly decorated. **showily** adverb, **showiness** noun

shrapnel noun pieces of metal scattered from an exploding shell. [named after H. Shrapnel, a British officer who invented it in about 1806]

shred noun (plural shreds)
1 a tiny piece torn or cut off something. 2 a small amount, *There is not a shred of evidence.*
shred verb (shreds, shredding, shredded) cut into shreds. **shredder** noun

shrew noun (plural shrews)
1 a small mouse-like animal.
2 (old use) a bad-tempered woman who is constantly scolding people. **shrewish** adjective

shrewd adjective having common sense and good judgement; clever. **shrewdly** adverb, **shrewdness** noun [from old sense of *shrew* = spiteful or cunning person]

shriek noun (plural shrieks) a shrill cry or scream.
shriek verb (shrieks, shrieking, shrieked) give a shriek. [imitating the sound]

shrill *adjective* sounding very high and piercing. **shrilly** *adverb*, **shrillness** *noun*

shrimp *noun* (*plural* **shrimps**) a small shellfish, pink when boiled.

shrine *noun* (*plural* **shrines**) an altar, chapel, or other sacred place. [originally = a container for holy relics; via Old English from Latin *scrinium* = a case or chest]

shrink *verb* (**shrinks**, **shrinking**, **shrank**, **shrunk**)
1 make or become smaller.
2 move back to avoid something.
3 avoid doing something because of fear, conscience, embarrassment, etc. **shrinkage** *noun*, **shrunken** *adjective*

shrivel *verb* (**shrivels**, **shrivelling**, **shrivelled**) make or become dry and wrinkled.

shroud *noun* (*plural* **shrouds**)
1 a cloth in which a dead body is wrapped. 2 each of a set of ropes supporting a ship's mast.

shrub *noun* (*plural* **shrubs**) a woody plant smaller than a tree; a bush. **shrubby** *adjective* [from Old English]

shrubbery *noun* (*plural* **shrubberies**) an area planted with shrubs.

shrug *verb* (**shrugs**, **shrugging**, **shrugged**) raise your shoulders as a sign that you do not care, do not know, etc. **shrug** *noun* **shrug something off** treat it as unimportant.

shudder *verb* (**shudders**, **shuddering**, **shuddered**)
1 shiver violently with horror, fear, or cold. 2 make a strong shaking movement. **shudder** *noun*

shuffle *verb* (**shuffles**, **shuffling**, **shuffled**)
1 walk without lifting the feet from the ground. 2 slide playing cards over each other to get them into random order. 3 shift or rearrange. **shuffle** *noun*

shun *verb* (**shuns**, **shunning**, **shunned**) avoid; deliberately keep away from something. [from Old English]

shunt *verb* (**shunts**, **shunting**, **shunted**) move a train or wagons on to another track; divert. **shunt** *noun*, **shunter** *noun*

shut *verb* (**shuts**, **shutting**, **shut**)
1 move a door, lid, or cover etc. so that it blocks an opening; make or become closed. 2 bring or fold parts together, *Shut the book.*
shut down 1 stop something working. 2 stop business.
shut up 1 shut securely.
2 (*informal*) stop talking or making a noise.

shutter *noun* (*plural* **shutters**)
1 a panel or screen that can be closed over a window. 2 the device in a camera that opens and closes to let light fall on the film. **shuttered** *adjective* [from *shut*]

shuttle *noun* (*plural* **shuttles**)
1 a holder carrying the weft-thread across a loom in weaving. 2 a train, bus, or aircraft that makes frequent short journeys between two points.
shuttle *verb* (**shuttles**, **shuttling**, **shuttled**) move, travel, or send backwards and forwards. [from Old English]

shy adjective (**shyer, shyest**) afraid to meet or talk to other people; timid. **shyly** adverb, **shyness** noun

SI noun an internationally recognized system of metric units of measurement, including the metre and kilogram. [short for French *Système International d'Unités* = International System of Units]

Siamese twins plural noun twins who are born with their bodies joined together. [after two famous twins born in Siam (now called Thailand), who were joined near the waist]

sick adjective
1 ill; physically or mentally unwell. **2** vomiting or likely to vomit, *I feel sick.* **3** distressed or disgusted. **4** making fun of death, disability, or misfortune in an unpleasant way.
sick of tired of.

sicken verb (**sickens, sickening, sickened**)
1 begin to be ill. **2** make or become distressed or disgusted, *Vandalism sickens us all.*
sickening adjective

sickle noun (plural **sickles**)
1 a tool with a narrow curved blade, used for cutting corn etc. **2** something shaped like this blade, e.g. the crescent moon.

sickly adjective
1 often ill; unhealthy. **2** making people feel sick, *a sickly smell.* **3** weak, *a sickly smile.*

sickness noun (plural **sicknesses**)
1 illness. **2** a disease. **3** vomiting.

side noun (plural **sides**)
1 a surface, especially one joining the top and bottom of something.
2 a line that forms part of the boundary of a triangle, square, etc. **3** either of the two halves into which something can be divided by a line down its centre. **4** the part near the edge and away from the centre. **5** the place or region next to a person or thing, *He stood at my side.* **6** one aspect or view of something, *Study all sides of the problem.* **7** one of two groups or teams etc. who oppose each other.
on the side as a sideline.
side by side next to each other.

side verb (**sides, siding, sided**)
side with take a person's side in an argument.

side effect noun (plural **side effects**) an effect, especially an unpleasant one, that a medicine has on you as well as the effect intended.

sidelight noun (plural **sidelights**)
1 a light at the side of a vehicle or ship. **2** light from one side.

sideline noun (plural **sidelines**)
1 something done in addition to the main work or activity. **2** a line at the side of a football pitch etc.; the area just outside this.

sidelong adjective towards one side; sideways, *a sidelong glance.* [from *side* + Old English *-ling* = extending in a certain direction]

sidetrack verb (**sidetracks, sidetracking, sidetracked**) take someone's attention away from the main subject or problem.

sideways adverb & adjective
1 to or from one side, *Move it sideways.* **2** with one side facing forwards, *We sat sideways in the bus.*

siding noun (plural **sidings**)
a short railway line by the side of
a main line.

siege noun (plural **sieges**) the
besieging of a place.

lay siege to begin besieging.

sieve (say siv) noun (plural
sieves) a device made of mesh or
perforated metal or plastic, used
to separate the smaller or soft
parts of something from the
larger or hard parts.

sieve verb (**sieves, sieving,
sieved**) put something through
a sieve.

sift verb (**sifts, sifting, sifted**)
1 sieve. **2** examine and analyse
facts or evidence etc. carefully.
sifter noun

sigh noun (plural **sighs**) a sound
made by breathing out heavily
when you are sad, tired, relieved,
etc.

sigh verb (**sighs, sighing, sighed**)
make a sigh.
[probably from Old English]

sight noun (plural **sights**)
1 the ability to see. **2** a thing that
can be seen or is worth seeing,
Our roses are a wonderful sight.
3 an unsightly thing, *You do look
a sight in those clothes!* **4** a device
looked through to help aim a gun
or telescope etc.

at sight or **on sight** as soon as
a person or thing has been seen.

in sight 1 visible. **2** clearly near,
Victory was in sight.

USAGE: Do not confuse with
site.

sight verb (**sights, sighting,
sighted**)
1 see or observe something. **2** aim
a gun or telescope etc.

sight-reading noun playing or
singing music at sight, without
preparation.

sightseeing noun visiting
interesting places in a town etc.
sightseer noun

sign noun (plural **signs**)
1 something that shows that
a thing exists, *There are signs of
decay.* **2** a mark, device, or notice
etc. that gives a special meaning,
a road sign. **3** an action or
movement giving information or
a command etc. **4** any of the
twelve divisions of the zodiac,
represented by a symbol.

sign verb (**signs, signing, signed**)
1 make a sign or signal. **2** write
your signature on something;
accept a contract etc. by doing
this. **3** use signing.

sign on 1 accept a job etc. by
signing a contract. **2** sign a form
to say that you are unemployed
and want to claim benefit.
[from Latin *signum* = sign]

signal noun (plural **signals**)
1 a device, gesture, or sound etc.
that gives information or
a command. **2** a message made up
of such things. **3** a sequence of
electrical impulses or radio
waves.

signal verb (**signals, signalling,
signalled**) make a signal to
somebody. **signaller** noun

USAGE: Do not use this word
in mistake for *single* in the
phrase *to single out.*

signal box noun (plural **signal
boxes**) a building from which
railway signals, points, etc. are
controlled.

signature *noun* (*plural signatures*) a person's name written by himself or herself. [from Latin *signare* = make a mark]

signature tune *noun* (*plural signature tunes*) a special tune always used to announce a particular programme, performer, etc.

significant *adjective*
1 having a meaning; full of meaning. **2** important, *a significant event*. **significantly** *adverb*, **significance** *noun*

signpost *noun* (*plural signposts*) a sign at a road junction etc. showing the names and distances of places down each road.

Sikh (*say* seek) *noun* (*plural Sikhs*) a member of a religion founded in northern India, believing in one God and accepting some Hindu and some Islamic beliefs. **Sikhism** *noun* [from Sanskrit *sisya* = disciple]

silence *noun* (*plural silences*) absence of sound or talk.

silence *verb* (*silences, silencing, silenced*) make a person or thing silent.

silencer *noun* (*plural silencers*) a device for reducing the sound made by a gun or a vehicle's exhaust system etc.

silent *adjective*
1 without any sound. **2** not speaking. **silently** *adverb* [from Latin *silere* = to be silent]

silhouette (*say* sil-oo-et) *noun* (*plural silhouettes*) a dark shadow seen against a light background. **silhouette** *verb* [named after a French author, É.

de Silhouette, who made paper cut-outs of people's profiles from their shadows]

silicon *noun* a substance found in many rocks, used in making transistors, chips for microprocessors, etc. [from Latin *silex* = flint or quartz]

silk *noun* (*plural silks*)
1 a fine soft thread or cloth made from the fibre produced by silkworm caterpillars for making their cocoons. **2** a length of silk thread used for embroidery. **silken** *adjective*, **silky** *adjective* [from Old English, probably from Latin]

silly *adjective* (*sillier, silliest*) foolish or unwise. **silliness** *noun* [from Old English *saelig* = happy, blessed by God, later = innocent, helpless]

silt *noun* sediment laid down by a river or sea etc.

silt *verb* (*silts, silting, silted*) **silt up** block or clog or become blocked with silt.

silver *noun*
1 a shiny white precious metal. **2** the colour of silver. **3** coins or objects made of silver or silver-coloured metal. **4** a silver medal, usually given as second prize. **silver** *adjective*, **silvery** *adjective*

silver *verb* (*silvers, silvering, silvered*) make or become silvery.

silver wedding *noun* (*plural silver weddings*) a couple's 25th wedding anniversary.

similar *adjective* nearly the same as another person or thing; of the same kind. **similarly** *adverb*, **similarity** *noun* [from Latin *similis* = like]

simile (say sim-il-ee) noun (plural similes) a comparison of one thing with another, e.g. *He is as strong as a horse. We ran like the wind.* [same origin as *similar*]

simmer verb (simmers, simmering, simmered) boil very gently.
simmer down calm down.

simper verb (simpers, simpering, simpered) smile in a silly affected way. **simper** noun

simple adjective (simpler, simplest)
1 easy, *a simple question.* 2 not complicated or elaborate. 3 plain, not showy, *a simple cottage.* 4 without much sense or intelligence. 5 not of high rank; ordinary, *a simple countryman.* **simplicity** noun

simple-minded adjective naive or foolish.

simplify verb (simplifies, simplifying, simplified) make a thing simple or easy to understand. **simplification** noun

simply adverb
1 in a simple way, *Explain it simply.* 2 without doubt; completely, *It's simply marvellous.* 3 only or merely, *It's simply a question of time.*

simulator noun (plural simulators) a machine or device for simulating actual conditions or events, often used for training, *a flight simulator.*

simultaneous (say sim-ul-tay-nee-us) adjective happening at the same time. **simultaneously** adverb [from Latin]

sin noun (plural sins)
1 the breaking of a religious or moral law. 2 a very bad action.
sin verb (sins, sinning, sinned) commit a sin. **sinner** noun

since conjunction
1 from the time when, *Where have you been since I last saw you?* 2 because, *Since we have missed the bus we must walk home.*
since preposition from a certain time, *She has been here since Christmas.*
since adverb between then and now, *He ran away and hasn't been seen since.*
[from Old English *sithon* = then]

sincere adjective without pretence; truly felt or meant, *my sincere thanks.* **sincerely** adverb, **sincerity** noun
Yours sincerely see *yours.*
[from Latin *sincerus* = clean or pure]

sine noun (plural sines) (in a right-angled triangle) the ratio of the length of a side opposite the one of the acute angles to the length of the hypotenuse. (Compare *cosine.*)

sinewy adjective slim, muscular, and strong.

sinful adjective
1 guilty of sin. 2 wicked. **sinfully** adverb, **sinfulness** noun

sing verb (sings, singing, sang, sung)
1 make musical sounds with the voice. 2 perform a song. **singer** noun

singe (say sinj) verb (singes, singeing, singed) burn something slightly.

single *adjective*
1 one only; not double or multiple. **2** suitable for one person, *single beds.* **3** separate, *We sold every single thing.* **4** not married. **5** for the journey to a place but not back again, *a single ticket.* **singly** *adverb*

single *noun* (*plural* **singles**)
1 a single person or thing. **2** a single ticket. **3** a record with one short piece of music on each side.

single *verb* (**singles, singling, singled**)
single out pick out or distinguish from other people or things.

single file *noun*
in single file in a line, one behind the other.

single-handed *adjective* without help.

single-minded *adjective* with your mind set on one purpose only.

singsong *adjective* having a monotonous tone or rhythm, *a singsong voice.*

singular *noun* (*plural* **singulars**) the form of a noun or verb used when it stands for only one person or thing, *The singular is 'man', the plural is 'men'.*

singular *adjective*
1 to do with the singular. **2** uncommon or extraordinary, *a woman of singular courage.*
singularly *adverb*,
singularity *noun*
[from Latin *singulus* = single]

sinister *adjective*
1 looking evil or harmful. **2** wicked, *a sinister motive.* [from Latin, = on the left (which was thought to be unlucky)]

sink *verb* (**sinks, sinking, sank, sunk**)
1 go or cause to go under the surface or to the bottom of the sea etc., *The ship sank. They sank the ship.* **2** go or fall slowly downwards, *He sank to his knees.* **3** dig or drill, *They sank a well.* **4** invest money in something.
sink in become understood.

sink *noun* (*plural* **sinks**) a fixed basin with a drainpipe and usually a tap or taps to supply water.

-sion *suffix* see **-ion.**

sip *verb* (**sips, sipping, sipped**) drink in small mouthfuls. **sip** *noun*

siphon *noun* (*plural* **siphons**)
1 a pipe or tube in the form of an upside-down U, arranged so that liquid is forced up it and down to a lower level. **2** a bottle containing soda water which is released through a tube.

siphon *verb* (**siphons, siphoning, siphoned**) flow or draw out through a siphon.
[Greek, = pipe]

sir *noun*
1 a word used when speaking politely to a man, *Please sir, may I go?* **2 Sir** the title given to a knight or baronet, *Sir John Moore.* [from French; related to *senior*]

siren *noun* (*plural* **sirens**)
1 a device that makes a long loud sound as a signal. **2** a dangerously attractive woman. [named after the Sirens in Greek legend, women who by their sweet singing lured seafarers to shipwreck on the rocks]

sissy noun (plural **sissies**) a timid or cowardly person. [from sis = sister]

sister noun (plural **sisters**)
1 a daughter of the same parents as another person. **2** a woman who is a fellow member of an association etc. **3** a nun. **4** a female hospital nurse in charge of others. **sisterly** adjective [from Old English]

sister-in-law noun (plural **sisters-in-law**)
1 the sister of a married person's husband or wife. **2** the wife of a person's brother.

sit verb (**sits, sitting, sat**)
1 rest with your body supported on the buttocks; occupy a seat, We were sitting in the front row. **2** seat; cause someone to sit. **3** (of birds) perch; stay on the nest to hatch eggs. **4** be a candidate for an examination. **5** be situated; stay. **6** (of Parliament or a lawcourt etc.) be assembled for business.

site noun (plural **sites**) the place where something happens or happened or is built etc., a camping site. [from Latin situs = position]

USAGE: Do not confuse with sight.

sit-in noun (plural **sit-ins**)
a protest in which people sit down or occupy a public place and refuse to move.

sitting room noun (plural **sitting rooms**) a room with comfortable chairs for sitting in.

situation noun (plural **situations**)
1 a position, with its surroundings. **2** a state of affairs at a certain time, The police faced a difficult situation. **3** a job. [same origin as site]

six adjective & noun (plural **sixes**) the number 6. **sixth** adjective & noun
at sixes and sevens in disorder or disagreement.

sixteen noun & adjective the number 16. **sixteenth** adjective & noun

sixty adjective & noun (plural **sixties**) the number 60. **sixtieth** adjective & noun

size noun (plural **sizes**)
1 the measurements or extent of something. **2** any of the series of standard measurements in which certain things are made, a size eight shoe.

size verb (**sizes, sizing, sized**) arrange things according to their size.
size up 1 estimate the size of something. **2** form an opinion or judgement about a person or thing.
[originally, a law fixing the amount of a tax: from old French assise = law, court session]

sizeable adjective large or fairly large.

sizzle verb (**sizzles, sizzling, sizzled**) make a crackling or hissing sound.

skate noun (plural **skates**)
1 a boot with a steel blade attached to the sole, used for sliding smoothly over ice. **2** a roller-skate.

skate verb (**skates, skating, skated**) move on skates. **skater** noun [from Dutch]

skateboard noun (plural
skateboards) a small board with
wheels, used for riding on (as
a sport) while standing.
skateboarder, skateboarding
nouns

skein noun (plural skeins) a coil
of yarn or thread. [from old
French]

skeleton noun (plural skeletons)
1 the framework of bones of the
body. 2 the shell or other hard
part of a crab etc. 3 a framework,
e.g. of a building. **skeletal**
adjective [from Greek skeletos
= dried-up]

sketch noun (plural sketches)
1 a rough drawing or painting.
2 a short account of something.
3 a short amusing play.

sketch verb (sketches,
sketching, sketched) make
a sketch.
[from Greek schedios = done
without practice or preparation]

sketchy adjective rough and not
detailed or careful.

skewer noun (plural skewers)
a long pin pushed through meat
to hold it together while it is
being cooked. **skewer** verb [origin
unknown]

ski (say skee) noun (plural skis)
each of a pair of long narrow
strips of wood, metal, or plastic
fixed under the feet for moving
quickly over snow.

ski verb (skies, skiing, skied)
travel on skis. **skier** noun
[Norwegian]

skid verb (skids, skidding,
skidded) slide accidentally.

skid noun (plural skids)
1 a skidding movement.
2 a runner on a helicopter, for

use in landing.
[probably from Old Norse skith
= ski]

skilful adjective having or
showing great skill. **skilfully**
adverb

skill noun (plural skills) the
ability to do something well.
skilled adjective [from Old Norse]

skim verb (skims, skimming,
skimmed)
1 remove something from the
surface of a liquid; take the
cream off milk. 2 move quickly
over a surface or through the air.
3 read something quickly. [from
old French escume = scum]

skimp verb (skimps, skimping,
skimped) supply or use less than
is needed, Don't skimp on the
food. [origin unknown]

skimpy adjective (skimpier,
skimpiest) scanty or too small.

skin noun (plural skins)
1 the flexible outer covering of
a person's or animal's body. 2 an
outer layer or covering, e.g. of
a fruit. 3 a skin-like film formed
on the surface of a liquid.

skin verb (skins, skinning,
skinned) take the skin off
something.

skinny adjective (skinnier,
skinniest) very thin.

skip¹ verb (skips, skipping,
skipped)
1 move along lightly, especially
by hopping on each foot in turn.
2 jump with a skipping rope. 3 go
quickly from one subject to
another. 4 miss something out,
You can skip chapter six.

skip noun (plural skips)
a skipping movement.

skip² noun (plural **skips**) a large metal container for taking away builders' rubbish etc. [from Old Norse *skeppa* = basket]

skipping rope noun (plural **skipping ropes**) a rope, usually with a handle at each end, that is swung over your head and under your feet as you jump.

skirt noun (plural **skirts**)
1 a piece of clothing for a woman or girl that hangs down from the waist. **2** the part of a dress below the waist.

skirt verb (**skirts**, **skirting**, **skirted**) go round the edge of something.

skittish adjective frisky; lively and excitable.

skulk verb (**skulks**, **skulking**, **skulked**) loiter stealthily.

skull noun (plural **skulls**) the framework of bones of the head.

skunk noun (plural **skunks**) a North American animal with black and white fur that can spray a bad-smelling fluid. [a Native American word]

sky noun (plural **skies**) the space above the earth, appearing blue in daylight on fine days. [from Old Norse]

skylight noun (plural **skylights**) a window in a roof.

skyline noun (plural **skylines**)
1 the horizon, where earth and sky appear to meet. **2** the outline of buildings etc. against the sky.

skyscraper noun (plural **skyscrapers**) a very tall building.

slab noun (plural **slabs**) a thick flat piece. [origin unknown]

slack adjective
1 not pulled tight. **2** not busy; not working hard. **slackly** adverb, **slackness** noun

slack verb (**slacks**, **slacking**, **slacked**) avoid work; be lazy. **slacker** noun

slacken verb (**slackens**, **slackening**, **slackened**) make or become slack.

slacks plural noun trousers for informal occasions.

slag noun waste material separated from metal in smelting. [from old German]

slag heap noun (plural **slag heaps**) a mound of waste matter from a mine etc.

slain past participle of **slay**.

slake verb (**slakes**, **slaking**, **slaked**) quench, *slake your thirst*.

slam verb (**slams**, **slamming**, **slammed**)
1 shut loudly. **2** hit violently. **slam** noun

slander noun (plural **slanders**) a spoken statement that damages a person's reputation and is untrue. (Compare **libel**.) **slanderous** adjective

slander verb (**slanders**, **slandering**, **slandered**) make a slander against someone. **slanderer** noun [from old French; related to *scandal*]

slang noun words that are used very informally to add vividness or humour to what is said, especially those used only by a particular group of people, *teenage slang*. **slangy** adjective [origin unknown]

slant *verb* (**slants, slanting, slanted**)

1 slope. 2 present news or information etc. from a particular point of view.

slap *verb* (**slaps, slapping, slapped**)

1 hit with the palm of the hand or with something flat. 2 put forcefully or carelessly, *We slapped paint on the walls*. **slap** *noun* [imitating the sound]

slapdash *adjective* hasty and careless.

slapstick *noun* comedy with people hitting each other, falling over, etc. [from *slap* + *stick*¹]

slash *verb* (**slashes, slashing, slashed**)

1 make large cuts in something. 2 cut or strike with a long sweeping movement. 3 reduce greatly, *Prices were slashed*. **slash** *noun* (*plural* **slashes**) a slashing cut. [probably from old French]

slate *noun* (*plural* **slates**)

1 a kind of grey rock that is easily split into flat plates. 2 a piece of this rock used in covering a roof or (formerly) for writing on. **slaty** *adjective*

slate *verb* (**slates, slating, slated**)

1 cover a roof with slates. 2 (*informal*) criticize severely.

slaughter *verb* (**slaughters, slaughtering, slaughtered**)

1 kill an animal for food. 2 kill people or animals ruthlessly or in great numbers. **slaughter** *noun* [from Old Norse]

slaughterhouse *noun* (*plural* **slaughterhouses**) a place where animals are killed for food.

slave *noun* (*plural* **slaves**) a person who is owned by another and obliged to work for him or her without being paid. **slavery** *noun*

slave *verb* (**slaves, slaving, slaved**) work very hard. [from Latin *sclavus* = captive]

slavish *adjective*

1 like a slave. 2 showing no independence or originality.

slay *verb* (**slays, slaying, slew, slain**) (*poetical*) kill. [from Old English]

sledge *noun* (*plural* **sledges**) a vehicle for travelling over snow, with strips of metal or wood instead of wheels. **sledging** *noun* [from old Dutch; related to *sled*]

sledgehammer *noun* (*plural* **sledgehammers**) a very large heavy hammer. [from Old English *slecg* = sledgehammer, + *hammer*]

sleek *adjective* smooth and shiny. [a different spelling of *slick*]

sleep *noun* the condition or time of rest in which the eyes are closed, the body relaxed, and the mind unconscious. **sleepy** *adjective*, **sleepily** *adverb*, **sleepiness** *noun*

sleep *verb* (**sleeps, sleeping, slept**) have a sleep.

sleeper *noun* (*plural* **sleepers**)

1 someone who is asleep. 2 each of the wooden or concrete beams on which the rails of a railway rest. 3 a railway carriage with beds or berths for passengers to sleep in; a place in this.

sleepwalker noun (plural **sleepwalkers**) a person who walks about while asleep. **sleepwalking** noun

sleet noun a mixture of rain and snow or hail.

sleeve noun (plural **sleeves**) 1 the part of a garment that covers the arm. 2 the cover of a record.
up your sleeve hidden but ready for you to use.

sleight (say as slight) noun sleight of hand skill in using the hands to do conjuring tricks etc.

slender adjective slim. **slenderness** noun [origin unknown]

sleuth (say slooth) noun (plural **sleuths**) a detective. [from Old Norse sloth = a track or trail]

slew past tense of slay.

slice noun (plural **slices**) 1 a thin piece cut off something. 2 a portion.

slice verb (slices, slicing, sliced) 1 cut into slices. 2 cut from a larger piece, Slice the top off the egg. 3 cut cleanly, The knife sliced through the apple.

slick adjective 1 quick and clever or cunning. 2 slippery.

slick noun (plural **slicks**) 1 a large patch of oil floating on water. 2 a slippery place. [from Old English]

slide verb (slides, sliding, slid) 1 move or cause to move smoothly on a surface. 2 move quietly or secretly, The thief slid behind a bush.

slide noun (plural **slides**) 1 a sliding movement. 2 a smooth surface or structure on which

people or things can slide. 3 a photograph that can be projected on a screen. 4 a small glass plate on which things are placed to be examined under a microscope. 5 a fastener to keep hair tidy. [from Old English]

slight adjective very small; not serious or important. **slightly** adverb, **slightness** noun

slim adjective (slimmer, slimmest) 1 thin and graceful. 2 small, a slim chance. **slimness** noun

slim verb (slims, slimming, slimmed) make yourself thinner. **slimmer** noun

slime noun unpleasant wet slippery stuff. **slimy** adjective, **sliminess** noun [from Old English]

sling noun (plural **slings**) 1 a loop or band placed round something to support or lift it. 2 a looped strap used to throw a stone etc.

sling verb (slings, slinging, slung) 1 support or lift with a sling. 2 (informal) throw. [from old Dutch or Old Norse]

slink verb (slinks, slinking, slunk) move in a stealthy or guilty way. **slinky** adjective [from Old English]

slip verb (slips, slipping, slipped) 1 slide accidentally; lose your balance by sliding. 2 move or put quickly and quietly, Slip it in your pocket. We slipped away from the party. 3 escape from, The dog slipped its leash. It slipped my memory.
slip up make a mistake.

slip noun (plural **slips**) 1 an accidental slide or fall.

2 a mistake. 3 a small piece of paper. 4 a petticoat. 5 a pillowcase.
give someone the slip escape or avoid him or her skilfully.

slipper noun (plural **slippers**)
a soft comfortable shoe to wear indoors.

slippery adjective smooth or wet so that it is difficult to stand on or hold. **slipperiness** noun

slipshod adjective careless; not systematic. [originally = wearing slippers or badly fitting shoes; from slip + shod]

slit noun (plural **slits**) a narrow straight cut or opening.

slit verb (**slits, slitting, slit**) make a slit or slits in something.

slither verb (**slithers, slithering, slithered**) slip or slide unsteadily. [from Old English]

sliver (say sliv-er) noun (plural **slivers**) a thin strip of wood or glass etc. [from Middle English slive = to split or to cut a piece off]

slog verb (**slogs, slogging, slogged**)
1 hit hard. 2 work or walk hard and steadily. **slog** noun, **slogger** noun

slogan noun (plural **slogans**)
a phrase used to advertise something or to sum up the aims of a campaign etc., Their slogan was 'Ban the bomb!' [from Scottish Gaelic sluagh-ghairm = battle-cry]

slope verb (**slopes, sloping, sloped**) lie or turn at an angle; slant.
slope off (informal) go away.

slope noun (plural **slopes**)
1 a sloping surface. 2 the amount

by which something slopes. [origin unknown]

sloppy adjective (**sloppier, sloppiest**)
1 liquid and splashing easily.
2 careless or slipshod, sloppy work. 3 weakly sentimental, a sloppy story. **sloppily** adverb, **sloppiness** noun [from slop]

slot noun (plural **slots**) a narrow opening to put things in. **slotted** adjective [from old French]

sloth (rhymes with both) noun (plural **sloths**)
1 laziness. 2 a South American animal that lives in trees and moves very slowly. **slothful** adjective [from slow]

slot machine noun (plural **slot machines**) a machine worked by putting a coin in the slot.

slouch verb (**slouches, slouching, slouched**) stand, sit, or move in a lazy awkward way, not with an upright posture. **slouch** noun

slovenly (say sluv-en-lee) adjective careless or untidy. **slovenliness** noun

slow adjective
1 not quick; taking more time than is usual. 2 showing a time earlier than the correct time, Your watch is slow. 3 not clever; not able to understand quickly or easily. **slowly** adverb, **slowness** noun

slow adverb slowly, Go slow.

slow verb (**slows, slowing, slowed**) go more slowly; cause to go more slowly, The storm slowed us down.

slow-worm noun (plural **slow-worms**) a small European legless lizard that looks like a snake, and gives birth to live young.

sludge noun thick mud. [origin unknown]

slug noun (plural **slugs**)
1 a small slimy animal like a snail without a shell. 2 a pellet for firing from a gun.

sluggish adjective slow-moving; not alert or lively. [from slug]

sluice-gate noun (plural **sluice-gates**) a sliding barrier for controlling a flow of water.

slum noun (plural **slums**) an area of dirty overcrowded houses.

slumber verb (**slumbers, slumbering, slumbered**) sleep.
slumber noun, **slumberer** noun, **slumberous** or **slumbrous** adjective

slump verb (**slumps, slumping, slumped**) fall heavily or suddenly.
slump noun (plural **slumps**) a sudden great fall in prices or trade.

slur verb (**slurs, slurring, slurred**)
1 pronounce words indistinctly by running the sounds together.
2 mark with a slur in music.
slur noun (plural **slurs**)
1 a slurred sound. 2 discredit, It casts a slur on his reputation.
3 a curved line placed over notes in music to show that they are to be sung or played smoothly without a break.

slush noun partly melted snow on the ground. **slushy** adjective [imitating the sound when you walk in it]

sly adjective (**slyer, slyest**)
1 unpleasantly cunning or secret.
2 mischievous, a sly smile. **slyly** adverb, **slyness** noun [from Old Norse]

smack[1] noun (plural **smacks**)
1 a slap. 2 a loud sharp sound, It hit the wall with a smack.
3 (informal) a hard hit or blow.
smack verb (**smacks, smacking, smacked**)
1 slap. 2 hit hard.
smack your lips close and then part them noisily in enjoyment.
smack adverb (informal) forcefully or directly, The ball went smack through the window. [from German or old Dutch]

smack[2] noun (plural **smacks**) a slight flavour of something; a trace.
smack verb (**smacks, smacking, smacked**) have a slight flavour or trace, His manner smacks of conceit.
[from Old English]

small adjective not large; less than the usual size. **smallness** noun **the small of the back** the smallest part of the back (at the waist).

smallholding noun (plural **smallholdings**) a small area of land used for farming.
smallholder noun

small hours plural noun the early hours of the morning, after midnight.

small-minded adjective selfish; petty.

small print noun the details of a contract, especially if in very small letters or difficult to understand.

small talk noun conversation about unimportant things.

smart adjective
1 neat and elegant; dressed well.
2 clever. 3 forceful; brisk, She ran at a smart pace. **smartly** adverb, **smartness** noun

smarten verb (**smartens**, **smartening**, **smartened**) make or become smarter.

smash verb (**smashes**, **smashing**, **smashed**)
1 break noisily into pieces. **2** hit or move with great force.
3 destroy or defeat completely.

smash noun (plural **smashes**)
1 the action or sound of smashing. **2** a collision.
3 a disaster.

smashing adjective (informal) excellent or beautiful. **smasher** noun

smear verb (**smears**, **smearing**, **smeared**)
1 rub something greasy or sticky or dirty on a surface. **2** try to damage someone's reputation.
smeary adjective

smear noun (plural **smears**)
1 smearing; something smeared.
2 material smeared on a slide to be examined under a microscope.
3 a smear test.
[from Old English]

smell verb (**smells**, **smelling**, **smelt** or **smelled**)
1 be aware of something by means of the sense organs of the nose, *I can smell smoke*. **2** give out a smell.

smell noun (plural **smells**)
1 something you can smell; a quality in something that makes people able to smell it. **2** an unpleasant quality of this kind.
3 the ability to smell things.
smelly adjective
[origin unknown]

smile noun (plural **smiles**) an expression on the face that shows pleasure or amusement, with the lips stretched and turning upwards at the ends.

smile verb (**smiles**, **smiling**, **smiled**) give a smile.

smirk noun (plural **smirks**) a self-satisfied smile.

smirk verb (**smirks**, **smirking**, **smirked**) give a smirk.
[from Old English]

smite verb (**smites**, **smiting**, **smote**, **smitten**) hit hard. [from Old English]

smith noun (plural **smiths**)
1 a person who makes things out of metal. **2** a blacksmith. [from Old English]

smithereens plural noun small fragments. [from Irish]

smock noun (plural **smocks**)
1 an overall shaped like a very long shirt. **2** a loose top worn by a pregnant woman.

smog noun a mixture of smoke and fog. [from *smoke* + *fog*]

smoke noun
1 the mixture of gas and solid particles given off by a burning substance. **2** a period of smoking tobacco, *He wanted a smoke*.
smoky adjective

smoke verb (**smokes**, **smoking**, **smoked**)
1 give out smoke. **2** have a lighted cigarette, cigar, or pipe between your lips and draw its smoke into your mouth; do this as a habit.
3 preserve meat or fish by treating it with smoke, *smoked haddock*. **smoker** noun
[from Old English]

smokescreen noun (plural **smokescreens**)
1 a mass of smoke used to hide

the movement of troops.
2 something that conceals what is happening.

smooth *adjective*
1 having a surface without any lumps, wrinkles, roughness, etc. **2** moving without bumps or jolts etc. **3** not harsh, *a smooth flavour.* **smoothly** *adverb*, **smoothness** *noun*

smooth *verb* (**smooths, smoothing, smoothed**) make a thing smooth.

smote *past tense of* **smite**.

smother *verb* (**smothers, smothering, smothered**)
1 suffocate. **2** cover thickly, *The buns were smothered in sugar.* **3** restrain or conceal, *She smothered a smile.* [from Old English]

smoulder *verb* (**smoulders, smouldering, smouldered**)
1 burn slowly without a flame. **2** continue to exist inwardly, *Their anger smouldered.*

smudge *noun* (*plural* **smudges**) a dirty mark made by rubbing something. **smudgy** *adjective*

smudge *verb* (**smudges, smudging, smudged**) make a smudge on something; become smudged.
[origin unknown]

smug *adjective* self-satisfied; too pleased with your own good fortune or abilities. **smugly** *adverb*, **smugness** *noun* [from old German *smuk* = pretty]

smuggle *verb* (**smuggles, smuggling, smuggled**) bring something into a country etc. secretly or illegally.
smuggler *noun*

snack *noun* (*plural* **snacks**)
1 a small meal. **2** food eaten between meals. [from old Dutch]

snag *noun* (*plural* **snags**)
1 a difficulty. **2** a sharp projection. **3** a tear in material that has been caught on something sharp.

snail *noun* (*plural* **snails**) a small animal with a soft body and a shell. [from Old English]

snake *noun* (*plural* **snakes**) a reptile with a long narrow body and no legs. **snaky** *adjective* [from Old English]

snap *verb* (**snaps, snapping, snapped**)
1 break suddenly or with a sharp sound. **2** bite suddenly or quickly. **3** say something quickly and angrily. **4** take something or move quickly. **5** take a snapshot of something.

snap *noun* (*plural* **snaps**)
1 the action or sound of snapping. **2** a snapshot. **3** Snap *noun* a card game in which players shout 'Snap!' when they see two similar cards.

snappy *adjective*
1 snapping at people. **2** quick and lively. **snappily** *adverb*

snapshot *noun* (*plural* **snapshots**) an informal photograph.

snare *noun* (*plural* **snares**) a trap for catching birds or animals.

snare *verb* (**snares, snaring, snared**) catch in a snare. [from Old English]

snarl *verb* (**snarls, snarling, snarled**)
1 growl angrily. **2** speak in a bad-tempered way. **snarl** *noun* [imitating the sound]

snatch verb (snatches, snatching, snatched) seize; take quickly, eagerly, or by force.

snatch noun (plural snatches) 1 snatching. 2 a short and incomplete part of a song, conversation, etc.

sneak verb (sneaks, sneaking, sneaked) 1 move quietly and secretly. 2 (informal) take secretly, He sneaked a biscuit from the tin. 3 (slang) tell tales.

sneak noun (plural sneaks) a tell-tale. **sneaky** adjective, **sneakily** adverb

sneer verb (sneers, sneering, sneered) speak or behave in a scornful way. **sneer** noun [probably from Old English]

sneeze verb (sneezes, sneezing, sneezed) send out air suddenly and uncontrollably through the nose and mouth in order to get rid of something irritating the nostrils. **sneeze** noun [from Old English fneosan, imitating the sound]

sniff verb (sniffs, sniffing, sniffed) 1 make a sound by drawing in air through the nose. 2 smell something. **sniff** noun, **sniffer** noun [imitating the sound]

sniffle verb (sniffles, sniffling, sniffled) 1 sniff slightly. 2 keep on sniffing. **sniffle** noun [imitating the sound]

snigger verb (sniggers, sniggering, sniggered) giggle slyly. **snigger** noun

snip verb (snips, snipping, snipped) cut with scissors or shears in small cuts. **snip** noun

snipe verb (snipes, sniping, sniped) shoot at people from a hiding place. **sniper** noun

snippet noun (plural snippets) a small piece of news, information, etc. [from snip]

snivel verb (snivels, snivelling, snivelled) cry or complain in a whining way.

snob noun (plural snobs) a person who despises those who have not got wealth, power, or particular tastes or interests. **snobbery** noun, **snobbish** adjective

snooker noun a game played with cues and 21 balls on a special cloth-covered table.

snoop verb (snoops, snooping, snooped) pry; ask or look around secretly. **snooper** noun [from Dutch]

snooze noun (plural snoozes) a nap. **snooze** verb [origin unknown]

snore verb (snores, snoring, snored) breathe very noisily while sleeping. **snore** noun [imitating the sound]

snort verb (snorts, snorting, snorted) make a rough sound by breathing forcefully through the nose. **snort** noun

snout noun (plural snouts) an animal's projecting nose, or nose and jaws. [from old German or old Dutch]

snow noun frozen drops of water that fall from the sky in small white flakes.

snow verb (snows, snowing, snowed) send down snow. **be snowed under** be overwhelmed with a mass of letters or work etc.

snowdrop noun (plural **snowdrops**) a small white flower that blooms in early spring.

snowdrift noun (plural **snowdrifts**) a large heap or bank of snow piled up by the wind.

snowflake noun (plural **snowflakes**) a flake of snow.

snowshoe noun (plural **snowshoes**) a frame rather like a tennis racket for walking on soft snow.

snowstorm noun (plural **snowstorms**) a storm in which snow falls.

snub verb (**snubs, snubbing, snubbed**) treat in a scornful or unfriendly way.

snub noun (plural **snubs**) scornful or unfriendly treatment.

snub-nosed adjective having a short turned-up nose.

snuff[1] noun powdered tobacco for taking into the nose by sniffing. [from old Italian *snuffen* = snuffle]

snuff[2] verb (**snuffs, snuffing, snuffed**) put out a candle by covering or pinching the flame. **snuffer** noun [origin unknown]

snuffle verb (**snuffles, snuffling, snuffled**) sniff in a noisy way. **snuffle** noun [same origin as *snuff*[1]]

snug adjective (**snugger, snuggest**)
1 cosy. 2 fitting closely. **snugly** adverb, **snugness** noun [probably from Dutch]

snuggle verb (**snuggles, snuggling, snuggled**) press closely and comfortably; nestle. [from *snug*]

so adverb
1 in this way; to such an extent, *Why are you so cross?* 2 very, *Cricket is so boring.* 3 also, *I was wrong but so were you.*
or so or about that number.
so far up to now.
so long! (*informal*) goodbye.
so what? (*informal*) that is not important.

so conjunction for that reason, *They threw me out, so I came here.* [from Old English]

soak verb (**soaks, soaking, soaked**) make a person or thing very wet. **soak** noun
soak up take in a liquid in the way that a sponge does.

soap noun (plural **soaps**)
1 a substance used with water for washing and cleaning things. 2 a soap opera. **soapy** adjective

soap opera noun (plural **soap operas**) a television serial about the everyday lives of a group of people. [originally American, where they were sponsored by soap manufacturers]

soar verb (**soars, soaring, soared**)
1 rise high in the air. 2 rise very high, *Prices were soaring.* [from old French; related to *aura*]

sob verb (**sobs, sobbing, sobbed**) make a gasping sound when crying. **sob** noun [probably from old Dutch]

sober adjective
1 not drunk. 2 serious and calm. 3 (of colour) not bright. **soberly** adverb, **sobriety** (say so-bry-it-ee) noun

sober verb (**sobers, sobering, sobered**) make or become sober. [from Latin]

so-called *adjective* named in what may be the wrong way, *This so-called gentleman slammed the door.*

soccer *noun* Association football. [short for *Association*]

sociable *adjective* liking to be with other people; friendly. **sociably** *adverb*, **sociability** *noun* [same origin as *social*]

social *adjective*
1 living in a community, not alone, *Bees are social insects.* **2** of life in a community, *social science.* **3** concerned with people's welfare, *social worker.* **4** helping people to meet each other, *a social club.* **5** sociable. **socially** *adverb* [from Latin *sociare* = unite, associate]

socialism *noun* a political system where wealth is shared equally between people, and the main industries and trade etc. are controlled by the government. (Compare *capitalism*.) [from French; related to *social*]

socialist *noun* (*plural* **socialists**) a person who believes in socialism.

social security *noun* money and other assistance provided by the government for those in need through being ill, disabled, unemployed, etc.

social services *plural noun* welfare services provided by the government, including schools, hospitals, and pensions.

society *noun* (*plural* **societies**)
1 a community; people living together in a group or nation.
2 a group of people organized for a particular purpose, *the school dramatic society.* **3** company;

companionship, *We enjoy the society of our friends.* [same origin as *social*]

sock *noun* (*plural* **socks**) a short stocking reaching only to the ankle or below the knee. [from Old English]

socket *noun* (*plural* **sockets**)
1 a hollow into which something fits, *a tooth-socket.* **2** a device into which an electric plug or bulb is put to make a connection. [from old French]

soda water *noun* water made fizzy with carbon dioxide, used in drinks.

sodden *adjective* made very wet. [the old past participle of *seethe*]

sodium *noun* a soft white metal.

sofa *noun* (*plural* **sofas**) a kind of settee. [from Arabic *suffa* = long stone bench]

soft *adjective*
1 not hard or firm; easily pressed.
2 smooth, not rough or stiff.
3 gentle; not loud. **softly** *adverb*, **softness** *noun*

soft drink *noun* (*plural* **soft drinks**) a cold drink that is not alcoholic.

soften *verb* (**softens**, **softening**, **softened**) make or become soft or softer. **softener** *noun*

software *noun* computer programs, disks, etc. (Compare *hardware*.)

soggy *adjective* (**soggier**, **soggiest**) very wet and heavy, *soggy ground.* [from dialect *sog* = swamp]

soil *noun* (*plural* **soils**)
1 the loose earth in which plants grow. **2** territory, *on British soil.* [old French *soil*]

solar panel noun (plural **solar panels**) a panel designed to catch the sun's rays and use their energy for heating or to make electricity.

solar power noun electricity or other forms of power derived from the sun's rays.

solar system noun the sun and the planets that revolve round it. [from Latin sol = sun]

soldier noun (plural **soldiers**) a member of an army. [from old French]

sole[1] noun (plural **soles**)
1 the bottom surface of a foot or shoe. **2** a flat edible sea fish.
sole verb (**soles, soling, soled**) put a sole on a shoe.
[from Latin solum]

sole[2] adjective single; only, She was the sole survivor. **solely** adverb [from Latin solus]

solemn adjective
1 not smiling or cheerful. **2** dignified or formal. **solemnly** adverb, **solemnity** noun

solicitor noun (plural **solicitors**) a lawyer who advises clients, prepares legal documents, etc.

solid adjective
1 not hollow; with no space inside. **2** keeping its shape; not liquid or gas. **3** continuous, for two solid hours. **4** firm or strongly made; not flimsy, a solid foundation. **5** showing solidarity; unanimous. **solidly** adverb, **solidity** noun
solid noun (plural **solids**)
1 a solid thing. **2** a shape that has three dimensions (length, width, and height or depth).
[from Latin]

solids plural noun solid food; food that is not liquid, Is your baby eating solids yet?

soliloquy (say sol-il-ok-wee) noun (plural **soliloquies**) a speech in which a person speaks his or her thoughts aloud without addressing anyone. **soliloquize** verb [from Latin solus = alone + loqui = speak]

solitary adjective
1 alone, without companions. **2** single, a solitary example. **3** lonely, a solitary valley. [from Latin solus = alone]

solitary confinement noun a form of punishment in which a prisoner is kept alone in a cell and not allowed to talk to others.

solo noun (plural **solos**) something sung, played, danced, or done by one person. **solo** adjective & adverb, **soloist** noun [Italian, = alone]

soluble adjective
1 able to be dissolved. **2** able to be solved. **solubility** noun [same origin as solve]

solution noun (plural **solutions**)
1 a liquid in which something is dissolved. **2** the answer to a problem or puzzle. [same origin as solve]

solve verb (**solves, solving, solved**) find the answer to a problem or puzzle. [from Latin solvere = unfasten]

solvent adjective
1 having enough money to pay all your debts. **2** able to dissolve another substance. **solvency** noun

solvent noun (plural **solvents**) a liquid used for dissolving something.

sombre *adjective* dark and gloomy. [from *sub-* + Latin *umbra* = shade]

some *adjective*
1 a few; a little, *some apples; some sugar.* **2** an unknown person or thing, *Some fool left the door open.* **3** about, *We waited some 20 minutes.*
some time at some point in time, *Come and see me some time* (not 'sometime'). *They left some time ago.*

some *pronoun* a certain number or amount that is less than the whole, *Some of them were late.*

-some *suffix* forms
1 adjectives meaning 'quality or manner' (e.g. *handsome, quarrelsome*). **2** nouns from numbers, meaning 'a group of this many' (e.g. *foursome*). [from Old English]

somebody *pronoun*
1 some person. **2** an important or impressive person.

somehow *adverb* in some way.

someone *pronoun* somebody.

somersault *noun* (*plural* **somersaults**) a movement in which you turn head over heels before landing on your feet.
somersault *verb* [from Latin *supra* = above + *saltus* = a leap]

something *noun* some thing; a thing which you cannot do or do not want to name.
something like rather like, *It's something like a rabbit;* approximately, *It cost something like £10.*

sometimes *adverb* at some times but not always, *We sometimes walk to school.*

somewhat *adverb* to some extent, *He was somewhat annoyed.*

somewhere *adverb* in or to some place.

son *noun* (*plural* **sons**) a boy or man who is someone's child.

sonata *noun* (*plural* **sonatas**) a piece of music for one instrument or two, in several movements. [from Italian *sonare* = to sound]

song *noun* (*plural* **songs**)
1 a tune for singing. **2** singing, *He burst into song.*
a song and dance (*informal*) a great fuss.
for a song bought or sold very cheaply.

sonic boom *noun* (*plural* **sonic booms**) a loud noise caused by the shock wave of an aircraft travelling faster than the speed of sound. [from Latin *sonus* = sound]

son-in-law *noun* (*plural* **sons-in-law**) a daughter's husband.

sonnet *noun* (*plural* **sonnets**) a kind of poem with 14 lines. [from Italian *sonetto* = a little sound]

soon *adverb*
1 in a short time from now. **2** not long after something.
as soon as willingly, *I'd just as soon stay here.*
as soon as at the moment that.
sooner or later at some time in the future.

soot *noun* the black powder left by smoke in a chimney or on a building etc. **sooty** *adjective* [from Old English]

soothe verb (soothes, soothing, soothed)
1 calm. 2 ease pain or distress.
soothingly adverb [from Old English]

sop verb (sops, sopping, sopped)
sop up soak up liquid like a sponge.

sophisticated adjective
1 of or accustomed to fashionable life and its ways. 2 complicated, a sophisticated machine.
sophistication noun [from Latin sophisticare = tamper with, mix with something]

sopping adjective very wet; drenched. [from sop]

soppy adjective
1 very wet. 2 (informal) sentimental in a silly way. [from sop]

soprano noun (plural sopranos)
a woman, girl, or boy with a high singing voice. [Italian, from sopra = above]

sorcerer noun (plural sorcerers)
a wizard. **sorceress** noun, **sorcery** noun

sordid adjective
1 dirty and nasty. 2 dishonourable; selfish and mercenary, sordid motives.
sordidly adverb, **sordidness** noun [from Latin]

sore adjective
1 painful or smarting. 2 (informal) annoyed or offended. 3 serious or distressing, in sore need. **soreness** noun

sore noun (plural sores) a sore place.
[from Old English]

sorrow noun (plural sorrows)
unhappiness or regret caused by loss or disappointment. **sorrowful** adjective, **sorrowfully** adverb

sorry adjective (sorrier, sorriest)
1 feeling pity, regret, or sympathy. 2 wretched, His clothes were in a sorry state.

sort noun (plural sorts) a group of things or people that are similar; a kind or variety.
out of sorts slightly unwell or depressed.
sort of (informal) rather; to some extent, I sort of expected it.

USAGE: Correct use is this sort of thing or these sorts of things (not 'these sort of things').

sort verb (sorts, sorting, sorted)
arrange things in groups according to their size, kind, etc. **sorter** noun
sort out disentangle; select; (slang) deal with and punish someone.

sortie noun (plural sorties)
1 an attack by troops coming out of a besieged place. 2 an attacking expedition by a military aircraft. [from French sortir = go out]

SOS noun (plural SOSs) an urgent appeal for help. [the international Morse code signal of extreme distress, chosen because it is easy to recognize, but often said to stand for Save Our Souls]

sought past tense of seek.

soul noun (plural souls)
1 the invisible part of a person that is believed to go on living after the body has died.

2 a person's mind and emotions etc. **3** a person, *There isn't a soul about.*

sound[1] *noun* (*plural* **sounds**)
1 vibrations that travel through the air and can be detected by the ear; the sensation they produce. **2** sound reproduced in a film etc. **3** a mental impression, *We don't like the sound of his plans.*

sound *verb* (**sounds, sounding, sounded**)
1 produce or cause to produce a sound. **2** give an impression when heard, *He sounds angry.* **3** test by noting the sounds heard, *A doctor sounds a patient's lungs with a stethoscope.* [from Latin]

sound[2] *verb* (**sounds, sounding, sounded**) test the depth of water beneath a ship.
sound out try to find out what a person thinks or feels about something. [from *sub-* + Latin *unda* = a wave]

sound[3] *adjective*
1 in good condition; not damaged. **2** healthy; not diseased. **3** reasonable; correct, *His ideas are sound.* **4** reliable; secure, *a sound investment.* **5** thorough; deep, *a sound sleep.* **soundly** *adverb*, **soundness** *noun* [from Old English *gesund* = healthy]

sound barrier *noun* the resistance of the air to objects moving at nearly supersonic speed.

sound effects *plural noun* sounds produced artificially to make a play, film, etc. seem more realistic.

soundtrack *noun* (*plural* **soundtracks**) the sound that goes with a cinema film.

soup *noun* (*plural* **soups**) liquid food made from stewed bones, meat, fish, vegetables, etc.
in the soup (*informal*) in trouble.

sour *adjective*
1 tasting sharp like unripe fruit. **2** stale and unpleasant, not fresh, *sour milk.* **3** bad-tempered. **sourly** *adverb*, **sourness** *noun*

source *noun* (*plural* **sources**) the place from which something comes. [from old French; related to *surge*]

south *noun*
1 the direction to the right of a person who faces east. **2** the southern part of a country, city, etc.
south *adjective & adverb* towards or in the south.
southerly (*say* suth-er-lee) *adjective*, **southern** *adjective*, **southerner** *noun*, **southernmost** *adjective*

south-east *noun, adjective, & adverb* midway between south and east. **south-easterly** *adjective*, **south-eastern** *adjective*

southward *adjective & adverb* towards the south. **southwards** *adverb*

south-west *noun, adjective, & adverb* midway between south and west. **south-westerly** *adjective*, **south-western** *adjective*

souvenir (*say* soo-ven-eer) *noun* (*plural* **souvenirs**) something that you keep to remind you of a person, place, or event. [from French *se souvenir* = remember]

sovereign noun (plural sovereigns)
1 a king or queen who is the ruler of a country; a monarch. 2 an old British gold coin, originally worth £1. [from old French; related to super-]

sow¹ (rhymes with go) verb (sows, sowing, sowed, sown or sowed) put seeds into the ground so that they will grow into plants. **sower** noun [from Old English sawan]

sow² (rhymes with cow) noun (plural sows) a female pig. [from Old English sugu]

space noun (plural spaces)
1 the whole area outside the earth, where the stars and planets are. 2 an area or volume, This table takes too much space. 3 an empty area; a gap. 4 an interval of time, within the space of an hour.

space verb (spaces, spacing, spaced) arrange things with spaces between, Space them out. [from Latin spatium = a space]

spacecraft noun (plural spacecraft) a vehicle for travelling in outer space.

spaceship noun (plural spaceships) a spacecraft.

space shuttle noun (plural space shuttles) a spacecraft for repeated use to and from outer space.

space station noun (plural space stations) a satellite which orbits the earth and is used as a base by scientists and astronauts.

spacious adjective providing a lot of space; roomy. **spaciousness**

spade¹ noun (plural spades) a tool with a long handle and a wide blade for digging. [from Old English spadu]

spade² noun (plural spades) a playing card with black shapes like upside-down hearts on it, each with a short stem. [from Italian spada = sword]

spaghetti noun pasta made in long thin sticks. [Italian, = little strings]

span noun (plural spans)
1 the length from end to end or across something. 2 the distance from the tip of the thumb to the tip of the little finger when the hand is spread out. 3 the part between two uprights of an arch or bridge. 4 the length of a period of time.

spaniel noun (plural spaniels) a kind of dog with long ears and silky fur. [from old French espaigneul = Spanish (because it originated in Spain)]

spank verb (spanks, spanking, spanked) smack a person on the bottom as a punishment. [imitating the sound]

spanner noun (plural spanners) a tool for gripping and turning the nut on a bolt etc. [German, from spannen = tighten]

spar¹ noun (plural spars) a strong pole used for a mast or boom etc. on a ship. [from Old Norse]

spar² verb (spars, sparring, sparred)
1 practise boxing. 2 quarrel or argue. [from Old English]

spare verb (spares, sparing, spared)
1 afford to give something, Can you spare a moment?

2 be merciful towards someone; not hurt or harm a person or thing. **3** use or treat economically, *No expense will be spared. Spare the rod and spoil the child!*

spare *adjective*
1 not used but kept ready in case it is needed; extra, *a spare wheel.* **2** thin; lean. **sparely** *adverb*, **spareness** *noun*
go spare (*slang*) become very annoyed.

spare time *noun* time not needed for work.

sparing (*say* **spair**-ing) *adjective* economical; grudging. **sparingly** *adverb* [from *spare*]

spark *noun* (*plural* **sparks**)
1 a tiny glowing particle. **2** a flash produced electrically.

spark *verb* (**sparks**, **sparking**, **sparked**) give off a spark or sparks.

sparkle *verb* (**sparkles**, **sparkling**, **sparkled**)
1 shine with tiny flashes of light. **2** show brilliant wit or liveliness. **sparkle** *noun* [from *spark*]

sparkler *noun* (*plural* **sparklers**) a sparking firework.

spark plug *noun* (*plural* **spark plugs**) a device that makes a spark to ignite the fuel in an engine.

sparrow *noun* (*plural* **sparrows**) a small brown bird. [from Old English]

sparse *adjective* thinly scattered; not numerous, *a sparse population.* **sparsely** *adverb*, **sparseness** *noun* [from Latin *sparsum* = scattered]

spasm *noun* (*plural* **spasms**)
1 a sudden involuntary movement of a muscle. **2** a sudden brief spell of activity etc. [from Greek]

spasmodic *adjective*
1 to do with or caused by a spasm. **2** happening or done at irregular intervals. **spasmodically** *adverb*

spastic *noun* (*plural* **spastics**) a person suffering from spasms of the muscles and jerky movements, especially caused by cerebral palsy.

USAGE: Do not use this word to mean a clumsy or stupid person.

spat *past tense of* **spit**¹.

spate *noun* (*plural* **spates**) a sudden flood or rush. [origin unknown]

spatter *verb* (**spatters**, **spattering**, **spattered**)
1 scatter in small drops. **2** splash, *spattered with mud.* **spatter** *noun* [origin unknown]

spawn *noun*
1 the eggs of fish, frogs, toads, or shellfish. **2** the thread-like matter from which fungi grow.

spawn *verb* (**spawns**, **spawning**, **spawned**)
1 produce spawn. **2** be produced from spawn. **3** produce something in great quantities. [from old French]

speak *verb* (**speaks**, **speaking**, **spoke**, **spoken**)
1 say something; talk. **2** talk or be able to talk in a foreign language, *Do you speak French?*
speak up 1 speak more loudly. **2** give your opinion.

speaker noun (plural **speakers**)
1 a person who is speaking.
2 someone who makes a speech.
3 a loudspeaker.

the Speaker the person who controls the debates in the House of Commons or a similar assembly.

spear noun (plural **spears**)
a weapon for throwing or stabbing, with a long shaft and a pointed tip.

special adjective
1 of a particular kind; for some purpose, not general, *special training*. 2 exceptional, *Take special care of it.* [same origin as *species*]

special effects plural noun
illusions created for films or television by using props, trick photography, or computer images.

specialist noun (plural **specialists**) an expert in one subject, *a skin specialist*.

speciality noun (plural **specialities**)
1 a special quality or product.
2 something in which a person specializes.

specialize verb (**specializes, specializing, specialized**) give particular attention or study to one subject or thing, *She specialized in biology.* **specialization** noun

species (say spee-shiz) noun (plural **species**)
1 a group of animals or plants that are very similar. 2 a kind or sort, *a species of sledge.* [Latin, = appearance, form, or kind]

specific adjective definite or precise; of or for a particular thing, *The money was given for a specific purpose.* **specifically** adverb [same origin as *species*]

specific gravity noun the weight of something as compared with the same volume of water or air.

specimen noun (plural **specimens**)
1 a sample. 2 an example, *a fine specimen of an oak tree.* [Latin, from *specere* = to look]

speck noun (plural **specks**)
a small spot or particle. [from Old English]

speckle noun (plural **speckles**)
a small spot or mark. **speckled** adjective

spectacle noun (plural **spectacles**)
1 an impressive sight or display.
2 a ridiculous sight. [from Latin *spectaculum* = a public show]

spectacles plural noun a pair of lenses set in a frame, worn in front of the eyes to help the wearer to see clearly. **spectacled** adjective

spectacular adjective
impressive. [same origin as *spectacle*]

spectator noun (plural **spectators**) a person who watches a game, show, incident, etc. [from Latin *spectare* = to look at]

spectre noun (plural **spectres**)
a ghost. **spectral** adjective [same origin as *spectrum*]

spectrum noun (plural **spectra**)
1 the bands of colours seen in a rainbow. 2 a wide range of things, ideas, etc. [Latin, = image]

speculate verb (speculates, speculating, speculated)
1 form opinions without having any definite evidence. 2 make investments in the hope of making a profit but risking a loss. **speculation** noun, **speculator** noun, **speculative** adjective [from Latin speculari = spy out]

sped past tense of speed.

speech noun (plural speeches)
1 the action or power of speaking. 2 words spoken. 3 a talk to an audience.

speechless adjective unable to speak because of great emotion.

speed noun (plural speeds)
1 a measure of the time in which something moves or happens. 2 quickness or swiftness.
at speed quickly.

speed verb (speeds, speeding, sped (in senses 3 and 4 speeded))
1 go quickly, The train sped by. 2 send quickly, to speed you on your way. 3 travel too fast. 4 make or become quicker, This will speed things up.
[from Old English]

speed limit noun (plural speed limits) the maximum speed at which vehicles may legally travel on a particular road.

speedometer noun (plural speedometers) a device in a vehicle, showing its speed. [from speed + meter]

speedy adjective (speedier, speediest) quick or swift. **speedily** adverb

spell[1] noun (plural spells) a saying or action etc. supposed to have magical power. [from Old English spel = speech, story]

spell[2] noun (plural spells)
1 a period of time. 2 a period of a certain work or activity etc. [from Old English spelian = take someone's place, take over a task]

spell[3] verb (spells, spelling, spelled or spelt)
1 put letters in the right order to make a word or words. 2 have as a result, Wet weather spells ruin for crops. **speller** noun [via old French from Germanic]

spellbound adjective entranced as if by a magic spell.

spend verb (spends, spending, spent)
1 use money to pay for things. 2 use up, Don't spend too much time on it. 3 pass time, We spent a holiday in Spain.

sperm noun (plural sperms or sperm) the male cell that fuses with an ovum. [from Greek sperma = seed]

sphere noun (plural spheres)
1 a perfectly round solid shape; the shape of a ball. 2 a field of action or interest etc., That country is in Russia's sphere of influence. **spherical** adjective [from Greek sphaira = ball]

spice noun (plural spices) a substance used to flavour food, often made from dried parts of plants. **spicy** adjective [from old French]

spick and span adjective neat and clean. [span is from Old Norse; spick is probably from old Dutch]

spider noun (plural spiders) a small animal with eight legs that spins webs to catch insects on which it feeds. [from Old English spithra = spinner]

spike noun (plural **spikes**)
1 a pointed piece of metal; a sharp point. **2** a long narrow projecting part. **spiky** adjective

spill verb (**spills, spilling, spilt** or **spilled**)
1 let something fall out of a container. **2** become spilt, *The coins came spilling out.* **spillage** noun

spin verb (**spins, spinning, spun**)
1 turn round and round quickly. **2** make raw wool or cotton into threads by pulling and twisting its fibres. **3** (of a spider or silkworm) make a web or cocoon out of threads from its body.
spin a yarn tell a story.
spin out cause to last a long time.

spinach noun a vegetable with dark green leaves. [via Spanish and Arabic from Persian]

spinal cord noun (plural **spinal cords**) the thick cord of nerves enclosed in the spine, that carries impulses to and from the brain.

spindly adjective thin and long or tall. [from *spindle*]

spine noun (plural **spines**)
1 the line of bones down the middle of the back. **2** a thorn or prickle. **3** the back part of a book where the pages are joined together. [from Latin]

spineless adjective
1 without a backbone. **2** lacking in determination or strength of character.

spinney noun (plural **spinneys**) a small wood or thicket. [from old French]

spin-off noun (plural **spin-offs**) a by-product.

spinster noun (plural **spinsters**) a woman who has not married. [the original meaning was 'one who spins' (because many unmarried women used to earn their living by spinning, which could be done at home)]

spiny adjective covered with spines; prickly.

spiral adjective going round and round a central point and becoming gradually closer to it or further from it; twisting continually round a central line or cylinder etc. **spirally** adverb

spiral noun (plural **spirals**) a spiral line or course.

spiral verb (**spirals, spiralling, spiralled**) move in a spiral. [from Greek *speira* = winding]

spire noun (plural **spires**) a tall pointed part on top of a church tower.

spirit noun (plural **spirits**)
1 the soul. **2** a person's mood or mind and feelings, *He was in good spirits.* **3** a ghost or a supernatural being. **4** courage or liveliness, *She answered with spirit.* **5** a kind of quality in something, *the romantic spirit of the book.* **6** a strong distilled alcoholic drink.

spirit verb (**spirits, spiriting, spirited**) carry off quickly and secretly, *They spirited her away.* [from Latin *spiritus* = breath]

spirit level noun (plural **spirit levels**) a device consisting of a tube of liquid with an air bubble in it, used to find out whether something is level.

spiritual adjective
1 to do with the human soul; not physical. **2** to do with the Church

or religion. **spiritually** adverb, **spirituality** noun

spiritual noun (plural **spirituals**) a religious folk song, especially of Black people in America.

spiritualism noun the belief that the spirits of dead people communicate with living people. **spiritualist** noun

spit[1] verb (spits, spitting, spat or spit)
1 send out drops of liquid etc. forcibly from the mouth, *He spat at me.* **2** fall lightly, *It's spitting with rain.*

spit noun saliva.
[from Old English *spittan*]

spit[2] noun (plural **spits**)
1 a long thin metal spike put through them meat or vegetables to hold them together while they are being roasted. **2** a narrow strip of land sticking out into the sea.
[from Old English *spitu*]

spite noun a desire to hurt or annoy somebody. **spiteful** adjective, **spitefully** adverb, **spitefulness** noun
in spite of not being prevented by, *We went out in spite of the rain.* [same origin as *despite*]

spitting image noun an exact likeness.

splash verb (splashes, splashing, splashed)
1 make liquid fly about in drops. **2** (of liquid) be splashed. **3** wet by splashing, *The bus splashed us.*

splash noun (plural **splashes**)
1 the action or sound or mark of splashing. **2** a striking display or effect.

splay verb (splays, splaying, splayed) spread or slope apart.
[from *display*]

splendid adjective
1 magnificent; full of splendour. **2** excellent. **splendidly** adverb [from Latin *splendidus* = shining]

splendour noun a brilliant display or appearance. [from Latin *splendere* = shine brightly]

splint noun (plural **splints**) a straight piece of wood or metal etc. tied to a broken arm or leg to hold it firm.

splinter noun (plural **splinters**) a thin sharp piece of wood, glass, stone, etc. broken off a larger piece.

splinter verb (splinters, splintering, splintered) break into splinters.

splinter group noun (plural **splinter groups**) a group of people that has broken away from a larger group or movement.

split verb (splits, splitting, split)
1 break into parts; divide. **2** (slang) reveal a secret.

split noun (plural **splits**)
1 the splitting or dividing of something. **2** a place where something has split.
the splits an acrobatic position in which the legs are stretched widely in opposite directions.

split second noun a very brief moment of time; an instant.

splutter verb (splutters, spluttering, spluttered)
1 make a quick series of spitting sounds. **2** speak quickly but not clearly. **splutter** noun [imitating the sound]

spoil verb (spoils, spoiling, spoilt or spoiled)
1 damage something and make it

useless or unsatisfactory. **2** make someone selfish by always letting them have what they want.

spoke[1] *noun* (*plural* **spokes**) each of the bars or rods that go from the centre of a wheel to its rim.

spoke[2] *past tense of* **speak.**

spokesperson *noun* (*plural* **spokespersons**) a person who speaks on behalf of a group of people. **spokesman** *noun*, **spokeswoman** *noun*

sponge *noun* (*plural* **sponges**)
1 a sea creature with a soft porous body. **2** the skeleton of this creature, or a piece of a similar substance, used for washing or padding things.
3 a soft lightweight cake or pudding. **spongy** *adjective*

sponge *verb* (**sponges, sponging, sponged**)
1 wipe or wash something with a sponge. **2** live by cadging from people, *He sponged on his friends.* **sponger** *noun*

sponsor *noun* (*plural* **sponsors**) someone who provides money or help etc. for a person or thing, or who gives money to a charity in return for something achieved by another person. **sponsorship** *noun*

sponsor *verb* (**sponsors, sponsoring, sponsored**) be a sponsor for a person or thing. [from Latin *sponsum* = promised]

spontaneous (*say* spon-**tay**-nee-us) *adjective* happening or done naturally; not forced or suggested by someone else. **spontaneously** *adverb*, **spontaneity** *noun* [from Latin *sponte* = of your own accord]

spool *noun* (*plural* **spools**) a rod or cylinder on which something is wound. [via old French from Germanic]

spoon *noun* (*plural* **spoons**) a small device with a rounded bowl on a handle, used for lifting things to the mouth or for stirring or measuring things. **spoonful** *noun* (*plural* **spoonfuls**)

spoonerism *noun* (*plural* **spoonerisms**) an accidental exchange of the initial letters of two words, e.g. by saying *a boiled sprat* instead of *a spoiled brat.* [named after Canon Spooner (1844–1930), who made mistakes of this kind]

spore *noun* (*plural* **spores**) a tiny reproductive cell of a plant such as a fungus or fern. [from Greek *spora* = seed]

sport *noun* (*plural* **sports**)
1 an athletic activity; a game or pastime, especially outdoors.
2 games of this kind, *Are you keen on sport?* **3** (*informal*) a person who behaves fairly and generously, *Come on, be a sport!*

sporting chance *noun* a reasonable chance of success.

sports car *noun* (*plural* **sports cars**) an open low-built fast car.

sportsman *noun* (*plural* **sportsmen**)
1 a man who takes part in sport.
2 a person who shows sportsmanship.

sportsmanship *noun* sporting behaviour; behaving fairly and generously to rivals.

sportswoman *noun* (*plural* **sportswomen**)
1 a woman who takes part in sport. **2** a woman who shows sportsmanship.

spot *noun* (*plural* **spots**)
1 a small round mark. **2** a pimple. **3** a small amount, *We had a spot of trouble.* **4** a place. **5** a drop, *a few spots of rain.*

on the spot without delay or change of place; under pressure to take action, *This really puts him on the spot!*

spot *verb* (**spots**, **spotting**, **spotted**)
1 mark with spots. **2** (*informal*) notice, *We spotted her in the crowd.* **3** watch for and take note of, *train-spotting.* **spotter** *noun*

spotlight *noun* (*plural* **spotlights**)
1 a strong light that can shine on one small area. **2** public attention, *The Royal Family are used to being in the spotlight.*

spotty *adjective* marked with spots.

spouse *noun* (*plural* **spouses**)
a person's husband or wife. [from old French; related to *sponsor*]

spout *noun* (*plural* **spouts**)
1 a pipe or similar opening from which liquid can pour. **2** a jet of liquid.

spout *verb* (**spouts**, **spouting**, **spouted**)
1 come or send out as a jet of liquid. **2** (*informal*) speak for a long time.

sprain *verb* (**sprains**, **spraining**, **sprained**) injure a joint by twisting it. **sprain** *noun*

sprawl *verb* (**sprawls**, **sprawling**, **sprawled**)
1 sit or lie with the arms and legs

spread out loosely. **2** spread out loosely or untidily. **sprawl** *noun* [from Old English]

spray[1] *verb* (**sprays**, **spraying**, **sprayed**) scatter tiny drops of liquid over something.

spray *noun* (*plural* **sprays**)
1 tiny drops of liquid sprayed. **2** a device for spraying liquid. [origin unknown]

spray[2] *noun* (*plural* **sprays**)
1 a single twig with its leaves and flowers. **2** a small bunch of flowers. [from Old English]

spread *verb* (**spreads**, **spreading**, **spread**)
1 open or stretch something out to its full size, *The bird spread its wings.* **2** make something cover a surface, *We spread jam on the bread.* **3** become longer or wider, *The stain was spreading.* **4** make or become more widely known or felt or distributed etc., *We spread the news. Panic spread.*

spread *noun* (*plural* **spreads**)
1 the action or result of spreading. **2** a thing's breadth or extent. **3** a paste for spreading on bread. **4** (*informal*) a large or grand meal.
[from Old English]

spreadeagled *adjective* with arms and legs stretched out, *He lay spreadeagled on the bed.*
[originally = a picture of an eagle with legs and wings stretched out, used as an emblem on a knight's shield, inn sign, etc.]

spree *noun* (*plural* **sprees**) a lively outing. [origin unknown]

sprig *noun* (*plural* **sprigs**) a small branch; a shoot. [from old German]

sprightly *adjective* (**sprightlier, sprightliest**) lively and full of energy. [from *sprite*]

spring *verb* (**springs, springing, sprang, sprung**)
1 jump; move quickly or suddenly, *He sprang to his feet.*
2 originate or arise, *The trouble has sprung from carelessness.*
3 present or produce suddenly, *They sprang a surprise on us.*

spring *noun* (*plural* **springs**)
1 a springy coil or bent piece of metal. 2 a springing movement. 3 a place where water comes up naturally from the ground. 4 the season when most plants begin to grow. [from Old English]

springboard *noun* (*plural* **springboards**) a springy board from which people jump in diving and gymnastics.

spring-clean *verb* (**spring-cleans, spring-cleaning, spring-cleaned**) clean a house thoroughly in springtime.

springy *adjective* (**springier, springiest**) able to spring back easily after being bent or squeezed. **springiness** *noun*

sprinkle *verb* (**sprinkles, sprinkling, sprinkled**) make tiny drops or pieces fall on something. **sprinkler** *noun*

sprint *verb* (**sprints, sprinting, sprinted**) run very fast for a short distance. **sprint** *noun*, **sprinter** *noun* [from Old Norse]

sprout *verb* (**sprouts, sprouting, sprouted**) start to grow; put out shoots.

sprout *noun* (*plural* **sprouts**)
1 a shoot of a plant. 2 a Brussels sprout.

spruce¹ *noun* (*plural* **spruces**) a kind of fir tree. [from *Pruce*, the old name of Prussia, an area in central Europe, where it was grown]

spruce² *adjective* neat and trim; smart.

spruce *verb* (**spruces, sprucing, spruced**) smarten, *Spruce yourself up.*
[probably from *spruce jerkin*, made of leather from Prussia (see *spruce*¹)]

spry *adjective* (**spryer, spryest**) active, nimble, and lively.

spur *noun* (*plural* **spurs**)
1 a sharp device worn on the heel of a rider's boot to urge a horse to go faster. 2 a stimulus or incentive. 3 a projecting part.
on the spur of the moment on an impulse; without planning.

spur *verb* (**spurs, spurring, spurred**) urge on; encourage. [from Old English]

spurious *adjective* not genuine. [from Latin]

spurn *verb* (**spurns, spurning, spurned**) reject scornfully. [from Old English]

spurt *verb* (**spurts, spurting, spurted**)
1 gush out. 2 increase your speed suddenly.

spurt *noun* (*plural* **spurts**)
1 a sudden gush. 2 a sudden increase in speed or effort. [origin unknown]

spy *noun* (*plural* **spies**) someone who works secretly for one country, person, etc. to find out things about another.

spy *verb* (**spies, spying, spied**)
1 be a spy. 2 keep watch secretly.

3 see or notice, *She spied a house.*
4 pry.
[from old French *espier* = espy]

squabble verb (**squabbles,
squabbling, squabbled**) quarrel
or bicker. **squabble** *noun*

squad noun (*plural* **squads**)
a small group of people working
or being trained together. [from
old French; related to *squadron*]

squadron noun (*plural*
squadrons) part of an army,
navy, or air force. [from Italian;
related to *squad*]

squalid *adjective* dirty and
unpleasant. **squalidly** *adverb*,
squalor *noun* [from Latin
squalidus = rough, dirty]

squall noun (*plural* **squalls**)
1 a sudden storm or gust of wind.
2 a baby's loud cry.

squall verb (**squalls, squalling,
squalled**) (of a baby) cry loudly.
[probably from *squeal* and *bawl*]

squander verb (**squanders,
squandering, squandered**) spend
money or time etc. wastefully.

square noun (*plural* **squares**)
1 a flat shape with four equal
sides and four right angles. **2** an
area surrounded by buildings,
Leicester Square. **3** the number
produced by multiplying
something by itself, *9 is the
square of 3 (9 = 3 × 3).*

square *adjective*
1 having the shape of a square.
2 forming a right angle, *The desk
has square corners.* **3** equal or
even, *The teams are all square
with six points each.* **squarely**
adverb, **squareness** *noun*

square foot, square metre, etc.,
the area of a surface with sides

that are one foot or one metre etc.
long.

square verb (**squares, squaring,
squared**)
1 make a thing square. **2** multiply
a number by itself, *5 squared is
25.* **3** match; make or be
consistent, *His story doesn't
square with yours.* **4** (*informal*)
bribe.
[from old French; related to
quadrant]

square deal noun one that is
honest and fair.

square meal noun (*plural* **square
meals**) a good satisfying meal.

square root noun (*plural* **square
roots**) the number that gives
a particular number if it is
multiplied by itself, *3 is the
square root of 9 (3 × 3 = 9).*

squash verb (**squashes,
squashing, squashed**)
1 press something so that it loses
its shape; crush. **2** pack tightly.
3 suppress or quash.

squash noun (*plural* **squashes**)
1 a crowded condition. **2** a fruit-
flavoured soft drink. **3** a game
played with rackets and a soft
ball in a special indoor court.

squat verb (**squats, squatting,
squatted**)
1 sit on your heels; crouch. **2** use
an unoccupied building for living
in without permission. **squat**
noun, **squatter** *noun*

squat *adjective* short and fat.
[from *ex-* + old French *quatir*
= press down, crouch]

squawk verb (**squawks,
squawking, squawked**) make
a loud harsh cry. **squawk** *noun*

squeak verb (**squeaks, squeaking,
squeaked**) make a high-pitched

cry or sound. **squeak** noun, **squeaky** adjective, **squeakily** adverb [imitating the sound]

squeal verb (**squeals, squealing, squealed**) make a long shrill cry or sound. **squeal** noun [imitating the sound]

squeamish adjective easily disgusted or shocked. **squeamishness** noun [from old French]

squeeze verb (**squeezes, squeezing, squeezed**)
1 press something from opposite sides, especially to get liquid out of it. 2 force into or through a place, *We squeezed through a gap in the hedge.* **squeezer** noun
squeeze noun (plural **squeezes**)
1 the action of squeezing. 2 a drop of liquid squeezed out, *Add a squeeze of lemon.* 3 a time when money is difficult to get or borrow.
[origin unknown]

squelch verb (**squelches, squelching, squelched**) make a sound like someone treading in thick mud. **squelch** noun

squid noun (plural **squids**) a sea animal with eight short tentacles and two long ones. [origin unknown]

squint verb (**squints, squinting, squinted**)
1 be cross-eyed. 2 peer; look with half-shut eyes at something.
squint noun

squire noun (plural **squires**)
1 the man who owns most of the land in a country parish or district. 2 a young nobleman in the Middle Ages who served a knight. [from *esquire*]

squirm verb (**squirms, squirming, squirmed**) wriggle. [origin unknown]

squirrel noun (plural **squirrels**) a small animal with a bushy tail and red or grey fur, living in trees. [from Greek]

squirt verb (**squirts, squirting, squirted**) send or come out in a jet of liquid. **squirt** noun [imitating the sound]

St. or **St** abbreviation
1 Saint. 2 Street.

stab verb (**stabs, stabbing, stabbed**) pierce or wound with something sharp.
stab noun (plural **stabs**)
1 the action of stabbing.
2 a sudden sharp pain, *She felt a stab of fear.* 3 (informal) an attempt, *I'll have a stab at it.*

stability noun being stable.

stable[1] adjective
1 steady or firmly fixed; not likely to move or change.
2 sensible and dependable. **stably** adverb [from Latin *stare* = to stand]

stable[2] noun (plural **stables**) a building where horses are kept.
stable verb (**stables, stabling, stabled**) put or keep in a stable. [from old French; related to *stable*[1]]

stack noun (plural **stacks**)
1 a neat pile. 2 a haystack.
3 (informal) a large amount, *a stack of work.* 4 a single tall chimney; a group of small chimneys.
stack verb (**stacks, stacking, stacked**) pile things up.
[from Old Norse]

stadium noun (plural **stadiums**)
a sports ground surrounded by
seats for spectators. [Latin]

staff noun (plural **staffs** or, in
sense **4**, **staves**)
1 the people who work in an
office, shop, etc. **2** the teachers in
a school or college. **3** a stick or
pole used as a weapon or support
or as a symbol of authority. **4** a set
of five horizontal lines on which
music is written.

staff verb (**staffs**, **staffing**,
staffed) provide with a staff of
people, *The centre is staffed by
volunteers.*
[from Old English]

stag noun (plural **stags**) a male
deer. [probably from Old
English]

stage noun (plural **stages**)
1 a platform for performances in
a theatre or hall. **2** a point or part
of a process, journey, etc., *the
final stage.*

stage verb (**stages**, **staging**,
staged)
1 present a performance on
a stage. **2** organize, *We decided to
stage a protest.*

stagecoach noun (plural
stagecoaches) a horse-drawn
coach that formerly ran
regularly from one point to
another along the same route.

stage-manage verb (**stage-
manages**, **stage-managing**, **stage-
managed**)
1 be stage manager. **2** organize
and control an event so that it
has a particular effect.

stage manager noun (plural
stage managers) the person in
charge of the scenery, lighting,
sound, etc. during a performance.

stage-struck adjective fascinated
by the theatre and longing to be
an actor.

stagger verb (**staggers**,
staggering, **staggered**)
1 walk unsteadily. **2** shock
deeply; amaze, *We were staggered
at the price.* **3** arrange things so
that they do not coincide, *Please
stagger your holidays so that there
is always someone here.* **stagger**
noun

stagnant adjective
1 not flowing. **2** not active or
developing, *business is stagnant.*
[from Latin *stagnum* = a pool]

stain noun (plural **stains**)
1 a dirty mark on something.
2 a blemish on someone's
character or past record.
3 a liquid used for staining
things.

stain verb (**stains**, **staining**,
stained)
1 make a stain on something.
2 colour with a liquid that sinks
into the surface.
[from an old word *distain* = dye]

stained glass noun pieces of
coloured glass held together in
a lead framework to make
a picture or pattern.

stainless steel noun steel that
does not rust easily.

stair noun (plural **stairs**) each of
the fixed steps in a series that
lead from one level or floor to
another in a building. [from Old
English]

staircase noun (plural **staircases**)
a flight of stairs.

stake noun (plural **stakes**)
1 a thick pointed stick to be
driven into the ground. **2** the
post to which people used to be tied

for execution by being burnt alive. **3** an amount of money bet on something. **4** an investment that gives a person a share or interest in an enterprise.
at stake being risked.

stake verb (stakes, staking, staked)
1 fasten, support, or mark out with stakes. **2** bet or risk money etc. on an event.
stake a claim claim or obtain a right to something.

stalactite noun (plural stalactites) a stony spike hanging like an icicle from a cave roof. [from Greek *stalaktos* = dripping]

USAGE: See note at *stalagmite*.

stalagmite noun (plural stalagmites) a stony spike standing like a pillar on the floor of a cave. [from Greek *stalagma* = a drop]

USAGE: Remember that a *stalagmite* stands up from the ground, while a *stalactite* hangs down from the ceiling.

stale adjective not fresh. **staleness** noun [old French, = at a standstill]

stalemate noun
1 a drawn position in chess when a player cannot make a move without putting his or her king in check. **2** a deadlock; a situation in which neither side in an argument will give way. [from old French *stale* = at a standstill, + *mate²*]

stalk¹ noun (plural stalks) a stem of a plant etc. [from Old English *stalu*]

stalk² verb (stalks, stalking, stalked)
1 track or hunt stealthily. **2** walk in a stiff or dignified way. [from Old English *stealcian*]

stall¹ noun (plural stalls)
1 a table or counter from which things are sold. **2** a place for one animal in a stable or shed.

stall verb (stalls, stalling, stalled)
1 stop suddenly, *The car engine stalled.* **2** put an animal into a stall.
[from Old English]

stall² verb (stalls, stalling, stalled) delay things deliberately so as to avoid having to take action. [from an old word *stall* = a decoy or a pickpocket's helper]

stallion noun (plural stallions) a male horse. [from old French]

stalls plural noun the seats in the lowest level of a theatre.

stalwart adjective sturdy; strong and faithful, *my stalwart supporters.* [from Old English]

stamen noun (plural stamens) the part of a flower bearing pollen. [Latin, = thread]

stamina noun strength and ability to endure things for a long time. [Latin, plural of *stamen* (referring to the threads of life spun by the fates)]

stammer verb (stammers, stammering, stammered) keep repeating the same syllables when you speak. **stammer** noun

stamp noun (plural stamps)
1 a small piece of gummed paper with a special design on it; a postage stamp. **2** a small device for pressing words or marks on something; the words or marks made by this. **3** a distinctive

characteristic, *His story bears the stamp of truth.*

stamp *verb* (**stamps, stamping, stamped**)
1 bang a foot heavily on the ground. 2 walk with loud heavy steps. 3 stick a stamp on something. 4 press a mark or design etc. on something.
stamp out put out a fire etc. by stamping; stop something, *stamp out cruelty.*

stampede *noun* (*plural* **stampedes**) a sudden rush by animals or people. **stampede** *verb* [from Spanish *estampida* = crash, uproar]

stand *verb* (**stands, standing, stood**)
1 be on your feet without moving, *We were standing at the back of the hall.* 2 set or be upright; place, *We stood the vase on the table.* 3 stay the same, *My offer still stands.* 4 be a candidate for election, *She stood for Parliament.* 5 tolerate or endure, *I can't stand that noise.* 6 provide and pay for, *I'll stand you a drink.*
it stands to reason it is reasonable or obvious.
stand by be ready for action.
stand for 1 represent. 2 tolerate.
stand up for support or defend.
stand up to 1 resist bravely. 2 stay in good condition in hard use.

stand *noun* (*plural* **stands**)
1 something made for putting things on, *a music stand.* 2 a stall where things are sold or displayed. 3 a grandstand.
4 a stationary condition or position, *He took his stand near the door.* 5 resistance to attack, *We made a stand.*

standard *noun* (*plural* **standards**)
1 how good something is, *a high standard of work.* 2 a thing used to measure or judge something else. 3 a special flag, *the royal standard.* 4 an upright support.

standard *adjective*
1 of the usual or average quality or kind. 2 regarded as the best and widely used, *the standard book on spiders.*
[from old French]

stand-in *noun* (*plural* **stand-ins**) a deputy or substitute.

standing order *noun* (*plural* **standing orders**) an instruction to a bank to make regular payments, or to a trader to supply something regularly.

stand-offish *adjective* cold and formal; not friendly.

standpoint *noun* (*plural* **standpoints**) a point of view.

standstill *noun* a stop; an end to movement or activity.

staple[1] *noun* (*plural* **staples**)
1 a small piece of metal pushed through papers and clenched to fasten them together. 2 a U-shaped nail. **staple** *verb*, **stapler** *noun* [from Old English]

staple[2] *adjective* main or usual, *Rice is their staple food.* **staple** *noun* [from old French]

star *noun* (*plural* **stars**)
1 a large mass of burning gas that is seen as a speck of light in the sky at night. 2 a shape with rays from it; an asterisk. 3 an object or mark of this shape showing rank or quality, *a five-star hotel.*
4 a famous performer; one of the chief performers in a play or show etc.

star verb (stars, starring, starred)
1 perform or present as a star in a show etc. **2** mark with an asterisk or star symbol. [from Old English]

starboard noun the right-hand side of a ship or aircraft when you are facing forward. (Compare port¹.) [from Old English steor = paddle for steering (usually mounted on the right-hand side), + board]

starch noun (plural starches) **1** a white carbohydrate in bread, potatoes, etc. **2** this or a similar substance used to stiffen clothes. **starchy** adjective

starch verb (starches, starching, starched) stiffen with starch. [from Old English]

stare verb (stares, staring, stared) look at something intensely. **stare** noun

starfish noun (plural starfish or starfishes) a sea animal shaped like a star with five points.

stark adjective
1 complete or unmistakable, stark nonsense. **2** desolate and bare; without cheerfulness, the stark lunar landscape. **starkly** adverb, **starkness** noun

stark adverb completely, stark naked.

starling noun (plural starlings) a noisy black bird with speckled feathers.

starry adjective full of stars.

starry-eyed adjective made happy by foolish dreams or unrealistic hopes.

start verb (starts, starting, started) **1** begin or cause to begin. **2** begin a journey. **3** make a sudden movement because of pain or surprise. **starter** noun

start noun (plural starts) **1** the beginning; the place where a race starts. **2** an advantage that someone starts with, We gave the young ones ten minutes' start. **3** a sudden movement.

startle verb (startles, startling, startled) surprise or alarm someone.

starve verb (starves, starving, starved) **1** suffer or die from lack of food; cause to do this. **2** (informal) be very hungry. **starvation** noun [from Old English]

state noun (plural states) **1** the quality of a person's or thing's characteristics or circumstances; condition. **2** a grand style, She arrived in state. **3** an organized community under one government (the State of Israel) or forming part of a republic (the 50 States of the USA). **4** a country's government, Help for the earthquake victims was provided by the state. **5** (informal) an excited or upset condition, Don't get into a state about the robbery.

state verb (states, stating, stated) express something in spoken or written words. [same origin as stable¹]

stately adjective (statelier, stateliest) dignified, imposing, or grand. **stateliness** noun [from state]

statement noun (plural statements) **1** words stating something. **2** a formal account of facts, The witness made a statement to the *police*. **3** a written report of a financial account, *a bank statement*.

state school *noun* (*plural* **state schools**) a school which is funded by the government and which does not charge fees to pupils.

statesman *noun* (*plural* **statesmen**) a person, especially a man, who is important or skilled in governing a country. **statesmanship** *noun*, **stateswoman** *noun*

static *adjective* not moving or changing. [from Greek]

static electricity *noun* electricity that is present in something, not flowing as current.

station *noun* (*plural* **stations**)
1 a place where a person or thing stands or is stationed; a position. **2** a stopping place on a railway with buildings for passengers and goods. **3** a building equipped for people who serve the public or for certain activities, *the police station*. **4** a broadcasting establishment with its own frequency. [from Latin *statio* = a stand, standing]

stationary *adjective* not moving, *The car was stationary when the van hit it*.

USAGE: Do not confuse with *stationery*.

stationery *noun* paper, envelopes, and other articles used in writing or typing.

USAGE: Do not confuse with *stationary*.

statistician (*say* stat-is-**tish**-an) *noun* (*plural* **statisticians**) an expert in statistics.

statistics *noun* the study of information based on the numbers of things.

statue *noun* (*plural* **statues**) a model made of stone or metal etc. to look like a person or animal. [same origin as *stable*[1]]

statuette *noun* (*plural* **statuettes**) a small statue.

stature *noun*
1 the natural height of the body. **2** greatness because of ability or achievement. [same origin as *stable*[1]]

status (*say* **stay**-tus) *noun* (*plural* **statuses**)
1 a person's or thing's position or rank in relation to others. **2** high rank or prestige. [same origin as *stable*[1]]

statute *noun* (*plural* **statutes**) a law passed by a parliament.

statutory *adjective* [from Latin *statuere* = set up, decree; related to *stable*[1]]

staunch *adjective* firm and loyal, *our staunch supporters*. **staunchly** *adverb* [from old French]

stave *verb* (**staves**, **staving**, **staved** or **stove**) dent or break a hole in something, *The collision stove in the front of the ship*.

stave off keep something away, *We staved off the disaster*.

stay *verb* (**stays**, **staying**, **stayed**)
1 continue to be in the same place or condition; remain. **2** spend time in a place as a visitor. **3** satisfy temporarily, *We stayed our hunger with a sandwich*. **4** pause. **5** show endurance in a race or task.

stay put (*informal*) remain in place.

stay *noun* (*plural* **stays**)
1 a time spent somewhere, *We made a short stay in Rome.*
2 a postponement, *a stay of execution.*
[same origin as **stable**[1]]

stead *noun*
in a person's or **thing's stead** instead of this person or thing.
stand a person in good stead be very useful to him or her.

steadfast *adjective* firm and not changing, *a steadfast refusal.*

steady *adjective* (**steadier, steadiest**)
1 not shaking or moving; firm.
2 regular; continuing the same, *a steady pace.* **steadily** *adverb*, **steadiness** *noun* [from **stead**]

steak *noun* (*plural* **steaks**) a thick slice of meat (especially beef) or fish. [from Old Norse]

steal *verb* (**steals, stealing, stole, stolen**)
1 take and keep something that does not belong to you; take secretly or dishonestly. **2** move secretly or without being noticed, *He stole out of the room.* [from Old English]

stealthy (*say* stelth-ee) *adjective* (**stealthier, stealthiest**) quiet and secret, so as not to be noticed. **stealth** *noun*, **stealthily** *adverb*, **stealthiness** *noun* [probably from Old English and related to **steal**]

steam *noun*
1 the gas or vapour that comes from boiling water; this used to drive machinery. **2** energy, *He ran out of steam.* **steamy** *adjective*

steam *verb* (**steams, steaming, steamed**)
1 give out steam. **2** cook or treat by steam, *a steamed pudding.*
3 move by the power of steam, *The ship steamed down the river.*

steam engine *noun* (*plural* **steam engines**) an engine driven by steam.

steamroller *noun* (*plural* **steamrollers**) a heavy vehicle with a large roller used to flatten surfaces when making roads. [because the first ones were powered by steam]

steed *noun* (*plural* **steeds**) (*poetical*) a horse. [from Old English]

steel *noun* (*plural* **steels**)
1 a strong metal made from iron and carbon. **2** a steel rod for sharpening knives. [from Old English]

steely *adjective*
1 like or to do with steel. **2** cold, hard, and severe, *a steely glare.*

steep[1] *adjective*
1 sloping very sharply, not gradually. **2** (*informal*) unreasonably high, *a steep price.* **steeply** *adverb*, **steepness** *noun*

steep[2] *verb* (**steeps, steeping, steeped**) soak thoroughly; saturate [probably from a Scandinavian language]

steepen *verb* (**steepens, steepening, steepened**) make or become steeper.

steeple *noun* (*plural* **steeples**) a church tower with a spire on top.

steer verb (steers, steering, steered) make a car, ship, or bicycle etc. go in the direction you want; guide. **steersman** noun [from Old English *stieran*]

steering wheel noun (plural **steering wheels**) a wheel for steering a car, boat, etc.

stem[1] noun (plural **stems**) 1 the main central part of a tree, shrub, or plant. 2 a thin part on which a leaf, flower, or fruit is supported. 3 a thin upright part, e.g. the thin part of a wineglass between the bowl and the foot. 4 the main part of a verb or other word, to which endings are attached. 5 the front part of a ship, *from stem to stern*.

stem verb (stems, stemming, stemmed)
stem from arise from; have as its source.
[from Old English]

stem[2] verb (stems, stemming, stemmed) stop the flow of something. [from Old Norse]

stench noun (plural **stenches**) a very unpleasant smell.

stencil noun (plural **stencils**) a piece of card, metal, or plastic with pieces cut out of it, used to produce a picture, design, etc.

step noun (plural **steps**) 1 a movement made by lifting the foot and setting it down. 2 the sound or rhythm of stepping. 3 a level surface for placing the foot on in climbing up or down. 4 each of a series of things done in some process or action, *The first step is to find somewhere to practise.*
in step 1 stepping in time with others in marching or dancing. 2 in agreement.
watch your step be careful.

step verb (steps, stepping, stepped) tread or walk.
step in intervene.
step on it (*informal*) hurry.
step up increase something.
[from Old English *steppan*]

step- *prefix* related through remarriage of one parent. [from Old English *steop-*]

stepfather noun (plural **stepfathers**) a man who is married to your mother but was not your natural father.

stepladder noun (plural **stepladders**) a folding ladder with flat treads.

stepmother noun (plural **stepmothers**) a woman who is married to your father but was not your natural mother.

stepping stone noun (plural **stepping stones**) 1 each of a line of stones put into a shallow stream so that people can walk across. 2 a way of achieving something, or a stage in achieving it, *good exam results can be a stepping stone to a career.*

stereo noun (plural **stereos**) 1 stereophonic sound or recording. 2 a stereophonic record player or radio. [from *stereophonic*]

stereophonic adjective using sound that comes from two different directions so as to give a natural effect. [from Greek *stereos* = solid, three-dimensional + *phone* = sound]

stereotype noun (plural **stereotypes**) a standardized character; a fixed idea etc., *The* *stereotype of a hero* is one who is tall, strong, brave, and good-looking. [originally = a kind of printing which appeared three-dimensional: from Greek *stereos* = solid, three-dimensional, + *type*]

sterile *adjective*
1 not fertile; barren. **2** free from germs. **sterility** *noun* [from Latin]

sterilize *verb* (**sterilizes, sterilizing, sterilized**)
1 make a thing free from germs, e.g. by heating it. **2** make a person or animal unable to reproduce. **sterilization** *noun*, **sterilizer** *noun*

sterling *noun* British money.

sterling *adjective*
1 genuine, *sterling silver*. **2** excellent; of great worth, *her sterling qualities.* [probably from Old English *steorra* = star, + *-ling* (because some early coins had a star on them)]

stern[1] *adjective* strict and severe, not lenient or kindly. **sternly** *adverb*, **sternness** *noun*

stern[2] *noun* (*plural* **sterns**) the back part of a ship. [from Old Norse]

stew *verb* (**stews, stewing, stewed**) cook slowly in liquid.

stew *noun* (*plural* **stews**) a dish of stewed food, especially meat and vegetables.

in a stew (*informal*) very worried or agitated.

steward *noun* (*plural* **stewards**)
1 a man whose job is to look after the passengers on a ship or aircraft. **2** an official who keeps order or supervises the arrangements at an event. [from Old English *stig* = house or hall, + *ward*]

stewardess *noun* (*plural* **stewardesses**) a woman whose job is to look after the passengers on a ship or aircraft.

stick[1] *noun* (*plural* **sticks**)
1 a long thin piece of wood. **2** a walking stick. **3** the implement used to hit the ball in hockey, polo, etc. **4** a long thin piece of something, *a stick of rock*. [from Old English *sticca*]

stick[2] *verb* (**sticks, sticking, stuck**)
1 push a thing into something, *Stick a pin in it.* **2** fix or be fixed by glue or as if by this, *Stick stamps on the parcel.* **3** become fixed and unable to move, *The boat stuck on a sandbank.* **4** (*informal*) endure or tolerate, *I can't stick that noise!* **5** (*informal*) impose a task on someone, *We were stuck with the clearing up.*

stick out 1 come or push out from a surface; stand out from the surrounding area. **2** be very noticeable.

stick to 1 remain faithful to a friend or promise etc. **2** keep to and not alter, *He stuck to his story.*

stick together 1 stay together. **2** support each other.

stick up for (*informal*) stand up for.

stickler *noun* (*plural* **sticklers**) a person who insists on something, *a stickler for punctuality.* [from Old English *stihtan* = put in order]

sticky *adjective* (**stickier, stickiest**)
1 able or likely to stick to things. **2** (of weather) hot and humid, causing perspiration. **3** (*informal*) uncooperative, *She was very*

sticky about letting me come.
stickily *adverb*, **stickiness** *noun*
come to a sticky end die or end in
a painful or unpleasant way.

stiff *adjective*
1 not bending or moving or
changing its shape easily. **2** not
fluid; hard to stir, *a stiff dough.*
3 difficult, *a stiff examination.*
4 formal in manner; not friendly.
5 severe or strong, *a stiff breeze.*
stiffly *adverb*, **stiffness** *noun*
[from Old English]

stiffen *verb* (**stiffens, stiffening,
stiffened**) make or become stiff.
stiffener *noun*

stifle *verb* (**stifles, stifling, stifled**)
1 suffocate. **2** suppress, *She stifled
a yawn.*

stile *noun* (*plural* **stiles**) an
arrangement of steps or bars for
people to climb over a fence.
[from Old English]

stiletto heel *noun* (*plural* **stiletto
heels**) a high pointed shoe-heel.

still *adjective*
1 not moving, *still water.* **2** silent.
3 not fizzy. **stillness** *noun*

still *adverb*
1 without moving, *Stand still.*
2 up to this or that time, *He was
still there.* **3** in a greater amount
or degree, *You can do still better.*
4 nevertheless, *They've lost. Still,
they tried, and that was good.*

stillborn *adjective* born dead.
[from *still*[1] + *born*]

still life *noun* (*plural* **still lifes**)
a painting of lifeless things such
as ornaments and fruit.

stilted *adjective* stiffly formal.
[originally = raised on stilts]

stilts *plural noun* a pair of poles
with supports for the feet so that
the user can walk high above the
ground.

stimulate *verb* (**stimulates,
stimulating, stimulated**)
1 make more lively or active.
2 excite or interest. **stimulation**
noun

sting *noun* (*plural* **stings**)
1 a sharp-pointed part of an
animal or plant, often containing
a poison, that can cause a wound.
2 a painful wound caused by this
part.

sting *verb* (**stings, stinging,
stung**)
1 wound or hurt with a sting.
2 feel a sharp pain. **3** stimulate
sharply, *I was stung into
answering rudely.* **4** (*slang*) cheat
a person by overcharging; extort
money from someone.
[from Old English]

stingy (*say* stin-jee) *adjective*
(**stingier, stingiest**) mean, not
generous; giving or given in
small amounts. **stingily** *adverb*,
stinginess *noun* [from *sting*]

stink *noun* (*plural* **stinks**)
1 an unpleasant smell.
2 (*informal*) an unpleasant fuss
or protest.

stink *verb* (**stinks, stinking, stank**
or **stunk**) have an unpleasant
smell.

stint *noun* (*plural* **stints**)
1 a fixed amount of work to be
done. **2** limitation of a supply or
effort, *They gave help without
stint.*

stint *verb* (**stints, stinting,
stinted**) limit; be niggardly, *Don't
stint them of food.*

stir verb (stirs, stirring, stirred)
1 mix a liquid or soft mixture by moving a spoon etc. round and round in it. 2 move slightly; start to move. 3 excite or stimulate, *They stirred up trouble.*

stir noun
1 the action of stirring.
2 a disturbance; excitement, *The news caused a stir.*

stirrup noun (plural **stirrups**) a metal part that hangs from each side of a horse's saddle, for a rider to put his or her foot in. [from Old English]

stitch noun (plural **stitches**)
1 a loop of thread made in sewing or knitting. 2 a method of arranging the threads, *cross stitch.* 3 a sudden sharp pain in the side of the body, caused by running.

stitch verb (stitches, stitching, stitched) sew or fasten with stitches.

stoat noun (plural **stoats**) a kind of weasel also called an ermine.

stock noun (plural **stocks**)
1 a number of things kept ready to be sold or used. 2 livestock.
3 a line of ancestors, *a man of Irish stock.* 4 liquid made by stewing meat, fish, or vegetables, used for making soup etc.
5 a garden flower with a sweet smell. 6 shares in a business company's capital (see *share* 2).
7 the main stem of a tree or plant.
8 the base, holder, or handle of an implement etc. 9 a kind of cravat.

stock verb (stocks, stocking, stocked)
1 keep goods in stock. 2 provide a place with a stock of something.

stockade noun (plural **stockades**) a fence made of stakes. [from Spanish]

stockbroker noun (plural **stockbrokers**) a broker who deals in stocks and shares.

stock exchange noun (plural **stock exchanges**) a place where stocks and shares are bought and sold.

stocking noun (plural **stockings**) a garment covering the foot and part or all of the leg. [from *stock*]

stock market noun (plural **stock markets**)
1 a stock exchange. 2 the buying and selling of stocks and shares.

stockpile noun (plural **stockpiles**) a large stock of things kept in reserve. **stockpile** verb

stocks plural noun a wooden framework with holes for a seated person's legs, used like the pillory. [from *stock*]

stock-still adjective quite still.

stocktaking noun the counting, listing, and checking of a shop's stock or a company's goods and resources.

stocky adjective (stockier, stockiest) short and solidly built, *a stocky man.* [from *stock*]

stodgy adjective (stodgier, stodgiest)
1 (of food) heavy and filling. 2 dull and boring, *a stodgy book.* **stodginess** noun

stoical (say stoh-ik-al) adjective bearing pain or difficulties etc. calmly without complaining. **stoically** adverb, **stoicism** noun [named after ancient Greek philosophers called *Stoics*]

stoke verb (stokes, stoking, stoked) put fuel in a furnace or on a fire. **stoker** noun [from Dutch]

stole past tense of **steal**.

stolid adjective not excitable; not feeling or showing emotion. **stolidly** adverb, **stolidity** noun

stomach noun (plural stomachs) 1 the part of the body where food starts to be digested. 2 the abdomen.

stomach verb (stomachs, stomaching, stomached) endure or tolerate. [from Greek]

stone noun (plural stones) 1 a piece of rock. 2 stones or rock as material, e.g. for building. 3 a jewel. 4 the hard case round the kernel of plums, cherries, etc. 5 a unit of weight equal to 14 pounds, *She weighs 6 stone.*

stone verb (stones, stoning, stoned) 1 throw stones at somebody. 2 remove the stones from fruit. [from Old English]

stone- prefix completely, *stone-cold.*

Stone Age noun the earliest period of human history, when tools and weapons were made of stone.

stone-cold adjective extremely cold; completely without warmth.

stone-deaf adjective completely deaf.

stony adjective 1 full of stones. 2 like stone; hard. 3 not answering, *a stony silence.*

stool noun (plural stools) 1 a movable seat without arms or a back. 2 a footstool. 3 a lump of faeces.

stoop verb (stoops, stooping, stooped) 1 bend your body forwards and down. 2 lower yourself, *He would not stoop to cheating.* **stoop** noun [from Old English]

stop verb (stops, stopping, stopped) 1 bring or come to an end; not continue working or moving. 2 stay. 3 prevent or obstruct something. 4 fill a hole, especially in a tooth.

stop noun (plural stops) 1 stopping; a pause or end. 2 a place where a bus or train etc. regularly stops. 3 a punctuation mark, especially a full stop. 4 a lever or knob that controls pitch in a wind instrument or allows organ pipes to sound. [from Old English]

stopcock noun (plural stopcocks) a valve controlling the flow of liquid or gas in a pipe.

stopgap noun (plural stopgaps) a temporary substitute.

stoppage noun (plural stoppages) 1 an interruption in the work of a factory etc. 2 an amount taken off someone's wages. 3 a blockage.

stopper noun (plural stoppers) a plug for closing a bottle etc.

stopwatch noun (plural stopwatches) a watch that can be started and stopped when you wish, used for timing races etc.

store noun (plural stores) 1 a stock of things kept for future use; a place where these are kept. 2 a shop, especially a large one. **in store** 1 being stored. 2 going to

happen, *There's a surprise in store for you.*
set store by something value it greatly.
store verb (stores, storing, stored) keep things until they are needed. **storage** noun

storey noun (plural **storeys**) one whole floor of a building. [from Latin]

USAGE: Do not confuse with *story*.

stork noun (plural **storks**) a large bird with long legs and a long beak.

storm noun (plural **storms**)
1 a very strong wind usually with rain, snow, etc. **2** a violent attack or outburst, *a storm of protest.*
stormy adjective
storm in a teacup a great fuss over something unimportant.

storm verb (storms, storming, stormed)
1 move or behave violently or angrily, *He stormed out of the room.* **2** attack or capture by a sudden assault, *They stormed the castle.*

story noun (plural **stories**)
1 an account of a real or imaginary event. **2** the plot of a play or novel etc. **3** (*informal*) a lie, *Don't tell stories!* [from Latin *historia* = history]

USAGE: Do not confuse with *storey*.

stout adjective
1 rather fat. **2** thick and strong. **3** brave and determined, *a stout defender of human rights.* **stoutly** adverb, **stoutness** noun

stove[1] noun (plural **stoves**)
1 a device containing an oven or ovens. **2** a device for heating a room. [from old German or old Dutch]

stove[2] past tense of **stave**.

stow verb (stows, stowing, stowed) pack or store something away. **stowage** noun
stow away hide on a ship or aircraft so as to travel without paying. **stowaway** noun

straddle verb (straddles, straddling, straddled) be astride; sit or stand across something, *A long bridge straddles the river.*

straggle verb (straggles, straggling, straggled)
1 grow or spread in an untidy way. **2** lag behind; wander on your own. **straggler** noun, **straggly** adjective [origin unknown]

straight adjective
1 going continuously in one direction; not curving or bending. **2** tidy; in proper order. **3** honest and frank, *a straight answer.* **straightness** noun

straight adverb
1 in a straight line or manner. **2** directly; without delay, *Go straight home.*
straight away immediately. [old past participle of *stretch*]

USAGE: Do not confuse with *strait*.

straight away adverb
immediately.

straighten verb (straightens, straightening, straightened) make or become straight.

straightforward *adjective*
1 easy, not complicated. 2 honest and frank.

strain[1] *verb* (**strains, straining, strained**)
1 stretch tightly. 2 injure or weaken something by stretching or working it too hard. 3 make a great effort. 4 put something through a sieve or filter to separate liquid from solid matter.

strain *noun* (*plural* **strains**)
1 straining; the force of straining. 2 an injury caused by straining. 3 something that uses up strength, patience, resources, etc. 4 exhaustion. 5 a part of a tune.

strain[2] *noun* (*plural* **strains**)
1 a breed or variety of animals, plants, etc.; a line of descent. 2 an inherited characteristic, *There's an artistic strain in the family.* [from Old English]

strait *noun* (*plural* **straits**)
a narrow stretch of water connecting two seas. [from Latin *strictus* = tightened]

USAGE: Do not confuse with *straight*.

straits *plural noun*
1 a strait, *the Straits of Dover*. 2 a difficult condition, *We were in dire straits when we lost our money.*

strand[1] *noun* (*plural* **strands**)
1 each of the threads or wires etc. twisted together to form a rope, yarn, or cable. 2 a single thread. 3 a lock of hair.

strand[2] *verb* (**strands, stranding, stranded**)
1 run or cause to run onto sand or rocks in shallow water. 2 leave in a difficult or helpless position, *We were stranded when our car broke down.* [from Old English]

strange *adjective*
1 unusual or surprising. 2 not known or seen or experienced before. **strangely** *adverb*, **strangeness** *noun* [from Latin *extraneus* = extraneous]

stranger *noun* (*plural* **strangers**)
1 a person you do not know. 2 a person who is in a place or company that he or she does not know.

strangle *verb* (**strangles, strangling, strangled**)
1 kill by squeezing the throat to prevent breathing. 2 restrict something so that it does not develop. **strangler** *noun*

strap *noun* (*plural* **straps**) a flat strip of leather or cloth etc. for fastening things or holding them in place.

strap *verb* (**straps, strapping, strapped**) fasten with a strap or straps; bind.

strapping *adjective* tall and healthy-looking, *a strapping lad.*

strategy *noun* (*plural* **strategies**)
1 a plan or policy to achieve something, *our economic strategy.* 2 the planning of a war or campaign. (Compare *tactics*.) [from Greek *strategos* = a general]

stratosphere *noun* a layer of the atmosphere between about 10 and 60 kilometres above the earth's surface. [from *stratum* + *sphere*]

straw *noun* (*plural* **straws**)
1 dry cut stalks of corn. 2 a narrow tube for drinking through. [from Old English]

strawberry noun (plural strawberries) a small red juicy fruit, with its seeds on the outside. [probably because straw is put around the plants to keep slugs away]

stray verb (strays, straying, strayed) leave a group or proper place and wander; get lost.

stray adjective that has strayed; wandering around lost, a stray cat. **stray** noun [from old French]

streak noun (plural streaks) 1 a long thin line or mark. 2 a trace, a streak of cruelty. **streaky** adjective

streak verb (streaks, streaking, streaked) 1 mark with streaks. 2 move very quickly. 3 run naked in a public place for fun or to get attention. [from Old English]

stream noun (plural streams) 1 water flowing in a channel; a brook or small river. 2 a flow of liquid or of things or people. 3 a group in which children of similar ability are placed in a school.

stream verb (streams, streaming, streamed) 1 move in or like a stream. 2 produce a stream of liquid. 3 arrange schoolchildren in streams according to their ability.

streamline verb (streamlines, streamlining, streamlined) 1 give something a smooth shape that helps it to move easily through air or water. 2 organize something so that it works more efficiently. **streamlined** adjective

street noun (plural streets) a road with houses beside it in a city or village. [via Old English from Latin strata via = paved way]

strength noun (plural strengths) 1 how strong a person or thing is; being strong. 2 an ability or good quality, Patience is your great strength.

strengthen verb (strengthens, strengthening, strengthened) make or become stronger.

stress noun (plural stresses) 1 a force that acts on something, e.g. by pressing, pulling, or twisting it; strain. 2 emphasis, especially the extra force with which you pronounce part of a word or phrase. 3 distress caused by having too many problems or too much to do.

stress verb (stresses, stressing, stressed) put a stress on something; emphasize. [from distress]

stretch verb (stretches, stretching, stretched) 1 pull something or be pulled so that it becomes longer or wider or larger. 2 be continuous, The wall stretches right round the estate. 3 push out your arms and legs etc.

stretch noun (plural stretches) 1 the action of stretching. 2 a continuous period of time or area of land or water.

stretcher noun (plural stretchers) a framework for carrying a sick or injured person.

strict adjective 1 demanding obedience and good behaviour, a strict teacher.

2 complete or exact, *the strict truth*. **strictly** *adverb*, **strictness** *noun* [same origin as **strait**]

stride *verb* (**strides, striding, strode, stridden**) walk with long steps.

stride *noun* (*plural* **strides**)
1 a long step when walking or running. **2** progress.
get into your stride settle into a fast and steady pace of working.
take something in your stride manage or deal with something without difficulty.

strife *noun* conflict; fighting or quarrelling.

strike *verb* (**strikes, striking, struck**)
1 hit. **2** attack suddenly. **3** produce by pressing or stamping something, *They are striking some special coins*. **4** light a match by rubbing it against a rough surface. **5** sound, *The clock struck ten*. **6** make an impression on someone's mind, *She strikes me as truthful*. **7** find gold or oil etc. by digging or drilling. **8** stop work until the people in charge agree to improve wages or conditions etc. **9** go in a certain direction, *We struck north through the forest*.
strike off or **out** cross out.
strike up begin playing or singing; start a friendship etc.

strike *noun* (*plural* **strikes**)
1 a hit. **2** an attack. **3** a stoppage of work, as a way of making a protest (see sense **8** of the verb). **4** a sudden discovery of gold or oil etc.
on strike (of workers) striking.

striking *adjective*
1 that strikes. **2** noticeable.
strikingly *adverb*

string *noun* (*plural* **strings**)
1 cord used to fasten or tie things; a piece of this or similar material. **2** a piece of wire or cord etc. stretched and vibrated to produce sounds in a musical instrument. **3** a line or series of things, *a string of buses*.

string *verb* (**strings, stringing, strung**)
1 fit or fasten with string.
2 thread on a string. **3** remove the tough fibre from beans.
string out 1 spread out in a line.
2 cause something to last a long time.

strings *plural noun* musical instruments with strings.

stringy *adjective*
1 like string. **2** containing tough fibres.

strip[1] *verb* (**strips, stripping, stripped**)
1 take a covering or layer off something. **2** undress. **3** deprive a person of something.

strip *noun* the distinctive clothes worn by a sports team while playing.
[probably from Old English]

strip[2] *noun* (*plural* **strips**) a long narrow piece or area. [from old German]

strip cartoon *noun* (*plural* **strip cartoons**) a comic strip (see **comic**).

stripe *noun* (*plural* **stripes**)
1 a long narrow band of colour. **2** a strip of cloth worn on the sleeve of a uniform to show the

wearer's rank. **striped** *adjective*, **stripy** *adjective* [probably from old German and related to *strip²*]

striptease *noun* (*plural* **stripteases**) an entertainment in which a person slowly undresses.

strive *verb* (**strives, striving, strove, striven**) **1** try hard to do something. **2** carry on a conflict. [from old French]

stroke¹ *noun* (*plural* **strokes**) **1** a hit. **2** a movement or action. **3** the sound made by a clock striking. **4** a sudden illness that often causes paralysis. [from *strike*]

stroke² *verb* (**strokes, stroking, stroked**) move your hand gently along something. **stroke** *noun* [from Old English]

stroll *verb* (**strolls, strolling, strolled**) walk in a leisurely way. **stroll** *noun*, **stroller** *noun* [from German]

strong *adjective* **1** having great power, energy, effect, flavour, etc. **2** not easy to break, damage, or defeat. **3** having a certain number of members, *an army 5,000 strong*. **strongly** *adverb*

stronghold *noun* (*plural* **strongholds**) **1** a fortified place. **2** an area where many people live or think in a particular way, *a Tory stronghold*.

strove *past tense* of **strive**.

structure *noun* (*plural* **structures**) **1** something that has been constructed or built. **2** the way something is constructed or organized. **structural** *adjective*, **structurally** *adverb* [from Latin *struere* = build]

struggle *verb* (**struggles, struggling, struggled**) **1** move your arms, legs, etc. in trying to get free. **2** make strong efforts to do something. **3** try to overcome an opponent or a problem etc.

struggle *noun* (*plural* **struggles**) the action of struggling; a hard fight or great effort. [origin unknown]

strum *verb* (**strums, strumming, strummed**) **1** sound a guitar by running your fingers across its strings. **2** play badly or casually on a musical instrument.

strut *verb* (**struts, strutting, strutted**) walk proudly or stiffly.

strut *noun* (*plural* **struts**) **1** a bar of wood or metal strengthening a framework. **2** a strutting walk. [probably from old German]

stub *noun* (*plural* **stubs**) **1** a short stump left when the rest has been used or worn down. **2** a counterfoil.

stub *verb* (**stubs, stubbing, stubbed**) bump your toe painfully.

stub out put out a cigarette by pressing it against something hard.

stubble *noun* **1** the short stalks of corn left in the ground after the harvest is cut. **2** short hairs growing after shaving. [from old French]

stubborn *adjective* obstinate. **stubbornly** *adverb*, **stubbornness** *noun* [origin unknown]

stubby *adjective* short and thick.

stuck-up *adjective* (*informal*) conceited or snobbish.

stud *noun* (*plural* **studs**)
1 a small curved lump or knob.
2 a device like a button on a stalk, used to fasten a detachable collar to a shirt.

student *noun* (*plural* **students**) a person who studies a subject, especially at a college or university. [from Latin *studere* = to study]

studio *noun* (*plural* **studios**)
1 the room where a painter or photographer etc. works. 2 a place where cinema films are made.
3 a room from which radio or television broadcasts are made or recorded. [Italian; related to *study*]

studious *adjective*
1 keen on studying. 2 deliberate, *with studious politeness*. **studiously** *adverb*, **studiousness** *noun*

study *verb* (**studies, studying, studied**)
1 spend time learning about something. 2 look at something carefully.

study *noun* (*plural* **studies**)
1 the process of studying.
2 a subject studied; a piece of research. 3 a room where someone studies. 4 a piece of music for playing as an exercise. [from Latin *studium* = zeal]

stuff *noun*
1 a substance or material.
2 things, *Leave your stuff outside*.
3 valueless matter, *stuff and nonsense!*

stuff *verb* (**stuffs, stuffing, stuffed**)
1 fill tightly. 2 fill with stuffing.
3 push a thing into something, *He stuffed the notebook into his pocket*. 4 (*informal*) eat greedily. [from old French]

stuffing *noun*
1 material used to fill the inside of something; padding.
2 a savoury mixture put into meat or poultry etc. before cooking.

stuffy *adjective* (**stuffier, stuffiest**)
1 badly ventilated; without fresh air. 2 with blocked breathing passages, *a stuffy nose*. 3 formal and boring. **stuffily** *adverb*, **stuffiness** *noun*

stumble *verb* (**stumbles, stumbling, stumbled**)
1 trip and lose your balance.
2 speak or do something hesitantly or uncertainly. **stumble** *noun*
stumble across or **on** find accidentally.

stumbling block *noun* (*plural* **stumbling blocks**) an obstacle; something that causes difficulty.

stump *noun* (*plural* **stumps**)
1 the bottom of a tree trunk left in the ground when the rest has fallen or been cut down.
2 something left when the main part is cut off or worn down.
3 each of the three upright sticks of a wicket in cricket.

stump *verb* (**stumps, stumping, stumped**)
1 walk stiffly or noisily. 2 put a batsman out by knocking the bails off the stumps while he or she is out of the crease. 3 (of a question or problem) be too

difficult for somebody.

stump up (*informal*) produce the money to pay for something.

stumpy *adjective* short and thick. **stumpiness** *noun*

stun *verb* (**stuns, stunning, stunned**)

1 knock a person unconscious. **2** daze or shock, *She was stunned by the news.*

stunt¹ *verb* prevent a thing from growing or developing normally, *a stunted tree.* [probably from Old English]

stunt² *noun* (*plural* **stunts**) something unusual or difficult done as a performance or to attract attention. [originally American: origin unknown]

stupendous *adjective* amazing or tremendous. **stupendously** *adverb*

stupid *adjective*

1 not clever or thoughtful. **2** without reason or common sense. **stupidly** *adverb*, **stupidity** *noun* [from Latin *stupidus* = dazed]

sturdy *adjective* (**sturdier, sturdiest**) strong and vigorous or solid. **sturdily** *adverb*, **sturdiness** *noun* [from old French]

stutter *verb* (**stutters, stuttering, stuttered**) stammer. **stutter** *noun*

style *noun* (*plural* **styles**)

1 the way something is done, made, said, or written etc. **2** elegance. **3** the part of a pistil that supports the stigma in a plant. **stylistic** *adjective*

stylish *adjective* in a fashionable style.

sub- *prefix* (often changing to **suc-, suf-, sum-, sup-, sur-, sus-** before certain consonants)

1 under (as in *submarine*). **2** subordinate, secondary (as in *subsection*). [from Latin *sub* = under]

subconscious *adjective* to do with our own mental activities of which we are not fully aware. **subconscious** *noun*

subdivide *verb* (**subdivides, subdividing, subdivided**) divide again or into smaller parts. **subdivision** *noun*

subdue *verb* (**subdues, subduing, subdued**)

1 overcome; bring under control. **2** make quieter or gentler. [from old French]

subject *noun* (*plural* **subjects**)

1 the person or thing being talked about or written about etc. **2** something that is studied. **3** (in grammar) the word or words naming who or what does the action of a verb, e.g. '*the book*' in *the book fell off the table.* **4** someone who is ruled by a particular king, government, etc.

subject *adjective* ruled by a king or government etc.; not independent.

subject to 1 having to obey. **2** liable to, *Trains are subject to delays during fog.* **3** depending upon, *Our decision is subject to your approval.*

subject (*say* sub-jekt) *verb* (**subjects, subjecting, subjected**)

1 make a person or thing undergo something, *They subjected him to torture.* **2** bring a country under your control. **subjection** *noun* [from *sub-* + Latin *-jectum* = thrown]

subjective *adjective*
1 existing in a person's mind and not produced by things outside it. 2 depending on a person's own taste or opinions etc. (Compare *objective*.)

subjunctive *noun* (*plural* **subjunctives**) the form of a verb used to indicate what is imagined or wished or possible. There are only a few cases where it is commonly used in English, e.g. 'were' in *if I were you* and 'save' in *God save the Queen*. [from *sub*- + Latin *junctum* = joined]

sublime *adjective*
1 noble or impressive. 2 extreme; not caring about the consequences, *with sublime carelessness*. [from Latin]

submarine *adjective* under the sea, *We laid a submarine cable*.

submarine *noun* (*plural* **submarines**) a ship that can travel under water.

submerge *verb* (**submerges**, **submerging**, **submerged**) go under or put under water or other liquid. **submergence** *noun*, **submersion** *noun* [from *sub*- + Latin *mergere* = dip]

submit *verb* (**submits**, **submitting**, **submitted**)
1 let someone have authority over you; surrender. 2 put forward for consideration, testing, etc., *Submit your plans to the committee*. **submission** *noun* [from *sub*- + Latin *mittere* = send]

subnormal *adjective* below normal.

subordinate *adjective*
1 less important. 2 lower in rank.

subordinate *noun* (*plural* **subordinates**) a person working under someone's authority or control.

subordinate *verb* (**subordinates**, **subordinating**, **subordinated**) treat as being less important than another person or thing. **subordination** *noun* [from *sub*- + Latin *ordinare* = arrange]

subordinate clause *noun* (*plural* **subordinate clauses**) a clause which adds details to the main clause of the sentence, but cannot be used as a sentence by itself.

sub-plot *noun* (*plural* **sub-plots**) a secondary plot in a play etc.

subscribe *verb* (**subscribes**, **subscribing**, **subscribed**)
1 contribute money to a project or charity etc. 2 pay regularly so as to be a member of a society, get a periodical, have the use of a telephone, etc. 3 sign, *subscribe your name*. 4 say that you agree, *We cannot subscribe to this theory*. **subscriber** *noun*, **subscription** *noun* [from *sub*- + Latin *scribere* = write]

subsequent *adjective* coming after in time or order; later. **subsequently** *adverb* [from *sub*- + Latin *sequens* = following]

subside *verb* (**subsides**, **subsiding**, **subsided**)
1 sink. 2 become less intense, *Her fear subsided*. **subsidence** *noun* [from *sub*- + Latin *sidere* = settle]

subsidiary *adjective*
1 less important; secondary.
2 (of a business) controlled by another, *a subsidiary company*. [same origin as *subsidy*]

subsidize verb (**subsidizes, subsidizing, subsidized**) pay a subsidy to a person or firm etc.

subsidy noun (plural **subsidies**) money paid to an industry etc. that needs help, or to keep down the price at which its goods etc. are sold to the public. [from Latin subsidium = assistance]

subsoil noun soil lying just below the surface layer.

substance noun (plural **substances**)
1 matter of a particular kind.
2 the main or essential part of something, We agree with the substance of your report but not with its details. [from Latin substantia = essence]

substantial adjective
1 of great size, value, or importance, a substantial fee.
2 solidly built, substantial houses.
3 actually existing. **substantially** adverb [same origin as substance]

substitute noun (plural **substitutes**) a person or thing that acts or is used instead of another.

substitute verb (**substitutes, substituting, substituted**) put or use a person or thing as a substitute. **substitution** noun [from sub- + Latin statuere = to set up]

subterranean adjective underground. [from sub- + Latin terra = ground]

subtitle noun (plural **subtitles**)
1 a secondary or additional title.
2 words shown on the screen during a film, e.g. to translate a foreign language.

subtle (say sut-el) adjective
1 slight and delicate, a subtle perfume. 2 ingenious; not immediately obvious, a subtle joke. **subtly** adverb, **subtlety** noun

subtract verb (**subtracts, subtracting, subtracted**) deduct; take away a part, quantity, or number from a greater one. **subtraction** noun [from sub- + Latin tractum = pulled]

suburb noun (plural **suburbs**) a district with houses that is outside the central part of a city. **suburban** adjective [from sub- + Latin urbs = city]

subway noun (plural **subways**) an underground passage.

suc- prefix
1 under. 2 subordinate, secondary. see **sub-**.

succeed verb (**succeeds, succeeding, succeeded**)
1 be successful. 2 come after another person or thing; become the next king or queen, She succeeded to the throne; Edward VII succeeded Queen Victoria. [from suc- + Latin cedere = go]

success noun (plural **successes**)
1 doing or getting what you wanted or intended. 2 a person or thing that does well, The show was a great success. [same origin as succeed]

successful adjective having success; being a success. **successfully** adverb

succession noun (plural **successions**)
1 a series of people or things.
2 the process of following in order. 3 succeeding to the throne; the right of doing this. [same origin as succeed]

successive *adjective* following one after another, *on five successive days*. **successively** *adverb*

succumb (*say* suk-um) *verb* (**succumbs, succumbing, succumbed**) give way to something overpowering. [from *suc-* + Latin *cumbere* = to lie]

such *adjective*
1 of the same kind; similar, *Cakes, biscuits, and all such foods are fattening*. 2 of the kind described, *There's no such person.* 3 so great or intense, *It gave me such a fright!*

such-and-such *adjective* particular but not now named, *He promises to come at such-and-such a time but is always late.*

suck *verb* (**sucks, sucking, sucked**)
1 take in liquid or air through almost-closed lips. 2 squeeze something in your mouth by using your tongue, *sucking a toffee.* 3 draw in, *The canoe was sucked into the whirlpool.* **suck** *noun*
suck up to (*informal*) flatter someone in the hope of winning their favour.

suckle *verb* (**suckles, suckling, suckled**) feed on milk at the mother's breast or udder.

suction *noun*
1 sucking. 2 producing a vacuum so that things are sucked into the empty space, *Vacuum cleaners work by suction.*

sudden *adjective* happening or done quickly or without warning. **suddenly** *adverb*, **suddenness** *noun*

suds *plural noun* froth on soapy water.

sue *verb* (**sues, suing, sued**) start a lawsuit to claim money from somebody. [from old French]

suet *noun* hard fat from cattle and sheep, used in cooking.

suf- *prefix*
1 under. 2 subordinate, secondary. see **sub-**.

suffer *verb* (**suffers, suffering, suffered**)
1 feel pain or sadness.
2 experience something bad, *suffer damage.* 3 (*old use*) allow or tolerate. **sufferer** *noun*, **suffering** *noun* [from *suf-* + Latin *ferre* = to bear]

suffice *verb* (**suffices, sufficing, sufficed**) be enough for somebody's needs. [from *suf-* + Latin *facere* = make or do]

sufficient *adjective* enough. **sufficiently** *adverb*, **sufficiency** *noun* [same origin as *suffice*]

suffix *noun* (*plural* **suffixes**) a letter or set of letters joined to the end of a word to make another word (e.g. in forget*ful*, lion*ess*, rust*y*) or a form of a word (e.g. sing*ing*, wait*ed*). [from *suf-* + Latin *figere* = fix]

suffocate *verb* (**suffocates, suffocating, suffocated**)
1 make it difficult or impossible for someone to breathe. 2 suffer or die because breathing is prevented. **suffocation** *noun* [from *suf-* + Latin *fauces* = throat]

sugar *noun* a sweet food obtained from the juices of various plants (e.g. sugar cane, sugar beet). **sugar** *verb*, **sugary** *adjective*

suggest *verb* (**suggests, suggesting, suggested**)
1 give somebody an idea that you think is useful. 2 cause an idea or

possibility to come into the mind.
suggestion *noun*, **suggestive**
adjective [from Latin]

suicide *noun* (*plural* **suicides**)
1 killing yourself deliberately,
commit suicide. **2** a person who
deliberately kills himself or
herself. **suicidal** *adjective* [from
Latin *sui* = of yourself, + *-cide*]

suit *noun* (*plural* **suits**)
1 a matching jacket and trousers,
or a jacket and skirt, that are
meant to be worn together. **2**
clothing for a particular
activity, *a diving suit*. **3** any of
the four sets of cards (clubs,
hearts, diamonds, spades) in
a pack of playing cards.
4 a lawsuit.

USAGE: Do not confuse with
suite.

suit *verb* (**suits, suiting, suited**)
1 be suitable or convenient for
a person or thing. **2** make
a person look attractive.
[from Latin *sequi* = to go together
or follow]

suitable *adjective* satisfactory or
right for a particular person,
purpose, or occasion etc. **suitably**
adverb, **suitability** *noun*

suitcase *noun* (*plural* **suitcases**)
a rectangular container for
carrying clothes, usually with
a hinged lid and a handle.

suite (*say as* sweet) *noun* (*plural*
suites)
1 a set of furniture. **2** a set of
rooms. **3** a set of attendants. **4** a set
of short pieces of music. [French;
related to *suit*]

USAGE: Do not confuse with
suit.

sulk *verb* (**sulks, sulking, sulked**)
be silent and bad-tempered
because you are not pleased.
sulks *plural noun*, **sulky** *adjective*,
sulkily *adverb*, **sulkiness** *noun*

sullen *adjective* sulking and
gloomy. **sullenly** *adverb*,
sullenness *noun* [from old
French; related to *sole²*]

sulphur *noun* a yellow chemical
used in industry and in
medicine. **sulphurous** *adjective*
[from Latin]

sultry *adjective*
1 hot and humid, *sultry weather*.
2 suggesting passion or sexual
desire, *her sultry smile*. **sultriness**
noun

sum *noun* (*plural* **sums**)
1 a total. **2** a problem in
arithmetic. **3** an amount of
money.

sum *verb* (**sums, summing,
summed**)
sum up 1 summarize, especially
at the end of a talk etc. **2** form an
opinion of a person, *sum him up*.
[from Latin *summa* = main thing]

sum- *prefix*
1 under. **2** subordinate,
secondary. see **sub-**.

summarize *verb* (**summarizes,
summarizing, summarized**) make
or give a summary of something.

summary *noun* (*plural*
summaries) a statement of the
main points of something said or
written.

summary *adjective*
1 brief. **2** done or given hastily,
without delay, *summary
punishment*. **summarily** *adverb*
[same origin as *sum*]

summer *noun* (*plural* **summers**) the warm season between spring and autumn. **summery** *adjective*

summer house *noun* (*plural* **summer houses**) a small building providing shade in a garden or park.

summit *noun* (*plural* **summits**) 1 the top of a mountain or hill. 2 a meeting between the leaders of powerful countries, *a summit conference*. [from Latin *summus* = highest]

summon *verb* (**summons**, **summoning**, **summoned**) 1 order someone to come or appear, *summoned to court*. 2 request firmly, *He summoned the rebels to surrender*.

summon up gather or prepare, *Can you summon up the energy to get out of bed?* [from *sum-* + Latin *monere* = warn]

sumptuous *adjective* splendid and expensive-looking. **sumptuously** *adverb* [from Latin *sumptus* = cost, expense]

sun *noun* (*plural* **suns**) 1 the star round which the earth travels. 2 light and warmth from the sun, *Go and sit in the sun*. 3 any star in the universe round which planets travel.

sun *verb* (**suns**, **sunning**, **sunned**) warm something in the sun, *sunning ourselves on the beach*. [from Old English]

sunbathe *verb* (**sunbathes**, **sunbathing**, **sunbathed**) expose your body to the sun, especially to get a tan.

sunbeam *noun* (*plural* **sunbeams**) a ray of sun.

sunburn *noun* redness of the skin caused by the sun. **sunburnt** *adjective*

sundae (say sun-day) *noun* (*plural* **sundaes**) a mixture of ice cream and fruit, nuts, cream, etc. [from *Sunday* (because sundaes were originally sold then, possibly to use up ice cream not sold during the week)]

sundial *noun* (*plural* **sundials**) a device that shows the time by a shadow on a dial.

sundry *adjective* various or several.
all and sundry everyone.

sunglasses *plural noun* dark glasses to protect your eyes from strong sunlight.

sunken *adjective* sunk deeply into a surface, *Their cheeks were pale and sunken*.

sunlamp *noun* (*plural* **sunlamps**) a lamp which uses ultraviolet light to give people an artificial tan.

sunlight *noun* light from the sun. **sunlit** *adjective*

sunny *adjective* (**sunnier**, **sunniest**) 1 full of sunshine. 2 cheerful, *She was in a sunny mood*. **sunnily** *adverb*

sunrise *noun* (*plural* **sunrises**) the rising of the sun; dawn.

sunset *noun* (*plural* **sunsets**) the setting of the sun.

sunshade *noun* (*plural* **sunshades**) a parasol or other device to protect people from the sun.

sunshine *noun* sunlight with no cloud between the sun and the earth.

sunstroke *noun* illness caused by being in the sun too long.

sup- *prefix*
1 under. 2 subordinate, secondary. see **sub-**.

super *adjective* (slang) excellent or superb. [from *super-*]

super- *prefix*
1 over or on top (as in *superstructure*). 2 of greater size or quality etc. (as in *supermarket*). 3 extremely (as in *superabundant*). 4 beyond (as in *supernatural*). [from Latin *super* = over]

superb *adjective* magnificent or excellent. **superbly** *adverb* [from Latin *superbus* = proud]

superficial *adjective* on the surface; not deep or thorough. **superficially** *adverb*, **superficiality** *noun* [from *super-* + Latin *facies* = face]

superfluous *adjective* more than is needed. **superfluity** *noun* [from *super-* + Latin *fluere* = flow]

superhuman *adjective*
1 beyond ordinary human ability, *superhuman strength*. 2 higher than human; divine.

superimpose *verb* (**superimposes**, **superimposing**, **superimposed**) place a thing on top of something else. **superimposition** *noun*

superintend *verb* (**superintends**, **superintending**, **superintended**) supervise. [from *super-* + Latin *intendere* = direct, intend]

superintendent *noun* (plural **superintendents**)
1 a supervisor. 2 a police officer above the rank of inspector.

superior *adjective*
1 higher in position or rank, *She is your superior officer*. 2 better

than another person or thing.
3 conceited. **superiority** *noun*

superior *noun* (plural **superiors**) a person or thing that is superior to another.
[Latin, = higher]

superlative *adjective* of the highest degree or quality, *superlative skill*. **superlatively** *adverb*

superlative *noun* (plural **superlatives**) the form of an adjective or adverb that expresses 'most', *The superlative of 'great' is 'greatest'*. (Compare *positive* and *comparative*.)
[from Latin *superlatum* = carried above]

supermarket *noun* (plural **supermarkets**) a large self-service shop that sells food and other goods.

supernatural *adjective* not belonging to the natural world, *supernatural beings such as ghosts*.

supersonic *adjective* faster than the speed of sound.

superstition *noun* (plural **superstitions**) a belief or action that is not based on reason or evidence, e.g. the belief that it is unlucky to walk under a ladder. **superstitious** *adjective* [from Latin *superstare* = stand over]

supervise *verb* (**supervises**, **supervising**, **supervised**) be in charge of a person or thing and inspect what is done. **supervision** *noun*, **supervisor** *noun*, **supervisory** *adjective* [from *super-* + Latin *visum* = seen]

supper *noun* (plural **suppers**) a meal eaten in the evening.
[from old French *soper* = sup]

supple *adjective* bending easily; flexible. **supplely** *adverb*, **suppleness** *noun* [from *sup-* + Latin *plicare* = to fold, bend]

supplement *noun* (*plural* **supplements**)
1 something added as an extra.
2 an extra section added to a book or newspaper, *the colour supplement.* **supplementary** *adjective*

supplement *verb* (**supplements**, **supplementing**, **supplemented**) add to something, *She supplements her pocket money by working on Saturdays.* [same origin as *supply*]

supply *verb* (**supplies**, **supplying**, **supplied**) give or sell or provide what is needed or wanted. **supplier** *noun*

supply *noun* (*plural* **supplies**)
1 an amount of something that is available for use when needed.
2 the action of supplying something. [from *sup-* + Latin *-plere* = fill]

support *verb* (**supports**, **supporting**, **supported**)
1 keep a person or thing from falling or sinking. **2** give strength, help, or encouragement to someone, *Support your local team.* **3** provide with the necessities of life, *She has two children to support.* **supporter** *noun*, **supportive** *adjective*

support *noun* (*plural* **supports**)
1 the action of supporting.
2 a person or thing that supports. [from *sup-* + Latin *portare* = carry]

suppose *verb* (**supposes**, **supposing**, **supposed**) think that something is likely to happen or

be true. **supposedly** *adverb*, **supposition** *noun*

be supposed to be expected to do something; have as a duty.

suppress *verb* (**suppresses**, **suppressing**, **suppressed**)
1 put an end to something forcibly or by authority, *Troops suppressed the rebellion.* **2** keep something from being known or seen, *They suppressed the truth.* **suppression** *noun*, **suppressor** *noun* [from *sup-* + Latin *pressus* = pressed]

supreme *adjective*
1 most important or highest in rank. **2** greatest, *supreme courage.* **supremely** *adverb*, **supremacy** *noun* [from Latin *supremus* = highest]

sur-¹ *prefix* **1** under. **2** subordinate, secondary. see **sub-**.

sur-² *prefix* = super- (as in *surcharge*, *surface*). [from old French]

sure *adjective*
1 convinced; feeling no doubt.
2 certain to happen or do something, *Our team is sure to win.* **3** reliable; undoubtedly true. **sureness** *noun*
for sure definitely.
make sure 1 find out exactly.
2 make something happen or be true, *Make sure the door is locked.* [from old French; related to *secure*]

surf *noun* the white foam of waves breaking on a rock or shore. [origin unknown]

surface *noun* (*plural* **surfaces**)
1 the outside of something. **2** any of the sides of an object,

especially the top part. **3** an outward appearance, *On the surface he was a kindly man.*

surfboard *noun* (*plural* **surfboards**) a board used in surfing.

surfeit (*say* ser-fit) *noun* too much of something. **surfeited** *adjective* [from *sur-²* + Latin *facere* = do]

surfing *noun* balancing yourself on a board that is carried to the shore on the waves. **surfer** *noun*

surf-riding *noun* surfing. **surf-rider** *noun*

surge *verb* (**surges, surging, surged**) move forwards or upwards like waves. **surge** *noun* [from Latin *surgere* = rise]

surgeon *noun* (*plural* **surgeons**) a doctor who treats disease or injury by cutting or repairing the affected parts of the body.

surgery *noun* (*plural* **surgeries**) **1** the place where a doctor or dentist etc. regularly gives advice and treatment to patients. **2** the time when patients can visit the doctor etc. **3** the work of a surgeon. **surgical** *adjective*, **surgically** *adverb* [from Greek *cheirourgia* = handiwork]

surly *adjective* (**surlier, surliest**) bad-tempered and unfriendly. **surliness** *noun* [originally = majestic, haughty: from *sir* + *-ly*]

surname *noun* (*plural* **surnames**) the name held by all members of a family.

surpass *verb* (**surpasses, surpassing, surpassed**) do or be better than all others; excel.

surplus *noun* (*plural* **surpluses**) an amount left over after spending or using all that was needed. [from *sur-²* + Latin *plus* = more]

surprise *noun* (*plural* **surprises**) **1** something unexpected. **2** the feeling caused by something that was not expected.
surprise *verb* (**surprises, surprising, surprised**) **1** be a surprise to somebody. **2** come upon or attack somebody unexpectedly. **surprisingly** *adverb* [from old French]

surrender *verb* (**surrenders, surrendering, surrendered**) **1** give yourself up to an enemy. **2** hand something over to another person, especially when compelled to do so. **surrender** *noun* [from *sur-²* + French *rendre* = give, deliver]

surreptitious (*say* su-rep-tish-us) *adjective* stealthy. **surreptitiously** *adverb* [from Latin *surrepticius* = stolen, taken secretly]

surrogate mother *noun* (*plural* **surrogate mothers**) a woman who agrees to conceive and give birth to a baby for a woman who cannot do so herself, using a fertilized egg of the other woman or sperm from the other woman's partner.

surround *verb* (**surrounds, surrounding, surrounded**) come or be all round a person or thing; encircle. [from *sur-²* + Latin *undare* = rise in waves]

surroundings *plural noun* the things or conditions round a person or thing.

survey (say **ser**-vay) noun (plural **surveys**)
1 a general look at something.
2 an inspection of an area, building, etc.

survey (say **ser**-vay) verb (**surveys, surveying, surveyed**) make a survey of something; inspect. **surveyor** noun [from sur-² + Latin videre = see]

survival noun (plural **survivals**)
1 surviving; the likelihood of surviving. 2 something that has survived from an earlier time; a relic.

survive verb (**survives, surviving, survived**) stay alive; go on living or existing after someone has died or after a disaster. **survivor** noun [from sur-² + Latin vivere = to live]

sus- prefix
1 under. 2 subordinate, secondary. see sub-.

susceptible (say sus-**ept**-ib-ul) adjective likely to be affected by something, She is susceptible to colds. **susceptibility** noun [from Latin susceptum = caught up]

suspect (say sus-**pekt**) verb (**suspects, suspecting, suspected**)
1 think that a person is not to be trusted or has committed a crime; distrust. 2 have a feeling that something is likely or possible.

suspect (say **sus**-pekt) noun (plural **suspects**) a person who is suspected of a crime etc. **suspect** adjective
[from sus- + Latin specere = to look]

suspend verb (**suspends, suspending, suspended**)
1 hang something up. 2 postpone; stop something temporarily.

3 deprive a person of a job or position etc. for a time. [from sus- + Latin pendere = hang]

suspender noun (plural **suspenders**) a fastener to hold up a sock or stocking by its top.

suspense noun an anxious or uncertain feeling while waiting for something to happen or become known. [same origin as suspend]

suspension noun
1 suspending. 2 the springs etc. in a vehicle that lessen the effect of rough road surfaces. 3 a liquid containing small pieces of solid material which do not dissolve.

suspicion noun (plural **suspicions**)
1 suspecting or being suspected; distrust. 2 a slight belief. [same origin as suspect]

suspicious adjective feeling or causing suspicion. **suspiciously** adverb

sustain verb (**sustains, sustaining, sustained**)
1 support. 2 keep someone alive. 3 keep something happening. 4 undergo; suffer, We sustained a defeat. [from sus- + Latin tenere = hold, keep]

SW abbreviation
1 south-west. 2 south-western.

swab (say swob) noun (plural **swabs**)
1 a mop or pad for cleaning or wiping something; a small pad for cleaning a wound.
2 a specimen of fluid from the body taken on a swab for testing.

swab verb (**swabs, swabbing, swabbed**) clean or wipe with a swab.
[from Dutch]

swagger verb (swaggers, swaggering, swaggered) walk or behave in a conceited way; strut. **swagger** noun

swallow[1] verb (swallows, swallowing, swallowed) 1 make something go down your throat. 2 believe something that ought not to be believed. **swallow** noun

swallow up take in and cover; engulf, *She was swallowed up in the crowd.*
[from Old English *swelgan*]

swallow[2] noun (plural **swallows**) a small bird with a forked tail and pointed wings. [from Old English *swealwe*]

swamp noun (plural **swamps**) a marsh. **swampy** adjective

swamp verb (swamps, swamping, swamped) 1 flood. 2 overwhelm with a great mass or number of things. [origin unknown]

swan noun (plural **swans**) a large usually white swimming bird with a long neck. [from Old English]

swank verb (swanks, swanking, swanked) (*informal*) boast or swagger; show off.

swank noun (*informal*) showing yourself or your possessions off in a conceited way. [origin unknown]

swansong noun (plural **swansongs**) a person's last performance or work. [from the old belief that a swan sang sweetly when about to die]

swap verb (swaps, swapping, swapped) (*informal*) exchange. **swap** noun [formerly = seal

a bargain by slapping each other's hands; imitating the sound]

swarm noun (plural **swarms**) a large number of insects or birds etc. flying or moving about together.

swarm verb (swarms, swarming, swarmed) 1 gather or move in a swarm. 2 be crowded or overrun with insects, people, etc.
[from Old English]

swarthy adjective having a dark complexion. **swarthiness** noun [from Old English]

swastika noun (plural **swastikas**) an ancient symbol formed by a cross with its ends bent at right angles, adopted by the Nazis as their sign. [from Sanskrit *svasti* = well-being, luck]

swat verb (swats, swatting, swatted) hit or crush a fly etc. **swatter** noun [originally American, a different spelling of *squat*]

swathe verb (swathes, swathing, swathed) wrap in layers of bandages, paper, or clothes etc. [from Old English]

sway verb (sways, swaying, swayed) 1 swing gently; move from side to side. 2 influence, *His speech swayed the crowd.* **sway** noun [origin unknown]

swear verb (swears, swearing, swore, sworn) 1 make a solemn promise, *She swore to tell the truth.* 2 make a person take an oath, *We swore him to secrecy.* 3 use curses or coarse words in anger or surprise etc.

swear by have great confidence in something.

sweat (say swet) noun moisture given off by the body through the pores of the skin; perspiration.
sweaty adjective

sweat verb (sweats, sweating, sweated) give off sweat; perspire. [from Old English]

sweater noun (plural sweaters) a jersey or pullover.

sweatshirt noun (plural sweatshirts) a thick cotton jersey worn for sports or casual wear.

sweep verb (sweeps, sweeping, swept)
1 clean or clear with a broom or brush etc. 2 move or remove quickly, The floods swept away the bridge. 3 go smoothly, quickly, or proudly, She swept out of the room. **sweeper** noun

sweep noun (plural sweeps)
1 the process of sweeping, Give this room a good sweep.
2 a chimney sweep.
3 a sweepstake.
[from Old English]

sweeping adjective general or wide-ranging, He made sweeping changes.

sweet adjective
1 tasting as if it contains sugar; not bitter. 2 very pleasant, a sweet smell. 3 charming or delightful.
sweetly adverb, **sweetness** noun

sweet noun (plural sweets)
1 a small shaped piece of sweet food made with sugar, chocolate, etc. 2 a pudding; the sweet course in a meal. 3 a beloved person.

sweeten verb (sweetens, sweetening, sweetened) make or become sweet. **sweetener** noun

sweetheart noun (plural sweethearts) a person you love very much.

swell verb (swells, swelling, swelled, swollen or swelled) make or become larger in size or amount or force.

swell noun (plural swells)
1 the process of swelling. 2 the rise and fall of the sea's surface.

swelling noun (plural swellings) a swollen place.

swerve verb (swerves, swerving, swerved) turn to one side suddenly. **swerve** noun

swift adjective quick or rapid.
swiftly adverb, **swiftness** noun

swift noun (plural swifts) a small bird rather like a swallow.

swill verb (swills, swilling, swilled) pour water over or through something; wash or rinse.

swim verb (swims, swimming, swam, swum)
1 move the body through the water; be in the water for pleasure. 2 cross by swimming, She swam the Channel. 3 float.
4 be covered with or full of liquid, Our eyes were swimming in tears.
5 feel dizzy, His head swam.
swimmer noun

swim noun (plural swims) the action of swimming, We went for a swim. **swimsuit** noun
[from Old English]

swimming bath noun (plural swimming baths) a public swimming pool.

swimming pool noun (plural swimming pools) an artificial pool for swimming in.

swindle verb (swindles, swindling, swindled) cheat a person in business etc. **swindle**

noun, **swindler** *noun* [from German *Schwindler* = a fool, a cheat]

swine *noun* (*plural* **swine**)
1 a pig. 2 a very unpleasant person. 3 (*informal*) a difficult thing, *This crossword's a real swine!*

swing *verb* (**swings, swinging, swung**)
1 move to and fro while hanging; move or turn in a curve, *The door swung open.* 2 change from one opinion or mood etc. to another.

swing *noun* (*plural* **swings**)
1 a swinging movement. 2 a seat hung on chains or ropes etc. so that it can be moved backwards and forwards. 3 the amount by which votes or opinions etc. change from one side to another. 4 a kind of jazz music.
in full swing full of activity; working fully.

swirl *verb* (**swirls, swirling, swirled**) move round quickly in circles; whirl. **swirl** *noun* [probably from old Dutch]

swish *verb* (**swishes, swishing, swished**) move with a hissing sound. **swish** *noun*

Swiss roll *noun* (*plural* **Swiss rolls**) a thin sponge cake spread with jam or cream and rolled up.

switch *noun* (*plural* **switches**)
1 a device that is pressed or turned to start or stop something working, especially by electricity. 2 a change of opinion, policy, or methods. 3 a mechanism for moving the points on a railway track. 4 a flexible rod or whip.

switch *verb* (**switches, switching, switched**)
1 turn something on or off by means of a switch. 2 change or transfer or divert something. [probably from old German]

switchback *noun* (*plural* **switchbacks**) a railway at a fair, with steep slopes up and down alternately.

switchboard *noun* (*plural* **switchboards**) a panel with switches etc. for making telephone connections or operating electric circuits.

swivel *verb* (**swivels, swivelling, swivelled**) turn round.

swivel *noun* (*plural* **swivels**) a device joining two things so that one can revolve without turning the other.

swollen *past participle* of **swell**.

swoon *verb* (**swoons, swooning, swooned**) (*old use* or *poetical*) faint. **swoon** *noun* [from Old English]

swoop *verb* (**swoops, swooping, swooped**) come down with a rushing movement; make a sudden attack. **swoop** *noun* [probably from *sweep*]

sword (*say* sord) *noun* (*plural* **swords**) a weapon with a long pointed blade fixed in a handle or hilt. **swordsman** *noun*

swot *verb* (**swots, swotting, swotted**) (*slang*) study hard. **swot** *noun* [a dialect word for *sweat*]

sycamore *noun* (*plural* **sycamores**) a tall tree with winged seeds, often grown for its timber. [from Greek]

syl- *prefix*
1 with, together. 2 alike. see **syn-**.

syllable noun (plural **syllables**)
a word or part of a word that has
one vowel sound when you say it,
'Cat' has one syllable, 'el-e-phant'
has three syllables. **syllabic**
adjective [from syl- + Greek
lambanein = take]

syllabus noun (plural **syllabuses**)
a summary of the things to be
studied by a class or for an
examination etc. [from Greek]

sym- prefix
1 with, together. **2** alike. see **syn-**.

symbol noun (plural **symbols**)
1 a thing used as a sign, The cross
is a symbol of Christianity.
2 a mark or sign with a special
meaning (e.g. +, −, and ÷ in
mathematics). **symbolic** adjective,
symbolical adjective, **symbolically**
adverb [from Greek symbolon
= token]

USAGE: Do not confuse with
cymbal.

symbolize verb (**symbolizes**,
symbolizing, **symbolized**) make
or be a symbol of something.

symmetrical adjective able to be
divided into two halves which
are exactly the same but the
opposite way round, Wheels and
butterflies are symmetrical.
symmetrically adverb, **symmetry**
noun [from sym- + Greek metron
= a measure]

sympathize verb (**sympathizes**,
sympathizing, **sympathized**) show
or feel sympathy. **sympathizer**
noun

sympathy noun (plural
sympathies)
1 the sharing or understanding of
other people's feelings, opinions,
etc. **2** a feeling of pity or

tenderness towards someone
who is hurt, sad, or in trouble.
sympathetic adjective,
sympathetically adverb [from
sym- + Greek pathos = feeling]

symphony noun (plural
symphonies) a long piece of
music for an orchestra.
symphonic adjective [from sym-
+ Greek phone = sound]

symptom noun (plural
symptoms) a sign that a disease
or condition exists, Red spots are
a symptom of measles.
symptomatic adjective [from
Greek symptoma = chance,
accident]

syn- prefix (changing to **syl-** or
sym- before certain consonants)
1 with, together (as in
synchronize). **2** alike (as in
synonym). [from Greek]

synagogue (say sin-a-gog) noun
(plural **synagogues**) a place
where Jews meet for worship.
[from Greek synagoge
= assembly]

syndicate noun (plural
syndicates)
1 a group of people or firms who
work together in business.
2 a group of people who buy
something together, or who
gamble together, sharing the cost
and any gains. [from syn- + Greek
dike = judgement]

synonym (say sin-o-nim) noun
(plural **synonyms**) a word that
means the same or almost the
same as another word, 'Large'
and 'great' are synonyms of 'big'.
synonymous (say sin-on-im-us)
adjective [from syn- + Greek
onyma = name]

syntax (*say* sin-taks) *noun* the way words are arranged to make phrases or sentences. **syntactic** *adjective*, **syntactically** *adverb* [from *syn-* + Greek *taxis* = arrangement]

synthesizer *noun* (*plural* **synthesizers**) an electronic musical instrument that can make a large variety of sounds.

synthetic *adjective* artificially made; not natural. **synthetically** *adverb* [same origin as *synthesis*]

syringe *noun* (*plural* **syringes**) a device for sucking in a liquid and squirting it out. [from Greek *syrinx* = pipe, tube]

syrup *noun* a thick sweet liquid. **syrupy** *adjective* [from Arabic *sharab* = a drink]

system *noun* (*plural* **systems**) 1 a set of parts, things, or ideas that are organized to work together. 2 a way of doing something, *a new system of training motorcyclists*. [from Greek]

systematic *adjective* methodical; carefully planned. **systematically** *adverb*

Tt

tab *noun* (*plural* **tabs**) a small flap or strip that sticks out.

tabby *noun* (*plural* **tabbies**) a grey or brown cat with dark stripes. [originally = a kind of striped silk material: named after al-Attabiyya, a district of Baghdad where it was made]

table *noun* (*plural* **tables**) 1 a piece of furniture with a flat top supported by legs. 2 a list of

facts or figures arranged in order. 3 a list of the results of multiplying a number by other numbers, *multiplication tables*. [from Latin *tabula* = plank, tablet, or list]

tablecloth *noun* (*plural* **tablecloths**) a cloth for covering a table, especially at meals.

tablespoon *noun* (*plural* **tablespoons**) a large spoon for serving food. **tablespoonful** *noun*

tablet *noun* (*plural* **tablets**) 1 a pill. 2 a solid piece of soap. 3 a flat piece of stone or wood etc. with words carved or written on it. [from old French *tablete* = small table or slab]

table tennis *noun* a game played on a table divided by a net, over which you hit a small ball with bats.

taboo *adjective* not to be done or used or talked about. **taboo** *noun* [from Tongan *tabu* = sacred]

tack[1] *noun* (*plural* **tacks**) 1 a short nail with a flat top. 2 a tacking stitch. 3 (in sailing) the direction taken when tacking.

tack *verb* (**tacks, tacking, tacked**) 1 nail something down with tacks. 2 fasten material together with long stitches. 3 sail a zigzag course to take advantage of what wind there is.

tack on (*informal*) add an extra thing.

tack[2] *noun* harness, saddles, etc. [from *tackle* = equipment]

tackle *verb* (**tackles, tackling, tackled**) 1 try to do something that needs doing. **2** try to get the ball from someone else in a game of football or hockey.

tackle noun (plural **tackles**) **1** equipment, especially for fishing. **2** a set of ropes and pulleys. **3** tackling someone in football or hockey.

tacky adjective sticky, not quite dry, *The paint is still tacky.* **tackiness** noun [from **tack**[1] = a fastening]

tact noun skill in not offending people. **tactful** adjective, **tactfully** adverb, **tactless** adjective, **tactlessly** adverb [from Latin *tactus* = sense of touch]

tactics noun **1** the method of arranging troops etc. skilfully for a battle. **2** the methods you use to achieve something or gain an advantage. **tactical** adjective, **tactically** adverb, **tactician** noun [from Greek *taktika* = things arranged]

USAGE: *Strategy* is a general plan for a whole campaign, *tactics* is for one part of this.

tadpole noun (plural **tadpoles**) a young frog or toad that has developed from the egg and lives entirely in water. [from *toad* + *poll* = head]

tag[1] noun (plural **tags**) **1** a label tied on or stuck into something. **2** a metal or plastic point at the end of a shoelace.

tag verb (**tags**, **tagging**, **tagged**) **1** label something with a tag. **2** add as an extra thing, *A postscript was tagged on to her letter.* **3** (informal) go with other people, *Her sister tagged along.* [origin unknown]

tag[2] noun a game in which one person chases the others. [origin unknown]

tail noun (plural **tails**) **1** the part that sticks out from the rear end of the body of a bird, fish, or animal. **2** the part at the end or rear of something. **3** the side of a coin opposite the head, *Heads or tails?*

tail verb (**tails**, **tailing**, **tailed**) **1** remove stalks etc. from fruit, *top and tail gooseberries.* **2** (informal) follow a person or thing.

tail off become fewer, smaller, or slighter etc.; cease gradually.

tailor noun (plural **tailors**) a person who makes men's clothes.

taint noun (plural **taints**) a small amount of decay, pollution, or a bad quality that spoils something.

taint verb (**taints**, **tainting**, **tainted**) give something a taint. [from old French; related to *tint*]

take verb (**takes**, **taking**, **took**, **taken**) This word has many uses, including **1** get something into your hands or possession or control etc. (*take this cup*; *we took many prisoners*), **2** make use of (*take a taxi*) or indulge in (*take a holiday*), **3** carry or convey (*Take this parcel to the post*), **4** perform or deal with (*When do you take your music exam?*), **5** study or teach a subject (*Who takes you for maths?*), **6** make an effort (*take trouble*) or experience a feeling (*Don't take offence*), **7** accept; endure (*I'll take a risk*), **8** require (*It takes a strong man to lift this*),

9 write down (*take notes*), **10** make a photograph, **11** subtract (*take 4 from 10*), **12** assume (*I take it that you agree*). **taker** noun

take after be like a parent etc.

take in deceive somebody.

take leave of say goodbye to.

take off (of an aircraft) leave the ground and become airborne. **take-off** noun

take on 1 begin to employ someone. **2** play or fight against someone. **3** (*informal*) show that you are upset.

take over take control. **takeover** noun

take place happen or occur.

take up 1 start something. **2** occupy space or time etc. **3** accept an offer.

takeaway noun (*plural takeaways*)
1 a place that sells cooked meals for customers to take away. **2** a meal from this.

tale noun (*plural tales*) a story. [from Old English]

talent noun (*plural talents*) a special or very great ability. **talented** adjective [from Greek *talanton* = sum of money]

talk verb (**talks, talking, talked**) speak; have a conversation. **talker** noun

talk noun (*plural talks*) **1** talking; a conversation. **2** an informal lecture. [from Middle English; related to *tale*]

talkative adjective talking a lot.

tall adjective **1** higher than the average, *a tall tree*. **2** measured from the bottom to the top, *It is 10 metres tall*. **tallness** noun

tall story noun (*plural tall stories*) (*informal*) a story that is hard to believe.

tally verb (**tallies, tallying, tallied**) correspond or agree with something else, *Does your list tally with mine?*

talon noun (*plural talons*) a strong claw. [from Latin]

tambourine noun (*plural tambourines*) a circular musical instrument with metal discs round it, tapped or shaken to make it jingle. [from French]

tame adjective **1** (of animals) gentle and not afraid of people; not wild or dangerous. **2** not exciting; dull. **tamely** adverb, **tameness** noun

tame verb (**tames, taming, tamed**) make an animal become tame. **tamer** noun

tamper verb (**tampers, tampering, tampered**) meddle or interfere with something. [from *temper*]

tampon noun (*plural tampons*) a plug of soft material that a woman puts into her vagina to absorb the blood during her period. [French]

tan noun (*plural tans*) **1** a light brown colour. **2** a brown colour in skin that has been exposed to the sun.

tan verb (**tans, tanning, tanned**) **1** make or become brown by exposing skin to the sun. **2** make an animal's skin into leather by treating it with chemicals. [probably from Latin]

tandem noun (*plural tandems*) a bicycle for two riders, one behind the other. [Latin, = at length]

tang noun (plural **tangs**) a strong flavour or smell. [from Old Norse]

tangent noun (plural **tangents**) a straight line that touches the outside of a curve or circle. [from Latin *tangens* = touching]

tangerine noun (plural **tangerines**) a kind of small orange from Tangier in Morocco. [named after Tangier]

tangle verb (**tangles, tangling, tangled**) make or become twisted into a confused mass. **tangle** noun

tango noun (plural **tangos**) a ballroom dance with gliding steps.

tank noun (plural **tanks**) 1 a large container for a liquid or gas. 2 a heavy armoured vehicle used in war. [from Gujarati or Marathi, languages spoken in India]

tankard noun (plural **tankards**) a large mug for drinking beer from, usually made of silver or pewter. [origin unknown]

tanker noun (plural **tankers**) 1 a large ship for carrying oil. 2 a large lorry for carrying a liquid. [from *tank*]

tantalize verb (**tantalizes, tantalizing, tantalized**) tease or torment a person by showing him or her something good but keeping it out of reach. [from the name of Tantalus in Greek mythology, who was punished by being made to stand near water and fruit which moved away when he tried to reach them]

tantrum noun (plural **tantrums**) an outburst of bad temper.

tap[1] noun (plural **taps**) a device for letting out liquid or gas in a controlled flow.

tap verb (**taps, tapping, tapped**) 1 take liquid out of something, especially through a tap. 2 obtain supplies or information etc. from a source. 3 fix a device to a telephone line so that you can overhear conversations on it. [from Old English]

tap[2] noun (plural **taps**) 1 a quick light hit; the sound of this. 2 tap-dancing.

tap verb (**taps, tapping, tapped**) hit a person or thing quickly and lightly.
[from French]

tape noun (plural **tapes**) 1 a narrow strip of cloth, paper, plastic, etc. 2 a narrow plastic strip coated with a magnetic substance and used for making recordings. 3 a tape recording. 4 a tape-measure.

tape verb (**tapes, taping, taped**) 1 fix, cover, or surround something with tape. 2 record something on magnetic tape. **get** or **have something taped** (slang) know or understand it; be able to deal with it.

tape-measure noun (plural **tape-measures**) a long strip marked in centimetres or inches for measuring things.

taper verb (**tapers, tapering, tapered**) 1 make or become thinner towards one end. 2 make or become gradually less.

tape recorder noun (plural **tape recorders**) a machine for recording sounds or computer data on magnetic tape and reproducing them. **tape recording** noun

tapestry noun (plural **tapestries**) a piece of strong cloth with pictures or patterns woven or embroidered on it. [from French *tapis* = carpet]

tapeworm noun (plural **tapeworms**) a long flat worm that can live as a parasite in the intestines of people and animals.

tar noun a thick black liquid made from coal or wood etc. and used in making roads.

target noun (plural **targets**) something aimed at; a thing that someone tries to hit or reach.

tariff noun (plural **tariffs**) a list of prices or charges. [via French and Italian from Arabic]

tarmac noun an area surfaced with tarmacadam, especially on an airfield. [*Tarmac* is a trade mark]

tarnish verb (**tarnishes**, **tarnishing**, **tarnished**) 1 make or become less shiny, *The silver had tarnished.* 2 spoil or blemish, *The scandal tarnished his reputation.* **tarnish** noun [from French *terne* = dark, dull]

tarpaulin noun (plural **tarpaulins**) a large sheet of waterproof canvas. [from *tar* + *pall*[1]]

tarry[1] (say **tar**-ee) adjective covered with or like tar.

tarry[2] (say **ta**-ree) verb (**tarries**, **tarrying**, **tarried**) (old use) stay for a while longer; linger. [origin unknown]

tart[1] noun (plural **tarts**) 1 a pie containing fruit or sweet filling. 2 a piece of pastry with jam etc. on top. [from Latin]

tart[2] adjective 1 sour. 2 sharp in manner, *a tart reply.* **tartly** adverb, **tartness** noun [origin unknown]

tartan noun a pattern with coloured stripes crossing each other, especially one that is used by a Scottish clan. [probably from old French *tiretaine*, a kind of material]

tartar[1] noun (plural **tartars**) a person who is fierce or difficult to deal with. [named after the Tartars, warriors from central Asia in the 13th century]

tartar[2] noun (plural **tartars**) a hard chalky deposit that forms on teeth. [from Latin]

task noun (plural **tasks**) a piece of work to be done. **take a person to task** rebuke him or her. [from old French; related to *tax*]

tassel noun (plural **tassels**) a bundle of threads tied together at the top and used to decorate something. **tasselled** adjective [from old French]

taste verb (**tastes**, **tasting**, **tasted**) 1 take a small amount of food or drink to try its flavour. 2 be able to perceive flavours. 3 have a certain flavour.

taste noun (plural **tastes**) 1 the feeling caused in the tongue by something placed on it. 2 the ability to taste things. 3 the ability to enjoy beautiful things or to choose what is suitable, *Her choice of clothes shows her good taste.* 4 a liking, *I've developed quite a taste for skiing.* 5 a very small amount of food or drink.

tasteful *adjective* showing good taste. **tastefully** *adverb*, **tastefulness** *noun*

tasteless *adjective*
1 having no flavour. **2** showing poor taste. **tastelessly** *adverb*, **tastelessness** *noun*

tasty *adjective* (**tastier, tastiest**) having a strong pleasant taste.

tattered *adjective* badly torn; ragged. [from *tatters*]

tatters *plural noun* rags; badly torn pieces.
in tatters torn to pieces, *My coat was in tatters.*

tattoo[1] *verb* (**tattoos, tattooing, tattooed**) mark a person's skin with a picture or pattern by using a needle and some dye.

tattoo *noun* (*plural* **tattoos**) a tattooed picture or pattern. [from a Polynesian language]

tattoo[2] *noun* (*plural* **tattoos**)
1 a drumming or tapping sound. **2** an entertainment consisting of military music, marching, etc. [from Dutch]

taunt *verb* (**taunts, taunting, taunted**) jeer at or insult someone. **taunt** *noun* [from French *tant pour tant* = tit for tat]

taut *adjective* stretched tightly. **tautly** *adverb*, **tautness** *noun* [probably from *tough*]

tautology *noun* (*plural* **tautologies**) saying the same thing again in different words, e.g. *You can get the book free for nothing* (where *free* and *for nothing* mean the same). [from Greek *tauto* = the same + *logos* = word]

tavern *noun* (*plural* **taverns**) (*old use*) an inn or public house. [from Latin]

tawny *adjective* brownish-yellow. [from old French; related to *tan*]

tax *noun* (*plural* **taxes**)
1 money that people or business firms have to pay to the government, to be used for public purposes. **2** a strain or burden, *The long walk was a tax on his strength.*

tax *verb* (**taxes, taxing, taxed**)
1 put a tax on something. **2** charge someone a tax. **3** pay the tax on something, *I have taxed the car up to June.* **4** put a strain or burden on a person or thing, *Will it tax your strength?* **5** accuse, *I taxed him with leaving the door open.* **taxable** *adjective*, **taxation** *noun* [from Latin *taxare* = calculate]

taxi *noun* (*plural* **taxis**) a car that carries passengers for payment, usually with a meter to record the fare to be paid. **taxicab** *noun*

taxi *verb* (**taxies, taxiing, taxied**) (of an aircraft) move along the ground or water, especially before or after flying. [short for *taximeter cab*, from French *taxe* = tariff, charge + *mètre* = meter]

tea *noun* (*plural* **teas**)
1 a drink made by pouring hot water on the dried leaves of an evergreen shrub (the *tea-plant*). **2** these dried leaves. **3** a meal in the afternoon or early evening. **teacup** *noun*, **tea leaf** *noun*, **tea table** *noun*, **teatime** *noun* [via Dutch from Chinese]

tea bag *noun* (*plural* **tea bags**) a small bag holding about a teaspoonful of tea.

teach *verb* (**teaches, teaching, taught**)
1 give a person knowledge or

skill; train. **2** give lessons, especially in a particular subject. **3** show someone what to do or avoid, *That will teach you not to meddle!*

teacher noun (plural **teachers**) a person who teaches others, especially in a school.

team noun (plural **teams**) **1** a set of players forming one side in certain games and sports. **2** a set of people working together. **3** two or more animals harnessed to pull a vehicle or a plough etc.

teapot noun (plural **teapots**) a pot with a lid and a handle, for making and pouring tea.

tear[1] (say teer) noun (plural **tears**) a drop of the water that comes from the eyes when a person cries. **teardrop** noun
in tears crying.
[from Old English *taeher*]

tear[2] (say tair) verb (**tears, tearing, tore, torn**) **1** pull something apart, away, or into pieces. **2** become torn, *Newspaper tears easily.* **3** run or travel hurriedly.
tear noun (plural **tears**) a split made by tearing.
[from Old English *teran*]

tear gas noun a gas that makes people's eyes water painfully.

tease verb (**teases, teasing, teased**) **1** amuse yourself by deliberately annoying or making fun of someone. **2** pick threads apart into separate strands.
tease noun (plural **teases**) a person who often teases others.

teaspoon noun (plural **teaspoons**) a small spoon for stirring tea etc. **teaspoonful** noun

tea towel noun (plural **tea towels**) a cloth for drying washed dishes, cutlery, etc.

technical adjective **1** to do with technology. **2** to do with a particular subject and its methods, *the technical terms of chemistry.* **technically** adverb [from Greek *technikos* = skilled in an art or craft]

technical college noun (plural **technical colleges**) a college where technical subjects are taught.

technicality noun (plural **technicalities**) **1** being technical. **2** a technical word or phrase; a special detail.

technician noun (plural **technicians**) a person whose job is to look after scientific equipment and do practical work in a laboratory.

technique noun (plural **techniques**) the method of doing something skilfully. [French, related to *technical*]

technology noun (plural **technologies**) the study of machinery, engineering, and how things work. **technological** adjective, **technologist** noun [from Greek *techne* = craft, skill, + *-ology*]

teddy bear noun (plural **teddy bears**) a soft furry toy bear. [named after US President Theodore ('Teddy') Roosevelt, who liked hunting bears]

tedious adjective annoyingly slow or long; boring. **tediously** adverb, **tediousness** noun, **tedium** noun [from Latin *taedium* = tiredness]

tee noun (plural **tees**)
1 the flat area from which golfers strike the ball at the start of play for each hole. **2** a small piece of wood or plastic on which a golf ball is placed for being struck. [origin unknown]

teem verb (**teems**, **teeming**, **teemed**) be full of something, *The river was teeming with fish.* [from Old English]

-teen suffix a form of 'ten' added to numbers from *three* to *nine* to form *thirteen* to *nineteen*.

teenage adjective to do with teenagers.

teenager noun (plural **teenagers**) a person in his or her teens.

teens plural noun the time of life between 13 and 19 years of age.

teething noun (of a baby) having its first teeth beginning to grow through the gums.

teetotal adjective never drinking alcohol. **teetotaller** noun [from *total* with *tee* added for emphasis]

tele- prefix far; at a distance (as in *telescope*). [from Greek]

telecommunications plural noun communications over a long distance, e.g. by telephone, telegraph, radio, or television.

telegram noun (plural **telegrams**) a message sent by telegraph.

telegraph noun a way of sending messages by using electric current along wires or by radio. **telegraphic** adjective, **telegraphy** noun

telepathy (say til-ep-ath-ee) noun communication of thoughts from one person's mind to another without speaking, writing, or gestures. **telepathic** adjective [from *tele-* + Greek *pathos* = feeling]

telephone noun (plural **telephones**) a device or system using electric wires or radio etc. to enable one person to speak to another who is some distance away.

telephone verb (**telephones**, **telephoning**, **telephoned**) speak to a person on the telephone. [from *tele-* + Greek *phone* = sound, voice]

telescope noun (plural **telescopes**) an instrument using lenses to magnify distant objects. **telescopic** adjective

telescope verb (**telescopes**, **telescoping**, **telescoped**)
1 make or become shorter by sliding overlapping sections into each other. **2** compress or condense something so that it takes less space or time. [from *tele-* + Greek *skopein* = look at]

television noun (plural **televisions**)
1 a system using radio waves to reproduce a view of scenes, events, or plays etc. on a screen. **2** an apparatus for receiving these pictures. **3** televised programmes. **televise** verb

tell verb (**tells**, **telling**, **told**)
1 make a thing known to someone, especially by words. **2** speak, *Tell the truth.* **3** order, *Tell them to wait.* **4** reveal a secret, *Promise you won't tell.*

5 decide or distinguish, *Can you tell the difference between butter and margarine?* **6** produce an effect, *The strain began to tell on him.* **7** count, *There are ten of them, all told.*

tell off (*informal*) reprimand.

tell tales report something naughty or bad that someone has done.

telling *adjective* having a strong effect, *a very telling reply.*

tell-tale *adjective* revealing or indicating something, *There was a tell-tale spot of jam on his chin.*

temper *noun* (*plural* **tempers**)
1 a person's mood, *He is in a good temper.* **2** an angry mood, *She was in a temper.*

lose your temper lose your calmness and become angry.

temper *verb* (**tempers, tempering, tempered**)
1 harden or strengthen metal etc. by heating and cooling it.
2 moderate or soften the effects of something, *tempering justice with mercy.*
[via Old English from Latin *temperare* = mix]

temperament *noun* (*plural* **temperaments**) a person's nature as shown in the way he or she usually behaves, *a nervous temperament.* [same origin as *temper*]

temperamental *adjective*
1 likely to become excitable or moody suddenly. **2** to do with a person's temperament.
temperamentally *adverb*

temperate *adjective* neither extremely hot nor extremely cold, *Britain has a temperate climate.* [originally = not affected by strong emotions: same origin as *temper*]

temperature *noun* (*plural* **temperatures**)
1 how hot or cold a person or thing is. **2** an abnormally high temperature of the body. [from Latin *temperatus* = tempered]

tempest *noun* (*plural* **tempests**) a violent storm. [from Latin *tempestas* = weather]

temple¹ *noun* (*plural* **temples**) a building where a god is worshipped. [from Latin *templum* = consecrated place]

temple² *noun* (*plural* **temples**) the part of the head between the forehead and the ear. [from Latin *tempora* = sides of the head]

tempo *noun* (*plural* **tempos** or **tempi**) the speed or rhythm of something, especially of a piece of music. [Italian, from Latin *tempus* = time]

temporary *adjective* lasting for a limited time only; not permanent. **temporarily** (*say* tem-per-er-il-ee) *adverb* [from Latin *temporis* = of a time]

tempt *verb* (**tempts, tempting, tempted**) try to persuade or attract someone, especially into doing something wrong or unwise. **temptation** *noun*, **tempter** *noun*, **temptress** *noun* [from Latin *temptare* = test]

ten *adjective* & *noun* (*plural* **tens**) the number 10. [from Old English]

tenacious (*say* ten-ay-shus) *adjective*
1 holding or clinging firmly to something. **2** obstinate and

persistent. **tenaciously** adverb, **tenacity** noun [from Latin tenere = to hold]

tenant noun (plural **tenants**) a person who rents a house, building, or land etc. from a landlord. **tenancy** noun [French, = holding]

tend[1] verb (**tends**, **tending**, **tended**) have a certain tendency, Prices tend to rise. [same origin as tender[2]]

tend[2] verb (**tends**, **tending**, **tended**) look after, Shepherds were tending their sheep. [from attend]

tendency noun (plural **tendencies**) the way a person or thing is likely to behave, She has a tendency to be lazy.

tender[1] adjective
1 easy to chew; not tough or hard. **2** easily hurt or damaged; sensitive or delicate, tender plants. **3** gentle and loving, a tender smile. **tenderly** adverb, **tenderness** noun [from Latin tener = soft]

tender[2] verb (**tenders**, **tendering**, **tendered**) offer something formally, He tendered his resignation.

tender noun (plural **tenders**) a formal offer to supply goods or carry out work at a stated price, The council asked for tenders to build a school.

legal tender kinds of money that are legal for making payments, Are pound notes still legal tender? [from Latin tendere = stretch, hold out]

tendril noun (plural **tendrils**)
1 a thread-like part by which a climbing plant clings to

a support. **2** a thin curl of hair etc. [from French; related to tender[1]]

tennis noun a game played with rackets and a ball on a court with a net across the middle.

tenor noun (plural **tenors**) a male singer with a high voice.

tense[1] noun (plural **tenses**) the form of a verb that shows when something happens, e.g. he came (**past tense**), he comes or is coming (**present tense**), he will come (**future tense**). [from Latin tempus = time]

tense[2] adjective
1 tightly stretched. **2** nervous or worried and unable to relax. **tensely** adverb, **tenseness** noun

tense verb (**tenses**, **tensing**, **tensed**) make or become tense. [from Latin tensum = stretched]

tension noun (plural **tensions**)
1 how tightly stretched a rope or wire is. **2** a feeling of anxiety or nervousness about something that is just about to happen. **3** voltage, high-tension cables. [from Latin tensio = stretching]

tent noun (plural **tents**) a shelter made of canvas or other material. [from French; related to tense[2]]

tentacle noun (plural **tentacles**) a long flexible part of the body of certain animals (e.g. snails, octopuses), used for feeling or grasping things or for moving. [from Latin]

tentative adjective cautious; trying something out, a tentative suggestion. **tentatively** adverb [same origin as tempt]

tenth adjective & noun next after the ninth. [from Old English]

tenuous *adjective* very slight or thin, *tenuous threads; a tenuous connection*. [from Latin *tenuis* = thin]

tepid *adjective* only slightly warm; lukewarm, *tepid water*. [from Latin *tepere* = to be warm]

term *noun* (*plural* **terms**)
1 the period of weeks when a school or college is open. **2** a definite period, *a term of imprisonment*. **3** a word or expression, *technical terms*.

term *verb* (**terms, terming, termed**) name; call something by a certain term, *This music is termed jazz*.
[from French; related to *terminus*]

terminal *noun* (*plural* **terminals**)
1 the place where something ends; a terminus. **2** a building where air passengers arrive or depart. **3** a place where a wire is connected in an electric circuit or battery etc. **4** a device for sending information to a computer, or for receiving it.

terminal *adjective*
1 to do with or at the end or boundary of something. **2** in the last stage of a fatal disease, *terminal cancer*. **terminally** *adverb*
[same origin as *terminus*]

terminate *verb* (**terminates, terminating, terminated**) end; stop finally. **termination** *noun*
[same origin as *terminus*]

terminology *noun* (*plural* **terminologies**) the technical terms of a subject. **terminological** *adjective* [via German from Latin]

terminus *noun* (*plural* **termini**) the end of something; the last station on a railway or bus route. [Latin, = end, limit, or boundary]

termite *noun* (*plural* **termites**) a small insect that is very destructive to timber. [from Latin]

terms *plural noun*
1 a relationship between people, *They are on friendly terms*.
2 conditions offered or accepted, *peace terms*.

terrace *noun* (*plural* **terraces**)
1 a level area on a slope or hillside. **2** a paved area beside a house. **3** a row of houses joined together. **4** a series of steps for spectators at a sports-ground.
terraced *adjective*

terrestrial *adjective* to do with the earth or land.

terrible *adjective* very bad; distressing. **terribly** *adverb* [same origin as *terror*]

terrier *noun* (*plural* **terriers**) a kind of small lively dog. [from old French *chien terrier* = earth-dog (because they were used to dig out foxes from their earths)]

terrific *adjective* (*informal*)
1 very great, *a terrific storm*.
2 excellent. **terrifically** *adverb* [from Latin *terrificus* = frightening]

terrify *verb* (**terrifies, terrifying, terrified**) fill someone with terror. [same origin as *terrific*]

territory *noun* (*plural* **territories**) an area of land, especially one that belongs to a country or person. **territorial** *adjective*

terror noun (plural **terrors**)
1 very great fear. **2** a terrifying person or thing. [from Latin *terrere* = frighten]

terrorist noun (plural **terrorists**) a person who uses violence for political purposes. **terrorism** noun

terrorize verb (**terrorizes, terrorizing, terrorized**) fill someone with terror; frighten someone by threatening them. **terrorization** noun

test noun (plural **tests**)
1 a short examination. **2** a way of discovering the qualities, abilities, or presence of a person or thing, *a test for radioactivity*. **3** (*informal*) a test match.
test verb (**tests, testing, tested**) carry out a test on a person or thing. **tester** noun [from Latin]

testament noun (plural **testaments**)
1 a written statement. **2** either of the two main parts of the Bible, the Old Testament or the New Testament. [from Latin *testari* = act as a witness, make a will]

testicle noun (plural **testicles**) either of the two glands in the scrotum where semen is produced. [from Latin]

testify verb (**testifies, testifying, testified**) give evidence; swear that something is true. [from Latin *testis* = witness]

testimonial noun (plural **testimonials**)
1 ~~...~~ter describing someone's ~~...~~ character, etc. **2** a gift ~~...~~d to someone as a mark ~~...~~ct. [same origin as *testify*]

test match noun (plural **test matches**) a cricket or Rugby match between teams from different countries.

test tube noun (plural **test tubes**) a tube of thin glass with one end closed, used for experiments in chemistry etc.

tether verb (**tethers, tethering, tethered**) tie an animal so that it cannot move far.
tether noun (plural **tethers**) a rope for tethering an animal.
at the end of your tether unable to endure something any more.

tetra- prefix four. [from Greek]

tetrahedron noun (plural **tetrahedrons**) a solid with four sides (i.e. a pyramid with a triangular base). [from *tetra-* + Greek *hedra* = base]

text noun (plural **texts**)
1 the words of something written or printed. **2** a sentence from the Bible used as the subject of a sermon etc. [from Latin *textus* = literary style]

textbook noun (plural **textbooks**) a book that teaches you about a subject.

texture noun (plural **textures**) the way that the surface of something feels. [from Latin *textura* = weaving]

than conjunction compared with another person or thing, *His brother is taller than he is* or *taller than him*. [from Old English]

thank verb (**thanks, thanking, thanked**) tell someone that you are grateful to him or her.
thank you I thank you.

thankful adjective grateful.

thankfully adverb
1 in a grateful way. **2** I am grateful that; fortunately, *Thankfully, John remembered to lock the door.*

USAGE: Some people say it is incorrect to use *thankfully* to mean 'I am grateful that' or 'fortunately', and say that it should only be used to mean 'in a grateful way'. This first use is very common in informal language but you should probably avoid it when you are writing or speaking formally.

thankless adjective not likely to win thanks from people, *a thankless task.*

thanks plural noun
1 statements of gratitude.
2 (informal) thank you.
thanks to as a result of; because of, *Thanks to your help, we succeeded.*

that adjective & pronoun (plural **those**) the one there, *That book is mine. Whose is that?*

that adverb to such an extent, *I'll come that far but no further.*

that relative pronoun which, who, or whom, *This is the record that I wanted. We liked the people that we met on holiday.*

that conjunction used to introduce a wish, reason, result, etc., *I hope that you are well. The puzzle was so hard that no one could solve it.*

thatch noun straw or reeds used to make a roof.

thatch verb (**thatches, thatching, thatched**) make a roof with thatch. **thatcher** noun

thaw verb (**thaws, thawing, thawed**) melt; stop being frozen.

thaw noun (plural **thaws**) a period of warm weather that thaws ice and snow. [from Old English]

the adjective (called the *definite article*) a particular one; that or those.

theatre noun (plural **theatres**)
1 a building where plays etc. are performed to an audience.
2 a special room where surgical operations are done, *the operating theatre.* [from Greek *theatron* = place for seeing things]

theatrical adjective to do with plays or acting. **theatrically** adverb

thee pronoun (old use) the form of *thou* used as the object of a verb or after a preposition. [from Old English]

theft noun (plural **thefts**) stealing. [from Old English]

their adjective
1 belonging to them, *Their coats are over there.* **2** (informal) belonging to a person, *Somebody has left their coat on the bus.* [from Old Norse]

USAGE: Do not confuse with *there*.

theirs possessive pronoun belonging to them, *These coats are theirs.*

USAGE: It is incorrect to write *their's*.

them pronoun the form of *they* used as the object of a verb or after a preposition, *We saw them.*

theme noun (plural **themes**)
1 the subject about which a person speaks, writes, or thinks. 2 a melody. [from Greek]

themselves pronoun they or them and nobody else. (Compare herself.)

then adverb
1 at that time, We were younger then. 2 after that; next, Make the tea, then pour it out. 3 in that case, If this is yours, then this must be mine. [from Old English]

theology noun the study of religion. **theological** adjective, **theologian** noun [from Greek theos = a god, + -logy]

theorem noun (plural **theorems**) a mathematical statement that can be proved by reasoning. [from Greek theorema = theory]

theoretical adjective based on theory not on experience. **theoretically** adverb

theory noun (plural **theories**)
1 an idea or set of ideas put forward to explain something. 2 the principles of a subject rather than its practice. **in theory** according to what should happen rather than what may in fact happen. [from Greek theoria = thinking about, considering]

therapy noun (plural **therapies**) treatment to cure a disease etc. **therapeutic** adjective [from Greek therapeia = healing]

there adverb
1 in or to that place etc. 2 used to call attention to something (There's a good boy!) or to introduce a sentence where the verb comes before its subject (There was plenty to eat). [from Old English]

USAGE: Do not confuse with their.

thereabouts adverb near there.

therefore adverb for that reason. [from there + fore]

thermo- prefix heat. [same origin as therm]

thermodynamics noun the science dealing with the relation between heat and other forms of energy.

thermometer noun (plural **thermometers**) a device for measuring temperature.

thermostat noun (plural **thermostats**) a piece of equipment that automatically keeps the temperature of a room or piece of equipment steady. **thermostatic** adjective, **thermostatically** adverb [from thermo- + Greek statos = standing]

thesaurus (say thi-sor-us) noun (plural **thesauruses** or **thesauri**) a kind of dictionary containing sets of words grouped according to their meaning. [from Greek thesauros = storehouse, treasury]

these plural of this.

they pronoun
1 the people or things being talked about. 2 people in general, They say the show is a great success. 3 (informal) he or she; a person, I am never angry with anyone unless they deserve it. [from Old Norse]

they're (mainly spoken) they are.

USAGE: Do not confuse with their and there.

thick adjective
1 measuring a lot or a certain amount between opposite surfaces. 2 (of a line) broad, not fine. 3 crowded with things; dense, a thick forest; thick fog. 4 fairly stiff, thick cream. 5 (informal) stupid. **thickly** adverb, **thickness** noun [from Old English]

thicken verb (thickens, thickening, thickened) make or become thicker.

thicket noun (plural thickets) a number of shrubs and small trees etc. growing close together. [from Old English]

thief noun (plural thieves) a person who steals things. **thievish** adjective, **thievery** noun, **thieving** noun [from Old English]

thigh noun (plural thighs) the part of the leg between the hip and the knee. [from Old English]

thimble noun (plural thimbles) a small metal or plastic cap worn on the end of the finger to push the needle in sewing. [from Old English]

thin adjective (thinner, thinnest) 1 not thick; not fat. 2 feeble, a thin excuse. **thinly** adverb, **thinness** noun

thin verb (thins, thinning, thinned) make or become less thick. **thinner** noun

thine adjective & possessive pronoun (old use) belonging to thee. [from Old English]

thing noun (plural things) an object; something which can be seen, touched, thought about, etc.

think verb (thinks, thinking, thought)
1 use your mind; form connected ideas. 2 have as an idea or opinion, We think we shall win. **thinker** noun [from Old English]

third adjective next after the second. **thirdly** adverb

third noun (plural thirds)
1 the third person or thing. 2 one of three equal parts of something.

Third World noun the poorer countries of Asia, Africa, and South America, also called 'developing countries'.

thirst noun
1 a feeling of dryness in the mouth and throat, causing a desire to drink. 2 a strong desire, a thirst for adventure. **thirsty** adjective, **thirstily** adverb

thirteen adjective & noun the number 13. **thirteenth** adjective & noun

thirty adjective & noun (plural thirties) the number 30. **thirtieth** adjective & noun

this adjective & pronoun (plural these) the one here, This house is ours. Whose is this?

this adverb to such an extent, I'm surprised he got this far. [from Old English]

thistle noun (plural thistles) a prickly wild plant with purple, white, or yellow flowers. [from Old English]

thong noun (plural thongs) a narrow strip of leather etc. used for fastening things. [from Old English]

thorn noun (plural thorns)
1 a small pointed growth on the stem of a plant. 2 a thorny tree or shrub.

thorny adjective (**thornier, thorniest**)
1 having many thorns. 2 like a thorn. 3 difficult, a thorny problem.

thorough adjective
1 done or doing things carefully and in detail. 2 complete in every way, a thorough mess. **thoroughly** adverb, **thoroughness** noun [a different spelling of through]

thoroughbred adjective bred of pure or pedigree stock. **thoroughbred** noun

thoroughfare noun (plural **thoroughfares**) a public road or path that is open at both ends. [from an old sense of thorough = through + fare = to progress]

those plural of that.

thou pronoun (old use, in speaking to one person) you. [from Old English]

though conjunction in spite of the fact that; even if, We must look for it, though we probably shan't find it.

though adverb however, She's right, though.

thought[1] noun (plural **thoughts**)
1 something that you think; an idea or opinion. 2 the process of thinking, She was deep in thought. [from Old English; related to think]

thought[2] past tense of think.

thoughtful adjective
1 thinking a lot. 2 showing thought for other people's needs; considerate. **thoughtfully** adverb, **thoughtfulness** noun

thoughtless adjective
1 careless; not thinking of what may happen. 2 inconsiderate. **thoughtlessly** adverb, **thoughtlessness** noun

thousand adjective & noun (plural **thousands**) the number 1,000. **thousandth** adjective & noun [from Old English]

thrash verb (**thrashes, thrashing, thrashed**)
1 beat someone with a stick or whip; keep hitting very hard. 2 defeat someone thoroughly. 3 move violently, The crocodile thrashed its tail.

thread noun (plural **threads**)
1 a thin length of any substance. 2 a length of spun cotton, wool, or nylon etc. used for making cloth or in sewing or knitting. 3 the spiral ridge round a screw.

thread verb (**threads, threading, threaded**)
1 put a thread through the eye of a needle. 2 pass a strip of film etc. through or round something. 3 put beads on a thread.

threadbare adjective (of cloth) with the surface worn away so that the threads show.

threat noun (plural **threats**)
1 a warning that you will punish, hurt, or harm a person or thing. 2 a sign of something undesirable. 3 a person or thing causing danger. [from Old English]

threaten verb (**threatens, threatening, threatened**)
1 make threats against someone. 2 be a threat or danger to a person or thing.

three *adjective & noun* (*plural* **threes**) the number 3. [from Old English]

three-dimensional *adjective* having three dimensions (length, width, and height or depth).

threshold *noun* (*plural* **thresholds**)
1 a slab of stone or board etc. forming the bottom of a doorway; the entrance. **2** the beginning, *We are on the threshold of a great discovery.* [from Old English]

thrift *noun*
1 careful spending or management of money or resources. **2** a plant with pink flowers. **thrifty** *adjective*, **thriftily** *adverb* [Old Norse, = thriving]

thrill *noun* (*plural* **thrills**) a feeling of excitement.

thrill *verb* (**thrills**, **thrilling**, **thrilled**) have or give a feeling of excitement. **thrilling** *adjective* [from Old English]

thriller *noun* (*plural* **thrillers**) an exciting story, play, or film, usually about crime.

thrive *verb* (**thrives**, **thriving**, **throve**, **thrived** or **thriven**) grow strongly, prosper or be successful.

throat *noun* (*plural* **throats**)
1 the tube in the neck that takes food and drink down into the body. **2** the front of the neck. [from Old English]

throb *verb* (**throbs**, **throbbing**, **throbbed**) beat or vibrate with a strong rhythm, *My heart throbbed.* **throb** *noun*

thrombosis *noun* the formation of a clot of blood in the body. [from Greek *thrombos* = lump]

throne *noun* (*plural* **thrones**) a special chair for a king, queen, or bishop at ceremonies. [from Greek *thronos* = high seat]

throng *noun* (*plural* **throngs**) a crowd of people.

throng *verb* (**throngs**, **thronging**, **thronged**) crowd, *People thronged the streets.*

throttle *noun* (*plural* **throttles**) a device that controls the flow of fuel to an engine; an accelerator.

throttle *verb* (**throttles**, **throttling**, **throttled**) strangle. **throttle back** or **down** reduce the speed of an engine by partially closing the throttle. [from *throat*]

through *preposition*
1 from one end or side to the other end or side of, *Climb through the window.* **2** by means of; because of, *We lost it through carelessness.* **3** at the end of; having finished successfully, *He is through his exam.*

through *adverb*
1 through something, *We squeezed through.* **2** with a telephone connection made, *I'll put you through to the president.* **3** finished, *Wait till I'm through with these papers.*

through *adjective*
1 going through something, *No through road.* **2** going all the way to a destination, *a through train.* [from Old English]

throughout *preposition & adverb* all the way through.

throve *past tense of* **thrive**.

throw *verb* (**throws**, **throwing**, **threw**, **thrown**)
1 send a person or thing through the air. **2** put something in a place

carelessly or hastily. **3** move part of your body quickly, *He threw his head back.* **4** put someone in a certain condition etc., *It threw us into confusion.* **5** move a switch or lever in order to operate it. **6** shape a pot on a potter's wheel. **throw** *noun*, **thrower** *noun*
throw away 1 get rid of something because it is useless or unwanted. **2** waste, *You threw away an opportunity.*

thrush *noun* (*plural* **thrushes**) a songbird with a speckled breast. [from Old English]

thrust *verb* (**thrusts, thrusting, thrust**) push hard. **thrust** *noun* [from Old Norse]

thud *verb* (**thuds, thudding, thudded**) make the dull sound of a heavy knock or fall. **thud** *noun* [originally Scots; probably from Old English]

thug *noun* (*plural* **thugs**) a rough and violent person. **thuggery** *noun* [from Hindi; the Thugs were robbers and murderers in India in the 17th–19th centuries]

thumb *noun* (*plural* **thumbs**) the short thick finger set apart from the other four.
be under a person's thumb be completely under his or her influence.

thump *verb* (**thumps, thumping, thumped**)
1 hit or knock something heavily. **2** punch. **3** thud. **4** throb or beat strongly, *My heart was thumping.* **thump** *noun*

thunder *noun*
1 the loud noise that is heard with lightning. **2** a similar noise, *a thunder of applause.*

thunderous *adjective*, **thunderstorm** *noun*, **thundery** *adjective*

thunder *verb* (**thunders, thundering, thundered**)
1 sound with thunder. **2** make a noise like thunder; speak loudly. [from Old English]

thunderbolt *noun* (*plural* **thunderbolts**) a lightning flash thought of as a destructive missile.

thus *adverb*
1 in this way, *Hold the wheel thus.* **2** therefore. [from Old English]

thwart *verb* (**thwarts, thwarting, thwarted**) frustrate; prevent someone from achieving something. [from Old Norse]

thy *adjective* (*old use*) belonging to thee. [from *thine*]

tiara (*say* tee-ar-a) *noun* (*plural* **tiaras**) a woman's jewelled crescent-shaped ornament worn like a crown. [from Greek]

tic *noun* (*plural* **tics**) an unintentional twitch of a muscle, especially of the face.

tick[1] *noun* (*plural* **ticks**)
1 a small mark (usually ✓) put by something to show that it is correct or has been checked. **2** a regular clicking sound, especially that made by a clock or watch. **3** (*informal*) a moment, *Back in a tick.*
tick *verb* (**ticks, ticking, ticked**)
1 put a tick by something. **2** make the sound of a tick.
tick off (*informal*) reprimand someone.
[probably from old German or old Dutch]

tick² noun (plural **ticks**)
a bloodsucking insect. [from Old English]

ticket noun (plural **tickets**)
1 a printed piece of paper or card that allows a person to travel on a bus or train, see a show, etc. **2** a label showing a thing's price. [via French from old Dutch]

tickle verb (**tickles, tickling, tickled**)
1 touch a person's skin lightly in order to produce a slight tingling feeling and laughter. **2** (of a part of the body) have a slight tingling or itching feeling. **3** amuse or please somebody. [origin unknown]

ticklish adjective
1 likely to laugh or wriggle when tickled. **2** awkward or difficult, a ticklish situation.

tidal wave noun (plural **tidal waves**) a huge sea wave.

tide noun (plural **tides**)
1 the regular rise and fall in the level of the sea which usually happens twice a day. **2** (old use) a time or season, Christmas-tide.

tide verb (**tides, tiding, tided**)
tide a person over provide him or her with what is needed, for a short time.

tidy adjective (**tidier, tidiest**)
1 with everything in its right place; neat and orderly. **2** (informal) fairly large, It costs a tidy amount. **tidily** adverb, **tidiness** noun

tidy verb (**tidies, tidying, tidied**)
make a place tidy.
[originally = at the right time or season: from tide]

tie verb (**ties, tying, tied**)
1 fasten something with string, ribbon, etc. arrange something into a knot or bow. **3** make the same score as another competitor.

tie noun (plural **ties**)
1 a strip of material worn passing under the collar of a shirt and knotted in front. **2** a result when two or more competitors have equal scores.
[from Old English]

tier (say teer) noun (plural **tiers**) each of a series of rows or levels etc. placed one above the other. **tiered** adjective [from French tire = rank¹]

tiff noun (plural **tiffs**) a slight quarrel. [origin unknown]

tiger noun (plural **tigers**) a large wild animal of the cat family, with yellow and black stripes. [from Greek]

tight adjective
1 fitting very closely. **2** firmly fastened. **3** fully stretched; tense. **4** in short supply, Money is tight at the moment. **5** stingy, He is very tight with his money. **6** (slang) drunk. **tightly** adverb, **tightness** noun

tighten verb (**tightens, tightening, tightened**) make or become tighter.

tightrope noun (plural **tightropes**) a tightly stretched rope high above the ground, on which acrobats perform.

tights plural noun a garment that fits tightly over the feet, legs, and lower part of the body.

tile *noun* (*plural* **tiles**) a thin square piece of baked clay or other hard material, used in rows for covering roofs, walls, or floors. **tiled** *adjective*

till[1] *preposition & conjunction* until. [from Old English *til* = to]

USAGE: It is better to use *until* rather than *till* when the word stands first in a sentence (e.g. *Until last year we had never been abroad*) or when you are speaking or writing formally.

till[2] *noun* (*plural* **tills**) a drawer or box for money in a shop; a cash register. [origin unknown]

tilt *verb* (**tilts**, **tilting**, **tilted**) move into a sloping position. **tilt** *noun* a sloping position. **at full tilt** at full speed or force.

timber *noun* (*plural* **timbers**) 1 wood for building or making things. 2 a wooden beam. [from Old English]

time *noun* (*plural* **times**) 1 all the years of the past, present, and future; the continuous existence of the universe. 2 a particular point or portion of time, *the first time I saw him.* 3 an occasion, *the first time I saw him.* 4 a period suitable or available for something, *Is there time for a cup of tea?* 5 a system of measuring time, *Greenwich Mean Time.* 6 (*in Music*) rhythm depending on the number and stress of beats in the bar. 7 (*in Mathematics*) times multiplied by, *Five times three is 15 (5 × 3 = 15).* **in time** 1 not late. 2 eventually. **on time** punctual.

time *verb* (**times**, **timing**, **timed**) 1 measure how long something takes. 2 arrange when something is to happen. **timer** *noun* [from Old English]

timeless *adjective* not affected by the passage of time; eternal.

timely *adjective* happening at a suitable or useful time, *a timely warning.*

timetable *noun* (*plural* **timetables**) a list showing the times when things will happen, e.g. when buses or trains will arrive and depart, or when school lessons will take place.

timid *adjective* easily frightened. **timidly** *adverb*, **timidity** *noun* [from Latin *timidus* = nervous]

timpani *plural noun* kettledrums. [Italian]

tin *noun* (*plural* **tins**) 1 a silvery-white metal. 2 a metal container for food.

tinge *verb* (**tinges**, **tingeing**, **tinged**) colour something slightly; tint. **tinge** *noun* [same origin as *tint*]

tingle *verb* (**tingles**, **tingling**, **tingled**) have a slight pricking or stinging feeling. **tingle** *noun* [probably from *tinkle*]

tinker *verb* (**tinkers**, **tinkering**, **tinkered**) work at something casually, trying to improve or mend it. [origin unknown]

tinkle *verb* (**tinkles**, **tinkling**, **tinkled**) make a gentle ringing sound. **tinkle** *noun*

tinny *adjective* 1 like tin. 2 (of a sound) unpleasantly thin and high-pitched.

tinsel *noun* strips of glittering material used for decoration. [from old French; related to *scintillate*]

tint *noun* (*plural* **tints**) a shade of colour, especially a pale one.

tint *verb* (**tints, tinting, tinted**) colour something slightly. [from Latin *tingere* = to dye or stain]

tiny *adjective* (**tinier, tiniest**) very small. [origin unknown]

-tion *suffix* see **-ion**.

tip[1] *noun* (*plural* **tips**) the part right at the top or end of something.

tip *verb* (**tips, tipping, tipped**) put a tip on something. [from Old Norse]

tip[2] *noun* (*plural* **tips**)
1 a small present of money given to someone who has helped you. **2** a small but useful piece of advice; a hint. **3** a slight push.

tip *verb* (**tips, tipping, tipped**) **1** give a person a tip. **2** name someone as a likely winner, *Which team would you tip to win the championship?* **tipper** *noun* [probably from *tip*[1]]

tip[3] *verb* (**tips, tipping, tipped**) **1** tilt or topple. **2** empty rubbish somewhere.

tip *noun* (*plural* **tips**)
1 the action of tipping something. **2** a place where rubbish etc. is tipped. [probably from a Scandinavian language]

tipsy *adjective* slightly drunk. [from *tip*[3]]

tiptoe *verb* (**tiptoes, tiptoeing, tiptoed**) walk on your toes very quietly or carefully.
on tiptoe walking or standing on your toes.

tired *adjective* feeling that you need to sleep or rest.
tired of having had enough of something and impatient or bored with it.

tiresome *adjective* annoying.

tissue *noun* (*plural* **tissues**)
1 tissue paper. **2** a paper handkerchief. **3** the substance forming any part of the body of an animal or plant, *bone tissue*. [from old French; related to *textiles*]

tissue paper *noun* very thin soft paper used for wrapping and packing things.

tit[1] *noun* (*plural* **tits**) a kind of small bird. [probably from a Scandinavian language]

tit[2] *noun*
tit for tat something equal given in return; retaliation. [originally 'tip for tap': from *tip*[2] + *tap*[2]]

titbit *noun* (*plural* **titbits**) a nice little piece of something, e.g. of food, gossip, or information. [from a dialect word *tid* = tender, + *bit*[1]]

titillate *verb* (**titillates, titillating, titillated**) stimulate or excite you pleasantly. **titillation** *noun* [from Latin *titillare* = to tickle]

title *noun* (*plural* **titles**)
1 the name of a book, film, song, etc. **2** a word used to show a person's rank or position, e.g. *Dr, Lord, Mrs*. **3** a championship in sport, *the world heavyweight title*. **4** a legal right to something. [from Latin]

titter verb (titters, tittering, tittered) giggle. **titter** noun [imitating the sound]

to preposition This word is used to show
1 direction or arrival at a position (*We walked to school. He rose to power*), **2** limit (*from noon to two o'clock*), **3** comparison (*We won by six goals to three*), **4** receiving or being affected by something (*Give it to me. Be kind to animals*). Also used before a verb to form an infinitive (*I want to see him*) or to show purpose etc. (*He does that to annoy us*), or alone when the verb is understood (*We meant to go but forgot to*).

to adverb
1 to or in the proper or closed position or condition, *Push the door to.* **2** into a state of activity, *We set to and cleaned the kitchen.* **to and fro** backwards and forwards.
[from Old English]

toad noun (plural **toads**) a frog-like animal that lives mainly on land. [from Old English]

toadstool noun (plural **toadstools**) a fungus (usually poisonous) with a round top on a stalk.

toast verb (toasts, toasting, toasted)
1 heat bread etc. to make it brown and crisp. **2** warm something in front of a fire etc. **3** drink in honour of someone.

toast noun (plural **toasts**)
1 toasted bread. **2** the call to drink in honour of someone; the person honoured in this way.
[from Latin *tostum* = dried up]

tobacco noun the dried leaves of certain plants prepared for smoking in cigarettes, cigars, or pipes or for making snuff. [via Spanish from a Central American language]

toboggan noun (plural **toboggans**) a small sledge used for sliding downhill. **tobogganing** noun [via Canadian French from a Native American language]

today noun this present day, *Today is Monday.*

today adverb on this day, *Have you seen him today?*
[from *to* (preposition) + *day*]

toddler noun (plural **toddlers**) a young child who has only recently learnt to walk. **toddle** verb [origin unknown]

to-do noun (plural **to-dos**) a fuss or commotion.

toe noun (plural **toes**)
1 any of the separate parts (five in humans) at the end of each foot. **2** the part of a shoe or sock etc. that covers the toes.

toffee noun (plural **toffees**) a sticky sweet made from heated butter and sugar. [origin unknown]

together adverb with another person or thing; with each other, *They went to the party together.*

toil verb (toils, toiling, toiled)
1 work hard. **2** move slowly and with difficulty. **toiler** noun

toil noun hard work.
[from old French]

toilet noun (plural **toilets**)
1 a bowl-like object, connected by pipes to a drain, which you use to get rid of urine and faeces.

2 a room containing a toilet. **3** the process of washing, dressing, and tidying yourself.

token *noun* (*plural* **tokens**)
1 a piece of metal or plastic that can be used instead of money. **2** a voucher or coupon that can be exchanged for goods. **3** a sign or signal of something, *a token of our friendship.*

tolerable *adjective* able to be tolerated. **tolerably** *adverb*

tolerant *adjective* tolerating things, especially other people's behaviour, beliefs, etc. **tolerantly** *adverb*, **tolerance** *noun*

tolerate *verb* (**tolerates**, **tolerating**, **tolerated**) allow something without protesting or interfering. **toleration** *noun* [from Latin *tolerare* = endure]

toll¹ (rhymes with *hole*) *noun* (*plural* **tolls**)
1 a charge made for using a road, bridge, etc. **2** loss or damage caused, *The death toll in the earthquake is rising.* [via Old English and Latin from Greek *telos* = a tax]

toll² (rhymes with *hole*) *verb* (**tolls**, **tolling**, **tolled**) ring a bell slowly. **toll** *noun* [probably from Old English]

tom *noun* (*plural* **toms**) a male cat. **tomcat** *noun* [short for *Thomas*]

tomato *noun* (*plural* **tomatoes**) a soft round red or yellow fruit eaten as a vegetable. [via French, Spanish, or Portuguese from Nahuatl (a Central American language)]

tomb (*say* toom) *noun* (*plural* **tombs**) a place where someone is buried; a monument built over this. [from Greek]

tomboy *noun* (*plural* **tomboys**) a girl who enjoys rough noisy games etc. [from *tom* (short for *Thomas*) + *boy*]

tombstone *noun* (*plural* **tombstones**) a memorial stone set up over a grave.

tomorrow *noun & adverb* the day after today. [from *to* (preposition) + *morrow*]

ton *noun* (*plural* **tons**)
1 a unit of weight equal to 2,240 pounds or about 1,016 kilograms. **2** a large amount, *There's tons of room.* **3** (*slang*) a speed of 100 miles per hour. [a different spelling of *tun*]

tone *noun* (*plural* **tones**)
1 a sound in music or of the voice. **2** each of the five larger intervals between notes in a musical scale (the smaller intervals are *semitones*). **3** a shade of a colour. **4** the quality or character of something, *a cheerful tone.* **tonal** *adjective*, **tonally** *adverb*

tone *verb* (**tones**, **toning**, **toned**)
1 give a particular tone or quality to something. **2** be harmonious in colour.
tone down make a thing quieter or less bright or less harsh.
tone up make a thing brighter or stronger. [from Greek *tonos* = tension]

tongs *plural noun* a tool with two arms joined at one end, used to pick up or hold things.

tongue *noun* (*plural* **tongues**)
1 the long soft muscular part that moves about inside the mouth.
2 a language. **3** the leather flap on a shoe or boot underneath the laces. **4** a pointed flame.

tongue-tied *adjective* too shy to speak.

tonic *noun* (*plural* **tonics**)
1 a medicine etc. that makes a person healthier or stronger.
2 a keynote in music. **tonic** *adjective* [same origin as *tone*]

tonight *noun* & *adverb* this evening or night. [from *to* (preposition) + *night*]

tonne *noun* (*plural* **tonnes**)
a metric ton (1,000 kilograms). [French]

too *adverb*
1 also, *Take the others too.* **2** more than is wanted or allowed etc., *That's too much sugar for me.* [from Old English]

tool *noun* (*plural* **tools**) an object that helps you to do a particular job, *A saw is a tool for cutting wood or metal.* [from Old English]

tooth *noun* (*plural* **teeth**)
1 one of the hard white bony parts that are rooted in the gums, used for biting and chewing things. **2** one of a row of sharp parts, *the teeth of a saw.*
toothache *noun*, **toothbrush** *noun*, **toothed** *adjective*
fight tooth and nail fight very fiercely.

toothpaste *noun* (*plural* **toothpastes**) a paste for cleaning your teeth.

top[1] *noun* (*plural* **tops**)
1 the highest part of something.
2 the upper surface. **3** the covering or stopper of a bottle, jar, etc. **4** a piece of clothing for the upper part of the body.
on top of in addition to something.

top *adjective* highest, *at top speed.*

top *verb* (**tops**, **topping**, **topped**)
1 put a top on something. **2** be at the top of something, *She tops the list.* **3** remove the top of something.
top up fill up something that is half empty, *top up your glass.* [from Old English]

top[2] *noun* (*plural* **tops**) a toy that can be made to spin on its point. [origin unknown]

top hat *noun* (*plural* **top hats**) a man's tall stiff black or grey hat worn with formal clothes.

top-heavy *adjective* too heavy at the top and likely to overbalance.

topic *noun* (*plural* **topics**) a subject to write, learn, or talk about. [from Greek *topos* = place]

topical *adjective* connected with things that are happening now, *a topical film.* **topically** *adverb*, **topicality** *noun* [originally = covering a particular place or topic]

topmost *adjective* highest.

topple *verb* (**topples**, **toppling**, **toppled**)
1 fall over; totter and fall. **2** make something fall; overthrow. [from *top*[1]]

top secret *adjective* extremely secret, *top secret information.*

topsy-turvy *adverb* & *adjective* upside down; muddled. [probably from *top*[1] + Middle English *terve* = turn upside down]

torch noun (plural **torches**)
1 a small electric lamp that you can carry in your hand. **2** a stick with burning material on the end, used as a light.

torment verb (**torments, tormenting, tormented**)
1 make someone suffer greatly.
2 tease; keep annoying someone.
tormentor noun

torment noun (plural **torments**)
great suffering.
[from old French; related to *torture*]

tornado (say tor-**nay**-doh) noun (plural **tornadoes**) a violent storm or whirlwind. [from Spanish *tronada* = thunderstorm]

torpedo noun (plural **torpedoes**)
a long tube-shaped missile that can be fired under water to destroy ships. [Latin, = a large sea fish that can give an electric shock which causes numbness]

torrent noun (plural **torrents**)
1 a rushing stream; a great flow.
2 a heavy downpour of rain.
torrential adjective [from Latin]

torso noun (plural **torsos**) the trunk of the human body.
[Italian, = stump]

tortoise noun (plural **tortoises**)
a slow-moving animal with a shell over its body. [from Latin]

tortoiseshell (say tort-a-shell) noun (plural **tortoiseshells**)
1 the mottled brown and yellow shell of certain turtles, used for making combs etc. **2** a cat or butterfly with mottled brown colouring.

torture verb (**tortures, torturing, tortured**) make a person feel great pain or worry. **torture** noun, **torturer** noun

Tory noun (plural **Tories**)
a Conservative. **Tory** adjective
[from Irish *toraidhe* = an outlaw]

toss verb (**tosses, tossing, tossed**)
1 throw something, especially up into the air. **2** spin a coin to decide something according to which side of it is upwards after it falls. **3** move restlessly or unevenly from side to side. **toss** noun

toss-up noun (plural **toss-ups**)
1 the tossing of a coin. **2** an even chance.

tot[1] noun (plural **tots**)
1 a small child. **2** (informal) a small amount of spirits, *a tot of rum.* [originally a dialect word]

tot[2] verb (**tots, totting, totted**)
tot up (informal) add up.
[from *total*]

total adjective
1 including everything, *the total amount.* **2** complete, *total darkness.* **totally** adverb

total noun (plural **totals**) the amount you get by adding everything together.

total verb (**totals, totalling, totalled**)
1 add up the total. **2** amount to something, *The cost of the damage totalled £500.*
[from Latin *totum* = the whole]

totalitarian adjective using a form of government where people are not allowed to form rival political parties. [from *total*]

totem pole noun (plural **totem poles**) a pole carved or painted by Native Americans with the symbols (*totems*) of their tribes or families. [from Ojibwa, a Native American language]

totter verb (totters, tottering, tottered) walk unsteadily; wobble. **tottery** adjective

touch verb (touches, touching, touched)
1 put your hand or fingers etc. on something lightly. **2** be or come together so that there is no space between. **3** hit something gently. **4** move or meddle with something. **5** reach, *The thermometer touched 30° Celsius.* **6** affect someone's feelings, e.g. by making them feel sympathy, *The sad story touched our hearts.* **7** (slang) persuade someone to give or lend you money.
touch and go an uncertain situation.
touch down 1 (of an aircraft) land. **2** (in Rugby football) touch the ball on the ground behind the goal line.
touch up improve something by making small additions or changes.

touch noun (plural **touches**)
1 the action of touching. **2** the ability to feel things by touching them. **3** a small amount; a small thing done, *the finishing touches.* **4** a special skill or style of workmanship, *She hasn't lost her touch.* **5** communication with someone, *We lost touch with him.* **6** the part of a football field outside the playing area.
[from old French]

touching adjective causing you to have kindly feelings such as pity or sympathy.

touchline noun (plural **touchlines**) one of the lines that mark the side of a sports pitch.

touchstone noun (plural **touchstones**) a test by which the quality of something is judged. [formerly, a kind of stone against which gold and silver were rubbed to test their purity]

touchy adjective (touchier, touchiest) easily offended.
touchily adverb, **touchiness** noun [origin unknown]

tough adjective
1 strong; difficult to break or damage. **2** difficult to chew. **3** firm or stubborn; able to stand hardship. **4** difficult, *a tough decision.* **toughly** adverb, **toughness** noun

toughen verb (toughens, toughening, toughened) make or become tough.

tour noun (plural **tours**) a journey visiting several places.

tour verb (tours, touring, toured) make a tour.
[from old French; related to *turn*]

tourism noun the industry of providing services for people on holiday in a place.

tourist noun (plural **tourists**) a person who makes a tour or visits a place for pleasure.

tournament noun (plural **tournaments**) a series of contests. [from old French; related to *turn*]

tow (rhymes with *go*) verb (tows, towing, towed) pull something along behind you. **tow** noun [from Old English *togian*]

toward preposition towards.

towards preposition
1 in the direction of, *She walked towards the sea.* **2** in relation to; regarding, *He behaved kindly towards his children.*

3 as a contribution to, *Put the money towards a new bicycle.* **4** near, *towards four o'clock.*

towel *noun* (*plural* **towels**) a piece of absorbent cloth for drying things. **towelling** *noun*

tower *noun* (*plural* **towers**) a tall narrow building.

tower *verb* (**towers, towering, towered**) be very high; be taller than others, *Skyscrapers towered over the city.* [from Greek]

town *noun* (*plural* **towns**) a place with many houses, shops, offices, and other buildings. [from Old English *tun* = enclosure]

town hall *noun* (*plural* **town halls**) a building with offices for the local council and usually a hall for public events.

towpath *noun* (*plural* **towpaths**) a path beside a canal or river, originally for use when a horse was towing a barge etc.

toxic *adjective* poisonous; caused by poison. **toxicity** *noun*

toy *noun* (*plural* **toys**) a thing to play with.

toy *adjective*
1 made as a toy. **2** (of a dog) of a very small breed kept as a pet, *a toy poodle.*

toy *verb* (**toys, toying, toyed**)
toy with handle a thing or consider an action casually.

trace *noun* (*plural* **traces**)
1 a mark left by a person or thing; a sign, *There is no trace of the thief.* **2** a very small amount.

trace *verb* (**traces, tracing, traced**)
1 copy a picture or map etc. by drawing over it on transparent paper. **2** follow the traces of a person or thing; find, *The police have been trying to trace her.*

tracer *noun* [from old French; related to *tract*[1]]

tracery *noun* a decorative pattern of holes in stone, e.g. in a church window. [from *trace*]

track *noun* (*plural* **tracks**)
1 a mark or marks left by a moving person or thing. **2** a rough path made by being used. **3** a road or area of ground specially prepared for something (e.g. racing). **4** a set of rails for trains or trams etc. **5** one of the songs or pieces of music on a CD, tape, etc. **6** a continuous band round the wheels of a tank or tractor etc.
keep track of keep yourself informed about where something is or what someone is doing.

track *verb* (**tracks, tracking, tracked**)
1 follow the tracks left by a person or animal. **2** follow or observe something as it moves. **tracker** *noun*
track down find a person or thing by searching.

tract[1] *noun* (*plural* **tracts**)
1 an area of land. **2** a series of connected parts along which something passes, *the digestive tract.* [from Latin *tractus* = drawing, draught]

tract[2] *noun* (*plural* **tracts**) a pamphlet containing a short essay, especially about religion or politics. [via Old English from Latin]

tractor *noun* (*plural* **tractors**) a motor vehicle for pulling farm machinery or other heavy loads.

trade noun (plural **trades**)
1 buying, selling, or exchanging goods. **2** business of a particular kind; the people working in this. **3** an occupation, especially a skilled craft.

trade verb (**trades, trading, traded**) buy, sell, or exchange things. **trader** noun

trade in give a thing as part of the payment for something new, *He traded in his motorcycle for a car.*

trade mark noun (plural **trade marks**) a firm's registered symbol or name used to distinguish its goods etc. from those of other firms.

tradesman noun (plural **tradesmen**) a person employed in trade, especially one who sells or delivers goods.

trade union noun (plural **trade unions**) a group of workers organized to help and protect workers in their own trade or industry.

tradition noun (plural **traditions**)
1 the passing down of beliefs or customs etc. from one generation to another. **2** something passed on in this way. **traditional** adjective, **traditionally** adverb
[from Latin *tradere* = to hand on, deliver, or betray]

traffic noun
1 vehicles, ships, or aircraft moving along a route. **2** trading, especially when it is illegal or wrong, *drug traffic.*

traffic lights plural noun coloured lights used as a signal to traffic at road junctions etc.

traffic warden noun (plural **traffic wardens**) an official who assists police to control the movement and parking of vehicles.

tragedy noun (plural **tragedies**)
1 a play with unhappy events or a sad ending. **2** a very sad or distressing event.

tragic adjective
1 very sad or distressing. **2** to do with tragedies, *a great tragic actor.* **tragically** adverb

trail noun (plural **trails**)
1 a track, scent, or other sign left where something has passed.
2 a path or track made through a wild region.

trail verb (**trails, trailing, trailed**)
1 follow the trail of something; track. **2** drag or be dragged along behind; lag behind. **3** hang down or float loosely.
[from Latin *tragula* = net for dragging a river]

trailer noun (plural **trailers**)
1 a truck or other container pulled along by a vehicle. **2** a short piece from a film or television programme, shown in advance to advertise it. [from *trail*]

train noun (plural **trains**)
1 a railway engine pulling a line of carriages or trucks that are linked together. **2** a number of people or animals moving in a line, *a camel train.* **3** a series of things, *a train of events.* **4** part of a long dress or robe that trails on the ground at the back.

train verb (**trains, training, trained**)
1 give a person instruction or practice so that he or she becomes skilled. **2** practise,

She was training for the race.
3 make something grow in a particular direction. **4** aim a gun etc., *Train that gun on the bridge.* [from French; related to *traction*]

trainer *noun* (*plural* **trainers**)
1 a person who trains people or animals. **2** a soft rubber-soled shoe of the kind worn for running or by athletes etc. while exercising.

traitor *noun* (*plural* **traitors**)
a person who betrays his or her country or friends. **traitorous** *adjective* [from old French; related to *tradition*]

tram *noun* (*plural* **trams**) a public passenger vehicle running on rails in the road. [from old German or old Italian *trame* = plank, shaft of a cart]

tramp *noun* (*plural* **tramps**)
1 a person without a home or job who walks from place to place.
2 a long walk. **3** the sound of heavy footsteps.

tramp *verb* (**tramps, tramping, tramped**)
1 walk with heavy footsteps. **2** walk for a long distance. [probably from old Dutch]

trample *verb* (**tramples, trampling, trampled**) tread heavily on something; crush something by treading on it. [from *tramp*]

trampoline *noun* (*plural* **trampolines**) a large piece of canvas joined to a frame by springs, used by gymnasts for jumping on.

trance *noun* (*plural* **trances**) a dreamy or unconscious state rather like sleep.

tranquil *adjective* calm and quiet.
tranquilly *adverb*, **tranquillity** *noun* [from Latin]

tranquillizer *noun* (*plural* **tranquillizers**) a medicine used to make a person feel calm.

trans- *prefix*
1 across; through. **2** beyond. [from Latin *trans* = across]

transatlantic *adjective* across or on the other side of the Atlantic Ocean.

transcript *noun* (*plural* **transcripts**) a written copy. [from Latin *transcriptum* = written out]

transfer *verb* (**transfers, transferring, transferred**)
1 move a person or thing to another place. **2** hand over. **transferable** *adjective*, **transference** *noun*

transfer *noun* (*plural* **transfers**)
1 the transferring of a person or thing. **2** a picture or design that can be transferred onto another surface.
[from *trans-* + Latin *ferre* = carry]

transfigure *verb* (**transfigures, transfiguring, transfigured**)
change the appearance of something greatly.
transfiguration *noun* [from *trans-* + Latin *figura* = figure]

transfix *verb* (**transfixes, transfixing, transfixed**)
1 make a person or animal unable to move because of fear or surprise etc. **2** pierce and fix with something pointed. [from *trans-* + Latin *fixum* = fixed]

transform *verb* (**transforms, transforming, transformed**)
change the form or appearance

or character of a person or thing.
transformation noun [from trans-
+ Latin formare = to form]

transformer noun (plural
transformers) a device used to
change the voltage of an electric
current.

transfusion noun (plural
transfusions) putting blood taken
from one person into another
person's body. **transfuse** verb
[from trans- + Latin fusum
= poured]

transistor noun (plural
transistors)
1 a tiny semiconductor device
that controls a flow of electricity.
2 (also **transistor radio**) a portable
radio that uses transistors.
transistorized adjective [from
transfer + resistor]

transition noun (plural
transitions) the process of
changing from one condition or
form etc. to another. **transitional**
adjective [from trans- + Latin
itum = gone]

transitive adjective (of a verb)
used with a direct object after it,
e.g. change in change your shoes
(but not in change into dry shoes).
(Compare **intransitive**.)
transitively adverb [from Latin
transitivus = passing over]

translate verb (translates,
translating, translated) put
something into another
language. **translatable** adjective,
translation noun, **translator** noun
[from trans- + Latin latum
= carried]

transliterate verb (transliterates,
transliterating, transliterated)
write a word in the letters of

a different alphabet or language.
transliteration noun [from trans-
+ Latin littera = letter]

translucent (say tranz-loo-sent)
adjective allowing light to shine
through but not transparent.
[from trans- + Latin lucens
= shining]

transmission noun (plural
transmissions)
1 transmitting something.
2 a broadcast. 3 the gears by
which power is transmitted from
the engine to the wheels of
a vehicle.

transmit verb (transmits,
transmitting, transmitted)
1 send or pass on from one
person or place to another. 2 send
out a signal or broadcast etc.
transmitter noun [from trans-
+ Latin mittere = send]

transmute verb (transmutes,
transmuting, transmuted) change
something from one form or
substance into another.
transmutation noun [from trans-
+ Latin mutare = to change]

transparent adjective able to be
seen through. [from trans- + Latin
parens = appearing]

transplant verb (transplants,
transplanting, transplanted)
1 remove a plant and put it to
grow somewhere else. 2 transfer
a part of the body to another
person or animal. **transplantation**
noun

transplant noun (plural
transplants)
1 the process of transplanting.
2 something transplanted.
[from trans- + Latin plantare = to
plant]

transport verb (transports, transporting, transported) take a person, animal, or thing from one place to another.
transportation noun, **transporter** noun

transport noun the action or means of transporting people, animals, or things, *The city has a good system of public transport.* [from trans- + Latin *portare* = carry]

transpose verb (transposes, transposing, transposed)
1 change the position or order of something. 2 put a piece of music into a different key. **transposition** noun [from trans- + Latin *positum* = placed]

trap noun (plural **traps**)
1 a device for catching and holding animals. 2 a plan or trick for capturing, detecting, or cheating someone. 3 a device for collecting water etc. or preventing it from passing.
4 a two-wheeled carriage pulled by a horse.

trap verb (traps, trapping, trapped) catch or hold a person or animal in a trap. **trapper** noun [from Old English]

trapdoor noun (plural **trapdoors**) a door in a floor, ceiling, or roof.

trapeze noun (plural **trapezes**) a bar hanging from two ropes as a swing for acrobats. [French; related to *trapezium*]

trapezium noun (plural **trapeziums** or **trapezia**) a quadrilateral in which two opposite sides are parallel and the other two are not. [from Greek *trapeza* = table]

trash noun rubbish or nonsense.
trashy adjective

trauma (say traw-ma) noun (plural **traumas**) a shock that produces a lasting effect on a person's mind. **traumatic** adjective, **traumatize** verb [Greek, = a wound]

travel verb (travels, travelling, travelled) move from place to place. **travel** noun, **traveller** noun

traveller's cheque noun (plural **traveller's cheques**) a cheque for a fixed amount of money that is sold by banks and that can be exchanged for money in foreign countries.

trawl verb (trawls, trawling, trawled) fish by dragging a large net along the seabed. [from old Dutch; related to *trail*]

trawler noun (plural **trawlers**) a boat used in trawling.

tray noun (plural **trays**)
1 a flat piece of wood, metal, or plastic, usually with raised edges, for carrying cups, plates, food, etc. 2 an open container for holding letters etc. in an office.

treacherous adjective
1 betraying someone; disloyal.
2 not to be relied on; dangerous, *It's snowing and the roads are treacherous.* **treacherously** adverb, **treachery** noun [from old French *trechier* = to trick or deceive]

treacle noun a thick sticky liquid produced when sugar is purified.
treacly adjective [originally = ointment for an animal bite; from Greek *therion* = wild or poisonous animal]

tread *verb* (**treads, treading, trod, trodden**) walk or put your foot on something.

tread *noun* (*plural* **treads**)
1 a sound or way of walking. 2 the top surface of a stair; the part you put your foot on. 3 the part of a tyre that touches the ground.

treadmill *noun* (*plural* **treadmills**)
1 a wide mill-wheel turned by the weight of people or animals treading on steps fixed round its edge. 2 monotonous routine work.

treason *noun* betraying your country. **treasonable** *adjective*, **treasonous** *adjective* [from old French; related to *tradition*]

treasure *noun* (*plural* **treasures**)
1 a store of precious metals or jewels. 2 a precious thing or person.

treasure *verb* (**treasures, treasuring, treasured**) value greatly something that you have.

treasurer *noun* (*plural* **treasurers**) a person in charge of the money of a club, society, etc.

treasury *noun* (*plural* **treasuries**) a place where money and valuables are kept.
the Treasury the government department in charge of a country's income.

treat *verb* (**treats, treating, treated**)
1 behave in a certain way towards a person or thing. 2 deal with a subject etc. 3 give medical care in order to cure a person or animal. 4 put something through a chemical or other process, *The fabric has been treated to make it waterproof.* 5 pay for someone else's food, drink, or entertainment, *I'll treat you to an ice cream.*

treat *noun* (*plural* **treats**)
1 something special that gives pleasure. 2 the process of treating someone to food, drink, or entertainment.
[from Latin *tractare* = to handle or manage]

treatment *noun* (*plural* **treatments**) the process or manner of dealing with a person, animal, or thing.

treaty *noun* (*plural* **treaties**) a formal agreement between two or more countries. [from French; related to *treat*]

treble *adjective* three times as much or as many.

treble *noun* (*plural* **trebles**)
1 a treble amount. 2 a person with a high-pitched or soprano voice.

treble *verb* (**trebles, trebling, trebled**) make or become three times as much or as many. [from old French; related to *triple*]

tree *noun* (*plural* **trees**) a tall plant with a single very thick hard stem or trunk that is usually without branches for some distance above the ground. [from Old English]

trek *noun* (*plural* **treks**) a long walk or journey.

trek *verb* (**treks, trekking, trekked**) go on a long walk or journey.
[from Italian *trekken* = pull]

trellis *noun* (*plural* **trellises**) a framework with crossing bars of wood or metal etc. to support climbing plants.

tremble verb (trembles, trembling, trembled) shake gently, especially with fear.
tremble noun [from French; related to *tremulous*]

tremendous adjective
1 very large; huge. 2 excellent.
tremendously adverb [from Latin *tremendus* = making someone tremble]

trench noun (plural trenches) a long narrow hole cut in the ground.
trench verb (trenches, trenching, trenched) dig a trench or trenches.

trend noun (plural trends) the general direction in which something is going. [from Old English]

trendy adjective (informal) fashionable; following the latest trends. **trendily** adverb, **trendiness** noun

trespass verb (trespasses, trespassing, trespassed)
1 go on someone's land or property unlawfully. 2 (old use) do wrong; sin. **trespasser** noun
trespass noun (plural trespasses) (old use) wrongdoing; sin.
[from old French *trespasser* = go beyond]

tress noun (plural tresses) a lock of hair. [from French]

trestle noun (plural trestles) each of a set of supports on which a board is rested to form a table.
trestle-table noun [from old French; = small beam]

tri- prefix three (as in triangle). [from Latin or Greek]

trial noun (plural trials)
1 the trying of a person in a lawcourt. 2 testing a thing to see how good it is. 3 a test of qualities or ability. 4 an annoying person or thing; a hardship.
on trial 1 being tried in a lawcourt. 2 being tested.
trial and error trying out different methods of doing something until you find one that works. [from old French; related to *try*]

triangle noun (plural triangles)
1 a flat shape with three sides and three angles. 2 a percussion instrument made from a metal rod bent into a triangle.
triangular adjective [from *tri-* + Latin *angulus* = angle]

tribe noun (plural tribes)
1 a group of families living in one area as a community, ruled by a chief. 2 a set of people. **tribal** adjective, **tribally** adverb, **tribesman** noun [from Latin]

tribunal (say try-bew-nal) noun (plural tribunals) a committee appointed to hear evidence and give judgements when there is a dispute. [from Latin *tribunale* = tribune's seat]

tributary noun (plural tributaries) a river or stream that flows into a larger one or into a lake. [same origin as *tribute*]

tribute noun (plural tributes)
1 something said, done, or given to show respect or admiration.
2 payment that one country or ruler was formerly obliged to pay to a more powerful one. [from Latin *tribuere* = assign, grant, share]

trice noun (old use)
in a trice in a moment.
[from old Italian *trisen* = pull
quickly, tug]

trick noun (plural **tricks**)
1 a crafty or deceitful action;
a practical joke, *Let's play a trick
on Jo.* 2 a skilful action,
especially one done for
entertainment, *magic tricks.* 3 the
cards picked up by the winner
after one round of a card game
such as whist.

trick verb (**tricks**, **tricking**,
tricked)
1 deceive or cheat someone by
a trick. 2 decorate, *The building
was tricked out with little flags.*
[from old French]

trickery noun the use of tricks;
deception.

trickle verb (**trickles**, **trickling**,
trickled) flow or move slowly.
trickle noun [imitating the sound]

tricky adjective (**trickier**, **trickiest**)
1 difficult; needing skill, *a tricky
job.* 2 cunning or deceitful.
trickiness noun

tricycle noun (plural **tricycles**)
a vehicle like a bicycle but with
three wheels.

trifle noun (plural **trifles**)
1 a pudding made of sponge cake
covered in custard, fruit, cream,
etc. 2 a very small amount.
3 something that has very little
importance or value.

trifle verb (**trifles**, **trifling**, **trifled**)
treat a person or thing without
seriousness or respect, *She is not
a woman to be trifled with.*
[from old French]

trifling adjective small in value
or importance.

trigger noun (plural **triggers**)
a lever that is pulled to fire a gun.

trigger verb (**triggers**, **triggering**,
triggered)
trigger off start something
happening.
[from Italian *trekker* = puller]

trigonometry (say trig-on-om-it-
ree) noun the calculation of
distances and angles by using
triangles. [from Greek *trigonon*
= triangle + *metria*
= measurement]

trill verb (**trills**, **trilling**, **trilled**)
make a quivering musical sound.
trill noun [from Italian]

trim adjective neat and orderly.
trimly adverb, **trimness** noun

trim verb (**trims**, **trimming**,
trimmed)
1 cut the edges or unwanted parts
off something. 2 decorate a hat or
piece of clothing by adding lace,
ribbons, etc. 3 arrange sails to
suit the wind.

trim noun (plural **trims**)
1 condition, *in good trim.*
2 cutting or trimming, *Your
beard needs a trim.* 3 lace,
ribbons, etc. used to decorate
something.

Trinity noun God regarded as
three persons (Father, Son, and
Holy Spirit). [from Latin]

trinket noun (plural **trinkets**)
a small ornament or piece of
jewellery.

trio noun (plural **trios**)
1 a group of three people or
things. 2 a group of three
musicians or singers. 3 a piece of
music for three musicians.
[Italian, from Latin *tres* = three]

trip verb (trips, tripping, tripped)
1 catch your foot on something and fall; make someone do this. 2 move with quick light steps. 3 operate a switch.
trip up 1 stumble. 2 make a slip or blunder. 3 cause a person to do either of these things.
trip noun (plural trips)
1 a journey or outing. 2 the action of tripping. 3 a stumble. 3 (informal) hallucinations caused by taking a drug.

tripe noun
1 part of an ox's stomach used as food. 2 (slang) nonsense. [French]

triple adjective
1 consisting of three parts. 2 involving three people or groups, a triple alliance. 3 three times as much or as many. **triply** adverb
triple verb (triples, tripling, tripled) treble.
[from Latin triplus = three times as much]

triplet noun (plural triplets) each of three children or animals born to the same mother at one time. [from triple]

triplicate noun
in triplicate as three identical copies. [from tri- + Latin plicare = to fold]

tripod (say try-pod) noun (plural tripods) a stand with three legs, e.g. to support a camera. [from tri- + Greek podes = feet]

trite (rhymes with kite) adjective worn out by constant repetition; hackneyed, a few trite remarks. [from Latin tritum = worn by use]

triumph noun (plural triumphs)
1 a great success or victory; a feeling of joy at this. 2 a celebration of a victory. **triumphal** adjective, **triumphant** adjective, **triumphantly** adverb
triumph verb (triumphs, triumphing, triumphed)
1 be successful or victorious. 2 rejoice in success or victory. [from Latin]

trivia plural noun unimportant details or pieces of information. [same origin as trivial]

trivial adjective small in value or importance. **trivially** adverb, **triviality** noun [from Latin trivialis = commonplace]

troll (rhymes with hole) noun (plural trolls) (in Scandinavian mythology) a supernatural being, either a giant or a friendly but mischievous dwarf.

trolley noun (plural trolleys)
1 a small table on wheels or castors. 2 a small cart or truck. [probably from dialect troll = to roll or flow]

trombone noun (plural trombones) a large brass musical instrument with a sliding tube. [from Italian tromba = trumpet]

troop noun (plural troops)
1 an organized group of soldiers, Scouts, etc. 2 a number of people moving along together.

USAGE: Do not confuse with troupe.

troop verb (troops, trooping, trooped) move along as a group or in large numbers, They all trooped in.
[from Latin troppus = herd]

trooper noun (plural **troopers**)
a soldier in the cavalry or in an armoured unit. [from troop]

troops plural noun armed forces.

trophy noun (plural **trophies**)
a prize or souvenir for a victory or other success. [from Greek]

tropic noun (plural **tropics**)
a line of latitude about 23½° north of the equator (**tropic of Cancer**) or 23½° south of the equator (**tropic of Capricorn**).

the tropics the hot regions between these two latitudes. [from Greek trope = turning (because the sun seems to turn back when it reaches these points)]

tropical adjective to do with the tropics, tropical fish.

trot verb (**trots, trotting, trotted**)
1 (of a horse) run, going faster than when walking but more slowly than when cantering.
2 (informal) go, Trot round to the chemist.

trot out (informal) produce or repeat, He trotted out the usual excuses.

trot noun a trotting run.

on the trot (informal) one after the other without a break, She worked for ten days on the trot.

trouble noun (plural **troubles**)
1 difficulty, inconvenience, or distress. 2 a cause of any of these.

take trouble take great care in doing something.

trouble verb (**troubles, troubling, troubled**)
1 cause trouble to someone. 2 give yourself trouble or inconvenience etc., Don't trouble to reply.
[from old French]

troublesome adjective causing trouble or annoyance.

trough (say trof) noun (plural **troughs**)
1 a long narrow open container, especially one holding water or food for animals. 2 a channel for liquid. 3 the low part between two waves or ridges. 4 a long region of low air pressure. [from Old English]

troupe (say as troop) noun (plural **troupes**) a company of actors or other performers. [French, = troop]

USAGE: Do not confuse with troop.

trousers plural noun a piece of clothing worn over the lower half of the body, with a separate part for each leg. [from Irish or Scottish Gaelic]

trout noun (plural **trout**)
a freshwater fish that is caught as a sport and for food. [from Greek]

trowel noun (plural **trowels**)
1 a small garden tool with a curved blade for lifting plants or scooping things. 2 a small tool with a flat blade for spreading mortar etc. [from Latin trulla = scoop]

truant noun (plural **truants**)
a child who stays away from school without permission.
truancy noun
play truant be a truant.
[old French, = criminal, probably of Celtic origin]

truce noun (plural **truces**) an agreement to stop fighting for a while.

truck[1] noun (plural **trucks**)
1 a lorry. **2** an open container on wheels for transporting loads; an open railway wagon. **3** an axle with wheels attached, fitted under a skateboard. [probably from *truckle* = a pulley or castor]

truck[2] noun
have no truck with refuse to have dealings with, *I'll have no truck with fortune-tellers.* [origin unknown]

trudge verb (**trudges, trudging, trudged**) walk slowly and heavily. [origin unknown]

true adjective (**truer, truest**)
1 representing what has really happened or exists, *a true story.* **2** genuine or proper; not false, *He was the true heir.* **3** accurate. **4** loyal or faithful, *Be true to your friends.* **trueness** noun [from Old English]

truffle noun (plural **truffles**)
1 a soft sweet made with chocolate. **2** a fungus that grows underground and is valued as food because of its rich flavour. [probably from Dutch]

truly adverb
1 truthfully. **2** sincerely or genuinely, *We are truly grateful.* **3** accurately. **4** loyally or faithfully.
Yours truly see **yours**.

trump noun (plural **trumps**)
a playing card of a suit that ranks above the others for one game.

trump verb (**trumps, trumping, trumped**) beat a card by playing a trump.
trump up invent an excuse or an accusation etc.
[from *triumph*]

trumpet noun (plural **trumpets**)
1 a metal wind instrument with a narrow tube that widens near the end. **2** something shaped like this.

trumpet verb (**trumpets, trumpeting, trumpeted**)
1 blow a trumpet. **2** (of an elephant) make a loud sound with its trunk. **3** shout or announce something loudly.
trumpeter noun

truncheon noun (plural **truncheons**) a short thick stick carried as a weapon, especially by police. [from old French; related to *trunk*]

trundle verb (**trundles, trundling, trundled**) roll along heavily, *He was trundling a wheelbarrow. A bus trundled up.* [related to Old English *trendel* = ball]

trunk noun (plural **trunks**)
1 the main stem of a tree. **2** an elephant's long flexible nose. **3** a large box with a hinged lid for transporting or storing clothes etc. **4** the human body except for the head, arms, and legs. [from Latin]

trunk road noun (plural **trunk roads**) an important main road. [regarded as a 'trunk' from which smaller roads branch off]

trunks plural noun shorts worn by men and boys for swimming, boxing, etc.

truss noun (plural **trusses**)
1 a framework of beams or bars supporting a roof or bridge etc. **2** a bundle of hay etc. **3** a type of padded belt worn to support a hernia.

truss verb (**trusses, trussing, trussed**)
1 tie up a person or thing securely. 2 support a roof or bridge etc. with trusses.

trust verb (**trusts, trusting, trusted**)
1 believe that a person or thing is good, truthful, or strong. 2 let a person have or use something in the belief that he or she will behave responsibly, *Don't trust him with your CD player!* 3 hope, *I trust that you are well.*
trust to rely on, *trusting to luck.*

trust noun (*plural* **trusts**)
1 the belief that a person or thing can be trusted. 2 responsibility; being trusted, *Being a prefect is a position of trust.* 3 money legally entrusted to a person with instructions about how to use it.
trustful adjective, **trustfully** adverb, **trustworthy** adjective

trusty adjective (*old use*) trustworthy or reliable, *my trusty sword.*

truth noun (*plural* **truths**)
1 something that is true. 2 the quality of being true.

truthful adjective
1 telling the truth, *a truthful boy.* 2 true, *a truthful account of what happened.* **truthfully** adverb, **truthfulness** noun

try verb (**tries, trying, tried**)
1 attempt. 2 test something by using or doing it, *Try sleeping on your back.* 3 examine the accusations against someone in a lawcourt. 4 be a strain on, *Very small print tries your eyes.*
try on put on clothes etc. to see if they fit.

try noun (*plural* **tries**)
1 an attempt. 2 (in Rugby football) putting the ball down behind the opponents' goal line in order to score points.

trying adjective putting a strain on someone's patience; annoying.

tub noun (*plural* **tubs**) a round open container holding liquid, ice cream, soil for plants, etc.

tubby adjective (**tubbier, tubbiest**) short and fat. **tubbiness** noun [from *tub*]

tube noun (*plural* **tubes**)
1 a long hollow piece of metal, plastic, rubber, glass, etc., especially for liquids or air etc. to pass along. 2 a container made of flexible material with a screw cap, *a tube of toothpaste.* 3 the underground railway in London. [from Latin]

tuber noun (*plural* **tubers**) a short thick rounded root (e.g. of a dahlia) or underground stem (e.g. of a potato) that produces buds from which new plants will grow. [Latin, = a swelling]

tuberculosis noun a disease of people and animals, producing small swellings in the parts affected by it, especially in the lungs. **tubercular** adjective [from Latin *tuberculum* = little swelling]

tuck verb (**tucks, tucking, tucked**)
1 push a loose edge into something so that it is hidden or held in place. 2 put something away in a small space, *Tuck this in your pocket.*
tuck in (*informal*) eat heartily.

tuck noun (plural **tucks**)
1 a flat fold stitched in a garment. **2** (slang) food, especially sweets and cakes etc. that children enjoy. **tuck shop**

-tude suffix forms nouns meaning 'quality or condition' (e.g. altitude, solitude). [from French]

tuft noun (plural **tufts**) a bunch of threads, grass, hair, or feathers etc. growing close together. **tufted** adjective

tug verb (**tugs, tugging, tugged**)
1 pull something hard or suddenly. **2** tow a ship.

tug noun (plural **tugs**)
1 a hard or sudden pull. **2** a small powerful boat used for towing others.
[Middle English; related to tow]

tug of war noun a contest between two teams pulling a rope from opposite ends.

tulip noun (plural **tulips**) a large cup-shaped flower on a tall stem growing from a bulb. [from Persian dulband = turban (because the flowers are this shape)]

tumble verb (**tumbles, tumbling, tumbled**)
1 fall or roll over suddenly or clumsily. **2** move or push quickly and carelessly. **tumble** noun **tumble to** (informal) realize what something means.

tumbler noun (plural **tumblers**)
1 a drinking glass with no stem or handle. **2** a part of a lock that is lifted when a key is turned to open it. **3** an acrobat.

tummy noun (plural **tummies**) (informal) the stomach.
[imitating a small child trying to say 'stomach']

tumour (say tew-mer) noun (plural **tumours**) an abnormal lump growing on or in the body. [from Latin tumere = to swell]

tumult (say tew-mult) noun an uproar; a state of noisy confusion and agitation. [from Latin]

tune noun (plural **tunes**) a short piece of music; a pleasant series of musical notes. **tuneful** adjective, **tunefully** adverb
in tune at the correct musical pitch.

tune verb (**tunes, tuning, tuned**)
1 put a musical instrument in tune. **2** adjust a radio or television set to receive a certain channel. **3** adjust an engine so that it runs smoothly. **tuner** noun
[a different spelling of tone]

tunic noun (plural **tunics**)
1 a jacket worn as part of a uniform. **2** a garment reaching from the shoulders to the hips or knees. [from Latin]

tunnel noun (plural **tunnels**) an underground passage.

tunnel verb (**tunnels, tunnelling, tunnelled**) make a tunnel.
[from old French tonel = barrel]

turban noun (plural **turbans**) a covering for the head made by wrapping a strip of cloth round a cap. [from Persian]

turbine noun (plural **turbines**) a machine or motor driven by a flow of water, steam, or gas. [from Latin turbo = whirlwind, spinning top]

turbulent adjective
1 moving violently and unevenly, turbulent seas. **2** unruly. **turbulently** adverb, **turbulence** noun

turf *noun* (*plural* **turfs** or **turves**)
1 short grass and the earth round its roots. 2 a piece of this cut from the ground.
the turf horse racing.

turkey *noun* (*plural* **turkeys**)
a large bird kept for its meat. [originally the name of a different bird which was imported from Turkey]

turmoil *noun* wild confusion or agitation, *Her mind was in turmoil.* [origin unknown]

turn *verb* (**turns**, **turning**, **turned**)
1 move round; move to a new direction. 2 change in appearance etc.; become, *He turned pale.* 3 make something change, *You can turn milk into butter.* 4 move a switch or tap etc. to control something, *Turn that radio off.* 5 pass a certain time, *It has turned midnight.* 6 shape something on a lathe.
turn down 1 fold down. 2 reduce the flow or sound of something. 3 reject, *We offered her a job but she turned it down.*
turn out 1 send out. 2 empty something, especially to search or clean it. 3 happen. 4 prove to be, *The visitor turned out to be my uncle.*
turn up 1 appear or arrive. 2 increase the flow or sound of something.

turn *noun* (*plural* **turns**)
1 the action of turning; a turning movement. 2 a change; the point where something turns. 3 an opportunity or duty etc. that comes to each person in succession, *It's your turn to wash up.* 4 a short performance in an entertainment. 5 (*informal*) an

attack of illness; a nervous shock, *It gave me a nasty turn.*
good turn a helpful action.
in turn in succession; one after another.
[from Greek *tornos* = lathe]

turning *noun* (*plural* **turnings**)
a place where one road meets another, forming a corner.

turnip *noun* (*plural* **turnips**)
a plant with a large round white root used as a vegetable. [from Latin]

turnout *noun* (*plural* **turnouts**)
the number of people who attend a meeting, vote at an election, etc., *Despite the rain, there was a pretty good turnout.*

turnover *noun* (*plural* **turnovers**)
1 the amount of money received by a firm selling things. 2 the rate at which goods are sold or workers leave and are replaced. 3 a small pie made by folding pastry over fruit, jam, etc.

turnstile *noun* (*plural* **turnstiles**)
a revolving gate that lets one person in at a time.

turntable *noun* (*plural* **turntables**) a circular revolving platform or support, e.g. for the record in a record player.

turquoise *noun* (*plural* **turquoises**)
1 a sky-blue or greenish-blue colour. 2 a blue jewel. [from French *pierre turquoise* = Turkish stone]

turret *noun* (*plural* **turrets**)
1 a small tower on a castle or other building. 2 a revolving structure containing a gun.

turreted *adjective* [from old French *tourete* = small tower]

turtle *noun* (*plural* **turtles**) a sea animal that looks like a tortoise. **turn turtle** capsize. [probably from French *tortue* = tortoise]

turtle-dove *noun* (*plural* **turtle-doves**) a wild dove. [from Old English]

tusk *noun* (*plural* **tusks**) a long pointed tooth that sticks out from the mouth of an elephant, walrus, etc.

tussle *noun* (*plural* **tussles**) a struggle or conflict over something.

tussock *noun* (*plural* **tussocks**) a tuft or clump of grass. [origin unknown]

tutor *noun* (*plural* **tutors**)
1 a teacher who teaches one person or a small group, not in a school. **2** a teacher of students in a college or university. [Latin, = guardian]

TV *abbreviation* television.

twain *noun & adjective* (*old use*) two. [from Old English *twegen* = two]

twang *verb* (**twangs, twanging, twanged**)
1 play a guitar etc. by plucking its strings. **2** make a sharp sound like that of a wire when plucked. **twang** *noun*

tweak *verb* (**tweaks, tweaking, tweaked**) pinch and twist or pull something sharply. **tweak** *noun*

tweed *noun* thick woollen twill, often woven of mixed colours. [originally a mistake; the Scottish word *tweel* (= twill) was wrongly read as *tweed* by being confused with the River Tweed]

tweezers *plural noun* small pincers for picking up or pulling very small things. [from French *étui* = prison, in English = a case of surgical instruments, including tweezers]

twelve *noun & adjective* the number 12. **twelfth** *adjective & noun*

twenty *adjective & noun* (*plural* **twenties**) the number 20. **twentieth** *adjective & noun*

twice *adverb*
1 two times; on two occasions. **2** double the amount. [from Old English]

twiddle *verb* (**twiddles, twiddling, twiddled**) twirl or finger something in an idle way; twist something quickly to and fro. **twiddle** *noun*, **twiddly** *adjective* [origin unknown]

twig *noun* (*plural* **twigs**) a small shoot on a branch or stem of a tree or shrub. [from Old English]

twilight *noun* dim light from the sky just after sunset or just before sunrise. [from Old English *twi-* = twice, double, + *light*]

twin *noun* (*plural* **twins**)
1 either of two children or animals born to the same mother at one time. **2** either of two things that are exactly alike.

twin *verb* (**twins, twinning, twinned**)
1 put things together as a pair. **2** if a town is twinned with a town in a different country, the two towns exchange visits and organize cultural events together.

twine verb (twines, twining, twined) twist or wind together or round something.

twinge noun (plural twinges) a sudden pain; a pang. [from Old English]

twinkle verb (twinkles, twinkling, twinkled) shine with tiny flashes of light; sparkle. **twinkle** noun [from Old English]

twirl verb (twirls, twirling, twirled) twist quickly. **twirl** noun [origin unknown]

twist verb (twists, twisting, twisted)
1 pass threads or strands round something or round each other. 2 turn the ends of something in opposite directions. 3 turn round or from side to side, *The road twisted through the hills.* 4 bend something out of its proper shape. 5 (*informal*) swindle somebody. **twister** noun

twist noun (plural twists) a twisting movement or action. **twisty** adjective [from Old English]

twitch verb (twitches, twitching, twitched) move or pull with a slight jerk. **twitch** noun

twitter verb (twitters, twittering, twittered) make quick chirping sounds. **twitter** noun

two adjective & noun (plural twos) the number 2.
be in two minds be undecided about something.

two-faced adjective insincere or deceitful.

tycoon noun (plural tycoons) a rich and influential business person. [from Japanese *taikun* = great prince]

tying present participle of **tie**.

type noun (plural types)
1 a kind or sort. 2 letters or figures etc. designed for use in printing.

type verb (types, typing, typed) write something by using a typewriter. **typist** noun [from Greek *typos* = impression]

typewriter noun (plural typewriters) a machine with keys that are pressed to print letters or figures etc. on a piece of paper. **typewritten** adjective [the word *typewriter* at first meant the person using the machine, as well as the machine itself]

typhoon noun (plural typhoons) a violent hurricane in the western Pacific or East Asian seas. [from Chinese *tai fung* = great wind]

typical adjective
1 having the usual characteristics or qualities of a particular type of person or thing, *a typical school playground.* 2 usual in a particular person or thing, *He worked with typical carefulness.* **typically** adverb [same origin as *type*]

tyranny (say ti-rran-ee) noun (plural tyrannies)
1 government by a tyrant. 2 the way a tyrant behaves towards people. **tyrannical** adjective, **tyrannous** adjective

tyrant (say ty-rant) noun (plural tyrants) a person who rules cruelly and unjustly; someone who insists on being obeyed. [from Greek *tyrannos* = ruler with full power]

tyre *noun* (*plural* **tyres**) a covering of rubber fitted round a wheel to make it grip the road and run more smoothly. [from *attire*]

Uu

ubiquitous (*say* yoo-**bik**-wit-us) *adjective* found everywhere, *The ubiquitous television aerials spoil the view*. **ubiquity** *noun* [from Latin *ubique* = everywhere]

-uble *prefix* see **-able**.

udder *noun* (*plural* **udders**) the bag-like part of a cow, ewe, female goat, etc. from which milk is taken.

ugly *adjective* (**uglier**, **ugliest**) **1** unpleasant to look at; not beautiful. **2** hostile and threatening, *The crowd was in an ugly mood*. **ugliness** *noun* [from Old Norse *uggligr* = frightening]

UK *abbreviation* United Kingdom.

ulcer *noun* (*plural* **ulcers**) a sore on the inside or outside of the body. **ulcerated** *adjective*, **ulceration** *noun*

ulterior *adjective* beyond what is obvious or stated, *an ulterior motive*. [Latin, = further]

ultimate *adjective* furthest in a series of things; final, *Our ultimate destination is London*. **ultimately** *adverb* [from Latin *ultimus* = last]

ultimatum (*say* ul-tim-**ay**-tum) *noun* (*plural* **ultimatums**) a final demand or statement that unless something is done by a certain time action will be taken or war will be declared. [same origin as *ultimate*]

ultra- *prefix* **1** beyond (as in *ultraviolet*). **2** extremely; excessively (as in *ultramodern*). [from Latin *ultra* = beyond]

ultramarine *noun* a deep bright blue. [from *ultra-* + Latin *mare* = sea (because it was originally imported 'across the sea' from the East)]

ultraviolet *adjective* (of light-rays) beyond the violet end of the spectrum and so not visible to the human eye.

umbilical cord *noun* (*plural* **umbilical cords**) the tube through which a baby receives nourishment before it is born, connecting its body with the mother's womb.

umbrella *noun* (*plural* **umbrellas**) **1** a circular piece of material stretched over a folding frame with a central stick used as a handle, or a central pole, which you open to protect yourself from rain or sun. **2** a general protection. [from Italian *ombrella* = a little shade]

umpire *noun* (*plural* **umpires**) a referee in cricket, tennis, and some other games.

umpire *verb* (**umpires**, **umpiring**, **umpired**) act as an umpire. [from French *non* = not + *per* = an equal, *peer*]

UN *abbreviation* United Nations.

un- *prefix* **1** not (as in *uncertain*). **2** (before a verb) reversing the action (as in *unlock* = release from being locked. [from Old English]

NOTE: Many words beginning with this prefix are not listed here if their meaning is obvious.

unable *adjective* not able to do something.

unaccountable *adjective*
1 unable to be explained, *For some unaccountable reason I completely forgot your birthday.*
2 not accountable for what you do. **unaccountably** *adverb*

unanimous (say yoo-nan-im-us) *adjective* with everyone agreeing, *a unanimous decision.*
unanimously *adverb*, **unanimity** (say yoo-nan-im-it-ee) *noun* [from Latin *unus* = one + *animus* = mind]

unassuming *adjective* modest; not arrogant or pretentious. [from *un-* + *assume*]

unavoidable *adjective* not able to be avoided.

unawares *adverb* unexpectedly; without warning, *His question caught me unawares.*

unbearable *adjective* not able to be endured. **unbearably** *adverb*

unbecoming *adjective*
1 not making a person look attractive. 2 not suitable or fitting. [from *un-* + *become* (sense 2)]

unbelievable *adjective* not able to be believed; incredible.
unbelievably *adverb*

unbend *verb* (unbends, unbending, unbent)
1 change from a bent position; straighten up. 2 relax and become friendly.

unblock *verb* (unblocks, unblocking, unblocked) remove an obstruction from something.

unborn *adjective* not yet born.

unbroken *adjective* not broken or interrupted.

uncalled for *adjective* not justified; impertinent.

uncanny *adjective* (uncannier, uncanniest) strange or mysterious, *an uncanny coincidence.* **uncannily** *adverb*, **uncanniness** *noun* [from *un-* + an old sense of *canny* = knowing, able to be known]

uncertain *adjective*
1 not certain. 2 not reliable, *His aim is rather uncertain.*
uncertainly *adverb*, **uncertainty** *noun*

in no uncertain terms clearly and forcefully.

uncharitable *adjective* making unkind judgements of people or actions. **uncharitably** *adverb*

uncle *noun* (plural **uncles**) the brother of your father or mother; your aunt's husband. [from Latin *avunculus* = uncle]

uncomfortable *adjective* not comfortable. **uncomfortably** *adverb*

uncommon *adjective* not common; unusual.

uncompromising (say un-komp-rom-I-zing) *adjective* not allowing a compromise; inflexible.

unconcerned *adjective* not caring about something; not worried.

unconditional *adjective* without any conditions; absolute, *unconditional surrender.*
unconditionally *adverb*

unconscious *adjective* not conscious; not aware of things.
unconsciously *adverb*,
unconsciousness *noun*

uncouth (*say* un-kooth) *adjective* rude and rough in manner; boorish. [from *un-* + Old English *cuth* = known]

uncover *verb* (**uncovers, uncovering, uncovered**)
1 remove the covering from something. **2** reveal or expose, *They uncovered a plot to kill the king.*

undecided *adjective*
1 not yet settled; not certain. **2** not having made up your mind yet.

undeniable *adjective* impossible to deny; undoubtedly true.
undeniably *adverb*

under *preposition*
1 below or beneath, *Hide it under the desk.* **2** less than, *under 5 years old.* **3** governed or controlled by, *The country prospered under his rule.* **4** in the process of; undergoing, *The road is under repair.* **5** using, *He writes under the name of 'Lewis Carroll'.*
6 according to the rules of, *This is permitted under our agreement.*
under way in motion or in progress.

under *adverb* in or to a lower place or level or condition, *Slowly the diver went under.*

under *adjective* lower, *the under layers.*
[from Old English]

under- *prefix*
1 below or beneath (as in *underwear*). **2** lower; subordinate (as in *under-manager*). **3** not enough; incompletely (as in *undercooked*).

undercarriage *noun* (*plural* **undercarriages**) an aircraft's landing wheels and their supports.

undercover *adjective* done or doing things secretly, *an undercover agent.*

undercurrent *noun* (*plural* **undercurrents**)
1 a current that is below the surface or below another current. **2** an underlying feeling or influence, *an undercurrent of fear.*

undercut *verb* (**undercuts, undercutting, undercut**) sell something for a lower price than someone else sells it.

underdone *adjective* not thoroughly done; undercooked.

underestimate *verb* (**underestimates, underestimating, underestimated**) make too low an estimate of a person or thing.

undergo *verb* (**undergoes, undergoing, underwent, undergone**) experience or endure something; be subjected to, *The new aircraft underwent intensive tests.*

undergraduate *noun* (*plural* **undergraduates**) a student at a university who has not yet taken a degree.

underground *adjective & adverb*
1 under the ground. **2** done or working in secret.

underground *noun* a railway that runs through tunnels under the ground.

undergrowth *noun* bushes and other plants growing closely, especially under trees.

underhand *adjective* done or doing things in a sly or secret way.

underline *verb* (**underlines, underlining, underlined**)
1 draw a line under a word etc.
2 emphasize something.

underlying *adjective*
1 forming the basis or explanation of something, *the underlying causes of the trouble.*
2 lying under something, *the underlying rocks.*

undermine *verb* (**undermines, undermining, undermined**)
weaken something gradually.

underneath *preposition & adverb* below or beneath. [from *under-* + Old English *neothan* = beneath]

underpants *plural noun* a piece of men's underwear covering the lower part of the body, worn under trousers.

underprivileged *adjective* having less than the normal standard of living or rights in a community.

understand *verb* (**understands, understanding, understood**)
1 know what something means or how it works or why it exists.
2 know and tolerate a person's ways.
3 have been told, *I understand that you would like to speak to me.*
4 take something for granted, *Your expenses will be paid, that's understood.*
understandable *adjective*, **understandably** *adverb* [from Old English]

understanding *noun*
1 the power to understand or think; intelligence.
2 sympathy or tolerance.
3 agreement in opinion or feeling, *a better understanding between nations.*

understatement *noun* (*plural* **understatements**) an incomplete or very restrained statement of facts or truth, *To say they disagreed is an understatement; they had a violent quarrel.*

understudy *noun* (*plural* **understudies**) an actor who learns a part in order to be able to play it if the usual performer is ill or absent.

undertake *verb* (**undertakes, undertaking, undertook, undertaken**) agree or promise to do something.

undertaker *noun* (*plural* **undertakers**) a person whose job is to arrange funerals and burials or cremations.

undertone *noun* (*plural* **undertones**)
1 a low or quiet tone, *They spoke in undertones.*
2 an underlying quality or feeling etc., *His letter has a threatening undertone.*

underwear *noun* clothes worn next to the skin, under indoor clothing.

underweight *adjective* not heavy enough.

underwent *past tense* of **undergo**.

underworld *noun*
1 the people who are regularly involved in crime.
2 (in myths and legends) the place for the spirits of the dead, under the earth.

undeveloped *adjective* not yet developed.

undo verb (undoes, undoing, undid, undone)
1 unfasten or unwrap. **2** cancel the effect of something, *He has undone all our careful work.*

undoing noun
be someone's undoing be the cause of their ruin or failure.

undress verb (undresses, undressing, undressed) take your clothes off.

undue adjective excessive; too great. **unduly** adverb

undulate verb (undulates, undulating, undulated) move like a wave or waves; have a wavy appearance. **undulation** noun [from Latin *unda* = a wave]

undying adjective everlasting.

unearth verb (unearths, unearthing, unearthed)
1 dig something up; uncover something by digging. **2** find something by searching.

unearthly adjective
1 unnatural; strange and frightening. **2** (*informal*) very early or inconvenient, *We had to get up at an unearthly hour.*

uneasy adjective
1 worried or anxious. **2** uncomfortable. **uneasily** adverb, **uneasiness** noun

unemployed adjective without a job. **unemployment** noun

unerring (say un-er-ing) adjective making no mistake, *unerring accuracy.* [from *un-* + *err*]

uneven adjective
1 not level or regular. **2** unequal. **unevenly** adverb, **unevenness** noun

unfair adjective not fair; unjust. **unfairly** adverb, **unfairness** noun

unfaithful adjective not faithful; disloyal.

unfamiliar adjective not familiar. **unfamiliarity** noun

unfasten verb (unfastens, unfastening, unfastened) open the fastenings of something.

unfavourable adjective not favourable. **unfavourably** adverb

unfeeling adjective not caring about other people's feelings; unsympathetic.

unfit adjective
1 unsuitable. **2** not in perfect health because you do not take enough exercise.

unfit verb (unfits, unfitting, unfitted) make a person or thing unsuitable.

unfold verb (unfolds, unfolding, unfolded)
1 open; spread out. **2** make or become known slowly, *as the story unfolds.*

unfortunate adjective
1 unlucky. **2** unsuitable or regrettable, *an unfortunate remark.* **unfortunately** adverb

unfounded adjective not based on facts. [from *un-* + *found*²]

unfriendly adjective not friendly. **unfriendliness** noun

unfurl verb (unfurls, unfurling, unfurled) unroll; spread out, *They unfurled a large flag.*

ungainly adjective awkward-looking or clumsy; ungraceful. **ungainliness** noun [from *un-* + Middle English *gainly* = graceful]

ungodly adjective
1 not giving reverence to God; not religious.

2 (*informal*) outrageous; very inconvenient, *She woke me at an ungodly hour.* **ungodliness** *noun*

ungovernable *adjective* uncontrollable.

unguarded *adjective*
1 not guarded. **2** without thought or caution; indiscreet, *He said this in an unguarded moment.*

unhappy *adjective*
1 not happy; sad. **2** unfortunate or unsuitable, *an unhappy coincidence.* **unhappily** *adverb*, **unhappiness** *noun*

unhealthy *adjective* not healthy. **unhealthiness** *noun*

unheard-of *adjective* never known or done before; extraordinary.

unhinge *verb* (**unhinges**, **unhinging**, **unhinged**) cause a person's mind to become unbalanced.

uni- *prefix* one; single (as in *unicorn*). [from Latin *unus* = one]

unicorn *noun* (*plural* **unicorns**) (in legends) an animal that is like a horse with one long straight horn growing from its forehead. [from *uni-* + Latin *cornu* = horn]

uniform *noun* (*plural* **uniforms**) special clothes showing that the wearer is a member of a certain organization, school, etc.

uniform *adjective* always the same; not varying, *The desks are of uniform size.* **uniformly** *adverb*, **uniformity** *noun*
[from *uni-* + Latin *forma* = form]

unilateral *adjective* done by one person or group or country etc., *a unilateral decision.* [from *uni-* + *lateral*]

uninhabitable *adjective* unfit to live in.

union *noun* (*plural* **unions**)
1 the joining of things together; uniting. **2** a trade union. [from Latin *unio* = unity]

Union Jack *noun* (*plural* **Union Jacks**) the British flag.

unique (*say* yoo-**neek**) *adjective* being the only one of its kind, *This jewel is unique.* **uniquely** *adverb* [French, from Latin *unicus* = one and only]

> USAGE: *Unique* does not mean 'unusual' or 'remarkable', so avoid saying things like *very unique* or *most unique*.

unison *noun*
in unison 1 with all sounding or singing the same tune etc. together, or speaking in chorus. **2** in agreement.
[from *uni-* + Latin *sonus* = sound]

unit *noun* (*plural* **units**)
1 an amount used as a standard in measuring or counting things, *Centimetres are units of length; pence are units of money.* **2** a group, device, piece of furniture, etc. regarded as a single thing but forming part of a larger group or whole, *an army unit; a sink unit.* [from Latin *unus* = one]

unite *verb* (**unites**, **uniting**, **united**) join together; make or become one thing. [same origin as *unit*]

United Kingdom *noun* Great Britain and Northern Ireland.

> USAGE: See note at *Britain*.

unity *noun*
1 being united; being in agreement. **2** something whole that is made up of parts. **3** (in mathematics) the number one.

universal *adjective* to do with or including or done by everyone or everything. **universally** *adverb*

universe *noun* everything that exists, including the earth and living things and all the heavenly bodies. [from Latin *universus* = combined into one]

university *noun* (*plural* **universities**) a place where people go to study at an advanced level after leaving school. [from Latin *universitas*, literally = the universe, later = a community or group of people (i.e. the teachers and students)]

unjust *adjective* not fair or just.

unkempt *adjective* looking untidy or neglected. [from *un-* + an old word *kempt* = combed]

unkind *adjective* not kind. **unkindly** *adverb*, **unkindness** *noun*

unleaded *adjective* (of petrol) without added lead.

unleash *verb* (**unleashes**, **unleashing**, **unleashed**) **1** set a dog free from a leash. **2** let a strong feeling or force be released.

unless *conjunction* except when; if ... not, *We cannot go unless we are invited.*

unlike *preposition* not like, *Unlike me, she enjoys cricket.*

unlike *adjective* not alike; different, *The two children are very unlike.*

unlikely *adjective* (**unlikelier**, **unlikeliest**) not likely to happen or be true.

unlimited *adjective* not limited; very great or very many.

unload *verb* (**unloads**, **unloading**, **unloaded**) remove the load of things carried by a ship, aircraft, vehicle, etc.

unlock *verb* (**unlocks**, **unlocking**, **unlocked**) open something by undoing a lock.

unlucky *adjective* not lucky; having or bringing bad luck. **unluckily** *adverb*

unmask *verb* (**unmasks**, **unmasking**, **unmasked**) **1** remove a person's mask. **2** reveal what a person or thing really is.

unmentionable *adjective* too bad or embarrassing to be spoken of.

unmistakable *adjective* not able to be mistaken for another person or thing. **unmistakably** *adverb*

unmitigated *adjective* absolute, *an unmitigated disaster.* [from *un-* + *mitigate*]

unnatural *adjective* not natural or normal. **unnaturally** *adverb*

unnecessary *adjective* not necessary; more than is necessary.

unorthodox *adjective* not generally accepted, *an unorthodox method.*

unpack *verb* (**unpacks**, **unpacking**, **unpacked**) take things out of a suitcase, bag, box, etc.

unparliamentary *adjective* impolite or abusive.

USAGE: It is a rule of debates in Parliament that speakers must be polite to each other. Impolite language is 'unparliamentary'.

unpick *verb* (**unpicks, unpicking, unpicked**) undo the stitching of something.

unpleasant *adjective* not pleasant. **unpleasantly** *adverb*, **unpleasantness** *noun*

unpopular *adjective* not popular.

unprecedented (*say* un-press-id-en-tid) *adjective* that has never happened before. [from *un-* + *precedent*]

unprepared *adjective* not prepared beforehand; not ready or equipped.

unprintable *adjective* too rude or indecent to be printed.

unprofessional *adjective* not professional; not worthy of a member of a profession.

unqualified *adjective*
1 not officially qualified to do something. **2** not limited, *We gave it our unqualified approval.*

unravel *verb* (**unravels, unravelling, unravelled**)
1 disentangle. **2** undo something that is knitted. **3** investigate and solve a mystery etc. [from *un-* + an old word *ravel* = tangle]

unready *adjective* not ready; hesitating.

USAGE: In the title of the English king *Ethelred the Unready* the word means 'lacking good advice or wisdom'.

unreal *adjective* not real; existing in the imagination only. **unreality** *noun*

unreasonable *adjective*
1 not reasonable. **2** excessive or unjust. **unreasonably** *adverb*

unrelieved *adjective* without anything to vary it, *unrelieved gloom.*

unreserved *adjective*
1 not reserved. **2** without restriction; complete, *unreserved loyalty.* **unreservedly** *adverb*

unrest *noun* restlessness; trouble caused because people are dissatisfied.

unroll *verb* (**unrolls, unrolling, unrolled**) open something that has been rolled up.

unruly *adjective* difficult to control; disorderly. **unruliness** *noun* [from *un-* + *rule*]

unsavoury *adjective* unpleasant or disgusting.

unscrew *verb* (**unscrews, unscrewing, unscrewed**) undo something that has been screwed up.

unscrupulous *adjective* having no scruples about wrongdoing.

unseemly *adjective* not proper or suitable; indecent.

unseen *adjective* not seen; invisible.

unseen *noun* (*plural* **unseens**) a passage for translation without previous preparation.

unsettled *adjective*
1 not settled or calm. **2** (of weather) likely to change.

unshakeable *adjective* not able to be shaken; firm.

unshaven *adjective* (of a man) not recently shaved.

unsightly *adjective* not pleasant to look at; ugly. **unsightliness** *noun*

unskilled *adjective* not having or not needing special skill or training.

unsolicited *adjective* not asked for, *unsolicited advice*. [from *un- + solicit*]

unsound *adjective* not sound; damaged, unhealthy, unreasonable, or unreliable. [from *un- + sound*[b]]

unspeakable *adjective* too bad to be described; very objectionable.

unstable *adjective* not stable; likely to change or become unbalanced.

unstuck *adjective*
come unstuck 1 cease to stick. **2** (*informal*) fail or go wrong.

unthinkable *adjective* too bad or too unlikely to be worth considering.

unthinking *adjective* thoughtless.

untidy *adjective* (**untidier, untidiest**) not tidy. **untidily** *adverb*, **untidiness** *noun*

untie *verb* (**unties, untying, untied**) undo something that has been tied.

until *preposition & conjunction* up to a particular time or event.

USAGE: See the note on *till*[1].

untold *adjective*
1 not told. **2** too much or too many to be counted, *untold wealth* or *wealth untold*.

untruth *noun* (*plural* **untruths**) an untrue statement; a lie.
untruthful *adjective*, **untruthfully** *adverb*

unused *adjective*
1 (*say* un-**yoozd**) not yet used, *an unused stamp*. **2** (*say* un-**yoost**) not accustomed, *He is unused to eating meat*.

unusual *adjective* not usual; strange or exceptional. **unusually** *adverb*

unveil *verb* (**unveils, unveiling, unveiled**)
1 remove a veil or covering from something. **2** reveal.

unwarranted *adjective* not justified; uncalled for.

unwell *adjective* not in good health.

unwholesome *adjective* not wholesome.

unwieldy *adjective* awkward to move or control because of its size, shape, or weight.
unwieldiness *noun* [from *un- + wield*]

unwind *verb* (**unwinds, unwinding, unwound**)
1 unroll. **2** (*informal*) relax after a time of work or strain.

unwise *adjective* not wise; foolish.
unwisely *adverb*

unwrap *verb* (**unwraps, unwrapping, unwrapped**) open something that is wrapped.

up *adverb*
1 to or in a higher place or position or level, *Prices went up*. **2** so as to be upright, *Stand up*. **3** out of bed, *It's time to get up*. **4** completely, *Eat up your carrots*. **5** finished, *Your time is up*. **6** (*informal*) happening, *Something is up*.

up against 1 close to. **2** (*informal*) faced with difficulties, dangers, etc.

ups and downs 1 ascents and descents. **2** alternate good and bad luck.

up to 1 until. **2** busy with or doing something, *What are you up to?* **3** capable of, *I don't think I'm up to it*. **4** needed from, *It's up to us to help her*.

up to date 1 modern or fashionable. **2** giving recent information etc.

USAGE: Use hyphens when this is used as an adjective before a noun, e.g. *up-to-date information* (but *The information is up to date*).

up *preposition* upwards through or along or into, *Water came up the pipes.*
[from Old English]

upbringing *noun* the way someone is trained during childhood.

update *verb* (**updates, updating, updated**) bring a thing up to date.

upheaval *noun* (*plural* **upheavals**) a sudden violent change or disturbance. [from *up-* + *heave*]

uphill *adverb* up a slope.

uphill *adjective*
1 going up a slope. **2** difficult, *It was an uphill struggle.*

uphold *verb* (**upholds, upholding, upheld**) support or maintain a decision or belief etc.

upholster *verb* (**upholsters, upholstering, upholstered**) put covers, padding, and springs etc. on furniture. **upholstery** *noun*
[from *uphold* = maintain and repair]

upkeep *noun* keeping something in good condition; the cost of this.

uplifting *adjective* making you feel more cheerful.

upon *preposition* on. [from *up* (adverb) + *on* (preposition)]

upper *adjective* higher in place or rank etc.

upper class *noun* (*plural* **upper classes**) the highest class in society, especially the aristocracy. **upper-class** *adjective*

uppermost *adjective* highest.

uppermost *adverb* on or to the top or the highest place, *Keep the painted side uppermost.*
[from *upper* + *most*]

upright *adjective*
1 vertical or erect. **2** strictly honest or honourable.

upright *noun* (*plural* **uprights**) a post or rod etc. placed upright, especially as a support.

uprising *noun* (*plural* **uprisings**) a rebellion or revolt.

uproar *noun* an outburst of noise or excitement or anger.

uproot *verb* (**uproots, uprooting, uprooted**)
1 remove a plant and its roots from the ground. **2** make someone leave the place where he or she has lived for a long time.

upset *verb* (**upsets, upsetting, upset**)
1 overturn; knock something over. **2** make a person unhappy or distressed. **3** disturb the normal working of something; disrupt, *This has really upset my plans.*

upset *adjective*
1 unhappy or distressed.
2 slightly ill, *an upset stomach.*

upset *noun* (*plural* **upsets**)
1 a slight illness, *a stomach upset.*
2 an unexpected result or setback, *There has been a major upset in the quarter-finals.*

upshot *noun* (*plural* **upshots**) an outcome. [originally = the final shot in an archery contest]

upside down *adverb & adjective*
1 with the upper part underneath instead of on top. **2** in great disorder; very untidy, *Everything had been turned upside down.*

upstairs *adverb & adjective* to or on a higher floor.

upstart *noun (plural* **upstarts***)* a person who has risen suddenly to a high position, especially one who then behaves arrogantly. [from an old verb *upstart* = to spring up suddenly]

uptake *noun*
quick on the uptake quick to understand.
slow on the uptake slow to understand.

uptight *adjective (informal)* tense and nervous or annoyed.

upward *adjective & adverb* going towards what is higher. **upwards** *adverb* [from *up* + *-ward*]

uranium *noun* a heavy radioactive grey metal used as a source of nuclear energy. [named after the planet Uranus]

urban *adjective* to do with a town or city. [from Latin *urbis* = of a city]

urchin *noun (plural* **urchins***)*
1 a poorly dressed or mischievous boy. **2** a sea urchin. [from Latin *ericius* = hedgehog]

urge *verb* (**urges, urging, urged**)
1 try to persuade a person to do something. **2** drive people or animals onward.

urge *noun (plural* **urges***)* a strong desire.
[from Latin]

urgent *adjective* needing to be done or dealt with immediately.
urgently *adverb*, **urgency** *noun* [from Latin *urgens* = urging]

urinate (*say* yoor-in-ayt) *verb* (**urinates, urinating, urinated**) pass urine out of your body.
urination *noun*

urine (*say* yoor-in) *noun* waste liquid that collects in the bladder and is passed out of the body.
urinary *adjective* [from Latin]

urn *noun (plural* **urns***)*
1 a large metal container with a tap, in which water is heated. **2** a container shaped like a vase, usually with a foot, especially a container for holding the ashes of a cremated person. [from Latin]

US *abbreviation* United States (of America).

us *pronoun* the form of *we* used when it is the object of a verb or after a preposition.

USA *abbreviation* United States of America.

use (*say* yooz) *verb* (**uses, using, used**) perform an action or job with something, *Use soap for washing.* **user** *noun*
used to 1 was or were in the habit of doing, *We used to go by train.* **2** accustomed to or familiar with, *I'm used to his strange behaviour.*
use up use all of something.

use (*say* yooss) *noun (plural* **uses***)*
1 the action of using something; being used, *the use of computers in schools.* **2** the purpose for which something is used, *Can you find a use for this crate?* **3** the quality of being useful, *These scissors are no use at all.* [from Latin]

used *adjective* not new; second-hand, *used cars.*

useful *adjective* able to be used a lot or to do something that needs doing. **usefully** *adverb*, **usefulness** *noun*

useless *adjective* not useful; producing no effect, *Their efforts were useless.* **uselessly** *adverb*, **uselessness** *noun*

usher *noun* (*plural* **ushers**) a person who shows people to their seats in a public hall or church etc.

usher *verb* (**ushers, ushering, ushered**) lead someone in or out; escort someone as an usher. [from Latin *ostiarius* = doorkeeper]

usherette *noun* (*plural* **usherettes**) a woman who shows people to their seats in a cinema or theatre.

usual *adjective* such as happens or is done or used etc. always or most of the time. **usually** *adverb* [from Latin *usum* = used]

utensil (*say* yoo-**ten**-sil) *noun* (*plural* **utensils**) a tool, device, or container, especially one for use in the house, *cooking utensils.* [from Latin *utensilis* = fit for use]

utilitarian *adjective* designed to be useful rather than decorative or luxurious; practical. [from *utility*]

utility *noun* (*plural* **utilities**) **1** usefulness. **2** an organization that supplies water, gas, electricity, etc. to the community. [from Latin *utilis* = useful]

utilize *verb* (**utilizes, utilizing, utilized**) use; find a use for something. **utilization** *noun* [from French]

utmost *adjective* extreme or greatest, *Look after it with the utmost care.* **utmost** *noun* [from Old English *utemest* = furthest out]

Utopia (*say* yoo-**toh**-pee-a) *noun* (*plural* **Utopias**) an imaginary place or state of things where everything is perfect. **Utopian** *adjective* [Latin, = nowhere; used in 1516 as the title of a book by Sir Thomas More, in which he describes an ideal society]

utter[1] *verb* (**utters, uttering, uttered**) say or speak; make a sound with your mouth. **utterance** *noun* [from old Dutch]

utter[2] *adjective* complete or absolute, *utter misery.* **utterly** *adverb* [from Old English *uttra* = outer]

uttermost *adjective* & *noun* utmost.

U-turn *noun* (*plural* **U-turns**) **1** a U-shaped turn made in a vehicle so that it then travels in the opposite direction. **2** a complete change of policy.

Vv

vacant *adjective* **1** empty; not filled or occupied. **2** without expression; blank, *a vacant stare.* **vacantly** *adverb*, **vacancy** *noun* [from Latin *vacans* = being empty]

vacation (*say* vak-**ay**-shon) *noun* (*plural* **vacations**) **1** a holiday, especially between the terms at a university. **2** vacating a place etc.

vaccinate (*say* vak-sin-ayt) *verb* (**vaccinates, vaccinating, vaccinated**) inoculate someone with a vaccine. **vaccination** *noun*

vaccine (*say* vak-seen) *noun* (*plural* **vaccines**) a substance used to immunize a person against a disease. [from Latin *vacca* = cow (because serum from cows was used to protect people from the disease smallpox)]

vacuum *noun* (*plural* **vacuums**)
1 a completely empty space; a space without any air in it. **2** (*informal*) a vacuum cleaner. **vacuum** *verb* [from Latin *vacuus* = empty]

vacuum cleaner *noun* (*plural* **vacuum cleaners**) an electrical device that sucks up dust and dirt etc.

vagabond *noun* (*plural* **vagabonds**) a person with no settled home or regular work; a vagrant.

vagina (*say* va-jy-na) *noun* (*plural* **vaginas**) the passage that leads from the vulva to the womb. [Latin, = sheath]

vagrant (*say* vay-grant) *noun* (*plural* **vagrants**) a person with no settled home or regular work; a tramp. **vagrancy** *noun*

vague *adjective* not definite or clear. **vaguely** *adverb*, **vagueness** *noun* [from Latin *vagus* = wandering]

vain *adjective*
1 conceited, especially about your appearance. **2** useless, *They made vain attempts to save her.*

vainly *adverb*
in vain with no result; uselessly. [from Latin *vanus* = empty]

USAGE: Do not confuse with *vane* or *vein*.

valency *noun* (*plural* **valencies**) the power of an atom to combine with other atoms, measured by the number of hydrogen atoms it is capable of combining with. [from Latin *valentia* = power]

valiant *adjective* brave or courageous. **valiantly** *adverb* [from old French; related to *value*]

valid *adjective*
1 legally able to be used or accepted, *This passport is out of date and not valid.* **2** (of reasoning) sound and logical. **validity** *noun* [from Latin *validus* = strong]

valley *noun* (*plural* **valleys**)
1 a long low area between hills.
2 an area through which a river flows, *the Nile valley.* [from Latin]

valuable *adjective* worth a lot of money; of great value. **valuably** *adverb*

valuables *plural noun* valuable things.

value *noun* (*plural* **values**)
1 the amount of money etc. that is considered to be the equivalent of something, or for which it can be exchanged. **2** how useful or important something is, *They learnt the value of regular exercise.*
value *verb* (**values, valuing, valued**)
1 think that something is valuable. **2** estimate the value of

a thing. **valuation** noun, **valuer** noun [from Latin *valere* = be strong]

valve noun (plural **valves**)
1 a device for controlling the flow of gas or liquid through a pipe or tube. **2** a device that controls the flow of electricity in old televisions, radios, etc. **3** each piece of the shell of oysters etc. **valvular** adjective [from Latin *valva* = a panel of a folding door]

vampire noun (plural **vampires**) a ghost or revived corpse supposed to leave a grave at night and suck blood from living people. [from Serbo-Croat (a Slavonic language spoken in the Balkan countries)]

van noun (plural **vans**)
1 a covered vehicle for carrying goods. **2** a railway carriage for luggage or goods, or for the use of the guard. [short for *caravan*]

vandal noun (plural **vandals**) a person who deliberately breaks or damages things, especially public property. **vandalism** noun [named after the Vandals, a Germanic tribe who invaded the Roman Empire in the 5th century, destroying many books and works of art]

vandalize verb (**vandalizes**, **vandalizing**, **vandalized**) damage things as a vandal.

vane noun (plural **vanes**)
1 a weathervane. **2** the blade of a propeller, sail of a windmill, or other device that acts on or is moved by wind or water. [from Old English]

USAGE: Do not confuse with *vain* or *vein*.

vanilla noun a flavouring obtained from the pods of a tropical plant. [from Spanish *vainilla* = little pod]

vanish verb (**vanishes**, **vanishing**, **vanished**) disappear completely. [from Latin]

vanity noun conceit; being vain.

vanquish verb (**vanquishes**, **vanquishing**, **vanquished**) conquer. [from Latin *vincere* = conquer]

vantage point noun (plural **vantage points**) a place from which you have a good view of scenery or something interesting. [from Middle English *vantage* = advantage]

vaporize verb (**vaporizes**, **vaporizing**, **vaporized**) change or be changed into vapour. **vaporization** noun, **vaporizer** noun

vapour noun (plural **vapours**) a visible gas to which some substances can be converted by heat; steam or mist. [from Latin *vapor* = steam]

variable adjective likely to vary; changeable. **variably** adverb, **variability** noun

variable noun (plural **variables**) something that varies or can vary; a variable quantity.

variant adjective differing from something. '*Gipsy*' is a variant spelling of '*gypsy*'. **variant** noun

variation noun (plural **variations**)
1 varying; the amount by which something varies. **2** a different form of something.

varied adjective of different sorts; full of variety.

variegated (*say* vair-ig-ay-tid) *adjective* with patches of different colours. **variegation** *noun* [same origin as *various*]

variety *adjective* (*plural* **varieties**) **1** a quantity of different kinds of things. **2** the quality of not always being the same; variation. **3** a particular kind of something, *There are several varieties of spaniel.* **4** an entertainment that includes short performances of various kinds. [same origin as *various*]

various *adjective* **1** of several kinds; unlike one another, *for various reasons.* **2** several, *We met various people.* **variously** *adverb* [from Latin *varius* = changing]

varnish *noun* (*plural* **varnishes**) a liquid that dries to form a hard shiny usually transparent coating.

varnish *verb* (**varnishes**, **varnishing**, **varnished**) coat something with varnish.

vary *verb* (**varies**, **varying**, **varied**) **1** make or become different; change. **2** be different. [same origin as *various*]

vase *noun* (*plural* **vases**) an open usually tall container used for holding cut flowers or as an ornament. [from Latin *vas* = vessel]

vast *adjective* very great, especially in area, *a vast expanse of water.* **vastly** *adverb*, **vastness** *noun* [from Latin *vastus* = unoccupied, desert]

VAT *abbreviation* value added tax; a tax on goods and services.

vat *noun* (*plural* **vats**) a very large container for holding liquid.

vault *verb* (**vaults**, **vaulting**, **vaulted**) jump over something, especially while supporting yourself on your hands or with the help of a pole.

vault *noun* (*plural* **vaults**) **1** a vaulting jump. **2** an arched roof. **3** an underground room used to store things. **4** a room for storing money or valuables. **5** a burial chamber. [from Latin *volvere* = to roll]

vaulted *adjective* having an arched roof.

vaunt *verb* (**vaunts**, **vaunting**, **vaunted**) (*old use* or *poetical*) boast. **vaunt** *noun* [from Latin *vanus* = vain]

VDU *abbreviation* visual display unit.

veal *noun* calf's flesh used as food. [from Latin *vitulus* = calf]

vector *noun* (*plural* **vectors**) (*in Mathematics*) a quantity that has size and direction (e.g. velocity, = speed in a certain direction). **vectorial** *adjective* [Latin, = carrier, traveller]

veer *verb* (**veers**, **veering**, **veered**) change direction; swerve.

vegetable *noun* (*plural* **vegetables**) a plant that can be used as food. [from Latin *vegetare* = enliven, animate]

vegetarian *noun* (*plural* **vegetarians**) a person who does not eat meat. **vegetarianism** *noun* [from *vegetable* + *-arian*]

vegetation *noun* **1** plants that are growing. **2** vegetating. [from Latin *vegetatio* = the power to grow]

vehement (say **vee**-im-ent)
adjective showing strong feeling,
a vehement refusal. **vehemently**
adverb, **vehemence** *noun*

vehicle *noun* (plural **vehicles**)
a means of transporting people or
goods, especially on land. [from
Latin *vehere* = carry]

veil *noun* (plural **veils**) a piece of
thin material worn to cover the
face or head.

take the veil become a nun.

veil *verb* (veils, veiling, veiled)
1 cover something with a veil.
2 partially conceal something,
veiled threats.

vein *noun* (plural **veins**)
1 any of the tubes that carry
blood from all parts of the body to
the heart. (Compare *artery*.)
2 a line or streak on a leaf, rock,
insect's wing, etc. **3** a long deposit
of mineral or ore in the middle of
a rock. **4** a mood or manner, *She
spoke in a serious vein.* [from
Latin]

USAGE: Do not confuse with
vain or *vane*.

velocity *noun* (plural **velocities**)
speed in a given direction. [from
Latin *velox* = swift]

velvet *noun* a woven material
with very short soft furry fibres
on one side. **velvety** *adjective*
[from Latin *villus* = soft fur]

vendetta *noun* (plural **vendettas**)
a long-lasting bitter quarrel;
a feud. [Italian, from Latin
vindicta = vengeance]

vending machine *noun* (plural
vending machines) a slot
machine from which you can
obtain drinks, chocolate,
cigarettes, etc.

veneer *noun* (plural **veneers**)
1 a thin layer of good wood
covering the surface of a cheaper
wood in furniture etc. **2** an
outward show of some good
quality, *a veneer of politeness.* [via
German from French *fournir*
= furnish]

venerable *adjective* worthy of
being venerated, especially
because of great age.

venerate *verb* (venerates,
venerating, venerated) honour
with great respect or reverence.
veneration *noun* [from Latin
venerari = revere]

venereal disease *noun* (plural
venereal diseases) a disease
passed on by sexual intercourse.

vengeance *noun* revenge.
with a vengeance very strongly
or effectively. [from old French;
related to *vindictive*]

venison *noun* deer's flesh as food.
[old French, from Latin *venatio*
= hunting]

Venn diagram *noun* (plural **Venn
diagrams**) (in *Mathematics*)
a diagram in which circles are
used to show the relationships
between different sets of things.
[named after an English
mathematician, John Venn]

venom *noun*
1 the poisonous fluid produced
by snakes, scorpions, etc. **2** very
bitter feeling towards somebody;
hatred. **venomous** *adjective* [from
Latin *venenum* = poison]

vent *noun* (plural **vents**) an
opening in something, especially
to let out smoke or gas etc.
give vent to express your feelings
openly.

vent verb (vents, venting, vented)
1 make a vent in something.
2 give vent to feelings.
[from Latin ventus = wind]

ventilate verb (ventilates, ventilating, ventilated) let air move freely in and out of a room etc. **ventilation** noun, **ventilator** noun [same origin as vent]

ventriloquist noun (plural ventriloquists) an entertainer who makes his or her voice sound as if it comes from another source. **ventriloquism** noun [from Latin venter = abdomen + loqui = speak]

venture noun (plural ventures) something you decide to do that is risky.

venture verb (ventures, venturing, ventured) risk; dare to do or say something or to go somewhere, We ventured out into the snow.
[from adventure]

venturesome adjective ready to take risks; daring.

veracity (say ver-**as**-it-ee) noun truth. **veracious** (say ver-**ay**-shus) adjective [from Latin verus = true]

veranda noun (plural verandas) a terrace with a roof along the side of a house. [via Hindi from Portuguese varanda = railing, balcony]

verb noun (plural verbs) a word that shows what a person or thing is doing, e.g. bring, came, sing, were. [from Latin verbum = word]

verbal adjective
1 to do with or in words; spoken, not written, a verbal statement.
2 to do with verbs. **verbally** adverb [same origin as verb]

verdict noun (plural verdicts) a judgement or decision made after considering evidence, especially that made by a jury. [from Latin verus = true + dictum = said]

verge noun (plural verges)
1 the extreme edge or brink of something, on the verge of madness. **2** a strip of grass along the edge of a road or path etc.

verge verb (verges, verging, verged)
verge on border on something; be close to something, This puzzle verges on the impossible.

veritable adjective real; rightly named, a veritable villain. **veritably** adverb

vermin plural noun
1 pests (e.g. foxes, rats, mice) regarded as harmful to domestic animals, crops, or food.
2 unpleasant or parasitic insects, e.g. lice. **verminous** adjective [from Latin vermis = worm]

vernacular (say ver-**nak**-yoo-ler) noun (plural vernaculars) the language of a country or district, as distinct from an official or formal language. [from Latin vernaculus = domestic]

versatile adjective able to do or be used for many different things. **versatility** noun [from Latin versare = to turn]

verse noun (plural verses)
1 writing arranged in short lines, usually with a particular rhythm

and often with rhymes; poetry.
2 a group of lines forming a unit in a poem or song. **3** each of the short numbered sections of a chapter in the Bible. [via Old English from Latin *versus* = a line of writing]

version noun (*plural* **versions**)
1 a particular person's account of something that happened.
2 a translation, *modern versions of the Bible*. **3** a special or different form of something, *the latest version of this car*. [from Latin *versum* = turned, transformed]

versus preposition against; competing with, *Arsenal versus Liverpool*. [Latin, = against]

vertebra noun (*plural* **vertebrae**) each of the bones that form the backbone.

vertebrate noun (*plural* **vertebrates**) an animal that has a backbone. (The opposite is *invertebrate*.) [from *vertebra*]

vertical adjective at right angles to something horizontal; upright. **vertically** adverb

vertigo noun a feeling of dizziness and loss of balance, especially when you are very high up. [Latin, = whirling around]

verve (say verv) noun enthusiasm and liveliness. [French, = vigour]

very adverb
1 to a great amount or intensity; extremely, *It was very cold.*
2 (used to emphasize something), *on the very next day; the very last drop.*

very adjective
1 exact or actual, *It's the very thing we need.* **2** extreme, *at the very end.*
[from old French *verai* = true]

vessel noun (*plural* **vessels**)
1 a ship or boat. **2** a container, especially for liquid. **3** a tube carrying blood or other liquid in the body of an animal or plant. [from old French; related to *vase*]

vest noun (*plural* **vests**) a piece of underwear covering the trunk of the body.

vest verb (**vests, vesting, vested**)
1 give something as a right, *The power to make laws is vested in Parliament.* **2** (*old use*) clothe.
[from Latin *vestis* = a piece of clothing]

vested interest noun (*plural* **vested interests**) a strong reason for wanting something to happen, usually because you will benefit from it.

vet noun (*plural* **vets**) a person trained to give medical and surgical treatment to animals.

vet verb (**vets, vetting, vetted**) check a thing to see if it has any mistakes or faults.
[short for *veterinary surgeon*]

veteran noun (*plural* **veterans**) a person who has had long service or experience in something, *a war veteran*. [from Latin *vetus* = old]

veterinary (say vet-rin-ree) adjective to do with the medical and surgical treatment of animals, *a veterinary surgeon*. [from Latin *veterinae* = cattle]

veto (say vee-toh) noun (*plural* **vetoes**)
1 a refusal to let something

happen. **2** the right to prohibit
something.

veto *verb* (**vetoes, vetoing,
vetoed**) refuse or prohibit
something.
[Latin, = I forbid]

vex *verb* (**vexes, vexing, vexed**)
annoy; cause somebody worry.
vexation *noun*, **vexatious**
adjective [from Latin *vexare* = to
shake]

vexed question *noun* (*plural*
vexed questions)
a problem that is difficult or
much discussed.

VHF *abbreviation* very high
frequency.

via (*say* vy-a) *preposition* through;
by way of, *The train goes from
London to Exeter via Bristol.*
[Latin, = by way of]

viable *adjective* able to work or
exist successfully; practicable,
a viable plan. **viability** *noun*
[French, from *vie* = life]

viaduct *noun* (*plural* **viaducts**)
a long bridge, usually with many
arches, carrying a road or
railway over a valley or low
ground. [from Latin *via* = road
+ *ducere* = to lead]

vibrant *adjective* full of energy;
lively. [same origin as *vibrate*]

vibrate *verb* (**vibrates, vibrating,
vibrated**)
1 shake very quickly to and fro.
2 make a throbbing sound.
vibration *noun* [from Latin
vibrare = shake]

vicar *noun* (*plural* **vicars**)
a member of the clergy who is in
charge of a parish.

vice[1] *noun* (*plural* **vices**)
1 evil or wickedness. **2** an evil or
bad habit; a bad fault. [from
Latin *vitium* = fault]

vice[2] *noun* (*plural* **vices**) a device
for gripping something and
holding it firmly while you work
on it. [from Latin *vitis* = vine]

vice- *prefix*
1 authorized to act as a deputy or
substitute (as in *vice-captain,
vice-president*). **2** next in rank to
someone (as in *vice-admiral*).
[Latin, = in place of, by a change]

vice versa *adverb* the other way
round, *Which do you prefer—blue
spots on a yellow background or
vice versa?* [Latin, = the position
being reversed]

vicious *adjective*
1 cruel and aggressive. **2** severe
or violent. **viciously** *adverb*,
viciousness *noun* [same origin as
vice[1]]

vicious circle *noun* (*plural*
vicious circles) a situation where
a problem produces an effect
which itself produces the
original problem or makes it
worse.

victim *noun* (*plural* **victims**)
someone who is injured, killed,
robbed, etc. [from Latin *victima*
= a person or animal sacrificed to
a god]

victimize *verb* (**victimizes,
victimizing, victimized**) make
a victim of someone; punish
a person unfairly. **victimization**
noun

victor *noun* (*plural* **victors**) the
winner. [same origin as *victory*]

Victorian *adjective* belonging to
the time of Queen Victoria (1837–
1901). **Victorian** *noun*

victory noun (plural **victories**)
success won against an opponent
in a battle, contest, or game.
victorious adjective [from Latin
victum = conquered]

video noun (plural **videos**)
1 recorded or broadcast pictures.
2 a video recorder or recording.
3 a visual display unit. [Latin,
= I see]

video recorder noun (plural
video recorders) a machine for
recording a television
programme etc. on magnetic tape
for playing back later.

videotape noun (plural
videotapes) magnetic tape
suitable for recording television
programmes.

vie verb (**vies**, **vying**, **vied**)
compete; carry on a rivalry,
vying with each other. [probably
from envy]

view noun (plural **views**)
1 what can be seen from one
place, e.g. beautiful scenery.
2 sight; range of vision, The ship
sailed into view. **3** an opinion, She
has strong views about politics.
in view of because of.
on view displayed for inspection.
with a view to with the hope or
intention of.

view verb (**views**, **viewing**,
viewed)
1 look at something. **2** consider.
viewer noun
[from Latin videre = to see]

viewpoint noun (plural
viewpoints) a point of view.

vigorous adjective full of strength
and energy. **vigorously** adverb

Viking noun (plural **Vikings**)
a Scandinavian trader and pirate
in the 8th–10th centuries. [from
Old Norse]

vile adjective
1 extremely disgusting. **2** very
bad or wicked. **vilely** adverb,
vileness noun [from Latin vilis
= cheap, unworthy]

villa noun (plural **villas**) a house,
especially a holiday home
abroad. [Latin, = country house]

village noun (plural **villages**)
a group of houses and other
buildings in a country district,
smaller than a town and usually
having a church. **villager** noun
[old French; related to villa]

villain noun (plural **villains**)
a wicked person or a criminal.
villainous adjective, **villainy** noun
[from Latin villanus = villager]

vindicate verb (**vindicates**,
vindicating, **vindicated**)
1 clear a person of blame or
suspicion. **2** prove something to
be true or worthwhile.
vindication noun [from Latin
vindicare = set free]

vine noun (plural **vines**)
a climbing or trailing plant
whose fruit is the grape. [from
Latin vinum = wine]

vinegar noun a sour liquid used to
flavour food or in pickling.
[from Latin vinum = wine + acer
= sour]

vintage noun (plural **vintages**)
1 the harvest of a season's grapes;
the wine made from this. **2** the
period from which something
comes. [from French; related
to vine]

vintage car noun (plural **vintage cars**) a car made between 1917 and 1930.

viola (say vee-oh-la) noun (plural **violas**) a musical instrument like a violin but slightly larger and with a lower pitch. [Spanish or Italian]

violate verb (**violates, violating, violated**)
1 break a promise, law, or treaty etc. 2 break into somewhere; treat a person or place without respect. **violation** noun, **violator** noun [from Latin violare = treat violently]

violence noun force that does harm or damage. **violent** adjective, **violently** adverb [from Latin]

violet noun (plural **violets**)
1 a small plant that often has purple flowers. 2 purple.

violin noun (plural **violins**) a musical instrument with four strings, played with a bow. **violinist** noun [from Italian violino = small viola]

viper noun (plural **vipers**) a small poisonous snake. [from Latin vipera = snake]

virgin noun (plural **virgins**) a person, especially a girl or woman, who has never had sexual intercourse. **virginal** adjective, **virginity** noun

virgin adjective not yet touched or used, virgin snow.

virtual adjective being something in effect though not strictly in fact, His silence was a virtual admission of guilt. [same origin as virtue]

virtually adverb nearly or almost.

virtue noun (plural **virtues**)
1 moral goodness; a particular form of this, Honesty is a virtue. 2 a good quality or advantage, Jamie's plan has the virtue of simplicity. **virtuous** adjective, **virtuously** adverb
in virtue of because of. [from Latin virtus = worth]

virtuoso (say ver-tew-oh-soh) noun (plural **virtuosos** or **virtuosi**) a person with outstanding skill, especially in singing or playing music. **virtuosity** noun [Italian, = skilful]

virus noun (plural **viruses**)
1 a very tiny living thing, smaller than a bacterium, that can cause disease. 2 a disease caused by a virus. 3 a hidden set of instructions in a computer program that is designed to destroy data. [Latin, = poison]

visa (say vee-za) noun (plural **visas**) an official mark put on someone's passport by officials of a foreign country to show that the holder has permission to enter that country. [Latin, = things seen]

viscount (say vy-kownt) noun (plural **viscounts**) a nobleman ranking below an earl and above a baron. **viscountess** noun [from old French visconte = vice-count]

visible adjective able to be seen or noticed, The ship was visible on the horizon. **visibly** adverb, **visibility** noun [from Latin]

USAGE: Do not confuse with visual.

vision noun (plural **visions**)
1 the ability to see; sight.
2 something seen in a person's

imagination or in a dream.
3 foresight and wisdom in
planning things. **4** a person or
thing that is beautiful to see.
[from old French; related to
visible and *visual*]

visionary *adjective* extremely
imaginative or fanciful.

visionary *noun* (*plural*
visionaries) a person with
extremely imaginative ideas and
plans.

visit *verb* (**visits, visiting, visited**)
1 go to see a person or place.
2 stay somewhere for a while.
visitor *noun*

visit *noun* (*plural* **visits**)
1 going to see a person or place.
2 a short stay somewhere.
[from Latin *visitare* = go to see]

vista *noun* (*plural* **vistas**) a long
view. [Italian, = view]

visual *adjective* to do with or used
in seeing; to do with sight.
visually *adverb* [from Latin *visus*
= sight]

USAGE: Do not confuse with
visible.

visual aid *noun* (*plural* **visual
aids**) a picture, slide, film, etc.
used as an aid in teaching.

visual display unit *noun* (*plural*
visual display units) a device that
looks like a television screen and
displays data received
from a computer or fed into it.

visualize *verb* (**visualizes,
visualizing, visualized**) form
a mental picture of something.
visualization *noun*

vital *adjective*
1 connected with life; necessary
for life to continue, *vital
functions such as breathing.*

2 essential; very important.
vitally *adverb* [from Latin *vita*
= life]

vitality *noun* liveliness or energy.

vitamin (*say* vit-a-min *or* vy-ta-
min) *noun* (*plural* **vitamins**) any
of a number of substances that
are present in various foods and
are essential to keep people and
animals healthy. [from Latin *vita*
= life, + *amine*, a kind of chemical
related to amino acids, which
vitamins were once thought to
contain]

vivacious (*say* viv-ay-shus)
adjective happy and lively.
vivaciously *adverb*, **vivacity** *noun*
[from Latin *vivus* = alive]

vivid *adjective*
1 bright and strong or clear, *vivid
colours; a vivid description.*
2 active and lively, *a vivid
imagination.* **vividly** *adverb*,
vividness *noun* [from Latin
vividus = full of life]

vivisection *noun* doing surgical
experiments on live animals.
[from Latin *vivus* = alive + *sectio*
= cutting]

vixen *noun* (*plural* **vixens**)
a female fox. [from Old English]

vocabulary *noun* (*plural*
vocabularies)
1 a list of words with their
meanings. **2** the words known to
a person or used in a particular
book or subject etc. [from Latin
vocabulum = name]

vocal cords *plural noun* two
strap-like membranes in the
throat that can be made to
vibrate and produce sounds.
[from Latin *vocis* = of the voice]

vocalist noun (plural **vocalists**)
a singer, especially in a pop group.

vocation noun (plural **vocations**)
1 a person's job or occupation.
2 a strong desire to do a particular kind of work, or a feeling of being called by God to do something. [from Latin *vocare* = to call]

vocational adjective teaching you the skills you need for a particular job or profession, *vocational training*.

vodka noun (plural **vodkas**)
a strong alcoholic drink very popular in Russia. [from Russian *voda* = water]

vogue noun (plural **vogues**) the current fashion, *Very short hair for women seems to be the vogue.*
in vogue in fashion, *Stripy dresses are definitely in vogue.*

voice noun (plural **voices**)
1 sounds formed by the vocal cords and uttered by the mouth, especially in speaking, singing, etc. **2** the ability to speak or sing, *She has lost her voice.* **3** someone expressing a particular opinion about something, *Emma's the only dissenting voice.* **4** the right to express an opinion or desire, *I have no voice in this matter.*

void adjective
1 empty. **2** having no legal validity.

void noun (plural **voids**) an empty space or hole. [from old French; related to *vacant*]

volatile (say vol-a-tyl) adjective
1 evaporating quickly, *a volatile liquid.* **2** changing quickly from one mood or interest to another.

volatility noun [from Latin *volatilis* = flying]

volcano noun (plural **volcanoes**)
a mountain with an opening at the top from which lava and hot gases etc. flow. **volcanic** adjective
[Italian, from *Vulcan*, the ancient Roman god of fire]

vole noun (plural **voles**) a small animal rather like a rat.

volley noun (plural **volleys**)
1 a number of bullets or shells etc. fired at the same time.
2 hitting back the ball in tennis etc. before it touches the ground.

volley verb (**volleys**, **volleying**, **volleyed**) send or hit something in a volley or volleys.
[from Latin *volare* = to fly]

volt noun (plural **volts**) a unit for measuring electric force. [named after an Italian scientist, A. Volta, who discovered how to produce electricity by a chemical reaction]

voltage noun (plural **voltages**)
electric force measured in volts.

volume noun (plural **volumes**)
1 the amount of space filled by something. **2** an amount or quantity, *The volume of work has increased.* **3** the strength or power of sound. **4** a book, especially one of a set. [from Latin *volumen* = a roll (because ancient books were made in a rolled form)]

voluntary adjective
1 done or doing something willingly, not because you are forced to do it. **2** unpaid, *voluntary work.* **voluntarily** adverb

voluntary noun (plural **voluntaries**) an organ solo, often improvised, played before or after a church service. [from Latin *voluntas* = the will]

volunteer verb (**volunteers, volunteering, volunteered**) give or offer something of your own accord, without being forced to.

volunteer noun (plural **volunteers**) a person who volunteers to do something, e.g. to serve in the armed forces. [from French; related to *voluntary*]

vomit verb (**vomits, vomiting, vomited**) bring up food etc. from the stomach and out through the mouth; be sick. **vomit** noun

voodoo noun a form of witchcraft and magical rites, especially in the West Indies. [via American French from a West African language]

-vore suffix forms nouns meaning 'eating or feeding on something' (e.g. *carnivore*).

-vorous suffix forms adjectives corresponding to nouns in *-vore* (e.g. *carnivorous*).

vote verb (**votes, voting, voted**) show which person or thing you prefer by putting up your hand, making a mark on a paper, etc. **voter** noun

vote noun (plural **votes**)
1 the action of voting. **2** the right to vote.
[from Latin *votum* = a wish or vow]

vouch verb (**vouches, vouching, vouched**)
vouch for guarantee that something is true or certain,

I will vouch for his honesty. [from old French; related to *vocation*]

voucher noun (plural **vouchers**) a piece of paper that can be exchanged for certain goods or services; a receipt. [from *vouch*]

vow noun (plural **vows**) a solemn promise, especially to God or a saint.

vow verb (**vows, vowing, vowed**) make a vow. [from old French; related to *vote*]

vowel noun (plural **vowels**) any of the letters a, e, i, o, u, and sometimes y, which represent sounds in which breath comes out freely. (Compare *consonant*.) [from Latin *vocalis littera* = vocal letter]

voyage noun (plural **voyages**) a long journey on water or in space.

voyage verb (**voyages, voyaging, voyaged**) make a voyage. **voyager** noun [from old French]

vulgar adjective rude; without good manners. **vulgarly** adverb, **vulgarity** noun [from Latin *vulgus* = the common or ordinary people]

vulnerable adjective able to be hurt or harmed or attacked. **vulnerability** noun [from Latin *vulnus* = wound]

vulture noun (plural **vultures**) a large bird that feeds on dead animals.

vulva noun (plural **vulvas**) the outer parts of the female genitals.

vying present participle of **vie**.

Ww

W. abbreviation
1 west. 2 western.

wad (say wod) noun (plural **wads**)
a pad or bundle of soft material
or banknotes, papers, etc. [from
Dutch]

waddle verb (**waddles, waddling,
waddled**) walk with short steps,
swaying from side to side.
waddle noun [probably from
wade]

wade verb (**wades, wading,
waded**) walk through water or
mud etc. **wader** noun [from Old
English]

wafer noun (plural **wafers**) a kind
of thin biscuit. [from old French;
related to waffle¹]

waffle¹ (say wof-el) noun (plural
waffles) a small cake made of
batter and eaten hot. [from
Dutch]

waffle² (say wof-el) noun
(informal) vague wordy talk or
writing. **waffle** verb [from an old
word waff = to bark or yelp]

waft (say woft) verb (**wafts,
wafting, wafted**) carry or float
gently through the air or over
water. [from old German or
Dutch]

wag¹ verb (**wags, wagging,
wagged**) move quickly to and fro,
a dog wagging its tail. **wag** noun
[from Old English]

wag² noun (plural **wags**) a person
who makes jokes. [from an old
word waghalter = someone likely
to be hanged]

wage noun or **wages** plural noun
a regular payment to someone in
return for his or her work.

wage verb (**wages, waging,
waged**) carry on a war or
campaign.

wager (say way-jer) noun (plural
wagers) a bet. **wager** verb [from
old French; related to wage]

waggle verb (**waggles, waggling,
waggled**) move quickly to and
fro; wag. **waggle** noun [from wag]

wagon noun (plural **wagons**)
1 a cart with four wheels, pulled
by a horse or an ox. 2 an open
railway truck, e.g. for coal. [from
Dutch]

waif noun (plural **waifs**)
a homeless and helpless person,
especially a child. [from old
French]

wail verb (**wails, wailing, wailed**)
make a long sad cry. **wail** noun

waist noun (plural **waists**) the
narrow part in the middle of
your body.

USAGE: Do not confuse with
waste.

waistcoat noun (plural
waistcoats) a short close-fitting
jacket without sleeves, worn over
a shirt and under a jacket.

waistline noun (plural
waistlines) the amount you
measure around your waist,
which indicates how fat or thin
you are.

wait verb (**waits, waiting, waited**)
1 stay somewhere or postpone an
action until something happens;
pause. 2 be postponed, This
question must wait until our next
meeting. 3 wait on people.
wait on 1 hand food and drink to
people at a meal. 2 be an
attendant to someone.

wait noun an act or time of waiting, *We had a long wait for the train.*
[from old French; related to wake[1]]

waiter noun (plural **waiters**) a man who serves people with food and drink in a restaurant.

waiting list noun (plural **waiting lists**) a list of people waiting for something to become available.

waiting room noun (plural **waiting rooms**) a room provided for people who are waiting for something.

waitress noun (plural **waitresses**) a woman who serves people with food and drink in a restaurant.

wake[1] verb (**wakes, waking, woke, woken**)
1 stop sleeping, *Wake up! I woke when I heard the bell.* **2** stop someone sleeping, *You have woken the baby.*

wake noun (plural **wakes**) (in Ireland) a party held after a funeral.
[from Old English]

wake[2] noun (plural **wakes**)
1 the track left on the water by a moving ship. **2** currents of air left behind a moving aircraft.
in the wake of following.
[probably from Old Norse]

wakeful adjective unable to sleep.

waken verb (**wakens, wakening, wakened**) wake.

walk verb (**walks, walking, walked**) move along on your feet at an ordinary speed. **walker** noun

walk noun (plural **walks**)
1 a journey on foot. **2** the manner of walking. **3** a path or route for walking.

walking stick noun (plural **walking sticks**) a stick used as a support while walking.

walk of life noun (plural **walks of life**) a person's occupation or social position.

walkover noun (plural **walkovers**) an easy victory.

wall noun (plural **walls**)
1 a continuous upright structure, usually made of brick or stone, forming one of the sides of a building or room or supporting something or enclosing an area. **2** the outside part of something, *the stomach wall.*

wall verb (**walls, walling, walled**) enclose or block something with a wall, *a walled garden.*

wallet noun (plural **wallets**) a small flat folding case for holding banknotes, documents, etc.

wallflower noun (plural **wallflowers**) a garden plant with fragrant flowers, blooming in spring. [because it is often found growing on old walls]

wallow verb (**wallows, wallowing, wallowed**)
1 roll about in water, mud, etc. **2** get great pleasure by being surrounded by something, *wallowing in luxury.* **wallow** noun [from Old English]

wallpaper noun (plural **wallpapers**) paper used to cover the inside walls of rooms.

walnut noun (plural **walnuts**) an edible nut with a wrinkled surface.

walrus noun (plural **walruses**) a large Arctic sea animal with two long tusks. [probably from Dutch]

waltz *noun* (*plural* **waltzes**)
a dance with three beats to a bar.

waltz *verb* (**waltzes, waltzing, waltzed**) dance a waltz.
[from German *walzen* = revolve]

wand *noun* (*plural* **wands**) a thin rod, especially one used by a magician. [from Old Norse]

wander *verb* (**wanders, wandering, wandered**)
1 go about without trying to reach a particular place. **2** leave the right path or direction; stray. **wanderer** *noun*

wane *verb* (**wanes, waning, waned**)
1 (of the moon) show a bright area that becomes gradually smaller after being full. (The opposite is *wax*.) **2** become less, smaller, or weaker, *His popularity waned.*

want *verb* (**wants, wanting, wanted**)
1 wish to have something. **2** need, *Your hair wants cutting.* **3** be without something; lack.

want *noun* (*plural* **wants**)
1 a wish to have something. **2** lack or need of something.
[from Old Norse]

wanted *adjective* (of a suspected criminal) that the police wish to find or arrest.

war *noun* (*plural* **wars**)
1 fighting between nations or groups, especially using armed forces. **2** a serious struggle or effort against crime, disease, poverty, etc.
at war taking part in a war.

warble *verb* (**warbles, warbling, warbled**) sing with a trilling sound, as some birds do.
warble *noun*

ward *noun* (*plural* **wards**)
1 a room with beds for patients in a hospital. **2** a child looked after by a guardian. **3** an area electing a councillor to represent it.

ward *verb* (**wards, warding, warded**)
ward off keep something away.

-ward *suffix* forms adjectives and adverbs showing direction (e.g. *backward, forward, homeward*). [from Old English]

warden *noun* (*plural* **wardens**) an official who is in charge of a hostel, college, etc., or who supervises something. [from old French; related to *guardian*]

warder *noun* (*plural* **warders**) (*old use*) an official in charge of prisoners in a prison. [from old French; related to *guard*]

wardrobe *noun* (*plural* **wardrobes**)
1 a cupboard to hang clothes in. **2** a stock of clothes or costumes. [from old French *warder* = to guard, + *robe*]

-wards *suffix* forms adverbs showing direction (e.g. *backwards, forwards*). [from Old English *-weardes* = *-ward*]

warhead *noun* (*plural* **warheads**) the head of a missile or torpedo etc., containing explosives.

warlike *adjective*
1 fond of making war.
2 threatening war.

warm *adjective*
1 fairly hot; not cold or cool.
2 friendly or enthusiastic, *a warm welcome.* **warmly** *adverb*, **warmness** *noun*, **warmth** *noun*

warm *verb* (**warms, warming, warmed**) make or become warm.
[from Old English]

warm-blooded *adjective* having blood that remains warm permanently.

warn *verb* (**warns, warning, warned**) tell someone about a danger etc. that may affect them, or about what they should do, *I warned you to take your wellingtons.* **warning** *noun* [from Old English]

warp (*say* worp) *verb* (**warps, warping, warped**)
1 bend or twist out of shape, e.g. by dampness. 2 distort a person's ideas, judgement, etc., *Jealousy warped his mind.*

warrant *noun* (*plural* **warrants**) a document that authorizes a person to do something (e.g. to search a place) or to receive something.

warrant *verb* (**warrants, warranting, warranted**)
1 justify, *Nothing can warrant such rudeness.* 2 guarantee. [from old French; related to *guarantee*]

warren *noun* (*plural* **warrens**)
1 a piece of ground where there are many burrows in which rabbits live and breed.
2 a building or place with many winding passages. [from old French]

warrior *noun* (*plural* **warriors**) a person who fights in battle; a soldier.

warship *noun* (*plural* **warships**) a ship used in war.

wart *noun* (*plural* **warts**) a small hard lump on the skin, caused by a virus. [from Old English]

wary (*say* **wair**-ee) *adjective* cautious; looking carefully for possible danger or difficulty.
warily *adverb*, **wariness** *noun* [from Old English]

wash *verb* (**washes, washing, washed**)
1 clean something with water or other liquid. 2 be washable, *Cotton washes easily.* 3 flow against or over something, *Waves washed over the deck.* 4 carry along by a moving liquid, *A wave washed him overboard.*
5 (*informal*) be accepted or believed, *That excuse won't wash.*
wash out (*informal*) if an event is washed out, it is abandoned because of rain.
wash up wash dishes and cutlery etc. after use. **washing-up** *noun*

wash *noun* (*plural* **washes**)
1 the action of washing. 2 clothes etc. being washed. 3 the disturbed water behind a moving ship. 4 a thin coating of colour.

washable *adjective* able to be washed without becoming damaged.

washbasin *noun* (*plural* **washbasins**) a small sink for washing your hands etc.

washer *noun* (*plural* **washers**)
1 a small ring of rubber or metal etc. placed between two surfaces (e.g. under a bolt or screw) to fit them tightly together. 2 a washing machine.

washing *noun* clothes etc. being washed.

washing machine *noun* (*plural* **washing machines**) a machine for washing clothes etc.

wasn't (*mainly spoken*) was not.

wasp noun (plural **wasps**)
a stinging insect with black and
yellow stripes round its body.
[from Old English]

wastage noun loss of something
by waste.

waste verb (**wastes, wasting,
wasted**)
1 use something in an
extravagant way or without
getting enough results. 2 fail to
use something, *You wasted an
opportunity.* 3 make or become
gradually weaker or useless.

waste adjective
1 left over or thrown away
because it is not wanted. 2 not
used; not usable, *waste land.*
lay waste destroy the crops and
buildings etc. of an area.

waste noun (plural **wastes**)
1 wasting a thing, not using it
well, *a waste of time.* 2 things that
are not wanted or not used. 3 an
area of waste land, *the wastes of
the Sahara Desert.* **wasteful**
adjective, **wastefully** noun,
wastefulness noun
[from Latin *vastus* = empty]

USAGE: Do not confuse with
waist.

watch verb (**watches, watching,
watched**)
1 look at a person or thing for
some time. 2 be on guard or
ready for something to happen,
*Watch for the traffic lights to turn
green.* 3 take care of something.
watcher noun

watch noun (plural **watches**)
1 the action of watching. 2 a turn
of being on duty in a ship.
3 a device like a small clock,
usually worn on the wrist.

watchful adjective watching
closely; alert. **watchfully** adverb,
watchfulness noun

watchman noun (plural
watchmen) a person employed to
look after an empty building etc.,
especially at night.

water noun (plural **waters**)
1 a colourless odourless tasteless
liquid that is a compound of
hydrogen and oxygen. 2 a lake or
sea etc. 3 the tide, *at high water.*
pass water urinate.

water verb (**waters, watering,
watered**)
1 sprinkle or supply something
with water. 2 produce tears or
saliva, *It makes my mouth water.*
water down dilute.

watercolour noun (plural
watercolours)
1 paint made with pigment and
water (not oil). 2 a painting done
with this kind of paint.

waterfall noun (plural **waterfalls**)
a stream flowing over the edge of
a cliff or large rock.

waterlogged adjective
completely soaked or swamped
in water. [from *water* + *log*]
(because water was said to 'lie
like a log' in the hold of
a waterlogged ship]

waterproof adjective that keeps
out water, *a waterproof jacket.*
waterproof verb

water-skiing noun the sport of
skimming over the surface of
water on a pair of flat boards
(**water-skis**) while being towed by
a motor boat.

watertight adjective
1 made or fastened so that water
cannot get in or out.

2 that cannot be changed or set aside or proved to be untrue, *a watertight excuse.*

waterworks plural noun a place with pumping machinery etc. for supplying water to a district.

watery adjective
1 like water. **2** full of water. **3** containing too much water.

watt noun (plural **watts**) a unit of electric power. [named after James Watt, a Scottish engineer, who studied energy]

wave noun (plural **waves**)
1 a ridge moving along the surface of the sea etc. or breaking on the shore. **2** a wave-like curve, e.g. in hair. **3** the wave-like movement by which heat, light, sound, or electricity etc. travels. **4** the action of waving.

wave verb (**waves, waving, waved**)
1 move loosely to and fro or up and down. **2** move your hand to and fro as a signal or greeting etc. **3** make a thing wavy. **4** be wavy. [from Old English]

wavelength noun (plural **wavelengths**) the size of a sound wave or electromagnetic wave.

waver verb (**wavers, wavering, wavered**)
1 be unsteady; move unsteadily. **2** hesitate; be uncertain. [from Old Norse]

wavy adjective full of waves or curves. **wavily** adverb, **waviness** noun

wax¹ noun (plural **waxes**)
1 a soft substance that melts easily, used to make candles, crayons, and polish. **2** beeswax.
waxy adjective

wax verb (**waxes, waxing, waxed**) coat or polish something with wax.
[from Old English *waex*]

wax² verb (**waxes, waxing, waxed**)
1 (of the moon) show a bright area that becomes gradually larger. (The opposite is *wane*.)
2 become stronger or more important. [from Old English *weaxan*]

waxwork noun (plural **waxworks**) a model of a person etc. made in wax.

way noun (plural **ways**)
1 a line of communication between places, e.g. a path or road. **2** a route or direction. **3** a distance to be travelled. **4** how something is done; a method or style. **5** a respect, *It's a good idea in some ways.* **6** a condition or state, *Things were in a bad way.*
get or **have your own way** make people let you do what you want.
give way 1 collapse. **2** let somebody else move first. **3** yield.
in the way forming an obstacle or hindrance.
no way (*informal*) that is impossible!
under way see *under.*

waylay verb (**waylays, waylaying, waylaid**) lie in wait for a person or people, especially in order to talk to them or rob them.

-ways suffix forms adverbs showing direction or manner (e.g. *sideways*). [from *way*]

wayside noun
fall by the wayside fail to continue doing something.

wayward adjective disobedient; wilfully doing what you want. [from *away* + *-ward*]

we *pronoun* a word used by a person to refer to himself or herself and another or others.

weak *adjective* not strong; easy to break, bend, defeat, etc.
weakness *noun* [from Old English]

weaken *verb* (**weakens, weakening, weakened**) make or become weaker.

weakling *noun* (*plural* **weaklings**) a weak person or animal.

wealth *noun*
1 a lot of money or property; riches. 2 a large quantity, *The book has a wealth of illustrations.* [from Old English]

wealthy *adjective* (**wealthier, wealthiest**) having wealth; rich.
wealthiness *noun*

wean *verb* (**weans, weaning, weaned**) make a baby take food other than its mother's milk. [from Old English]

weapon *noun* (*plural* **weapons**) something used to harm or kill people in a battle or fight.
weaponry *noun*

wear *verb* (**wears, wearing, wore, worn**)
1 have clothes, jewellery, etc. on your body. 2 damage something by rubbing or using it often; become damaged in this way, *The carpet has worn thin.* 3 last while in use, *It has worn well.* **wearable** *adjective*, **wearer** *noun*
wear off 1 be removed by wear or use. 2 become less intense.
wear on pass gradually, *The night wore on.*
wear out 1 use or be used until it becomes weak or useless. 2 exhaust.

weary *adjective* (**wearier, weariest**)
1 tired. 2 tiring, *It's weary work.*
wearily *adverb*, **weariness** *noun*

weary *verb* (**wearies, wearying, wearied**) tire. [from Old English]

weasel *noun* (*plural* **weasels**) a small fierce animal with a slender body and reddish-brown fur. [from Old English]

weather *noun* the rain, snow, wind, sunshine etc. at a particular time or place.
under the weather feeling ill or depressed.

weather *verb* (**weathers, weathering, weathered**)
1 expose something to the effects of the weather. 2 come through something successfully, *The ship weathered the storm.*

weathercock or **weathervane** *noun* (*plural* **weathercocks, weathervanes**) a pointer, often shaped like a cockerel, that turns in the wind and shows from which direction it is blowing.

weave *verb* (**weaves, weaving, wove, woven**)
1 make material or baskets etc. by crossing threads or strips under and over each other. 2 put a story together, *She wove a thrilling tale.* 3 (*past tense & past participle* **weaved**) twist and turn, *He weaved through the traffic.* **weaver** *noun*

weave *noun* (*plural* **weaves**) a style of weaving, *a loose weave.*

web *noun* (*plural* **webs**)
1 a cobweb. 2 a network. [from Old English *webb* = a piece of woven cloth]

webbed or **web-footed** adjective
having toes joined by pieces of
skin, *Ducks have webbed feet; they
are web-footed.* [from *web*]

wed verb (**weds, wedding,
wedded**)
1 marry. **2** unite two different
things.

wedding noun (plural **weddings**)
the ceremony when a man and
woman get married.

wedge noun (plural **wedges**)
1 a piece of wood or metal etc.
that is thick at one end and thin
at the other. It is pushed between
things to force them apart or
prevent something from moving.
2 a wedge-shaped thing.
wedge verb (**wedges, wedging,
wedged**)
1 keep something in place with
a wedge. **2** pack tightly together,
Ten of us were wedged in the lift.

weed noun (plural **weeds**) a wild
plant that grows where it is not
wanted.
weed verb (**weeds, weeding,
weeded**) remove weeds from the
ground.
[from Old English *weod*]

weedy adjective (**weedier,
weediest**)
1 full of weeds. **2** thin and weak.

week noun (plural **weeks**)
a period of seven days, especially
from Sunday to the following
Saturday.
[from Old English]

weekday noun (plural **weekdays**)
a day other than Saturday or
Sunday.

weekend noun (plural
weekends) Saturday and Sunday.

weekly adjective & adverb
happening or done once a week.

weep verb (**weeps, weeping,
wept**)
1 shed tears; cry. **2** ooze moisture
in drops. **weep** noun, **weepy**
adjective

weeping adjective (of a tree)
having drooping branches,
a weeping willow.

weigh verb (**weighs, weighing,
weighed**)
1 measure the weight of
something. **2** have a certain
weight, *What do you weigh?* **3** be
important; have influence, *Her
evidence weighed with the jury.*
weigh anchor raise the anchor
and start a voyage.
weigh down 1 keep something
down by its weight. **2** depress or
trouble somebody.
weigh up estimate or assess
something. [from Old English]

weight noun (plural **weights**)
1 how heavy something is; an
object's mass expressed as
a number according to a scale of
units. (Compare *mass* 3.) **2** a piece
of metal of known weight,
especially one used on scales to
weigh things. **3** a heavy object.
4 importance or influence.
weighty adjective, **weightless**
adjective
weight verb (**weights,
weighting, weighted**) put a weight
on something.

weir (say weer) noun (plural
weirs) a small dam across a river
or canal to control the flow of
water.

weird *adjective* very strange; uncanny. **weirdly** *adverb*, **weirdness** *noun* [from Old English]

USAGE: When spelling this word, note that the 'e' comes before the 'i', not the other way round.

welcome *noun* (*plural* **welcomes**) a greeting or reception, especially a kindly one.

welcome *adjective*
1 that you are glad to receive or see, *a welcome gift*. **2** gladly allowed, *You are welcome to come.*

welcome *verb* (**welcomes**, **welcoming**, **welcomed**) show that you are pleased when a person or thing arrives.
[from *well*² + *come*]

weld *verb* (**welds**, **welding**, **welded**)
1 join pieces of metal or plastic by heating and pressing or hammering them together. **2** unite people or things into a whole.

welfare *noun* people's health, happiness, and comfort. [from *well*² + *fare*]

welfare state *noun* a system in which a country's government provides money to pay for health care, social services, benefits, etc.

well¹ *noun* (*plural* **wells**)
1 a deep hole dug to bring up water or oil from underground. **2** a deep space, e.g. containing a staircase.

well *verb* (**wells**, **welling**, **welled**) rise or flow up, *Tears welled up in our eyes.*

[from Old English *wella* = spring of water]

well² *adverb* (**better**, **best**)
1 in a good or suitable way, *She swims well.* **2** thoroughly, *Polish it well.* **3** probably or reasonably, *This may well be our last chance.*
well off 1 fairly rich. **2** in a good situation.

well *adjective*
1 in good health, *He is not well.*
2 satisfactory, *All is well.*
[from Old English *wel* = prosperously]

well-being *noun* good health, happiness, and comfort.

wellingtons *plural noun* rubber or plastic waterproof boots. **wellies** *plural noun* (*informal*) [named after the first Duke of Wellington, who wore long leather boots]

well-known *adjective*
1 known to many people. **2** known thoroughly.

well-mannered *adjective* having good manners.

well-meaning *adjective* having good intentions.

well-read *adjective* having read a lot of good books.

well-to-do *adjective* fairly rich.

weren't (*mainly spoken*) were not.

werewolf *noun* (*plural* **werewolves**) (in legends) a person who sometimes changes into a wolf. [from Old English *wer* = man, + *wolf*]

west *noun*
1 the direction where the sun sets, opposite east. **2** the western part of a country, city, etc.

west adjective
1 situated in the west, *the west coast.* 2 coming from the west, *a west wind.*

west adverb towards the west, *We sailed west.*

westerly adjective to or from the west.

western adjective of or in the west.

western noun (plural **westerns**) a film or story about cowboys or American Indians in western North America during the 19th and early 20th centuries.

westward adjective & adverb towards the west. **westwards** adverb

wet adjective (**wetter**, **wettest**)
1 soaked or covered in water or other liquid. 2 not yet dry, *wet paint.* 3 rainy, *wet weather.* **wetly** adverb, **wetness** noun

wet verb (**wets**, **wetting**, **wet** or **wetted**) make a thing wet.
[from Old English]

whale noun (plural **whales**) a very large sea animal.
a whale of a (*informal*) very good or great, *We had a whale of a time.*

whaling noun hunting whales.

what adjective used to ask the amount or kind of something (*What kind of bike have you got?*) or to say how strange or great a person or thing is (*What a fool you are!*).

what pronoun
1 what thing or things, *What did you say?* 2 the thing that, *This is what you must do.*
what's what (*informal*) which things are important or useful.

whatever pronoun
1 anything or everything, *Do whatever you like.* 2 no matter what, *Keep calm, whatever happens.*

whatever adjective of any kind or amount, *Take whatever books you need. There is no doubt whatever.*

wheat noun a cereal plant from which flour is made. **wheaten** adjective [from Old English]

wheedle verb (**wheedles**, **wheedling**, **wheedled**) coax. [probably from German]

wheel noun (plural **wheels**)
1 a round device that turns on a shaft that passes through its centre. 2 a horizontal revolving disc on which clay is made into a pot.

wheel verb (**wheels**, **wheeling**, **wheeled**)
1 push a bicycle or trolley etc. along on its wheels. 2 move in a curve or circle; change direction and face another way, *He wheeled round in astonishment.*
[from Old English]

wheelbarrow noun (plural **wheelbarrows**) a small cart with one wheel at the front and legs at the back, pushed by handles.

wheelchair noun (plural **wheelchairs**) a chair on wheels for a person who cannot walk.

wheeze verb (**wheezes**, **wheezing**, **wheezed**) make a hoarse whistling sound as you breathe. **wheeze** noun, **wheezy** adjective

when adverb at what time; at which time, *When can you come to tea?*

when *conjunction*
1 at the time that, *The bird flew away when I moved.* **2** although; considering that, *Why do you smoke when you know it's dangerous?*
[from Old English]

whence *adverb & conjunction* from where; from which.

whenever *conjunction* at whatever time; every time, *Whenever I see it, I smile.*

where *adverb & conjunction* in or to what place or that place, *Where did you put it? Leave it where it is.*

where *pronoun* what place, *Where does she come from?*

whereabouts *adverb* in or near what place, *Whereabouts are you going?*

whereabouts *plural noun* the place where something is, *Do you know the whereabouts of my radio?*

whereas *conjunction* but in contrast, *Some people enjoy sport, whereas others hate it.*

whereupon *conjunction* after which; and then.

wherever *adverb* in or to whatever place.

whet *verb* (**whets, whetting, whetted**)
whet your appetite stimulate it.
[from Old English *hwettan* = sharpen]

USAGE: Do not confuse with *wet*.

---

whether *conjunction* as one possibility; if, *I don't know whether to believe her or not.*
[from Old English]

which *adjective* what particular, *Which way did he go?*

which *pronoun*
1 what person or thing, *Which is your desk?* **2** the person or thing referred to, *The film, which is a western, will be shown on Saturday.*
[from Old English]

whichever *pronoun & adjective* no matter which; any which, *Take whichever you like.*

whiff *noun* (*plural* **whiffs**) a puff or slight smell of smoke, gas, etc.
[imitating the sound of a puff]

while *conjunction*
1 during the time that; as long as, *Whistle while you work.*
2 although; but, *She is dark, while her sister is fair.*

while *noun* a period of time, *a long while.*

while *verb* (**whiles, whiling, whiled**)
while away pass time, *We whiled away the afternoon on the river.*
[from Old English]

whim *noun* (*plural* **whims**) a sudden wish to do or have something.

whimper *verb* (**whimpers, whimpering, whimpered**) cry or whine softly. **whimper** *noun*

whimsical *adjective* impulsive and playful. **whimsically** *adverb*, **whimsicality** *noun* [from *whim*]

whine *verb* (**whines, whining, whined**)
1 make a long high miserable cry or a shrill sound. **2** complain in a petty or feeble way. **whine** *noun*
[from Old English]

whip *noun* (*plural* **whips**)
1 a cord or strip of leather fixed to a handle and used for hitting

people or animals. **2** an official of a political party in Parliament. **3** a pudding made of whipped cream and fruit or flavouring.

whip verb (whips, whipping, whipped)
1 hit a person or animal with a whip. **2** beat cream until it becomes thick. **3** move or take something suddenly, *He whipped out a gun.* **4** (*informal*) steal something.
whip up stir up people's feelings etc., *She whipped up support for her plans.*
[from old German or old Dutch]

whirl verb (whirls, whirling, whirled) turn or spin very quickly. **whirl** noun

whirlpool noun (plural whirlpools) a whirling current of water.

whirlwind noun (plural whirlwinds) a strong wind that whirls round a central point.

whirr verb (whirrs, whirring, whirred) make a continuous buzzing sound. **whirr** noun
[imitating the sound]

whisk verb (whisks, whisking, whisked)
1 move or brush something away quickly and lightly. **2** beat eggs etc. until they are frothy.

whisk noun (plural whisks)
1 a kitchen tool used for whisking things. **2** a whisking movement.
[from Old Norse]

whisker noun (plural whiskers)
1 a hair of those growing on a man's face, forming a beard or moustache if not shaved off.
2 a long bristle growing near the mouth of a cat etc. **whiskery** adjective [from *whisk*]

whisky noun (plural whiskies) a strong alcoholic drink. [from Scottish Gaelic *uisge beatha* = water of life]

whisper verb (whispers, whispering, whispered)
1 speak very softly. **2** talk secretly. **whisper** noun [from Old English]

whist noun a card game usually for four people.

whistle verb (whistles, whistling, whistled) make a shrill or musical sound, especially by blowing through your lips. **whistler** noun

whistle noun (plural whistles)
1 a whistling sound. **2** a device that makes a shrill sound when air or steam is blown through it. [from Old English]

White noun (plural Whites) a person with a light-coloured skin. **White** adjective

white noun (plural whites)
1 the very lightest colour, like snow or salt. **2** the transparent substance (albumen) round the yolk of an egg, which turns white when it is cooked.

white adjective
1 of the colour white. **2** very pale from the effects of illness or fear etc. **3** (of coffee) with milk. **whiteness** noun

white elephant noun (plural white elephants) a useless possession.

white-hot adjective extremely hot; so hot that heated metal looks white.

white lie noun (plural **white lies**)
a harmless or trivial lie that you
tell in order to avoid hurting
someone's feelings.

whiten verb (**whitens, whitening,
whitened**) make or become
whiter.

whitewash noun
1 a white liquid containing lime
or powdered chalk, used for
painting walls and ceilings etc.
2 concealing mistakes or other
unpleasant facts so that someone
will not be punished. **whitewash**
verb

whither adverb & conjunction (old
use) to what place. [from Old
English]

USAGE: Do not confuse with
wither.

whittle verb (**whittles, whittling,
whittled**)
1 shape wood by trimming thin
slices off the surface. 2 reduce
something by removing various
things from it, whittle down the
cost. [from Old English]

whiz verb (**whizzes, whizzing,
whizzed**)
1 move very quickly. 2 sound like
something rushing through the
air.

who pronoun which person or
people; the particular person or
people, This is the boy who stole
the apples. [from Old English]

whoever pronoun
1 any or every person who. 2 no
matter who.

whole adjective
1 complete. 2 not injured or
broken.

whole noun
1 the full amount. 2 a complete
thing.
on the whole considering
everything; mainly.

wholemeal adjective made from
the whole grain of wheat etc.
[from whole + meal]

whole number noun (plural
whole numbers) a number
without fractions.

wholesale noun selling goods in
large quantities to be resold by
others. (Compare retail.)
wholesaler noun

wholesale adjective & adverb
1 on a large scale; including
everybody or everything,
wholesale destruction. 2 in the
wholesale trade.

wholesome adjective good for
health; healthy, wholesome food.
wholesomeness noun [from an
old sense of whole = healthy,
+ -some]

wholly adverb completely or
entirely.

whom pronoun the form of who
used when it is the object of
a verb or comes after
a preposition, as in the boy whom
I saw or to whom we spoke.

whoop (say woop) noun (plural
whoops) a loud cry of
excitement. **whoop** verb

whooping cough (say hoop-ing)
noun an infectious disease that
causes spasms of coughing and
gasping for breath. [because of
the sound the person makes
gasping for breath]

whopper noun (plural **whoppers**)
(slang) something very large.
[from Middle English whop = to
strike or beat]

whopping *adjective* (*slang*) very large or remarkable, *a whopping lie*. [from *whopper*]

who's (*mainly spoken*) who is; who has.

USAGE: Do not confuse with *whose*.

whose *pronoun* belonging to what person or persons; of whom; of which, *Whose house is that?* [from Old English]

USAGE: Do not confuse with *who's*.

why *adverb* for what reason or purpose; the particular reason on account of which, *This is why I came.* [from Old English]

wick *noun* (*plural* **wicks**)
1 the string that goes through the middle of a candle and is lit. **2** the strip of material that you light in a lamp or heater etc. that uses oil. [from Old English]

wicked *adjective*
1 morally bad or cruel. **2** very bad; severe, *a wicked blow*.
3 mischievous, *a wicked smile*. **wickedly** *adverb*, **wickedness** *noun* [from Old English *wicca* = witch]

wicket *noun* (*plural* **wickets**)
1 a set of three stumps and two bails used in cricket. **2** the part of a cricket ground between the wickets. [via old French from Germanic]

wicketkeeper *noun* (*plural* **wicketkeepers**) the fielder in cricket who stands behind the batsman's wicket.

wide *adjective*
1 measuring a lot from side to side; not narrow. **2** measuring from side to side, *The cloth is one metre wide*. **3** covering a great range, *a wide knowledge of birds*.
4 fully open, *staring with wide eyes*. **5** far from the target, *The shot was wide of the mark*. **widely** *adverb*, **wideness** *noun*

wide *adverb*
1 widely. **2** completely or fully, *wide awake*. **3** far from the target, *The shot went wide*. [from Old English]

widen *verb* (**widens, widening, widened**) make or become wider.

widespread *adjective* existing in many places or over a wide area, *a widespread belief*.

widow *noun* (*plural* **widows**) a woman whose husband has died. **widowed** *adjective* [from Old English]

widower *noun* (*plural* **widowers**) a man whose wife has died. [from *widow*]

width *noun* (*plural* **widths**) how wide something is; wideness. [from *wide*]

wield *verb* (**wields, wielding, wielded**) hold something and use it, *wielding a sword*. [from Old English]

wife *noun* (*plural* **wives**) the woman to whom a man is married. [from Old English *wif* = woman]

wig *noun* (*plural* **wigs**) a covering made of real or artificial hair, worn on the head. [short for *periwig*, from old French *perruque*]

wigwam *noun* (*plural* **wigwams**) a tent formerly used by Native Americans, made by fastening skins or mats over poles. [a Native American word]

wild adjective
1 living or growing in its natural state, not looked after by people. 2 not cultivated, *a wild landscape*. 3 not civilized, *the Wild West*. 4 not controlled; very violent or excited. 5 very foolish or unreasonable, *these wild ideas*. **wildly** adverb, **wildness** noun [from Old English]

wilderness noun (plural **wildernesses**) a wild uncultivated area; a desert. [from Old English *wild deor* = wild deer, + *-ness*]

wildlife noun wild animals.

wilful adjective
1 obstinately determined to do what you want, *a wilful child*. 2 deliberate, *wilful murder*. **wilfully** adverb, **wilfulness** noun [from *will²* + *-ful*]

will¹ auxiliary verb used to express the future tense, questions, or promises. [from Old English *wyllan*]

USAGE: See the entry for **shall**.

will² noun (plural **wills**)
1 the mental power to decide and control what you do. 2 a desire; a chosen decision, *I went to the party against my will*. 3 determination to do something, *They set to work with a will*. 4 a written statement of how a person's possessions are to be disposed of after his or her death. **at will** whenever you like, *You can come and go at will*.

will verb (**wills**, **willing**, **willed**) use your will-power; influence something by doing this, *I was willing you to win!* [from Old English *willa*]

willing adjective ready and happy to do what is wanted. **willingly** adverb, **willingness** noun [from *will²*]

willow noun (plural **willows**) a tree or shrub with flexible branches, usually growing near water.

will-power noun strength of mind to control what you do.

willy-nilly adverb whether you want to or not. [from *will I, nill I* (= will I, will I not)]

wilt verb (**wilts**, **wilting**, **wilted**) lose freshness or strength; droop. [originally dialect; probably from old Dutch]

wily (say wy-lee) adjective cunning or crafty. **wiliness** noun [from *wile*]

win verb (**wins**, **winning**, **won**)
1 defeat your opponents in a battle, game, or contest. 2 get or achieve something by a victory or by using effort or skill etc., *She won the prize*.

win noun (plural **wins**) a victory. [from Old English]

wince verb (**winces**, **wincing**, **winced**) make a slight movement because of pain or embarrassment etc. [from old French]

wind¹ (rhymes with *tinned*) noun (plural **winds**)
1 a current of air. 2 gas in the stomach or intestines that makes you feel uncomfortable. 3 breath used for a purpose, e.g. for running or speaking. 4 the wind instruments of an orchestra. **get** or **have the wind up** (slang) feel frightened.

wind verb (winds, winding, winded) put a person out of breath, *The climb had winded us.* [from Old English *wind*]

wind² (rhymes with *find*) verb (winds, winding, wound)
1 go or turn something in twists, curves, or circles. 2 wind up a watch or clock etc. **winder** noun
wind up 1 make a clock or watch work by tightening its spring. 2 close a business. 3 (*informal*) end up in a place or condition, *He wound up in jail.* [from Old English *windan*]

windfall noun (plural **windfalls**)
1 a piece of unexpected good luck, especially a sum of money. 2 a fruit blown off a tree by the wind.

wind instrument noun (plural **wind instruments**) a musical instrument played by blowing, e.g. a trumpet.

windmill noun (plural **windmills**) a mill worked by the wind turning its sails.

window noun (plural **windows**)
1 an opening in a wall or roof etc. to let in light and often air, usually filled with glass. 2 the glass in this opening. 3 an area on a VDU screen used for a particular purpose. [from Old Norse *vind* = wind, air + *auga* = eye]

windpipe noun (plural **windpipes**) the tube by which air passes from the throat to the lungs.

windscreen noun (plural **windscreens**) the window at the front of a motor vehicle.

windy adjective with much wind, *It's windy outside.*

wine noun (plural **wines**)
1 an alcoholic drink made from grapes or other plants. 2 a dark red colour. [same origin as *vine*]

wing noun (plural **wings**)
1 one of the pair of parts of a bird, bat, or insect, that it uses for flying. 2 one of the pair of long flat parts that stick out from the side of an aircraft and support it while it flies. 3 a part that sticks out at one end or side of something; **the wings** the sides of a theatre stage out of sight of the audience. 4 the part of a motor vehicle's body above a wheel. 5 a player at either end of the forward line in football or hockey etc. 6 a section of a political party, with more extreme opinions than the others.
on the wing flying.
take wing fly away.

wing verb (wings, winging, winged)
1 fly; travel by means of wings, *The bird winged its way home.* 2 wound a bird in the wing or a person in the arm.

winged adjective having wings.

wink verb (winks, winking, winked)
1 close and open your eye quickly, especially as a signal to someone. 2 (of a light) flicker or twinkle.

wink noun (plural **winks**)
1 the action of winking. 2 a very short period of sleep, *I didn't sleep a wink.*

winkle verb (winkles, winkling, winkled)
winkle out extract; prise a thing out, *I managed to winkle out some information.*

winner *noun* (*plural* **winners**)
1 a person or animal etc. that wins. **2** something very successful, *Her latest book is a winner.*

winnings *plural noun* money won.

winter *noun* (*plural* **winters**) the coldest season of the year, between autumn and spring. **wintry** *adjective*

wipe *verb* (**wipes, wiping, wiped**) dry or clean something by rubbing it. **wiper** *noun*
wipe out 1 cancel, *wipe out the debt.* **2** destroy something completely.

wire *noun* (*plural* **wires**)
1 a strand or thin flexible rod of metal. **2** a piece of wire used to carry electric current. **3** a fence etc. made from wire. **4** a telegram.

wire *verb* (**wires, wiring, wired**)
1 fasten or strengthen something with wire. **2** fit or connect something with wires to carry electric current.

wireless *noun* (*plural* **wirelesses**) (*old use*) a radio. [because it does not need wires to conduct sound]

wiry *adjective*
1 like wire. **2** lean and strong.

wisdom *noun*
1 being wise. **2** wise sayings. [from Old English *wis* = wise, + -*dom*]

wisdom tooth *noun* (*plural* **wisdom teeth**) a molar tooth that may grow at the back of the jaw of a person aged about 20 or more.

wise *adjective* knowing or understanding many things; judging well. **wisely** *adverb* [from Old English *wis*]

-wise *suffix* forms adverbs meaning 'in this manner or direction' (e.g. *otherwise, clockwise*). [from Old English *wise* = way or manner]

wish *verb* (**wishes, wishing, wished**)
1 feel or say that you would like to have or do something or would like something to happen. **2** say that you hope someone will get something, *Wish me luck!*

wish *noun* (*plural* **wishes**)
1 something you wish for; a desire. **2** the action of wishing, *Make a wish when you blow out the candles.*
[from Old English]

wishbone *noun* (*plural* **wishbones**) a forked bone between the neck and breast of a bird (sometimes pulled apart by two people; the person who gets the bigger part can make a wish).

wishful thinking *noun* believing something because you wish it were true rather than on the facts.

wisp *noun* (*plural* **wisps**)
1 a few strands of hair or bits of straw etc. **2** a small streak of smoke or cloud etc. **wispy** *adjective* [origin unknown]

wistful *adjective* sadly longing for something. **wistfully** *adverb*, **wistfulness** *noun* [from Middle English *whist* = quiet, + -*ful*]

wit *noun* (*plural* **wits**)
1 intelligence or cleverness, *Use your wits.* **2** a clever kind of humour. **3** a witty person.
at your wits' end not knowing what to do. [from Old English]

witch noun (plural **witches**)
a person, especially a woman, who uses magic to do things.
[from Old English]

witchcraft noun the use of magic, especially for evil purposes.

witch-hunt noun (plural **witch-hunts**) a campaign to find and punish people who hold views that are considered to be unacceptable or dangerous.

with preposition used to indicate
1 being in the company or care etc. of (Come with me), **2** having (a man with a beard), **3** using (Hit it with a hammer), **4** because of (shaking with laughter), **5** feeling or showing (We heard it with pleasure), **6** towards or concerning (I was angry with him), **7** in opposition to; against (Don't argue with your father), **8** being separated from (We had to part with it). [from Old English]

withdraw verb (**withdraws, withdrawing, withdrew, withdrawn**)
1 take back or away; remove, She withdrew money from the bank. **2** go away from a place or people, The troops withdrew from the frontier. **withdrawal** noun [from Old English with- = away, back, + draw]

wither verb (**withers, withering, withered**)
1 shrivel or wilt. **2** make something shrivel or wilt. [a different spelling of weather]

USAGE: Do not confuse with whither.

withering adjective scornful or sarcastic, a withering remark.

within preposition & adverb
inside; not beyond something.

without preposition
1 not having, without food. **2** free from, without fear. **3** (old use) outside, without the city wall.

without adverb (old use) outside, We looked at the house from within and without.
[from Old English]

withstand verb (**withstands, withstanding, withstood**) endure something successfully; resist.
[from Old English with- = against + stand]

witness noun (plural **witnesses**)
1 a person who sees or hears something happen, There were no witnesses to the accident.
2 a person who gives evidence in a lawcourt.

witness verb (**witnesses, witnessing, witnessed**)
1 be a witness of something, Did anyone witness the accident? **2** sign a document to confirm that it is genuine.
[from wit]

witticism noun (plural **witticisms**) a witty remark.

witty adjective (**wittier, wittiest**) clever and amusing; full of wit. **wittily** adverb, **wittiness** noun

wizard noun (plural **wizards**)
1 a male witch; a magician.
2 a person with amazing abilities. **wizardry** noun [from an old sense of wise = a wise person]

wobble verb (**wobbles, wobbling, wobbled**) stand or move unsteadily; shake slightly.
wobble noun, **wobbly** adjective

woe noun (plural **woes**)
1 sorrow. 2 misfortune. **woeful** adjective, **woefully** adverb [from Old English]

woebegone adjective looking unhappy. [from woe + an old word bego = attack, surround]

wok noun (plural **woks**) a Chinese cooking pan shaped like a large bowl. [from Chinese]

wolf noun (plural **wolves**) a fierce wild animal of the dog family.

wolf verb (**wolfs**, **wolfing**, **wolfed**) eat something greedily. [from Old English]

woman noun (plural **women**) a grown-up female human being. **womanhood** noun [from Old English]

womanly adjective having qualities that are thought to be typical of women.

womb (say woom) noun (plural **wombs**) the hollow organ in a female's body where babies develop before they are born. [from Old English]

women's lib or **women's liberation** noun the freedom of women to have the same rights, opportunities, and status as men.

wonder noun (plural **wonders**)
1 a feeling of surprise and admiration or curiosity.
2 something that causes this feeling; a marvel.
no wonder it is not surprising.

wonder verb (**wonders**, **wondering**, **wondered**)
1 feel that you want to know; try to form an opinion, We are still wondering what to do next.
2 feel wonder.
[from Old English]

wonderful adjective marvellous or excellent. **wonderfully** adverb

won't (mainly spoken) will not.

woo verb (**woos**, **wooing**, **wooed**) (old use)
1 court a woman. 2 seek someone's favour. **wooer** noun [from Old English]

wood noun (plural **woods**)
1 the substance of which trees are made. 2 many trees growing close together.

wooded adjective covered with growing trees.

wooden adjective
1 made of wood. 2 stiff and showing no expression or liveliness. **woodenly** adverb

woodlouse noun (plural **woodlice**) a small crawling creature with seven pairs of legs, living in rotten wood or damp soil etc.

woodpecker noun (plural **woodpeckers**) a bird that taps tree trunks with its beak to find insects.

woodwind noun wind instruments that are usually made of wood, e.g. the clarinet and oboe.

woodwork noun
1 making things out of wood.
2 things made out of wood.

woody adjective
1 like wood; consisting of wood.
2 full of trees.

wool noun (plural **wools**)
1 the thick soft hair of sheep and goats etc. 2 thread or cloth made from this.

woollen adjective made of wool.

woolly adjective
1 covered with wool or wool-like hair. 2 like wool; woollen.

3 not thinking clearly; vague or confused, *woolly ideas.*

woolliness *noun*

word *noun* (*plural* **words**)
1 a set of sounds or letters that has a meaning, and when written or printed has no spaces between the letters. **2** a promise, *He kept his word.* **3** a command or spoken signal, *Run when I give the word.* **4** a message; information, *We sent word of our safe arrival.*

word for word in exactly the same words.

word *verb* (**words**, **wording**, **worded**) express something in words, *Word the question carefully.*

wording *noun* the way something is worded.

word of honour *noun* a solemn promise.

word-perfect *adjective* having memorized every word perfectly, *He was word-perfect at the rehearsal.*

word processor *noun* (*plural* **word processors**) a kind of computer used for editing and printing words typed into it.

wordy *adjective* using too many words; not concise.

wore *past tense of* **wear**.

work *noun* (*plural* **works**)
1 something you have to do that needs effort or energy, *Digging is hard work.* **2** the use of effort or energy to do something (contrasted with *play* or *recreation*). **3** a job; employment. **4** something produced by work, *The teacher marked our work.* **5** a piece of writing, painting, music, etc., *the works of William Shakespeare.*

at work working.

out of work having no work; unable to find paid employment.

work *verb* (**works**, **working**, **worked**)
1 do work. **2** have a job; be employed, *She works in a bank.* **3** act or operate correctly or successfully, *Is the lift working?* **4** make something act; operate, *Can you work the lift?* **5** shape or press etc., *Work the mixture into a paste.* **6** make a way; pass, *The grub works its way into timber.*

work out 1 find an answer by thinking or calculating. **2** have a particular result.

work up make people become excited; arouse.

workable *adjective* that can be used or will work.

worker *noun* (*plural* **workers**)
1 a person who works. **2** a member of the working class. **3** a bee or ant etc. that does the work in a hive or colony but does not produce eggs.

working class *noun* (*plural* **working classes**) people who work for wages, especially in manual or industrial work.

workman *noun* (*plural* **workmen**) a man employed to do manual labour; a worker.

workmanship *noun* a person's skill in working; the result of this.

work of art *noun* (*plural* **works of art**) a fine picture, building, etc.

workshop *noun* (*plural* **workshops**) a place where things are made or mended.

world noun (plural **worlds**)
1 the earth with all its countries and peoples.
2 a planet, *creatures from another world*. **3** the people or things belonging to a certain activity, *the world of sport*.
4 a very great amount, *It will do him a world of good. She is worlds better today.*

worm noun (plural **worms**)
1 an animal with a long small soft rounded or flat body and no backbone or limbs. **2** an unimportant or unpleasant person. **wormy** adjective

worm verb (**worms**, **worming**, **wormed**) move along by wriggling or crawling.

worm out gradually get someone to tell you something by constantly and cleverly questioning them, *We eventually managed to worm the truth out of them.*

worn past participle of **wear**.

worn-out adjective
1 exhausted. **2** damaged by too much use.

worried adjective feeling or showing worry.

worry verb (**worries**, **worrying**, **worried**)
1 be troublesome to someone; make a person feel slightly afraid. **2** feel anxious. **3** hold something in the teeth and shake it, *The dog was worrying a rat.*
worrier noun

worry noun (plural **worries**)
1 the condition of worrying; being uneasy. **2** something that makes a person worry.

worse adjective & adverb more bad or more badly; less good or less well. [from Old English; related to *war*]

worship verb (**worships**, **worshipping**, **worshipped**)
1 give praise or respect to God or a god. **2** love or respect a person or thing greatly. **worshipper** noun

worship noun (plural **worships**)
1 worshipping; religious ceremonies. **2** a title of respect for a mayor or certain magistrates, *his worship the mayor*.
[from Old English *weorth* = worth, + *-ship*]

worst adjective & adverb most bad or most badly; least good or least well. [from Old English]

worth adjective
1 having a certain value, *This stamp is worth £100.* **2** deserving something; good or important enough for something, *That book is worth reading.*

worthwhile adjective important or good enough to deserve the time or effort needed, *a worthwhile job.* [from *worth the while* = worth the time]

worthy adjective having great merit; deserving respect or support, *a worthy cause.*
worthiness noun
worthy of deserving, *This charity is worthy of your support.* [from *worth*]

would auxiliary verb used
1 as the past tense of *will*[1] (*We said we would do it*), in questions (*Would you like to come?*), and in polite requests (*Would you come in, please?*). **2** with *I* and *we* and the verbs *like*, *prefer*, *be glad*, etc. (e.g. *I would like to come, we*

would be glad to help), where the strictly correct use is *should*, **3** of something to be expected (*That's just what he would do!*).

USAGE: For sense **2**, see the note on *should* **4**.

would-be *adjective* wanting or pretending to be, *a would-be comedian.*

wouldn't (*mainly spoken*) would not.

wound[1] (*say* woond) *noun* (*plural* **wounds**)
1 an injury done by a cut, stab, or hit. **2** a hurt to a person's feelings.

wound *verb* (**wounds, wounding, wounded**)
1 cause a wound to a person or animal. **2** hurt a person's feelings, *She was wounded by these remarks.*

wound[2] (*say* wownd) *past tense of* **wind**[2].

wrap *verb* (**wraps, wrapping, wrapped**) put paper or cloth etc. round something as a covering.

wrapper *noun* (*plural* **wrappers**) a piece of paper etc. wrapped round something.

wreath (*say* reeth) *noun* (*plural* **wreaths**)
1 flowers or leaves etc. fastened into a circle, *wreaths of holly.*
2 a curving line of mist or smoke. [from Old English *writhan* = writhe]

wreathe (*say* reeth) *verb* (**wreathes, wreathing, wreathed**)
1 surround or decorate something with a wreath. **2** cover, *Their faces were wreathed in*

smiles. **3** move in a curve, *Smok wreathed upwards.* [from *wreath* and *writhe*]

wreck *verb* (**wrecks, wrecking, wrecked**) damage or ruin something so badly that it canno be used again.

wreck *noun* (*plural* **wrecks**)
1 a wrecked ship or building or car etc. **2** a person who is left very weak, *a nervous wreck.* **3** th wrecking of something.

wreckage *noun* the pieces of a wreck.

wren *noun* (*plural* **wrens**) a very small brown bird.

wrench *verb* (**wrenches, wrenching, wrenched**) twist or pull something violently.

wrench *noun* (*plural* **wrenches**)
1 a wrenching movement. **2** pai caused by parting, *Leaving hom was a great wrench.* **3** an adjustable tool rather like a spanner, used for gripping an turning bolts, nuts, etc. [from Old English]

wrestle *verb* (**wrestles, wrestling wrestled**)
1 fight by grasping your opponent and trying to throw him or her to the ground.
2 struggle with a problem etc.
wrestle *noun*, **wrestler** *noun* [from Old English]

wretch *noun* (*plural* **wretches**)
1 a person who is very unhapp or who you pity. **2** a person wh is disliked; a rascal. [from Old English]

wretched *adjective*
1 miserable or unhappy. **2** of ba quality. **3** not satisfactory; causing a nuisance, *This*

wretched car won't start.
wretchedly *adverb,* **wretchedness**
noun [from *wretch*]

wriggle *verb* (**wriggles, wriggling,
wriggled**) move with short
twisting movements. **wriggle**
noun, **wriggly** *adjective*
wriggle out of avoid work or
blame etc. cunningly.

wring *verb* (**wrings, wringing,
wrung**)
1 twist and squeeze a wet thing to
get water etc. out of it. **2** squeeze
something firmly or forcibly.
3 get something by a great effort,
We wrung a promise out of him.
wring *noun*
wringing wet so wet that water
can be squeezed out of it.

wrinkle *noun* (*plural* **wrinkles**)
1 a small furrow or ridge in the
skin. **2** a small crease in
something.
wrinkle *verb* (**wrinkles,
wrinkling, wrinkled**) make
wrinkles in something; form
wrinkles.
[origin unknown]

wrist *noun* (*plural* **wrists**) the
joint that connects the hand and
arm.

wristwatch *noun* (*plural*
wristwatches) a watch for
wearing on the wrist.

write *verb* (**writes, writing, wrote,
written**)
1 put letters or words etc. on
paper or another surface. **2** be the
author or composer of
something, *write books or music.*
3 send a letter to somebody.
writer *noun,* **writing** *noun* [from
Old English]

writhe *verb* (**writhes, writhing,
writhed**)
1 twist your body because of
pain. **2** wriggle. **3** suffer because
of great shame.

wrong *adjective*
1 incorrect; not true, *the wrong
answer.* **2** morally bad; unfair;
unjust, *It is wrong to cheat.* **3** not
working properly, *There's
something wrong with the engine.*
wrongly *adverb,* **wrongness** *noun*
wrong *adverb* wrongly, *You
guessed wrong.*
wrong *noun* (*plural* **wrongs**)
something morally wrong; an
injustice.
in the wrong having done or said
something wrong.
wrong *verb* (**wrongs, wronging,
wronged**) do wrong to someone;
treat a person unfairly.
[probably from Old Norse]

wrought *adjective* (of metal)
worked by being beaten out or
shaped by hammering or rolling
etc., *wrought iron.* [the old past
participle of *work*]

wry *adjective* (**wryer, wryest**)
1 slightly mocking or ironic,
a wry smile. **2** twisted or bent out
of shape. (Compare *awry.*) **wryly**
adverb, **wryness** *noun*

Xx

-xion *suffix* see *-ion.*

Xmas *noun* Christmas. [the X
represents the Greek letter called
chi, the first letter of *Christos*
= Christ]

X-ray *noun* (*plural* **X-rays**)
a photograph or examination of
the inside of something,

especially a part of the body, made by a kind of radiation (called **X-rays**) that can penetrate solid things.

X-ray verb (**X-rays, X-raying, X-rayed**) make an X-ray of something.

xylophone (say zy-lo-fohn) noun (plural **xylophones**) a musical instrument made of wooden bars that you hit with small hammers. [from Greek xylon = wood + phone = sound]

Yy

-y[1] and **-ie** suffixes form names showing fondness, or diminutives (e.g. daddy, pussy). [origin unknown]

-y[2] suffix forms adjectives meaning 'to do with' or 'like' (e.g. angry, horsy, messy, sticky). [from Old English]

yacht (say yot) noun (plural **yachts**)
1 a sailing boat used for racing or cruising. 2 a private ship.
yachting noun, **yachtsman** noun, **yachtswoman** noun [from Dutch jaghtschip = fast pirate ship]

yak noun (plural **yaks**) an ox with long hair, found in central Asia. [from Tibetan]

yank verb (**yanks, yanking, yanked**) (informal) pull something strongly and suddenly. **yank** noun [origin unknown]

Yankee noun (plural **Yankees**) an American, especially of the northern USA. [probably from Dutch Janke = Johnny]

yap verb (**yaps, yapping, yapped**) bark shrilly. **yap** noun

yard[1] noun (plural **yards**)
1 a measure of length, 36 inches or about 91 centimetres. 2 a long pole stretched out from a mast to support a sail. [from Old English gerd]

yard[2] noun (plural **yards**) an enclosed area beside a building or used for a certain kind of work, a timber yard. [from Old English geard]

yarn noun (plural **yarns**)
1 thread spun by twisting fibres together, used in knitting etc.
2 (informal) a tale or story. [from Old English]

yawn verb (**yawns, yawning, yawned**)
1 open the mouth wide and breathe in deeply when feeling sleepy or bored. 2 form a wide opening, A pit yawned in front of us. **yawn** noun [from Old English]

ye pronoun (old use, in speaking to two or more people) you. [from Old English]

year noun (plural **years**)
1 the time the earth takes to go right round the sun, about 365¼ days. 2 the time from 1 January to 31 December; any period of twelve months. **yearly** adjective & adverb

yearn verb (**yearns, yearning, yearned**) long for something. [from Old English]

yeast noun a substance that causes alcohol and carbon dioxide to form as it develops, used in making beer and wine and in baking bread etc. [from Old English]

yell verb (yells, yelling, yelled) give a loud cry; shout. **yell** noun

yellow noun (plural **yellows**) the colour of buttercups and ripe lemons.

yellow adjective
1 of yellow colour. **2** (informal) cowardly. **yellowness** noun [from Old English]

yellow pages plural noun a special telephone directory giving addresses and telephone numbers of businesses, arranged according to what services they provide.

yelp verb (yelps, yelping, yelped) give a shrill bark or cry. **yelp** noun [from Old English gielpan = to boast]

yen[1] noun (plural **yen**) a unit of money in Japan. [from Japanese en = round]

yen[2] noun (plural **yens**) a longing for something. [from Chinese]

yes adverb used to agree to something (= the statement is correct) or as an answer (= I am here). [from Old English]

yesterday noun & adverb the day before today. [from Old English]

yet adverb
1 up to this time; by this time, The post hasn't come yet. **2** eventually, I'll get even with him yet! **3** in addition; even, She became yet more excited.

yet conjunction nevertheless, It is strange, yet it is true.

yew noun (plural **yews**) an evergreen tree with dark green needle-like leaves and red berries.

yield verb (yields, yielding, yielded)
1 give in or surrender. **2** agree to do what is asked or ordered; give way, He yielded to persuasion. **3** produce as a crop or as profit etc.

yoga (say yoh-ga) noun a Hindu system of meditation and self-control. [Sanskrit, literally = union]

yoghurt (say yog-ert) noun milk thickened by the action of certain bacteria, giving it a sharp taste. [from Turkish]

yoke noun (plural **yokes**)
1 a curved piece of wood put across the necks of animals pulling a cart or plough etc.
2 a shaped piece of wood fitted across a person's shoulders, with a pail or load hung at each end.
3 a close-fitting upper part of a piece of clothing, from which the rest hangs.

yoke verb (yokes, yoking, yoked) harness or join things by means of a yoke.
[from Old English]

USAGE: Do not confuse with yolk.

yolk (rhymes with coke) noun (plural **yolks**) the round yellow part inside an egg. [from Old English geolu = yellow]

USAGE: Do not confuse with yoke.

yonder adjective & adverb over there.

you pronoun
1 the person or people being spoken to, Who are you? **2** anyone or everyone; one, You can't tell what will happen next.

young *adjective* having lived or existed for a short time; not old.

youngster *noun* (*plural* **youngsters**) a young person; a child.

your *adjective* belonging to you. [from Old English]

USAGE: Do not confuse with *you're*.

you're (*mainly spoken*) you are.

USAGE: Do not confuse with *your*.

yours *possessive pronoun* belonging to you.
Yours faithfully, Yours sincerely, Yours truly ways of ending a letter before you sign it. (*Yours faithfully* and *Yours truly* are more formal than *Yours sincerely*.)

USAGE: It is incorrect to write *your's*.

yourself *pronoun* (*plural* **yourselves**) you and nobody else. (Compare *herself*.)

youth *noun* (*plural* **youths**)
1 being young; the time when you are young. **2** a young man. **3** young people. **youthful** *adjective*, **youthfulness** *noun*

youth hostel *noun* (*plural* **youth hostels**) a place, often in the countryside, where young people can stay cheaply when they are on holiday.

yo-yo *noun* (*plural* **yo-yos**) a round wooden or plastic toy that moves up and down on a string that you hold. [probably from a language spoken in the Philippines]

Yule *noun* (*old use*) the Christmas festival, also called **Yuletide**.

Zz

zap *verb* (**zaps, zapping, zapped**) (*slang*)
1 attack or destroy something forcefully. **2** change quickly from one section of a videotape etc. to another. [imitating the sound of a blow or shot]

zeal *noun* enthusiasm or keenness. **zealous** (*say* zel-us) *adjective*, **zealously** *adverb* [from Greek]

zebra (*say* zeb-ra) *noun* (*plural* **zebras**) an African animal of the horse family, with black and white stripes all over its body. [Italian, Spanish, or Portuguese]

zebra crossing *noun* (*plural* **zebra crossings**) a place for pedestrians to cross a road safely, marked with broad white stripes.

zero *noun* (*plural* **zeros**)
1 nought; the figure 0. **2** the point marked 0 on a thermometer etc. [from Arabic *sifr* = cipher]

zero hour *noun* the time when something is planned to start.

zest *noun* great enjoyment or interest. **zestful** *adjective*, **zestfully** *adverb*

zigzag *noun* (*plural* **zigzags**) a line or route that turns sharply from side to side.
zigzag *verb* (**zigzags, zigzagging, zigzagged**) move in a zigzag. [via French from German]

zinc *noun* a white metal. [from German]

zip noun (plural **zips**)
1 a zip fastener. 2 a sharp sound like a bullet going through the air. 3 liveliness or vigour. **zippy** adjective

zip verb (**zips, zipping, zipped**)
1 fasten something with a zip fastener. 2 move quickly with a sharp sound.
[imitating the sound]

zip fastener or **zipper** noun (plural **zip fasteners, zippers**) a fastener consisting of two strips of material, each with rows of small teeth that interlock when a sliding tab brings them together.

zodiac (say zoh-dee-ak) noun a strip of sky where the sun, moon, and main planets are found, divided into twelve equal parts (called **signs of the zodiac**),

each named after a constellation.
[from Greek zodiion = image of an animal]

zone noun (plural **zones**) an area of a special kind or for a particular purpose, a war zone; a no-parking zone. [Greek, = girdle]

zoo noun (plural **zoos**) a place where wild animals are kept so that people can look at them or study them. [short for zoological gardens]

zoology (say zoh-ol-o-jee) noun the study of animals. **zoological** adjective, **zoologist** noun [from Greek zoion = animal, + -logy]

zoom verb (**zooms, zooming, zoomed**)
1 move very quickly, especially with a buzzing sound. 2 rise quickly, Prices had zoomed. **zoom** noun [imitating the sound]

APPENDIX 1
Prefixes and Suffixes

Prefixes

A prefix is placed at the beginning of a word to change its meaning or to form a new word. The following prefixes have entries at their alphabetical places in the dictionary.

a-	apo-	contra-	equi-	infra-	octa-	pro-	sur-
ab-	ar-	cor-	eu-	inter-	of-	proto-	sus-
abs-	arch-	counter-	ex-	intra-	omni-	pseudo-	syl-
ac-	as-	cross-	extra-	intro-	op-	psycho-	sym-
ad-	at-	de-	for-	ir-	ortho-	quadri-	syn-
aero-	auto-	deca-	fore-	iso-	out-	quasi-	tele-
af-	auto-	deci-	geo-	kilo-	over-	radio-	tetra-
Afro-	be-	demi-	hecto-	mal-	pan-	re-	thermo-
ag-	bene-	di-	hepta-	mega-	para-	retro-	trans-
al-	bi-	dia-	hetero-	micro-	penta-	se-	tri-
ambi-	bio-	dif-	hexa-	milli-	per-	self-	ultra-
amphi-	cata-	dis-	homo-	mini-	peri-	semi-	un-
an-	cath-	dys-	hydr-	mis-	phil-	step-	under-
ana-	centi-	e-	hydro-	mono-	philo-	sub-	uni-
Anglo-	circum-	ef-	hyper-	multi-	photo-	suc-	vice-
ant-	co-	electro-	hypo-	neo-	poly-	suf-	
ante-	col-	em-	il-	non-	post-	sum-	
anti-	com-	en-	im-	ob-	pre-	sup-	
ap-	con-	epi-	in-	oc-		super-	

Suffixes

A suffix is placed at the end of a word to form another word or to form a plural, past tense, comparative, superlative, etc. The following suffixes have entries at their alphabetical places in the dictionary.

-able	-cracy	-ette	-hood	-ification	-kin	-or	-vorous
-arch	-crat	-faction	-ible	-ing	-less	-pathy	-ward
-archy	-cule	-ferous	-ic	-ion	-ling	-phobia	-wards
-arian	-cy	-fold	-ical	-ise	-logical	-ship	-ways
-ary	-dom	-ful	-ician	-ish	-logist	-sion	-wise
-ate	-ed	-fy	-icity	-ism	-logy	-some	-xion
-ation	-ee	-gen	-ics	-ist	-ly	-teen	-y
-bility	-er	-gon	-ier	-ite	-most	-tion	
-ble	-esque	-gram	-iest	-itis	-ness	-tude	
-cide	-ess	-graph	-iferous	-ive	-oid	-uble	
-cle	-est	-graphy	-ize	-ology	-vore		

Some foreign words and phrases used in English

ad hoc done or arranged only when necessary and not planned in advance. [Latin, = for this]

ad infinitum (*say* in-fin-I-tum) without limit; for ever. [Latin, = to infinity]

ad nauseam (*say* naw-see-am) until people are sick of it. [Latin, = to sickness]

aide-de-camp (*say* ayd-der-kahm) a military officer who is the assistant to a senior officer. [French, = camp-helper]

à la carte ordered and paid for as separate items from a menu. (Compare *table d'hôte*.) [French, = from the menu]

alfresco *adjective* & *adverb* in the open air, *an alfresco meal*. [from Italian *al fresco* = in the fresh air]

alter ego another, very different, side of someone's personality. [Latin, = other self]

au fait (*say* oh fay) knowing a subject or procedure etc. well. [French, = to the point]

au gratin (*say* oh grat-an) cooked with a crisp topping of breadcrumbs or grated cheese. [French]

au revoir (*say* oh rev-wahr) goodbye for the moment. [French, = to be seeing again]

avant-garde *noun* people who use a very modern style in art or literature etc. [French, = vanguard]

bête noire (*say* bayt nwahr) a person or thing you greatly dislike. [French, = black beast]

bona fide (*say* boh-na fy-dee) genuine; without fraud, *Are they bona fide tourists or spies?* [Latin, = in good faith]

bona fides (*say* boh-na fy-deez) honest intention; sincerity, *We do not doubt his bona fides.* [Latin, = good faith]

bon voyage (*say* bawn vwah-yahzh) pleasant journey! [French]

carte blanche (*say* kart blahnsh) freedom to act as you think best. [French, = blank paper]

c'est la vie (*say* sel la vee) life is like that. [French, = that is life]

chef-d'oeuvre (*say* shay dervr) a masterpiece. [French, = chief work]

compos mentis (*say* in your right mind; sane. (The opposite is non compos mentis.) [Latin, = having control of the mind]

cordon bleu (*say* kor-dawn bler) (of cooks and cookery) first-class. [French, = blue ribbon]

corps de ballet (*say* kor der bal-ay) the whole group of dancers (not the soloists) in a ballet. [French]

corps diplomatique (*say* kor dip-lom-at-eek) the diplomatic service. [French]

coup de grâce (*say* koo der grahs) a stroke or blow that puts an end to something. [French, = mercy-blow]

coup d'état (say koo day-**tah**) the sudden overthrow of a government. [French, = blow of State]

crème de la crème (say krem der la krem) the very best of something. [French, = cream of the cream]

curriculum vitae (say **veet**-I) a brief account of a person's education, career, etc. [Latin, = course of life]

déjà vu (say day-zha vew) a feeling that you have already experienced what is happening now. [French, = already seen]

de rigueur (say der rig-**er**) proper; required by custom or etiquette. [French, = of strictness]

de trop (say der **troh**) not wanted; unwelcome. [French, = too much]

doppelgänger (say **dop**-el-geng-er) noun the ghost of a living person. [German, = double-goer]

dramatis personae (say dram-a-tis per-**sohn**-I) the characters in a play. [Latin, = persons of the drama]

en bloc (say ahn **blok**) all at the same time; in a block. [French]

en masse (say ahn **mass**) all together. [French, = in a mass]

en passant (say ahn pas-**ahn**) by the way. [French, = in passing]

en route (say ahn **root**) on the way. [French]

entente (say ahn-**tahnt** or on-**tont**) noun a friendly understanding between nations. [French]

esprit de corps (say es-pree der **kor**) loyalty to your group. [French, = spirit of the body]

eureka (say yoor-**eek**-a) interjection I have found it! [Greek]

exeunt (say eks-ee-unt) verb they leave the stage. [Latin, = they go out]

ex gratia (say eks **gray**-sha) given without being legally obliged to be given, an ex gratia payment. [Latin, = from favour]

faux pas (say foh **pah**) an embarrassing blunder. [French, = false step]

hara-kiri noun a form of suicide formerly used by Japanese officers when in disgrace. [from Japanese hara = belly, kiri = cutting]

hoi polloi the ordinary people; the masses. [Greek, = the many]

Homo sapiens human beings regarded as a species of animal. [Latin, = wise man]

hors-d'oeuvre (say or-dervr) noun food served as an appetizer at the start of a meal. [French, = outside the work]

in camera in a judge's private room, not in public. [Latin, = in the room]

in extremis (say eks-**treem**-iss) at the point of death; in very great difficulties. [Latin, = in the greatest danger]

in memoriam in memory (of). [Latin]

in situ (say sit-yoo) in its original place. [Latin]

joie de vivre (say zhwah der veevr) a feeling of great enjoyment of life. [French, = joy of life]

laissez-faire (*say* lay-say-**fair**)
noun a government's policy of not
interfering. [French, = let (them)
act]

maître d'hôtel (*say* metr doh-**tel**)
a head waiter. [French, = master
of house]

milieu (*say* meel-**yer**) *noun*
environment; surroundings.
[French, from *mi* = mid + *lieu* =
place]

modus operandi (*say* moh-dus
op-er-**and**-ee) **1** a person's way of
working. **2** the way a thing
works. [Latin, = way of working]

nem. con. *abbreviation*
unanimously. [short for Latin
nemine contradicente = with
nobody disagreeing]

nom de plume a writer's
pseudonym. [French, = pen-name
(this phrase is not used in
France)]

non sequitur (*say* non sek-wit-er)
a conclusion that does not follow
from the evidence given. [Latin,
= it does not follow]

nota bene (*say* noh-ta ben-ee)
(usually shortened to NB) note
carefully. [Latin, = note well]

nouveau riche (*say* noo-voh
reesh) a person who has only
recently become rich. [French, =
new rich]

objet d'art (*say* ob-*zh*ay dar)
a small artistic object.
[French, = object of art]

par excellence (*say* par eks-el-
ahns) more than all the others; to
the greatest degree.
[French, = because of special
excellence]

pas de deux (*say* pah der der)
a dance (e.g. in a ballet) for two
persons. [French, = step of two]

pâté de foie gras (*say* pat-ay der
fwah grah) a paste or pie of goose-
liver.
[French, = paste of fat liver]

per annum for each year; yearly.
[Latin]

per capita (*say* **kap**-it-a) for each
person. [Latin, = for heads]

persona grata (*say* per-soh-na
grah-ta) a person who is
acceptable to someone, especially
a diplomat acceptable to a foreign
government. (The opposite is
persona non grata).
[Latin, = pleasing person]

pièce de résistance (*say* pee-ess
der ray-zees-**tahns**) the most
important item. [French]

placebo (*say* plas-**ee**-boh) *noun*
(placebos) a harmless substance
given as if it were medicine,
usually to reassure a patient.
[Latin, = I shall be pleasing]

poste restante (*say* rest-**ahnt**)
a part of a post office where
letters etc. are kept until called
for.
[French, = letters remaining]

prima facie (*say* pry-ma **fay**-shee)
at first sight; judging by the first
impression.
[Latin, = on first appearance]

quid pro quo (*say* kwoh)
something given or done in
return for something.
[Latin, = something for
something]

raison d'être (*say* ray-zawn detr)
the purpose of a thing's existence.
[French, = reason for being]

rigor mortis (*say* ry-ger mor-tis)
stiffening of the body after death.
[Latin, = stiffness of death]

RIP *abbreviation* may he or she (or they) rest in peace. [short for Latin *requiescat* (or *requiescant*) *in pace*]

sang-froid (*say* sahn-**frwah**) *noun* calmness in danger or difficulty. [French, = cold blood]

savoir faire (*say* sav-wahr **fair**) *noun* knowledge of how to behave socially. [French, = knowing how to do]

sotto voce (*say* sot-oh **voh**-chee) in a very quiet voice. [Italian, = under the voice]

status quo (*say* stay-tus **kwoh**) the state of affairs as it was before a change. [Latin, = the state in which]

sub judice (*say* **joo**-dis-ee) being decided by a judge or lawcourt. [Latin, = under a judge]

table d'hôte (*say* tahbl **doht**) a restaurant meal served at a fixed inclusive price. (Compare **à la carte**.) [French, = host's table]

terra firma dry land; the ground. [Latin, = firm land]

tête-à-tête (*say* tayt-ah-**tayt**) *noun* a private conversation, especially between two people. [French, = head to head]

vis-à-vis (*say* veez-ah-**vee**) *adverb* & *preposition* 1 in a position facing one another; opposite to. 2 as compared with. [French, = face to face]

viva voce (*say* vy-va **voh**-chee) in a spoken test or examination. [Latin, = with the living voice]

volte-face (*say* volt-**fahs**) *noun* a complete change in your attitude towards something. [French]

APPENDIX 3
List of Countries

Country	People	Country	People
Afghanistan	Afghans	Congo Democratic Republic	Congolese
Albania	Albanians	Costa Rica	Costa Ricans
Algeria	Algerians	Croatia	Croats
Andorra	Andorrans	Cuba	Cubans
Angola	Angolans	Cyprus	Cypriots
Antigua and Barbuda	Antiguans, Barbudans	Czech Republic	Czechs
Argentina	Argentinians	Denmark	Danes
Armenia	Armenians	Djibouti	Djiboutians
Australia	Australians	Dominica	Dominicans
Austria	Austrians	Dominican Republic	Dominicans
Azerbaijan	Azerbaijanis	Ecuador	Ecuadoreans
Bahamas	Bahamians	Egypt	Egyptians
Bahrain	Bahrainis	El Salvador	Salvadoreans
Bangladesh	Bangladeshis	Equatorial Guinea	Equatorial Guineans
Barbados	Barbadians	Eritrea	Eritreans
Belarus	Belorussians	Estonia	Estonians
Belgium	Belgians	Ethiopia	Ethiopians
Belize	Belizians	Falkland Islands	Falkland Islanders
Benin	Beninese	Fiji	Fijians
Bhutan	Bhutanese	Finland	Finns
Bolivia	Bolivians	France	French
Bosnia-Herzegovina	Bosnians	Fyrom (Former Yugoslavia Rep of Macedonia)	Macedonians
Botswana	Batswana		
Brazil	Brazilians		
Brunei Darussalam	People of Brunei	Gabon	Gabonese
Bulgaria	Bulgarians	Gambia	Gambians
Burkina Faso	Burkinans	Georgia	Georgians
Burundi	People of Burundi	Germany	Germans
Cambodia	Cambodians	Ghana	Ghanaians
Cameroon	Cameroonians	Gibraltar	Gibraltarians
Canada	Canadians	Greece	Greeks
Central African Republic	People of the Central African Republic	Grenada	Grenadians
		Guatemala	Guatemalans
Chad	Chadians	Guinea	Guineans
Chile	Chileans	Guinea-Bissau	People of Guinea-Bissau
China, People's Republic of	Chinese		
China, Republic of	Taiwanese	Guyana	Guyanese
Colombia	Colombians	Haiti	Haitians
Congo	Congolese	Honduras	Hondurans
		Hungary	Hungarians

Country	People	Country	People
Iceland	Icelanders	Nepal	Nepalese
India	Indians	Netherlands	Dutch
Indonesia	Indonesians	New Zealand	New Zealanders
Iran	Iranians	Nicaragua	Nicaraguans
Iraq	Iraqis	Niger	Nigeriens
Ireland, Republic of	Irish	Nigeria	Nigerians
Israel	Israelis	North Korea	North Koreans
Italy	Italians	Norway	Norwegians
Ivory Coast	People of the Ivory Coast	Oman	Omanis
Jamaica	Jamaicans	Pakistan	Pakistanis
Japan	Japanese	Panama	Panamanians
Jordan	Jordanians	Papua New Guinea	Papua New Guineas
Kazakhstan	Kazakhs	Paraguay	Paraguayans
Kenya	Kenyans	Peru	Peruvians
Kirgyzstan	Kirgyz	Philippines	Filipinos
Kuwait	Kuwaitis	Poland	Poles
Laos	Laotians	Portugal	Portuguese
Latvia	Latvians	Qatar	Qataris
Lebanon	Lebanese	Romania	Romanians
Lesotho	Basotho	Russia (Russian Federation)	Russians
Liberia	Liberians		
Libya	Libyans	Rwanda	Rwandans
Liechtenstein	Liechtensteiners	St Kitts-Nevis	People of St Kitts-Nevis
Lithuania	Lithuanians		
Luxembourg	Luxembourgers	St Lucia	St Lucians
Madagascar	Malagasies	St Vincent and the Grenadines	St Vincentians
Malawi	Malawians		
Malaysia	Malaysians	São Tomé and Principe	People of São Tomé and Principe
Mali	Malians		
Malta	Maltese	Saudi Arabia	Saudi Arabians
Mauritania	Mauritanians	Senegal	Senegalese
Mauritius	Mauritians	Sierra Leone	Sierra Leoneans
Mexico	Mexicans	Singapore	Singaporeans
Moldavia, Moldava	Moldavians	Slovakia	Slovaks
Monaco	Monégasques	Slovenia	Slovenes
Mongolia	Mongolians	Solomon Islands	Solomon Islanders
Montserrat	Montserratians	Somalia	Somalis
Morocco	Moroccans	South Africa	South Africans
Mozambique	Mozambicans	South Korea	South Koreans
Myanmar (until 1989 called *Burma*)		Spain	Spaniards
		Sri Lanka	Sri Lankans
Namibia	Namibians	Sudan	Sudanese
Nauru	Nauruans	Suriname	Surinamers

	People	Country	People
	Swazis	United Kingdom	British
	Swedes	United States of America	Americans
	Swiss		
Sy...	Syrians	Uruguay	Uruguayans
Tajikistan	Tajiks	Uzbekistan	Uzbeks
Tanzania	Tanzanians	**V**anuatu	People of Vanuatu
Thailand	Thais	Venezuela	Venezuelans
Togo	Togolese	Vietnam	Vietnamese
Trinidad and Tobago	Trinidadians and Tobagans	**W**estern Samoa	Western Samoans
Tunisia	Tunisians	**Y**emen, Republic of	Yemenis
Turkey	Turks	Yugoslavia	Yugoslavs
Turkmenistan	Turkmens	(Montenegro and Serbia)	(Montenegrins)
Uganda	Ugandans		
Ukraine	Ukrainians	**Z**ambia	Zambians
United Arab Emirates	People of the United Arab Emirates	Zimbabwe	Zimbabweans

APPENDIX 4

Weights and Measures

Note The conversion factors are not exact unless so marked. They are given only to the accuracy likely to be needed in everyday calculations.

1. METRIC, WITH BRITISH EQUIVALENTS

Linear Measure

1 millimetre		= 0.039 inch
1 centimetre	= 10 mm	= 0.394 inch
1 decimetre	= 10 cm	= 3.94 inches
1 metre	= 10 dm	= 1.094 yards
1 decametre	= 10 m	= 10.94 yards
1 hectometre	= 100 m	= 109.4 yards
1 kilometre	= 1,000 m	= 0.6214 mile

Square Measure

1 square centimetre	= 0.155 sq.inch	
1 square metre	= 10,000 sq.cm	
	= 1.196 sq. yards	
1 are	= 100 sq.m.	= 119.6 sq.yards
1 hectare	= 100 ares	= 2.471 acres
1 square kilometre	= 100 hectares	
	= 0.386 sq. mile	

Cubic Measure

1 cubic centimetre	= 0.061 cu.inch
1 cubic metre	= 1,000,000 cu.cm
	= 1.308 cu. yards

Capacity Measure

1 millilitre		= 0.002 pint (British)
1 centilitre	= 10 ml	= 0.018 pint
1 decilitre	= 10 cl	= 0.176 pint
1 litre	= 10 dl	= 1.76 pints
1 decalitre	= 10 l	= 2.20 gallons
1 hectolitre	= 100 l	= 2.75 bushels
1 kilolitre	= 1,000 l	= 3.44 quarters

Weight

1 milligram		= 0.015 grain
1 centigram	= 10 mg	= 0.154 grain
1 decigram	= 10 cg	= 1.543 grains
1 gram	= 10 dg	= 15.43 grains
1 decagram	= 10 g	= 5.63 drams
1 hectogram	= 100 g	= 3.527 ounces
1 kilogram	= 1,000 g	= 2.205 pounds
1 tonne (metric ton)	= 1,000 kg	
	= 0.984 (long) ton	

2. BRITISH AND AMERICAN, WITH METRIC EQUIVALENTS

Linear Measure

1 inch	= 25.4 mm exactly
1 foot	= 12 inches	= 0.3048 metre
1 yard	= 3 feet	= 0.9144 metre exactly
1 (statute) mile	= 1,760 yards	= 1.609 km

Square Measure

1 square inch		= 6.45 sq. cm
1 square foot		
	= 144 sq. in.	= 9.29 sq. dm
1 square yard		
	= 9 sq. ft.	= 0.836 sq. metre
1 acre		
	= 4,840 sq. yd.	= 0.405 hectare
1 square mile		
	= 640 acres	= 259 hectares

Cubic Measure

1 cubic inch		= 16.4 cu. cm
1 cubic foot		
	= 1,728 cu. in.	= 0.0283 cu. metre
1 cubic yard		
	= 27 cu. ft.	= 0.765 cu. metre

Avoirdupois Weight

1 grain		= 0.065 gram
1 dram		= 1.772 grams
1 ounce	= 16 drams	= 28.35 grams
1 pound	= 16 ounces	= 7,000 grains
		= 0.4536 kilogram
		(0.45359237 exactly)
1 stone		
	= 14 pounds	= 6.35 kilograms
1 quarter		
	= 2 stones	= 12.70 kilograms
1 hundredweight		
	= 4 quarters	= 50.80 kilograms
1 (long) ton		
	= 20 hundredweight	= 1.016 tonnes
1 short ton		
	= 2,000 pounds	= 0.907 tonne

Capacity Measure

British

1 pint	= 20 fluid oz.	
	= 34.68 cu. in.	= 0.568 litre
1 quart	= 2 pints	= 1.136 litres
1 gallon	= 4 quarts	= 4.546 litres
1 peck	= 2 gallons	= 9.092 litres
1 bushel	= 4 pecks	= 36.4 litres
1 quarter	= 8 bushels	
		= 2.91 hectolitres

American dry

1 pint	= 33.60 cu. in.	= 0.550 litre
1 quart	= 2 pints	= 1.101 litres
1 peck	= 8 quarts	= 8.81 litres
1 bushel	= 4 pecks	= 35.3 litres

American liquid

1 pint	= 16 fluid oz.	
	= 28.88 cu. in.	= 0.473 litre
1 quart	= 2 pints	= 0.946 litre
1 gallon	= 4 quarts	= 3.785 litres

TEMPERATURE

Fahrenheit: Water boils (under standard conditions) at 212° and freezes at 32°.

Celsius or Centigrade: Water boils at 100° and freezes at 0°.

Kelvin: Water boils at 373.15 K and freezes at 273.15 K.

Celsius	Fahrenheit	Celsius	Fahrenheit
−17.8°	0°	50°	122°
−10°	14°	60°	140°
0°	32°	70°	158°
10°	50°	80°	176°
20°	68°	90°	194°
30°	86°	100°	212°
40°	104°		

To convert Celsius into Fahrenheit: multiply by 9, divide by 5, and add 32.

To convert Fahrenheit into Celsius: subtract 32, multiply by 5, and divide by 9.

METRIC PREFIXES

Abbreviation or symbol	Factor		Abbreviation or symbol	Factor
da	10	deci-	d	10^{-1}
h	10^2	centi-	c	10^{-2}
k	10^3	milli-	m	10^{-3}
M	10^6	micro-	μ	10^{-6}
G	10^9	nano-	n	10^{-9}
T	10^{12}	pico-	p	10^{-12}
P	10^{15}	femto-	f	10^{-15}
E	10^{18}	atto-	a	10^{-18}

The prefixes may be applied to any units of the metric system:
hectogram (abbreviated hg) = 100 grams;
kilowatt (abbreviated kW) = 1,000 watts.

5. SI UNITS

Basic SI units

Quantity	Unit	Symbol
Length	Metre	m
Mass	Kilogram	kg
Time	Second	s
Electric current	Ampere	A
Temperature	Kelvin	K
Light intensity	Candela	cd
Amount of substance	Mole	mol

Derived SI units

Quantity	Unit	Symbol
Area	Square metre	m^2
Volume	Cubic metre	m^3
Frequency	Hertz	Hz
Force	Newton	N
Pressure	Pascal	Pa
Energy	Joule	J
Power	Watt	W
Electric potential	Volt	V
Electrical resistance	Ohm	V
Electric charge	Coulomb	C
Radioactivity	Becquerel	Bq

Basic SI units and derived SI units

The seven basic SI units have scientific standards that define the size of the units with great precision. All derived units are related to the basic SI units. Each unit has its own entry in the dictionary.

Note: SI stands for Système International, the international system of units of measurement.